# ECONOMIC DEVELOPMENT

---

THEORIES,

EVIDENCE,

AND POLICIES

---

# ECONOMIC DEVELOPMENT

---

THEORIES,

EVIDENCE,

AND POLICIES

---

**PETER HESS**
DAVIDSON COLLEGE

**CLARK ROSS**
DAVIDSON COLLEGE

THE DRYDEN PRESS
HARCOURT BRACE COLLEGE PUBLISHERS

FORT WORTH   PHILADELPHIA   SAN DIEGO   NEW YORK   AUSTIN   ORLANDO   SAN ANTONIO
TORONTO   MONTREAL   LONDON   SYDNEY   TOKYO

|                                     |                              |
| ----------------------------------: | ---------------------------- |
|                 Acquisitions Editor | Emily Barrosse               |
|                 Developmental Editor | Stacey Sims                  |
|                      Project Editor | Kathryn Stewart              |
|                 Production Manager  | Carlyn Hauser                |
|                    Product Manager  | R. Paul Stewart              |
|                       Art Director  | Linda Wooton                 |
|         Art & Literary Rights Editor | Adele Krause                 |
|    Electronic Publishing Coordinator | Cathy Spitzenberger          |
|                         Copy Editor | Kathy Nevils Bunnell         |
|                         Proofreader | Sheryl Nelson                |
|                     Critical Reader | Milt Silver                  |
|                             Indexer | Sonsie Conroy                |
|                           Text Type | 9.5/12 Palatino              |
|              Text and Cover Design  | Beverly Baker                |
|                         Cover Image | Earth Imaging/Tony Stone Images |

Copyright © 1997 by Harcourt Brace & Company

All rights reserved. No part of this publication may be reproduced or transmitted in any form or by any means, electronic or mechanical, including photocopy, recording, or any information storage and retrieval system, without permission in writing from the publisher.

Requests for permission to make copies of any part of the work should be mailed to: Permissions Department, Harcourt Brace & Company, 6277 Sea Harbor Drive, Orlando, FL 32887-6777.

*Address for Editorial Correspondence*
The Dryden Press, 301 Commerce Street, Suite 3700, Fort Worth, TX 76102

*Address for Orders*
The Dryden Press, 6277 Sea Harbor Drive, Orlando, FL 32887
1-800-782-4479, or 1-800-433-0001 (in Florida)

ISBN: 0-03-010081-X

Library of Congress Catalog Card Number: 96-84774

Printed in the United States of America

6 7 8 9 0 1 2 3 4 5   039   9 8 7 6 5 4 3 2 1

The Dryden Press
Harcourt Brace College Publishers

*To my parents, George and Jane Hess,*
*with love, admiration, and gratitude,*
*I dedicate this work.*

PETER HESS

*To the memory of my nephew,*
*Stephen Blaine Ross (1978–1993),*
*I dedicate this work.*

CLARK ROSS

# THE DRYDEN PRESS SERIES IN ECONOMICS

Baldani, Bradfield, and Turner
*Mathematical Economics*

Baumol and Blinder
*Economics: Principles and Policy*
Seventh Edition (Also available in micro and macro paperbacks)

Baumol, Panzar, and Willig
*Contestable Markets and the Theory of Industry Structure*
Revised Edition

Berch
*The Endless Day: The Political Economy of Women and Work*

Breit and Elzinga
*The Antitrust Casebook: Milestones in Economic Regulation*
Third Edition

Brue
*The Evolution of Economic Thought*
Fifth Edition

Demmert
*Economics: Understanding the Market Process*

Dolan and Lindsey
*Economics*
Seventh Edition (Also available in micro and macro paperbacks)

Edgmand, Moomaw, and Olson
*Economics and Contemporary Issues*
Third Edition

Gardner
*Comparative Economic Systems*
Second Edition

Glahe
*Microeconomics: Theory and Application*
Second Edition

Green
*Macroeconomics: Analysis and Applications*

Gwartney and Stroup
*Economics: Private and Public Choice*
Eighth Edition (Also available in micro and macro paperbacks)

Gwartney and Stroup
*Introduction to Economics: The Wealth and Poverty of Nations*

Heilbroner and Singer
*The Economic Transformation of America: 1600 to the Present*
Second Edition

Hess and Ross
*Economic Development: Theories, Evidence, and Policies*

Hirschey and Pappas
*Fundamentals of Managerial Economics*
Fifth Edition

Hirschey and Pappas
*Managerial Economics*
Eighth Edition

Hyman
*Public Finance: A Contemporary Application of Theory to Policy*
Fifth Edition

Kahn
*The Economic Approach to Environmental and Natural Resources*

Kaserman and Mayo
*Government and Business: The Economics of Antitrust and Regulation*

Kaufman
*The Economics of Labor Markets*
Fourth Edition

Kennett and Lieberman
*The Road to Capitalism: The Economic Transformation of Eastern Europe and the Former Soviet Union*

Kreinin
*International Economics: A Policy Approach*
Seventh Edition

Lott and Ray
*Applied Econometrics with Data Sets*

Marlow
*Public Finance: Theory and Practice*

Nicholson
*Intermediate Microeconomics and Its Application*
Seventh Edition

Nicholson
*Microeconomic Theory: Basic Principles and Extensions*
Sixth Edition

Puth
*American Economic History*
Third Edition

Ragan and Thomas
*Principles of Economics*
Second Edition (Also available in micro and macro paperbacks)

Ramanathan
*Introductory Econometrics with Applications*
Third Edition

Rukstad
*Corporate Decision Making in the World Economy: Company Case Studies*

Rukstad
*Macroeconomic Decision Making in the World Economy: Text and Cases*
Third Edition

Samuelson and Marks
*Managerial Economics*
Second Edition

Scarth
*Macroeconomics: An Introduction to Advanced Methods*
Third Edition

Stockman
*Introduction to Economics*
(Also available in micro and macro paperbacks)

Thomas
*Economics: Principles and Applications*
(Also available in micro and macro paperbacks)

Walton and Rockoff
*History of the American Economy*
Seventh Edition

Welch and Welch
*Economics: Theory and Practice*
Fifth Edition

Yarbrough and Yarbrough
*The World Economy: Trade and Finance*
Fourth Edition

# PREFACE

In 1920 the great economist, Alfred Marshall, wrote in the eighth edition of his *Principles of Economics,* "The study of the causes of poverty is the study of the causes of the degradation of a large part of mankind." His characterization of the poor: "Overworked and undertaught, weary and careworn, without quiet and without leisure, they have no chance of making the best of their mental faculties," remains true today.[1]

As we approach the twenty-first century, one fifth of the human race, more than one billion people, live in absolute poverty. On every continent, we see signs of environmental deterioration. The world's population is projected to increase 50 percent by the year 2025, with 90 percent of this growth expected to occur in the less developed countries. The world is becoming smaller. More than ever before, we are aware of the welfare of those living in other nations. Perhaps no subject in the social sciences deserves our attention more than economic development.

*Economic Development: Theories, Evidence, and Policies* is intended both for undergraduates with only economic principles as background and for graduate students in masters programs in business, public policy, or international affairs. While the emphasis is on the progress and prospects of the developing nations of Asia, Africa, the Middle East, and Latin America, we also address two related challenges: the conversion of the former socialist nations of Eastern Europe to market economies, and the generation of sustainable global development that encompasses the universal fulfillment of basic human needs and the effective stewardship of common resources and the environment.

## THE INTENTION

The ultimate objective of economic theory should be enlightened policy. Therefore, we begin with the theories of economic development. Throughout the text, we try to show not only how each theory added to our understanding of the complex process of economic development, but how the limitations of a theory and perceived shortcomings of the derived policies contributed to new theories. For example, the growth model approach of the 1950s and 1960s was followed by basic needs strategy of the 1970s. Then, in the 1980s, we saw a reemphasis on economic growth and market orientation. The "market-friendly" strategy, an assimilation of four decades of development theory and experience, has been promoted by the World Bank in the 1990s.

The theories are confronted with the evidence. Beginning with Chapter 1 and continuing throughout the text, indicators of development are presented for all countries

---

[1]Alfred Marshall, *Principles of Economics,* 8th ed., London: Macmillan, 1920, page 3 (reprinted in 1927).

grouped according to the World Bank's per capita income classification (low-income, middle-income, and high-income economies); and for the less developed countries grouped by regions (sub-Saharan Africa, Middle East and North Africa, Europe and Central Asia, South Asia, East Asia and the Pacific, and Latin America and the Caribbean). In addition, seven less developed countries are selected to highlight the diversity within income classes and regions: Ghana, Sri Lanka, Egypt, Poland, Costa Rica, Brazil, and South Korea.

A dozen case studies or country profiles, drawn from all regions of the developing world, are provided to illustrate different paths in development. We will see not only common tendencies and shared concerns, but how each country is uniquely defined by its geographical, historical, cultural, political, and economic conditions.

Moreover, to illustrate how theories are tested, the fundamentals of simple regression analysis and interpreting multiple regression equations are presented in an appendix to Chapter 1. Then, in the appendices to two other chapters, multiple regression estimates, based on cross-sections of less developed countries, are discussed. In Chapter 3, the relationship between economic growth and physical capital deepening is assessed. In Chapter 7, equations for the total fertility rate and infant mortality rate are estimated. Such empirical verification of theories is crucial for effective policy making. For instance, do family planning programs—holding constant other socioeconomic factors—have a statistically significant influence on fertility rates in less developed countries?

From the theories, and based on the evidence, policy implications are derived. What should be done to promote economic development? Many issues in economic development are unsettled, and some are controversial. We seek to provide a balanced treatment of these issues. Further, we believe that development theories and policies should be evaluated in historical context. To this end, we refer to significant events of the post-World War II era, when economic development was first recognized as a distinct discipline in economics.

In short, the organizing principle of specifying the theory, reviewing the evidence, and discussing the policy implications promotes a natural progression within, and consistency across, the chapters of the text. Our goal is to impart not only a better understanding of the phenomenon of economic development, but an appreciation for the importance of achieving sustainable development in all parts of the world.

## CHAPTER OUTLINE

We begin in Chapters 1 and 2 with the concepts and measurement of economic growth, economic development, and population growth. Common economic and demographic features of the less developed countries are illustrated.

In Part II, Theories of Economic Growth and Development, the progression of thought in economic development theory is outlined, starting in Chapters 3 and 4 with the early growth models that initially dominated the field and progressing to the more recent endogenous growth theory. In Chapter 5, we consider alternative approaches, including criticisms of mainstream development theory—from the radical (Marxist) school, E. F. Schumacher's philosophy of Buddhist economics, and Herman Daly's model of steady-state economics. These three chapters provide the theoretical core for the subsequent analyses of issues in economic development. Chapter 6 deals with the role of government and relates economic systems to development strategies.

In Part III of the text, we cover human and capital resources: theories of fertility behavior and population policy in Chapter 7; human capital formation in Chapter 8; labor markets and employment in Chapter 9; and physical capital formation in Chapter 10. Policy options are discussed: for curbing the rapid population growth that may be hindering economic development in many countries; for improving the quality of life and increasing labor productivity through investments in nutrition, health, and education; for expanding employment opportunities; and for generating the saving and investment needed to raise the physical capital-to-labor ratios and per capita incomes.

In Part IV, we study of the sectors of agriculture, natural resources, industry and services. Economic development entails the transformation of traditional, agrarian economies into diversified economies, with vibrant industrial and service sectors. In Chapter 11, the key role played by agriculture in economic development is examined. In Chapter 12 we address the natural resource-intensive sectors of mining, fishing, and forestry, as well as policies that promote sustainable development. The growth of industry and modern services is the subject of Chapter 13.

International integration is the focus of Part V, although international issues are treated throughout the text. In Chapter 14, we illustrate the basis for, and the gains from, international trade. The trends in trade liberalization are also reviewed. Balance of payments adjustment, exchange rate systems, and the external debt problems of the developing nations are covered in Chapter 15. Two of the more controversial topics in economic development, foreign direct investment and foreign aid, are examined in Chapter 16.

In Part VI, Development Paths, we apply the theories and policies of the earlier chapters by profiling three regions of the developing world. In Chapter 17 we explore the economic achievements in East Asia and the economic transitions in Eastern Europe. Chapter 18 is devoted to the special development challenges facing the region of sub-Saharan Africa. In the final chapter, we address the global concerns with militarization, environmental preservation, and the management of common resources. We review the international cooperation in these areas and offer an agenda for global development.

## ADDITIONAL FEATURES OF THE TEXT

At the end of each chapter are summaries of the main points, questions, a list of key terms, and suggested readings. The summaries, intended as concise reviews of the chapters, should serve as a useful study guide. The questions offer a mixture of analytical problems and reflection/discussion. Working through these exercises should enhance understanding of the underlying theoretical models and concepts. Answers to the numerical problems are provided at the end of the text. Also, definitions of over 250 key terms are provided in a glossary.

The suggested readings, selected in part for their accessibility to students, complement the material in the text and allow for further exploration in areas of interest. In particular, we recommend the annual *World Development Reports* of the World Bank and *Human Development Reports* of the United Nations Development Programme for lending currency and concreteness to the academic study of economic development. Accompanying the text is a recent edition of the *World Bank Atlas,* a colorful series of maps and current data on economic development, population, and the environment.

## SUPPLEMENTS

The Dryden Press will provide complimentary supplements or supplement packages to those adopters qualified under our adoption policy. Please contact your sales representative to learn how you may qualify. If as an adopter or potential user you receive supplements you do not need, please return them to your sales representative or send them to:

ATTN: Returns Department
Troy Warehouse
465 South Lincoln Drive
Troy, MO 63379

## ACKNOWLEDGMENTS

We have enjoyed writing *Economic Development: Theories, Evidence, and Policies.* Our labors have benefited from the advice and fine work of many others. We are fortunate to have good students and fine colleagues at Davidson College. We appreciate the generous and always timely assistance of Hansford Epes in software troubleshooting. We are grateful to Dennis Appleyard for his counsel and steadfast support. We thank Murray Simpson, a former student of ours, and now a fellow faculty member, for his contribution of the case studies on Brazil, Costa Rica, and Jamaica. Especially, we would like to acknowledge our friend and former chairman, Charles E. Ratliff, Jr., Kenan Professor Emeritus, who has represented all that is right and good with higher education.

The staff at The Dryden Press is top-notch. We consider it both a privilege and pleasure to work with the Dryden team. Jeanie Anirudhan and Stacey Sims, our developmental editors, and Kathryn Stewart, our project editor, have been terrific. We also acknowledge Emily Barrosse, executive editor; Linda Wooton, art director; Carlyn Hauser, production manager; and Cathy Spitzenberger, electronic publishing coordinator, for their efforts in this endeavor.

We would like to thank Dennis D. Miller, Baldwin-Wallace College; Bryan Taylor, California State University–Los Angeles; Henry Thompson, Auburn University; Amin V. Sarkar, SUNY–Fredonia; Don Wells, University of Arizona; Charles Johnston, University of Michigan at Flint; Ray Canterbery, Florida State University; Sharmila Vishwasrao, University of Kentucky; Edwin A. Sexton, Virginia Military Institute; Henrik van den Berg, University of Nebraska–Lincoln; Stephen L. Smith, Gordon College; and Rathin Basu, Ferrum College for their insightful and helpful comments.

Numerous others have contributed to our project, and although we are not able to thank each individually, we do acknowledge their efforts. Finally, we hope that the students who use this text will become motivated not only to continue their study of economic development, but to work toward the goal of global development. We welcome comments and suggestions. Our email addresses are pehess@davidson.edu and clross@davidson.edu.

Peter Hess and Clark Ross
*Davidson, North Carolina*

In addition, I would like to thank Boo, Jamie, and Joey. Everyday, I realize just how lucky I am. **PH**

# ABOUT THE AUTHORS

Peter Hess and Clark Ross are professors of economics at Davidson College and coauthors of *Principles of Economics: An Analytical Approach* (West 1993). Their collaboration on this development text reflects again their complementary teaching interests and research experiences. At Davidson, Professor Hess teaches courses in economic development, international economics, and macroeconomic theory. Professor Ross teaches courses in comparative systems, labor economics, and microeconomic theory.

A graduate of Bowdoin College (1972), Hess received his Ph.D. in economics from the University of North Carolina at Chapel Hill in 1982. He has been teaching at Davidson College since 1980, with the exception of 1986–1988 when he was a visiting schoolar at the Carolina Population Center. The author of *Population Growth and Socioeconomic Progress in Less Developed Countries* (Praeger 1988), Hess has also written journal articles on the fertility transition in developing economies and the determinants and consequences of military spending in less developed countries. Hess has traveled and studied in Sri Lanka, India, and South Korea.

A graduate of the University of Pennsylvania (1971), Ross received his Ph.D. from Boston College (1976). From 1976 to 1979, Ross worked as a research scientist for the Center for Economic Development at the University of Michigan, primarily on grain transactions in Senegal. In 1979 Ross came to Davidson College. He also served as an economist for the Organization for the Development of the Gambia River Basin from 1978 to 1985 and consulted with the United Nations Development Programme and the U.S. Agency for International Development in other parts of West Africa. In addition to his work in Africa, Professor Ross has made two professional trips to Russia.

# CONTENTS IN BRIEF

## I   INTRODUCTION   1

**Chapter 1**   Economic Development: Concepts and Measurements   3
**Chapter 2**   Population Growth   31

## II   THEORIES OF ECONOMIC GROWTH AND DEVELOPMENT   57

**Chapter 3**   The Growth Model Approach and Steady-State Equilibrium   59
**Chapter 4**   Initiating and Sustaining Economic Growth   89
**Chapter 5**   Alternative Approaches to Economic Development   117
**Chapter 6**   Economic Systems, Development Strategies, and the Role of the State   155

## III   HUMAN AND CAPITAL RESOURCES   183

**Chapter 7**   Population Policy   185
**Chapter 8**   Human Capital Formation   219
**Chapter 9**   Employment   251
**Chapter 10**   Physical Capital Formation   283

## IV   SECTORS IN DEVELOPMENT   321

**Chapter 11**   Agriculture   323
**Chapter 12**   Natural Resources and the Environment   353
**Chapter 13**   Industry and Services   387

## V   INTERNATIONAL INTEGRATION   419

**Chapter 14**   Trade and Development   421
**Chapter 15**   Balance of Payments, Exchange Rates, and External Debt   451
**Chapter 16**   Foreign Direct Investment and Foreign Aid   489

# VI DEVELOPMENT PATHS 521

**CHAPTER 17** Profiles in Development: Economic Achievement in East Asia and Economic Transition in Eastern Europe 523
**CHAPTER 18** Development Challenge: Poverty in sub-Saharan Africa 559
**CHAPTER 19** Global Development 587

GLOSSARY 611
ANSWERS TO SELECTED NUMERICAL QUESTIONS 623
CREDITS 629
INDEX 631

# CONTENTS

PREFACE

## I INTRODUCTION

**CHAPTER 1**    Economic Development: Concepts and Measurements    3
     ECONOMIC GROWTH    6
         Sources of Output Growth    6
         Gross Domestic Product and Gross National Product    7
     ECONOMIC DEVELOPMENT    8
     INDICATORS OF GROWTH AND DEVELOPMENT    9
         Classification of Nations    9
         Characteristics of Developing Economies    11
         Differences in Development    14
     APPENDIX: Testing Theory    22

**CHAPTER 2**    Population Growth    31
     COMPONENTS OF POPULATION CHANGE    32
         Indicators of Mortality    35
         Indicators of Fertility    37
     POPULATION MOMENTUM    40
         An Illustration of Population Momentum    42
     THE DEMOGRAPHIC TRANSITION    43
         The Western Experience    44
         The Demographic Transition of the LDCs    47
     CALDWELL'S NET INTERGENERATIONAL WEALTH FLOWS    49
     APPENDIX: The Growth Rate in Population    55

## II THEORIES OF ECONOMIC GROWTH AND DEVELOPMENT    57

**CHAPTER 3**    The Growth Model Approach and Steady-State Equilibrium    59
     PRODUCTION FUNCTIONS    60
         Fixed-Coefficients Production Function    60
         Production Functions with Factor Substitution    62
     HARROD-DOMAR GROWTH MODEL    64
         The "Knife-Edge" Problem    67
     THE SAVING RATE AND THE DISTRIBUTION OF INCOME    68
         Japan's Savings and Growth    69
     SOLOW'S SOLUTION TO THE KNIFE-EDGE PROBLEM: FACTOR SUBSTITUTION    71
     POLICY IMPLICATIONS OF THE EARLY GROWTH MODELS    75
     OTHER CONSTRAINTS ON GROWTH: FOREIGN EXCHANGE AND HUMAN CAPITAL    76

APPENDIX A: Numerical Example of the Harrod-Domar Growth Model   82
APPENDIX B: Economic Growth and Physical Capital Deepening   85

**CHAPTER 4   Initiating and Sustaining Economic Growth   89**

LOW-LEVEL EQUILIBRIUM TRAP   89
   Growth Rate of Physical Capital   90
   Growth Rate of Labor   91
   Escaping the Low-Level Equilibrium Trap   92

ROSTOW'S TAKE-OFF INTO SELF-SUSTAINING GROWTH   96
   Classification of Economies   97
   The Take-Off   99

LEWIS' TWO-SECTOR MODEL   101
   Growth of the Modern Sector   103
   Policy Implications of the Lewis Model   103

SUSTAINING ECONOMIC GROWTH   105
   Variable Population Growth   106
   Growth in Labor Productivity   108
   Endogenous Growth Theory   109

**CHAPTER 5   Alternative Approaches to Economic Development   117**

ECONOMIC GROWTH AND THE DISTRIBUTION OF INCOME   118

ADELMAN'S DEPAUPERIZATION   120
   Growth with Equity   121
   Agricultural Demand-Led Industrialization   122

THE BASIC NEEDS APPROACH   123
   Basic Needs Policies   123
   Implementation of the Basic Needs Approach   128

EVIDENCE ON ECONOMIC GROWTH AND INCOME INEQUALITY   130

THE RADICAL CRITIQUE   132
   The Marxian Foundation   132
   The Radical School   133

SCHUMACHER'S BUDDHIST ECONOMICS   135
   The Sarvodaya Shramadana Movement   138

DALY'S STEADY-STATE ECONOMICS   140
   Institutions for a Steady-State Economy   141

CASE STUDIES
   South Korea   146
   Sri Lanka   150

**CHAPTER 6   Economic Systems, Development Strategies, and the Role of the State   155**

ECONOMIC SYSTEMS AND DEVELOPMENT STRATEGIES   156
   Laissez-faire Capitalism   156
   Managed or Authoritarian Capitalism   158
   Centralized Socialism   160

POSSIBLE ROLES FOR GOVERNMENT   162
   Resource Allocation   162
   Economic Regulation   163
   Income Maintenance and Redistribution   166
   Macroeconomic Stability   167
   Policy Coordination   168

THE CHOICE OF AN ECONOMIC SYSTEM   169

CASE STUDIES

China 174
Ghana 177
Brazil 179

# III  HUMAN AND CAPITAL RESOURCES  183

**CHAPTER 7**  Population Policy  185

POTENTIAL CONSEQUENCES OF RAPID POPULATION GROWTH IN LESS DEVELOPED COUNTRIES  186
   Historical Setting  186
   The Cycle of Poverty and Rapid Population Growth  187

A RANGE OF PERSPECTIVES ON POPULATION GROWTH AND ECONOMIC DEVELOPMENT  190

THE DEMAND FOR CHILDREN  193
   Determinants of the Demand for Children  198

EASTERLIN'S SUPPLY-DEMAND SYNTHESIS  201
   Evidence from sub-Saharan Africa on Contraceptive Use  204

THE SELECTION OF POPULATION POLICIES  205
   Range of Policies  205
   Birth Control in China  208

APPENDIX: Determinants of Fertility: Cross-Country Evidence  214

**CHAPTER 8**  Human Capital Formation  219

HUMAN CAPITAL FORMATION AND ECONOMIC DEVELOPMENT  220

NUTRITION  222
   The Importance of Nutrition  222
   Nutrition Policy  224

HEALTH  227
   Health Conditions in the Less Developed Countries  227
   Health-Care Policy  231

EDUCATION  238
   Current Educational Efforts in the Low-Income Countries  239
   Education as a Human Capital Investment  239
   Educational Policy Reform  245

**CHAPTER 9**  Employment  251

THE THEORY OF THE COMPETITIVE LABOR MARKET  252
   The Demand for Labor  252
   Labor Supply  254
   Labor-Market Equilibrium  255

LABOR MARKETS IN DEVELOPING COUNTRIES  256
   Rural Labor Markets  256
   Urban Informal Labor Markets  259
   Modern-Sector Employment  260

UNEMPLOYMENT AND UNDEREMPLOYMENT  261
   Unemployment Defined  261
   Macroeconomic Analysis of Unemployment  262
   Microeconomic Explanations of Unemployment  266

MIGRATION  268
   Economic Migration  268
   Political Migration  272

POLICIES TO PROMOTE EMPLOYMENT  272
    Labor-Market Policy  273
    Education  275
    Macroeconomic Policy  275

CASE STUDY
    Egypt  278

**CHAPTER 10** Physical Capital Formation  283

MONEY AND FINANCIAL CAPITAL  284
    Functions of Money  284

THE SAVING RATE AND ECONOMIC GROWTH  286
    Incremental Capital–Output Ratios  287

SOURCES OF FUNDS FOR DOMESTIC INVESTMENT  288
    Basic Macroeconomic Identity  288
    Foreign Saving  291
    Gross Domestic Investment and Growth in National Output  291

FINANCIAL INTERMEDIATION  294
    Financing Government Budget Deficits  295
    Efficiencies in Financial Intermediation  296
    Interest Rate Ceilings  298
    Informal Credit Markets  299
    Effects of Inflation on the Market for Loanable Funds  300

CONSTRAINTS ON DOMESTIC SAVING IN LESS DEVELOPED COUNTRIES  302
    Household Saving  302
    Business Saving  305
    Government or Public Saving  306

NET PRESENT VALUE CRITERION FOR DEVELOPMENT PROJECTS  307

IMPROVING POPULAR ACCESS TO CREDIT  311

MEASURES TO PROMOTE DOMESTIC INVESTMENT  313

# IV  SECTORS IN DEVELOPMENT  321

**CHAPTER 11** Agriculture  323

IMPORTANCE OF AGRICULTURE  324

THE TRANSFORMATION OF THE AGRICULTURAL SECTOR  326

CHARACTERISTICS OF AGRICULTURE IN THE LDCS  327
    Type and Size of Farms  327
    The Seasonality and Risk of Agriculture  330
    Long-Run Trend in the Agricultural Terms of Trade  332
    The Income-Inelasticity of Food  334

CONSTRAINTS TO AGRICULTURAL DEVELOPMENT  336
    Access to Fertile Land  336
    Agricultural Pricing Policy  337
    Availability of Inputs and Credit  340

POLICY REFORM  341
    Clear Policy Objectives  342
    Land Access  342
    Increasing the Profitability of Agriculture  343

CASE STUDY

Costa Rica   349

**CHAPTER 12**   Natural Resources and the Environment   353

NATURAL RESOURCES AND ECONOMIC GROWTH   354
Resource Scarcity   355
Agriculture and Other Natural Resource-Intensive Sectors   357
Exports of Natural Resource-Intensive Products   360
Dutch Disease: A Development Distortion   363

SUSTAINABLE DEVELOPMENT   369
Market Failures and Government Regulation   369
Diversity in Resource Endowment and Utilization   375
Policies for Sustainable Development   377

CASE STUDY
Jamaica   383

**CHAPTER 13**   Industry and Services   387

THE IMPORTANCE OF INDUSTRY AND SERVICES   388
The Industrial Sector   388
The Service Sector   390
Public Production of Industry and Services   391

SECTORAL LINKAGES WITHIN AN ECONOMY   392
An Input-Output Model   392

GLOBAL INDUSTRIAL INTEGRATION   398
Free Trade   398
Import Substitution   399
An Evaluation of Import Substitution   405

POLICY ISSUES CONCERNING INDUSTRY   407
Regulation of Industry   407
Investment in Economic Infrastructure   409

CASE STUDY
India   416

# V   INTERNATIONAL INTEGRATION   419

**CHAPTER 14**   Trade and Development   421

ILLUSTRATION OF THE GAINS FROM TRADE   422
International Factor Mobility   425
The International Terms of Trade and the Gains from Trade   427
General Principles of Trade   430
The Product Cycle Theory of Trade   433
Recent Experience in Trade   434
Export Expansion   436
Implementing the Trade Strategy   442
GATT and Trade Liberalization   443

**CHAPTER 15**   Balance of Payments, Exchange Rates, and External Debt   451

BALANCE OF PAYMENTS ACCOUNT   451
Current Account   452
Capital Account   454
Official Settlements Account   456

RELATIONSHIP BETWEEN THE BALANCE OF PAYMENTS
AND EXCHANGE RATE   458

The Demand for Foreign Exchange   459
The Supply of Foreign Exchange   460

DETERMINING THE EQUILIBRIUM EXCHANGE RATE   461
Flexible Exchange Rates   462
Fixed Exchange Rates   462
Fixed versus Flexible Exchange Rates   466
Hybrid Exchange Rate Systems   469
Present Exchange Rate Arrangements   469
Choosing an Exchange Rate System   471

THE EXTERNAL DEBT PROBLEM   473
Brief History of Less Developed Country Debt   473
The Debt Crisis and Aftermath   476
Resolving the Debt Problem   482

**Chapter 16**  Foreign Direct Investment and Foreign Aid   489

FOREIGN DIRECT INVESTMENT   490
Transnational Corporations   492
Foreign Direct Investment and the Less Developed Countries   494

FOREIGN AID   498
The Case for Foreign Aid   499
The Case Against Aid   501
A Brief History of Official Development Assistance (ODA)   505
Multilateral Aid Agencies   510
Assessing the Effectiveness of Official Development Assistance   514
Reforms in Foreign Aid   515

# VI  DEVELOPMENT PATHS   521

**Chapter 17**  Profiles in Development: Economic Achievement in East Asia and Economic Transition in Eastern Europe   523

MARKET-FRIENDLY STRATEGY OF DEVELOPMENT   523
Stable Macroeconomy   524
Competitive Domestic Markets   524
Investments in Human Capital   526
International Integration   528
Implementing the Market-Friendly Strategy of Development   529
Concerns with the Market-Friendly Strategy   531

EAST ASIAN ECONOMIES: RAPID GROWTH WITH EQUITY   532
Keys to Economic Success in East Asia   534
Reservations about the East Asian Developments   538

ECONOMIC TRANSITION OF THE FORMER SOCIALIST STATES   538
Centralized Socialism   539
The Economics of Transition   541
Country Studies   548

**Chapter 18**  Development Challenge: Poverty in sub-Saharan Africa   559

FROM COLONIZATION TO ECONOMIC STAGNATION   561
Colonization   561
The Hopeful Decade of the 1960s   563
Economic Stagnation: 1970s to the Present   565

THE ECONOMIC PROBLEMS OF AFRICA   566
Failures of the African Governments and the Donor Community   566

Excessive Population Growth   569
Poor Agricultural Performance   571
Basic Needs: Education and Health Care   575
Lack of Economic Diversity in Africa   576

THE AFRICAN DEVELOPMENT AGENDA   577
Structural Adjustment   578
More Radical Approaches   582

**CHAPTER 19** Global Development   587

DEFINING GLOBAL DEVELOPMENT   588

MILITARY SPENDING   590
Recent Trends   590

NATURAL RESOURCES AND THE ENVIRONMENT   596

INTERNATIONAL COOPERATION   600
Security Agreements   601
Agreements on Natural Resources and the Environment   602

AN AGENDA FOR GLOBAL DEVELOPMENT   603
Regional Groups   604
Trade   604
Finance   605
Economic Assistance   605
The Environment   606
Security   606
Reforming the International Order   607

**GLOSSARY**   611
**ANSWERS TO SELECTED NUMERICAL QUESTIONS**   623
**CREDITS**   629
**INDEX**   631

# PART I

# INTRODUCTION

# CHAPTER 1

# ECONOMIC DEVELOPMENT: CONCEPTS AND MEASUREMENTS

The achievement of sustained and equitable development remains the single greatest challenge facing the human race. Despite good progress over the past generation, more than 1 billion people still live in acute poverty and suffer grossly inadequate access to the resources—education, health services, infrastructure, land and credit—required to give them a chance for a better life.[1]

The opening of the final decade of the twentieth century brought reason for optimism. With the end of the Cold War, superpower confrontation gave way to cooperation. With the Start II Treaty, the United States and Russia set in motion a two-thirds reduction in their nuclear arsenals. More than 120 nations had signed an international treaty banning chemical weapons. Demilitarization raised anticipation for a peace dividend—the release of resources for improving standards of living. Many nations turned toward more market-oriented economies and more democratic systems. A more cohesive United Nations emerged. The Uruguay Round of the General Agreement on Tariffs and Trade (GATT) finally concluded with the promise of trade liberalization and enhanced growth. The world population growth rate was declining. The international debt crisis had been defused. The Earth Summit in Rio de Janeiro signalled, at the very least, an increased awareness of the environment and the desirability of policies that promoted "sustainable development," meaning development that would meet the needs of the present generation without compromising the needs of future generations.[2]

Notwithstanding these encouraging signs, reasons existed for continuing concern. Even after the dramatic reductions of Start II, the United States and Russia would still possess over 6,000 nuclear warheads. Indeed, with the dissolution of the Soviet Union, the nuclear weapons were distributed across several independent republics. Other

---

[1]World Bank, *World Development Report 1992,* New York: Oxford University Press, 1992, page 1.
[2]Ibid., page 8.

nations seek to join the nuclear club, even as increasingly potent conventional weapons proliferate. While declining from the peak levels of the early 1980s, 3.4 percent of the collective national incomes of the less developed countries (LDCs) in 1990 went for military expenditures—more than half again as much as these governments spent on education and health.[3] Ethnic conflict within nations has replaced the ideological struggle between East and West as a major cause of turmoil.

Effective economic reforms with tangible improvements in the standards of living prove elusive in most of the nations of Eastern Europe and the former Soviet Union. The possibility that some of these states could slip back toward totalitarianism has to be recognized. With more than one-fifth of the human race living in absolute poverty, clearly the benefits of the impressive economic growth and increased international trade since World War II have not been equally shared. In brief, the developed economies of the United States, Canada, Japan, Australia, New Zealand, and the nations of Western Europe, while having only 15 percent of the world population, account for nearly 80 percent of the global gross domestic products and 70 percent of merchandise exports. See Figure 1.1.[4]

While the global population growth rate is declining, in absolute numbers the annual increases are enormous. Over 90 million people, more than the combined populations of France and Canada, are being added each year. Under even the most optimistic scenarios, the world population would still increase by 50 percent over the next few decades—from 5.5 billion in 1993 to over 8 billion. Ninety percent of this increase is expected to occur in the less developed countries, where rapid population growth hinders economic development, perpetuates poverty, and threatens the natural resource base and environment.

Signs of global environmental stress are evident.

> [Since 1970] ... the world has lost nearly 200 million hectares of tree cover, an area roughly the size of the United States east of the Mississippi River. Deserts expanded by some 120 million hectares, claiming more land than is currently planted to crops in China. Thousands of plant and animal species with which we shared the planet in 1970 no longer exist ...
>
> During the eighties the amount of carbon pumped into the atmosphere from the burning of fossil fuels climbed to a new high, reaching nearly 6 billion tons in 1990 ... the eighties [were] the warmest decade since record-keeping began more than a century ago.[5]

The concerns with population pressure, environmental thresholds, and economic stagnation are not new. Nearly two centuries ago Thomas Malthus warned that, unless checked, population growth would ultimately overwhelm the food supply, imposing a

---

[3]United Nations Development Programme, *Human Development Report 1993*, New York: Oxford University Press, 1993, Table 2.

[4]These figures are the estimated shares in the world totals in 1993 for the 19 high-income economies of the Organization of Economic Cooperation and Development (OECD) with populations of 1 million or more: Australia, Austria, Belgium, Canada, Denmark, Finland, France, Germany, Ireland, Italy, Japan, Netherlands, New Zealand, Norway, Spain, Sweden, Switzerland, United Kingdom, and United States. For the United States alone, the shares are approximately 5 percent of the population, 27 percent of the output, and 13 percent of the merchandise exports. The calculations are from data in World Bank, *World Development Report 1995*, New York: Oxford University Press, 1995, Tables 1, 3, and 13.

[5]Lester Brown, "The New World Order," in *State of the World 1991*, Worldwatch Institute, New York: W. W. Norton, 1991, pages 3 and 8.

## FIGURE 1.1   SHARES IN WORLD POPULATION, OUTPUT, AND MERCHANDISE EXPORTS, 1993

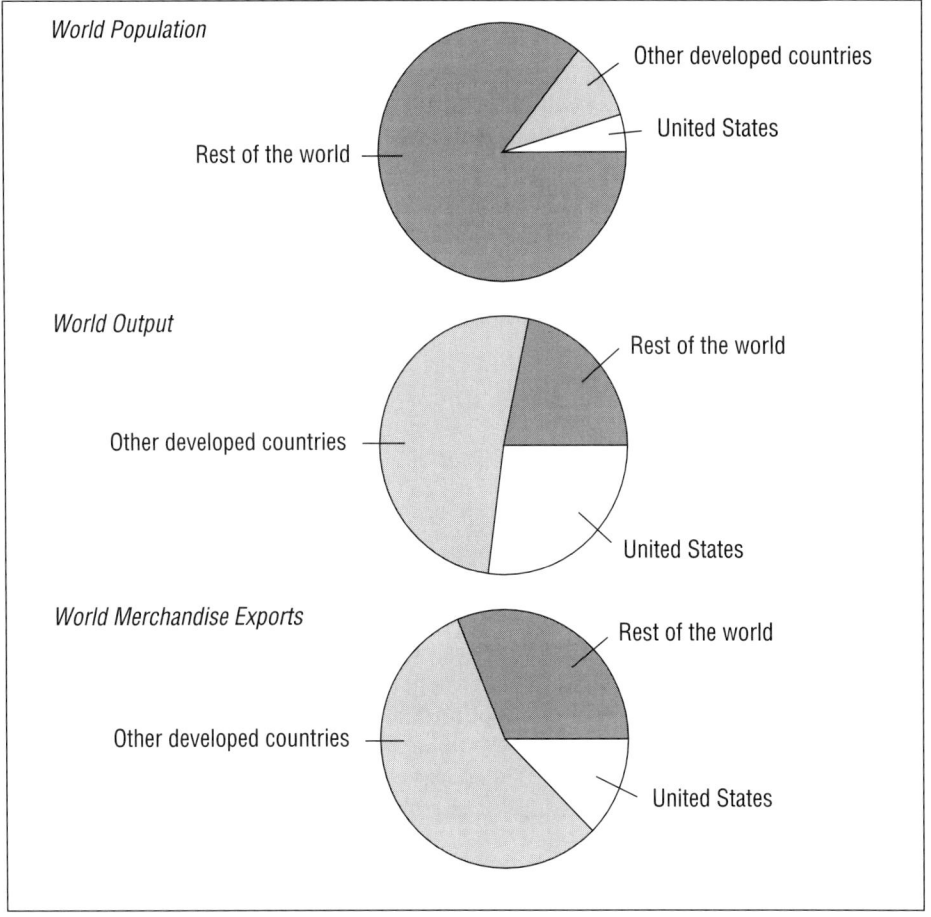

FROM World Bank, *World Development Report 1995*, New York: Oxford University Press, 1995, Tables 1, 3, and 13.

subsistence level of living on the human race. The Malthusian specter has yet to come to pass, however. Currently world food supplies are more than sufficient to ensure adequate diets for all. The malnutrition and hunger present today reflect not an inability to produce food, but economic inequality and political upheaval. While poverty remains the major cause of chronic malnutrition, the World Bank observes that military conflict has been "far and away the most important cause of famine in developing countries in recent years."[6]

In this text we will focus on the contemporary developing nations of Africa, the Middle East, Asia and the Pacific, and Latin America and the Caribbean as they strive to achieve sustainable development. These regions account for three-fourths of the

---

[6]World Bank, *World Development Report 1991*, New York: Oxford University Press, 1991, page 2.

world population. While much of the discussion will be relevant for the former socialist states of Eastern Europe and the Soviet Union, we will also address the specific circumstances these countries face in their transitions to more market-oriented economies.

In this first chapter we begin by drawing the distinction between economic growth and development. Then, to get our bearings and to appreciate better the concept of "less developed," we present summary statistics on growth and development. It will become evident that, although we will note common characteristics and patterns of development, no stereotypical "less developed country" exists. Each country is defined by a unique blend of geographical, historical, cultural, political, and economic conditions. In the appendix to the chapter we illustrate a basic statistical technique used in the text to evaluate hypotheses about economic development.

## ECONOMIC GROWTH

Although related and sometimes used interchangeably, economic growth and economic development are distinct phenomena. **Economic growth** refers to quantitative change and is usually measured as increases in per capita output or income.

Recall from economic principles the concept of a **production possibilities boundary (PPB),** a curve that represents the combinations of outputs of final goods and services that could be produced over a given period of time in an economy using all of the available resources fully and efficiently. Expansion of a PPB, indicating output growth, results from increases in the quantity and quality of the available resources and technological progress. If the production of output increases faster than population, then output per capita rises and economic growth occurs.

### SOURCES OF OUTPUT GROWTH

Taking the nation as the basic unit of analysis and national output as the measure of interest, we can identify the sources of aggregate output growth. To begin, there are three primary factors of production: human resources (labor), human-made resources (physical capital), and natural resources.

The input of **physical labor** refers to the employed labor force. The size of the labor force is directly related to the size of the population and the labor force participation rates (the percentage of the population working or actively seeking employment). The demand for labor ultimately determines the percentage of the labor force employed. Investments in human capital such as education, health care, and nutrition increase the average quality of labor.

Different types of labor exist. One especially important type, the entrepreneur, should be noted. An **entrepreneur** is an individual willing and able to organize factors of production. Essential to any dynamic economy, entrepreneurs seek out profitable opportunities to produce output.

The **physical capital stock** for the economy comprises the plant, equipment, and machinery; the residential structures and other buildings; and the economic infrastructure of the transportation and communication networks in the nation. Increases in the capital stock result from investment in the production of capital goods, that is, those goods intended not for present consumption but for the production of other goods and services. Advances in technology are often embodied in new capital goods (for example, more energy-efficient machinery and more powerful computers), and so tend to increase the quality of capital.

**Natural resources** are the land, forests, minerals, energy sources, lakes, oceans, and waterways available for use in production. All nations are endowed with natural resources, the utilization of which will depend, in part, on the efforts required to recover such resources. The quality of the natural resources encompasses the fertility of the land, health of the forests, richness of the mineral deposits, and the inherent productivity of the water resources. Pollution and poor conservation practices can reduce the quality of the natural resource base.

**Technology** is represented by the stock of knowledge useful for the production of goods and services. Technological progress through inventions and innovations in technique allows greater output to be produced from a given set of inputs.

Increases in **total factor productivity** (or gains in output not directly attributable to higher levels of inputs) can occur with technological progress, improvements in the quality of the inputs, and through increasing returns to scale and economies of scale. **Increasing returns to scale** are the efficiencies gained in production when a proportionate increase in all inputs results in a more than proportionate increase in output. **Economies of scale,** a reduction in the unit costs of production achieved with greater volumes of output, contribute to economic growth. In the isolated, small markets of traditional economies, individuals are more self-sufficient, and the standard of living tends to be lower. With increases in population and consumer demand and improvements in transportation that widen the extent of the market, specialization and the division of labor become economical.[7] Individuals specialize in occupations (e.g., brain surgery, auto mechanics, teaching, and engineering) and become more proficient as they learn and practice their skills. Large-scale production also makes feasible the division of labor whereby production is broken into small stages (such as workstations on the assembly line and suppliers of specialized component parts). Such division increases labor productivities and encourages the substitution of high-speed machinery. Output increases and products become more standardized.

In sum, population growth, to be addressed in Chapter 2, can increase the potential supply of labor. Increases in labor, along with increases in the physical capital and natural resources available, technological progress, increasing returns to scale, and economies of scale generate output growth. When output increases faster than population, economic growth occurs.

## GROSS DOMESTIC PRODUCT AND GROSS NATIONAL PRODUCT

The most widely used measure of national output is **Gross Domestic Product (GDP),** defined as the market value of the final goods and services produced in an economy during a year. A related measure is **Gross National Product (GNP),** which is the market value of the final goods and services produced by residents of a nation during a year. Residents of a nation are the individuals, businesses, institutions, and

---

[7]Note the distinction between *increasing returns to scale*, where a given percentage increase in all inputs produces a greater percentage increase in output, and *economies of scale*, where the expansion of output reduces the unit costs of production. With returns to scale, the relative factor proportions remain constant. In contrast, with economies of scale, capital may be substituted for labor if the use of high-speed automated machinery and equipment is warranted with increases in the volume of production.

government agencies for whom the nation is legal domicile. GDP equals GNP plus **net factor payments,** or the payments for the services of foreign labor and capital used in the production of domestic output less the receipts by residents of the nation for the services of labor and capital used to produce foreign output.

For numerous developing countries, a significant source of national income (and foreign exchange) is the remittance of labor income from workers abroad. Thus, their GNPs tend to exceed their GDPs. For example, a Mexican migrant working in Texas would contribute to the Gross Domestic Product of the United States and the Gross National Product of Mexico. Conversely, the interest earned by a United States resident on bonds issued by a Mexican corporation would contribute to the GNP of the United States and the GDP of Mexico.

For purposes of employment and the productive capacity of an economy, Gross Domestic Product is a better measure of national output. The percentage change in per capita GDP is an appropriate indicator of economic growth. For purposes of the income earned and purchasing power of the residents of a nation, Gross National Product is the preferred aggregate measure. The level of per capita GNP is often used as an indicator of economic development and the average standard of living in a nation; however, as we will discuss below, such an interpretation is not always appropriate.

## ECONOMIC DEVELOPMENT

Economic development is a more difficult concept to define and measure than economic growth. **Economic development** has a qualitative dimension; entails structural change; and encompasses the reduction of poverty and widespread gains in nutrition, health, education, and the standard of living. Economic development also involves the transformation of poor, stagnant, primarily agrarian economies into diversified, urban-based economies capable of sustained growth. In short, economic development implies a diffusion of economic growth and an expansion of economic opportunities.

It is possible to have growth without much development—a skewed growth where the gains in income are highly concentrated and economic mobility is very limited. It is unlikely, however, that significant economic development will occur without, at least, moderate economic growth. In other words, economic growth may be a necessary, but not a sufficient, condition for economic development.

While a conventional measure of growth exists—the percentage change in per capita output—numerous indicators of development have been suggested. In the next section we will discuss several of these statistical measures. Before doing so, we make an observation: although we focus on economic development in this text, we should not forget other dimensions necessary to the quality of life. One is political freedom, the enjoyment of basic civil rights and the opportunity to participate fully in the political process. Another is security from harm, not just in terms of national security, but security from violence and personal injury. A third is the freedom to practice one's religion or beliefs. Fourth, the enjoyment of leisure and the absence of unhealthy stress contribute to the quality of life. Last, there is an environmental dimension, crystallized in the concept of sustainable development and manifested by the safeguarding of the environment, the conservation of resources, and the preservation of species.

# INDICATORS OF GROWTH AND DEVELOPMENT

The presentation of statistics on growth and development needs to be prefaced with a note of caution. Aggregate data, especially at the national level for the less developed countries, have varying degrees of reliability. Many developing nations, facing severe budget constraints, cannot afford the comprehensive surveys and data collection necessary to compile accurate aggregate statistics. Therefore, international agencies, like the World Bank, often must supplement the reported national statistics.

For international comparisons the difficulties are compounded. Countries may have different definitions for key measures (e.g., unemployment, literacy, "urban" versus "rural"). The level and composition of government expenditures may be considered politically or strategically sensitive and so not reported with accuracy. Both GDP and GNP measure market activity and, for the less developed countries, a comparatively large percentage of economic activity may not enter the formal market (e.g., subsistence farming and barter activity) and thus go unrecorded. Converting data based on national currencies into a common currency like the U.S. dollar often poses a problem, since the official exchange values of currencies may not reflect the relative purchasing powers of the currencies. In this text we rely largely, although not exclusively, on the most recent data published by the World Bank in the annual *World Development Reports*, which may be the best source of comparable cross-country economic and demographic data readily accessible. Although the World Bank goes to considerable lengths to ensure accuracy, the data presented should be regarded as approximations, not as precise magnitudes. Furthermore, due to the time involved in collecting and processing the data, lags of two or more years in the statistics published are common. This means, for example, that the international data published in 1995 usually are for the years 1993 or earlier. Nevertheless, statistics on the economy and population, albeit based on incomplete data, are important, not only for measuring socioeconomic progress over time, but for guiding policy.

## CLASSIFICATION OF NATIONS

Notwithstanding the uniqueness of each country, it has been common practice to delineate groups of nations according to some shared characteristic. In terms of economic achievement, the most basic split is between the **developed countries (DCs)** and **less developed countries (LDCs).** We hasten to add that the terms "developed" and "less developed" refer only to relative economic progress. No social or cultural connotations should be inferred. Indeed, many of the early great civilizations were centered in what are now called "less developed countries."

A related division is intended by the labels **North** and **South,** since most of the developed countries are located in the northern hemisphere, while many of the LDCs are in the southern hemisphere. While "North" and "South" may be more colorful and less value-laden, many exceptions are found. For example, the developed countries of Australia and New Zealand are south of the equator, while the LDCs in Asia, the Middle East, the upper half of Africa, and Central America are above the equator.

## TABLE 1.1  SELECTED STATISTICS ON ECONOMIC GROWTH AND DEVELOPMENT: COUNTRIES CLASSIFIED BY INCOME GROUP

|  | LOW-INCOME ECONOMIES | | | MIDDLE-INCOME ECONOMIES | HIGH-INCOME ECONOMIES | WORLD |
|---|---|---|---|---|---|---|
|  | CHINA | INDIA | OTHER |  |  |  |
| Population—1993 (millions) | 1178 | 898 | 1016 | 1596 | 812 | 5502 |
| Population growth rate (average annual)—1980–1993 | 1.4% | 2.0% | 2.5% | 1.7% | .6% | 1.7% |
| GNP per capita—1993 | $490 | $300 | $300 | $2480 | $23,090 | $4420 |
| GNP per capita growth rate (average annual)—1980–1993 | 8.2% | 3.0% | .1% | .2% | 2.2% | 1.2% |
| Infant mortality rate—1993 | 30 | 80 | 89 | 39 | 7 | 48 |
| Female secondary school enrollment rate—1992 | 45% | 32% | 21% | ... | ... | ... |
| % of Population Urban—1993 | 29% | 26% | 27% | 60% | 78% | 44% |

NOTES: These statistics are based on weighted averages for the countries in the designated income groups. The weights are population shares. The per capita income groups set by the World Bank for 1993 are low-income ($695 or less); middle-income ($696 to $8625); and high-income ($8626 or more). Lack of data is indicated by ...

The *High-Income Economies* include the OECD (Organization for Economic Cooperation and Development) nations of Australia, Austria, Belgium, Canada, Denmark, Finland, France, Germany, Iceland, Ireland, Italy, Japan, Luxembourg, Netherlands, New Zealand, Norway, Spain, Sweden, Switzerland, United Kingdom, and United States; and the developing nations of Israel, Hong Kong, Kuwait, Singapore, and the United Arab Emirates. Greece, Mexico, Portugal, and Turkey are OECD members, but are included with the *Middle-Income Economies*. Also included with the *Middle-Income Economies* are the republics of the former Soviet Union.

The *Infant Mortality Rate* is the number of infants who die before reaching one year of age per thousand live births in a given year.

The *Female Secondary School Enrollment Rate* is the ratio of females enrolled in secondary school to the female population of secondary school–age (generally 12 to 17 years of age).

FROM World Bank, *World Development Report 1995*, New York: Oxford University Press, 1995, Tables 1, 25, 27, 28, 31.

Another designation has been in terms of "worlds." The **First World** refers to the industrial market economies of the United States, Canada, Western Europe, Japan, Australia, and New Zealand, or the high-income member countries of the Organization for Economic Cooperation and Development (OECD). The developing economies of Asia, Africa, the Middle East, and Latin America make up the **Third World.**

The **Second World** was used to denote the nonmarket economies of Eastern Europe and the Soviet Union. With the breakdown of communism, the dissolution of the Soviet Union, and the conversion of the former socialist economies of Eastern Europe, the label "Second World" has become less pertinent.

Sometimes the term **Fourth World** has been applied to the least developed economies or the poorest economies, primarily in, but not restricted to, sub-Saharan Africa and South Asia. To distinguish those developing countries that have been more successful in generating economic growth and development, the term **Newly Industrializing Countries (NICs)** was coined. The East Asian nations of South Korea, Hong Kong, Singapore, and Taiwan are the leading NICs. Malaysia, Thailand, and the Latin American nations of Brazil and Mexico have also been included in the NICs by some observers.

The World Bank classifies nations on the basis of per capita income. **Low-income, middle-income,** and **high-income economies** are the primary categories. In this text we use developed countries (DCs), advanced economies, and high-income economies interchangeably to refer to the group of nations of the so-called "First World." Less developed countries (LDCs), developing economies, and low- and middle-income economies will be used to designate all other nations unless otherwise indicated. We also find it useful to group the LDCs by region and speak of sub-Saharan Africa, the Middle East and North Africa, Europe and Central Asia, South Asia, East Asia and the Pacific, and Latin America and the Caribbean.

We begin with the World Bank income classifications. See Table 1.1 for summary statistics and the per capita income ranges. China and India are separated from the other low-income economies, since with over 21 percent and 16 percent of the total world population, respectively, these two nations dominate any summary statistics weighted by population shares.

China and, to a lesser extent, India have been highly successful in generating economic growth over the last decade—this in marked contrast to many of the other developing countries. In fact, for the other low-income and the middle-income economies, growth was minimal: average annual increases of .1 percent and .2 percent respectively in per capita GNPs over the period 1980 to 1993. To explore further, refer to Table 1.2 on page 13, where summary measures for the LDCs based on geographical region are presented. The nations of Asia, particularly East Asia, have achieved impressive growth rates. On average, though, the developing nations in sub-Saharan Africa, the Middle East and North Africa, Europe and Central Asia, and Latin America and the Caribbean experienced declines in per capita income. Some observers have labelled the 1980s as a "lost decade of development," in recognition of the missed opportunities—even real slippage—for many nations in promoting economic development.

## CHARACTERISTICS OF DEVELOPING ECONOMIES

We observe, in general, an inverse relationship between population growth and per capita income. That is, often the highest rates of population growth are found in the poorest nations. Notable exceptions are China and, to a lesser degree, India, where birth-control programs have moderated population growth.

In truth, per capita GNP is not always an accurate measure of the level of economic development or the average standard of living. Recall that Gross National Product measures the income generated by residents of a nation in the production of final goods and services. Aside from the inevitable errors in measuring national incomes and populations and the problems with conversion to a common currency, per capita GNP is an aggregate statistic that does not control for differences in the distribution of income or the composition of expenditures across countries. For example, if the distribution of income were highly concentrated or very unequal, then a nation with a high per capita

GNP might also have a large percentage of the population living in poverty.[8] Or, if a nation allocated a large percentage of income toward military expenditures, then per capita GNP might overstate the average level of personal consumption. Differences in the cost of living across nations will also affect consumer welfare for any given per capita income. And, as suggested earlier, other dimensions important to the quality of life are not captured by per capita income.

One widely used indicator of development is the **infant mortality rate (IMR),** or the number of infants who die before reaching one year of age per thousand live births. Unlike the statistic of per capita income, in which the weights individuals receive in the calculation are directly proportional to their incomes (for example, an individual with an annual income of $1 million would have a weight 5000 times that of an individual with an income of $200), the infant mortality rate is a very egalitarian measure (every infant death receives an equal weight). The IMR seems to be sensitive to the level and distribution of per capita income; popular access to health care; and the general sanitary conditions, including access to clean water, treatment of sewage, and disposal of wastes.

For the least developed economies (Fourth World), infant mortality rates in excess of 100 are still common, meaning that one out of every 10 infants dies before reaching his or her first birthday. With economic development the IMR declines. For the developed countries, represented in Table 1.1 by the high-income economies, infant mortality rates are under 10 (per thousand live births). In 1993 Japan recorded the lowest IMR of 4 (per thousand).

Another indicator of economic development, one that captures the status of women, is the **female secondary school enrollment rate.** Promoting the socioeconomic mobility of young women through education may not only boost labor productivity, but can be a key to reducing the high birth rates found in many of the LDCs. For the low-income economies, frequently less than one-fourth of the eligible females are enrolled in secondary school. For the developed countries, female secondary school enrollment rates are usually in excess of 85 percent.

Structural change, an integral component of the economic development process, involves shifts in population and resources from rural areas and agriculture to urban centers and industry. In low-income economies, three-fourths of the populations can still be found in rural areas, despite massive rural-to-urban migrations that have overwhelmed the capacities of many cities to absorb the population increases.

Turning to Table 1.2, we can see significant regional differences in economic development. The sub-Saharan African and South Asian regions (the latter dominated by India) lag well behind in infant mortality and female secondary school enrollment. Despite much lower average incomes, the success of the East Asian and Pacific region

---

[8]To illustrate this possibility, consider two populations, A and B, with five individuals in each. The incomes of the individuals are listed below.

| POPULATION A | | POPULATION B | |
|---|---|---|---|
| INDIVIDUAL | INCOME | INDIVIDUAL | INCOME |
| 1A | $ 100 | 1B | $ 200 |
| 2A | $ 200 | 2B | $ 400 |
| 3A | $ 500 | 3B | $ 600 |
| 4A | $1200 | 4B | $ 800 |
| 5A | $3000 | 5B | $1000 |
| Per Capita Income | $1000 | Per Capita Income | $ 600 |

If the cost of living were the same for both populations and the poverty level were $300, then despite a higher per capita income, the poverty rate is twice as high in Population A (40 percent) as in Population B (20 percent).

| TABLE 1.2 | SELECTED STATISTICS ON ECONOMIC GROWTH AND DEVELOPMENT: THE LESS DEVELOPED COUNTRIES BY REGION | | | | | |
|---|---|---|---|---|---|---|
| | SUB-SAHARAN AFRICA | MIDDLE EAST & N. AFRICA | EUROPE & CENTRAL ASIA | SOUTH ASIA | EAST ASIA & PACIFIC | LATIN AMERICA & THE CARIBBEAN |
| Population—1993 (millions) | 559 | 263 | 495 | 1194 | 1714 | 466 |
| Population growth rate (average annual)—1980–1993 | 2.9% | 3.0% | .8% | 2.1% | 1.5% | 2.0% |
| GNP per capita—1993 | $520 | ... | $2450 | $310 | $820 | $2950 |
| GNP per capita growth rate (average annual)—1980–1993 | −.8% | −2.4% | −.3% | 3.0% | 6.4% | −.1% |
| Infant mortality rate—1993 | 93 | 52 | 25 | 84 | 36 | 43 |
| Female secondary school enrollment rate—1992 | 16% | 51% | ... | 29% | 46% | 54% |
| % of Population Urban—1993 | 30% | 55% | 65% | 26% | 31% | 71% |

NOTES: These statistics are based on weighted averages for the countries in the designated regions. The weights are population shares. Lack of data is indicated by ...

*Sub-Saharan Africa* comprises all African countries south of the Sahara.

*Middle East & North Africa* comprises the low- and middle-income economies of Algeria, Bahrain, Egypt, Iran, Iraq, Jordan, Lebanon, Libya, Morocco, Oman, Saudi Arabia, Syrian Arab Republic, Tunisia, and Republic of Yemen.

*Europe & Central Asia* comprises the middle-income economies of Albania, Bulgaria, Czech Republic, Gibraltar, Greece, Hungary, Isle of Man, Malta, Poland, Portugal, Romania, Slovak Republic, Turkey, former Yugoslavia, and the newly independent economies of the former Soviet Union.

*South Asia* comprises Afghanistan, Bangladesh, Bhutan, India, Maldives, Nepal, Pakistan, and Sri Lanka.

*East Asia & the Pacific* comprises all the low- and middle-income economies of East and Southeast Asia and the Pacific, including China.

*Latin America & the Caribbean* comprises all American and Caribbean economies south of the United States.

FROM World Bank, *World Development Report 1995*, New York: Oxford University, 1995, Tables 1, 25, 27, 28, 31.

(dominated by China) in human capital formation is comparable to the Latin American and Caribbean, and the Middle East and North African regions. The middle-income countries of Europe and Central Asia (including the former socialist states of Eastern Europe and the newly independent economies of the former Soviet Union) have the highest average income and have made the most progress in infant mortality and secondary education (although the average enrollment for this region was not available).

We should not forget, however, that poverty exists in all nations. While destitute people are present in even the most advanced economies, what characterizes the less developed countries is the pervasiveness and depth of the poverty. Unless one has travelled in a low-income nation and witnessed the conditions under which many in the population exist, it may be difficult to visualize underdevelopment. In the *World Development Report 1990*, which focused on poverty, the World Bank provided an account of a subsistence farm household in Ghana, a small nation located on the east coast of Africa.

In Ghana's Savannah region a typical family of seven lives in three one-room huts made from mud bricks, with earthen floors. They have little furniture and no toilet, electricity, or running water. Water is obtained from a stream a fifteen-minute walk away. The family has few possessions, apart from three acres of unirrigated land and one cow, and virtually no savings.

The family raises sorghum, vegetables, and groundnuts on its land. The work is seasonal and physically demanding. At peak periods of tilling, sowing, and harvesting, all family members are involved, including the husband's parents, who are sixty and seventy years old. The soil is very low in quality, but the family lacks access to fertilizer and other modern inputs. Moreover, the region is susceptible to drought; the rains fail two years out of every five. In addition to her farm work, the wife has to fetch water, collect firewood, and feed the family. The market town where the husband sells their meager cash crops and buys essentials is five miles away and is reached by dirt tracks and an unsealed road that is washed away every time the rains come.

None of the older family members ever attended school, but the eight-year-old son is now in the first grade. The family hopes that he will be able to stay in school, although there is pressure to keep him at home to help with the farm in the busy periods. He and his two younger sisters have never seen a doctor.[9]

Many variations on this personal plight in the developing economies are found—families picking through garbage dumps on the outskirts of large cities; beggars lying in the gutters; homeless boys roaming back alleys; young girls sold into prostitution rings; refugees dislocated by civil war; and workers laid off from state factories during the transition to more market-oriented systems. Many success stories also are evident—peasant farmers innovating with new seeds and methods of cultivation; first-generation graduates from high school; entrepreneurs opening new businesses; and migrants to urban areas hustling to earn income to send back to families in the rural villages.

To illustrate the variety of country experiences, in Table 1.3 we present the indicators on growth and development for seven nations: Ghana, Sri Lanka, Egypt, Poland, Costa Rica, Brazil, and South Korea. Drawn from all regions of the developing world, the nations in this sample range from the small to the very large, from the low-income to the upper middle-income, and from the low to the high achievers in generating economic development. We will continue to highlight these seven, along with China and India, throughout the text. In addition, we introduce two indicators: one, a more comparable measure of per capita income, and two, an index of human development.

## DIFFERENCES IN DEVELOPMENT

Earlier we noted that per capita GNP can be a misleading measure of economic development. One reason is the difficulty in comparing the purchasing powers of different national incomes. The exchange rates used for conversion into a common currency, even when market-determined and not officially set, reflect the prices of traded goods, services and assets. In developing economies many goods and services that do not enter into international trade (except when consumed by foreign tourists) are relatively inexpensive. For example, the prices for local foods, clothing, and basic services can be quite low, due not only to the low wage costs of production with the abundance of labor, but to the relatively depressed demands with the low levels of income. In short,

---

[9]This excerpt is from the World Bank, *World Development Report 1990,* New York: Oxford University Press, 1990, page 24.

| TABLE 1.3 | SELECTED STATISTICS ON ECONOMIC GROWTH AND DEVELOPMENT: SEVEN LESS DEVELOPED COUNTRIES | | | | | | |
|---|---|---|---|---|---|---|---|
| | GHANA | SRI LANKA | EGYPT | POLAND | COSTA RICA | BRAZIL | SOUTH KOREA |
| Population—1993 (millions) | 16.4 | 17.9 | 56.4 | 38.3 | 3.3 | 156.5 | 44.1 |
| Population growth rate (average annual)—1980–1993 | 3.3% | 1.5% | 2.0% | .6% | … | 2.0% | 1.1% |
| GNP per capita—1993 | $430 | $600 | $660 | $2260 | $2150 | $2930 | $7660 |
| GNP per capita growth rate (average annual)—1980–1993 | .1% | 2.7% | 2.8% | .4% | 1.1% | .3% | 8.2% |
| Infant mortality rate—1993 | 79 | 17 | 64 | 15 | 14 | 57 | 11 |
| Female secondary school enrollment rate—1992 | 29% | 77% | 73% | 86% | 45% | (39%) (male and female) | 91% |
| % of Population Urban—1993 | 35% | 22% | 44% | 64% | 49% | 71% | 78% |
| GNP per capita—1993 (international $) | $1970 | $2990 | $3780 | $5000 | $5520 | $5370 | $9630 |
| Human Development Index—1992 | .482 | .704 | .613 | .855 | .883 | .804 | .882 |

NOTES: GNPs per capita in international dollars are the Gross National Products per capita adjusted for the domestic purchasing power of the national currencies to account for cost of living differences across countries. Lack of data is indicated by …

FROM World Bank, *World Development Report 1995*, New York: Oxford University Press, 1995, Tables 1, 25, 27, 28, 29, 30, and 31.

The *Human Development Index (HDI)*, devised by the United Nations Development Programme, is an indicator of the average standard of living in a country based on life expectancy at birth; the adult literacy rate; the combined primary, secondary, and tertiary school enrollment ratios; and GDP per capita (in international dollars and adjusted to reflect an assumption that contributions to human development of incomes above an average level are sharply diminishing). The theoretical range for the HDI is from 0 to 1.0. A country's HDI score reflects its relative achievement in these performance measures.

FROM United Nations Development Programme, *Human Development Report 1995*, New York: Oxford University Press, 1995, Table 1.

an individual could live fairly well on $200 a month in many developing economies, but would struggle on the same income in a developed economy.

The United Nations International Comparison Programme has attempted to estimate per capita Gross National Product on the basis of the domestic purchasing powers of the national currencies. The estimates for the seven nations for 1993, expressed in international dollars, are also shown in Table 1.3.[10] In general, the lower costs of living in the less developed countries would boost their per capita GNPs when valued in

---

[10]See World Bank, *World Development Report 1995*, pages 242–244, for a discussion of the methodology in estimating Gross National Products in internationally comparable dollars. To obtain the estimates

*continued*

internationally comparable dollars. For example, Sri Lanka's per capita GNP in 1993 is estimated to be $600, while its per capita GNP in 1993 in international dollars is estimated to be $2990. The difference is due to the much lower cost of living in Sri Lanka compared to the United States. For Costa Rica, the estimated 1993 per capita GNP (in international dollars) is 150 percent above the 1993 estimate of per capita GNP (in dollars).

The second indicator is the **Human Development Index (HDI),** which is designed by the United Nations Development Programme (UNDP) to "measure... people's ability to live a long and healthy life, to communicate and to participate in the life of the community, and to have sufficient resources to obtain a decent living."[11] The components of this index are the life expectancy at birth (the average number of years a newborn could expect to live given the current mortality conditions); the adult literacy rate; the combined primary, secondary, and tertiary school enrollment ratios; and per capita Gross Domestic Product (in international dollars and adjusted to reflect an assumption that the marginal contributions of incomes above the poverty level to human development are sharply diminishing). The HDI has been tabulated for 174 nations. The value of the HDI, which can range from 0 to 1.0, reflects a nation's relative achievement (measured between minimum and maximum values) in education, health, and income.[12] For 1992 (the latest year presented), Canada had the highest HDI at .950. The United States was second at .938. The lowest HDI was Niger at .207.

Comparing a country's ranking in the human development index with its ranking in per capita national income among the 174 nations may provide some insight into its development policy. For example, for Costa Rica and Madagascar, the HDI rankings are significantly higher than their respective rankings in per capita national income, indicating their success in meeting the basic needs in education and health with relatively modest incomes. Other nations, like Oman and Gabon, have per capita national income rankings that are significantly higher than their HDI rankings, indicating considerable potential remains for translating their incomes into improving the well-being of their populations.[13] The UNDP observes that the publication of the human development

---

of national GNPs in international dollars, a conversion factor reflecting purchasing-power parity is used. The conversion factor is "the number of units of a country's currency required to buy the same amount of goods and services in the domestic market as one dollar would buy in the United States." See page 243.

[11]United Nations Development Programme, *Human Development Report 1993,* New York: Oxford University Press, 1993, page 104. For a discussion of the underlying philosophy of the Human Development Index, refer to pages 100–114. For a description of the construction of the most recently revised Human Development Index, see United Nations Development Programme, *Human Development Report 1995,* New York: Oxford University Press, 1995, pages 15–22 and 134–135.

[12]The minimum and maximum values for adult literacy are 0% and 100%; for life expectancy at birth, 25 years and 85 years; for combined primary, secondary, and tertiary enrollment ratios, 0% and 100%; and for per capita Gross Domestic Product in international dollars, $100 and $40,000. For example, a nation with an adult literacy rate of 50% would receive a .5 score for the literacy component of the HDI.

[13]See United Nations Development Programme, *Human Development Report 1995,* Table 1.2 and pages 21–22. Debate continues on how to measure economic development. See, for example, Paul Streeten, "Human Development: Means and Ends," pages 232–237; T. N. Srinivasan, "Human Development: A New Paradigm or Reinvention of the Wheel?" pages 238–243; and Harsha Aturupane, Paul Glewwe, and Paul Isenman, "Poverty, Human Development and Growth: An Emerging Consensus?" (pages 244–249), all in *American Economic Review,* vol. 84, no. 2 (May 1994). Streeten, recognizing the limitations of any statistical index to capture all the dimensions of economic development, finds indexes like the HDI to be "useful in focusing attention and simplifying the problem" (page 235). Srinivasan

indexes has "opened healthy competition among countries to improve their human development status."[14]

Aggregate statistics for nations, however, can mask substantial differences within the nations—across demographic groups (e.g., by gender or ethnicity) and across regions. For example, the UNDP estimated HDIs for regions of China for 1992: Shanghai ranked first with a HDI of .865, and Tibet ranked last with a HDI of .404.[15] Such discrepancies in the HDI may inform national policy in terms of regional or demographic priorities for social investment.

## Gender Equity

Discrimination in any form hinders human development and socioeconomic progress. In its *Human Development Report 1993*, the UNDP concluded that, "No country treats its women as well as its men." Elaborating, the UNDP stated that,

> In industrial countries, gender discrimination (measured by the HDI) is mainly in employment and wages, with women often getting less than two-thirds of the employment opportunities and about half the earnings of men.
> 
> In developing countries, the great disparities, besides those in the job market, are in health care, nutritional support, and education.[16]

In its *Human Development Report 1995*, the UNDP cites evidence that in both developed and developing economies, women—compared to men—tend to work longer hours (in part due to bearing the burden of childrearing and household responsibilities). In addition, businesswomen do not enjoy the same access to credit as businessmen. In many countries, women face legal discrimination in marital, inheritance, and property rights. The UNDP also observes tragically that "An estimated one million children, mostly girls in Asia, are forced into prostitution annually. And an estimated 100 million girls suffer genital mutilation."[17]

---

takes a more critical view; in particular, he finds the HDI to be "conceptually weak and empirically unsound" (page 241). Aturupane, Glewwe, and Isenman compare the approaches of the World Bank (through the annual *World Development Reports*) and the United Nations Development Programme (through the annual *Human Development Reports*) to measuring and promoting economic development. They argue that progress is best indicated by percentage changes over time (e.g., the percentage decrease in the infant mortality rate in a country from 1980 to 1993). We should note that these three articles were written before the 1994 and 1995 revisions in the HDI. For an interesting commentary on the 1995 HDI, see "Different Roads to Development," *The Economist* (August 19, 1995), pages 35–36.

[14]United Nations Development Programme, *Human Development Report 1995*, page 119.

[15]United Nations Development Programme, *Human Development Report 1994*, New York: Oxford University Press, 1994, page 100. In the revised calculation of the HDI in 1995, the combined primary, secondary, and tertiary enrollment ratios replaced mean years of schooling for the population aged 25 years and older as an indicator of education. The HDI calculations for regions of China reflect the 1994 formulation, however.

[16]United Nations Development Programme, *Human Development Report 1993*, pages 16–17. In 1995 the UNDP devised a gender-related human development index (GDI), in which the national HDI was adjusted to reflect differential achievements by gender. For a given HDI, the generally lower attainments in education, health, and income by females would reduce the score for the GDI.

[17]See United Nations Development Programme, *Human Development Report 1995*, in particular, "The Revolution for Gender Equality," pages 1–10. This quotation is from page 7.

PER CAPITA INCOME AND DEVELOPMENT

Using some of the countries in Table 1.3 as examples, we can illustrate the earlier points on the relationship between per capita income and economic development. In general, a direct association exists between per capita GNP and economic development, as indicated by the infant mortality rate and the female secondary school enrollment rate. Some exceptions merit further examination.

For example, Brazil's per capita GNP in 1993 is nearly five times Sri Lanka's. Even when adjusted for relative purchasing power, Brazil's per capita GNP in international dollars is 80 percent greater than Sri Lanka's. Sri Lanka's infant mortality rate is one-third of Brazil's, however. The anomaly largely reflects the different strategies of development pursued by the two nations. Sri Lanka is a widely cited example of a basic-needs orientation in which the early emphasis in the development process was on human capital formation—providing for the education, health, and nutritional needs of the population—even at a sacrifice of higher economic growth rates. Brazil, in contrast, has placed a premium on economic growth, which produced a relatively high per capita income. The impressive growth, however, has not translated into a significant improvement in the standard of living for many in the nation. Brazil has one of the most unequal distributions of income in the world.[18] Indicative of the different approaches might be the mean years of schooling for the female population of age 25 years or more in 1992: for Sri Lanka, 6.3 years, while for Brazil, only 3.9 years.[19] The lesson may be that economic growth does not automatically result in reduced poverty or, more specifically, that rapidly rising per capita income need not translate into human capital formation with widespread gains in economic opportunity.

We observed how differences in the composition of expenditures could skew the linkage between per capita income and economic development. Consider Oman, a small, oil-producing nation in the Middle East. The estimated per capita GNP in 1993 (in international dollars) for Oman was $9020, over 60 percent greater than for Costa Rica, yet the infant mortality rate in Costa Rica (14 per thousand) was half that in Oman (29 per thousand). One contributing factor, among others, might be the differences in the military burden (the share of military expenditures in Gross Domestic Product) in the two nations. In 1992, for Oman, located in a tension-filled, heavily armed region of the world, the military burden was 17.5 percent. In Costa Rica, a nation noted for not having a standing army, military expenditures accounted for only .9 percent of GDP.[20] The lesson here may be that differences in national priorities (reflected in government budget allocations) may be just as, if not more, important than differences in income

---

[18]It was estimated in 1989 that the top 10 percent of the population in Brazil had over 50 percent of the personal income, while the poorest 40 percent earned just 7 percent of the personal income. The disparities in wealth in Brazil are likely to be even greater. See the World Bank, *World Development Report 1995*, Table 30.

[19]See United Nations Development Programme, *Human Development Report 1994*, Table 5, for the mean years of education for adult females.

[20]For 1993 per capita GNPs (in international dollars) and 1993 infant mortality rates, see World Bank, *World Development Report 1995*, Tables 30 and 27, respectively. For Costa Rica in 1990–1991, military expenditures were equal to 5 percent of public expenditures on education and health. For Oman in 1990–1991, military expenditures were 293 percent of public expenditures on education and health. The shares of military expenditures in national income for 1992 and the ratios of military expenditures to combined education and health expenditures for 1990–1991, are from United Nations Development Programme, *Human Development Report 1995*, Table 14.

in explaining differential success in economic development. In the 1970s Costa Rica launched a comprehensive public health campaign, effectively extending primary health-care services to the rural population. By the mid-1980s Costa Rica was spending over 20 percent of its government budget on health—a share made possible, in part, by its low military burden.[21] With an HDI for 1992 of .884, Costa Rica ranked 28th among the 174 nations of the world listed. With a 1992 HDI of .715, Oman ranked 91st.[22]

## CONCLUDING NOTE

Care is warranted in drawing inferences about relative levels of economic development based solely on differences in per capita incomes. We should never forget that behind the myriad of statistics lie unique development experiences.

Since a fundamental difference between the developed and less developed countries centers on population growth, we turn in Chapter 2 to the components of population change. Demographic transition theory provides a framework for comparing the current rapid population growth of the less developed countries with the historical experiences of the developed countries.

## SUMMARY OF MAIN POINTS

1. The end of the Cold War, progress in trade liberalization, reduced population growth rates, and greater environmental awareness augur well for the world as the twenty-first century draws near. Significant challenges, however, include dismantling the existing nuclear arsenals, resolving ethnic conflicts, and alleviating the abject poverty experienced by one-fifth of the world's population.
2. Economic growth refers to rising output per capita. Technological progress and increases in the quantity and quality of labor, capital, and available natural resources are the primary sources of output growth.
3. Gross National Product (GNP) and Gross Domestic Product (GDP) are two measures of national output and national income. GNP measures the market value of all final goods and services produced by the residents of a nation, regardless of where the output was produced. GDP measures the market value of all final goods and services produced within the borders of a nation, regardless of who supplied the factors used to produce the output.
4. Economic development refers to a general improvement in the standard of living for a population. With economic development comes structural change—a transformation from a primarily agrarian economy to a diversified industrial economy.

---

[21]World Bank, *World Development Report 1990*, pages 74–75.
[22]See United Nations Development Programme, *Human Development Report 1995*, Table 1.2.

5. A comparison of per capita GNPs may not accurately capture relative economic development due to differences in the distribution of national incomes; the extent of nonmarket activities; the composition of national outputs; and the costs of living. The conversion of national currencies into a common value such as the U.S. dollar is another potential source of measurement error.
6. Indicators of economic development include the infant mortality rate (IMR), female secondary school enrollment rate, and the percentage of the population that is urban.
7. Nations can be grouped according to common features or tendencies, such as the levels of income, degree of economic development, or geographical region. One basic division reflects relative economic progress and is between the developed countries (DCs) and the less developed countries (LDCs). The LDCs are also referred to as the developing economies, the South, and the Third World.
8. In general, the LDCs are characterized by relatively low per capita incomes; high rates of population growth; high infant mortality; low levels of education, and high percentages of the population living in rural areas.
9. An improved measure of per capita national incomes for cross-country comparisons is based on internationally comparable dollars. Differences in the costs of living across nations are considered. Generally for the LDCs, their per capita GNPs in international dollars are greater than their per capita GNPs in (unadjusted) U.S. dollars due to their lower costs of living (compared to the United States).
10. The United Nations Development Programme has devised a human development index (HDI) to measure the relative progress of nations in health care, education, and per capita income. Comparing a nation's HDI ranking with its ranking in per capita GNP indicates how well the nation has translated its income into meeting the basic needs of its population in education and health. As with per capita GNP, the HDI may mask significant variations within a nation with respect to gender, ethnic groups, or regions.
11. While common characteristics may exist for the less developed countries, it is important to remember that each nation is unique.

## KEY TERMS

developed countries (DCs)
economic development
economic growth
economies of scale
entrepreneur
female secondary school enrollment rate
First World
Fourth World
Gross Domestic Product (GDP)
Gross National Product (GNP)
high-income economies
Human Development Index (HDI)
increasing returns to scale
infant mortality rate (IMR)
less developed countries (LDCs)
low-income economies
middle-income economies
natural resources
net factor payments
Newly Industrializing Countries (NICs)
North
physical capital stock
physical labor
production possibilities boundary (PPB)
Second World
South
technology
Third World
total factor productivity

## QUESTIONS

1. Does negative economic growth necessarily mean that national output has declined? Explain. What economic factors could account for decreases in national output? Be specific.
2. Using the latest available *World Development Report* from the World Bank, collect the following statistics for Kenya and Cameroon: population growth; GNP per capita (in U.S. dollars); GNP per capita (in international dollars); growth rate in per capita GNP; infant mortality rate; female secondary school enrollment rate; and percentage of the population that is urban. Which country would you regard as more developed? Discuss why.
3. Economic growth may be a necessary, but not sufficient, condition for economic development. Do you agree? Discuss.
4. Are economic growth and sustainable development incompatible? Discuss.
5. Suppose for a country, Atlantica, that GNP equals $100 million; labor income earned by residents of Atlantica working abroad equals $1.5 million; labor income earned by foreigners (nonresidents) working in Atlantica equals $.6 million; interest and dividends payed by Atlantica to foreign investors equal $.8 million; and interest and dividends received by residents of Atlantica from foreign investments equal $.1 million. Calculate Atlantica's GDP.
6. Suppose for a country, Pacifica, that GNP per capita is 5000 rupees and that the official exchange rate between the rupee and U.S. dollar is 10 rupees to $1.00. What would be the per capita GNP for Pacifica expressed in U.S. dollars at the official exchange rate?

    If prices in Pacifica are exactly 40 percent of prices for similar commodities in the United States (i.e., any item costing $1 in the United States costs 4 rupees in Pacifica), estimate the per capita GNP for Pacifica in international dollars.
7. In 1994 the United Nations Development Programme estimated 1992 human development indexes for Egypt as a nation (.551); for Cairo, the capital of Egypt (.738); and for rural upper Egypt (.444). (See *Human Development Report 1994*, pages 99–100.) What might account for these differences within Egypt?
8. How would you extend the UNDP's human development index to capture other dimensions of the quality of life? Why hasn't a more comprehensive HDI been devised?

## SUGGESTED READINGS

Aturupane, Harsha, Paul Glewwe, and Paul Isenman, "Poverty, Human Development and Growth: An Emerging Consensus?" *American Economic Review,* vol. 84, no. 2 (May 1994), pages 244–249.

Brown, Lester, "The New World Order," in *State of the World 1991,* Worldwatch Institute, New York: W. W. Norton, 1991.

Durning, Alan, "Ending Poverty," in *State of the World 1990,* Worldwatch Institute, New York: W. W. Norton, 1990.

Sen, Amartya, "The Concept of Development," in *Handbook of Development Economics,* Vol. 1, edited by H. Chenery and T. N. Srinivasan, Amsterdam, Netherlands: Elsevier Science Publishers, 1988.

Srinivasan, T. N., "Human Development: A New Paradigm or Reinvention of the Wheel?" *American Economic Review,* vol. 84, no. 2 (May 1994), pages 238–243.

Stern, Nicholas, "The Economics of Development: A Survey," *Economic Journal,* vol. 99, no. 3 (September 1989), pages 597–685.

Streeten, Paul, "Human Development: Means and Ends," *American Economic Review,* vol. 84, no. 2 (May 1994), pages 232–237.

United Nations Development Programme, "Trends in Human Development," Chapter 1 in *Human Development Report 1993,* New York: Oxford University Press, 1993.

United Nations Development Programme, "Towards Sustainable Development," Chapter 1 in *Human Development Report 1994,* New York: Oxford University Press, 1994.

United Nations Development Programme, *Human Development Report 1995,* New York: Oxford University Press, 1995.

World Bank, "What Do We Know About the Poor?" Chapter 2 in *World Development Report 1990,* New York: Oxford University Press, 1990.

In general, the latest annual editions of the World Bank's *World Development Report* and the United Nations Development Programme's *Human Development Report* are recommended.

# APPENDIX

## TESTING THEORY

The title of this book, *Economic Development: Theories, Evidence, and Policies,* illustrates a basic organization and use of knowledge. With theories we seek to explain how the world—or a small part of it—works. We construct models with equations that express the hypothesized relationships among the carefully defined variables of interest. From the models we derive predictions, or statements on what we expect to observe in practice. To test the predictions of the model, we collect and assess evidence or data.

As social scientists dealing with human behavior and social institutions, economists usually rely on uncontrolled experiments to test their theories. That is, the data gathered are from the actual economic systems in operation. Statistical procedures allow us to organize and evaluate the evidence. Theories that regularly receive confirmation from the evidence form the basis for informed policymaking. Policymaking involves the selection of the appropriate means to achieve a given objective.

In this appendix we illustrate one of the most basic empirical methodologies used to test economic theory. For our purposes it is not important to understand the derivation of the statistical tests but, rather, to acquire an intuition into the process. Further, we do not propose to construct large-scale models, but to present simple statistical tests of selected, specific hypothesized relationships in economic development.

The dynamic process of economic development is complex, and in each country evolves over many years. Unfortunately, few if any developing countries have aggregate time series data of sufficient length and reliability to test directly for the changes that define economic development. Researchers rely on cross-sections of nations at different stages of development to test hypotheses about the process of development. The relevance of the inferences drawn for any developing economy is subject to debate; however, given the data constraints, there is little recourse. While one is mindful of the uniqueness of each nation's development experience, one can nevertheless learn from identifying trends and common patterns. The varying degrees of data reliability and small sizes of the developing country samples warrant caution in interpreting the results. In particular, sensitivity analysis to assess the robustness or stability of the empirical estimates should be done. That is, are the estimated relationships highly sensitive to the constellation of nations in the sample? Does the inclusion of one or several nations in the sample significantly influence the results? We will subject our findings to such sensitivity analysis.

Let us begin with a simple hypothesis:

> In the less developed countries the infant mortality rate is inversely related to per capita income.

That is, developing nations with higher incomes, ceteris paribus, should have healthier and better nourished populations.[1] As the average level of income rises, so should the ability to afford medical care and adequate diets. The specified causality is from per capita income (the explanatory or independent variable) to the infant mortality rate (the dependent variable).

To measure per capita income, we select Gross National Product per capita. We specify, unless theory or subsequent evidence suggests otherwise, a linear relationship.

$$IMR_i = a_o + a_1 (Y/P)_i + u_i$$

where $IMR_i$ = the infant mortality rate for Country $i$

$(Y/P)_i$ = GNP per capita for Country $i$

$u_i$ = error term for Observation $i$

We would expect the intercept term, $a_o$, to be positive; in theory, $a_o$ would represent the average infant mortality rate if per capita income were zero. We have hypothesized that the influence of per capita GNP on the infant mortality rate is negative, so we expect the sign of $a_1$ to be negative. The error term, $u_i$, is unobserved and is assumed to be unrelated to the explanatory variable (here $Y/P$). The error term captures the combined impact of other influences on the dependent variable, including random or chance events.

We now need to take a sample of less developed countries and collect data on the infant mortality rate (*IMR*) and per capita Gross National Product (*Y/P*) for a given year, say 1991. Generally, for cross-country studies, the sample should include all the developing nations for which reliable and comparable data are available. Here, for illustrative purposes we restrict the sample to the developing nations of sub-Saharan Africa. The data for *IMR* and *Y/P* are listed in Table 1A.1 on p. 24, along with the data for two other explanatory variables, which will be added to the model later. The sample means and ranges for the variables and the data sources are also given in Table 1A.1.

As can be seen with a scanning of the data, higher infant mortality rates tend to be found in nations with lower per capita incomes, although clear exceptions occur. To obtain a better sense of the relationship, we can plot a *scatter diagram*. See Figure 1A.1 on page 25. The ordered pairs of data for each observation are plotted, with the values of the dependent variable (*IMR*) measured on the vertical axis and the values

---

[1]*Ceteris paribus* is a Latin expression meaning "other things being equal." We use the expression to isolate a relationship of interest, here between per capita income and the infant mortality rate. The assumption is that all other relevant influences on the dependent variable (here the infant mortality rate) do not change.

| TABLE 1A.1 | DATA FOR THE SAMPLE OF SUB-SAHARAN AFRICAN NATIONS | | | |
|---|---|---|---|---|
| Country | IMR | Y/P | FED | DPT |
| Mozambique | 149 | 80 | 1.2 | 19 |
| Tanzania | 115 | 100 | 1.3 | 79 |
| Ethiopia | 130 | 120 | 0.7 | 44 |
| Uganda | 118 | 170 | 0.6 | 77 |
| Burundi | 107 | 210 | 0.2 | 83 |
| Chad | 124 | 210 | 0.1 | 18 |
| Madagascar | 114 | 210 | 1.7 | 46 |
| Sierra Leone | 145 | 210 | 0.4 | 75 |
| Malawi | 143 | 230 | 1.1 | 81 |
| Rwanda | 111 | 270 | 0.5 | 89 |
| Mali | 161 | 280 | 0.1 | 35 |
| Burkina Faso | 133 | 290 | 0.1 | 37 |
| Niger | 126 | 300 | 0.1 | 18 |
| Nigeria | 85 | 340 | 0.5 | 65 |
| Kenya | 67 | 340 | 1.3 | 36 |
| Benin | 111 | 380 | 0.3 | 67 |
| Central African Republic | 106 | 390 | 0.5 | 82 |
| Ghana | 83 | 400 | 2.2 | 39 |
| Togo | 87 | 410 | 0.8 | 73 |
| Zimbabwe | 48 | 650 | 1.7 | 89 |
| Côte d' Ivoire | 95 | 690 | 0.9 | 48 |
| Senegal | 81 | 720 | 0.4 | 60 |
| Cameroon | 64 | 850 | 0.8 | 56 |
| Sample mean | 109 | 341 | 0.8 | 57 |
| Maximum | 161 (Mali) | 850 (Cameroon) | 2.2 (Ghana) | 89 (Rwanda, Zimbabwe) |
| Minimum | 48 (Zimbabwe) | 80 (Mozambique) | 0.1 (Chad, Mali, Burkina Faso, Niger) | 18 (Chad, Niger) |

IMR = Infant mortality rate in 1991 (per thousand live births) (World Bank, *World Development Report 1993*, New York: Oxford University Press, 1993, Table 28).

Y/P = Gross National Product per capita in 1991 in U.S. dollars ($) (World Bank, *World Development Report 1993*, New York: Oxford University Press, 1993, Table 1).

FED = Mean years of schooling for female population aged 25 years and over in 1990 (United Nations Development Programme, *Human Development Report 1993*, New York: Oxford University Press, 1993, Table 5).

DPT = Percentage of children of age one or less immunized with three completed doses of vaccine against diphtheria, pertussis, and tetanus in 1990–1991 (World Bank, *World Development Report 1993*, Table A-8).

### FIGURE 1A.1  SCATTER DIAGRAM FOR *IMR* AND *Y/P*

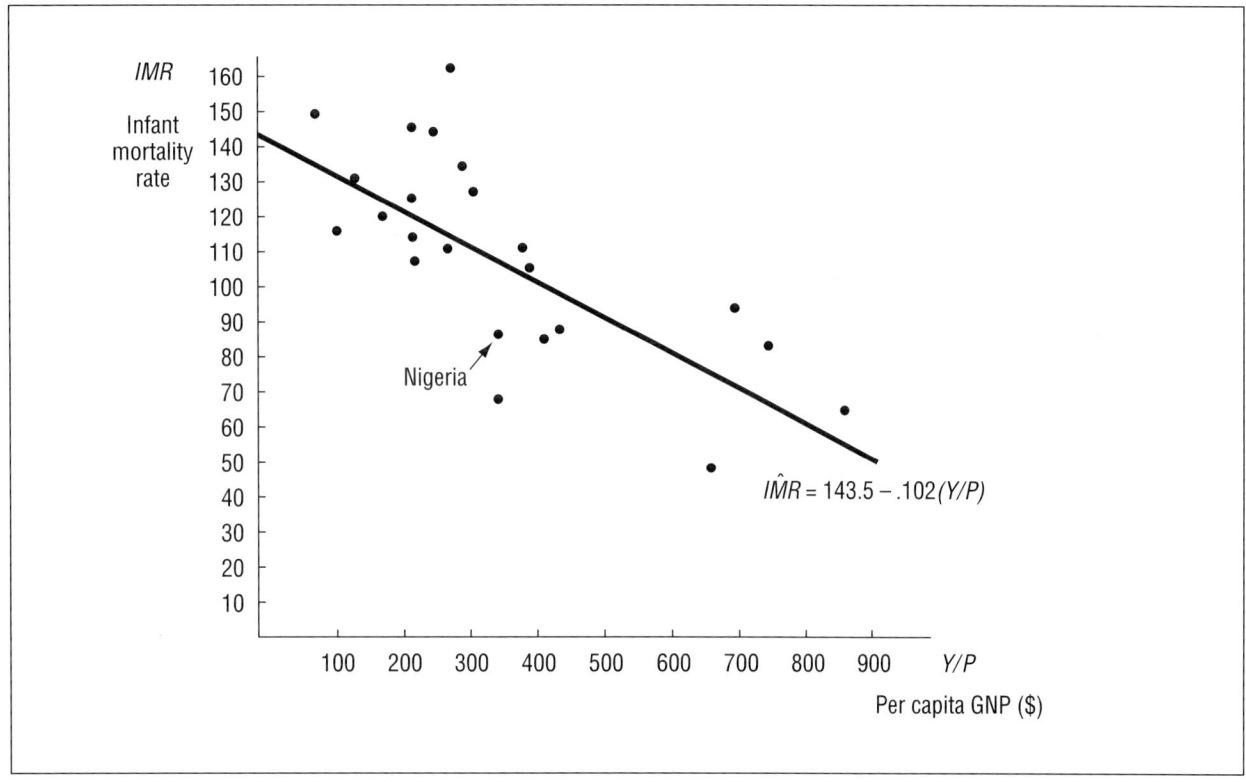

of the explanatory variable *(Y/P)* measured on the horizontal axis. (For example, see the plotted point for Nigeria, where *IMR* = 85 and *Y/P* = 340.) The visual plot also seems to support the hypothesized inverse relationship. If no relationship existed, the points on the scatter diagram would appear to be randomly dispersed. Even if the infant mortality rate were negatively related to per capita GNP, we would not expect to find all the plotted points lying on a straight line with a negative slope. For one, there may be a nonlinear relationship. That is, the infant mortality rate may fall, but at a diminishing rate as per capita GNP rises.[2]

In addition, recall the error term included in the specification. In any empirical analysis, errors in measurement occur and explanatory variables are omitted. Suppose we assume that the dependent variable, *IMR*, is measured accurately.[3] We have already discussed the problems in measuring national incomes across countries, including the differential degrees in nonmarket activities and the difficulties in converting to a common currency. Such errors in measurement of the explanatory variable can contribute

---

[2] In fact, we tested for diminishing returns to per capita income by using the square root of per capita GNP as the explanatory variable. Since the explanatory power of the model did not improve, we stayed with the simpler linear specification. Given the low levels of per capita income found in sub-Saharan Africa, it may not be surprising that diminishing returns to per capita income in reducing the infant mortality rate have not yet set in.

[3] In practice, the vital registration systems of all countries will be less than perfect, so some births and deaths—especially infant deaths—will be missed.

to the dispersion of the plotted points around a line, even if the true relationship between IMR and Y/P were linear and negative. Moreover, other important influences on the infant mortality rate may exist that have not been included in the model. (We will extend the analysis later to consider some additional explanatory variables.)

Given the scatter diagram for the 23 sub-Saharan African nations in the sample, we estimate a line through the plotted points that best fits the data. The estimated *line of best fit* or the *sample regression equation* is:

$$\hat{IMR}_i = e_o + e_1 (Y/P)_i$$

where $\hat{IMR}_i$ = predicted infant mortality rate for Country $i$
$e_o$ = estimated value for the intercept term $a_o$
$e_1$ = estimated value for the coefficient term $a_1$

The criterion we use to derive the estimates $e_o$ and $e_1$ is to minimize the sum of the squares of the prediction errors *(SSE)*. That is, we find the values of $e_o$ and $e_1$ that minimize the following expression:

$$SSE = \sum_{i=1}^{n} (IMR_i - \hat{IMR}_i)^2$$

where $IMR_i - \hat{IMR}_i$ = the *prediction error* for Country $i$

The prediction error for any Observation $i$ is the difference between the actual or observed value of the dependent variable and the value for the dependent variable that is predicted from the regression equation. We square the prediction errors over all $n$ observations (where $n$ is the size of the sample; here $n$ = 23) so that negative prediction errors ($IMR_j < \hat{IMR}_j$) will not offset positive prediction errors ($IMR_k > \hat{IMR}_k$) and $j$ and $k$ are any two such observations in the sample. In other words, the least squares criterion minimizes the sum of the distances of the plotted points from the line of best fit.

Return to Figure 1A.1 in which the scatter diagram is illustrated for the 23 observations in the sample. The estimated line of best fit or the regression equation is:

1. $\hat{IMR}_i = 143.5 - .102(Y/P)_i$ $\qquad R^2 = .49$

We need not concern ourselves with the mechanics of the estimation procedure. The least squares criterion we use is a basic procedure found in most statistical packages available for computers. Of concern is using the estimated regression equation to test our hypothesis. The estimated coefficient of per capita GNP is –.102, which is consistent with our hypothesis of a negative relationship. Ceteris paribus, an increase of $100 in per capita GNP is associated with a decline in the infant mortality rate of 10.2 deaths per thousand live births. ($\Delta\hat{IMR} = -.102\Delta(Y/P)$, and if $\Delta(Y/P) = 100$, then $\Delta\hat{IMR} = -.102(100) = -10.2$.)

There is a statistic, $R^2$, called the *coefficient of determination*, that indicates the percentage of the variation in the values of the dependent variable that is "explained" or "accounted for" by variation in the values of the independent or explanatory variable over the sample.[4] For this regression of the 23 sub-Saharan African nations, $R^2 = .49$—

49 percent of the variation in the 1991 infant mortality rates is explained by variation in the 1991 per capita GNPs. Note that if $R^2 = 1.0$, then all of the variation in the dependent variable would be accounted for by the variation in the independent variable. In such a case, all the plotted points in the scatter diagram would lie on a straight line. For example, the predicted value for the infant mortality rate for Nigeria from the regression equation is 109: $\hat{IMR} = 143.5 - .102(340) = 109$, which is greater than the actual value of 85. The prediction error equals –24. If the coefficient of determination equalled 1.0, then the predicted value for the infant mortality rate would equal the actual value for Nigeria; and for every other nation in the sample, the predicted value would equal the actual value of the infant mortality rate.

We can extend the analysis to include other possible determinants of the infant mortality rate. Suppose we hypothesize that the infant mortality rate is also inversely related to the average level of education in the nation. Intuitively, with education individuals are more knowledgeable about health, hygiene, and child care and may be more prone to seek medical assistance when needed. To measure this influence we use the average level of education of adult females, the primary caregivers in the nation. Let

$FED_i$ = mean years of schooling for the female population aged 25 years and older in 1990 in Country $i$

(Note: The latest year of data available at the time of this analysis was 1990. Given that the mean years of schooling for the adult female population is unlikely to change very much from one year to the next, this one-year difference between the data for female education and infant mortality is not believed to be significant.)

Another hypothesis is that the infant mortality rate is inversely related to popular access to health care. To measure this influence for infants we use an immunization rate. Let

$DPT_i$ = percentage of children of age less than one year in Country $i$ immunized with three completed doses of vaccine against diphtheria, pertussis (whooping cough), and tetanus in 1990–1991.

---

[4]The coefficient of determination is equal to

$$R^2 = 1 - \frac{SSE}{TSS} = 1 - \frac{\text{sum of squared errors}}{\text{total sum of squares}}$$

where $SSE = \sum_{i=1}^{n} (IMR_i - \hat{IMR}_i)^2$

$TSS = \sum_{i=1}^{n} (IMR_i - \overline{IMR})^2$

$\overline{IMR}$ = average or mean of the $n$ values of $IMR_i$ in the sample.

The numerator in the quotient term ($SSE$) is the sum of the squares of the prediction errors. The denominator ($TSS$) is the total sum of squares and indicates the total variation in the dependent variable over the sample of $n$ observations, or the dispersion of the values of the infant mortality rate around the mean. If, for the $n$ observations in the sample, the values of the dependent variable are exactly predicted by the estimated regression equation (i.e., $IMR_i = \hat{IMR}_i$ for $i = 1 \ldots n$), then the numerator would equal zero and the coefficient of determination ($R^2$) would equal one.

The data for these two new explanatory variables, along with the sample means and ranges, are given in Table 1A.1. Again, the diversity in development within sub-Saharan Africa is apparent, as is the generally low level of education for females.

When we add these two explanatory variables to the model, we can no longer plot a scatter diagram with the dependent variable on one axis and an explanatory variable on each of the three other axes. Doing so would require a four dimensional diagram. Statistical analysis, however, is not bound by any dimensional constraint. The least squares criterion can easily be extended to include other explanatory influences. Our hypothesized equation is

$$IMR_i = a_0 + a_1(Y/P)_i + a_2 FED_i + a_3 DPT_i + u_i$$

where $a_0$, $a_1$, $a_2$, and $a_3$ are the coefficients to be estimated and $u_i$ is the error term associated with the regression equation. In particular, $a_1$, $a_2$, and $a_3$ represent the hypothesized influences of per capita GNP, mean years of female education, and the infant immunization rate respectively on the infant mortality rate, other things being equal. The regession equation to be estimated is

$$\hat{IMR}_i = e_0 + e_1(Y/P)_i + e_2 FED_i + e_3 DPT_i$$

where $e_0$, $e_1$, $e_2$, and $e_3$ are the estimates for $a_0$, $a_1$, $a_2$, and $a_3$, respectively. The least squares criterion is, as before, to find the values for $e_0$, $e_1$, $e_2$, and $e_3$ that minimize the sum of the squared prediction errors *(SSE)*.

$$\text{minimize } SSE = \sum_{i=1}^{n} (IMR_i - \hat{IMR}_i)^2$$

The estimated regression equation is:

2.  $\hat{IMR}_i = 165.9 - .094(Y/P) - 17.1\ FED - .21\ DPT$     $\bar{R}^2 = .61$
    \*\*\*            \*\*\*            \*\*

The signs of all the estimated coefficients are consistent with the hypothesized negative influences of the explanatory variables on the infant mortality rate. The statistic $\bar{R}^2$, called the *adjusted coefficient of determination*, is used for multiple regressions, or when more than one explanatory variable is included in the regression equation.[5] For this sample, 61 percent of the variation in the infant mortality rate is accounted for by the variation in the explanatory variables for per capita GNP, female education, and infant immunization.

Statistical tests can identify which, if any, of the explanatory variables are important influences on the dependent variable. Using these tests, we indicate with the star symbol "*" the level of confidence we have in accepting the hypothesis that an explanatory variable has a statistically significant, systematic influence on the dependent

---

[5]The adjusted coefficient of determination, $\bar{R}^2$, is a standardized measure of the explanatory power of an equation. You can always increase the $R^2$ by adding explanatory variables. The $\bar{R}^2$, however, will decline in value if irrelevant explanatory variables are added to the model.

variable.[6] In particular, the number of stars indicates how confident we can be in accepting the hypothesis that the coefficient of an explanatory variable is not equal to zero. One star (*) indicates a 90 percent level of confidence, or that the chances are less than 10 in a hundred that the explanatory variable has no systematic influence on the dependent variable. Two stars (**) indicate a 95 percent level of confidence, or chances of less than five in a hundred. Three stars (***) indicate a 99 percent level of confidence, or chances of less than 1 in a 100 that the explanatory variable does not systematically influence the dependent variable.

In the regression equation here, two of the explanatory variables are statistically significant influences on the infant mortality rate: per capita GNP $(Y/P)$ at the 99 percent level of confidence, and mean years of education of adult females $(FED)$ at the 95 percent level of confidence. The infant immunization rate $(DPT)$, however, is statistically not a significant influence on the infant mortality rate for this sample of 23 sub-Saharan African nations.

Before we interpret the significant coefficient estimates, it is important to assess the robustness of the regression equation. In small samples with varying degrees of data reliability, the estimation results may be "unstable," or highly sensitive to the presence of one or several observations in the sample. Tests can identify influential observations or, in this case, the countries whose inclusion in the sample significantly affects the value of one or more of the estimated coefficients. If the estimates are highly conditional, depending on the presence of one or several nations in the sample, then the inferences drawn from the regression may not be representative of the general behavior in the sample of nations under analysis.

Of the 23 countries in the sample, Kenya is the most influential observation. To assess the sensitivity of the estimates, we deleted Kenya from the sample. The regression equation without Kenya is

$$3. \ \widehat{IMR}_i = 169.8 \underset{***}{} - .094 \underset{***}{(Y/P)_i} - 13.9 \underset{**}{FED_i} - .29 \underset{*}{DPT_i} \qquad \overline{R}^2 = .67$$

The explanatory variables for per capita GNP and female education are still statistically significant influences at the 99 percent and 95 percent levels, respectively. In contrast to the regression for the full sample, the infant immunization rate becomes a statistically significant influence on the infant mortality rate, albeit at the 90 percent level. The explanatory power of the regression $(\overline{R}^2)$ improves somewhat; 67 percent of the variation in the 1991 infant mortality rate is accounted for by the regression equation. Overall, the coefficient estimates are fairly robust, or stable. Generalizing from the second and third regressions and rounding off to the nearest integer for the infant mortality rate, we can interpret the estimated coefficients as follows. Ceteris paribus, for this sample of sub-Saharan African nations:

- An increase of $100 in per capita GNP $(\Delta(Y/P) = +100)$ is associated with a decrease in the infant mortality rate of 9 (infant deaths per thousand live births).

---

[6]The statistical tests are called *t tests*. The *t statistic* for an estimated coefficient is the value of the estimated coefficient divided by its estimated standard error (a measure of the expected dispersion of the coefficient estimate). The higher the absolute value of the *t* statistic, the more confident we are that the estimated coefficient does not equal zero and the associated explanatory variable is a statistically significant influence on the dependent variable.

- An increase of 1 year in the mean years of education for females of age 25 or older ($\Delta$FED = +1) is associated with a decrease in the infant mortality rate of 14 to 17 (infant deaths per thousand live births).
- An increase of 10 percentage points in the infant immunization rate ($\Delta$DPT = +10) is associated with a decrease in the infant mortality rate of 2 to 3 (infant deaths per thousand live births). The statistical significance of this influence, however, may be marginal.

While suggestive, one regression study for a small sample of sub-Saharan African nations for one year is not a sufficient basis for drawing policy conclusions. Bigger samples, better data, different years, larger models (e.g., additional equations and variables), and more sophisticated statistical estimations would be needed. Moreover, it is important to complement cross-country studies like this with micro-level investigations based on surveys of household behavior within countries. If such analyses regularly support the hypotheses, then the derived policy implications are well grounded. In this example, infant mortality rates appear to be lowered by economic growth (increases in per capita GNP); improvements in female education; and greater access to health care (e.g., immunizations for infants and children). By estimating multiple regression models, we can better assess the expected individual contributions of economic growth, education, and health care.

Finally, a benefit of cross-country studies is the identification of *outliers*, or nations where the predicted values for the dependent variable from the regression equation are significantly different from the values observed in practice. For example, in this sample of sub-Saharan African nations, Malawi is an "underachiever." The recorded infant mortality rate in 1991 for Malawi is significantly greater than the infant mortality rate predicted from the regression equation. Interesting case studies may follow to investigate the underlying reasons for the deviate or extraordinary performances of the outliers. To be addressed are factors that account for Malawi's underachievement in reducing infant mortality.

At other points in this text we again present statistical tests of hypotheses on economic development. The tests are offered as evidence, albeit partial, to help us better understand the complex process of economic development.

# CHAPTER 2

# POPULATION GROWTH

For the vast span of human existence on planet Earth, population growth rates have been minimal. An estimated 1 out of every 18 human beings ever born is alive today.[1] It took over 500 centuries for the human population to reach one billion (circa 1800 A.D.). It took only 13 decades to add the second billion (circa 1930), and three additional decades for the world population to grow to three billion (circa 1960). Fifteen years more brought the size of the world population to four billion (circa 1975). Twelve years later the world reached five billion (circa 1987).

With a simple numerical exercise we can demonstrate that the current rate of global population growth is unsustainable. If we divide the estimated population of the world in 1993 (5.5 billion) into the total land area of the earth, approximately 269,000 square feet would exist per person (or an area roughly the size of 4.5 football fields). Extrapolating the average annual world population growth rate of 1.7 percent for the period 1980 to 1993 (a doubling time of 41 years), 260 square feet would exist per person around the year 2400, and less than one square foot per person by the year 2750. Forty-one years later there would be more than two persons per square foot of land area on earth. Clearly such a scenario is unreal. Moreover, eight hundred years is a long time, or so it seems. In the 500 centuries of Homo sapiens' life on this planet, however, 800 years is comparable to 23 minutes in a day. Doomsday projections aside, the point is that anything other than minimal population growth is a recent aberration in human history—one that is unlikely to last much longer. How much longer, though, is open to speculation.

Demographer Wolfgang Lutz identified three major certainties for the world population over the next 35 years. First, the size of the world population will increase by at least 50 percent, and may even double. Second, by the year 2030, the contemporary developing countries (excluding Russia and the former socialist states of Eastern

---

[1]This is an estimate by Carl Haub, "How Many People Have Ever Lived on Earth?" *Population Today*, vol. 23, no. 2 (February 1995).

Europe) will account for approximately 85 percent of the world population. Third, all populations will become older; in particular, the percentages of the populations that are over 65 years of age will increase.[2]

As noted in Chapter 1, a fundamental difference between the developed and less developed countries is the rate of population growth. For the low-income and middle-income economies, the average annual rate of population growth for the 1980 to 1993 period was 1.9 percent, or more than three times the rate for the high-income economies.[3] Recall that economic growth is the difference between output growth and population growth. In Chapter 1 we discussed the sources of output growth, primarily technological progress and increases in the quantity and quality of human labor, physical capital, and the available natural resources. In this chapter we explore the phenomenon of population growth and the reasons for the rapid population growth in the contemporary developing nations.

We begin with the measurement of the components of population change: births, deaths, and net in-migration. Presented are standardized measures of fertility and mortality that can be used for comparisons across countries at different stages of development. We then illustrate the concept of population momentum to show that even if every nation in the world were to attain replacement-level fertility now, the world population would still increase by at least half again.

To place the rapid population growth of the LDCs in historical context, we turn to demographic transition theory, or an explanation of the transition from a demographic equilibrium of high birth rates and high death rates to one of low birth rates and low death rates. Two centuries ago the political economist Thomas Malthus warned that, unless population growth were checked, eventually there would be a stationary state of zero population growth at a subsistence level of income. The developed countries of Western Europe, the United States, Canada, Japan, Australia, and New Zealand have checked their population growth. Russia and the former socialist countries of Eastern Europe also have low rates of population growth. We contrast this with the differential progress made by the regions of the developing world in demographic transition. We conclude this second chapter with a theory of net intergenerational wealth flows, which suggests that current high fertility in less developed economies may be economically rational behavior. In Chapter 7 we return to population matters, examining the consequences of rapid population growth for economic development, theories of fertility, and policies to address the high birth rates in developing economies.

## COMPONENTS OF POPULATION CHANGE

For a given geographical area (e.g., a city, state, country, or region), the components of population change are births, deaths, and net in-migration. Net in-migration is the difference between immigration (movement into an area) and emigration (movement out of an area). The size of a population in an area at the end of a period of time (e.g., one year) is equal to the initial population in the area, plus the births, less the deaths,

---

[2]Wolfgang Lutz, "The Future of World Population," *Population Bulletin,* vol. 49, no. 1 (June 1994), page 34.
[3]These population growth rates are from World Bank, *World Development Report 1995,* New York: Oxford University Press, 1995, Table 25.

## INDICATORS OF MORTALITY

The crude death rate is a weighted average over all ages of the age-specific death rates, whereby the weights are the percentage shares of each age group in the total population.

$$CDR = \sum_a ASDR_a\,(POP_a/POP)$$

where $ASDR_a$ = age-specific death rate for age interval $a$

$$= \frac{\text{deaths to population of age interval } a \text{ during a year}}{\text{mid-year population of age interval } a} \times 1000$$

$POP_a$ = mid-year population of age interval $a$

$POP$ = total mid-year population

and $\sum_a$ refers to the summation over all age intervals

Due to high fertility in the past, the less developed countries have young populations; that is, a relatively high percentage of the populations (40 percent or more) is under age 15 and a small percentage is over age 65 (5 percent or less). In contrast, in the developed countries birth rates have been low for over two decades (and much longer if the baby boom following World War II is excluded). Consequently the populations of the DCs are older, with 20 percent or less of the populations under age 15 and 10 percent or more over age 65.

A common pattern is found, however, for age-specific death rates across all populations. The ASDR is relatively high for the first year of life, then drops sharply through childhood, reaching a low for the early adolescent years (10 to 14 years of age). The ASDR then rises gradually through adolescence and young adulthood, picking up as middle age approaches. The ASDR accelerates further after age 50. See Figure 2.1 on page 36, in which the female ASDRs for the United States for 1960 and 1990 are plotted.

Developing nations with young populations, therefore, have a comparatively high percentage of their populations in the low-mortality years. In fact, as we will illustrate, it is possible for one nation to have higher ASDRs for all age intervals than a second nation, yet have a lower crude death rate. Consider two populations, A and B, that are representative of the age structures of a less developed country and a developed country, respectively. The ASDRs (per thousand mid-year population), population distributions, and age brackets are given below.

| Age Interval | Population A (LDC) % of Population | Population A (LDC) ASDR | Population B (DC) % of Population | Population B (DC) ASDR |
| --- | --- | --- | --- | --- |
| Less than 1 | 5 | 20 | 2 | 10 |
| 1–14 | 40 | 2 | 18 | 1 |
| 15–44 | 35 | 4 | 35 | 2 |
| 45–64 | 15 | 10 | 30 | 5 |
| 65 and over | 5 | 100 | 15 | 50 |

$CDR_A = .05(20) + .40(2) + .35(4) + .15(10) + .05(100) = 9.7$

$CDR_B = .02(10) + .18(1) + .35(2) + .30(5) + .15(50) = 10.1$

FIGURE 2.1 | AGE-SPECIFIC DEATH RATES (ASDRs) FOR THE FEMALE POPULATION OF THE UNITED STATES: 1960 AND 1990

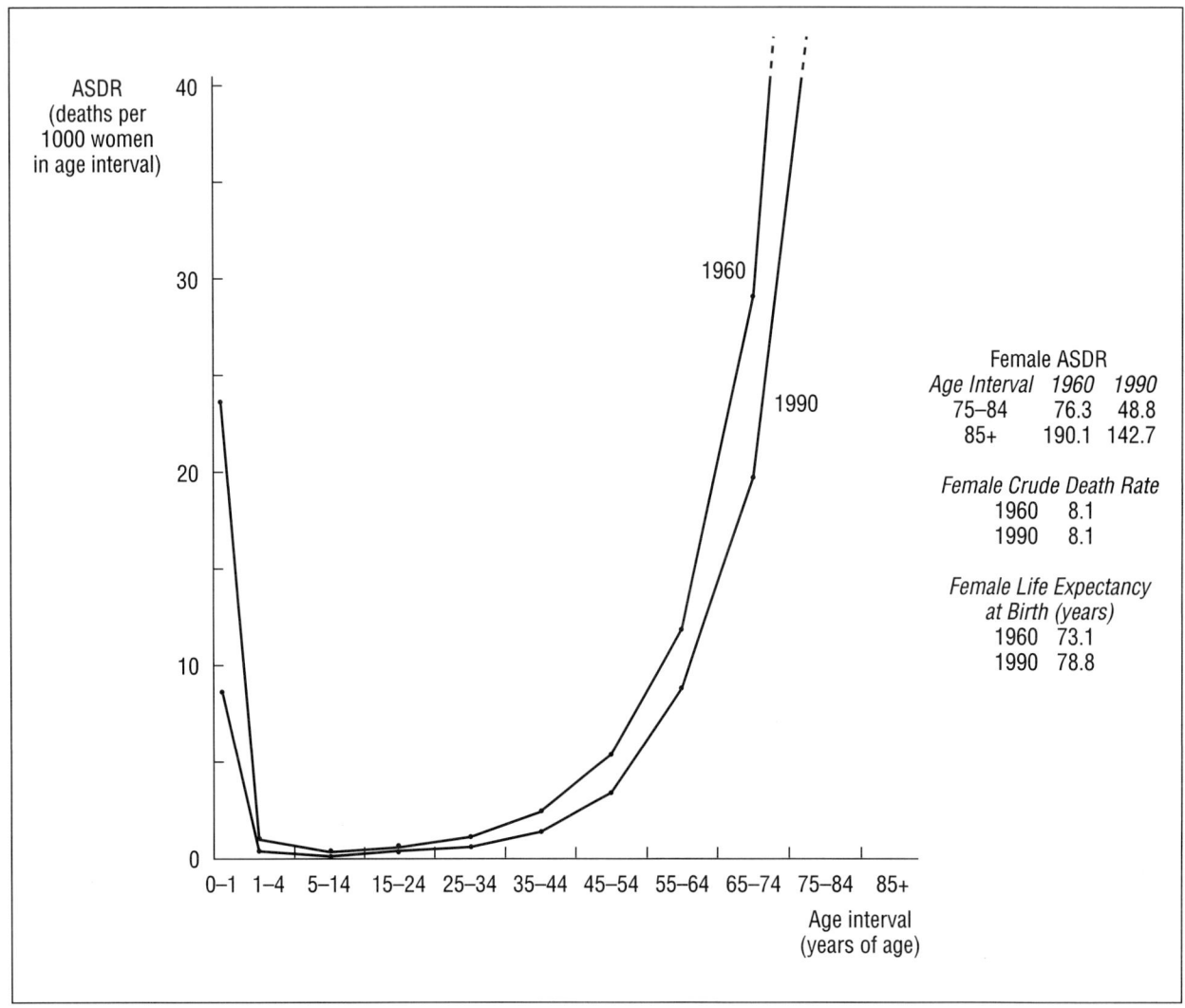

Even though the age-specific death rates for each age interval are twice as high in Population A, the crude death rate is slightly lower. Indeed, referring to Figure 2.1, the female age-specific death rates are uniformly lower for the United States in 1990 than in 1960, indicating improved mortality conditions, while the female crude death rate is 8.1 in both years.

In short, crude death rates are not reliable indicators of the relative mortality conditions in nations with different age structures. The infant mortality rate and the life expectancy at birth are measures of mortality that are independent of the age distribution of the population. **Life expectancy at birth** is the average number of years a newborn could expect to live if subjected to the currently prevailing age-specific death rates. Since age-specific death rates also differ between males and females, it is better to use life expectancy at birth for one sex for international comparisons. (Between 1960 and 1990 the female life expectancy at birth in the United States increased by nearly six years.) Referring to Table 2.1, we see that the female life expectancy at birth ranges from 57 years for the low-income economies to 80 years for the high-income economies.

## INDICATORS OF FERTILITY

In any society the two primary factors that determine fertility are exposure to the risk of conception and fecundity, or the biological capacity to bear children. For the representative or average female, exposure to the risk of conception is socially determined by the average age when sexual activity is initiated and the frequency of sexual union (each, in turn, a function of marriage customs and norms on sexual activity). The risk of conception also depends on the effective practice of contraception and birth control. Fecundity varies with the age of the female, and in general reflects the health of the female population, for example, the incidence of sterility and the prevalence of miscarriage.

Age-specific birth rates or age-specific fertility rates reflect the probability of giving birth at each age. Across populations a general parabolic pattern is evident in the age-specific birth rates. Biology limits most child-bearing to between the ages of 15 and 45. The peak fertility years typically occur in the mid-twenties. In Figure 2.2 on page 38, we plot the age-specific birth rates (ASBRs) for the United States population for 1960 (a few years after the peak of the post-war baby boom) and for 1990. Formally, the age-specific birth rates are defined as:

$$ASBR_a = \text{age-specific birth rate for women in age interval } a$$

$$= \frac{\text{births to women in age interval } a \text{ during a year}}{\text{mid-year population of women of age interval } a} \times 1000$$

Typically age-specific birth rates are presented for 5-year age intervals and expressed as per thousand women. For example, for the United States in 1960 the ASBR for age interval 20 to 24 years was 258.1. That is, in 1960 there were 258.1 births per thousand women of ages 20 through 24. Roughly one out of every four women in this age interval were giving birth that year. In contrast, by 1990 the ASBR for women of ages 20 to 24 had decreased to 116.5 (or less than one in eight women giving birth).

A standardized measure of fertility is the total fertility rate. The **total fertility rate (TFR)** is the average number of children that would be born to a woman if she were to live to the end of the childbearing years and bear children at each age in accordance with the prevailing age-specific birth rates. The TFR is equal to the sum of the age-specific birth rates, times the length of the age interval. In Table 2.2 on page 39, we illustrate the TFR for the United States for 1990.

The total fertility rate is similar to the life expectancy in that each represents the experience of a hypothetical individual exposed to the prevailing fertility or mortality conditions. The TFR indicates the cumulative consequences of the present age-specific fertility rates for the representative female. This is not to imply that all women bear children according to the ASBRs in a given year, just as not all women can expect to live the number of years given by the female life expectancy at birth.

## FIGURE 2.2 — AGE-SPECIFIC BIRTH RATES (ASBRs) FOR THE POPULATION OF THE UNITED STATES: 1960 AND 1990

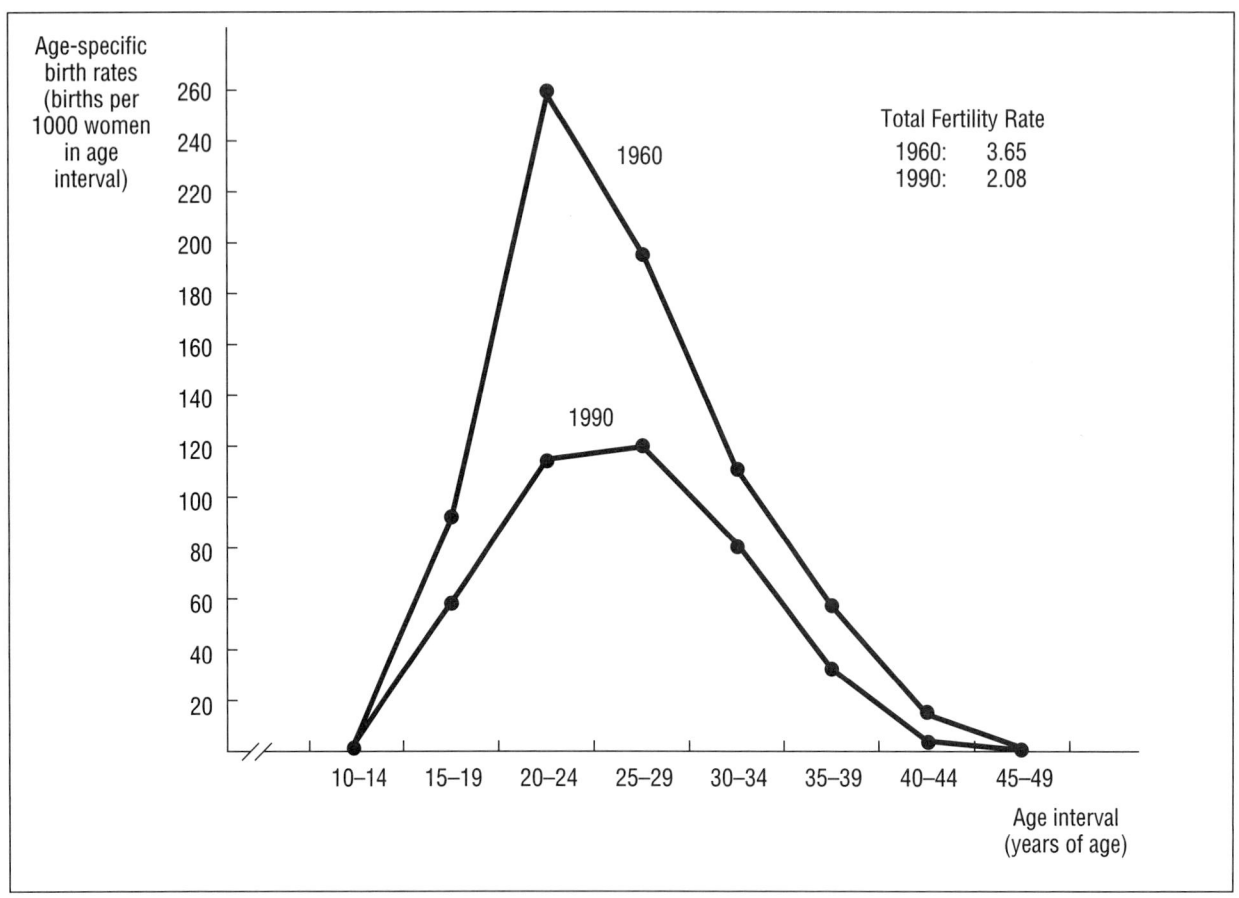

**Replacement-level fertility** refers to the fertility rate in which, for given mortality conditions, each generation just replaces itself, so that in the long run the crude rate of natural increase equals zero. For a developed country in which more than 95 percent of newborn girls survive through the childbearing years (i.e., reach age 49), replacement-level fertility would correspond to a total fertility rate of 2.05 to 2.1. For most of the contemporary developing nations, in which the probability of a newborn girl surviving to the end of the childbearing years is significantly lower (survival rates in the range of 70 to 85 percent), replacement-level fertility would be a TFR of between 2.3 and 2.5.

The 1990 U.S. total fertility rate of 2.08 is consistent with replacement-level fertility; however, because of the post-war baby boom the crude rate of natural increase still exceeds zero. Referring back to Table 2.1, we can see the ranges in the total fertility rates. For the other low-income economies, a woman, on average, had 5.5 children in 1993, implying a more than doubling of the size of each generation. Among the regions of the developing world, sub-Saharan Africa stands out with a total fertility rate of 6.2. In the high-income nations the TFR in 1993 was 1.7; each generation is not even replacing itself, which, in the long run, would mean a decrease in population size.

| TABLE 2.2 | CALCULATION OF THE TOTAL FERTILITY RATE |

| AGE INTERVAL OF MOTHER (5-YEAR RANGE) | $ASBR_a$ |
|---|---|
| 10–14 years | 1.4 |
| 15–19 | 59.9 |
| 20–24 | 116.5 |
| 25–29 | 120.2 |
| 30–34 | 80.8 |
| 35–39 | 31.7 |
| 40–44 | 5.5 |
| 45–49 | .2 |

TFR = length of age interval times the sum of the age-specific birth rates

$$TFR_{1990} = 5 \sum_a ASBR = 5(1.4 + 59.9 + 116.5 + 120.2 + 80.8 + 31.7 + 5.5 + .2)$$
$$= 2081$$

or expressed per woman,

$$TFR_{1990} = 2.08$$

Age-specific birth rates ($ASBR_a$) for the United States in 1990 are the births per thousand women in the age interval $a$.

FROM U.S. Bureau of the Census, *Statistical Abstract of the United States 1993,* 113th edition, Washington, DC: 1993, Table 119.

A strong correlation exists between the CBR and TFR. Since the total fertility rate is independent of the age distribution of females in the population, it is the preferred measure for comparisons of fertility across countries. For determining population growth rates, however, the crude birth rate is used.

The total fertility rate is a period measure; that is, the TFR is affected by conditions prevailing in each period. Short-term fluctuations in the TFR may simply reflect timing decisions, without any change in desired family sizes. For example, consider the "Year of the Fiery Horse," which occurs every 60 years. In Japan superstition holds that girls born in that year would have difficult dispositions, such as a proclivity for murdering their husbands. Understandably, girls born in Fiery Horse years might find it harder to marry. The most recent occurrence was 1966, and in Japan the recorded fertility rates dipped sharply in that year. In 1906, the previous Fiery Horse year, Japanese fertility rates also dropped, even though modern contraception was not available.[5]

Economic conditions may affect the timing of marriage and the spacing of children from one year to the next. Nevertheless, aside from possible short-term fluctuations, the total fertility rate is largely determined by the demand for children, the average health of the population, and the degree to which effective contraception is practiced.

---

[5]See John Weeks, *Population: An Introduction to Concepts and Issues,* 5th ed., Belmont, CA: Wadsworth, 1994, page 148.

## POPULATION MOMENTUM

We have alluded to the fact that populations attaining replacement-level fertility may continue to grow for some time. The phenomenon is known as **population momentum**, which is the potential inherent in the age-sex structure of a population for future growth after the onset of replacement-level fertility. The reason for population momentum can be found in past high rates of fertility—relative to mortality—which produce a young and growing population. With fertility above the replacement level, successive generations are larger. Even if women in the reproductive years, on average, begin to have just enough children to replace themselves and their partners, the population would continue to increase for a while.

A summary measure of the age structure of a population is the **burden of dependency (BD),** defined as:

$$BD = \frac{\text{population under age 15} + \text{population over age 64}}{\text{population from ages 15 through 64}} \times 100$$

$$= \frac{\text{pop}(0-14) + \text{pop}(65+)}{\text{pop}(15-64)} \times 100$$

The burden of dependency, expressed as an index with a base of 100, can be disaggregated into a youth burden of dependency ($YBD$) and an elderly burden of dependency ($EBD$).

$$BD = 100 \times \frac{\text{pop}(0-14)}{\text{pop}(15-64)} + 100 \times \frac{\text{pop}(65+)}{\text{pop}(15-64)}$$

$$BD = YBD + EBD$$

In the aggregate the burden of dependency gives the ratio of net consumers (the population generally too young or too old to be in the labor force and so produce enough to meet their consumption needs) to net producers (the population in the prime labor force years of 15 to 64). A value of 80 for the index means that for every 100 people in the prime labor force ages, 80 others exist who are younger or older. While labor force participation rates differ across countries and are not confined to the ages 15 through 64, the burden of dependency does represent the potential "drag" of the age structure of a population on the production possibilities of an economy.

Reflecting their high rates of population growth, the LDCs have high youth burdens of dependency. Conversely, in the developed countries low fertility and declining rates of population growth have resulted in an aging of their populations and relatively high elderly burdens of dependency. Overall the less developed countries have significantly greater burdens of dependency, on the order of 80 to 100 net consumers per 100 net producers, compared to 45 to 60 net consumers per net producers in the developed countries. As we will discuss in Chapter 7, a high burden of dependency may impair economic growth and development.

The age-sex structure of a population can be illustrated with a **population pyramid**, a bar graph for the population in each age group, with males on the left, and females on the right, of the vertical axis. Rapidly growing populations with high fertility have expansive population pyramids; that is, the bases of the pyramids are broad. For example, see Figure 2.3 and the population pyramid for Mali, a low-income African

FIGURE 2.3   POPULATION PYRAMIDS: MALI AND SWEDEN, 1990

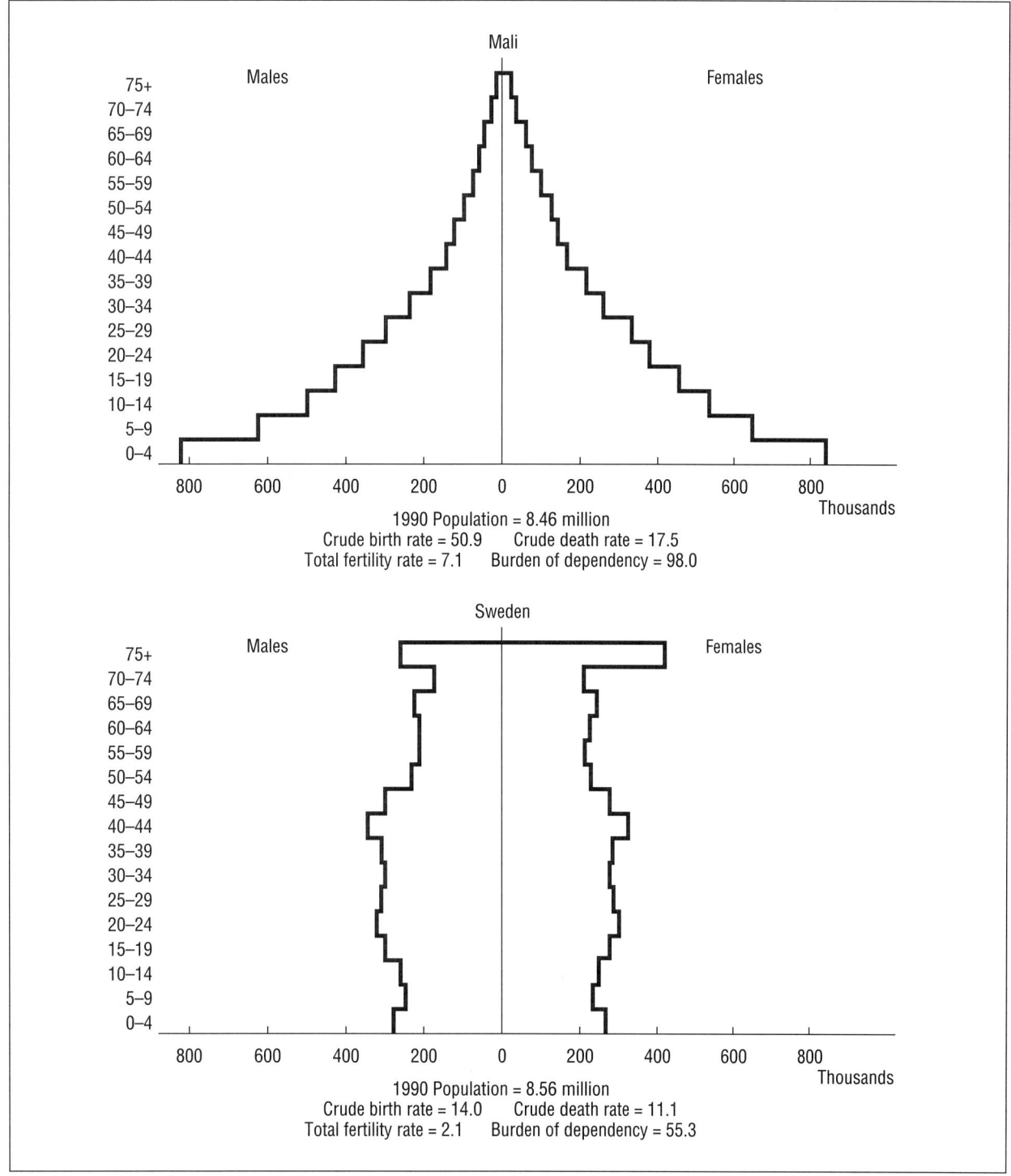

FROM World Bank, *World Population Projections 1994–95,* Baltimore, MD: The Johns Hopkins Press, 1994, pages 330 and 460.

## TABLE 2.3  ILLUSTRATION OF POPULATION MOMENTUM

Assumptions:
1. There is a 100 percent survival rate from birth through age 44 years. All individuals die on their 45th birthday.
2. The initial population is evenly distributed across all ages, with an equal number of males and females in each age.
3. All births occur to the population that begins in the middle age interval.
4. The total fertility rate is 2.0 for all periods, past and future, except the second and third periods, when the TFR increases to 4.0.
5. The periods of projection are 15 years and equal to the length of each age interval.

|  |  | POPULATION AT THE END OF THE PERIOD | | | | |
|---|---|---|---|---|---|---|
| AGE GROUP | INITIAL POPULATION | PERIOD 1 | PERIOD 2 | PERIOD 3 | PERIOD 4 | PERIOD 5 |
| 0–14 | 100 | 100 | 200 | 200 | 200 | 200 |
| 15–29 | 100 | 100 | 100 | 200 | 200 | 200 |
| 30–44 | 100 | 100 | 100 | 100 | 200 | 200 |
| **Total** | 300 | 300 | 400 | 500 | 600 | 600 |
| TFR |  | 2.0 | **4.0** | **4.0** | 2.0 | 2.0 |

nation with a total fertility rate of 7.1 and burden of dependency of 98.0 in 1990. Mali has substantial population momentum—even if younger generations begin only to replace themselves, Mali's population will continue to increase for several decades at least. In contrast, the population pyramid for Sweden, a high-income European nation of roughly the same-size population as Mali, is shaped more like a rectangle. Sweden has been near replacement-level fertility for some time; consequently, population momentum in Sweden is minimal. Sweden's aging population, however, is evident by the bulging bars for its population of ages 75 years and above.

## AN ILLUSTRATION OF POPULATION MOMENTUM

We can illustrate the consequences of population momentum with a simple example. Consider a population divided into three age groups: 0 to 14, 15 to 29, and 30 to 44 years of age. Within each age group there is an equal number of males and females and the distribution of population is uniform across single-year ages. To make the mathematics easier, assume that the survival rate is 100 percent through age 44, but that all deaths occur immediately at age 45. Assume that all childbearing occurs to those who are in the middle age interval (15 through 29) at the beginning of the period and is evenly spread over the population in that interval. We begin with an initial population (period 0) that has been subject to replacement-level fertility for some time. Note that under these assumptions replacement-level fertility corresponds to a total fertility rate of exactly two *(TFR* = 2.0).

We will project the initial population forward in 15-year intervals under given total fertility rates and will calculate the population size. See Table 2.3 for the projections.

The initial population aged 0 to 14 survives intact over the 15-year projection to become the population aged 15 to 29 at the end of period 1. (See the diagonal arrow labeled (*a*) in Table 2.3.) So too the initial population aged 15 to 29 survives forward to become the population aged 30 to 44 at the end of the first period. (See the arrow labeled (*b*) in Table 2.3.) This age bracket is responsible for the 100 births over the period. All of the initial population aged 30 to 44 dies out over the 15-year interval. With replacement-level fertility and a population with a uniform age distribution, zero population growth occurs and there is no population momentum. In fact, a stationary population results, with 33.3 percent of the population younger than 15 years.

For the second projection, suppose the total fertility rate doubles to four *(TFR* = 4.0). There would now be 200 births from the 100 people of the childbearing cohort. The population increases to 400 in size, and there is now population momentum. Fifty percent of the population is under age 15, and will move into childbearing in the future. Suppose the total fertility rate remains at 4.0 in the third period. Then, in the third period 200 births would also occur (from the 100 people of ages 15 to 29 at the beginning of the period), and the population size increases to 500. Now, in the fourth period and all subsequent periods, assume that fertility returns to the replacement level (here *TFR* = 2.0). Even though parents are now only replacing themselves (the 200 people beginning in the age interval 15 to 29), population momentum increases the size of the population to 600. At the end of the fourth period the population momentum has been spent and we return to a stationary population with a uniform age distribution. Thus, a two-period spurt in the total fertility rate beyond replacement level produces population growth that continues for one extra period due to the population momentum.

We re-emphasize a point made in Chapter 1. The relevance of population momentum should be clear. The LDCs have young populations and have built up considerable population momentum. Even if every country were to attain replacement-level fertility today, the population of the world would increase by another 2 to 3 billion. Whether these additions will strain the available resources, put pressure on the environment, or hinder economic development is open to speculation. The fact is that few developing countries are even close to replacement-level fertility. We are, therefore, likely to add significantly more than 2 or 3 billion before the world population stabilizes. To assess the prospects for the less developed countries in reducing fertility, we turn to the theory of the demographic transition.

## THE DEMOGRAPHIC TRANSITION

The **demographic transition** refers to the movement from a state of high birth and high death rates, characteristic of traditional societies, to one of low birth and low death rates, characteristic of modern, industrial economies. All of the high-income developed countries have made this transition. The less developed countries are currently undergoing their transitions with varying degrees of progress.

For the vast majority of the human experience, a demographic equilibrium has existed of high, fairly stable birth rates offsetting high, volatile death rates. Population growth, on average, was minimal. Periods of population increases would alternate with intervals of depopulation. From 8000 B.C., the time of the first Agricultural Revolution with the cultivation of crops and domestication of animals, to the mid-eighteenth century and the Industrial Revolution, the world population is estimated to have increased a hundredfold, from 8 million to 800 million. The average annual increase works out to less than half an additional person per thousand population.

The volatility in death rates reflects the impact of exogenous shocks. Populations were vulnerable to crop failures and famine from pests, blight, and sudden shifts in weather. Epidemics and wars also took their toll. Fertility behavior was dictated by custom, with little or no individual discretion. Indeed, with the high mortality, birth rates had to be high to ensure the survival of families and societies. Moreover, in traditional agrarian societies, large families are advantageous. Extra hands to work the fields and do chores are always welcome. With no social security net, parents depend on their children for old-age support.

## THE WESTERN EXPERIENCE

During the last half of the eighteenth century, first in England, then on the European continent, and later in North America, there began sustained declines in death rates. A second agricultural revolution was underway, with significant increases in crop yields through the adoption of better techniques of cultivation, improved strains of seeds and plants, advances in irrigation and fertilizer use. The growth of markets with freer trade and improvements in transportation meant that food shortages from local crop failures could be averted. The greater food supplies, along with the increased demand for labor with the Industrial Revolution, pulled up real wages and the average standard of living. The gains in nutrition made populations hardier and more resistant to sickness and disease.[6] With the gains in health, fecundity increased. With unchanging fertility behavior, birth rates rose. Improvements in economic conditions that resulted in a fall in death rates and a rise in birth rates were not unusual. They were also not expected to last.

### MALTHUSIAN POPULATION THEORY

Thomas Malthus, a professor of political economy at East India College in England, helped set the tone for classical economics with his *Essay on the Principle of Population*, first published anonymously in 1798. Malthus observed that population growth, when unchecked, increases in a geometric ratio: 2, 4, 8, 16, 32 ... $2^N$, where $N$ refers to a generation of approximately 25 years. He speculated that the means of subsistence or the production of food, at best, could only increase in an arithmetic ratio: 1, 2, 3, 4, 5 ... $N$. The supply of arable land was finite, and further increases in agricultural output would require using less fertile fields. Malthus concluded that

---

[6]In the nineteenth century, advances in medicine (e.g., smallpox vaccinations and the use of antiseptics during surgery) and public health measures (e.g., improvements in sanitation and hygiene) contributed to the declining mortality.

population growth, unless checked, would inevitably outstrip the food supply, yielding a stationary state of subsistence.

Malthus identified two kinds of population checks. **Positive checks**, operating through the death rate, were manifested either as "vice" (increases in the death rate brought on by humans through wars, violence, and infanticide) or "misery" (increases in the death rate due to the laws of nature such as disease, natural disasters, and famine). **Preventative checks** operated through decreases in the birth rate. Immoral relations and birth control were also labelled by Malthus as "vice."[7] In later editions Malthus allowed that "moral restraint," or the postponement of marriage and children until one could adequately support a family, was a virtuous preventative check to population growth.

For Malthus, education was the key—to enlightenment, the exercise of moral restraint, and the curbing of population growth. Otherwise, the long-run equilibrium would be a stationary state of zero population growth at subsistence-level wages. The ultimate check on population growth would be famine. Any improvement in the standard of living would be temporary. For example, a favorable harvest might lower food prices and boost real wages. Death rates would fall, and with earlier marriage and family formation possible, birth rates might rise. The ensuing population growth would increase the demand for food, necessitating that marginal lands of lower productivity be brought under cultivation. The price of food would rise, which together with the greater population, would lower real per capita incomes back to a subsistence level.

Malthus underestimated, however, the reduction in fertility that would follow the sustained declines in mortality, as well as the subsequent technological progress in agriculture that increased the ability to produce food. By the end of the nineteenth century birth rates were declining throughout Western Europe and North America. Combining to reduce the advantages of large families were shifts in population to cities; the institution of child-labor laws; the recognition that education was important for economic mobility; and increased consumption aspirations. The practice of fertility limitation, first adopted by the upper class then the middle class, spread. Once begun, the declines in fertility persisted, and by the mid-1930s, birth rates had reached near parity with death rates. In fact, during the Great Depression years, concerns were expressed that the low population growth rates of the industrialized nations were contributing to the economic stagnation.

### Stages of the Demographic Transition

The three stages of the demographic transition are illustrated in Figure 2.4. In the traditional, or Malthusian, stage that has characterized most of human history, birth rates are high and fairly stable, while death rates are high and sensitive to external shocks. Populations are young; that is, life expectancy is short and a relatively high

---

[7]Malthus included among immoral relations, prostitution, homosexuality, and sexual acts that could not result in conception. Malthus opposed birth control and admonished that "promiscuous intercourse to such a degree as to prevent the birth of children seems to lower, in the most marked manner, the dignity of human nature" (*An Essay on the Principle of Population*, vol. 1, 7th ed., London: J. M. Dent and Sons, 1927, page 13). For an interesting account of Malthus, see "The Gloomy Presentiments of Parson Malthus and David Ricardo," pages 40–73 in Robert Heilbroner, *The Worldly Philosophers*, Fourth edition, New York: Simon and Schuster, 1972 (or subsequent editions).

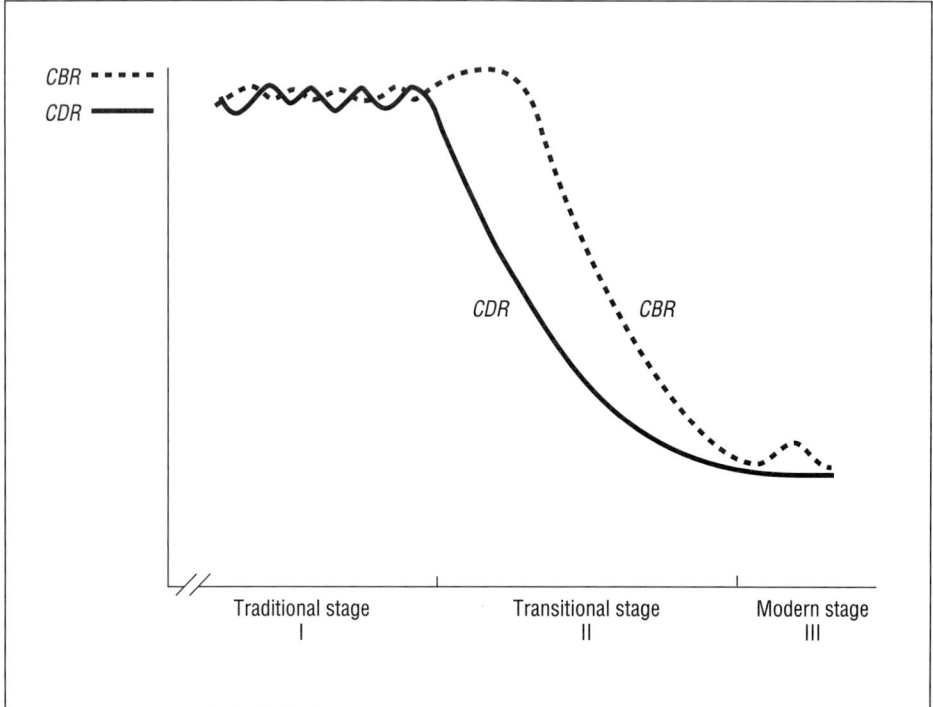

**FIGURE 2.4** DEMOGRAPHIC TRANSITION

percentage of the population is under age 15. Stage II is the transitional stage of population disequilibrium. Declines in death rates precede declines in birth rates, opening up historically high rates of population growth. Eventually, falling birth rates catch up with the lower death rates and the modern demographic equilibrium is reached. In this third, or modern, stage, birth rates, while low and somewhat responsive to economic cycles, again offset death rates.[8] Population growth is minimal, average life expectancy is high, and populations are older.

Upon further investigation, however, the evidence from Europe offers a mixed picture of the demographic transition. In fact, to label the generalized account of the transition experiences of the developed countries a theory may be misleading. The implication is that the declines in mortality, particularly in infant and child mortality rates, were a necessary, and even a sufficient, condition for declines in fertility. Lower child mortality would mean that to attain a desired family size, fewer births would be required. While mortality would respond quickly to economic development and improvements in nutrition and health, the response of fertility would be delayed. It

---

[8]In the first 20 years following World War II, the developed countries did experience baby booms, with birth rates soaring. By the mid-1970s, however, birth rates had declined back to the lows of the 1930s, and even below replacement-level fertility in the United States and a number of Western European nations. Nevertheless, populations continued to increase due to the population momentum from the earlier baby booms and immigration.

would take time for the customs underpinning high fertility to be replaced by the innovative practice of birth control. The lag in fertility decline produced the significant population growth.

As might be expected, nations had different experiences. In some, notably France and Germany, the decline in fertility largely coincided with the decline in mortality. Knodel and van de Walle note that, "Fertility declines took place under a wide variety of social, economic and demographic conditions."[9] Birth rates began to fall in rural France in the face of high infant mortality, nearly a century before the fertility declines in England (the home of the Industrial Revolution) and other Western nations. The onset and diffusion of family limitation in Western Europe appears to be more related to cultural factors (common language, customs, and mores) than to socioeconomic thresholds (child mortality and urbanization).[10] Traditional methods of birth control (abstinence, coitus interruptus, and abortion) were initially relied upon for family limitation. Furthermore, there is evidence that the high infant mortality may have been, in part, an accommodation to high fertility. Abusive child care, even infanticide, may have been the response of some parents to "extra births."[11]

## THE DEMOGRAPHIC TRANSITIONS OF THE LDCS

The developing economies of Asia, Africa, the Middle East, and Latin America are currently in the disequilibrium stage of their transitions, whereby the declines in mortality have outpaced the declines in fertility, producing rapid population growth. It is instructive, despite the rather loose framework offered by demographic transition theory, to compare the situations of the LDCs with the earlier experience of the Western European nations.[12]

One major difference is the source of the mortality declines. Recall that greater food supplies were primarily responsible for improving the average standard of living and initiating the sustained declines in mortality in the West in the latter half of the eighteenth century. In contrast, medical technologies, financed and administered by the West, especially after the Second World War, were responsible for the sharply reduced death rates in the LDCs. Disease control (for example, malaria eradication campaigns and vaccinations for polio, diphtheria, and tetanus) and antibiotics were able to improve survival rates significantly without much economic development in these regions.

Moreover, the pace of the declines in mortality was much faster. An early account is given by the sociologist-demographer Kingsley Davis.

---

[9]John Knodel and Etienne van de Walle, "European Transition," *International Encyclopedia of Population*, vol. 1, edited by John Ross, New York: The Free Press, 1982, page 268.

[10]See Ansley Coale, "The Demographic Transition," *International Population Conference, Liege,* vol. 1, Liege, Belgium: International Union for the Scientific Study of Population, 1973, pages 53–72.

[11]See Knodel and van de Walle, page 271.

[12]For a concise overview, see Michael Teitelbaum, "Relevance of Demographic Transition Theory for Developing Countries," *Science*, vol. 188 (May 1975), pages 420–425, reprinted in *Population: Dynamics, Ethics, and Policy*, edited by Priscilla Reining and Irene Tinker, Washington, DC: American Association for the Advancement of Science, 1975, pages 174–179.

> The rapidity with which the death rate has declined in most of the underdeveloped areas, including many areas with a high ratio of population to resources, has been unprecedented. It has never been matched at any time in the now advanced countries ...
>
> The best known case is that of Ceylon [now Sri Lanka]. There the crude death rate fell by 34 percent in one year (from 1946 to 1947)! This was no fluke, because the death rate continued to fall....
>
> The main cause of the spectacular decline of mortality in Ceylon is well known. It was the use of DDT as a residual spray in the control of malaria. For centuries this disease was the major cause of death and illness on the island.[13]

Crude birth rates in Western Europe at the time of the transition were comparatively low—in the range of 30 to 35 per thousand—suppressed by the practice of late marriage and a high incidence of celibacy or never marrying. To an extent this reflected land constraints and the custom of primogeniture, in which the eldest son often would delay marriage until he took over the family farm. Other siblings, who may have eventually migrated to the cities, would also have to postpone marriage.

In contrast, when death rates began to fall in the developing nations of Africa, Asia, the Middle East, and Latin America, birth rates were much higher, bolstered by the practice of early and near-universal marriage. Thus the period of childbearing for the average couple was considerably longer, and crude birth rates were in the range of 45 to 50 per thousand.

The combination of the sharper declines in mortality and the initially higher fertility has produced explosive population growth in the less developed regions. Whereas the nations of Western Europe experienced population doubling times from 50 to 100 years during their transitions, the doubling times for the LDCs in the early decades following World War II were 20 to 30 years. Moreover, unlike the European nations, which had the outlet of emigration to the Americas, Australia, and New Zealand, the contemporary developing nations have to deal with their higher population growth largely on their own. International migration is more restricted than in the eighteenth and nineteenth centuries.

To see how the developing regions are progressing through the demographic transition, refer to Figure 2.5. For all regions the crude birth rates (*CBRs*) exceed the crude death rates (*CDRs*). The highest birth rates are found in sub-Saharan Africa, a region where the signs of fertility decline are still minimal. The East Asian and Pacific and Latin American and the Caribbean areas have similar trends over the past two decades, despite the much higher incomes in the latter. The East Asian nations, in particular, have been very successful in reducing fertility—a reflection of effective birth-control policies and perhaps the pragmatic cultures. Similarly, despite lower average incomes and higher mortality rates, the South Asian region has made more progress in reducing fertility than the Middle East and North Africa, a difference that may be explained, in part, by more family planning in the former and the lower status of females in the latter.

There is diversity not only across regions, but within each region of the developing world. To illustrate, consider the following crude birth rates (in parentheses) for low-income economies for 1993: Niger (52) and Kenya (36) in sub-Saharan Africa; Pakistan (40) and Sri Lanka (20) in South Asia; and Lao PDR or Laos (44) and China (19) in East

---

[13]Kingsley Davis, "The Amazing Decline of Mortality in Underdeveloped Areas," *American Economic Review*, vol. 46, no. 2 (May 1956), pages 305–318. These quotations are from pages 306–307 and 311.

## FIGURE 2.5  PROGRESS IN THE DEMOGRAPHIC TRANSITION (1970–1993)

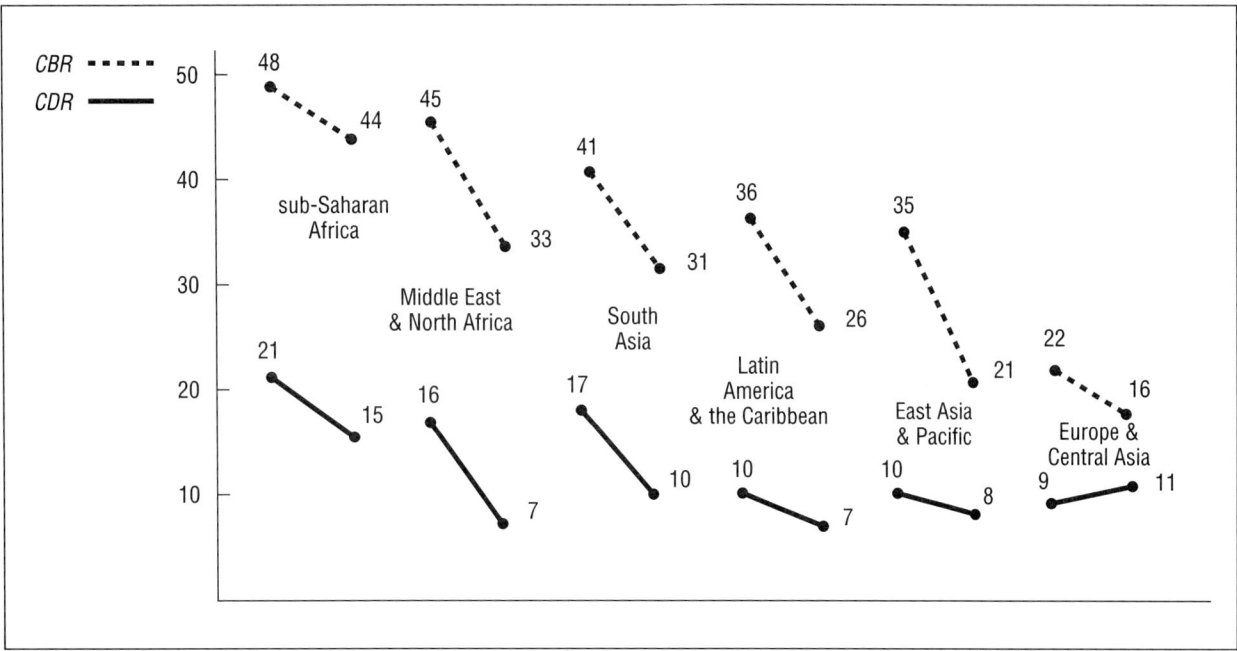

FROM World Bank, *World Development Report 1995*, Table 26.

Asia and Pacific. For middle-income economies, examples of the range of crude birth rates for 1993 are Oman (43) and Morocco (28) in the Middle East and North Africa; Uzbekistan (31) and Greece (10) in Europe and Central Asia; and Guatemala (38) and Uruguay (17) in Latin America and the Caribbean region.[14]

Given that zero population growth is a likely long-run equilibrium for planet Earth, the ultimate size of the world's population largely depends on how soon the developing nations complete their demographic transitions. While the determinants of fertility will be considered in detail in Chapter 7, we present here one theory for the high fertility rates found in the less developed countries—Caldwell's theory of net intergenerational wealth flows.

## CALDWELL'S NET INTERGENERATIONAL WEALTH FLOWS

With a disarmingly simple theory, John Caldwell offers an explanation for the transition from the high fertility of traditional societies to the low fertility in modern

---

[14] These statistics are from the World Bank, *World Development Report 1995*, Table 26.

societies. An important premise is that rational behavior, that is, behavior consistent with attaining given objectives, must be judged in the sociocultural context. For Caldwell,

> [T]he fundamental issue in demographic transition ... is the direction and magnitude of intergenerational wealth flows or the net balance of the two flows—one from parents to children and the other from children to parents.[15]

In traditional, especially agrarian, societies, children are put to work at an early age in the fields or around the household. Even in urban areas of developing economies many children work long hours in sweatshops or odd-jobbing on the streets. Older siblings or grandparents watch after the children too young to work. Moreover, in the absence of social security systems, parents rely on their children for old-age support.[16] As an example, consider the following excerpts from a newspaper article from New Delhi, India.

> According to an unofficial ILO [International Labor Office] estimate, there are 138 million working children in India....
>
> Nuruslam and Shabum are two brothers who spend their day gathering and selling paper from 8 A.M. to 6 P.M. One brother is ten years old while the other is eight. They manage to make Rs20 every day [approximately $1], an important fact since their father made them leave school for these 20 rupees....
>
> According to the Catholic Hospital Association of India spokesman, 35,000 children work in the slate industry. Dust enters their lungs causing fibrosis—a disease deadlier than tuberculosis. The life expectancy is 30 years. Children at the age of 12 or less are forced into this fatal work to sustain their dying parents—only to learn that they too will die soon. Since the children are married early and the husbands die young, this area is known as the land of the child widows ... [despite the fact that] the Constitution has forbidden employment of children under the age of 14 in factories, mines, and other hazardous occupations.[17]

In short, in addition to the universal psychic and emotional satisfaction children bring, children may be economic assets in developing countries. With relatively high rates of child mortality, more births are required to ensure surviving sons; and with more sons, parents increase the chances of being adequately supported in old age. Under such conditions, where wealth flows are, on net, from children to parents, high fertility is economically rational behavior.

In the high-income Western cultures, in contrast, the net flow of wealth is decidedly from parents to children. Children are expensive. Primary and secondary schooling are required, and costly higher education is widely perceived as the key to economic mobility. With affluence, consumer aspirations rise, and children would naturally share in the higher standards of living. Children are not expected to gener-

---

[15]John Caldwell, "Toward a Restatement of Demographic Transition Theory," *Population and Development Review*, vol. 2, no. 3–4 (September/December 1976), pages 321–366. This quotation is from page 344.

[16]In some traditional societies daughters are not considered as economically valuable as sons. Not only might the dowry be expensive to marry them off, but, once married, the daughters "belong" to their husbands' families.

[17]Seema Sarin, "Child Victims of Industrialization," *The Statesman*, New Delhi, India (September 23, 1989).

ate much income, however, and with social security systems, parents need not depend on their children for old-age support. While the emotional and psychic satisfaction derived from children may be just as strong, in Western industrial societies the economic advantages of children are usually far outweighed by the costs. It is not surprising that in the West lower fertility is economically rational behavior.[18]

Caldwell argues that the small-family norm is largely a Western phenomenon, one that nevertheless can be transmitted to developing economies. Mass education and the mass media, both heavily influenced by Western culture, are the means of transmission. In less developed countries the school curriculum, texts, and instruction are typically based on the Western model. Advertising and entertainment on television, the radio, and in popular magazines promote the Western lifestyle. The elite, urban, educated women will be the first in the developing economies to limit fertility. Their examples will be emulated by other women as education and economic mobility increase, and rising consumer aspirations conflict with large families.

In sum, when net flows of wealth shift from "from children to parents" (as in traditional societies and developing economies) to "from parents to children" (as in Western societies and developed economies), then economically rational behavior shifts from high fertility to low fertility. Accompanying the demographic transition, according to Caldwell, is a wealth transition. (In Chapter 7 we will discuss other theories of fertility.)

## CONCLUDING NOTE

In the first two chapters we have discussed the concepts and measurements of economic growth, economic development, and population growth. As we will see throughout the text, economic growth, economic development, and population growth are inextricably linked in ways that are still not entirely understood. In the contemporary developing nations, rapid population growth may be both a cause and a consequence of the low levels of economic development. Consequently, while a common goal is economic development, the policies prescribed to achieve that goal may differ or even conflict, thus sparking controversy and debate. We turn in Section II (Chapters 3 through 6) to strategies of economic development, beginning with the growth model approach and proceeding more or less as development theory has evolved over time.

---

[18]The rising elderly burden of dependency in the developed countries, largely a consequence of the low fertility rates over the last quarter century, combined with generous social support systems, is beginning to squeeze the populations of working age. For example, in the United States, Social Security (and to some extent, Medicare) is funded on a "pay-as-you-go" basis, with tax revenues on current labor incomes used to pay for the benefits of current recipients. Increasingly, in the aggregate, net wealth is flowing from young and middle-aged parents to their children and to the elderly. The implications for future fertility are speculative. Consider that in the United States the percentage of the population 65 years or older, estimated at 12.6% in 1990, is projected to rise to 15.3% by the year 2015. The corresponding shares of the elderly in the total population are projected to rise from 17.8% in 1990 to 20.4% in 2015 in Sweden, and from 11.9% in 1990 to 24.1% in 2015 in Japan. These elderly burdens of dependency are derived from World Bank, *World Population Projections 1994–95*, by Eduard Bos, My T. Vu, Ernest Massiah, and Rodolfo Bulatao, Baltimore: The Johns Hopkins University Press, 1994 (pages 284, 460, and 494).

## SUMMARY OF MAIN POINTS

1. For the human race, significant population increases are a relatively recent phenomenon. With a finite earth, zero population growth—where, on average, crude birth rates offset crude death rates—would appear to be necessary for long-run equilibrium.
2. Currently the highest rates of population growth are found in the less developed countries, producing young populations with substantial population momentum.
3. The growth rate for a population in a given area is equal to the sum of the crude rate of natural increase (the crude birth rate less the crude death rate) and the net in-migration rate. To approximate the doubling time (in years) of a population, divide the annual population growth rate (expressed in percentage points) into 72.
4. The crude death rate is not a good indicator for comparisons of mortality conditions across populations with significantly different age structures. Better measures for cross-country comparisons are the infant mortality rate and the female life expectancy at birth.
5. The total fertility rate, the average number of children that would be born to a woman living to the end of the childbearing years and experiencing the current age-specific birth rates, is a standardized measure of present fertility, useful for comparisons across countries or over time. Replacement-level fertility—for the developed countries, a total fertility rate of between 2.05 and 2.1, and somewhat higher for less developed countries—is consistent with zero population growth in the long run.
6. The age-sex structure of a population can be illustrated with a population pyramid. A summary measure of the age structure of a population is the burden of dependency, roughly giving the ratio of the dependent population to the population of working age. Countries with high rates of fertility have expansive population pyramids, high youth burdens of dependency, and considerable population momentum.
7. The demographic transition is the evolution from a traditional demographic equilibrium of high birth and death rates, low life expectancies, and young populations to a modern equilibrium of low birth and death rates, high life expectancies, and older populations. Historically, in between the two equilibrium states of minimal or zero population growth is a disequilibrium stage of rapid population growth.
8. The demographic transition experiences of the contemporary developing economies have been qualitatively and quantitatively different from the earlier experiences of Western Europe. After World War II, death rates fell sharply in the developing economies, largely from imported disease-control technologies. In the face of high fertility, population growth rates soared.
9. Malthus held that, in the absence of positive checks (through higher death rates) or preventative checks (through lower birth rates), in the long run population growth would outpace increases in food supply, dooming the human race to a subsistence level of living. The key to curbing population growth was "moral restraint," whereby family sizes would be conscientiously limited to the numbers that could be adequately provided for.

10. Most of the contemporary developing nations are in the transition stage of the demographic transition, where declining fertility has not caught up with the declining mortality. Regionally, outside of Europe and Central Asia, the East Asian nations are the closest to attaining replacement-level fertility. At the other extreme, the high fertility rates in sub-Saharan Africa are only beginning to show signs of a sustained decline.

11. According to Caldwell, high fertility may be economically rational behavior in those societies where the net flow of wealth is from children to parents. In developing economies, children are often economic assets—generating current income and providing old-age security. Under such circumstances, with high rates of infant and child mortality, high rates of fertility are required to achieve the desired family size.

## KEY TERMS

burden of dependency (BD)
crude birth rate (CBR)
crude death rate (CDR)
crude rate of natural increase (CRNI)
demographic transition
life expectancy at birth
net in-migration rate

population momentum
population pyramid
positive checks
preventative checks
replacement-level fertility
total fertility rate (TFR)

## QUESTIONS

1. Compare the indices for the crude death rate and life expectancy at birth. In particular, how does each index capture a dimension of the mortality in a nation? What is the most appropriate use of each index?

2. Compare the indices for the crude birth rate and total fertility rate. In particular, how does each index capture a dimension of the fertility in a nation? What is the most appropriate use of each index?

3. Calculate the crude death rate for the following population given its age structure and the age-specific death rates (ASDRs).

| Age Interval (Years) | % of Population | ASDR |
|---|---|---|
| Under age 1 | 4 | 30 |
| 1–14 | 35 | 4 |
| 15–44 | 30 | 10 |
| 45–64 | 26 | 40 |
| 65 and over | 5 | 120 |

If the crude birth rate were 50 (births per thousand mid-year population) and the net in-migration rate were –2 (net in-migrants per thousand mid-year population), find the annual population growth rate and estimate the population doubling time.

4. Given the following age-specific birth rates (ASBRs), calculate the total fertility rate for the population.

| Age Interval of Mother (Years) | ASBR |
|---|---|
| 10–14 | 2 |
| 15–19 | 120 |
| 20–24 | 230 |
| 25–29 | 200 |
| 30–34 | 150 |
| 35–39 | 80 |
| 40–44 | 10 |
| 45–49 | 1 |

5. Given the three population pyramids below,

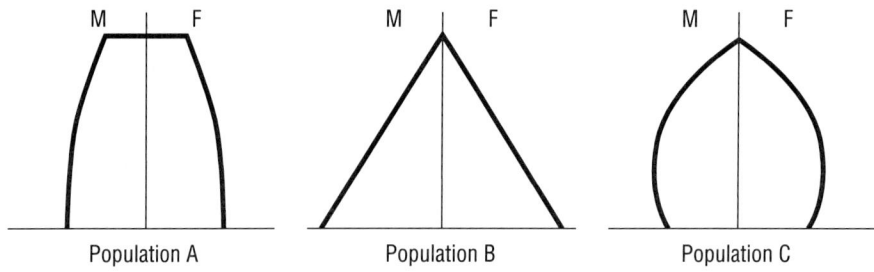

which age structure most resembles a developing economy? Why?
Can you infer anything about the total fertility rates in the three populations? In particular, in which population is the total fertility rate below replacement level?

6. Generally, during the transitional stage of the demographic transition, the decline in death rates has preceded the decline in birth rates. Discuss whether or not it would be possible or likely for a sustained decline in fertility to precede the decline in mortality for a nation during the transition stage.

7. Can Malthus's theory of population ever be proven wrong? Discuss.

## SUGGESTED READINGS

Caldwell, John, "Toward a Restatement of Demographic Transition Theory," *Population and Development Review*, vol. 2, no. 3–4 (September/December 1976), pages 321–366.

Coale, Ansley, "The Demographic Transition," *International Population Conference, Liege*, vol. 1, Liege, Belgium: International Union for the Scientific Study of Population, 1973, pages 53–72.

Davis, Kingsley, "The Amazing Decline of Mortality in Underdeveloped Areas," *American Economic Review*, vol. 46, no. 2 (May 1956), pages 305–318.

Heilbroner, Robert, "The Gloomy Presentiments of Parson Malthus and David Ricardo," in *The Worldly Philosophers*, 4th ed., New York: Simon and Schuster, 1972, pages 40–73.

Knodel, John and Etienne van de Walle, "European Transition," *International Encyclopedia of Population*, vol. 1, edited by John Ross, New York: The Free Press, 1982, pages 268–275.

Lutz, Wolfgang, "The Future of World Population," *Population Bulletin*, vol. 49, no. 1 (June 1994), Washington, DC: Population Reference Bureau.

Teitelbaum, Michael, "Relevance of Demographic Transition Theory for Developing Countries," *Science*, vol. 188 (May 1975), pages 420–425.

# APPENDIX

## THE GROWTH RATE IN POPULATION

To derive the equation for the growth rate in the population for an area, let

$P_T$ = population of an area at time $T$, the beginning of a period of duration $t$ (where $t$ equals one year)

$P_{T+t}$ = population of the area at time $T + t$, the end of the period

$B_t$ = births during the period to the population

$D_t$ = deaths during the period to the population

$NM_t$ = net in-migration to the area during the period

The size of a population at a point in time is a stock variable. Births, deaths, and net in-migration, defined over a period of time, are flow variables.

In Equation 1 the population size at time $T + t$, the end of the period, is equal to the population size at the beginning of the period plus the difference between births and deaths plus net in-migration to the area over the period. Subtracting the initial, or beginning of period, population from both sides of the equation gives an expression for population change over the period. See Equation 2. Dividing both sides of this equation by one-half of the sum of the initial and final populations (or the mid-year population, assuming a uniform flow of births, deaths, and net in-migration over the period) yields an expression for the growth rate of population.

1. $P_{T+t} = P_T + B_t - D_t + NM_t$

2. $P_{T+t} - P_T = B_t - D_t + NM_t$

3. $\dfrac{P_{T+t} - P_T}{.5(P_{T+t} + P_T)} = \dfrac{B_t}{.5(P_{T+t} + P_T)} - \dfrac{D_t}{.5(P_{T+t} + P_T)} + \dfrac{NM_t}{.5(P_{T+t} + P_T)}$

4. $r_t = CBR_t - CDR_t + NMR_t$

population growth rate = crude birth rate − crude death rate + net in-migration rate

To illustrate, consider a small country with 200,000 inhabitants at the beginning of the year. Suppose that over the year there are 5000 births and 3000 deaths in this population. In addition, there are 400 immigrants and 600 emigrants. At the end of the year, then, the population of the country is 201,800 = 200,000 + 5000 − 3000 + (400 − 600). Assuming even flows of births, deaths, immigration, and emigration over the year, the mid-year population size is 200,900 (or the average of the populations at the beginning and end of the year). In terms of rates, the crude birth rate is .0249 = 5000/200,900 (or 24.9 births per thousand population); and the crude death rate is .0149 = 3000/200,900 (or 14.9 deaths per thousand population). The crude rate of natural increase is .010 = 1.0 percent (or 10 per thousand population). The net in-migration rate is −.001 = −200/200,900 (or −1 per thousand population). Thus, the population growth rate is .9 percent or 9 per thousand population. At this rate, the doubling time for this population would be approximately 80 years.

PART II

# THEORIES OF ECONOMIC GROWTH AND DEVELOPMENT

# CHAPTER 3

# THE GROWTH MODEL APPROACH AND STEADY-STATE EQUILIBRIUM

Only in designing a world economic order to follow the Second World War and in considering the situation of countries which would be making their own economic policies for the first time, did expressions like the underdeveloped countries and the Third World come into use. Once the subject was identified, there arose a separate field of economics known as "development economics." The ideas of the first development economists were tremendously influential and are crucial to understanding actual policies adopted by LDCs in the 1950s, many of which remain in place today.[1]

Early efforts in development economics centered on modeling economic growth. The growth model approach is distinguished by an emphasis on physical capital accumulation. The implied assumption is that economic growth and increases in per capita income invariably yield economic development. Indeed, for poor countries, economic growth would seem to be a necessary condition for economic development. Several considerations may help to explain the thrust of these models.

First, the attention of the International Bank for Reconstruction and Development (World Bank) in the early post–World War II era was focused on the reconstruction of the war-torn economies of Europe and Japan.[2] In these nations, educated populations and skilled labor forces existed; hence, the overwhelming need was to rebuild the economic infrastructure and invest in new plant, equipment, and machinery. Second, with

---

[1]Richard Pomfret, *Diverse Paths of Economic Development,* New York: Prentice-Hall, 1992, page 4.

[2]Three major international economic institutions established in the mid-1940s are as follows: the International Bank for Reconstruction and Development (World Bank), designed to channel financial capital to nations for rebuilding and developing their economies; the International Monetary Fund (IMF), charged with monitoring a code of conduct for exchange rate practices and assisting in balance of payments adjustments; and the General Agreement on Tariffs and Trade (GATT), intended to provide a framework for liberalizing international trade. The subsequent roles played by these institutions in fostering economic growth and development will be discussed in later chapters.

the rapid population growth associated with the sharp declines in mortality rates, an abundance of labor and a scarcity of capital seemed to be common features of the developing economies of Asia, the Middle East, Africa, and Latin America. Third, it is much easier to model economic growth—a concept that can be conveyed through an aggregate production function—than it is to capture quantitatively the more complex phenomenon of economic development. Moreover, given the dimensional constraint imposed by graphical analysis, a two-factor production function, with capital and labor, augmented by technological progress, offered a useful abstraction. Thus, the form and content of the growth models of the 1950s are not surprising.

In the next two chapters we examine some of the models in this tradition. We will see in later chapters the influence of these models on development policy. As necessary background, however, we first review properties of production functions.

## PRODUCTION FUNCTIONS

Recall from Chapter 1, in which the sources of economic growth were identified, that the growth rate of output depends on technological change and the growth rates of the inputs. The underlying relationship between output, inputs, and technology is represented by a production function. One of the simplest, yet most restrictive, is the **fixed-coefficients production function**, where a fixed and inflexible relationship between output and the required input mix is assumed. We begin with this type of production function, which not only was a key feature of the early growth models, but which forms the basis for input-output analysis (to be discussed in Chapter 13). We then consider a more general production function that allows for substitution between the inputs.

### FIXED-COEFFICIENTS PRODUCTION FUNCTION

To illustrate, assume there are only two factors, capital and labor, and that technological progress is neutral, affecting total factor productivity, but not the relative marginal productivities of the factors. Let

$$Y = \text{real national output}$$
$$K = \text{physical capital stock}$$
$$L = \text{labor}$$
$$A = \text{index of technology}$$

The fixed-coefficients production function can be written as:

$$Y = A \cdot \min[K/v, L/u]$$

where

$$v = \text{fixed capital–output ratio } (v = K/Y)$$
$$u = \text{fixed labor–output ratio } (u = L/Y)$$

The level of output is determined by the minimum (min) of the ratios $K/v$ and $L/u$. Exactly $v$ units of capital and $u$ units of labor are required to produce $A$ units of output. For example, if $A = 1$, $v = 5$, and $u = 10$, then 5 units of capital and 10 units of labor would be required to produce 1 unit of output. Similarly, 10 units of capital and 20 units of labor would be required to produce 2 units of output. With a fixed-coefficients production function, no substitution between capital and labor is possible. The capital–labor ratio is constant and equal to $v/u$ (here $v/u = 5/10 = .5$).

We will also assume **constant returns to scale.** A doubling (halving) of inputs yields a doubling (halving) of output. More formally, if all the inputs are multiplied by a factor $c$ ($c > 0$), then the output will be multiplied by the same factor $c$. That is, given

$$Y = A \cdot \min[K/v, L/u]$$

then

$$A \cdot \min[cK/v, cL/u] = cY$$

The production function is characterized by constant returns to scale.

Graphically, a fixed-coefficients production function generates right-angled isoquants. An **isoquant** is the locus of points representing all the combinations of inputs capable of producing a given level of output. Continuing with our example, where $A = 1$, $v = 5$, and $u = 10$, the isoquants for three levels of output are shown in Figure 3.1 on page 62. Only the corner points on these isoquants are technically efficient input combinations.[3] For example, with 10 units of labor and 5 units of capital, 1 unit of output could be produced (see point $e_1$ on the isoquant labeled $Y = 1$). Adding only labor would not increase output (see point $e'_1$, with $L = 15$ and $K = 5$ on $Y = 1$). In other words, the marginal product of labor (the change in output associated with a change in labor) equals zero along the horizontal portion of an isoquant. Similarly, beginning with 5 units of capital and 10 units of labor and adding only capital would not increase output (see point $e''_1$ on the isoquant $Y = 1$, with $K = 7.5$ and $L = 10$). The marginal product of capital equals zero along the vertical portion of an isoquant. With a fixed-coefficients production function, the **output-expansion path,** representing the least-cost combinations of the technically efficient input mixes associated with varying levels of output, is a ray from the origin with a slope equal to the constant capital–labor ratio (see the ray 0E in Figure 3.1). Unless capital and labor increase at the same rate, the faster-growing factor will be underutilized, and output growth will be constrained by the slower-growing factor.

Technological change is indicated here by a change in the value of $A$, the index of technology. Technological progress, an increase in $A$, means that for any level of inputs, more output can be produced. Graphically, technological progress would be indicated by a shift of the isoquants in toward the origin: Fewer inputs would be required to produce any level of output.

---

[3]**Technical efficiency** means that the marginal products of all the inputs or factors used in production are positive. More simply put, an additional unit of a factor would not be used unless it increased output. **Economic efficiency** refers to the least-cost combination of inputs for a given set of input prices. Technical efficiency is a necessary condition for economic efficiency.

## FIGURE 3.1 — ISOQUANTS FOR FIXED-COEFFICIENTS PRODUCTION FUNCTION

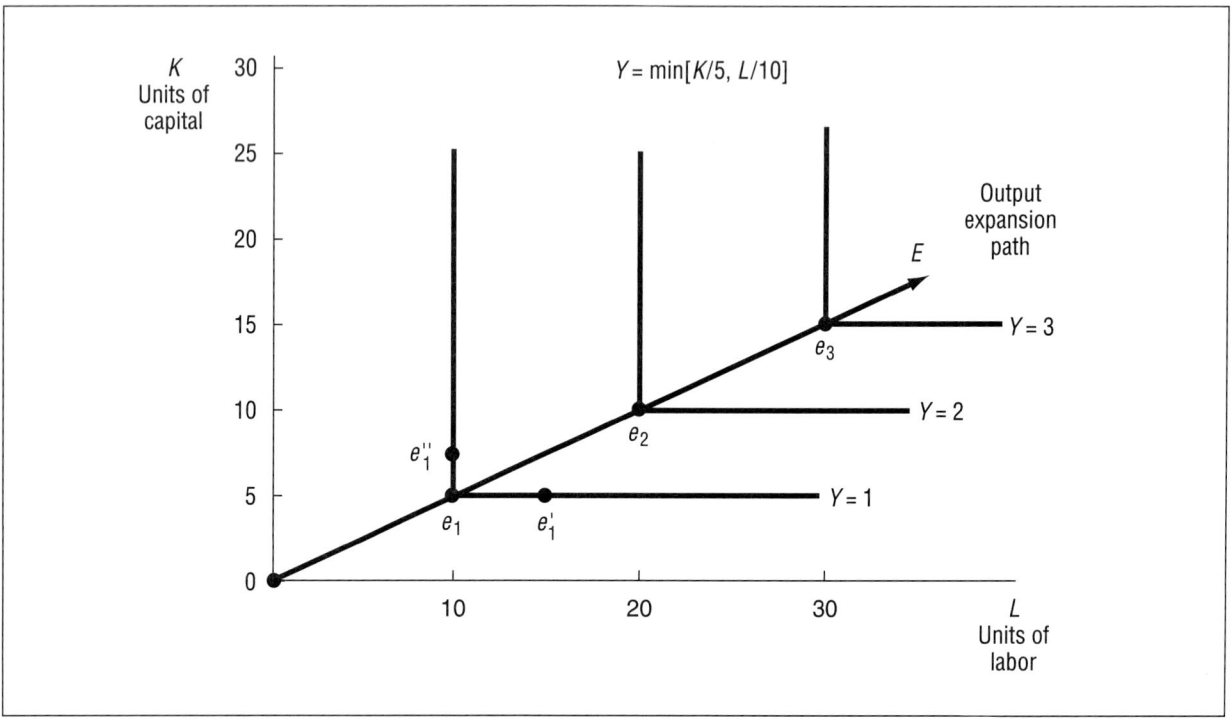

### PRODUCTION FUNCTIONS WITH FACTOR SUBSTITUTION

A less restrictive assumption about production functions is to allow for substitution between capital and labor. We can illustrate, while retaining the constant returns-to-scale property. Assume now that the production function can be written as:

$$Y = A \cdot (K/v)^a (L/u)^b$$

where $\quad 0 < a < 1 \text{ and } 0 < b < 1 \text{ and } a + b = 1$

The exponents $a$ and $b$ (assumed here to sum to one) can be shown to equal the partial output elasticities of capital and labor, respectively.[4] The **partial output elasticity** of an input indicates the responsiveness of output to a small change in the use of the input, holding constant the levels of all other inputs and technology.

For comparison to the earlier fixed-coefficients production function, let $A = 1$, $a = .5$, and $b = .5$.

$$Y = (K/5)^{.5} (L/10)^{.5}$$

In Figure 3.2 we sketch two isoquants for this production function. In contrast to the right-angled isoquants of a fixed-coefficients production function, the isoquants are smooth curves, reflecting the assumption of factor substitution. To confirm that the

## FIGURE 3.2    Isoquants for Production Function with Factor Substitution

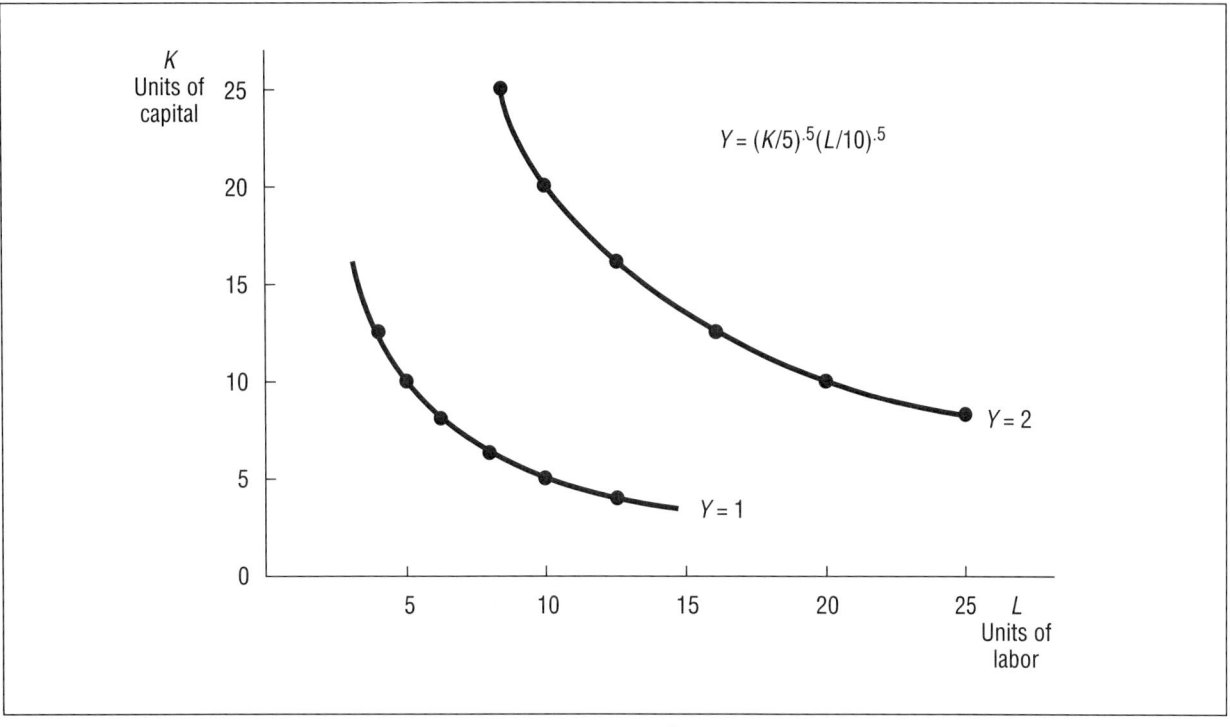

[4]Formally, the partial output elasticity of capital (labor) is the instantaneous change in output due to an infinitesimal change in capital (labor), ceteris paribus. Using derivative calculus and the production function in the example, $Y = A(K/v)^a (L/u)^b$, to derive the partial output elasticity of capital, we partially differentiate the production function with respect to capital.

$$\partial Y / \partial K = aA(K/v)^{a-1} (L/u)^b (1/v)$$

then dividing through by $Y/K$, we obtain

$$(\partial Y / \partial K)/(Y/K) = a = \text{partial output elasticity of capital.}$$

Similarly, the partial output elasticity of labor can be derived as:

$$(\partial Y / \partial L)/(Y/L) = b = \text{partial output elasticity of labor.}$$

Less formally, and allowing for discrete changes in the inputs, the partial output elasticity of capital (labor) is the ratio of the percentage change in output to the percentage change in capital (labor), holding constant labor (capital). Rearranging the terms and allowing for discrete changes (indicated by $\Delta$), gives:

$$(\partial Y/\partial K)/(Y/K) = (\partial Y/Y)/(\partial K/K) \doteq (\Delta Y/Y)/(\Delta K/K) = \frac{\%\ \text{change in } Y}{\%\ \text{change in } K} = a$$

$$(\partial Y/\partial L)/(Y/L) = (\partial Y/Y)/(\partial L/L) \doteq (\Delta Y/Y)/(\Delta L/L) = \frac{\%\ \text{change in } Y}{\%\ \text{change in } L} = b$$

In this example we use a Cobb-Douglas production function that has some nice properties, including factor substitution and constant returns to scale (since the sum of the exponents, $a$ and $b$, equals one). Other more complicated production functions exist.

property of constant returns to scale holds, multiply the inputs by a scalar $c$, $(c>0)$, and note that output is also multiplied by $c$.

$$(cK/5)^{.5} (cL/10)^{.5}$$
$$= (c)^{.5+.5} (K/5)^{.5} (L/10)^{.5}$$
$$= c^1 (K/5)^{.5} (L/10)^{.5} = cY$$

From the example in Figure 3.2, we can see that doubling the levels of capital and labor exactly doubles the output produced. Our understanding of these two types of production functions will be important for the analysis of the growth models. We start with a version of the Harrod-Domar model.

## HARROD-DOMAR GROWTH MODEL

One of the first and best-known growth models is Harrod-Domar.[5] The model consists of five equations listed below.

| | | |
|---|---|---|
| H1) | $K = vY$ | (full capacity condition) |
| H2) | $L = uY$ | (full employment condition) |
| H3) | $I = S$ | (investment equals saving equilibrium) |
| H4) | $S = sY$   $0 < s < 1$ | (saving equation) |
| H5) | $\Delta L/L = n$ | (natural growth rate of the labor force) |

The first two equations represent the fixed-coefficients aggregate production function $Y = A \cdot \min[K/v, L/u]$, where, for simplicity, $A = 1$. With the assumed fixed capital–output ratio $(v)$ and labor–output ratio $(u)$, to produce a given level of output, $Y_o$, would require exactly $vY_o$ units of capital $(K)$ and $uY_o$ units of labor $(L)$. Any change in output $(\Delta Y)$ would require fixed changes in inputs $(\Delta K$ and $\Delta L)$.

H1') $\Delta K = v\Delta Y$

H2') $\Delta L = u\Delta Y$

---

[5] See Roy Harrod, "An Essay in Dynamic Theory," *Economic Journal* (March 1939), pages 14–33, and Evsey Domar, "Capital Expansion, Rate of Growth, and Employment," *Econometrica* (April 1946), pages 137–147, for the seminal articles from which this basic Harrod-Domar model has been derived. A more formal presentation of the growth models discussed in this chapter can be found in R. G. D. Allen, "Simple Growth Models" and "Neoclassical Growth Models," Chapters 11 and 14 in *Macroeconomic Theory: A Mathematical Treatment*, New York: St. Martin's Press, 1968. For a less technical treatment of the sources of economic growth, refer to any intermediate macroeconomics text, for example, Richard Froyen, "The Supply Side: Intermediate and Long-Term Economic Growth," Chapter 17 in *Macroeconomics: Theories and Policies*, 5th ed., New York: Macmillan, 1996.

Dividing the terms in Equations H1') and H2') by the corresponding terms in Equations H1) and H2) yields:

$$\Delta K/K = v\Delta Y/vY = \Delta Y/Y \quad \text{and} \quad \Delta L/L = u\Delta Y/uY = \Delta Y/Y$$

where $\Delta Y/Y$, $\Delta K/K$, and $\Delta L/L$ are the growth rates in output, capital, and labor, respectively.

That is, given that the capital stock and labor force are initially fully utilized, then to maintain the full capacity and full employment conditions, the capital stock and labor force would have to grow at the same rate as output—which makes sense for a fixed-coefficients production function.

The third equation in the model, $I = S$, is the equilibrium condition in the product market. In a simple one-sector model with no government and no foreign trade, the macroeconomic equilibrium reduces to the condition that investment $(I)$ equals saving $(S)$. Investment is the production of national output not used for present consumption. Saving is the income generated in the production of national output that is not used for consumption. When investment equals saving, desired aggregate expenditures on national output equal the national output produced.[6]

The fourth equation, $S = sY$, states that real saving $(S)$ is a constant proportion of real national income $(Y)$. The coefficient $s$ is the fixed propensity to save, assumed to be

---

[6]From the basic macroeconomic identity, we have:
$$C + I + G + X - M = Y = C + S + T + R + F$$

- $C$ = personal consumption expenditures
- $I$ = gross private domestic investment
- $G$ = government purchases of goods and services
- $X$ = exports of goods and services
- $M$ = imports of goods and services
- $Y$ = national output (gross domestic product)
- $S$ = gross private domestic saving
- $T$ = net taxes (tax receipts less government transfer payments)
- $R$ = net unilateral transfer payments to the rest of the world
- $F$ = net factor payments to the rest of the world

The left-hand side of the identity represents the disaggregation of national output by expenditures. The right-hand side represents the disposition of the income generated in the production of national output. Setting the two sides equal and cancelling the common consumption expenditures term $(C)$ gives:
$$I + G + X - M = S + T + R + F$$
Solving for $I$ gives
$$I = S + (T - G) + (M - X + R + F)$$
or gross private domestic investment $(I)$ must be covered by gross private domestic saving $(S)$, net public saving (indicated by the government budget balance, $T - G$), and net foreign saving (represented by the deficit on current account, $M - X + R + F$). If we simplify to an economy with no government ($G = T = 0$) and no foreign trade, foreign aid, or foreign investment ($X = M = 0$, $R = 0$, and $F = 0$), the macroeconomic identity reduces to $I = S$. Alternatively, we could incorporate the government sector by including the difference between tax receipts and current expenditures of the government with $S$ to obtain gross domestic saving and adding the capital expenditures by the government to gross private domestic investment to obtain gross domestic investment. In Chapter 10 we examine the sources of funding for gross domestic investment in detail.

determined by factors outside the model such as the level of interest rates, distribution of income, and age distribution of the population.

Using these four equations, we can derive an expression for the growth rate in output consistent with the full employment of capital and labor and the maintenance of macroeconomic equilibrium. Given the fixed capital–output ratio, $v$, from Equation H1) $K = vY$, it follows that the change in the capital stock required for a given change in output is:

$$\Delta K = v\Delta Y$$

Any change in the capital stock, however, is due to investment.[7]

$$\Delta K = I$$

To maintain the macroeconomic equilibrium $(I = S)$ with the assumed saving function $(S = sY)$ implies that

$$\Delta K = I = S = sY$$

Equating all the terms gives

$$v\Delta Y = \Delta K = I = S = sY$$

Thus,

$$v\Delta Y = sY$$

Solving for the growth rate in output, $\Delta Y/Y$, by dividing both sides by $vY$, yields

$$v\Delta Y/vY = sY/vY$$

$$\Delta Y/Y = s/v$$

Therefore, the ratio of the propensity to save to the capital–output ratio gives the **warranted growth rate** in output—and, correspondingly, the required growth rate in capital and labor.

The fifth and last equation of the Harrod-Domar growth model specifies the "natural" growth rate of the labor force $(n)$. The natural growth rate of the labor force is considered to be given, determined by the exogenous population growth rate, age-sex composition of the population, and the labor force participation rates.

**Steady-state equilibrium** in the model requires maintaining full capacity use of the capital stock, full employment of the labor force, and equilibrium in the product market. These simultaneous conditions imply that the warranted growth rate in output $(s/v)$—which, according to the fixed-coefficients production function, gives the growth

---

[7]Note that here we are abstracting from depreciation of the capital stock, and regarding $I$ and $S$ as equivalent to net fixed investment and net private domestic saving, respectively. In order for the physical capital stock to increase, net fixed investment must be positive. Then, if $I > 0$, $\Delta K > 0$.

rate required for capital and labor—must equal the natural growth rate in the labor force *(n)*. That is, for steady-state equilibrium, $s/v = n$.

## THE "KNIFE-EDGE" PROBLEM

There is no reason, however, to expect that the natural growth rate of the labor force, determined by earlier birth rates and current death rates, international migration rates, and labor force participation rates, would always equal the warranted growth rate of the labor force, set by the saving rate and capital–output ratio.

To elaborate, assume the economy begins in a full capacity–full employment equilibrium. Focusing on labor, to maintain steady-state equilibrium, the growth rate in the demand for labor (given by the warranted growth rate of $s/v$) must equal the growth rate in the supply of labor (given by the natural growth rate *n*). Otherwise, one of the factors would be underutilized. For example, if the natural growth rate of the labor force exceeded the warranted growth rate, $n > s/v$, there would be a surplus of labor and unemployment. The growth rate in output would be equal to $s/v$, and would be constrained by the available capital. The excess labor would not be absorbed into employment, and the unemployment would grow in successive periods. Given the assumptions of a fixed-coefficients production function and the exogenously determined saving propensity and natural growth rate of labor, no adjustment mechanism exists in the model.

Conversely, if the warranted growth for labor exceeds the natural growth rate, $s/v > n$, a shortage of labor or an excess demand for labor would occur. The growth rate in output would be equal to *n*, and constrained by the amount of labor available. Moreover, there would be excess capacity or a surplus of capital that would continue to increase over time.

The Harrod-Domar model is said to be dynamically unstable. Unless the condition $s/v = n$ is always met—and there is no reason to expect that it would be—the economy would depart from a steady-state equilibrium. There would be either growing unemployment or excess capacity with no subsequent corrections—a property of the model known as the **knife-edge problem**. Simply stated, the Harrod-Domar model is overdetermined. Too many fixed parameters *(s, v, u,* and *n)* exist and no adjustment mechanism. To escape the knife-edge problem, some flexibility must be introduced.

Below we discuss two modifications. In the first, the saving rate becomes a function of the distribution of income. In the second, the fixed-coefficients production function is replaced by one that allows for factor substitution. We will see that, while both of these approaches "solve" the knife-edge problem, the policy implications for economic growth are similar to those derived from the Harrod-Domar model. In this chapter's Appendix A we illustrate the knife-edge problem with a numerical example.

We should note that in this steady-state equilibrium, economic growth is equal to zero. The growth rates in output and labor are equal, so output per unit of labor and, in general, output per capita, are constant. In fact, economic growth is a desirable disequilibrium of the growth model. Following World War II, capital was commonly regarded as the factor limiting economic growth in the developing economies of Asia, Africa, the Middle East, and Latin America, where dramatic improvements in mortality rates had yielded historically rapid rates of population growth. Unemployment and underemployment of labor appeared to be a problem. An emphasis on saving, investment, and physical capital accumulation seemed appropriate.

## THE SAVING RATE AND THE DISTRIBUTION OF INCOME

Given the condition for steady-state equilibrium in the Harrod-Domar model, $s/v = n$, Nicholas Kaldor allows for variation in the saving rate as an adjustment mechanism.[8] National income $(Y)$ is disaggregated into returns to labor, or wage income $(W)$, and returns to capital, or profits $(P)$. $Y = W + P$.

Kaldor assumes that the marginal propensity to save out of profits $(s_p)$ exceeds the marginal propensity to save out of wages $(s_w)$.

$$0 < s_w < s_p < 1$$

In general, for laborers in low-income economies the marginal propensity to consume is relatively high and close to unity. Compared to labor, capitalists, by their very nature, would be inclined to save more of any dollar of income earned, and, with their higher incomes, would be able to save a higher proportion of income.

Total saving $(S)$ equals the sum of the savings from wages and profits.

$$S = s_w W + s_p P$$

Dividing through both sides of the saving equation by national income, $Y$, we obtain the saving rate, $s$. Thus, we derive Equation K4), which replaces Equation H4) in the Harrod-Domar model.

K4) $\quad s = S/Y = s_w(W/Y) + s_p(P/Y)$

The national saving rate is a weighted average of the assumed fixed saving rates out of wages and profits, with the weights being the variable shares of wages $(W/Y)$ and profits $(P/Y)$ in national income. By shifting the distribution of income, we can change the saving rate associated with any given level of national income.

Using the fact that $(W/Y) + (P/Y) = 1$ or $W/Y = 1 - (P/Y)$, we can substitute for the share of wages in national income in Equation K4) and solve for the relationship between the national saving rate and the share of profits.

$$s = s_w(1 - P/Y) + s_p(P/Y)$$
$$s = s_w + (s_p - s_w)(P/Y)$$

Clearly, under the assumption of a greater marginal propensity to save out of profits than wages, the saving rate is directly related to the share of profits in national income. To increase the saving rate, a given level of national income could be redistributed in favor of capitalists. To illustrate, return to the steady-state condition and suppose $v = 5$, $n = .02$, $s = .10$, and let $s_w = .02$, $s_p = .42$, $(W/Y) = .80$, and $(P/Y) = .20$. (Note: These saving propensities and income distribution yield an aggregate saving rate of 10 percent: $s = .02(.80) + .42(.20) = .10$).

---

[8]See Nicholas Kaldor, "Alternative Theories of Distribution," *Review of Economic Studies*, vol. 23, no. 2 (1955–1956), pages 83–100.

We begin in steady-state equilibrium: $s/v = .10/5 = .02 = n$. Now, suppose the natural growth rate in the labor force increases to $n' = .03$, or 3 percent. Under the assumptions of the Harrod-Domar model (fixed-coefficients production function and a constant saving rate), the economy would depart from steady-state equilibrium with an excess supply of labor and increasing unemployment. With Kaldor's modification, however, raising the saving rate to $s' = .15$ could restore the steady-state equilibrium: $s'/v = .15/5 = .03 = n'$.

That is, to absorb the greater labor force growth, a higher saving rate and more capital formation are required. To achieve the higher saving rate, the distribution of income could be shifted in favor of the high savers, the capitalists. In fact, such a redistribution might naturally occur. With the scarcity of capital constraining output growth, the returns to capitalists and profit rates would tend to rise; in contrast, surplus labor would depress the wage rate. In this example, given the propensities to save out of wages and profits of .02 and .42, respectively, an increase from 20 percent to 32.5 percent in the share of national income accounted for by profits would raise the saving rate to 15 percent.

$$s' = .15 = s_w + (s_p - s_w)(P/Y)'$$
$$.15 = .02 + (.42 - .02)(P/Y)'$$
$$.15 = .02 + .40(P/Y)'$$
$$.13 = .40(P/Y)'$$
$$.325 = (P/Y)'$$

Real national output, employment, and the capital stock are all now increasing at 3 percent—leaving, as before, a constant output per unit of labor. Labor income per capita, however, has declined with the fall in the share of wages in national income (from 80 percent to 67.5 percent).

Conversely, a drop in the natural growth rate of the labor force could be accommodated by a decrease in the saving rate and shift in the distribution of income from capitalists to laborers. As noted, for the developing economies in the post–World War II era, increasing population growth rates and "surplus" labor were common. Consequently, policy measures to boost saving rates and capital formation were promoted. The example of Japan may be illustrative.

## JAPAN'S SAVINGS AND GROWTH

Japan has experienced impressive economic growth in the post-war era, fueled in part by its high rates of saving and investment. A number of factors have contributed to Japan's success in generating saving. Fiscal policies stressed low budget deficits, and low rates of taxation promoted private saving. The absence of a generous system of social security, combined with very high life expectancies, has forced Japanese citizens to provide for their retirement with household savings. Moreover, Japan reached replacement-level fertility over a quarter century ago. Japan's burden of dependency is under 45 (the dependent population per hundred producer population). In addition, a relatively large percentage of Japan's population is currently in the prime saving years of the life cycle, ages 40 to 65, when savings are accumulated for retirement.

Banks in Japan play a major role in providing equity financing to private enterprises, and are relatively less involved with consumer loans for automobiles and houses.

Consequently, Japanese households tend to save for their major purchases. Finally, employees of large corporations in Japan often receive a significant portion of their compensation as biannual bonuses, much of which is saved.

For 1993, the share of gross domestic saving in gross domestic product for Japan was 33 percent, more than half again as great as the average share (20 percent) for all the high-income economies. Japan's high domestic saving rate even exceeded its high share of gross domestic investment in GDP (30 percent), so that Japan was a net lender to the rest of the world.[9] Japan's growth rate in GDP over the past two decades has similarly exceeded the average for the high-income economies by more than one full percentage point.[10]

As critical as the high rates of saving and investment are, other factors lie behind Japan's impressive economic growth over the past half-century. In Chapter 17 we will discuss key features of the East Asian nations' developments.

## SOLOW'S SOLUTION TO THE KNIFE-EDGE PROBLEM: FACTOR SUBSTITUTION

While Kaldor introduced variation in the saving rate as an adjustment mechanism, Robert Solow addressed the knife-edge problem by modifying the production function. Solow's adjustment mechanism is the capital–labor ratio.[11] While retaining the property of constant returns to scale, Solow replaced the assumption of fixed coefficients with one of factor substitution. In particular, output per unit of labor is a function of the capital–labor ratio. Given $Y = A \cdot F(K,L)$ and $cY = A \cdot F(cK, cL)$ due to constant returns to scale, let $c = 1/L$, then

$$(1/L)Y = A \cdot F((1/L)K, (1/L)L)$$

$$Y/L = A \cdot F(K/L, L/L)$$

$$y = A \cdot f(k, 1)$$

$$y = A \cdot f(k)$$

where
- $y$ = output per unit of labor $(Y/L)$
- $k$ = capital–labor ratio $(K/L)$
- $A$ = index of technology

---

[9]Gross domestic saving is calculated as gross domestic product (GDP) less the sum of private consumption and general government consumption. The statistics are from World Bank, *World Development Report 1995*, New York: Oxford University Press, 1995, Table 9.

[10]Ibid., Table 2. The average annual growth rates for GDP for 1970–1980 and 1980–1993 for Japan are 4.3% and 4.0%, respectively. The corresponding averages for the high-income economies are 3.2% and 2.9%, respectively.

[11]See Robert Solow, "A Contribution to the Theory of Economic Growth," *The Quarterly Journal of Economics*, vol. 70, no. 1 (February 1956), pages 65–94. Solow won the Nobel Prize in Economics in 1987 primarily for his work in economic growth theory.

Output per unit of labor (the average product of labor) is a positive, but decreasing, function of the capital–labor ratio. As an example, let

$$Y = K^{.5} L^{.5} \quad \text{(here } A = 1\text{)}$$

Dividing through by $L$ gives

$$Y/L = K^{.5}/L^{.5} = (K/L)^{.5}$$
$$y = k^{.5}$$

In Figure 3.3 on page 72, we sketch the corresponding production function, which is concave (i.e., the slope of the production function is positive, but becomes flatter as capital per unit of labor increases). Output per unit of labor rises with the capital–labor ratio, but at a diminishing rate. A quadrupling of the capital–labor ratio from 1 to 4 to 16 results in only a doubling of output per unit of labor from 1 to 2 to 4.

We can show that the instantaneous growth rate in the capital–labor ratio $(dk/k)$ equals the difference between the instantaneous growth rates in capital $(dK/K)$ and labor $(dL/L)$.

$$dk/k = dK/K - dL/L$$

where the $d$ is the derivative operator, the continuous counterpart to the discrete symbol $\Delta$ denoting a "change in" a quantity.[12] Intuitively, if the capital stock is increasing faster than labor $(dK/K > dL/L)$, then the capital–labor ratio would be rising $(dk/k > 0$ and $k\uparrow)$.

Rewriting the growth model, with Solow's production function (Equation S1) replacing the Harrod-Domar fixed-coefficients production function (Equations H1 and H2), we have

S1) $y = A \cdot f(k)$ (output per unit of labor)

S2) $I = S$ (investment equals saving equilibrium)

S3) $S = sY \quad 0 < s < 1$ (saving equation)

S4) $dL/L = n$ (natural growth rate of the labor force)

---

[12]Differentiating both sides of the expression for the capital–labor ratio and then dividing through by the capital–labor ratio gives the instantaneous growth rate of the capital–labor ratio, $dk/k$.

$$k = K/L$$
$$dk = \frac{dK \cdot L - K \cdot dL}{L^2} = dK/L - (K/L)(dL/L)$$
$$dk/k = (dK/L)(L/K) - (K/L)(dL/L)(L/K)$$
$$dk/k = dK/K - dL/L$$

Strictly speaking, this equation for the instantaneous growth rate for the capital–labor ratio holds only for infinitesimal changes in the capital stock or labor. For discrete changes in capital or labor ($\Delta K$ or $\Delta L$), the relationship is only an approximation. With the smoothly curved isoquants of the Solow model, where continuous factor substitution is allowed, the derivative operator is appropriate.

## FIGURE 3.3 | OUTPUT PER UNIT OF LABOR AND THE CAPITAL–LABOR RATIO

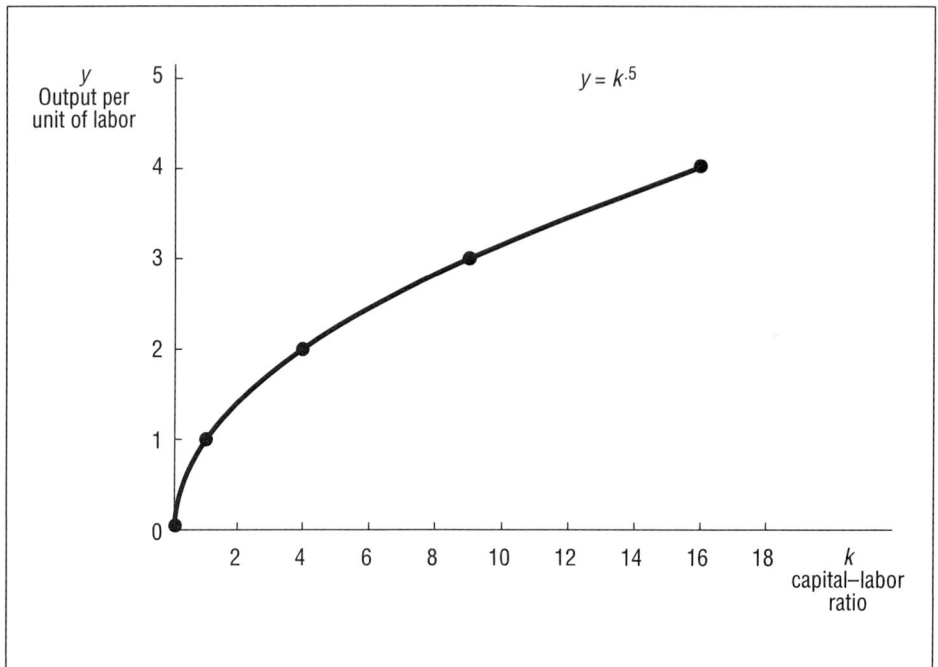

We can show that the **fundamental equation of the Solow model** is:

$$dk = sy - nk$$

where $dk$ is the change in the capital–labor ratio.[13] The term $sy$ represents the saving per unit of labor forthcoming. The term $nk$ represents the investment per unit of labor needed to maintain the capital–labor ratio for the given natural growth rate of the labor

---

[13]Beginning with the expression for the growth rate in the capital–labor ratio,
$$dk/k = dK/K - dL/L$$
and multiplying through both sides by $k$, we find
$$dk = dK/L - k(dL/L)$$
Incorporating the other equations of the model into this expression, we can derive the condition for steady-state equilibrium.
$$dk = I/L - k(dL/L) = S/L - k(dL/L) = sY/L - k(dL/L)$$
Recall that investment $(I)$ is, by definition, equal to the change in the capital stock $(dK)$; and to maintain product market equilibrium, investment must equal saving $(I = S)$, where saving is a fixed proportion of income $(sY)$. Replacing $Y/L$ with $y$ and substituting the natural growth rate of the labor force $(n)$ for $(dL/L)$, we obtain the fundamental equation of the Solow model.
$$dk = sy - nk$$

force (n). Since in steady-state equilibrium the capital stock, employment, output, and the labor force are all growing at the same rate, the capital–labor ratio would be constant: $dk = 0$. Therefore, in steady-state equilibrium the fundamental equation of the Solow model reduces to:

$$0 = sy - nk, \quad \text{or} \quad sy = nk$$

In other words, in steady-state equilibrium the saving generated is just equal to the investment required to maintain the capital–labor ratio. A little rearranging of this expression reveals the condition for steady-state equilibrium growth in the Harrod-Domar model.

$$sy = nk$$
$$s(Y/L) = n(K/L)$$
$$s(Y/L)/(K/L) = n$$
$$s(Y/K) = n$$
$$s/v = n \qquad \text{since } (K/Y) \text{ is the capital–output ratio } v$$

The difference is that in Solow's model the capital–output ratio ($v$) is flexible, since factor substitution is allowed. In the Harrod-Domar model the capital–output ratio (along with the saving rate and natural growth rate of the labor force) is fixed. The flexibility gained through factor substitution allows Solow to escape the knife-edge problem. The adjustment mechanism is the capital–labor ratio.

We can illustrate graphically the dynamic stability of the Solow model. In Figure 3.4 on page 74, we place the capital–labor ratio $k$ on the horizontal axis. On the vertical axis we measure the two terms on the right-hand side of the fundamental equation: saving per unit of labor ($sy$) and investment per unit of labor ($nk$). Recall from Figure 3.3 that output per unit of labor ($y$) rises at a diminishing rate with the capital–labor ratio. Multiplying output per unit of labor (or, equivalently, income per unit of labor) by the constant saving rate ($0 < s < 1$) simply rotates the curve down proportionally. The graph of the term $nk$ against $k$ is a ray from the origin with a slope equal to $n$, the natural growth rate of the labor force. Steady-state equilibrium occurs where the curve $sy$ intersects the ray $nk$ (i.e., $sy = nk$), giving a constant equilibrium capital–labor ratio $k^*$.

Suppose the capital–labor ratio were too low, such as $k_1 < k^*$ in Figure 3.4. At $k_1$ there is an excess of saving over the investment needed to maintain the capital–labor ratio ($sy_1 > nk_1$, where $y_1 = f(k_1)$), indicated by the line segment CD. The excess supply of loanable funds would tend to drive down the market rate of interest, encouraging more investment and the adoption of more capital-intensive production processes. Consequently the capital–labor ratio would increase ($k\uparrow$). As the capital–labor ratio rises, output and income per unit of labor rise and saving per unit of labor increases (indicated by the movement from point C to point E along the curve $sy$). Saving increases, however, at a slower rate than the investment needed given the natural growth rate of the labor force (indicated by the movement from point D to point E along the ray $nk$), until the steady-state capital–labor ratio is reached at $k^*$, where $sy^* = nk^*$, with $y^* = f(k^*)$.

## FIGURE 3.4  STEADY-STATE EQUILIBRIUM IN SOLOW MODEL

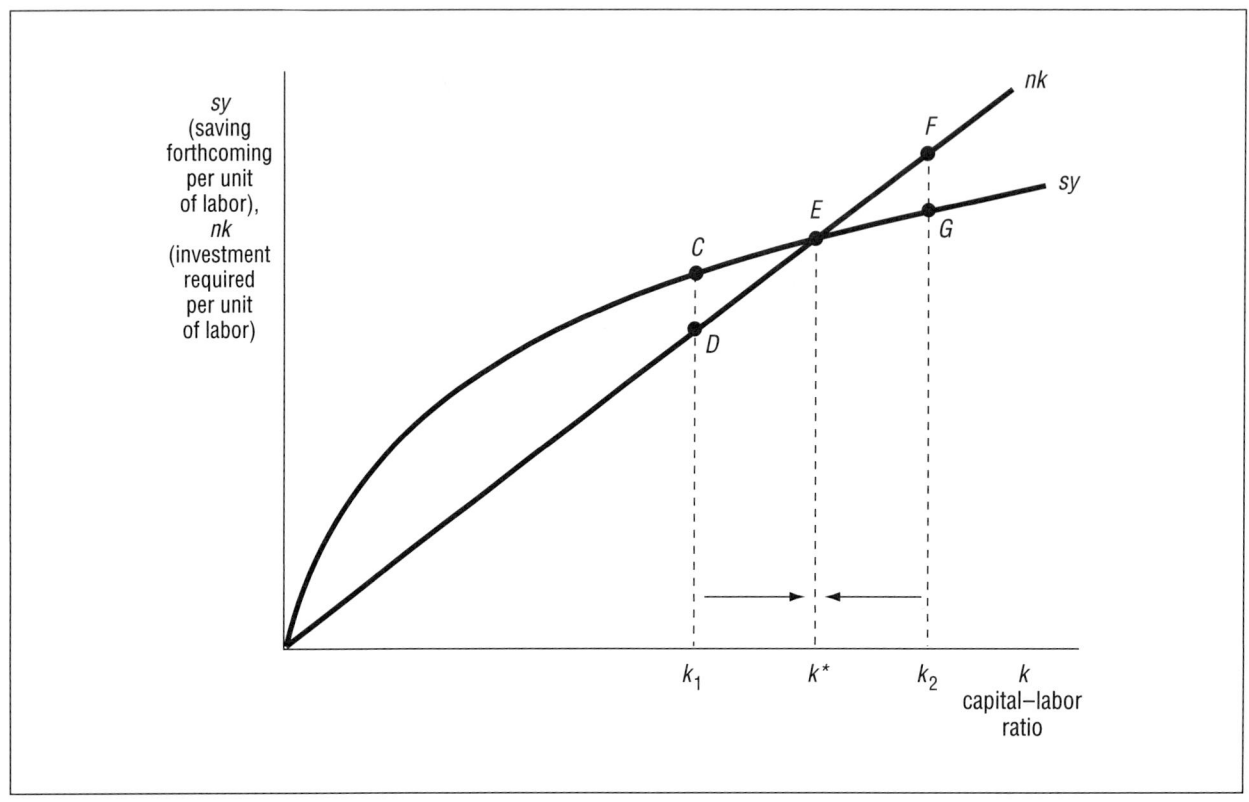

Conversely, too high a capital–labor ratio (e.g., $k_2$ in Figure 3.4) would mean that the saving forthcoming was insufficient for the investment needed. The excess demand for loanable funds would push up the interest rate, discourage investment in new capital, and result in the adoption of more labor-intensive production processes. The capital–labor ratio would fall from $k_2$ to $k^*$, with the required investment per unit of labor falling faster (from point $F$ to point $E$ along the ray $nk$) than saving per unit of labor (from point $G$ to point $E$ along the curve $sy$).

Derived from the Solow model is a primary explanation for the lower levels of per capita output and income in less developed economies: the lower capital–labor ratios, which reflect, in part, the relatively abundant supplies of labor. Moreover, labor-abundant nations need to use relatively labor-intensive production processes to employ the available labor.

In sum, allowing for factor substitution and adjustment through the capital–labor ratio also solves the knife-edge problem of the Harrod-Domar model. As we have observed, steady-state equilibrium is characterized by full use of the available capital and labor, a constant capital–labor ratio, and a constant output per unit of labor. Economic growth, however, is indicated by increases in per capita output. Thus, economic growth is a disequilibrium state in these growth models. Given a goal of generating economic growth, what insights can we draw from these models?

# POLICY IMPLICATIONS OF THE EARLY GROWTH MODELS

While a discussion of specific policy instruments will have to wait until later, it is useful now to outline the broad policy implications of these models for generating economic growth and, by presumption, economic development. For this purpose we return to the fundamental equation of the Solow growth model: $dk = sy - nk$.

In the absence of technological progress, in order to increase output per unit of labor, the capital–labor ratio must rise $(dk > 0)$. This, in turn, means that the saving forthcoming must be greater than the investment needed to maintain the present capital–labor ratio. Beginning with a steady-state equilibrium indicated by $k_0^*$ in Figure 3.5, where $sy_0^* = nk_0^*$, either increasing the saving rate (resulting in a counterclockwise rotation of the $sy$ curve as illustrated in Figure 3.5A) or decreasing the natural growth rate of the labor force (resulting in a clockwise rotation of the $nk$ ray as illustrated in Figure 3.5B) would raise the capital–labor ratio and generate economic growth. In each case economic growth would be temporary, indicated by the movement from one steady-state equilibrium $(E$ at $k_0^*)$ to another $(E'$ at $k_1^*)$. The higher equilibrium capital–labor ratio, however, would produce a higher equilibrium level of per capita output $(y_1^* > y_0^*$, where $y_1^* = f(k_1^*)$ and $y_0^* = f(k_0^*))$.

FIGURE 3.5  INCREASE IN THE EQUILIBRIUM CAPITAL–LABOR RATIO

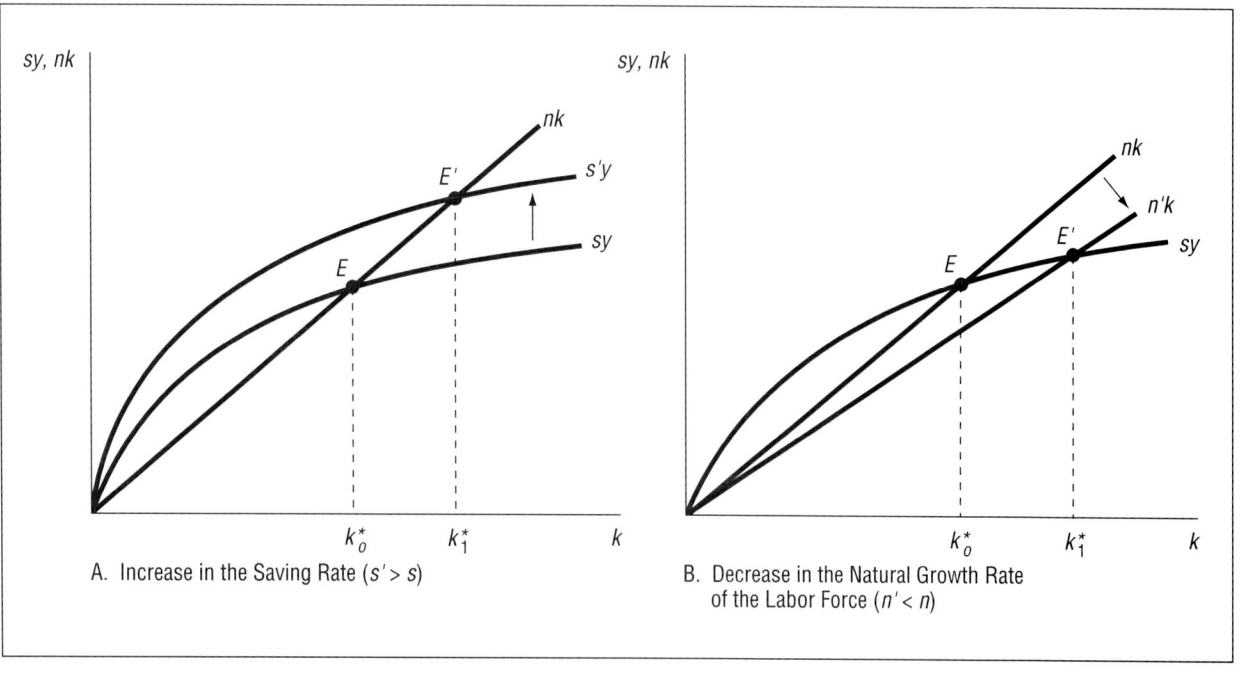

A. Increase in the Saving Rate $(s' > s)$

B. Decrease in the Natural Growth Rate of the Labor Force $(n' < n)$

Consistent with Kaldor's formulation, increases in the saving rate could be achieved at any level of income by shifting the distribution of income in favor of capitalists, who are assumed to have the higher propensity to save. Indeed, in the pursuit of economic growth in the 1950s and 1960s, policies to stimulate investment and capital formation, including subsidized interest rates and overvalued exchange rates, were adopted by many less developed countries. In later chapters we will discuss consequences of these growth policies.

In the short term, at least, reducing the natural growth rate of the labor force proves to be more difficult. Needless to say, increasing the death rates of the population of labor force age is not an appropriate policy option for reducing labor surplus conditions. Emigration rates depend, at least in part, on foreign country migration policies, although nations can adjust immigration and emigration policies to affect the natural growth rates of their labor forces.

As noted, the growth rate of the current labor force reflects not only current labor force participation rates, death rates, and international migration rates, but prior birth rates. Any changes in birth rates will not have consequences for the potential growth of the labor force for roughly a decade and a half, given the earliest age when labor force participation typically begins. (In some poor economies, however, labor force participation may actually be significant for children under age 15. Also, decreases in current fertility rates will probably have consequences for current female labor force participation rates.) Nevertheless, in the longer run, family-planning programs and birth control were promoted as a means of reducing the growth rate in the natural labor force and increasing the capital–labor ratio.

Finally, technological change, which, for given levels of inputs, could increase output, was advocated to spur economic growth. (In the production functions discussed earlier, technological progress would be indicated by a rise in $A$, the index of technology. Technological progress could also take the form of new production functions with innovation; invention of new products and inputs; improvements in management and decision-making processes; and better-quality physical capital.) For the less developed countries, transfers of technology from the developed nations were sought.

Graphically, technological progress would tend to rotate the $sy$ curve in a counterclockwise direction: For any given capital–labor ratio the average product of labor $(y)$ would rise. Indeed, given an upper bound on feasible saving rates and probable lower bounds on the natural growth rate of the labor force, technological progress seemed to offer the best strategy for sustained economic growth over the long run.

In Chapter 4 we address some of the subsequent work in modeling the role of technological progress in economic growth. Before we conclude this present chapter, however, we extend the analysis to two other potential constraints to economic growth: the availability of foreign exchange and human capital.

## OTHER CONSTRAINTS ON GROWTH: FOREIGN EXCHANGE AND HUMAN CAPITAL

While the early growth models emphasized the importance of increasing saving and investment to relieve the constraint imposed by the scarcity of physical capital, other bottlenecks to economic growth were recognized. In particular, the lack of foreign exchange (to import needed capital goods and inputs) and human capital (specific labor skills and entrepreneurship) could limit the growth of output in developing economies. The potential role played by foreign assistance in relaxing these constraints was highlighted by Hollis Chenery and Alan Strout in an article written in the mid-1960s.

> A country setting out to transform its economy without external assistance must provide for all of the requirements of accelerated growth from its own resources or from imports paid by exports. Success thus requires a simultaneous increase in skills, domestic saving, and export earnings as well as the allocation of these increased resources in such a way as to satisfy the changing demands resulting from rising levels of income.... By relieving these constraints, foreign assistance can make possible fuller use of domestic resources and hence accelerate growth.[14]

For example, another source of loanable funds for domestic investment is foreign saving, indicated by a deficit on the nation's current account balance.[15] In Chapter 15 we will examine in detail the balance of international payments account for a nation. Suffice it to note here that a nation can cover its imports of goods and services either with export revenues; net income earned from its foreign investments; net receipts of foreign assistance (i.e., unilateral transfers); the sale of its assets to foreigners; or borrowing from foreigners. The sale of a nation's assets to foreigners and borrowing from foreigners, both considered as foreign investment in the nation, serve to make foreign exchange available to the nation.

Nations, particularly less developed countries with limited domestic manufacturing capacity, may depend on imports of equipment and machinery, spare parts and intermediate goods, as well as on imports of key raw materials. With no domestic substitutes for these imported inputs, a lack of foreign exchange may force a decrease in domestic production and employment.

In addition, a complementary relationship may exist between physical and human capital. Physical capital may be underutilized or misused if the labor force does not possess the skills required to operate the machinery efficiently or to make the necessary repairs in the case of breakdowns. Similarly, a deficiency in entrepreneurship may restrict the realization of the full productive potential of the available resources.

The human capital in a nation depends on investments in education, health care, and job training. Nations can import human capital, however. In the case of the foreign direct investment through transnational corporations, nations may receive not only human capital (in particular, skilled labor and management), but foreign technology, some of which will be embodied in the physical capital equipment transferred by the transnational corporation. The inflow of technical expertise could also be provided through foreign aid.

In sum, given that neither physical capital, human capital, and physical labor, nor imported and domestic inputs into production, are perfect substitutes, then economic growth in any period may be limited by any one of the following: physical capital (reflecting a shortage of saving and investment); physical labor (due to relatively slow growth in the labor force); human capital (from insufficient investment in labor skills

---

[14]See Hollis Chenery and Alan Strout, "Foreign Assistance and Economic Development," *American Economic Review*, vol. 56, no. 4 (September 1966), pages 679–733. The quotation is from page 680.

[15]Return to Note 6 and the expression for gross private domestic investment, $I = S + (T - G) + (M - X + R + F)$. Gross private domestic investment can be funded by gross private domestic saving $(S)$, net public saving $(T - G)$, or net foreign saving $(M - X + R + F)$.

or shortfalls in entrepreneurship); or imported inputs (due to foreign exchange constraints). Consequently, the policy implications come down to increasing the supply of the factor currently constraining economic growth.

For labor-abundant developing economies, the most pressing constraints on growth are often the supply of domestic saving and foreign exchange. As we will discuss in Chapter 8, human capital, despite seeming to be relatively scarce in the less developed countries, often has migrated to the developed countries. It is important to reiterate that economic growth, a rise in per capita income, involves a departure from steady-state equilibrium. In addition to increasing the domestic saving rate or decreasing the natural growth rate of the labor force to achieve physical capital deepening, measures to stimulate economic growth should address the constraints set by human capital and foreign exchange. Since developing nations may not be able to rely continually on foreign capital—and would eventually want to reduce their dependence on foreign saving and the accumulation of foreign debt—the generation of foreign exchange will involve the expansion of exports and some substitution of domestic production for imports. In Chapter 14 we will examine export expansion strategies of development.

Finally, we should observe that the focus of the discussion in this chapter has been on the supply side. The implication is that the product market is always in equilibrium. Steady-state growth encompasses the full employment of labor and capital and assumes that production of output would necessarily translate into a demand for that output. In Chapter 9 we will explore this assumption, since an additional constraint to economic growth may be insufficient aggregate demand.

## CONCLUDING NOTE

The Harrod-Domar growth model set forth a condition for steady-state equilibrium. Output, the capital stock, and employed labor all had to grow at a pace equal to the saving rate divided by the capital–output ratio. Moreover, this warranted rate of growth had to match the given natural growth rate of the labor force. Otherwise, the model would be thrown out of equilibrium, with either rising unemployment or increasing excess capacity over time.

Two solutions to this knife-edge problem of the Harrod-Domar model were to allow for flexibility in the aggregate saving rate (through the incorporation of the distribution of income) and to allow for flexibility in the capital–output ratio (through factor substitution in the production function). Economic growth, however, is a disequilibrium state, where output and income increase faster than the labor force and population. A common feature of these growth models is the emphasis on physical capital accumulation as the key to economic growth, and presumably economic development. For a given state of technology, capital deepening or increases in the capital–labor ratio are required for increasing output per capita. The attendant policy prescriptions center on raising the aggregate saving rate through a redistribution of income from the low-savers (laborers) to the high-savers (capitalists). In the longer run, reducing the natural growth rate of the labor force would also enhance capital deepening. We also discussed other constraints to economic growth, in particular, foreign exchange and human capital. At any point in time, then, one of several factors may be limiting the growth of output.

In Appendix B to this chapter we use a sample of less developed countries to test two hypotheses central to the growth model approach. First, is per capita income directly related to the physical capital–labor ratio? Second, can the variation in economic growth rates across developing nations be explained by variation in the rates of capital deepening? In Chapter 4 we extend the analysis to models that address the challenge of initiating and sustaining economic growth.

## SUMMARY OF MAIN POINTS

1. Development economics as a distinct field of study in economics began after World War II. Early efforts focused on economic growth. For the developing economies of Asia, Africa, the Middle East, and Latin America, shortages of physical capital appeared to be constraining the growth in national output.
2. An influential early theoretical framework for the analysis of economic growth was the Harrod-Domar model. Key features of this model were a fixed-coefficients production function and exogenously determined saving rate and natural growth rate of the labor force. Steady-state equilibrium in the Harrod-Domar model required that output, capital, and labor all grow at the same rate. This rate, called the warranted rate of growth, is equal to the ratio of the saving rate to the capital–output ratio.
3. The Harrod-Domar model, however, is dynamically unstable. No adjustment mechanism exists. If the natural growth rate of the labor force does not equal the warranted rate of growth for labor, capital, and output, the model is thrown off the steady-state equilibrium growth path, with either continually rising unemployment or excess capacity of capital resulting. This inherent instability of the Harrod-Domar model is known as the knife-edge problem.
4. Kaldor's solution to the knife-edge problem was to introduce flexibility through the saving rate, which he wrote as a function of the distribution of income. Assuming two types of income, wages and profits, and a higher marginal propensity to save out of profits than wages, the aggregate saving rate (thus the warranted rate of growth) could be adjusted by varying the distribution of income.
5. Solow's solution to the knife-edge problem was to replace the fixed-coefficients production function of the Harrod-Domar model with one that allows for substitution between capital and labor. The adjustment mechanism in the Solow model is the capital–labor ratio. If the natural rate of growth of the labor force exceeds the warranted rate of growth for labor, a surplus of labor would be available. Wages would fall and firms would absorb the surplus labor by shifting to a more labor-intensive method of production. The steady-state equilibrium capital–labor ratio and output per capita would decline.
6. The fundamental equation of the Solow model, characterizing steady-state equilibrium, is that the per capita saving forthcoming equals the per capita investment necessary to maintain the capital–labor ratio for the given natural growth rate of the labor force.
7. In steady-state equilibrium, economic growth is zero, since output and labor are growing at the same rate. Thus, economic growth, a rise in per capita output, is a

desirable disequilibrium. To generate economic growth from a steady-state equilibrium, the saving rate could be increased or the natural growth rate of the labor force could be decreased. In either case, in the Solow model the equilibrium capital–labor ratio and output per unit of labor would increase until a new steady-state equilibrium were attained. Continual technological progress, however, could produce sustained economic growth.

8. Factors other than the supplies of physical capital and labor that could constrain output growth in an economy include the availability of foreign exchange (needed to import required inputs) and human capital (the labor skills and entrepreneurship that complement the other factors of production).

## KEY TERMS

constant returns to scale
economic efficiency
fixed-coefficients production function
fundamental equation of the Solow model
isoquant
knife-edge problem

output-expansion path
partial output elasticity
steady-state equilibrium
technical efficiency
warranted growth rate

## QUESTIONS

1. Using the following Harrod-Domar model:

   H1) $K = 4Y$ (full capacity condition)

   H2) $L = 12Y$ (full employment condition)

   H3) $I = S$ (investment equals saving equilibrium)

   H4) $S = .06Y$ (saving equation)

   H5) $\Delta L/L = .015$ (natural growth rate of the labor force)

   and given the initial levels of capital and labor: $K_0 = 100$ and $L_0 = 300$

   a. Assuming steady-state equilibrium growth, fill in the blanks for the table below. Show your work.

   |  | CAPITAL (K) | UNITS OF LABOR (L) | OUTPUT (Y) |
   |---|---|---|---|
   | Time period 0 | 100 | 300 | ___ |
   | Time period 1 | ___ | ___ | ___ |

   b. If instead the natural growth rate of the labor force were equal to .02, or 2 percent, specifically what would be the consequences in Period 1? What factor would be constraining output growth? Why?

2. Modify the savings equation in the above model as Kaldor suggested.

$$S = s_w W + s_p P$$

where $s_w$ and $s_p$ are the marginal propensities to save out of wages (W) and profits (P), respectively. Suppose that $s_w = .02$ and $s_p = .18$ and initially that $(W/Y) = .75$ and $(P/Y) = .25$.

Find the new distribution of income that can maintain steady-state equilibrium growth when the natural growth rate of the labor force increases from .015 to .02. Show your work.

3. Given the Solow growth model:

   S1) $Y = 2K^{.5}L^{.5}$      (aggregate production function)

   S2) $I = S$      (investment equals saving equilibrium)

   S3) $S = .10Y$      (saving equation)

   S4) $dL/L = .025$      (natural growth rate of the labor force)

   **a.** Derive the fundamental equation of the Solow model. Plot and graphically solve for the steady-state equilibrium capital–labor ratio, $k^*$. What are the associated output per unit of labor $(y)$ and capital–output ratio $(v)$?

   **b.** Find the new steady-state equilibrium capital–labor ratio when the saving rate increases to .15. Determine the new output per unit of labor and capital–output ratio.

   **c.** Return to the saving rate in Question 3a, and find the new steady-state equilibrium capital–labor ratio when the natural growth rate of the labor force falls to .02. Determine the new output per unit of labor and capital–output ratio.

4. Using the Solow model, graphically illustrate the effects of technological progress that increases the per capita output associated with any capital–labor ratio. Describe the process of adjustment to a new steady-state equilibrium.

5. Shortages in physical capital, labor, human capital, or foreign exchange might each limit output growth. How could the policymakers tell which factor was constraining output growth in an economy? For each of the four factors listed above, discuss short-term and longer-run policies to increase their supply.

## SUGGESTED READINGS

Allen, R. G. D., "Simple Growth Models," in *Macroeconomic Theory: A Mathematical Treatment*, New York: St. Martin's Press, 1968.

Kaldor, Nicholas, "Alternative Theories of Distribution," *Review of Economic Studies*, vol. 23, no. 2 (1955–1956), pages 83–100.

Pomfret, Richard, "Pioneers in Development Economics," *Diverse Paths of Economic Development*, New York: Prentice-Hall, 1992, pages 14–24.

Solow, Robert, "A Contribution to the Theory of Economic Growth," *The Quarterly Journal of Economics*, vol. 70, no. 1 (February 1956), pages 65–94.

World Bank, "Paths to Development," *World Development Report 1991*, New York: Oxford University Press, 1991, Chapter 2.

## APPENDIX A

### NUMERICAL EXAMPLE OF THE HARROD-DOMAR GROWTH MODEL

In this appendix we illustrate the knife-edge problem of the Harrod-Domar model. Assuming the following values for the parameters: $v = 5$, $u = 10$, $s = .10$, and $n = .02$, and given the initial values of the capital stock and labor of $K_0 = 20$ and $L_0 = 40$, the Harrod-Domar model becomes:

H1) $K = 5Y$

H2) $L = 10Y$

H3) $I = S$

H4) $S = .10Y$

H5) $\Delta L/L = .02$

From H1) and H2) the production function is $Y = \min[K/5, L/10]$. With the initial values for the model, we begin in steady-state equilibrium with full utilization of the capital stock and full employment of the labor force.

$$Y_0 = \min[20/5, 40/10] = \min[4, 4] = 4$$
$$K_0 = vY_0 = (5)(4) = 20$$
$$L_0 = uY_0 = (10)(4) = 40$$

In Table 3A.1 the values for output, capital, and labor are listed for the initial and next periods. In this initial period the level of saving is $S_0 = .10(Y_0) = .10(4) = .4$; and given the equilibrium condition of saving equals investment, all saving is assumed to be channeled into investment. Therefore the increase in the capital stock is $\Delta K = I_0 = S_0 = .4$.

For the next period the capital stock is $K_1 = K_0 + \Delta K = 20 + .4 = 20.4$. The labor force has increased by 2 percent: $\Delta L/L = .02$, so $\Delta L = .02L$ and $L_1 = L_0 + \Delta L = 40 + .02(40) = 40.8$. The new level of output is $Y_1 = \min[(20.4)/5, (40.8)/10] = \min[4.08, 4.08] = 4.08$. Steady-state equilibrium is maintained. In particular, the quantity demanded of labor, $L_1^d = 10Y_1 = 10(4.08) = 40.8$ units, is equal to the quantity supplied of labor, $L_1^s = 40.8$

### TABLE 3A.1

| | Capital (K) | Units of Labor (L) | Output (Y) | Condition |
|---|---|---|---|---|
| Time period 0 | 20 | 40 | 4 | steady-state equilibrium |
| Time period 1 | 20.4 | 40.8 | 4.08 | steady-state equilibrium |

## TABLE 3A.2

|  | CAPITAL (K) | UNITS OF LABOR (L) | OUTPUT (Y) | CONDITION |
|---|---|---|---|---|
| Time period 0 | 20 | 40 | 4 | steady-state equilibrium |
| Time period 1 | 20.4 | 41.2 | 4.08 | surplus labor |

units. As long as the warranted growth rate equals the natural growth rate, $s/v = .10/5 = .02 = n$, the economy would remain along the steady-state growth path. In this example, output, the capital stock, and the labor force are all growing at a rate of 2 percent. If, for some reason, these rates differ, the economy would fall off the knife-edge growth path and face either increasing unemployment or excess capacity.

To illustrate, suppose in Period 1 the natural growth rate of the labor force increases from 2 percent to 3 percent. With labor supply now growing faster than labor demand, unemployment results. Refer to Table 3A.2, where the labor force increases from 40 to 41.2 units of labor in Period 1. Output growth at 2 percent is constrained by the amount of capital.

In Period 1 the natural growth rate of labor increases from .02 to .03.

$Y_1 = \min[(20.4)/5, (41.2)/10] = \min[4.08, 4.12] = 4.08.$

The quantity demanded of labor is $L_1^d = 10(4.08) = 40.8$ units.

The quantity supplied of labor is $L_1^s = 40 + .03(40) = 41.2$ units.

Unemployment (excess quantity supplied of labor) equals .4 units.

Given the assumption of a fixed-coefficients production function, the surplus labor could not be used to produce more output. Furthermore, assuming a constant saving rate and a constant natural growth rate for the labor force, the unemployment would increase in subsequent periods. (You should be able to confirm that the unemployed labor rises to .82 units in Period 2.)

On the other hand, a decrease in the natural growth rate of the labor force from $n = .02$ to $n' = .01$ would also push the economy off a steady-state growth path to disequilibria characterized by increasing excess capacity. See Table 3A.3, where output growth at 1 percent is now constrained by the available labor supply. In Period 1 excess capacity is equal to .2 units of capital.

## TABLE 3A.3

|  | CAPITAL (K) | UNITS OF LABOR (L) | OUTPUT (Y) | CONDITION |
|---|---|---|---|---|
| Time period 0 | 20 | 40 | 4 | steady-state equilibrium |
| Time period 1 | 20.4 | 40.4 | 4.04 | surplus capital |

In Period 1 the natural growth rate of labor decreases from .02 to .01.

$Y_1 = \min[(20.4)/5, (40.4)/10] = \text{minimum}[4.08, 4.04] = 4.04$

The quantity of capital used is: $K_1^d = 5(4.04) = 20.2$ units.

The quantity of capital available is: $K_1^s = 20.4$ units.

The excess capacity (surplus capital stock) equals .2 units.

## APPENDIX B

### ECONOMIC GROWTH AND PHYSICAL CAPITAL DEEPENING

The fundamental relationship to be tested is between economic growth and physical capital deepening. First, do nations with higher capital–labor ratios have higher per capita incomes (as measured by Gross National Product per capita)? Second, do nations with higher growth rates in the capital–labor ratio have higher growth rates in per capita output (as measured by the percentage change in Gross Domestic Product per capita)? Data on per capita income and economic growth rates are readily available for the contemporary developing nations. Comparable data on physical capital stocks and labor forces, however, are not as available. Therefore, to measure the capital–labor ratio, we use per capita energy consumption (in kilograms of oil equivalent) to indicate the flow of factor services yielded by the capital stock.

In Table 3B.1 we present per capita Gross National Products (GNPs) and energy consumptions for the standard three groups of nations for 1991. In general, a positive relationship appears to exist. For example, the average per capita GNP for the middle-income economies is approximately 7 times the average for the other low-income economies; and the average energy consumption per capita is nearly 8 times the average for the other low-income economies. While also appearing to be direct, the relationship between the average annual growth rates in per capita GDPs and energy consumption for 1980 to 1991 is not as clear.

To better assess these relationships, data on the variables for a sample of less developed countries were collected from the *World Development Report 1993*. All low-income and middle-income economies for which the data were available are included in the sample.[1]

---

[1] In ascending order of 1991 per capita GNPs, the 78 nations included in the sample are Mozambique, Tanzania, Ethiopia, Guinea, Burundi, Chad, Madagascar, Sierra Leone, Bangladesh, Malawi, Rwanda, Mali, Burkina Faso, Niger, India, Kenya, Nigeria, China, Haiti, Benin, Central African Republic, Ghana, Pakistan, Togo, Nicaragua, Sri Lanka, Mauritania, Honduras, Indonesia, Egypt, Zimbabwe, Bolivia, Côte d'Ivoire, Senegal, Philippines, Papua New Guinea, Cameroon, Guatemala, Dominican Republic, Ecuador, Morocco, Jordan, Peru, El Salvador, Congo, Syria, Colombia, Paraguay, Jamaica, Romania, Tunisia, Thailand, Turkey, Poland, Bulgaria, Costa Rica, Panama, Chile, Iran, Mauritius, Czechoslovakia, Malaysia, Botswana, South Africa, Hungary, Venezuela, Argentina, Uruguay, Brazil, Mexico, Trinidad and Tobago, Gabon, Portugal, Oman, Puerto Rico, South Korea, Greece, and Saudi Arabia.

Algeria was included in the initial sample, but was subsequently deleted as an influential observation. That is, including Algeria in the sample significantly deflated the estimated coefficient for the growth rate of per capita energy consumption, and overstated the negative coefficient for the oil-exporter variable in the regression for the growth rate of per capita GDP. Algeria, an oil-exporting nation, had an annual average growth rate of .0 percent in GDP per capita and an annual average growth rate of 12.1 percent in per capita energy consumption over the period 1980 to 1991.

| TABLE 3B.1 | PER CAPITA INCOMES AND ENERGY CONSUMPTION | | | |
|---|---|---|---|---|
| | GNP PER CAPITA, 1991 ($) | ENERGY CONSUMPTION PER CAPITA, 1991 | AVERAGE ANNUAL GROWTH RATES, 1980–1991 | |
| | | | GDP PER CAPITA (%) | ENERGY CONSUMPTION PER CAPITA (%) |
| INCOME GROUP | | | | |
| India | 330 | 337 | 3.3 | 5.1 |
| China | 370 | 602 | 7.9 | 3.8 |
| Other low-income economies | 350 | 173 | 1.1 | 2.1 |
| Middle-income economies | 2480 | 1351 | .5 | 1.5 |
| High-income economies | 21,050 | 5106 | 2.3 | .9 |
| REGION | | | | |
| sub-Saharan Africa | 350 | 135 | –1.0 | .4 |
| Middle East & North Africa | 1940 | 1185 | –1.1 | 4.1 |
| Europe & Central Asia | 2670 | 2387 | 1.2 | .8 |
| South Asia | 320 | 289 | –.7 | 5.0 |
| East Asia & Pacific | 650 | 571 | 6.1 | 3.7 |
| Latin America & the Caribbean | 2390 | 1051 | –.3 | .7 |
| SELECTED COUNTRIES | | | | |
| Ghana | 400 | 130 | .0 | –2.8 |
| Sri Lanka | 500 | 177 | 2.6 | 3.5 |
| Egypt | 610 | 594 | 2.3 | 2.1 |
| Poland | 1790 | 3165 | –.9 | –.9 |
| Costa Rica | 1850 | 570 | .4 | 1.0 |
| Brazil | 2940 | 908 | 1.8 | 4.0 |
| South Korea | 6330 | 1936 | 8.5 | 6.8 |

NOTES:
Energy consumption per capita is measured in kilograms of oil equivalent. Included are all commercial forms of energy—petroleum and natural gas liquids, natural gas, solid fuels (coal, lignite, and so on) and primary electricity (nuclear, geothermal, and hydroelectric power)—all converted into oil equivalents. The use of firewood, dried animal excrement, and other traditional fuels, although substantial in some developing countries, is not taken into account because reliable and comprehensive data are not available.

The average annual growth rates for per capita GDP and energy consumption are equal to the average annual growth rates in GDP and energy consumption less the average annual growth rates in population, respectively.

SOURCE: World Bank, *World Development Report 1993,* New York: Oxford University Press, 1993, Tables 1, 2, 5, and 26, and page 309.

In Table 3B.2 sample statistics are given for the 78 countries. The diversity of development experience represented is indicated by the range between the maximum and minimum values of the variables.

For the regression for per capita GNP in 1991, using the square root of the variable for per capita energy consumption gives a better fit, and is consistent with the property of diminishing returns to capital intensity. (That is, per capita income rises, but at a diminishing rate, with the capital–labor ratio.) The estimated equation is:

| TABLE 3B.2 | Selected Sample Statistics for the 78 Less Developed Countries |

| Variable | Mean | Minimum | Maximum |
| --- | --- | --- | --- |
| Y/P (GNP per capita, 1991) | $1569 | $80 (Mozambique) | $7820 (Saudi Arabia) |
| E/P (energy consumption per capita, 1991, in kilograms of oil equivalent) | 867 | 17 (Chad) | 4907 (Trinidad and Tobago) |
| GYP (average annual growth rate in GDP per capita, 1980–1991) | .2% | –6.2% (Jordan) | 8.7% (South Korea) |
| GEP (average annual growth rate in energy consumption per capita, 1980–1991) | .6% | –4.6% (Senegal) | 6.8% (South Korea) |

$$(\widehat{Y/P}) = -196.9 + \underset{***}{74.1} \, (E/P)^{.5} \qquad \overline{R}^2 = .56$$

$(\widehat{Y/P})$ = predicted value for per capita GNP in 1991

$(E/P)^{.5}$ = square root of per capita energy consumption in 1991

Recall from the Appendix to Chapter 1 that the statistical significance of the estimated coefficient is indicated by the number of stars. Three stars (***) indicate that the estimated coefficient is statistically significant at the .01 level. The coefficient of determination of .56 indicates that 56 percent of the variation in 1991 per capita GNP for this sample of 78 countries was explained, or accounted for, by the variation in per capita energy consumption. The estimated coefficient of 74.1 can be interpreted to show that an increase of 100 kilograms of per capita energy consumption is associated with an increase of $741; that is, 741 = (74.1)(100)$^{.5}$, in per capita GNP, ceteris paribus.

The identified underachievers in the sample (i.e., nations whose actual per capita GNPs in 1991 were significantly lower than the per capita GNPs predicted by the regression equation) are the former Eastern bloc nations of Romania, Poland, Bulgaria, and Czechoslovakia. This underachievement may reflect the entrenched inefficiencies in their former socialist economies and the difficulties in making the transition to more market-oriented systems. The overachievers, with significantly better than predicted per capita GNPs in 1991 are the 6 highest-income nations in the sample: Portugal, Oman, Puerto Rico, South Korea, Greece, and Saudi Arabia. In fact, the poorest of the six still has a per capita GNP that is nearly 4 times the average for the full sample of 78 nations. These higher-income developing economies may have different aggregate production functions, characterized by more advanced levels of technology.

The estimated equation for the dynamic counterpart estimation of the growth rate in per capita GDP is shown below.

$$\hat{GYP} = -.20 + .61 \underset{***}{GEP} \qquad \bar{R}^2 = .25$$

where

$\hat{GYP}$ = predicted average annual growth rate in per capita GDP for 1980–1991

$GEP$ = average annual growth rate in per capita energy consumption for 1980–1991

The estimated effect of a 1 percentage point increase in the growth rate of per capita energy consumption is to increase the growth rate in per capita GDP by .61 percentage points, ceteris paribus. One quarter, or 25 percent, of the variation in the average annual economic growth rate over 1980 to 1991 for this sample of 78 less developed countries is accounted for by the variation in the average annual growth rate of per capita energy consumption.

We then added a second explanatory variable to the regression equation; since over the decade of the 1980s—in contrast to the 1970s—world oil prices sharply declined, which depressed the economies of those nations dependent on oil export revenues. Eight nations in the sample are designated by the World Bank as oil exporters: Nigeria, Congo, Iran, Venezuela, Trinidad and Tobago, Gabon, Oman, and Saudi Arabia. To control for the attribute of an oil exporter, we use a "dummy variable."[2] Let $DOE$ = dummy variable for oil exporter, where $DOE = 1$ (0 otherwise) if 50 percent or more of the nation's exports of goods and services were fuel.

The estimated equation for the average annual growth rate in per capita GDP for 1980 to 1991 then becomes

$$\hat{GYP} = .05 + .65 \underset{***}{GEP} - 2.75 \underset{***}{DOE} \qquad \bar{R}^2 = .33$$

The coefficients of both explanatory variables are statistically significant at the .01 level. An increase of 1 percentage point in the growth rate of per capita energy consumption is associated with an increase of .65 percentage points in the growth rate of per capita GDP for this sample of less developed countries. Ceteris paribus, oil-exporting developing nations had growth rates in per capita GDPs that were 2.75 percentage points lower than non-oil exporters. Three nations qualified as underachievers were Nicaragua, Jordan, and Saudi Arabia. Two nations qualified as overachievers were China and Botswana. The variation in per capita growth rates in GDP now accounted for by the regression equation increases to 33 percent.

In sum, these limited tests do provide some support for the positive relationship between economic growth and physical capital deepening. There are, of course, other factors that influence economic growth, including human capital formation; technological change; the role played by private enterprise; trade policies; scale economies;

---

[2] A *dummy variable* is a special type of explanatory variable used in regression analysis to indicate an attribute or characteristic. A dummy variable usually assumes only two values: 1 if the given characteristic is present for that observation, and 0 if the characteristic is not present.

and exogenous shocks such as civil wars and natural disasters. In the following chapters we address these factors.

## DATA SOURCES

All the data used in the empirical analysis were derived from "World Development Indicators," *World Development Report 1993*, World Bank, New York: Oxford University Press, 1993.

- $Y/P$ = Gross National Product per capita in 1991 (in dollars), Table 1
- $E/P$ = energy consumption per capita in 1991 (in kilograms of oil equivalent), Table 5
- $GYP$ = average annual growth rate in GDP per capita, 1980–1991
  $GYP = GY - GP$, where
  $GY$ = average annual growth rate in Gross Domestic Product, 1980–1991, Table 2
  $GP$ = average annual growth rate in population, 1980–1991, Table 26
- $GEP$ = average annual growth rate in per capita energy consumption, 1980–1991 (in kilograms of oil equivalent)
  $GEP = GE - GP$, where
  $GE$ = average annual growth rate in energy consumption 1980–1991 (in kilograms of oil equivalent), Table 5
- $DOE$ = dummy variable for exporters of fuel (mainly oil)
  If exports of fuel accounted for 50 percent or more of total exports of goods and services in the period 1987–1989, then $DOE = 1$ (otherwise $DOE = 0$). (*World Development Report 1993*, pages 328–329.)

# CHAPTER 4

# INITIATING AND SUSTAINING ECONOMIC GROWTH

Economic policy-makers face the difficult question of how best to promote rapid, sustainable economic growth in the face of depletable stocks of irreproducible natural resources. Improvements in technology are the best chance we have to overcome the apparent "limits to growth." ... if mankind continues to discover ways to produce more output (or better output) while conserving on those inputs that cannot be accumulated or regenerated, then there seems no reason why living standards cannot continue to rise for many centuries to come.[1]

In Chapter 3 we derived the conditions for steady-state growth, whereby output, the capital stock, and labor all increase at the same rate, consistent with the maintenance of full employment and product market equilibrium (investment equals saving). We also observed that economic growth, a rise in per capita output and income, actually represents a desired disequilibrium state. For the less developed countries following World War II, however, sustained economic growth could not be considered a given. The possibility that economies were stagnating at low levels of income, unable to generate sustained growth, had to be addressed. In this chapter we examine how to initiate and then sustain economic growth. We begin with the theory of the low-level equilibrium trap.

## LOW-LEVEL EQUILIBRIUM TRAP

Recall the traditional stage of the demographic transition, where high and volatile death rates are offset, on average, by high and relatively stable birth rates.

---

[1] Gene Grossman and Elhanan Helpman, "Endogenous Innovation in the Theory of Growth," *Journal of Economic Perspectives,* vol. 8, no. 1 (winter 1994), pages 23–44. This quotation is from page 42.

Accompanying this low-level demographic equilibrium might be a low-level economic equilibrium. The high fertility rates produce a large youth burden of dependency, restricting the ability of the economy to generate saving. The corresponding low rates of investment translate into modest capital–labor ratios; low average products of labor; and depressed per capita incomes. The economy is mired in a subsistence state. Any improvement in income, perhaps due to a favorable harvest, is temporary. The gains in the standard of living, which may induce increased saving and investment and raise the capital–labor ratio, are overwhelmed by the population growth from the falling death rates. Any increase in the capital–labor ratio is reversed, with per capita income pulled back to a subsistence level. The dilemma is how to break out of the stagnant state of poverty and engage self-sustaining economic growth. To illustrate we draw on a model of the **low-level equilibrium trap** set forth by Richard Nelson.[2]

As with the Solow model, we employ an aggregate production function characterized by constant returns to scale and factor substitution. Doing so permits us to write output per unit of labor (or more generally per capita income) as a positive, but decreasing, function of the capital–labor ratio.

$$y = A \cdot f(k) \text{ where } A \text{ is an index of technology}$$

In order for the capital–labor ratio *(k)* to rise, the growth rate in the capital stock must exceed the growth rate in the labor force. In Nelson's model, the growth rates of capital and labor are functions of per capita income *(y)*.

## GROWTH RATE OF PHYSICAL CAPITAL

The growth rate in the physical capital stock *(dK/K)* is assumed to be a positive function of per capita income above a zero net saving level.

$$\text{N1)} \quad dK/K = g(y \overset{+}{-} x)$$

where $x$ = level of per capita income where the (net) saving rate equals zero. If $y < x$, then dissaving and disinvestment take place, and $dK/K < 0$. The capital stock would be wearing out faster than it could be replaced. An extreme example would be peasant farmers facing starvation who eat the seeds intended for the next crop's planting. If $y > x$, then the saving forthcoming exceeds the investment necessary just to maintain the capital stock. Consequently the capital stock grows $(dK/K > 0)$.

In Figure 4.1 we sketch the *dK/K* curve. To the left of point $x$, per capita income is so low that the capital stock is decreasing. To the right of point $x$, capital formation rises with per capita income, initially at an increasing rate as marginal propensities to save rise with income and profitable investment outlets expand with economic growth. Eventually the rate of growth in the capital stock may taper off as higher consumption aspirations stabilize saving rates and as the growth in new investment opportunities slows.

The *dK/K* curve is drawn holding constant, among other factors, the distribution of income and net foreign capital inflows. For example, as in the Kaldor model, shifts in

---

[2]See Richard Nelson, "A Theory of the Low-Level Equilibrium Trap in Underdeveloped Economies," *American Economic Review*, vol. 46, no. 1 (December 1956), pages 894–908.

## FIGURE 4.1 | GROWTH RATE OF CAPITAL STOCK

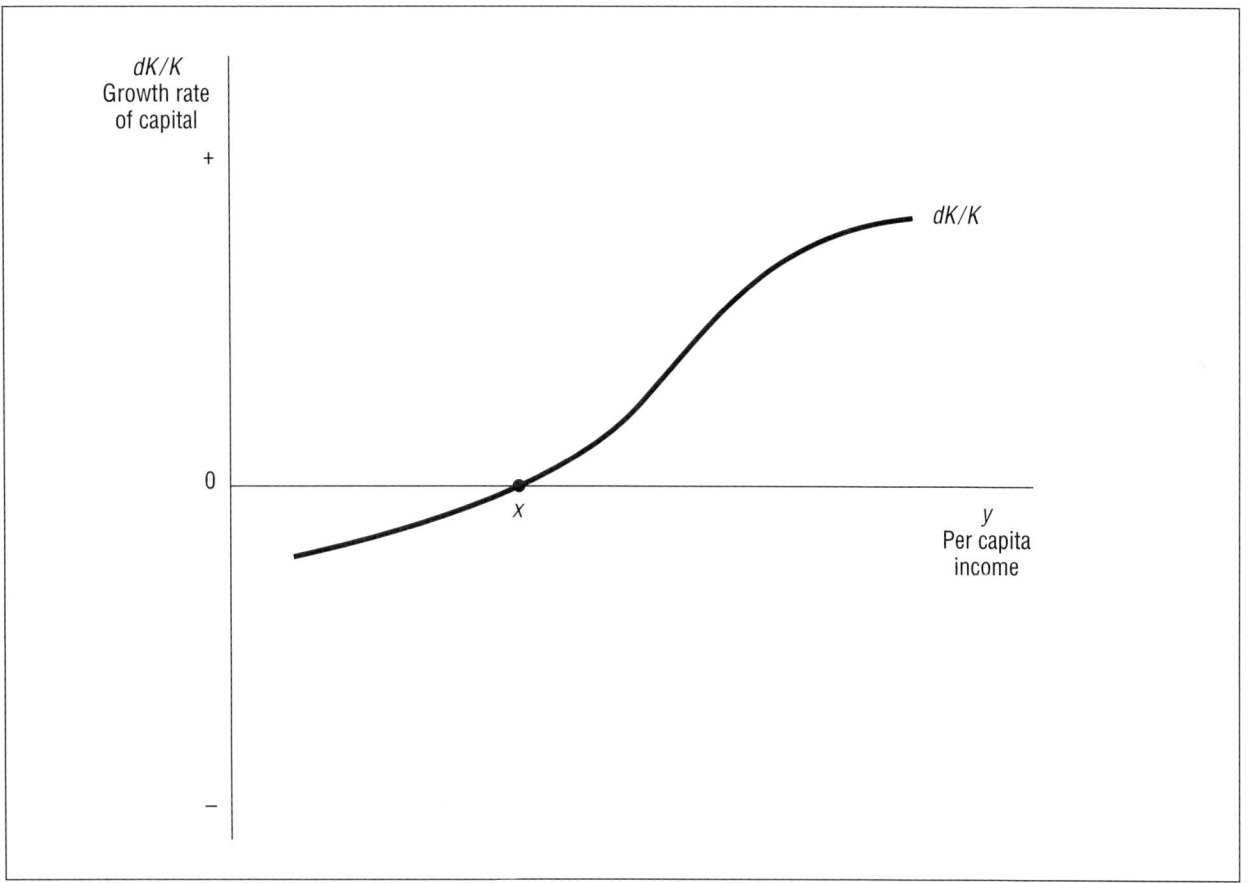

the distribution of income in favor of capitalists would increase the aggregate saving rate for any level of per capita income. Here such a redistribution of income would shift the $dK/K$ curve up (or leftward). Foreign capital inflows, whether in the form of foreign aid or foreign investment, could also contribute to capital formation at any given level of income.

## GROWTH RATE OF LABOR

The growth rate in the labor force is assumed to be directly related to per capita income above the subsistence level. That is,

$$\text{N2)} \quad dL/L = h(y \overset{+}{-} z)$$

where $z$ = the subsistence level of per capita income.

At low levels of per capita income, birth and death rates are high. Outside of fluctuations in migration, the variation in population growth rates largely reflects changing mortality conditions. Moreover, current labor forces are assumed to be unaffected

## FIGURE 4.2 | GROWTH RATE OF LABOR

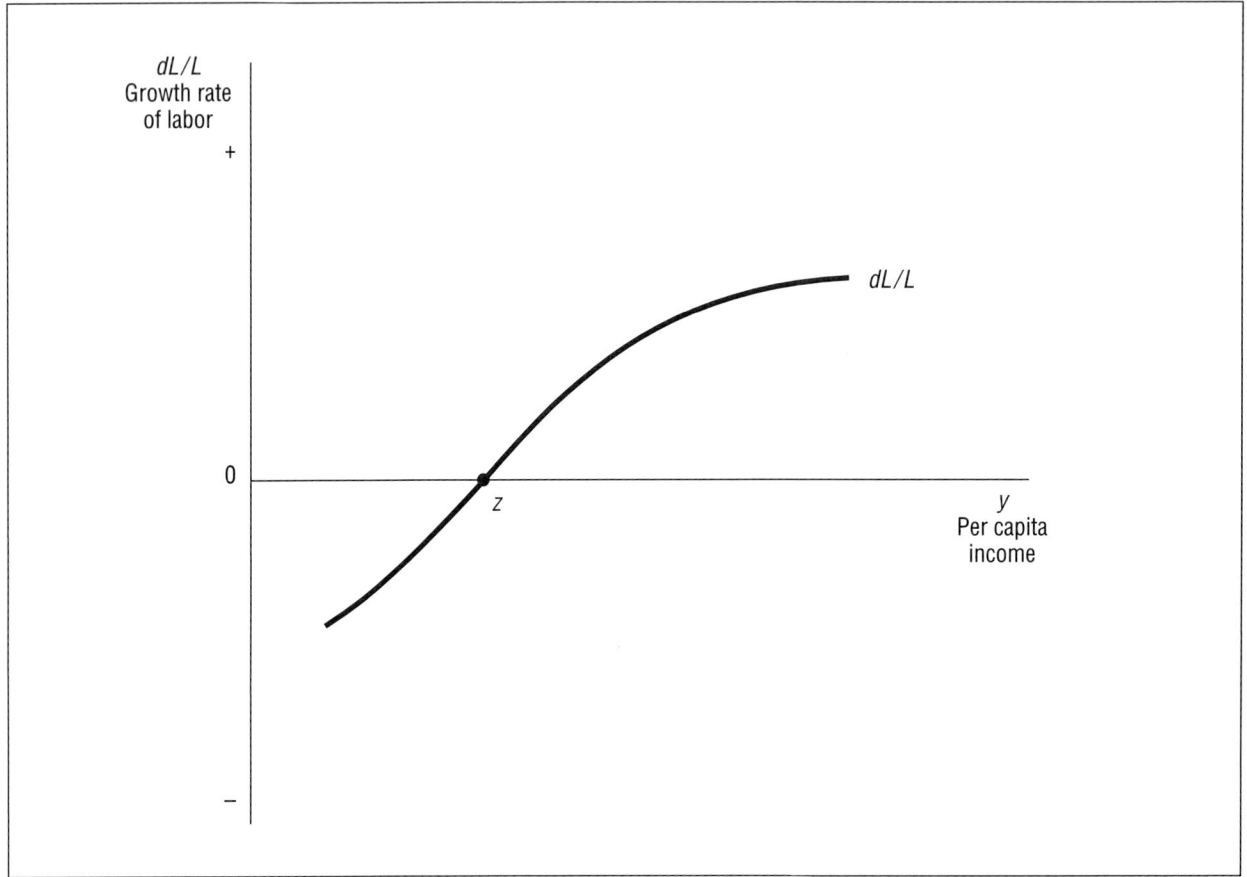

by the current birth rates. If $y < z$, then average income is below the subsistence level. Death rates (and perhaps out-migration rates) rise, and labor force growth is negative. If $y > z$, then the improvement in income lowers death rates (and perhaps induces net in-migration), so the labor force grows. The slope of the $dL/L$ curve, depicted in Figure 4.2, may taper off as per capita income rises as further reductions in mortality become more difficult to achieve from higher income alone.

The $dL/L$ curve is drawn holding constant public health measures (e.g., malaria eradication campaigns and inoculation programs) and environmental conditions (including the Malthusian positive checks of adverse weather conditions, natural disasters, and war).

### ESCAPING THE LOW-LEVEL EQUILIBRIUM TRAP

We now combine the two curves on one graph (see Figure 4.3). We will assume that $x = z$; that is, at the subsistence level of per capita income, where labor force growth is zero,

## FIGURE 4.3  LOW-LEVEL EQUILIBRIUM TRAP

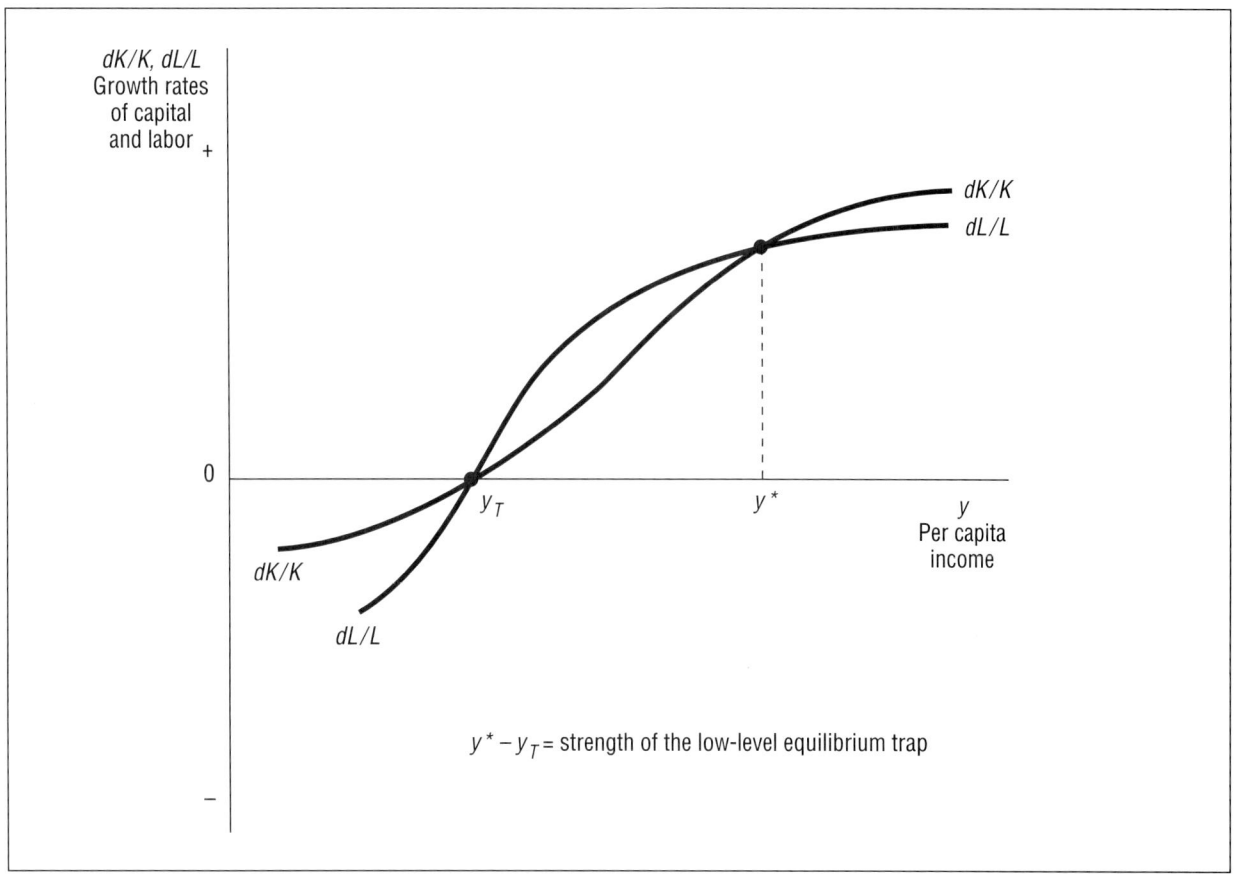

$y^* - y_T$ = strength of the low-level equilibrium trap

the net saving rate is zero.[3] Moreover, we need to assume that in the neighborhood of this level of per capita income, the growth rate in the labor force is more sensitive to changes in per capita income than is the growth rate of the capital stock. In other words, the $dL/L$ curve is steeper than the $dK/K$ curve around the $x = z$ level of per capita income. Given the configuration of the two curves, two steady-state equilibria exist: where $dK/K = dL/L$ and the capital–labor ratio and per capita income are constant. At the level of per capita income labelled $y_T$, where $x = z$, the equilibrium is stable. For per capita incomes below $y_T$, the labor force is declining faster than the capital stock, thus raising the capital–labor ratio and pulling per capita income back up to $y_T$.

---

[3]*Note:* It is not necessary to assume that the subsistence level of per capita income $(z)$ is the same as the level where the net saving rate is zero $(x)$. If the subsistence level exceeds the zero net saving level of per capita income $(z > x)$, then the low-level equilibrium trap would be characterized by a positive growth rate for the labor force. The low-level equilibrium trap could, for a while at least, be characterized by negative growth in the labor force (if $z < x$). Required, however, in the neighborhood of the low-level equilibrium trap is that the response of labor force growth to changes in per capita income is greater than the response of capital formation.

If $y < y_T$, then $dL/L < dK/K < 0$ and $k\uparrow$, resulting in $y\uparrow$ to $y_T$

Conversely, for per capita incomes between $y_T$ and $y^*$, the second steady-state equilibrium, the capital stock is not growing as fast as the labor force. The capital–labor ratio falls and pulls per capita income back to $y_T$.

If $y_T < y < y^*$, then $dL/L > dK/K > 0$, and $k\downarrow$ resulting in $y\downarrow$ to $y_T$

The point $y_T$ represents the low-level equilibrium trap. The strength of the trap is indicated by the distance between $y^*$ and $y_T$.

To escape the trap, per capita income has to rise beyond $y^*$. This second equilibrium of $y^*$ is unstable.

If $y > y^*$ then $dK/K > dL/L > 0$, and $k\uparrow$, resulting in $y\uparrow$

Once beyond $y^*$, economic growth should be self-sustaining. Moreover, at significantly higher levels of per capita income (not shown in the graphs) birth rates may decline, which, with a lag of 15 years or so, would reduce the growth rate of the labor force.

Technological progress, which increases output and income for any given levels of capital and labor, or foreign aid, which improves the standard of living, could boost the economy beyond this threshold level. It is ironic to note that the imported medical technologies which dramatically reduced mortality rates in the developing nations after World War II initially may have increased the strength of the low-level equilibrium trap. The drop in death rates at all levels of per capita income would shift up the $dL/L$ curve, reducing the income level associated with the low-level equilibrium trap and increasing the threshold level of income. This is not to suggest that the improvements in mortality conditions were unwelcome. Indeed, aside from the obvious welfare gains from raising the average life expectancy, significantly lower child mortality rates may be a precondition for reducing high fertility rates. In hindsight, however, the advances in public health might have been better complemented with foreign assistance that generated economic development.

In contrast, upward shifts in the $dK/K$ curve will diminish, and may even break entirely, the low-level equilibrium trap (see Figure 4.4). Here the strength of the trap is reduced from $y^* - y_T$ to $y^{*\prime} - y_T'$. In the tradition of the growth models discussed in the last chapter, the policy implications of the theory of the low-level equilibrium trap center on physical capital formation as the key to economic growth and, by extension, economic development. Measures to encourage saving and investment are advocated. Foreign aid and foreign direct investment are desirable, not only as contributors to capital formation, but as vehicles for the transfer of foreign technology. Moreover, if superior technologies are embodied in the new machinery and equipment, then technological change would accompany the capital formation. Thus, as the $dK/K$ curve shifted up, per capita output ($y$) would be rising.

Birth-control programs not only have the beneficial, if delayed, effect of slowing labor force growth (eventually shifting down the $dL/L$ curve), but also work to reduce the current youth burden of dependency. Resources that would have been used for the social welfare maintenance of the young (e.g., education, health care, and housing) are freed up for more directly productive investments in physical capital (e.g., transportation systems, power generation, and factories).

To illustrate, see Table 4.1, and consider two hypothetical populations, with the same initial age structure and size. (For a similar example, refer back to Table 2.3.) To

| FIGURE 4.4 | REDUCING THE STRENGTH OF THE LOW-LEVEL EQUILIBRIUM TRAP |

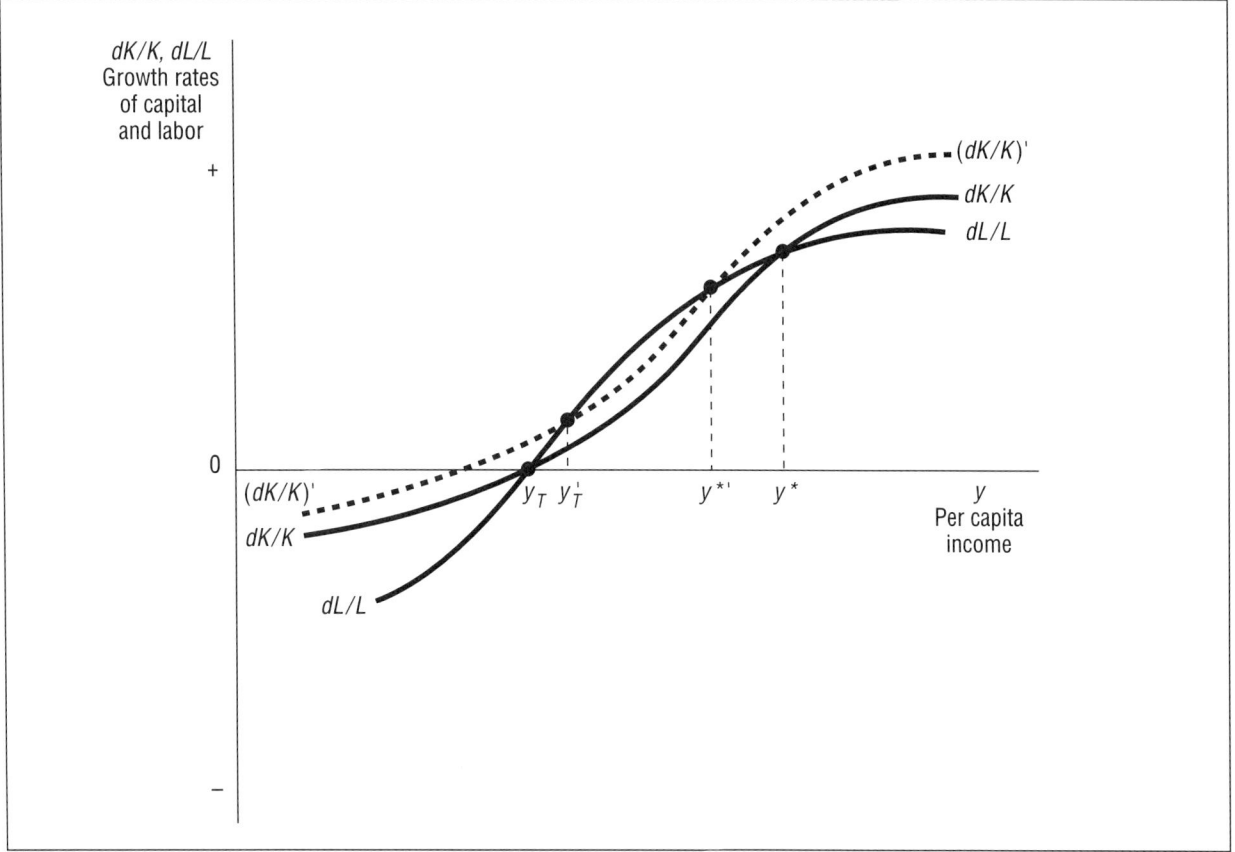

make the mathematics easier, we assume all the adult population (ages 15 through 44 years) is employed and that each adult produces $700 worth of output and income.

For the initial populations the per capita income is $350 (400 adults each earning $700 equals $280,000 in total income, divided by a population of 800). For Population A, the total fertility rate for the 15-year projection is assumed to equal 4. Therefore, the 200 childbearing individuals of ages 15 to 29 would have 400 births over the 15-year projection, and the population size would grow to 1000. In this example, the per capita income rises to $420 due to the relatively large increase in the working adult population (aging up from the 0 to 14 interval).

For Population B, the total fertility rate for the 15-year projection is lower and assumed to be equal to 3. Hence, only 300 births in Population B occur over the period, giving a total population size of 900. With a smaller population under age 15 (compared to Population A), but with the same working adult population, per capita income in Population B rises to $467.

In sum, a decline in fertility can boost per capita income since the increase in the population under age 15 is immediately reduced, while the population in the labor force years is unaffected for 15 years. The output and income that would have been allocated for the maintenance of the young dependents can now be used to increase per

| TABLE 4.1 | ILLUSTRATION OF THE GAINS FROM REDUCED FERTILITY |

Assumptions:

1. There is a 100 percent survival rate from birth through age 44 years. All individuals die on their 45th birthday.
2. In each age interval the population is evenly distributed across all ages with an equal number of males and females.
3. All births occur to the population that begins in the middle age interval.
4. All adults (ages 15–44) work and earn $700 each.
5. The period of projection is fifteen years and is equal to the length of each age interval.
6. The total fertility rate (TFR) is equal to 4 for Population A and 3 for Population B.

| AGE GROUP | POPULATION A INITIAL | POPULATION A END OF PERIOD 1 | POPULATION B INITIAL | POPULATION B END OF PERIOD 1 |
|---|---|---|---|---|
| 0–14 | 400 | 400 | 400 | 300 |
| 15–29 | 200 | 400 | 200 | 400 |
| 30–44 | 200 | 200 | 200 | 200 |
| Total Population | 800 | 1000 | 800 | 900 |
| Total Income ($) | 280,000 | 420,000 | 280,000 | 420,000 |
| Income per capita ($) | 350 | 420 | 350 | 467 |
| Total Fertilty Rate (TFR) | 4.0 | | 3.0 | |

capita consumption and to invest in physical and human capital. Moreover, the gains in per capita output from the reduced fertility may be even greater than illustrated, since we assumed here that all adults were employed. In fact, lower fertility rates may increase female labor force participation rates, somewhat offsetting the effects of reduced fertility on future labor force growth.

From another perspective, past high fertility rates virtually guarantee significant growth in the labor forces of the less developed countries—for the next few decades, at least. The challenge will be in generating the resources for the physical and human capital investments needed to accompany the increases in the labor forces and to improve the levels of labor productivity.

We turn now to Rostow's stages-of-growth theory, which is an attempt to describe the process of economic growth and development drawing from the experiences of the industrialized nations.

## ROSTOW'S TAKE-OFF INTO SELF-SUSTAINING GROWTH

The key concept in W. W. Rostow's theory is the "take-off," or the escape from a low-level equilibrium trap. Rostow hypothesized that the process of economic growth can usefully be regarded as centering on a relatively brief interval of two or three decades when the economy and society of which it is a part transform themselves in such ways that economic growth is, subsequently, more or less automatic.[4]

## CLASSIFICATION OF ECONOMIES

Rostow classifies economies according to four types.[5] In the **traditional economy** conditions are similar to the economic stagnation found in the low-level equilibrium trap. The economy is largely agrarian; production techniques are primitive; incomes are low; saving and capital formation are modest; and population growth is minimal. Socioeconomic activity is bound by tradition and custom.

In the **pre-take-off** economy some improvement occurs in the standard of living with the beginnings of economic growth and structural transformation. Population growth increases as death rates fall; meanwhile, the economic, social, and political preconditions for self-sustaining economic growth are put into place.

While the traditional economy may have persisted for centuries, and the preconditions for take-off evolve over a number of decades, the third stage of the **take-off** is relatively brief, lasting a generation or less. During the take-off, the pull of the low-level equilibrium trap is broken, and the economy is transformed so that economic growth can be maintained. Relating back to Figure 4.3, the traditional economy would operate in the neighborhood of the low-level equilibrium trap; the pre-take-off economy would be between the trap and threshold levels of per capita income ($y_T$ to $y^*$); and the take-off economy would have escaped the trap ($y > y^*$).

When successful, the take-off leads to the final, ongoing stage of an increasingly diversified **growing economy,** with rising levels of per capita consumption and investment. While business cycles may dampen, and even periodically reverse economic growth, a secure foundation is in place for continued, widespread improvements in the average standard of living.

In Figure 4.5 we depict the four stages outlined by Rostow. Time is represented on the horizontal axis, and per capita income ($y$) is on the vertical axis. The graph is a mirror image of the demographic transition theory. (Refer back to Figure 2.4 in Chapter 2.) On average, economic growth and population growth are minimal in the traditional economy—although intervals of economic growth and population increase alternate with intervals of economic decline and depopulation. As in the Malthusian stage of high birth rates and high death rates, economies and populations are especially vulnerable to exogenous shocks, such as extremes in weather, natural disasters, and plagues. The pre-take-off economy parallels the early transition stage in which

---

[4]See W. W. Rostow, "The Take-Off into Self-Sustained Growth," *Economic Journal*, vol. 46, no. 1 (March 1956), reprinted in *The Economics of Underdevelopment*, edited by A. N. Agarwala and S. P. Singh, New York: Oxford University Press, 1970, pages 154–186. The following quotation is from page 154 in Agarwala and Singh.

[5]Rostow elsewhere delineates five stages of growth: the traditional society, the preconditions for take-off, the take-off, the drive to maturity, and the age of high mass consumption. See W. W. Rostow, "The Stages of Economic Growth," *Economic History Review*, vol. 12, no. 1 (1959), pages 1–16. In this chapter our main focus is on the requirements for a successful take-off, so we combine the fourth and fifth stages into a "growing economy."

## FIGURE 4.5   STAGES OF GROWTH

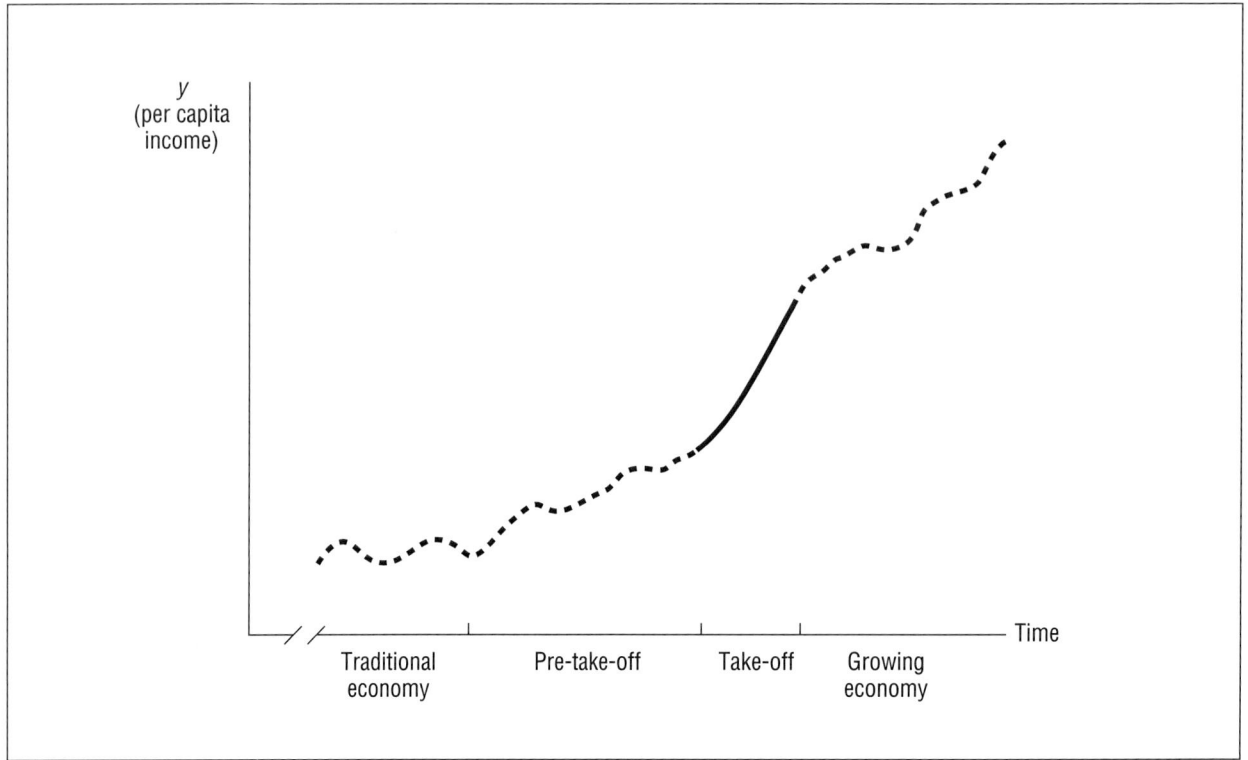

improvements in mortality conditions in the face of unchanging fertility behavior translate into significant population growth. The burst in economic growth, general rise in the standard of living, and expansion of economic opportunities during the take-off may induce the declines in fertility needed to complete the demographic transition. Finally, the counterpart of the growing, diversified economy with high rates of human and physical capital formation is the modern demographic equilibrium of low birth and death rates and high life expectancies.

## THE TAKE-OFF

As indicated, the key to Rostow's model is the take-off. The colorful analogy is that of a heavy cargo plane, lumbering down the runway, accelerating to the speed necessary to become airborne. Given the mechanical soundness of the plane, the technical expertise of the pilots, the absence of poor weather conditions, and a clear path on the runway, the plane should successfully take off, quickly escaping the pull of gravity. The plane would then climb to a comfortable cruising altitude, albeit occasionally buffeted by pockets of turbulence.

### PRECONDITIONS

Rostow identifies three crucial developments during the pre-take-off stage. First is stepped-up investment in the economic infrastructure, particularly in transportation.

New railroads, highways, waterways, and airports must be built. Improvements in the transportation network, along with income and population growth, widen the extent of the market, permitting greater labor specialization and enhancing total productivity. Often beyond the budgetary constraints of the developing nation governments, these infrastructural investments may have to be largely funded by foreign capital.

Second, agricultural productivity must be significantly improved in order to feed the growing urban-industrial population. The adoption of new seeds, fertilizers, and methods of cultivation, along with increased orientation to the market, not only raises crop yields, but releases farm labor to the industrial workforce.

Third, in the early stages of economic development domestic firms will not likely be capable of producing the capital goods (machinery and equipment) needed for expanding the manufacturing base and increasing capital–labor ratios. Therefore, imports of capital goods are required. These imports may be funded by the exportation of natural resources and primary products.

## Initiating a Take-Off

Given that an economy has met the preconditions (increases in infrastructural investment, agricultural productivity, and imports of capital goods), the initiation of take-off may come through a sharp stimulus. A political revolution that establishes a new government committed to economic development and capable of marshalling the forces for change may trigger a take-off. An example would be the Republic of Korea (South Korea), which entered the 1960s as a low-income nation with rapid population growth; poor natural resource endowments; a corrupt and ineffective government; and an economy virtually dependent on United States aid. Student uprisings led to a military coup in 1961 and the formation of the authoritarian government of General Park Chung Hee. Economic reforms were quickly implemented and a coherent strategy of development put in place. South Korea then experienced sustained and rapid economic growth. (In the next chapter we provide a brief case study of South Korea.)

Examples of political revolution in the last two decades that may have set back economic development—at least from a Western perspective—would include the devastation under the Khmer Rouge in Cambodia (then Kampuchea) and the rise to power of the Ayatollah Khomeini and Islamic fundamentalism in Iran.

Technological change could also be the spark igniting a take-off. The Industrial Revolution underway in the latter half of the eighteenth century in England brought forth a series of inventions and innovations that unleashed entrepreneurial energies and began the modern factory system. Some two centuries later the Green Revolution in agriculture introduced high-yielding varieties of seeds and improvements in fertilizers and herbicides, significantly raising agricultural productivity in many less developed countries. While highly beneficial to the nations involved, the Green Revolution technology has not triggered the take-off that the earlier Industrial Revolution did for England. One reason might be the substantial trade barriers and policy distortions that have hindered agricultural development. Another would be the income inelasticity of demand for most agricultural commodities (i.e., the percentage increases in demand lag behind the percentage increases in income, so that the share of total expenditures for agricultural commodities declines with economic growth).

Foreign investment through transnational corporations may provide the capital, technology, and expertise to develop the natural resources and initiate take-offs in some less developed countries.

SUSTAINING A TAKE-OFF

Whatever the fuse, once begun, a take-off needs to be sustained. Rostow lists requirements for a successful take-off. First, echoing the growth model emphasis on capital accumulation, an increase in the rate of net investment (i.e., gross investment less depreciation) from 5 percent, or less, to 10 percent, or more, of national income is needed. Such an increase would permit capital deepening (a rise in the capital–labor ratio) and raise labor productivity and per capita income. The sources for investment are domestic saving (achieved, for example, with a shift in the distribution of income in favor of capitalists or with public saving from increased taxation) and foreign saving.

Inflation, up to a point, it was argued, might contribute to a higher domestic saving rate. Profits may increase faster than wages during an inflationary period since wages may be set in labor contracts and, thus, relatively fixed. A rise in the share of profits in national income would tend to increase the saving rate. (Recall the Kaldor model in Chapter 3.) A progressive income tax with marginal tax rates rising with nominal income would allow the government to increase the share of taxes in national income during inflationary times.[6] Foreign saving, either in the form of foreign aid or foreign investment, could also serve as a source for new capital formation.

Second, Rostow cites the need to develop one or more manufacturing sectors with high growth potential that are capable of leading the industrialization of the economy. Rostow distinguishes between primary growth, supplementary growth, and derived growth sectors.

**Primary growth sectors,** often in agriculture and natural resources, tend to be especially important during the pre-take-off stage in initiating the economic growth and generating the foreign exchange needed for the importation of capital goods. The emphasis may shift from subsistence farming and the growing of food crops for domestic consumption to commercial agriculture and the export of cash crops. Nations favorably endowed with the resources may step up the extraction of minerals or the harvesting of timber for export. Given the natural resource intensity of the production and the importance of export revenues, the domestic government and foreign corporations may be directly involved in the development of these primary growth sectors (for example, large plantations for growing tea or rubber, and capital-intensive mining companies). Rostow claims that railroads, important for the expansion of the domestic market, have been a key sector of early growth. Textiles and apparel also have traditionally been among the initial group of manufacturing sectors to be developed.

Ideally, linkages to other sectors could be fostered. Forward linkages may exist in the case of processing raw materials or primary products like petroleum, timber, or coffee. Backward linkages may exist to manufacture the inputs needed in the primary sectors, as in the case of fertilizers and farm implements, textile looms, and mining equipment. These **supplementary growth sectors** would feed off the expansion of the primary sectors. For example, the development of a railway system might stimulate the domestic production of steel. Other supplementary growth sectors could be promoted through import substitution. Here trade barriers are used to reduce foreign competition and redirect domestic demand to domestic production. In addition to textiles and apparel, commodities such as shoes and simple consumer electronics can be relatively easily manufactured with domestic labor and little capital. One or more of these sectors

---

[6]This bracket-creep effect of inflation, however, may be offset by the loss in purchasing power from the delay in collecting the tax revenues on current income. In general, inflation is not recommended as a policy to promote saving and growth, for reasons that will become clearer in Chapters 10 and 12.

may even emerge during the take-off as an "engine of growth," with rapidly expanding output, employment, and income.

With the general expansion of the economy through the take-off and into the growing stage, increasingly **derived growth sectors** will be stimulated. The diversification of the manufacturing base and the multiplier effects from rising incomes and expenditures would increase the demands for both consumer goods and capital goods—from appliances and furniture to machinery and capital equipment; from housing and public utilities to education and health care; and from financial services to entertainment. Structural change with new markets and new products becomes pervasive. In short, the foundation for economic growth and economic development is in place.

The third requirement in Rostow's scheme for a successful take-off is the establishment of institutions to sustain and expand capital formation. Effective financial intermediation (with commercial banks, thrift institutions, bond and stock markets, insurance companies, and even pension funds) is needed to mobilize and channel loanable funds into productive investments. A growing supply of entrepreneurs, crucial for initiating the take-off, is also needed to start new businesses; expand existing enterprises; reinvest profits; and engineer the ongoing structural change. Rostow observes that often the ranks of entrepreneurs are filled with oppressed minorities or ethnic groups who, finding the traditional avenues of socioeconomic mobility blocked, are willing to initiate new ventures.

Rostow's theory, because of the important role assigned to physical capital formation, may be placed within the growth model tradition. Unlike the other models discussed, each of which can be represented with mathematical equations and reduced to equilibrium conditions, Rostow's theory is more descriptive. He attempts to flesh out the dynamic processes of economic growth and development, incorporating difficult-to-quantify factors such as political revolutions and entrepreneurship. Rostow's model of the take-off has been criticized, however, like demographic transition theory, as less of a theory complete with specific assumptions and testable hypotheses, and more of a generalized account fashioned from the diverse experiences of developed economies.

Indeed, given the unique historical, cultural, political, and economic circumstances that define each country, capturing the process of economic development with a general model has proven to be elusive. It is important to remember that to be useful and manageable, theoretical models in the social sciences will necessarily be abstractions from reality, not exact reproductions of it. Identifying general tendencies or common patterns across countries, however, does yield insight into the complex phenomenon of economic development.

We now extend the analysis of the initiation of economic growth and development to explicit consideration of two sectors, agriculture and industry. A universal feature of the economic development process has been the transfer of resources out of agriculture and into industry—along with a shift in population from rural to urban areas. A model by Lewis addresses this basic structural change.

## LEWIS'S TWO-SECTOR MODEL

The transformation of primarily agrarian, traditional economies into modern, industrial economies epitomizes economic development. In a classic article, W. Arthur Lewis set out a two-sector model to explain the growth and function of the capitalist surplus under the labor-abundant conditions typical of less developed economies.[7] Reflecting the tenor of the growth model approach, Lewis states,

> The central problem in the theory of economic development is to understand the process by which a community which was previously saving and investing 4 or 5 percent of its national income or less, converts itself into an economy where voluntary saving is running at about 12 to 15 percent of national income or more. This is the central problem because the central fact of economic development is rapid capital accumulation (including knowledge and skills with capital).[8]

The two sectors identified by Lewis are the subsistence (traditional) and capitalist (modern) sectors. The **subsistence sector** consists predominantly of family farmers using traditional, labor-intensive techniques of production on small plots of land.[9] Surplus labor exists. The capital–labor ratio is low, resulting in a low average product of labor and incomes near the subsistence level. The marginal product of labor (the change in output associated with a change in labor) approaches zero. Labor could be withdrawn from the traditional sector with no loss in output, provided that the remaining labor picked up the slack by working a bit longer, or harder, or more efficiently. Consequently, in the traditional sector the wage is based on the average product of labor (total output divided by labor) rather than on the marginal product of labor, which, near zero, is well below the subsistence level.

In contrast, in the **capitalist sector,** which emerges when entrepreneurs seize upon the profitable opportunities for investment that arise in the early stages of economic growth, the capital–labor ratio is significantly higher, a reflection of the more capital-intensive technologies required in manufacturing.[10] The capitalist, or modern, sector wage will exceed that found in the subsistence, or traditional, sector—even adjusting for the higher cost of living in urban areas—due not only to the greater labor productivity in the modern sector, but also to the need to attract labor from the traditional sector. That is, given that the majority of the population in less developed economies is found in rural areas, a real wage premium must exist in the urban, modern sector to cover the costs of migration—the direct costs (transportation and relocation); opportunity cost (lost income from not working during migration and relocation); and psychic cost (the stress from moving from the familiar to a new environment). In Chapter 9 rural-to-urban labor migration will be examined in more detail.

---

[7]See W. Arthur Lewis, "Economic Development with Unlimited Supplies of Labour," *The Manchester School* (May 1954), reprinted in Agarwala and Singh (1970). In 1979 Lewis and Theodore Schultz shared the Nobel Prize in Economics for their work in economic development.

[8]Ibid., page 416.

[9]The traditional sector may also encompass urban informal employment—the myriad of economic activities found on the fringe of the modern sector, such as rickshaw operators, vendors, odd-jobbers, self-employed guides, street performers, and even small shops and retail establishments.

[10]This simple twofold classification of a traditional-rural-agricultural sector and a modern-urban-industrial sector, while overdrawn, is useful to illustrate the dualistic nature of economic development. In practice, along with the existence of urban informal economic activity (more akin to the traditional sector), fairly capital-intensive agriculture may be found on large estates producing cash crops for export (a rural extension of the modern sector).

## GROWTH OF THE MODERN SECTOR

Lewis assumes that, at least in the early stages of economic growth and development, an unlimited supply of labor can be drawn from the traditional sector into the modern sector at the modern-sector real wage. Assuming a marginal product of zero, this labor can be shifted without any loss of output in the traditional sector. The transferred labor could be used to produce capital goods, increasing the capital stock and productivity of labor in the modern sector. Increases in the **capitalist surplus** (the total revenues from the sale of output less the labor costs) allow additional labor to be drawn in from the traditional sector. The essential idea is that by redistributing labor from lower-productivity employment (in the traditional sector) to higher-productivity employment (in the modern sector), aggregate output can be increased, with some of the increased output taking the form of capital goods that further enhance labor productivity in the modern sector.

In Figure 4.6 we illustrate. The supply of labor to the capitalist sector is assumed to be perfectly elastic at the real wage $(w_m)$, which exceeds the subsistence-sector wage $(w_t)$. The initial marginal-product-of-labor curve (indicated by $MP_L$) is drawn for a given capital stock and technology of the capitalist sector. The downward slope of the $MP_L$ curve reflects diminishing returns to labor. That is, the contribution of additional units of labor to the production of modern-sector output decreases in the short run.

The profit-maximizing employment in the modern sector will occur where the marginal product of labor equals the real wage (see point $M_1$ in Figure 4.6). At this level of employment, $L_1$, the last unit of labor hired adds as much to the output of the capitalist sector as the real wage that must be paid (or the command over goods and services received by labor). Hiring any more or less labor than $L_1$ would reduce profits in the modern sector. Total real wage payments equal $(w_m)(L_1)$ or the area labeled $w_m M_1 L_1 0$. The value of the output produced by labor is given by the area under the $MP_L$ curve up to $L_1$ (or the area labeled $V_1 M_1 L_1 0$). The capitalist surplus, out of which must be paid the fixed costs of capital and materials costs, is equal to the area $V_1 M_1 w_m$. Any residual from the capitalist surplus after costs would be profits, which could be reinvested in the production of new capital goods (plant, equipment, and machinery). The resulting increase in the stock of capital goods would shift out the $MP_L$ curve to $MP'_L$, allowing more labor from the traditional sector to be employed in the modern sector. Given the modern-sector real wage of $w_m$, now $L_2$ units of labor would be hired. The capitalist surplus grows to $V_2 M_2 w_m$ and the process of capital accumulation and growth in the modern sector continues.

We have oriented the discussion to modern-sector manufacturing and, implicitly, private capitalists. In the case of public entrepreneurship, the government may use surplus labor from the traditional sector for construction projects (e.g., roads, bridges, railways, seaports, airports, power plants, and dams) that add to the physical infrastructure of the economy and complement the private capital formation in manufacturing.

Indeed, a certain amount of economic infrastructure may need to be in place before much private capital formation is profitable. Lewis notes that in the early stages the capitalist surplus may not yield sufficient profits for the reinvestment required to boost labor productivity (shift the $MP_L$ curve right) and start the expansion process. Initially, the government may need to generate the required funds.

## POLICY IMPLICATIONS OF THE LEWIS MODEL

To extract funds directly from the traditional sector through income taxes may prove difficult, given the low level of incomes in the traditional sector. The government,

## FIGURE 4.6  CAPITALIST SURPLUS IN THE MODERN SECTOR

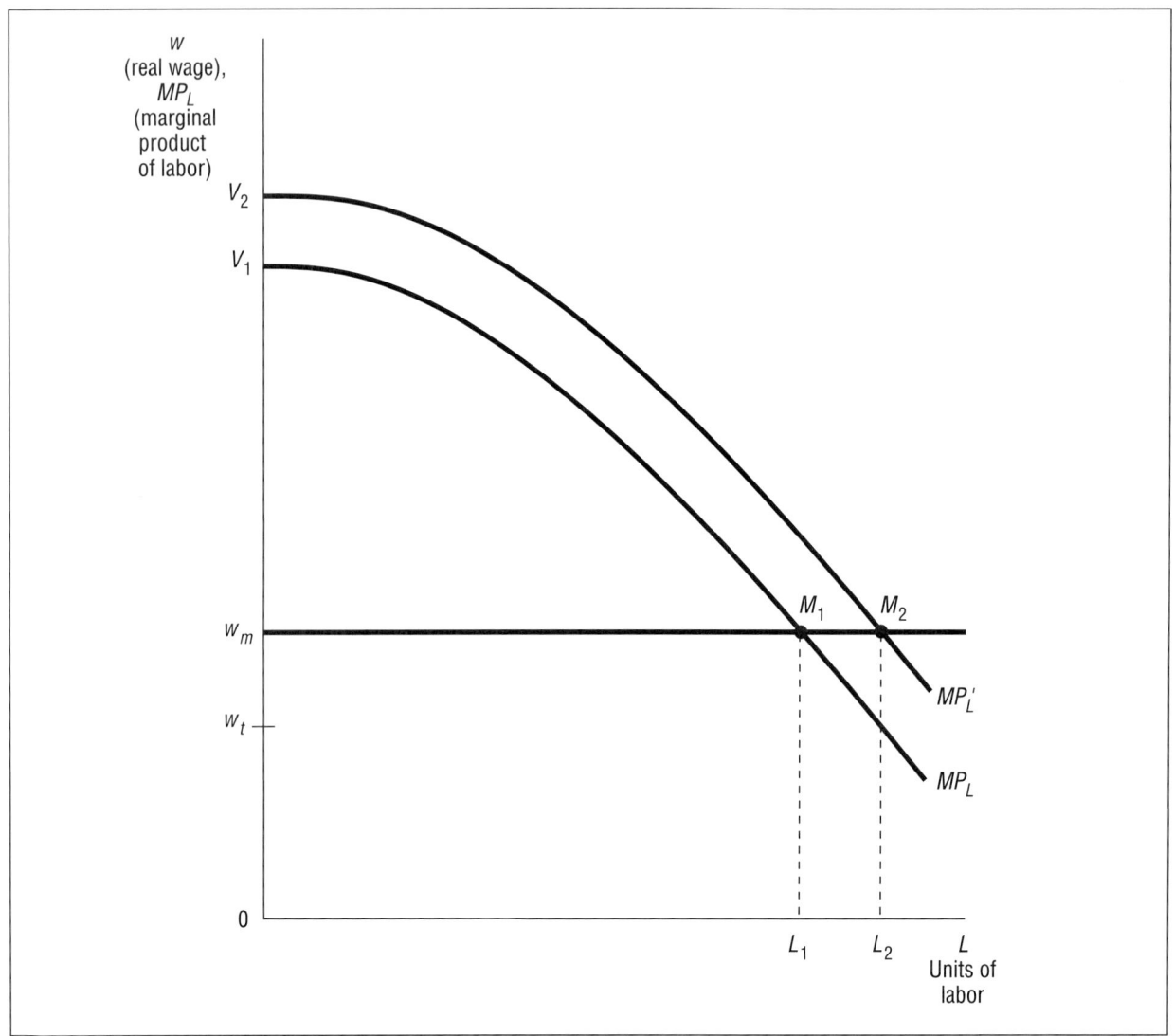

however, could control the prices paid to farmers for their produce. State agricultural boards would pay farmers prices below world market levels. The state could then sell the agricultural produce in urban areas for a profit. If the prices paid to domestic farmers were significantly depressed, then the food prices to urban consumers might still be less than world market levels—in effect subsidizing the modern-sector real wage. The government could use the revenues to fund capital projects.

Public-sector capital formation may also be funded through budget deficits financed by printing money. While initially inflationary, the capital formation would eventually increase the productive capacity of the nation, stimulating economic growth and moderating the inflation. Moreover, for the reasons noted earlier, inflation—if not allowed to spin out of control—might increase the aggregate saving rate and further boost capital formation.

The process of capital formation in the modern sector would, at some point, slow down. Eventually, all of the surplus labor in the traditional sector would have been drawn into the modern sector, so the marginal product of labor in the traditional sector would rise above zero. No longer will the supply of labor to the modern sector be perfectly elastic.[11] Further transfers of labor would be at a sacrifice of traditional-sector output. The terms of trade will move against the modern sector. The relative price of agricultural goods (compared to manufactured goods) will rise, putting upward pressure on the modern-sector real wage and cutting into the capitalist surplus. Labor unions and minimum-wage laws may also exert upward pressure on the modern-sector real wage, reducing the labor hired, the capitalist surplus, and the profits available for reinvestment in the modern sector. Finally, an underlying assumption is that the capitalist surplus is actually reinvested in domestic capital formation. If instead the profits are used to finance high levels of domestic consumption or reinvested abroad (capital flight), the expansion of the modern sector would be stifled.

Lewis's model is useful in illustrating the dualistic nature of economic development: how a modern industrial sector can arise in a traditional, agrarian-based economy. Lewis recognized the importance of a healthy agricultural base for industrial development. The policy implications of his model—transfers of surplus labor and income from the traditional to the modern sector—were seized upon. Often, in the pursuit of industrialization, developing nations squeezed agriculture too hard. Agricultural prices that were kept artificially low discouraged farmers from producing for the market. The low rural incomes may have accelerated the migration to urban areas—beyond the capacities of the urban areas to provide adequate employment and amenities. Investment in agriculture and rural development were slighted in favor of industrialization and urbanization. As a result, agricultural production failed to keep pace with the requirements of a growing economy. Some developing nations ended up using scarce foreign exchange to import foodstuffs that could have been produced domestically—if there had been earlier investments in agriculture and sufficient incentives for farmers. In short, without a viable agricultural sector, industrial development may be quite limited.

In Chapter 11 we will examine the role of agriculture in economic development. In the final section of the present chapter, we extend the basic Solow growth model introduced in Chapter 3.

## SUSTAINING ECONOMIC GROWTH

We saw in Chapter 3 how Solow's variable capital–labor ratio provided an adjustment mechanism that solved the knife-edge problem of the Harrod-Domar model and

---

[11]Even before the exhaustion of the surplus labor, the selectivity of rural out-migration may deprive the traditional sector of its most productive labor. That is, rural-to-urban migration rates have tended to be relatively high for younger and more educated labor.

allowed a steady-state equilibrium to be maintained. As we have noted, however, economic growth is zero in this steady-state equilibrium. The more interesting and relevant question is how to generate sustained economic growth with income regularly rising faster than population. Indeed, in the modern era, economic growth has been the norm for the developed countries, as well as for many of the less developed countries.

Given diminishing returns to the capital–labor ratio (i.e., per capita output that rises at a diminishing rate with the capital–labor ratio), and given a constant saving rate and a constant natural growth rate of the labor force, economic growth in the Solow model occurs only between steady-state equilibria. For example, a rise in the saving rate, or a fall in the natural growth rate of the labor force, or exogenous technological progress could each result in economic growth until the new equilibrium capital–labor ratio was attained.

We now extend the Solow framework in three ways. First, as in the low-level equilibrium trap model, variable population growth is considered. Second, exogenous growth in labor productivity is incorporated to illustrate a steady-state equilibrium with rising per capita income. Third, the recent work in endogenous growth theory, highlighting the importance of technological progress, is reviewed.

## VARIABLE POPULATION GROWTH

In his seminal article, Solow addressed the possibility of population growth rates dependent on per capita income.[12] In the low-level equilibrium trap model, recall, death rates were assumed to vary inversely with per capita income. Further, according to demographic transition theory, presented in Chapter 2, birth rates fall with economic development, bringing down the growth rate in population and, eventually, the labor force growth rate.

Specifically, at low levels of per capita income (and the physical capital–labor ratio), the natural growth rate of the labor force may even be negative, due to high death rates and, perhaps, labor emigration. As income rises and death rates fall, the natural growth rate of the labor force rises. At still higher levels of income, birth rates begin to decline; thus, the population growth rate and, with a lag, the natural growth rate of the labor force, fall.

In Figure 4.7 we illustrate. The graph of $nk$, representing the per capita investment necessary to maintain the capital–labor ratio, $k$, given the natural growth rate of the labor force, $n$, is no longer a ray from the origin. The variation in $n$ makes the graph of $nk$ curvelinear.[13] Contrast with Figure 3.4 of the previous chapter. We retain the other assumptions of the Solow model, in particular the diminishing returns to the capital–labor ratio, the constant saving rate, $s$, and exogenous technological change, $A$.

In Figure 4.7 two equilibria are depicted: One is stable and one is unstable. The stable equilibrium is $E_o$, with a capital–labor ratio of $k_o^*$. Below $k_o^*$ the per capita saving forthcoming $(sy)$ exceeds the per capita investment required $(nk)$. Consequently, as capital formation outpaces labor force growth, the capital–labor ratio and per capita

---

[12]See Robert Solow, "A Contribution to the Theory of Economic Growth," *Quarterly Journal of Economics*, vol. 70, no. 1 (February 1956), pages 65–94.

[13]We are assuming that the economy is operating well beyond the low-level equilibrium trap. Recall, the low-level equilibrium trap model is concerned primarily with traditional, low-income societies breaking free from economic stagnation. The implication from Figure 4.3 is that beyond $y^*$ sustained

## FIGURE 4.7    VARIABLE POPULATION GROWTH IN THE SOLOW MODEL

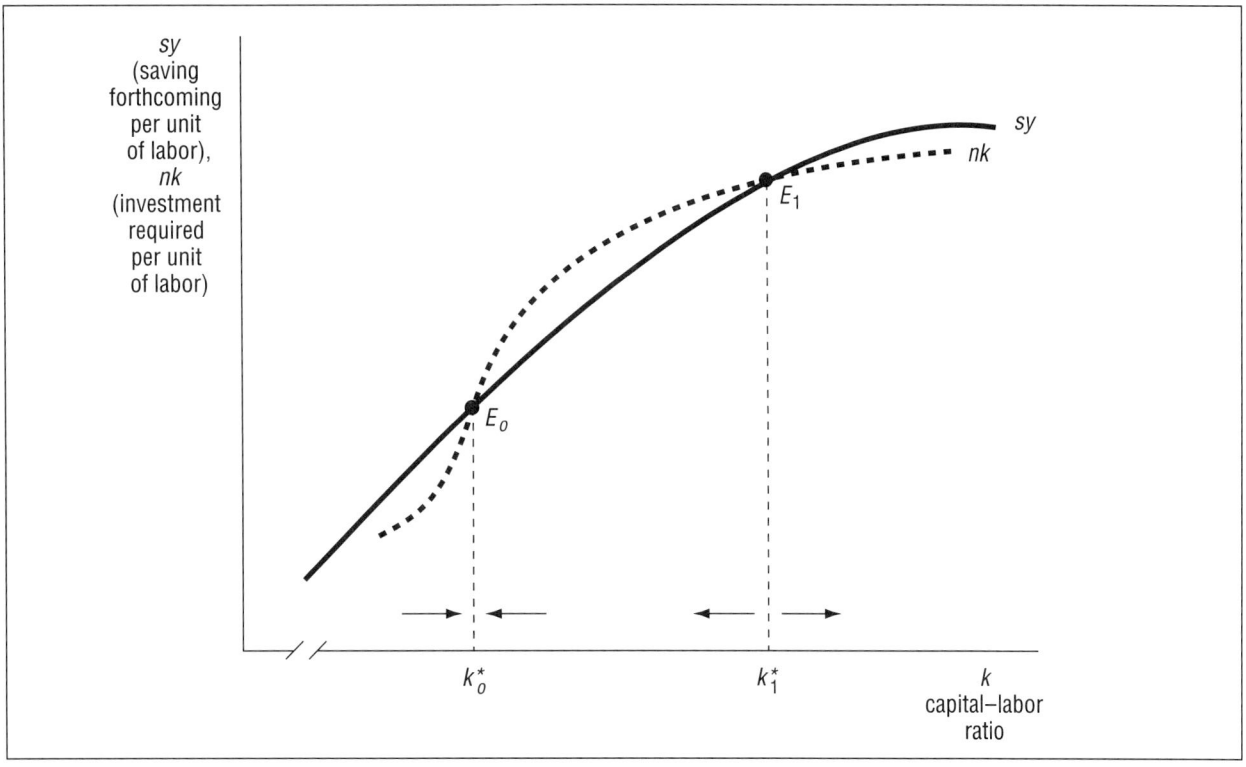

income rise until $k_0^*$ is reached. Between $k_0^*$ and $k_1^*$, a shortage of saving and upward pressure on the interest rate occur. As labor is substituted for capital, the capital–labor ratio falls back to $k_0^*$. At some point, lower fertility rates dominate lower mortality rates, and the natural growth rate of the labor force decreases (i.e., the slope of the $nk$ curve becomes flatter, but remains positive as long as the labor force is increasing in size). If the economy can push the capital–labor ratio beyond $k_1^*$, then per capita saving would exceed the required per capita investment and economic growth with capital deepening could be achieved. Eventually, though, depending on the natural growth rate of the labor force, diminishing returns to the capital–labor ratio could move the economy to a higher steady-state equilibrium. We add that achieving sustained increases in per capita income from a rising capital–labor ratio presumes no other binding constraints to economic growth exist, whether from the available natural resources, human capital, or foreign exchange.

---

economic growth would be generated. At higher levels of per capita income, however, the natural growth rate in the labor force may again rise before falling. In Figure 4.7, the increase in the slope of the $nk$ curve as the economy approaches $k_0^*$ may reflect not only population momentum but an increase in female labor force participation rates as fertility falls. If so, then, ceteris paribus, the economy would move toward a new steady-state equilibrium at $k_0^*$.

## GROWTH IN LABOR PRODUCTIVITY

Until now, we have assumed that technological change is neutral, affecting the total output that can be produced from given levels of capital and labor, but not affecting the relative productivities of capital and labor. Suppose we now allow for growth in labor productivity due to education, experience, or technological change that raises the output produced by each unit of physical labor, ceteris paribus. Specifically, consider the concept of **effective labor,** defined to be the product of physical labor $(L)$ and an index of labor productivity $(q)$. That is, let

$$E = q \cdot L, \text{ where } E \text{ refers to units of effective labor}$$

In the base period, the index of labor productivity, $q_0$, is set equal to 1.0 (or 100 percent). With a growth rate in labor productivity of, say, 2 percent, then in the next period, the index, $q_1$, would equal 1.02. In other words, 100 units of physical labor, e.g., person hours, in Period 1 would produce as much output, ceteris paribus, as 102 units of physical labor did in the base period. Thus, the effective labor force can increase due to growth in the physical labor force (more workers) or to growth in the average productivity of labor (better workers). In fact, we can show that the growth rate of effective labor, $dE/E$, is equal to the sum of the growth rates of physical labor $(dL/L)$ and labor productivity $(dq/q)$.[14]

$$dE/E = dL/L + dq/q$$

We rewrite the Solow model in terms of effective labor, the capital–effective labor ratio ($\bar{k} = K/E$) and output per unit of effective labor ($\bar{y} = Y/E$).

| | | | |
|---|---|---|---|
| S1') | $\bar{y}$ | $= A \cdot f(\bar{k})$ | (output per unit of effective labor) |
| S2') | $I$ | $= S$ | (investment equals saving equilibrium) |
| S3') | $S$ | $= sY \quad 0 < s < 1$ | (saving equation) |
| S4') | $dE/E$ | $= n + \bar{q}$ | (growth rate of the effective labor force) |

In Equation S4') the growth rate in the effective labor force is equal to the sum of the exogenous natural growth rate, $dL/L = n$, determined by the population growth rate and labor force participation rates, and the exogenous growth rate in labor productivity, $dq/q = \bar{q}$. The steady-state equilibrium condition now becomes

$$d\bar{k} = s\bar{y} - (n + \bar{q})\bar{k} = 0$$

or

$$s\bar{y} = (n + \bar{q})\bar{k}$$

---

[14]From the expression for effective labor $E = q \cdot L$, totally differentiating, then dividing through by $E$ and simplifying, we obtain

$$dE/E = dL/L + dq/q$$

which, strictly speaking, represents the instantaneous growth rate of effective labor and holds only for infinitesimal changes in physical labor or labor productivity.

That is, because the capital–effective labor ratio $(\bar{k})$ is constant in steady-state equilibrium, so is output per unit of effective labor $(\bar{y})$.[15] This equilibrium requires that the saving per unit of effective labor forthcoming $(s\bar{y})$ is just equal to the investment per unit of effective labor required to maintain the capital–effective labor ratio, given the natural growth rate in the physical labor force and the growth rate in labor productivity.

Note that in steady-state equilibrium, output $(Y)$ and the physical capital stock $(K)$ are increasing at the rate $(n + \bar{q})$, while the physical labor force $(L)$ is increasing at the rate $n$. Therefore, output per unit of labor is rising at the rate $\bar{q}$, and steady-state equilibrium now is characterized by economic growth.

Further, with the incorporation of effective labor and positive growth in labor productivity $(\bar{q} > 0)$, the requirements for the saving rate for steady-state equilibrium for any capital-output ratio $(v = K/Y)$ are greater. That is, as long as labor productivity is rising, the growth rate of the effective labor force will exceed the natural growth rate of the physical labor force; a higher percentage of national income, therefore, will have to be saved and invested to maintain the physical capital–effective labor ratio.[16]

Refer to Figure 4.8, where the components of the steady-state equilibrium condition are illustrated. Note that the key variable now is $\bar{k}$, the capital–effective labor ratio. If the growth rate in labor productivity were zero (i.e., $\bar{q} = 0$), then the steady-state equilibrium capital–effective labor ratio, given the saving rate, $s$, would be $\bar{k}^*_{o'}$ (see point $E_o$ in Figure 4.8). An increase in labor productivity, $\bar{q} > 0$, rotates the ray from the origin, representing the required investment needed to keep the capital–effective labor ratio constant, counterclockwise. At the original equilibrium capital–effective labor ratio, $\bar{k}^*_{o'}$ there would be insufficient saving (indicated by the line segment $E_o'E_o$). In order to prevent the capital–effective labor ratio from decreasing to $\bar{k}_1$, the saving rate would have to increase to $s'$, where, at $\bar{k}^*_{o'}$ we have $s'\bar{y} = (n + \bar{q})\bar{k}$.

In sum, human capital formation or labor-augmenting technological change increases the effective labor force, ceteris paribus, and requires more saving, investment, and physical capital formation to maintain the equilibrium capital–effective labor ratio. In Figure 4.8, the higher saving rate, $s'$, maintains the equilibrium capital–effective labor ratio at $\bar{k}^*_o$. The increase in labor productivity, however, increases the growth rate of output per unit of physical labor in steady-state equilibrium.

## ENDOGENOUS GROWTH THEORY

Endogenous growth theory originated in the 1980s, stimulated by both theoretical concerns with, and evidence contrary to, the implications of the standard neoclassical

---

[15]Formally, differentiating the expression $k = K/E$ gives

$$d\bar{k} = \frac{dK \cdot E - K \cdot dE}{E^2} = dK/E - \bar{k}(dE/E)$$

Now, substituting in $sY$ for $I = dK$ (to maintain the investment equals saving equilibrium) and $(n + \bar{q})$ for $dE/E$ gives

$$d\bar{k} = s\bar{y} - (n + \bar{q})\bar{k}$$

[16]From the condition for steady-state equilibrium $s\bar{y} = (n + \bar{q})\bar{k}$, we divide through by $\bar{y} = Y/E$ and simplify

$$s = (n + \bar{q})(\bar{k}/\bar{y}) = (n + \bar{q})(K/E)/(Y/E) = (n + \bar{q})(K/Y)$$
$$s = (n + \bar{q})v \quad \text{where } v = K/Y, \text{ the flexible capital-output ratio}$$

An increase in $\bar{q}$ requires an increase in $s$ to maintain steady-state equilibrium.

## FIGURE 4.8    Growth in Labor Productivity and Steady-State Equilibrium

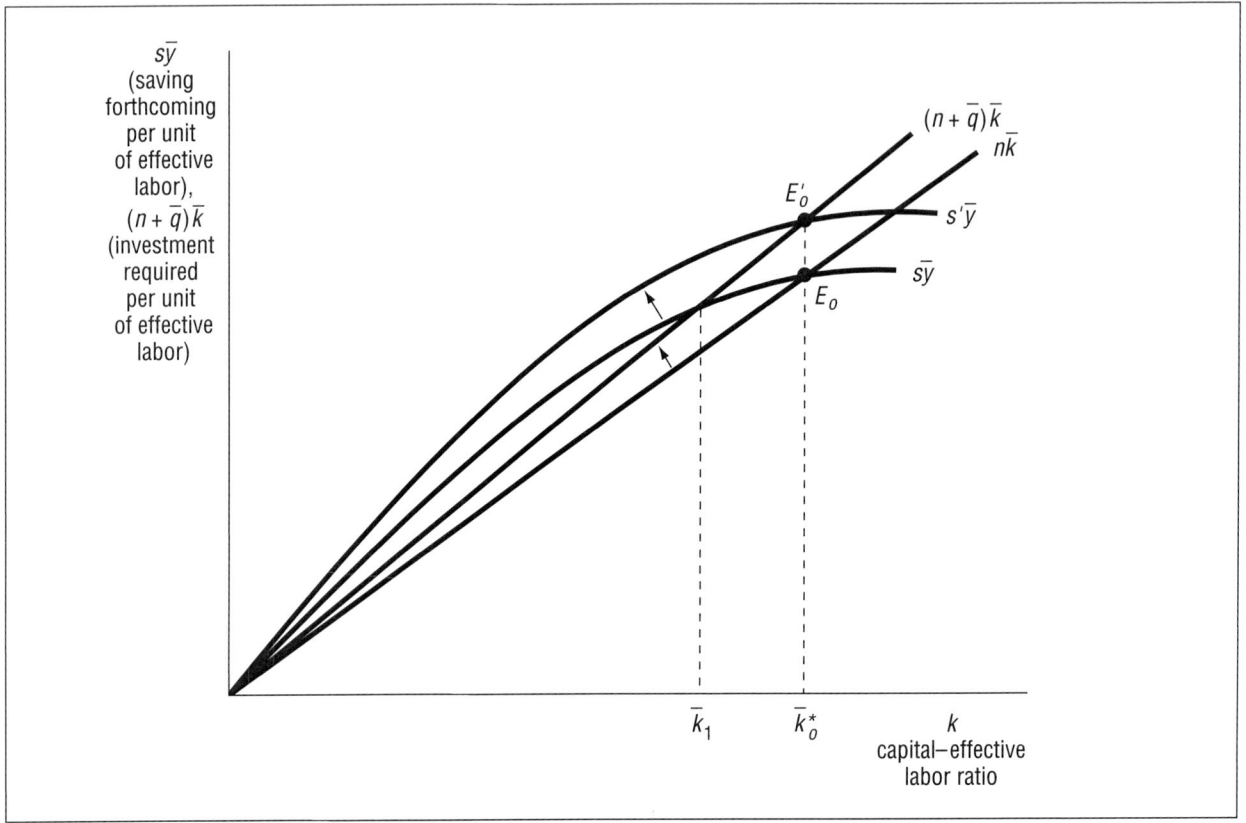

growth model that had been set forth three decades earlier by Solow.[17] Theoretically, the combination of a production function characterized by diminishing returns to physical capital intensity, a constant saving rate and a constant natural growth rate for the labor force, would bring an economy eventually to a steady-state equilibrium. Whether this equilibrium was characterized by zero or positive economic growth depended on whether the exogenous technological change was zero or positive. (Refer back to the illustration of effective labor with the exogenous growth in labor productivity.)

Variable population growth and the tendency for birth rates and population growth rates to fall at higher levels of income could allow for a rising capital–labor ratio and serve to postpone a steady-state equilibrium. However, given likely upper

---

[17] A recommended collection of articles on the new growth theory is found in the *Journal of Economic Perspectives*, vol. 8, no. 1 (winter 1994). See the four articles by Romer, Grossman and Helpman, Solow, and Pack listed as suggested readings at the end of this chapter. Our discussion draws on these four articles. Solow and Pack provide good overviews of the assumptions underlying the neoclassical growth model.

limits on saving rates and lower limits on the natural growth rate of the labor force, diminishing returns to physical capital intensity ultimately would lead to a steady-state equilibrium. Indeed, the best hope for continual economic growth was technological change. Thus, efforts to explain technological change seemed in order.

Second, if we assume that information is universally accessible and the same production functions are used by all economies, then given their lower physical capital–labor ratios, the marginal product of capital should be greater in the less developed countries. Hence, greater investment should take place in the LDCs, raising their capital–labor ratios and closing the per capita income gaps with the developed countries. (As we will discuss in Chapters 10 and 16, other obstacles to physical capital formation and foreign direct investment are found in the less developed countries.) That per capita incomes, in general, between the developed and less developed countries did not seem to be converging cast doubt on the standard assumptions underlying the neoclassical growth model.

In particular, access to modern technology may differ across countries. Less developed countries may not be able to afford or use the latest technologies. The technological gaps may be due to differences in income levels (affecting the funding of research and development); human capital (reflecting the ability to understand and apply the new technologies); and institutions (determining the environment for invention, innovation, and entrepreneurship through patent laws, property rights, and antitrust activity). In short, while higher saving rates and lower population growth rates are able to explain some of the growing income disparities between the few developed and many less developed countries, superior technology seemed to be the dominant factor.

The contribution of technological progress to economic growth can be seen not only in the invention of new products (e.g., personal computers) and procedures (e.g., word processing and spreadsheet accounting), but in the continual improvements in plant, equipment, and machinery (e.g., the automobile assembly line) and even intermediate goods (e.g., maintenance-free automobile batteries). Moreover, increasing returns to investment in physical capital may occur—a form of positive externality—as the new technologies embodied in the most recent generation of capital goods diffuse throughout the economy, not only adding to the existing stock of knowledge, but prompting new skills and encouraging further research. Paul Romer refers to "knowledge spillovers," where

> each unit of capital not only increases the stock of physical capital but also increases the level of technology for all firms in the economy....

and

> an increase in the total supply of labor causes negative spillover effects because it reduces the incentives for firms to discover and implement labor-saving innovations that also have positive spillover effects on production throughout the economy.[18]

---

[18]Paul Romer, "The Origins of Endogenous Growth," *Journal of Economic Perspectives*, vol. 8, no. 1 (winter 1994), pages 3–22. This quotation is from page 7.

## FIGURE 4.9 CONTINUAL TECHNOLOGICAL PROGRESS

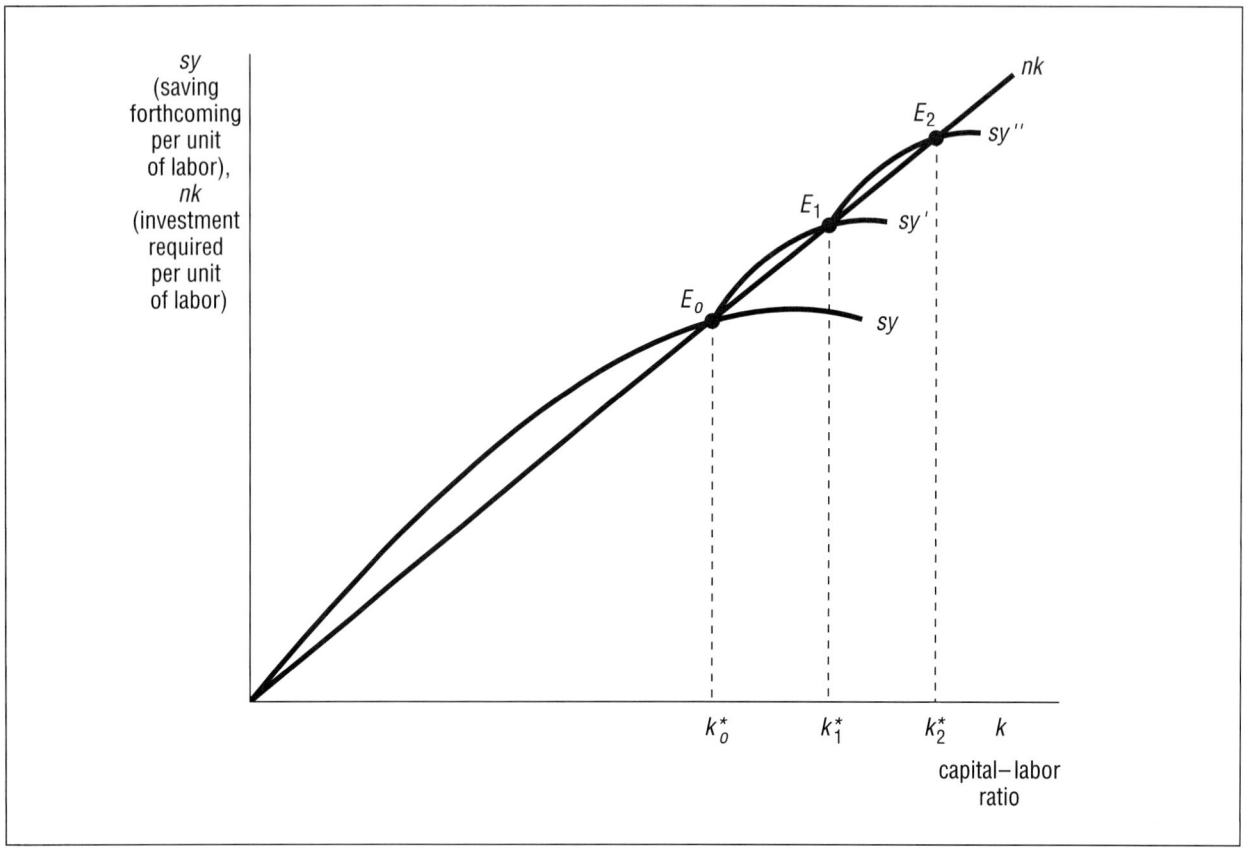

In fact, as illustrated in Figure 4.9, the diminishing returns to physical capital intensity for a given production function may be overwhelmed as the capital–labor ratio rises by the ongoing improvements from the latest technologies embodied in the new capital. Continuous technological change may ratchet up both the production function (from $sy$ to $sy'$ to $sy''$, etc.) and steady-state capital–labor ratio (from $k_0^*$ to $k_1^*$ to $k_2^*$, etc.).

The key for long-run growth, then, is to develop new technologies. For the less developed countries, policies that facilitate the adoption of new technologies should be pursued. Included would be human capital formation, the encouragement of entrepreneurship, and international integration that increases the exposure to modern technologies. As Gene Grossman and Elhanan Helpman put it,

> Whereas many firms in the industrialized North race to bring out the latest innovative products, most firms in the developing South confine their technological efforts to imitating products developed abroad.[19]

---

[19] Gene Grossman and Elhanan Helpman, "Endogenous Innovation in the Theory of Growth," *Journal of Economic Perspectives*, vol. 8, no. 1 (winter 1994), pages 23–44. This quotation is from page 41.

Indeed, advantages may exist for latecomers, who are able to reap the benefits from the technologies embodied in the latest generation of products. This seems especially true with the rapid advances in information technology, as the following excerpts from a *Wall Street Journal* article on personal computers (PCs) illustrate.

> Less developed countries, locked for years out of the technology market because of the high cost, are gaining entry via today's more-affordable, more-powerful personal computers and networks. From Poland and Indonesia to Uganda and Bangladesh, PCs are becoming crucial. And throughout the emerging world, sales are sizzling....
>
> One company at a time, personal computers are narrowing the competitiveness gap between the more-advanced and less-advanced societies....
>
> In fact, the technological backwardness of companies in developing nations is working in their behalf: They don't have huge investments in old systems, as many American companies do. Thus, they are purchasing the most-advanced systems without wrestling with mainframes that are wearing out.[20]

We will discuss in Chapter 14 a product cycle theory of trade that reflects such technological transfers. We will also relate the advantages of an export-oriented strategy of development for innovation and efficiency.

## CONCLUDING NOTE

Given the importance attributed to physical capital accumulation in initiating economic growth, the contributions of Nelson, Rostow, and Lewis fall within the growth model tradition. In hindsight, the conventional wisdom that drove development policies in the 1950s and 1960s may have overemphasized the constraint to economic growth imposed by physical capital scarcity. As we noted in Chapter 3, another factor that seemed to be binding was human capital—in the forms of labor forces sufficiently disciplined and adept to work with modern machinery; entrepreneurs able to exploit the profitable opportunities through the formation of new businesses; public officials and administrators capable of facilitating the structural change that accompanies economic development; and the numerous specific skills from electrical engineers to secondary-school teachers, and from agricultural extension agents to nurses—all required for a modern economy. Moreover, the recent work in endogenous growth theory has emphasized the importance of technological change for sustaining economic growth.

The presumption, however, that economic growth invariably produces economic development was challenged in the 1970s. Evidence abounded that for many less developed countries the push for capital formation, even when generating considerable economic growth, had not significantly reduced poverty.

In Chapter 5 we explore alternative approaches to economic development that, for various reasons, discount the notion that the benefits of growth will eventually "trickle down" to improve the general standard of living. Further, we examine the issue of the appropriate level of technology for less developed countries with an abundance of labor.

---

[20]Scott McCartney and Jonathan Friedland, "Computer Sales Sizzle as Developing Nations Try to Shrink PC Gap," *Wall Street Journal* (June 29, 1995), pages A1 and A8.

## SUMMARY OF MAIN POINTS

1. The low-level equilibrium trap describes an economy stagnating at low per capita incomes and unable to generate sufficient investment to raise the capital–labor ratio above a critical threshold where economic growth can be sustained.
2. By increasing the rate of physical capital formation and raising per capita income, increased domestic saving (through shifts in the distribution of income in favor of the high-saving classes or through birth-control programs that lower the youth burden of dependency) along with foreign capital inflows (foreign aid and foreign investment) may break the hold of the low-level equilibrium trap and engage self-sustaining economic growth.
3. Rostow's stages of growth theory describes the transition from a low-income, traditional economy to a growing, industrial economy. According to Rostow, the key to successful economic development is the "take-off," a period of intense structural change lasting up to two or three decades, when all the conditions necessary for sustained economic growth coalesce.
4. Preconditions for a take-off include the development of the economic infrastructure, especially the transportation system; improved productivity in agriculture; and imports of the capital goods needed for the expansion of industry.
5. The take-off may be initiated by a political revolution, rapid technological progress, or massive foreign investment. The keys to sustaining a take-off, once begun, are raising the rate of net investment to 10 percent or more of national income; developing leading sectors in industry; and establishing the financial institutions for mobilizing and channeling domestic saving into productive investment.
6. In the Lewis model, there exist a subsistence, or traditional, sector (primarily agriculture), and a capitalist, or modern, sector (primarily industry). Excess labor is withdrawn from the subsistence sector at a constant real wage for employment in the capitalist sector. A capitalist surplus emerges—the difference between the value of the output in the capitalist sector and the wages paid to labor. Any profits left over from the capitalist surplus after the fixed costs of capital and materials costs can be reinvested to generate more capital and employment.
7. The expansion of the capitalist sector in the Lewis model will slow down, and may even stop, as the surplus labor from the subsistence sector is exhausted. The rising real wages that must then be paid to draw labor into the capitalist sector will cut into the capitalist profits.
8. One of the most influential policy implications from the Lewis model is the need to shift labor and extract saving from the subsistence sector. Often governments of the less developed countries, in their desire to industrialize, have discouraged agricultural development by indirectly taxing the incomes of farmers through depressed official prices for farm produce.
9. With variable population growth, where birth rates and eventually labor force growth rates decline at higher incomes, rising capital–labor ratios and economic growth may be sustained. Diminishing returns to the capital–labor ratio, however, ultimately could move the economy again into a steady-state equilibrium.
10. Allowing for growth in labor productivity, due to human capital formation or labor-augmenting technological change, gives a steady-state equilibrium with

positive economic growth. That is, output per unit of physical labor would be increasing at the rate of labor productivity growth.

11. Endogenous growth theory highlights the role of technological progress in sustaining economic growth. Technological advances occur not only with new products and production techniques, but are also embodied in the continually improving capital and intermediate goods. Moreover, increasing returns to investment in new physical capital may occur as the latest technologies are disseminated throughout economies.

12. For less developed countries unable to generate new technologies, efforts should center on learning and adapting the technologies created by the developed countries. Human capital formation and international integration through the expansion of trade and receptiveness to foreign direct investment are important.

## KEY TERMS

**capitalist sector**
**capitalist surplus**
**derived growth sector**
**effective labor**
**growing economy**
**low-level equilibrium trap**

**pre-take-off economy**
**primary growth sector**
**subsistence sector**
**supplementary growth sector**
**take-off**
**traditional economy**

## QUESTIONS

1. *a.* Sketch the graph of an economy in a low-level equilibrium trap when $x$ (the level of per capita income at which the net saving rate is zero) is less than $z$ (the subsistence level of per capita income). Identify the low-level equilibrium trap.
   *b.* Now illustrate the effects of imported medical technologies that lower the death rates of the population. Assuming the economy began in the initial low-level equilibrium trap, discuss the transition to the new low-level equilibrium trap. Does anything seem unusual about the new low-level equilibrium trap? Discuss.
2. Is it likely that a low-income traditional economy could achieve a successful take-off, as in Rostow's theory, in isolation (i.e., without any foreign assistance or intervention)? Discuss.
3. According to the Lewis model, what is the role of agriculture in the economic development process?
4. Identify and discuss the key insight as well as the main limitation of each of the following:
   *a.* the low-level equilibrium trap model
   *b.* Rostow's stages-of-growth theory
   *c.* Lewis's two-sector model
5. Is it possible for income per unit of physical labor to rise while income per unit of effective labor falls? Discuss. Illustrate with an example.
6. Is it possible for economic growth to continue indefinitely? If not, why not? If so, what would be required?

## SUGGESTED READINGS

Grossman, Gene and Elhanan Helpman, "Endogenous Innovation in the Theory of Growth," *Journal of Economic Perspectives*, vol. 8, no. 1 (winter 1994), pages 23–44.

Lewis, W. Arthur, "Economic Development with Unlimited Supplies of Labour," *The Manchester School* (May 1954), reprinted in *The Economics of Underdevelopment*, edited by A. N. Agarwala and S. P. Singh, New York: Oxford University Press, 1970, (pages 400–449).

Nelson, Richard, "A Theory of the Low-Level Equilibrium Trap in Underdeveloped Economies," *American Economic Review*, vol 46, no. 1 (December 1956), pages 894–908.

Pack, Howard, "Endogenous Growth Theory: Intellectual Appeal and Empirical Shortcomings," *Journal of Economic Perspectives*, vol. 8, no. 1 (winter 1994), pages 55–72.

Romer, Paul, "The Origins of Endogenous Growth," *Journal of Economic Perspectives*, vol. 8, no. 1 (winter 1994), pages 3–22.

Rostow, W. W., "The Take-Off into Self-Sustained Growth," *Economic Journal*, vol. 46, no. 1 (March 1956); reprinted in *The Economics of Underdevelopment*, edited by A. N. Agarwala and S. P. Singh, New York: Oxford University Press, 1970, (pages 154–186).

Solow, Robert, "Perspectives on Growth Theory," *Journal of Economic Perspectives*, vol. 8, no. 1 (winter 1994), pages 45–54.

# CHAPTER 5

# ALTERNATIVE APPROACHES TO ECONOMIC DEVELOPMENT

Poverty is the greatest threat to political stability, social cohesion, and the environmental health of the planet.[1]

In contrast with the general growth in national outputs and expansion of international trade over the 1950s and 1960s, the decade of the 1970s witnessed economic turbulence. The post-war international monetary system set up at Bretton Woods, New Hampshire, in 1944 broke down, only to be replaced by a "nonsystem" of diverse exchange-rate practices. Poor harvests across the world in the early 1970s led to shortfalls and rising prices for agricultural commodities. Later, the sharp increases in oil prices triggered by the embargo of the Organization of Petroleum Exporting Countries (OPEC) produced stagflation (a combination of rising unemployment and inflation) in the oil-importing nations and massive transfers of income to the oil-exporting nations.

The assumption that economic growth would yield economic development and reduce poverty was increasingly called into question. Indeed, in his pioneering article published in 1954, W. Arthur Lewis had observed,

> The fact that the wage level in the capitalist sector depends upon earnings in the subsistence sector is sometimes of immense political importance, since its effect is that capitalists have a direct interest in holding down the productivity of the subsistence workers.... In actual fact the record of every imperial power in Africa in modern times is one of impoverishing the subsistence economy, either by taking the people's land, or by demanding forced labor in the capitalist sector, or by imposing taxes to drive people to work for capitalist employers.[2]

---

[1] United Nations Development Programme, *Human Development Report 1994*, New York: Oxford University Press, 1994, page 20.

[2] W. Arthur Lewis, "Economic Development with Unlimited Supplies of Labour," *The Manchester School* (May 1954), reprinted in *The Economics of Underdevelopment*, edited by A. N. Agarwala and S. P. Singh, New York: Oxford University Press, 1970, pages 409–410.

By the 1970s it was becoming apparent that, in spite of economic growth and rising per capita incomes, the numbers of poor in the less developed countries were increasing. Moreover, in those nations where the benefits of the economic growth were highly concentrated (e.g., Brazil, Mexico), the conditions of the poorest appeared to be deteriorating not only relatively, but absolutely. The disparities, in part, were attributed to the policies derived from the growth model approach, in which, to spur physical capital formation, measures were adopted to shift income in favor of the capitalists. The inequities also reflected the vested interests of the elites in the less developed countries, who not only sought to enhance their positions, but were the most able to take advantage of the emerging economic opportunities.

In this chapter we discuss some of the alternative approaches to economic development, beginning with Irma Adelman's dynamic growth-with-equity strategy; then the basic needs orientation that directly addresses poverty; and followed by the Marxist critique of capitalism; the philosophy of "Buddhist economics" espoused by E. F. Schumacher; and, finally, the "limits to growth" argument presented by Herman Daly. While different in terms of policy prescriptions, these approaches have a common rejection of the growth model emphasis on physical capital accumulation and economic growth as the key to economic development. We begin with an overview of the ways disparities in income and economic mobility could arise in the early stages of economic growth.

## ECONOMIC GROWTH AND THE DISTRIBUTION OF INCOME

To encourage investment and physical capital accumulation, governments in the developing economies often maintained interest rates below the market equilibrium level. Refer to Figure 5.1, which illustrates the demand and supply of loanable funds (or credit). The supply of loanable funds primarily comes from household saving (or the income not used for present consumption). Foreign saving or net inflows of financial capital can add to this domestic supply of loanable funds. The demand for loanable funds reflects the desire for credit both by business to finance purchases of physical capital (plant, equipment, and machinery) and by the government to finance budget deficits. The market-clearing interest rate is $i_o$. To subsidize investment, however, the government would set an official interest rate at $i^*$. Doing so results in an excess demand for loanable funds (equal to $F_2 - F_1$) and the need to ration the available credit ($F_1$). Favored investors, often capitalists in the modern sector, would obtain the low-interest credit. The artificially low interest rates encourage capital-intensive methods of production, reducing the employment of labor. Smaller investors and entrepreneurs, who tend to be more inclined toward labor-intensive production methods, would not be able to obtain credit at the official rate of $i^*$.

Similarly, to subsidize the imports of capital goods, a government could maintain an official exchange rate that overvalues the domestic currency. For example, suppose the market equilibrium exchange rate for the domestic currency, the peso, were 25 pesos = $1.00 (or 1 peso = $.04). The government sets an official exchange rate of 20 pesos = $1.00 (or 1 peso = $.05). The official peso is overvalued (i.e., worth $.01 more than justified by the market demand and supply of foreign exchange, here dollars, in

## FIGURE 5.1 THE DEMAND AND SUPPLY OF LOANABLE FUNDS

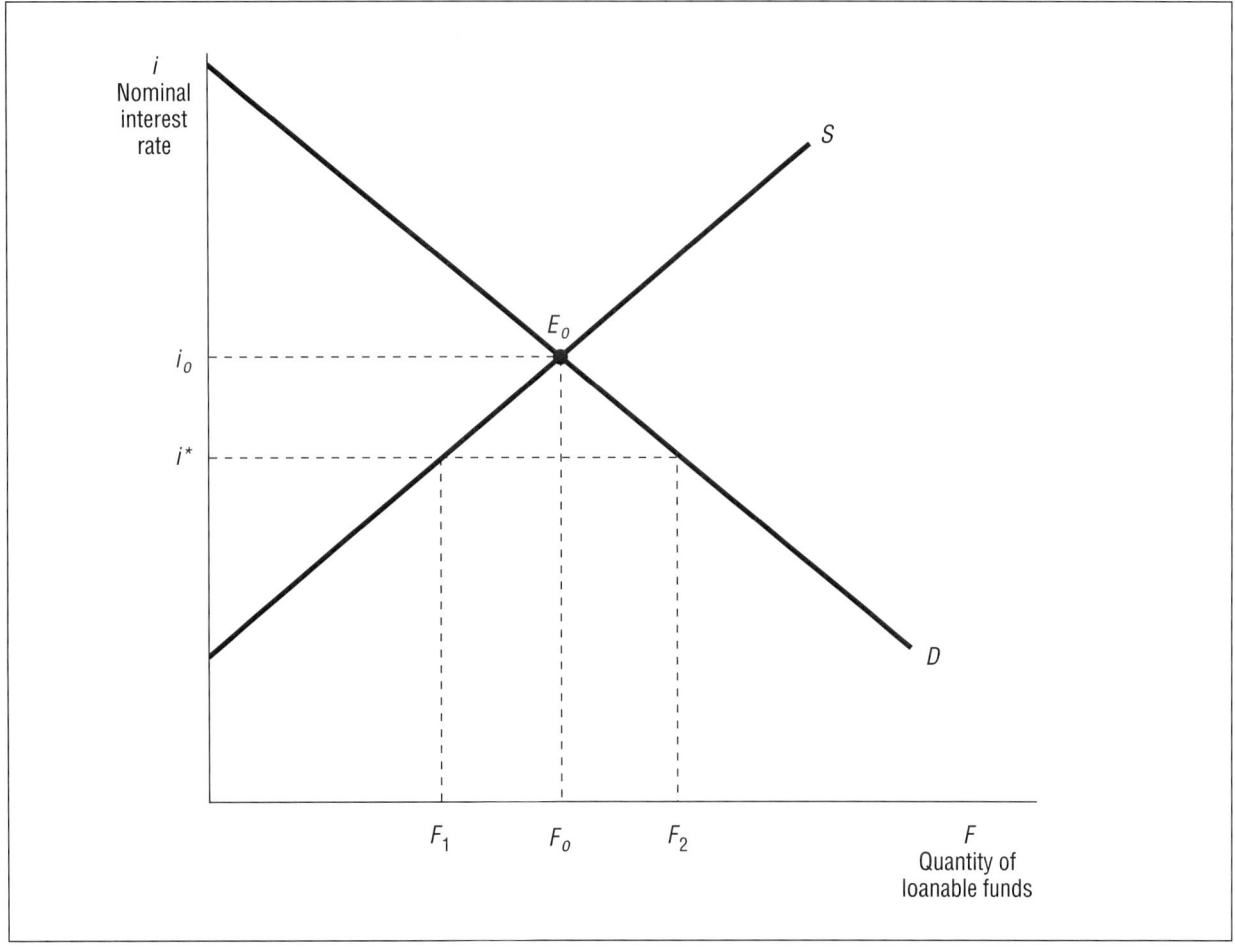

the nation). An excess demand for dollars would result. The government could ration the available dollars needed for imports with import licenses. To import a machine costing $1000 would only require 20,000 pesos at the official exchange rate, or 5000 pesos less than at the market equilibrium exchange rate. Thus the favored holders of import licenses (again likely to be those capitalists with connections) would benefit from being able to purchase capital goods imports at subsidized prices. As with the artificially low interest rates, the subsidized capital imports encourage capital-intensive production methods. Furthermore, the capital goods imported may embody a technology that is inappropriate for the labor-abundant conditions found in the less developed countries. Subsidizing credit and capital imports, intended to boost investment, often has the effect of reducing the share of wages in national income.

In line with the policy implications of the Lewis model, governments set up agricultural marketing boards to extract the surplus from the traditional sector and foster capital accumulation in the modern sector. Prices paid to farmers growing food crops for domestic consumption are set below market equilibrium levels—indirectly taxing the modest incomes of the farmers, while possibly subsidizing the wages paid in the modern sector with low food prices.

Overall, a distinct urban bias characterized development policy in the 1950s and 1960s. Industrialization was favored over agricultural development. If agriculture were promoted, for example, with access to credit, technical and marketing assistance, or government-funded irrigation projects, the benefits went primarily to the large estates producing cash crops for export (e.g., tea, coffee, and rubber) and using relatively capital- and land-intensive methods of production.

The better health-care services and schools were found in the urban areas. Primary health care for the rural population was often slighted in favor of the higher profile, but less cost-effective, health care provided through urban hospitals. So too, resources for education were disproportionately allocated for university students, benefiting mostly the children of wealthier families who could afford to take advantage of the heavily subsidized tuitions. Primary education, in contrast, was underfunded. Consequently the quality of primary education was typically low. Even when schooling was "free," poor families could not afford the opportunity cost of having their children attend schools, rather than working. Absenteeism and attrition were high. Civil servant employment in the expanding government sector, when not reserved for those with political connections, was effectively restricted to those with higher education.

Foreign investment through transnational corporations, while welcome as a source of capital, management expertise, and technology, usually was concentrated in modern-sector enclaves with few linkages to the rest of the economy. Mining companies and large-scale manufacturing were favored with access to credit and public investment in the economic infrastructure in transportation, communication, and power generation. These modern-sector islands may have discouraged local entrepreneurship, inflated wage scales, and introduced inappropriate labor-saving technologies—each of which limited employment of the rapidly growing labor forces.

Thus, it was argued that much of the populations in the less developed countries had been shut off from the benefits of economic growth. In particular, left behind in the drive to industrialize were legions of small farmers operating on marginal family plots, or working as tenants for subsistence shares of the crops, or employed as landless laborers on plantations. Many in the rural areas, pushed off the land by population pressure on the resources or the increased mechanization of large-scale agriculture, and pulled by the hopes for modern-sector employment, migrated to the urban areas, where they joined the expanding pools of workers in the informal sector.

Were the perceived inequities in the growth of the less developed countries inevitable costs of the structural changes that accompany industrialization? Is the process of economic development necessarily a Darwinian evolution of the fittest—a race where the rewards appropriately go to the most able and where the promise of a higher standard of living provides incentive enough for progress? Or is it possible to have equitable growth in which the rising tide of economic development lifts all boats? By the 1970s, questions like these became charged issues of debate.

## ADELMAN'S DEPAUPERIZATION

Based on an analysis of cross-section data for 43 less developed countries for the period 1950 to 1963, Irma Adelman concluded:

for the longest part of the development process—corresponding to the transition from the state of development of sub-Saharan Africa to that of the least developed Latin American countries—the primary impact of economic development on income distribution is, on the average, to decrease both the absolute and the relative incomes of the poor. Not only is there no automatic trickle-down of the benefits of development; on the contrary, the development process leads typically to a trickle-up in favor of the middle classes and the rich.[3]

Adelman's research had convinced her that a reorientation of development strategy was needed whereby "in each nation the proper long-term goal of national development policy must be the successive relaxation of the systematic obstacles to the full realization of the human potential of its members."[4] She called her approach **depauperization,** and she set out a three-stage strategy modeled after five nations (Israel, Japan, South Korea, Singapore, and Taiwan) that had successfully combined economic growth with equity.

## GROWTH WITH EQUITY

In Adelman's first stage a redistribution of assets occurs—not only to level the playing field, but to expand economic opportunities. Given that most of the populations in less developed countries live in rural areas and are engaged in farming, asset redistribution implies land tenure reform. Large estates, whether the legacy of earlier colonial policies or the product of the current skewed distribution of wealth, are broken up and distributed to peasant farmers. By extending to these farmers a stake in the future—secure title to the land—incentives are provided to save and invest in the land. Moreover, small-scale agriculture tends to be labor-intensive, thus consistent with the labor-abundant conditions found in the developing economies.

Land tenure reform requires a strong government, one that is capable of overcoming the opposition of the large landholders whose estates are to be redistributed. Often such reform is easiest after liberation from a colonial power. For example, upon gaining independence from Japan following World War II, South Korea, under the guidance of a transitional American administration, redistributed the large colonial estates to small Korean farmers.

The second stage entails an ambitious accumulation of human capital. Building upon the redistribution of assets in the first stage is the formation of human capital. Primarily through investments in education, the foundation for self-sustaining growth and development is solidified. In fact, the creation of a literate and skilled labor force may be a prerequisite for rapid industrialization. South Korea, for example, instituted universal primary education, complemented by adult literacy campaigns, soon after liberation from Japanese rule.

Adelman notes that during these first two stages, which may require two to three decades, economic growth may be slow, and social tensions and political instability may run high. Nevertheless, the preconditions for the third stage are in place.

---

[3]Irma Adelman, "Development Economics—A Reassessment of Goals," *American Economic Review,* vol. 65, no. 2 (May 1975), page 302.

[4]Ibid., page 306.

In the third stage, rapid, human resource-intensive growth takes place. For the East Asian nations of Japan, South Korea, Singapore, and Taiwan, the expansion of labor-intensive manufactured exports served as the engine of growth. Labor-abundant developing countries should have a comparative advantage in labor-intensive manufacturing, especially if earlier investments in human capital have yielded a literate and productive labor force. By producing for the world market, smaller countries can attain the lower unit costs from the economies of scale in large-volume outputs. Commodities with standardized technologies and modest investments in physical capital, like shoes, clothing, textiles, toys, and simple consumer electronics, have typically been among the leading exports in the early stages. To achieve success with this export-oriented growth, the nation must have a competitive exchange rate and competitive unit labor costs (given by the ratio of the wage rate to the average product of labor). Moreover, success is contingent upon international cooperation and access to foreign markets. In the appendix to this chapter we profile South Korea and how it became one of the economic success stories of the post–World War II era with this three-stage strategy.

Adelman recognizes that the five nations she identifies as typifying equitable growth may be special cases. These nations are all small, natural resource-poor countries with culturally homogeneous populations. In the East Asian countries, the populations share a Confucian tradition—embodying, among other attributes, a desire for education and respect for authority; a willingness to sacrifice and work hard; and a receptiveness to change and modernization. Each nation benefited from considerable economic assistance from the West, in particular from the United States. Each nation had strong and stable governments that were capable of managing a comprehensive strategy of economic development. National identities were galvanized by external threats; for example, South Korea with North Korea, Taiwan with China, and Israel with her Arab neighbors.

## AGRICULTURAL DEMAND–LED INDUSTRIALIZATION

Writing a decade later, Adelman revised her recommended strategy.[5] Where the healthy expansion in the world economy during the 1960s favored an outward orientation, the international recessions in the mid-1970s and early 1980s and the subsequent rise in protectionism in the developed countries had since reduced the viability of a strategy of export-led growth. Thus, for those less developed countries that did not have a foothold in the foreign markets for manufactures, Adelman advocated a strategy of **agricultural demand–led industrialization (ADLI)**.

Building upon the first stage of her earlier strategy, investment would be channeled into agriculture to increase the productivity of small- to medium-scale farming. Improvements in irrigation systems, access to credit, assistance in land terracing and crop rotation, dissemination of new seeds and fertilizers, better roads to markets, and fair prices for agricultural produce would not only energize a major sector in the economy, but would enhance industrialization. With increasing incomes in the rural sector, the effective demand for domestic manufactured goods would be bolstered. Scarce

---

[5]See Irma Adelman, "Beyond Export-Led Growth," *World Development,* vol. 12, no. 9 (1984), pages 937–949.

foreign exchange that had been used to import foodstuffs would be conserved by increasing domestic agricultural production. Moreover, the growth in agricultural output would also increase the demand for agricultural inputs—from fertilizers to water pumps. Linkages to capital goods industries would be fostered, another derived demand for industrial output. Thus, in direct contrast to the Lewis model, in which the emphasis was on extracting a surplus from the traditional/agricultural sector to subsidize industrialization, with Adelman's ADLI strategy, agriculture is developed as a leading sector in the industrialization process.

We note here, and will expand further in Chapters 14 and 17, that trade liberalization in the 1990s (e.g., the successful completion of the GATT-sponsored Uruguay Round and the North American Free Trade Agreement) may renew the appeal of Adelman's initial three-stage strategy of depauperization.

## THE BASIC NEEDS APPROACH

As noted, poverty in the developing economies was receiving renewed attention in the 1970s. Doubts were mounting that the benefits of the economic growth in the earlier decades had trickled down, or would necessarily trickle down, to improve the conditions of the poor. The explosive population growth in the less developed countries and the proliferation of urban slums made the plight of the poor all the more obvious.

The basic human needs approach was introduced in 1976 at the World Employment Conference of the International Labour Organization, an affiliate of the United Nations.[6] In direct contrast to the top-down approach of the growth models (e.g. Solow, Rostow, and Lewis), the basic needs orientation is a bottom-up strategy of development. An underlying premise is that the most direct way to address poverty in developing economies is to provide for the basic needs of the population. The five core **basic needs** for a decent human existence are food, water, shelter, clothing, and health care.

Advocates maintain that the approach is not anti-growth. Clearly, increased per capita output is needed to provide for the basic needs of the population. Rather, the approach represents a reorientation of priorities. Economic surpluses are not just funneled back to the capitalists for reinvestment, so much as used to expand economic opportunities. By involving the larger population in the development process from the beginning and by investing in human capital, the surest foundation for sustainable growth is laid.

### BASIC NEEDS POLICIES

The basic needs approach is not a massive welfare program that relies on a redistribution of wealth. Instead, it emphasizes the creation of conditions whereby many

---

[6]For a useful overview of this strategy, see Michael Crosswell, "Basic Human Needs: A Development Planning Approach," in *Basic Needs and Development*, edited by Danny Leipzeiger, Cambridge, MA: Oelgeschlager, Cunn, and Hain, 1981, pages 1–25.

people can initiate and sustain improvements in their standard of living. These conditions consist of employment generation, access to resources, and human capital formation.

### EMPLOYMENT GENERATION

The best anti-poverty program may be productive employment. Employment opportunities can be expanded by getting factor prices right (i.e., ending the subsidization of physical capital formation through artificially low interest rates and overvalued exchange rates) and using appropriate technologies (i.e., labor-intensive rather than labor-saving).

Employment in the modern sector is directly restricted when the wage is set by institutional factors above the market equilibrium level. Transnational corporations, in an attempt to skim off the top talent in the labor pool, may pay a wage above the market-clearing rate.[7] Government employment may also be characterized by an inflated pay scale—either a carryover from colonial times when high wages were paid to expatriate administrators or due to the influence of labor unions.

To illustrate, refer to Figure 5.2, in which an isoquant-isocost line diagram is presented for a firm in the modern sector. Recall that in the long run, when both capital and labor are variable factors of production, a profit-maximizing firm will select the input combination for producing the selected level of output where the marginal product per dollar spent on each factor is equal.

$$MP_L/w = MP_K/i$$

where $MP_L$ = marginal product of labor

$MP_K$ = marginal product of capital

$w$ = the user cost of a unit of labor, indicated by the wage rate

$i$ = the user cost of a dollar of capital, indicated by the interest rate

Alternatively, this profit-maximizing or cost-minimizing condition can be written as:

$$MP_L/MP_K = w/i$$

That is, to minimize the total cost of producing a given level of output, the firm should equate the ratio of the marginal products with the ratio of factor prices. The negative ratio of the marginal products is the **marginal rate of factor substitution,** which equals the slope of the isoquant at any combination of capital and labor. The negative ratio of factor prices gives the slope of the isocost line, which represents the combinations of capital and labor obtainable for a given cost. The cost-minimizing factor combination will occur at the tangency of the selected isoquant with the lowest isocost line.

---

[7]According to the efficiency wage theory, firms may pay a wage above the market-clearing level not only to screen out the best workers among the surplus of job applicants, but to provide an incentive to employees to remain with the firm and to work hard. The underlying assumption is that worker productivity is directly related to the wage received.

## FIGURE 5.2 — FACTOR PRICE RATIOS AND THE LEAST-COST FACTOR COMBINATIONS

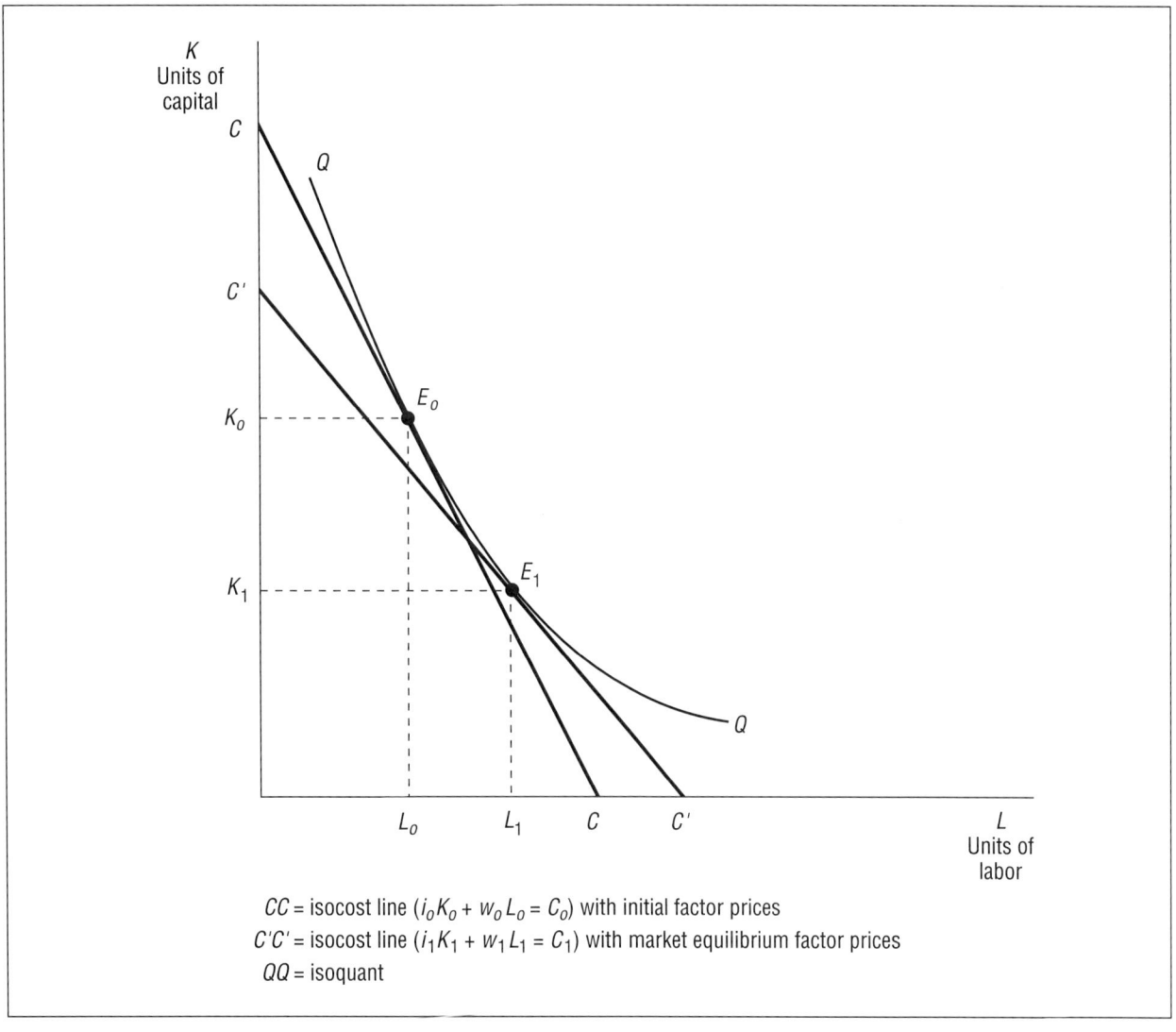

$CC$ = isocost line ($i_0 K_0 + w_0 L_0 = C_0$) with initial factor prices
$C'C'$ = isocost line ($i_1 K_1 + w_1 L_1 = C_1$) with market equilibrium factor prices
$QQ$ = isoquant

Let

$w_0$ = institutionally set wage rate paid by a firm in the modern sector

$i_0$ = subsidized interest rate to a firm in the modern sector

$w_1$ = market equilibrium wage rate that reflects the opportunity cost of labor

$i_1$ = market equilibrium interest rate that reflects the opportunity cost of capital

where $w_0 > w_1$ and $i_0 < i_1$

and $QQ$ = isoquant for producing a given level of output

If we begin with the output and technology (reflected in the $QQ$ isoquant) and factor prices (reflected in the isocost line $CC$), the cost-minimizing combination of capital and labor would be $K_o$ and $L_o$ (see point $E_o$ in Figure 5.2 at which the isocost line $CC$ is tangent to the isoquant $QQ$). Now, if we allow for factor prices that indicate the relative factor scarcities, the modern-sector wage would fall (from $w_o$ to $w_1$), and the interest rate would rise (from $i_o$ to $i_1$). The new isocost line, $C'C'$, is tangent to the isoquant $QQ$ at point $E_1$. Therefore, "getting factor prices right" results in more employment (from $L_o$ to $L_1$) and a conservation of capital (from $K_o$ to $K_1$) as the firm shifts to a more labor-intensive input mix.

Further gains in employment (and conservation of capital) may be achieved by adopting a technology more consistent with the labor-abundant conditions. For example, a textile factory could use several hand looms instead of one highly automated power loom, thereby employing more labor with a smaller investment in capital.

To elaborate, a transnational corporation establishing a foreign subsidiary in a less developed country to manufacture textiles may bring in a modern, capital-intensive technology that is ideally suited for the labor-scarce conditions in the home country. While seeking to maximize profits, the corporation may discount, or even be unaware of, the potential benefits from using a lower-level, more labor-intensive technology (perhaps older, less automated looms). Or the transnational corporation may overestimate the ability of the local labor force to use the modern technology; or believe that success in international competition requires that its foreign subsidiary use the latest technology from the beginning. On the other hand, the government of the host developing nation may insist, as a condition of entry for the foreign subsidiary, that only the latest technology be used. Or, domestic firms in the developing nation may have a preference for the most modern technology and, given some internal market power, may not have to minimize the costs of production to remain in business.

In any case, suppose that a more labor-intensive technology is available, illustrated in Figure 5.3 by the isoquant $Q''Q''$, which represents the same level of output as the initial isoquant $QQ$. The isoquant $Q''Q''$ illustrates a more labor-intensive technology since any ratio of the unit price of labor to the unit price of capital (the slope of an isocost line) would yield a cost-minimizing factor combination with a lower capital–labor ratio on $Q''Q''$ than on $QQ$.

The shift to the more labor-intensive technology is illustrated by the tangency of the $Q''Q''$ isoquant with the lower isocost line $C''C''$ (see point $E_2$ in Figure 5.3). Not only is additional employment generated (from $L_1$ to $L_2$) and a further saving of capital (from $K_1$ to $K_2$), but the total cost of producing the firm's output has been reduced. See the parallel shift in the isocost line in to the origin from $C'C'$ to $C''C''$. The firm becomes more profitable; and, in the aggregate, the nation may become more competitive in international trade.

In general, it may make sense for less developed countries to adopt initially lower-level, labor-intensive technologies, consistent with their labor-abundant conditions, especially if the output produced is intended for domestic consumption. With additional human capital formation and the gains in labor productivity that come from "learning by doing," the developing economy would graduate to more sophisticated, capital-intensive technologies.

Thus, advocates of the basic needs approach support increasing employment through "freeing up" institutionally set factor prices in the modern sector and shifting to more appropriate technologies. Increasing employment not only raises the share of wages in national income—consistent with a more equitable distribution of income and

## FIGURE 5.3    SHIFTS IN TECHNOLOGY

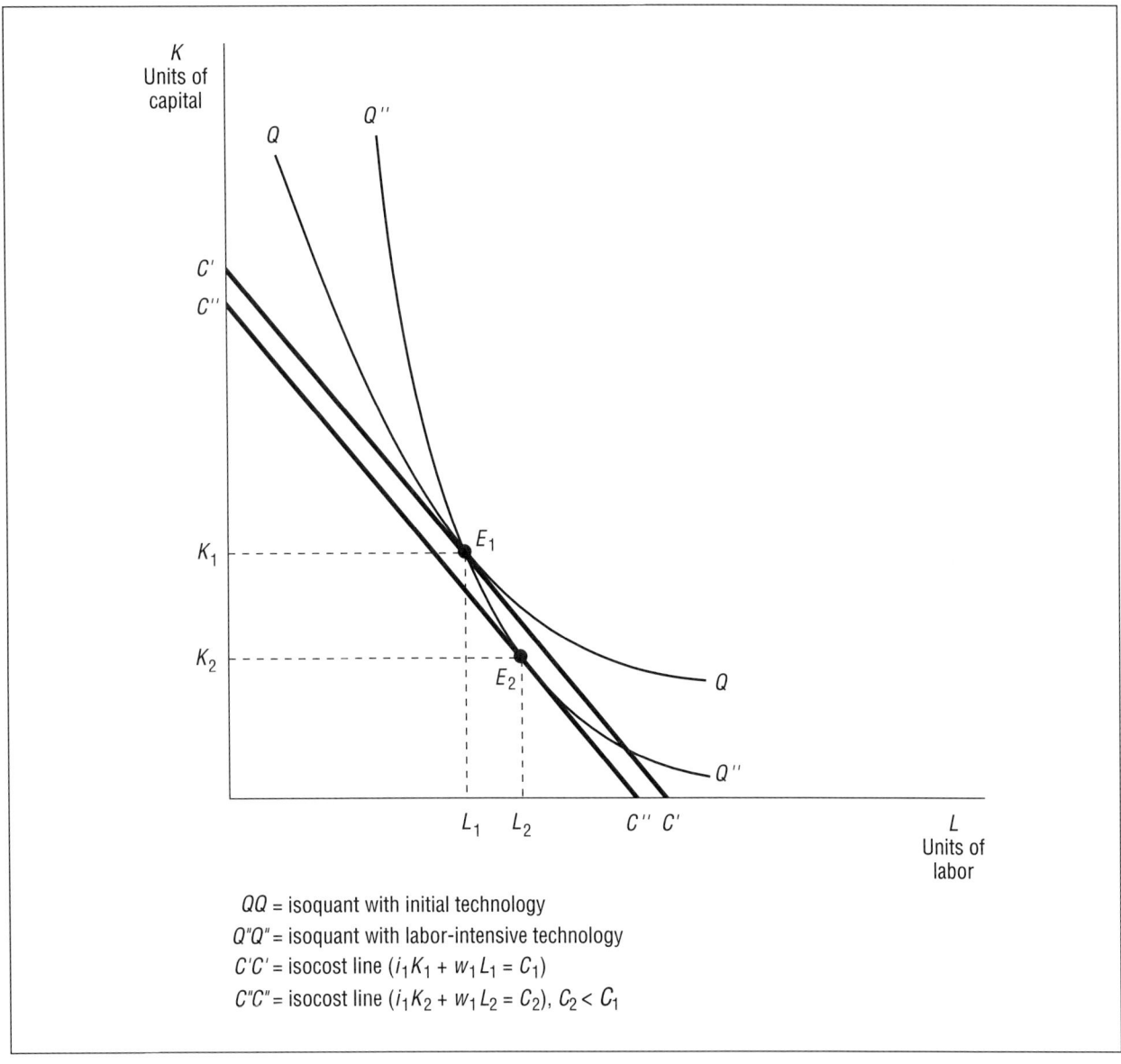

$QQ$ = isoquant with initial technology
$Q"Q"$ = isoquant with labor-intensive technology
$C'C'$ = isocost line ($i_1 K_1 + w_1 L_1 = C_1$)
$C"C"$ = isocost line ($i_1 K_2 + w_1 L_2 = C_2$), $C_2 < C_1$

expanding economic opportunities—but promotes economic growth and enhances international competitiveness.

### ACCESS TO RESOURCES

The second policy focus in the basic needs approach is a more equitable access to resources. Similar to the first stage of Adelman's depauperization and her subsequent agricultural demand–led industrialization strategy, the emphasis is on rural development. Land redistribution, access to credit, technical assistance, and investment in rural infrastructure all should contribute to improving agricultural productivity and the quality of life of the rural population. Some public projects (e.g., rural electrification and construction of roads, irrigation systems, health clinics, and schools) could draw on the surplus rural labor that often exists during the off-seasons in agriculture.

### Human Capital Formation

Third, the basic needs orientation in development seeks to sustain the improvements in the standard of living through human capital formation. While initially some of the core basic needs of the poor in food and housing may have to be directly provided through income or income-in-kind transfers, in the longer run investments in the quality of the population through education, health care, and nutrition will be required for sustainable economic development. Increasing access to a high-quality primary education and to basic health care through preventative measures is stressed, achieved in part through a reallocation of resources away from the expensive university education and the cost-ineffective, urban-based, curative hospital care. Priorities include increasing basic literacy; greater knowledge of hygiene; access to family planning; and control of diseases and illness through immunizations and improved sanitation. (In Chapter 8 we discuss human capital formation in more detail, including policy reforms in education and health care.)

In sum, the basic needs philosophy incorporates the larger population in the development process from the beginning—not just as eventual recipients of the benefits of economic growth, but as full participants. Concerns exist, however, over the viability of such an approach.[8]

## IMPLEMENTATION OF THE BASIC NEEDS APPROACH

The first concern some economists have is with the definition of basic needs. At one extreme, the five core needs of food, shelter, clothing, water, and health care could be narrowly defined in terms of the minimums needed for human survival. For example, the least expensive diet capable of ensuring the minimum requirements in calories and nutrients would probably be very bland and devoid of variety. Or, for a family of four the basic need in shelter may be defined as a 400-square-foot room with a roof. At the other extreme, additional basic needs could be set for education (how many years?); employment (at what minimum compensation?); security from crime and violence; and political freedom. Moreover, if the basic needs standards are relative (for example, a poverty line set as a percentage of mean income), then with economic development the requirements for basic needs would increase.

A second concern is the related problem of dependency. Any transfer program has to weigh the desirable objective of helping the recipients with the undesirable consequence of fostering dependency. Rephrasing the parable: Give people fish and you feed

---

[8]See, for example, Paul Streeten, "Basic Needs: Some Unsettled Questions," *World Development*, vol. 12, no. 9 (1984), pages 973–978.

them for a day. Teach them to fish and to make fishing poles and they are able to feed themselves. A successful assistance program is one that eventually is no longer needed. In the long run, investments in education and expansion of employment are the keys to reducing poverty. In any case, there will always be some segments in a society (e.g., the elderly, disabled, infirm) who, unable to provide for their basic needs, will require assistance.

A third concern: Given that resources are limited and that it may be impossible to meet the basic needs of all in the society at once, the question arises of which groups to target. The "most deserving" may be the chronically poor (e.g., landless peasants and the urban homeless). Considerable expenditures may be needed, however, before any significant improvements are evident in the conditions of the most destitute in the population. Greater early returns may be achieved by targeting the marginal groups (e.g., small farmers and laborers in the urban informal sector) who, with a little help, may significantly increase their productivities and incomes, thus escaping the poverty trap.

Critics of the basic needs strategy cite the opportunity costs of the expenditures for assistance and human capital formation. Proponents of the growth model approach maintain that the best way to generate employment is through physical capital formation in the private sector. (Recall in Lewis's model the expansion of the modern sector through the reinvestment of the capitalist surplus.) Implementing the basic needs program would increase the role of the government in directing resources—and may discourage private enterprise. Investments in the private sector may be further dampened if government capital expenditures on the infrastructure (e.g., electrical power plants, transportation and communication systems) are reduced to allow for current expenditures on basic needs. Whereas the payoffs in the form of greater output from physical capital formation come relatively soon, the economic benefits of human capital formation (in particular, increases in labor productivity) are often delayed and the costs are up-front. Barring generous foreign assistance, the very economic growth required for meeting the basic needs of the population is reduced when scarce resources are diverted from investments in physical capital.

As a development strategy, the basic needs approach has proven difficult and expensive to implement on a large scale. In part a reflection of the frustration over stagflation, the conservative Reagan and Thatcher administrations were in power in the 1980s in the United States and Great Britain, respectively, and general policy shifted back to an emphasis on economic growth. In an appendix to this chapter we profile Sri Lanka, a country noted for its successful basic needs development in the post–World War II era. Even Sri Lanka, however, by the end of the 1970s, had shifted to more growth-oriented policies.

We conclude this discussion on basic needs with an observation and a look at some evidence. First, the observation: No fixed relationship exists among economic growth, the alleviation of absolute poverty, and income inequality. Proponents of the growth model approach argue that economic growth and increases in per capita income make it possible to reduce absolute poverty even as the distribution of income becomes less equal. Moreover, it is possible to have a more equitable distribution of income, little or no growth, and no reduction in poverty. Proponents of the basic needs approach argue, however, that it is preferable to reduce poverty with a more equitable access to resources, even at the sacrifice of present growth, if the foundation for sustained economic development is put into place.

## EVIDENCE ON ECONOMIC GROWTH AND INCOME INEQUALITY

Evidence on the relationship among economic growth, inequality, and poverty is, at best, fragmentary. Household surveys on income and expenditures are expensive and subject to considerable measurement error. Comparable data on the distribution of income, the numbers of poor, and depth of poverty are scarce—especially time series for less developed countries. It is possible, however, to compare income distributions of LDCs at different stages of development.

In Table 5.1 we list the percentage shares of income for the lowest 40 percent of the populations for the 14 low-income and middle-income economies for which data are available for the period from 1989 to 1992. The countries are ranked by 1993 per capita GNPs in international dollars. In Figure 5.4 we plot the ordered pairs for the percentages shares of the poorest 40 percent of the population against the 1993 per capita GNPs.

Given the small size of the sample and the nature of the data, we need to exercise caution in drawing conclusions. Not much support for the "U-shaped" relationship between income shares and per capita GNPs, however, can be garnered here. The former socialist economies of Bulgaria, Poland, and Hungary have relatively equal income distributions. In contrast, the nine Latin American nations in the sample have

### TABLE 5.1  SHARES OF INCOME OF THE LOWEST 40 PERCENT OF THE POPULATION: SELECTED COUNTRIES (1989–1992)

|  | % SHARE OF INCOME RECEIVED BY POOREST 40% OF POPULATION | GNP PER CAPITA IN 1993 (INTERNATIONAL $) |
|---|---|---|
| Honduras (1989) | 8.7 | 1910 |
| China (1990) | 17.4 | 2330 |
| Guatemala (1989) | 7.9 | 3350 |
| Dominican Republic (1989) | 12.1 | 3630 |
| Bulgaria (1992) | 21.4 | 4100 |
| Poland (1989) | 23.0 | 5000 |
| Brazil (1989) | 7.0 | 5370 |
| Colombia (1991) | 11.2 | 5490 |
| Costa Rica (1989) | 13.1 | 5520 |
| Panama (1989) | 8.3 | 5840 |
| Hungary (1989) | 25.7 | 6050 |
| Malaysia (1989) | 12.9 | 7930 |
| Venezuela (1989) | 14.3 | 8130 |
| Chile (1992) | 10.2 | 8400 |

NOTES:
The dates in parentheses refer to the year of reference for the income distribution data. The 1993 per capita GNPs (Gross National Products) are expressed in international dollars (i.e., adjusted for differences in the domestic purchasing powers of the national currencies).

FROM World Bank, *World Development Report 1995*, New York: Oxford University Press, 1995, Table 30.

## FIGURE 5.4 — INCOME DISTRIBUTION AND PER CAPITA GNPs

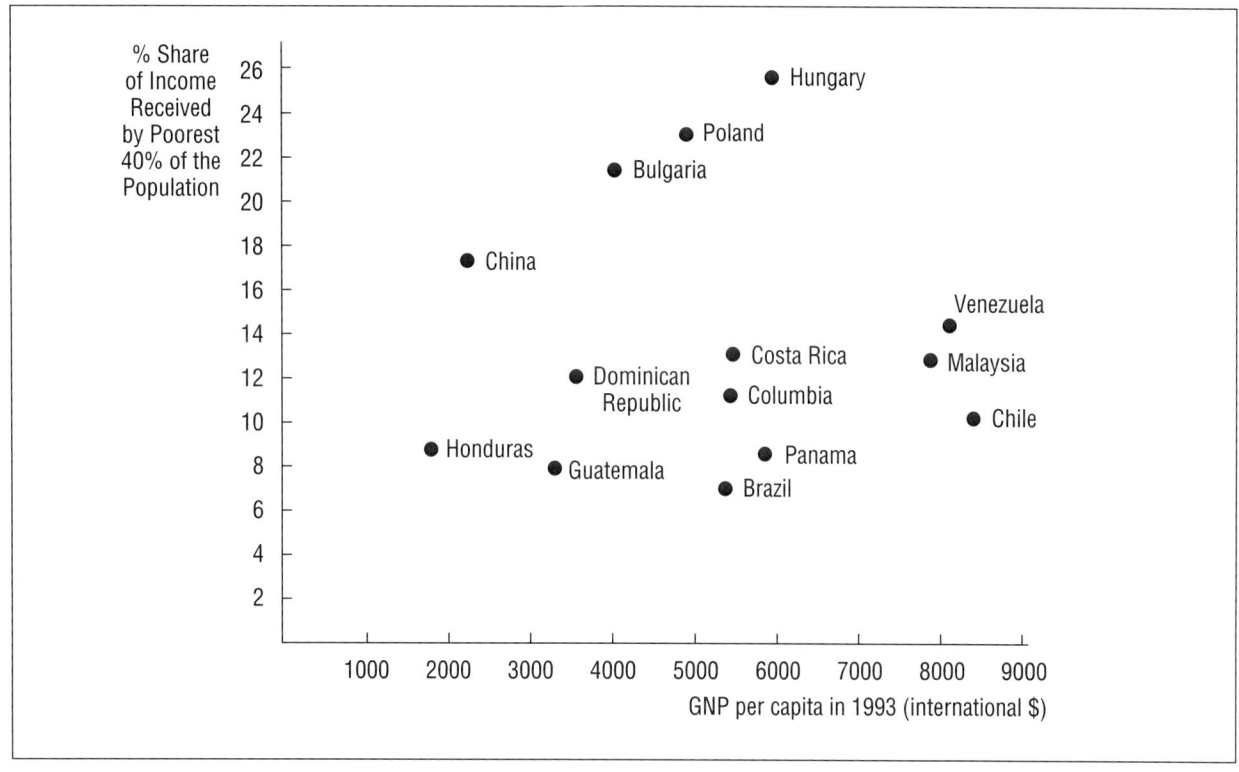

comparatively unequal distributions of income. A decline in the share of income accounted for by the poorest 40 percent of the population need not indicate a decline in the absolute incomes of the poorest 40 percent. For example, a 50 percent increase in per capita income would more than offset a decline in the income share of the bottom 40 percent of the population from 20 to 15 percent. On the other hand, using the bottom 40 percent of the population may not adequately capture the conditions of the poorest in the nation.

In the *World Development Report 1990*, an issue devoted to poverty, the World Bank found no support for the hypothesis that economic growth in the less developed countries resulted in an increase in poverty or even a deterioration in the distribution of income.

> In the 1980s the link between growth and poverty reduction is still there, but it is weaker than before. By and large, economic growth reduces poverty and economic decline increases it. Fluctuations in inequality, however, were larger in the 1980s....[9]
>
> A key conclusion ... [is that] ... the countries that have been most successful in attacking poverty have encouraged a pattern of growth that makes efficient use of labor and have invested in the human capital of the poor.[10]

---

[9]See World Bank, *World Development Report 1990*, New York: Oxford University Press, 1990, page 48.
[10]Ibid., page 51.

We turn now to the radical critique of economic development, which maintains that impoverishment of the masses is to be expected with development under capitalism.

## THE RADICAL CRITIQUE

The radical school views Western economic development based on capitalism and free enterprise as exploitative. The underdevelopment of Third World nations, to a large degree, is a consequence of exploitation by the developed capitalist nations.

### THE MARXIAN FOUNDATION

The intellectual origins of the radical school can be found in the writings of Karl Marx (1818–1883), who authored the *Communist Manifesto* (1848) and *Das Kapital* (volume 1, published in 1867). Marx believed that conflict was the essential fact of history, and that conflict was necessary for change.[11]

In any period, society is defined by the conditions of production—reflected in the technology utilized, the ownership of property, and the organization of labor. With the exception of the final classless state under communism, in every society a dominant class (bourgeoisie) and an oppressed class (proletariat) exist. In the case of capitalism there are the capitalists (the owners of the factories) and the laborers (workers in the factories). According to Marx, class struggle is the force that generates change.

In general, an economy is able to produce a surplus above the subsistence needs of the workers and the value of the raw materials and capital used up in production. This surplus is captured by the capitalist class as net profits, interest, and rent. In particular, only part of the worker's day is needed to produce the output required for the compensation of labor. During the remainder of the day the worker toils for the capitalist, creating **surplus value.** The goal of the capitalist is to increase the surplus value, which can be accomplished by extending the working day, reducing wages to the subsistence level, or raising the productivity of labor.

Competition and the pursuit of higher labor productivity drive the capitalists to invest in new technologies embodied in machinery with a labor-saving bias. Here is the conflict, however. Capitalists need labor to create surplus value, out of which comes the profits for reinvestment. The passion for capital accumulation, however, has the effect of displacing the labor that creates the surplus value. Capitalists continue to expand production without any reference to the effective demand for output. The displaced labor, which swells the ranks of Marx's "industrial reserve army" of the unemployed, does not have the income to purchase the output. The excessive capital accumulation diminishes the marginal product of capital and the return on investment. The tendency for overproduction and excess capacity not only reduces profits, but results in economic recession. Smaller firms are taken over by larger

---

[11]For a colorful account of Marx and an overview of his critique of capitalism, see Robert Heilbroner, "The Inexorable System of Karl Marx," in *The Worldly Philosophers*, 4th ed., New York: Simon and Schuster, 1972, pages 131–163.

capitalists. Eventually, depressed wages and the depreciation of the capital stock reduce the costs of production, and profitability rebounds. Firms recover, wages rise, and the quest for capital accumulation begins anew. The process of overproduction, excess capacity, and unemployment repeats itself. Each business cycle ends with a more severe recession.

As domestic conditions worsen, capitalists look abroad for profitable investment outlets. Colonies serve as cheap sources of raw materials and primary products as well as markets for manufactured goods. Vladimir Lenin, who rose to power in Russia in 1917, expanded Marx's analysis to **imperialism,** or the economic and political domination of less developed countries. In their race for colonies, the capitalist powers carve up the developing world.

Ultimately, however, capitalism would be abolished. The system produces exploitation, colonial expansion, and wars. While destined to fail, capitalism, nevertheless, is a necessary stage in the evolution to communism. At some point, the oppressed workers—that is, the proletariat—would rise up and strike down the capitalists. A classless, rational society under communism would eventually emerge, where collective ownership of the means of production replaces private property and where a more egalitarian distribution of income replaces exploitation and unemployment.

## THE RADICAL SCHOOL

Drawing on the theories of Marx and Lenin, radical economists argue that

> the central problem of underdevelopment ... was that during the era of imperialism, a high proportion of the economic surplus potentially available for domestic investment was transferred abroad in the form of uncompensated exports or was used locally to pay for the cost of colonial administration, the maintenance of large standing armies and police forces, and the high standard of luxury consumption of the expatriate ruling class.[12]

Former colonies, upon gaining independence after the Second World War, found it difficult to escape the legacy of colonialism. Even today, many Third World nations rely on a few primary commodities for the bulk of their export earnings. These commodities (e.g., coffee, cocoa, sugar, bananas) are subject to short-term volatility in export revenues (due to shifts in supply and price-inelastic demands) and long-term deterioration in the terms of trade (due to income-inelastic demands). Linkages of these sectors to the rest of the economy have been limited, in part due to the lack of earlier investments in complementary sectors and, in part due to the protectionist policies of the developed countries that discouraged the processing of these primary products.

For those developing nations favorably endowed with oil or minerals (e.g., copper, bauxite, tin ore), export revenues have been similarly concentrated. Here the instability in export revenue is due to the shifts in demand characteristic of the international business cycle.

---

[12]See Keith Griffin and John Gurley, "Radical Analyses of Imperialism, the Third World, and the Transition to Socialism: A Survey Article," *Journal of Economic Literature*, vol. 23, no. 3 (September 1985), pages 1089–1143. This quotation is from page 1109. In this article Griffin and Gurley provide a good overview of the radical literature.

Even though the labor-abundant developing nations should have the comparative advantage in labor-intensive manufactures, attempts to industrialize also have been frustrated by the protectionist policies of the developed countries. Despite significant progress in the post–war era in reducing international tariffs through the multilateral trade negotiations sponsored by the General Agreement on Tariffs and Trade (GATT), the products of greatest interest to the less developed countries have been among the most heavily protected in the world.[13] In addition to agricultural commodities, examples include textiles and apparel, shoes, and steel.

Radical economists see the rise of the transnational corporation as the clearest manifestation of neocolonialism, or what has been called "imperialism without colonies."[14] Headquartered in the advanced capitalist nations, transnational corporations establish foreign subsidiaries to continue the expropriation of the economic surpluses of the less developed countries. Export enclaves are set up to draw on the cheap labor, yet employment is limited by the use of inappropriate (i.e., capital-intensive) technologies. Harmful consumption patterns are introduced by expatriate managers. Governments are co-opted as the elite and policymakers in the host developing nations align themselves with the interests of the foreign capitalists.

Radical economists also identify the international monetary system as an arena of domination. Less developed countries, due to their inferior positions in trade, become net debtors. To finance their import surpluses, the LDCs either surrender control over domestic assets (as in the case of foreign investment in their economies) or borrow from foreign creditors. As the interest burdens accumulate, the capitalist creditor nations are able to extract the economic surpluses from the LDCs. When the LDCs fall behind in their debt repayments, the International Monetary Fund (IMF), controlled by the same capitalist nations, intervenes and mandates policy reforms as a condition for further credit.[15] The IMF medicine involves an austerity program with tighter monetary policy, higher taxes, less government spending, and privatization of state-owned enterprises. The burden of the adjustment typically falls most heavily on the poorest in the developing nations.

Foreign aid, as viewed by the radical school, is yet another instrument of control exercised by the capitalist nations. Bilateral aid is intended less to enhance the development of the recipient nations and more to further the economic and strategic interests of the donor countries. For example, much of the aid given by the Western capitalist nations, particularly the United States, in the 1950s and 1960s was for the purpose of containing communism. Moreover, such aid flows are not highly correlated with poverty. Channelled to "friendly governments" that were often more concerned with solidifying their positions of power, the aid seemed to do little to improve the conditions of the poor. As related by Griffin and Gurley,

---

[13]The General Agreement on Tariffs and Trade was the international institution established in 1947 to promote trade liberalization. To this end GATT sponsored several multilateral trade negotiations. The success in reducing tariffs, however, was offset somewhat by a proliferation of nontariff barriers to trade, such as import quotas, voluntary export restraints, government procurement policies, and discriminatory regulations. In Chapter 14 we will discuss GATT and the role of international trade in economic development in greater detail. In 1995 GATT was replaced by the World Trade Organization.

[14]See Griffin and Gurley (1985), page 1089, for this definition of neocolonialism.

[15]The International Monetary Fund is the international institution that was formed in 1944 to administer the international monetary system devised for the post–World War II era.

the economic forces that lie at the heart of imperialism are underlined by capitalism's acceptance of military dictatorships and other anti-democratic regimes as members of the "free world," provided these nations are open to foreign investment and other capitalist incursions into their economies.[16]

The World Bank is similarly seen as an agent of capitalism. Run by the capitalist nations, the World Bank's primary purpose is to lend money for large-scale development projects.[17] Radicals point to many of the funded projects in the less developed countries as suffering from the same capital-intensive bias that does little to generate employment and economic development, but much to promote the interests of foreign investors.

Like Marx, who over a century ago predicted that the inevitable destruction of capitalism would pave the way for communism, the radical school of economic development has heralded a workers' revolution as an end to exploitation. Also like Marx, radical economists have concentrated their firepower on exposing the defects of capitalism, and have failed to provide a viable socialist model of development. Indeed, with the dissolution of the Soviet Union and related upheavals in the Eastern European nations in the late 1980s, it appears that it was communism that had self-destructed. As the former socialist nations turned to more market-oriented systems and more democratic forms of government, some observers maintained that Marx and the radical school could safely be relegated to the history of economic thought. The subsequent difficulties experienced by these nations as they tried to convert their political-economic systems and their disenchantment with some aspects of capitalism, however, suggest that such an assessment may be premature.

## SCHUMACHER'S BUDDHIST ECONOMICS

The late British economist E. F. Schumacher was also highly critical of Western economics, which he equated with capitalism. As held by the basic needs approach, Schumacher believed that economic development begins with the people. Similar to the Marxian view, Schumacher believed that capitalism is not a sustainable system.

In his *Small Is Beautiful: Economics As If People Mattered,* a book written before the energy crises of the 1970s, Schumacher castigates Western economics as justifying a lifestyle that is selfish and narrow—the single-minded pursuit of materialism, a quest

---

[16]See Griffin and Gurley (1985), page 1103. In Chapter 16 we explore the controversies surrounding foreign aid.

[17]The World Bank (the International Bank for Reconstruction and Development) was established, along with the International Monetary Fund, in 1944 by a conference at Bretton Woods, New Hampshire. In the early years the World Bank focused on the reconstruction of the war-torn economies of Europe and Japan. Later, the Bank turned its attention to the less developed countries. In addition to making loans, the World Bank is a leading center for research and technical assistance on economic development.

that is without limits and is, therefore, inconsistent with a finite physical environment. For Schumacher, capitalism, relying on private enterprise and the market mechanism, is the "institutionalization of individualism and nonresponsibility."[18]

The central conflict is that Western individuals do not see themselves as part of nature, but as a force to dominate and control nature.[19] Therefore, Schumacher argues, Western-style development, with its emphasis on the quantitative goal of maximizing per capita output and income, is not an appropriate model for developing countries.

Schumacher proposes an alternative, which he calls **Buddhist economics.** By no means restricted to practitioners of any one philosophy or religion, Buddhist economics is Schumacher's generic term for a type of development that is not only compatible with the underlying culture and spiritual values, but where "people matter"; the environment is respected; and scarce natural resources are conserved.[20] The principles of Buddhist economics are simplicity and nonviolence. The orientation is small-scale. The goal is qualitative growth whereby individuals seek the maximum wellbeing with the minimum of consumption.

Specifically, Schumacher argues that dependence on natural capital, especially non-renewable resources, should be minimized and that the beauty, value, and sustainability of land and renewable resources should be preserved. To achieve this, land should be more equally distributed.

> [M]en organized in small units will take better care of *their* bit of land or other natural resources than anonymous companies or megalomaniac governments which pretend to themselves that the whole universe is their legitimate quarry.[21]

Schumacher decries the unbridled pursuit of economic growth that fosters modern technologies based on an extreme division of labor. While assembly-line production may yield the greatest output (permitting the greatest per capita consumption), the human workers are reduced to small cogs in an impersonal process. The fragmented, isolated workstations on the assembly line require continuous repetition of specific tasks. The problem is that in the West, work has been reduced to a "means to an end"—the end being the generation of income for consumption. In Buddhist economics, work has a threefold function: to provide an opportunity for using and developing one's faculties; to enable one to overcome egocenteredness by joining with others in a common task; and to bring forth the goods and services for a becoming existence.[22]

From the beginning Buddhist economics plans for full employment. In labor-abundant developing nations the need is for workplaces—large numbers of decentralized, small-scale workplaces capable of being created within a short time with modest investments in physical capital and minimal reliance on scarce resources, and utilizing technologies that are consistent with the natural intelligence, drive,

---

[18]E. F. Schumacher, *Small Is Beautiful: Economics As If People Mattered,* New York: Harper and Row, 1973, page 44.
[19]Ibid., page 14.
[20]See Chapter 4, "Buddhist Economics," in Schumacher pages 53–62.
[21]Schumacher, page 36.
[22]Ibid., pages 54–55.

and creative energy of the workers. The goal should be to maximize work opportunities, not output per employed worker. Production by the masses is better than mass production.[23]

The appropriate technology to use is an **intermediate technology**—between the traditional, or primitive, methods and the capital-intensive, commercial energy-dependent, labor-saving technologies that define Western workplaces.

Schumacher writes:

> the apparent shortage of entrepreneurs in many developing countries today is precisely the result of the "negative demonstration effect" of a sophisticated technology infiltrated into an unsophisticated environment."[24]

Schumacher favors tools that complement, not displace, human effort, and that return craftsmanship and a sense of pride to work. With an intermediate technology the full potential of the abundant labor in the less developed countries could be realized. For example, intermediate to wooden hoes and diesel tractors are steel plows drawn with oxen, which may be an appropriate technology for peasant farmers working small plots of land. A hand calculator is intermediate to an abacus and a personal computer. Inexpensive solar cookers are intermediate to cutting down branches for fuelwood and a microwave oven.

Ultimately Schumacher is calling for a more humane development with spiritual growth.

> Simplicity and nonviolence are obviously closely related. The optimal pattern of consumption, producing a high degree of human satisfaction by means of a relatively low rate of consumption, allows people to live without great pressure and strain and to fulfil the primary injunction of Buddhist teaching: "Cease to do evil; try to do good." As physical resources are everywhere limited, people satisfying their needs by means of a modest use of resources are obviously less likely to be at each other's throats than people depending upon a high rate of use. Equally, people who live in highly self-sufficient local communities are less likely to get involved in large-scale violence than people whose existence depends on world-wide systems of trade.
>
> From the point of view of Buddhist economics, therefore, production from local resources for local needs is the most rational way of economic life ...[25]

In Figure 5.5 on page 138, we present a model of Buddhist economics. For each individual there would not be the distinction found in the West between the economic identity and the spiritual identity. Rather, each individual would seek "right livelihood," or a dignified, satisfying existence consistent with our place in nature. For the individual, education and spiritual growth produce enlightenment, which, combined with an optimal pattern of consumption and fulfilling work yield, and are influenced by, right livelihood. Right livelihood is cultural-specific.

Schumacher's approach to development is clearly from the bottom up. Enlightened individuals build enlightened communities, which form enlightened nations. Communities and nations, all relatively autonomous and self-sufficient, would be

---

[23]Ibid., page 74.
[24]Ibid., page 185.
[25]Ibid., pages 58–59.

### FIGURE 5.5 — A MODEL OF BUDDHIST ECONOMICS: RIGHT LIVELIHOOD FOR THE INDIVIDUAL

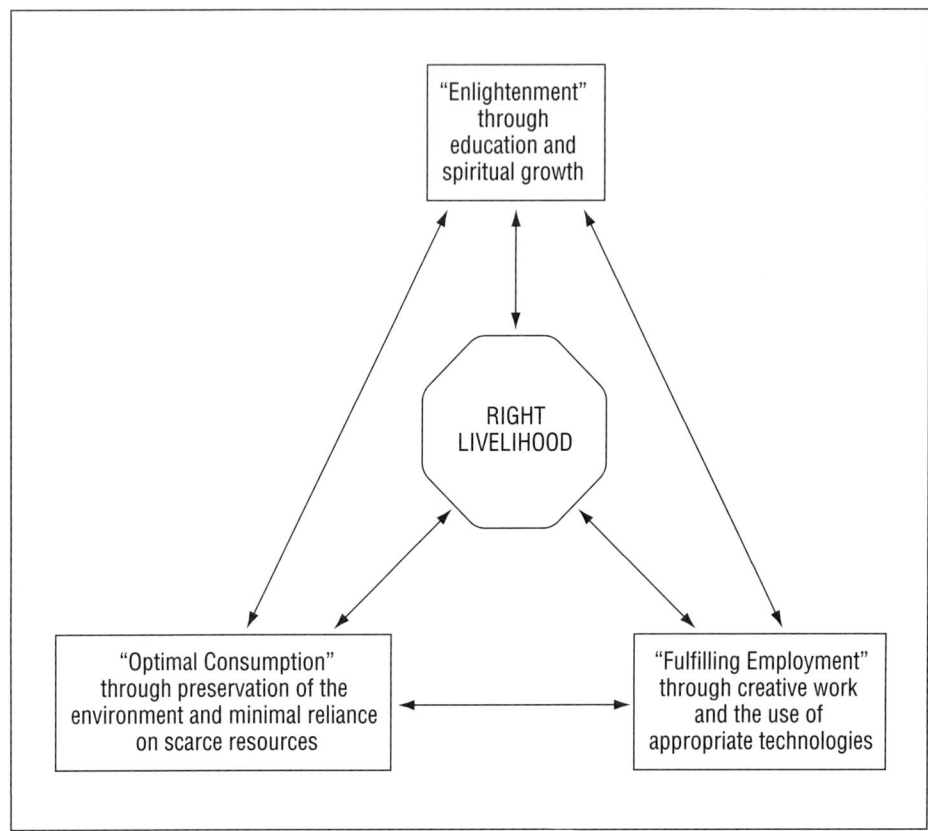

connected by an intellectual superstructure for the exchange of ideas and insights into attaining right livelihood.

Does Buddhist economics offer a viable strategy for economic development in the less developed countries? *Small Is Beautiful*, while striking a responsive chord among many readers, was largely discounted by the economics profession. Elements of Schumacher's philosophy are very appealing—the concern with the environment; the use of appropriate technologies; and the qualitative dimensions of development. Any wholesale adoption as a development strategy, however, would require fundamental changes in attitudes and priorities. Nevertheless, Schumacher's Buddhist economics may provide a useful model for initiating economic development in communities in less developed countries. As an example, consider the Sarvodaya Shramadana Movement in Sri Lanka.

## THE SARVODAYA SHRAMADANA MOVEMENT

The Sarvodaya Shramadana Movement began in the late 1950s when a young high school teacher, A. T. Ariyaratne, together with students and friends, visited a poor, socially isolated, rural village to learn, to initiate communication, and to assist in community development. By the 1980s, Sarvodaya had become the largest nongovernmental organization in Sri Lanka, covering several thousand villages, with a network of educational and training centers, an international reputation, and external funding.[26]

The literal meaning of "Sarvodaya Shramadana" is "the awakening of all in society by the mutual sharing of one's time, thought, and energy."[27] Intellectually and spiritually inspired by Gandhian movements in India, Sarvodaya, from the outset, has attempted to assist in the self-development of the rural poor in Sri Lanka. The effort arose from the desire to preserve and enrich the cultural traditions of rural life in Sri Lanka, a heritage that Ariyaratne felt had been trampled on during the colonial experience and then shunted aside in the ensuing process of economic development.

The Sarvodaya approach begins with the technique of a *shramadana*, or "the mutual sharing of labor." A village, assisted by experienced Sarvodaya personnel and community volunteers, would organize a work camp designed to "satisfy the biggest felt need of the community which can be completed with voluntary labor and for which the capital expenditure involved is the least possible."[28] Examples of modest projects include the repair of a village road, improvements to the local irrigation system, and construction of latrines. The emphasis at all times is on personal involvement in a group cause. The idea is to "awaken" the village to its potential—first, by undertaking a common task that provides for some of the basic needs of the villagers, and then by identifying and training young leaders who can carry on after the initial work camp. The role of the Sarvodaya team is to initiate, facilitate, and encourage. From preparing for the first shramadana to implementing future village projects, participation of the members of the village is stressed. Involvement cuts across all social classes, ages, and occupations. Village interest groups, starting with one for preschoolers, are formed to furnish input into village decision making.

Besides initiating the shramadanas, Sarvodaya assists in setting up community kitchens, child-care centers, and inoculation programs. Through its education and training centers, village youth acquire needed community skills, and useful information is dispensed on nutrition, health care, and home gardening. Village-level organizations are set up so that community development will be a self-sustaining process. Sarvodaya also has established model farms, not only as a natural extension of its activity in the rural areas, but to provide ongoing training in agricultural techniques. These farms benefit from rural credit cooperatives set up through Sarvodaya and from Sarvodaya's success in securing the services of government agricultural extension agents.

While special attention is given to the basic economic needs of the villagers—especially the health, nutritional, and educational needs of preschoolers and young mothers—the spiritual needs of the people are also part of the Sarvodaya philosophy. From

---

[26]There have been a number of studies on the Sarvodaya Shramadana Movement. For example, see Denis Goulet, *Survival With Integrity: Sarvodaya at the Crossroads*, Colombo, Sri Lanka: Marga Institute, 1981; and Joanna Macy, *Dharma and Development: Religion As Resource in the Sarvodaya Self-Help Movement*, West Hartford, CT: Kumarian Press, 1983. In addition, A. T. Ariyaratne has written extensively. See Ariyaratne's *Collected Works, Volumes I and II*, Colombo, Sri Lanka: Sarvodaya Research Institute, printed in the Netherlands, 1979 and 1980, respectively. Both of these volumes have been edited by Nandesena Ratnapala of the Sarvodaya Research Institute, Sri Lanka.

[27]See Ariyaratne, *Collected Works, Volume I*, page 23.

[28]Ibid., page 62.

the first shramadana, the cultural, social, and moral aspects of community development are explored. Incorporating the teachings of Buddhism, Sarvodaya emphasizes the four cardinal principles of social life: Dana (sharing), which promotes an exploitation-free society and an equitable distribution of wealth; Priya Vachana (pleasant speech), which encourages harmonious and respectful interpersonal relations; Artha Charya (constructive activity), which is the advancement of activities that improve material well-being but do not infringe on spiritual development, such as a shramadana; and Samanathmatha (equality), which means the absence of social discrimination.[29]

Like Schumacher's Buddhist economics, the Sarvodaya Shramadana Movement should not be viewed as confined to Buddhists. The Movement has cut across ethnic groups and social classes in Sri Lanka. Rather, Sarvodaya represents a way of providing for early basic needs by drawing on indigenous resources, while maintaining rich cultural traditions.[30] More important, by encouraging the participation of all in the communities in fashioning development, Sarvodaya taps one of the greatest underutilized resources in the developing world—the talents and energies of the rural populations.[31]

Literally thousands of nongovernmental organizations are working in less developed countries. In Chapter 16 we discuss the role of nongovernmental organizations in economic development. We conclude this chapter with a critique of the growth model approach to development based on resource limitations.

## DALY'S STEADY-STATE ECONOMICS

Another attack on the growth model orthodoxy came in Herman Daly's *Steady-State Economics: The Economics of Biophysical Equilibrium and Moral Growth* (1977). Daly, who later joined the World Bank as a senior economist, argues that

> a steady-state economy is a necessary and desirable future state of affairs and that its attainment requires quite major changes in values, as well as radical, but nonrevolutionary, institutional reforms.[32]

Daly modernizes the Malthusian specter of unchecked population growth outpacing the means of subsistence. The ultimate limit to economic and population growth, according to Daly, is the supply of low entropy.[33] **Entropy** is a measure of the energy

---

[29] Ibid., pages 51–53.

[30] For example, Sarvodaya has effectively incorporated into its development strategy the Buddhist monk, traditionally a respected and esteemed leader in village life in Sri Lanka. See Chapter 5 in Macy, *Dharma and Development: Religion As Resource in the Sarvodaya Self-Help Movement*.

[31] Unfortunately, Sarvodaya's efforts in rural development, indeed socioeconomic progress in Sri Lanka, has been impeded by over a decade of ethnic conflict and civil war.

[32] Herman Daly, *Steady-State Economics: The Economics of Biophysical Equilibrium and Moral Growth*, San Francisco: W. H. Freeman, 1977. This quotation is from page 2.

[33] Ibid., pages 21–22.

that is no longer capable of being converted into work. Daly invokes the first and second laws of thermodynamics to support his thesis. First, neither matter nor energy can be created or destroyed. Second, energy cannot be recycled and matter can be recycled only at less than 100 percent efficiency.

In a finite environment with a finite amount of matter and energy available (from fossil fuels and other natural resources and from solar, wind, and tidal power), there are limits to increases in population and consumption. Simply put, if inputs are ultimately limited, so must be output. Moreover, the use of resources to produce goods and services involves the return to nature of high-entropy matter (with decreased potential for energy conversion into work). The ability of the environment to absorb and recycle the wastes is limited. Thus, Daly proposes a **steady-state economy (SSE),** defined as

> an economy with constant stocks of people and artifacts, maintained at some desired, sufficient levels by low rates of maintenance "throughput," that is, by the lowest feasible flows of matter and energy from the first stage of production (depletion of low-entropy materials from the environment) to the last stage of consumption (pollution of the environment with high-entropy wastes and exotic materials).[34]

Like Schumacher, Daly believes that a system founded on materialism and economic growth is not sustainable. Continued economic growth (increases in per capita output) coupled with population growth requires increased drawdowns of energy and resources to supply the greater stocks of people and artifacts. While technological change may reduce the depletion rates of energy sources and increase the ability of the environment to absorb wastes, it cannot eliminate the rise in entropy. Given the limits imposed by the available resources and environmental thresholds, Daly questions whether it is feasible for even the present world population (85 percent of which live in the less developed countries) to aspire to the standard of consumption enjoyed by the average citizen of a developed country. Realizing that, under the most optimistic scenarios for the less developed countries to complete their demographic transitions, the world population would increase by half-again to more than 8 billion, and that consumer aspirations show no signs of abating, a steady-state economy seems inevitable. If so, Daly urges, we had better begin preparing for such an economy.

Therefore, we need to turn away from Western economics and the addiction to economic growth. The solution to absolute scarcity is not more growth. Once we withdraw the hollow promise of more growth as a solution to poverty, we must confront the gross inequities in the distributions of income and wealth. For Daly, the first step is replacing the attitude of "more is better" with one of "enough is best.[35]

## INSTITUTIONS FOR A STEADY-STATE ECONOMY

Daly proposes a blueprint for a steady-state economy, which combines "macrostability" (obtained by setting absolute bounds for population size, resource use, income, and wealth) with "microvariability" (obtained by allowing for resource allocations within

---

[34]Ibid., page 17.
[35]Ibid., page 2.

these bounds to be determined by the market mechanism).[36] Three institutions define his SSE. To stabilize population, marketable birth licenses would be issued. Consistent with zero population growth in the long run, each woman would be given licenses for 2.1 births, divisible into units of .1 births. Those who desired additional children could purchase deciles of births in the market from those women not using their full quotas.

To stabilize the stocks of renewable natural resources and to reduce the use of non-renewable resources, quotas would be set and depletion licenses would be auctioned off by the government. The depletion of renewable resources would be held to rates consistent with their long-run sustainability (e.g., the regeneration of forests). Restricting access to nonrenewable resources would drive up the market prices of the depletion licenses, encouraging conservation and the substitution of renewable resources (e.g., solar energy for fossil fuels). The government would capture the quota rents or the revenues from the sale of the depletion licenses. Limiting the use of resources should reduce pollution and the return of high-entropy matter to the environment.

Limiting the use of resources would also restrain the production of goods and services and the generation of real income for the present population. To address poverty and the issue of equity, Daly proposes minimum and maximum limits to individual income and a maximum limit on individual wealth. Income above the maximum would be taxed at 100 percent and redistributed to those below the minimum. Revenues from the auctioning of the depletion quotas could also be used, if needed, for the required income transfers.

Clearly, Daly's steady-state economics would involve a large role for the government and a sacrifice of individual freedom in reproduction, the earning of income, and the accumulation of wealth. Enforcement would be a problem—especially with unlicensed births and undeclared income. Just as with Schumacher's Buddhist economics, Daly's SSE would require fundamental changes in attitudes. While economic growth would be zero, economic development could continue. Reducing the resources needed to attain a given level of satisfaction, or, alternatively, deriving more satisfaction from a given utilization of resources, would constitute economic development. More enlightened use of leisure time would substitute for greater consumption of goods.

Given the present international disparities in per capita incomes and resource utilization, Daly argues that the developed countries should be the first to adopt SSE.

> It is absolutely a waste of time as well as morally backward to preach steady-state doctrines to under-developed countries before the overdeveloped countries have taken any measure to reduce their own population growth or the growth of their per capita resource consumption.[37]

While the developed countries have been below replacement-level fertility for some time (the slow growth occurring in their populations is due to population momentum and net in-migration), there are no signs of a voluntary downward trend in per capita consumption.

It is easy to dismiss Daly as an alarmist.[38] His proposed three SSE institutions would never be willingly accepted. At the very least, however, his thesis raises important

---

[36]Ibid., Chapter 3, pages 50–76.

[37]Ibid., page 148.

[38]Daly was not alone, however, in the 1970s in warning of limits to growth. Simulation models were constructed that predicted "crashes" in the global economy due to resource constraints and increased pollution. See, for example, D. H. Meadows et al., *The Limits to Growth,* New York: Universe Books, 1972. For an earlier, incisive article on population growth, see Garrett Hardin, "The Tragedy of the Commons," *Science,* vol. 162 (December 1968), pages 1243–1248.

questions. Is it possible for economic growth to continue indefinitely? Will technological progress save the day, allowing us to "do more with less"? What price do we put on the extinction of a species or the permanent loss of rain forest? Do future generations have rights to ecosystems as productive and viable as present generations? The answers given to these questions may have a profound impact on the future economic policies of both developed and less developed countries.

## CONCLUDING NOTE

We might organize the approaches to economic development in the first three decades following World War II into three camps. The growth model approach emphasized economic growth through investment, physical capital accumulation, and industrialization. The Harrod-Domar, Kaldor, Solow, Nelson, Rostow, and Lewis models are in this tradition and dominated development theory and policy in the 1950s and 1960s. The growth-with-equity approach promoted in the 1970s shifted the emphasis to employment, human capital formation, and rural development. Adelman's depauperization and agricultural demand–led industrialization strategies and the basic needs orientation all fall in this camp. The third camp is united by its rejection of conventional Western economic thinking. For different reasons, the radical school (Marxism), Schumacher (Buddhist economics), and Daly (steady-state economics) criticize capitalism and the related emphasis on economic growth. While the radical school may be perceived as less relevant to the current development policy debate, the work of Schumacher and Daly foreshadowed the attention that would be given in the 1990s to sustainable development. In Chapters 12 and 19 we discuss policies for sustainable development.

Since the 1980s, however, a general movement has occurred back to the more conservative growth model approach with a greater reliance on the market mechanism. In particular, endogenous growth theory emphasizes the importance of technological progress. In the 1990s the World Bank began recommending an eclectic market-friendly strategy of development with four major components: a stable macroeconomy; competitive domestic markets; investment in human capital; and integration with the international economy through trade and investment.[39] We explore these and other components of economic development in more detail in the following chapters. To conclude this section of the text on approaches to economic development, we turn in Chapter 6 to the role of the state—a role that both defines and is defined by the development strategy pursued.

## SUMMARY OF MAIN POINTS

1. Re-examined in the 1970s, a period characterized by severe shocks to the international economy, was the issue of whether the economic growth in the less developed countries during the 1950s and 1960s resulted in economic development

---

[39]See World Bank, *World Development Report 1991*, New York: Oxford University Press, 1991. For an overview of this strategy see pages 1–11.

and reduced poverty. New approaches to economic development that shifted the emphasis from economic growth and physical capital formation were advanced. In particular, concern that both the relative and absolute incomes of the poorest might decline during the initial stages of economic growth motivated greater attention to human capital formation and employment generation.

2. Reasons for increasing discrepancies in income and economic mobility during the initial stages of economic growth included policies to subsidize investment and physical capital formation (e.g., setting official interest rates below market equilibrium levels, maintaining overvalued currencies, and depressing the prices paid to farmers) and a bias in public expenditures on education and health care in favor of the higher income, urban populations.

3. Adelman's depauperization approach is based on the experiences of five countries that successfully generated equitable economic growth. The three stages in this development strategy are a redistribution of assets; human capital formation; and human resource-intensive economic growth.

4. In the mid-1980s, a decade after proposing her depauperization strategy, Adelman recast her recommendations. Under agricultural demand–led industrialization (ADLI), investment in agriculture and rural development are promoted.

5. The basic needs approach is a bottom-up strategy of development. The first priority is meeting the core basic needs of the population for food, water, shelter, clothing, and health care. Human capital formation and employment generation are emphasized as providing the surest foundation for sustainable development. Gains in employment in the less developed countries can be realized by allowing input prices (especially interest rates and wage rates) to reflect input scarcities and by using labor-intensive technologies. In human capital formation, primary education and basic preventative health care are stressed.

6. There are concerns with the feasibility of a basic needs strategy of development. The first is agreeing on a definition of basic needs that has clear policy implications. Second is promoting economic mobility, while avoiding the dependencies that can arise with transfer programs. Third, the resources for funding and administering a comprehensive basic needs strategy are limited. Fourth, investment in the physical capital needed for economic growth can be crowded out by the basic needs expenditures.

7. Evidence on the relationship among economic growth, income inequality, and poverty is limited and far from conclusive. In general, however, it appears that economic growth is a necessary, but not sufficient, condition for poverty reduction.

8. Marx criticized capitalism as a system of exploitation in which capitalists, driven by profits and a passion for capital accumulation, took advantage of labor. According to Marx, capitalism was bound to fail. Oppressed workers would revolt and a classless system of communism would emerge.

9. Radical-school economists, inspired by the writings of Marx, argue that the underdevelopment of the contemporary less developed countries is a result of exploitation by the developed, capitalist countries—in the past during colonialism and in the present under dominant international institutions, such as the International Monetary Fund and the World Bank. In international trade, finance, investment, and aid, the interests of the LDCs have been subordinate.

10. Schumacher castigates Western economics as an unsustainable system based on materialism, unsuitable for emulation by the less developed countries. Schumacher's alternative, called Buddhist economics, represents an approach to development in which the orientation is small-scale, the environment is

respected, and right livelihood is pursued—a blend of fulfilling employment, optimal consumption, and enlightenment.

11. Daly rejects Western economics with its priority on growth as inconsistent with a finite environment and a limited supply of low entropy (potential energy available for work). Daly proposes a steady-state economic system based on three institutions: marketable birth licenses to ensure zero population growth; depletion quotas for natural resources to ensure sustainable development; and a maximum limit for individual wealth with upper and lower bounds for individual incomes.

## KEY TERMS

agricultural demand–led industrialization (ADLI)
basic needs
Buddhist economics
depauperization
entropy

imperialism
intermediate technology
marginal rate of factor substitution
steady-state economy (SSE)
surplus value

## QUESTIONS

1. Identify and discuss the key insight as well as the main limitation of each of the following:
   *a.* Adelman's depauperization
   *b.* the basic needs strategy of development
   *c.* the radical (Marxist) school
   *d.* Schumacher's Buddhist economics
   *e.* Daly's steady-state economics
2. Compare and contrast Rostow's four types of economies (presented in Chapter 4) with Adelman's three-stage growth-with-equity strategy.
3. Compare and contrast Lewis's treatment of the capitalist surplus (presented in Chapter 4) with Marx's treatment of surplus value.
4. Compare the approach of endogenous growth theory (presented in Chapter 4) with Daly's steady-state economics.
5. Discuss how the radical (Marxist) school and E. F. Schumacher (Buddhist economics) each reject the Western approach to economic development. Note any common ground as well as the important differences.
6. Discuss the difficulties in implementing the following strategies of development:
   *a.* Adelman's depauperization
   *b.* basic needs
   *c.* Schumacher's Buddhist economics
   *d.* Daly's steady-state economics

## SUGGESTED READINGS

Adelman, Irma, "Development Economics—A Reassessment of Goals," *American Economic Review*, vol. 65, no. 2 (May 1975), pages 302–309.

Adelman, Irma, "Beyond Export-Led Growth," *World Development*, vol. 12, no. 9 (1984), pages 937–949.
Crosswell, Michael, "Basic Human Needs: A Development Planning Approach," in *Basic Needs and Development*, edited by Danny Leipzeiger, Cambridge, MA: Oelgeschlager, Cunn, and Hain, 1981, pages 1–25.
Daly, Herman, *Steady-State Economics: The Economics of Biophysical Equilibrium and Moral Growth*, San Francisco: W. H. Freeman, 1977.
Goulet, Denis, *Survival With Integrity: Sarvodaya at the Crossroads,* Colombo, Sri Lanka: Marga Institute, 1981.
Griffin, Keith and John Gurley, "Radical Analyses of Imperialism, the Third World, and the Transition to Socialism: A Survey Article," *Journal of Economic Literature*, vol. 23, no. 3 (September 1985), pages 1089–1143.
Hardin, Garrett, "The Tragedy of the Commons," *Science*, vol. 162 (December 1968), pages 1243–1248.
Heilbroner, Robert, "The Inexorable System of Karl Marx," in *The Worldly Philosophers*, 4th ed., New York: Simon and Schuster, 1972, pages 131–163.
Schumacher, E. F., *Small Is Beautiful: Economics As If People Mattered,* New York: Harper and Row, 1973.
Streeten, Paul, "Basic Needs: Some Unsettled Questions," *World Development*, vol. 12, no. 9 (1984), pages 973–978.

## CASE STUDIES

### SOUTH KOREA

Until 1876, when regular contact with the outside world began following its forced signing of a commerce treaty with Japan, Korea was known as the "hermit kingdom," a largely self-sufficient, feudalistic society.[1] During the period from 1876 to 1904, Japan, China, and Russia competed for control over the Korean peninsula. After defeats of China in the Sino-Japanese War of 1894 and then Russia in the Russo-Japanese War of 1904, Japan emerged as the dominant power. In 1910 Korea was formally annexed and remained a Japanese colony until liberation at the end of World War II.

Under Japanese rule Korea experienced considerable economic development. A central bank and a system of taxes were established. The economic infrastructure, particularly in transportation and communications, was improved. Important advances occurred in agriculture through improvements in seeds, fertilizers, and irrigation. The share of manufacturing in gross domestic product increased significantly, and the Korean economy became more open, although almost all trade was with Japan.

Koreans were exploited by the Japanese, however, and had few civil rights and little economic mobility. Despite many schools serving the Japanese in Korea, the vast

---

[1]The main sources for this case study are Peter Hess, *Demographic Factors in South Korean Economic Development: 1963-1977*, Ph.D. dissertation, The University of North Carolina, Chapel Hill, NC, 1982; and Byung-Nak Song, *The Rise of the Korean Economy*, Hong Kong: Oxford University Press, 1990. A "Survey of South Korea," appearing in *The Economist* (June 3, 1995) has also been helpful. To put South Korean economic development in a regional context, see the World Bank's *The East-Asian Miracle: Economic Growth and Public Policy*, New York: Oxford University Press, 1993. We will again highlight South Korea in Chapter 17, along with several other of the East Asian nations, as examples of the World Bank's "market-friendly" strategy of development.

majority of Koreans received no formal education. The Japanese disproportionately owned the agricultural estates and factories. Initially regarded as a cheap source of raw materials and rice, Korea was subsequently developed to be part of the Japanese empire.

The Korean economy was in poor shape when the Japanese left in 1945. The infrastructure had significantly deteriorated during the war; factories were operating at a fraction of capacity; managers, technicians, and skilled labor were all in short supply; and inflation was accelerating. Moreover, a political vacuum had been created.

Korea was temporarily partitioned at the 38th parallel, with the United States administering the southern part of the country, and Russia the northern half, until the situation could be stabilized. Not only was the division of Korea contrary to the desires of the Korean people for a unified and independent nation, it was economically counterproductive. First, nature and then Japanese development had created a complementary relationship between the country's two halves. Because most of the hydroelectric power sources and mineral deposits were located in the north, the Japanese had concentrated the heavy industry there. In the south, agriculture and light industry were prevalent. Partitioning the country negated this regional comparative advantage, since commerce between the two halves effectively ceased.

With the Cold War, the division of Korea became permanent. Then, in June of 1950, North Korean troops invaded South Korea. The bitter Korean War followed, ending in the summer of 1953 with an armistice. North Korea became the Democratic People's Republic of Korea and a communist state. South Korea became the Republic of Korea.

Under the American administration (1945–1948) two important initiatives were undertaken in the south before the Korean War. First, compulsory primary education was introduced, not only as part of a campaign for human capital formation, but to promote democratic principles. Rapid expansion in school enrollments followed, creating the human capital that has been the foundation of South Korean economic development. Second, under an extensive land-tenure reform program the large estates previously owned by the Japanese were redistributed to Korean peasant farmers. In fact, all landholdings were divided into small farms. Combined with subsequent investments in rural development, agriculture, still dominated by small family farms, has significantly contributed to Korea's economic growth.

After the cessation of hostilities with the north, South Korea began the reconstruction of its economy and the resettlement of its population. During the 1950s, however, South Korea was dependent on U.S. foreign aid. The government of Syngman Rhee was ineffective—concerned more with solidifying its power base than generating economic development. South Korea entered into the 1960s as a poor, densely populated country with few natural resources and no clear development strategy. Student demonstrations over the political corruption led to a change in government, and eventually a military coup in 1961, which brought General Park Chung Hee to power. In 1963 Park was elected as President of South Korea.

No longer able to rely on U.S. aid to bolster the economy, the Park government implemented an outward-looking strategy of growth to be led by the expansion of labor-intensive manufactured exports. The human capital formation begun in the late 1940s provided a literate labor force that was prepared for rapid industrialization. Devaluation of the Korean currency, the won, and export subsidies signalled the new direction. Tighter fiscal and monetary policies were implemented to enhance South Korea's international competitiveness. Large firms were given annual export targets, which, if met, were rewarded with tax breaks, preferential credit, and access to foreign exchange for imports of capital and intermediate goods.

The South Korean economy took off. From 1963 to 1977, the average annual growth rates for Gross National Product and for exports of goods and services were 9.7 percent and 30.3 percent, respectively. From less than 4 percent of GNP in 1963, exports of goods and services grew to over 40 percent by 1977.[2] The government actively promoted industry. For example, in the 1970s an ambitious program to develop heavy and chemical industries, including steel and shipbuilding, was initiated. However, overextension of the Korean economy and poor timing (the international oil price hikes and stagflation) led to initially disappointing results. In late 1979 President Park, who had been re-elected in 1972, was assassinated by the head of the Korean Central Intelligence Agency.

In 1980 South Korea was plagued by recession, high inflation, internal unrest, poor harvests, and mounting external debt. General Chun Doo Hwan seized power under martial law. After aggressive stabilization measures that included a devaluation, the Korean economy recovered vigorously—led by renewed growth in manufactured exports that were becoming more physical capital- and skill-intensive as Korean labor productivity increased. By 1987, South Korea experienced its first trade surplus. Yet domestic turmoil again struck, with student riots and labor unrest. In 1988 Roh Tae-Woo, another former general in the South Korean army, was elected as president. Then, in 1993, a civilian and long-time opponent of military rule, Kim Young Sam, became South Korea's president.

South Korea is widely regarded as one of the most impressive economic success stories of the modern era. As observed in *The Economist* (June 3, 1995), "Three decades ago the average Korean earned around $100 a year, less than the average Indian or Ghanaian. Today, South Korea's GNP per head is $8,500, 30 times India's and 20 times Ghana's."[3] Whether South Korea can serve as a model for other developing nations, however, is less clear.

South Korea's economic achievement reflects a number of factors, some unique and some more easily transferable. Several of the most salient are noted here. First, the Korean population is very homogeneous in terms of culture, language, and common experience.[4] Underlying the culture is a Confucian ethic, which fosters respect for authority, a desire for education, and a strong sense of familial responsibility. In particular, education is perceived as the key to economic mobility.[5] Parents willingly sacrifice for their children's education, expecting the investments to pay off also in terms of their own old-age security.

Second, South Korea's modern experience has been defined by its close ties with Japan (first as a colony, then on a more equal basis after the normalization of relations in 1965) and the United States (as a political and military ward after liberation, a recipient of massive aid, and a subsequent close ally). Japan and the United States are the major trading partners of South Korea, and are important sources of investment and technology transfers. Although significant differences exist (for example, the burden of

---

[2] These statistics are from the Bank of Korea, *Economic Statistics Yearbook,* 1979.
[3] "A Survey of South Korea," *The Economist,* (June 3, 1995), page 3.
[4] See Chapter 4, "East Asian Culture and the New Confucian Ethic," in Song.
[5] The secondary school and tertiary enrollment rates for South Korea in 1992 were 90 percent and 42 percent, respectively, comparable to enrollment rates in high-income economies (from World Bank, *World Development Report 1995,* New York: Oxford University Press, 1995, Table 28).

expenditures on national defense), South Korea's development strategy has much in common with Japan's. South Koreans' exposure to the United States has been diverse, including education at American universities, joint military training, and emulation of American consumer behavior.

Third, South Korea's development has been very human-capital intensive. The gains in education have been remarkable and contributed not only to South Korea's rapid progress through the demographic transition, but to an export-led growth, characterized by continual improvement in the technological sophistication of the products exported.[6]

Fourth, a fairly equitable distribution of income has been maintained during the accelerated pace of the economic growth. In part, South Korea's broad-based development strategy emphasized employment through the expansion of labor-intensive manufactures. Deliberate policies to promote equity have also been implemented, beginning with the comprehensive land-tenure reform after the Second World War. Later, in the 1970s, concerns over growing gaps between the incomes of the urban and rural populations led to an emphasis on rural development. Farm prices have been subsidized, and farmers have been protected from international competition.

Fifth has been the role played in South Korea's development by strong government and public entrepreneurship. From the time of the Park regime in the early 1960s, the government has directed and guided the economy—albeit with attention to market fundamentals. In particular, the financial sector has been tightly controlled. The primary goal, though, has been rapid growth through exports, and the underlying principle has been to reward economic performance. Large businesses, the Korean conglomerates known as *jaebol* (or *chaebol*) have been favored. As a result, Korean industry is heavily concentrated. Labor unions have been suppressed and, for some time, the Korean work week has been among the longest in the world. With the success of private enterprise, the Korean government should no longer need to be as actively involved in the micromanagement of the economy.

Political liberalization in South Korea, however, still lags behind the economic liberalization. The threat posed by North Korea and the need to focus on a strong economy have been used by successive governments to justify authoritarian rule. With gains in the material standard of living, South Koreans are increasingly demanding more leisure and more political rights. Moreover, with the recent change in leadership in North Korea, reunification, long desired by all Koreans, may be more than a distant dream.

From one of the poorest nations in the world less than four decades ago, South Korea stands ready to join the ranks of the developed countries. Perhaps Byung-Nak Song best sums up the prospects.

> In all likelihood, [South] Korea will continue to have a highly motivated, industrious, and disciplined labour force, experienced and venturesome entrepreneurs, effective cooperation between government and business, and competent and flexible policymakers attuned to changing domestic and international circumstances.[7]

---

[6]Heavy manufactures, including steel, automobiles, and chemicals, account for approximately two-thirds of all South Korea's exports. See World Bank, *Trends in Developing Economies 1994*, Washington, DC, 1994, page 261.

[7]Song, page 236.

## SRI LANKA

Sri Lanka, known until 1972 as Ceylon, is an island of roughly the same land size but with four times the population of Ireland. Located 22 miles south of India, Sri Lanka was a feudal society consisting of three kingdoms, with a traditional economy centered on the cultivation of rice, until the beginning of the sixteenth century when the Portuguese conquered the coastal regions of the island.[1] Trade with the outside world, predominantly spices and precious stones for silk, was expanded by the Portuguese and then the Dutch, who followed in the mid-1600s. Near the end of the eighteenth century, the British arrived in force, and in 1815 the entire island, for the first time, came under one foreign authority.

The British developed an export economy based on large plantations using Tamil labor (most of whom were indentured) imported from south India. Coffee, initially the major crop, was destroyed by disease, and replaced by tea. Sri Lanka's production of tea increased from 10 million pounds in 1885 to 150 million pounds in 1900 (one-fourth of the world's production).[2] Coexisting with, but separate from, the plantation economy were the subsistence rice farmers, whose paddy lands were subject to seizure by the colonial authorities for nonpayment of taxes.

Rubber became the second major export crop, when rubber trees were planted on the British-owned and -managed plantations. Coconuts developed into a third export crop; however, unlike tea and rubber, coconuts were largely grown by the indigenous population on smaller landholdings. The modest industrialization on the island was related to the plantation economy, primarily processing and shipping the tea and rubber. Although part of the British empire, Sri Lanka did enjoy some measure of self-rule. In 1931 universal suffrage was adopted—except for the Indian Tamils on the plantations. Upon gaining its independence in 1948, Sri Lanka inherited a dualistic agrarian economy, heavily dependent on the export of the plantation crops and the importation of food, particularly rice.[3]

Three themes have run through the political economy of Sri Lanka since independence. First is the importance of the plantation export crops. The plantation sector provided an attractive source of tax revenues that could be used to fund social services. In fact, Sri Lanka is widely cited for its early and sustained attention to the basic needs of its population through food subsidies and free education (through the university level) and health care. On the other hand, for a long time, Sri Lanka was neither able to fully develop its plantation agriculture, nor diversify its economic base.

Second, for cultural as well as economic and political reasons, a long-term objective of government policy has been to achieve self-sufficiency in rice production. With food subsidies centered on the provision of rice, significant portions of the government budget and Sri Lanka's foreign exchange earnings have been expended

---

[1] The main sources for this case study are Satchi Ponnambalam, *Dependent Capitalism in Crisis: The Sri Lankan Economy 1948–1980,* London: Zed Press, 1980; and Henry Bruton, in collaboration with Gamini Abeysekera, Nimal Sanderatne, and Zainal Aznam Yusof, *The Political Economy of Poverty, Equity, and Growth: Sri Lanka and Malaysia,* A World Bank Comparative Study, New York: Oxford University Press, 1992. Also helpful is World Bank, *Trends in Developing Economies 1994,* Washington, DC, 1994.

[2] Ponnambalam, page 9.

[3] In 1950 more than 90 percent of Sri Lanka's exports were accounted for by tea, rubber, and coconut products. See Bruton et al., page 31.

on rice imports. After independence, programs were implemented to increase the land under rice production, primarily through reclamation of uncultivated land and resettlement of landless farmers. Moreover, with the majority of the population in rural areas and much of the indigenous agrarian economy involved in rice farming, increasing the production of rice would promote both economic growth and income equality.

Third, ethnic tensions, always a sensitive issue, became volatile in the early 1980s with the outbreak of terrorist activity and then civil war. The major ethnic group, accounting for over 70 percent of the population, is the Sinhalese, who are predominantly Buddhists. Tamils, roughly split between the Sri Lankan Tamils and the Indian Tamils on the plantations, are predominantly Hindus and make up nearly 20 percent of the population. The Indian Tamils, in general, have the lowest standard of living and limited civil rights. Muslims constitute the majority of the remaining 10 percent of the population.

Post-independence Sri Lanka has also been characterized by revolving-door, though democratically elected, governments. The two dominant parties, the more conservative United National Party (UNP) and the more radical Sri Lanka Freedom Party (SLFP) have rotated in and out of power, making it difficult to implement consistent, long-range, economic policy. Moreover, the two parties have usually been identified closely with powerful families (in particular, the SLFP with the Bandaranaike family).

From 1948 to 1956, the UNP governed, with support generally drawn from the upper-income, propertied classes. Initially, the Sri Lankan government was flush with funds, not only from the expenditures by the British military on the island during the war years, but from the strong export tax revenues from tea and rubber in the early 1950s. The liberal social welfare program of food subsidies, free education and health care, however, became a burden when export prices fell—with the end of the Korean War and the decline in the demand for rubber. The government's attempt at abolishing the rice subsidy in late 1953 met with popular protest and led to the resignation of the prime minister. During this period no comprehensive strategy of development existed and, in particular, no effective policy to promote industrialization.

The Sri Lanka Freedom Party was elected in 1956 under the leadership of S. W. R. D. Bandaranaike. The new government did attempt some industrialization as part of an import substitution strategy, although public corporations, rather than private enterprise, were favored. In agriculture, increased attention was paid to rice farming, with investments in fertilizers and mechanization and with credit and measures to improve the security of tenant farmers. Consequently, rice yields and production rose. Replanting in higher-yielding varieties of tea and rubber trees was also encouraged on the plantations.

Bandaranaike was assassinated in 1958, however. After elections in 1960, his widow, Sirimavo, succeeded him, becoming the world's first woman prime minister. Under Mrs. Bandaranaike, the Sri Lankan government nationalized petroleum distribution and insurance and imposed a new tax on business.[4] Further, with a decline in export prices and revenues, the government resorted to import restrictions to control the growing trade deficits.

---

[4]Ponnambalam, page 48, notes that, "By 1965, Sri Lanka had emerged as the most heavily taxed of the world's Less Developed Countries."

The UNP returned to power in the election of 1965, and began to rely on foreign borrowing to cover the import surpluses. Loans from Western commercial banks as well as credit from the International Monetary Fund increased Sri Lanka's external indebtedness. In 1967 the Sri Lankan rupee was devalued. Government budget deficits continued to grow, not only from the social welfare expenditures, but from the subsidies to rice farmers and the interest on the public debt. Inflation increased from the expansion in the money supply involved in financing the budget deficits. Nevertheless, economic growth was strong, as the adoption of Green Revolution technology (improved seeds, fertilizers, irrigation) significantly boosted rice yields.

The 1970s saw Mrs. Bandaranaike and the SLFP back in office, just as the international economy experienced turbulence. Sri Lanka was hurt by the rising prices for food and oil imports. As part of the contractionary economic policies adopted, the government reduced rice subsidies. Land-reform legislation led to the nationalization of the large plantations. Construction began on the Mahaweli Ganga Development Scheme, a massive dam project to irrigate the drylands (increasing the area under rice production) and generate hydroelectric power. Other measures to stimulate industry and promote rural development were tried, but with little success. Continuing to hamper Sri Lankan industrialization was the lack of private entrepreneurship, whether directly crowded out by government attempts to industrialize through public corporations or discouraged by the lack of a coherent policy and conducive climate for private investment. Unemployment, a chronic problem since independence, especially among the educated youth, grew worse in the 1970s, as did inflation, the government budget deficit, and the trade balance.

True to form, the election of 1977 brought a change in government. The UNP, under J. R. Jayewardne, won in a landslide. The new government quickly moved to change the direction of the Sri Lankan economy, adopting a pro-growth strategy. Income tax rates were reduced. Imports were liberalized and foreign investment was solicited. The rupee was devalued substantially. A Free Trade Zone (or export-processing zone) was established to promote manufactured exports. Sri Lanka's increased openness, embraced by the International Monetary Fund, the World Bank, and Western donor nations, was rewarded with new loans and foreign assistance. With the election mandate, Jayewardne revised the food subsidy policy, eventually replacing the subsidized rice rations with food stamps restricted to low-income households. Income inequality increased with the change in economic strategy. In the first few years under the new regime, imports soared, while exports improved little. The trade deficits were again covered by foreign borrowing. Then, in 1983, simmering ethnic unrest erupted into violence between militant Tamils, who ultimately sought a Tamil homeland in the northern part of Sri Lanka, and the Sinhalese government. Besides the tragic loss in life and the destruction of property, the ongoing conflict has impeded economic development and increased the government budget deficits.

The annual growth rate in real Gross Domestic Product in Sri Lanka from 1980 to 1993 averaged 4.0 percent. Industry grew faster than agriculture, yet the share of industry in national output, 26 percent in 1993, was little changed from the 24 percent of 1970. The economy has been able to diversify its exports: In 1993 the share of manufactures in merchandise exports reached 73 percent (compared to only 1 percent in 1970). Most of the manufactured exports, however, consist of textiles and clothing. The reliance on imported foodstuffs, particularly rice, has been reduced. Sri Lanka is well-known for its impressive human capital formation (e.g., a female life expectancy at birth of 74 years in 1993 and a female secondary school enrollment rate of 77 percent in 1992), despite its ranking as a low-income economy (per capita GNP in 1993 of

$600). The investments in education, nutrition, and health care contributed to lowering Sri Lanka's total fertility rate from 4.3 in 1970 to 2.4 in 1993.[5]

The UNP governed from 1977 to 1994, an unprecedented stretch for one party in post-independence Sri Lanka. While the thrust of economic policy has been on liberalizing the economy through private enterprise, government budget deficits and foreign trade deficits remain large, and inflation persists.[6] In 1993 the president of Sri Lanka was assassinated and, in August of 1994, the UNP lost the general election. Chandrika Kumaratunga became the president and appointed her mother, Sirimavo Bandaranaike, as the new prime minister.[7] Sri Lanka may turn again to a more interventionist approach to development. The prospects for development depend crucially on adhering to sound economic policies and resolving the long and bitter civil war.

---

[5]These statistics are from the World Bank, *World Development Report 1995*, New York: Oxford University Press, 1995; Tables 1, 2, 3, 15, 26, 28, and 29.

[6]The recent performance of the Sri Lankan economy is concisely reviewed in World Bank, *Trends in Developing Economies 1994*, pages 466–470.

[7]Under a constitutional change in 1978, the head of state in Sri Lanka is now the president, not the prime minister.

# CHAPTER 6

# ECONOMIC SYSTEMS, DEVELOPMENT STRATEGIES, AND THE ROLE OF THE STATE

> The extent and efficiency of the state's involvement in the economy has been critical ... the quality of government matters as much as the quantity.[1]

The government of a developing country plays a pivotal role in affecting the direction and pace of economic growth and development. Opinions vary concerning the appropriate policies that governments or states should advance. Many economists advocate a "free market" capitalist approach that calls for minimal government intervention in the economy; others tend to support a highly mixed economy in which the government takes a more active role in guiding resources. Following the demise of the Soviet Union, very few economists today argue for a highly centralized, socialist system in which the government directly allocates resources.

In this chapter, we first give an overview of three economic systems, each having a very different role for government: laissez-faire capitalism, managed or authoritarian capitalism, and command socialism. We consider the consistency of each system with possible development strategies. We then discuss the areas of economic activity potentially involving governments, commenting on the degree of consensus concerning the appropriateness of such governmental involvement. The development strategy chosen by the country will define, to a great extent, the acceptable parameters for government intervention in the economic system. Finally, we comment on the role that history and culture may play in the choice of an economic system and development policy. We conclude the chapter with three case studies on the role of government within the economies of China, Ghana, and Brazil.

---

[1] World Bank, *World Development Report 1991*, New York: Oxford University Press, 1991, page 31.

# ECONOMIC SYSTEMS AND DEVELOPMENT STRATEGIES

The nation's economic system largely prescribes the role of government in the economy. Not surprisingly, advantages and disadvantages are associated with each economic system.

## LAISSEZ-FAIRE CAPITALISM

**Laissez-faire capitalism** is grounded in the sanctity of the private ownership of the means of production—land and capital assets. In competitive input and output markets, individuals (often acting jointly as households or firms) freely enter into purchases (as demanders) and sales (as suppliers). Economic agents are presumably motivated by self-interest. Firms seek to maximize economic profits; households and individuals seek to maximize utility. The result of these voluntary actions is a set of market prices that serve to allocate resources. The goods and services produced are those demanded by households earning income from supplying the inputs.

Economists, from Adam Smith onward, have tended to be impressed by the efficient working of a competitive market system comprised of many small buyers and sellers. The "invisible hand" of self-interest leads to the production of the goods desired by those with income; and, in the long run, the goods will be produced at minimum unit cost. Competitive capitalism leads to a specialization of resources with inputs channeled into those activities whose economic returns are the highest.

The actual distribution of income and resulting output is a function of the factors that individuals supply to the market. Those with significant amounts of highly valued labor and financial assets will be more rewarded. Equality of income is highly unlikely, since individual talent and work effort are not equally distributed and assets tend to be concentrated. To the extent that income is unequally distributed, a bias could exist toward saving and investment, since higher-income individuals (often enjoying significant capital income) are apt to have higher saving rates, as in the Kaldor model. Enhanced capital formation will promote growth in national income. In true laissez-faire capitalism, the market-determined income distribution is accepted with little role for the government to address poverty or income inequality. Concern for the poor is a matter of individual choice or conscience.

The protection of property rights and the production of public goods (those goods such as national defense that cannot be efficiently produced by the private market) are the accepted roles for government in the pure system of laissez-faire capitalism. Secure property rights are vital to the efficient working of a capitalist system. The legal rights to acquire property or assets and to use that property for individual gain provide incentives for the creation of wealth and the production of output. For instance, a farmer who has clear title to his land will have greater incentive to care for the land than would a farmer who is simply using land owned by the state. Governments protect property rights through a fair and independent judiciary that adjudicates ownership disputes and enforces contracts between consenting parties.

In fact, many would argue that the sanctity of property rights is a vital precondition for the functioning of a capitalist system. We will return to this issue when we discuss the economic transition to capitalism of the former socialist countries.

Proponents of laissez-faire capitalism as a development approach stress the efficiency of free-market decision making. By definition, laissez-faire capitalism is consistent with free trade. A country will produce and export those goods in which it has a comparative advantage (lower opportunity cost of production), importing those goods in which it has a comparative disadvantage. Any use of tariffs or nontariff barriers that interfere with the workings of the free market will lead to a reduction in aggregate economic welfare. Economic growth will be determined, in large part, by the spending decisions of consumers. Individual households will determine the division of income between current consumption and savings (investment) as they weigh the desirability of present versus future consumption. Government spending is limited within laissez-faire capitalism. Thus, advocates argue that a reduced probability exists that a country will experience large fiscal deficits that require either increased government borrowing—crowding out private-sector investment—or growth of the money supply—generating inflation.

In the post–World War II years, many developing countries have intervened in various aspects of the economy. Often called **dirigism,** this intervention is a form of economic policy in which the state exerts significant influence, both direct and indirect, on the allocation of resources. Common examples of such government intervention into resource allocation are the use of quotas to block imports and promote domestic industry; the nationalizing of private industry; and the setting of unremunerative producer prices in agriculture. Within the last 15 years, international agencies such as the World Bank and the International Monetary Fund have been encouraging developing countries to pursue more open, market-friendly strategies that reduce the role of government in the economy. This approach reflects that "The literature in development economics has now turned full circle from the unquestioning dirigism of the early 1950s to the gory neoclassical accounts in recent years of the failures and disasters of regulatory, interventionist states."[2] (In Chapter 17 we discuss the World Bank's market-friendly strategy in some detail.)

Opponents of laissez-faire capitalism point to significant opportunity costs to government inaction. In reality, laissez-faire capitalism may experience imperfect competition and market failures such as externalities. As discussed below, government intervention would be desirable to address such concerns. Some argue that advertising and materialism can introduce a consumption bias into modern capitalism, reducing the rate of savings at all levels of income. Government policy to encourage greater investment and more rapid economic growth may be needed to counter this bias. Others advocate an income-maintenance role for government that provides for the basic needs of all citizens. Finally, some propose that governments, especially in less developed countries, should target and develop sectors with promising future economic potential, reducing the countries' reliance on exporting agricultural commodities and raw materials, the goods in which developing countries often have a comparative advantage. Those wary of laissez-faire capitalism for any of the above reasons favor a more managed capitalism.

---

[2]Pranab Bardhan, "Symposium on the State and Economic Development," *Journal of Economic Perspectives*, vol. 4 no. 3 (summer 1990), page 3.

## MANAGED OR AUTHORITARIAN CAPITALISM

Advocates of **managed capitalism** feel that government intervention to promote certain key development objectives is warranted and preferable to a laissez-faire capitalism. Usually, the authority of government is viewed as insulating the economy from elements that can retard economic growth and development, such as a consumption bias or a neglect of the basic needs of the poor.

Most developing countries are best characterized by a form of managed capitalism, even though some state ownership of the means of production may concurrently exist. At a minimum, developing countries often have development plans that identify key objectives. These plans can be very broad, with a simple listing of goals, such as increasing mean years of educational attainment or reducing the incidence of a debilitating disease. Or plans can be more specific, actually setting production goals for key commodities, such as steel or rice. (In Chapter 13 we will discuss the use of sectoral planning.)

Below we consider how the government, within a managed capitalist framework, can use policy tools to influence the path of economic development. Unfortunately, some government leaders have often used the authority of government in self-serving ways that have been detrimental to economic performance and equity. We will return to the issue of government reform at different times in later chapters. Here, we concentrate on the power of government to achieve legitimate economic objectives.

### Promoting Investment and Growth

As noted, some argue that laissez-faire capitalism contains a consumption bias that leads to reduced investment and growth in the capital stock. For instance, let us assume that capital is the limiting factor in the growth process in a decentralized capitalist economy. As in the Kaldor model, if the marginal propensity to save from capital income is higher than from labor income, policies to redistribute income from labor to capital will increase saving, investment, the capital stock, and the rate of economic growth.

Similarly, if high-income groups have a greater marginal propensity to save, income redistribution from low- to high-income groups could foster saving and investment. More precisely, in this case, government may try to avoid using progressive taxation, such as graduated income taxes, that disproportionately impact high-income groups. Rather, governments might favor sales taxes and payroll taxes that are less progressive (and even regressive) in incidence. Moreover, the government can tax to raise funds to undertake infrastructure investments (broadly defined to include the transportation and communications sectors, power grids, and other capital improvements) that enhance private-sector investment. Thus, within a managed capitalist economy, government may take initiatives that increase the rate of capital formation and the growth of real output.

### Providing Basic Needs

The basic needs strategy that was reviewed in Chapter 5 argues that economic development is a process of expanding opportunities and improving the quality of life for all citizens. While the actual priorities of a basic needs strategy will vary, particular attention is given to providing core basic needs, usually defined to include food, water, shelter, clothing, and health care. Government intervention may be needed to accomplish these goals. Labor market policies that generate employment and expand the wage share of national income will allow families themselves to provide for many basic needs. Initially, governments may need to tax wealthier individuals to increase the opportunities for lower-income individuals. In many cases, government may even produce the good or service, such as public education or sanitation and primary health care in rural areas. In other cases, a form of public-private partnership (as in the provision of family-planning services in some Latin American countries) can be an effective means to enhance the welfare of individuals. The *World Development Report 1991* states that "The evidence shows that investing heavily in people makes sense not just in human terms, but also in hard-headed economic terms."[3]

INDUSTRIAL POLICY OR SECTORAL DEVELOPMENT

Many of the Asian countries, particularly Japan and South Korea, have pursued a development strategy aimed at identifying key sectors or industries that promise to contribute to an export-led growth process. To serve as leading sectors, these industries should have significant linkages to the rest of the economy. To promote long-term development of these **infant industries,** the government pursues an industrial policy that provides credit, tax concessions, or other subsidies aimed at stimulating these industries.

Since the early 1960s, South Korea has pursued such a strategy. As Larry Westphal describes:

> For nearly three decades, the Korean government has selectively intervened to promote targeted infant industries, typically by supporting the creation of large-scale establishments which were accorded temporary monopolies. Notable examples include cement, fertilizer, and petroleum refining in the early 1960s; steel and petrochemicals in the late 1960s and early 1970s; shipbuilding, other chemicals, capital goods, and durable consumer items in the mid-to-late 1970s; and more recently, critical electronic and other components previously sourced from Japan. At their inception, targeted industries have received preferential access to long- and short-term credit on preferential terms as well as reductions or exemptions with respect to most or all direct and indirect taxes (including tariffs).[4]

Underlying this industrial policy is a belief that the government is better able to assess profitable long-term economic opportunities than is the private market and, further, that the government can enhance the development of the targeted industries. Economists, however, have vigorously debated the contribution of industrial policy to economic development, particularly for Japan. Opponents feel that governments often have had a poor record in identifying winning industries and that development has actually occurred in spite of, and not because of, industrial policy.[5] (In Chapter 17

---

[3]World Bank, *World Development Report 1991*, page 69.

[4]Larry E. Westphal, "Industrial Policy in an Export-Propelled Economy: Lessons from South Korea's Experience," *Journal of Economic Perspectives*, vol. 4, no. 3 (summer 1990), page 47.

[5]For a critical overview of industrial planning in Japan, see: "Picking Losers in Japan," *The Economist*, (February 26, 1994), page 69. This work draws on Richard Beason and David Weinstein, "Growth, Economies of Scale, and Targeting in Japan (1955–90)," Discussion Paper 1644 of the Harvard Institute of Economic Research, 1994.

we assess in some detail the newly industrialized economies of Asia that are often credited with successful use of industrial policy.)

In sum, government can be called upon to intervene within a predominantly capitalist framework to promote specific development strategies. The actual policy tools (types of taxes and expenditures) are determined by the strategy of the government. The central thesis of managed capitalism is that laissez-faire capitalism will not fulfill the development objectives of the society.

As stated, intervention in developing countries has also been used in self-serving ways by corrupt governments not truly pursuing a development strategy for the benefit of the population. Examples of the predatory state can be found in the Mobutu government of Zaire (1965 to the present); Haiti under the Duvaliers (1957–1986); and the Philippines under Marcos (1966–1986).[6] Even in relatively "honest" governments, inefficient and self-seeking bureaucracies can waste scarce resources and interfere with the development process. Thus, there is a fear that with government intervention, inappropriate policies will be pursued, or that the intervention will be inefficient and, at its worst, highly corrupt. (In Chapter 18 we discuss the failures of many African governments to promote sustained economic development.)

In surveying the experience of government and its role in the development process (primarily for the managed capitalist countries), Anne Krueger has concluded, "Government failure may have consisted as much in failing to provide the infrastructure in which government has a large comparative advantage as it has in providing poorly things in which it does not have a comparative advantage."[7] Many developing countries have tried to improve the performance of government with reform programs aimed both at reducing waste and improving the efficiency of markets. Joan Nelson, in analyzing the experience of Third World countries in promoting economic reform, cites three influences that affect the government's success: "the strength of political leaders' commitment to the program, the government's capacity to implement the program and manage political responses, and the political response the program evokes from influential groups."[8] While not all countries have had successful reform programs, and while a mixed record of intervention and reform exists within managed capitalism, some government involvement in the economy may be necessary to promote well-chosen development objectives.

## CENTRALIZED SOCIALISM

The extreme model of government intervention is the command model of **centralized socialism,** as practiced most notably by the Soviet Union during the 1930 to 1985 period. Command economies are grounded in Marxist ideology and usually introduced by revolution (as in Russia in 1917 or China in 1949) or imposed from the outside (Soviet influence in Eastern Europe after World War II). The means of production are typically owned and controlled by the state. In fact, within a fully socialist state, individual ownership of land or capital is illegal.

---

[6]Bardhan, page 5.

[7]Anne O. Krueger, "Government Failures in Development," *Journal of Economic Perspectives,* vol. 4, no. 3 (summer 1990), page 17.

[8]Joan M. Nelson, "The Political Economy of Stabilization: Commitment, Capacity, and Public Response," *World Development,* vol. 12, no. 10 (1984), page 985.

With this centralized socialist model, the government, through a series of economic plans, allocates the publicly owned resources by command, or fiat. Typically, emphasis is placed on national defense and industrial development at the expense of private consumption. With the totalitarian conditions that tend to accompany centralized socialism, the citizenry has few legal outlets to contest this allocation of resources. Moreover, the centralized model tends to be insulated from international contact and economic exchange. It is the most inward-looking of the development models, largely eschewing the potential gains from international trade.

The ability of the government to channel inputs and resources toward infrastructure and capital-intensive heavy industry tends to lead initially to rapid economic growth. Called **extensive growth,** this policy relies on the increased use of inputs to increase output with no change in productivity. With public ownership of firms and virtually guaranteed employment and wages for the population, little economic incentive or opportunity exists for individuals to allocate inputs to their most productive use. Even though governments have tried to use bonuses to stimulate production, wages have tended to be divorced from individual effort and productivity. As a result, centralized socialism tends to be highly inefficient, generating little **intensive growth** (increase in output per unit of input). Nevertheless, for a country possessing significant natural resources that can insulate itself from the rest of the world (as did the former Soviet Union), centralized socialism can unleash impressive industrial growth—at least for some period of time.

The demise of the Soviet system primarily resulted from its inability to provide increasing living standards and a freer society. The inefficiencies of the Soviet model, manifested in shortages, poor-quality products, and stagnant consumption levels finally became too burdensome. With the rise to power of Mikhail Gorbachev, a leader who recognized the serious problems of his country, greater political openness and criticism came to exist. Support for the old system crumbled, and the Soviet Union fragmented in 1991.

In addition to the Soviet Union and China, other countries that have used the centralized socialist system include North Korea, Cuba, and the Eastern European countries of Albania, Bulgaria, the former Czechoslovakia, the Democratic Republic of Germany (East Germany), Hungary, Poland, and Romania. Hungary and Poland had introduced economic and political reforms in their countries prior to the breakdown of centralized socialism in the late 1980s. In the mid-1990s only North Korea and Cuba still cling to a Soviet-style command economy. Finally, many African countries pursued, at different times, a mixed socialist economy with significant nationalization, state planning, and direct resource allocation. In the African cases, the limited economic and planning expertise and the absence of a true commitment to national development rendered the centralized model ineffective in generating economic growth.

The transition of economies from centralized socialism to a more market-oriented capitalist system is a major challenge for the nations of the former Soviet bloc. We discuss economic transition in Chapter 17, where we focus on the economies of Eastern Europe. Moreover, many developing countries, particularly those in Africa, are trying to introduce more market elements into their economies.

The four primary issues in the transition of economies are (1) the privatization of previously nationalized assets, such as land and factories; (2) the establishment of property rights with an independent judicial system to enforce these rights; (3) the freeing of controlled prices; and (4) the integration of previously closed economies into world trade and finance. Different views exist concerning the appropriate speed with which economic transition should be accomplished. Rapidly decontrolled prices can impose significant hardships on fixed-income groups. Given that state-owned firms tend toward overemployment, rapid privatization can lead to significant unemployment, as assets are reorganized for profit-seeking activities. Thus, added to the contemporary challenge of economic development are the vexing issues of economic transition.

Having provided this overview of three economic systems and their philosophies for development, let us now consider specific roles for government.

## POSSIBLE ROLES FOR GOVERNMENT

The state may intervene in the economy with both microeconomic and macroeconomic policies. In the microeconomic realm, these include direct resource allocation and public production of goods and services; economic regulation; and income maintenance and redistribution. Macroeconomic policy initiatives are aimed at stabilization and international economic coordination.[9] Below we review these different options, commenting on their compatibility with the previously discussed roles for government.

### RESOURCE ALLOCATION

The state can influence the allocation of resources and the resulting output mix, either by direct production or by using subsidies (taxes) to encourage (discourage) production. Even within laissez-faire capitalism, a role exists for government production of certain goods, called pure public goods.

A **pure public good** has two distinguishing characteristics. First, one individual's consumption of the good does not diminish the potential consumption of others (nonrival consumption). Second, it is difficult or impossible to exclude nonpayers from consuming the good. National defense and lighthouses are two examples of public goods. National defense is jointly and equally consumed; moreover, it would be difficult to exclude from protection those citizens wishing not to pay their share. For such public goods, public production with compulsory taxation is appropriate, even in laissez-faire capitalism. Of contention is the level of production (i.e., the type and quantity of national defense) and the form of taxation (e.g., income taxes or sales taxes) to pay the costs of production.

Within capitalism, most goods are produced privately, with the interaction of demand (willingness to pay) and supply (marginal costs of production) determining the output mix. It should also be noted that governments enter into private markets as purchasers of goods and services. Government expenditure for goods or services will usually have some impact on the allocation of resources. For example, as the

---

[9]Reviews of the role of the state in the development process can be found in "Rethinking the State," Chapter 7 of the *World Development Report 1991*, pages 128–147; and "The Role of Government," Chapter 4 of the *World Development Report 1987,* pages 58–77.

government purchases more computers, the computer industry will draw resources from other sectors of the economy. Consumer sovereignty (including government as a consumer) will determine the exact quantities of privately produced goods.

Within managed capitalism, governments can use subsidies and taxes to guide private production toward national goals. Often, these goals are sectoral in nature or product-specific. For instance, within a managed capitalist system, input subsidies (on labor, intermediate goods, or credit) or reduced levels of corporate taxation could be provided for products destined for the export market. Coffee in El Salvador, peanuts in Senegal, or personal computers in South Korea could receive preferential treatment to encourage both domestic production and exports to generate foreign exchange.

Opportunity costs for the inputs directed toward export production exist; often, there will be reduced national production of other products, such as food crops in the cases of El Salvador and Senegal. In these instances, if imported food is not made available at reasonable prices to domestic consumers, there could be significant income distribution effects.

Finally, in those systems in which there is public ownership of the means of production, such as centralized socialism, the government will directly determine the levels of output that form the core of the economy's operating plan. In such cases, the government will also set prices for the commodities. Several potential inefficiencies are prevalent in this type of nationally directed resource allocation. First, the output mix usually does not correspond to the desires of consumers; often, insufficient quantities of consumer goods are produced, as resources are disproportionately allocated toward heavy industry. Second, the controlled prices will neither serve to clear the market nor to direct production toward those goods most desired by consumers. Often in command economies, prices are set below market-clearing levels, leading to shortages and illegal parallel (or black) markets.

## ECONOMIC REGULATION

To promote the general welfare of its citizens, even relatively laissez-faire capitalist governments may justifiably intervene to regulate economic activity. Of particular interest in developing countries is regulation aimed at correcting externalities; labor market policies aimed at promoting employment and/or higher wages; and anti-trust policies to encourage competition.

### EXTERNALITIES

For some goods a divergence can exist between the private and social benefits and costs. Firms and consumers make decisions based on private benefits and costs. In the event that benefits accrue or costs shift to other members of the society not directly involved in the consumption or production of the good, an **externality** exists. For instance, if the production of coal leads to environmental degradation or air pollution, a social cost not borne by the producing firm will result in a negative externality. In the case of basic research that has wide uses within the economy (e.g., development of transistors), social benefits not reaped by the contractor (buyer) of the research occur—a positive externality. With externalities, laissez-faire capitalism does not efficiently allocate resources, and the resulting output mix is inefficient.

With a negative externality, the private marginal cost of production of a good is less than the social marginal cost. Thus, in a competitive industry, the short-run market

### FIGURE 6.1   ILLUSTRATION OF A NEGATIVE EXTERNALITY

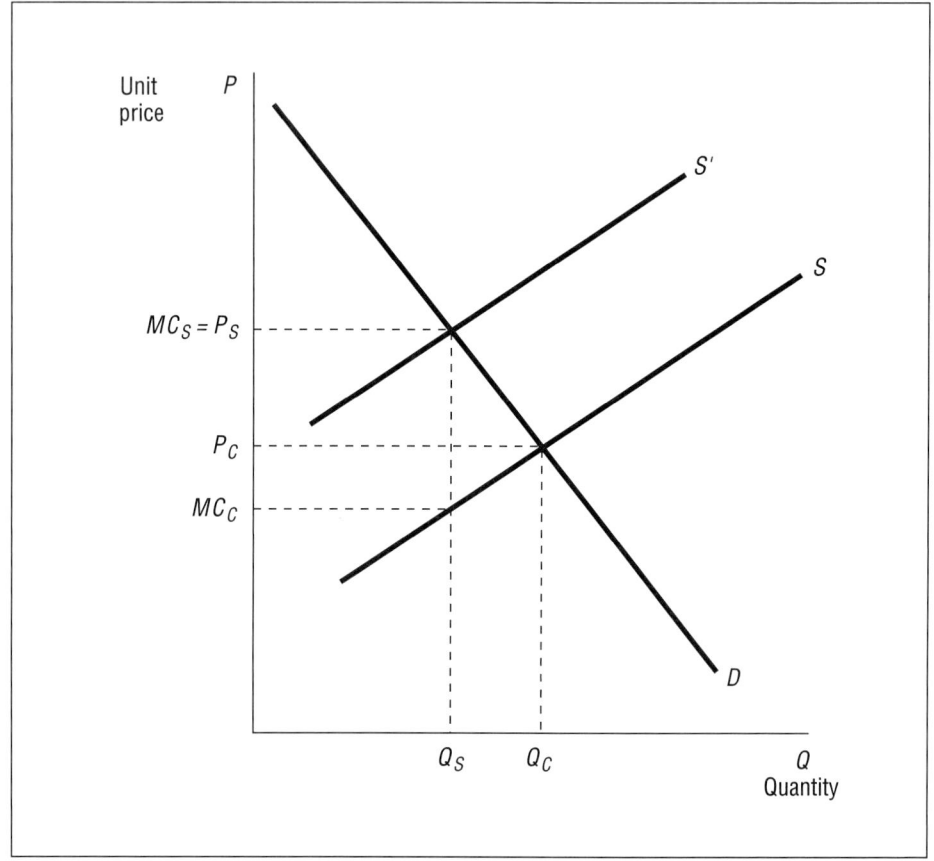

supply curve (S), the sum of the individual firms' short-run marginal cost curves, will lie below the sum of marginal cost curves that include all costs, including social costs, S' (see Figure 6.1).[10] For a given demand curve, the equilibrium price will be lower ($P_c < P_s$) and the equilibrium quantity higher ($Q_c > Q_s$) with the supply curve that contains only private costs. From an efficiency perspective, less output at a higher price should be produced—at the intersection of the supply curve with all costs (S') and the demand curve.

Remedies for a negative externality involve quantity reductions and price increases. Within a capitalist market system, a per-unit tax that raises private marginal cost ($MC_c$) to the level of social marginal cost ($MC_s$) will result in less output and a higher price, promoting economic efficiency. In Figure 6.1, a per-unit tax of ($MC_s - MC_c$) would raise the producers' marginal cost, internalizing the externality and leading to the efficient output ($Q_s$) and per-unit price ($P_s$). Within a centrally

---

[10]More precisely, within perfect competition, the short-run supply curve of the individual firm is the rising portion of its marginal cost curve above the average variable cost curve.

planned economy, however, output restrictions through the planning process, with commensurately higher product prices, would address the negative externality. In a theoretical sense, one could argue that addressing negative externalities might be easier in a planned socialist economy, which is less concerned with satisfying immediate consumer preferences. In reality, the economies of the former Soviet Union and Eastern Europe, in their zeal to industrialize and increase output, tended not to pay adequate attention to environmental problems. (See also Chapter 12 for a more detailed treatment of negative externalities.)

Developing countries that wish to increase available output for their citizens are also faced with policy decisions concerning pollution and externalities. For instance, are clean air and water luxury goods that should be pursued only after a certain level of development has been reached? Should the low-income consumers of developing countries be forced to pay higher output prices to promote a cleaner environment? Clearly, benefits and costs are associated with pollution abatement. While achieving a totally pollution-free environment would not be a cost-effective objective, unrestrained pollution will have health costs and will impose, in many cases, irreparable environmental damage that cannot be addressed in the future at a higher level of development. Moreover, air and water pollution will cross national borders, imposing costs on neighboring countries. For this reason, developed countries should be supportive, both politically and financially, of efforts to address pollution problems in the developing world. Internationally coordinated efforts such as the 1992 United Nations–sponsored Conference on Environment and Development in Rio de Janeiro can be effective vehicles to mobilize support for addressing global environmental degradation.

With a positive externality, the social benefits of a good exceed the private benefits. Basic health care such as immunizations, disease control, and sanitation projects are apt to have societal benefits beyond those accruing to direct consumers of the goods. An unregulated market will produce too little of such goods at too high a price. With a positive externality, it is appropriate to provide a subsidy that will reduce private marginal costs and increase market supply (an outward shift), leading to greater production and a lower per-unit price.

## Labor Markets

Governments may attempt to intervene in the allocation and compensation of labor. While full employment at remunerative wage levels is clearly a goal for most societies, unemployment tends to characterize market economies in both developed and developing nations. Of particular concern for developing countries is the fact that low levels of capital, coupled with less educated labor forces, result in productivity levels that do not often justify wages above subsistence. Improved health care and better education are two important means to increase labor productivity, wages, and the quality of life.

Unemployment may increase when societies attempt to raise wages above market-clearing levels or introduce reforms aimed at providing job security. Nations often consider using macroeconomic policy to target the aggregate level of employment (and resulting unemployment). We shall discuss the limitations of using macro policy to reduce unemployment in Chapter 9.

In the model of centralized socialism, full employment usually exists, as labor is allocated through the planning apparatus to firms. Unemployed labor will always be assigned to some firm. The primary goal for a firm is to meet its production quota; and, as long as the marginal product of labor is positive, an additional unit of labor will increase output. With this process, however, labor is not necessarily allocated most efficiently. In some sectors, the marginal productivity of the assigned labor will be less than its marginal cost or wage. Other areas of the economy may experience labor shortages. Thus, in the centralized socialist model, the efficiency of the allocation of labor and worker motivation are issues of concern.

## INCOME MAINTENANCE AND REDISTRIBUTION

While a truly laissez-faire capitalist system is neither apt to recognize any right to a minimum living standard (or claim to basic needs) nor promote income redistribution, most nations consider economic equity as a legitimate concern for government. Since equity, or fairness, is really a value judgment, no universally accepted standard exists that can be applied in determining the optimal degree of income inequality. The pursuit of equity can include providing a minimum level of income for each citizen, ensuring basic needs such as food, education, and health care; and limiting income differentials through progressive income taxation with transfers to lower-income individuals.

Measures to provide minimum income levels are defended on moral and humanistic grounds. Additionally, positive economic impacts can result from income maintenance. A better educated and healthier citizenry will provide a more productive labor force, increasing real output. Finally, reducing income inequalities can lead to reduced levels of crime, resentment, and social discord—the negative externalities of significant income inequality and alienation.

Arguments exist, however, against redistribution. From the perspective of laissez-faire capitalism, the forcible taxing of income to transfer to others is considered a form of unjust confiscation. While supporting some degree of income redistribution, most neoclassical economists caution against the inefficiencies that tend to accompany tax and transfer schemes. First, those taxed will receive a lower after-tax (or take-home) pay; economic theory suggests that a lower wage is accompanied by reduced work effort. Also, those who receive a transfer are apt to reduce work effort. Income redistribution can lead to a reduction in the aggregate level of investment, as high-income individuals with high marginal propensities to save are taxed, with funds transferred to poorer individuals with higher marginal propensities to consume.

Programs aimed at reducing the price per unit of basic commodities have been used in many developing countries. Using food aid to supplement the domestic food supply can lower food prices, a benefit for the poor consumer. However, the lower price of food can reduce incentives for local farmers to produce food, lowering their incomes and increasing the country's dependency on imports of food. Price controls below the market-clearing price for basic needs such as food will lead to shortages and disincentives for production.

The society or nation must assess the benefits and costs of income redistribution, attempting to implement tax and transfer schemes consistent with the collective judgment of a socially desirable distribution of income. Income redistribution is an issue typically found in a managed capitalist system, such as Sri Lanka or Israel. Within laissez-faire market capitalism, redistribution is not sympathetically considered; however, providing basic needs like education and health care might be advanced as productivity-augmenting, human capital investments. For many developing countries, the budgetary costs of education and health care can be a major constraint.

Yet, international development assistance can effectively contribute to providing for these basic needs.

Within centralized socialism, a societal commitment to meeting the basic needs for all citizens has normally existed. In the absence of personal property or capital income, usually income differentials were less than in capitalist societies. Often the state provided all citizens with free medical care and education. Frequently, to keep prices low, basic consumer goods were rationed (either formally with ration coupons or effectively through waiting in lines) at below market-clearing prices. Centralized socialist societies had many efficiency concerns: motivational problems, poor-quality goods, as well as significant shortages of consumer goods. Moreover, there was considerable inequality in outcome, as politically favored bureaucrats and particularly talented individuals received access to quality goods denied the general public.

In conclusion, it is not obvious how best to promote an equitable society. Some equity in opportunity and in outcome (income or basic needs) needs to be present. Given the inefficiencies that can be associated with well-meaning tax and transfer schemes, implementing such a goal is a significant challenge for any government.

## MACROECONOMIC STABILITY

Within primarily capitalist countries, economists are in considerable disagreement over the appropriate policies to promote macroeconomic stability, usually defined as low levels of unemployment and inflation with healthy economic growth. Classical and neoclassical economists argue that an economy with competitive markets and little government intervention will tend toward full employment with price stability. Keynesians have argued that with deficient aggregate demand, the economy can be mired in a macro-equilibrium with high unemployment; activist Keynesians then argue that fiscal and monetary policy can be used to stimulate aggregate demand, promoting employment. Keynesian policies to stimulate the economy and to promote employment can have short-run political appeal. They include tax cuts, government expenditure increases, and expansionary monetary policy. The persistent use of these policies, however, can lead to government budget deficits and escalating inflation. With high levels of public indebtedness and weak credit ratings, developing countries find it difficult to sell new bonds to finance government deficits. Rather, they are apt to borrow from their central banks, directly increasing the money supply and the rate of inflation. As we shall discuss in Chapter 9, expansionary economic policy has serious limitations as a stimulus to aggregate employment creation. For these reasons, many international development agencies have been encouraging developing countries to have a less expansionary fiscal and monetary policy mix and, instead, to pursue policies that will reduce their fiscal deficits and lower their rates of inflation.

Within a centrally planned socialist economy, macroeconomic stability is a less crucial issue. Full employment is normally assured through the assigning of labor to firms requesting additional labor. Since the firm's overall profitability is not usually an indicator of success, firms will continue to demand labor even when the marginal revenue product of labor is less than the wage rate. As previously discussed, this type of planned labor allocation can lead to serious labor market inefficiencies. Price stability can be achieved by fiat, as controlled prices can eliminate inflation as an explicit problem. Repressed inflation, however, will be manifested in product shortages, poor-quality products, and parallel markets (often illegal) with transactions at prices above controlled levels.

## POLICY COORDINATION

In the broadest sense, the role of the government is to coordinate policies. Even in laissez-faire capitalism, the government must define and defend property rights, while promoting competitive markets. Clearly, in more managed capitalism, the government assumes additional roles, directing resources when certain sectors or industries are favored, promoting employment, and redistributing income. In centralized socialism, the annual plan for the economy becomes the tool of coordination. Consistent with the nation's development objectives, the plan sets sectoral outputs, input allocations, and both input and output prices.

An additional coordinating role that the government has assumed in developing countries is that of interacting with international development agencies. Many developing countries are receiving grants or concessionary loans directly from other countries (bilateral aid) or from international agencies like the World Bank and the United Nations (multilateral aid). Donors almost always provide policy guidance to developing countries; and, frequently, donors try to negotiate formal conditions for the continued disbursement of development assistance. The Structural Adjustment Agreements (SAA) of the World Bank, a relatively formal covenant with the developing country, provide an example of conditionality. An SAA can include a range of economic policy variables, such as the exchange rate, trade barriers, taxes and government expenditures, labor market regulations, and product market pricing.[11] Negotiating SAAs can be a very complicated and time-consuming task for governments; the subsequent monitoring of compliance with the SAA requires additional resources.

Developing nations need to coordinate the advice and policy agreements that different donors are proposing. Otherwise, the government may find it difficult to maintain a coherent development strategy. For instance, one donor's suggestion to provide a social safety net for the very poor can conflict with another donor's insistence that the national budget deficit be reduced. Or, suggesting that import tariffs be introduced to limit imports of consumption items and to raise government funds can conflict with the idea that the economy should be more open, subject to more international competition. A potentially effective means for promoting coordination is the donor council that meets with important local government officials to discuss development strategies and the ways in which international assistance can support a coherent strategy. Some developing countries have become wary of such groups and the potential loss of autonomy when such a coordinated effort by donors occurs. (Official development assistance will be discussed in more detail in Chapter 16.) Given the importance of development assistance for some countries, particularly those in Africa, a significant reduction in national sovereignty can result when donors coordinate.

Within both developed and developing nations, discussion continues as to the level of government (national, state, or local) that should be responsible for public-sector activities. In recent years, many developed countries have opted for a policy of **devolution,** in which a function of government is transferred from the national to a more local level, presumably promoting greater efficiency and accountability. In developing

---

[11]Joan Nelson has introduced the idea that economic reform can be viewed as a continuum from stabilization or demand-side policies (shorter term) to structural adjustment or supply-side policies (longer term). See Nelson, page 984.

countries, this process is often hindered by the lack of trained personnel at local levels of government. Thus, in many developing countries, a large proportion of public-sector activity is centralized at the state level, within the capital city.

## THE CHOICE OF AN ECONOMIC SYSTEM

Is there an optimal political-economic system that will best promote economic development? What degree of income inequality is most conducive to economic growth? Finally, what are the obstacles that countries face in implementing an ideal system?

With the demise of the Soviet Union and the transition of the former Soviet-bloc countries toward market capitalism, greater consensus now exists among economists that an economic system with the following characteristics will provide conditions that are conducive to economic growth: secure property rights; appropriate incentives; competitive markets and prices; openness to foreign trade; relatively low budget deficits; and moderate money supply growth.[12] In this sense, market capitalism may be the best economic system. Yet, as discussed in this chapter, variants to capitalism exist, primarily differentiated by the role of government. As Partha Dasgupta says, each society must find "the right mix of government, market, community, and household activities."[13]

While economists may agree that the characteristics of market capitalism are conducive to economic growth, the role of democracy in promoting growth is less clear. With democracy, elections provide for orderly changes in government. Democracy also enhances the participation of various groups in national decision making, leading to more consensus and possibly greater economic growth. It is that very participation, however, that can lead to special interest groups' receiving favorable political and economic treatment that can be costly to growth. Alberto Alesina and Roberto Perotti state "there seems to be no obvious correlation between democracy and growth."[14]

Empirical results are consistent with this observation. Some dictatorships have better records of economic growth than do democracies, and some have worse records. Alesina and Perotti do find that political instability, as measured by the collapse and total change of government, regardless of the type of political system, reduces incentives to save and invest, lowering economic growth.[15] For example, nations in political transition, such as Russia and the countries of Eastern Europe, might initially experience economic downturns as new forms of government emerge.

---

[12]Two recent analyses that support the positive contributions of property rights, free markets, and open economies to economic growth are Robert Barro, "Democracy: A Recipe for Growth?" *Wall Street Journal* (December 1, 1994), page A-18; and Kim Holmes, "In Search of Free Markets," *Wall Street Journal* (December 12, 1994), page A-14.

[13]Partha Dasgupta, *An Inquiry into Well-Being and Destitution,* Oxford, UK: Clarendon Press, 1995, page 26.

[14]Alberto Alesina and Roberto Perotti, "The Political Economy of Growth: A Critical Survey of the Recent Literature," *The World Bank Economic Review,* vol. 8, no. 3 (September 1994), page 353.

[15]Ibid., pages 355–359.

The issue of an optimal degree of income inequality is also debated. With higher-income individuals saving a greater proportion of their income, income inequality often has been seen as conducive to greater investment and income growth. Yet Alesina and Perotti summarize several arguments which suggest that greater income equality may be associated with stronger economic growth.[16] Lower- and middle-income groups who have more purchasing power will help boost consumer demand and stimulate economic activity. Also, with imperfect capital markets in many developing countries, individuals must use their own resources to finance their education. In a society with significant income inequality, education will then be limited to a smaller number of people. The resulting reduced level of human capital will negatively affect productivity and national income. Finally, a political linkage may exist between income inequality and economic performance. With significant income inequality, the lower-income majority will favor high income taxes that fall disproportionately on the wealthy, resulting in a decreased incentive to save and invest. According to Alesina and Perotti, a survey of empirical studies shows "evidence that initial income inequality and subsequent growth are inversely related."[17]

The above discussion has suggested that market capitalism, limited inequality, and political stability are all conducive to promoting economic growth. In reality, the process of moving to a political-economic system with these attributes is complicated by the fact that when introducing significant changes, policymakers must constantly confront trade-offs among worthy objectives. For instance, in providing for basic needs—a strategy that will reduce income inequality and set the stage for future growth—near-term costs may result, such as reduced incentives to work and earn income, both for those being taxed and those receiving transfers. Moreover, the role of the government and the size of the budget deficit may increase. Or, in promoting a more open economy with lower tariffs and increased imports, domestic producers may no longer be competitive. Labor in contracting sectors may face some unemployment until they find work in expanding industries. Thus, each country must confront trade-offs among policy objectives as it designs the policies that will characterize its economic system.

In reality, the design of these policies may be further constrained, at least for some period of time, by the country's level of economic development, its history, and its culture. In commenting on the role of government within the economic system, Dasgupta states

> It isn't possible to comment on how extensive a government's actual reach should be if we don't know something of the wealth of the country and its distribution, the reliability of its administrative capability, the motivation of the political authorities, and the performance of its markets and of existing patterns of communal security provided through the family, the village, the temple or mosque or church, whatever.[18]

Many of the differences referred to by Dasgupta seem to exist among the developing countries. For instance, are Asian societies, by nature, thriftier than other countries? Is there a stronger individual work effort and appreciation for education within those societies? In such cases pro-growth policies that stress human and physical capital

---

[16]Ibid., pages 359–361.
[17]Ibid., page 364.
[18]Dasgupta, page 26.

formation may have more rapid and higher returns. In a country such as Russia, characterized by centuries of autocratic rule by Tsars followed by nearly 75 years of Communist rule, can orderly decentralized economic and political decision making be quickly adopted? Serfs under the Tsars and workers under communism were provided with many basic needs. How quickly can a population be expected to live without the economic security that had been provided to the generations of the past? Some feel that African village society is strongly influenced by the promoting of the collective good and the rapid sharing of any surplus with those in financial need. In this case, encouraging the private accumulation of savings through financial intermediaries must be approached carefully and in ways that may differ from successful savings initiatives in Asia.

Economists cannot agree on the actual impacts that culture has on the latitude of policy design or on the actual economic performance within a country. We can recognize that some policies and changes may simply be outside the opportunity set for a country at a particular moment of time. We can also acknowledge that some policies that work well in one developing country may not produce the same result in another developing country. Addressing these issues is yet another of the challenges facing government policymakers.

## CONCLUDING NOTE

In this chapter we reviewed the range of political-economic approaches to foster economic development. While precise suggestions for the role of government in promoting growth and development are highly situation-specific, we can advance a few general conclusions. First, the role of government is related to the economic system that characterizes the nation. The role of government tends to be clearer and more concretely defined in the polar cases of laissez-faire capitalism and centralized socialism. However, few contemporary developing countries have such pure economic systems. Most countries pursue some form of managed capitalism, frequently with a dose of public ownership of some means of production. Second, no consensus exists on the type and degree of government intervention that will optimally promote economic development. Some guiding principles, however, seem to emerge from research on this issue.

The degree of commitment that the government brings to any policy action will influence its success. For example, the resoluteness of the South Korean government in promoting key sectors has a beneficial impact; in contrast, many African states have not always been faithful to policy commitments, particularly those involving reforms, such as limiting government expenditures and public-sector employment to reduce fiscal deficits. Insulating the government from special-interest groups that wish to subvert certain policies seems to be a key to consistently pursuing a policy goal. Respecting the culture and the history of a people can also mean the difference between a successful and an unsuccessful policy initiative.

The issue of quality versus quantity of government intervention is most relevant. Pursuing a few policy objectives may be more effective than advancing a less focused, broader agenda. Limited government resources, both human and financial, require the identification of a truly manageable set of government interventions; this set may well be relatively modest at first. Finally, external support, such as funding for health and education initiatives, appropriate food aid, environmental programs, budgetary support, and public-sector debt relief, may be vital for governments as they strive to achieve sound developmental objectives. We now turn to three case studies illustrating government intervention, commenting on the successes and failures of each. Finally, we should keep in mind Mrinal Datta-Chaudhuri's challenge: "The important question for developing societies is how to develop a mutually supportive structure of market and non-market institutions, which is well-suited to promote economic development."[19]

## SUMMARY OF MAIN POINTS

1. The actions and policies of the government of a developing country have significant effects on the direction and pace of economic growth and development.
2. Countries tend to be characterized by their reliance on one of three economic systems: laissez-faire capitalism, managed capitalism, and centralized, command socialism.
3. Within laissez-faire capitalism, individual households and firms, in pursuing their self-interest, make purchases and sales that allocate available inputs and determine outputs within competitive markets. There is little role for the government in laissez-faire capitalism. Proponents cite the efficiency of market capitalism. Critics, however, point to the potential for a concentration of economic power (e.g., monopoly) and income inequality.
4. A system of managed capitalism combines a market orientation with national development objectives promoted by state policy. Such objectives could include greater investment, the provision of basic needs, or an industrial policy aimed at promoting certain industries.
5. The Soviet model of command socialism was developed in the early 1930s and persisted until the demise of the Soviet Union in 1991. Given the rigidity and totalitarian nature of command socialism, this model has little appeal for contemporary developing countries.
6. Even in market capitalism, a role exists for governments in allocating resources. For example, pure public goods, such as national defense, are best produced by government and funded through general tax revenues.
7. Governments often promote competition with anti-trust laws and regulate product quality, wages, and working conditions. When externalities exist, governments may intervene to reduce (increase) market output when there is a negative (positive) externality.
8. To reduce poverty and income inequality, governments redistribute income from the wealthy to the poor. This role of government is particularly contentious, since no absolute standard exists for measuring equity and the optimal degree of income redistribution.

---

[19]Mrinal Datta-Chaudhuri, "Market Failure and Government Failure," *Journal of Economic Perspectives*, vol. 4, no. 3 (summer 1990), page 38.

9. Macroeconomic stability, defined to include low unemployment and a stable price level, is a legitimate objective for an economy. Within a market system, various macroeconomic schools differ in their advocacy of policies to promote stability.
10. An important role for government in the development process is to promote policy coordination. Third World countries can ill afford to mismanage their resources and need to have efficient governments to coordinate development efforts.
11. Economists tend to agree that secure property rights, competitive output and input markets, political stability, and modest income inequality are all conducive to economic growth.
12. To some degree, governments have a choice in their economic and political systems, as well as the degree of income inequality that prevails. Implementing these choices, however, is complicated by trade-offs between worthy development objectives and the cultural and historical setting of the country.

## KEY TERMS

centralized socialism
devolution
dirigism
extensive growth
externality
infant industries
intensive growth
laissez-faire capitalism
managed capitalism
pure public good

## QUESTIONS

1. In the absence of any governmental activity within market capitalism, discuss whether increased economic growth could be expected. Discuss whether the promotion of economic development would be enhanced without government activity.
2. As vehicles for economic development, managed capitalism and centralized socialism can be used to direct economic resources. Compare these two approaches.
3. Discuss whether the optimal role of government is likely to vary at different stages of the development process.
4. Why might the government of a developing country have difficulty in promoting policies and programs aimed at improving health and educational status?
5. From the three case studies that follow, do you see any common themes concerning the "optimal" role for government in the development process? Are there any lessons for limiting the government's role in economic development? Discuss.

## SUGGESTED READINGS

Alesina, Alberto and Roberto Perotti, "The Political Economy of Growth: A Critical Survey of the Recent Literature," *The World Bank Economic Review*, vol. 8, no. 3 (September 1994), pages 351–371.

Bardhan, Pranab, "Symposium on the State and Economic Development," *Journal of Economic Perspectives*, vol. 4, no. 3 (summer 1990), pages 3–7.

Dasgupta, Partha, *An Inquiry into Well-Being and Destitution*, Oxford, UK: Clarendon Press, 1995, Chapter 2.

Datta-Chaudhuri, Mrinal, "Market Failure and Government Failure," *Journal of Economic Perspectives*, vol. 4, no. 3 (summer 1990), pages 25–39.

Gregory, Paul R. and Robert C. Stuart, *Comparative Economic Systems*, 5th ed., Boston: Houghton Mifflin, 1995, Chapters 1–4.

Krueger, Anne O., "Government Failures in Development," *Journal of Economic Perspectives*, vol. 4, no. 3 (summer 1990), pages 9–23.

Nelson, Joan M., "The Political Economy of Stabilization: Commitment, Capacity, and Public Response," *World Development*, vol. 12, no. 10 (1984), pages 983–1006.

Westphal, Larry E., "Industrial Policy in an Export-Propelled Economy: Lessons from South Korea's Experience," *Journal of Economic Perspectives*, vol. 4, no. 3 (summer 1990), pages 41–59.

World Bank, "The Role of Government," *World Development Report 1987*, New York: Oxford University Press, 1987, Chapter 4.

World Bank, "Rethinking the State," *World Development Report 1991*, New York: Oxford University Press, 1991, Chapter 7.

World Bank, "The Roles of the Government and the Market in Health," *World Development Report 1993*, New York: Oxford University Press, 1993, Chapter 3.

## CASE STUDIES

We have chosen three case studies that show different experiences and philosophies associated with government direction of a developing economy. China provides a useful example of an economy that has been in transition for 40 years, from centralized socialism to aggressive market reform. Ghana provides an example of the challenge of development in Africa, where, for many nations, the enthusiasm of national independence has not translated into sustained economic development. Finally, Brazil is an example of managed capitalism with a strong emphasis on economic growth to the detriment of some other aspects of economic development.

### CHINA

The Chinese empire dates to the Qin dynasty (221–207 B.C.), when various feudal states were placed under central control.[1] The dynasty system survived until the twentieth century. The modern history of China begins in 1911 with the establishment of a republic under the leadership of Sun Yat-sen and his Nationalist (Guomindang) Party. In the early 1920s a communist party was formed, and by the early 1930s, Mao Zedong became the leader of this party. Following Sun Yat-sen's death in 1925, the country was unified under a new leader, Chiang Kai-shek. The national government then began an aggressive campaign against the communists. The fighting, however, was interrupted by the Japanese invasion of China in 1937. The communists then retreated to the north of China with their "Long March" and remained there until the end of World War II in 1945. At that time, civil war between the Nationalist forces of Chiang Kai-shek and Mao's communists resumed. In 1949 the communists, having driven the Nationalist forces to the island of Taiwan, established the People's Republic of China.

---

[1] A helpful reference for the economic history of China is Chapter 16 of *Comparative Economic Systems*, by H. Stephen Gardner, Chicago: The Dryden Press, 1988, pages 363–387.

In the early years, 1949 to 1957, Mao, with Soviet advisors and assistance, introduced central planning and other features of centralized socialism within the industrial sector. Unlike the Soviet Union, the Chinese did not introduce large-scale collective agriculture on a widespread basis. The government confiscated land from large landholders and redistributed much of this land as small holdings to peasants. Additionally, the government began a program of social reform stressing education, health care, and equality for women. During this time, GNP per capita nearly doubled.

With the Great Leap Forward (1958–1960), Chairman Mao encouraged a movement away from the centralized Soviet model. During this period the Soviets, disagreeing with Mao's policies, withdrew their aid and advisors. Mao's "leftist" scheme was aimed at developing the "communist" citizen and encouraging sacrifice for the country. The government paid particular attention to the promotion of small-scale industry and the improvement of rural living conditions. A system of people's communes with a hierarchical division of each commune into brigades, teams, and households was introduced. This effort led to more collective decision making in the rural areas. Generally speaking, however, the Great Leap Forward was an economic failure, with an estimated average annual rate of decrease in GNP of 10 to 20 percent. On the positive side, the departure of the Soviets and the attention to rural development may have paved the way for the more meaningful economic reforms begun in the late 1970s.

The 1961–1976 period was one of significant policy shifts. The early 1960s saw a return to a more centrally directed economy with greater emphasis on planning. The ideological fervor of the Great Leap Forward was replaced with a more practical commitment to economic growth. The government began its campaign to reduce population growth by introducing various disincentives to family size. By 1964 the economy had returned to its pre-Great Leap Forward output. Political and economic inequality, however, began to appear. Bureaucrats and enterprise leaders gained in economic and political influence.

The least-well-understood period in modern Chinese history is the Cultural Revolution of 1966 to 1976. Seemingly the aims of the Cultural Revolution were ideological, reducing the power of the industrial bureaucrats; expunging both Western and traditional Chinese influences; and instilling a socialist consciousness in the population.[2] The campaign against the bourgeoisie led to the banishment of elites to the countryside for forced re-education; a closing of the society to Westerners; and the reversing of the established order (for example, the students became the teachers of the professors). Mao was near death when the Cultural Revolution finally ended. By 1980 economic reform had begun and a "re-educated" Deng Xiaoping emerged as the most powerful Chinese leader.

Under Deng Xiaoping sweeping economic reforms were introduced, first in the rural sector (1979–1984), and then in the urban industrial sectors (1984 to the present).[3] The commune system was broken up and individual households farmed their own land under a "household contract responsibility system." Farmers' output above a state quota could be sold for profit at market-clearing prices. Agricultural output doubled between 1979 and 1984. Concurrently, small-scale, collectively-owned enterprises, operating outside of the system of central planning, were encouraged. By 1991 these enterprises employed nearly 25 percent of the labor force.

---

[2]Gardner, page 372.
[3]United Nations Development Programme, *Human Development Report 1993*, "Liberalization Study: China," page 56.

In the second round of economic reforms, after 1984, the government encouraged private-sector, urban development. Private foreign direct investment led to joint ventures. International trade has steadily increased. From 1980 to 1993, the average annual growth of GDP has been a remarkable 9.3 percent; the industrial sector has grown at an annual average rate of 11.5 percent during this time period.[4] With population growth averaging approximately one percent per year, per capita GDP has grown at an annual rate of 8.2 percent.[5] With such economic growth, living standards in China have steadily increased. The 1993 per capita GNP is estimated at $490; however, when the purchasing power of that income is considered, the estimate rises to $2330 (in international dollars).[6] (See Chapter 1 for an explanation of the purchasing power parity estimates of GNP.)

Inequality, however, has been accentuated with market reform. Both within regions and across regions, greater variance now exists in income levels. Successful businesspeople have emerged at the top of the income scale; residents in the coastal regions have tended to do better than those in the interior of China. Moreover, housing and health care, two basic needs previously provided by the government at heavily subsidized prices, are either being privatized or priced closer to average cost to reduce government outlays. Thus, inequality in living standards is increasing at a rate that is disturbing to those who feel that relative equality had been an important achievement of the Chinese system.

The privatizing of large state enterprises has continued to be a problem for the Chinese. The output of many of these large, inefficient factories is not economically competitive with the production from new private firms or with imported products. Thus, many of these firms are being subsidized by the government to avoid large layoffs and resulting unemployment. With the rapid growth of the private sector, the share of GDP accounted for by these state firms is steadily decreasing.

By most accounts, China's economic reform program has been remarkably successful as the government has led a transition from centralized socialism toward a system with many capitalist features. Dwight Perkins concludes:

> China has gone a long way toward a market system, especially in agriculture, foreign trade, and small-scale firms. Most of the problems that stand between a partially reformed Chinese economy of the early 1990s and a full market system reside in the large-scale enterprise sector, and in the partial nature of the reform of the banking system.[7]

Despite success in economic reform, five primary areas of concern, however, have yet to be satisfactorily addressed. First, as stated, the slow pace of reform in the banking sector, both with the central bank and with burgeoning commercial banks, has led to excessive monetary growth and high inflation. Second, there has been insufficient attention to the pollution problems that have accompanied the rapid growth. Third, income inequality, both within and across regions, is a concern in a society that had

---

[4]World Bank, *World Development Report 1995*, Tables 1 and 2.
[5]Ibid., Table 1.
[6]Ibid., Tables 1 and 30.
[7]Dwight Perkins, "Completing China's Move to the Market," *Journal of Economic Perspectives*, vol. 8, no. 2 (spring 1994), page 43. See the same volume for other recent articles on Chinese reform: "Symposia, China," pages 23–92. Also, see "China's Reforms: Structural and Welfare Aspects," a series of articles in *American Economic Review*, vol. 84, no. 2 (May 1994), pages 266–284.

previously stressed egalitarianism. Fourth, population growth in this country with over one billion people remains an important issue. Finally, the government has not concurrently introduced political reforms aimed at promoting a multiparty democracy. China still operates as a one-party dictatorship, albeit one that has dramatically changed the course of its economic policy over the last 15 years.

## GHANA

Ghana, a former British colony, became an independent nation on March 6, 1957.[1] The country's name originates with the ancient West African kingdom of Ghana, situated northwest of present-day Ghana. The current territory of Ghana is a combination of the British colonies of the Gold Coast and Ashanti, as well as British Togoland. The area has been settled since the third or fourth century.

Until about 1600 most of West Africa was directly or indirectly controlled by a series of Sudanic empires to the north of Ghana. Sudanese traders extended their activities to the Gold Coast as early as the thirteenth century, thereby contributing to the development of this area. Exports from the Gold Coast to the Sudan consisted primarily of gold and kola nuts.

In 1471 the Portuguese reached the Gold Coast and established a monopoly on the export of gold to Europe. By 1700, however, the French, the Dutch, and the English had joined the Portuguese and were each profitably exporting gold and slaves from the Gold Coast. Following the outlawing of the slave trade in the early part of the nineteenthth century, the European powers, with the exception of the British, gradually lost interest in this part of Africa. In 1874 the British declared the Gold Coast a British colony.

The colony advanced economically with the export of cocoa and forest products. After 1925 the British gave Africans some limited representation in the colonial legislative councils. The colonial government, however, retained all significant political powers. Following agitation and riots in 1948, Africans were given greater political rights in administering the territory. With the elections of 1951, Kwame Nkrumah and his Convention People's Party, advocating self-government, emerged as the dominant political force among the Africans and led the country to independence.

The economy of Ghana in 1957 was relatively prosperous and stable, with significant foreign exchange reserves, as a result of high world prices for cocoa. By 1966, when Nkrumah was deposed in a coup, the economy of Ghana had deteriorated and the government had considerable foreign debt. An expanding public sector, a large-scale public construction program of relatively uneconomic projects, and lower world cocoa prices all contributed to the rapid decline of Ghana's economy.

Under a series of military rulers and councils from 1966 to 1979, Ghana's economy continued to decline. Expanding military expenditures, alleged corruption, droughts, and continued low world commodity prices impoverished the economy and produced rampant inflation. In June 1979, a junior military officer, Jerry Rawlings, seized power with the pledge to fight corruption and government inefficiency. Following elections, a civilian government was in place from September of 1979 to December

---

[1] A helpful reference for the history of the Gold Coast and Ghana can be found in J. D. Fage, "Ghana," in *Encyclopedia Americana*, vol. 12, Danbury, CT: Grolier, 1990, pages 713–719.

of 1981. Then, in the midst of continued economic chaos, Rawlings again seized power. In 1983, he began an economic reform program that has continued, under his leadership, to the present.

The Rawlings Economic Recovery Program, with support from the International Monetary Fund and the World Bank, has included price liberalization; lowered import duties; currency devaluation; reform of the banking system; a new stock exchange; elimination of government subsidies; and a reformed tax structure.[2] While private-sector investment has increased modestly, entrepreneurs are still wary of the government's commitment to market capitalism. Capital markets and financial intermediaries are not well developed, leading to a scarcity of investment funds. Moreover, despite the privatization of 80 enterprises from 1987 to 1992, a significant number of firms are still nationalized, requiring large fiscal outlays from the government.

The rural sector still suffers from a lack of investment in schools, health facilities, and roads. A large number of rural inhabitants are small-scale farmers using labor-intensive methods of cultivation with resulting low per-hectare yields. These farmers are growing food crops primarily for subsistence, supplementing their earnings with some cash crops such as cocoa.

By some measures, the economy has done reasonably well in recent years, with GDP growing at an annual average rate of 3.5 percent between 1980 and 1993.[3] In contrast, the rate of output growth for all of sub-Saharan Africa was only 1.6 percent during this time.[4] An encouraging sign is that Ghanaian industrial growth averaged 4.2 percent per year from 1980 to 1993; however, the annual rate of growth of agriculture was only 1.3 percent.[5] Given the low economic base after two decades of neglect, per capita GNP is only an estimated $430 per year.[6] With population increasing at a 3.3 percent annual rate, per capita GNP has only increased at an annual average rate of .1 percent from 1980 to 1993. Yet, within sub-Saharan Africa, the change in per capita income has been –.8 percent per year over the same time period.[7]

Recent tax and expenditure changes show the incremental nature of the reform process in Ghana. During the 1992 elections, the granting of civil-servant wage increases by the Rawlings government, a politically popular move, strained the government's budget.[8] More recently, in 1994, the government imposed an unpopular value-added tax to increase state revenues and to discourage consumption. Yet, with a relatively sustained commitment to economic reform and democracy, Ghana is considered by some development experts as a success in sub-Saharan Africa.[9]

---

[2]United Nations Development Programme, *Human Development Report 1993,* "Liberalization Study: Ghana," page 58.
[3]World Bank, *World Development Report 1995,* Table 2.
[4]Ibid.
[5]Ibid.
[6]Ibid., Table 1.
[7]Ibid., Tables 1 and 30.
[8]Ajay Chhibber and Chad Leechor, "Ghana: 2000 and Beyond," *Finance and Development,* vol. 30, no. 3 (September 1993), page 25.
[9]Tim Carrington, "Amid Africa's Agony, One Nation, Ghana Shows Modest Gains," *Wall Street Journal* (January 26, 1994), page A-1.

## BRAZIL

Brazil, the fifth largest country in the world, covers almost half of South America. Rich in mineral resources, the country has an extensive river system that provides substantial hydroelectric potential. The population was estimated at 156 million in 1994, making Brazil the world's sixth most populous nation. Nearly 47 percent of the population resides in the southeast, near the cities of São Paulo and Rio de Janeiro.[1]

Claimed as a Portuguese colony in 1500, Brazil acquired its name from its first export good. The colony abounded in brazilwood desired by Europeans for the red dye derived from its bark. Export cycles in sugar and gold stimulated Brazil's economic growth during the colonial period. Sugar cultivation was introduced in northeastern Brazil in 1520, and sugar exports grew steadily for over a century. The discovery of gold in the state now known as Minas Gerais in 1695 initiated a gold rush and a second great export boom. The gold cycle waned in the 1770s, however, with the depletion of the gold deposits.

Brazil declared its independence from Portugal in 1822. Around that time coffee consumption expanded in Europe and North America as living standards rose following the Industrial Revolution. Having produced coffee since the early 1700s, Brazil increased its output of coffee to satisfy world demand. An export boom ensued, with coffee becoming the principal force driving Brazil's economic growth.

The federal government of Brazil instituted several policies in the nineteenth century to stimulate economic development. Railroad construction was promoted by government subsidies and guaranteed rates of return to firms constructing the railroads. The state also encouraged immigration, which grew rapidly after the abolition of slavery in 1888.[2]

A spurt of manufacturing growth tied to the coffee sector began in the 1880s and continued for three decades. The railroads, power stations, and other infrastructural investments that serviced the coffee sector generated a demand for spare parts produced by local manufacturers. Moreover, the immigrant population employed in the coffee sector created a large market for inexpensive consumer goods, giving rise to light industries such as textiles, clothing, shoes, and food processing.[3]

The interruption of shipping during both World Wars and the reduced output of the industrialized nations during the Great Depression sharply curtailed Brazilian imports during these periods. Shortages of imported manufactured goods, and rising prices for these goods spurred domestic manufacturing production. In addition, during the Depression, world coffee demand fell, while Brazil's coffee output rose. To protect Brazil's economy from declining coffee prices, the federal government guaranteed minimum coffee prices by purchasing all coffee produced and destroying any that could not be sold or stored. By maintaining employment and income levels in the coffee sector and related sectors, the price-support program also maintained domestic demand for manufactured goods.[4] Agriculture, however, was still the leading growth sector of the economy.

---

[1] Werner Baer, *The Brazilian Economy: Growth and Development*, 4th ed., Westport, CT: Praeger, 1995, page 7.
[2] Ibid., pages 20–21.
[3] Ibid., page 27.
[4] Ibid., pages 36–37.

At the end of World War II, Brazil was heavily dependent on agricultural exports for its economic wellbeing. This dependence made Brazil's economy sensitive to fluctuations in the world economy. Moreover, the outlook for future growth in food and raw material markets was not favorable. Brazilian policymakers in the 1950s decided to develop the nation's manufacturing sector rapidly through a policy of import-substitution industrialization (ISI). The government used tariffs, quotas, and exchange-rate controls to establish protective barriers against many imported products. The goal was to create a large, protected market that would stimulate local investments by private domestic firms and foreign multinational corporations in the production of manufactured products that Brazil previously imported.

Since Brazil's financial markets were not well developed, the government established the National Economic Development Bank to finance projects in the industrial sector. To ease inflationary pressures and to promote industrial growth through low input prices, the government controlled prices for electricity, telecommunications, and railroad transportation. The low prices did not provide a sufficient rate of return to encourage multinational firms to remain in these sectors and to modernize their operations. As a result, state-owned companies gradually took control of the power generation, telecommunication, and railroad transportation networks.

Policymakers believed that greater productive capacity in Brazil's steel industry would foster rapid industrialization and the development of a capital goods sector. Since neither the private sector nor state governments had the financial resources to build modern steel mills, the federal government constructed such enterprises as state-owned companies. Lastly, the government prohibited foreign firms from entering certain sectors of the economy for national security reasons and to prevent foreign exploitation of important nonrenewable resources. As a result, state-owned companies came to dominate the mining, petroleum, and chemicals industries.[5] In sum, ISI transformed Brazil into a heavily managed, capitalistic economy.

The industrialization process yielded high rates of economic growth over the 1956 to 1962 period. However, it worsened an already unequal distribution of income and failed to create enough jobs for the expanding urban population. The economy stagnated from 1963 to 1967 because consumers lacked the income to purchase the high-priced manufactured goods produced by relatively inefficient firms in the protected market.[6] In sharp contrast, the 1968–1974 period is called the "Brazilian economic miracle" because record rates of growth were achieved, with increases in real GDP averaging 11.3 percent on an annual basis.[7] Factors contributing to this growth were an effective stabilization plan that brought inflation under control; large government investments in infrastructure projects and the mining and petrochemical industries; a system of tax incentives that encouraged private investment; financial sector reforms that stimulated savings; the diversification of exports; and small devaluations of the Brazilian currency on a frequent, but unpredictable, basis.

---

[5]Ibid., pages 248–249.
[6]Ibid., pages 74–75.
[7]Ibid., page 77.

A series of external and internal shocks over the 1973–1985 period followed the miracle years. At the time of the first oil price shock in 1973, Brazil satisfied 80 percent of its petroleum consumption with imports.[8] The country continued to import the non-oil inputs needed for industrial production and borrowed abroad to pay for oil imports. Economic growth continued, but Brazil's foreign debt increased substantially. A second oil price shock in 1979, coupled with domestic agricultural shortages and rising food prices, contributed to a surge in Brazil's rate of inflation in 1980. In the United States, the monetary authorities implemented a tight monetary policy that subsequently led to higher world interest rates in the early 1980s. Since Brazil had contracted most of its foreign debt on an adjustable-interest-rate basis, this interest-rate shock significantly increased the cost of both new debt and servicing outstanding debt.

From 1987 to 1993, the Brazilian economy experienced severe stagflation, with an average annual growth rate of 0.6 percent and inflation rates reaching record four-digit levels.[9] Policymakers implemented a series of "heterodox" inflation stabilization plans that temporarily froze wages, prices, and the exchange rate, while the fiscal authorities tried to reduce the government's large budget deficits. These plans failed to bring inflation under control, however. The acceleration of inflation resulted from the high degree of indexation characterizing the Brazilian economy. Formal and informal indexation mechanisms pitted different segments of the economy in a struggle to maintain their shares of national income. Producers employed markup pricing techniques to pass on any cost increases to customers. Wage earners, through their unions and in accordance with legal wage-adjustment formulas, passed on cost-of-living increases to their employers. The indexation of financial assets protected savers from any inflationary erosion of their wealth. Regular mini-devaluations of the exchange rate provided protection to exporters, while importers pressured the government for subsidies and tax credits. Even the government maintained its share in national income by increasing nominal government expenditures. The Brazilian economy became locked into an inflationary "fight for shares." No consensus existed about how national income should be distributed.[10]

Such a consensus, however, has gradually emerged in the first half of the 1990s. The force driving this consensus is the acknowledgment by policymakers that excessive state intervention in the economy has been increasingly detrimental since the mid-1970s. The response has been a continual effort to liberalize the economy and to allow national income and its distribution to be determined by a freer, more open-market economy. Consequently, since the early 1990s, a large-scale program to privatize state-owned enterprises has been underway. Trade liberalization has focused on the gradual reduction of import tariffs; the elimination of export incentive programs; and the encouragement of foreign direct investment. Lastly, the Real Plan—

---

[8]Ibid., page 89.

[9]Ibid., page 177. For a discussion and explanation of Brazil's inflation experience since 1960, see Murray S. Simpson, *The Distributive Effects of Inflation Stabilization Policies in Brazil: A CGE Modeling Approach,* Ph.D. Dissertation, University of Illinois at Urbana-Champaign, 1994, pages 6–24.

[10]For more details, see Werner Baer, "Social Aspects of Latin American Inflation," in *Latin America: The Crisis of the Eighties and the Opportunities of the Nineties,* Werner Baer, Joseph Petry, and Murray Simpson, eds. Bureau of Economic and Business Research, University of Illinois at Urbana-Champaign, 1991, pages 45–57.

an inflation stabilization program implemented in December 1993—has proven effective in bringing Brazil's chronically high rate of inflation under control.[11] Thus, in the mid-1990s, experts are hopeful that the Brazilian economy is on a more stable development path.

---

[11]The Real Plan reduced the budget deficit with an across-the-board tax increase and reductions in government expenditures. It also introduced a stable unit of account called the Unit of Real Value (URV), which exchanged for dollars on a one-to-one basis. As Brazil's currency (the *cruzeiro real*) depreciated against the dollar in line with inflation, the daily quotation of the URV in *cruzeiros reais* increased. Gradually, more and more prices began to be expressed in URVs rather than cruzeiros reais. Transactions, however, were still conducted in cruzeiros reais. On July 1, 1994, the government replaced the cruzeiro real with a new currency called the *real* that had a value of one URV, or one dollar, or 2750 cruzeiros reais. The government also instituted a tight monetary policy that raised interest rates. The combination of a new currency, that Brazilians believed would retain its purchasing power, and high interest rates, that precluded a consumption boom, successfully reduced Brazil's monthly inflation rate from 47 percent in June 1994 to 1.5 percent in September 1994. See Werner Baer, *The Brazilian Economy: Growth and Development*, 4th ed., pages 377–379, for more details about the Real Plan.

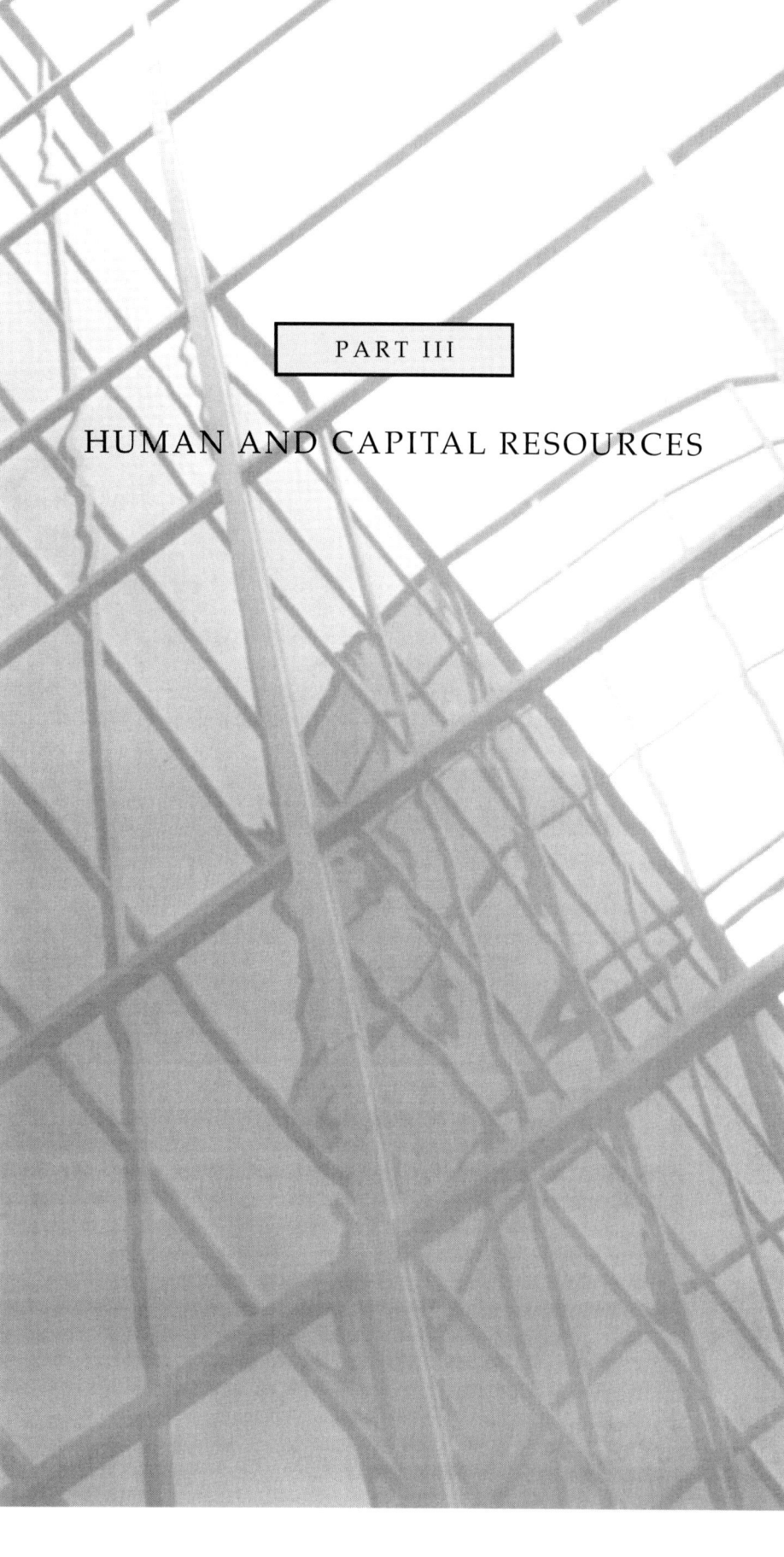

PART III

HUMAN AND CAPITAL RESOURCES

# CHAPTER 7

## POPULATION POLICY

Many biologists, who see the world as a finite system able to support finite numbers, warn that the 10 billion people who the United Nations project will live on the planet in 2050 will strain water, soil, and other resources to the breaking point, causing horrific environmental damage, widespread hunger, and global misery. Many economists counter that free markets will keep supplies of even scarce commodities in line with demand and will stimulate the search for substitutes, much as fiber optics are now replacing copper wires in communications. And science, they believe, will always come through with technological fixes like the green revolution.[1]

With few exceptions outside of Eastern Europe and the former Soviet Union, the less developed countries are experiencing significant population growth. The consequences for economic development depend not only on the rate of population increase, but on the average levels of human capital, the available technologies, and the existing ratios of natural resources and physical capital to population.

In this chapter we begin with an overview of the potentially adverse consequences of rapid population growth for low-income economies. We follow with a review of the range of positions on the relationship between population growth and economic development. Before discussing the policy options, however, we need to examine more closely the determinants of fertility behavior in less developed countries. A microeconomic model of utility-maximization offers a useful framework for explaining why the demand for children declines with economic development. An explanation for the increased motivation for fertility control that accompanies economic development is provided by Easterlin's supply–demand synthesis model. We conclude with a discussion of fertility policy options, ranging from laissez-faire to state control. The authoritarian population policy of China is profiled. In the appendix to the chapter a

---

[1]Sharon Begley, "Can More = Better?" *Newsweek* (September 12, 1994), page 27.

simultaneous model for the total fertility rate and infant mortality rate is estimated for a cross-section of less developed countries.

## POTENTIAL CONSEQUENCES OF RAPID POPULATION GROWTH IN LESS DEVELOPED COUNTRIES

As discussed in Chapter 2, the demographic transition experiences of the nations of Africa, the Middle East, Asia, and Latin America in the post–World War II era are qualitatively and quantitatively different from the earlier transitions of the nations of Western Europe and the United States. The differences reflect historical, economic, and cultural factors. We begin with the historical setting.

### HISTORICAL SETTING

For example, the rapid population growth in the United States during its demographic transition enhanced economic growth and development. Land and natural resources in America were abundant, and the increases in population encouraged investments in the economic infrastructure, especially in the railway system. Population centers grew and markets were linked, promoting gains in efficiency through greater specialization of labor. The natural increases in population (with the excess of births over deaths) were augmented by heavy inflows of migrants, primarily from Europe. Since many of the migrants were of labor-force age and possessed valuable skills, the stock of human capital grew with the population. So too, for the European nations during their demographic transitions, economic growth and development seemed to coincide with rapid population growth. In fact, during the economic depression of the 1930s, there were concerns in the industrialized nations that, with fertility near replacement levels, the low rates of population growth were contributing to the economic stagnation.[2]

In contrast, for the less developed countries of the post–World War II era, not only have the population growth rates been higher, but the economic conditions have not been as favorable. True, the LDCs experienced considerable economic growth with their population growth in the 1950s and 1960s. Impressive gains in human capital formation were also achieved—evidenced by increases in average life expectancies and higher school enrollment rates. However, even then, the common perception of the developing economies was one of surplus labor, with shortages of physical and human capital constraining further economic growth and development.

---

[2]See, for example, Alvin Hansen, "Economic Progress and Declining Population Growth," *American Economic Review*, vol. 29, no. 1 (March 1939), pages 1–15. The subsequent post–World War II baby booms in the developed nations relieved the anxieties over insufficient population growth. The rise in birth rates, however, did not last, and by the 1970s fertility rates in the United States and Europe had dropped to below replacement levels. Now there is renewed concern in Europe and Japan over the low birth rates, which eventually will not only translate into slower, even negative, growth in the population of labor-force age, but will also sharply increase the elderly burden of dependency (the ratio of the population 65 years and over to the population of ages 15 through 64).

The international economic turbulence of the 1970s (e.g., the breakdown of the international monetary system, the sharp hikes in oil prices, the subsequent inflation and soaring interest rates) contributed to external debt crises in the 1980s that, in turn, hampered the economic progress of many developing nations, especially in sub-Saharan Africa and Latin America. While in numerous countries the rates of population growth were declining, in absolute numbers the increases in populations were greater than ever. At the First International Population Conference, held in Bucharest, Romania, in 1974, the less developed countries rallied around the slogan "Economic development is the best contraceptive." By the time of the Second International Population Conference in Mexico City in 1984, however, a consensus had emerged that both economic development and family planning programs were important for lowering the high rates of fertility found in the LDCs. Thus, it was surprising and controversial that the Reagan administration downplayed family planning, arguing that the key to reducing problematic population growth was to promote private enterprise and capitalism.[3] Ten years later, the Third International Population Conference, in Cairo, Egypt, in 1994, not only re-emphasized family planning and birth control, but highlighted the importance of empowering women through education and socioeconomic mobility.[4]

Relatively few developing nations exist today that are not subject to population pressures. In some of the poorer, more densely populated nations, the pressures on the natural resource base and the overcrowding of cities have become serious. Given the poverty that helps sustain high fertility, these nations can expect continued high rates of population growth over the next few decades. Indeed, the built-up population momentum virtually guarantees substantial increases in population.

In Figure 7.1 we outline the potential consequences of rapid population growth for low-income economies. In general, the consequences will be more adverse the higher the rates of population growth and the higher the current ratios of population to natural resources and physical capital.

## THE CYCLE OF POVERTY AND RAPID POPULATION GROWTH

The combination of poverty and rapid population growth can be devastating to the environment and natural resource base of a developing economy. The ultimate constraints on agricultural production set by the finite supply of land can be exacerbated by harsh climates (e.g., extremes in temperature and precipitation) and poor land management. Where popular access is restricted by a heavy concentration of ownership (often dominated by large estates producing cash crops for export), pressure on the available supply of land is intensified. Pushed onto marginal land, peasant farmers may use fragile hillsides that, without the proper terracing, will severely erode with heavy rains, or may cut down forests to expand the land under cultivation. With the resulting deforestation, the ability of the land to hold water is diminished and soil

---

[3]See "U.S. Policy Statement for the International Conference on Population," *Population and Development Review*, vol. 10, no. 3 (September 1984), pages 574–579.

[4]The Cairo conference will also be remembered for the strong positions taken by the Vatican against birth control (especially abortion), and by some predominantly Muslim nations against the influence of Western culture on their traditional family values.

### FIGURE 7.1 — POTENTIAL EFFECTS OF RAPID POPULATION GROWTH ON LESS DEVELOPED COUNTRIES

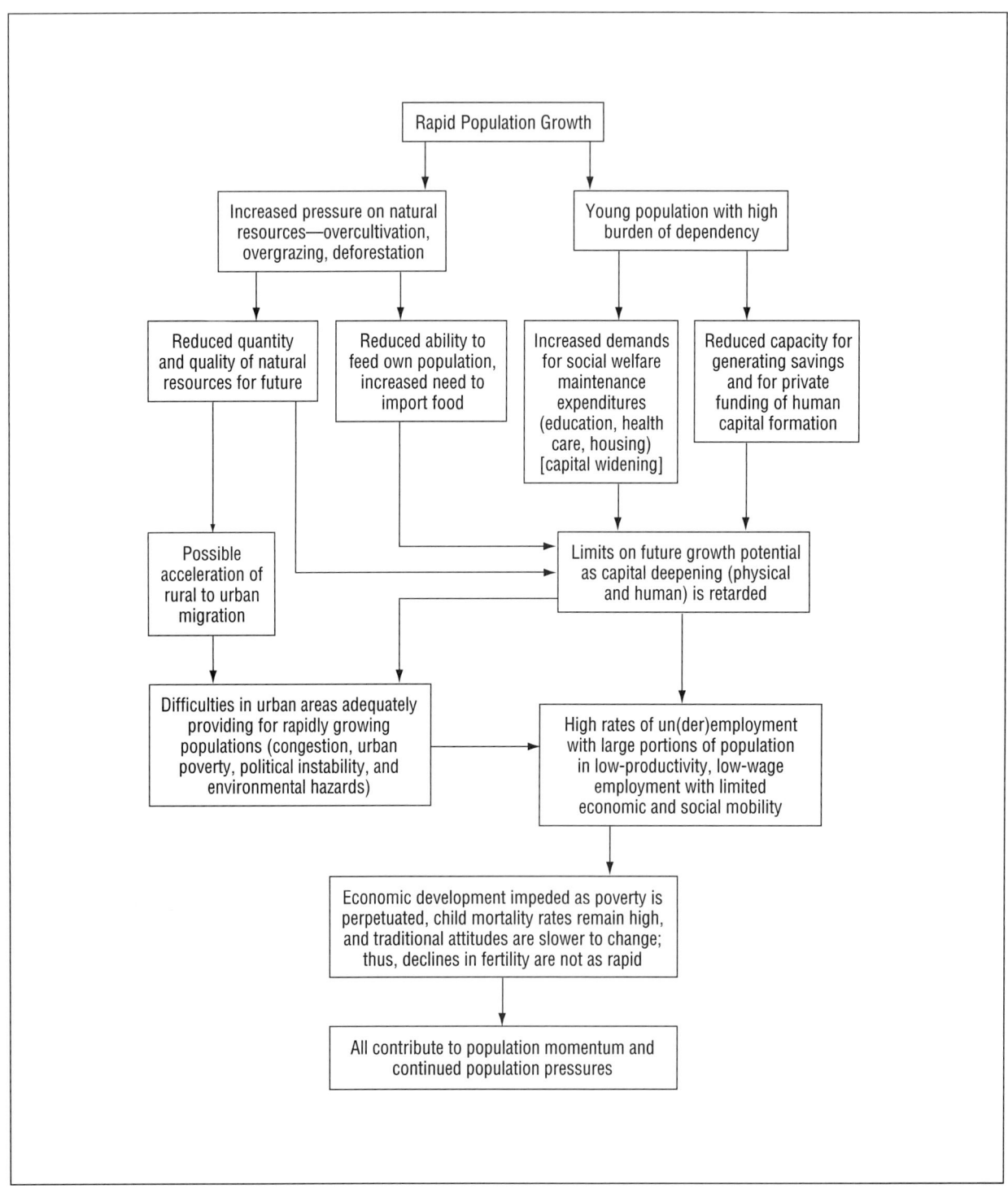

erosion is accelerated. Population pressure on forests also occurs when the poor cut down young trees for fuelwood.

> Some 2 billion people rely on fuelwood for cooking and heating, yet in many developing countries demand is far greater than supply. In many areas of Western and sub-Saharan Africa, fuelwood consumption is running 30 to 200 percent ahead of the average increase in the stock of trees.[5]

Increases in population and livestock can result in the overgrazing of pastures and desertification. With the low productivities of land, farm output and income remain low. Poor farmers do not have the resources to invest in improving the quality of the land. Moreover, without secure title to the land, they would not have the inclination to invest even if their means were sufficient. The loss of forests and mining of soils decrease the quality and quantity of the natural resource base, restricting the potential for economic growth. Sounding a note of alarm over a decade ago, the Worldwatch Institute warned:

> There is now evidence that population growth may be driving climatic change in Africa. The sheer number of people seeking to survive on arid, marginal land may be driving a self-reinforcing process of dessication, literally drying out the continent. Coming at a time of declining food output, this suggests a breakdown in the relationship between people and environmental support systems that could lead Africa into a crisis of historic dimensions—one that goes beyond short-term emergency food relief.[6]

A reduced ability to grow food domestically increases the reliance on imports. The opportunity costs of the foreign exchange used to import food would include the forgone imports of the raw materials, intermediate goods, and capital goods needed for the expansion of manufacturing. Unable to make a living off the land, small farmers join the exodus to urban areas. The cities, already congested and strained, are unable to provide for their mushrooming populations adequate housing, employment, and public services (water, electricity, sewerage, and solid waste disposal). Squatter settlements and shanty towns proliferate. The urban informal sector of low-wage, labor-intensive activities swells, offering a myriad of services and merchandise, from vendors of handicrafts and food, to day laborers, guides, street performers, and workers in sweatshops. Conditions for crime, unrest, exploitation, and pollution are ripe.

As an example, consider these *Time* magazine statistics for Mexico City in 1984—with 17 million people, the second largest city in the world at the time.

> More than 2 million of the city's people have no running water in their homes ...

---

[5] See *World Resources 1994–95: A Guide to the Global Environment,* A Report by the World Resources Institute in collaboration with the United Nations Environment Programme and the United Nations Development Programme, New York: Oxford University Press, 1994, page 33.

[6] Lester Brown, "A False Sense of Security," in *State of the World 1985,* Worldwatch Institute, New York: W.W. Norton & Company, 1985, pages 3–22. This quotation is from page 4. For more recent evidence of land degradation in Africa, see World Bank, *World Development Report 1991,* New York: Oxford University Press, 1991, page 61. In several countries, population pressure on the land has shortened fallow periods, resulting in diminished soil fertility and reduced crop yields.

More than 3 million residents have no sewage facilities ...

Mexico City produces about 14,000 tons of garbage every day but processes only 8,000. Of the rest, about half gets dumped in landfill, and half is left to rot in the open. One result: legions of rats.

Three million cars and 7,000 diesel buses, many of them old and out of repair, spew contamination into the air. So do the approximately 130,000 nearby factories that represent more than 50% of all Mexican industry. The daily total of chemical air pollution amounts to 11,000 tons. Just breathing is estimated to be equivalent to smoking two packs of cigarettes a day.[7]

Nonetheless, the population growth of Mexico City has continued at a rapid pace. Moreover, numerous other cities are found in nations poorer than Mexico, where conditions are no better, if not worse.

High fertility produces a young age structure, where 40 percent or more of the population is under 15 years of age. Consequently the demand for social welfare expenditures—education, health care, and housing—is great, while the ability to fund such expenditures is restricted by the generally low incomes. Public budgets and resources are stretched just to maintain the modest levels of per capita expenditures on education and health care, leaving little for the expansion and improvement of the economic infrastructure (i.e., the transportation system, telecommunications network, and public utilities) essential for a modern economy.

Low ratios of human and physical capital to labor translate into low labor productivities and low earnings. The lack of economic mobility perpetuates poverty. Child mortality rates remain high, and so do fertility rates—if, as Caldwell maintains, the net flow of wealth is from children to parents. Rapid population growth continues and, with the increasing size of generations, population momentum builds. To prevent such a cycle from emerging, or to stop a cycle once underway, is a primary challenge of economic development. Without significant economic development, population growth rates will probably remain high, and high rates of population growth in a low-income nation can be an obstacle to economic development.

## A RANGE OF PERSPECTIVES ON POPULATION GROWTH AND ECONOMIC DEVELOPMENT

The potentially adverse consequences of rapid population growth in a low-income economy were just highlighted. We reiterate that whether population growth is regarded as advantageous or not depends on the particular circumstances. A high rate of population growth may contribute to economic development in a natural resource–abundant nation with considerable human and physical capital formation;

---

[7]These statistics are from "A Proud Capital's Distress," by Otto Friedrich, *Time* (August 6, 1984), pages 14–15.

while in a resource-poor, low-income nation with little human and physical capital formation, the same rate of population growth may be detrimental to economic progress.

Let us now step back and sample the diversity of positions on the relationship between population growth and economic development. By *population growth* we refer to annual population growth rates between 1 and 4 percent, a range which encompasses nearly all of the developing economies, save the former socialist states of Eastern Europe and the Soviet Union.[8]

Advocates of population growth emphasize:

- The beneficial effects of efficiency through greater labor specialization and scale economies
- The increased returns to public investment in the economic infrastructure
- The boost to private investment with growing consumer demands
- The stimulus to technological progress that comes with a greater awareness of natural resource constraints
- The vitality of a youthful population, especially when succeeding generations are more educated
- Enhanced national security

In a review of the economic consequences of population growth, Allen Kelley notes

> It is in agriculture where the positive benefits of population size have been most discussed. Higher population densities can decrease per unit costs and increase the efficiency of transportation, irrigation, extension services, markets, and communications.

Kelley later adds that

> it is frequently found that institutional conditions—such as land ownership patterns, poorly developed capital markets, and government policies—restrict the exploitation of technologies embodying positive scale effects. It is probably the differences between institutional conditions that most differentiate the putative favorable historical experience with scale effects in some developed countries with the apparently less favorable experience in many Third World nations.[9]

---

[8]For the 105 low- and middle-income economies with populations of 1 million or more with data, the distributions of population growth rates are:

| Average Annual Population Growth Rate for 1980–1993 | Number of Countries |
|---|---|
| Under 0% | 1 (Hungary) |
| 0% through 1% | 21 (15 are former socialist states of Eastern Europe and the Soviet Union) |
| Over 1% through 2% | 21 |
| Over 2% through 3% | 46 |
| Over 3% through 4% | 13 |
| Over 4% | 3 (Jordan, Oman, Saudi Arabia) |

The tabulations are from World Bank, *World Development Report 1995,* New York: Oxford University Press, 1995, Table 25.

[9]See Allen Kelley, "Economic Consequences of Population Change in the Third World," *Journal of Economic Literature,* vol. 26, no. 4 (December 1988), pages 1685–1728. These quotations are from pages 1703 and 1704 respectively.

On opposite sides are the Marxist and free market ideologies. According to Marxists, with the correct economic and political system in place, overpopulation and surplus labor would not be a problem. Capitalism exploits labor and requires a large industrial reserve army of the unemployed. Under socialism, workers would no longer be oppressed, and society would adequately provide for the needs of the population.

In contrast is the argument advanced by the Reagan administration at the Second International Conference on Population in Mexico City in 1984. According to this view,

> localized crises of population growth are, in part, evidence of too much government control and planning....
>
> [There was] a demographic overreaction in the 1960s and 1970s.... [T]oo many governments pursued population control measures without sound economic policies that create the rise in living standards historically associated with decline in fertility rates.[10]

Another perspective is that the expressed concern over rapid population growth in the LDCs is a smokescreen. Binding resource constraints and environmental deterioration can be attributed not so much to overpopulation in the developing economies as to overconsumption by the developed countries. If the relatively few in the wealthy nations did not exploit the world's resources to maintain their excessively high levels of consumption, poverty could be alleviated, the environment safeguarded, and sustainable development achieved. Thus the real issue should be the gross inequities in the consumption of resources, not the numbers of people in the low-income nations. The emphasis of the more developed economies on birth control for the less developed economies is yet another attempt to subjugate the weaker nations. Supporting evidence for this position can be drawn from an observation by the World Resources Institute:

> The North has had a greater impact on the global commons than the South has had, by dominating the marine fisheries of the open ocean, many of which are now endangered, and contributing a larger share of industrial chemicals now degrading the Earth's stratospheric ozone shield. Northern consumption of fossil fuel has contributed disproportionately to the buildup of carbon dioxide in the atmosphere and hence to the threat of global climatic change.[11]

While rapid population growth may be recognized as both a cause and a consequence of poverty, formal opposition to birth control, especially abortion, is found in religion. The sanctity of the family and adherence to moral precepts are more important than economic advancement and a higher material quality of life. These principles were clearly voiced by the Vatican at the 1994 International Population Conference. The high birth rates generally found in Muslim populations also reflect traditional values.

The position advanced by the less developed countries at the First International Population Conference in 1974 was grounded in demographic transition theory. That is, with economic development, population growth will adjust. Reductions in child mortality rates, increases in education, and greater economic opportunities will promote lower fertility.

---

[10]The quotations are from "U.S. Policy Statement for the International Conference on Population," *Population and Development Review,* vol. 10, no. 3 (September 1984), pages 574–579.

[11]See *World Resources 1994–95: A Guide to the Global Environment,* A Report by the World Resources Institute in collaboration with the United Nations Environment Programme and the United Nations Development Programme, New York: Oxford University Press, 1994. This quotation is from page 3.

A more activist approach recommends the incorporation of population policy in the overall development strategy. Measures to reduce high fertility should be part of the provision of basic health-care services. Economic development and fertility control are not only complementary, but reinforcing processes in alleviating poverty and improving the general standard of living.

Finally, an extreme position is that uncontrolled population growth is the principal cause of underdevelopment, resource depletion, and environmental deterioration. Therefore, governments are justified in imposing strict birth-control measures to reduce population growth.

Clearly, the issue of population growth and economic development is contentious. It is important to keep in mind, however, that the vast majority of the less developed countries can expect significant population growth over the next few decades, at least. The uncertainty is when these nations will complete their demographic transitions. The related policy question is how actively should governments intervene to accelerate this transition.

For a policy to be effective, there should be an understanding of the underlying behavior to be modified—in this case, fertility. Ansley Coale set out three preconditions for a sustained decline in fertility.[12]

First, fertility must be considered subject to individual discretion. That is, couples must perceive they have some control over the number and spacing of their children. Second, there must be perceived advantages to smaller family sizes. In other words, individuals must be motivated to reduce their fertility. Third, there must be effective methods available for limiting fertility. Traditional methods of contraception (e.g., rhythm method and coitus interruptus) and abortion have always been available, although not always used effectively. More modern methods of contraception (e.g., birth-control pills and intrauterine devices) when used correctly have significantly lower failure rates.

Population policy can influence all three of Coale's preconditions for lower fertility. We begin our discussion of the determinants of fertility with a model of the demand for children based on the theory of consumer behavior.

## THE DEMAND FOR CHILDREN

The seminal application of the utility–maximization framework to the analysis of the demand for children is associated with Gary Becker.[13] The underlying rationale is that the decision to have children implies a substantial commitment of resources for

---

[12] Ansley Coale, "The Demographic Transition," in *International Population Conference, Liege, 1973*, vol. 1, Liege, Belgium: International Union for the Scientific Study of Population, 1973, pages 53–72. The three preconditions are on page 65.

[13] See Gary Becker, "An Economic Analysis of Fertility," in *Demographic and Economic Change in Developed Countries*, National Bureau of Economic Research, Princeton, NJ: Princeton University Press, 1960, pages 209–231. Although initially receiving mixed reviews, Becker's analysis stimulated much research in the economics of fertility. In 1992 he was awarded the Nobel Prize in Economics for his innovative applications of economic theory to human behavior. Becker's initial focus was on fertility in developed countries. The model presented in this chapter for less developed countries is derived from Becker's framework.

their upbringing—with the opportunity costs being other expenditures unrelated to childrearing. Universally, children are a source of satisfaction as well as a necessity to preserve family lines. As incomes rise, however, average family sizes tend to decrease—as though children were inferior goods. Microeconomic theory can shed some light on this negative correlation of income and fertility.

Consider a representative couple at the beginning of their planning horizon, at a point where they are contemplating family size and lifestyle choices.[14] We assume the couple seeks to maximize their lifetime satisfaction or total utility from the consumption or enjoyment of children and other goods and services. The objective is to

$$\text{maximize } U = U(\overset{+}{C}, \overset{+}{X})$$

where
$U$ = lifetime total utility of the couple

$C$ = number of children

$X$ = quantities of other goods and services unrelated to childrearing

and the plus signs over the arguments $C$ and $X$ indicate the positive marginal utilities associated with children and other consumption.

Total expenditures of the couple, however, are limited to their expected lifetime or **permanent income**.[15] The income constraint is given by

$$Q \cdot C + P \cdot X = I$$

where
$Q$ = expenditures per child or "quality of children"

$P$ = price index of goods and services unrelated to childrearing

$I$ = permanent income

Becker referred to expenditures per child as the **quality of children,** intended to signify not a moral judgment, but the intensity of resource commitment. An increase in $Q$ indicates "child-deepening."

In developing economies children may be put to work at an early age, and so generate income for their parents. Children may also be a source of old-age security. Here we will regard $Q$, then, as "net expenditures per child," or average expenditures on children less the average income earned by the children. We will assume that the quality of children is predetermined by the parents and is a function of their expectations of, and aspirations for, them. The desired quality of children is influenced by the social reference group with which the parents identify. For example, poor parents in a developing economy may typically expect their children to attend only a few years of primary school before beginning work and contributing to the family's income. With economic development, parental aspirations for their children rise (e.g., more education), while their expectations of income generation fall—consistent with an increase in child quality.

---

[14]Clearly, Becker's analysis presupposes that the representative couple perceives that they can exert some control over their fertility. Thus, Coale's first precondition for reducing fertility is met.

[15]*Permanent income* is an estimate of the discounted future income of the couple based on their education, labor force participation, job prospects, and financial wealth.

## FIGURE 7.2  INDIFFERENCE MAPPING AND INCOME CONSTRAINT

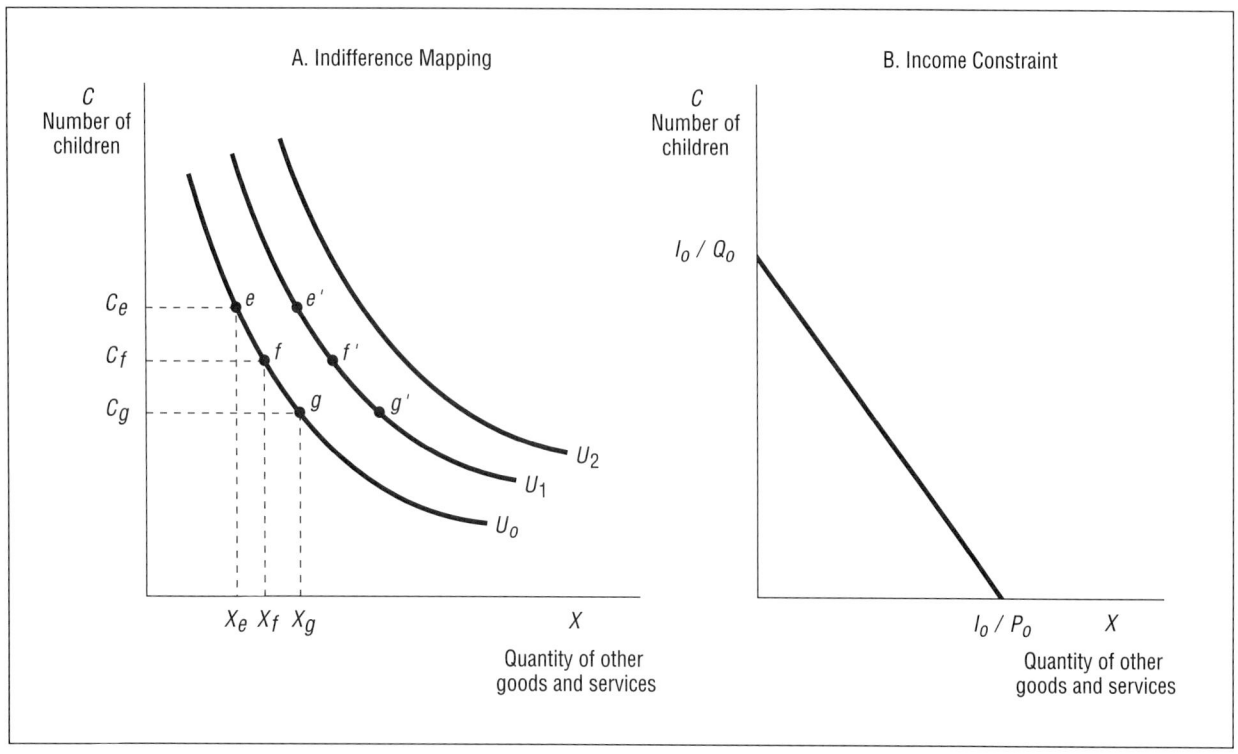

Also assumed to be given are permanent income (predetermined by the couple along with the quality of children) and the price index for other goods and services (exogenously set in the marketplace). Thus, a couple seeks to choose the combination of family size $(C)$ and other consumption $(X)$ that maximizes their total utility $(U)$, given their permanent income $(I)$, their desired quality of children $(Q)$, and the price index for other goods and services $(P)$.

We can illustrate this constrained optimization problem with indifference curves and a budget line. If we return to the utility function, indifference curves can be derived that show the combinations of the number of children and consumption of other goods and services yielding the same total utilities. For example, in Figure 7.2A the representative couple is indifferent between any two combinations of $C$ and $X$ on the indifference curve $U_0$. The combinations of children and other goods represented by points $e$, $f$, and $g$ all yield the same total utility $(U_0)$. As we move out from the origin to higher indifference curves (such as $U_1$ and $U_2$), the total utilities rise. Therefore, while the couple is indifferent between combinations $e'$, $f'$, and $g'$ on indifference curve $U_1$, any combination on $U_1$ is preferred to any combination on $U_0$, a lower indifference curve.

The indifference curves are negatively sloped and convex to the origin. The negative slope indicates the trade-off between family size and other consumption. Given that additional children or other goods always contribute to total utility (formally, the marginal utilities of $C$ and $X$ are assumed always to be positive), then along an indifference curve, a couple would be willing to have fewer children only if their consumption of other goods increased.

The slope of an indifference curve, called the **marginal rate of substitution,** indicates the rate that a couple is willing to trade off or substitute children for other goods. The hypothesis of diminishing marginal utility accounts for the convexity of the curves. As increasing amounts of other goods are consumed (as $X$ rises), the additional satisfaction received from the consumption of another unit of $X$ decreases (the marginal utility of $X$ falls). Conversely, as the number of children declines, the willingness to reduce further family size decreases. Thus, as a couple moves down and to the right along an indifference curve, the quantity of other goods required to replace each child increases. The slope of the indifference curve becomes flatter. In Figure 7.2A, in moving from combinations $e$ to $f$ to $g$ along indifference curve $U_o$, the decrease in the number of children is equal $(C_e - C_f = C_f - C_g)$, but the increase in other goods required to maintain the total utility of the parents is rising $(X_g - X_f > X_f - X_e)$.

A set of indifference curves, called an *indifference mapping*, is drawn for the given tastes and preferences of the couple. A change in tastes and preferences would rotate the indifference curves. For example, an increase in consumer aspirations or a shift in tastes in favor of smaller families would rotate the indifference curves in a clockwise fashion (the indifference curves would become steeper). The couple would be more willing to "give up" children (accept a smaller family) for a given increase in the consumption of other goods and services.

The maximization of total utility is constrained by permanent income. The income constraint, plotted in Figure 7.2B, represents all the combinations of children and other goods the couple can afford given the permanent income $(I_o)$, the predetermined quality of children $(Q_o)$, and price index for other goods $(P_o)$. At one extreme, if all income were devoted to children, the maximum number of children would be $(I_o/Q_o)$. At the other extreme, if there were no children, the maximum quantity of other goods would be $(I_o/P_o)$. The slope of the income constraint is equal to the negative of the ratio of the price index to the quality of children $(-P_o/Q_o)$. An increase in permanent income would shift the income constraint out to the right in a parallel fashion. A change in the desired quality of children (expenditures per child) or in the price index for other goods, however, would affect the slope of the income constraint.

The maximization of total utility of the couple occurs at the tangency of the income constraint with the highest indifference curve. In Figure 7.3 the income constraint $BB$ is tangent to the indifference curve $U_o$ at point $e_o$, giving an optimal combination of children and other goods of $C_o$ and $X_o$. An increase in permanent income, ceteris paribus, would shift the income constraint out to the right in a parallel fashion, allowing the couple to attain greater consumption levels. If normal goods, then the increase in income results in increases in the demands for children and other goods (see the increase from $C_o$ to $C_1$ and from $X_o$ to $X_1$ in Figure 7.3). Thus, the widely observed negative correlation between fertility and income must be due to other factors, such as changes in tastes and preferences, and to relative increases in the desired quality of children.

Indeed, with economic development there are factors which contribute to the decline in the demand for children even as incomes rise. In particular, with gains in education the economic mobility of females is enhanced. Women are more likely to postpone marriage and participate in the labor force as the wages they could earn rise with their education. As the opportunity cost of a woman's time increases, child care—a time-intensive activity—becomes more expensive. Consequently the time spent by more-educated women on childrearing becomes more valuable, and can be modeled as an increase in the quality of children.

Also, as individuals become more educated, their appreciation for the value of schooling and their aspirations for their children rise. Couples decide to spend more on

| FIGURE 7.3 | CONSUMER EQUILIBRIUM |

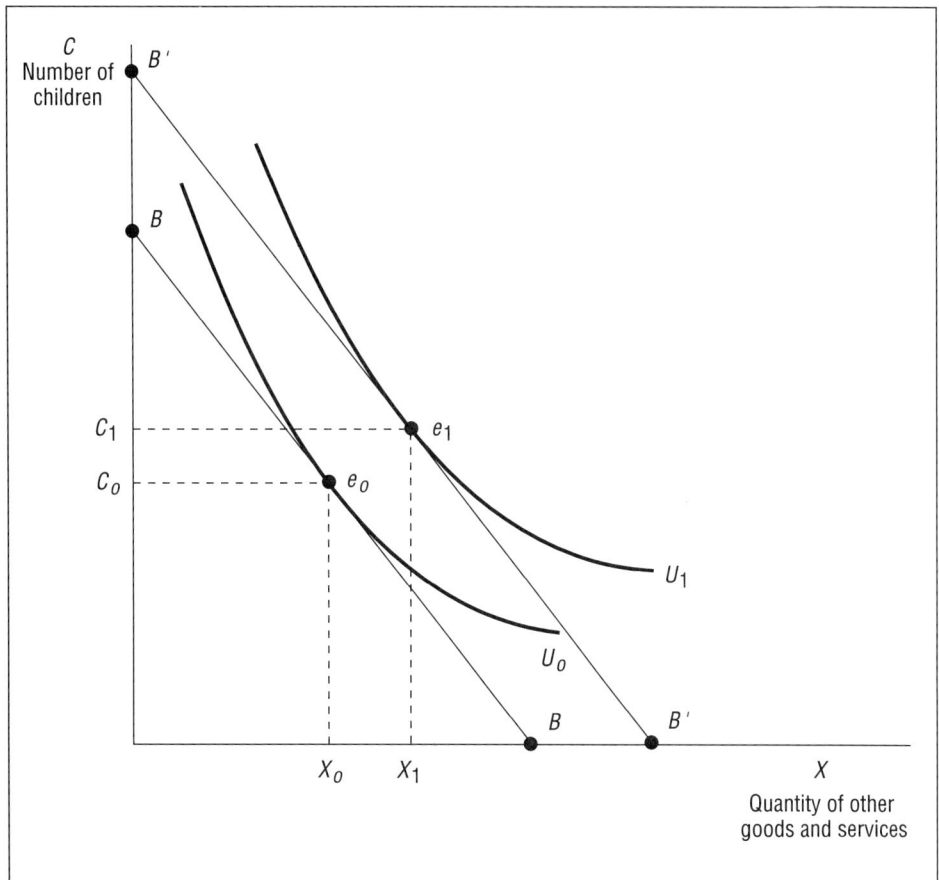

each child—an investment in human capital that makes more economic sense as child survival rates increase with economic development. In short, with education couples become more inclined to substitute "quality" for "quantity" of children.

With the gains in income that accompany economic development, consumer aspirations may be stimulated. In order to afford an improved lifestyle, therefore, couples may have to limit family size. This shift in tastes and preferences in favor of higher consumption standards and smaller families is reflected in a rotation of the indifference mapping in a clockwise manner; that is, at any combination of children and other goods, the slope of the relevant indifference curve becomes steeper.

In Figure 7.4 we summarize the effects of economic development on the demand for children. At low levels of development the representative couple's utility-maximizing combination of children and other goods is given by $C_o$ and $X_o$, respectively (see point $e_o$, where the indifference curve $U_o$ is tangent to the income constraint $BB$). As incomes rise with economic development, the income constraint shifts out to the right $(B'B')$. The shift, however, is not parallel, since there is a relative increase in the desired quality of children compared to the price index for other goods. (The slope of the new income constraint is flatter. Indeed, with economic development, consumer goods may become relatively plentiful, moderating the rise in $P$.) The new utility-maximizing combination for the couple, based on the increase in income and the relative rise in the

### FIGURE 7.4 A DECREASE IN THE DEMAND FOR CHILDREN WITH ECONOMIC DEVELOPMENT

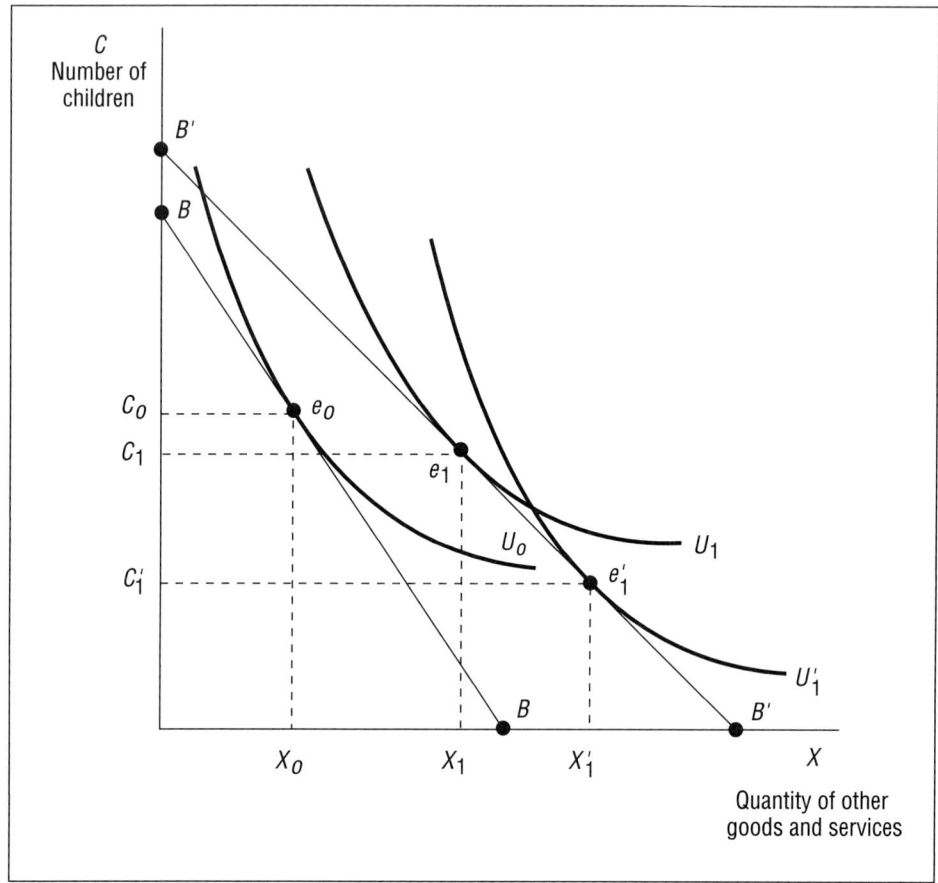

desired quality of children, would be at point $e_1$. The change in tastes and preferences in favor of higher consumption standards and smaller families, however, rotates the indifference mapping. (Compare the indifference curves $U_1'$ with $U_1$.) As a result, the new utility-maximizing combination of children and other goods becomes $C_1'$ and $X_1'$, represented by point $e_1'$ at the tangency of the income constraint $B'B'$ with the indifference curve $U_1'$. In sum, with economic development the demand for children declines.

As we will see, a decrease in the demand for children, by itself, need not translate into lower fertility. We need to consider "supply-side" fertility factors and the costs of birth control. First, we will expand the theoretical framework presented above and discuss evidence on the demand for children in Mexico.

## DETERMINANTS OF THE DEMAND FOR CHILDREN

We extend the model of utility-maximization to consider relative status and other influences on a couple's decision making. Individuals may derive satisfaction from more than just the absolute consumption of goods and services—they may measure their consumption against that of some reference group. Attaining or exceeding some aspired-to standard of performance may add to total utility.

## Relative Status

Return to the representative couple at the outset of their planning process, when choices about family size and lifestyle are first contemplated. Assessing their education and labor skills, their perceptions of job prospects, and their financial wealth, the couple will project their permanent income. Within this income constraint and given their expectations (or aspirations) for the quality of their children, the couple will etch plans for the number of children and their lifetime consumption of other goods and services. These initial plans, likely to be tentative, are not made in a vacuum. The couple's choices are influenced by the benchmark performance of a social reference group. For example, with respect to the quantity of children, the economist Leibenstein writes:

> To a considerable degree people take their cues about the correct number of children from others in the same social status. Something like a "bandwagon effect" occurs. Thus, if most households are having between 2 and 3 children, that fact influences the desired number.[16]

In traditional, agrarian societies with limited educational opportunities and restricted economic mobility, high fertility can be easily perpetuated. Social pressures encourage conformity to the conventional behavior. Alternative role models, especially in remote villages, are few, if present at all. The expected life pattern is well established. The typical young woman is confronted by minimal education, marriage at a young age, early and frequent childbearing, and the primary responsibility for the maintenance of the family, as well as expectations for contributing to the income of the household (for example, working in the fields).

With economic development and the structural change of urbanization and industrialization, however, the cohesiveness of such high-fertility regimes tends to break down. Increased access to education, health care, and family planning programs, along with improved employment opportunities, yield new options. Fertility behavior becomes more discretionary, and the demand for children falls. Recall Caldwell's theory (discussed in Chapter 2), in which economic development reverses the net flow of intergenerational wealth such that the desire for smaller families becomes economically rational.

## Evidence from Mexico

Data from the 1982 National Demographic Survey of Mexico were used to assess the determinants of the demand for children, in particular, the influence of community factors.[17] The demand for children was measured by the response to a question on the "ideal number of children." Over 20,000 households in 99 metropolitan, urban, and

---

[16]See Harvey Leibenstein, "The Economic Theory of Fertility Decline," *Quarterly Journal of Economics*, vol. 89, no. 1 (1975), pages 1–31. This quotation is from page 22.

[17]This analysis is from "The Demand for Children: Evidence from Mexico," by Peter Hess, David Guilkey, and Boone Turchi, Carolina Population Center Working Paper, The University of North Carolina at Chapel Hill, June 1988.

rural communities in Mexico were sampled. While some 10,500 eligible women (i.e., women between the childbearing years of 15 and 49) were extensively interviewed, only currently married or cohabiting women in their original unions were used in the regression analysis. Consequently, the relevant sample size was reduced to 4468 women. Data on the characteristics of the communities in which the women lived were also collected. From the household survey, community averages for both income and children ever born were calculated.

In general, the survey found that the demand for children increased with the age of the female respondent. For married women in original unions, the means for the ideal number of children were 2.9 for women 15 to 24 years of age; 3.7 for women 25 to 34 years of age; and 4.9 for women of ages 35 to 49 years. Indeed, there may be a bias in response by age or marital duration to the ideal-number-of-children question. Older women may not only have experienced different economic and social conditions during their prime childbearing years, but because of longer unions may have produced more "unintended" children. The responses of older women, then, may inflate their true demand for children as they "rationalize" their excess fertility.

A multiple regression analysis was conducted with the eligible woman's response to the question "What is the ideal number of children?" used to indicate the demand for children, the dependent variable. The explanatory variables on the individual level were the age of the eligible woman; her education (years of schooling); and the income earned by the adult males (16 years or older) in the woman's household, divided by the size of the household. Controls were included for the woman's employment before her marital union (prior labor force participation); home ownership (a proxy for household wealth); and access to piped water (a proxy for basic amenities).[18]

To measure relative income, the per capita male income of the woman's household was divided by the mean per capita male income for surveyed households in the community. As individual incomes rise relative to the community average, consumer aspirations may be stimulated and tastes and preferences may shift in favor of smaller families.[19]

Two community measures were included as explanatory influences on the demand for children. One variable was the community birth rate, a measure of the total fertility rate for the community, based on the recent fertility of all women of ages 15 to 49 in the surveyed households in the community. The hypothesis is that high-birth-rate communities perpetuate a strong demand for children, if only through a pervasive demonstration effect. The second variable was a measure of community access to secondary education. The variable constructed was based on physical distance to secondary schools, adjusted for mean per capita income in the community. Higher-income communities may have better-quality schools since the local tax base can support more public education expenditures. Greater access to education may, in effect, raise the cost of children to parents if there are increased pressures to send children to school. Not only would there be the direct expenses of books and school clothes, but there are the opportunity costs of the income that could have been earned by the children if not in school. Moreover, if education were perceived as necessary for socioeconomic mobility, parents would be more likely to invest in each child, substituting quality for quantity of children.

---

[18]Data on child mortality for the eligible women were not collected. The variable for access to piped water may pick up some of this effect, however, as poor sanitary conditions are highly correlated with child morbidity and mortality.

[19]See Eva Mueller and Kathleen Short, "Effects of Income and Wealth on the Demand for Children," in *Determinants of Fertility in Developing Countries,* Volume 1, edited by Rodolfo Bulatao and Ronald Lee, with Paula Hollerbach and John Bongaarts, New York: Academic Press, 1983.

For the full sample of 4468 women of ages 15 to 49 in original unions, the regression results confirmed the hypothesized relationships.[20] Age of the female and the absence of piped water were statistically very significant positive influences on the ideal number of children. Education of the woman and prior work experience were statistically very significant negative influences. The effect of income on the demand for children was especially interesting. Per capita male income in the woman's household was a highly significant positive influence. As relative income rose, however, the demand for children declined, up to a point. At very high levels of relative income (over 400 percent of the community mean), the demand for children increased. Thus, while children appeared to be a "normal good" (evidenced by the positive absolute income effect), initial gains in relative income could raise consumer aspirations and prompt a shift in preferences to smaller families. For the wealthiest households in a given community, however, children may have become a "superior good." In other words, maintaining high consumption standards in large families may be the ultimate status symbol.[21]

With respect to the community variables, the average birth rate was an important determinant of the demand for children. Controlling for the individual-level characteristics of the eligible women (i.e., age, education, and prior work experience; household access to piped water; per capita income earned by adult males [both absolute and relative]; and home ownership), women in communities with high fertility did have significantly higher demands for children. In contrast, as hypothesized, community access to secondary education was a negative and statistically very significant influence on the ideal number of children. These results suggest that the social environment (community birth rates and access to education, as well as relative income) needs to be considered when modeling the demand for children.[22]

## EASTERLIN'S SUPPLY–DEMAND SYNTHESIS

As suggested earlier, the demand for children does not alone determine actual fertility. There are supply-side factors, as well as the costs of birth control, to consider. In an innovative use of the concepts of supply and demand, Richard Easterlin devised a framework for explaining the declines in fertility that occur with economic development.[23]

---

[20]Given the presence of community influences (the common values for the community birth rate and access-to-education variables for all the women in a community), a generalized least squares regression was run. See Hess, Guilkey, and Turchi (1988) for the empirical analysis.

[21]The only explanatory variable that was not found to be a statistically significant influence on the ideal number of children was the control for home ownership. Given an inability to determine the monetary value of the equity in the home, this lack of significance may not be surprising.

[22]When the regression equation was estimated for the 906 eligible women in small communities (i.e., communities with populations of 20,000 or less), the results were very similar.

[23]See Richard Easterlin, "An Economic Framework for Fertility Analysis," *Studies in Family Planning*, vol. 6 (March 1975), pages 54–63, for an early exposition of the model. A more complete presentation with empirical analysis can be found in *The Fertility Revolution: A Supply–Demand Analysis*, by Richard Easterlin and Eileen Crimmins, Chicago: The University of Chicago Press, 1985.

Since we have discussed why the demand for children declines with development, we now focus on the supply side. We begin with the concept of **natural fertility,** which may be defined as the average number of live births a woman would have if she did nothing deliberately to influence her fertility. Natural fertility is consistent with passive decision making, where a woman adheres to the prevailing social customs and practices concerning fertility.

The main determinants of natural fertility are exposure to the risk of conception and fecundity. Exposure to the risk of conception is influenced by marriage customs; sanctions on premarital and extramarital sexual unions; social practices with respect to abstinence within unions; and the effective use of contraception. Under a natural fertility regime there is no discretionary use of contraception or conscious birth control. Fecundity is the biological capacity to bear children, which extends from menarche to menopause.

Natural fertility differs across societies. In many of the contemporary, less developed countries, marriage still tends to be at an early age, which increases the period of exposure to the risk of conception. Often there are customs, however, that reduce this exposure and serve to dampen the natural fertility. In some traditional societies women retreat to their parents' homes for a considerable period of time after giving birth. Women may cease sexual activity after becoming grandmothers, and with early marriage and childbearing, a woman may become a grandmother well before the age of menopause. Another reason is the separation of couples with the migration of males to urban areas, or even out of the country, for employment. Furthermore, the practice of breastfeeding, prevalent in traditional societies, can act as a natural contraceptive.

Fecundity is affected by health and nutrition. In low-income economies with inadequate health care and poor nutrition, the incidences of sterility and miscarriage are high. Consequently, fecundity is suppressed.

With economic development, however, improvements in health and nutrition and the erosion of practices which had limited exposure to the risk of conception (such as extensive breastfeeding and prolonged periods of postpartum abstinence) can increase natural fertility. Without greater individual control over fertility, the increase in natural fertility translates into higher birth rates. Given that survival rates of infants and children also improve with economic development, the potential supply of children rises even faster.

In Figure 7.5 Easterlin's supply–demand synthesis is illustrated. On the vertical axis is the average number of surviving children per woman. On the horizontal axis is an index of economic development. While the demand for children ($C^d$) declines with development, the potential supply of children ($C^s$) increases. There are essentially two fertility regimes: supply-driven and demand-driven.

To the left of point $M$ in Figure 7.5 there is an excess demand for children. The actual number of surviving children ($\overline{C}$) is constrained by supply factors, such as suppressed fecundity and high rates of infant and child mortality. With an excess demand for children, there is little motivation to use birth control. As such, family planning programs and other measures to increase the use of contraception would not likely meet with much success. Although largely determined by supply factors, the actual number of surviving children will be less than the potential supply as long as some women in the society are practicing effective birth control (contraception and abortion). In a completely natural fertility regime, the actual number of surviving children ($\overline{C}$) would coincide with the potential supply of children ($C^s$).

## FIGURE 7.5  Easterlin's Supply–Demand Synthesis

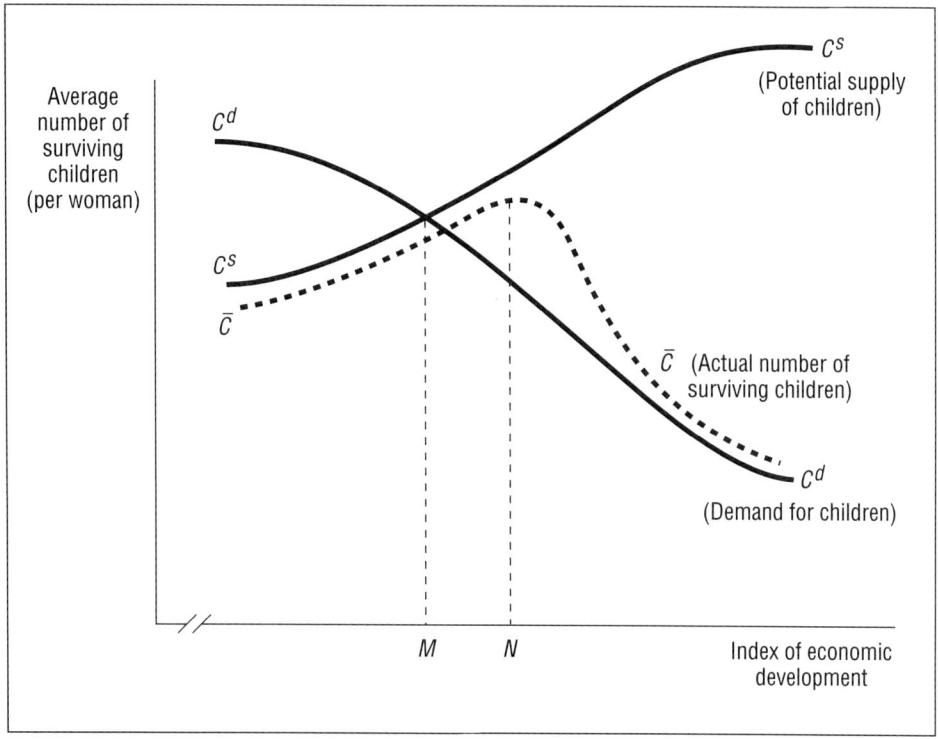

To the right of point M, at higher levels of economic development, there is a potential excess supply of children. Consequently the motivation to use birth control increases. As Easterlin notes, even when the motivation exists, a couple may not practice birth control due to the associated costs. Therefore, the actual number of surviving children may continue to rise even when there is a potential excess supply of children (see the interval between point M and N in Figure 7.5).

There are two basic types of costs of using birth control. One is the direct or monetary cost, including expenditures on contraceptive methods (e.g., pills, IUDs, condoms) or abortion, and for visits to the doctor and pharmacy to secure services and prescriptions. The other is the psychic cost or emotional stress. The practice of contraception (especially the more modern techniques) may be an innovative behavior in traditional societies, and thus meet with the disapproval of authority figures—the parents of couples desiring many grandchildren, the husbands whose self-esteem may be tied to their number of sons, and the churches for moral reasons. Moreover, any new behavior carries with it uncertainty and risk. Women with minimal education may be fearful of the reported (and often exaggerated) side-effects of modern contraception. Visits to a doctor may evoke apprehension. Women may be anxious about even discussing sexual practices. Where illegal or back-alley abortions are the primary means of birth control, the fears are clearly credible. Indeed, one of the benefits of education is an increased awareness of, and receptivity to, new types of behavior.

Educated individuals feel more in control of their lives and are more able to practice effective contraception.

With economic development, not only does the potential excess supply of children rise, but the costs of contraception fall. Family planning programs, in particular, increase the availability of modern contraceptive techniques (reducing the direct costs) and, by providing information and encouragement, lend a legitimacy to the practice of modern contraception (reducing the psychic costs). Therefore, the increased motivation to practice birth control, combined with the reduced costs, brings down birth rates.

In Figure 7.5 the actual number of surviving children (the $\overline{C}$ curve) declines (past point $N$) and begins to follow the demand-for-children curve $(C^d)$. The fertility regime becomes demand-driven. Nevertheless, the demand for children would not completely determine fertility unless the costs of birth control were zero. The actual number of surviving children, however, will approach the demand for children as the motivation to use birth control increases and the costs of using birth control decrease.

Easterlin's model provides insight into why, in the absence of economic development, family planning programs might not have much impact on reducing fertility. At low levels of development there tends to be an excess demand for children, hence little motivation for using contraception. Easterlin's model also explains why older women who desire to cease childbearing are often among the first to practice birth control.

There are, however, other points in the life cycle where contraception is used even though there is an excess demand for children.[24] Contraception may be used to avoid unwanted fertility (for instance, outside of marital unions), to postpone the first birth, or to increase the interval between births.

### EVIDENCE FROM SUB-SAHARAN AFRICA ON CONTRACEPTIVE USE

Among the reasons cited in a study by John Caldwell, I. O. Orubuloye, and Pat Caldwell for the generally high birth rates in Africa are the importance of ancestry and preserving the family line (which requires high fertility in the face of high infant and child mortality); the practice of polygyny (which works to reduce the economic responsibility of fathering children); and the advantages of large families (for example, greater claims on communal land and the increased influence of family contacts in business).[25] In the sub-Saharan African countries with evidence of declining fertility, however, increased female education and economic mobility are inducing greater contraceptive use at all ages.

Specifically, given the relatively high prevalence of premarital sexual activity in Africa and the desire to continue schooling and pursue modern-sector employment, the practice of birth control (including abortion) is rising among young women. With modernization and a shortening of the traditional periods of postpartum abstinence, there is a growing demand for contraception to extend birth intervals not only to enhance the survival prospects of infants, but to alleviate the economic burdens of too

---

[24]See Peter Hess, "An Eclectic Model of the Fertility Transition," in *Population Growth and Socioeconomic Progress in Less Developed Countries*, New York: Praeger, 1988, pages 111–125, for an adaptation of the Easterlin framework to the life cycle of a representatve female in a developing economy.

[25]See John Caldwell, I.O. Orubuloye, and Pat Caldwell, "Fertility Decline in Africa: A New Type of Transition," *Population and Development Review*, vol. 18, no. 2 (June 1992), pages 211–242.

closely spaced births. African women who have become grandmothers and wish to remain sexually active are using contraception and cutting down on unwanted pregnancies once the decision to cease childbearing is reached. In addition, the AIDS epidemic in Africa has stimulated the use of condoms. Finally, the shift in government policy to advocating family planning has both increased the supply of contraceptives and encouraged the practice of family limitation. The authors of the study surmise that

> the African fertility decline is likely to present the world with a new type of demographic transition, one where a similarity in contraceptive use and fertility decline is found at all ages. Among unmarried young women there will be a demand for contraceptives to prevent pregnancies and enforced marriage, and this will probably be the main reason for a rise in the age at marriage.... Among married women there is likely to be little practice of contraception between marriage and first birth, but a demand for contraception between succeeding births.... Finally, a host of reasons, increasingly including the economic burden of the large family, will undoubtedly foster behavioral change aimed at limiting fertility.[26]

# THE SELECTION OF POPULATION POLICIES

**Population policy** involves the selection of measures to influence the growth rate, composition, or distribution of a population. What type of population policy is *warranted* in a nation largely depends on the relationship between the current rate of population growth and national objectives. What type of population policy is *possible* depends on the economic, political, social, and cultural conditions in the nation. Once implemented, the effectiveness of any population policy depends on the commitment of the government and the receptiveness of the targeted groups.

Here we are concerned with those LDCs in which rapid population growth is considered to be hampering economic development.[27] Raising mortality rates is clearly not an option, nor is promoting emigration. Other nations must agree to accept the emigrants, and often the more capable in the nation are disproportionately represented among the emigrants. Thus, we focus on measures to reduce the fertility rate.

## RANGE OF POLICIES

With a laissez-faire or "hands-off" approach, the government does not attempt to influence fertility rates. Such neutrality could reflect a failure to recognize the consequences of rapid population growth; or the belief that the government cannot, or should not,

---

[26]Ibid., page 219.

[27]While most governments in developing nations now recognize the benefits of curbing rapid population growth, in the past many did not. Some governments, especially in Africa, even followed pronatalist policies.

intervene in population matters; or opposition from churches or other powerful constituencies in the nation.

### Family Planning Programs

A more activist approach that combines measures to control fertility with personal choice is family planning. Whether state-sponsored or privately operated through nongovernmental organizations, **family planning programs (FPP)** are designed to provide information and advice on contraception; to promote the use of effective contraception; and to increase the variety and supplies of contraceptive techniques available. A fundamental tenet of family planning is that a couple's decision on the number and spacing of children is a basic human right. Evidence suggests there is a large unmet demand for contraception (especially among women) in developing economies, which translates into excess fertility. Family planning programs can help parents realize their desired family sizes by lowering the direct and psychic costs of contraception. Often incorporated into the health-care system, FPP also provide instruction on infant and child care. In particular, by encouraging breastfeeding and longer birth intervals, the nutrition and health of infants are enhanced.

The family planning movement is heavily involved in both the research to understand the determinants of fertility behavior and the development of contraceptive techniques that are cheaper and more reliable (i.e., with a lower user-failure rate). In many cases, FPP offer abortion along with a range of contraceptive techniques, including condoms, IUDs, pills, immunizations, injectibles, and male and female sterilization. The goal, however, is to promote the practice of effective contraception so that abortions can be reduced, if not eliminated.

A recent World Bank study estimated that about half of the married women of reproductive age in developing nations practice contraception.[28] Annually, public and private expenditures on family planning in the developing world have totalled $4 to $5 billion, or about $1 to $1.25 per capita. Since user payments cover only a quarter of the costs, the heavy reliance on donor contributions and government funding is expected to continue.

Considerable differences exist among (and within) the developing regions of the world in contraceptive prevalence. South Asia had some of the earliest family planning programs (notably in India), but the combination of low levels of development and poor implementation hindered the widespread adoption of contraception. Significant progress in birth control has been made in East Asia—a reflection of the rapid economic growth, relative political stability, and effective population policies. In Latin America, the private sector, rather than the government, took the lead in meeting the demand for family planning. Cultural barriers and the subordinate status of females have hurt family planning efforts in much of North Africa and the Middle East. Finally, in sub-Saharan Africa the demand for contraception has been generally weak, and family planning has not been a priority for most governments.

Indeed, family planning programs have not always been successful. Some of the problems have been insufficient funding; long lines and poor service at the clinics; and inadequate training and supervision of the FPP's workers. In the mid-1970s a

---

[28]See Rodolfo Bulatao, "Effective Family Planning Programs," Washington, DC: The World Bank, 1993, page 11. Much of the following three paragraphs is drawn from this study.

sterilization campaign in India got out of hand, not only damaging the family planning movement but contributing to the downfall of the Indira Gandhi government. Lessons have been learned from both the failures and the successes.

At the national level, a first priority is information and education. Public service messages on television, radio, billboards, and in the print media can not only reach many people, but demonstrate the national commitment to family planning. Popular slogans addressing the number of children, such as "Three is enough, two is better," can promote the idea of quality over quantity of children. School curricula can include sex education. More emphasis on convincing males to practice contraception is needed, since males typically exercise the dominant influence in traditional societies and male sterilization (vasectomies) is less expensive than female sterilization (tubal ligation).

The efforts of national government can be complemented by the major international organizations involved in family planning (for example, the United Nations Population Fund and the International Planned Parenthood Federation), as well as by local non-governmental organizations and the private sector. Many of the family planning services can be provided by nurses and community health workers when appropriately trained and supervised, reserving the more complicated procedures for qualified doctors. Pharmacies can be used to distribute contraceptive supplies.

Advocates of FPP argue that family planning is an effective compromise between maintaining individual choice and working toward the socially desirable goals of reducing rapid population growth and promoting economic development. Critics counter that FPP do not go far enough and that stronger measures are needed to reduce fertility. It is true that family planning programs work best when there is a strong demand for contraception. Improving the socioeconomic mobility of females and reducing infant and child mortality are almost prerequisites for increasing the demand for contraception.

### ECONOMIC INCENTIVES AND OTHER MEASURES

Economic incentives have often been components of population policies. Payments to individuals for adopting contraception are made, with the amounts adjusted for the age of the acceptor and the effectiveness of the contraceptive method. Benefits for smaller families may include preferential access to public housing; scholarships for schooling; and state pensions or social security for parents who limit their fertility. Economic incentives can be costly, adding to the demands on government budgets.

Economic disincentives are designed to make certain behavior more expensive. Among the disincentives would be higher taxes or the withdrawal of welfare and maternity benefits to families with higher-birth-order children. Indeed, the burden of disincentives may fall on the higher-birth-order children in large families.

More direct government intervention can come in the form of induced social change. To promote lower fertility, governments may legislate minimum ages for marriage. National service commitments (e.g., two years in the military) may be required for all youth. Measures to improve the status of females may include scholarships and subsidies for education; greater opportunities and fairer remuneration in the labor market; and less discriminatory laws on divorce, inheritance, and property rights.

*The Economist* recently reported on an innovative policy adopted in one state of India to combat the discrimination in education and health care faced by girls. As in many traditional societies, in India daughters are an economic burden to parents. First, there are the expenses of childrearing; then, a dowry must be provided for marriage, at which point the daughter "belongs" to the family of her husband. Under the plan, for each newborn girl, the state government would deposit 2500 rupees in a savings account. The account would increase to 25,000 rupees and could be claimed by the parents if the girl is still unmarried on her 18th birthday. The program is limited to low-income families with no more than two children. If successful in raising the average age of marriage and encouraging parental investment in the education and health of their daughters, thereby reducing fertility, the plan may be extended to all of India.[29]

At the other extreme from laissez-faire would be authoritarian birth control policy. If population growth is regarded as the major obstacle to economic growth and development, governments may turn to more coercive measures. State-issued birth licenses may be used to regulate fertility in each year. Unauthorized pregnancies would be terminated with abortions. There could be forced sterilization for couples upon reaching their allowed quota on children. Clearly the implementation of such measures requires a strong government and would be contrary to democratic principles. Few nations would even consider, much less enact, such a policy. Below, we profile one nation that has.

## BIRTH CONTROL IN CHINA

With an estimated population of 1.2 billion in 1994, China has more than one out of every five people in the world. On the other hand, China has only 7 percent of the world's arable land, with very limited, if any, potential for increasing the land under cultivation.[30]

A quarter of a century ago, the leaders of China forecast an inability to feed China's rapidly expanding population. Thus, a series of aggressive population control measures was begun. At the time the total fertility rate (TFR) was near six. Despite low per capita incomes and a predominantly rural population, China succeeded in lowering the total fertility rate to replacement level in one decade.[31] Because of the population momentum from the previous high fertility, China still faces the real prospect of a population of nearly 1.5 billion by the year 2025, well above the 1.2 billion estimated by the government as the largest population China could support.[32]

---

[29]See "India's Rich Little Poor Girls," *The Economist* (March 11, 1995), page 40.

[30]See H. Yuan Tien with Zhang Tianlu, Ping Yu, Li Jingneng, and Liang Zhongtang, "China: Demographic Billionaire," *Population Bulletin*, vol. 38, no. 2 (April 1983), page 5. Another useful article is Nathan Keyfitz, "The Population of China," *Scientific American*, vol. 250, no. 2 (February 1984), pages 38–47. Tien provides a good account of the population history of China after the Communist Revolution. Keyfitz focuses more on the implications of China's population policy. A more recent account is H. Yuan Tien et al., "China's Demographic Dilemmas," *Population Bulletin*, vol. 47, no. 1 (June 1992).

[31]The total fertility rate fell from 5.8 in 1970 to 2.2 in 1980, where it more or less stabilized. The 1992 TFR was also 2.2. See Susan Kalish, "In China, the Peak Childbearing Years Have Peaked," *Population Today* (January 1993), page 5. Recent evidence indicates the Chinese TFR may have declined further to slightly below 2.

[32]The 1.5 billion is a World Bank projection for China. See *World Development Report 1994*, Table 25. See Keyfitz (page 38) for the official estimate of 1.2 billion for the maximum population that could be adequately supported. (Note: the World Bank's projection for India's population in the year 2025 is 1.4 billion.)

The rapid population growth in China was triggered in the 1930s by sharp declines in mortality.[33] After the establishment of the People's Republic in 1949, China implemented a massive public campaign to control diseases and provide basic health care to the population through the proliferation of "barefoot doctors" (paramedics with additional training in preventative medicine) and the expansion of rural medical facilities. Birth rates remained high, due in part to a cultural predisposition to large families bolstered by a strong preference for sons. In the early 1950s the first birth-control measures, including the legalization of abortion, were adopted. By the latter half of the decade, birth rates were declining. With the economic dislocation of the Great Leap Forward in 1958 to 1959 (a development strategy of industrial decentralization), followed by the crop failures and famine in 1960 to 1961, the crude birth rate (CBR) fell to under 20 (births per thousand population).

China then experienced a brief baby boom. The CBR doubled in one year and peaked at 44 in 1963. Consequently, China mounted a second attempt at birth control, which moderated fertility but was undermined by the chaos of the Cultural Revolution of 1966 to 1969. The crude birth rate remained above 33 for the rest of the decade.

In 1970, with a crude rate of natural increase of 26 (per thousand), China's leaders recognized the need, even urgency, for a comprehensive plan to reign in population growth. The Marriage Law of 1950, which had set a minimum legal age of marriage of 18 for women and 20 for men, was tightened to 23 and 25 years of age for women and men in rural areas; and to 25 and 28 years of age in urban areas.[34] The CBR fell during the 1970s from 34 to 18, but even this decline was deemed insufficient given the scarcity of agricultural land and the prospect of continued population increase. So, in 1979 China instituted the "One Child Campaign" in an attempt to reverse population momentum.[35]

The key feature of the new population policy was a system of birth licenses. Consistent with central planning, the state would set a target fertility rate, which was translated into birth quotas at the local level. Licenses for authorized pregnancies were distributed. Unlicensed couples were expected to use contraception. Contraceptive techniques and services were available free of charge. IUDs became popular among younger couples, and sterilization was relied on by older couples who had completed their families. Unauthorized pregnancies were to be terminated by abortion.

There has been constant propaganda to promote the "one child" norm, a policy that is not popular, particularly given the traditional preference for sons. Economic incentives and disincentives have also been used to compel socially responsible reproduction. "Only" children may receive free medical care and school tuition. Preferential treatment in housing and old-age pensions may be provided to couples who so limit

---

[33]From 1930 to 1950 the crude death rate (CDR) in China was halved, from over 40 to under 20 (deaths per thousand population). By the mid-1960s the CDR had declined to under 10. This reduction in the Chinese CDR is comparable to the decline in the CDR in the United States over the period from 1800 to 1970. See Tien (1983, page 12). The historical summary given here is also drawn from Tien (1983).

[34]As Tien (1983, pages 20–22) relates, premarital fertility is rare in China, so raising the legal age of marriage would effectively reduce exposure to the risk of conception.

[35]Indeed, a shift in emphasis from delaying marriage and childbearing to reducing family size was warranted. In 1980 marriage laws were liberalized, a recognition of the considerable frustration and social unrest caused by the high legal minimum ages for marriage. See Tien (1983, pages 20–21).

their fertility. Income penalties and discrimination in housing, schooling, and employment have been used to punish couples who do not conform.

China's population policy, viewed by many as coercive and harsh, is justified by proponents as necessary for the nation's economic survival. A comprehensive "one-child norm" may be the most equitable way to distribute the burden and ensure sustainable development.

There are, however, problems with the policy. For one, the authoritarian birth-control program has fallen short of its goals. There has been the inevitable slippage in realizing the birth rate targets. In all likelihood, China's population will continue to grow well beyond the earlier goal of 1.2 billion and may even approach 1.7 billion before becoming stationary.[36] Strictly enforcing the one-child norm has proven to be difficult, especially in rural areas. That traditional son preference remains is evidenced by China's high male–female birth ratio. As Tien notes:

> Male preference has resurfaced strongly with the one child campaign. The recent rise in the sex ratio could be partly due to underreporting of female births by parents who deliberately avoid registering a firstborn female child in order to have another chance. Also reports of female infanticide are increasingly frequent.[37]

The one-child policy, an attempt to move well below replacement level fertility and reduce the final size of the population, will have dramatic effects on the age distribution in China, even if only partially successful. Initially the youth burden of dependency will shrink. Within two decades, labor force growth will decline. Then, as the cohorts born before the strict birth control regime begin to retire, the old-age burden of dependency will soar. The rapid aging of the Chinese population may bring a rigid, overly conservative society, where seniority rules and frustrated youth confront blocked upward mobility. Of more immediate concern may be the social implications of generations of one-child families. Single children, lavished with attention and gifts from two sets of grandparents and being the beneficiaries of preferential treatment in school, may become spoiled—unaccustomed to sharing and sacrifice and unfamiliar with the normal give-and-take of growing up with siblings.[38]

China's experiment in authoritarian birth control is still unfolding. The implications for the rest of the world of China's striving to cope with its population growth are profound. Will other nations face a similar predicament in the future? In fact, sometime in the twenty-first century India may surpass China as the most populous nation. Can China's population policy be replicated? Should it?

---

[36]The 1.7 billion is the World Bank's projected stationary population for China. See World Bank, *World Development Report 1994*, Table 25. Tien et al. (1992, page 2) note that the Chinese population is officially projected to exceed 1.3 billion by the year 2000.

[37]Tien (1983, page 20). Tien et al. (1992, page 11) observe that the total fertility rate did not fall below 2.5 births in rural areas, although it dropped to 1.2 births in urban areas. In the late 1980s, couples in the rural areas were generally permitted to have a second child, if the first had been a girl. From the outset, ethnic minorities were granted special dispensation for second, and even third, births. Even so, the sex ratios at birth in China over the past decade have been extraordinarily high.

[38]If restricted to one child, then parents would want to ensure the chances of a healthy child. Another consequence of the one-child policy may have been the proposed legislation in China to prevent births of children with disabilities, whether from a history of mental illness in the family or hereditary diseases. See Kathy Chen, "China's Idea for 'Better' Babies Welcomed," *Wall Street Journal* (December 30, 1993), page A6.

## CONCLUDING NOTE

Population policy is clearly an important and controversial area, especially for the less developed countries where rapid population growth is making it more difficult to sustain economic development. A key—if not, *the* key—to reducing high fertility and lowering the rate of population growth is economic development. Government intervention—whether through family planning programs, economic incentives, induced social change, or more authoritarian birth-control measures—can enhance the transition to lower fertility. As the role of the government increases beyond family planning services, however, individual choice in reproduction may be sacrificed.

In Chapter 8 we address another facet of population policy: human capital formation resulting from gains in nutrition, health, and education. Human capital formation can be considered as both an investment in the productivity of the labor force and as consumption in the form of an improved quality of life. After all, the primary objective of economic development, when all is said and done, is better-nourished, healthier, more-educated individuals living longer.

## SUMMARY OF MAIN POINTS

1. The effects of population growth on the economic development of a country depend on the rate of population increase, the natural resource base, the stocks of physical and human capital, and the available technology.
2. For low-income economies, rapid population growth can seriously impede economic development, primarily by taxing the natural resource base and limiting the physical and human capital deepening required to improve labor productivity and generate economic growth.
3. A wide range of perspectives exists on the relationship between population growth and economic development in the less developed countries, from population growth promoting economic development to its being the primary cause of underdevelopment.
4. Fertility rates decline with economic development and increases in per capita income, but not because children are "inferior goods." Rather, with education and improved economic mobility, parents opt for having fewer children and investing more in each child. Also, large families conflict with satisfying the rise in consumer aspirations.
5. Natural fertility refers to the number of births, on average, to a woman who follows the prevailing social customs and does not consciously attempt to control her fertility.
6. According to Easterlin, there are basically two fertility regimes. One is a natural fertility regime, characteristic of developing economies, in which there is an excess demand for children and, consequently, little motivation to use birth control. The second, characteristic of developed economies, is a discretionary fertility regime, where the demand for children is the dominant influence on fertility.
7. With economic development, the motivation for using birth control increases with the potential excess supply of children. Family planning programs (FPP), by

reducing the monetary and psychic costs of using contraception, can enhance a decline in fertility, once underway.

8. The type of population policy appropriate for a particular country depends on the perceived relationship between the current population growth and the desired social, cultural, and economic objectives. The range of policy options includes laissez-faire, family planning programs, economic incentives and disincentives, social legislation, and population control through birth licenses.

9. China has instituted an authoritarian birth-control policy in an attempt to reverse the considerable population momentum that had built up in the 1950s and 1960s. The government of China hopes to stabilize the population at a level consistent with its natural resource endowment and economic goals. The centerpiece of the policy is a system of birth licenses to promote the one-child norm.

## KEY TERMS

**family planning programs**
**marginal rate of substitution**
**natural fertility**

**permanent income**
**population policy**
**quality of children**

## QUESTIONS

1. Given the following utility-maximizing model for a representative couple in a developing economy:

$$\text{maximize } U = U(C, X) \text{ subject to } Q \cdot C + P \cdot X = I$$

where
- $U$ = lifetime total utility of the couple
- $C$ = number of children
- $X$ = quantities of other goods and services unrelated to childrearing
- $Q$ = expenditures per child (desired quality of children)
- $P$ = price index of goods and services unrelated to childrearing
- $I$ = permanent income

   *a.* Assume that initially $I_0 = 100$, $P_0 = 1$ and $Q_0 = 10$.
   Assume also that the couple is indifferent among the following 10 combinations of $C$ and $X$ on one of its indifference curves, $U_0$

   | C | 10 | 9 | 8 | 7 | 6 | 5 | 4 | 3 | 2 | 1 |
   |---|----|----|----|----|----|----|----|----|-----|-----|
   | X | 20 | 22 | 26 | 32 | 40 | 52 | 68 | 90 | 115 | 150 |

   Using a large graph and graph paper, carefully sketch the couple's indifference curve, $U_0$, placing $C$ on the vertical axis. Graphically determine the utility-maximizing combination of children and other goods and services.

   *b.* Using Easterlin's supply–demand synthesis, discuss whether the demand for children found in 1a will necessarily equal the actual fertility of the representative couple.

c. Suppose that with economic development, permanent income rises to $I_1 = 330$; the price index for other goods and services doubles, $P_1 = 2$; and a representative couple triples the desired quality of children to $Q_1 = 30$.

Assume also that the tastes and preferences of a representative couple change (i.e., a new indifference mapping is relevant) and that the following combinations of C and X are on indifference curve $U'_1$, given below.

| C | 10 | 9  | 8  | 7  | 6  | 5  | 4   | 3   | 2   | 1   |
|---|----|----|----|----|----|----|-----|-----|-----|-----|
| X | 77 | 78 | 80 | 84 | 90 | 98 | 108 | 120 | 138 | 160 |

On the same graph, sketch the new indifference curve, $U'_1$, and determine the new utility-maximizing combination of children and other goods and services. With economic development and the rise in income, what has happened to the relative preference for children? Specifically, how can you tell?

2. The per capita GNPs (in international dollars) and total fertility rates in 1993 are listed below for four countries.

|             | 1993 Per Capita GNP | 1993 Total Fertility Rate |
|-------------|---------------------|---------------------------|
| Congo       | $2440               | 6.2                       |
| Philippines | $2670               | 3.9                       |
| Indonesia   | $3150               | 2.8                       |
| Peru        | $3220               | 3.3                       |

(Statistics are from the World Bank, *World Development Report 1995*, Tables 26 and 30.)

   a. Discuss the factors that might explain the difference between the total fertility rates for Congo and the Philippines. Check the World Bank's *World Development Report 1995* for evidence supporting your hypotheses.
   b. Repeat 2a for Indonesia and Peru.
   c. Based on these two pairs of countries, can you draw any conclusions about the determinants of fertility in developing countries? Discuss.
3. Uganda's total fertility rate is estimated to have risen from 6.9 in 1970 to 7.2 in 1993 (World Bank, *World Development Report 1995*, Table 26).
   a. Using Easterlin's framework, explain how this rise in fertility might have occurred.
   b. Outline a strategy for reducing fertility in Uganda. Be specific.
4. Bangladesh succeeded in lowering its total fertility rate dramatically from 7.0 to 4.3 between 1970 and 1993 (World Bank, *World Development Report 1995*, Table 26), despite having a low level of economic development. What might explain this?
5. Which of the eight positions outlined in the chapter on the relationship between population growth and economic development do you think is most relevant for developing countries today? Discuss why. Do you believe any of the positions may be counterproductive or even harmful? Discuss.

## SUGGESTED READINGS

Becker, Gary, "An Economic Analysis of Fertility," in *Demographic and Economic Change in Developed Countries*, National Bureau of Economic Research, Princeton, NJ: Princeton University Press, 1960, pages 209–231.

Bulatao, Rodolfo, "Effective Family Planning Programs," Washington, DC: The World Bank, 1993.

Caldwell, John, I. O. Orubuloye, and Pat Caldwell, "Fertility Decline in Africa: A New Type of Transition," *Population and Development Review*, vol. 18, no. 2 (June 1992), pages 211–242.

Easterlin, Richard and Eileen Crimmins, *The Fertility Revolution: A Supply–Demand Analysis*, Chicago: The University of Chicago Press, 1985.

Hess, Peter, "An Eclectic Model of the Fertility Transition," in *Population Growth and Socioeconomic Progress in Less Developed Countries*, New York: Praeger, 1988, pages 111–125.

Kelley, Allen, "Economic Consequences of Population Change in the Third World," *Journal of Economic Literature*, vol. 26, no. 4 (December 1988), pages 1685–1728.

Keyfitz, Nathan, "The Population of China," *Scientific American*, vol. 250, no. 2 (February 1984), pages 38–47.

Mueller, Eva and Kathleen Short, "Effects of Income and Wealth on the Demand for Children," in *Determinants of Fertility in Developing Countries*, vol. 1, edited by Rodolfo Bulatao and Ronald Lee, with Paula Hollerbach and John Bongaarts, New York: Academic Press, 1983.

Tien, H. Yuan, "China: Demographic Billionaire," *Population Bulletin*, vol. 38, no. 2 (April 1983).

Tien, H. Yuan, with Zhang Tianlu, Ping Yu, Li Jingneng, and Liang Zhongtang, "China's Demographic Dilemmas," *Population Bulletin*, vol. 47, no. 1 (June 1992).

"U.S. Policy Statement for the International Conference on Population," *Population and Development Review*, vol. 10, no. 3 (September 1984), pages 574–579.

World Bank, "The Consequences of Rapid Population Growth," Chapter 5, and "Slowing Population Growth," Chapter 6, in *World Development Report 1984*, New York: Oxford University Press, 1984.

# APPENDIX

## DETERMINANTS OF FERTILITY: CROSS-COUNTRY EVIDENCE

To assess the determinants of fertility in less developed countries, we estimate a simultaneous model for the total fertility rate and infant mortality rate for a cross-section of low- and middle-income economies. The policy implications of the regression analysis are briefly discussed.

According to demographic transition theory, declines in infant and child mortality trigger declines in fertility. In traditional societies children are economic assets, producers of income and providers of old-age security. For any given demand for children, increased survival rates would be necessary before parents would willingly cut back on fertility. High rates of fertility, however, can contribute to high infant and child mortality. With closely spaced births (i.e., under two years), infants may be weaned too soon and thereby deprived of the complete nutritional and immunological benefits of breastfeeding. Too little space between children may stretch the resources of the household and reduce the attention and quality of care each child receives. Moreover, the ability of the mother to recover physically may be impaired by too-short birth intervals. Thus, fertility and infant mortality are directly related and simultaneously determined. The two dependent variables in the model are the national total fertility rate (TFR) and infant mortality rate (IMR) for 1991.

Two other determinants of fertility tested are female education and family planning program effort. For the reasons discussed earlier in the chapter, we expect a negative relationship between female education and fertility. To review briefly, education increases a woman's economic mobility and the wages she can earn. Consequently, having and rearing children become more expensive. Moreover, educated women are more likely and better able to use effective contraception. The explanatory variable for education is the mean years of schooling for adult females, FED, in the nation in 1990.

To measure family planning program effort, we select a widely used assessment of the comparative strengths of family planning programs.[1] National family planning programs were evaluated for 1989 on the basis of criteria such as official support for family planning and the coverage and quality of family planning services provided. The family planning program effort (FPP) of the nation is rated as either strong, moderate, or weak.[2]

For the independent determinants of the infant mortality rate we use female education; per capita Gross Domestic Product valued in international dollars; and an infant immunization rate. More-educated women would probably have better knowledge of hygiene and preventative health care and would be more likely to recognize illness and seek medical assistance when required. Per capita Gross Domestic Product (GDP), a measure of the average income generated in the nation in 1991, is expressed here as an index, based on the Gross Domestic Product per capita for the United States in 1991 ($22,130), which is set equal to 100. Increases in per capita income would permit better diets, sanitary conditions, and health care. Access to basic health-care services for infants may be captured by the percentage of infants fully immunized against diphtheria, pertussis, and tetanus (DPT) in 1990–1991.

In Figure 7A.1 we illustrate the basic model, with the definitions and data sources for the variables also listed. The two dependent variables, TFR and IMR, are circled, with the plus sign over the double arrow between them indicating the positive feedback relationship. Recall that the total fertility rate (TFR) measures the average number of children that would be born to a woman who survived through the childbearing years and gave birth according to the prevailing schedule of age-specific fertility rates. The infant mortality rate (IMR) is the number of infant deaths (before age 1) per thousand live births. Nations with a high infant mortality rate would be expected to have a high total fertility rate and vice versa. The independent variables are enclosed in rectangles. Female education (FED) is hypothesized to be inversely related to both the total fertility rate and the infant mortality rate. The negative influences of the other exogenous explanatory variables are indicated by the minus signs along the directed arrows: FPP for the total fertility rate; GDP and DPT for the infant mortality rate.

The sample consists of 61 low- and middle-income economies—all the less developed countries for which comparable data on the variables in the model could be assembled. In Table 7A.1 we present some sample statistics (mean and range) for the variables. Of the 61 LDCs in the sample, 10 had strong family planning programs; 18 were judged to have moderate family planning program efforts; and 33 nations were ranked as having weak or nonexistent family planning programs.[3]

---

[1] See Rodolfo Bulatao, "Family Planning: The Unfinished Revolution," *Finance and Development*, vol. 29, no. 4 (December 1992), page 5. For a discussion of the original index of family planning program effort, see W. Parker Mauldin and Robert J. Lapham, "Measuring Family Planning Program Effort in Developing Countries, 1972 and 1982," in *The Effects of Family Planning Programs on Fertility in the Developing World*, World Bank Staff Working Papers, No. 677, Nancy Birdsall, ed., Washington, DC: 1985.

[2] The two-year lag for family planning program effort (1989) and one-year lag for adult female schooling (1990), which reflected the data availability at the time of the study, should not significantly affect the regression estimates for the 1991 total fertilty rate and infant mortality rate.

[3] The 10 nations in the sample classified as having a strong family planning program effort are Bangladesh, India, China, Sri Lanka, Indonesia, El Salvador, Tunisia, Thailand, Mexico, and South

*continued*

### FIGURE 7A.1 — FLOW CHART OF SIMULTANEOUS MODEL

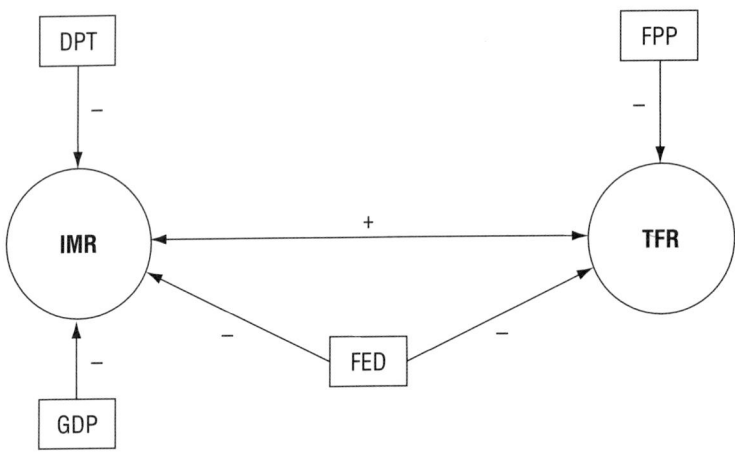

TFR = Total fertility rate in 1991
(from World Bank, *World Development Report 1993*, Table 27)

IMR = Infant mortality rate in 1991
(from World Bank, *World Development Report 1993*, Table 28)

FED = Mean years of schooling for adult females (age 25 years or older) in 1990 (from United Nations Development Programme, *Human Development Report 1993*, Table 5)

FPP = Family planning program effort in 1989
  1 if family planning program effort is strong
FPP = 0 if family planning program effort is moderate
  −1 if family planning program effort is weak or nonexistent
(From Rodolfo Bulatao, "Family Planning: The Unfinished Revolution," *Finance and Development*, vol. 29, no. 4 (December 1992), page 5)

DPT = Percentage of children under age one immunized in 1990–1991 with three completed doses of vaccine against diphtheria, pertussis (whooping cough), and tetanus.
(From World Bank, *World Development Report 1993*, Table A8)

GDP = Gross Domestic Product per capita in 1991 in international dollars—adjusted for domestic purchasing powers of national currencies and indexed to U.S. per capita GDP in 1991 (100).
(From World Bank, *World Development Report 1993*, Table 30)

The regression results from estimating the two equations simultaneously are presented in Table 7A.2. We observe that 74 percent and 77 percent of the variation in the 1991 total fertility rates and infant mortality rates, respectively, are explained by the regression equations. (See the adjusted coefficients of determination, $\bar{R}^2$.) Consistent with our hypothesis, the total fertility rate and infant mortality rate are interdependent,

---

Korea. The 18 nations with a moderate family planning program effort are Nepal, Kenya, Ghana, Pakistan, Honduras, Egypt, Zimbabwe, Philippines, Guatemala, Dominican Republic, Ecuador, Morocco, Peru, Colombia, Chile, Iran, Malaysia, and Venezuela. The 33 nations with a weak or nonexistent family planning program effort are Mozambique, Tanzania, Ethiopia, Uganda, Burundi, Chad, Madagascar, Sierra Leone, Lao PDR, Malawi, Rwanda, Mali, Burkina Faso, Niger, Nigeria, Haiti, Benin, Central African Republic, Togo, Bolivia, Côte d'Ivoire, Senegal, Papua New Guinea, Cameroon, Jordan, Syria, Paraguay, Turkey, Algeria, Argentina, Uruguay, Brazil, and Saudi Arabia.

### TABLE 7A.1  Selected Sample Statistics for the 61 LDCs

| Variable | Mean | Minimum | Maximum |
|---|---|---|---|
| TFR<br>1991 total fertility rate | 5.0 | 1.8<br>(S. Korea) | 7.6<br>(Malawi) |
| IMR<br>1991 infant mortality rate | 73.0 | 15<br>(Malaysia) | 161<br>(Mali) |
| FED<br>mean years of schooling<br>for adult females in 1990 | 2.6 | .1<br>(4 nations) | 8.9<br>(Argentina) |
| GDP<br>1991 per capita Gross Domestic<br>Product (U.S. GDP = 100) | 13.5 | 1.7<br>(Ethiopia) | 49.0<br>(Saudi Arabia) |
| DPT<br>Infant immunization rate in<br>1990–1991 | 69.4% | 18%<br>(Chad) | 95%<br>(China) |

### TABLE 7A.2  Regression Results (Simultaneous Model)

$$\widehat{TFR} = \underset{***}{4.45} + \underset{*}{.013}\,IMR - \underset{***}{.73}\,FPP - \underset{***}{.27}\,FED \qquad \overline{R}^2 = .74$$

$$\widehat{IMR} = \underset{*}{58.3} + \underset{***}{11.25}\,TFR - \underset{*}{.25}\,DPT - 2.26\,FED - \underset{***}{1.34}\,GDP \qquad \overline{R}^2 = .77$$

\* = Estimated coefficient is statistically significant at the 10% level.
\*\* = Estimated coefficient is statistically significant at the 5% level.
\*\*\* = Estimated coefficient is statistically significant at the 1% level.

with the influence of fertility on infant mortality appearing to be more significant. In fact, without incorporating the simultaneity, the estimated influence of TFR on IMR would be understated.[4]

Ceteris paribus, across this sample of LDCs, a decrease of one birth in the total fertility rate is associated with a decrease of 11.25 infant deaths in the infant mortality rate. The influence of the infant mortality rate on the total fertility rate is statistically only marginally significant (at the 10 percent level). A decrease of 10 (infant deaths per

---

[4]The estimated coefficient for TFR when the IMR equation is independently estimated with ordinary least squares (not shown here) is equal to 7.89, as compared with the estimated coefficient for TFR (11.25) in the simultaneous model estimation with two-stage least squares.

thousand live births) in the IMR is associated with a decrease of .13 births in the predicted TFR.

For the TFR estimation, both the female education and family planning program variables are statistically very significant influences (at the 1 percent level) on the total fertility rate. An increase of 1 year in the mean schooling of adult females in the nation would reduce the total fertility rate by .27 births, ceteris paribus. Controlling for female education and the infant mortality rate, a nation with a strong (weak) family planning program effort would have a predicted TFR that is lower (higher) by .73 births compared to a nation with a moderate effort in family planning.

For the IMR estimation, other than the total fertility rate, the statistically most significant influence on the infant mortality rate is per capita GDP.[5] An increase of 10 points (roughly $2100 in internationally comparable dollars) in per capita GDP is associated with a decrease of 13.4 (infant deaths) in the predicted value for the infant mortality rate. The influence of female education on infant mortality is statistically insignificant with the simultaneous estimation.[6] The infant immunization rate is marginally significant: A 10 percentage point increase in the proportion of infants vaccinated against diphtheria, pertussis, and tetanus, ceteris paribus, is associated with a decrease of 2.5 (infant deaths) in the predicted IMR.

Overall, the regression results are robust. There are no observations in the sample that seriously distort the estimated regression coefficients. In sum, there is cross-country support for the importance of economic development (lowering infant mortality rates and increasing schooling for females) and family planning programs for reducing fertility in developing nations. Moreover, reducing total fertility rates and increasing birth intervals may be a key to reducing the high rates of infant mortality.

---

[5]We might add that including per capita Gross Domestic Product as an explanatory variable in the total fertility regression does not add to the explanatory power of the model and has no significant impact on the other estimated coefficients.

[6]Using ordinary least squares to estimate the IMR equation independently, the estimated coefficient for the female education variable (FED) was equal to −3.72, and statistically significant at the 5 percent level. The implication is that increases in female schooling work indirectly (through lowering the total fertility rate) to reduce the infant mortality rate.

CHAPTER 8

# HUMAN CAPITAL FORMATION

The Nobel-laureate economist Theodore Schultz once observed:

> The decisive factors of production in improving the welfare of poor people are not space, energy, and cropland; the decisive factors are the improvement in population quality and advances in knowledge.[1]

Human capital formation, reflected in improvements in nutrition and health and gains in knowledge and skills, not only translates into increased productivity, but directly enhances the quality of life. The increased productivity from investing in human capital is measured by the rise in output from a given physical amount of labor, holding constant the uses of all nonhuman factors and the level of technology. Enhancement in the quality of life refers to the additional utility individuals receive from living longer, feeling better, and knowing more.

We begin this chapter with an overview of the importance of human capital formation for economic development. The related areas of nutrition, health, and education are examined in detail. We review the progress the developing nations have made, as well as the considerable gaps that remain between the developed and less developed economies in human capital formation. While considerable resources have been devoted to human capital formation in the LDCs, the returns have not always justified the costs. Consequently, we discuss the need for policy reform.

---

[1]Theodore Schultz, *Investing in People: The Economics of Population Quality*, Berkeley, CA: The University of California Press, 1981, page 4.

## HUMAN CAPITAL FORMATION AND ECONOMIC DEVELOPMENT

Investments in population quality, like all commitments of resources, have opportunity costs in the forms of forgone consumption, physical capital formation, or expenditures on national defense. On the other hand, human capital formation often has positive externalities. For example, better-nourished and healthier individuals are less likely to become ill and pass on communicable diseases. Education may stimulate entrepreneurship and the creation of economic opportunities and employment. Literate populations may contribute to political stability and the safeguarding of democratic rights.

In many cases the benefits of investments in human capital can be measured. For instance, ensuring that expectant mothers receive adequate nutrition and health care reduces the incidence of low-birth-weight babies and the attendant intensive medical care then required. Well-nourished and healthy children not only are more likely to attend school regularly (reducing absenteeism and dropout rates that diminish the returns on public education expenditures), but perform better while in school. Educational productivity, measured, for example, by standardized test scores, should rise. Better-educated students should become more productive workers and more knowledgeable parents.

One of the most evident signs of human capital formation is increased life expectancy, which extends the "pay-off" period for investments in population quality. As the World Bank notes, impressive progress has been made.

> Over the past forty years life expectancy has improved more than during the entire previous span of human history. In 1950 life expectancy in developing countries was forty years; by 1990 it had increased to sixty-three years.[2]

Yet great gaps between the North and South remain.

> If death rates among children in poor countries were reduced to those prevailing in rich countries, 11 million fewer children would die each year. Almost half of these preventable deaths are a result of diarrheal and respiratory illness, exacerbated by malnutrition. In addition, every year 7 million adults die of conditions that could be inexpensively prevented or cured; tuberculosis alone causes 2 million of these deaths. About 400,000 women die from the direct complications of pregnancy and childbirth. Maternal mortality ratios are, on average, thirty times as high in developing countries as in high-income countries.[3]

Some of the benefits of human capital formation, however, are difficult to quantify, though no less important. Consider improvements in nutrition that contribute to declines in morbidity rates or the incidence of disease. Reducing morbidity enhances the physiological and psychological capacities for work, study, and play. Healthier

---

[2]World Bank, *World Development Report 1993: Investing in Health,* New York: Oxford University Press, 1993, page 1.
[3]Ibid.

#### FIGURE 8.1   THE EFFECTS OF HUMAN CAPITAL FORMATION ON A COHORT OF NEWBORNS

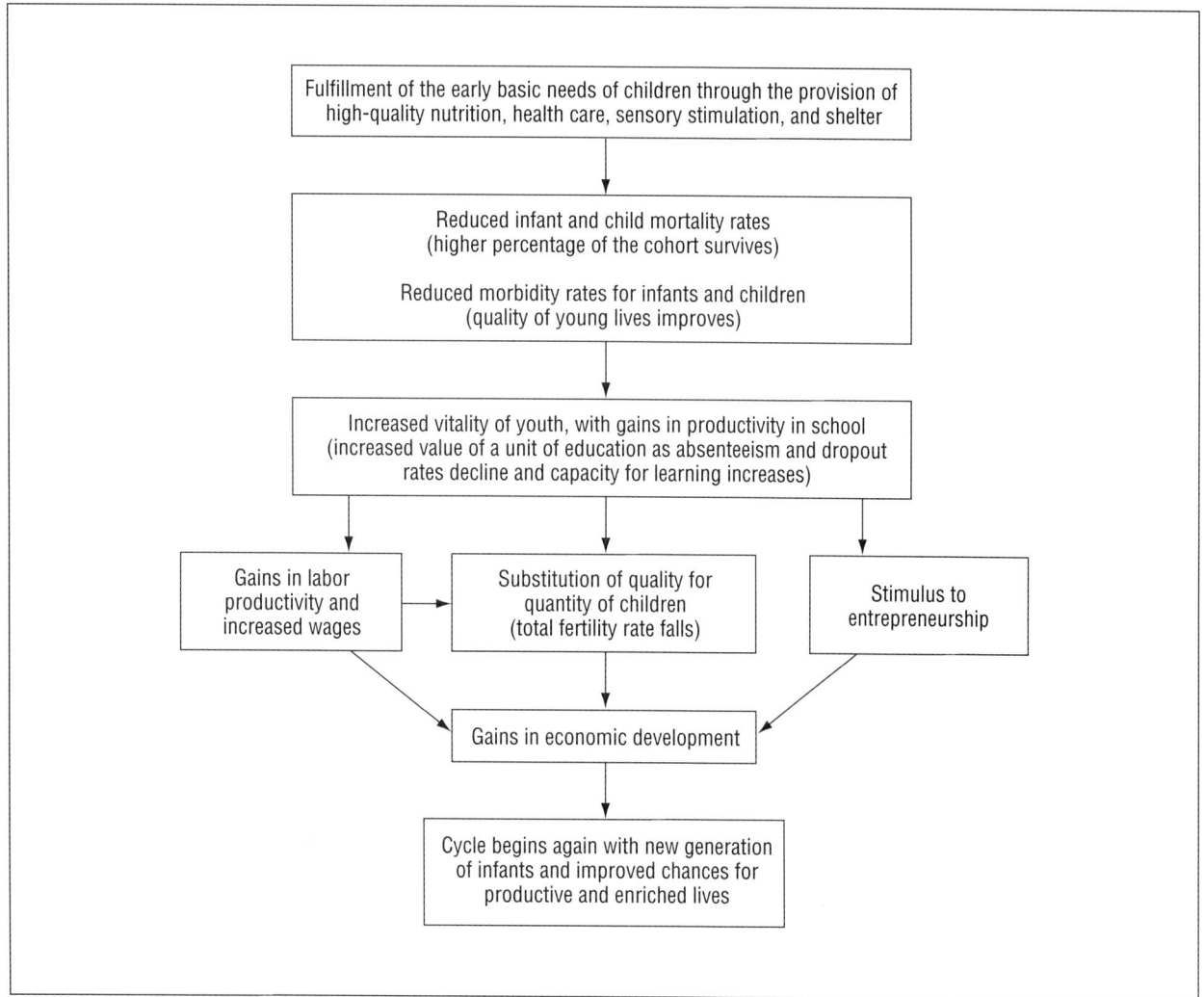

individuals tend to have more positive outlooks, greater confidence, and are more willing and able to accept challenges.

In Figure 8.1 the effects of investing in a cohort of newborns are summarized. The benefits of human capital formation accumulate over the life cycle and can be passed from one generation to the next.

Nevertheless, because investments in human capital are typically less tangible than investments in physical capital (e.g., the purchase of a new machine), and because the contributions to economic growth from investments in nutrition, health, and education may be significantly delayed, while the costs are more immediate, human capital formation often has not received its due emphasis in development strategies. Recall the growth-model approach to economic development, with its stress on physical capital formation, that dominated theory and policy in the first two decades following World

War II. By the mid-1960s, however, human capital was increasingly recognized as an important factor constraining economic growth and development. With the basic needs orientation in the 1970s, the importance of human capital formation was further highlighted.

Indeed, skilled labor and physical capital are complementary factors of production. Literate, healthy workers are required to operate and maintain modern machinery and equipment. Educated and well-trained personnel are needed to provide the services in public administration, finance, education, health care, and communications that are essential to a modern economy. Education increases the willingness to take calculated risks. From the farmers who adopt new seeds to the entrepreneurs who open new businesses, innovators are the protagonists of economic development.

We turn now to the major components of human capital formation: nutrition, health, and education. As we progress through the chapter, keep in mind that these three are mutually reinforcing investments in population quality. Referring back periodically to Figure 8.1 will be helpful for its illustration of the progressive cycle of improvement in human capital.

## NUTRITION

Nutrition refers to the use of food for the growth (before adulthood), maintenance, and functioning of the mind and body. Adequate nutrition is a basic human need, the neglect of which can seriously diminish productivity and the quality of life. **Undernutrition** occurs when across-the-board deficits exist in the essential nutrients. **Malnutrition** is related more to inefficiencies in the allocation of nutrients (poor choice in diet) or in the processing and use of food (with illness or poor hygiene).

### THE IMPORTANCE OF NUTRITION

Good nutrition is especially important for infants and young children. Protein deficiencies can have an adverse impact on cognitive development. In the case of severe malnutrition at an early age, irreversible damage may occur to the central nervous system. Milder forms of malnutrition are evidenced by apathetic behavior and listlessness, which dull the responsiveness of children to environmental stimuli. Poorly nourished children are more susceptible to disease and are less able to recover once afflicted.

The World Bank has recently catalogued some of the more grave nutrient disorders found in the developing nations.[4]

---

[4]Ibid., pages 75–77.

Iron deficiency is the most common micronutrient disorder. It reduces physical productivity and children's capacity to learn in school. By reducing appetite, it may diminish children's intake and growth. Women suffer especially because menstruation and childbearing raise their need for iron, and anemia, a shortage of iron in the blood, increases the risk of death from hemorrhage in childbirth. The problem is worst in India, where 88 percent of pregnant women are anemic ...

Iodine deficiency causes mental retardation, delayed motor development, and stunting, as well as neuromuscular, speech, and hearing disorders. It is the leading preventable cause of intellectual impairment in the world. Cretinism from iodine deficiency affects 5.7 million people, and lack of iodine causes another 20 million to be mentally retarded.

Vitamin A deficiency causes varying degrees of vision loss and is the primary cause of acquired blindness in children. It also increases the severity of and mortality from a variety of infections, especially measles and diarrhea. WHO (World Health Organization) calculates that 13.8 million children have some degree of eye damage because of vitamin A deficiency; of these, 250,000 to 500,000 go blind each year and two-thirds of the blinded children die. Both vitamin A and iodine deficiency are particularly common in Asia and sub-Saharan Africa.

In short, an erosion in human capital can be triggered by early deprivation. Inadequate nutrition for infants and young children impairs their abilities to function and learn, reducing the returns from investments in health and education, consequently limiting future labor productivity and earning capacity, and ultimately perpetuating poverty.

In Table 8.1 summary statistics on malnutrition for 1980 to 1990 are presented. The focus of the World Bank's *World Development Report 1993* was on health. In reporting these statistics on health and nutrition, the World Bank identified eight demographic regions, a grouping that is slightly different from that used throughout the text. The demographic regions are: sub-Saharan Africa, India, China, Other Asia and Islands, Latin America and the Caribbean, Middle Eastern Crescent, Formerly Socialist Economies of Europe, and Established Market Economies. Since the summary statistics for Established Market Economies are not available, we present the data for the United States.

Two indicators of malnutrition are illustrated in Table 8.1 and graphically in Figure 8.2. **Stunting,** defined as low height for age (for children of ages 24 to 59 months), indicates chronic malnutrition. Low incomes, unsanitary conditions, and poor nutritional practices largely explain stunting. **Wasting,** defined as low weight for height (for children of ages 12 to 23 months), indicates acute or short-term malnutrition. Moderate to severe stunting/wasting occurs where the child's height-for-age/weight-for-height profile is more than two standard deviations below the median set by the U.S. National Center for Health Statistics.[5] Crises such as crop failures and upheaval from civil wars are the primary causes of wasting. From the data presented, stunting appears to be significantly more prevalent across the developing nations. More than half of the young children in Asia (outside of China) are afflicted; for China and sub-Saharan Africa, two out of every five children between the ages of two and five years are affected by stunting.

---

[5]Ibid., pages 196–197.

| TABLE 8.1 | SELECTED STATISTICS ON NUTRITION | |
|---|---|---|
| | PERCENTAGE OF CHILDREN AFFECTED BY: | |
| | STUNTING, 1980–1990 (AGES 24–59 MONTHS) | WASTING, 1980–1990 (AGES 12–23 MONTHS) |
| sub-Saharan Africa | 39 | 10 |
| India | 65 | 27 |
| China | 41 | 8 |
| Other Asia & Islands | 53 | 11 |
| Latin America & the Caribbean | 26 | 5 |
| Middle Eastern Crescent | ... | ... |
| Formerly Socialist Economies of Europe | ... | ... |
| Established Market Economies | ... | ... |
| United States | 2 | 2 |

NOTES: Lack of data is indicated by ...
*Stunting* is defined as low height for age.
*Wasting* is defined as low weight for height.
Sub-Saharan Africa comprises all the countries south of the Sahara Desert, including Madagascar and South Africa, but excluding Mauritius, Reunion, and Seychelles, which are in the Other Asia and Islands group.
Other Asia & Islands includes the low- and middle-income economies of Asia (excluding India and China) and the islands of the Indian and Pacific Oceans except for Madagascar.
Latin America & the Caribbean comprises all American and Caribbean economies south of the United States, including Cuba.
Middle Eastern Crescent consists of the group of economies extending across North Africa through the Middle East to the Asian Republics of the former Soviet Union and including Israel, Malta, Pakistan, and Turkey.
Formerly Socialist Economies of Europe include the Eastern republics of the former Soviet Union and the formerly socialist economies of Eastern and Central Europe.
Established Market Economies includes all the countries of the Organization for Economic Cooperation and Development (OECD) except Turkey, as well as a number of small, high-income economies in Europe.
FROM: World Bank, *World Development Report 1993*, Table A.6.

## NUTRITION POLICY

One of the best ways to ensure adequate nutrition for infants is breastfeeding. Mother's milk not only is the optimal source of essential nutrients, but provides immunological benefits to infants. In contrast to infant formula, breastmilk is free and does not need to be mixed with water, which is often contaminated in low-income households. Moreover, as noted in the last chapter, breastfeeding can act as a natural contraceptive, helping to lengthen birth intervals.

In general, infants should be breastfed for the first year or 18 months, with solid foods introduced as a complement after six months. (Exceptions would be for those mothers incapable of producing enough breastmilk to nourish the infants and for those mothers afflicted with the AIDS virus. In these cases bottle feeding would be required from the outset.) Unfortunately, the practice of breastfeeding has been declining in many developing nations, especially among women with some education. Contributing factors are urbanization, with the increased female labor force participation in the modern sector,

## FIGURE 8.2 — INCIDENCES OF STUNTING AND WASTING

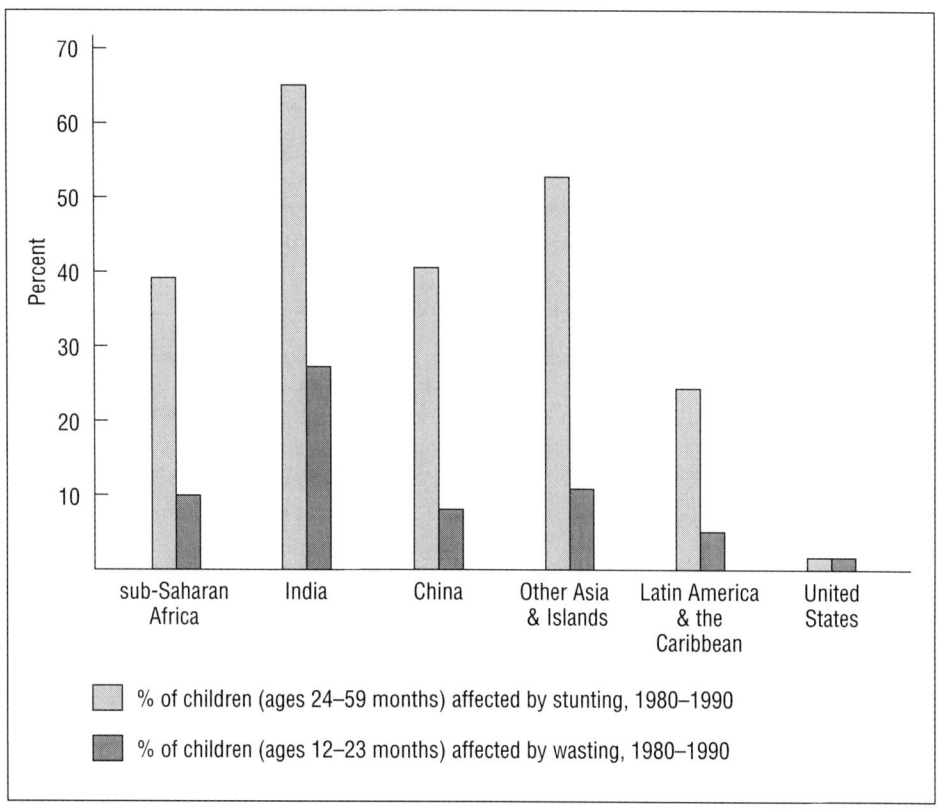

- % of children (ages 24–59 months) affected by stunting, 1980–1990
- % of children (ages 12–23 months) affected by wasting, 1980–1990

and aggressive marketing of infant formula. A first priority of nutrition policy, then, may be to promote the practice of breastfeeding.

Poverty, reflected in an inability to afford an adequate diet, is perhaps the primary explanation for chronic undernutrition. Globally there is more than sufficient capacity in agriculture to provide a balanced diet for every individual. Even some developing nations that are net exporters of food grains have high percentages of their populations undernourished. Low incomes and insufficient purchasing power, not aggregate production constraints, explain widespread undernutrition. On a micro level the problem can be exacerbated by an unequal distribution of food within households. In some societies, during times when food is scarce (whether due to high food prices in the offseason or low incomes), the working males in the family may enjoy priority access to the available food at the expense of women and children, particularly young girls.

Economic growth and rising incomes that are more equitably distributed help to alleviate undernutrition. Agricultural development, including investment in irrigation, research and technical assistance, and improvements in the rural infrastructure, would increase domestic food supplies and moderate food prices. Sometimes, however, with increases in income, households purchase less nutritious, albeit tastier and more varied, diets. Malnutrition may remain a problem even as undernutrition is reduced.

In the short run, governments can directly intervene to improve nutritional levels. For example, subsidies can lower food prices to low-income households. Food stamps can be distributed, allowing qualifying individuals to purchase certain foods at discounted prices. For school children, free or heavily subsidized meals can be provided. One problem with school meals, however, is that households may then cut back on the food portions for the children at home, thereby undermining the goal of improving their nutrition.

Food subsidy programs can be very expensive unless the target population is limited and well-defined. When food subsidies become universal entitlements, not only are current government budgets strained, but any attempts to pare back the subsidies as populations grow will be resisted, sometimes violently. If, to reduce costs, governments lower the prices paid to farmers, less incentive exists for farmers to produce. Consequently, the nation may have to import foodstuffs, with the attendant drain on foreign exchange. Some foreign aid, though, has taken the form of "food-for-work" programs that help meet the nutritional needs of poor workers on public projects while conserving on foreign exchange.

Food fortification is another option. Here nutrients are directly added to processed food. For example, iodine could be added to salt and vitamin A to tea. Two related problems arise. One, the additives will be consumed by all who purchase the fortified food, even those with otherwise healthy diets. Second, those most likely in need of the nutrients, namely the rural poor, may buy little processed food, relying on home-grown produce or informal farmers' markets.

Along with encouragement of breastfeeding, more effective education is needed on nutrition and basic hygiene, from instruction on balanced diets and the sanitary preparation of foods to the debunking of traditional practices that undermine good nutrition. For instance, the World Bank notes that, "In a number of Asian and African countries, children and women, especially pregnant women, are discouraged from eating eggs and fruit."[6] Nutrition education can be integrated into the school curriculum and prenatal and infant health care.

On the macro level, public campaigns can promote sound nutritional practices and distribute medicine to cure parasitic worms such as roundworms and hookworms, which compete for food with the host body. Public projects to increase popular access to safe water and to provide proper sewerage would also contribute to better nutrition. Finally, if civil wars and internal strife could be prevented, so could a primary cause of the famine and wasting produced by the disruption to agriculture, the breakdown of distribution networks, and the movement of refugees.

Thus, measures to address the widespread undernutrition and malnutrition in the less developed countries are possible. To what extent governments should directly intervene to promote good nutrition, however, is controversial. As with any resource commitment, programs to improve nutrition should be subject to benefit-cost analysis. Later in this chapter we will illustrate a benefit-cost analysis for investment in education.

---

[6]Ibid., page 79. For a good overview of the nutritional challenges and policies in the LDCs, see pages 75–82 of the *World Development Report 1993*. For an exhaustive survey of the literature on nutrition and health, see Jere Behrman and Anil Deolalikar, "Health and Nutrition," pages 631–711 in *Handbook of Development Economics, Volume 1,* edited by Hollis Chenery and T. N. Srinivasan, Amsterdam: North Holland, 1988.

## HEALTH

Like nutrition, good health is essential for individuals to realize their full potentials—whether working on the job, learning in school, performing the necessary tasks at home, or simply enjoying leisure time. Poor nutrition can lead to poor health, just as poor health can contribute to poor nutrition. As cited earlier, the main causes of mortality in young children in developing economies are diarrheal diseases and respiratory infections (e.g., influenza and pneumonia). A major reason these and other curable diseases end in death is their interaction with malnutrition, which lowers the child's resistance and weakens their ability to recover once ill.

The World Bank lists four ways that improved health contributes to economic growth.[7] First, healthier workers have fewer absences from the job and greater physiological capacities for work. Hence, there are output gains associated with good health. Similarly, healthier children are absent less from school and, when feeling good, perform better in school. Third, the eradication of diseases (e.g., malaria and riverblindness) allows for the reclamation of land, such as fertile river banks, that may have been abandoned due to earlier infestation. Fourth, to the extent diseases can be prevented, the resources that would have been used for treatment are saved. A dramatic example is AIDS (Acquired Immune Deficiency Syndrome). As reported by the World Bank:

> Although it [AIDS] remains much less common in the developing world than diseases such as malaria, its economic impact per case is greater for two reasons: it mainly affects adults in their most productive years, and the infections resulting from it lead to heavy demand for expensive health care.... Research in nine developing and seven high-income countries suggests that preventing a case of AIDS saves, on average, about twice GNP per capita in discounted lifetime costs of medical care; in some urban areas the saving may be as much as five times GNP per capita.[8]

As we will discuss later, many less developed countries have not sufficiently emphasized preventative measures in health care.

## HEALTH CONDITIONS IN THE LESS DEVELOPED COUNTRIES

High rates of mortality and morbidity are directly related to poverty. Low-income households are more likely to live in areas where diseases are endemic, sanitary conditions inadequate, and medical assistance deficient. Disease-carrying insects, such as mosquitoes (malaria) and tsetse flies (sleeping sickness) thrive in the hot, humid conditions found in many developing countries. Restricted access to safe water and the

---

[7]World Bank, *World Development Report 1993*, page 17.
[8]Ibid., page 20. Globally, deaths from AIDS in 1994 were estimated to be 1.5 million, one third of whom were women. The incidence of AIDS is, by far, the highest in sub-Saharan Africa, where nearly 1.3 million died from AIDS in 1994 and where, unlike the rest of the world, more female (40%) deaths occurred than male (37%). Deaths to children from AIDS accounted for the remaining 23% of the total. From "Women, Children, and AIDS," *Population Today* (April 1995), page 3.

lack of proper treatment of sewage perpetuate the diseases transmitted by human feces, including dysentary, cholera, and typhoid fever. Intestinal and parasitic disorders are also common under such conditions. The congestion and attendant air pollution in many urban areas further contribute to health problems, particularly respiratory infections and cancers.

The poor, who tend to have little education and cannot afford decent shelter and diets, are more vulnerable to diseases since they often fail to take basic precautionary measures. Many who then become ill cannot afford the necessary medicines even when available. Many in the rural areas are effectively cut off from medical care. The loss of income when a working adult becomes sick can financially devastate households living on the margin, thereby plunging families into abject poverty.

While decreasing slowly in the developed countries, per capita consumption of tobacco and alcohol is on the rise in many developing countries.[9] Smoking and alcohol abuse not only are unhealthy, but are a drain on household budgets. Negative externalities also exist. The incidence of respiratory problems is higher for nonsmokers in the presence of smokers—the ill effects of passive smoking. Safety issues arise: Alcohol abuse disproportionately contributes to injury and death on the highways. Intoxicated workers not only are less productive, but are more prone to accidents.

For reasons not entirely understood, females generally live longer than males. The female advantage in life expectancy increases with economic development and is evident in Table 8.2, which presents data for male and female life expectancies at birth for 1970 and 1993. (*Note:* We return to the standard regional grouping of nations.) Several factors may help to explain the varying differentials.

As discussed in Chapter 7, high rates of fertility are directly related to high rates of infant and child mortality. Early marriage and short birth intervals, combined with poor access to health care, contribute to the high rates of maternal mortality. In male-dominant societies, abuse of females may be more tolerated. In many LDCs, especially in Asia, strong preferences for sons persist. Economically, daughters are less of an asset to parents. Young girls may face discrimination in nutrition, health care, and education. Female economic mobility is limited. So too, in Middle Eastern and North African nations females are traditionally subservient. In some parts of Africa, a painful and unhealthy ritual of circumcision for young girls is often performed under unsanitary conditions. With economic development, life expectancy improves, as well as the rights of females.

In Table 8.3 on page 230, we present statistics on health care using the regional grouping of nations in Table 8.1. One measure of health-care inputs is medical doctors per thousand population. While professional requirements for medical certification may vary across countries, very large regional differences are found in the doctor/population ratios. Sub-Saharan Africa and Asia (with the exception of China) stand out as well below average. These two regions also have the lowest average life expectancies at birth (refer back to Table 8.2). On the other hand, the average doctor/population ratios for the Formerly Socialist Economies of Europe are half again as high as for the Established Market Economies. The low doctor/population ratios in sub-Saharan Africa and Asia are somewhat offset by the high ratios of nurses to doctors. Caution, however, is warranted in drawing inferences about access to health care from comparisons of doctor/population ratios. For one, most of the doctors in the LDCs live in the urban areas and may not be easily available to the rural population. Second, the

---

[9]Ibid., pages 86–89.

| TABLE 8.2 | MALE AND FEMALE LIFE EXPECTANCIES AT BIRTH: 1970 AND 1993 | | | | | |
|---|---|---|---|---|---|---|
| | MALE | | FEMALE | | FEMALE ADVANTAGE | |
| | 1970 | 1993 | 1970 | 1993 | 1970 | 1993 |
| INCOME GROUP | | | | | | |
| India | 50 | 61 | 49 | 61 | −1 | 0 |
| China | 61 | 68 | 63 | 71 | +2 | +3 |
| Other low-income | 45 | 54 | 47 | 57 | +2 | +3 |
| Middle-income | 58 | 65 | 63 | 71 | +5 | +6 |
| High-income | 68 | 74 | 75 | 80 | +7 | +6 |
| REGION | | | | | | |
| sub-Saharan Africa | 42 | 50 | 46 | 53 | +4 | +3 |
| Middle East & North Africa | 52 | 65 | 54 | 67 | +2 | +2 |
| Europe & Central Asia | 64 | 65 | 71 | 74 | +7 | +9 |
| South Asia | 50 | 60 | 48 | 60 | −2 | 0 |
| East Asia & Pacific | 58 | 66 | 60 | 70 | +2 | +4 |
| Latin America & the Caribbean | 58 | 66 | 63 | 72 | +5 | +6 |
| SELECTED COUNTRIES | | | | | | |
| Ghana | 48 | 55 | 51 | 58 | +3 | +3 |
| Sri Lanka | 64 | 70 | 66 | 74 | +2 | +4 |
| Egypt | 50 | 63 | 52 | 65 | +2 | +2 |
| Poland | 67 | 67 | 74 | 76 | +7 | +9 |
| Costa Rica | 65 | 74 | 69 | 79 | +4 | +5 |
| Brazil | 57 | 64 | 61 | 69 | +4 | +5 |
| South Korea | 58 | 68 | 63 | 75 | +5 | +7 |

NOTES:
Life expectancy at birth measures the number of years a newborn infant would live if prevailing patterns of mortality at the time of its birth were to stay the same throughout its life.

FROM: World Bank, *World Development Report 1995*, Table 29.

urban hospitals in which many of these doctors practice concentrate more on curative medicine. As we will discuss later, the greater potential for improving health conditions in the LDCs (as well as in many developed countries) lies with preventative medicine. Many of the basic preventative health-care services can be provided by nurses and trained community health workers.

A second indicator of health-care inputs is the share of total health expenditures, both public and private, in Gross Domestic Product. With the exception of India, the ratio of total health expenditures to GDP is fairly uniform (approximately 4 percent) across the developing regions. Outside of Asia (again excluding China), public expenditures on health (including government and parastatal expenditures and development assistance for health) exceed private expenditures. International comparisons here, too, become complicated if significant variation occurs either in the composition of expenditures across countries (for example, the relative importance of curative versus preventative health care) or in the efficiency with which the health-care services are

## TABLE 8.3   Selected Statistics on Health

| | Doctors per 1000 Population (1988–1992) | Nurse to Doctor Ratio (1988–1992) | Total Health Expenditures as % of GDP (1990) | Percentage of Infants Immunized (1990–1991) | Disability-Adjusted Life Years per 1000 Population (1990) |
|---|---|---|---|---|---|
| sub-Saharan Africa | .12 | 5.1 | 4.5 | 52 | 574 |
| India | .41 | 1.1 | 6.0 | 83 | 344 |
| China | 1.37 | .5 | 3.5 | 95 | 178 |
| Other Asia & Islands | .31 | 3.0 | 4.5 | 81 | 259 |
| Latin America & the Caribbean | 1.25 | .5 | 4.0 | 71 | 232 |
| Middle Eastern Crescent | 1.04 | 1.5 | 4.1 | 75 | 287 |
| Formerly Socialist Economies of Europe | 4.07 | 2.2 | 3.6 | 77 | 168 |
| Established Market Economies | 2.52 | 2.1 | 9.2 | 80 | 117 |

NOTES:
*Doctor* is defined to include only individuals with the professional degree of medical doctor. The definition of *nurse* includes only registered nurses and registered midwives. The statistics are for one year in the period 1988–1992.

Health expenditures include outlays for prevention, promotion, rehabilitation and care; population activities; nutrition activities; program food aid; and emergency aid specifically for health. It does not include water and sanitation. Total expenditures include public and private expenditures.

Infant immunization rate is for three completed doses of vaccine against diphtheria, pertussis (whooping cough), and tetanus. The denominator is the number of surviving infants of age one year.

Disability-Adjusted Life Years (DALYs) per thousand population is a standardized measure for a population of the loss in productive years of life due to death and disease relative to a low-mortality population.

FROM: World Bank, *World Development Report 1993*, Tables A.8, A.9, and B.1.

provided. The uniformity in the ratios of health expenditures to GDP across developing regions masks significant differences in per capita outlays on health.

A more comparable measure of access to health care is the immunization rate for infants (used earlier in the regression analyses for the infant mortality rate in the appendices to Chapters 1 and 7). Perhaps surprisingly, the LDCs, outside of sub-Saharan Africa, have infant vaccination rates for diphtheria, pertussis (whooping cough), and tetanus close to the coverage in the Established Market Economies.

The final statistic in Table 8.3 (shown graphically in Figure 8.3) represents an attempt by the World Bank, in collaboration with the World Health Organization, to estimate the total burden of disease in a population.[10] An estimate of the total number of healthy years of life lost in a given population due to mortality and morbidity is made for each nation. The morbidity rates are weighted by the severity of the disease, with the disability weights for the diseases ranging from 0 (perfect health) to 1 (death). The adjusted number of life years lost is calculated with reference to the expectation of life at each age for a hypothetical low-mortality population. The total number of **disability-adjusted life years (DALYs)** is divided by the population size

---

[10]See pages 26 and 213–214 in World Bank, *World Development Report 1993* for the derivation of this statistic.

## FIGURE 8.3 — DISABILITY-ADJUSTED LIFE YEARS

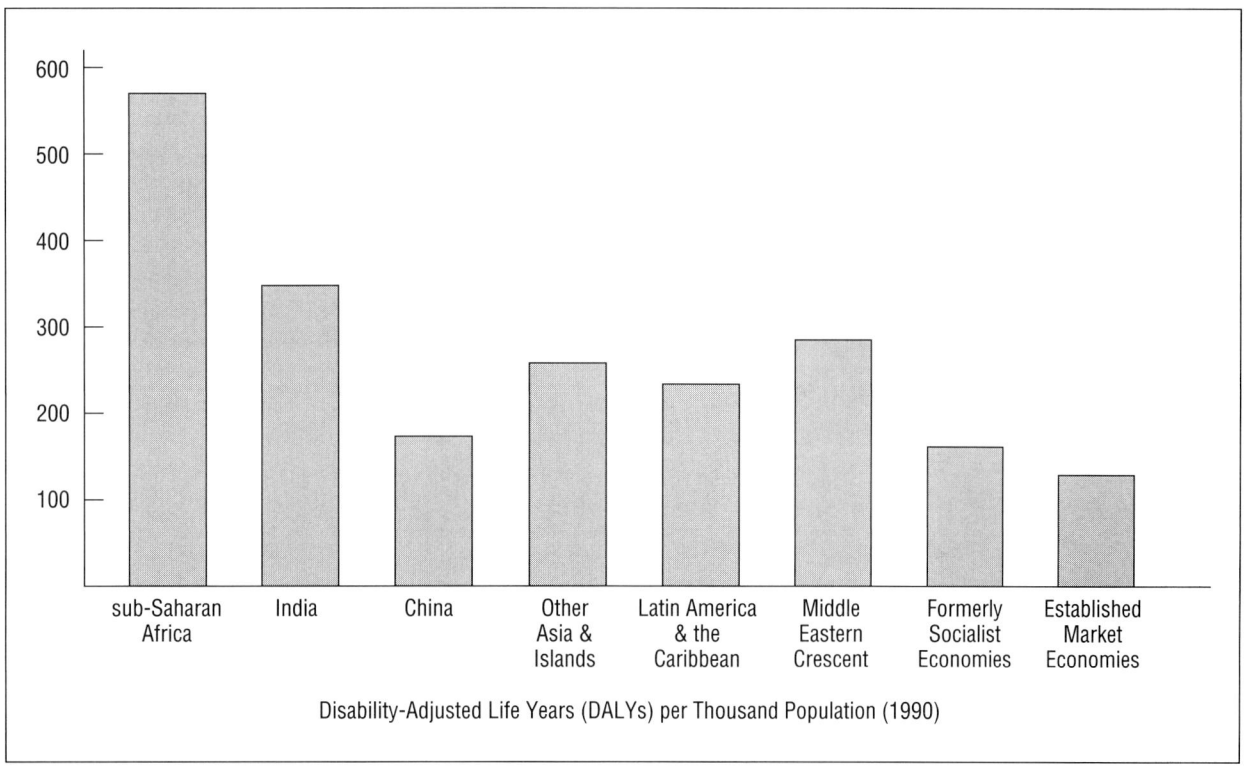

Disability-Adjusted Life Years (DALYs) per Thousand Population (1990)

and expressed as DALYs per thousand population, which gives a comprehensive measure of the loss of productive life due to death and disease. The regional aggregates in Table 8.3 are the population-weighted averages for the nations in the region. The highest DALYs per thousand population for 1990 are for sub-Saharan Africa, a reflection of the generally low levels of development and inadequate health care. Among the developing nations, China, despite a low per capita income, does quite well, in part due to a comprehensive health-care system that has emphasized preventative medicine.

### HEALTH-CARE POLICY

As implied, additional resource commitments to reduce mortality and morbidity rates in developing countries could have high payoffs, not only in raising human productivities and the overall quality of life in any given year, but, with greater life expectancies, in extending the number of years over which the benefits are realized. Many of the deaths and disabilities caused by diseases can be readily prevented. The medical technologies exist; it is a question of mobilizing the resources to improve health. Given the positive externalities (e.g., immunization against communicable diseases) and public good nature (e.g., disease control through insecticide spraying as in malaria eradication) of some critical health-care expenditures, governments must be involved. Yet, in many less developed countries, public expenditures on health care have not been a high priority.

Part of the reason for the relative neglect may be the flows of benefits and costs of investments in health care. The costs are upfront and substantial. Not only are there capital expenditures on facilities (hospitals and clinics) and equipment, but there is the expensive training of doctors, nurses, and other medical staff. The benefits from expenditures on health care, especially for preventative services, however, may be difficult to perceive. For example, increasing the life expectancy at birth from 50 years to 55 years, indicative of significant improvements in survival rates, may not be appreciated by, or even evident to, the general population until a generation passes and the perception takes hold that proportionally more children are surviving to adulthood. While the expense and inconvenience of getting innoculated against measles are obvious, less so is the benefit from the absence of the disease or the greatly reduced probability of affliction in the future. Yet immunizations against communicable diseases are highly cost-effective. Finally, in nations with rapid population growth, aggressive measures to reduce mortality rates may be resisted, given the subsequent short-run surge in the rate of natural increase. In the long run, however, lower mortality rates may be a precondition for the adoption of contraception and lower fertility.

### The Need for Reform

Often there are biases in the allocation of public health expenditures in favor of urban populations and curative medicine.[11] Perhaps these biases should not be surprising. Policymakers for the national and state governments tend to reside in urban areas. The demands for employment, housing, basic amenities, education, and health-care services are more evident in the urban areas. Rural populations, naturally more dispersed, are less organized and politically less influential. Consequently rural populations receive disproportionately fewer services. Moreover, if economies of scale exist in providing some health-care services (consider the substantial initial investments required in training, facilities, and equipment) then on a per capita basis it becomes much more expensive to provide for the health needs of the rural population.

The second bias is the emphasis placed on modern curative medicine provided through high-profile, urban hospitals. Foreign-aid donors and recipient governments in the developing economies often prefer funding impressive, new medical centers. The opportunity cost of such resource commitments may be better provision for the primary health-care needs of the larger population—needs that could be adequately addressed by small health clinics and disease-control campaigns.

Akin and Birdsall, writing for the World Bank in the late 1980s, identified three common problems in health care in the less developed countries: misallocation of resources, internal inefficiencies, and inequities.[12] The misallocation problem can be succinctly stated as too much social spending on costly services and too little on cost-effective services. With cost-effective services, the contribution to improved health

---

[11]In 1990 the World Bank estimated that 70 to 85 percent of total health expenditures (public and private) in the less developed countries went for curative care. Only 10 to 20 percent of spending was for preventative care, and just 5 to 10 percent was for community services such as mosquito control and health education. See World Bank, *World Development Report 1990*, New York: Oxford University Press, 1990, page 77.

[12]John Akin and Nancy Birdsall, "Financing of Health Services in LDCs," *Finance and Development*, vol. 24, no. 2 (June 1987), pages 40–43.

(lower mortality and morbidity rates) per dollar spent is higher. Included would be projects for the control of communicable diseases; immunization campaigns; health education; family planning; maternal and child care; and the provision of affordable, effective drugs for the most prevalent diseases. Akin and Birdsall cited Bangladesh as an example of resource misallocation, where

> the Government subsidizes specialized orthopedic, cardiovascular, and eye institutions catering to a relatively small number of persons, while each year an estimated 324,000 active tuberculosis patients above the age of ten receive no treatment, at least 90,000 children under age five die of pneumonia, and 136,000 infants die of tetanus.[13]

The internal inefficiencies stem from a misuse of the health-care services that are available. The perception and reality are that the superior health-care services are found in the urban areas. Urban hospitals have the better-trained staffs and more modern equipment, and are better stocked with the necessary supplies and medicines. In contrast, health clinics in rural areas and small towns are typically understaffed and underfinanced. Too often individuals bypass the local health clinics, which could effectively treat many of the maladies. As a result, the local clinics are underutilized, while the urban hospitals are overcrowded. A similar phenomenon occurs in the United States whereby poor families with no health insurance or means to pay for medical care rely on emergency rooms in public hospitals for all types of ailments, even those that could be much less expensively attended to by local physicians.

The equity problem refers to the heavy government subsidization of curative health care offered by urban hospitals and mainly consumed by relatively well-off patients. Poorer households, especially in rural areas and isolated towns, are not only effectively cut off from these subsidized services, but are forced to accept lower value for the health-care services they can purchase locally.[14]

## Recommendations for Reform

With economic growth, better health care can be purchased. Moreover, the demand for health care appears to be income-elastic. As per capita incomes rise, so do the shares of private and public expenditures on health in national income. High-income households can afford the care provided by private physicians; low-income households typically cannot. In less developed countries budget constraints severely limit public spending on health care—which should be more than enough incentive for choosing wisely and seeking efficiencies in the public health-care services provided.

Any discussion of public expenditure priorities will be somewhat normative. Often the allocation of public resources reflects political leverage and special economic interests rather than the underlying needs of the larger population. If the goal is to improve

---

[13]Ibid., page 40.

[14]As with inefficiency, the problem of inequity is not unique to the LDCs. In the United States in 1990–1991 only two out of every three infants under age one were completely immunized against diphtheria, pertussis, and tetanus—a lower ratio than for every developing region of the world, save sub-Saharan Africa (from World Bank, *World Development Report 1993*, Table A.8). The infants not immunized were predominantly from low-income households. Every year in the United States, however, billions of dollars are spent on expensive treatments for individuals in the last stages of terminal illnesses; and much of the cost of these procedures is not borne entirely by the patients, many of whom are from high-income households.

the average quality of life by extending life expectancies and reducing the incidence of morbidity, then a reallocation of resources in favor of a universal package of basic health-care services may be in order.

The World Bank has outlined an essential public health package.[15] A key component is the Expanded Programme on Immunization, an effort to immunize young children against diphtheria, pertussis, tetanus, polio, measles, and tuberculosis. Innoculations against other diseases, such as hepatitis B and yellow fever, could be added. Consistent with the priority on early health care are treatment of schoolchildren for worm infections and micronutrient deficiencies in vitamin A and iodine. Further, as part of the primary school curriculum, children should receive instruction on health care, including the prevention, recognition, and treatment of communicable diseases. In Bolivia radio lessons have been effectively used for this purpose.

> In 1993 more than 1000 third- and fourth-grade classrooms will receive broadcasts of a new curriculum that includes lessons on cholera, personal and dental hygiene, acute respiratory infections, immunizations, infectious diseases, and accident prevention. Nutrition, environmental health, and self-esteem are to be added in 1994. In response to parents' requests, a complementary community-based radio program is also being developed and tested.[16]

Other elements of the essential public health package are the provision of family planning services; measures to reduce the consumption of tobacco, alcohol, and illicit drugs; and programs for the prevention of AIDS and sexually-transmitted diseases, such as syphilis and gonorrhea.

Governments also must assume the responsibility for the environmental control of diseases spread through common carriers such as mosquitoes. Few governments in the developing nations can mount the necessary projects alone. Foreign assistance, not only for funding but for technical expertise, is usually essential. One successful international collaboration is the Onchocerciasis Control Programme.[17]

Onchocerciasis, or riverblindness, results in physical debilitation and eventually the loss of sight. Transmitted by a parasitic worm through the bites of blackflies that breed in rapidly flowing waters, riverblindness was particularly common in West Africa. In 1974 the World Health Organization, the United Nations Development Programme, and the World Bank joined forces with international donors and seven countries in West Africa in a massive project to reduce the incidence of riverblindness. At the time, roughly 10 percent of the 15 million total population in the area were afflicted with the disease, with 100,000 completely blind. Biodegradeable, ecologically-safe chemicals were used in widespread aerial spraying of larvicide against the blackflies. While funded by foreign donors, organized by international agencies, and incorporating modern technology, the Onchocerciasis Control Programme was staffed largely by personnel from the seven West African nations, who assumed greater responsibility for the operation of the project over time.

Roughly a decade later, the effort was hailed as "the largest and most successful health program in sub-Saharan Africa."[18] Transmission of the disease had been

---

[15]See World Bank, *World Development Report 1993*, Chapter 4, "Public Health," pages 72–107.
[16]World Bank, *World Development Report 1993*, page 48.
[17]This account is from Shuja Nawaz, "Riverblindness Controlled," *Finance and Development*, vol. 23, no. 2 (June 1986), pages 32–34.
[18]Ibid., page 33.

stopped in more than 90 percent of the project area. Fertile river banks, previously infested by the onchocerciasis-carrying blackflies, had been reclaimed for agriculture.[19] Similar efforts were planned for other areas of Africa and the developing world. In 1992 the pharmaceutical giant Merck announced that it would provide millions of doses of the drug ivermectin for free to treat riverblindness, which still afflicted an estimated 17 million people in the world.[20] Logistical problems, however—from inadequate transportation and distribution networks to political instability—hampered the delivery of the medicine to those in need. Riverblindness continues as a major health hazard in many parts of the world.

Unless aggressive efforts are sustained until eradication, such tropical diseases return. Vectors become more resistant to larvicides, and drugs may lose their potency as new strains of the disease develop. Malaria, once believed to be under control, has resurged. More than 100 million cases are reported annually, with 1 to 2 million attributed deaths.[21]

Related to the health problems associated with the environment are measures to increase popular access to safe water and improve sanitation. More than 1 billion people in the less developed countries do not have access to safe water. More than 1.7 billion do not have adequate sewage facilities.[22] The following account illustrates the "haves" and "have nots" in the consumption of this basic public utility.

> A daily occurrence in the pueblos jovenes of Lima: A poor family, living in an illegal squatter settlement, waits for the water truck to arrive. When it does, the family members fill a few buckets with water of dubious quality, paying $3 per cubic meter, which often amounts to 10 percent of household income. Because the price is so high, they use little water, cutting down, particularly, on "discretionary uses," such as washing and bathing. They defecate in a fly- and insect-infested open toilet. The economic, health, and human consequences of these miserable sanitary conditions are tremendous. As a result of diarrhea and other hygiene-related diseases, for example, almost one in ten children dies before its first birthday.
>
> Five miles away in the upper-class district of Miraflores, the situation could not be more different. Elegant houses have dishwashers, washing machines, and, in a city where it never rains, luscious gardens that are watered several times a day. The publicly run water supply company is supposed to charge its customers about 30 cents for a cubic meter of treated water available on tap in the house, but the actual amounts paid are much lower. Many households pay a low flat rate because the meters do not work or are not read, and many simply ignore their bills.
>
> With variations of degree and detail, the Lima story—and the challenge implicit in it—is one that faces most developing countries.[23]

Equity argues for a reallocation of resources and reorientation of user fees. The story of unequal exchange is a familiar one, whether it be access to water, health care, higher

---

[19]The World Bank notes that by the end of the century, when the Onchocerciasis Control Programme is concluded, some 25 million hectares of land will have been reclaimed for settlement and agriculture, with the main beneficiaries being subsistence farmers. Also, when done, the project is estimated to have prevented some 500,000 cases of blindness. *World Development Report 1993,* page 19.

[20]Elyse Tanouye, "Merck's 'River Blindness' Gift Hits Snags," *Wall Street Journal* (September 23, 1992), page B1.

[21]From Bernhard Liese and Paramjit Sachdeva, "Organizing Tropical Disease Control," *Finance and Development,* vol. 30, no. 4 (December 1993), pages 44–46.

[22]John Briscoe, "Poverty and Water Supply: How to Move Forward," *Finance and Development,* vol. 29, no. 4 (December 1992), pages 16–19.

[23]Ibid., page 16.

education, or credit. User fees should reflect the marginal cost of providing the service. Uniform fees would actually lower the prices paid by the urban poor, while raising the prices paid by the previously subsidized, wealthier households.

### AN INTEGRATED HEALTH-CARE SYSTEM

To increase popular access to basic health-care services, improvements in the number and quality of rural health facilities are needed. Within each village there should be a community health worker, functioning as an extension of the rural clinic to monitor local health conditions and treat common health problems, such as through oral rehydration therapy to prevent the dehydration in children caused by diarrhea. To be effective, the health clinics must be adequately staffed (for example, with an attending nurse and paramedic) and sufficiently stocked with equipment and medical supplies. The staffs must be trained to handle primary health-care needs, including first aid; delivery of births; family planning; the care of sick children; and immunizations. More serious medical cases should be referred to the second-tier district hospitals, located in the larger towns and small cities. Staffed by doctors and nurses, with more sophisticated equipment and greater variety in medicines and drugs, the district hospitals should provide a higher order of health services, including the treatment of tuberculosis, minor surgeries, and other in-patient curative medicine. The district hospitals should also supervise the rural health clinics within their regions. Also required are additional investments in the rural infrastructure, especially the transportation system, communications network, and generation of electrical power.

On the highest level are the tertiary hospitals in the major urban areas, where the specialists offer the full range of modern medicine with state-of-the-art facilities and equipment. These tertiary hospitals should also serve as medical schools and engage in health research.

In sum, the most common health problems can be treated in the clinics at the local level. The appropriate emphasis is on preventative care, the provision of which might be subsidized to reduce the need for more expensive curative medicine. (Recall the old adage, "An ounce of prevention is worth a pound of cure.") Advanced treatment for more serious health problems would be through referral to the district and urban hospitals. Fees would be adjusted according to the cost-effectiveness of the services provided and, perhaps, to the patient's ability to pay. More of the burden of curative care should be borne by the patients, especially for elective procedures and advanced treatments for illnesses related to individual lifestyles. Examples include lung cancer due to smoking, liver failure due to alcohol consumption, or sexually-transmitted diseases contracted through unprotected sex. Revenues could be collected and consumption discouraged by stiff excise taxes on alcohol and tobacco. A system of health insurance may be needed, especially for illnesses that are curable, but beyond the means of households. Akin and Birdsall suggest, as a start, that health insurance premiums collected through payroll taxes be mandatory for employees in the modern sectors of the developing economies.[24]

Even more important than the physical facilities are the personnel. In many developing countries shortages of primary care providers, especially in the rural areas, coexist with surpluses of medical specialists practicing in the cities. The imbalance reflects

---

[24]Akin and Birdsall, page 42.

the higher salaries, superior amenities, and greater prestige associated with urban hospitals and specialized medicine. The more pressing needs in the LDCs are for general practitioners, nurses, public health officials, and administrators of clinics, who are well-trained and willing to work in rural areas.

To correct this imbalance, a first step may be to modify the medical school curriculum, placing a greater emphasis on the awareness and treatment of the diseases prevalent in the less developed countries. Entrance of medical students to the specialties may have to be restricted. Doctors who choose to specialize in areas of lower social benefit, such as oncology and heart surgery, would be expected to bear most of the expenses of their training. On the other hand, the training of those doctors and nurses entering the fields of public health might continue to be subsidized. To reduce the burden on the government budget, the recipients of the subsidized medical school training could be required to pay back the public investment with service in designated rural areas.

With a shift in emphasis to preventative care and basic health services, an even greater demand will arise for administrators of health clinics, nurses, and community health workers. The training of these personnel should also reflect the needs of the developing countries. For example, in some cultures, females beyond puberty are not to be seen by male physicians. Thus more women should be encouraged to enter medicine to fill this need.

In many developing countries practitioners of traditional medicine far outnumber those certified in modern (Western) medicine. Rather than being dismissed as primitive, traditional practitioners could be incorporated into the primary health-care system, wherein, with additional training, they may effectively serve as community health workers. Moreover, the knowledge of these indigenous medicine men and women of folk remedies and natural drugs found locally may be a valuable resource for modern science.[25]

To keep the costs of drugs and equipment down, developing countries can use international clearinghouses for their purchases.[26] For example, the World Health Organization (WHO) has compiled a list of essential drugs that are available in generic form, and the United Nations Children's Fund (UNICEF) offers assistance to developing nations in purchasing drugs at competitive prices.[27] Significant savings can be realized when the needed drugs are regularly procured through such channels. Current information, however, must be available to doctors who prescribe, and the pharmacists who dispense, the drugs so that misuses or abuses can be reduced. The World Bank also notes the savings possible through better selection and operation of medical equipment, much of which is underutilized because of malfunctions or improper maintenance. International agencies can help developing nations secure better prices on their equipment purchases, too.

Finally, there is an agenda for research—in addition to the reorientation to preventative medicine and primary health care; the efforts in disease control; improvements in

---

[25]Transnational pharmaceutical companies are paying increasing attention to traditional medicine, especially as practiced indigenously in the tropical rainforests. See, for example, Thomas Burton, "Drug Company Looks to 'Witch Doctors' to Conjure Products," *Wall Street Journal* (July 7, 1994), pages A1 and A8.

[26]See Thomas Catsambas and Susan Foster, "Spending Money Sensibly: The Case of Essential Drugs," *Finance and Development*, vol. 23, no. 4 (December 1986), pages 29–32. See also World Bank, *World Development Report 1993*, pages 145–148.

[27]World Bank, *World Development Report 1993*, pages 137–138.

facilities and staffing; and savings in the purchases of drugs and medical equipment. Vaccinations for children in the Expanded Programme on Immunization could be improved such that fewer doses are required for the complete coverage, and the vaccines are less expensive and easier to store. The development of highly effective, but safe, larvicides for the tropical diseases carried by vectors is a high priority, as are easy-to-administer drugs to treat parasitic worms. Simple diagnostic tests to recognize the onset of disease that can be used in rural health clinics are another priority. Inexpensive and sanitary latrines need to be designed for those low-income families still deprived of indoor plumbing.

Much progress in improving health and extending life expectancies in the developing nations has been made over the past few decades. Yet much still remains to be done. From the 1990 World Summit for Children nearly 150 nations pledged to specific targets in reducing child and maternal mortality rates; eradicating diseases like polio; and improving nutrition, access to safe water, and sanitation.[28] To achieve these goals, not only will the developing nations have to place a higher priority on health care, but the developed countries have to be willing to provide more assistance. In a world of resource constraints, however, not all of the desirable initiatives can be funded. Which of the programs in health care will be implemented should depend on assessments of the associated benefits and costs.

We have examined nutrition and health and now move to the third component of human capital formation. The contributions of education to improved nutrition and health have been noted. The importance of education for economic development, however, extends far beyond these contributions.

## EDUCATION

Education is the process by which human capital is enhanced through increases in knowledge and the development of skills. Like nutrition and health, education is both a consumption good and an investment that yields a stream of benefits into the future. As a consumption good, education provides utility. We assume that individuals gain satisfaction and self-esteem from the challenge of learning and intellectual growth. As an investment, education is an engine of economic growth, leading to a more skilled and productive workforce. Education also enhances labor mobility and technological progress. As T. P. Schultz has summarized:

> Studies across persons, households, farms, and firms have documented, first generally in the United States and then in many low income countries, strong empirical regularities between educational attainment of populations and their productivity and performance in both market and nonmarket (home) production activities.[29]

---

[28]Ibid., page 14.

[29]T. Paul Schultz, "Education Investments and Returns," Chapter 13, *Handbook of Development Economics, Volume 1,* edited by Hollis Chenery and T. N. Srinivasan, Amsterdam: North Holland, 1988, page 544. Schultz's work provides a review of the literature on education and economic growth in developing countries.

## CURRENT EDUCATIONAL EFFORTS IN THE LOW-INCOME COUNTRIES

In general, the less developed countries have articulated ambitious educational goals. Most nations have compulsory primary education as an official policy, if not a reality. In Table 8.4 we present selected statistics on education.

Education is a normal good. With increases in income, enrollment rates tend to rise and student-teacher ratios (a rough proxy for the quality of education) tend to fall. In general, for all levels of education in the developing economies, enrollment rates increased from 1970 to 1992—an impressive achievement given the rapid growth in the populations of school-age children. India appears to have accommodated the rise in enrollment rates, in part, by increasing the student-teacher ratio. Sub-Saharan Africa lags well behind the other regions in primary and secondary enrollment coverage and, as with the other low-income economies, has essentially only been able to maintain its high student-teacher ratios.

In Table 8.4 on page 240, we note also the high attrition rates in education, particularly for the other low-income economies (other than China and India), where the 1992 enrollment rates dropped from 74 percent in primary school to 26 percent in secondary school. For sub-Saharan Africa the decrease is from 67 percent in primary school to 18 percent in secondary school.

Illiteracy rates are still very high—especially in South Asia, Africa, and the Middle East, where roughly half of the adults are illiterate. Illiteracy rates are usually higher for females than for males, a reflection of the lower priority often accorded to female education.

In reality, the growth of educational achievement in developing countries has been slower than that in the high-income countries. Adriaan Verspoor identifies several areas of concern in the effective provision of education in the LDCs, including rapid population growth; inefficient budgetary support; high rates of absenteeism in primary school; poor quality of education; high dropout and repetition rates; and insufficient attention to science and technology.[30] Educational policy reform, discussed later in this chapter, should address these issues.

## EDUCATION AS A HUMAN CAPITAL INVESTMENT

As with health care, nutrition, or any other commitment of resources, opportunity costs associated with education exist, measured by the goods and services that could have been produced with the resources used for education. Thus, the benefits must be compared to the costs in order to assess the desirability of an investment in education. The monetary value of the consumption of education is quite difficult to estimate. Thus, most economic assessments tend to treat education as an investment with future benefits and more immediate costs.[31] Any assessment of education (or health care or nutrition) is further complicated by differences between private and social benefits and

---

[30]Adriaan Verspoor, "Educational Development: Priorities for the Nineties," *Finance & Development* (March 1990), vol. 27, no. 1, pages 20–23.

[31]The pioneering work in assessing the returns to education as an investment in human capital was done by the Nobel-laureate economist Gary Becker in the early 1970s. See Becker's *Human Capital*, New York: National Bureau of Economic Research, 1975.

## TABLE 8.4  Selected Statistics on Education

| | Adult Illiteracy Rates (1990) | | Percentage of Age Group Enrolled in Education | | | | | | Pupil–Teacher Ratio | |
|---|---|---|---|---|---|---|---|---|---|---|
| | | | Primary | | Secondary | | Tertiary | | | |
| | Total | Female | 1970 | 1992 | 1970 | 1992 | 1970 | 1992 | 1970 | 1992 |
| **Income Group** | | | | | | | | | | |
| India | 52% | 66% | 73 | 102 | 26 | 44 | ... | ... | 41 | 63 |
| China | 27% | 38% | 89 | 121 | 24 | 51 | 1 | 2 | ... | 22 |
| Other low-income | 49% | 61% | 50 | 74 | 12 | 26 | 3 | 5 | 42 | 41 |
| Middle-income | 17% | ... | ... | 104 | ... | ... | ... | ... | ... | ... |
| High-income | ... | ... | ... | 103 | ... | ... | 36 | 51 | 24 | ... |
| **Region** | | | | | | | | | | |
| sub-Saharan Africa | 50% | 62% | 50 | 67 | 7 | 18 | 1 | 4 | 42 | 40 |
| Middle East & North Africa | ... | 57% | 68 | 97 | 24 | 56 | 10 | 15 | 34 | 26 |
| Europe & Central Asia | 5% | ... | ... | 99 | ... | ... | ... | ... | ... | ... |
| South Asia | 54% | 69% | 67 | 94 | 24 | 39 | ... | ... | 42 | 59 |
| East Asia & Pacific | 24% | 34% | 88 | 117 | 24 | 52 | 4 | 5 | ... | 23 |
| Latin America & the Caribbean | 15% | 18% | 95 | 106 | 28 | 45 | 15 | 18 | 34 | 26 |
| **Selected Countries** | | | | | | | | | | |
| Ghana | 40% | 49% | 64 | 74 | 14 | 38 | 2 | 2 | 30 | 29 |
| Sri Lanka | 12% | 17% | 99 | 107 | 47 | 74 | 3 | 6 | ... | 29 |
| Egypt | 52% | 66% | 72 | 101 | 35 | 80 | 18 | 19 | 38 | 26 |
| Poland | ... | ... | 101 | 98 | 62 | 83 | 18 | 23 | 23 | 17 |
| Costa Rica | 7% | 7% | 110 | 105 | 28 | 43 | 23 | 28 | 30 | 32 |
| Brazil | 19% | 20% | 82 | 106 | 26 | 39 | 12 | 12 | 28 | 23 |
| South Korea | 5% | 7% | 103 | 105 | 42 | 90 | 16 | 42 | 57 | 33 |

Notes: Lack of data is indicated by ...
*Adult illiteracy* is defined as the proportion of the population over the age of 15 who cannot, with understanding, read and write a short, simple statement on their everyday life.
   Primary school enrollment data are estimates of children of all ages enrolled in primary school, including pupils younger and older than the country's standard primary school age, typically 6 to 11 years. Secondary school age typically is from 12 to 17 years. The tertiary enrollment ratio is calculated by dividing the number of pupils enrolled in all post-secondary schools and universities by the population in the 20–24 age group.
   The pupil–teacher ratio is the number of pupils enrolled in school in a country, divided by the number of teachers in the education system.

From: World Bank, *World Development Report 1995*, Tables 1 and 28.

costs. In other words, the production of education is subject to externalities. As shown in Chapter 6, when externalities are present, the unregulated competitive market will not produce the optimal social output.

### The Benefits of Education

Economists tend to distinguish between education or training that is general in nature and that which is firm-specific. General education, such as primary and secondary schooling, is useful for a range of employment opportunities. Firm-specific training, such as learning the work process of a particular employer, is less useful outside the firm. Our discussion of the benefits to education primarily relates to general education.

The private benefits to education are mainly higher wages and expanded employment opportunities. As the human capital of an individual increases, the output per unit of labor should also increase. Primary education that teaches basic reading and writing will permit an individual to work in those semi-skilled jobs that require literacy. Secondary schooling and university study further expand the earnings capabilities and job options of individuals. Careers in management, finance, education, and government are available to those with more advanced levels of education. Unfortunately, in many countries, the creation of jobs for those with advanced degrees has not kept pace with the number of graduates, leading to discouragement for those unable to find appropriate work. (In Chapter 9 we will discuss labor markets and employment creation.)

Estimates of earnings differentials in developing countries among unskilled, semi-skilled, and skilled labor vary according to country and time period. The estimates tend to understate the advantages of jobs with higher educational requirements, which usually have more fringe benefits and better working conditions.

Beyond the private benefits of higher wages, there are social benefits not captured by individuals investing in education. Education provides a "screening" function, for example, making it less costly for employers to find individuals appropriate for job vacancies. For instance, with an opening in the sales department of an electronics firm, it would be reasonable to consider only those individuals with a high-school diploma. Those without that level of education would not be placed in the applicant pool, saving the firm both time and cost in its search process. A college diploma not only indicates higher educational attainment, but the major fields of concentration provide additional information on the skills and knowledge of the job applicants.

Second, if a country has an income tax, the higher incomes that accompany increased education will result in enhanced government tax revenues. That is, in the labor market, a more educated and productive labor force leads to an outward shift in the labor demand function, raising both the wage rate and the level of employment, and increasing incomes and tax collections.

Third, education should lead to a healthier population. Recall that education, particularly for females, is associated with lower fertility and child mortality.

> Demographic and health surveys in twenty-five developing countries show that, all else being equal, even one to three years of maternal schooling reduces child mortality by about 15 percent, whereas a similar level of paternal schooling achieves a 6 percent reduction. The effects increase when mothers have had more education.[32]

## The Costs of Education

The principal costs of education are the direct outlays for the teachers, buildings, and materials used in the educational process and the opportunity costs of any lost earnings for the individuals receiving education. The direct costs vary with the level of education offered. Primary education at the village level, using local teachers and basic materials

---

[32] World Bank, *World Development Report 1993*, page 42.

such as mimeographed texts, has a low cost per pupil. In contrast, higher education requiring libraries, computers, and science laboratories can be very expensive.

Since most students do not pay the full direct costs, a divergence exists between the social and private costs of education. Students or their parents usually pay fees (tuition) and purchase some needed materials (pencils, paper, books). These outlays by students, however, are invariably less than the direct costs of providing the education. Some government subsidy or private contribution is used to offset the difference. For instance, assume that educating an elementary student costs the government $85 per year, the social cost of providing the education. If the parents are paying school fees of $25 per year (the private cost of education), then the subsidy element equals $60 per year per child. Given that education is a good whose social benefits exceed the private benefits, some subsidy is typically warranted.

The opportunity cost of education is the value of the lost wages or the forgone contribution to output when an individual is enrolled in the education process instead of working. For instance, a 16-year-old high school student might have given up the opportunity to earn $80 per month as an agricultural laborer to remain in school, resulting in an opportunity cost of $80 per month or $720 for a nine-month school year.

Typically, opportunity cost varies directly with the level of education. For instance, the forgone earnings of a six-year-old primary school child in a rural area are very low. Lost earnings would simply be any reduction in the child's contribution to household tasks or participation in any family farm or business. In fact, a school calendar that provides some time off during planting and harvesting—periods of peak labor demand—would permit children to participate in the agricultural production process, reducing the opportunity cost of education. Clearly older children and young adults will have higher opportunity costs, since they are more valuable in household production or have other employment prospects. At the level of higher education, the opportunity costs can increase significantly. For example, a mid-level production manager of a textile plant who decides to pursue a college degree in accounting would have a relatively high opportunity cost if she had to give up her job to enroll in the university.

### THE RETURNS TO EDUCATION

The World Bank in the *World Development Report 1990* asserts:

> The principal asset of the poor is labor time. Education increases the productivity of this asset. The result at the individual level, as many studies show, is higher income. More recent research also points to a strong link between education and economic growth.[33]

In this section, we will show how the economic returns to education can be calculated and provide empirical support for the contention that the poor significantly benefit from educational investments.

The returns to education require a comparison of the benefits and costs associated with the educational process. With the divergence between social and private benefits and costs for education, we must consider both the private and the social rates of return. Given that the benefits of education, such as an enhanced earnings profile, accrue over time, the purest calculation of the returns to education would be the **net present value (NPV)** in which future benefits and costs are discounted by an

---

[33] World Bank, *World Development Report 1990,* page 80.

| TABLE 8.5 | RETURNS TO AN EDUCATIONAL INVESTMENT | | | | |
|---|---|---|---|---|---|
| | YEAR: | | | | |
| | 1 | 2 | 3 | 4 | SUM |
| Nominal net benefit | −$10,000 | $3300 | $4000 | $4200 | $1500 |
| (8% discount factor) | (.926) | (.857) | (.794) | (.735) | |
| Net Present Value | −$9260 | $2828 | $3176 | $3087 | −$169 |
| (7% discount factor) | (.935) | (.873) | (.816) | (.763) | |
| Net Present Value | −$9350 | $2881 | $3264 | $3205 | $0 |
| (6% discount factor) | (.943) | (.890) | (.840) | (.792) | |
| Net Present Value | −$9430 | $2937 | $3360 | $3326 | $193 |

appropriate measure of the cost of capital. The NPV calculation, however, does not lend itself to comparing the returns to education across levels or countries. Thus, many researchers use the **internal rate of return (IRR),** solving for the interest rate that equates benefits and costs over time, such that the NPV = 0.

Formally, the net present value of an investment is the sum of the discounted net benefits:

$$NPV = \sum_{t=1}^{n} \frac{(B_t - C_t)}{(1+i)^t}$$

where   $B_t$ = benefits from the investment in year $t$
        $C_t$ = costs of the investment in year $t$
        $i$ = opportunity cost of capital

For instance at an 8 percent (6 percent) opportunity cost of capital, a dollar payable in one year has a present value of $.926 ($.943). A dollar payable in three years with an 8 percent (6 percent) opportunity cost of capital has a present value of $.794 ($.840). Clearly, the present value of a given sum of money will be lower the further into the future the sum is received and the higher the rate of interest used to discount. The sum of the discounted future values gives the net present value of the investment.

A simple example of the use of NPV and IRR is found in Table 8.5. Consider a one-year basic training course that costs $10,000 in year 1 and will lead to a net increase in annual earnings in years 2 through 4 of $3300, $4000, and $4200 respectively. At the interest rate of 8 percent, the net present value of the hypothetical investment is −$169; and the investment should be rejected since the net present value is negative. At 7 percent, the net present value equals 0; thus, 7 percent is the internal rate of return of this investment. At a 6 percent rate of interest, the net present value is positive ($193), and the investment should be undertaken.

The IRR provides a useful reference. If the internal rate of return exceeds (is less than) the cost of capital, then the investment should be undertaken (rejected), since the NPV will be positive (negative). Also, investment projects can be ranked by their internal rates of return, showing their relative attractiveness.

A study for the World Bank by George Psacharopoulos summarizes the returns to investment in schooling by educational level. The averages for the rates of return from

## TABLE 8.6  Returns to Investment in Education by Level

| | Social Returns (%) | | | Private Returns (%) | | |
|---|---|---|---|---|---|---|
| | Primary | Secondary | Higher | Primary | Secondary | Higher |
| **Income Group** | | | | | | |
| Low-income | 23 | 15 | 11 | 35 | 19 | 24 |
| Lower middle-income | 18 | 13 | 11 | 30 | 19 | 19 |
| Upper middle-income | 14 | 11 | 10 | 21 | 13 | 15 |
| High-income OECD | 14 | 10 | 9 | 22 | 12 | 12 |
| **Region** | | | | | | |
| sub-Saharan Africa | 24 | 18 | 11 | 41 | 27 | 28 |
| Asia | 20 | 13 | 12 | 39 | 19 | 20 |
| Europe & Middle East & North Africa | 16 | 11 | 11 | 17 | 16 | 22 |
| Latin America & the Caribbean | 18 | 13 | 12 | 26 | 17 | 20 |

NOTES:
The above table shows arithmetic averages, rounded to the nearest percentage, of individual country studies that consistently measured returns to education by level (primary, secondary, and higher) for the economy as a whole (i.e., not by sector).

FROM: "Returns to Investment in Education: A Global Update," by George Psacharopoulos, Policy Research Working Paper #1067, The World Bank, April 1993, Table 1 (p. 7) and Table 2 (p. 12).

This work is an update of Psacharopoulos, G., "Returns to Education: A Further International Update and Implications," *The Journal of Human Resources*, vol. 20, no. 4 (fall 1985), pages 583–604.

---

studies done in different countries are shown in Table 8.6. (Note that the country aggregates are somewhat different from the standard presentation used throughout this text. Refer to Table 8.4 for a comparison.)

With the exception of the social rate of return for higher education in the the high-income OECD countries (at 9 percent), all rates of return are at least equal to 10 percent. The private rate of return is an indicator of the desirability of an individual using his or her own resources to acquire additional education. The returns reported in Table 8.6 suggest that education is an extremely attractive private investment. The social rate of return is an indicator of the relative effectiveness of investment in education, permitting the government to compare the desirability of investment projects in different sectors of the economy. For instance, in the low-income economies the social rates of return for primary education are very high, suggesting that additional public funds should be invested in this level of education.

From the data in Table 8.6, we might draw several conclusions. First, the private rates of return to education seem consistently higher than the social rates of return. Recall that the private rate of return includes only the direct cost of education paid by the student; the social rate of return considers the total resource cost. These data suggest that the subsidy element to education is quite high.

Second, the rates of return, both social and private, decline with the level of education, suggesting diminishing returns to investment in education. Rates of return are highest for primary education. The benefits of basic literacy tend to be relatively high compared to the costs. Fewer educational materials and lower salaries for primary teachers suggest that direct costs are relatively low. Moreover, the opportunity costs for younger children are relatively low. Thus, in all parts of the world primary education is apt to be one of the higher returning investments available within a society.

Third, the returns to education tend to decrease as the average income level rises. Again, we can observe the effects of the law of diminishing returns. In societies in which the average level of education is higher (the high-income countries), the return to additional education tends to be lower.

Psacharopoulos has found that the rate of return to education for females (12 percent) slightly exceeds that for males (11 percent) worldwide.[34] While males have a higher return for primary education, the greater rates of return for females in secondary and higher education dominate. A recent World Bank Discussion Paper reinforces this finding:

> The economic and social returns to education for women are substantial; the latter are on the whole probably greater than those for men. Education raises the productivity and earnings of both men and women. Educated parents have healthier children and, while the father has some influence on their health, the mother has far more. Educated mothers have more educated children. Educating women slows population growth by creating new economic opportunities that compete with childbearing and child care.... Thus by educating its women, a country can reduce poverty, improve productivity, ease population pressure, and offer its children a better future. Yet, paradoxically, many countries invest less in educating women than they do in educating men.[35]

Finally, given that the returns to education in much of the developing world are quite attractive and undoubtedly above the cost of capital (such as in sub-Saharan Africa, where the social return to primary education is estimated at 24 percent), many nations are underinvesting in education. Moreover, in many countries, as with health care, misallocation of resources invested in education occurs. Higher education, frequently for the benefit of the wealthy, tends to be overfunded, whereas investments in primary and secondary education, which more directly benefit the poor, are underfunded. For instance, *The Economist* reports that according to World Bank calculations, in sub-Saharan Africa during the 1980s "only $1 of official development assistance (ODA) went on each primary pupil; $11 on each secondary pupil; and $575 on each university student."[36] Donors and the developing countries themselves should reallocate educational resources toward primary schooling and education for women.

## EDUCATIONAL POLICY REFORM

Many developing countries, with rapidly growing populations, are falling farther behind the developed countries in educational achievement. This is particularly disturbing since relatively less productive labor forces reduce the ability of developing countries to compete in international markets and to adopt new technologies and production processes.[37]

---

[34]George Psacharopoulos, "Returns to Investment in Education: A Global Update," Policy Research Working Paper #1067, The World Bank, April 1993, Table 7, page 15.

[35]Barbara Herz, K. Subbarao, Masooma Habib, and Laura Raney, "Letting Girls Learn: Promising Approaches in Primary and Secondary Education," World Bank Discussion Paper #133, The World Bank, Washington, DC, 1991, page iii.

[36]"Foreign Aid: The Kindness of Strangers," *The Economist* (May 7, 1994), pages 19–21. The quote is from page 20.

[37]Verspoor, page 21.

A first priority in education in the less developed countries might be the widespread attainment of basic literacy and numeracy. For adults, remedial education classes may be necessary. In Ecuador, as part of the requirements for graduation, high school seniors have tutored adults in reading and writing. Renewed efforts are warranted to ensure that high-quality primary education is available and affordable to all. In many nations elementary class sizes are too large, materials are outdated (and even then in short supply), and teachers are both underpaid and underqualified. Consequently, absenteeism and dropout rates are high.

Significant economic gain can be compromised by the lack of a small expenditure, whether in the form of textbooks, chalkboards, or pencils and paper. Both country governments and donors need more effective planning, particularly in rural areas, to avoid interruptions in the educational process. The direct transfer of materials, supplies, and perhaps even used textbooks, from the developed countries to the developing countries could remove burdensome bottlenecks. Increasing the training of primary school teachers, particularly women, who are willing to teach in rural areas would lead to both employment growth and an increase in the number of rural students (particularly girls) attending school. With respect to the primary school curriculum, the integration of instruction in nutrition and health care was advocated earlier in the chapter.

Attention should be paid to poor households, where even modest fees for books and the expenses of school clothes, not to mention the opportunity cost of the lost work from children in school, are a financial burden. Even if willing, these households are usually not able to borrow funds to pay for their children's education.[38] Direct subsidies or low-interest loans should be available to allow all children to attend primary school.

It also may be possible to promote entrepreneurship. Economists argue that **entrepreneurship,** a willingness and ability to initiate and organize businesses, is vital to private-sector development and modernization. Some have maintained that certain attitudes are positively correlated with entrepreneurial initiative. These attitudes include

> a disposition to accept new ideas and try new methods; a readiness to express opinions; a time sense that makes men [and women] more interested in the present and future than in the past; a better sense of punctuality; a greater concern for planning, organization and efficiency; a tendency to see the world as calculable; a faith in science and technology; and, finally, a belief in distributive justice.[39]

Of crucial importance is how these attitudes are developed and adopted. Is it possible that education, particularly at the primary level, can influence behavioral tendencies? Evidence suggests that education with properly designed curricula can be effective in creating a receptivity to entrepreneurship.[40] Ways of promoting success include textbooks that highlight achievement; role models who demonstrate risk taking and initiative; and the rewarding of hardworking and enterprising students.

---

[38]Paul Glewwe and Hanan Jacoby, "Estimating the Determinants of Cognitive Achievement in Low-Income Countries: The Case of Ghana," Living Standards Measurement Study Working Paper Number 91, World Bank, Washington, DC, 1992, page 51.

[39]McClelland refers to this set of qualities as "N Achievement." See "Achievement Motive and Entrepreneurship" by David C. McClelland and David G. Winter, Leading Issues in Economic Development, 2d ed., edited by Gerald M. Meier, New York: Oxford University Press, 1970, pages 663–673. The quotation is from page 664 and is excerpted from David C. McClelland and David G. Winter, Motivating Economic Achievement, New York: The Free Press, 1969.

[40]McClelland and Winter, 1970, page 672.

Parental reinforcement of these attitudes would be a helpful complement to developing achievement and self-confidence.

With respect to secondary education, while a general or liberal arts curriculum should typically remain as standard pedagogy, there should also be attention to vocational training in those skills in high demand in developing economies (e.g., machine operators, data processors, electricians, plumbers, and paramedics). Subsidized apprenticeships and on-the-job training in the private sector would enhance the instruction provided in vocational schools.

Typically public universities in the less developed countries are overcrowded, a reflection of both the low tuitions and the artificially high salaries for the relatively few jobs attractive to college graduates. To free resources to improve primary and secondary education, enrollments in universities may have to be more strictly limited. The cost of a year of university education is far greater than that for secondary and primary schooling. Frequently tuitions to public universities, if not free, are heavily subsidized. Even so, it is primarily the children from the wealthier families who can afford the opportunity cost of attending. These students then seek to bolster their job prospects by obtaining more education. The process devolves into what has been called the "diploma disease," where positions are filled by individuals with one more degree than required to adequately perform the job.

It may seem ironic that in many developing countries there is a shortage of jobs for the educated, an issue to which we will return in the next chapter on employment and unemployment. In some cases inappropriate school curricula contribute to this unemployment. Examples include an excess of Ph.D.'s in English literature or philosophy that coexists with an undersupply of well-trained business managers, or agricultural economists, or secondary-school mathematics teachers. Of particular concern are the shortages of scientists, engineers, and technicians. Curriculum reform in higher education that provides training consistent with the skills demanded in the labor market would assist in reducing unemployment among the educated.

Some of the unemployed and highly educated migrate to the developed countries, adding to the "brain drain." Some governments in the less developed countries try to absorb the surplus college graduates by creating positions in the public sector, an imbalance that not only adds to the official bureaucracy, but may perpetuate the system of "tips" required to get government employees to render their services in a timely fashion. That is, civil servants may seek to supplement their regular salaries in order to bring their compensation in line with their aspirations.

Therefore, one needed reform would be a fairer pricing of higher education. For instance, it might be appropriate to increase tuitions to universities so that students bear more of the costs of their education. To promote equity, talented students from poor families could be given scholarships or subsidized loans. Payback could be required in the form of future social service, for example teaching primary school; serving as a nurse; working as an agricultural extension agent; or managing a credit cooperative in rural areas.

Scholarship programs for study in the high-income countries are a form of development assistance for education to help those of more modest means. These grants often tend to be for university and professional studies, such as medicine, science, or business. This type of support for students from developing countries is often more cost-effective than establishing professional programs within the low-income country. A concern with such scholarship programs, however, is that professionally trained graduates might not return to their countries, preferring to remain in the host country where employment opportunities are more attractive. The remitted labor earnings from these emigrants only provide partial compensation for the loss in human capital.

A possible resolution to this "brain drain" is the establishment of regional professional schools that attract students from neighboring countries. Establishing a medical school in one West African country that would proportionately accept students from neighboring countries would still be more cost-effective than establishing medical schools in each country. Moreover, the student's reluctance to return to his or her nation of origin should be reduced.

Finally, there is a research agenda for universities in the less developed countries. We noted earlier the need for more research and instruction in medical schools on the prevention and treatment of the diseases endemic to low-income economies. Similarly, there is a call to develop intermediate technologies or technologies appropriate to the conditions in the countries. From wind and solar energies, to low-cost construction materials and methods for housing, to improved seeds, fertilizers, and small-scale irrigation pumps: The possibilities are limitless.

## CONCLUDING NOTE

Economic development is manifested in a general improvement in the standard of living. Human capital formation—through increases in the average levels of nutrition, health, and education—is both a cause and a consequence of economic development. Despite the rapid population growth and uneven economic growth over the past half century, many less developed countries have made impressive progress in human capital formation. Yet, for too many nations, the average levels of human capital are still very low.

The high rates of return reported in this chapter for education suggest that more resources should be devoted to this type of human capital formation. So, too, the potential exists for cost-effective programs that significantly reduce mortality and morbidity rates in the developing nations. Even without substantial increases in resource commitments, a reorientation in resource allocations is warranted—from the oversubsidization of higher education provided by universities and the curative care provided by urban hospitals in favor of primary education, primary health care, and meeting the basic nutritional needs of children. Reductions in population growth through a combination of expanding economic opportunities and family planning would help to achieve the desired human capital deepening.

In Chapter 9 we address employment and labor markets in the less developed countries. The generation of productive employment is perhaps the best way to expand economic opportunities.

## SUMMARY OF MAIN POINTS

*1.* The effects of human capital formation on economic development are pervasive and cumulative. Appropriate investments in nutrition, health, and education will not only increase labor productivity, but directly improve the quality of life.

2. The incidences of malnutrition and undernutrition are high in many of the less developed countries. Poor nutrition can adversely affect, sometimes permanently, the health and development of infants and young children.
3. Regular breastfeeding is important for ensuring adequate nutrition for infants. Breastmilk, more economical and sanitary than infant formula in developing nations, also offers immunological benefits to infants.
4. Food subsidies, food fortification, and nutrition education are among the policy options for dealing with malnutrition. Undernutrition is largely a reflection of poverty.
5. Many unnecessary deaths and illnesses occur in the less developed countries from diseases and afflictions that are easily controlled when preventative measures are taken and environmental conditions improved.
6. Perhaps the best-known measure of general health conditions in a nation is the life expectancy at birth. In most nations, the life expectancy at birth for females exceeds that for males. Another general indicator of health is disability-adjusted life years (DALYs) per thousand population, which measures the average number of productive years of life lost due to disabling illness and early death.
7. Public health expenditures have not been a high priority for most developing countries. Moreover, public health policies have often been biased in favor of large urban hospitals specializing in expensive curative medicine, rather than numerous small clinics providing cost-effective primary health-care services.
8. Health-care reform in developing countries will usually include increased immunization of infants and children; greater access to family planning services; instruction in basic hygiene and health care; information campaigns and programs to prevent sexually-transmitted diseases; improved access to safe water and sanitation; and renewed efforts to eradicate diseases spread by vectors like mosquitoes.
9. Rural health clinics, adequately equipped with supplies and medicines and staffed by trained community health workers, should be the first line of defense in health-care systems in developing economies.
10. Education is both a consumption good, providing utility, and an investment good, enhancing labor productivity. As an investment, education should be subject to net present value and internal-rate-of-return assessments.
11. The private economic returns from education are higher wages and expanded employment opportunities. Private costs include the direct outlays for tuition and materials, as well as the opportunity cost of lost earnings. Social benefits from education must additionally account for more efficient labor markets, higher income tax revenues, and a healthier population. Also, greater educational opportunities for women should result in reduced fertility rates. Social costs include the subsidy element typically accorded education.
12. Rates of return calculations show that within the developing world, education is a good investment from both a private and social perspective. Given the diminishing returns to education, the highest returns are found in primary education and in lower-income countries.
13. Developing countries (as well as foreign-aid donors) need both to increase their financial commitments to education and to introduce needed educational reforms. Such policy changes would include a shift in resources toward primary education; the use of more appropriate classroom materials; a fairer pricing of higher education; and a greater emphasis on entrepreneurship and science within the curriculum.

## KEY TERMS

disability-adjusted life years (DALYs)
entrepreneurship
human capital formation
internal rate of return (IRR)
malnutrition

net present value (NPV)
stunting
undernutrition
wasting

## QUESTIONS

1. For each of the three areas, what do you think should be the highest priority in the less developed countries in terms of public policy: (a) nutrition; (b) health; (c) education. For each, explain why.
2. Why have adequate nutrition and good health not been higher priorities for governments in most of the less developed countries?
3. How can equity and efficiency be improved simultaneously in the public expenditures on nutrition and health care? Discuss.
4. What are the obstacles in the less developed countries to reforming health-care policies that are biased in favor of urban populations and curative medicine? How can these obstacles be overcome?
5. Discuss the role of education in improving nutrition and health in the less developed countries.
6. Explain why it is not surprising that the economic return, both social and private, will probably be higher when providing primary education to a 10-year-old female in a rural area than providing college education to a 20-year-old urban male.
7. Should governments in less developed countries try to promote entrepreneurship in the primary and secondary school curricula? Discuss.
8. What does the emigration of educated labor from a less developed country to a developed country (i.e., the "brain drain") suggest about the returns to education in the two countries? Is the brain drain necessarily bad? What policy reforms, if any, would you recommend? Why?

## SUGGESTED READINGS

Akin, John and Nancy Birdsall, "Financing of Health Services in LDCs," *Finance and Development*, vol. 24, no. 2 (June 1987), pages 40–43.

Becker, Gary, *Human Capital*, New York: National Bureau of Economic Research, 1975.

Ehrenberg, Ronald G. and Robert S. Smith, *Modern Labor Economics: Theory and Public Policy*, 5th ed., Chapter 9, "Investments in Human Capital: Education and Training," New York: HarperCollins, 1994, pages 279–325.

Herz, Barbara, K. Subbarao, Masooma Habib, and Laura Raney, "Letting Girls Learn: Promising Approaches in Primary and Secondary Education," World Bank Discussion Paper #133, The World Bank, Washington, DC, 1991.

Psacharopoulos, George, "Returns to Investment in Education: A Global Update," Policy Research Working Paper #1067, The World Bank, April 1993.

Verspoor, Adriaan, "Educational Development: Priorities for the Nineties," *Finance & Development*, vol. 27, no. 1 (March 1990), pages 20–23.

World Bank, *World Development Report 1990: Poverty*, Chapter 5, "Delivering Social Services to the Poor," New York: Oxford University Press, 1990, pages 74–89.

World Bank, *World Development Report 1993: Investing in Health*, New York: Oxford University Press, 1993.

CHAPTER 9

# EMPLOYMENT

High levels of unemployment spawn a host of problems: growing inequality and social exclusion, the waste of forgone output and unutilized human resources ... In contrast, a high and stable rate of productive job creation is the mainspring of equitable economic and social development.[1]

A primary macroeconomic goal of any nation is full employment. No economy can thrive for very long without operating near full employment. For most households, the employment of one or more adult members at decent wages is the surest way to avoid poverty.

A by-product of the rapid population growth experienced by the less developed countries over the past half-century is rapid labor force growth. From 2.1 billion in 1995, the labor forces in the LDCs are estimated to increase to 3.3 billion by the year 2025.[2] Many of these nations, especially after the slow economic growth and lagging physical capital formation in the 1980s, will be hard-pressed to provide their labor forces with productive employment. Moreover, most of the employment growth must be in industry and services. In 1992, some 58 percent of the labor forces in the developing economies were in agriculture, with only about 15 percent in industry and 27 percent in services. The comparable figures for the developed countries are 9 percent in agriculture, 33 percent in industry, and 58 percent in services.[3]

---

[1]International Labour Organization, *World Employment 1995: An ILO Report,* International Labour Office, Geneva, 1995, page v.

[2]World Bank, *World Development Report 1995,* New York: Oxford University Press, 1995, Table 1.1, page 9. This report, titled "Workers in an Integrating World," discusses many issues related to employment growth. It also contains an extensive bibliography of labor market studies; see pages 133–142.

[3]These statistics on the composition of the labor force for 1990–92 are from Table 51 in the *Human Development Report 1994* of the United Nations Development Programme, New York: Oxford University Press, 1994. Typically the category of agriculture includes forestry, hunting, and fishing. Industry encompasses manufacturing, mining, construction, and electricity, water, and gas.

In assessing current employment prospects in the developing world, a recent International Labour Organization report states:

> The economic performance of developing countries in different regions of the world has diverged significantly since the early 1980s and employment performance has varied accordingly. In East and Southeast Asia high and sustained rates of economic growth have led to rapid growth of modern-sector jobs, rising real wages and, in some cases, even labour shortages. By contrast, in sub-Saharan Africa economic stagnation or retrogression has led to a collapse of modern-sector employment, falling labour earnings, rising urban unemployment and a bloating of low-productivity informal-sector employment. In Latin America, there was also a similar deterioration of employment conditions during the 1980s though the situation has begun to improve in recent years.[4]

In this chapter we will explain why developing countries have had such varied success in generating employment. We begin with the perfectly competitive labor market that generates full employment and provides a reference case for departures from it. Following a review of the types of labor markets within developing economies, we discuss the specific macroeconomic and microeconomic explanations for the serious problems of unemployment and underemployment found in many developing countries. Rural to urban migration, with its impact on employment and unemployment, is also investigated. We then review policies to promote employment. We conclude this chapter with a case study of Egypt, a country that has had difficulties in generating attractive employment opportunities for the newly educated.

## THE THEORY OF THE COMPETITIVE LABOR MARKET

We first consider wage and employment determination within a competitive market with many buyers and sellers of homogeneous labor services.[5] Recall that in the labor market, firms demand labor to produce output, and households supply labor services to earn income. Such labor-market conditions describe, to a large extent, the market for farm laborers, as well as the informal urban labor markets that employ large numbers of individuals, often at relatively low wages.

### THE DEMAND FOR LABOR

Individual employers or firms use labor and other inputs to produce output with the aim of maximizing their economic profits. The value to a firm derived from

---

[4]International Labour Organization, *World Employment 1995: An ILO Report*, pages 9–10.
[5]A comprehensive discussion of the competitive labor market can be found in *Modern Labor Economics: Theory and Public Policy*, 5th ed., by Ronald Ehrenberg and Robert Smith, New York: HarperCollins, 1994, Chapters 3 and 6–8.

### FIGURE 9.1 | THE FIRM'S VALUE OF MARGINAL PRODUCT OF LABOR

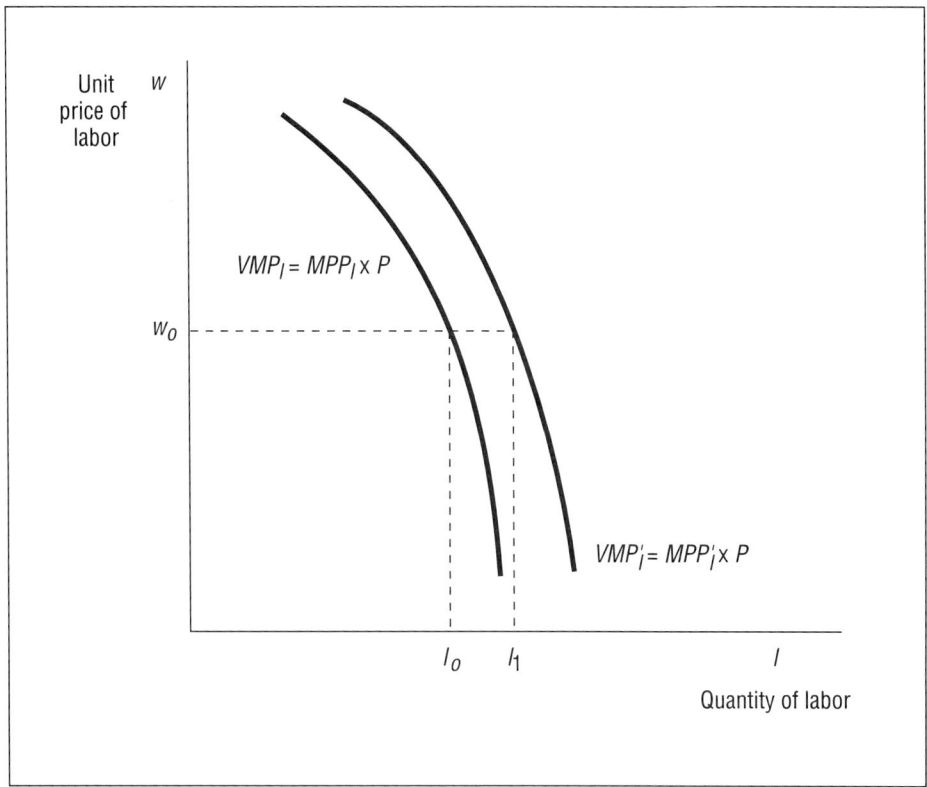

employing any unit of labor is a function of the increment to total revenues from selling the output produced by the labor. Consider a relatively small farm producing a standardized product, such as corn, the price of which is determined in a competitive output market. In this case, the extra revenue generated from employing an additional unit of labor, called the **value of marginal product of labor (VMP$_l$)**, equals the marginal physical product of labor (MPP$_l$) multiplied by the price of output (corn in this case), or MPP$_l \times$ P.[6]

The individual firm's employment decision will involve a comparison of the additional cost per unit of labor with the additional benefit from employing labor, illustrated by the VMP$_l$ curve in Figure 9.1. For instance, if the labor market is competitive and the firm may employ all the labor it wishes at the prevailing market wage, $w_o$, the profit-maximizing firm will hire $l_o$ units of labor at the equality of the wage and the

---

[6]Formally, the value of the additional contribution from a unit of labor is called the *marginal revenue product of labor (MRP$_l$)*, which equals the marginal physical product of labor multiplied by the marginal revenue of output. Recall that in a competitive output market, a firm is a price taker; thus, the firm's marginal revenue coincides with the market price of output. In this case, the firm's marginal revenue product of labor (MRP$_l$) is equal to the marginal physical product of labor (MPP$_l$) multiplied by the price of output (P), which economists call the value of marginal product (VMP$_l$).

value of marginal product of labor. Thus, the value-of-marginal-product-of-labor curve becomes the firm's labor demand function. The firm's demand curve for labor is downward sloping, consistent with the law of diminishing returns.

For a given wage or price of labor, the firm will employ more (less) labor as the $VMP_l$ curve shifts rightward (leftward). The $VMP_l$ curve will shift with either a change in the marginal product of labor or the price of output. Were the firm to have more of the fixed inputs (land and machinery for the farmer), each unit of labor would have a higher marginal physical product, shifting rightward the $VMP_l$ curve. For instance, as shown in Figure 9.1, the firm's marginal product of labor increases from $MPP_l$ to $MPP_l'$, shifting out the $VMP_l$ curve to $VMP_l'$. At the given wage, $w_o$, the firm increases its hiring of labor from $l_o$ to $l_1$. A higher output price would also shift rightward the $VMP_l$ curve, increasing the quantity of labor employed. Conversely, less of the fixed inputs or a lower output price would reduce the value of marginal product of labor, shifting leftward the $VMP_l$ curve, reducing employment.

The market demand for labor, $D_L$, assumed in this case to be units of unskilled labor measured in hours per month, is inversely related to the wage rate per hour $(w)$, as shown in Figure 9.2. As the wage rate falls, profit-maximizing firms employ more labor and produce more output. The market demand for labor is an aggregation of all individual firms' demands for labor and shows the quantity demanded for labor at different wage rates.

## LABOR SUPPLY

Labor is supplied by households to generate income to purchase goods and services, to pay taxes, and, when possible, to save for the future. As they allocate time among formal employment, other earnings opportunities, and leisure, individuals are assumed to maximize their satisfaction or utility. Thus, at higher wage rates individuals tend to supply more labor, reducing the time spent in other activities.

Actually, a higher wage will have two impacts on an individual. First, the opportunity cost of non–labor market activity (represented by the wage rate or the forgone earnings) will increase; individuals will be likely to allocate more time toward the labor market and less time toward individual earning opportunities (such as their own plots of land) and leisure. Economists refer to this reallocation of time as a **substitution effect.** The substitution effect of a higher (lower) wage will be an increase (decrease) in desired working hours or labor supplied.

A second expected response by an individual is called the **income effect.** With a higher wage rate per hour worked, an individual would receive higher income for the same work effort. This additional income could be spent on goods and services desired by families. There also may be a tendency to "purchase" more leisure with the additional income, following a wage increase. With relatively low per capita incomes and with high marginal propensities to consume food and other necessities in developing countries, the income effect of a wage increase is apt to be very weak. Note, however, that the income effect leads to a negative relationship between the wage rate and the quantity of labor supplied.

The market supply of labor is the sum of the quantities of labor supplied by each individual at each wage rate. As shown in Figure 9.2, the supply of labor, $S_L$, is generally assumed to be upward sloping; at higher wage rates a greater quantity of labor is supplied. Clearly, with an upward-sloping labor supply, economists are assuming that the substitution effect dominates the income effect of a wage change. As the wage rate

FIGURE 9.2 | THE COMPETITIVE LABOR MARKET

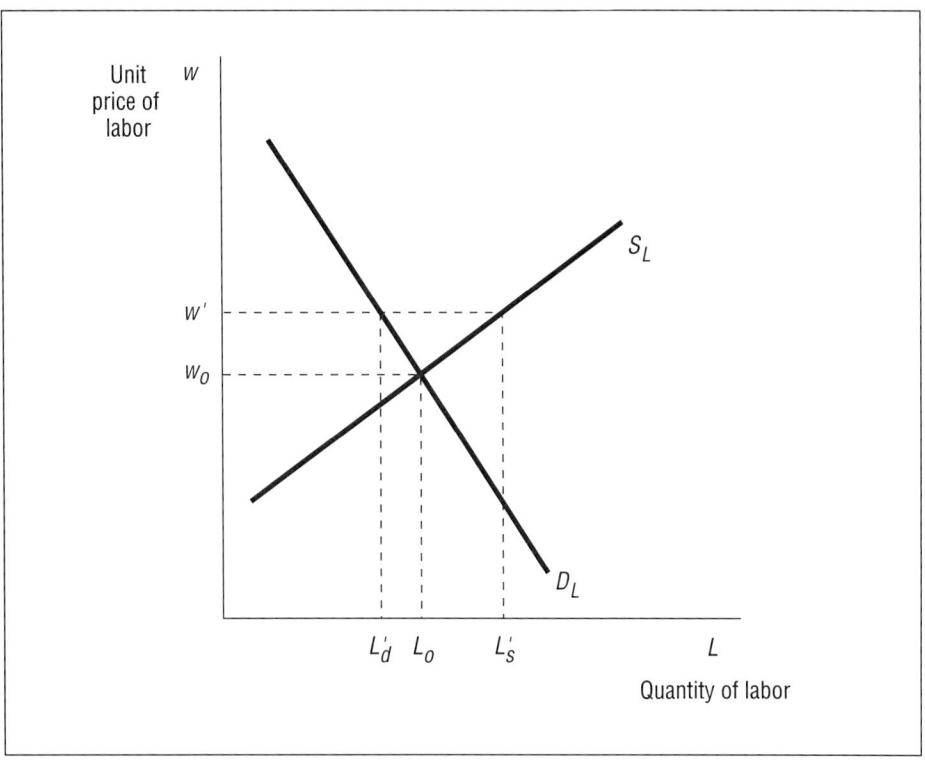

increases, individuals will wish to work more hours. Moreover, some individuals not previously in the labor market will be induced to become labor-market participants and supply labor hours. This latter point merits additional consideration. In the absence of effective compulsory schooling and child labor laws, higher wages may induce children to enter the labor market at a longer-run cost to themselves and to their society.

## LABOR-MARKET EQUILIBRIUM

The equilibrium wage is found where the quantity demanded of labor equals the quantity supplied of labor; see $w_o$ and $L_o$ in Figure 9.2. At a wage higher than $w_o$, such as $w'$, the quantity supplied of labor $(L_s')$ would exceed the quantity demanded $(L_d')$. There would be an excess supply of labor, with a tendency for the wage rate to fall to $w_o$. At any wage lower than $w_o$, there will be an excess demand for labor; the wage will be bid up to $w_o$, clearing the labor market.

The wage rate and level of employment will vary with changes in the demand or supply of labor. For instance, a greater capital stock would increase the marginal product of each unit of labor, leading to an outward (rightward) shift in labor demand. This increase in demand would lead to a higher wage and additional employment. Capital deepening and other productivity-augmenting measures are the primary contributors to higher wages and rising living standards. Labor-force growth that increases the supply of labor at each wage rate tends to lower wages, inducing firms to hire the additional labor supplied.

In the competitive labor market there will be no **involuntary unemployment;** all individuals wishing to work at the prevailing wage, $w_o$, will be employed. We have made no prediction about the level or adequacy of the equilibrium wage. In many developing countries, where labor markets are relatively competitive, wages for unskilled labor, for instance, can be very low.

## LABOR MARKETS IN DEVELOPING COUNTRIES

In developing countries, three basic types of labor markets exist: rural, urban informal, and urban formal (modern-sector). In this section, we discuss the characteristics of each of these markets.

### RURAL LABOR MARKETS

Analyses of rural labor markets tend to fall into three categories: the competitive model, the surplus labor model, and the household-producer model.[7] Given that a large proportion of the populations of developing countries lives in rural areas, an understanding of rural labor markets is crucial to designing effective development policies. Another important feature of rural labor markets is their seasonality. Rural economic activity is disproportionately agricultural; labor demands will vary widely during the year. Periods of peak labor demand include planting and harvesting. At other times, labor demand may be very weak. In this situation, workers are considered underemployed in that they would like to work more hours than offered by employers. Clearly, wages, earnings, and employment can vary significantly during the year.

#### THE COMPETITIVE RURAL LABOR MARKET

In those areas where many farmers employ nonfamily unskilled labor, the competitive market model may be applicable. With few effective minimum-wage laws and an absence of unions in rural areas, wages would tend toward the market-clearing, or equilibrium, level. A primary concern is that the average wage may be near subsistence level. Low ratios of capital to labor mean that the value of marginal product of labor and resulting labor demand are low. Moreover, if farm product prices are relatively low, the $VMP_l$ will be further depressed. A relatively large supply of labor, including children, may also lead to low wage levels.

To increase wage levels, the productivity of labor should be increased, both through basic education and with greater use of nonlabor inputs. Given that wage levels are

---

[7]A helpful review of the literature concerning labor markets in developing countries can be found in Chapter 15 (by Mark R. Rosenzweig) of the *Handbook of Development Economics, Volume 1*, edited by Hollis Chenery and T. N. Srinivasan, Amsterdam: North-Holland, 1988.

relatively low, labor-intensive techniques that use appropriate capital inputs should be attractive. For instance, equipping farm labor with better hand tools could lead to a more productive use of labor in harvesting crops; wages and employment should increase. Highly capital-intensive techniques, such as those found on U.S. farms, while raising the wages of those who remain employed, are likely to result in a substitution of capital for labor, reducing the overall rate of employment.

Lifting restraints on product prices would also stimulate the hiring of labor.[8] Output price increases will shift out labor's value of marginal product curve, raising both wages and employment. International economic integration that leads to increased demand for basic commodities, typically exported by developing countries, will have similar effects. Finally, increasing school attendance may reduce the supply of child labor, pushing up wage levels.

## Surplus Labor Models

Even when competitive labor market conditions appear to exist, there may be surplus labor (or involuntary unemployment), suggesting that an equilibrium wage rate does not hold. We consider two explanations for surplus labor: the Lewis model and more recent work on efficiency wages.

One of the earliest development models to include surplus labor in the rural sector was the Lewis model, discussed in Chapter 4. In this model, there was surplus labor in the sense that the marginal product of the last units of agricultural labor employed was zero. Nevertheless, all labor was employed and paid a wage equal to the average product of labor. Lewis further assumed that there were job vacancies in the urban sector that paid a wage equal to the marginal product of labor in the urban manufacturing sector, and that the real value of this urban wage exceeded the rural wage. Transferring labor from the rural sector to the urban sector would yield a net gain in output for the economy. There would be no loss of output in the rural area as long as the marginal product of labor was zero, and there would be a gain in output in the urban sector since the marginal product of urban labor is positive. Indeed, the development process is characterized by the transfer of labor from the rural to the urban areas.

The Lewis model of surplus rural labor, however, is probably not relevant in the contemporary developing countries. Most LDCs today have seasonal labor shortages in rural areas, at times of peak labor demands, while having labor surpluses in urban areas, particularly for modern-sector employment. Accounting for these labor imbalances is excessive rural-to-urban migration, to be discussed later in this chapter.

A second explanation for a labor surplus with explicit unemployment is the efficiency wage argument. To explain the co-existence of high rates of unemployment with relatively competitive rural labor markets (i.e., the absence of minimum wages and labor unions), economists have hypothesized a link between nutrition and wage levels.[9] Specifically, at low wage levels workers could not afford a sufficiently nutritious

---

[8]Recall that one of the policy implications of the Lewis model (see Chapter 4) was to control the prices paid to farmers at below–market equilibrium levels.

[9]See "Economics of Development and the Development of Economics" by Pranab Bardhan, in *Journal of Economic Perspectives*, vol. 7, no. 2 (spring 1993), pages 129–142. The first works that linked nutrition to rural wages are H. Leibenstein, *Economic Backwardness and Economic Growth: Studies in the Theory of Economic Development*, New York: Wiley, 1957; and D. Mazumdar, "The Marginal Productivity Theory of Wages and Disguised Unemployment," *Review of Economic Studies*, vol. 26, no. 71 (June 1959),

*continued*

diet to sustain a work effort worth employing. Employers would have to pay an above-equilibrium wage so that workers would have sufficient endurance and strength. Of course, the supply of labor would then exceed the demand at this wage, leaving surplus labor.

In recent years the efficiency wage argument has been bolstered with other explanations showing that the profit-maximizing firm may rationally pay a higher-than-market equilibrium wage. With an above-equilibrium wage and excess labor wishing to be employed, those working will feel compelled to perform better, fearing that they could be fired and easily replaced. Thus, the firm has an interest in paying this higher wage to discourage shirking or sub-par performance. With an excess supply of labor, the employer is able to choose among competing laborers, hiring those considered to be the best workers. Finally, the higher wage may boost morale and increase labor productivity.

### Labor As a Producer

In much of the Third World, particularly in Africa and Asia, a majority of rural residents have access to land that they cultivate, growing crops for home consumption and for sale. The household must decide on the allocation of time among different activities: growing its own crops, doing other household tasks, working off the farm as a wage laborer, and enjoying leisure.

As a producer, the household acts as a firm that must decide on the levels of outputs to produce and the inputs to use. In theory, the household would produce output to the equality of marginal revenue and marginal cost. In assessing its marginal cost, the household must have some estimate of the "opportunity cost" of its own labor, since its own labor contribution to crop production does not receive an explicit wage. The household, like a firm, claims the residual or accounting profit after explicit expenses are subtracted from total revenues. Post-harvest, the household can estimate its return (an "effective" wage rate) to compare with the opportunity cost of labor, usually the given market wage. In the future, the household may elect to devote more (less) labor to on-farm activities if its expected return is greater (less) than the opportunity cost of labor.

When rural labor activity is viewed from a producer point of view, development policy becomes directed toward increasing the profitability of small farming. Policy options concern land tenure; the availability of credit; the provision of appropriate seeds, fertilizer, and pesticides; storage practices; and marketing outlets. Rural labor markets are clearly affected by the profitability of small farming. Greater profits for small farmers will reduce the time they allocate to wage-paying labor activities (often as farm laborers for larger farmers). This reallocation of landholders' time toward their own farms will then increase the wage rate for those workers without land.

Particularly in Africa, where nearly 70 percent of the workforce is still engaged in agriculture, rural labor markets, regardless of the particular economic model applied, merit additional attention from policymakers. Low rural incomes and seasonal underemployment retard the development process. In arguing for continued support of small farmers in developing countries, the International Labour Organization states:

---

pages 190–197. Additional discussion of the efficiency wage argument within developing countries can be found in J. E. Stiglitz, "The Efficiency Wage Hypothesis, Surplus Labor and the Distribution of Income in LDCs," *Oxford Economic Papers*, vol. 28, no. 2 (July 1976), pages 185–207.

In the first place, to neglect the small farm sector would be to aggravate problems of rural poverty and underemployment. The poor who are concentrated in that sector would face reduced prospects for raising their productivity and incomes. This is especially harmful since it is unlikely that better alternative employment opportunities can be generated for all those who are displaced by falling incomes or the growth of capital-intensive and mechanized agriculture.

The main objective of rural policies in countries where there is still substantial employment in the small farm sector should therefore be to upgrade production in that sector and to increase its integration into the economic mainstream.[10]

We shall return to the challenge of promoting improved rural living standards both in Chapter 11 on agriculture and in Chapter 18 on Africa.

## URBAN INFORMAL LABOR MARKETS

The urban informal market is characterized by low-wage jobs with little job security and usually no fringe benefits. Often individuals do not work their desired number of hours. Some are underemployed and part-time, offered fewer working hours than desired. Others, given their income needs or the demands of the job, are required to work very long hours. The urban informal labor market usually includes a large number of small vendors, often reselling smaller lots of products, including food, clothing, handicrafts, and newspapers. Remuneration for the small sellers is simply the difference between their sale price and their own purchase price multiplied by the number of units sold.

Others work on a payment-by-piece basis, such as washing cars, running errands, or transporting people (e.g., rickshaw operators). Finally, many individuals work for an hourly wage in small factories or restaurants and other service activities. Depending on the labor laws of the country and the compliance of the employer, these workers may or may not be subject to enforced labor regulations concerning minimum wages, job security, and safe working conditions. As a result, many workers in the urban informal labor market may be working for very low wages in unsafe sweatshop conditions.

The informal labor market does offer employment opportunities that would not otherwise exist. The jobs are typically labor-intensive and have modest skill requirements. Also, the informal labor market provides a safety net for those who have not been successful in finding more attractive employment. Still, there is concern with the low value-added of these jobs. Productivity is low, and opportunities for advancement are relatively nonexistent. As a result, the annual labor payment per worker can be quite low, and employees will have little attachment to these jobs.

The use of child labor, at very low wages and often in dangerous conditions, is a particularly unattractive aspect of the informal labor market. Many children, particularly in parts of Asia, work long, tedious hours in textile and rug factories. While providing needed income for their families, these children are deprived of an education and subject to physical and mental developmental problems. International agreements concerning child labor have yet to be effective. To this point, the actual design of such regulations has been difficult. At the recent GATT Uruguay Round, completed in 1993, nations could not agree on suitable and enforceable regulations concerning child labor.

---

[10]International Labour Organization, *World Employment 1995: An ILO Report,* page 95.

The WTO (World Trade Organization), the successor organization to GATT, is committed to continued discussion of this issue. Ultimately, rising family incomes and compulsory elementary education will be the most effective deterrents to child labor.

The plight of these children was poignantly dramatized by a twelve-year-old Pakistani, Iqbal Masih, who had worked as a carpet weaver from the ages of four to ten, before becoming an internationally known spokesperson against child labor. In April of 1995, under circumstances that are still not clear, he was murdered outside of Lahore, Pakistan.

Informal-sector employment is very important in most developing countries. For instance, in sub-Saharan Africa, the informal sector accounts for 60 percent of the urban workforce.[11] For those with little education and experience, the informal sector is the primary employer. Moreover, unemployed modern-sector workers find temporary employment in the informal sector. A challenge for economic development is to improve informal-sector jobs without reducing employment, a subject we shall turn to in the final section of this chapter.

## MODERN-SECTOR EMPLOYMENT

Modern-sector employment opportunities are jobs that are characterized by above-subsistence wages, fringe benefits, job security, and advancement potential. Typically, these jobs are in urban areas. While the government is often a major provider of this type of employment, the private sector also offers both manufacturing and service-sector jobs that can be considered modern. Nearly always, a job classified as modern would require basic literacy; frequently, there will be more demanding educational requirements.

In nearly all developing countries, the supply of workers for modern employment exceeds the demand, suggesting that the wage levels are above the market-clearing level, as at the wage $w'$ in Figure 9.2. As will be further discussed in the next section, this excess supply of labor, generated by the above-equilibrium wages, can be considered a measure of unemployment. The most common explanations for the above-market-equilibrium wages are minimum wage laws, unionization, and the efficiency wage arguments discussed earlier in the context of rural employment. Moreover, in the public sector, governments have had a tendency, often as a legacy of colonialism, to pay attractive wages that exceed equilibrium levels. Often, modern-sector unemployment is directly related to the level of education. In most developing countries, an insufficient number of jobs exists for those with secondary and higher education. Frequently found is a surplus of individuals trained as lawyers and college professors, accompanied by a shortage of engineers and scientists.[12]

Expanding modern-sector employment is a primary development objective. Often, developing countries have overrelied on the public sector to provide these opportunities. Greater reliance on the private sector has become a major priority within the contemporary developing world. As previously mentioned, many Asian countries have

---

[11]United Nations Development Programme, *Human Development Report 1993,* New York: Oxford University Press, 1993, page 41.

[12]For some rough estimates of unemployment rates for different categories of educational achievement in India, see United Nations Development Programme, *Human Development Report 1993*, page 39. It should be noted that the rates of return to education used in Chapter 8 were based on the assumption that an individual was employed. For those who are unemployed, the return to education is clearly reduced.

been relatively successful in creating modern-sector manufacturing employment. The ILO credits this to "the maintenance of macroeconomic stability, high levels of savings and investment, a liberal trading regime, an export-oriented industrialization strategy, and the successful attraction of foreign direct investment."[13] Other developing countries may well emulate these Asian economies in creating attractive employment opportunities.

## UNEMPLOYMENT AND UNDEREMPLOYMENT

**Unemployment,** the absence of a job for someone willing to work at current wages; and **underemployment,** the mismatching of an individual's potential and actual labor contribution, reduce society's output. Lost income and diminished self-esteem accompany both unemployment and underemployment. Within developing countries, the incidence of unemployment typically exceeds that of the high-income countries. While industrial economies confront unemployment levels that usually vary from 5 to 10 percent, unemployment rates in developing countries can reach 20 percent or more.[14]

In this section, we define both unemployment and underemployment, discussing its measurement within a country. While this measurement is more accurately done within the high-income countries, knowledge of this process is important for an understanding of the functioning of labor markets. We will then consider the contributing factors to unemployment, both macroeconomic—those related to a deficiency of aggregate demand—and microeconomic—those related to factor price distortions.

### UNEMPLOYMENT DEFINED

For a given population *(WP)* above a certain appropriate working age (usually 16 years of age), individuals are classified as in the **labor force *(L)*** if they are **employed *(E)*** or **unemployed *(U)*.** To be officially counted as unemployed, an individual, while not working, must be actively seeking employment. Individuals are not in the labor force (and not officially considered unemployed) for varying reasons including school; home responsibilities; discouragement about job prospects; sufficient nonlabor market income; poor health; and retirement.

Economists use different measures to consider labor-market activity. The **rate of labor force participation (LFP)** is defined as the percentage of the population over 16 years of age that is either working or unemployed yet searching for work.

$$LFP = (E + U)/WP$$

---

[13]International Labour Organization, *World Employment 1995: An ILO Report,* page 63.

[14]For some rough estimates of unemployment rates in developing countries see United Nations Development Programme, *Human Development Report 1993,* page 35; and International Labour Organization, *World Employment 1995: An ILO Report,* page 67.

The **rate of unemployment (UNP)** is defined as the percentage of the labor force that is unemployed:

$$UNP = U/L = U/(E+U)$$

The unemployment rate tends to understate the nonutilization of labor within an economy for several reasons. First, those who are too discouraged to even look for work, even though they might well accept employment at the prevailing wage, are not included in the unemployment rate. Second, there are individuals who are underemployed in the sense of working fewer hours than they would desire (e.g., working only six hours per day when preferring to work nine hours). Another form of underemployment exists when an individual has a job which is not commensurate with her skills or training (e.g., a university professor working as a taxi driver). Finally, poor health that prevents an individual from either seeking employment or working full time, constitutes another cause of underutilization of labor.

Further complications arise in making calculations because actual unemployment rates for developing countries are not particularly reliable. In the developed economies, the unemployment rate is frequently calculated by a survey process. A government agency, such as the department or ministry of labor, will survey a sample of households on a regular basis. For each household the number of working-age individuals who are employed, seeking work, or not in the labor force is recorded. The national unemployment rate is then extrapolated from the survey results.

In developing countries, few governments can afford to devote the resources to reliable surveys and a careful processing of the data. Often, the political will does not exist to acknowledge poor economic performance and high unemployment rates. Of greater relevance is the fact that unemployment rates in developing economies are less meaningful. A significant understating of unemployment would occur because of the very high degree of underemployment. In informal labor markets, many individuals, including children under age 16, while attempting to work longer hours, may effectively be working only a few hours per day. By most definitions, this labor force activity is classified as employment, leading to an understatement of the actual unemployment. Additionally, in many developing countries, individuals will often be employed in situations that do not correspond to their educational backgrounds. The dearth of high-skilled and high-wage jobs leads to an underutilization of many educated people.

## MACROECONOMIC ANALYSIS OF UNEMPLOYMENT

The macroeconomic analysis of unemployment is modeled within the context of an economy-wide aggregate demand and aggregate supply framework. Aggregate demand measures the desired spending for the goods and services produced within the economy. Typically, aggregate demand is divided into four components: personal consumption expenditures, investment, government spending, and net exports (or exports less imports of goods and services). The **aggregate demand (AD)** curve illustrates the inverse relationship between desired spending on real national output $(Y)$ and the aggregate or average price level $(P)$ prevailing within the economy (see Figure 9.3).

An increase in the average price level reduces the aggregate quantity demanded for primarily three reasons. First, the purchasing power of the given nominal assets of

### FIGURE 9.3 | AGGREGATE DEMAND AND SUPPLY

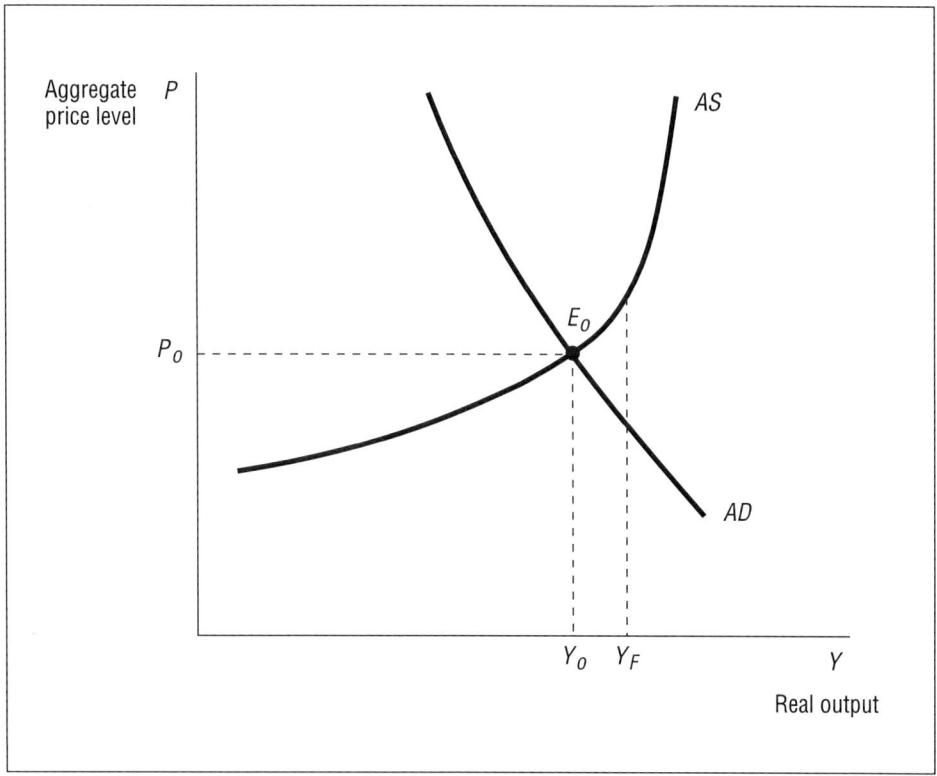

individuals decreases with a higher price level, reducing personal consumption. Second, a higher price level increases the demand for money, which tends to push up interest rates and thereby reduce interest-sensitive expenditures. Finally, for a given exchange rate, a higher price level tends to decrease the foreign quantity demanded for domestic goods and services (exports) and increase the domestic quantity demanded of foreign goods and services (imports).

Fiscal and monetary policy can be used to shift the aggregate demand curve. An expansionary fiscal policy, such as a reduction in tax rates or an increase in discretionary government spending, is intended to increase aggregate demand at every price level—shifting the *AD* curve rightward. An increase in the money supply, which lowers the rate of interest and increases investment, would also shift the aggregate demand curve rightward. The money supply can be increased by the central bank's purchasing government bonds and increasing bank reserves. Increased bank reserves would lead to an increased money supply, which would lower interest rates, increasing, at any aggregate price level, interest-sensitive expenditures such as business and residential fixed investment and consumer durables. In contrast, contractionary fiscal and monetary policy will shift the aggregate demand curve to the left.

**Aggregate supply (AS)** shows the real value of goods and services that will be supplied by all firms *(Y)* as the aggregate price level *(P)* varies. The short-run aggregate supply curve *(AS)*, shown in Figure 9.3, is upward sloping. Increases in the price level are associated with increases in the real national output supplied. With rising marginal costs of production, due to diminishing returns to labor, higher output prices are needed to induce increased production. Moreover, as production increases and labor demand shifts outward, wage rates could be bid up, further pushing up output prices. At some point on the aggregate supply curve is the quantity of real output corresponding to **full employment,** $Y_F$. The full-employment unemployment rate, while tending to be low (between 4 and 7 percent in the developed countries), does not equal zero. Even at full employment, some individuals will be between jobs (the **frictionally unemployed**) and some will have skills not currently in demand (the **structurally unemployed**).

At full-employment real output, $Y_F$, the labor market clears with an equilibrium wage rate. At output levels below full employment, there will be some excess supply of labor, or unemployment. The economy can not operate for long with an above-full employment output produced, as there will be strong inflationary pressures. At some level of real output, beyond $Y_F$, all resources are fully utilized, and no additional output can be produced in the short run. At this point, the short-run aggregate supply function is vertical.

The interaction of aggregate demand and aggregate supply determines an equilibrium aggregate price level, $P_0$, and level of real output, $Y_0$ (see Point $E_0$ in Figure 9.3). An associated employment of labor will also occur. For a given labor force, the unemployment rate will be inversely related to real output.

Expansionary fiscal and monetary policies have been advocated to raise the real level of output and reduce unemployment. Opponents of such interventionist policy, however, argue that expansionary fiscal and monetary policy will be ineffective in reducing unemployment over the longer run and will primarily result in a higher price level. Generally, noninterventionists believe that competitive input and output markets will lead the economy toward full employment without the need for government action. In particular, while expansionary policy could temporarily increase real output and employment, the resulting upward pressure on the price level would lead workers to demand higher nominal wages for any quantity of labor supplied. In this case the labor supply curve would shift inward (upward) raising nominal wage rates and shifting upward the aggregate supply function, reducing real output at each price level.

To illustrate, suppose the economy begins in equilibrium at $Y_0$ and $P_0$ in Figure 9.4. Assume that expansionary fiscal policy shifts the aggregate demand curve from $AD_0$ to $AD'$. Output and the price level increase to $Y_1$ and $P_1$ (see the move from $E_0$ to $E_1$). With the increase in the price level, labor may expect higher nominal wages, shifting up the aggregate supply curve from $AS_0$ to $AS'$. The level of real output would fall back toward the original level, $Y_0$, and the price level would rise further from $P_1$ to $P_2$ (see the move from $E_1$ to $E_2$). Here the expansionary policy has no impact on real output, but has led to a higher price level. Those favoring the use of discretionary fiscal policy contend that the labor supply response (the move from $E_1$ to $E_2$) may be rather slow and the benefits of an expansionary fiscal policy (the move from $E_0$ to $E_1$) can persist for some time. Clearly, the speed of the labor supply adjustment to the higher price level is a key issue of contention in this debate.

An additional criticism against discretionary policy is that policymakers have a very limited understanding of the aggregate economy. In this case, it is nearly impossible to discern the proper policy mix to promote full employment. In fact, economists do not agree on the actual full-employment unemployment rate. Limited economic understanding is particularly relevant in developing countries where complete and accurate aggregate economic models are apt to be lacking. Moreover, in these countries, additional constraints exist on the use of fiscal and monetary policy.

## FIGURE 9.4 | EXPANSIONARY FISCAL POLICY

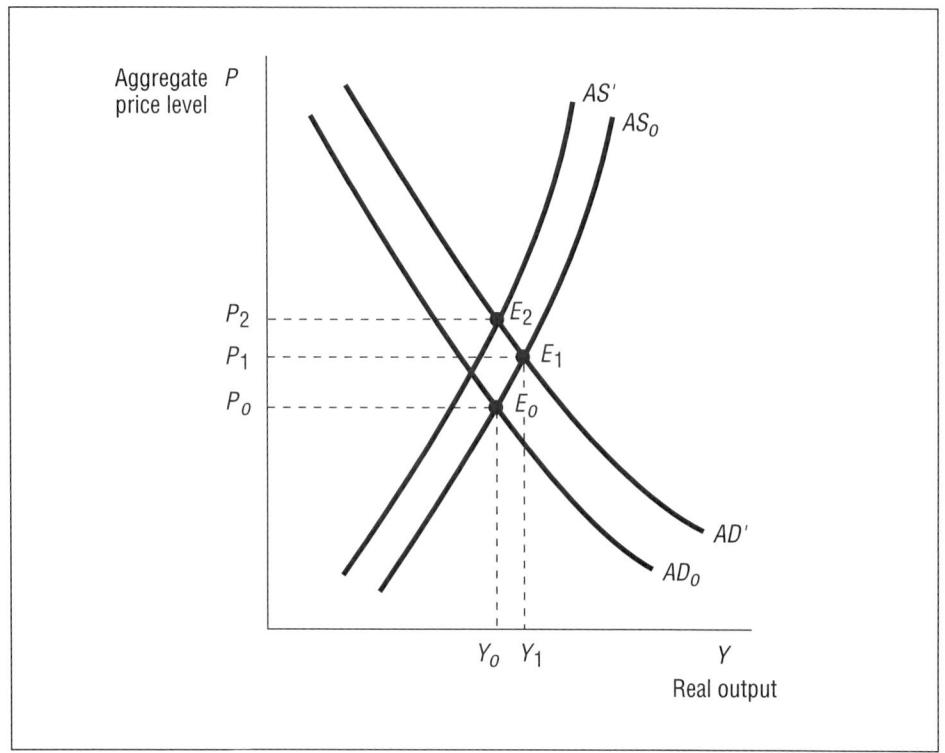

Expansionary fiscal policies usually result in government budget deficits that are typically funded through government borrowing with the issue of government bonds. To the extent that governments in developing countries are perceived as more risky borrowers, the interest rate on the bond issues is apt to be very high, forcing these countries to finance deficits through central bank borrowing that increases the money supply and leads to inflation. Currently, major development agencies like the World Bank and the International Monetary Fund with their structural adjustment programs are discouraging demand-management fiscal policies with the associated budget deficits, while encouraging more private-sector development. Further, income taxation is not a widely developed source of government revenues in many Third World countries. It is difficult and expensive to establish an income tax when compliance is based on the voluntary reporting of actual incomes. Small farmers, often illiterate, are unable to complete the tax forms. Often, rural household income, primarily from farming activities, is difficult to calculate in an exact manner. Finally, particularly for high-income individuals, strong incentives exist for noncompliance and underreporting of income. Without a system of income taxation, therefore, tax changes are not a readily available policy tool for many developing countries. Thus, developing countries have less flexibility in designing expansionary fiscal policies.

Also, demand-management monetary policy is not often a viable option for developing countries. Frequently, they do not have a banking system that is sufficiently organized and regulated by central authorities to permit a targeting of the aggregate money supply. Overexpansion of the money supply has been the source of significant inflation in many countries. Government budget deficits have been accommodated either through direct increases in the money supply (leading to inflation) or through increases in government debt. As will be discussed in Chapter 10, increased government borrowing can raise interest rates and "crowd-out" private-sector, interest-sensitive expenditures such as business investment. Current structural adjustment programs tend to impose monetary controls on developing countries.

While some agreement exists that the level of aggregate demand affects real output and employment in the short run, no consensus exists concerning the exact mix of macroeconomic policies necessary to promote full employment in either the developed or developing countries. However, the macroeconomic environment is clearly important to job creation. Those developing countries that have been most successful at creating modern-sector employment have had high rates of savings and investment, low rates of inflation, and relatively open economies.

We now turn to a discussion of the microeconomic distortions in the labor market that can inhibit employment.

## MICROECONOMIC EXPLANATIONS OF UNEMPLOYMENT

As illustrated in Chapter 5 with the basic needs approach, non–market-clearing input prices can bias economic decision making. An artificially high price of labor (or low price of capital) will lead to a reduced usage of labor, creating unemployment. Consider a farmer who uses land, labor, and machinery to produce corn. There are different combinations of the inputs that produce a given level of output. In the long run, the farmer will be able to substitute one input for another in the production process without changing total output; the production function will determine the rate at which this input substitution can occur. For instance, a higher price of labor could lead the farmer to use more machinery, such as replacing workers with a power tiller. Artificially low prices for capital goods, due to subsidized credit or an overvalued currency, could have the same effect.

### Minimum Wages, Social Security, and Unions

Many countries have minimum-wage laws that keep the price of labor higher than would exist in a competitive setting. As suggested, there would be a tendency to substitute capital for labor in this case. Alternatively, any tax on, or compulsory contribution from, labor to fund social security or health care will put upward pressure on the firm's cost per unit of labor and lead to reduced employment. Finally, regulations that prevent the release of labor, either in times of reduced activity or for incompetence, will raise the effective cost per unit of labor, reducing employment.

Above-market-equilibrium wages for civil servants have been quite common in the developing world. Government activity tends not to be subject to the discipline of the market. Governments often continue to pay wages in excess of those needed to employ people. Whether a legacy from colonialism, a desire to placate important political or ethnic groups, or a response to labor union demands, Third World governments have generally not been cost-effective in their labor practices. Government programs and projects have been overstaffed with individuals receiving high wages and generous fringe benefits. To the extent that this high wage structure spills over into the private sector, a further reduction in aggregate employment will occur.

In most instances, minimum-wage legislation, social security and health programs, and employment security legislation have laudable purposes. Unfortunately, they do introduce rigidity into the labor market and, on balance, contribute to less employment. Ideally, the government should try to provide minimum income and health benefits through programs that introduce less distortion into the economy. Cash grants to the poor elderly or the provision of basic health-care services to the poor are examples of less distorting interventions aimed at helping low-income citizens. Also, international development agencies, such as the World Bank and the International Monetary Fund, have been encouraging governments to reduce public-sector employment and wages and to rely more on markets to promote employment in the private sector.

Labor unions have both positive and negative effects within an economy. Supporters argue that unions increase productivity, protect workers' rights, and reduce income inequality. Detractors, however, feel that unions are simply trying to achieve above-equilibrium wages for their members. As a result of higher wages, total employment will fall. Most labor economists concur that the positive aspects of unions tend to be enhanced when unions operate in competitive product markets and when collective bargaining occurs at the local level, between a single union and a single employer.[15] In competitive product markets, unions are unable to achieve substantial wage increases without significantly reducing demand for the employer's output and total employment.

## BIAS TOWARD CAPITAL-INTENSIVE PROJECTS

Often both private- and public-sector investment decisions will be influenced by a bias or preference for more capital-intensive (i.e., less labor-intensive) techniques. The prestige associated with larger-scale or more modern (often imported) techniques, usually capital-intensive production, can lead to an investment decision that is not cost-minimizing for the scale of output, and uses relatively less labor. Irrigation projects in West Africa that rely on expensive dam schemes have often been favored over smaller-scale, more cost-effective rainfed agricultural developments. In the case of public investment decisions, both local governments and donor agencies have often been too encouraging of more capital-intensive production methods.

In addition, in many countries the price of capital has been kept artificially low. With either direct subsidies or preferential tax treatment, the effective rate of interest has often been below the market-clearing level, leading to a preference for capital-intensive projects and requiring credit rationing.

Further, an overvalued exchange rate will encourage more capital-intensive production techniques. Typically, less developed countries import machinery and capital equipment. The import prices of the capital goods will directly influence the firm's domestic production costs. To the extent that a country's currency is overvalued, imports are artificially cheap in terms of the domestic currency prices. In particular, the prices of imported capital goods would be correspondingly reduced, introducing a bias toward capital and away from labor in the production process. (An example of an overvalued currency reducing the price of capital imports was given in Chapter 5.)

---

[15]World Bank, *World Development Report 1995,* page 86.

Both the prestige of modern technology and artificially low capital prices lead to a bias toward capital-intensive production methods that reduce aggregate employment in the modern sector. The ILO reports:

> Whereas once it was thought that labour market imperfections were at the root of relative factor price distortions—i.e. that formal-sector workers received too high a wage—today it is widely accepted that the problem arises in the capital market, and specifically in many developing countries interest rate policy is strongly biased against the employment of labour.
>
> The problem is that interest rates in the commercial banking system are often too low, while they are often too high in the informal credit markets, assuming that credit is available at all. The result is that capital-intensity is raised in the formal sector, reducing the number of jobs created there. At the same time, capital–labour ratios outside the formal sector are too low and the productivity of labor is depressed. People may be employed, but their average incomes may leave them in poverty.[16]

Thus, capital-market reforms may be as important as labor-market reforms in promoting employment. We return to this topic in Chapter 10.

### LIMITED FACTOR SUBSTITUTION

Finally, with restricted factor substitution—an extreme case being the fixed-coefficients production function in the Harrod-Domar growth model discussed in Chapter 3—employment may be limited by a shortage of a critical complementary input. A shortage of a needed input, such as capital, highly skilled labor, or entrepreneurship could limit production and the employment of the abundant factor, typically unskilled labor.

## MIGRATION

The migration of individuals has always existed. With the structural change that defines economic development, there occurs a reallocation of labor from agriculture to industry and a shift in population from rural to urban areas. Much of the migration is motivated by the search for better employment opportunities. The migration of skilled labor and professionals from the Third World to high-income countries—"the brain drain"—is an example of employment-driven international migration. Recently, migration aimed at avoiding strife, violence, and famine has become more common.

### ECONOMIC MIGRATION

The economic development literature has focused primarily on labor migration, from rural to urban areas, both within and across national borders.[17] For example, workers

---

[16]International Labour Organization, *World Employment 1995: An ILO Report,* pages 90 and 91.

[17]A helpful review of the literature concerning migration can be found in Chapter 11, "Migration and Urbanization," by Jeffrey G. Williamson, in *Handbook of Development Economics Volume 1,* edited by Hollis Chenery and T.N. Srinivasan, Amsterdam: North-Holland, 1988.

from Bangladesh have long migrated to India, and Mauritanians to Senegal. Neoclassical economic theory holds that labor mobility from labor surplus areas to labor deficit areas will increase total output and, often, will lead to remittances of income to the families of migrants that remain at home. Unfortunately, the migration phenomena can have other consequences.

The less attractive story of migration is that of talented and ambitious young people leaving rural areas, reducing agricultural output and hindering the formation of a new generation of farmers. These individuals arrive in overcrowded urban areas unlikely to be employed in higher-paying, modern-sector employment. They survive on the low-wage, unsteady employment found in the urban informal sector and on the generosity of relatives or friends, reducing any potential savings that the benefactors might enjoy. Moreover, negative externalities are associated with rapid urbanization and growing youth unemployment, as the supply of workers exceeds the number of urban jobs.

How can these two views of migration be reconciled? In both cases, individuals may be making utility-maximizing, rational decisions. The first case assumes market-clearing wages with no unemployment. The individual simply compares the earnings differential, netting out any migration costs, both monetary and nonmonetary. A positive differential will lead to migration; and this migration benefits society, moving labor from areas of lower to higher productivity.

In the second case, however, market-clearing wages don't exist, and an individual faces some probability of not finding employment in the higher-wage, modern urban labor market. The individual then must evaluate whether the expected return from migration exceeds the expected cost of migration.[18]

Consider the case of an individual who is contemplating leaving the rural area and migrating to a city in search of better employment. As discussed, there are two basic urban labor markets: a modern sector with non-market-clearing wages and an excess supply of labor, and an informal sector with a competitive labor market having low wage levels. The modern-sector wage ($w_m^*$) is institutionally determined and several times greater than the market-clearing informal-sector wage. The expected urban wage for individuals seeking employment is a weighted average of the modern-sector real wage and the informal-sector real wage, where the weights are the perceived probabilities of securing employment in each sector. Since the informal labor market is assumed to be perfectly competitive, all urban labor not hired in the modern sector is absorbed in the informal sector. (This assumption can be relaxed and the probability of unemployment in the informal sector introduced.)

The prospective migrant has to consider not only the expected urban-rural real wage differential, but the costs of migration and relocation to the urban area, and other perceived advantages in the urban area, such as better schooling, health care, and amenities.

Aggregating overall potential migrants, the net migration from rural to urban areas ($NM_{r-u}$) will be a function of the expected economic gain and the perceived advantages of urban life.

$$NM_{r-u} = N(vw_m^* \overset{+}{+} (1-v)w_i - w_r, \overset{-}{C}, \overset{+}{Z})$$

---

[18] The model of comparing expected gains from labor migration to expected costs was first developed by Michael Todaro in "A Model of Labor, Migration and Urban Unemployment in Less Developed Countries," *American Economic Review*, vol. 59, no. 1 (March 1969), pages 138–148.

where:  $NM_{r-u}$ = net migration from rural to urban areas

$w_m^*$ = modern-sector real wage (institutionally set above market equilibrium)

$w_i$ = informal-sector real wage (market-clearing)

$w_r$ = rural-sector real wage (market-clearing)

$v$ = expected probability of securing a job in the modern sector

$1-v$ = expected probability of employment in the informal sector

$C$ = direct costs of migration to, and relocation in, urban area

$Z$ = other perceived urban advantages

Net migration will be directly related to the expected economic advantage from migrating, which itself will be positively related to the urban real wages (both $w_m^*$ and $w_i$) and the probability of finding work in the modern sector $(v)$, and negatively related to the rural real wage, $w_r$. Net migration is inversely related to the direct costs of migration $(C)$, which includes the monetary costs of transportation and relocation and the psychic costs (emotional stress) of moving. Moreover, a positive relationship exists between migration and other perceived advantages of urban life $(Z)$, including the attraction of the "bright city lights."[19]

Even when individuals correctly estimate the above parameters and rationally decide to migrate when the expected net private benefits exceed the expected net private costs, the migration process may impose social costs not included in the private calculation. Primarily, the costs of urban congestion and the straining of urban services and infrastructure are negative externalities not included in the private decision making.

Under certain circumstances, a "nonrational" migration decision may occur on the part of rural residents. First, if an individual overstates the probability of being hired in the modern sector $(v)$, a migration bias will exist. To the extent that imperfect information encourages optimism, more migration and more urban unemployment will occur than would otherwise. Also, if individuals, not finding work in the modern sectors are also unable to find work in the informal sector, then the expected gains from migration will be overstated. The model is no longer a "full-employment" model, as the combined probabilities of finding work in the urban area are less than one. In many of the African countries, despite high urban unemployment, the migration of individuals to the cities persists.

Second, if individuals are "risk lovers," attracted by the prospects of high incomes, even when the probability of success is very low, they could elect to migrate even if the expected urban income is less than the "relatively sure" rural income. Many young Africans find the near-certainty of low rural incomes coupled with few rural services

---

[19]In theory a prospective migrant should discount monetary benefits and costs over the time frame that the migration would cover (or the time period working in the urban area). In this case the migrant would be looking at the net present value of the permanent income gain from migration.

most uninviting. Thus, even though they face both low probabilities of finding modern-sector employment and an expected financial loss from migration, they may prefer to migrate, escaping the monotony of rural life.

In summary, when wages are market-clearing and indicate the relative scarcities of labor, a net gain will result with migration from lower-wage (and lower-productivity) to higher-wage (and higher-productivity) areas. Migration poses a problem when individuals are attracted to higher modern-sector wages in labor markets that have a significant excess supply of labor. In these cases, net costs are borne directly by the individuals who migrate and indirectly by the society as a whole.

To the extent that a country is concerned with rapid population growth in urban areas due to excessive migration, policymakers may attempt to influence the above parameters to reduce migration. Often it is thought that a wage subsidy to modern-sector firms, increasing their level of employment, would be appropriate. In this model, such a subsidy would increase the probability of finding modern-sector employment and would increase the economic return from migration, leading to more migration. Freeing the modern-sector wage, $w_m^*$, would have mixed results with respect to migration, since a lower, market-clearing wage in the modern sector would generate more employment, raising the probability of securing a modern-sector job $(v)$. Raising the costs of migration $(C)$, such as making urban housing less available by bulldozing urban squatter settlements, may not be a politically viable option. In many of the former socialist countries, however, rural-to-urban migration was often prohibited. Exceptions were sometimes given for those who had arranged in advance for both a job and for housing. Rural-sector development programs that increase the productivity of rural labor and provide services in the rural areas, affecting $w_r$ and $Z$, will increase the relative attractiveness of rural life, reducing net migration to urban areas. Ultimately, the best course of action is to increase rural living standards.

The extent to which rural–urban migration is a major economic problem depends on the particular circumstances of the developing country. Is the country able to accommodate a significant movement of people from rural to urban areas, or is the pace of migration overwhelming the urban areas? The answers are both time- and country-specific.

Africa is one of the areas where rural-to-urban migration continues to be a serious concern. The ILO states:

> Unless production conditions in [African] agriculture are improved, "push" factors are likely to lead to a continuation of high rates of rural-to-urban migration. This in turn will lead to a further swelling of the already large urban informal sector and an intensification of urban poverty and squalor. The consequences of this are likely to be frightening; a further rise in crime, and social and political unrest, could occur given the large numbers, including many educated young people, who face faint prospects of advancing into modern-sector jobs.[20]

Labor migration across national borders seems to be less of a problem. With respect to the international movement of labor, David Bloom and Adi Brender have concluded that

---

[20]International Labour Organization, *World Employment 1995: An ILO Report,* pages 65 and 66.

the level of migration around the world has been relatively small compared with the size and growth of the global labor force. Although migration may have a sizeable effect on labor markets in some countries or sub-national areas, its ultimate effect on the global distribution of labor is likely to be quite small.[21]

## POLITICAL MIGRATION

In the 1990s, political migration—individuals and families fleeing strife and famine—has become a major problem. Refugees migrate both within their own countries and to other countries; however, with governments increasingly regulating and limiting immigration, the number of displaced refugees within their own countries has been rising dramatically. The U.N. High Commissioner for Refugees estimated that in early 1995, 27.4 million people were displaced from their homes. Of this number, 14.5 million were refugees living outside of their country of nationality; the remaining 12.9 million were individuals who were displaced within their own country, such as in the former Yugoslavia and in Rwanda.[22]

Internal wars and famine are the primary causes of this population displacement. For instance, in 1995 more than 4 million were displaced in Sudan; more than 1.3 million in Bosnia; 1 million in the Philippines; and 800,000 in Azerbaijan.

The costs of this type of migration and displacement are very high. Large numbers of households disengage from any gainful economic activity and move into areas where they must be supported. For instance, in Rwanda during 1994 and 1995, significant disruption of agricultural activity occurred as families, seeking safety, abandoned their farms and left their villages. Providing sanitary facilities and feeding large numbers of people in refugee camps are beyond the capabilities of the involved governments. In many cases (for instance, Somalia) there is neither a will nor a capacity to address the costs of this movement of people. Beyond the human misery, loss of potential development assistance occurs as international agencies direct funds to emergency relief efforts. The long-term resolution to this type of migration is a sustained and participatory economic development that minimizes famine and violence.

## POLICIES TO PROMOTE EMPLOYMENT

Given the numbers of unemployed and underemployed and the projected growth of the labor forces, effective employment creation is vitally needed in the developing world. The United Nations Development Programme in *The Human Development Report 1993* observed that

---

[21]David Bloom and Adi Brender, "Labor and the Emerging World Economy," *Population Bulletin*, vol. 48, no. 2 (October 1993), page 3.

[22]Eduardo Lachica, "Africa Tops Asia in Refugee Numbers; More Europeans are Seeking U.N. Aid," *Wall Street Journal* (July 6, 1995), page A5-B.

In developing countries, the total labour force increased by more than 400 million during 1960–90. This was due to rapid population growth (2.3% a year), an increase in the proportion of people of working age, and greater numbers of women joining the ranks of job-seekers.

Without substantial policy changes, the employment outlook for these people is bleak. The labour force in developing countries will continue to increase by 2.3% a year in the 1990s, requiring an additional 260 million jobs. Women's participation in the labour force is likely to increase. And there will be a steady migration of people to urban areas in search of work: the annual rate of net migration is likely to be about 4.6% by the year 2000.

Taking into account the number of people unemployed or underemployed, the total requirement for the next decade is around one billion new jobs. This would imply increasing total employment in developing countries by more than 4% a year in the 1990s, compared with less than 3% in the 1980s.[23]

In Table 9.1 on page 274, we present selected statistics on population and the labor force. While the definition of "urban" differs across nations, in general, the percentage of the population living in urban areas increases with economic development. Among the developing regions, Asia and sub-Saharan Africa are the least urbanized; Latin America and the Caribbean have the highest percentage of the population that is urban. Despite lower birth rates in urban areas, the growth rates of urban populations exceed those of rural populations—largely a result of the substantial rural-to-urban migration. In the LDCs urban populations are increasing rapidly. With an annual population growth rate of 4 percent, an urban population would double within 18 years. Given these trends most of the future employment generation will be in the urban areas of the LDCs.

The percentage of the population in the labor force in the developing nations, while varying due to differences in the age structure of the populations and labor force participation rates, tends to fall in the range of 30 to 50 percent. China has 60 percent of the population in the labor force, a reflection of its high female labor force participation rates. The average annual growth rates in the labor forces of the LDCs, outside of Europe and Central Asia, largely fall between 2 and 3 percent. Reduced rates of population growth, while eventually translating into slower labor force growth, initially may yield more rapid growth in the labor force if lower fertility rates increase female labor force participation rates.

In sum, healthy rates of economic growth and investment along with direct measures to increase employment are needed to accommodate the projected growth in the labor forces of the LDCs. Economists agree that viable policies exist to promote employment. These include flexible labor markets, education, and sound macroeconomic policies.

## LABOR-MARKET POLICY

First, flexible labor markets in which wages adjust to market-clearing levels will promote more employment than labor markets in which wages are set at above-equilibrium levels. A justifiable concern is that flexible labor markets in developing countries will result in very low wage levels. Low labor productivity combined with large labor

---

[23]United Nations Development Programme, *Human Development Report 1993*, page 37.

## TABLE 9.1  Selected Statistics on Population and the Labor Force

| | Total Population 1993 (Millions) | % Urban | % Labor Force | Average Annual Growth Rates (%) (1980–1993) | | |
|---|---|---|---|---|---|---|
| | | | | Total Population | Urban Population | Labor Force |
| **Income Group** | | | | | | |
| India | 898 | 26 | 38 | 2.0 | 3.0 | 1.9 |
| China | 1178 | 29 | 60 | 1.4 | 4.3 | 2.0 |
| Other low-income | 1015 | 27 | 38 | 2.5 | 4.2 | 2.4 |
| Middle-income | 1597 | 60 | ... | 1.7 | 2.8 | ... |
| High-income | 812 | 78 | 47 | .6 | .8 | .7 |
| **Region** | | | | | | |
| sub-Saharan Africa | 559 | 30 | 41 | 2.9 | 4.8 | 2.5 |
| Middle East & North Africa | 262 | 55 | 27 | 3.0 | 4.1 | 3.2 |
| Europe & Central Asia | 495 | 65 | ... | .8 | 1.7 | ... |
| South Asia | 1194 | 26 | 37 | 2.1 | 3.3 | 2.1 |
| East Asia & Pacific | 1714 | 31 | 55 | 1.5 | 4.2 | 2.1 |
| Latin America & the Caribbean | 465 | 71 | 36 | 2.0 | 2.7 | 2.5 |
| **Selected Countries** | | | | | | |
| Ghana | 16 | 35 | 38 | 3.3 | 4.2 | 2.7 |
| Sri Lanka | 18 | 22 | 39 | 1.5 | 1.6 | 1.5 |
| Egypt | 56 | 44 | 29 | 2.0 | 2.1 | 2.6 |
| Poland | 38 | 64 | 53 | .6 | 1.3 | .6 |
| Costa Rica | 3 | 49 | 33 | ... | 3.7 | ... |
| Brazil | 156 | 71 | 38 | 2.0 | 2.5 | 2.2 |
| South Korea | 44 | 78 | 46 | 1.1 | 3.6 | 2.3 |

NOTES: Lack of data is indicated by ...
Population and labor force growth rates are exponential period averages calculated from midyear populations and total labor force estimates.
  Total labor force is the "economically active" population, including the armed forces and the unemployed, but excluding homemakers and other unpaid caregivers.
  Estimates of the urban population are based on different national definitions of what is urban. Cross-country comparisons should be made with caution.

FROM: World Bank, *World Development Report 1995,* Tables 25 and 31.

supplies could generate subsistence-level wages. The long-term remedy for this problem is increased investment in both physical and human capital that will shift outward the demand for labor, and reduced population growth that will moderate the growth in labor supply. Investment in rural areas that succeeds in generating attractive employment opportunities would aid in reducing excessive rural-to-urban migration. Encouraging appropriate union activity in the modern sector will protect workers' rights and may contribute to enhanced labor productivity.

In the short term, development assistance may be used to augment the earnings of low-income workers. For instance, food-aid allotments and public health initiatives that are not tied to labor–market activity can raise living standards without generating unemployment. In any case, above-equilibrium wages that generate unemployment are not effective in addressing the problems of low-income workers.

## EDUCATION

Investing in high-quality primary education will provide basic literacy and essential skills that will raise the productivity of labor and wage levels. Thus, compulsory school attendance laws that require children through some reasonable age, such as 14, to secure education can have beneficial effects in the labor market. Children will be less apt to be in the labor market; this, in itself, will reduce the labor supply and place upward pressure on wage rates. Second, children with education will be more productive adult workers, shifting out the labor demand in the future, raising wage rates. If there is a compulsory school attendance law, developing countries must make the educational investment to provide schooling for all children. Additionally, the school calendar should be sufficiently flexible to permit students in rural areas to help with family farm tasks at times of peak labor demand, such as plantings and harvests.

## MACROECONOMIC POLICY

We have argued that macroeconomic fine-tuning to eliminate unemployment would not be highly effective in developing countries, nor, for that matter, in the high-income market economies. Nevertheless, a role does exist for macroeconomic policy to promote employment. Generally, low inflation, political stability, and fairly secure property rights appeal to private investors, both local and foreign. A sound macroeconomic policy that avoids large fiscal deficits and maintains monetary discipline will contribute, over the longer run, to increased investment, higher wages, and greater employment. Market-determined interest rates and exchange rates—as opposed to interest rates set artificially low and overvalued official exchange rates—will lead to a more efficient use of inputs. For the typical developing country, market-determined rates will stimulate employment.

An open economy that allows countries to produce and export goods in which they have a comparative advantage is an effective environment for sustained job creation. Moreover, with an open economy, foreign investment can augment a country's capital stock and increase the demand for labor.[24]

When employment growth is an important priority, governments may wish to take a more active role. For instance, tax breaks to encourage labor-intensive industries may be justified as a way of offsetting a bias toward "sophisticated" and "leading-edge" technologies that are more capital intensive. Also, governments may find it appropriate to subsidize labor-intensive enterprises in rural areas and in informal urban sectors, although care must be taken that the enterprises become efficient and not dependent on government subsidies.

---

[24]See World Bank: "Is International Integration an Opportunity or a Threat to Workers?" *World Development Report 1995,* pages 49–68.

## CONCLUDING NOTE

A primary indicator of economic development is the provision of jobs that pay decent wages for those in the labor force. As discussed, specific labor-market policies can promote higher wages and greater employment. The most viable economic development, however, will be one that balances physical capital formation and human capital formation with appropriate technologies, and that combines the efficiency of the market mechanism with the social concerns of expanding economic opportunities and alleviating poverty.

In Chapter 8, we addressed human capital formation; with Chapter 10, we turn to physical capital formation.

## SUMMARY OF MAIN POINTS

1. Understanding the functioning of labor markets within developing countries is vital. Steady employment with adequate wages is both a cause and an effect of economic development.
2. In a competitive labor market, profit-maximizing firms continue to employ labor as long as the value of marginal product of labor exceeds the wage rate. Higher wages induce workers to supply more labor, as the opportunity cost of leisure increases (the substitution effect). With higher wages, individuals have higher incomes (for the same number of hours worked), leading them to elect more leisure (the income effect). The upward-sloping labor supply function is drawn on the premise that the substitution effect dominates the income effect. At the equilibrium wage, the quantity of labor demanded equals the quantity of labor supplied, and there is no involuntary unemployment.
3. Many rural labor markets are characterized by relatively competitive conditions. In other cases, surplus labor or involuntary unemployment may exist. Both the Lewis model and the theory of efficiency wages are consistent with an excess supply of labor. Particularly in rural Africa, disturbing levels of poverty and periodic underemployment exist. Expanding rural opportunities should be a priority of policymakers.
4. While urban informal labor markets provide employment for large numbers of unskilled workers, these jobs tend to be low paying and unstable. A challenge for policymakers is to aid in increasing the productivity and attractiveness of these jobs without significantly reducing employment.
5. Modern-sector employment tends to have high wages, greater job security, and some fringe benefits. Often modern-sector wages have been kept artificially high, leading to unemployment. Also, artificially low interest rates lead to the use of more capital-intensive techniques in the modern sector. With stable macroeconomies, many Asian countries recently have been successful in creating modern-sector manufacturing jobs.
6. The unemployment rate is typically calculated as the number of individuals not working but actively seeking employment divided by the number of people in

the labor force (the employed and the unemployed). Often, this rate understates labor-market inefficiencies by not counting those who are too discouraged to seek employment and not counting those who are underemployed. Reliable unemployment rates rarely exist for developing countries.

7. The aggregate rate of employment and a corresponding rate of unemployment can be assessed with aggregate demand and aggregate supply analysis. With significant unemployment caused by deficient aggregate demand, expansionary monetary and fiscal policies may have short-term potential to raise the output of the economy. Continued use of these policies, however, is apt to lead to inflation with little or no long-term gain in real output or employment.

8. Common microeconomic causes of unemployment include mandated wages that are above market-clearing levels, excessive labor market regulation, overvalued exchange rates, and bias toward capital-intensive projects.

9. Excessive rural-to-urban migration, common in many developing countries, can place strains on urban services and lead to additional urban unemployment. The migration decision is a function of the expected benefits (higher wages and urban amenities) and expected costs (lost rural-sector earnings, higher urban living expenses, and transportation expenses). Often migrants overestimate the expected net benefits from migration. In recent years political migration has been of increasing concern.

10. Flexible labor markets, appropriate educational initiatives, a dynamic rural sector, a receptiveness to foreign investment, a stable macroeconomy, and an open economy seem to be the best policies to promote employment growth in developing countries.

## KEY TERMS

**aggregate demand**
**aggregate supply**
**employed**
**frictionally unemployed**
**full employment**
**income effect**
**involuntary unemployment**
**labor force**
**rate of labor force participation**
**rate of unemployment**
**structurally unemployed**
**substitution effect**
**underemployment**
**unemployed**
**unemployment**
**value of marginal product of labor (VMP$_l$)**

## QUESTIONS

1. Assume that a developing country producing corn has a competitive labor market for agricultural workers. Show the effects on the equilibrium wage and level of employment following:
    a. the decontrol of the country's domestic corn price that had been kept artificially low to help urban consumers;
    b. the arrival of significant shipments of surplus rice given as food aid (corn and rice are substitute goods);
    c. the negotiating of trade agreements by which the country exports corn to other countries.

2. Discuss whether the model of the competitive labor market has more relevance for a developing country like Mexico or for a developed country like the United States.
3. Try to devise a set of policies that would increase both employment and wage levels in a developing country's rural sector.
4. How easily can other developing countries replicate the success of the Asian countries in creating modern-sector manufacturing employment?
5. Are there conditions under which developing countries should be encouraged to use expansionary monetary and fiscal policy to reduce unemployment? Discuss.
6. Which policy measures to reduce rural-to-urban migration are apt to be the most effective?
7. Choose a developing country and assess labor-market conditions within that country. Try to determine the binding constraints to employment growth, and propose effective policies to improve the functioning of that country's labor market.

## SUGGESTED READINGS

Bardhan, Pranab, "Economics of Development and the Development of Economics," *Journal of Economic Perspectives*, vol. 7, no. 2 (spring 1993), pages 129–142.

Bloom, David and Adi Brender, "Labor and the Emerging World Economy," *Population Bulletin*, vol. 48, no. 2 (October 1993), pages 1–30.

International Labour Organization, *World Employment 1995: An ILO Report*, International Labour Office, Geneva, 1995. See Part 2, "Developing Countries."

United Nations Development Programme, *Human Development Report 1993*, New York: Oxford University Press, 1993, Chapter 3.

World Bank, "Workers in an Integrating World," *World Development Report*, New York: Oxford University Press, 1995, Chapters 1 and 11–14.

## CASE STUDY

### EGYPT

All developing countries are unique, yet this study of Egypt alludes to many of the major issues that developing countries face: the appropriate role for government; the need to address population growth; the challenge of finding employment for the educated; the destructive forces of war; the burden of excessive military spending; and the role of foreign assistance.

Situated in the northeastern corner of Africa is the Arab Republic of Egypt. This country, in 1995 with a population of approximately 55 million people and a per capita income of $650, traces its roots as a unified nation back to 3100 B.C. Experts speak of the strong, shared heritage of the Egyptian people.

> Perhaps the first and most important quality that typified this civilization was continuity. In every aspect of Egyptian life, in every manifestation of its culture, a deep conservatism can be observed. This clinging to the traditions and ways of earlier generations was the particular strength of the Egyptians. It can also be regarded as a

weakness; but for a relatively primitive culture there was more to be gained than lost in attachment to the past. Regularity was a built-in characteristic of Egypt; life in the Nile Valley was determined to a greater extent by the behavior of the river itself. The patter of inundation and falling water, of high Nile and low Nile, established the Egyptian year and controlled the lives of the Egyptian farmers—and most Egyptians were tied to a life on the land—from birth to death, from century to century.[1]

Egypt's strategic location provides access to Europe toward the northwest, to the Far East via the Indian Ocean, and to the interior of Africa via the Nile. With the 1869 opening of the Suez Canal connecting the Mediterranean and the Red Seas, Egypt became increasingly important in world affairs. With significant debt from the building of the canal, Egypt was forced to turn to Britain for financial help. Eventually, the British occupied Cairo and the country received Protectorate status within the British Empire during World War I. For the next 35 years, during which time Egypt was a parliamentary kingdom under British influence, tension and conflict between the British and those desiring greater autonomy prevailed.

Egyptian nationalism surged in the post–World War II period. In 1952 the monarchy was overthrown, and in June 1953 Egypt became a republic. Colonel Gamal Abdel Nasser seized power, becoming the first leader of the modern Egyptian state. In the ensuing years, Nasser entered into an arms agreement with the Soviet Union and nationalized the Suez Canal. The latter action led to the Suez crisis and a short war in 1956 between Egypt and the British, French, and Israelis.

Following the Suez war and his official election as president of Egypt, Nasser began a more radical, state-directed growth strategy. While industrial growth during the early 1960s was impressive, agriculture received little attention. With rapid population growth, there was only a modest increase in per capita living standards. Finally, with Egypt's quick defeat by the Israelis in the June 1967 Six-Day War, Nasser temporarily resigned. Upon returning to power, Nasser's government was weak and ineffective. In 1970 Nasser, at his death, was succeeded by his vice president, Anwar Sadat, who seemingly shifted Egyptian domestic and foreign policy in more conservative directions—toward market capitalism and integration with the West. Progress toward a truly open, capitalistic economy, however, has been very slow.

In 1973, a second Arab-Israeli war occurred, in which Egypt lost a large portion of the Sinai Desert to Israel. An Israeli-Egyptian peace treaty in 1979, brokered by U.S. President Jimmy Carter, led to the Israeli withdrawal from the Sinai. Egypt's willingness to negotiate with Israel resulted in its relative isolation within the Arab world, increasing Egypt's financial and security dependence on the United States. In 1981 Sadat was assassinated and replaced by his vice president, Hosni Mubarak, who is the current president. In recent years, Egypt has been able to re-establish harmonious relations with most Arab states. Middle Eastern politics have clearly preoccupied Egypt during its 45 years as an independent republic.

Egypt's economic development has been skewed both by significant military expenditures and by the high level of foreign aid annually received, primarily from the United States. For instance, in 1991 official development assistance (ODA) to Egypt equalled 15.2 percent of its GDP, compared to ODA receipts of only 2.7 percent of GDP for all low-income countries.[2] The government has taken a very active role in the economy. Public enterprises and government activity have accounted for approximately

---

[1] "Egypt," *The New Encyclopedia Britannica, Volume 18,* Chicago: Encyclopedia Britannica, Inc., 1985, page 132.
[2] World Bank, *World Development Report 1994*, Table 19.

50 percent of GDP since the 1970s. Moreover, price controls, including interest rate ceilings, and other regulations have distorted the Egyptian economy.

Since the signing of the 1979 peace treaty, however, Egypt has been able to reduce its defense expenditures and concentrate more on economic development. Both the infusions of U.S. foreign aid and foreign investment from other Arab nations have contributed to the modernization of the Egyptian economy. Nonetheless, the country has had significant problems: high population growth (still around 2.5 percent per year); chronic unemployment; a large and relatively inefficient public sector; and serious social tensions related to Islamic fundamentalism.

Largely desert, the country still has nearly 50 percent of its population engaged in agriculture, primarily in the fertile Nile delta and valley. Egyptian agriculture has relatively strong subsistence and commercial sectors, accounting for approximately 20 percent of the 1995 GDP. The country exports significant quantities of cotton, rice, and citrus fruits.

During the 1970 to 1985 period, economic growth was relatively impressive, led by substantial public expenditures and supported by increased oil revenues. Nevertheless, the country's development strategy was geared toward import substitution within industry. Potential export activities, with the exception of oil, clothing, and agriculture, were neglected. During this period, the role of the government in the economy increased.

By the late 1980s, as a result of fiscal mismanagement and declining oil revenues, the economy had deteriorated to a crisis stage. Egypt was unable to service its public debt. The annual rate of inflation was roughly 20 percent and the rate of unemployment was officially 15 percent.[3] Egypt introduced structural adjustment programs in the spring of 1990 and again in 1993. These programs have stressed fiscal reform; the elimination of distorting price controls; and the promoting of a more open economy. Debt restructuring and financial support from both the World Bank and the International Monetary Fund have been accorded to Egypt.

Egypt has been relatively successful with structural adjustment. Both the rate of inflation and the ratio of the government budget deficit to GDP have been reduced, and the balance of payments has improved.[4] Also, a comprehensive reform of the income tax system has been introduced. Most price controls and government subsidies have been eliminated. Tariffs and nontariff trade barriers have been lowered. Industrial licensing requirements that had hindered the introduction of new firms have been greatly reduced.

A reorganization of the public enterprise system has also occurred, with a timetable for the privatization of more than 70 firms. Actual privatizations began in 1993. With as many as 1.3 million people employed in public firms in the early 1990s, privatization risks increasing the already high Egyptian unemployment rate.[5]

Despite this progress, the Egyptian economy is still fragile. The country has made good progress in the provision of education; in 1991 the secondary school enrollment rate was 80 percent, with a 73 percent rate for females.[6] With the economic restructuring, however, particularly the reduction of public-sector activity, appropriate employment opportunities have not been available for graduates of high school and college.

---

[3]World Bank, "Arab Republic of Egypt," *Trends in Developing Economies, 1994,* page 145.
[4]United Nations Development Programme, "Egypt," *Human Development Report 1993,* page 57.
[5]Ibid.
[6]World Bank, *World Development Report 1994,* Table 28.

Also, Islamic fundamentalism continually challenges the government's alliance with the West, especially the security arrangements with the United States and the economic involvement of the World Bank and the IMF. The privileged position of government elites and other modern-sector employees with relatively high-paying jobs is contrasted with the large numbers of poor within Egypt's principal cities. Finally, any significant effort at population planning affronts Islamic fundamentalists. Thus, despite its continuity over 5000 years, Egypt faces a very uncertain future.

# CHAPTER 10

# PHYSICAL CAPITAL FORMATION

> The biggest difference between rich and poor [countries] is the efficiency with which they have used their resources. The financial system's contribution to growth lies precisely in its ability to increase efficiency.[1]

Physical capital formation involves the diversion of resources from the production of goods and services for present consumption to enhancing the capacity for producing goods and services in the future. Physical capital formation encompasses net additions to the stocks of business plant, equipment, and machinery; residential housing, schools, and hospitals; and the economic infrastructure of the transportation system, telecommunications network, and public utilities. The role of physical capital formation in initiating and sustaining economic growth was highlighted in Chapters 3 and 4. Increased physical capital–labor ratios are a major reason for higher per capita incomes. As discussed in Chapter 8, another factor is human capital formation, where the average unit of labor is better nourished, healthier, and more educated. Physical capital formation and human capital formation are complementary; both contribute to labor productivity.

We begin this chapter on physical capital formation with an overview of the roles played by money and financial capital in the efficient operation of an economy. Next we review the relationship between saving rates and economic growth. The sources of funds for domestic investment are examined using the basic macroeconomic identity. The importance of effective financial intermediation for physical capital formation is noted. We then address the common constraints on physical capital formation in the less developed countries, including high inflation and rapid population growth. The net present value criterion for public investment projects is illustrated. We also

---

[1] World Bank, *World Development Report 1989: Financial Systems and Development*, New York: Oxford University Press, 1989, page 26.

look at recent attempts to improve popular access to credit. The chapter concludes with a discussion of policy measures to increase the level and productivity of domestic investment.

## MONEY AND FINANCIAL CAPITAL

Along with the structural changes in output and labor force composition, the technological improvements in production, and the opening of new markets at home and abroad, economic development is defined by advances in the financial sector, including the increased monetization of the economy and more effective financial intermediation. To begin, we should be clear on the distinctions among income, money, financial capital, and physical capital.

**Income** is generated in the production of output. For example, individuals supply their labor in exchange for wages, or labor income. The labor employed, together with other factors (primarily natural resources and physical capital), produce goods and services. **Money** is used for both the payment of income and the purchase of goods and services. **Financial capital** refers to the money funds available for investment. Firms raise financial capital through new issues of stocks and bonds and with loans from banks. Firms add to their financial capital through the funds set aside for depreciation and by retaining some of their profits after taxes. The financial capital is used by firms to fund inventories and purchases of **physical capital,** or the plant, equipment, and machinery needed to produce the goods and services.

Thus, income, money, financial capital, and physical capital are related. At any point in time, part of the income generated (flow) over the period will be held as money balances (stock). Money balances in excess of expenditures constitute a type of saving and contribute to the supply of financial capital, the source of funds for investment in inventories and physical capital. In this chapter, although we focus on physical capital formation, the underlying relationships with money and financial capital also will be examined.

### FUNCTIONS OF MONEY

Money is an asset serving three functions. As a **medium of exchange,** money facilitates the transactions of goods and services. Without money as a readily acceptable means of payment, all transactions would be reduced to barter. A very inefficient method of exchange, bartering requires a "double coincidence of wants" for any transaction—each of the parties involved must have something to exchange that is desired by the other. The use of money reduces transaction costs: Money or purchasing power is exchanged for the desired good or service.

One narrow definition of the aggregate money supply, known as $M1$ in the United States, consists of the currency in circulation (the coins and paper notes declared by the government to be legal tender and held outside the vaults of banks and the monetary authorities) and checkable deposits (accounts on which checks can be written to transfer money funds to designated parties). On some checkable deposits a modest rate of interest is earned.

The second function of money is a **store of value.** Money represents a stock of purchasing power or command over goods and services. The money funds are the most liquid of all assets.[2] Saving accounts and time deposits (with explicit maturity dates) are less liquid than checking accounts and are included in broader definitions of the money supply. To compensate for the sacrifice in liquidity, these assets pay a higher return to the owner than the money funds.

The third function of money is to provide a **unit of account,** or common denominator for measuring value. For the United States monetary value is expressed in dollars and cents. Knowing the money prices of individual items allows for an easy calculation of relative values. For example, suppose that one gallon of gasoline costs $1.50, one token for a subway costs $.75, and a bus ticket costs $.50. Then three bus tickets have the same value as two subway tokens and one gallon of gasoline. In contrast, under a barter system the terms of trade would have to be determined for every pair of commodities.

Money is crucial for the efficient operation of an economy, and as an economy expands so should the money supply. If the money supply does not increase as fast as real income and the transaction needs of the economy, then output growth can be hindered and unemployment may rise—especially if wages and prices are not downwardly flexible. Too rapid an expansion of the money supply, however, tends to be inflationary. The store-of-value function of assets whose nominal yields are not indexed to the price level is undermined by inflation. High rates of inflation or hyperinflation can even wreak havoc with the medium of exchange and unit-of-account functions of money. To illustrate, consider the following excerpts from a news article on Bolivia in early 1985, when inflation threatened to accelerate beyond the previous year's rate of 2700 percent:

> Planeloads of money arrive twice a week from printers in West Germany and Britain. Purchases of money cost Bolivia more than $20 million last year, making it the third-largest import, after wheat and mining equipment.
>
> The 1,000 peso bill, the most commonly used, costs more to print than it purchases. It buys one bag of tea. To purchase an average size television set with 1,000 peso bills, customers have to haul money weighing more than 68 pounds into the showroom. (The inflation makes use of credit cards impossible here, and the merchants generally don't take checks, either.) To ease the strain, the government in November came out with a new 100,000 peso note, worth $1. But there aren't enough in circulation to satisfy demand.... Food shortages abound, and fights break out as people try to squeeze into line to buy sugar at several times the official price. Some companies have resorted to barter.
>
> The situation has upset all phases of life in Bolivia. Private banks were closed a few days ago because of worries about executive safety. Strikes frequently close the factories. Many shops have closed. Because pesos are practically worthless, dollars are now being demanded for big-ticket purchases. People get their dollars from the 800 or so street-side money vendors who line Avenida Camacho, long La Paz's Wall Street. Banking, in effect, has moved outside.[3]

---

[2]The liquidity of an asset is measured by the ease with which it can be transferred into a medium of exchange without a loss in value. For example, a house serves as a store of value, but it is not a very liquid asset. Ownership of a house represents wealth; however, in order to obtain money funds for use as a medium of exchange, a house would have to be sold. The greater the urgency of the sale, the more likely the house would be sold for less than full value.

[3]From Sonia Nazario, "When Inflation Rate is 116,000 %, Prices Change by the Hour," *Wall Street Journal* (February 7, 1985), page A1.

Later in this chapter we will discuss the main cause of inflation in the less developed countries. Moreover, we will see that inflation can also erode the incentive to save, reducing both the supply of loanable funds and the ability to finance investment and physical capital formation.

## THE SAVING RATE AND ECONOMIC GROWTH

Recall from Chapter 4 the steady-state condition from the growth model with exogenous growth in labor productivity. The level of labor productivity is indicated by output per unit of labor, $y = Y/L$. Further, assume that the capital–output ratio is constant. Given a growth rate in labor productivity of $\bar{q}$, then in steady-state equilibrium the growth rate in real national output and real national income $(dY/Y)$ is equal to the national saving rate $(s)$ divided by the aggregate capital–output ratio $(v)$, which, in turn, is equal to the sum of the natural growth rate of the labor force $(n)$ and the growth rate in labor productivity $(\bar{q})$.[4] That is,

$$dY/Y = s/v = n + \bar{q}$$

In steady-state equilibrium the physical capital stock and output are growing at this warranted rate of growth $(s/v)$, and the physical labor force is growing at the natural rate of $n$. Full employment of capital and labor are maintained. Economic growth, indicated here by the growth rate of output per unit of labor, $dy/y$, the difference between the growth rate in output $(dY/Y)$ and the growth rate in the labor force $(dL/L)$, is equal to $\bar{q}$.

Solving for the saving rate $(\bar{s})$ required to maintain the growth rate in output per unit of labor gives

$$\bar{s}/v = n + \bar{q}$$
$$\bar{s} = v(n + \bar{q})$$

Thus, the saving rate required to maintain a given growth rate in output per unit of labor (or labor productivity) is directly related to the capital–output ratio and the natural growth rate of the labor force.

To illustrate, suppose that the growth rate in labor productivity is 2.5 percent: $(dy/y) = \bar{q} = .025$. In Table 10.1 we calculate the required saving rates for given combinations of the capital–output ratio (here $v = 2$ and $4$) and labor force growth rates (here $dL/L = n = .01, .02$, and $.03$). Ceteris paribus, higher labor force growth rates and higher capital–output ratios require higher national saving rates to achieve a given growth rate in output per unit of labor.

---

[4]Recall, here $s$ refers to the net saving rate, i.e., the gross saving rate less the depreciation rate of the physical capital stock.

| TABLE 10.1 | SAVING RATE REQUIRED FOR ATTAINING GIVEN ECONOMIC GROWTH RATE |

REQUIRED SAVING RATE ($\bar{s}$) FOR A GROWTH RATE
IN OUTPUT PER UNIT OF LABOR OF 2.5%

|  |  | CAPITAL–OUTPUT RATIO | |
|---|---|---|---|
|  |  | $v = 2$ | $v = 4$ |
| LABOR FORCE | .01 | .07 | .14 |
| GROWTH RATE | .02 | .09 | .18 |
| $(dL/L) = n$ | .03 | .11 | .22 |

$$\bar{s} = v(n + \bar{q})$$

Example: $(dy/y) = \bar{q} = .025,\ v = 2,\ \text{and}\ n = .03$
$\bar{s} = 2(.025 + .03) = 2(.055) = .11$

## INCREMENTAL CAPITAL–OUTPUT RATIOS

As discussed in earlier chapters, for developing economies in the second stage of the demographic transition, population and labor force growth rates are high. The heavy youth burden of dependency produced by the high fertility not only increases the demand for social welfare expenditures on education and health care, but constrains the ability to fund such expenditures, let alone generate saving.

Furthermore, developing economies tend to have high physical capital–output ratios. In the early stages of economic development, substantial investments in the infrastructure are necessary: the roads, highways, railways, bridges, canals, seaports, and airports that constitute the transportation system; telephones, cables, antennas, and postal facilities that form the core of the telecommunications network; and public utilities in power generation, water supply, sewage and trash disposal; along with the construction of buildings for the police, courts, public schools, and hospitals. Consequently, the aggregate capital–output ratio is high, reflecting the initial investments in physical capital needed to begin providing these essential services. The **incremental capital–output ratio** (ICOR = $\Delta K / \Delta Y$, or the change in the capital stock needed to generate another unit of output), however, may be declining. As the core of the economic infrastructure is established, more of the physical capital formation will take the form of directly productive investments in the plant, equipment, and machinery used to produce goods and services.

In sum, developing economies typically confront rapid population and labor force growth rates and high capital–output ratios, each of which increases the saving rate required to achieve any target rate of economic growth. We should emphasize, though, that it is not simply a matter of increasing the saving rate. Other factors must also be considered.

At any stage of development, incremental capital–output ratios will vary across, even within, sectors of the economy. Other things being equal, investing in the projects with the lowest ICORs will increase output the most for a given capital expenditure. The ICORs, however, are only estimates and will depend on the particular circumstances. The gain in output realized from additions to the capital stock depends on the efficiency with which the new capital is used. This is, in turn, a function of the availability and quality of the complementary factors—from the fuel needed to run generators, to the foreign exchange to import intermediate inputs, to the technical expertise to operate and maintain the physical capital. It may seem paradoxical in developing economies with overall shortages of capital, that some plant, equipment, and machinery may be underutilized, and even lie completely idle—a consequence of deficiencies in the supply or quality of complementary factors.

Investment in the economic infrastructure is usually the responsibility of the government. Numerous public projects may be worthy of funding, from building a bridge or tunnel to shorten the travel distance between two cities to constructing a dam to generate electricity for rural areas. The distribution of the benefits and costs of the capital project must be assessed. As we will discuss later in the chapter, the criteria for evaluating public investment projects can be complex and controversial. Finally, the financing of public investment may crowd out some private investment. To address this concern, we turn to the funding of domestic investment.

## SOURCES OF FUNDS FOR DOMESTIC INVESTMENT

A major constraint on physical capital formation in less developed countries is the ability to generate the funds for investment. From the basic macroeconomic identity we can derive the sources of funding for gross domestic investment.

### BASIC MACROECONOMIC IDENTITY

Recall that gross domestic product (GDP) measures the market value of all final goods and services produced in an economy during a year. The **basic macroeconomic identity,** written out below, is an accounting of the expenditures on national output and the disposition of the income generated in the production of national output.

$$C + I + G + X - M = GDP = C + S + T + R + F$$

where

- $C$ = personal consumption expenditures
- $I$ = gross private domestic investment
- $G$ = government purchases of goods and services
- $X$ = exports of goods and services
- $M$ = imports of goods and services

and

- $S$ = gross private domestic saving
- $T$ = net taxes (tax revenues less government transfers)
- $R$ = net transfers to foreigners (or the rest of the world)
- $F$ = net factor payments to foreigners (or the rest of the world)

On the left-hand side of the identity are the expenditures on national output by major type: by households for personal consumption *(C)*; by businesses for investment *(I)*; by the government *(G)*; and by the rest of the world (exports, *X*). Subtracted out from each of these expenditure components are those expenditures for goods and services produced abroad (imports, *M*). Gross private domestic investment *(I)* includes business purchases of new plant, equipment, and machinery; the value of new residential construction; and the change in business inventories over the year.

On the right-hand side of the identity are the uses of the income generated in the production of national output. The income can be used for personal consumption expenditures *(C)*, gross private domestic saving by households and businesses *(S)*, net taxes *(T)*, net transfers to the rest of the world *(R)*, and net factor payments to the rest of the world *(F)*. Net transfers to the rest of the world equal the difference between the total transfers (public and private) made to foreigners and the total transfers received from foreigners. Most developing nations are net recipients of transfers (due in large part to foreign aid); thus *R* tends to be negative in the basic macroeconomic identity. Net factor payments to the rest of the world *(F)* refer to the payments of factor income (primarily labor earnings and interest) to foreigners for the production of national output less the receipts of factor income from foreigners for the services of the labor and financial capital provided by residents of the nation. Recall that the difference between gross domestic product *(GDP)* and gross national product *(GNP)* is net factor payments to the rest of the world. GDP = GNP + F. For those less developed countries with heavy interest payments on foreign debt, *F* tends to be positive. For some LDCs, remittances of labor income from residents working abroad are a major source of foreign exchange and may even offset the interest payments to foreigners; thus *F*, on net, could be negative.

By equating the left- and right-hand sides of the identity and then cancelling out the common personal consumption expenditure term, we obtain:

$$I + G + X - M = S + T + R + F$$

Solving for gross private domestic investment, then grouping related terms yield:

$$I = S + (T - G) + (M - X + R + F)$$

| Gross private domestic investment | = | Gross private domestic saving | + | Net public saving | + | Net foreign saving |

Therefore, gross private domestic investment must be covered or offset by gross private domestic saving, net public saving, and net foreign saving. Gross private domestic saving primarily consists of the disposable personal income of households not used for consumption and business saving (capital consumption allowances and undistributed corporate profits). Net public saving is reflected in the government budget balance *(T − G)*. If net taxes exceed government purchases of goods and services, then the government budget is in surplus, which is equivalent to public saving. If negative, the government budget balance is in deficit and must be financed. (Later in this chapter we will review the financing of government budget deficits.)

Part of the physical capital formation that takes place in a nation occurs outside the private sector. Some of the government expenditures are for capital projects—not only on economic infrastructure, but plant, equipment, and machinery purchases by state-owned enterprises.[5] If we subtract from $G$ (government purchases of goods and services) these capital expenditures, $G_I$, we can derive an expression for gross domestic investment.

$$I + G_I = S + (T - G_C) + (M - X + R + F)$$

| Gross domestic investment | = | Gross private domestic saving | + | Current government budget balance | + | Deficit on current account balance |

where $G_C$ equals government consumption expenditures, so $(T - G_C)$ can be regarded as the current government budget balance, i.e., net of government capital expenditures.

Note that public and private expenditures on education, health, and nutrition are classified as consumption ($G_C$ and $C$). By excluding these expenditures on human capital, however, the statistics on saving and investment understate the actual capital formation taking place in an economy. Similarly, purchases of consumer durables, such as automobiles, appliances, and furniture, that yield a flow of services over time, may be better regarded as a type of household investment.

The other major source of funds for domestic investment is foreign saving. The term $(M - X + R + F)$ measures the nation's current account balance. (In Chapter 15 we will examine the international balance of payments accounts in detail.) If a nation has a current account deficit $(M - X + R + F > 0)$, then during that year the nation is a net debtor with respect to the rest of the world. Imports of goods and services plus net transfers and net factor payments to foreigners have exceeded exports of goods and services. A current account deficit indicates that foreign saving is being made available to the nation and that, on net, foreigners are acquiring claims on the nation's assets. In contrast, if a nation has a current account surplus $(M - X + R + F < 0)$, then the nation is a net creditor over that year and would be, on net, acquiring claims on foreign assets.

Consider two examples of how an increase in gross domestic investment could be offset in the identity. First, suppose a private business in a less developed country imports $10 million worth of new machinery and equipment. Then gross private domestic investment would rise by $10 million ($\Delta I = +10$), as would imports of goods and services ($\Delta M = +10$). The deficit in the nation's current account balance, ceteris paribus, would increase by $10 million.

Alternatively, suppose the government of the less developed country imports the $10 million worth of new machinery and equipment and that the government purchases are funded by foreign aid. Gross domestic investment rises by $10 million from the government capital expenditures ($\Delta G_I = +10$). Imports rise by $10 million, as before. Net transfers to the rest of the world decline by $10 million ($\Delta R = -10$) with the receipt of the foreign aid, which is regarded as government tax revenues ($\Delta T = +10$). Here, the offsetting increases in gross domestic investment and imports do not add to the nation's deficit on the current account.

---

[5]The capital expenditures by the government for national defense, e.g., military bases and equipment, are classified as government consumption, not as public investment.

## FOREIGN SAVING

Most LDCs, especially in the initial stages of development, run balance of trade deficits, that is, imports of goods and services *(M)* exceed exports of goods and services *(X)*. These trade deficits $(M - X > 0)$ are usually not offset by net receipts of transfers and factor income from the rest of the world $(R + F < 0)$, and so, result in current account deficits $(M - X + R + F > 0)$.

Outside of foreign aid, without the ability to run a deficit on the current account, a nation would have to fund its domestic investment entirely with domestic saving, either from the private sector *(S)* or from the public sector $(T - G_C)$. Consequently, foreign saving has tended to bolster physical capital formation in the developing economies. Inflows of foreign saving, however, depend on the willingness of the rest of the world to extend credit and to invest in the nation. In addition, overreliance on foreign saving may create an external indebtedness that becomes unsustainable. In the absence of debt cancellation or rescheduling, the only way for a nation to reduce its external indebtedness is to generate current account surpluses. The external debt crises of the 1980s sharply reduced the inflows of foreign saving and forced many developing countries to cut back on domestic investment. As a result, incomes and economic growth suffered. In the 1990s, however, rapidly growing mutual funds in the United States and other developed nations have invested heavily in the emerging markets of the developing economies. While welcome as an additional source of finance, these foreign capital flows to the LDCs are very volatile, since the mutual funds are driven largely by short-term profits. Managers of the major mutual funds may influence, directly and indirectly, the economic policies of these developing nations.[6]

## GROSS DOMESTIC INVESTMENT AND GROWTH IN NATIONAL OUTPUT

In Table 10.2 on page 292, we present statistics on gross domestic investment (GDI) and gross domestic saving (GDS). Here the difference between GDI and GDS is equal to the deficit on the balance of trade.[7] Although there is considerable variation in these shares in GDP, for the LDCs, gross domestic investment generally exceeds gross domestic saving, indicating trade deficits and net inflows of foreign saving.

Gross domestic investment is an important component of gross domestic product, one that affects both aggregate demand and aggregate supply. An increase in GDI not only increases expenditures on national output (shifting the aggregate demand curve to the right), but would increase the capital stock—assuming the gross

---

[6]See Craig Torres and Thomas Vogel, Jr., "Some Mutual Funds Wield Growing Clout in Developing Nations," *Wall Street Journal* (June 14, 1994), pages A1 and A6.

[7]If we define gross domestic saving (GDS) as private domestic saving *(S)* plus the current government budget balance $(T - G_C)$, then the difference between GDI and GDS is equal to the deficit on the current account balance (i.e., the deficit on the balance of trade, $M - X$, plus net transfers [R] and payments of factor income [F] to foreigners). In Table 10.2, gross domestic saving is derived as gross domestic product less personal consumption expenditures *(C)* and government consumption $(G_C)$; so the difference between GDI and GDS is simply the trade deficit.

## TABLE 10.2 — Selected Statistics on Gross Domestic Investment (GDI) and Gross Domestic Saving (GDS)

| | % of Gross Domestic Product | | | | Average Annual Growth Rate (%) | | | |
|---|---|---|---|---|---|---|---|---|
| | Gross Domestic Saving | | Gross Domestic Investment | | Gross Domestic Product | | Gross Domestic Investment | |
| | 1970 | 1993 | 1970 | 1993 | 1970–1980 | 1980–1993 | 1970–1980 | 1980–1993 |
| **INCOME GROUP** | | | | | | | | |
| India | 16 | 24 | 17 | 24 | 3.4 | 5.2 | 4.5 | 5.7 |
| China | 29 | 40 | 28 | 41 | 5.5 | 9.6 | 7.6 | 11.1 |
| Other low-income | 12 | 10 | 14 | 17 | 4.4 | 2.9 | 7.4 | –.2 |
| Middle-income | … | 22 | … | 23 | 5.5 | 2.1 | … | .8 |
| High-income | 24 | 20 | 23 | 19 | 3.2 | 2.9 | 2.3 | 3.4 |
| **REGION** | | | | | | | | |
| sub-Saharan Africa | 18 | 15 | 21 | 16 | 3.8 | 1.6 | 4.3 | –2.8 |
| Middle East & North Africa | … | 27 | … | 28 | … | 2.2 | … | … |
| Europe & Central Asia | … | 17 | … | 21 | 5.4 | 0.4 | … | … |
| South Asia | 15 | 21 | 16 | 23 | 3.5 | 5.2 | 4.6 | 5.5 |
| East Asia & Pacific | 28 | 35 | 27 | 36 | 6.9 | 7.8 | 9.8 | 9.6 |
| Latin America & the Caribbean | 20 | 19 | 22 | 20 | 5.4 | 1.9 | 6.6 | .1 |
| **SELECTED COUNTRIES** | | | | | | | | |
| Ghana | 13 | –1 | 14 | 15 | –.1 | 3.5 | –2.5 | 9.8 |
| Sri Lanka | 16 | 16 | 19 | 25 | 4.1 | 4.0 | 13.8 | 2.4 |
| Egypt | 9 | 6 | 14 | 17 | 9.5 | 4.3 | 18.7 | 1.2 |
| Poland | … | 13 | … | 16 | … | .7 | … | –1.1 |
| Costa Rica | 14 | 25 | 21 | 30 | 5.7 | 3.6 | 9.2 | 5.5 |
| Brazil | 20 | 21 | 21 | 19 | 8.1 | 2.1 | 8.9 | –.3 |
| South Korea | 15 | 35 | 24 | 34 | 10.1 | 9.1 | 14.1 | 11.8 |

NOTES: Data not available is indicated by …

Gross domestic savings are calculated by deducting personal consumption expenditures and government consumption from gross domestic product. Government consumption includes all current expenditures for purchases of goods and services by all levels of government. Capital expenditures on national defense and security are regarded as government consumption.

Gross domestic investment consists of outlays on additions to the fixed assets of the economy plus net changes in the level of inventories.

FROM: World Bank, *World Development Report 1995*, Tables 2, 8, and 9.

domestic investment expenditures are greater than depreciation—and add to the productive capacity of the nation (shifting the aggregate supply curve to the right). (Refer back to Figure 9.3 in the previous chapter for the graphical framework.) While the demand side effects of a change in GDI usually dominate in the short run, the long-run impacts of a change in GDI on the aggregate price level and real national output depend on the relative magnitudes of the shifts in the aggregate demand and supply curves.

FIGURE 10.1   AVERAGE ANNUAL GROWTH RATES IN GROSS DOMESTIC INVESTMENT

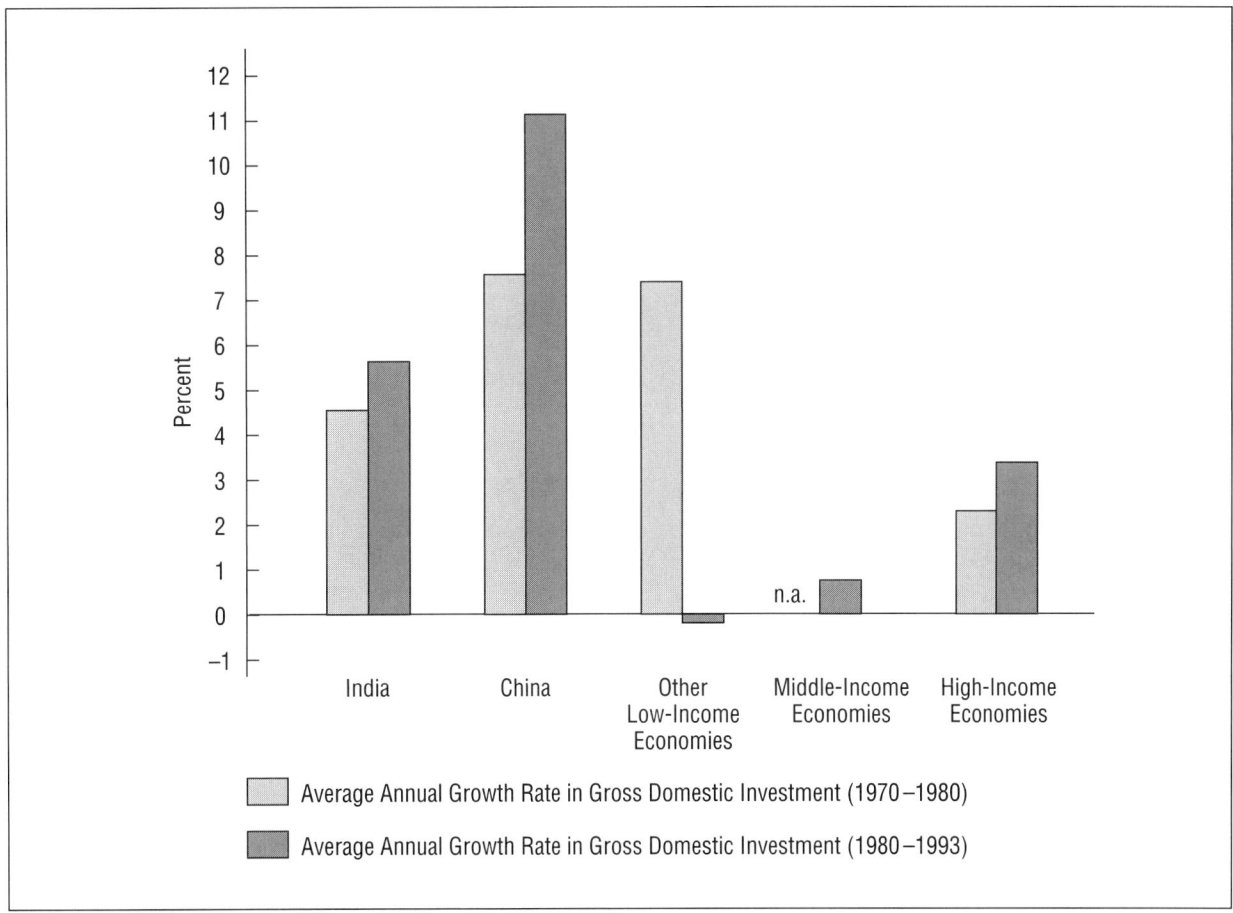

In Table 10.2 the growth rates for GDP and GDI for 1970–1980 and 1980–1993 are also given. Figure 10.1 illustrates the investment growth rates by income group. A positive correlation between growth in investment and growth in national output is evident, both across nations and over time. East Asian nations (especially China and South Korea) were able to maintain very high rates of growth in gross domestic investment over the 1980s, not only contributing to the expansion of current output, but adding to the potential for future growth. South Asia, dominated by India, also performed fairly well. In contrast, for the other low-income economies, and for sub-Saharan Africa in particular, the average growth rates for gross domestic investment for 1980 to 1993 were negative—a reflection of, among other factors, coping with external debt crises. (Illustrating once again the diversity in development experiences, the average annual growth rate in gross domestic investment for Ghana increased dramatically from −2.5 percent for 1970 to 1980 to 9.8 percent for 1980 to 1993.)

## FINANCIAL INTERMEDIATION

In Rostow's model (see Chapter 4), a key factor in transforming the take-off into self-sustaining economic growth is the establishment of institutions for mobilizing and channeling saving into productive investment. As described by the World Bank:

> Before World War II, developing country governments had a poor record on financial development. In Latin America and the Mediterranean countries, they failed to create sound legal and regulatory systems and maintain macroeconomic stability. Borrowers relied excessively on foreign capital, and financial systems were undermined by imprudence. In Africa and Asia the restricted use of bank credit, the limited spread of the banking habit, and the persistence of the hoarding habit were all legacies of the colonial banking systems that had failed to reach the indigenous population.
> 
> After World War II, governments began to take a greater interest in the financing of high priority sectors such as industrial investment, exports, and housing. They created, or helped to create, credit institutions that specialized in long-term finance.[8]

**Financial intermediation** is the process of matching the supply of loanable funds with the demand for loanable funds. For example, banks serve as financial intermediaries by accepting deposits from those whose current incomes exceed their expenditures, and extend credit through loans to others whose desired expenditures exceed their current incomes. To the extent the loanable funds are directed to more productive users of the financial capital, gains in efficiency and income will be realized. In Figure 10.2 we illustrate the sources of the supply and demand for loanable funds and the types of financial intermediaries.

On net, households are suppliers of loanable funds. From keeping their savings in jars, to maintaining savings accounts at banks, to investing in stocks and bonds, households can hold their financial wealth in various ways. Households also hold tangible wealth, mainly in the equity in their homes and consumer durables. (*Note:* Producer households, such as family farms, are considered as businesses.)

On net, businesses are demanders of loanable funds. Some of the funds for inventories and the purchases of new plant, equipment, and machinery are generated internally from earnings. Much of business investment, however, is financed through credit obtained through bank loans or, for major corporations, the issuance of bonds. Corporations also raise financial capital by issuing stock, or shares of ownership in the business, especially when the enterprise is formed.

For most developing nations, governments run budget deficits, and so are net demanders of loanable funds. When government expenditures exceed revenues (or government purchases of goods and services, $G$, exceed net taxes, $T$, tax revenues less government transfers), a budget deficit results.

Finally, as noted earlier, most developing economies tend to run current account deficits. The foreign saving that results is an important source of loanable funds.

Financial markets in many developing economies are still weak. The banking network may not extend to rural areas, depriving many households of suitable instruments for saving, like passbook savings accounts. Consequently, any saving rural

---

[8]World Bank, *World Development Report 1989*, page 49.

## FIGURE 10.2  LOANABLE FUNDS AND FINANCIAL INTERMEDIATION

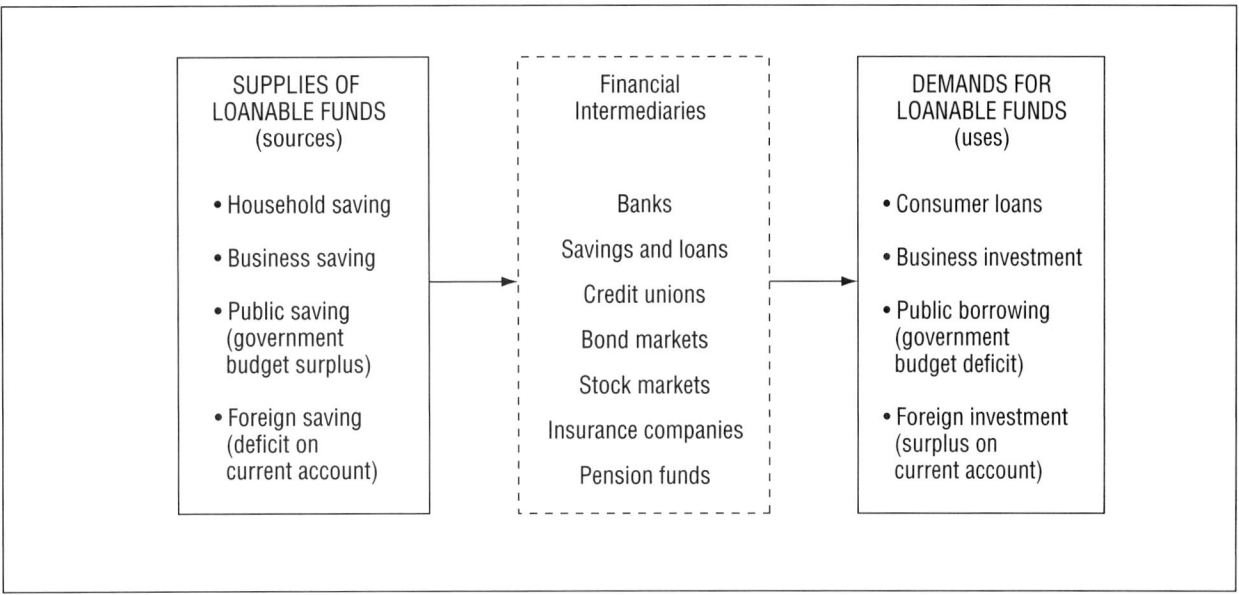

households can muster may take the form of currency kept in a jar, gold jewelry, or other items of value that nevertheless do not contribute to the supply of loanable funds. Farm households often save by adding to their livestock or inventories of grain or by acquiring additional land—investing at the same time. Bond markets and stock markets may be thin, although with the growing internationalization of financial markets, even in the least developed countries these asset markets are rapidly emerging. For wealthy households in urban areas, banks may be available, but high inflation, a depreciating domestic currency, or political instability may push them to send their savings abroad in the purchase of foreign stocks, bonds, certificates of deposit, or even real estate. For some developing nations, this capital flight significantly reduces the domestic supply of loanable funds.

### FINANCING GOVERNMENT BUDGET DEFICITS

To finance a deficit the treasury or finance ministry prints up government bonds, which are then offered for sale. The consequences of the bond sales for the economy largely depend on who purchases them.

If the government bonds are purchased by private parties (e.g., individuals, commercial banks, or pension funds), there would be upward pressure on the market rate of interest. The government, in competition with other demanders of credit, would have to increase the return offered on the government bonds to attract purchasers. The rise in interest rates would "crowd out" some private investment. As credit becomes more expensive, businesses may postpone, or even cancel, plans to purchase new plant, equipment, and machinery. A more direct form of crowding out occurs when the government requires banks to invest a certain percentage of their asset portfolios in government bonds.

On the other hand, if the government bonds are purchased by the central bank (monetary authorities) of the nation, then the initial upward pressure on interest rates could be avoided. The central bank can, in effect, print up new money to cover its bond purchases. This is known as "monetizing the debt." The consequence of such an increase in the money supply, not surprisingly, is usually inflation. In fact, accommodating monetary policy combined with chronic budget deficits is the primary source of inflation in less developed countries.

## EFFICIENCIES IN FINANCIAL INTERMEDIATION

The importance of efficiency in financial intermediation can be illustrated. Consider the market for bank credit in an economy. For ease of exposition, simply assume that domestic households make deposits in savings accounts from which the banks make loans to businesses for investment expenditures on capital goods. Let

$S^d$ = supply of loanable funds (here the savings deposits of households)

$D$ = demand for loanable funds (here loans to businesses)

$i$ = nominal rate of interest (or the user cost per \$1 of loanable funds)

Banks earn income primarily by maintaining a spread between the interest rate charged on loans and the interest rate paid on deposits. Let

$i^l$ = nominal interest rate charged by banks on loans.

$i^d$ = nominal interest rate paid by banks on savings deposits.

$i^l > i^d$

The difference between the lending and deposit rates covers the bank's costs of operation (including the administrative costs of making loans and expected losses from bad loans) and a profit margin. In developing nations, banks may have very high administrative costs due to inefficiencies in operation. Examples include the recording by pencil and paper of bank deposits and withdrawals; cumbersome clearinghouse mechanisms that delay the transfers of funds between banks when checks are drawn; inadequate and expensive credit investigations on potential borrowers; and excess holding of reserves to meet high required reserve ratios set by the central bank.[9] There may also be considerable write-offs of bad loans due to the relatively risky nature of investments in developing economies. Therefore, the spread between lending and deposit rates in banks may be quite large. In addition, the lack of competition in the banking system would not compel banks to be efficient and reduce the interest spread.

---

[9]The reserves held by banks, whether as cash in their vaults or deposits with the central bank, generally do not earn interest. Therefore, there is an opportunity cost to holding reserves, represented by the income that banks could have earned if the funds had been loaned or otherwise invested. Central banks or the monetary authorities set minimum reserve requirements (mainly on checkable deposits) to maintain more control over the money supply. In developing economies, central banks may set relatively high required reserve ratios in order to increase their access to credit for the purchase of the government bonds. Also, as noted, banks may be required to allocate a percentage of their deposits directly to the purchase of government bonds. In both cases, the effect is to reduce the inflationary consequences that would result from the central bank's printing money to finance government budget deficits. There is still a crowding out of private investment expenditures and banks are generally less profitable under such requirements.

## FIGURE 10.3  A MARKET FOR LOANABLE FUNDS: COMMERCIAL BANK CREDIT

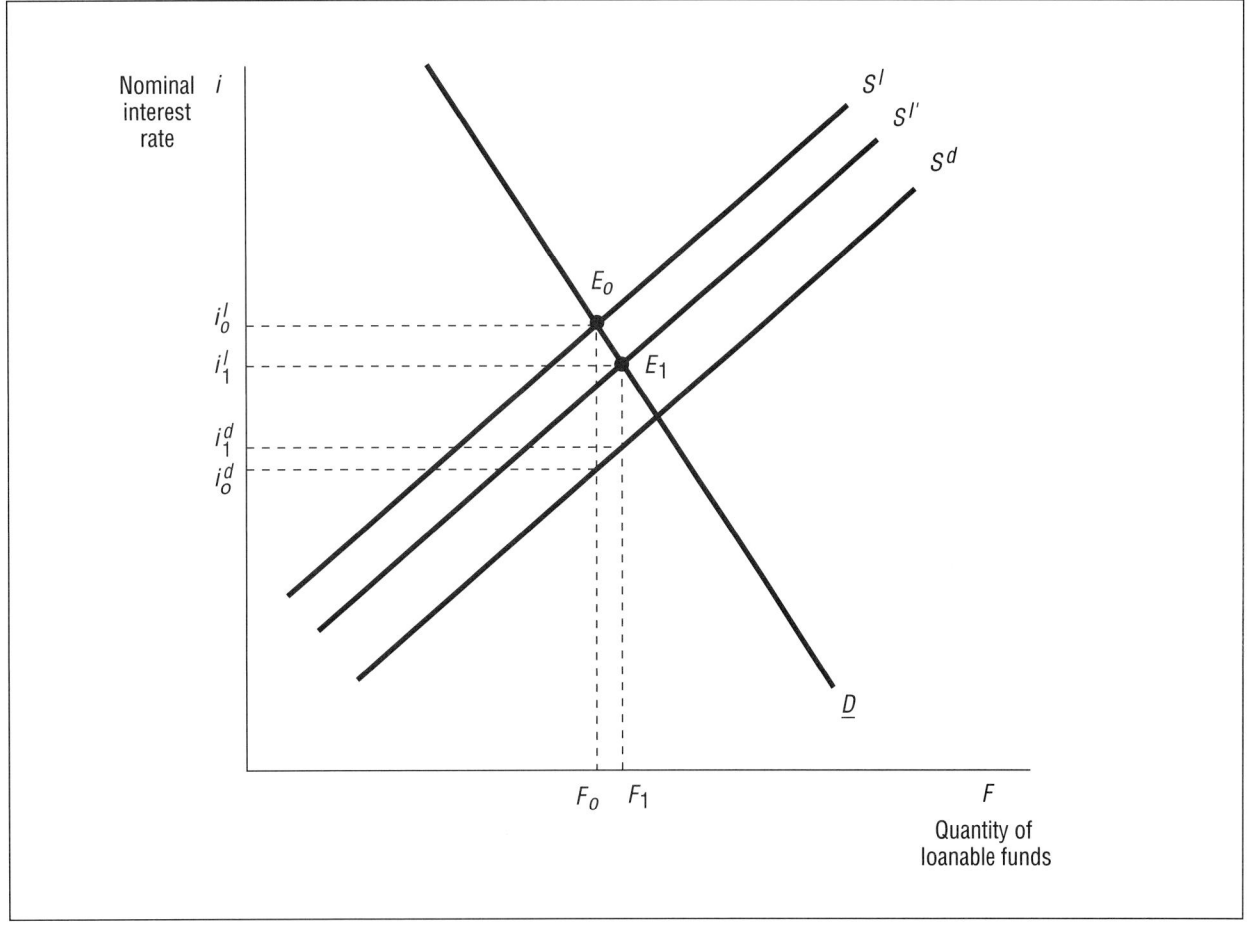

In Figure 10.3 the market for bank credit is illustrated. The difference between the $S^l$ curve (the effective supply of credit offered by banks) and the $S^d$ curve (the supply of loanable funds placed in banks as deposits) reflects the interest rate spread of the banks. Initially the market-clearing lending rate is $i_0^l$ and the associated deposit rate is $i_0^d$. The amount of bank credit extended is $F_0$. If banks can become more efficient, e.g., by processing the transfer of funds more quickly, reducing the administrative costs of making loans, or improving the credit checks to decrease the income loss from default, then for the given supply of loanable funds, $S^d$, there would be an increase in the supply of bank credit. The $S^l$ curve would shift down to $S^{l\prime}$ as banks would be able to reduce their interest spread. As the number of banks and other financial intermediaries increases with economic development, greater competition may force such a reduction in the interest rate spread.

The increase in the supply of credit not only reduces the equilibrium lending rate ($i_0^l$ to $i_1^l$), but raises the equilibrium deposit rate (from $i_0^d$ to $i_1^d$). The amount of bank credit increases from $F_0$ to $F_1$. Thus, with no changes in the underlying supply or demand for loanable funds, greater efficiencies in financial intermediation can increase the quantities of saving and investment in the system.

With the development of bond and stock markets, the ability to raise funds for investment is further enhanced. In fact, with these additional outlets for saving there is greater competition in the capital markets, hence more pressure on banks to become efficient. For example, to raise the financial capital to fund an expansion in plant and machinery, a corporation has options of obtaining a loan from a bank, issuing bonds, or selling more shares of stock. The profit-maximizing firm would select the least-cost option of raising funds.

## INTEREST RATE CEILINGS

In an effort to encourage investment and to channel credit to priority sectors, governments in developing economies have often held interest rates below market equilibrium levels, in effect setting **interest rate ceilings.** One consequence of an interest rate ceiling, however, is that the quantity of investment financed by bank credit falls.

Consider Figure 10.4, where we illustrate the market for loanable funds and the effect of an interest rate ceiling. To simplify the diagram, only the supply of bank credit (at the bank lending rate) is represented; the underlying supply of loanable funds (at the bank deposit rate) is not shown. The market equilibrium interest rate on loans is $i_o$, with an associated quantity of bank credit extended of $F_o$. An interest rate ceiling set at $i^*$ reduces the quantity of bank credit supplied to $F_1$, while increasing the quantity of credit demanded to $F_2$. A credit shortage equal to $F_2 - F_1$ is created. A method of allocating the available credit $(F_1)$ must be implemented. The government could designate high-priority borrowers, likely to be among the powerful industrialists and state-owned enterprises. To secure access to the scarce credit, prospective borrowers may bribe the bank officers or government officials determining the loan allocations. In fact, with a binding price ceiling and less than complete compliance, a black market inevitably arises. A **black market** transaction is one that takes place at a price above the legally-set ceiling. At one extreme, if all the available credit were diverted through the black market, the interest rate would rise to $i'$, with the differential $i' - i^*$ equal to the illegal interest premium or bribe. Recall from Chapter 5, however, that some favored borrowers will be able to obtain the subsidized credit at $i^*$. For those borrowers, the artificially low interest rate encourages the use of more capital-intensive production processes than is warranted by the true relative scarcity of capital.

In sum, as a policy to increase investment and capital formation, interest rate ceilings fail. Not only is the available amount of bank credit reduced, but the effective interest rate paid (on the black market), rather than falling, may rise. Moreover, with an interest rate ceiling and the restricted access to credit, there is no guarantee that the investments that are funded will be the most productive. As described by the World Bank, experiences with directed credit have been generally disappointing.

> The financial and industrial policies pursued by many countries during the 1960s and 1970s left their financial systems weak and vulnerable to change. Banks were often directed to provide subsidized credit to firms in favored regions or sectors. In some countries firms in priority sectors have been consistently unprofitable. In others they were profitable only as long as they were protected; today such firms account for a large proportion of nonperforming loans.[10]

---

[10]World Bank, *World Development Report 1989,* page 75.

## FIGURE 10.4  INTEREST RATE CEILING

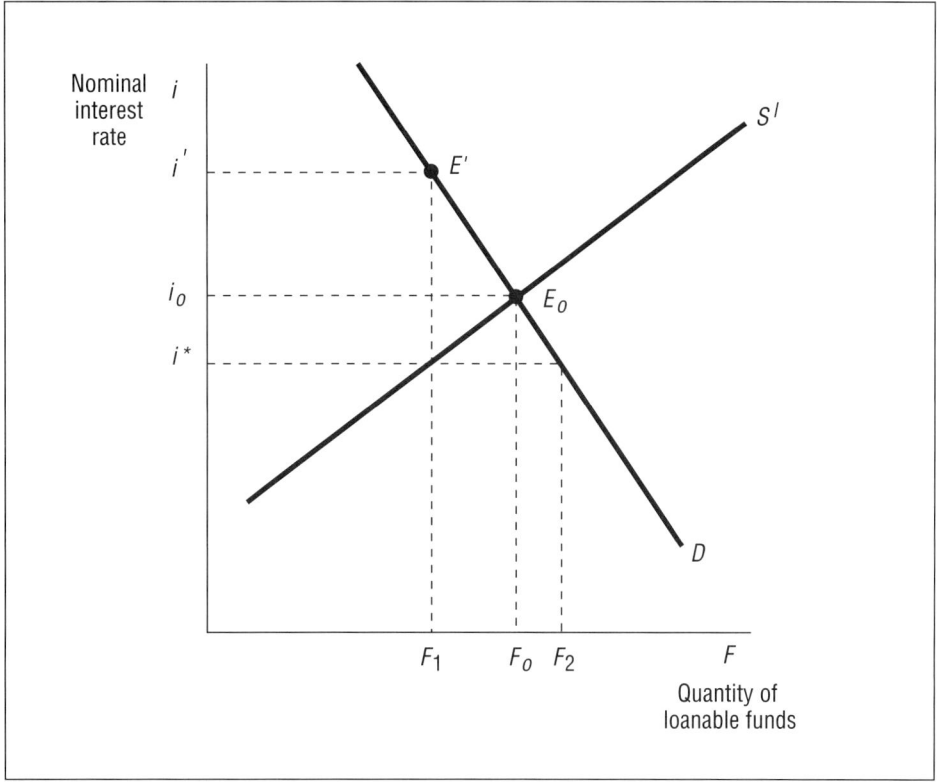

## INFORMAL CREDIT MARKETS

With credit rationing, **informal credit markets** are important in the developing countries. As in the developed countries, prospective borrowers unable to secure bank credit would have to turn to the informal credit market, which operates outside the banking system. Unregulated, these vendors of credit (including professional moneylenders, pawnbrokers, and merchants) are able to charge very high interest rates—more than justified by the overflow of demand from the formal credit markets and possibly even more than justified by the perceived greater riskiness of the loan clientele.

Not surprisingly, informal credit-market transactions take a variety of forms. One common arrangement is the credit extended by retailers to finance consumer and small-business purchases. Suppose an individual wanted to buy a bicycle for transportation to work. Unable to pay the purchase price of $50 in cash, the individual might agree to pay $10 a month for six months. The total payments are $60, for an annual interest rate of 40 percent (i.e., $10 interest on a $50 purchase for half a year).[11]

---

[11]Actually, given that the buyer is making monthly installments of $10, reducing the principal outstanding, the effective annual interest rate is more than 40 percent.

Other important sources of credit in the informal market are families and friends, who tend to charge low interest rates, if any. In fact, these informal loans may serve not only to extend credit in times of need—whether for emergencies (e.g., sickness or crop failure), special occasions (e.g., weddings or funerals), or business opportunities (e.g., purchases of raw materials or equipment)—but are a form of insurance. Personal creditors, by making funds available to family members and friends, gain the right to expect reciprocal treatment, if needed in the future. A network of obligations is established that reduces individual risk.

## EFFECTS OF INFLATION ON THE MARKET FOR LOANABLE FUNDS

Inflation drives a wedge between the real and nominal rates of interest. The real return to saving, before any taxes on interest income, is given by:

$$r^d = \frac{1 + i^d}{1 + INF} - 1$$

where
$r^d$ = real rate of interest on savings deposits

$i^d$ = nominal rate of interest on savings deposits

$INF$ = inflation rate

For low rates of inflation, a useful approximation for the real rate of interest on deposits is the difference between the nominal rate of interest and the inflation rate: $r^d \doteq i^d - INF$. For example, if $i^d = .10$ and $INF = .06$, then $r^d = (1 + .10)/(1 + .06) - 1 = .038 \doteq .04 = .10 - .06$.

Similarly, the real interest rate on a loan is given by:

$$r^l = \frac{1 + i^l}{1 + INF} - 1$$

where
$r^l$ = real rate of interest on loan

$i^l$ = nominal rate of interest on loan

With inflation expected, depositors and creditors would require a higher nominal interest rate to retain the same real return. In particular, creditors typically add a premium equal to the expected rate of inflation to the desired real return on the loan. Conversely, expected inflation reduces the real cost of borrowing for any given nominal interest rate charged on loans and thus increases the demand for credit.

Return to the market for loanable funds, illustrated in Figure 10.5 by the supply curve of loanable funds ($S^l$) based on the nominal interest rate charged by banks on loans and the demand curve for loanable funds ($D$). If market-determined, the initial equilibrium nominal interest rate on loans would be $i_o^l$ and $F_o$ would be the market quantity of loanable funds. If there were an interest rate ceiling set at $i^*$, then the excess demand for credit would be equal to $F_2 - F_1$, with $F_1$ being the quantity of loanable funds available. The demand and supply curves for loanable funds are drawn for given, and not necessarily equal, expectations of the inflation rate.

| FIGURE 10.5 | EFFECTS OF INFLATION ON THE MARKET FOR LOANABLE FUNDS |

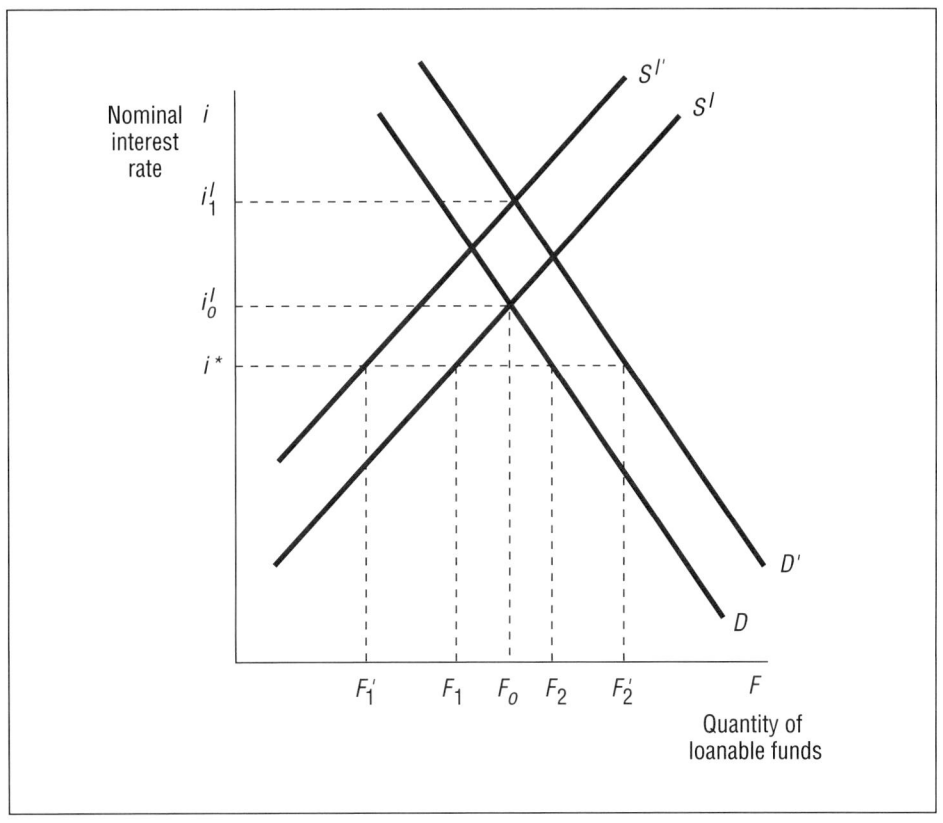

Suppose, due to a rise in the current rate of inflation, higher inflation is expected. The demand for loanable funds increases from $D$ to $D'$ (since, at any nominal interest rate, the real cost of borrowing is less). The supply of bank credit, however, falls (shifts left) from $S^l$ to $S^{l'}$ (since, for any nominal interest rate, the real return on a loan is less). Put another way, banks would try to add the increase in expected inflation to the current nominal interest rate charged on a loan. For any given rise in the current inflation rate, the upward shifts in the demand and supply curves for credit depend on how inflationary expectations are formed.

Under a free market for credit, the equilibrium nominal interest rate would rise to $i_1^l$, with the consequences for the quantity of credit available dependent on the relative shifts in the $D$ and $S^l$ curves. Under an interest rate ceiling set in nominal terms and not indexed to the rate of inflation, the quantity of loanable funds available would be reduced (from $F_1$ to $F_1'$) and the excess demand for credit would increase to $F_2' - F_1'$. The black market rate of interest would probably rise beyond $i_1^l$. Those favored borrowers able to obtain the scarce credit at $i^*$ may even end up paying negative real rates of interest (if the actual rate of inflation exceeded the nominal interest rate charged on the loans).

In sum, inflation tends to reduce the incentive to save, especially when nominal interest rates paid to depositors lag well behind the expected increase in the price level.

If banks are quicker to recognize changes in inflation (and so adjust their expectations) than the demanders of credit, then even when nominal interest rates are free to vary, inflation would reduce the quantity of credit extended.

In particular, with high and variable inflation, little long-term lending takes place. Just as it erodes the store-of-value function of money balances, inflation compels individuals to seek other ways to hold their wealth. Individuals may shift to gold or consumer durables or land, assets that better maintain their value during inflation. High rates of inflation may encourage speculation. A bias develops toward investment projects with quick payoffs. For example, in a number of developing countries, a highly profitable venture is the construction of luxury residential housing and apartment complexes catering to foreigners stationed there, whether as managers of transnational corporations, embassy staff, or employees of international aid agencies. The demand for housing of these expatriates and their families is typically very price-inelastic. Consequently, the rents that can be charged yield attractive returns on these investments.

Nominal interest rate ceilings that become increasingly out of equilibrium with inflation induce greater efforts to obtain the scarce credit through bribes. Wealthy individuals may also shift their wealth from domestic financial assets to foreign stocks, bonds, and certificates of deposit. Moreover, to the extent that not all factor prices are free to vary with changes in the aggregate price level, inflation will distort relative prices, thereby affecting the allocation of resources.

## CONSTRAINTS ON DOMESTIC SAVING IN LESS DEVELOPED COUNTRIES

To the extent that it is not the lack of private and public investment opportunities that constrains physical capital formation in the LDCs, but the ability to generate funding for the investments, it is important to examine the determinants of domestic saving. Three major components of domestic saving exist: personal saving or the saving of households, business saving, and net public saving. We begin with household saving.

### HOUSEHOLD SAVING

The difference between disposable personal income (i.e., personal income after taxes paid and transfers received) and personal consumption expenditures is personal saving. The ability of a household to save is largely determined by its level of real income and the size and composition of the household. Given the ability to save, the incentive to save depends on the time preference of the household and the reward for postponing present consumption.

#### Demographic Factors

We have discussed how rapid population growth produces a high youth burden of dependency. In low-income economies there are often more than two child dependents per adult worker. Household budgets are stretched to meet the basic needs of the members, leaving little discretionary income for saving or investing in human capital. Lower fertility may help to stimulate saving not only by reducing the youth burden of dependency, but by freeing adult females for more active participation in the labor force.

Whether for children's education or downpayments on a house, some saving is required for the major expenditures that occur during the life cycle. In traditional societies, a major motivation for household saving may be for dowries of daughters and the expenses of weddings, funerals, and other important ceremonies. In the absence of adequate social security systems or children for old-age support, individuals need to provide for their dissaving during retirement. In addition, parents may want to leave some inheritance for their children.

The **life cycle theory** of consumption, and by extension, saving, stresses the importance of the age composition of the population. The ability and inclination of individuals to save varies over the life cycle. Individuals move through stages of life: from dependents as children; to net borrowers as young adults beginning to form households; to net savers in the peak earnings years of middle age (when debts incurred earlier are paid off and savings are set aside for retirement); and finally to dissavers living off the wealth generated during the working years.

In the aggregate, as nations undergo the transition from high to low fertility, there would be a rising percentage of the population moving into the peak saving years, usually ages 40 to 60, over the first two or three decades following the decline in birth rates. Consequently, the personal saving rate should increase. Nations with prolonged low fertility (i.e., at or near replacement level) would find a relatively high percentage (10 percent or more) of the population in the dissaving years (age 65 or older). This, in itself, would tend to depress the national saving rate. On the other hand, increases in life expectancy, especially after age 65, may force individuals to save more during their working years in order to provide for the increased years of retirement.

## Income Effects

With respect to income, the effect on saving may depend not only on the level, but the distribution and growth rate of income. Higher-income households, ceteris paribus, have the ability (and tendency) to save more since the basic needs of the members are likely to be addressed. Moreover, some consumption expenditures (such as food) are income-inelastic. Therefore, as real per capita incomes rise, the percentage that could be allocated to saving increases.

The propensity to save may differ by type of income. Recall that a key assumption of the Kaldor model (in Chapter 3) is that the propensity to save out of profits (the income of capitalists) exceeds the propensity to save out of wages (labor income). If so, then for a given level of national income, a redistribution of income from wages to profits would boost the aggregate saving rate. For example, consistent with this proposition, a nation may have relatively favorable tax treatment for profits compared to wages.

The **permanent income hypothesis** of consumption holds that unexpected variations in income primarily affect the propensity to save. That is, households project their **permanent income,** the income expected to be available for spending and saving—based on the human capital, employment prospects, and financial wealth of the members of the household. In any period household consumption expenditures are largely determined by this estimate of permanent income. The difference between the actual income received and permanent income is called **transitory income.** According to the theory, the marginal propensity to consume (save) out of transitory income is close to zero (unity). Thus, transitory income, if positive, is mostly saved. If transitory income is negative, then households seek to maintain their level of consumption by dissaving. Over time the swings in transitory income would probably cancel out so that, on average, transitory income would be close to zero. Household estimates of permanent income would be revised as circumstances changed (e.g., increased education of household members; improved employment opportunities; or a significant drop in wealth). In the long run, however, household consumption would be a fairly stable percentage of permanent income. In the short run, the share of actual income going for consumption expenditures could vary.

The significance of the permanent income hypothesis for saving rates in developing economies is that during periods of rapid economic growth, transitory income may be positive and relatively large. That is, the actual income received by households may consistently and substantially exceed estimates of permanent income. Consequently, the saving rates of households may rise sharply, boosting gross domestic saving and the ability to finance capital formation. Conversely, during recessions (and the type of economic stagnation that confronted many developing nations during the 1980s as they wrestled with their external debts), household saving rates may fall precipitously, and more than suggested by the actual declines in real per capita incomes.

The relevance of the permanent income hypothesis for less developed countries, however, is open to question. For low- and middle-income households in developing countries, the general rise in income with economic development may stimulate consumer aspirations so much that the saving rate initially does not rise. Recall from Chapter 7 that increases in the desired quality of children (expenditures per child) and consumption unrelated to children prompted by gains in income were an important factor in reducing the demand for children.

### RETURN TO SAVING

The return to saving is the expected real interest rate after taxes. For savings deposits, adding the tax rate on interest income, $t_s$ (usually assessed on nominal interest) and letting $INF^e$ be the expected rate of inflation held by savers, then the expected real interest rate after taxes is:

$$(r^d)^e = \frac{1 + (1 - t_s)i^d}{1 + INF^e} - 1$$

Increases in the tax rate on interest income or in the expected rate of inflation would reduce the incentive to save at any nominal interest rate ($i^d$). In Figure 10.3, an increase in $t_s$ or $INF^e$ would shift the underlying supply of loanable funds curve ($S^d$) to the left.

To illustrate the calculation of the expected real interest rate after taxes, let

$$i^d = .08, t_s = .15, \text{ and } INF^e = .05.$$

$$(r^d)^e = \frac{1 + (1 - .15)(.08)}{1 + .05} - 1 = \frac{1.068}{1.05} - 1 = .017 = 1.7\%$$

If the time preference of savers were such that $1.017 of real consumption in one year were valued more than (less than) $1.00 of present consumption, then there would be (not be) an incentive to save. If there were an increase in the expected inflation rate from 5 percent to 10 percent (i.e., $INF^{e\prime} = .10$), then to preserve the same expected real interest rate after taxes, the nominal interest rate on savings deposits would have to rise to 14 percent ($i^{d\prime} = .14$).

$$(r^d)^e = .017 = \frac{1 + (1 - .15)(.14)}{1 + .10} - 1 = 1.7\%$$

In general, we assume that the quantity of savings or loanable funds supplied increases with the nominal interest rate, given the expected rate of inflation and the tax rate on interest income. In other words, the supply curve for loanable funds ($S^d$ in Figure 10.3) is upward sloping. The possibility that individuals are target savers, however, should be noted. For instance, if an individual has a goal of $20,000 in wealth or accumulated savings by retirement, then a rise in the nominal interest rate on saving, ceteris paribus, would allow the individual to set aside less income for saving in each period and still attain the saving target. By drawing the supply curve for saving as positively sloped, we are assuming that the substitution effect (higher nominal interest rates induce a substitution away from present consumption) dominates the income effect (higher nominal interest rates allow less income to be saved for a given saving target).

### INSTRUMENTS FOR HOUSEHOLD SAVING

While the ability to save is directly related to income, and the incentive to save is directly related to the expected real return after taxes, another important factor is attractive instruments for saving. As noted earlier, banking services may not extend to all rural areas of a developing country. Even if such services are available, many households in developing economies may not be used to saving regularly in banks. To the extent that minimum balances are required to open or maintain accounts, there may be a disincentive to save in banks. In small towns and villages, credit cooperatives may be an effective way to induce saving, as well as extend credit. In a **credit cooperative,** the individuals who hold the accounts own shares in the enterprise. Loans are made to cooperative members from the pool of deposits.

While the focus has been on saving deposits, other outlets exist for household financial saving, including stocks and bonds. The expected yield on an asset (the given interest rate on a bond or dividend rate on a stock plus the anticipated capital gains) is directly related to the riskiness of the asset (the possible loss in value due to a decrease in the market price of the bond or stock). With savings deposits, to the extent insured, the nominal principal or the amount on deposit is protected. In contrast, stocks and bonds are riskier, having the potential for swings in market values from changes in market conditions and investor perceptions. As noted, in many of the less developed countries, bond and stock markets are still emerging, and there is not yet much active trading.

### BUSINESS SAVING

As noted earlier, business investment is funded, in part, from business saving. When a business is established, an initial investment is made in the necessary plant, equipment, and machinery. Over time the physical capital depreciates, or loses value due to the wear and tear from use and with technological obsolescence. **Depreciation,** a cost to the firm, is a measure of the contribution of the firm's capital stock to its output. The funds set aside by firms for depreciation are a major source of business saving. Business profits, after taxes and distribution to owners, are another type of business saving.[12]

To encourage business saving and investment directly, governments could reduce the tax rate on profits; institute investment tax credits that subsidize purchases of capital goods; and allow for more liberal write-offs of depreciated capital. Indirectly, promoting economic growth should boost business profits as the demands for output rise with per capita incomes. Economic growth may also open up new opportunities for investment.

Inflation may increase the share of profits in national income at the expense of wages. During an economic expansion firms may have greater flexibility to raise output prices than labor has to raise wage rates, often fixed in labor contracts. Inflation, however, as a policy to stimulate business profits and saving is not recommended. Unless checked, price increases can easily spiral out of control. Moreover, as discussed earlier, inflation tends to reduce the supply of loanable funds. The ill effects of inflation are compounded when nominal interest rates are held below market-clearing levels, since the quantity of loanable funds supplied would be reduced and access to credit would be restricted.

## GOVERNMENT OR PUBLIC SAVING

If we restrict our attention to the current government budget (i.e., after subtracting capital expenditures from total government purchases of goods and services), then net public saving is defined as a surplus on the current government budget balance. Typically, in the less developed countries, governments tend to run budget deficits and so add to the demand for loanable funds.

We have discussed earlier the heavy demands for social welfare expenditures when incomes are low and a high percentage of the population is young. While counted as government consumption, public expenditures on education, health, and nutrition are also investments in human capital. To contribute to economic growth and development, however, human capital deepening is required in the forms of increases in the average levels of education, health, and nutrition. Rapid population growth makes achieving this all the more challenging. In addition, there are current expenditures for public administration (e.g., salaries of civil servants and the operation of the government and judicial system) and for national defense. (In Chapter 19 we discuss the burden of defense expenditures in the LDCs.)

Overall, government revenues usually fall short of government expenditures. The generally low levels of income may limit the revenue potential from a comprehensive income tax. Even if there were a broad income tax base, the ability to administer such a system may be hampered by, first, the difficulties in understanding the income tax forms when illiteracy rates are high and, second, the logistics in collecting the income

---

[12]In the national income accounts gross fixed investment is made up of business fixed investment (expenditures by businesses on new plant, equipment, and machinery) and residential fixed investment (the value of new residential construction). Net fixed investment is equal to gross fixed investment less depreciation or capital consumption. If net fixed investment is positive, then the physical capital stock is increasing. In this part of the chapter on business saving, we are focusing on business fixed investment. Residential fixed investment is largely financed by banks through home mortgages.

taxes owed when the use of withholding from paychecks is not widespread. Furthermore, the successful implementation of an income tax requires a competent and honest corps of tax officials to provide assistance in filing and to process the tax forms and payments.

The significant degree of nonmarket activity (whether bartering or simply underreporting of monetary transactions) reduces the potential revenues from sales taxes. The desire not to discourage business investment combined with relatively few large corporations (who nevertheless may exert considerable influence over tax legislation) limits the use of corporate profits taxes.

Often, then, foreign trade has been relatively heavily taxed. Consistent with an import substitution strategy in which tariffs and other trade barriers are used to protect domestic producers from foreign competition, revenues can be generated from taxes and fees on imports. Taxes on exports can also be used and, if the nation enjoys some degree of international market power, part of the tax burden can be shifted to foreign consumers. As we will discuss in Chapter 13, taxes on foreign trade, while attractive to governments when other sources of revenues are insufficient, may create distortions and inefficiencies.

To illustrate, consider the tax reform that has been an important part of the economic liberalization that has taken place in Latin America over the past decade.

> At the beginning of the 1980s, most Latin American tax systems were complex and cumbersome—loaded with hundreds of taxes, with little revenue being collected from any of them. Consumption and production taxes suffered from multiple rates and were difficult to administer. These taxes were also inefficient because of "cascading," that is, they taxed not only the value of production but also taxes paid in earlier stages of production. Often levied at the manufacturing, rather than the retail stage, they harmed competitiveness by adding to production costs. Income taxes were riddled with high and multiple rates, exemptions, and incentives, and were generally not indexed to inflation—leading to narrow tax bases, inequities, and low revenue productivity...
>
> Reform-minded countries simplified their tax systems by focusing on income taxation in the early years of the reform process and, increasingly, on the taxation of production and consumption in later years.[13]

In general, increased use of value added taxes has occurred with less reliance on export and import tariffs. Greater sophistication of financial markets in Latin America has also contributed to improved tax collection.

## NET PRESENT VALUE CRITERION FOR DEVELOPMENT PROJECTS

Given the tight budgets faced by governments in most developing economies, care in the allocation of public investment expenditures is clearly warranted. In particular, it is important that criteria be in place for evaluating development projects. Below we

---

[13]Parthasarathi Shome, "Tax Reform in Latin America," *Finance and Development*, vol. 32, no. 1 (March 1995), pages 14–16. The quotations are from pages 14 and 15.

illustrate one such criterion: net present value (refer back to Chapter 8 for an earlier example).

With respect to private investment expenditures, the usual assumption is that firms invest in projects that are expected to contribute to profits. For public investments and development projects, the objectives are less obvious. For any development project, governments must consider who benefits and who bears the brunt of the costs. Moreover, assessing the social benefits and costs is usually more difficult than measuring private benefits and costs.

For example, is it better to fund the construction of a large dam for the generation of electricity and irrigation of farmland in a rural area or to fund the building of 10 new elementary schools to serve a rapidly growing urban population? What do we mean by "better?"

**Net present value (NPV)** measures the discounted value of a future stream of net benefits (i.e., benefits less costs) associated with a project over its life. If NPV is positive, then the project is worth funding. If NPV is negative, the investment is not worthwhile. Given limited funds for public investment, projects with higher net present values would receive priority.

To determine net present value, let

$B_t$ = estimated benefits in year $t$ from the development project

$C_t$ = estimated costs in year $t$ of the development project

$n$ = estimated useful life (in years) of the development project

If we assume simple annual compounding, where the discounted value of the benefits and costs are calculated at the end of each year, then the net present value of the development project is given by:

$$NPV = \sum_{t=1}^{n} \frac{(B_t - C_t)}{(1+i)^t} \qquad \text{where } i \text{ is the discount rate}$$

The discount rate can reflect either the interest rate charged on loans or simply the rate at which policymakers wish to discount future net benefits.

Suppose there were two development projects under consideration. Only one can be funded in the next period. The discount rate selected is 10 percent (i.e., $i = .10$). The estimated benefits and input requirements are given in Table 10.3. For simplicity we assume that each project has a useful life of two years.

Although the sums of the undiscounted benefits over the two years of the projects are equal, for Project A most of the benefits come in the second year, in direct contrast to Project B. The higher the discount rate used, the more favored will be projects where the benefits come earlier (and the costs later).

The two projects also differ on the mix of required inputs. Project B is relatively intensive in physical capital $(K)$ and imported inputs $(M)$. Project A is relatively labor-intensive. (Note: In this example the physical capital requirements in both projects decrease from the first to the second year—which may be normal for projects with initial construction and set-up costs.)

To determine the costs associated with the projects, we need to multiply the physical input requirements by the unit prices of the inputs. Recall the common practice in

## TABLE 10.3 — ILLUSTRATION OF NET PRESENT VALUES FOR TWO PROJECTS

|  | ESTIMATED BENEFITS | REQUIRED INPUTS (UNITS) | | |
|---|---|---|---|---|
|  |  | CAPITAL (K) | LABOR (L) | IMPORTS (M) |
| **PROJECT A** |  |  |  |  |
| Year 1 | $40,000 | 100 | 400 | 10 |
| Year 2 | $100,000 | 50 | 400 | 10 |
| **PROJECT B** |  |  |  |  |
| Year 1 | $100,000 | 200 | 150 | 25 |
| Year 2 | $40,000 | 150 | 150 | 25 |

$K$ = units of physical capital
$L$ = units of labor
$M$ = units of imported inputs
Assume a discount rate of 10 percent ($i = .10$)

I. UNIT PRICES OF FACTORS (AT CURRENT USER COSTS)

$P_K = \$200$
$P_L = \$100$
$P_M = \$400$

II. UNIT PRICES OF FACTORS (AT OPPORTUNITY COSTS)

$P'_K = \$250$
$P'_L = \$75$
$P'_M = \$500$

I. NET PRESENT VALUES

$NPV_A = +\$16,199$
$NPV_B = +\$19,421$

II. NET PRESENT VALUES

$NPV'_A = +\$25,206$
$NPV'_B = +\$6,302$

---

LDCs of maintaining artificially low interest rates (subsidizing investments in physical capital); overvalued currencies (subsidizing imports); and inflated wages in the modern sector (institutionally-set above market equilibrium levels, thus limiting employment). Suppose this to be the case here. The prevailing user costs for physical capital, labor, and imported inputs are: $P_K = \$200$, $P_L = \$100$, and $P_M = \$400$, respectively, as given by Set I in Table 10.3. The net present values for Projects A and B can now be determined.

$$NPV_A = \frac{\$40,000 - [\$200(100) + \$100(400) + \$400(10)]}{(1+.1)^1}$$

$$+ \frac{\$100,000 - [\$200(50) + \$100(400) + \$400(10)]}{(1+.1)^2}$$

$$NPV_A = -\$21,818 + \$38,017 = +\$16,199$$

$$NPV_B = \frac{\$100{,}000 - [\$200(200) + \$100(150) + \$400(25)]}{(1+.1)^1}$$

$$+ \frac{\$40{,}000 - [\$200(150) + \$100(150) + \$400(25)]}{(1+.1)^2}$$

$$NPV_B = +\$31{,}818 + -\$12{,}397 = +\$19{,}421$$

Since both NPVs are positive, both projects should be funded. If there are budget constraints, however, then Project B, with the higher NPV, would have priority.

While the net present value criterion seems straightforward, we should nevertheless be sensitive to the underlying assumptions. First, we assume that all the benefits and costs can be accurately estimated. The longer the expected life of the project, the harder it may be to project future benefits and costs. Moreover, as we discussed in Chapter 8, the benefits from some investments in human capital, such as improved mental and physical capacities for work and changed attitudes toward fertility, can be difficult to quantify. Many of the benefits of human capital formation, while increasing with time, are delayed: for example, high-quality primary education, which leads to secondary education and later improved labor productivity and reduced fertility as an adult. The costs are up-front. The higher the discount rate selected, the less likely that projects in human capital formation will be funded, ceteris paribus. As policymakers, politicians have short-run horizons: reap the benefits now and pay the costs later. Similarly, foreign-aid donors often prefer tangible "bricks and mortar" projects, where the benefits are immediate and highly visible.

Even if all the benefits could be accurately measured, the question then arises as to the distribution of benefits. Project A may be a rural health center that significantly improves access to basic health services for 500 households. Project B may be a new runway at a major airport that significantly increases the export capacity of the nation. Should preference be given to the project that addresses the basic needs of low-income households even if the estimated net present value is less than the project that generates income and foreign exchange? To the extent that the beneficiaries of the development project are concentrated and identifiable, then user fees may be charged to help defray some of the costs.

Other considerations in project evaluation would be factor constraints. For labor-abundant nations, projects that create more employment may be favored—Project A in this example. Or, if foreign exchange is scarce, projects that require fewer import expenditures may receive preference. Relative factor scarcities, however, should be reflected in relative factor prices. This need not be so if factor prices are controlled at nonmarket-clearing levels.

To illustrate, instead of the prevailing factor prices (Set I), let us use the opportunity costs (or underlying market equilibrium factor prices). The unit price of capital would be higher (say, $P'_K = \$250 > \$200 = P_K$), as would the unit price of imported inputs (say, $P'_M = \$500 > \$400 = P_M$). The unit price of labor, in contrast, would be less (say, $P'_L = \$75 < \$100 = P_L$). Recalculating the net present values reveals Project A (the more labor-intensive project) to have the higher NPV (an increase from $16,199 to $25,206). The NPV for Project B (relatively intensive in the now more expensive physical capital and imported inputs) falls from $19,421 to $6,302.

$$NPV'_A = \frac{\$40{,}000 - [\$250(100) + \$75(400) + \$500(10)]}{(1 + .1)^1}$$

$$+ \frac{\$100{,}000 - [\$250(50) + \$75(400) + \$500(10)]}{(1 + .1)^2}$$

$$NPV'_A = -\$18{,}182 + \$43{,}388 = +\$25{,}206$$

$$NPV'_B = \frac{\$100{,}000 - [\$250(200) + \$75(150) + \$500(25)]}{(1 + .1)^1}$$

$$+ \frac{\$40{,}000 - [\$250(150) + \$75(150) + \$500(25)]}{(1 + .1)^2}$$

$$NPV'_B = +\$23{,}864 + -\$17{,}562 = +\$6{,}302$$

Thus, holding down nominal interest rates may not only discourage domestic saving, but could result in an inefficient allocation of resources. Similarly, maintaining an overvalued currency would contribute to an import surplus. In this example, using the current subsidized prices of capital (reflecting a below-market equilibrium interest rate) and imports (reflecting an overvalued currency) inflates the NPV of Project B. As a consequence, Project B might be funded over Project A, a project that makes more efficient use of the available resources.

In sum, the selection of development projects to fund and the allocation of public investment expenditures are highly conditional on the criteria used for evaluation. In the case of the net present value criterion, the decision depends on the accuracy of the projected future benefits and the choices of the discount rate and relevant factor prices. Ideally, the factor prices used would reflect the opportunity costs of the factors.

## IMPROVING POPULAR ACCESS TO CREDIT

E. F. Schumacher in his book *Small Is Beautiful: Economics As If People Mattered* argued that an investment priority to promote economic opportunity in the less developed countries should be the creation of workplaces. With fairly modest investments in capital, large numbers of workplaces could be created—in rural areas, small towns, and even on the outskirts of major cities—using labor-intensive technologies compatible with the skills of the population.[14]

---

[14] E. F. Schumacher, *Small Is Beautiful: Economics As If People Mattered,* New York: Harper and Row, 1973, pages 174–176.

Indeed, there have been dramatic success stories where small loans have enabled individuals, who by all conventional wisdom would be deemed uncreditworthy, to start or expand profitable businesses. For a well-known example—the Grameen Bank in Bangladesh—the World Bank provides this account:

> While the government struggled to create a viable rural banking system in Bangladesh, a small private initiative was started in 1976 to help the landless without normal bank collateral to obtain credit. This program has become the Grameen (Rural) Bank.... The bank's customers, who are restricted to the very poor, are organized into five-person groups, and each group member must establish a regular pattern of weekly saving before seeking a loan. The first two borrowers in a group must make several weekly payments on their loans before other group members can borrow. Most loans are to finance trading and the purchase of livestock.
>
> By February 1987 the Grameen Bank was operating 300 branches covering 5,400 villages. Nearly 250,000 persons were participating, among them an increasing number of women, who accounted for about 75 percent of the total. The membership included about 13 percent of households with less than half an acre of land in the areas in which the bank was operating. Loans are small—on average, about 3,000 taka ($100) in 1985....
>
> In sharp contrast to the Bangladesh commercial banking system, the Grameen Bank has experienced excellent loan recovery. As of February 1987 about 97 percent of loans had been recovered within one year after disbursement and almost 99 percent within two years. This good performance is reportedly attributable to a combination of factors: close supervision of field operations, dedicated service by bank staff, borrowing for purposes that generate regular income, solidarity within groups, and repayment in weekly installments. Another factor which encourages repayment is the borrower's knowledge that the availability of future loans depends on the repayment of borrowed funds.
>
> Bank staff meet weekly with groups to disburse loans, collect savings deposits and loan repayments, and provide training in financial responsibility. This means high operating costs. The ratio of expenses to loans rose from 9 percent in 1984 to 18 percent in 1986. These high costs have been partially offset by low-cost funds from international agencies.[15]

Another example is in Bolivia, where a private commercial bank, BancoSol, has specialized in making loans to the poor at market rates of interest. Having evolved from an earlier nonprofit finance company that had been supported, in part, by foreign aid, BancoSol began to extend credit to street vendors and other tradespeople in the capital city of La Paz in early 1992. As with the Grameen Bank, most of the borrowers are women. To secure a loan from BancoSol, an individual has to be a member of a small group of similar vendors or neighbors that guarantees repayment. Despite the high rates of interest charged and the poverty of the loan recipients, the loan recovery rate has been excellent. By 1994 BancoSol expected to turn a profit on the venture.[16]

---

[15]World Bank, *World Development Report 1989*, page 117. By 1991 the Grameen Bank was operating nearly 900 branches, covering more than 23,000 villages across Bangladesh. Some one million households had received loans (averaging $60 at an interest rate of 16 percent). See United Nations Development Programme, *Human Development Report 1993*, New York: Oxford University Press, 1993, page 95.

[16]From Jeb Blount, "Profit's Not a Dirty Word at Bolivia's Bank for the Poor," *Wall Street Journal* (April 10, 1992), page A17.

In fact, in the developing nations more credit is being extended to women, long discriminated against not only in terms of lending, but in wages and working conditions. The *Wall Street Journal* provided one such report in 1994.

> [Development agencies and multilateral banks] are increasingly funding women-led businesses and farming projects based on the assumption that women—more than men—are the critical players in the fight to relieve poverty....
>
> A recent World Bank study found that women head half the households in rural sub-Saharan Africa. And a study of village life in Cameroon found that women work an average of 64 hours a week, compared with 32 for men. And women's earnings are more likely to be used for health and education of the next generation....
>
> The focus on women's economic activities coincides with a growing interest in financing the thousands of tiny businesses that make up the developing world's vast "informal sector." Many of these so-called microenterprises, ranging from food sellers on street corners to one-person apparel makers, are run by women.
>
> Though statistics are shaky, it is estimated that informal-sector businesses make up as much as half of all economic activity in many developing countries. Yet, until recently, the international institutions have funneled nearly all development funds to governments and state enterprises for projects that often did little for the poorest population segments.[17]

The clear implication from these and other accounts is that tremendous potential exists for improving the efficiency of resource allocation and for alleviating poverty by allowing equal access to credit to those traditionally shut off, namely women and the poor.

## MEASURES TO PROMOTE DOMESTIC INVESTMENT

In general, economic growth enhances the supply of domestic saving, thus making more funds available for investment and physical capital formation. Healthy rates of economic growth combined with political stability may also attract foreign capital, as well as reduce the flight overseas of domestic savings. In addition, specific policy measures might be taken to raise the level and productivity of domestic investment. Five areas for possible reform are discussed below.

First, interest rates should reflect the scarcity of financial capital. Removing interest rate ceilings and allowing the nominal interest rates to rise to market-clearing levels would increase the quantity of loanable funds available. Similarly, credit should be allocated by the market, not rationed to favored sectors by government directive. Toward this end, competition in financial markets should be promoted. As summarized by the World Bank, "Competition ensures that transactions costs are held down,

---

[17]Tim Carrington, "In Developing World, International Lenders Are Targeting Women," *Wall Street Journal* (June 22, 1994), pages A1, A6.

that risk is allocated to those most willing to bear it, and that investment is undertaken by those with the most promising opportunities."[18]

While this proposal seems straightforward in theory, in practice there may well be resistance. Recall the emphasis on physical capital accumulation in the growth-model approach to development. In the desire to stimulate investment and promote industrialization, governments have held down interest rates and channelled the available credit. Those in positions to determine access to credit enjoy considerable power. Moreover, the relationship between the government and the banking system is frequently close, with political appointees in charge of the banks. Efforts to liberalize the banking system through market competition would be opposed by those who prospered under the earlier system—both the distributors and recipients of the subsidized credit.

Second, inflation needs to be kept under control in order to maintain positive real rates of interest (where the after-tax nominal interest rate exceeds the inflation rate). Even when nominal interest rates are set by the market, high and variable inflation rates can reduce the amount of credit made available, especially for long-term financing. Positive real rates of interest have been associated with economic growth, not only through the incentive to save, but through increases in the overall productivity of investment, as funds for weaker investment projects are less likely to be sought.[19]

To keep inflation down, monetary discipline needs to be exerted. The growth of the money supply should correspond, on average, to the real growth in output and income. To avoid real interest rates so high that significant amounts of private investment are crowded out, fiscal discipline is also in order. The chronic practice of running large budget deficits must come to an end. Improved tax systems would help, as would better collection of the taxes that are owed. Progressive taxes on income and wealth (including land), along with substantial sales taxes on luxury items and labor-saving appliances, might be considered. Government expenditures must be reined in so that increased revenues will bring down the deficits. By trimming government budget deficits, the exercise of restraint in monetary policy is made easier.

Clearly, raising taxes will not be popular. So too, while there may be savings in reducing waste and fraud in government programs, the difficulty in curbing government expenditures should not be underestimated. Attempts to cut back in any area will be opposed by the current beneficiaries of the government spending. Administrations that are not politically stable would naturally be reluctant to adopt contractionary fiscal policies.

Third, to conserve on the capital stock that is presently available, and to stretch future investments in physical capital, labor-intensive (or capital-saving) technologies should be used wherever possible—or as long as the nation's underlying comparative advantages are not compromised. Freeing up factor markets (removing interest rate ceilings, phasing out institutionally set money wages in the modern sector, and devaluing overvalued currencies) would tend to promote the adoption of more labor-intensive production processes. Similarly, when evaluating public investment expenditures and development projects, costs should be based on the opportunity costs of the factors of production.

Here, too, opposition to reform can be expected from those who benefit from interest rate ceilings, high modern-sector wages, and overvalued currencies. The adoption

---

[18]World Bank, *World Development Report 1989,* page 25.
[19]Ibid., pages 31–33.

of intermediate technologies and labor-intensive production processes might be rejected by some as inferior and uncompetitive.

Fourth, stock and bond markets need to be developed to provide additional outlets for saving and investment. Stock markets are important for raising venture capital, particularly in those industries that are capital-intensive and relatively risky, for example, steel, cement, petrochemicals, and heavy manufacturing. Bond markets are important for long-term financing. These capital markets need to operate under well-defined rules of regulation and supervision. Developing countries may want to encourage more joint ventures with foreign banks and financial institutions, not only to increase competition in the domestic market, but to introduce new technologies and skills in financial management. The recent rapid growth in emerging market mutual funds suggests that developing nations may be able to attract increasing amounts of foreign capital.

Fifth, more effective financial intermediation should be made available to the small savers and borrowers typically shut out of the formal credit markets. Households in the rural areas and small towns may be an important source of domestic saving. Small businesses, especially those run by women, can often make good use of credit. To secure funds, they would be willing to pay market rates of interest, rates that nevertheless may be lower than those charged in the informal market. The success of the Grameen Bank in Bangladesh is instructive and encouraging. Some initial subsidization by the government (or foreign donors) of rural credit cooperatives and even private banks that expand into rural areas may be necessary where overhead and personnel training costs are high. Subsidized group loans for capital improvements in villages and neighborhoods might be considered, with user charges assessed for the repayment of the loans.

Funds need to be mobilized for savings and loan associations and other thrift institutions for use in the long-term financing of mortgages. The World Bank notes that housing typically accounts for 20 to 30 percent of a nation's physical capital stock. A result of high inflation, interest rate ceilings, and underdeveloped capital markets, the shortage of long-term financing for mortgages contributes to the poor quality and inadequate stock of housing in many of the less developed countries.[20]

To encourage long-term saving, employees in the modern sector could be required to contribute a set percentage of their wages to retirement accounts or pension funds. Chile, which began to privatize its social security system in 1981, is widely cited as a model. Employees contribute a fixed proportion of their salaries to personal pension accounts managed by private investment companies operating under government regulation. The Chilean pension system has bolstered private saving and contributed to the development of securities markets in the economy.[21]

## CONCLUDING NOTE

The chapters in Part III addressed population policy (measures to influence the growth rate, composition, or distribution of a population); human capital formation (resources

---

[20]Ibid., pages 101–102.
[21]See G. A. Mackenzie, "Reforming Latin America's Old Age Pension Systems," *Finance and Development*, vol. 32, no. 1 (March 1995), pages 10–13.

devoted to improving the nutrition, health, and education of a population); employment (the use of human labor to produce goods and services); and physical capital formation (expenditures on infrastructure and on plant, equipment, and machinery for use in the production of other goods and services). The investments a nation makes in human and physical capital formation affect its prospects for economic growth and development. The less developed countries have been challenged by high rates of population growth to provide employment for their rapidly expanding labor forces, while increasing their human capital–labor and physical capital–labor ratios in order to raise labor productivities and promote economic growth and development.

As discussed in these four chapters, policy options exist to reduce the rate of population growth, expand employment, encourage human capital formation, and stimulate physical capital formation. The appropriate role of the government in directing development and allocating resources remains controversial. In the developing economies, policies, whether well-intentioned or the product of special interests, have sometimes contributed to inefficient and inequitable resource allocations.

In Part IV we examine economic development from another perspective, that of the major sectors of the economy: agriculture, natural resources, manufacturing, and services. Not surprisingly, the issues of efficiency and equity in resource allocations will re-emerge. We begin in Chapter 11 with agriculture.

## SUMMARY OF MAIN POINTS

1. Effective financial intermediation, by increasing the level and productivity of the funds allocated to investment, contributes to economic growth.
2. Money functions as a medium of exchange, store of value, and unit of account, thereby promoting the efficient operation of an economy. Overexpansion of the money supply, however, can result in inflation which, in the extreme form of hyperinflation, undermines these functions.
3. The direct relationship between economic growth and the saving rate depends, in part, on the capital–output ratio and growth rate of the labor force. Ceteris paribus, the high capital–output ratios and rapid labor force growth characteristic of developing economies increase the saving rate required to achieve a given rate of growth in output per unit of labor.
4. Gross domestic investment can exceed gross domestic saving with the inflow of foreign saving, reflected in a deficit on the nation's current account balance. Gross domestic investment increases aggregate demand (with public and private expenditures on capital goods and inventories) and aggregate supply (with net additions to the physical capital stock).
5. For most economies the primary source of loanable funds is household saving. On net, business and the government are demanders of loanable funds. Financial intermediaries, such as banks and deposit institutions, stock markets and bond markets, serve to coordinate and allocate the available loanable funds.
6. Increases in the efficiency of financial intermediaries can promote investment by lowering the transaction costs—thereby increasing the net return for the suppliers of loanable funds, while reducing the net cost for the demanders of loanable funds.

7. Interest rate ceilings reduce the quantity of loanable funds supplied and create shortages of bank credit. The available loanable funds have to be rationed. Often a black market for credit is created. In addition, informal credit markets develop to accommodate those unable to borrow from the banks in the formal market.
8. For a given nominal rate of interest, inflation reduces the real rate of interest. Consequently, expectations of inflation, ceteris paribus, increase the demand and reduce the supply of loanable funds.
9. Household saving in the less developed countries is constrained by the generally low incomes; high youth burdens of dependency; low or negative real rates of interest; and limited access to banks and depository institutions.
10. Governments in the less developed countries tend to run budget deficits due to the heavy demands for government expenditures and the limited abilities for raising revenues. The financing of the government budget deficits either crowds out private investment (through higher interest rates or preferential access to the available credit) or leads to an inflationary expansion of the money supply.
11. The net present value criterion can be used to evaluate development projects. Difficulties in applying this criterion include accurately estimating the benefits and costs of a project over its life; selecting an appropriate discount rate; and weighing the distribution of the benefits and costs across the population.
12. Evidence (e.g., the Grameen Bank) suggests that the poor in developing economies may make good use of loans and may be good credit risks.
13. Measures to promote domestic saving and investment include allowing factor prices to reflect factor scarcities (in particular, removing interest rate ceilings); controlling inflation to keep real interest rates positive; developing financial markets; and increasing the access of the rural population to depository institutions.

## KEY TERMS

basic macroeconomic identity
black market
credit cooperative
depreciation
financial capital
financial intermediation
income
incremental capital–output ratio (ICOR)
informal credit markets
interest rate ceiling

life cycle theory
medium of exchange
money
net present value
permanent income
permanent income hypothesis
physical capital
store of value
transitory income
unit of account

## QUESTIONS

1. Find the saving rate required for maintaining a steady-state growth rate in output per unit of labor (or labor productivity) of 2 percent, when the capital–output ratio is 3 and the natural growth rate of the labor force is 1 percent.

    a. Suppose the natural growth rate of the labor force increases to 2 percent. Find the new steady-state saving rate. Discuss why a less developed country might find it difficult to increase the saving rate with the higher growth rate of the labor force. What might happen if the saving rate did not increase?

**b.** Suppose instead that the growth rate in labor productivity increased to 3 percent. Find the new steady-state saving rate. Would an economy find it easier to increase the saving rate in response to an increase in labor productivity growth or labor force growth? Discuss.

2. Explain how higher interest rates may help, rather than hurt, a developing economy.

3. How can you tell whether a nation is using foreign saving to fund its domestic investment?

4. Given the following demand and supply curves in the market for loanable funds:

$$D = 80 - 4i \quad \text{(demand for loanable funds)}$$
$$S^l = -30 + 6i \quad \text{(banks' supply of loanable funds)}$$
$$S^d = -12 + 6i \quad \text{(banks' supply of deposits)}$$

where $i$ is the nominal interest rate and the difference between the $S^l$ and $S^d$ curves reflects the interest rate spread of banks (i.e., the difference between the rate of interest charged by banks on loans, $i^l$, and the rate of interest paid by banks on deposits, $i^d$).

**a.** Sketch the above curves and determine the market equilibrium rate of interest on loans, $i^l_o$, and the equilibrium quantity of loanable funds, $F_o$. Also determine the equilibrium rate of interest received by depositors, $i^d_o$.

**b.** Illustrate the effects on the market equilibrium of an increase in the efficiency of banks that, given the supply of loanable funds deposited, $S^d$, increases the supply of loanable funds offered by banks to:

$$S^{l\prime} = -20 + 6i$$

5. Return to question 4. Now impose an interest rate ceiling on the nominal rate of interest charged by banks of $i^* = 10$ percent. Find the new quantity of loanable funds available, $F_1$, and the resulting excess quantity demanded of credit, $F_2 - F_1$. What is the new rate of interest on bank deposits?

6. In 1993 the ratio of gross domestic saving to GDP in Egypt was only 6 percent, compared to 16 percent for Sri Lanka, another low-income economy. What might account for the lower rate of gross domestic saving in Egypt?

7. Suppose the government of a less developed country is considering funding only one of the following development projects. Each of the projects has a two-year time horizon. Assume that all benefits and costs are valued at the end of the year. Assume also that the discount rate $(i)$ used is 10 percent.

**a.** Given the following information, under the net present value criterion, which project should the government fund?

i. assuming the unit factor prices in Set I.

ii. assuming the unit factor prices in Set II.

**b.** Discuss some of the limitations in using the net present value criterion for selecting among development projects.

|  | ESTIMATED BENEFITS | REQUIRED INPUTS (UNITS) | | |
|---|---|---|---|---|
|  |  | CAPITAL (K) | LABOR (L) | IMPORTS (M) |
| PROJECT A |  |  |  |  |
| Year 1 | $1100 | 50 | 300 | 15 |
| Year 2 | $2000 | 40 | 400 | 10 |
| PROJECT B |  |  |  |  |
| Year 1 | $1800 | 30 | 500 | 10 |
| Year 2 | $1200 | 25 | 600 | 5 |

I. UNIT FACTOR PRICES
    Capital   $P_K = \$10$
    Labor    $P_L = \$2.0$
    Imports  $P_M = \$12$

II. UNIT FACTOR PRICES
    Capital   $P'_K = \$15$
    Labor    $P'_L = \$1.5$
    Imports  $P'_M = \$30$

## SUGGESTED READINGS

Gersovitz, Mark, "Saving and Development," *Handbook of Development Economics,* Volume 1, edited by H. Chenery and T. N. Srinivasan, Amsterdam, Netherlands: Elsevier Science Publishers, 1988, pages 381–424.

World Bank, *World Development Report 1989: Financial Systems and Development,* New York: Oxford University Press, 1989.

# PART IV

# SECTORS IN DEVELOPMENT

# CHAPTER 11

# AGRICULTURE

> Thus in sum and substance, the man who is bound by traditional agriculture cannot produce much food no matter how rich the land. Thrift and work are not enough.... To produce an abundance of farm products requires that the farmer has access to and has the skill and knowledge to use what science knows about soils, plants, animals, and machines.... The knowledge that makes the transformation possible is a form of capital, which entails investment—investment not only in material inputs in which a part of this knowledge is embedded but importantly also investment in farm people.[1]

So observed Theodore Schultz in his pioneering work on agriculture and economic development written more than 30 years ago. Unfortunately, his concern that policymakers ignore the important role of agriculture in economic development is still relevant in parts of the Third World.

A majority of the labor forces in the LDCs works in agriculture, and output from this sector meets a large portion of domestic food needs. For many low- and middle-income countries, the bulk of export earnings are generated from agriculture. Indeed, economic development is often indicated by the transformation of traditional farming into modern agriculture, as productivity gains free rural labor for employment in the urban-industrial sector.

In the developing world, however, progress in agriculture has been uneven. A World Resources Institute report states

> Even though the world's food production has to date far outpaced its population growth, some regional and national data show reason for concern. The 22 percent increase in Africa's food production between 1980–82 and 1990–92 fell short of meeting demand; per capita food production dropped by 5 percent. Somali, Malawi, and

---

[1]Theodore W. Schultz, *Transforming Traditional Agriculture,* New Haven: Yale University Press, 1964, pages 205–206.

Liberia experienced the most serious declines in food production over the 10 year period. In Asia, South America, Europe, and the former U.S.S.R., food production grew faster than the population.[2]

From 1980 to 1993 the average annual growth rate of agriculture was over 5 percent in China, nearly 4 percent in Costa Rica, but barely 1 percent in Ghana (see Table 11.1). How do we account for such differences in agricultural performance? How do we transfer the lessons from the successful countries to those with less impressive performances? These are some of the issues that we address in this chapter.

We will first discuss the importance of agriculture to economic development. Then, we turn to the transformation of agriculture from small-scale subsistence farming to modern market-oriented agriculture. In the third section of the chapter, the prevailing characteristics of agriculture in the developing countries, such as the small size of most farms and the seasonality and risk of production, are analyzed. Then we elaborate on the primary constraints to promoting successful agricultural development in the Third World. In the final section, we discuss policy reforms that may contribute to the development of agriculture and economic growth. A case study of economic development in Costa Rica concludes the chapter.

## IMPORTANCE OF AGRICULTURE

Progress in the agricultural sector is a precondition for stimulating growth in the modern sector. A surplus of agricultural products from the rural sector is needed to feed the expanding urban population and sustain the growth of the industrial sector. Moreover, the growth in agricultural productivity releases rural workers to move to the urban areas as industrial labor. Once a successful development process has been initiated, however, agriculture tends to grow more slowly than the manufacturing and service sectors. C. P. Timmer, in a survey of agriculture in the development process, concludes:

> The share of agriculture in a country's labor force and total output declines in both cross-section and time-series samples as incomes per capita increase. The declining importance of agriculture is uniform and pervasive, a tendency obviously driven by powerful forces inherent in the development process, whether in socialist or capitalist countries, Asian, Latin American, or African, currently developed or still poor.[3]

We shall see that two of these powerful forces are the income-inelastic nature of the demand for agricultural commodities and the powerful technological progress (for example, the Green Revolution) that has greatly increased agricultural production.

In Table 11.1 we confirm that the percentage of GDP accounted for by agriculture declines with income. For the low-income countries agriculture accounts for 37 percent

---

[2]World Resources Institute, *World Resources 1994–95*, New York: Oxford University Press, 1994, page 291.
[3]C. P. Timmer, "The Agricultural Transformation," *Handbook of Development Economics, Volume 1*, edited by H. Chenery and T. N. Srinivasan, Amsterdam: North Holland, 1988, page 276.

| TABLE 11.1 | SELECTED STATISTICS ON AGRICULTURE | | | | | | |
|---|---|---|---|---|---|---|---|
| | AGRICULTURE AS PERCENT OF GDP | | AVERAGE ANNUAL GROWTH RATE IN AGRICULTURE (%) | | CEREAL IMPORTS (KG. PER CAPITA) | FOOD-AID CEREALS (KG. PER CAPITA) | FERTILIZER CONSUMPTION (100G PER HECTARE) |
| | 1970 | 1993 | 1970–1980 | 1980–1993 | 1993 | 1992–1993 | 1992–1993 |
| INCOME GROUP | | | | | | | |
| India | 45 | 31 | 1.8 | 3.0 | .8 | .31 | 720 |
| China | 34 | 19 | 2.6 | 5.3 | 6.2 | .1 | 3005 |
| Other low-income | 31 | 37 | ... | 2.2 | 26.0 | 7.8 | 352 |
| Middle-income | ... | ... | ... | 1.6 | 72.2 | 3.8 | 603 |
| High-income | 4 | ... | ... | ... | 95.5 | 0.0 | 1115 |
| REGION | | | | | | | |
| sub-Saharan Africa | 27 | 20 | 1.7 | 1.7 | 23.5 | 9.1 | 149 |
| Middle East & North Africa | ... | ... | ... | 4.4 | 145.4 | ... | 641 |
| Europe & Central Asia | ... | ... | ... | –.2 | 69.6 | 8.9 | 570 |
| South Asia | 44 | 30 | 1.8 | 3.1 | 5.2 | 1.4 | 737 |
| East Asia & Pacific | 34 | 17 | 3.1 | 4.0 | 17.5 | .3 | 2055 |
| Latin America & the Caribbean | 12 | ... | 3.4 | 2.1 | 59.6 | 3.4 | 524 |
| SELECTED COUNTRIES | | | | | | | |
| Ghana | 47 | 48 | –.3 | 1.3 | 24.8 | 4.7 | 38 |
| Sri Lanka | 28 | 25 | 2.8 | 2.1 | 63.8 | 13.8 | 964 |
| Egypt | 29 | 18 | 2.8 | 1.3 | 128.7 | 8.6 | 3392 |
| Poland | ... | 6 | 0 | –.5 | 82.7 | 5.3 | 811 |
| Costa Rica | 23 | 15 | 2.5 | 3.6 | 162.0 | 28.8 | 2354 |
| Brazil | 12 | 11 | 4.2 | 2.5 | 50.3 | .1 | 608 |
| South Korea | 25 | 7 | 2.7 | 2.0 | 256.2 | 0.0 | 4656 |

NOTES: Lack of data is indicated by ...

Agriculture covers forestry, hunting, and fishing. In developing countries with high levels of subsistence farming, much agricultural production is either not exchanged or not exchanged for money. This increases the difficulty of measuring the contribution of agriculture to Gross Domestic Product (GDP) and reduces the reliability and comparability of such numbers.

Per capita cereal imports and food aid, measured in grain equivalents, are in metric tons per thousand population or kilograms per person. Food aid in the form of cereals covers wheat and flour, bulgur, rice, coarse grains, and the cereal component of blended foods. Due to the differences in the reporting and receipt of the food aid, the figures on cereal imports and food aid are not directly comparable.

Fertilizer consumption (in hundreds of grams of plant nutrient per hectare of arable land) measures the plant nutrients used in relation to arable land. Fertilizer products cover nitrogenous, potash, and phosphate fertilizers. Arable land is defined as land under temporary crops (double-cropped areas are counted once), temporary meadows for mowing or pasture, land under market or kitchen gardens, and land temporarily fallow or lying idle, as well as land under permanent crops.

FROM: World Bank, *World Development Report 1995*, Tables 1, 2, 3, and 4.

of GDP in 1993; in contrast, for the high-income countries, the comparable figure would be less than 5 percent. From another perspective, between 1970 and 1993, the share of agriculture in the low-income countries declined as per capita income grew; for instance, in India the share fell from 45 percent to 31 percent.

The development of the agricultural sector is vital to increasing the incomes and quality of life of those who remain in rural areas. A majority of the populations of the contemporary LDCs reside in rural areas, highly dependent on earnings from agriculture. A critical need exists for agricultural productivity improvements that raise rural incomes. Also, higher living standards in rural areas will moderate the migration to cities that has been problematic in many countries.

Finally, agricultural products are a staple export of many developing countries, which depend on these earnings to repay foreign debt and to import needed consumption and investment goods. Many LDCs import basic food items, and dynamic agricultural development can reduce these imports and conserve needed foreign exchange.[4]

Thus, agriculture plays a pivotal role in the economy of the typical developing country as a supplier of labor for the industrial workforce; a provider of food for the urban population; a source of income for rural residents; and a critical earner of foreign exchange. Let us now see how that role changes within the development process.

## THE TRANSFORMATION OF THE AGRICULTURAL SECTOR

The transformation of agriculture is characterized by a progressive movement to higher-yielding stages of production.[5] During the first phase, a country moves from **subsistence agriculture,** where farmers simply produce for their own needs and have little marketable surplus. Rising output per worker leads to an agricultural surplus that will support nonagricultural activities, such as industry. As in the Lewis model, higher-paying industrial employment opportunities attract workers from agriculture. The Green Revolution, a term used to describe the successful new grains introduced in Asia in the late 1960s, with accompanying higher-yielding seeds and effective pesticides and herbicides, has helped many of today's developing countries move beyond subsistence agriculture.[6]

In the post-subsistence or second phase, governments tend to take a more active role to capture part of the agricultural surplus. Most developing countries are in this phase of agricultural development. Consistent with the traditional capital-scarce development models (recall the Lewis model in Chapter 4), agriculture is often taxed to transfer economic resources to government-assisted industrial development. Such taxation

---

[4]Clearly, if the reduction in imports is at the expense of another developing country's exports, the net gain for the developing world is reduced. For instance, were The Gambia to succeed in growing more domestic rice, reducing its rice imports from Thailand, The Gambia would conserve foreign exchange, but Thailand would lose export earnings.

[5]Timmer, pages 279–283.

[6]The term *Green Revolution* was first used by William Gaud of the U.S. Agency for International Development when he described the greatly increased harvests from new wheat varieties during the late 1960s in India and Pakistan. Since then, the term has been more broadly used to refer to the highly successful technological change with the growing of cereal grains (wheat, rice, and corn). See George W. Norton and Jeffrey Alwang, *Introduction to Economics of Agricultural Development,* New York: McGraw-Hill, 1993, page 281.

can be either direct, with individual income taxes or even confiscation of agricultural output, or indirect, with pricing policies aimed at keeping urban food prices low. In recent years, awareness has grown that the excessive taxation of the agricultural sector is not an effective vehicle for an economic development that stresses enhanced opportunities for all citizens. The greater concern now is for a more balanced development that includes improving living standards in rural areas with a more gradual reallocation of resources from agriculture to modern-sector activities.

In phase three of the transformation of agriculture, an integration of agriculture and industry occurs. Agriculture becomes highly mechanized, and the most efficient farm size tends to increase. Rural and urban factor markets, particularly for financial capital, are linked. Agriculture becomes more susceptible to the macroeconomic swings of the aggregate economy, such as credit-market conditions. Also, the differences in living standards between urban and rural areas tend to narrow. Middle-income countries with relatively prosperous farms of modest size would have an agricultural sector in phase three of the transformation process.[7] We now turn to those characteristics of agriculture that must, at least for the near term, be considered as given and beyond the control of policymakers.

## CHARACTERISTICS OF AGRICULTURE IN THE LDCs

Agriculture in contemporary developing countries is significantly influenced by the small size of the average farm; the risk and seasonal nature of production; the beneficial effects of the Green Revolution; and the income inelasticity of demand for agricultural output. Rural development efforts should be designed with an understanding of these given characteristics. Of course, the developing countries exhibit considerable diversity with respect to their potential agricultural productivity (land quality and the suitability of the climate), their current degree of mechanization, and the policy environment in which agriculture operates.

### TYPE AND SIZE OF FARMS

The family or household farm characterizes much of the rural sector in Asia and Africa. In contrast, agriculture in Latin America is more dualistic, with subsistence farms of suboptimal size coexisting with larger plantations that depend on hired labor.

---

[7]Timmer suggests that high-income countries enter a fourth phase of agricultural development. Capital–labor ratios become very high, and the relative importance of agriculture falls dramatically. He says that "the role of agriculture in industrialized economies is little different from the role of the steel, housing, or insurance sectors" (Timmer, page 292). Some qualification to this observation is in order, however, for in the United States, Europe—particularly France—and Japan, farmers assert political influence that is disproportionate to their declining economic importance. Thus, even in the industrialized economies, agriculture can continue to be a highly visible sector.

HOUSEHOLD AS PRODUCER

A large proportion of rural residents in Africa, Asia, and Latin America cultivate their own small landholdings. While few reliable figures exist about the size distribution of such small farms, it is safe to assume that a large majority of households farm less than 15 hectares, with many operating on less than one hectare (approximately 2.47 acres), compared to an average in excess of 50 hectares in Western Europe and the United States.

> Farms of less than a hectare characterize China, Bangladesh, and Java; even in Japan average farm size is still only slightly greater than one hectare. The average in India is only about 1 to 2 hectares, and in Africa and Latin America farms tend to be less than 10 to 20 hectares in size.[8]

Many farmers have direct title to their land; in other cases they have traditional use rights that tend to be respected year after year. Clear title to property can be very important in encouraging proper care of, and longer-term investments in, the land.

The larger proportion of these small holdings are involved in rainfed agriculture, or production that is dependent on direct rainfall levels. Irrigated agriculture varies greatly in its technological sophistication, from the relatively inexpensive pumping of groundwater to large-scale dams that can hold enough water to irrigate thousands of hectares of land. In general, however, irrigation requires substantial investments in infrastructure (dams and canals) and mechanization (pumping). In many developing countries, greater use of irrigated agriculture is not cost-effective with current world-market crop prices and the small size of the typical farm. For instance, the cost per ton of producing irrigated rice in West Africa is likely to exceed the world market price of rice that is being exported from South Asia.

In most cases, farmers have some discretion in choosing among different crops. Often crops are divided into three categories: those destined purely for consumption; those intended for either consumption or sale; and those targeted at commercial outlets. For instance, a West African farmer may be growing some garden vegetables like tomatoes, exclusively for home consumption; some corn that will be divided between home consumption and sale; and a cash crop like cotton or peanuts that is intended for the market. Generally, farmers, like profit-maximizing firms, attempt to assess the incremental benefits (primarily the expected market prices) and costs from different combinations of plantings and then decide on the optimal allocation of land and labor to different crops.

Two additional considerations can enter into the farmer's decision making. The farmer may be constrained by the necessity to rotate crops. For instance, continually planting peanuts in a field may soon exhaust the productivity of the land; thus, the farmer must periodically either lay fallow the land or cultivate a different crop, such as a grain like millet. Second, risk-averse farmers may wish to achieve some minimum level of food self-sufficiency biasing them toward food crops, at the expense of cash crops.

The family farm in developing countries tends to be a highly labor-intensive operation. Land clearing, plowing, planting, weeding, and harvesting are typically done by family members using draft animals and relatively simple tools. The work tends to be

---

[8]Timmer, page 292.

highly seasonal, with peak labor demands at planting and harvesting, and a period of reduced activity in the interim. Typically, the marketing of crops, the repair of homes, and the clearing of fields must be done after the harvest and before the next planting season. Finally, in many of the parts of the developing world, **mixed agriculture,** which includes farming and livestock raising, exists. Many advantages to this mixed system exist, such as the ready availability of animal feed from crop residue and of fertilizer from the animals. Land availability, particularly in Asia, is a primary constraint to a greater use of mixed farming. Also, cultural factors can limit the extent of mixed farming. Certain groups, such as the Hutus in Rwanda and Burundi, have traditionally concentrated on farming, leaving livestock to other groups.

Models that integrate the rural household's production and consumption decisions, as well as decisions concerning family size, can be useful in analyzing the effectiveness of agricultural policies.[9] Since the farming unit is simultaneously a producer and consumer of food, the production decision cannot always be viewed in isolation. Also, the household's decisions concerning family size (i.e., number of children) have implications for both labor supply (production) and consumption. Moreover, as discussed in Chapter 9, the rural-to-urban migration decision, itself a function of rural economic opportunities, affects family size and the resulting production and consumption of food.

## LARGE-SCALE AGRICULTURE

In many Latin America countries significant variation exists in farm size as well as in inequality in landholdings. Many very small holdings, or **minifundias** (less than 1 hectare), coexist with a small number of very large landholdings, called **latifundias.** Usually, there is a middle group of family farms in the 5 to 20 hectare range. In countries such as Argentina, Brazil, Colombia, Ecuador, Guatemala, and Peru, the degree of inequality is striking. For instance, in Peru, one percent of the farmers have owned nearly 80 percent of the farmland.

For a variety of reasons, the large farms in Latin America are not always efficient. In fact, output per hectare may be greater, on average, on the small family units. In some cases, large farms do not fully utilize their land; for instance, it can be difficult to find qualified day-labor at the low wages offered. The reservation wage (the lowest wage that will generate any labor supply) of unskilled labor can exceed the marginal revenue product of labor, creating a disequilibrium in the labor market. That is, the wages that can be offered are too low to attract any workers. The young are frequently drawn by the potential of higher wages to the cities. Also, the costs of supervising relatively unskilled labor can be high, limiting the extent to which wages for unskilled labor can be raised. Often, the large farms are more a source of conspicuous wealth and power than a profit-driven enterprise. With lowered profitability, there tends to be a reduced effort to improve the productivity of land.

Given that smaller farms in Latin America appear to offer some productivity advantages, calls for land reform can be justified on both equity and efficiency grounds. Land-reform effects can be significant. Breaking up larger holdings into smaller operations can actually lead to an increase in total output and rural employment as small

---

[9]See Howard Barnum and Lyn Squire, *A Model of an Agricultural Household: Theory and Evidence,* World Bank Staff Occasional Papers (27), Baltimore: The Johns Hopkins University Press, 1979.

farms tend to be cultivated in a more labor-intensive manner. Greater equality results in the distribution of land, and a reduction occurs in the number of people either landless or trying to farm on the less-than-efficiently-sized holdings. Under different circumstances in the twentieth century, Mexico, Bolivia, and Cuba have all instituted major land-reform programs. It should be noted that land reform has been done both with or without compensation to former owners.

Norton and Alwang argue that strong resolve from an honest government is needed for successful land reform.[10] The government must be able to counter large landholders who will resist land reform and urban consumers who often wrongly believe that land reform will result in higher food prices. Frequently, land reform follows a revolution or is aimed at addressing serious social tensions that could threaten the stability of the government. Land-reform programs must be implemented quickly to prevent large landowners from lowering the potential productivity of their land, either by selling capital assets, such as irrigation pumps, or farming the land too intensively prior to the actual redistribution. Finally, supporting institutions that provide credit and agricultural extension to farmers must be strengthened so that they can adequately address the needs of new, smaller farmers. Through implementing such land-reform policy, the government can increase its political legitimacy with the rural population.

## THE SEASONALITY AND RISK OF AGRICULTURE

Agriculture, particularly traditional rainfed, tends to have highly defined seasons, the months of which tend to vary across countries. Typically, planting occurs in spring, with a harvest in the fall. The pattern of rainfall and the growing days required per crop often limit rainfed agriculture to a single crop per year. In parts of the developing world, however, it is possible to have two rainfed seasons, usually relying on faster growing plants, like garden vegetables, for the second crop, frequently grown on secondary plots nearer to the farmer's house. Labor requirements for such double-cropping match or even exceed the available labor supply, and during the season, farmers tend to work long hours. Off-season, farmers market crops, prepare fields, maintain and repair equipment, and do other household tasks; however, the farmers are often underemployed and search for other income-generating activities.

In some parts of the world, particularly Asia, the greater availability of irrigation regularly permits double-cropping. As indicated, more extensive use of irrigation tends to be limited by its cost. Large-scale irrigation tends to increase both the size of the cultivated surfaces and the yields per hectare. These changes, in turn, can contribute to significant income inequality and conflict for the rights to cultivate the irrigated land. In these cases, policymakers have to confront a trade-off between equity and efficiency.

Agriculture, particularly when dependent on direct rainfall, is highly risky. The quantity and timing of rains will clearly affect a farmer's yield per hectare. The overall impact of a changed harvest, whether an increase or decrease in output, depends on the size of the market and the number of producers affected.

In a highly integrated world market, local changes in the supply of output will have no consequences of significance for world-market supply. A poor cotton harvest in Chad, for instance, will have no real impact on the international price of cotton.

---

[10]Norton and Alwang, pages 201–203.

## FIGURE 11.1 PRODUCT PRICE INSTABILITY

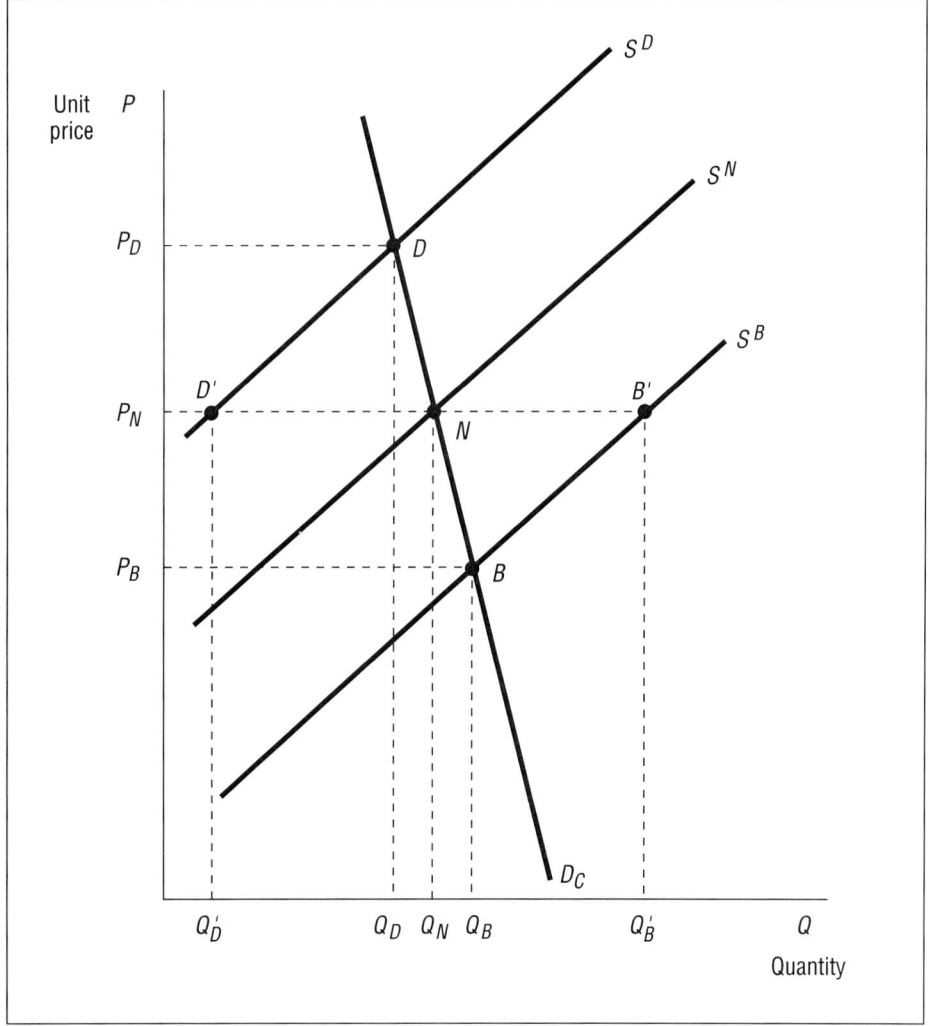

Product prices will be unchanged; only the local farmers' outputs will change. In a good year, the affected farmers will receive higher incomes; in a poor year, the farmers will experience income losses. For many export crops for which a country is a small supplier, market price is likely to be insensitive to local production. Crop diseases, pests, adverse rainfall patterns, and temperature changes can have relatively localized effects. Clearly, farmers may be subject to considerable income instability in integrated markets when their local production varies significantly.

In contrast, when local producers are an important or influential portion of the market for a product, as with local food crops, a good or bad harvest will shift market supply and affect both the equilibrium price and the quantity. In Figure 11.1, suppose a normal crop or harvest of corn results in a per unit price of $P_N$ and quantity $Q_N$ (point N). A particularly good or bumper crop will shift out the market supply to $S^B$; the price will fall to $P_B$; and the quantity will increase to $Q_B$ (point B). A particularly bad crop, as in a drought year, will shift in the market supply left to $S^D$; the price will rise to $P_D$; and the quantity will decrease to $Q_D$ (point $D$). The effect on farmers' total revenues in each of these cases depends on the price elasticity of demand.

In most instances, the demand for food and other primary products is price-inelastic; the change in quantity demanded is proportionately less than the change in price. With inelastic demand, total revenues will be higher in the drought year than in the normal year; the percentage increase in price exceeds the percentage decrease in quantity. In the bumper year, total revenues will fall when compared to the normal year.

Given that farmers' costs tend to be relatively constant in good and in bad harvests, programs to promote revenue stability have often appealed to farmers. Economists have advocated storage schemes that keep **buffer stocks** of grain or other products that are affected by supply instability. Assume that the use of a buffer stock is aimed at keeping prices and revenues stable at $P_N$ and $(P_N)(Q_N)$ in Figure 11.1. In bumper-crop years, authorities would purchase wheat and store it; they would purchase the excess supply at the normal price, the amount $NB'$ in Figure 11.1. Price would then rise up to $P_N$. In years of poor harvest, grain from the buffer stock would be sold to augment local supplies and maintain the normal price. They would sell a quantity equal to the excess demand at $P_N$, equal to the amount $D'N$. Price would then fall back to $P_N$.

Buffer schemes are not always effective, however. Often governments cannot afford the costs of maintaining and funding these storage programs. Poor storage practices can result in losses, leaving the government with insufficient grain to meet the shortages and excess demand of poor years. Finally, trying to maintain a "normal" price is very problematic. The normal price as viewed by consumers tends to be lower than the normal price as viewed by producers. Most important, over time, the normal price should fall, as increased production leads to lower, long-run food prices. Decreases in the accepted "normal" price will be resisted by farmers. Finally, when buffer-stock programs are international, involving more than a few nations, serious coordination problems can result. Disagreements concerning price targets and the cost sharing of crop storage hamper the smooth operation of international price stabilization efforts.

We now turn to the agricultural productivity gains that are associated with economic development.

## LONG-RUN TREND IN THE AGRICULTURAL TERMS OF TRADE

In this section we discuss the underlying factors behind changes in the market supply and demand for agricultural products. Significant increases in market supply have resulted from the rapid technological progress in agriculture during the post–1950 period. As indicated, the aggregation of this technological progress in the less developed countries has been referred to as the **Green Revolution.** Generally speaking, this revolution refers to the development of high-yielding seed varieties (corn, rice, and wheat, especially) that usually are most effective when accompanied by special fertilizers, pesticides, herbicides, and dependable water sources. The advantages of the Green Revolution are the significant increases in factor productivity (both land and labor) and the benefit to small farmers who, with a modest investment, reap the rewards of technological developments. Unlike technological progress in machinery (more efficient tractors or combines), which tends to increase the minimum efficient farm size, the use of the inputs of the Green Revolution does not necessarily lead to an increase in efficient farm size.

The Green Revolution has been particularly successful in raising the output of farmers in Asia. The World Bank reports

> More than 22 million hectares were brought under irrigation in South and Southeast Asia between 1966 and 1982, which raised the proportion of total irrigated agricultural land from about 20 percent to more than 28 percent. By the late 1970s, modern rice varieties covered 80 percent of the cultivated areas in China, more than 70 percent of the cultivated land in the Philippines and Sri Lanka, and more than 50 percent of such land in Indonesia and Pakistan. Modern varieties of wheat expanded to cover two-thirds of the total wheat area in India. Between 1966 and 1982, total fertilizer consumption increased more than sixfold in Southeast Asia and more than fourfold in South Asia.[11]

In Africa, the adoption of the tenets of the Green Revolution has been hindered by several factors. New seed varieties have not been as successfully developed for indigenous African crops such as millet and sorghum. More than the other continents, Africa has been plagued by periodic droughts in the last 20 years. These droughts not only reduce current output, but introduce greater uncertainty into the production process, making farmers more risk-averse and discouraging the adoption of new techniques. New agricultural inputs and processes must be properly explained by knowledgeable and credible agricultural extension workers. Often, however, African countries have not had effective agricultural extension programs. Agents are not well trained, and often have been given their positions as a political reward. Moreover, with high rates of illiteracy, written materials are not as useful in Africa.

A very important consideration in the introduction of new seed varieties is the proper use of complementary inputs. Unless the new seeds are combined with the proper fertilizers and pesticides, the output per unit of land can actually be lower than with more traditional techniques. Often these inputs are not available as a result of either government inefficiency in the delivery process or a lack of farmer credit to purchase them. For instance, as reported in Table 11.1, fertilizer consumption per hectare in the East Asia and Pacific region is now over 200 kilograms per hectare, in contrast with less than 15 kilograms in Africa. Farmers with a negative experience with a "portion" of the Green Revolution subsequently become resistant to technological progress. Clearly, to be effective the Green Revolution must be accompanied by competent agricultural extension services and the full complement of needed inputs.

Policymakers need to be sensitive to other concerns with the Green Revolution. First, the distribution of rural income may become more unequal if the improved techniques are not introduced to all of the farmers. Those without access to the benefits of the Green Revolution would particularly be disadvantaged if price decreases, triggered by increases in supply from the technological progress, lowered their revenues and profits. Thus, it is incumbent on policymakers that they ensure that all farmers have access to the new technology. Also, new technologies need to be tested for their environmental suitability. A pesticide or fertilizer that is environmentally safe in Asia may not have the same benign effects in parts of Africa.

In sum, the Green Revolution has the potential for being an engine of growth in the rural areas. Moreover, it can help developing countries transform the structure of their economies and move toward the relatively more intensive manufacturing and service-sector growth that characterizes developed economies.

---

[11]World Bank, *World Development Report 1986*, New York: Oxford University Press, 1986, page 78.

## THE INCOME-INELASTICITY OF FOOD

The nineteenth-century statistician Ernst Engel (1821–1896) observed that the share of food expenditures varied inversely with family income. Demand for food products increased proportionately less than any increase in income that families earned; therefore, the demand for food could be considered income-inelastic. Families tended to spend relatively more of any additional income on other goods, such as clothing and better housing, and the proportion of income spent on food declined.

A large proportion of the output of the rural sector is food or other commodities for which demand is income-inelastic. Thus, income growth coupled with supply increases can reduce the rural sector's terms of trade, lowering the ratio of prices received for farm goods to prices paid for manufacturing products. For instance, in Figure 11.2, if population growth and per capita income growth successively shift out the demand for food from $D_0$ to $D_1$ to $D_2$, while supply shifts out from $S_0$ to $S_1$ to $S_2$, the price for agricultural output will fall from $P_0$ to $P_1$ to $P_2$. In this case, the outward shift in demand, resulting from the growth in population and per capita income, is proportionately less than the outward shift in supply resulting from technological

**FIGURE 11.2**     THE DECLINING PRICE OF AGRICULTURAL OUTPUT

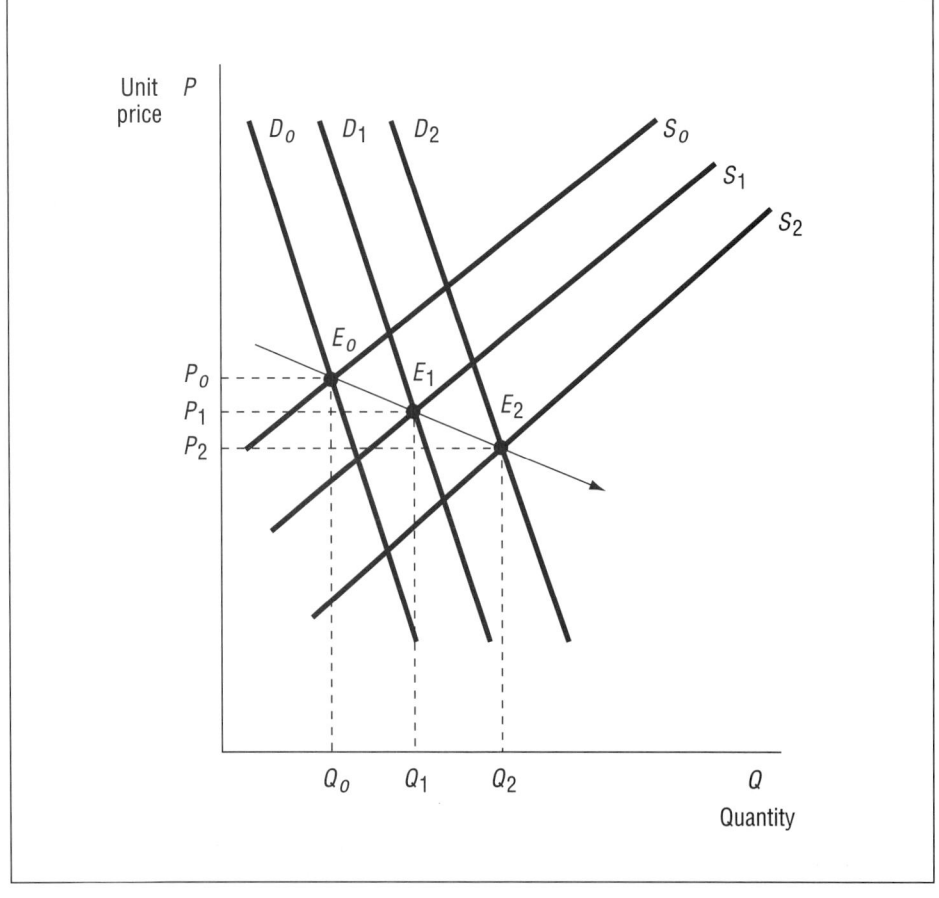

| TABLE 11.2 | WORLD COMMODITY PRICE INDEXES (1990 = 100) | | | | |
|---|---|---|---|---|---|
|  | 1975 | 1980 | 1985 | 1990 | 1992 |
| Total Agriculture | 185 | 193 | 151 | 100 | 85 |
| Timber | 62 | 129 | 94 | 100 | 112 |
| Metals and Minerals | 135 | 134 | 105 | 100 | 83 |
| Petroleum | 113 | 199 | 183 | 100 | 76 |

DEFINITIONS:
  Total Agriculture: total food and nonfood agricultural products
  Timber: logs
  Metals and Minerals: copper, tin, nickel, bauxite, aluminum, iron ore, lead, zinc, and phosphate rock.

SOURCE: World Resources Institute, *World Resources, 1994–95,* New York: Oxford University Press, 1994, Table 15.4.

improvement or an increased number of producers. A primary consequence of the income-inelasticity of food demand is that as a proportion of total output, agricultural output will decline with economic growth.

Since 1980 there has been a downward trend in world commodity prices for agricultural output (see Table 11.2). In contrast, world prices for timber and petroleum have tended to be more variable. With decreasing agricultural prices, both the domestic terms of trade and the international terms of trade will turn against agriculture. In fact, given the income-inelasticity of worldwide demand for most primary products, for developing countries relying on primary exports, the ratio of import prices to export prices will tend to fall over time. In other words, the country will have to export a greater quantity of primary products to import a given quantity of manufacturing products. After World War II, given the prospects of declining terms of trade, many developing countries pursued strategies aimed at rapid industrialization. Without comparative advantage in industrial output, however, the less developed countries were limiting their potential consumption and growth with their reduced participation in international trade.

To the extent that productivity gains in agriculture increase outputs, the effects of a decline in international terms of trade can be mitigated. Also, qualitative improvements in manufacturing goods may partially offset adverse changes in the LDCs' terms of trade. Nevertheless, the terms-of-trade consideration is a strong argument for developed countries to be open to the products of the developing countries. Any tariffs or other barriers to trade impose undue hardship on low-income countries that already confront a declining relative price for their primary exports. With more open markets, the high-income countries need to be willing to accept additional shifts of resources from agriculture to other economic activities. Unfortunately, as previously mentioned, powerful farm lobbies in the high-income countries have resisted imports of primary products. In fact, the farm lobbies have encouraged domestic agricultural support programs, as well as food-aid and export subsidies, to widen markets for surplus production. Predictably, during the recent Uruguay Round of GATT-sponsored trade talks, agricultural trade policy was a contentious issue.

In summary, developing agriculture in the Third World is a major challenge. Most farm households have a very small surface to cultivate; some households, particularly in Latin America, even lack access to an amount of land adequate for their own food needs. Moreover, the income-inelasticity of food demand places agriculture at a price disadvantage as rapid technological progress increases agricultural production.

## CONSTRAINTS TO AGRICULTURAL DEVELOPMENT

While varying across nations, key constraints to agricultural development confront a large percentage of Third World farmers. In this section, we shall consider the problem of land access and degradation; inappropriate pricing policies and incentives; and problems in the provision of inputs and credit. In the concluding section of this chapter, policy reforms to address these constraints are discussed.

### ACCESS TO FERTILE LAND

Throughout the developing world, as evidenced by the small size of most agricultural holdings, farmers face shortages of fertile land. Population growth and the degradation of land, two interrelated issues, contribute to this problem.

As indicated in Chapter 2, the average annual rate of population growth in the Third World is just under 2 percent, more than three times the rate in the high-income countries. With such population growth, demands for farm land increase as children mature and desire their own land. Clearly, limits exist to the subdividing of a given family plot. At some point, the continued subdividing compromises the economic viability of the resulting smaller farms. Particularly in Latin America, land shortages lead people to become day laborers, driving down the wages for agricultural labor. These lower rural wages intensify rural-to-urban migration. (Recall the migration model in Chapter 9: a decrease in the expected rural wage [or farm income] would increase the flow of migrants from the rural areas.) Finally, excessive population growth and land shortages often lead to deforestation and overcultivation, primary causes of the land degradation found in the Third World.

The Worldwatch Institute estimates that annually the earth's forest cover diminishes by 17 million hectares (an area the size of Austria) and that the annual loss of topsoil from cropland is 24 billion tons (the amount on Australia's wheatland). In the last 25 years, the world's deserts have expanded by some 120 million hectares (more than the cultivated land in China).[12] This degradation has occurred in both the developed and the developing countries. Deforestation is a major problem in Latin America, Africa, and parts of Asia; for example, the expansion of the Sahara desert has hindered agriculture in West Africa. Developing countries can least afford the environmental destruction that results from overcultivation, inadequate crop rotation, and the overcutting of trees. Reduced population growth and a better stewardship of resources are vitally needed to address the environmental damage of the last few decades. (We will return to these issues in Chapter 12.)

---

[12]Lester R. Brown, *State of the World 1991*, Worldwatch Institute, New York: W. W. Norton, 1991, pages 3 and 7.

## AGRICULTURAL PRICING POLICY

Providing incentives to agricultural producers is a necessary condition for the development of agriculture and the raising of rural living standards. Unfortunately, few of the less developed countries have consistently provided farmers with appropriate price incentives. In a landmark study of agricultural price policy in developing countries, the World Bank observed:

> Industrial and developing countries treat agriculture in very different ways. Industrial countries generally intervene to raise agricultural prices; developing countries tend to intervene to reduce prices below their international level. Because agriculture is usually the largest single economic sector in many developing countries, agricultural price policies have become a major instrument for influencing the economy. For that reason, agricultural price policies often have different objectives, many of which may be conflicting and few of which may be explicitly stated. These include encouraging food production to reduce food imports and achieve self-sufficiency, stabilizing food prices for producers or reducing them for urban consumers, generating revenue for the government by taxing the sector, increasing foreign exchange reserves by encouraging exports, and making raw materials available to the industrial sector at prices lower than would otherwise prevail.[13]

It should not be surprising that the rural sector is exploited for varying economic purposes. As previously discussed, in the second phase of the transformation of agriculture, governments have often taxed the agricultural sector to transfer resources to industrial activities. Often this taxation is indirect, aimed at raising the profitability of industry and concurrently reducing the profitability of agriculture. In other cases, the taxation is not intended to adversely affect agriculture; rather, governments are simply raising general budgetary revenues from a major sector of the economy.

Examples of the indirect taxation of domestic agriculture include official producer prices that are lower than their world-market equivalent **farm gate prices;** taxes levied on agricultural exports; overvalued currencies; subsidies provided to food imports; and sales of food aid to the general public.[14] In each of these cases, there occurs a negative impact on the profitability of domestic agriculture and a deterioration of the internal terms of trade between agriculture and industry. The agricultural sector is at a disadvantage with these "distorted" prices when compared to world-market prices. The farmers will receive a lower producer price and, given an upward-sloping, short-run supply curve, will, therefore, reduce their output. Total revenues clearly fall with both a lower price and lower output.

On occasion, to increase the profitability of agriculture, countries have supported farmers with direct producer subsidies for crops or with tariffs that raise the price of imported substitutes. A **subsidy** is accorded when the official producer price exceeds

---

[13]Schiff, Maurice and Alberto Valdes, *The Political Economy of Agricultural Pricing Policy, Volume 4: A Synthesis of the Economics in Developing Countries*, published for the World Bank, Baltimore: Johns Hopkins University Press, 1992, page 3. Other volumes in this very helpful five-volume study include *Volume 1: Latin America; Volume 2: Asia;* and *Volume 3: Africa and the Mediterranean,* all edited by Anne O. Krueger, Maurice Schiff, and Alberto Valdes. Also see Anne O. Krueger, *Volume 5: A Synthesis of the Political Economy in Developing Countries.*

[14]The local *farm gate price* is derived by subtracting local transportation costs from the world market price of the product landed as an import in a major consumption center within the country.

its farm gate equivalent. A tariff on an imported substitute will increase the demand for the local product, increasing both the market price and quantity. With both subsidies and tariffs, the total revenues of farmers will increase.

We now consider how these methods of taxation affect domestic production. With **official producer prices** that are lower than world-market prices, governments can directly profit by purchasing a crop at one price and reselling at a premium. Governments will make a profit on this operation as long as the price differential exceeds the per-unit transactions and storage costs associated with the sales. To increase their profit margins and resulting revenues, governments may increase the consumer prices of the food products that they purchase above the import price.

In order to pay lower-than-farm-gate prices, governments must be able to maintain a legal "monopsony" (that is, act as a sole buyer of output) on the marketing of the crop. Typically, producer marketing boards exist, and farmers are legally obliged to sell to these boards. In response to a lower official producer price, farmers will reduce their output of the crop, reallocating land and labor to other crops or, in the extreme, giving up farming altogether. To the extent that an official producer price exceeds the world-market price, a subsidy is accorded producers and they will increase their output. In this case, the government must be prepared to sell output at a loss, or unwanted surpluses of output will accumulate.

An **export tax** is a per-unit levy on the volume of output destined for export. For example, if the producers of coffee in a small country face a demand for their coffee that is perfectly elastic at the world-market price of $1.80 per pound, a $.15 per pound export tax lowers the producer price to $1.65 per pound, reducing farmer output.

An **overvalued currency** serves as an "indirect" tax on exporters. Consider a country like Chad, which exports a small amount of cotton, at a given world-market price expressed in dollars. Assume that the world-market price of cotton is $2 per bale and that the domestic producer price in Chad is 800 CFA (Currency unit of Francaphone Africa) per bale of cotton. At an overvalued exchange rate of 300 CFA per dollar, Chad's exports of cotton would cost $2.67 and not be competitive in the world market. Now, assume that the equilibrium exchange rate were 400 CFA per dollar; at this rate Chad could export cotton at the world price of $2.00. Thus, with an overvalued currency a small country will export less output and have reduced export earnings.

An **import subsidy** on a commodity that is competitive (a substitute good) with a locally-produced commodity will reduce the demand for local production. The availability of **food aid** at low prices will also reduce the demand for local food crops. In both cases, the price of the local commodity falls, as does the quantity produced, reducing farmers' total revenues. In contrast, if food aid were provided to the very poor, who would not otherwise be significant demanders of food since they lack the ability to pay for food, the negative impact on domestic producer prices would be less pronounced.

Fortunately, not all countries are net taxers of the rural sector. The World Bank reports that in the late 1970s and 1980s, countries pursued a variety of price policies with respect to the agricultural sector.[15] Côte d'Ivoire, for instance, used marketing boards and low producer prices to tax cocoa, an export crop, as a source of government funding. In contrast, to promote domestic rice production with an aim of reducing rice imports, the Côte d'Ivoire subsidized domestic rice production. Similarly, Korea heavily supported its domestic wheat and rice producers. On balance, more countries—particularly those in Africa—taxed agriculture products than granted producer

---

[15]World Bank, *World Development Report 1986*, pages 64–65.

support or subsidy. As a general rule, however, economic efficiency will be improved when both producer prices and exchange rates are at equilibrium levels.

## Example of the Use of Price Policy

As indicated from the discussion above, the pricing of agricultural products can be used to achieve different objectives. In this example, we first show a country that, with an equilibrium exchange rate, is a rice exporter. We then show this country operating with an overvalued exchange rate and becoming a rice importer in order to lower the consumer rice price. Finally, we show a pricing scheme that combines the efficiency of market prices with a concern for equity.

Consider a country that grows rice, a crop that is also traded internationally. The domestic demand for rice $(D_d)$ and the supply of rice by domestic producers $(S_d)$ is shown in Figure 11.3. In the absence of any trade, the domestic price will be $P_o$. With an equilibrium exchange rate, the world market price of rice, expressed in the domestic currency, is $P_w$. This country now becomes an exporter of rice. Domestic production is equal to $Q_s$, with domestic quantity demanded of only $Q_d$; the difference, $DS$ or $Q_s - Q_d$ is the quantity exported. Export revenues would equal $(P_w)(Q_s - Q_d)$. While producers increase their total revenues with these exports, domestic consumers, many of whom live in urban areas, pay a higher price for rice, since $P_w$ is greater than $P_o$.

As a means to subsidize imports and reduce its general price level, the country could use an overvalued currency. In this case, the world price of rice, expressed in the domestic currency, will be lower, say $P_w'$ in Figure 11.3. Let us assume that the government only pays farmers $P_f$. In this case domestic quantity demanded will be $Q_d'$ and domestic production will be $Q_f$; the country now imports a quantity of rice equal to $W'D'$ or $Q_d' - Q_f$. Import payments will equal $(P_w')(Q_d' - Q_f)$, but the government earns profits (tax revenues) on the sale of domestically produced rice equal to $(P_d - P_f)(Q_f)$. With this overvalued currency, the country's balance of trade deteriorates as it moves from being an exporter of rice to being an importer of rice. Farmers' revenues decrease from $(P_w)(Q_s)$ to $(P_f)(Q_f)$. With the lower consumer price of a basic food item, the urban real wage increases, being subsidized by farmers.

The government could consider a third pricing option that combines a concern for both efficiency and equity. To increase efficiency, the exchange rate returns to its equilibrium level, leading to a domestic producer price of $P_w$; domestic farmers then produce $Q_s$. To address the equity concern, the government purchases a certain quantity of rice, $DG$ or $Q_g - Q_d$ at the price $P_w$, for resale to the poor at the price $P_d$. At this price there will be excess demand equal to $N'D'$, and the government will have to introduce some form of rationing. The cost to the government of this food subsidy will be $(P_w - P_d)(Q_g - Q_d)$. Domestic rice consumption will then equal $Q_g$, or the quantity purchased in the market by consumers $(Q_d)$ plus the quantity redistributed $Q_g - Q_d$. The country exports the quantity $Q_s - Q_g$ so export earnings are equal to that quantity multiplied by the export price $P_w$.

With this pricing scheme domestic farmers receive the same total revenues $(P_w)(Q_s)$ as in the first option. The urban poor benefit as they pay the lower food price, $P_d$, of option two. However, unsubsidized consumers pay the higher price $(P_w)$ of option one. The trade balance is less than in option one but is greater than in option two when the country becomes a rice importer. Finally, unlike option two with a budget surplus, the government has a budget deficit since it subsidizes rice.

This discussion of price policy has shown that different groups within a society—consumers, producers, and taxpayers—will have different preferences with respect to food

## FIGURE 11.3 PRICING POLICY OPTIONS

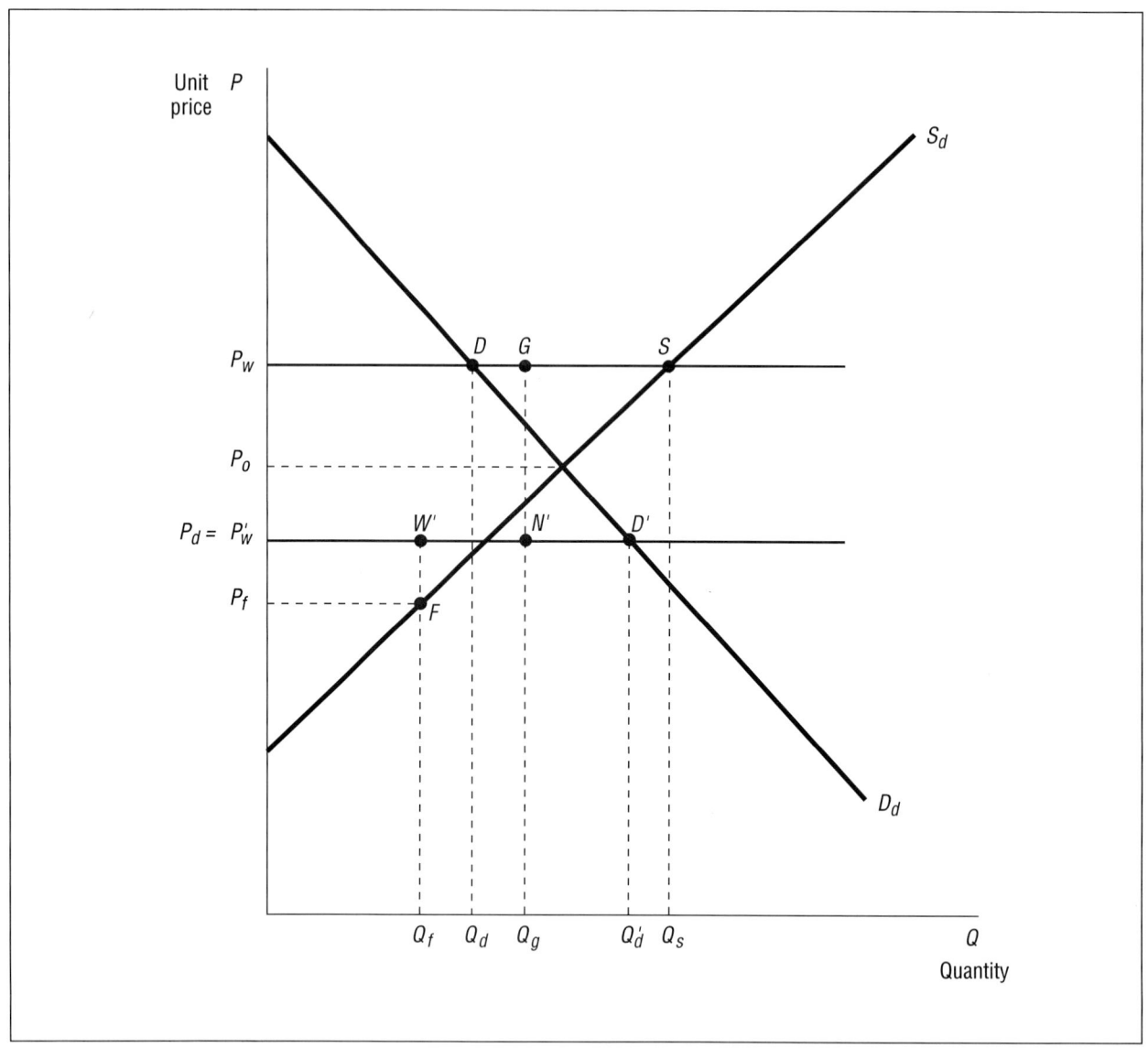

prices. Given the relative importance of food in developing countries, issues of price policy will be contentious, challenging governments to balance efficiency and equity.

### AVAILABILITY OF INPUTS AND CREDIT

Given the seasonal nature of agriculture, both the timely delivery of inputs and access to credit are vital to successful production. The key issues associated with inputs are their suitability, availability, and affordability. The Green Revolution has been very successful in developing high-yielding seed varieties with a complement of other inputs. Yet, for some parts of the world, particularly areas subject to drought, more appropriate seeds, fertilizers, pesticides, and herbicides still need to be developed. Local research agencies need to allocate additional resources to the development of appropriate technologies. Moreover, extension agents must be trained to explain the new methods to farmers who may initially be skeptical.

On-farm storage at the village level is also an input into the production and marketing of food. Often storage losses are high, due to spoilage from exposure and pests. Better storage methods could reduce losses in much of the developing world. Also, village-level storage schemes, where small warehouses are constructed, with each farmer being allocated a slot, could be profitable. To be successful, however, such village schemes must be operated honestly and efficiently or farmers will quickly be alienated.

Inputs must be available at critical times in the agricultural process. The absence of a key input can result in a significant reduction in yield per hectare. Government agencies have frequently been used to supply inputs to farmers. While often offering inputs at subsidized prices, the government delivery networks have not always provided a sufficient quantity of inputs at the appropriate time in the production process. Competitive private-sector input delivery offers a greater opportunity for timely delivery in many cases. Frequently, however, in more remote rural areas, input prices are higher due both to the absence of competition and the higher transport costs.

Finally, inputs must be affordable. An input should be used as long as its marginal benefit to production exceeds its marginal cost. Often, this calculation is difficult to make for fertilizers and other inputs. Farmers may tend to underestimate the marginal benefits of pesticides and herbicides, particularly when they are relatively expensive. To ensure that profitable inputs are used, agricultural credit should be available.

Farmers throughout the world tend to borrow working capital at planting time to purchase needed inputs and then to repay following the sale of the crops at harvest. In much of the Third World, for reasons discussed in the previous chapter, effective financial intermediation does not exist in rural areas. While there is some intravillage lending in times of hardship, a predictable source of farm credit at planting time does not always exist. Seed is often borrowed, as it can be more easily repaid following the harvest. Financial credit to purchase other inputs is often available only at very high rates of interest. Developing countries, themselves short on domestic savings, have not succeeded in making credit available to a significant percentage of farmers.

Having reviewed the main characteristics and constraints of agriculture in the contemporary developing countries, we now turn to the critical issue of policy reform.

## POLICY REFORM

The specific policy reforms that offer the greatest promise for agricultural development may vary across the developing countries. Nevertheless, common themes characterize these policy initiatives: clear government objectives with respect to agriculture; greater access to land; increased profitability of agriculture; and enhanced quality of life in rural areas.

## CLEAR POLICY OBJECTIVES

Often countries have not had clear policy objectives for agriculture. International donor agencies frequently contribute to this policy confusion. For instance, a country, despite the high domestic cost of growing food, may have a stated policy of food self-sufficiency. At the same time, it neglects the production of a potential export product, such as peanuts or cotton, in which it has a comparative advantage. In such a case, the country could more cheaply acquire food through international trade—by exporting peanuts or cotton and importing food. The reality, however, is often that a country wants to be food self-sufficient, neither dependent on the external world for basic food items, nor concerned about having the foreign exchange to import food.

In discussing the pursuit of food self-sufficiency the World Bank reports:

> Substantial gains from trade can be forgone in its pursuit. Such losses were evident in China when each province aimed to become self-sufficient in food grains. The same losses can occur if a country restricts trade in world markets. Take the case of Sri Lanka, where research spending, pricing policies, input subsidies, and investment in irrigation have all been geared to achieving self-sufficiency in rice. Many components of the effort were appropriate, but, from an economic point of view, the policies may have been pushed too far.... the high cost of self-sufficiency has often been underwritten by grants or concessionary loans from donors. Taken in isolation, many components of each country's policies may have been logical. Taken together, however, they add up to a bias against a well-integrated world agriculture capable of capturing the full benefits from trade.[16]

Countries can also receive conflicting advice from donors about rural development. For instance, one international development agency may be promoting growth through trade, by an importing of food when trade is a cheaper means to acquire food, while another agency may be promoting food self-sufficiency. In attempting to satisfy both agencies, an incoherent policy results. Other times, as a legacy from colonialism, countries continue to produce cash crops (even in the absence of a comparative advantage for the product) for export to the detriment of food crops for the domestic market.

In general, a departure from production with specialization according to world market prices should only be done when there are clear benefits to justify such departures. For instance, a food-importing country might have long-run comparative advantage in food production if proper technologies were used. In this case, some policy to protect, temporarily, domestic food production could be justified. A coherent agricultural policy is a precondition for a country to have credible and successful agricultural development.

## LAND ACCESS

Our discussion of land access has pointed to some clear policy recommendations. First, a reduced rate of population growth would mitigate the pressures on land found in many, if not most, of the less developed countries. Education and expanded opportunities for women are key components of a strategy to reduce population growth.

---

[16]World Bank, *World Development Report 1986,* page 78.

Second, land reclamation measures, including the protection of forests and better crop rotation practices, would slow the deterioration of agricultural lands. For instance, in Mexico, poor Indian farmers near the Guatemalan border have been working with the government to address the significant local deforestation caused by excessive cultivation and overgrazing by ranchers. Their efforts have culminated in a program of sustainable agriculture that stresses natural fertilizers, reforestation, and the promoting of nonfarming income activities.[17] Key ingredients of this program are community involvement and continual dialogue with the government, as well as the recognition that if some agricultural practices are to be limited (cultivation without sufficient fallow time and tree cutting), some other income-generating activities must be substituted (sale of forest products and of local animals and hides).

Land reform, particularly in Latin America, could achieve a more equitable access to land among rural inhabitants. As discussed, such land transfers could actually increase total output and employment, given the relatively more efficient and intensive use of land by smaller farmers. Finally, secure land titles would give farmers the incentive to make investments in land, instilling confidence that the land will not be confiscated and that they will reap the longer-run economic gains from such investments.

## INCREASING THE PROFITABILITY OF AGRICULTURE

The above discussion of agriculture has identified several areas where governments can contribute to increasing the profitability of agriculture and making rural life more attractive: price policy; credit; infrastructure, health, education, and research; agricultural extension; full employment in the off-season; and opportunities for women.

### PRICE POLICY

Appropriate price policy is a major ingredient to successful agricultural development. Agricultural output should not be taxed directly with export duties or indirectly with overvalued currencies. Moreover, import subsidies for food products and the extensive, regular use of food aid should be avoided lest domestic producer prices be reduced. Also, the developed countries should avoid export subsidies that can depress domestic prices in the LDCs. To encourage developing countries to use market prices to signal resource allocation, the developed countries must be willing to import more agricultural commodities. Quotas, tariffs, and other barriers to free trade often prevent developing countries from specializing according to comparative advantage—and from increasing their consumption possibilities through trade. For example, the United States has restricted lower-cost imports of sugar, peanuts, and beef from developing countries.

### CREDIT

Small producers have continual problems receiving credit for seeds and inputs at reasonable rates of interest. While the direct subsidizing of credit can be problematic, governments should encourage financial intermediation in rural areas. Cooperatives and

---

[17]United Nations Development Programme, *Human Development Report 1993*, page 85.

small banks that earn the confidence and trust of rural residents could succeed in receiving deposits from savers and loaning these funds to farmers. The example of the Grameen Bank in Bangladesh (in Chapter 10) may be emulated in other developing countries.

### INFRASTRUCTURE, HEALTH, EDUCATION, AND RESEARCH

Often the absence of good roads and other rural infrastructure interferes with both the timely delivery of inputs and the marketing of crops. A direct cost of inadequate transportation is higher transactions costs that both lower the effective price received by producers for their output and raise the delivered price of inputs, thereby reducing agricultural profits. The lack of effective transportation reduces the integration of rural and urban areas, isolating rural residents. An improved transportation network will also benefit the urban industrial sector. Food prices will be lower in urban areas and manufactured goods will be cheaper in rural areas.

Other infrastructure investments in education and health care can increase the productivity of rural residents and improve their quality of life. With these improvements, a reduction will occur in the rural-to-urban migration generated simply by the desire to avoid the hardships of rural life. Also, over time, these investments should contribute to reduced population growth.

Continued research into appropriate technology, seed varieties, and other complementary inputs is needed. For instance, risk-averse farmers in West Africa might find drought-resistant varieties more helpful than slightly higher-yielding, but more rain-dependent, varieties. New techniques and capital equipment that are appropriate for small farms are still needed. Ideally, new equipment would increase productivity by complementing labor effort during times of peak labor demand—planting and harvesting. Equipment that displaces labor in the production process is not apt to be cost-effective at market-equilibrium input prices. Moreover, such mechanization will increase minimum efficient farm size, leaving more households landless.

Research into better use of groundwater supplies and smaller-scale irrigation can lead to both production increases and a reduction in drought-related instability of output. As previously indicated, large-scale irrigation can be very expensive and disruptive to community life. Intermediate technologies do exist; the task is to refine and then to introduce them where profitable. Greater use of natural organic fertilizers and biogasification (the use of energy stored in crop residues) are examples of potentially profitable new technologies that are appropriate for many developing countries. The successful introduction of any new input or technology, however, requires competent agricultural extension.

### AGRICULTURAL EXTENSION

Agricultural extension services, particularly in Africa and Latin America, have been relatively ineffective. Frequently, research stations grow crops with only slightly modified traditional methods, yet obtain two to three times greater yields per hectare than farmers in neighboring villages. The inability to transfer the improved techniques to local farmers is a very costly failure.

Good agricultural extension should include five elements:

*1.* Individual agents should be credible and knowledgeable about farming. Gaining the trust of local people is an absolute precondition for effective agricultural extension. Training agents from the same region and same ethnic group can contribute to credibility and trust.

2. The benefits, costs, and risks of new techniques should be carefully explained to farmers. Any deception of farmers can compromise future credibility, which, once lost, is very difficult to regain. Experimenting with some type of subsidized crop insurance for innovative farmers who use the full complement of new inputs may be an appropriate way to reduce the risk to farmer income.
3. Agricultural extension should include some ideas for dry-season income-generating activities.
4. Education and health improvements should be incorporated into agricultural extension services, assuming that the additional tasks do not compromise the basic mission of the agents. For instance, the merits of basic literacy and sanitation practices could be reinforced by the agricultural extension agents.
5. Considering that women are heavily involved in farming in less developed countries, training female extension agents may be a very effective way of disseminating knowledge.

### Promoting Full Employment in the Off-Season

An imaginative approach to rural development using traditional village work groups has been launched in Burkina Faso. "Groupements Naam," with the motto "development without damage," organizes additional agricultural efforts in the rainy season, such as vegetable gardens and communal fields with traditional crops such as millet and peanuts. Proceeds from these common efforts are shared by participating members. Of particular interest are the activities undertaken in the dry season, when families have few income-earning opportunities. From textiles to soap-making, a range of projects contributes to increasing household incomes. Also, community work, including road repair, forestation projects, and building water-storage facilities, are aimed at improving rural living standards.[18] Projects of this nature using local labor and local resources should be encouraged to supplement and to complement traditional farming.

### Opportunities for Women

All studies of labor utilization in rural areas demonstrate the extraordinarily high labor contribution of females. In addition to assuming nearly all household tasks—cooking, cleaning, and washing—women are actively engaged in farming. Often, agricultural tasks are apportioned according to gender with differences across societies. In Africa, women are more often engaged in small-scale vegetable gardening and rice cultivation. Men are more engaged in producing the basic food staple, millet or sorghum, and the cash crops. In Asia, women may be more engaged in cash crops, as men try to supplement income with off-farm day labor at larger farms or in other capacities. In all cases, women's contributions to the agricultural production process are vital.

Unfortunately, rural development programs have tended to be aimed more at males and their income-generating activities. Programs to enhance female opportunities, and particularly labor-saving innovations, have been less prevalent. In recent years, international development agencies have become more aware of the contributions and burdens of females in the rural areas and have been designing programs that either include females or are directed exclusively at females. Often these efforts are aimed at women in both rural and urban areas. Such programs can include special saving and credit cooperatives for women; marketing outlets for goods produced by

---

[18]Ibid., page 94.

females; legal services for women; and lobbying for changes in the laws and government policies that discriminate against women.[19] Women are generally receptive to participating in projects. For example, in a review of projects in the Côte d'Ivoire, the World Bank concluded that women were more receptive than men to the introduction of new farming methods.[20]

Many of the above policy recommendations, such as pricing policy reform and infrastructure investment, will be costly and resisted by urban consumers, who wish to pay neither higher food prices nor higher taxes. High-income countries and international development agencies have an obligation to support developing-nation governments as they implement difficult initiatives.

## CONCLUDING NOTE

We have shown the importance of agriculture both as a provider of employment and as a key sector in sustaining economic development. Much remains to be done if agriculture is to reach its potential within the contemporary developing countries. Governments need to create a policy environment in which rural-sector activities will be more profitable and self-generating. With successful agricultural development, living standards will rise, opportunities for women will increase, and population growth should slow. As the development process continues, manufacturing and services increase in relative importance. In Chapter 13 we turn to an analysis of these two sectors. In the next chapter, natural resources and the environment are addressed.

## SUMMARY OF MAIN POINTS

1. With a majority of the Third World living in rural areas, the agricultural sector must be developed successfully to promote modern-sector growth. Increasing agricultural productivity frees labor for industrial growth and increases rural purchasing power. Moreover, growth in the production of agricultural commodities is needed to feed the expanding urban labor force. Also, many developing countries depend on the export of primary commodities to earn foreign exchange.

2. The transformation of the agricultural sector has been characterized as a movement through different stages. The first phase is the transition from subsistence agriculture; generating an agricultural surplus to support nonagricultural activities is a precondition for this change. In the second phase, governments often intervene in

---

[19]A review of some efforts on behalf of women can be found in United Nations Development Programme, "People in Community Organizations," Chapter 5, *Human Development Report 1993*, pages 84–99.

[20]Carrington, Tim, "In Developing World, International Lenders Are Targeting Women," *Wall Street Journal* (June 22, 1994), page A1.

the agricultural sector, taxing farm output to support industrial activities. The third phase is characterized by a relatively high level of mechanization and an integration of the agricultural and industrial sectors.
3. Most Third World farmers can be considered household producers who allocate land, labor, and other inputs to maximize their economic profits. Latin America illustrates a greater incidence of large-scale plantation agriculture. In these circumstance landholdings are unequally distributed and often inefficiently used. Many rural residents are landless and become day laborers on the large plantations. In countries with a high degree of inequality in land ownership, carefully designed land-reform programs have the potential to increase both efficiency and equity.
4. Agriculture is subject to significant production risk. The actual impact on a farmer from output variation depends on the size of the market. In a smaller local market, for example, price changes that are inversely related to the output change lead to revenues and income that are more stable than when the farmer is part of a larger market whose price is not affected by output changes in the local area. Buffer stock schemes can be used to try to stabilize revenues.
5. The long-run trend is for declining terms of trade for the agricultural sector. Production increases resulting from the Green Revolution and the income-inelastic nature of commodity demand lead to declining real prices for agricultural output.
6. Many developing countries have pursued agricultural pricing policies aimed at taxing the rural sector. Combining to benefit the urban consumer, but reduce the profitability of agriculture are low official producer prices; export taxes on farm commodities; overvalued currencies that reduce export demand; and subsidies on imported food.
7. Third World governments must commit themselves to policy reform aimed at improving incomes and living standards in the rural areas where a large proportion of their populations work.
8. While each country's agricultural constraints vary, the basic elements to a policy reform package can be identified: programs to ensure greater access to land for farmers; market-pricing for agricultural commodities to increase producer incentives; provision of credit in those areas not served by competitive commercial lenders; research into appropriate production technologies; competent agricultural extension; and rural health and educational initiatives.

## KEY TERMS

**buffer stocks**
**export tax**
**farm gate price**
**food aid**
**Green Revolution**
**import subsidy**
**latifundias**

**minifundias**
**mixed agriculture**
**official producer prices**
**overvalued currency**
**subsidy**
**subsistence agriculture**

## QUESTIONS

1. Choose a developing country. Research its agricultural sector and place its position in the transformation of agriculture. Discuss the major constraints facing the development of the country's rural sector.

2. Show how the impacts of increased food-aid deliveries on rural-sector development can vary depending on the assumptions made concerning the performance of a country's agricultural sector.
3. Discuss all the negative impacts from taxing agriculture to subsidize urban consumers.
4. Why do you think that developed countries, like France and Japan, heavily subsidize agriculture, while developing countries, like Mali and Kenya, have taxed their agricultural sectors? *(Hint:* Consider both political and economic influences in your answer.)
5. Choose two developing countries from different continents. Compare them based on the following criteria:
   a. importance of their agricultural sector
   b. average farm size and its variation
   c. principal crops
   d. agricultural price policy and the openness of the economy to trade
   e. degree of government intervention into agriculture
   f. principal constraints and prospects for agriculture
6. Assume that the domestic demand and supply schedules for rice in a developing country are given by:

$$Q^d = 50 - 6P \quad \text{and} \quad Q^s = -10 + 4P$$

where the quantities demanded and supplied are in millions of bushels and the unit price $P$ is in rupees per bushel. Assume that the developing nation is a price-taker on the world market for rice, and that the world price for rice is $.70 per bushel.
   a. If the equilibrium exchange rate is $1.00 = 10 rupees:
      Find the domestic quantities demanded and supplied of rice under free trade.
      Calculate the export revenues (import payments) in both dollars and rupees.
      Calculate the total revenues of domestic rice farmers and total expenditures for domestic consumers of rice in rupees.
   b. If the government of the developing nation is maintaining an overvalued exchange rate of $1.00 = 8 rupees, and controls the price paid to domestic rice farmers at 5 rupees per bushel:
      Given that the government purchases all the rice supplied by domestic farmers at 5 rupees per bushel and resells the rice to domestic consumers at the world price under the overvalued exchange rate, find the domestic quantities demanded and supplied.
      Calculate the export revenues (or import payments) in both dollars and rupees.
      Calculate the total revenues of domestic rice farmers and total expenditures of domestic consumers of rice in rupees.
      Calculate the revenues collected by the government.
   c. If the government devalues the domestic currency to restore the equilibrium exchange rate of $1.00 = 10 rupees and allows the domestic rice farmers to receive the world price for rice, and then purchases 4 million bushels of rice from the domestic farmers at the world price to resell to the poor households in the nation at the previously subsidized domestic price found in Question 6b:
      Find the domestic quantities demanded and supplied of rice.
      Calculate the export revenues (import payments) in both dollars and rupees.
      Calculate the total revenues of domestic rice farmers and total expenditures of domestic consumers of rice in rupees.

Calculate the cost of the government rice subsidy program in rupees.
*d.* Discuss the three options (a,b,c) in terms of the impacts on the developing nation's balance of trade and government budget and in terms of the impacts on domestic rice farmers, urban consumers, and the poor.

## SUGGESTED READINGS

Norton, George W. and Jeffrey Alwang, *Introduction to Economics of Agricultural Development,* New York: McGraw-Hill, 1993.

Schultz, Theodore W., *Transforming Traditional Agriculture,* New Haven: Yale University Press, 1964.

World Bank, *World Development Report 1986,* New York: Oxford University Press, 1986.

---

## CASE STUDY

### COSTA RICA

Costa Rica, a notable exception among Latin American countries, is a strong democracy with no standing army. With a well-educated labor force and a comprehensive system of social security and public services, the country also has a relatively equal distribution of income. As a result, Costa Rica's social indicators in the 1990s rank high when compared to those of 19 other Latin American nations. Costa Rica has the highest life expectancy (along with Cuba), the lowest infant mortality rate (along with Cuba and Jamaica), and the fifth lowest adult illiteracy rate.[1]

Christopher Columbus discovered Costa Rica in 1502, and Spain ruled the territory as a colony until 1821. Because the colony lacked gold and silver deposits, most settlers established self-sufficient farms and engaged in subsistence agriculture. Coffee exports stimulated economic growth after Costa Rica gained independence. Unable to satisfy the increasing demand for Costa Rican coffee in Europe and North America, coffee plantation owners had to buy coffee from smaller producers to meet their export contracts. They also had to pay high wages to farm laborers, who had the alternative of farming unsettled land. The mutual interdependence among the large exporters, the small growers, and the plantation workers contributed to a sharing of coffee revenues. These relationships were institutionalized in 1933 when the government established a Coffee Board to set the prices that the large exporters paid to the smaller producers.[2]

---

[1] The 19 Latin American nations considered (with populations of one million or more) are Argentina, Bolivia, Brazil, Chile, Colombia, Cuba, Dominican Republic, Ecuador, El Salvador, Guatemala, Haiti, Honduras, Jamaica, Mexico, Panama, Paraguay, Peru, Uruguay, and Venezuela. Life expectancy and infant mortality rates are compared for 1993 (except for Cuba and Haiti, whose infant mortality rates are for 1992). Adult illiteracy rates are compared for 1990. All figures, excluding the infant mortality rates of Cuba and Haiti, are from the World Bank, *World Development Report 1995,* New York: Oxford University Press, 1995, Table 1, Table 10, and Table 27. The infant mortality rates of Cuba and Haiti are from the United Nations Development Programme, *Human Development Report 1994,* New York: Oxford University Press, 1994, Table 11.

[2] Claudio González-Vega and Víctor Hugo Céspedes, "Costa Rica," in *The Political Economy of Poverty, Equity, and Growth: Costa Rica and Uruguay,* Simon Rottenberg, ed., New York: Oxford University Press, 1993, pages 62–66.

Bananas were second to coffee in generating export revenues. The multinational United Fruit Company started growing bananas on the Atlantic coast and first exported them in 1878. Another multinational corporation entered the banana trade in 1956, with two more following in 1965. Domestic producers sold their bananas to the multinationals at prices fixed by long-term contracts. By 1975, the domestic producers were supplying 41 percent of the bananas exported.[3] A long history of labor strikes culminated in the multinationals' abandonment of banana production in the 1980s. Leaving such production to domestic firms, the foreign companies began growing less labor-intensive pineapples and African oil palms on their former banana plantations.

The National Production Council (NPC) was created in 1943 to promote the production and stabilize the prices of staples such as rice, corn, sorghum, and beans. The NPC stimulated production by setting minimum prices for producers and purchasing the quantities supplied at those prices. It stabilized consumer prices by setting maximum prices at which it sold the staples in the domestic market. When producer prices were set higher than consumer prices, the resulting NPC deficits were financed by the profits of the state-owned liquor monopoly and credit from the Central Bank.[4]

In general, for rice and corn, producer-support prices set above international prices generated surpluses that the NPC exported at a loss. The NPC incurred additional losses when it sold rice and corn to domestic consumers at prices below the support price. The NPC typically had to import beans and sorghum to offset domestic shortages. As the sole legal importer of these staples, it earned a profit by selling sorghum to domestic consumers at a price above the international price and incurred a loss by selling beans to domestic consumers at a price below the international price.

Elected in 1940, a reformist administration favored greater government intervention in the economy. Besides creating the NPC, it enacted labor legislation and introduced a progressive income tax. The administration also created a social security system to provide benefits for sickness, maternity, work-related injuries, disability, and old age.[5]

Mounting opposition to the reformist group's alliance with the antidemocratic Communist Party and the group's annulment of the election of the opposition candidate in 1948 led to civil war. After winning the war in six weeks, the opposition forces abolished the Costa Rican army and promised to hold free and open elections. Continuing to increase the government's role in the economy, the new leaders nationalized the banking system; granted control of power generation, telecommunications, and the Pacific Railway to autonomous government institutions; undertook investments to develop highways and roads; and initiated the expansion of publicly provided services, including secondary education, health care, water supply, sewage disposal, and electricity.

Reacting to fluctuations in the international prices of bananas and coffee, policy-makers pursued a strategy of import-substitution industrialization (ISI) in the late 1950s in an attempt to develop the economy's manufacturing base. Costa Rica, however, was not able to establish as strong a protective barrier against imported manufactured products as did larger nations like Argentina and Brazil. Powerful agricultural exporters opposed the use of tariffs, quotas, and manufacturing subsidies. Costa Rica's

---

[3] Ibid., page 137.
[4] Ibid., page 116.
[5] John Sheahan, *Patterns of Development in Latin America: Poverty, Repression and Economic Strategy*, Princeton, NJ: Princeton University Press, 1987, page 290.

small population and relatively low income per capita limited the size of the domestic market, providing little stimulus for local manufacturing investments by private domestic firms and foreign multinational corporations.[6] In short, ISI failed to generate rapid growth in the manufacturing sector. On the other hand, gains were made in diversifying agricultural exports. Beef and sugar increased their shares of export earnings; the latter following the 1959 revolution in Cuba, which led the United States to impose an embargo on trade with Cuba and, therefore, to reallocate a portion of its sugar quota to Costa Rica.[7]

In the early 1960s, policymakers viewed membership in the Central American Common Market as a means to overcome Costa Rica's small size and continue the protectionist strategy of ISI. The common market established free regional trade among the five member nations and imposed common external tariffs on imports from all other countries.[8] Costa Rica stood to benefit from the large, protected regional market because its manufacturing sector was more developed than those of other member nations and its better-educated labor force could attract multinational corporations eager to gain access to the protected market.[9]

Costa Rica's manufacturing output grew rapidly during the 1960s in response to the significant increase in Central American trade. The growth slowed, however, in the early 1970s. The Central American market was not large enough for efficient diversification and expansion of industry. Moreover, the 1969 war between El Salvador and Honduras reduced regional trade.

Costa Rica's economy was adversely affected by a series of external shocks over the period 1973 to 1982. The first oil-price shock in 1973 greatly increased the prices of imported goods. A sharp drop in coffee prices in 1978 and a second oil-price shock in 1979 contributed to mounting trade deficits. Instead of devaluing the currency, policymakers opted to increase foreign borrowing. Most of the foreign debt was contracted on the basis of adjustable interest rates, and the rise in world interest rates in the early 1980s increased the cost of servicing this debt. During the 1973 to 1982 period, domestic and foreign private investment in Costa Rica contracted because of wars and uprisings in the Central American region. The government sought to fill the gap with public investments by the state-owned Costa Rican Development Corporation. These large public investments, the expansion of publicly provided services, and a drive to make social security coverage universal, however, generated large fiscal deficits.

Economic conditions deteriorated in the early 1980s as a result of the external shocks, trade deficits, and fiscal imbalances. In 1982, unemployment rose to 9.4 percent; real gross domestic product declined by more than 7 percent; and inflation jumped to

---

[6]Ibid., page 292.

[7]González-Vega and Céspedes, page 95.

[8]El Salvador, Guatemala, Honduras, and Nicaragua signed the treaty governing the formation of the common market in December 1960. Costa Rica delayed signing the treaty until July 1962. The value of intraregional exports grew considerably between 1960 and 1970. Reacting to the unequal distribution of benefits from the common market, and in the aftermath of its 1969 war with El Salvador, Honduras withdrew its membership in 1970 and began imposing tariffs on all imports from the region. Guatemala imposed trade restrictions in 1983 as well. By the mid-1980s free trade within the region had practically disappeared, a consequence of internal political instability, border conflicts, and mounting external debts.

[9]Sheahan, page 292.

90 percent.[10] In response to this crisis, successive governments throughout the 1980s and early 1990s implemented stabilization and structural adjustment programs. Effective in renewing economic growth, these programs lessened but did not eliminate Costa Rica's inflation problem.

Future economic growth in Costa Rica depends on the promotion of exports. Bananas generate the largest export revenues, but recently, tourism has surpassed coffee as the second leading source of foreign exchange.[11] For the policy of export-led growth to be successful, Costa Rica must expand its tourist industry and continue to develop other nontraditional exports.

---

[10]World Bank, "Costa Rica," in *Trends in Developing Countries 1994*, Washington, DC, 1994, page 121.
[11]Ibid.

# CHAPTER 12

# NATURAL RESOURCES AND THE ENVIRONMENT

Environmental protection is one area in which government must maintain a central role. Private markets provide little or no incentive for curbing pollution.[1]

In the less developed countries the issues of how to manage the natural resources to promote economic growth and development and how to meet the basic needs of their populations for clean water, food, and energy would seem to take precedence over concerns with the environment. In promoting economic development and addressing their widespread poverty, can these nations afford not to pay attention to the environment? As suggested in Chapter 7, a harmful cycle may unfold of poverty, rapid population growth, pressure on the natural resource base, and environmental deterioration. Usually the poorest in a nation suffer the most from degradation of the environment—whether from the consumption of unsafe water, the indoor air pollution from cooking over wood fires, or the erosion of soils as fragile lands are overcultivated. At the same time, poverty and population pressures contribute to environmental deterioration as young trees are cut down for fuelwood; rivers and streams are used for bathing and washing; pastures are overgrazed; and proper investments in farmland are unaffordable. Furthermore, with economic growth and development come not only greater rates of resource utilization, but the challenges of the proper disposal of increasing industrial and consumer wastes, including the exhaust emissions from automobiles.

In this chapter the role of natural resources in economic growth and development is examined. The distinction between renewable and nonrenewable natural resources is drawn. Having focused on agriculture in Chapter 11, we now turn to mining, fishing, and forestry, although we briefly compare these other natural resource-intensive sectors with agriculture. We discuss how natural resources have been exported to

---

[1]World Bank, *World Development Report 1992: Development and the Environment,* New York: Oxford University Press, 1992, page 1.

generate foreign exchange and government revenues. We also illustrate how a distorted type of development, known as the *Dutch disease,* can result from an overreliance on natural resource exports. We then explore the concept of sustainable development, and how nations might successfully manage their natural resources both to promote economic growth and development and to preserve, if not enrich, the quality of the environment. At the end of the chapter is a case study on Jamaica and its natural resource-intensive development.

## NATURAL RESOURCES AND ECONOMIC GROWTH

**Natural resources** encompass the wildlife, land, forests, mineral deposits, bodies of water, and energy sources available to a society. Even the atmosphere and weather may be considered part of the natural resources that define the environment shared by humans, their domesticated animals, and the cultivated plants.

Natural resources are a primary factor of production, along with human labor and physical capital. Increases in the quantity or quality of natural resources available to an economy will enhance the productive capacity of the nation, shifting out the production possibilities boundary.

Natural resource endowments vary across nations. Extensive mineral deposits (e.g., copper, iron ore, bauxite, diamonds) and significant reserves of petroleum, coal, and natural gas tend to be concentrated in parts of the world. Coastal nations clearly have greater access to the fish and resources in the oceans. Tropical rainforests are found mostly in Latin America; the tropical dry forests are mainly in Africa. The unevenness of natural resource endowments provides a basis for international trade. Indeed, for some nations the export of natural resources has been a leading sector of economic growth.

To use natural resources in the production of goods and services, the factors of human labor and, usually, physical capital have to be applied—to cultivate the land, catch the fish, harvest the forests, and extract the minerals. As raw materials, natural resources can be processed into intermediate goods, capital goods, and final goods. For example, diamonds are mined for use in industry in precision cutting machines and for personal consumption as fine jewelry. Timber can be cut and processed into lumber for home construction and for baseball bats and hockey sticks.

The quality of the available resources reflects their intrinsic values in production and consumption. The value of petroleum reserves differs according to the costs of refining into oil. Some nations, due to favorable climates and geography, have especially fertile farmland—whereas for other nations, the natural beauty of mountains and seashores gives them an advantage in tourism and recreation.

Natural resources can be classified as renewable or nonrenewable. With **renewable resources,** the stocks can be regenerated through proper use and management—farmland, forests, and fisheries are examples. **Nonrenewable resources,** in contrast, have finite stocks—at least for any foreseeable planning horizon. Mineral deposits and reserves of petroleum are examples of nonrenewable resources. Some forms of energy (solar, tidal, and wind) are renewable, but their current availability depends on the forces of nature.

The quality and quantity of natural resources are affected by human behavior. For instance, fertilizers can improve the productivity of the soil. New trees can be planted. On the other hand, overuse, mismanagement, or pollution can decrease the quantity and quality of the natural resource base. Overgrazing can turn a viable pasture into barren scrub land. Air pollution and acid rain can diminish forests. Improper disposal of industrial wastes can poison bodies of water. Such environmental deterioration not only reduces the production possibilities of a nation, but may directly diminish the quality of life by posing health hazards and impairing aesthetic enjoyment.

## RESOURCE SCARCITY

As noted, natural resource endowments are not evenly distributed across nation-states. For example, in Table 12.1 on page 356, we list the shares of the top four countries in the 1992 world production of selected minerals. To illustrate the nonrenewable nature of these resources, we also present a **world reserve base life index,** which is an estimate of the number of years of known reserves remaining, given the 1992 world production rates. *(Note:* These estimates should not be regarded as forecasts, but rather as projections of the current rates of utilization given the known reserves of the resources.) Represented are 16 different nations: 4 developed countries and 12 less developed countries. China appears in the top four 4 times; Australia, Canada, Russia, and Brazil appear 3 times each; and Indonesia, twice. The global shares of the top four producers for 1992 vary from 49 percent (zinc) to 79 percent (mercury). The projected number of years of production left ranges from 46 years (zinc) to 270 years (bauxite).

For renewable natural resources a balance must be found between present consumption and future availability. Without proper management, fishing stocks can easily be depleted and water tables can be quickly drawn down. Harvesting of forests without sufficient replanting may result in deforestation, which, in turn, contributes to soil erosion and desertification.

For nonrenewable resources, finite supplies exist by definition. Conservation and the substitution of synthetic for natural materials can reduce the use of nonrenewable resources.

It may seem ironic, but the greater concern now is with the adequacy of renewable resources. As the World Bank recently observed:

> Whereas fears that the world would run out of metals and other minerals were fashionable even fifteen years ago, the potential supply of these resources is now outstripping demand. Prices of minerals have shown a fairly consistent downward trend over the past hundred years. They fell sharply in the 1980s, leading to gluts that threatened to impoverish countries dependent on commodity exports.
>
> With some natural resources, by contrast, demand often exceeds supply. This is true of the demand for water, not only in the arid areas of the Middle East but also in northern China, east Java, and parts of India....
>
> The reason some resources—water, forests, and clean air—are under seige while others—metals, minerals, and energy—are not is that the scarcity of the latter is reflected in market prices and so the forces of substitution, technical progress, and structural change are strong. The first group is characterized by open access, meaning that there are no incentives to use them sparingly....

| TABLE 12.1 | COUNTRY SHARES IN THE WORLD PRODUCTION OF SELECTED MINERALS, 1992 | |
|---|---|---|
| MINERAL | SHARE IN ANNUAL WORLD PRODUCTION OF TOP FOUR NATIONS (%) | WORLD RESERVE BASE LIFE INDEX (YEARS) |
| BAUXITE | 73 | 270 |
| Australia (39%), Guinea (13%), Jamaica (11%), Brazil (10%) | | |
| COPPER | 53 | 64 |
| Chile (21%), United States (19%), Canada (8%), Zambia (5%) | | |
| NICKEL | 64 | 119 |
| Russia (23%), Canada (21%), New Caledonia (12%), Indonesia (8%) | | |
| TIN | 64 | 56 |
| China (24%), Brazil (17%), Indonesia (14%), Bolivia (9%), | | |
| ZINC | 49 | 46 |
| Canada (18%), Australia (14%), China (9%), Peru (8%) | | |
| IRON ORE | 59 | 247 |
| China (21%), Brazil (16%), Australia (13%), Russia (9%) | | |
| MERCURY | 79 | 80 |
| China (30%), Mexico (23%), Algeria (13%), Russia (13%) | | |

NOTES:
The country figures may not exactly sum to the totals due to rounding error.
   The reserve base is the portion of the mineral resource that meets grade, quality, thickness, and depth criteria defined by current mining and production processes. It includes both measured and indicated reserves and refers to those resources that are both currently economic and marginally economic, as well as some of those that are currently subeconomic.
   The world reserve base life index, expressed in years remaining, is computed by dividing the 1992 world reserve base by the world production rate for 1992. The underlying assumption is that world production remains constant at the 1992 rate.

FROM: *World Resources 1994–95: A Guide to the Global Environment*, A Report by the World Resources Institute in collaboration with the United Nations Environment Programme and the United Nations Development Programme, New York: Oxford University Press, 1994, Table 21.4.

[T]he environmental debate has rightly shifted away from concern about *physical limits* to growth toward concern about incentives for *human behavior* and policies that can overcome *market and policy failures*.[2]

While generalizations about natural resources—availability, use, and conservation—can be made, it is important to realize that important differences exist across the natural resource-intensive sectors of an economy.

---

[2]Ibid., pages 9 and 10.

## AGRICULTURE AND OTHER NATURAL RESOURCE-INTENSIVE SECTORS

To illustrate the diversity across natural resource-intensive sectors, we compare the characteristics of agriculture and mining. Then we extend the analysis to fishing and forestry.

### MINING

To begin, we observe that the extraction of minerals is more capital-intensive than agriculture. It is true that modern agriculture as practiced in the developed countries and on the large plantations in the LDCs tends to be capital- and land-intensive. However, as discussed in Chapter 11, the economies of scale in farming are fairly modest. Labor-intensive farming on small plots of land can be economically feasible in the less developed countries. The Green Revolution technology, with the improved seeds and the required complements of fertilizer and dependable water supplies, has significantly increased the productivity of small-scale farming.

Several differences are noted. First, most mining activity is large-scale, although small operations may be working on the fringe, prospecting for gold and precious stones. The start-up costs in mining are considerable and include the exploration of mineral reserves and the heavy equipment needed to extract and transport the minerals. Mining has been a leading sector for foreign direct investment in many less developed countries. Transnational corporations from the developed countries have the technical expertise, capital equipment, and funds to finance large-scale mining operations. Because mineral deposits can be considered as "gifts of nature," national governments have often been involved in the mining sector—either directly through state-owned mining companies and joint ventures with foreign corporations or indirectly through taxation of the revenues generated from mining.

Second, for nations with significant deposits of minerals, especially developing economies, domestic demands will fall far short of production capacities. Consequently, from the outset there may be a heavy reliance on foreign markets. This export orientation of mining has provided additional incentive for governments to get involved, to secure a share of the foreign exchange generated. While many developing nations also rely on cash crops for export revenues, usually a large part of the agricultural produce is for domestic consumption.

Third, whereas farmland, if properly cultivated and maintained, can yield agricultural produce on a regular basis, most mineral deposits can be considered to be nonrenewable. Therefore, an important concern in mining is the appropriate rate of depletion. As will be discussed below, a factor that tempers the long-run demand for minerals has been the development of synthetic substitutes, such as plastic or fiberglass for steel in automobiles.

### FISHING

Although obvious differences exist, fishing might be considered more akin to agriculture, and forestry more like mining. As in farming, small-scale fishing operations can be economically viable, especially in developing economies. The necessary capital investment (mainly boats and nets) may be fairly modest for fishing in rivers, lakes, or near the seacoast. Deep-sea fishing, where the fish are caught, processed, and frozen on board factory ships, is a more capital-intensive venture. As with plantation agriculture, such large-scale fishing is often geared to exporting.

Fishing stocks can be sustained when properly managed, that is, when not fished beyond the potential for regeneration or destroyed by pollution. However, here is where an important difference with agriculture exists. In agriculture, access to the land is usually well-defined, whether or not farmers actually working the land also own it. In contrast, property rights in fishing are less clearly established, especially in international waters.[3] In some traditional fishing communities, the fishing grounds may be communally "owned," with access determined by mutual agreement. Such common property resources, however, can break down with population growth (more fishermen competing for a livelihood) or technological change (yielding increased catches per fisherman). Unless carefully managed, common property can deteriorate into open access; and here, the potential exists for a serious depletion of the fishing stocks.

As evidence of this problem, consider the following excerpt:

> The oceans are emptying. From Iceland to India, from Namibia to Norway, fish catches are decreasing every year. The global marine catch has been declining in fits and starts since 1989, after increasing fivefold since 1950.
> 
> New fishing technology, lax regulation, a hodgepodge of conflicting government policies and an overall failure to manage the world's marine resources have combined to accelerate the world-wide decline of fish stocks.
> 
> ... About 60% of the fish types tracked by the Food and Agricultural Organization of the United Nations are categorized as fully exploited, over-exploited, or depleted....
> 
> Climate changes and other conditions account for some of this reduction, but one reason predominates: overfishing.[4]

While conservation through limiting access to fishing grounds and restrictions on fish catches may be required to replenish the vulnerable fish stocks, in agriculture the challenge will be to increase the productivity of the existing land under cultivation. The World Bank predicts that world consumption of cereal grains will almost double by the year 2030.

> To protect fragile soils and natural habitats, almost all of this increase will have to be achieved by raising yields on existing cropland rather than by extending the area under cultivation. There is little doubt that cultivated soils have the capacity to meet future increases in world agricultural demand so long as they are well managed. But intensification of production will involve the application of much higher levels of fertilizer and pesticides, as well as significant improvements in the allocation of water for agricultural use.[5]

---

[3]We should note the existence of fish farming, also known as *aquaculture,* where fish are cultivated in managed environments, ranging from ponds to flooded rice fields to sophisticated hatcheries, and where property rights tend to be more clearly defined. Fish farming accounts for approximately 10 percent of the world's annual commercial fish catch. China is the leading aquaculture producer. This information is derived from *The World Book Encyclopedia,* Volume F, Chicago: World Book, 1990, page 183.

[4]Anne Swardson, "Oceans Are Emptying All Around the Globe," *Charlotte Observer* (August 28, 1994), page 13A.

[5]World Bank, *World Development Report 1992,* page 42.

FORESTRY

Forestry is a major economic activity in many countries. With respect to logging, the primary commercial activity in forests, similarities to mining are found. Logging tends to be capital-intensive, given the heavy equipment needed to harvest and transport the timber. While forests are a renewable resource and should be managed with sustainability as a goal, the cycles for many trees from seedlings to mature growth cover several decades. Consequently, in the short to medium run, individual tree stands can be considered as nonrenewable. For those nations well endowed with forests, the export of timber can be a major source of foreign exchange.

One fairly distinguishing feature of forestry is noted by Tietenberg.

> Trees, when harvested, provide a salable commodity, but left standing they are a capital good, providing for increased growth the following year [until reaching maturity]. Each year the forest manager must decide whether to harvest a particular stand of trees or to wait for the additional growth.[6]

Forests provide much more than lumber. Indeed, a second distinguishing feature are the externalities associated with forests. Forests are an integral part of the environment, including the regional hydrologic cycles. Forests recycle carbon dioxide, helping to cleanse the earth's atmosphere. Tropical forests are home to roughly half of the plant and insect species on earth, and may hold untold potential for advances in science and medicine. Temperate forests are widely used for recreation such as hiking and camping.

As the World Bank notes, deforestation has become a major concern, not just in the nations directly experiencing the losses, but globally as part of the larger environmental deterioration.

> Forests (especially moist tropical forests), coastal and inland wetlands, coral reefs, and other ecosystems are being converted or degraded at rates that are high by historical standards. Tropical forests have declined by one-fifth in this century, and the rate has accelerated.... [I]n the 1980s tropical deforestation occurred at a rate of 0.9 percent a year, with Asia's rate slightly higher (1.2 percent) and sub-Saharan Africa's lower (0.8 percent). The loss of forests has severe ecological and economic costs—lost watershed protection, local climate change, lost coastal protection and fishing grounds—and affects people's lives. African women have to walk farther for fuelwood, indigenous forest dwellers in the Amazon have succumbed to settlers' diseases, and 5,000 villagers in the Philippines were recently killed by flooding caused in part by the deforestation of hillsides.[7]

Resource pressures in one area frequently spill over. An estimated 60 percent of the deforestation in the less developed countries is due to expansion for agriculture,

---

[6]Tom Tietenberg, *Environmental and Natural Resource Economics*, 3d ed., New York: HarperCollins, 1992, page 279. Further, as Tietenberg notes, the decision to harvest is affected not only by the expected price of the timber when harvested, but the intended use of the land afterward—in particular, whether to replant and begin a new cycle of trees. The costs of replanting clearly affect this decision (pages 284–286).

[7]World Bank, *World Development Report 1992*, page 6.

particularly in Latin America and Africa.[8] Reliance on firewood for cooking and heating accounts for the "largest share of wood use in developing countries, [mainly in the] tropical dry forests and nonforest wooded areas around dense human settlements in Africa and South Asia."[9] Tietenberg describes the dilemma facing some developing nations:

> Peasants see unclaimed forest land as an opportunity to become landowners. Nations confronted with masses of peasants see unowned or publicly owned forests as a politically more viable source of land for the landless than taking it forcibly from the rich. Without land, peasants descend upon the urban areas in search of jobs in larger numbers than can be accommodated by urban labor markets. Politically explosive tensions, created and nourished by the resulting atmosphere of frustration and hopelessness, force governments to open up forested lands to the peasants or at least look the other way as peasants stake their claims.[10]

## EXPORTS OF NATURAL RESOURCE-INTENSIVE PRODUCTS

Nations with substantial stocks of natural resources, especially mineral deposits and forest reserves, will enjoy a degree of international market power. That is, these nations will be price setters, since the demand curves for their exports of the natural resources will be downward-sloping. As with agriculture, considerable volatility can occur in revenues. The source of the export revenue instability, however, stems from the demand side, and reflects the economic conditions in foreign markets.

Minerals and timber are basically inputs into further stages of production (e.g., iron ore used in the steel for automobiles, or timber processed into boards for construction). When the international economy is healthy, with expanding industrial outputs and construction activity, the derived demands for minerals and lumber will increase. Revenues from mining and forestry will rise as market-clearing prices and quantities rise. In contrast, in periods of recession, industrial output and construction activity will decline. The derived demands for minerals and lumber will fall, pulling down market prices and quantities sold.

In Figure 12.1 we illustrate the potential for the procyclical boom-and-bust conditions in export revenues for a nation with forest reserves. With demand shifts, market prices and quantities move in the same direction. Over an international business cycle, annual export revenues from logging for this nation could go from $TR_N = (P_N)(Q_N)$ in an average or normal year to $TR_B = (P_B)(Q_B)$ in a boom year or period of economic expansion $(P_B > P_N, Q_B > Q_N)$ to $TR_R = (P_R)(Q_R)$ in a recession year $(P_R < P_N, Q_R < Q_N)$. If import expenditures are stable, the volatility in export revenues results in instability in the trade balance, which can lead to other difficulties, including exchange-rate variability. If, on the other hand, imports vary directly with exports, then the associated fluctuations in imports can be disruptive to the domestic economy. In periods when foreign demand is depressed and the inflow of foreign exchange from exports declines, the output of the domestic industries that depend on imported inputs may have to be cut back,

---

[8]Ibid., pages 134–135.

[9]Ibid., page 58.

[10]Tietenberg, page 288.

### FIGURE 12.1 — Export Revenue Instability in Natural Resources

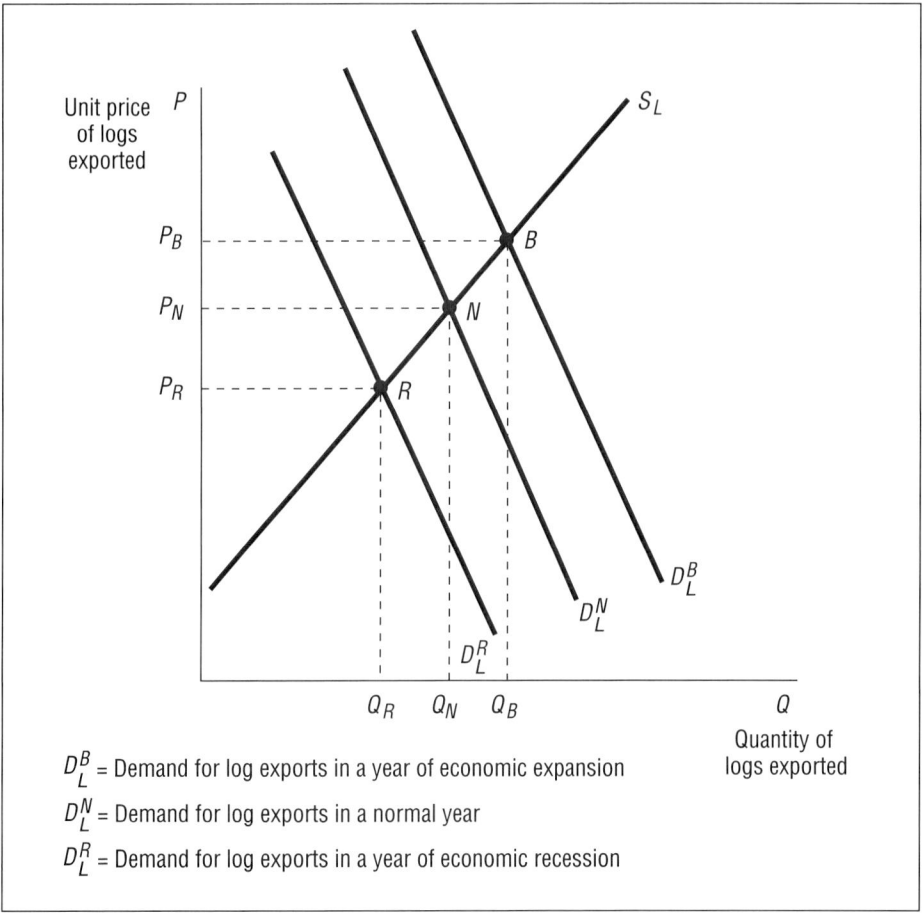

$D_L^B$ = Demand for log exports in a year of economic expansion
$D_L^N$ = Demand for log exports in a normal year
$D_L^R$ = Demand for log exports in a year of economic recession

increasing unemployment and reducing incomes in the nation. So too, shortages of foreign exchange may curtail development projects that depend on imported inputs.

Conversely, in boom periods when export revenues are rising sharply, the nation may overextend itself—with inflation, budget deficits, and external debt becoming problematic. (We will illustrate this phenomenon, known as the *Dutch disease*, below.) In short, nations with a high percentage of export revenues based on natural resources may be especially vulnerable to changing international economic conditions. Consequently, economic planning in the nation becomes more difficult.

In the long run the trend in real prices for many natural resources (i.e., the purchasing power of a physical unit of natural resources) has been downward. On the supply side, advances in technology and transportation have led to the discovery, recovery, and availability of greater quantities of natural resources. On the demand side, during the periods when natural resource prices have risen sharply, renewed efforts are made to conserve and to develop synthetic substitutes (or commodities that serve the same function but can be produced with fewer or cheaper resources). Two examples are plastic shutters replacing wood shutters on houses, and fiber optics replacing copper wire in telecommunications.

## FIGURE 12.2   CONSEQUENCES OF EXPORT TAX

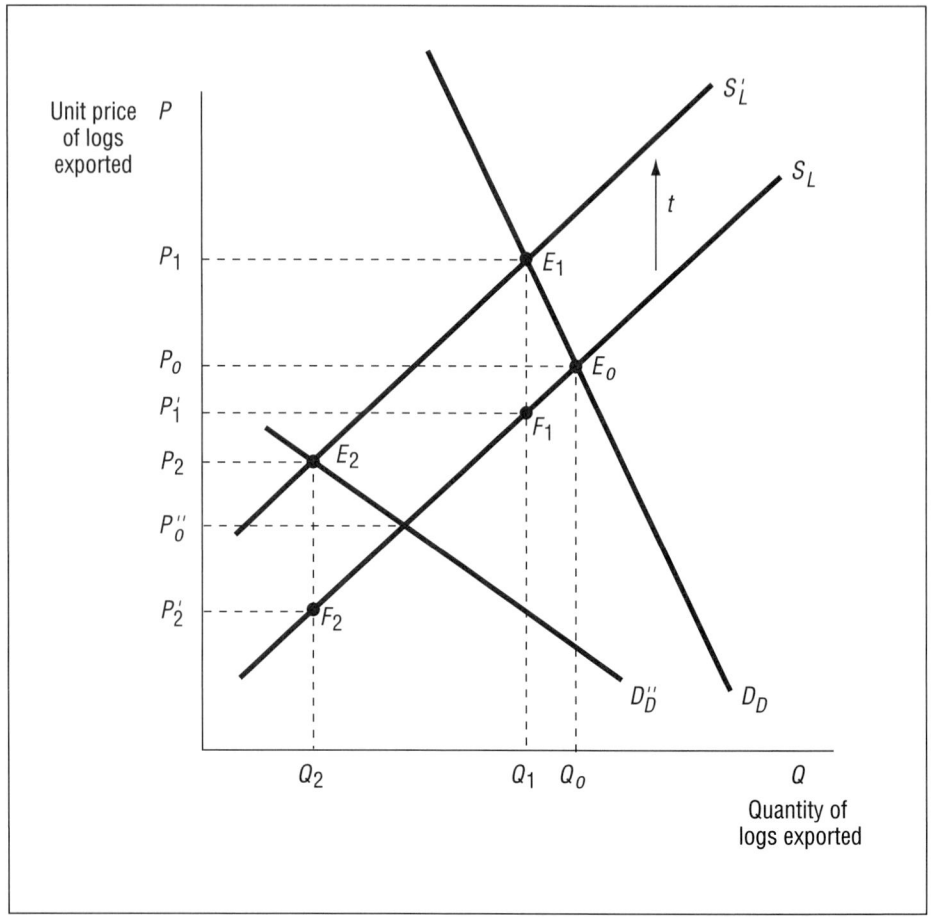

### TRADE-OFFS IN THE SHORT RUN AND LONG RUN

To illustrate the potential trade-off between the short-run and long-run revenues, consider a nation with extensive reserves of mahogany. Refer to Figure 12.2, in which the supply and demand curves for the mahogany logs exported by a nation are depicted. $S_L$ refers to the sum of the supply curves of the individual logging firms in the nation. $D_L$ is the aggregation of the demand curves of the foreign consumers of the nation's mahogany wood. Suppose that the initial market price is $P_o$, and that the nation is operating in the inelastic region (lower half) of the foreign demand curve for its log exports, at $E_o$. By levying a tax on the exports of logs, the nation can increase total export revenues while reducing the quantity of logs exported.

A specific tax of $\$t$ per log shifts the supply curve up in a parallel manner by $\$t$ from $S_L$ to $S'_L$. The quantity of logs exported during the period declines from $Q_o$ to $Q_1$, while the unit price foreign consumers pay rises from $P_o$ to $P_1$ (although not by the full amount of the tax). Total export revenues increase from $TR_o = (P_o)(Q_o)$ to $TR_1 = (P_1)(Q_1)$. The price received by domestic loggers falls from $P_o$ to $P'_1$, and their total revenues decline to $(P'_1)(Q_1)$ from $TR_o$. The government collects tax revenues of $(P_1 - P'_1)Q_1 = tQ_1$, with foreign consumers' share of the tax revenues equal to $(P_1 - P_o)Q_1$. The share of the tax revenues borne by domestic loggers is equal to $(P_o - P'_1)Q_1$.

As long as the foreign demand is price-inelastic, raising the tax on exports will increase total export revenues in the current period.[11] In the long run, however, relatively higher prices for log exports will encourage conservation and substitution. For example, here mahogany panelling may be replaced by sheetrock. Similarly, brick home exteriors or aluminum siding may become more common, and cedar siding less common. Oak and other hardwood floors may become very expensive, resulting in a boon to the carpet industry.[12]

Returning to Figure 12.2, in the long run conservation and substitution may reduce the foreign demand for logs to $D''_L$ (from $D_L$). Not only might the demand fall but, over time, with the greater possibilities for substitution, the demand curve would become more price-elastic. Assuming an unchanged supply curve and specific tax, the quantity of log exports would decline to $Q_2$ and the price paid by foreign consumers would decrease to $P_2$. Total export revenues are greatly reduced, from $TR_1 = (P_1)(Q_1)$ to $TR_2 = (P_2)(Q_2)$. The price received by domestic loggers is lowered to $P'_2$. Tax revenues are reduced to $(P_2 - P'_2)Q_2$, with the amount paid by foreign consumers falling to $(P_2 - P''_o)Q_2$.

Thus, nations with market power in natural resources may face a trade-off. The more aggressive they are in raising prices and generating export revenues in the short run, the more incentive provided to foreign consumers to conserve and develop substitutes. In the long run, export revenues may be greatly reduced.

## DUTCH DISEASE: A DEVELOPMENT DISTORTION

Another problem associated with an overreliance on export revenues and taxes on natural resources is known as the *Dutch disease*.[13] Before we illustrate this phenomenon, we need to understand the distinction between nominal and real exchange rates.

### Real and Nominal Exchange Rates

In order to purchase goods or services from another nation, it is usually necessary to purchase the currency of that nation in the foreign exchange market. The **nominal exchange rate** is the price of one currency expressed in units of a foreign currency.

---

[11]The OPEC (Organization of Petroleum Exporting Countries) cartel achieved much the same effect in the 1970s with quotas on oil production. With a price-inelastic demand for oil in the short run, oil prices and revenues sharply increased.

[12]In the case of petroleum, individuals not only turned down thermostats and car-pooled more often, but insulated their homes and switched to more fuel-efficient automobiles. Alternative sources of energy were used, including solar and natural gas. Finally, the sharply higher prices for gasoline and home heating oil during the 1970s and early 1980s prompted more exploration and recovery of petroleum reserves. Petroleum supplies on the market increased, not only with non-OPEC nations producing more, but as the OPEC members exceeded their quotas. By the end of the 1980s, world prices for petroleum (outside of the sudden spike during the Gulf War crisis) had declined back to the levels of the mid-1970s, and in real terms, were significantly less.

[13]This phenomenon was first applied to the Netherlands, when rapid increases in export revenues with the development of natural gas reserves during the 1960s and 1970s led to unbalanced growth, reducing the competitiveness of other sectors of the Dutch economy. For a brief description of the Dutch case, as well as case studies for Indonesia, Mexico, and Nigeria, see *Economics of Development*, 2d ed., Malcolm Gillis, Dwight Perkins, Michael Roemer, and Donald Snodgrass, New York: W. W. Norton, 1987, pages 535–539.

(As we will discuss further in Chapter 15, nominal exchange rates can be determined in the market or set by governments.) Changes in the exchange rate will affect the relative prices of domestic versus foreign commodities.

For example, suppose that the nominal exchange rate between the Mexican peso (p) and the U.S. dollar ($) is 200p = $1.00 (the peso price of the dollar), or equivalently, $.005 = 1p (the dollar price of the peso). A nominal **depreciation** of the peso is indicated by an increase in the peso price of the dollar, say from 200 pesos to 250 pesos to the dollar (or $.004 = 1 peso). This depreciation of the peso means that it costs 25 percent more pesos to purchase one dollar (or a dollar's worth of U.S. goods and services). Consequently we would expect fewer exports from the United States to Mexico. The depreciation of the peso, however, lowers the dollar price of any peso-denominated Mexican good or service, and should boost exports from Mexico to the United States.

Conversely, a nominal **appreciation** of the peso (a decrease in the peso price of the dollar, say from 200p = $1.00 to 160p = $1.00) should make Mexican goods and services less competitive internationally. (The dollar price of a Mexican good selling for 200 pesos increases from $1.00 to $1.25 with this appreciation of the peso from 1 peso = $.005 to 1 peso = $.00625.) As the peso appreciates, the Mexican balance of trade should deteriorate: Mexican exports decline and imports rise.

The **real exchange rate** is the nominal exchange rate adjusted for the relative price levels of internationally traded goods and services in the two countries. Let

$er$ = nominal exchange rate (e.g., the peso price of the dollar)

$er^*$ = real exchange rate (also expressed as pesos per dollar)

$P_M$ = a price index for traded goods and services in Mexico

$P_{US}$ = a price index for traded goods and services in the United States

The price indices $P_M$ and $P_{US}$ represent the average price levels for goods and services in Mexico and the United States, respectively, that are internationally traded. The real exchange rate is equal to

$$er^* = er \left[ \frac{P_{US}}{P_M} \right]$$

The real exchange rate $(er^*)$ can change either due to a change in the nominal exchange rate $(er)$, or a change in the relative price levels for traded goods and services $(P_{US}/P_M)$. In particular, a real depreciation of the peso could reflect a rise in the peso price of the dollar $(er \uparrow)$, a rise in the United States price index for traded goods and services $(P_{US} \uparrow)$, or a fall in the price index for traded goods and services in Mexico $(P_M \downarrow)$. A real depreciation of the peso makes Mexican goods and services more attractive internationally.

For example, let $er_o$ = 200 (i.e., 200p = $1.00) and begin in the base year, with $P_{US}$ and $P_M$ both equal to 100. Then in the base year, the nominal and real exchange rates are equal.

$$er^*_o = 200(100/100) = 200 = er_o$$

A depreciation of the real exchange rate to 250 (pesos to the dollar) could result from (1) a depreciation in the nominal exchange rate to 250 $(er_1 = 250)$; or (2) an increase in the United States price index from 100 to 125 ($P'_{US}$ = 125); or (3) a decrease in the Mexican price index from 100 to 80 ($P'_M$ = 80).

$$er_1^* = 250(100/100) = 200(125/100) = 200(100/80) = 250$$
$$\qquad\quad (1) \qquad\qquad\quad (2) \qquad\qquad\quad (3)$$

In contrast, a real appreciation of the peso ($er^*$ ↓), meaning fewer pesos are needed to purchase an inflation-adjusted dollar's worth of U.S. goods and services, would tend to weaken the Mexican balance of trade. Imports from the United States should rise and exports to the United States should fall with the stronger peso. A real appreciation of the peso could be caused by a nominal appreciation ($er$ ↓), a rise in the average level of prices for traded goods and services in Mexico ($P_M$ ↑), or a fall in the U.S. price index for traded goods and services ($P_{US}$ ↓).

For assessing the international price competitiveness of a nation's goods and services, the real exchange rate is relevant. Generally, nations with comparatively high rates of inflation experience nominally depreciating currencies (for reasons to be elaborated further in Chapter 15). Whether the real exchange rate depreciates, however, depends on the relative rate of inflation versus the rate of nominal depreciation of the domestic currency.

To illustrate, return to the example in which $er_o$ = 200, $P_{US}$ = 100, $P_M$ = 100, and $er_o^*$ = 200(100/100) = 200. If a bushel of tomatoes costs 400 pesos to produce in Mexico, then at the nominal exchange rate of 200 pesos to the dollar, the export price (border price from Mexico) to the United States would be $2.00 per bushel.[14] Suppose that Mexico experiences 15 percent inflation ($P'_M$ = 115) and the domestic cost of production for a bushel of tomatoes in Mexico rises to 460 pesos. Assume that the United States has an inflation rate of only 5 percent ($P'_{US}$ = 105), and the cost of producing a bushel of tomatoes in the United States rises by 5 percent. Therefore, the relative price level in Mexico has increased by 9.5 percent (115/105 = 1.095).

In order for Mexico to maintain a real exchange rate of 200 pesos to the dollar—and maintain its current price competitiveness—the peso would have to depreciate nominally, here from 200 to 219 pesos to the dollar.

$$er_1^* = er_1 \, (P'_{US}/P'_M) = 219(105/115) = 200 = er_o^*$$

If the peso depreciated nominally beyond 219 pesos to the dollar, say to 230p = $1.00, then in real terms the peso has also depreciated, here to 210 = 230(105/115). On the other hand, if the peso nominally depreciated by less, say to only 212.5p = $1.00, then in real terms the peso has appreciated, here to 194 = 212.5(105/115). A real appreciation of the peso would make Mexican goods and services less competitive internationally.

## An Illustration of the Dutch Disease

As already mentioned, a problem associated with an overreliance on export revenues and taxes on natural resources is called the **Dutch disease.** To illustrate, consider a nation with substantial reserves of petroleum, which is the beneficiary of sharply rising world prices for petroleum, as, for example, triggered by the OPEC oil embargo in

---

[14]Transportation costs and trade barriers will increase the import price to the United States beyond the Mexican export price. Here we ignore transportation costs, trade barriers, and any other factors that drive a wedge between the export and import prices of a commodity.

late 1973. Suppose further that this nation is not a member of OPEC and so is not bound by any agreement to restrict output in order to boost prices.[15]

The surge in petroleum export revenues initially results in a surplus in the nation's balance of trade. Flush with foreign exchange and tax revenues from petroleum exports, the government embarks on an ambitious program of spending and development projects. The rise in spending even outpaces the gain in revenues, and to cover the rising budget deficits the government turns to borrowing, both domestic and foreign. The central bank finances much of the domestic borrowing by printing money (monetizing the debt). While reducing the direct crowding-out effect on private investment spending from higher real interest rates, the expansion of the money supply induces inflation, which undermines the international competitiveness of the nation. Meanwhile, the robust export growth has triggered an acceleration of imports. In anticipation of the export boom continuing, the nation readily incurs foreign debt.

Because of the strong export earnings from petroleum, depreciation in the nominal exchange rate of the nation is modified. The high inflation, however, appreciates the real exchange rate. Sectors of the economy not involved in the petroleum trade (e.g., agriculture and light manufacturing) suffer a loss in international competitiveness and may find their output and employment declining. These sectors may also find their access to credit and foreign exchange restricted as the rapidly growing sectors linked to petroleum receive preferential treatment. Those sectors benefiting from the rapid growth in the economy (e.g., transportation and heavy manufacturing) will encounter, at some point, sharply higher marginal costs of production as bottlenecks and capacity constraints arise. More inflation is generated as the economy moves out toward the highly inelastic region of the aggregate supply curve.

Eventually the export boom ends and oil prices subside. Increased conservation by oil-importing countries and the expansion of alternative energy sources (coal, natural gas, solar) temper the demand for petroleum, while the discovery and recovery of new international petroleum reserves increase the market supply. With the significant decrease in export revenues, the nation is left with mushrooming budget deficits (the aggressive spending set in motion overwhelming the tax revenues, now greatly reduced); high inflation; a currency that has appreciated in real terms (undermining the nation's competitiveness); increased foreign debt; and weakened sectors of the economy. (As we will discuss in Chapter 15, the measures proposed for dealing with the foreign debt often impose austerity conditions on the nation.) In short, with the Dutch disease, the nation goes from heady rates of economic growth to stagnation.

### Evidence from Mexico

Mexico offers an example of this boom-to-bust cycle. Buoyed by extraordinary growth in oil export revenues in the late 1970s, Mexico overextended government spending

---

[15]We should note that the primary reason for the OPEC oil embargo in October of 1973 was political. To punish the United States for supporting Israel in the Yom Kippur War, the OPEC nations, dominated by the Arab states of the Middle East and North Africa, placed an embargo on oil exports to the United States. The contrived shortage of oil led to panic in the world market, nearly quadrupling the price of a barrel of oil. The OPEC nations recognized their collective market power and have attempted since, albeit with decreasing success, to keep the world price of oil up by restricting their outputs.

| TABLE 12.2 | SELECTED STATISTICS FOR MEXICO: 1973 AND 1981 | |
|---|---|---|
| | 1973 | 1981 |
| Merchandise exports (billions of U.S. dollars) | $2.6 | $20.0 |
| Share of fuels in merchandise exports (%) | 1 | 69 |
| Merchandise imports (billions of dollars) | $4.1 | $24.2 |
| External debt (total) (billions of U.S. dollars) | $9.0 | $78.2 |
| Ratio of government budget deficit to gross national product | 3.8 | 6.6 |
| Gross domestic product price deflator | | |
|     Mexico | 100 | 488 |
|     United States | 100 | 190 |
| Nominal exchange rate: pesos per dollar | 12.5 | 24.5 |
| Real exchange rate: pesos per dollar | 12.5 | 9.5 |

NOTES:
The real exchange rate is equal to the nominal exchange rate times the ratio of the GDP price deflator for the United States to the GDP price deflator for Mexico.

FROM: World Bank, *World Tables 1989–90,* Baltimore: The Johns Hopkins University Press, 1990, pages 392–395.

(including social programs, subsidies, and capital projects). The government deficits were financed by printing money and borrowing from foreign banks. Consequently, the impressive rates of economic growth Mexico enjoyed were accompanied by accelerating inflation and rising debt. Then, with the oil price declines in the 1980s, the Mexican economy hit the shoals. In August of 1982, Mexico, nearly out of international reserves, announced that it could not meet the scheduled payments on its foreign debt. Additional loans, a moratorium of payments on the principal owed to commercial banks, and debt rescheduling were requested. Mexico also approached the International Monetary Fund for assistance.

Mexico's announcement focused attention on the larger international debt crisis, a topic also to be examined in detail in Chapter 15. For our purposes here, we can refer to Table 12.2, where selected indicators for the Mexican economy are given for 1973 (the year of the OPEC oil embargo) and 1981 (the year before the Mexican crisis). We see that in 1973 only one percent of Mexico's merchandise exports was accounted for by fuels. The escalating world price for petroleum provided Mexico and other nations with an incentive to increase the exploration for, and recovery of, petroleum. Mexico discovered large oil deposits, and by the latter half of the 1970s had emerged as a major exporter of oil. Not a member of OPEC, and so free to increase production,

Mexico benefited from the second surge in world oil prices in late 1979, set off by the Iranian Revolution and the fall of the Shah of Iran.

In 1981 more than two-thirds of Mexico's merchandise exports were fuel. While export revenues, led by petroleum, grew rapidly, imports grew faster. The merchandise trade deficit increased from $1.5 billion in 1973 to $4.2 billion in 1981. Mexico's external debt exploded from under $10 billion to nearly $80 billion. The government budget deficit increased from 3.8 percent of gross national product in 1973 to 6.6 percent in 1981 due to the rapid expansion in spending on capital projects. (In fact, until 1982 the current government budget balance [excluding capital expenditures] was in surplus.)

In Mexico, real national output increased by over 60 percent from 1973 to 1981, but the money supply (defined as currency in circulation plus checkable deposits) rose by over 650 percent. Not surprisingly, inflation soared, as measured by the percentage change in the price deflator for gross domestic product (GDP). The GDP price deflator for Mexico increased 150 percent more than the GDP price deflator for the United States. The Mexican peso depreciated nominally from 12.5 pesos to the dollar in 1973 to 24.5 pesos to the dollar in 1981. In real terms, however, the peso appreciated from 12.5 to 9.5 pesos to the dollar.[16]

In response to its external debt problem, Mexico adopted tighter economic policies, including measures to reduce inflation, improve the trade balance, and attract foreign investment. Over the 1980s Mexico did manage to reform its economy, albeit with considerable hardships for large segments of its population. In the early 1990s Mexico joined the United States and Canada in the North American Free Trade Agreement (NAFTA).

### Avoiding the Dutch Disease

The lessons to be learned from the Dutch disease might be summarized as follows. First, if a nation experiences boom conditions for one or more of its exports, it should exercise self-discipline. In particular, an overly aggressive expansion of government spending on capital projects that exceed the absorptive capacity of the domestic economy should be avoided. Too rapid a push in investment, public or private, will encounter resource constraints and result in sharply escalating costs of production.

Second, a more balanced strategy may be called for, including more diversified exports. Clearly the temptation for a nation with exceptional growth in the exports of a sector is to "make hay while the sun shines." Too rapid an expansion in one sector, especially one like petroleum, which is capital-intensive and has limited linkages to the other production sectors of the economy, may cause severe distortions by drawing resources away from these other sectors. Furthermore, when the export boom ends, these relatively neglected sectors may be weakened and internationally less competitive.

Third, the real exchange rate needs to be monitored. A depreciation in the nominal exchange rate need not translate into a depreciation of the real exchange rate. Often less developed countries set the nominal exchange rate and then fail to adjust frequently enough to compensate for their comparatively high rates of inflation. The result is a chronic overvaluation of the domestic currency and a loss in international price competitiveness. Fiscal and monetary discipline (i.e., avoiding large budget deficits and excessive expansion in the money supply) are needed to keep inflation down and maintain a competitive real exchange rate.

---

[16]To calculate the real exchange rate here, we use the ratio of the price deflators for GDP, which include the prices of all final goods and services produced in the economies. If the data had been available, indices measuring the prices of only traded goods and services would have been used.

In sum, avoiding the Dutch disease, where initially conditions for growth seem especially favorable, requires self-restraint and foresight. We now turn to the issue of managing natural resources for sustainable development.

## SUSTAINABLE DEVELOPMENT

As introduced in Chapter 1, **sustainable development** refers to development where the needs of the present generations are met without compromising the ability to meet the needs of future generations. To remedy environmental deterioration requires additional resource commitments or a modification of current practices (such as reducing consumption). With the loss of biodiversity that comes with the extinction of species, remedies are too late.

It is important to note, however, that the depletion of nonrenewable resources need not imply an unsustainable development. Indeed, within the market mechanism, rising scarcities should be reflected in rising relative prices, which, in turn, encourage conservation and the development of substitutes. Moreover, technological progress, which allows for outputs to be produced with fewer inputs, and increases in the stocks of physical and human capital can enhance the economic development prospects of future generations—even as the stocks of nonrenewable resources are drawn down.[17]

We hasten to add that technological progress and increases in the average levels of consumption do not warrant a cavalier attitude toward natural resources and the environment. Even in the most advanced economies, where the knowledge and means to preserve the environment are readily available, signs of land, water, and air degradation are all too frequent. In fact, some technological progress may introduce new threats to the environment (e.g., the disposal of hazardous wastes from the generation of nuclear power).

Below we will consider the environmental conditions in the less developed countries, especially with respect to water, land use, air quality, and energy consumption. Policies to promote sustainable development will be discussed. We begin, however, with a review of *externalities*, or activities where the net private benefits diverge from the net social benefits.

### MARKET FAILURES AND GOVERNMENT REGULATION

Free markets, driven by the individual pursuit of self-interest (utility maximization for consumers and profit maximization for producers) do not always capture all the

---

[17]As noted earlier, with nonrenewable resources, the question of the optimal rate of depletion arises. The present value of the future net income (revenues less costs) generated from the use of a resource over its expected lifetime could be maximized. Such a calculation requires estimates of the future prices of the resources (which will depend on the future demands and supplies) and estimates of the future costs of extracting and processing the resource (which will depend on the technologies available). Moreover, to convert future net incomes into a present value, a discount rate must be selected, thereby implicitly assigning a premium to present consumption over future consumption.

consequences of the private economic activities in question. As discussed in Chapter 6, there may exist externalities or spillover effects on other parties not directly involved. With respect to the environment, negative externalities, or adverse consequences, seem to be more prevalent.

Consider: a logging company's clear-cutting of a hillside forest that, with the heavy spring rains, leads to erosion of the nearby farmland; a chemical company's dumping wastes in a river that threaten the fish and waterfowl; industrial air pollution that contributes both to acid rain that damages forests and to respiratory problems that impair human health; the expansion of slash-and-burn agriculture into the tropical rainforests that adds to the greenhouse effect and global warming; the aggressive use of large nets for tuna fishing that also ensnare dolphins, seriously depleting the stocks of this gentle and highly intelligent creature; the radioactive wastes generated by nuclear energy that are temporarily stored while awaiting better solutions to be found by future generations. In each case the full costs of production are not borne by the producers and consumers. The understating of the social costs of production result in market prices that are too low, with quantities produced and consumed that are too high.

Refer to Figure 12.3, where the market demand and supply curves for a commodity whose production or consumption creates negative externalities are illustrated. As an example, consider leaded gasoline, consumption of which by motor vehicles contributes to air pollution. The World Bank observes that

> High levels of lead, primarily from vehicle emissions, have been identified as the greatest environmental danger in a number of large cities in the developing world. Estimates for Bangkok suggest that the average child has lost four or more IQ points by the age of seven because of elevated exposure to lead, with enduring implications for adult productivity. In adults the consequences include risks of higher blood pressure and higher risks of heart attacks, strokes, and death. In Mexico City lead exposure may contribute to as much as 20 percent of the incidence of hypertension.[18]

In Figure 12.3 the market supply curve $S$ reflects the private costs of producing leaded gasoline. The supply curve $S'$ incorporates the additional social costs, here associated with the reduced air quality in congested areas that is unhealthy. (*Note:* In some cases the social costs from the negative externalities are borne by future generations who may inherit greatly reduced supplies of renewable resources, environmental blight, less biodiversity, or stockpiles of hazardous wastes.)

The free market would clear at $P_0$ and $Q_0$, with consumers' surplus of $HE_0P_0$ and producers' surplus of $P_0E_0G$. The social costs of the negative externality are equal to the area $GG'F_0E_0$. Some of the social costs are captured by the producers of leaded gasoline as producers' surplus ($GG'VE_0$). Some of the social costs are part of consumers' surplus ($E_1VE_0$). The social costs not accounted for or not redistributed are given by the area $E_1F_0E_0$.

If the additional costs from the reduced health caused by the air pollution from the burning of leaded gasoline were included, then the relevant supply curve would be $S'$. (*Note:* If the adverse health consequences increase with the production and consumption of leaded gasoline, then the supply curve $S'$ would have a greater slope than the market supply curve $S$.) The "social market-clearing" price would rise to $P_1$ and the quantity transacted (here gallons of leaded gasoline per day) would fall to $Q_1$.

---

[18]World Bank, *World Development Report 1992*, page 5.

### FIGURE 12.3 | MARKET FAILURE: A NEGATIVE EXTERNALITY

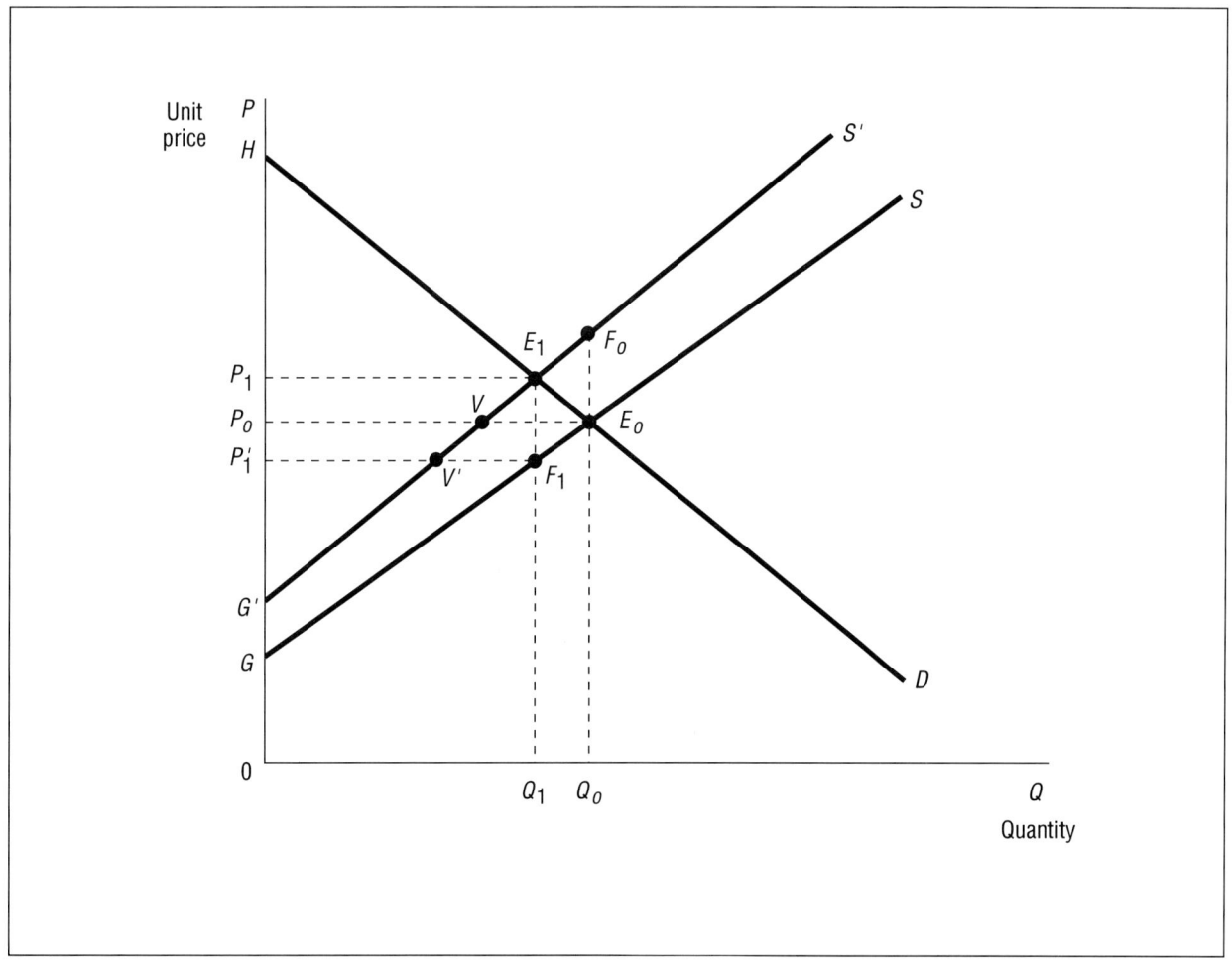

PRIVATE MARKET (WITHOUT CONSIDERATION OF THE NEGATIVE EXTERNALITY)
Price = $P_o$   Quantity = $Q_o$
Consumers' surplus = $HP_oE_o$   Producers' surplus = $GP_oE_o$
Social costs of negative externality = $GG'F_oE_o$
  Captured as producers' surplus ($GG'VE_o$) and consumers' surplus ($E_1E_oV$)
  Not captured = $E_1F_oE_o$

SOCIAL MARKET (WITH CONSIDERATION OF NEGATIVE EXTERNALITY)
Price consumers pay = $P_1$   Price producers receive = $P_1'$   Quantity = $Q_1$
Consumers' surplus = $HP_1E_1$   Producers' surplus = $GP_1'F_1$
Government revenues (from excise tax) = $P_1E_1F_1P_1'$
Social costs of negative externality = $GG'E_1F_1$
  Captured as producers' surplus ($GG'V'F_1$) and consumers' surplus (none)
  Captured as government revenues ($V'E_1F_1$)
  Not captured = none

Consumers' surplus would decrease to $HP_1E_1$ and producers' surplus would become $P_1E_1G'$. There would be a gain to society, however, from the reduced production and consumption of this commodity due to the reduced social costs, represented by the area $E_1F_1E_0F_0$. Furthermore, the resources released when less of this commodity is produced could be used elsewhere in the economy, creating additional output. For example, more unleaded gasoline could be produced as the output of leaded gasoline declined.

To deal with this market failure (i.e., an overproduction and overconsumption of this commodity due to the negative externalities), the government has two sets of options. Suppose the goal is to reduce the daily quantity consumed of leaded gasoline to $Q_1$, a level that is socially allocatively efficient; that is, the point at which the marginal social cost of production is equal to the price consumers are willing to pay for this last gallon of leaded gasoline consumed.

### Measures to Reduce Supply

One approach would be to reduce the supply from $S$ to $S'$. Moral suasion could be employed to encourage the producers of gasoline to develop and market less polluting brands of leaded gasoline, incurring the research and development costs of so doing. Other than the favorable publicity that might be gained from cooperating with the government's request, profit-maximizing producers would have little incentive to incur these additional costs—especially when competitors might not go along. Stronger measures might have to be taken, such as a phase-in of stricter standards on the lead content of gasoline.

The government could impose an excise tax on the producers of leaded gasoline, shifting the supply curve up from $S$ to $S'$. The tax revenues, here given by the area $P_1E_1F_1P_1'$, could be used to fund research into cleaner brands of gasoline or improved fuel efficiency of motor vehicles. Unless imposed on luxury or income-elastic commodities, excise taxes, however, tend to be regressive, taking a larger share of the incomes of poorer households. Nevertheless, if the supply can be shifted to $S'$ with a tax, the additional social costs associated with the production and consumption of this commodity are internalized in the market. Consumers' surplus falls to $HP_1E_1$; producers' surplus decreases to $GP_1'F_1$. The government captures the tax revenues $P_1E_1F_1P_1'$, which, as noted, could be used to fund research and development to improve the environment. The reduction in the social costs from the use of leaded gasoline is given by the area $E_1F_0E_0F_1$, which is a measure of the gains in health from improved air quality. Note the redistribution effects of the imposition of the excise tax on the suppliers of leaded gasoline. With the reduction of output to $Q_1$, all of the social costs of production from the negative externalities are captured: $GG'V'F_1$, as part of producers' surplus, and $V'E_1F_1$ as part of government revenues. The area $E_1F_0E_0$ represents the net gain in social welfare from the reduced production and consumption of leaded gasoline.

A variant of the supply-side approach is for the government to set a quota on the production of leaded gasoline. The quota could be set at $Q_1$, and the rights to produce leaded gasoline could be auctioned off. The market value of a license to produce one gallon of leaded gasoline could rise to $P_1 - P_1'$. In this way, as with an excise tax, the government could collect the revenues from the auctioning of the licenses. The initial consequences for the market price, consumers' and producers' surpluses, and the gain in air quality from a quota set at $Q_1$ would be the same as with a tax that shifted the supply curve up to $S'$. However, if the demand for leaded gasoline increased over time, an excise tax would permit increases in the production and consumption of leaded gasoline and, accordingly, increases in the social costs from the negative externalities. In contrast, an output quota set at $Q_1$ would freeze the production and consumption of leaded gasoline, and given the underlying supply curves $S$ and $S'$, the social costs associated with the externality.

## Measures to Reduce Demand

The second set of options involves reducing demand. See Figure 12.4, on page 374, in which the market demand curve shifts down from $D$ to $D'$ to intersect the private market supply curve at $Q_1$, the socially allocatively efficient level of output. To reduce the demand for leaded gasoline, the government (or public interest groups) could try to educate the population about the adverse health consequences of burning leaded gasoline. Carpooling, greater use of public transportation, purchasing more fuel-efficient automobiles, and switching to the lower-octane, but cleaner, unleaded gasoline could be encouraged.

The major problem with moral suasion and volunteerism is that the total response may be insufficient. That is, the decrease in demand may fall far short of that required to reduce consumption to $Q_1$. A related difficulty is with dysfunctional selection. Those conscientious citizens who do cut back on their consumption of leaded gasoline will help lower the market price—to the benefit of those individuals who do not cut back. Therefore, to reduce demand the government may attempt to regulate consumer behavior. For example, some cities have tried to ration the use of automobiles by restricting driving to certain days of the week: Cars with license plates ending in even numbers could be driven in the cities on Mondays, Wednesdays, and Fridays; cars with license plates ending in odd numbers or letters could be driven on Tuesdays, Thursdays, and Saturdays. The government could require all new automobiles to use only unleaded gasoline. The standards for annual inspections of motor vehicles could be tightened to require the use of emission controls. Public transit could be subsidized to encourage a substitution away from private transportation.

If the demand in Figure 12.4 could be reduced to $D'$, then for the market supply curve $S$, which only includes the private costs of production, the quantity transacted is reduced to $Q_1$. The market price falls to $P_1'$. The producers' and consumers' surpluses associated with the sales and use of leaded gasoline are lower ($P_1'F_1G$ and $H'P_1'F_1$ respectively); however, as before, there is a gain in the health benefits from the cleaner air enjoyed by the general public. The reduction in the quantity transacted from $Q_0$ to $Q_1$ decreases the social costs associated with the production and consumption of leaded gasoline by the area $E_1F_oE_oF_1$. Note that with the reduction in demand to $D'$, there are still social costs not captured (the area $E_1WF_1$), which, if accounted for, would reduce the quantity transacted further to $Q_2$. See the point $W$ in Figure 12.4, where the demand curve $D'$ intersects the supply curve $S'$ that incorporates the social costs.

In sum, where negative externalities associated with the production or consumption of a commodity are present, too much of the commodity at too low a price tends to be produced in a free market. As illustrated above, policy options can address these negative externalities and reach the socially allocatively efficient levels of output. While the selection of the specific policy would be dependent on the particular situation at hand, in general, a combination of supply-side and demand-side approaches may be required. Unfortunately, in some of the less developed countries, government policies may have undermined environmental preservation and sustainable development.

### FIGURE 12.4  A NEGATIVE EXTERNALITY AND A REDUCTION IN DEMAND

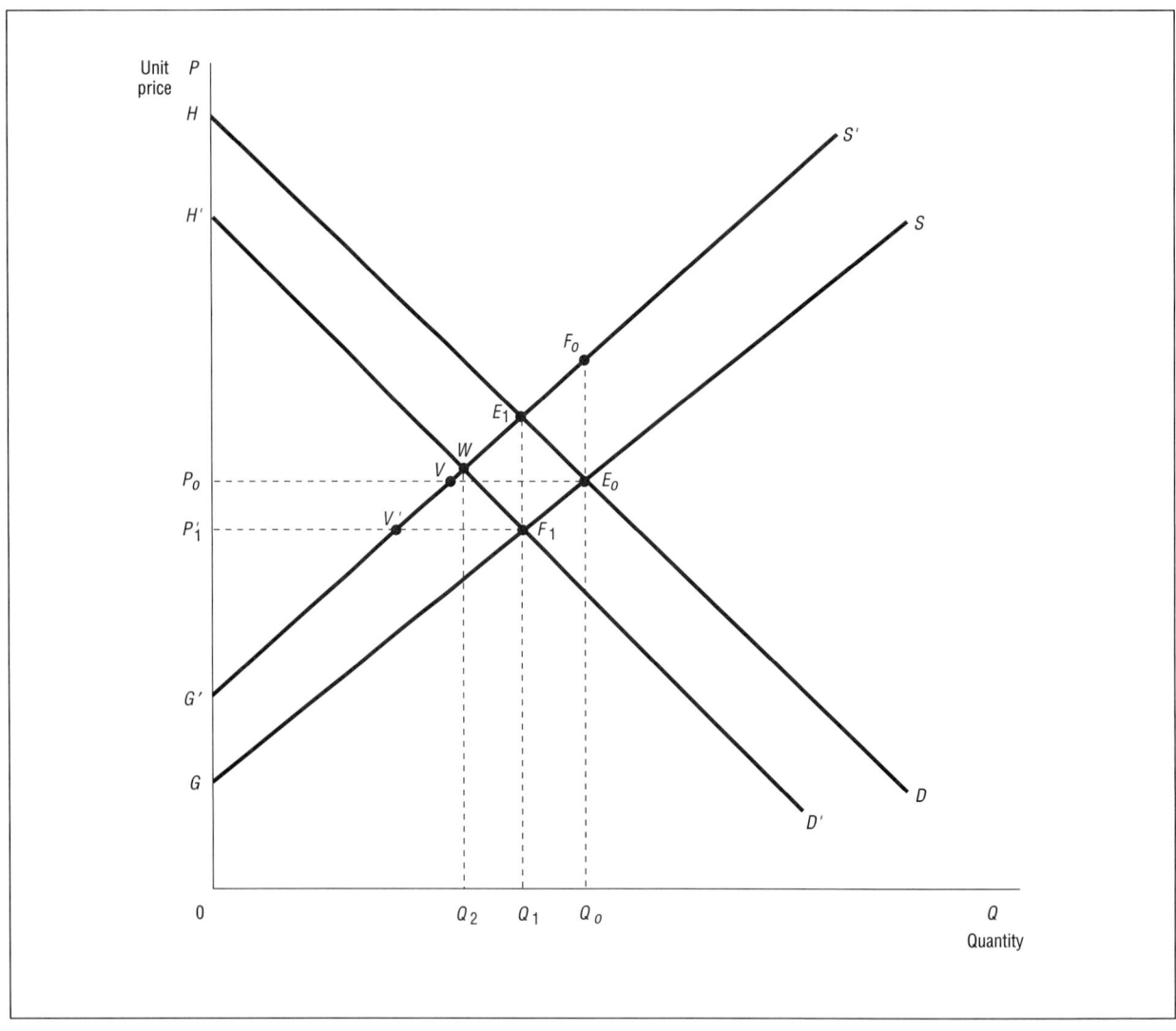

INITIAL DEMAND (D) IN PRIVATE MARKET
Price = $P_o$    Quantity = $Q_o$
Consumers' surplus = $HP_oE_o$    Producers' surplus = $GP_oE_o$
Social costs of negative externality = $GG'F_oE_o$
   Captured as producers' surplus $(GG'VE_o)$ and consumers' surplus $(E_1E_oV)$
   Not captured = $E_1F_oE_o$

REDUCED DEMAND (D') in Private Market
Price = $P'_1$    Quantity = $Q_1$
Consumers' surplus = $H'P'_1F_1$    Producers' surplus = $GP'_1F_1$
Social costs of negative externality = $GG'E_1F_1$
   Captured as producers' surplus $(GG'VF_1)$ and consumers' surplus $(VWF_1)$
   Not captured = $E_1F_1W$

| TABLE 12.3 | SELECTED STATISTICS ON LAND AND WATER | | | | | | | |
|---|---|---|---|---|---|---|---|---|
| | POPULATION DENSITY 1990 | SHARE OF TOTAL LAND AREA (%) | | | PER CAPITA WATER (CUBIC METERS) 1990 | SECTORAL WITHDRAWAL OF WATER (%) | | |
| | | AGR. | PERM. PAST. | FOREST | | AGR. | DOM. | INDUS. |
| sub-Saharan Africa | 22.1 | 7 | 33 | 30 | 7,488 | 88 | 8 | 3 |
| Middle East & North Africa | 22.7 | 6 | 22 | 3 | 1,071 | 89 | 6 | 5 |
| Europe | 93.6 | 39 | 16 | 29 | 2,865 | 45 | 14 | 42 |
| Other economies | 14.3 | 10 | 17 | 43 | 13,976 | 66 | 6 | 28 |
| South Asia | 240.1 | 45 | 4 | 23 | 4,236 | 94 | 2 | 3 |
| East Asia & Pacific | 103.9 | 11 | 30 | 25 | 5,009 | 86 | 6 | 8 |
| Latin America & the Caribbean | 21.6 | 9 | 28 | 48 | 24,390 | 72 | 16 | 11 |
| High-income OECD | 26.0 | 12 | 26 | 30 | 10,781 | 39 | 14 | 47 |

NOTES:
*Population density* is the mid-1990 population of the region per square kilometer of total land area.

*Agricultural land* (Agr.) includes both arable land (land under temporary crops, temporary meadows, market and kitchen gardens, and land temporarily fallow or lying idle) and permanent crop land (land occupied by crops such as cocoa, coffee, and rubber that are in place for long periods and need not be replanted after each harvest). Also included are lands under shrubs, fruit trees, nut trees and vines.

*Permanent pasture* (Perm. Past.) refers to land used permanently (five years or more) for herbaceous forage crops, either cultivated or growing wild.

*Forest and woodland* (Forest) refers to land under natural or planted stands of trees, whether subject to harvesting or not, and includes land from which forests have been cleared but that will be reforested in the forseeable future.

*Other land,* the residual category (not shown) includes unused but potentially productive land, built-on areas, wasteland, parks, ornamental gardens, roads, lanes, barren land, and any other land not specifically listed in the three categories.

*Per capita water* is annual per capita internal renewable water resources in 1990 (in cubic meters) and refers to the average annual flow of rivers and of aquifers generated from rainfall within the region divided by the population of the region.

Sectoral withdrawal of water resources is divided into *agriculture* (Agr.) for irrigation and livestock; *domestic* (Dom.) for drinking water, private homes, commercial establishments, public services, and municipal use or provision; and *industry* (Indus.), including water for cooling thermoelectric plants.

Regional data on water resources and utilization should be used with care. Average annual figures may conceal significant annual variations.

*Other economies* are Cuba, Democratic People's Republic of Korea, and the former Union of Soviet Socialist Republics.

*Europe* comprises the middle-income European economies of Albania, Bulgaria, former Czechoslovakia, Greece, Hungary, Poland, Portugal, Romania, Turkey, and former Yugoslavia.

FROM: World Bank, *World Development Report 1992*, Tables A3, A6, and 1.

## DIVERSITY IN RESOURCE ENDOWMENT AND UTILIZATION

To illustrate the diversity in resource endowment and utilization across regions of the developing world, refer to Table 12.3, which presents selected statistics on land and water use. By far, South Asia is the most densely populated region, with 240 persons per square kilometer of total land area, more than twice as high as in East Asia and the Pacific or the middle-income economies of Europe. The population densities of sub-Saharan Africa, the Middle East and North Africa, and Latin America and the Caribbean are virtually identical—at approximately 22 persons per square kilometer. Remember, however, that regional averages can mask significant variations in population density and the quality of the land within regions.

Concerning land use, the share of total land area accounted for by agriculture is generally 12 percent or less, the exceptions being South Asia (45 percent) and the middle-income economies of Europe (39 percent). The high share of agriculture in South Asia would appear to restrict severely the land area available for permanent pasture. Sub-Saharan Africa has the highest percentage of land used for permanent pasture (33 percent). With the extreme exception of the Middle East and North Africa, a region with much desert, from one-quarter to one-half of the total land areas is accounted for by forest and woodlands. Due largely to the vast Amazon Rain Forest in South America, Latin America and the Caribbean not only have 48 percent of land area in forests and woodlands but have, by far, the highest per capita water resources—more than 20 times the average for the Middle East and North Africa (see also Figure 12.5). Again, we note that average per capita levels of water resources for a year (1990) may obscure significant variation across countries within a region and over time. Moreover, a high level of per capita water resources need not mean that the water is always available at the appropriate times. For example, for some countries, the monsoon rains in several months may account for nearly all of the rainfall received during the year.

With respect to the allocation of water across sectors, for the developing countries of Africa, the Middle East, and Asia, agriculture accounts for approximately 90 percent of the water withdrawals. With economic development, however, the share of water going to industry rises, at the expense of agriculture.

With this overview, we turn to policies for the efficient utilization of natural resources and the preservation of the environment. Four interdependent areas are addressed: land, water, air, and energy.

## POLICIES FOR SUSTAINABLE DEVELOPMENT

The primary objectives of the proposed natural resource and environmental policies are to encourage efficiency in the use of the available resources; to ensure, at a minimum, a level of access to meet the basic needs of the population; and to promote sustainable development. The policy proposals fall into three areas: price signals, property rights, and technology.

### PRICE SIGNALS

Earlier we discussed how the presence of externalities in the production or consumption of a commodity could constitute a market failure. In the case of a negative externality, government intervention in the form of a tax or regulation of the activity in question would be warranted. With positive externalities, where there are socially beneficial consequences from the private activities, government subsidization may be justified. For example, the World Bank has observed that "Investments in providing clean water and sanitation have some of the highest economic, social, and environmental returns anywhere."[19]

Too often, however, in less developed countries government subsidies have resulted in inefficiencies and inequities in the use of natural resources and have unnecessarily added to budget deficits.

> Logging fees in a sample of five African countries ranged from 1 to 33 percent of the costs of replanting. Irrigation charges in most Asian countries covered less than 20

---

[19]Ibid., page 15.

| FIGURE 12.5 | RENEWABLE WATER RESOURCES PER CAPITA |

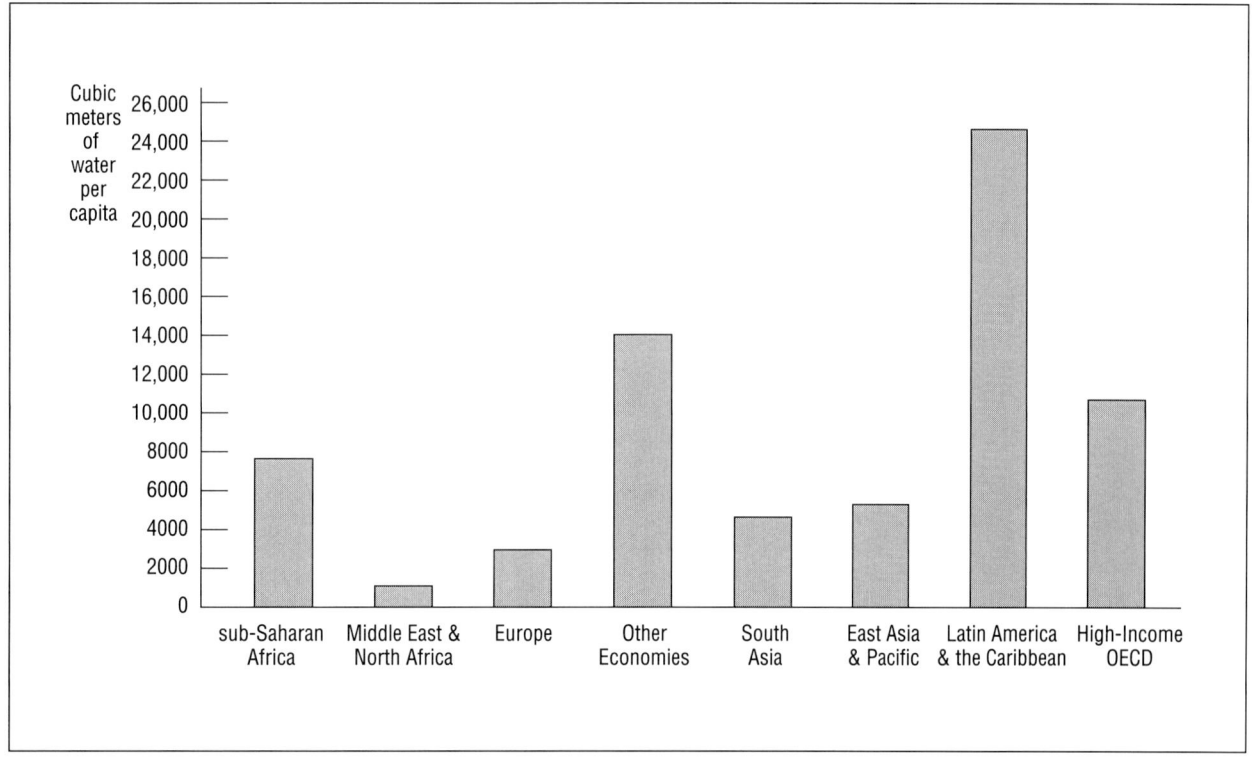

percent of the costs of supplying the water. And pesticide subsidies in a sample of seven countries in Latin America, Africa, and Asia ranged from 19 to 83 percent of costs.[20]

At present, underpricing of electricity is the rule, not the exception, in most developing countries. Prices, on average, are barely more than one-third of supply costs and are half those in industrial countries.[21]

In Europe and Japan, gasoline prices range from $3.00 to $4.00 per U.S. gallon. In the United States and in the developing countries, prices are less than one-third to one-half of that range.[22]

Thus, a first priority in natural resource policy would be "to get prices right." When the gains from an activity accrue to the private parties directly involved, then artificially low prices (either below world market levels or insufficient to cover the costs of production) provide incorrect signals to producers and consumers, resulting in a misallocation of resources. Further inequities arise when the subsidies enhance the

---

[20]Ibid., page 12.
[21]Ibid., page 116.
[22]Ibid., page 125.

incomes and consumption of the relatively well-off, rather than providing more modest, but widespread, improvements in the general level of incomes and consumption. In other words, in the above examples the primary beneficiaries of the subsidization usually are the owners of the logging companies, the larger farmers, industrialists, and the urban elite.

Tietenberg suggests that, as a general principle, public utilities should set rates that reflect the marginal costs of the services provided. For example, as found in the United States, power companies could charge different rates depending on the demands on the system: premium rates would be charged for the consumption of electricity during peak load periods. In the case of water, block pricing could be adopted to reduce the financial burden on poor households of the consumption of water for essentials, while encouraging conservation among wealthier and heavier users. For example, the charge for the first thousand gallons of water consumed per month might be 80 cents; 90 cents for the next thousand gallons, and so on.[23]

PROPERTY RIGHTS

To encourage the conservation of scarce resources and the proper maintenance of renewable resources, property rights may need to be more carefully established. Traditionally common property rights enforced by convention or social sanctions may have been sufficient in small villages or agrarian communities as long as resources were relatively abundant. With economic growth and population increases, however, resource pressures can develop which, on one hand, may stimulate technological progress and the recovery of new resources, but may also require new forms of property rights.

With the assignment of private property rights, individuals have the incentive to invest in and improve the resources under their ownership—the fertility of the land, stocks of fish, stands of trees. In the case of common resources considered as property of the state, access fees could be auctioned off to mine the minerals, harvest the forests, and fish the oceans within the nation's territorial boundaries. Refundable deposits could be required to ensure environmentally responsible behavior (e.g., proper disposal of wastes; replanting of forests; restoration of the landscape after strip mining; or limiting fish catches to levels consistent with the regeneration potential of the fish stocks). State-owned enterprises often lack the market incentives to be efficient, and may be staffed with political appointees with little interest in renewable resource management or environmental preservation. Therefore, greater reliance should be placed on private enterprise operating with carefully prescribed incentives for socially responsible behavior.

One example of local management of common resources comes from Mexico, where, in 1993, the government ceded control over a 2800-square-mile forest reserve in the southeastern region of the country to a nonprofit organization, Pronatura Peninsula Yucatan. Previously degraded by logging, the reserve is to be used by the indigenous population, with a protected area in the center to remain natural. As described by the *Wall Street Journal,*

> Federal, state, local and Pronatura workers have trained residents to manage and protect timber and other resources they still remove illegally to make ends meet. Where

---

[23]Tietenberg, pages 239–241.

logging is permitted—outside the reserve's virgin nucleus—residents practice reforesting methods. From their own nurseries, they plant mahogany and other native precious woods to harvest, as a family trust fund, in 25 to 50 years. They learn intensive organic agriculture methods that boost to 10 years from three the land's cultivability while bolstering staple corn and bean yields. They also plant commercial fruit and vegetables and develop apiaries employing the local high-yield Africanized bees....

This sustainable development process is beginning to provide residents a dignified, stable livelihood.[24]

With resources, like the atmosphere, where property rights are less clearly defined, environmental standards need to be set and enforced. One way to incorporate the market into the process of environmental regulation is to auction off pollution rights. For example, in the case of the atmosphere, the optimal amount of pollution to be allowed would be determined, whereby the marginal benefits equal the marginal costs of improving air quality. An equivalent number of licenses to discharge pollutants into the atmosphere would be auctioned off by the government. Firms operating within the set environmental standards could sell any unused pollution rights to other firms unable to meet the standards. Not only would the government generate revenues (which could be used for other environmental projects such as public investments in sanitation and water quality), but businesses would have an incentive to curb pollution.

## Technology

Continued, if not accelerated, research and development of new technologies that conserve on scarce resources and preserve the environment are needed. With their projected growth in population and the increases in per capita income and consumption required to alleviate poverty, the less developed countries will become the major force driving the sharply higher global demands for resources and commercial energy over the next few decades.

> By 2010 the share of total energy consumption accounted for by the rich countries will have fallen below 50% for the first time in the industrial era. Eastern Europe and the former Soviet Union will consume a sixth. The share of developing countries will have climbed from 27% now to 40%, and be rushing upwards faster than ever. The growth in energy consumption in developing countries between 2000 and 2010 will be greater than today's consumption in Western Europe. By 2010 their emissions of carbon dioxide, the main contributor to global warming, will be almost as big as those of the whole world in 1970 [according to the International Energy Agency].[25]

Considerable potential remains to be realized from renewable and environmentally sound sources of energy, such as solar, wind, and tidal. At present, some of the technologies most appropriate to the conditions prevalent in much of the developing world are available, but not widely disseminated. For example, we noted the environmental and health costs associated with cooking over wood (or in the case of poor farm households, cooking with dried animal dung that could have been used to fertilize

---

[24]Holly Neumann, "Mexico Adopts a Bottom-Up Environmental Policy," *Wall Street Journal* (June 25, 1993), page A11.

[25]"A Survey of Energy," *The Economist* (June 18, 1994), page 3.

the fields). There exists a simple solar box cooker, described as "an isolated box-within-a-box, 3 by 4 feet, large enough to capture four square feet of sunshine ... weighing about 16 pounds ... and easily made from inexpensive materials such as cardboard or wood, one sheet of glass, and aluminum foil," that can economically and safely be used in sunny climates. Not only would the solar box cooker reduce the deforestation caused by the burning of wood, but there would be savings in the time spent collecting the wood and a decrease in the indoor pollution from cooking over an open fire. Moreover, the solar energy requirement is modest ("solar ovens can cook anything as long as there is 15 minutes of sunshine every hour"); the cooked food is more nutritous ("a solar cooker can reduce or eliminate the bacterial contamination of food and can pasteurize water"); food requires less time and attention to prepare; and is reported to taste better than food cooked over wood.[26]

Numerous other examples can be found of intermediate technologies that may significantly improve the quality of life and environmental conditions for the poor in the LDCs. Simple latrines may provide an effective way to upgrade sanitation for the poorest households. Contour-based agriculture may help prevent soil erosion. Drip systems can improve the efficiency and equity in water use for irrigation. For example, in the Middle East, an area of the world where water supplies are especially tight, Israel has been a leader in conservation.

> Israel over the past 30 years has increased five-fold the value of the crops it can grow with a given amount of water. In a flooded or spray-irrigated field, at least half the water never reaches plant roots, but seeps underground or evaporates. Systems such as drip irrigation—from long lengths of hose containing pin-holes that drip water close to roots—cut this loss by half. Yet, even in water-starved countries, such systems are still the exception.[27]

In some cases, local knowledge, grounded in decades of experience, can be tapped to complement modern science. One well-known example is the traditional irrigation system for rice farming on the island of Bali. Regarded by development experts and Western engineeers as primitive and steeped in ritual and ceremony, the Balinese system involved high priests of water temples divining the allocation of water for irrigation and schedules for the planting and harvesting of rice. In the early 1980s the Balinese rice farmers were encouraged to adopt more modern methods, including high-yielding rice strains, larger dams and canals, and chemical fertilizers and pesticides. After experimentation with the new techniques (and experiencing disappointing harvests), it was discovered that under their traditional system the Balinese had been "practicing state-of-the-art resource management" in which water had been efficiently allocated, soil fertility had been preserved, and pests had been controlled. Since then, the two systems have been blended together, drawing on experience and modern science, to improve rice farming in Bali.[28]

The point is not that modern technology has little to offer developing economies. On the contrary, the less developed countries have been, and will continue to be, the beneficiaries of the research of the developed countries. Rather, it is a mistake to dismiss

---

[26]This information and the embedded quotations are from "Hot Box," by Alice Ainsworth, *Christian Science Monitor* (October 27, 1988), page 21.

[27]*The Economist* (August 12, 1995), page 36.

[28]"The Electronic Goddess: Computerizing Bali's Ancient Irrigation Rites," by Geoffrey Cowley, *Newsweek* (March 6, 1989), page 50.

automatically the current practices of indigenous peoples in poor countries as primitive, irrational, or unproductive. Lessons can be learned from all sources.

## CONCLUDING NOTE

Clearly many challenges face the LDCs, not the least of which is natural resource management. While viewed by some as lower priorities than economic growth and the alleviation of poverty, the effective stewardship of natural resources and the care of the environment are crucial elements of economic development.

The protection of the environment and the preservation of species, however, are obligations shared by the present generations of all nations. International cooperation is essential. In Chapter 19 we will examine the progress that has been realized from international cooperation, as well as the challenges that remain. To conclude this section of the text on sectors in development, we turn to manufacturing and services in Chapter 13.

## SUMMARY OF MAIN POINTS

1. Natural resources, along with human labor and physical capital, are a primary factor of production. Agriculture, fishing, forestry, and mining are natural resource-intensive sectors of the economy.
2. With proper management, renewable natural resources (e.g., farmland) can be replenished. Stocks are finite, however, for nonrenewable natural resources (e.g., mineral deposits). Conservation, recycling, and the development of renewable substitutes can extend the available supplies of nonrenewable natural resources.
3. Mining operations, with the exception, perhaps, of some precious stones, tend to be capital-intensive. In those less developed countries favorably endowed, the extraction and export of minerals have often attracted foreign direct investment and have been a major source of foreign exchange earnings.
4. For coastal nations, fishing is usually an important economic activity—accommodating both large-scale fishing fleets and numerous small fishermen. Globally, fish catches seem to be declining, due, in part, to overfishing.
5. Many developing nations, especially in the tropics, possess large reserves of forests. Forests serve many functions, ranging from the economic (e.g., timber for logging) to the environmental (e.g., recycling of carbon dioxide). During the last half-century, poverty and population pressure, along with extensive logging, have contributed to high rates of deforestation, with the consequent loss of some species and disturbance of ecological balances.
6. Nations that are well endowed with minerals or forests may be able to generate significant foreign-exchange earnings and tax revenues through exports. These export revenues, however, may be quite volatile, that is, dependent on swings in foreign demand with the international business cycle. Nations need to manage

their natural resources carefully, avoiding, first, export taxes so high that foreign consumers begin both to conserve and to develop substitute products, and, second, the Dutch disease brought on by overextending the domestic economy during an export boom.

7. The real exchange rate for a currency (say, the rupee) is equal to the nominal exchange rate (the rupee price of a U.S. dollar) times the ratio of the foreign (U.S.) price index to the domestic price index. A real depreciation (appreciation) of the currency increases (decreases) the nation's international price competitiveness.

8. Market failures in the form of negative (positive) externalities mean that some of the social costs (benefits) of an economic activity are not captured in the market's allocation of resources. With negative externalities (e.g., pollution) too much of a commodity is being produced and consumed at too low a price. Moral suasion, taxes, and government regulation are some of the options for dealing with negative externalities.

9. Sustainable development preserves, if not enhances, the ability of future generations to develop. It can be consistent with the depletion of some nonrenewable resources if compensated by technological progress or increases in other natural resources, physical capital, or human labor.

10. Policies for sustainable development fall into three basic categories. First, market incentives should be used, whenever possible, to allocate resources. Market failures such as externalities would be an exception requiring government intervention. Second, clearly defined property rights tend to promote careful management of resources. Where ownership of resources is highly concentrated, however, equity and efficiency may dictate some redistribution of assets. Third, continued research is needed to develop new technologies that conserve resources and protect the environment.

## KEY TERMS

**appreciation**
**depreciation**
**Dutch disease**
**natural resources**
**nominal exchange rate**

**nonrenewable resources**
**real exchange rate**
**renewable resources**
**sustainable development**
**world reserve base life index**

## QUESTIONS

1. Natural resources are sometimes referred to as "gifts of nature." Does this imply that the natural resources within a country belong to the state and should be regarded as public property? Should there be a distinction here between renewable and nonrenewable natural resources? In general, what should be the role of the government in developing and managing the natural resources of a nation? Discuss.

2. Suppose a country is well endowed with petroleum reserves. Does this imply a particular development strategy? Discuss.

3. Suppose a nation is well endowed with tropical rain forests. Does this imply a particular development strategy? Discuss.

4. Suppose a country experiences a boom in export revenues due to sharply higher foreign demand for its primary export, bauxite, which is used in the production of aluminum. What strategy should be adopted to avoid the Dutch disease?
5. Given a nominal exchange rate of 40 rupees equal to one U.S. dollar and domestic and foreign price indices equal to 100 (i.e., $P_D = 100$ and $P_F = 100$), first determine the dollar price of a rupee. Then calculate the new real exchange rate (both in terms of the rupee price of the dollar and the dollar price of the rupee) for each of the following changes:
   *a.* a depreciation in the nominal exchange value of the rupee by 10 percent
   *b.* an increase in the foreign price level by 10 percent
   *c.* an increase in the domestic price level by 10 percent
   Which of the above changes improves the international price competitiveness of the rupee-currency country?
6. Given a perfectly competitive market with the following demand and supply curves for a commodity whose production involves a negative externality:

$$D = 40 - 5P \quad \text{(market demand)}$$
$$S = -5 + 4P \quad \text{(market supply based on the private costs of production)}$$
$$S' = -8 + 3P \quad \text{(market supply based on the social costs of production)}$$

   *a.* Sketch the market demand and supply curves, and determine graphically the market equilibrium price and quantity transacted. Identify and label the consumers' surplus, producers' surplus, and the social costs not captured by the market.
   *b.* Now suppose the government levies an excise tax on the producers of this commodity so that the new market supply curve becomes $S' = -8 + 3P$ (effectively accounting for the negative externality). Determine graphically the new market equilibrium price and quantity transacted. Account for the changes in consumers' surplus and producers' surplus. Is there a net gain to society with the government tax? Discuss.

## SUGGESTED READINGS

"A Survey of Energy," *The Economist* (June 18, 1994).

Tietenberg, Tom, *Environmental and Natural Resource Economics*, 3d ed., New York: HarperCollins, 1992, Chapters 1, 2, 3, 11, and 22.

World Bank, *World Development Report 1992: Development and the Environment*, New York: Oxford University Press, 1992.

## CASE STUDY

### JAMAICA

The third largest island in the Caribbean, Jamaica is located about 90 miles south of Cuba and 100 miles west of Haiti. The country's population was approximately 2.5 million in 1994; nearly 55 percent of the population resides in urban areas, most notably the capital city of Kingston.[1] Driven by sugar cultivation, agriculture was the principal economic activity until the middle of the twentieth century. Although agriculture is still an important source of employment, this case study focuses on Jamaica's efforts to develop its natural resource base in the mining and tourism industries.

Jamaica experienced an economic boom from 1952 to 1972, driven largely by foreign investments in the bauxite-alumina and tourist industries. During the 1950s, the United States government sought to build up its strategic stockpile of aluminum ingots. In response, three transnational corporations—Alcoa, Reynolds, and Kaiser—developed bauxite mines in Jamaica to supply their aluminum processing plants in the United States. Also, Alcan, a Canadian transnational, built its own processing plant in Jamaica. As a result, the share of bauxite and alumina in total Jamaican exports grew from 11.4 percent in 1953 to 62.7 percent in 1972.[2] The bauxite-alumina industry became the leading source of foreign exchange and a major source of government revenues. Other than stimulating the construction and transportation sectors, the industry had few linkages to other sectors of the economy and failed to create a large number of new jobs.[3]

Foreign investment flowed into the construction of new hotels in the 1950s to accommodate the growing number of tourists traveling to Jamaica to enjoy its pleasant climate, exceptional beaches, and beautiful scenery. However, political uncertainty surrounding Jamaica's independence from Great Britain in 1962 slowed the rate of growth in tourist traffic. After independence, tourism expanded throughout the remainder of the decade. In 1972, approximately 494,000 tourists visited Jamaica, more than four times the number recorded in 1955, and total tourist receipts increased by more than 160 percent over the same period.[4] Jamaica's tourist industry generated significant foreign exchange, although its high imported input requirements somewhat offset the export earnings. In 1968, for example, Jamaican hotels imported 69.4 percent of their food supplies and 62.3 percent of their beverages and cigarettes.[5] Tourism also created employment opportunities for local residents, but the jobs were often seasonal and paid low wages.

Real gross domestic product grew at an average annual rate of 6.3 percent over the period 1950 to 1972.[6] Despite this impressive growth, unemployment and income inequality remained persistent problems. The unemployment rate in 1972 was 23.5 percent, almost the same as that recorded for 1953.[7] As previously mentioned, the capital-intensive bauxite industry did not create many new jobs, and the tourist industry was subject to seasonal unemployment. Moreover, the growing demand for bauxite contributed to an appreciation of the Jamaican currency, which limited agricultural exports and employment in that sector as well. The stagnation of the agricultural

---

[1]Population Reference Bureau, Inc., *1994 World Population Data Sheet* (April 1994); and World Bank, "Jamaica," *Trends in Developing Countries 1994*, Washington, DC, 1994, page 239.

[2]Carl Stone and Stanislaw Wellisz, "Jamaica," *The Political Economics of Poverty, Equity, and Growth: Five Small Open Economies*, Ronald Findlay and Stanislaw Wellisz, editors, New York: Oxford University Press for the World Bank, 1993, page 167.

[3]Ibid., page 166.

[4]Ibid., page 162.

[5]François J. Belisle, "Tourism and Food Imports: The Case of Jamaica," *Economic Development and Cultural Change*, vol. 32, no. 4 (July 1984), page 820.

[6]Stone and Wellisz, page 156.

[7]Omar Davies, "An Analysis of the Management of the Jamaican Economy: 1972–1985," *Social and Economic Studies*, vol. 35, no. 1 (March 1986), page 75.

sector precluded any improvement in the relative income position of rural households. In short, rural households did not benefit from the economic growth occurring in the mining and tourist industries.

Michael Manley, leader of the People's National Party, held the office of prime minister from 1972 to 1980 and committed Jamaica to a course of democratic socialism. The state became a majority stockholder in the bauxite mining operations of Kaiser and Reynolds and a minority stockholder in Alcoa and Alcan. The government purchased foreign-owned public utilities in electricity, telephone communication, and urban transportation. Majority ownership in the cement, gypsum, and steel industries passed to the government, and some banks were nationalized. A land-reform program addressed rural poverty by leasing public lands to landless peasants at low rental rates. In a similar vein, the government purchased several foreign-owned sugar estates and transformed them into workers' cooperatives. Expanded public health services, an adult literacy program, and a housing construction project sought to alleviate the widespread problems of low nutrition, illiteracy, and inadequate housing.[8]

The move toward socialism divided the country, however. Riots and political violence led to a decline in tourism. The recession in the United States following the 1973 oil price shock compounded the decline, highlighting the sensitivity of the tourist industry to economic conditions in the United States. From 1972 to 1977, Jamaican tourist receipts fell by more than 60 percent.[9]

The bauxite-alumina industry stagnated as well. Jamaican bauxite supplied aluminum refineries and smelters in the United States. The 1973 and 1979 oil price shocks raised the costs of producing aluminum in these refineries and smelters. In response, the transnational aluminum companies shifted their operations to countries such as Australia and Brazil, which were rich in both bauxite reserves and domestic energy resources, such as coal and hydroelectric power. Jamaica's bauxite-alumina industry declined further as a result of a levy imposed by the Manley government. Since Jamaica was dependent on imported oil to provide 98 percent of its energy needs, the government wanted to increase its foreign exchange earnings from the transnational aluminum companies to compensate for the foreign exchange losses resulting from the oil price shocks.[10] While initially reducing Jamaica's balance of payments problem, revenues from the bauxite levy did not keep pace with the cost of oil imported for the non-bauxite sector. Bauxite production declined from 15.3 thousand metric tons when the levy was imposed in 1974 to 11.6 thousand metric tons in 1975.[11]

Mounting budget deficits associated with the government's socialist programs and a deterioration in Jamaica's balance of payments resulting from the oil price shocks forced the Manley administration to enter into two loan agreements with the International Monetary Fund (IMF), the first lasting from July to December 1977 and the second lasting from May 1978 to December 1979. In exchange for the IMF loans, the government promised to devalue the Jamaican currency, limit wage increases, remove price controls, and reduce government spending. Both loan agreements were terminated, however, when Jamaica failed to meet performance criteria set by the IMF.

Under the Manley regime, real gross domestic product fell in every year except one between 1974 and 1980, and unemployment continually worsened.[12] The Jamaican

---

[8]Stone and Wellisz, pages 180–181.
[9]Ibid., page 191.
[10]Davies, page 81.
[11]Stone and Wellisz, page 183.
[12]Davies, pages 84 and 88.

Labour Party, under the leadership of Edward Seaga, won a landslide victory in the violent 1980 election. Arguing that the private sector should be the driving force in the economy, the Seaga administration removed the price controls, subsidies, and import restrictions established during the Manley regime and divested the government's holdings in some, but not all, businesses. However, to prevent an acceleration of food and energy price inflation and to contain unemployment, the Seaga administration vowed not to devalue the currency nor to dismiss government employees.

Loan agreements with the IMF were to provide the foreign exchange necessary to finance the rise in imports following liberalization—at least until Jamaica's traditional exports returned to their projected growth paths. Exports, however, declined while imports soared. A fixed exchange rate policy pursued in the presence of an inflation rate higher than that of Jamaica's trading partners led to an overvalued currency and a decline in the competitiveness of Jamaican exports. The international recession of the early 1980s hit bauxite exports particularly hard, and cuts in United States' import quotas hindered the expansion of sugar exports. The only bright spot was tourism. The return of political and social stability after the 1980 election and the economic expansion in the United States during the 1980s helped the industry recover. The number of tourists nearly doubled from 529,000 in 1980 to 1,031,000 in 1987.[13] Given the decline in other export sectors, tourism became the leading source of foreign exchange, and its share of gross domestic product increased sharply. Negative externalities, however, accompanied the economic ascent of tourism. Children skipped school in order to make money serving as personal guides to foreigners. Prostitution became more prevalent, and illegal drug transactions increased.

As Jamaica's merchandise trade balance deteriorated, the IMF attached stronger conditions to its loans. In 1983, the IMF insisted that the Seaga government reduce aggregate demand, shrink government expenditures, and devalue the Jamaican dollar. In response, the administration imposed new taxes, capped wage increases of government employees, dismissed a number of civil servants, and devalued the currency. These austerity measures coupled with the poor performance of exports depressed the economy, generating low or negative economic growth rates over the 1983 to 1986 period. By raising import prices, the rapid devaluation of the currency accelerated the rate of inflation. Aided by the devaluation, the labor-intensive tourist industry expanded, contributing to a reduction in the unemployment rate and an improvement in Jamaica's current account balance. Heavy foreign borrowing, however, increased debt service as a percentage of exports from 19.3 percent in 1980 to 49.4 percent in 1987.[14] These disappointing results and Michael Manley's repudiation of socialism allowed him to win the 1989 election and return to office.

This time, pursuing a program of reforms based on free market principles, the Manley administration accelerated the privatization of state-owned enterprises, the liberalization of trade, and the stabilization of the economy. Sound economic policies and improved terms of trade generated growth rates of real gross domestic product that averaged 1.1 percent per year from 1991 to 1993.[15] With the government budget in surplus, foreign direct investment increasing, and international oil prices remaining low, Jamaica has a good chance of sustaining this growth.

---

[13]Stone and Wellisz, page 202.

[14]Ibid., page 206.

[15]World Bank, "Jamaica," *Trends in Developing Countries 1994*, page 242.

# CHAPTER 13

# INDUSTRY AND SERVICES

Economic development can be viewed as a set of interrelated changes in the structure of an economy that are required for its continued growth. They involve the composition of demand, production, and employment as well as the external structure of trade and capital flows. Taken together, these structural changes define the transformation of a traditional to a modern economic system.[1]

Having studied both agriculture and natural resources, we now consider industry and services, the remaining sectors within the economy. In a classic work, *Structural Change and Development Policy*, Hollis Chenery analyzed structural change within the development process. He wrote of several common characteristics that countries share, including predictable changes in consumer demand with economic growth; increased investment; a move toward similar technological processes across nations; and increased international trade.[2] In this chapter we emphasize the growing importance of industry and services within a country that is on a sustained development path. The demands for the outputs of these sectors are typically income-elastic, so the growth of per capita income more than proportionately increases expenditures on the products of these sectors.

We begin with an overview of industry and services, highlighting changes in these sectors within the development process. The production linkages among agriculture, industry, and services are examined. We will see how increases in final demands in one sector will themselves require output increases in all sectors. Then we turn to international integration and the issue of import substitution as a policy to promote industry.

---

[1] Hollis Chenery, *Structural Change and Development Policy*, New York: Oxford University Press, 1979, page xvi.
[2] Ibid., pages 6 and 7.

We conclude with a discussion of economic infrastructure and its critical contribution to economic growth.

## THE IMPORTANCE OF INDUSTRY AND SERVICES

As an economy develops, resources are shifted from agriculture into industry, typically defined to include mining, manufacturing, construction, electricity, water, and gas.[3] Included in manufacturing are light industries such as textiles and food processing, as well as heavier industries such as steel and automobiles. Agriculture (including fishing, hunting, and forestry) and natural resources (excluding mining) generally are not part of the industrial sector.

The contemporary developing countries have seen a relative increase in their industrial sectors. For instance, from 1970 to 1993, the share of agriculture in GDP for all low-income countries fell from 37 to 28 percent, while the share of industry increased from 28 to 35 percent.[4] We see that this general trend holds for most of the low-income countries within the sample selected for Table 13.1.

The role of services, both private and public, in the development process is less clear. In the high-income developed economies, services have grown more rapidly than industry over the last 20 years. Note the increased share of services in the GDPs of those high-income countries shown in Table 13.1. For the developed nations, the combination of the income-elastic nature of services, coupled with a loss of comparative advantage in some types of industrial production, has resulted in a more rapid growth of the service sector.

In Japan, manufacturing, which accounted for 36 percent of GDP in 1970, accounted for only 24 percent in 1993. With agriculture declining in relative importance during this time period, from 6 percent of GDP to 2 percent, services have been increasing in relative magnitude from 47 to 57 percent. Finance, health care, data processing, insurance, real estate, and government have been the primary activities of service-sector growth in the developed countries.[5]

### THE INDUSTRIAL SECTOR

Within a predominately capitalist economy, industry is primarily a private-sector activity; however, government or public production of industrial output, such as electricity,

---

[3]World Bank, *World Development Report 1995*, New York: Oxford University Press, 1995, page 232.

[4]International data on the division of output and employment among the different sectors, agriculture, industry, and services, are incomplete and inconsistent. After defining agriculture and industry, the World Bank defines services as "value added in all other branches of economic activity, including imputed bank service charges, import duties, and any statistical discrepancies noted by national compilers." *World Development Report 1995*, pages 232 and 233. Given the absence of complete data on sectoral shares by country, we use a sample of countries in Table 13.1.

[5]The growth rates for these different service activities vary significantly within the developed countries.

| TABLE 13.1 | DATA ON SECTORAL SHARES FOR SELECTED COUNTRIES: 1970 AND 1993 | | | | | | | |
|---|---|---|---|---|---|---|---|---|
| | DISTRIBUTION OF GROSS DOMESTIC PRODUCT (%) | | | | | | | |
| | AGRICULTURE | | INDUSTRY | | MANUFACTURING | | SERVICES | |
| | 1970 | 1993 | 1970 | 1993 | 1970 | 1993 | 1970 | 1993 |
| **LOW-INCOME** | | | | | | | | |
| India | 45 | 31 | 22 | 27 | 15 | 17 | 33 | 41 |
| Nigeria | 41 | 34 | 14 | 43 | 4 | 7 | 45 | 24 |
| Pakistan | 37 | 25 | 22 | 25 | 16 | 17 | 41 | 50 |
| Ghana | 47 | 48 | 18 | 16 | 11 | 8 | 35 | 36 |
| China | 34 | 19 | 38 | 48 | 30 | 38 | 28 | 33 |
| Sri Lanka | 28 | 25 | 24 | 26 | 17 | 15 | 48 | 50 |
| Honduras | 32 | 20 | 22 | 30 | 14 | 18 | 45 | 50 |
| Egypt | 29 | 18 | 28 | 22 | ... | 16 | 42 | 60 |
| **MIDDLE-INCOME** | | | | | | | | |
| Senegal | 24 | 20 | 20 | 19 | 16 | 13 | 56 | 61 |
| Colombia | 25 | 16 | 28 | 35 | 21 | 18 | 47 | 50 |
| Algeria | 11 | 13 | 41 | 43 | 15 | 11 | 48 | 43 |
| Poland | ... | 6 | ... | 39 | ... | ... | ... | 55 |
| Costa Rica | 23 | 15 | 24 | 26 | ... | 19 | 53 | 59 |
| Brazil | 12 | 11 | 38 | 37 | 29 | 20 | 49 | 52 |
| Mexico | 12 | 8 | 29 | 28 | 22 | 20 | 59 | 63 |
| South Korea | 25 | 7 | 29 | 43 | 21 | 29 | 46 | 50 |
| **HIGH-INCOME** | | | | | | | | |
| Australia | 6 | 3 | 39 | 29 | 24 | 15 | 55 | 67 |
| Finland | 12 | 5 | 40 | 31 | 27 | 28 | 48 | 64 |
| Austria | 7 | 2 | 45 | 35 | 34 | 26 | 48 | 62 |
| Japan | 6 | 2 | 47 | 41 | 36 | 24 | 47 | 57 |

NOTE: Lack of data is indicated by ...

FROM: World Bank, *World Development Report 1995*, Table 3.

often occurs. Issues related to the public production of economic infrastructure will be discussed in the policy section of this chapter. The growth of the industrial sector is considered an indicator of economic development. Within most countries, the industrial sector tends to be more capital-intensive than either the agricultural or service sectors. As a result of the higher capital–labor ratio, wage rates within industry tend to exceed those in other sectors. Furthermore, with income growth, consumer aspirations for manufactured goods, from clothing to bicycles, increase. Thus, it is understandable that countries associate industrial growth with economic development.

The pursuit of industrial growth, however, can bring its own set of economic and social concerns. Industrial activity tends to be located in urban areas, drawing on the financial, transport, and public services that exist in cities. The presence of higher-paying manufacturing employment is likely to intensify rural-to-urban migration, even when sufficient job vacancies are lacking for all migrants. (Recall the costs of excessive migration, discussed in Chapter 9.) Industrial growth is associated with increased pollution, a negative externality. The release of toxic substances can damage air, land, and water. As stressed in Chapters 6 and 12, while economic remedies exist to address negative externalities, governments, especially in poor countries, frequently are unwilling to take measures that result in reduced output and employment.

While industrial wage levels may be relatively attractive, working conditions in industry, both within developed and developing nations, can be arduous and even unsafe. Long hours under sweatshop conditions often characterize light industry such as textiles, the assembly of components, and food processing. For instance, a burgeoning textile industry might be located in cramped, poorly ventilated warehouses with workers using noisy and dangerous machines. In such conditions, workers can be subject to long-term health hazards ranging from hearing loss to lung disease. Industrial accidents are common. In many developing countries children work for long hours at very low wages in manufacturing. We note that today's high-income countries, such as the United States and Great Britain, experienced many of the same abuses during their own industrial revolutions in the eighteenth and nineteenth centuries.

Often, laws to protect workers are either nonexistent or unenforced. In some cases, industrial operations owned by foreign investors or subsidiaries of foreign corporations are not responsible actors in the domestic economy. These foreign enterprises often rely on expatriate managers and skilled labor, bring in their own physical capital, and simply locate in the developing country to take advantage of low-cost unskilled labor. In these cases, the net benefits to the developing country are reduced. Thus, while industrial development is a necessary, and even a desirable, component of economic development, the governments of developing countries should be aware of the possible negative consequences of industry and be prepared to take offsetting actions. The regulation of industry will be addressed in the policy section of this chapter.

## THE SERVICE SECTOR

A broad range of activities is found in the service sector, including retail sales, health care, financial and legal services, public administration, and education. Services are provided in both the informal and modern (or formal) sectors. Each sector has its own specific characteristics and growth pattern within the development process.

### INFORMAL SERVICE SECTOR

Within a developing country, the informal service sector tends to be highly visible. As discussed in Chapter 9, informal service sector employment is very important within low-income countries. Activities range from the retail selling of newspapers and food items to car washing and delivery services. Employment is typically unstable, with low remuneration either in wages or commissions. The **value added** of this type of activity tends to be modest, with value added being defined as the difference between the selling price of output and the cost of the intermediate goods used in the production process.[6]

---

[6]Value added can also be expressed as the sum of factor payments including any profit. For instance, if an individual pays $.20 for a newspaper that she eventually sells for $.25, the value added by her labor, assuming no other intermediate expenses, would be $.05.

As development proceeds, the informal service sector becomes less important, displaced by modern services and industry. Expanding employment opportunities in these modern sectors are more attractive to workers. For instance, in the higher-income countries newspapers are not sold by individuals but offered through vending machines, an example of labor being reallocated from informal services to modern manufacturing. Bookkeepers are replaced by computer programmers within accounting firms.

## Modern Service Sector

The modern service sector includes private-sector activities that are more formally organized and tend to have higher levels of value added. Ranging from corporate law practices to medical laboratories, modern service activity, while relatively labor-intensive, tends to combine skilled labor with physical capital to provide those services demanded in a growing economy. Additionally, modern service activity, such as information technology, tourism, and banking, can be an export earner.

For the high-income countries, the growth of the modern service sector has been rapid. Even considering some variation in the definition and measurement across these countries, the service sector accounts for between 55 and 65 percent of GDP for nearly all the high-income countries.[7] Thus, the growth of the modern service sector can be expected and encouraged within the development process.

## PUBLIC PRODUCTION IN INDUSTRY AND SERVICES

As discussed in Chapter 6, governments, even within a relatively market-capitalist framework, produce needed goods or services. Typically included are **merit goods,** those goods, like education and health care, that society deems all individuals should consume, regardless of income level. Often with merit goods, positive externalities exist. Some of these goods and services could be provided by the private sector and, in fact, are to varying degrees within some countries. Recall that with private production of a good for which positive externalities exist, the unregulated market will produce too little of the good at too high a price, compared to the socially optimal quantity and price.

With a positive externality, to promote economic efficiency, the government should either subsidize private production to increase output and lower price, or provide the service directly, setting a higher, more efficient output level. The exact mix of public and private production is subject to debate, as is the appropriate level of aggregate production. (Recall the discussion in Chapter 8 concerning health care and education.) Given the income-elastic nature of these services, countries can expect them to grow in relative importance within the development process.

A second justification for government production is the case of a **natural monopoly.** Some goods, often those with large network or transmission costs (e.g., electricity and water distribution) are produced with significant economies of scale (or decreasing long-run average cost) compared to market demand. Therefore, when a natural

---

[7]World Bank, *World Development Report 1995*, Table 3.

monopoly exists, it can be more efficient to have a single producer of the good, producing the total market output at a lower average cost than would occur with several producers serving segments of the market.

In many countries, the government acts as the sole producer, for example, in building and maintaining roads or electric utility plants. In other cases, governments accord a monopoly to a private producer and regulate the pricing and output decision of the firm, avoiding the inefficiency of monopoly pricing. In the policy section of this chapter, we return to the issues of providing economic infrastructure and regulating natural monopolies.

# SECTORAL LINKAGES WITHIN AN ECONOMY

Economists are concerned with the linkages of the sectors of the economy within the production process. An understanding of these relationships is complicated by the fact that the output of each sector may be used (or demanded) both as a final good and as an intermediate good. For instance, electricity is used as an intermediate product in the production of most goods, including electricity itself. Also, electricity is used by consumers as a final good, to generate light and heat. Clearly, consistency must exist between the sources of a good (typically production and imports within an open economy) and the uses of a good (typically intermediate goods, final consumption, and exports).

## AN INPUT-OUTPUT MODEL

**Input-output analysis,** developed by Wassily W. Leontief, is a tool to capture these sectoral interrelationships within the production process.[8] In input-output analysis, the output of each sector or industry may be used as an intermediate good for each sector and as a source of final consumption. A complete input-output model would be disaggregated to include each major industry, such as electricity, coal, and steel, as well as particular agricultural products and major services. Also, a complete model would include both imports and exports, as well as any inventory changes.

Input-output analysis can be useful **ex post,** or after transactions have been completed, as an accounting or record of production relationships. With aggregate economic data it is possible to reconstruct the uses of inputs in producing output. Thus, even in market economies, in which sectoral planning is not used to allocate resources, input-output analysis can be a helpful tool. In market economies, equilibrium prices equate uses (demand) and sources (supply). With an ex post input-output analysis, outputs tend to be expressed in currency values, like millions of dollars of steel, found

---

[8]Wassily W. Leontief, *The Structure of the American Economy 1919–1939: An Empirical Application of Equilibrium Analysis,* 2d ed., White Plains, NY: International Arts and Sciences Press, 1951. Leontief's initial work on input-output modeling was done in the early 1940s.

by multiplying units of steel sold times the average price per unit. In command economies that do not rely on market-clearing prices, planners have used input-output analysis **ex ante** to allocate resources in a consistent manner for future production. For this type of planning, inputs and outputs tend to be expressed in physical units, like tons of steel.

Before discussing further the utility of input-output analysis, let us work through a simple example of the technique.[9] In the following example we will assume that only three sectors exist in the economy: agriculture (Sector 1), industry (Sector 2), and services (Sector 3). The output of each sector is used both as intermediate goods and for final consumption or demand. For instance, the agricultural sector will use some of its own output as an input (e.g., corn used as seed). Agriculture will also use the output of industry (e.g., plows) and the output of the service sector (e.g., transportation). We assume a closed economy with no imports or exports. A given technology and fixed-coefficients production functions exist. (Refer back to Chapter 3 for a review of fixed-coefficients production functions.)

In this case we will have three equations. For each, the value of the uses (intermediate goods and final consumption) equals the value of the sources (domestic production) for the sector.

1. $a_{11}X_1 + a_{12}X_2 + a_{13}X_3 + d_1 = X_1$
2. $a_{21}X_1 + a_{22}X_2 + a_{23}X_3 + d_2 = X_2$
3. $a_{31}X_1 + a_{32}X_2 + a_{33}X_3 + d_3 = X_3$

where $a_{ij}$ = the \$ requirement of Sector $i$ to produce \$1 of output in Sector $j$

$d_i$ = the final consumption of the output of Sector $i$ in \$

$X_i$ = the gross production of Sector $i$ in \$

Each $a_{ij}$ coefficient indicates the input requirement from Sector $i$ to produce a unit of Sector $j$'s output, or the share of the value of the output of Sector $j$ contributed by inputs from Sector $i$. For instance, $a_{11}$ shows the value of agricultural inputs needed to produce one dollar's worth of final agricultural output. The coefficients $a_{12}$ and $a_{13}$ show, respectively, the value of agricultural inputs used in producing one dollar's worth of output in industry and in services. With fixed-coefficients production functions, the substitution of inputs or of one intermediate good for another is not possible. In other words, for a given technology, the $a_{ij}$ coefficients are fixed.

Clearly, each of the $a$'s must be less than one; it would be illogical to use more than one dollar's worth of an intermediate good to produce a dollar's worth of output. In fact, the sum of the $a$'s for any Sector $j$ (or column) must be less than one. That sum ($a_{11} + a_{21} + a_{31}$ for agriculture) shows the total dollar requirement of intermediate goods needed to produce one dollar's worth of agricultural output. Subtracting the sum of the value of intermediate goods from one dollar of output will then give the value added by labor and capital per dollar of output for the sector. The final use of agricultural

---

[9]A theoretical discussion of the input-output production function can be found in Pan Yotopoulos and Jeffrey Nugent, *Economics of Development: Empirical Investigations*, New York: HarperCollins, 1976, pages 55–61.

goods is for final consumption, $d_1$, expressed in dollars of value. The sum of the intermediate uses and the final demand equals the dollar value of production of agriculture, $X_1$ (see Equation 1).

The above system of equations can be rewritten by combining like terms and then isolating the final demands on the right-hand side, as follows:

$$1'. \quad (1-a_{11})X_1 - a_{12}X_2 - a_{13}X_3 = d_1$$
$$2'. \quad -a_{21}X_1 + (1-a_{22})X_2 - a_{23}X_3 = d_2$$
$$3'. \quad -a_{31}X_1 - a_{32}X_2 + (1-a_{33})X_3 = d_3$$

With Equations 1' through 3', the final consumption values (for both private and public uses), $d_i$, are expressed as residuals, found by subtracting the intermediate use of each sector from its gross production. Planners could set the final consumption targets for each sector and then solve for the total production of each sector, $X_i$. For instance, assume the following coefficients, $a_{ij}$, and final consumption values, $d_i$.

$$a_{11} = .2 \quad a_{12} = .15 \quad a_{13} = .25 \quad d_1 = 1200$$
$$a_{21} = .2 \quad a_{22} = .3 \quad a_{23} = .1 \quad d_2 = 2300$$
$$a_{31} = .1 \quad a_{32} = .05 \quad a_{33} = .2 \quad d_3 = 1600$$

The term $a_{11}$ shows that each dollar of agricultural output requires $.2 of agricultural output as an intermediate good; $a_{13}$ shows that to produce each dollar of services requires $.25 of agricultural output. Here the final demands are set as $1200, $2300, and $1600 for the outputs of agriculture, industry, and services.

The value added in agriculture will be $.5 per $1 of output produced $[1-(.2+.2+.1)=.5]$; in industry $.5 and in services $.45. This value added represents payments to labor and to capital (including any economic profits that accrue to these inputs). In the following illustration we will assume the following division of value added between labor $(L)$ and capital $(K)$ in each sector (agriculture, industry, and services).

$$v_{LA} = .4 \quad v_{LI} = .3 \quad v_{LS} = .3$$
$$v_{KA} = .1 \quad v_{KI} = .2 \quad v_{KS} = .15$$

SECTORAL CONSISTENCY WITH INPUT-OUTPUT ANALYSIS

Using Equations 1' through 3' we can solve for the production values $X_i$ that are consistent with the intermediate uses and the final consumptions.[10] These values, shown in Table 13.2, are $3199, $4583, and $2686 for agriculture, industry, and services. Verify these results by substituting the production values for the $X$'s in Equations 1' through 3'. When sources equal uses, as in this example, the result is a **consistent plan**.

---

[10]A system of linear equations can be solved by substitution or the elimination of variables. In general, computers are used to solve the system of equations generated with an input-output model of more than a few sectors.

### TABLE 13.2     INPUT-OUTPUT RELATIONSHIPS

|  | \multicolumn{3}{c}{INTERMEDIATE-USER PURCHASES BY SECTOR ($)} | | | FINAL DEMAND ($) | TOTAL DEMAND ($) |
|---|---|---|---|---|---|---|
|  | AGR. | IND. | SERV. |  |  |  |
| Sales by: |  |  |  |  |  |  |
| Agriculture (Agr.) | 640 | 687 | 672 |  | 1200 | 3199 |
| Industry (Ind.) | 640 | 1375 | 268 |  | 2300 | 4583 |
| Services (Serv.) | 320 | 229 | 537 |  | 1600 | 2686 |
|  |  |  |  |  | Sum = 5100 |  |
| Value added: | 1599 | 2292 | 1209 |  | Sum = 5100 |  |
| Payments to labor | 1279 | 1375 | 806 |  | 3460 |  |
| Payments to capital | 320 | 917 | 403 |  | 1640 |  |
| Total Supply: | 3199 | 4583 | 2686 |  |  |  |

NOTE: These figures are rounded to the nearest dollar.

From Table 13.2, we can see the values of intermediate uses of each sector's output. For instance, the uses of agricultural output (shown in the first row of the sectoral matrix) as inputs in the production of agriculture, industry, and services are $640, $687, and $672 respectively. When these intermediate uses are added to the $1200 of final demand, the $3199 of gross, or total, output for agriculture is obtained.

The sum of any column shows the value of the intermediate goods used in the production of any sector's output. For instance, industry uses $687 of agricultural output as an intermediate good. Subtracting the sum of the intermediate goods from the value of total output gives the value added for the sector, $2292 in industry [$4583−($687+$1375+$229)=$2292]. This value added is divided between payments to labor ($1375) and to capital ($917). The sum of the value added in each sector ($1599 + $2292 + $1209) equals the sum of the final demands ($1200 + $2300 + $1600) and both, in this simple example, are equal to the Gross Domestic Product of the nation ($5100).

### PLAN FEASIBILITY

For ex ante planning, the feasibility of a consistent plan must be verified. For instance, does the economy have enough labor and capital to produce the output levels that would be required for the final consumption targets (the $d$'s) and the intermediate uses of the good? The feasibility check requires a comparison of the availability of inputs with the planned output requirements. From Table 13.3 on page 396, we see that $3460 of labor and $1640 of capital are required to produce the desired final consumption values for each sector.

Assume that, at the current prices of labor and capital, the country has $3900 of labor available and $1400 of capital available. In this case the plan would not be feasible, as the capital requirements exceed the availability of capital; there is a shortage of $240 of capital (or $1400−$1640). The fact that an excess of labor exists ($3900 − $3460 = $440)

| TABLE 13.3 | INPUT-OUTPUT FOLLOWING A CHANGE IN THE FINAL DEMAND FOR AGRICULTURAL OUTPUT OF $100 | | | | |
|---|---|---|---|---|---|
| | INTERMEDIATE-USER PURCHASES BY SECTOR ($) | | | | |
| | AGR. | IND. | SERV. | FINAL DEMAND ($) | TOTAL DEMAND ($) |
| Sales by: | | | | | |
| Agriculture (Agr.) | 668 (+28) | 694 (+7) | 677 (+5) | 1300 (+100) | 3339 (+140) |
| Industry (Ind.) | 668 (+28) | 1388 (+13) | 271 (+3) | 2300 | 4627 (+44) |
| Services (Serv.) | 334 (+14) | 231 (+2) | 541 (+4) | 1600 | 2706 (+20) |
| | | | | Sum = 5200 (+100) | |
| Value added: | 1669 (+70) | 2314 (+22) | 1217 (+8) | Sum = 5200 (+100) | |
| Payments to labor | 1335 (+56) | 1388 (+13) | 811 (+5) | 3534 (+74) | |
| Payments to capital | 334 (+14) | 926 (+9) | 406 (+3) | 1666 (+26) | |
| Total Supply: | 3339 (+140) | 4627 (+44) | 2706 (+20) | | |

does not remedy the capital shortage, for the given technology. With the capital shortage and fixed-coefficients production function, the country would not be able to produce the sectoral outputs consistent with the final consumption targets.

To reduce the aggregate capital requirement of a plan, the country could scale back its targets for final goods. Production levels consistent with the new, lower targets would be recalculated; then the new, lower capital requirements would be calculated and compared to the availability of capital. Similarly, with an expanded analysis allowing for more sectors and factors of production, feasibility checks would be needed for land, natural resources, and foreign exchange. Generally, developing countries encounter capital and foreign exchange constraints before encountering labor constraints. In other words, capital and foreign exchange are more likely to be limiting factors in expanding output.

The economy, over time, could attempt to reduce capital requirements (and foreign exchange requirements) by using more labor-intensive technologies. Substituting labor for capital in the production process to reduce the capital requirement of a plan may be possible. Given that most developing countries have labor surpluses (either visible or disguised, as discussed in Chapter 9), aggregate output can most likely be increased by adopting more labor-intensive production techniques. Since the input-output model assumes fixed-coefficient isoquants, a new input-output model would have to be constructed. Finally, if the level of savings in sufficiently high that net investment is positive, a country will have additional capital available in subsequent time periods. Whether this would be sufficient to absorb the growth in labor depends on the relative growth rates for capital and labor, as well as the production technologies used.

### CHANGE IN FINAL DEMANDS

Input-output analysis can be useful in assessing the sensitivity of each individual economic sector to a change in the final demand of one sector. For instance, assume that planners wish to increase the final consumption of agricultural output from $1200 to $1300. What will be the impact on the required production of agriculture, industry, and services? Substituting $1300 for $1200 as $d_1$ in Equation 3' and recalculating the final production levels shows that output in each of the three sectors would need to increase (see Table 13.3). Agricultural production would need to increase by $140 from $3199 to $3339, industry by $44 from $4583 to $4627, and services by $20 from $2686 to $2706. While no increase occurs in the final consumption of industry and services, the gross output of these two sectors must increase to support the increase in agricultural output. Note that value added also rises to $5200 with an increase in both labor and capital requirements. With ex ante planning, a country would need to verify that it had the necessary quantities of labor and capital to fulfill the higher production levels.

### CURRENT USES OF INPUT-OUTPUT ANALYSIS

A modified version of ex ante input-output planning, called the **material balance process,** was used to allocate resources by the former Soviet Union from the mid-1920s until the late 1980s, and by other command economies. With the demise of the Soviet command-style economies, input-output planning is little used in the direct allocation of resources. Today, input-output techniques are used in more limited, but still important ways in developing economies. An ex post, product-specific, input-output model permits decision makers to understand the interactions of economic activity within a society.

With this knowledge, the government can assess the overall effects on different industries of a policy intervention. Chenery points out that this type of interindustry analysis can identify bottlenecks in the development process.[11] For instance, if the government desired to increase available rice output by $x$ percent, a disaggregated input-output analysis could be used to show the corresponding increases in intermediate goods and services, such as rice for rice seed, fertilizer, pipes for canals, and energy for pumping water. The needed production levels for each of these intermediate goods could then be calculated based on the desired increase in rice output. If domestic production could not produce the required level of an input, a country could then make arrangements to increase its imports of that input or to scale back its planned increase of rice output.

Also, the aggregate input requirements, for labor, capital, and foreign exchange could be calculated, permitting a comparison of needs to available supplies of these

---

[11]Chenery, page 334.

inputs. With these feasibility assessments, policymakers can understand the limiting inputs to increasing overall economic activity. For instance, if foreign exchange is the binding constraint preventing an increase in gross output, as discussed in Chapter 3, the government could take offsetting actions. Policies to increase exports, to limit imports, or to increase the flow of foreign investment or assistance could be implemented. In contrast, if skilled labor were the binding constraint, the government could design particular educational initiatives to increase the availability of skilled labor.

Caution must be exercised, however, in using input-output analysis. The assumptions of fixed-coefficients production functions and constant returns to scale are restrictive and limiting. Also, accurate data needed to construct such a model are often not available. Further, as the model becomes more disaggregated, allowing for specific products, as opposed to broad sectors of the economy, the data requirements significantly increase. Finally, a given model does not allow for technological progress; rather, the model must be reconstructed with new coefficients.

Having discussed the interactions of economic sectors within an economy, we now turn to economic integration among economies.

## GLOBAL INDUSTRIAL INTEGRATION

The proportion of world trade accounted for by manufactured goods is quite high and increasing. The share of machinery, transportation equipment, textiles, and other manufacturing goods in global merchandise exports rose from 69 percent in 1970 to 83 percent in 1992.[12] Much of the trade is overlapping. For example, electrical appliances are exported and imported by Japan. Steel is exported by the industrialized economies, as well as by some of the more advanced LDCs, like South Korea and Brazil. Textiles are produced and exported by many developing countries. Usually, manufactured goods are not perishable, and, while shipping costs can represent a high portion of total costs, fear of spoilage, as with food products, is not a primary concern. The exporting of manufacturing goods stimulates local industry and employment; export revenues permit a country to import final goods and services, needed intermediate goods, and capital equipment. As discussed in Chapter 14, global integration and trade can serve as an engine of economic growth and development.

### FREE TRADE

In a world with competitive product and factor markets, as well as market-determined exchange rates, world prices, expressed in local currency equivalents, will give an indication of products for which a country has **comparative advantage.** This is defined as

---

[12]World Bank, *World Development Report 1994*, New York: Oxford University Press, 1994, Table 15.

the ability to produce output at a lower domestic opportunity cost than its trading partners. Within this model of free trade, a country will specialize in the production and export of those goods in which it has a comparative advantage, generating foreign exchange to import those goods in which it does not have a comparative advantage.

Consider the case of a small country, that is a price taker, with a textile industry, illustrated in Figure 13.1A (on page 400). In *autarky*, or the absence of any trade, domestic demand $(D_d)$ and domestic supply $(S_d)$ interact to produce an equilibrium price, $P_o$, and quantity transacted, $Q_o$. Now allow for international trade. Assume that the world market price of textiles expressed in the domestic currency is $P_M$, lower than the market-clearing domestic price. With the lower price of textiles, the country will import textiles. At $P_M$, the domestic quantity demanded will be $Q_1$; domestic producers will only supply $Q_2$; the country will import $Q_1 - Q_2$, or $GH$ units of textiles. In this case, consumers receive a greater quantity of textiles $(Q_1 > Q_o)$ and pay a lower per unit price $(P_M < P_o)$; domestic producers, however, produce less output $(Q_2 < Q_o)$. The domestic textile industry will contract, freeing resources for use in other industries for which the country currently has a comparative advantage. Export receipts from these industries should be available to pay for the imports of textiles, the cost of which equals $(Q_1 - Q_2)P_M$.

In contrast, as in Figure 13.1B, assume that the domestic equivalent of the world market price is $P_X$, higher than the domestic price in the absence of trade. With the higher price of textiles, the country will export textiles. At $P_X$, domestic demand will be $Q_3$; domestic producers will supply $Q_4$; the country will export $Q_4 - Q_3$, or $AB$ units of textiles. In this case, the country's domestic textile industry will expand, increasing output and employment. Export receipts, the equivalent of $(Q_4 - Q_3)P_X$, will be available to import goods in which the country does not have a comparative advantage.

Often developing countries, using world market prices, have a comparative advantage in the production of primary products. In this case, primary products would be exported and manufacturing products imported. Given that prices for primary products tend to be more variable than those for industrial goods and the demands for primary products tend to be income-inelastic, Third World countries have been reluctant to rely on primary exports. Also, developing countries have associated a growing industrial sector with economic modernization and have sought to reduce their dependence on the higher-income countries for manufactures. As a result, developing countries have often intervened to affect trade flows.

Usually, policies to redirect trade are aimed at limiting imports (import substitution) and increasing exports (export expansion). We will focus on the former strategy in this chapter; yet, in reality, countries have often tried simultaneously, to reduce imports and to increase exports.

## IMPORT SUBSTITUTION

Countries attempt to limit imports and favor domestic production, a process called **import substitution,** for different reasons. First, limiting some imports will conserve foreign exchange, enhancing the country's ability to import needed capital goods. The desire to conserve foreign exchange is particularly relevant when a country has an overvalued currency. These countries usually have a trade deficit, an excess of imports over exports. Moreover, the governments of LDCs may not believe that their young industries initially are competitive with more experienced foreign producers. The strategy of import substitution is often used as a means to quickly establish an industrial base.

## FIGURE 13.1 — A SMALL PRICE-TAKER COUNTRY WITH A TEXTILE INDUSTRY

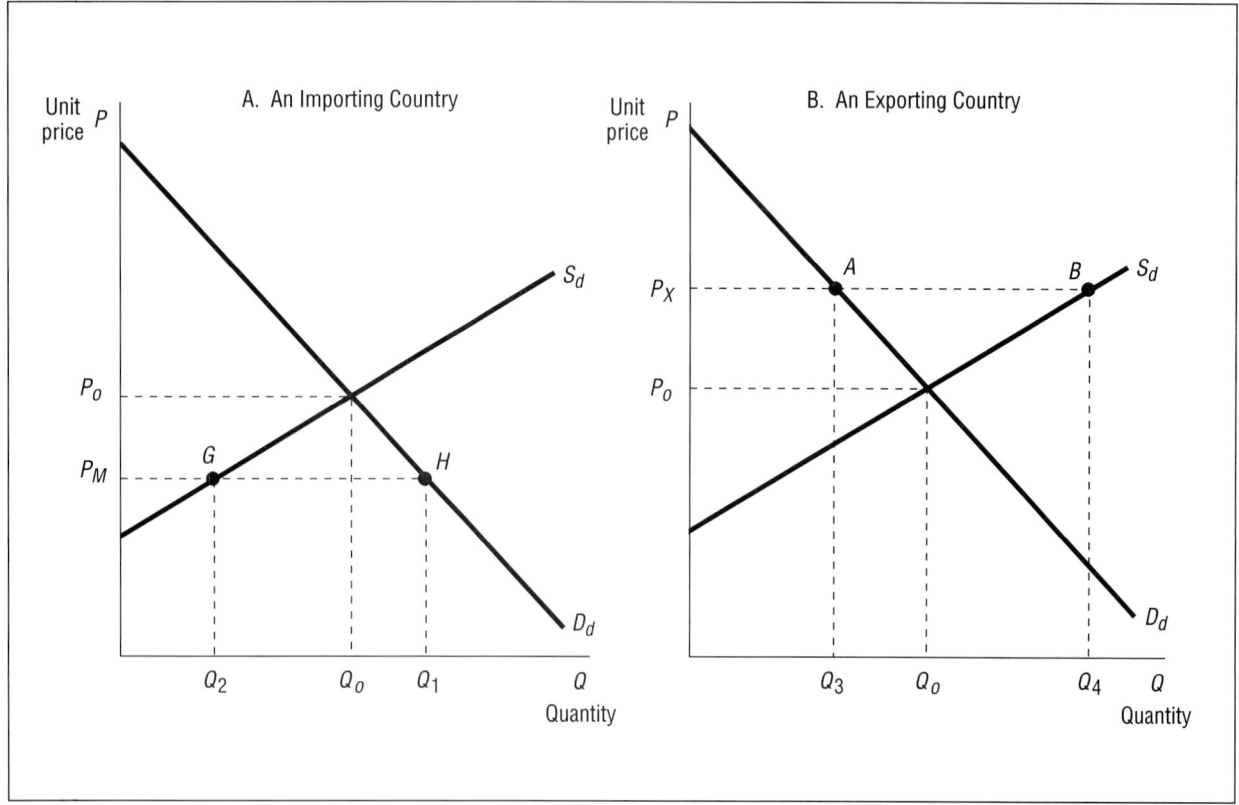

Third, countries with significant urban- or modern-sector unemployment have viewed import substitution as a means to create industrial employment.[13] Finally, nations have often held that with temporary protection, the domestic firms could ultimately gain a comparative advantage and become exporters. This approach, called the **infant-industry strategy,** presumes that with protection, local production will increase and the average cost of producing output will fall as the country's local industry expands and gains experience.[14] The basic means to reduce imports of a commodity, such as cotton shirts, include tariffs (and other trade barriers such as import quotas and subsidies to domestic textile producers).

---

[13] In the aggregate it is not clear that import-substituting policies will increase the level of employment. In theory, a country that limits imports will move along its production possibilities boundary (PPB) producing more of the previously imported good and less of other goods with no change in total employment. Thus, an employment gain occurs in one industry, and an employment loss in other sectors. In reality, nations do not operate at full employment (or on the PPB). With trade barriers, the loss of employment (from reduced exports) could exceed the gain in employment (from reduced imports); the import-substitution policy then reduces aggregate employment.

[14] Average cost in the long run can fall for two reasons. First, if firms in the industry experience economies of scale (a decreasing long-run average cost), output increases will lead to a reduced average or per-unit cost. Also, with greater experience in producing the good, overall factor productivity can increase, shifting down each firm's long-run average cost curve.

## TARIFFS

Tariffs can be expressed either as a particular levy or tax in the local currency (a **specific tariff**) or as a percentage of the import price (an **ad valorem tariff**). Assume the case of a small country such as Mali, to which the import price of a cotton shirt is perfectly elastic at 2400 CFA (the currency unit of Francophone Africa). Imposing a tariff of 600 CFA per shirt, a specific tariff, would raise the import price to 3000 CFA. Alternatively, a 25 percent tax on the imported shirt, an ad valorem tariff, would raise the import price to 3000 CFA.

In Figure 13.2 (on page 402), at the free trade price, $P_M$, the quantity of shirts consumed is $Q_1$; local production is $Q_2$ while imports are $Q_1 - Q_2$ or $GH$. A specific tariff of $t_o$ would raise the price to $P_M + t_o$, or $P'_M$ in Figure 13.2. At this higher price for shirts, consumers would reduce their purchases from $Q_1$ to $Q'_1$; domestic producers, moving along the domestic supply curve ($S_d$) would increase their quantity supplied from $Q_2$ to $Q'_2$; imports would fall to $Q'_1 - Q'_2$ or $G'H'$. Government tax revenues would equal the per unit tariff multiplied by the quantity of textiles imported, or $t_o(Q'_1 - Q'_2)$, given by the area $G'H'FF'$.

Thus, the tariff succeeds in substituting domestic production for imports, but at the expense of consumers who pay a higher per-unit price and purchase less output. Two deadweight efficiency losses occur. One, the consumption effect, is equal to $FH'H$; previously part of the consumer surplus, this area is now lost. Also, the area $GG'F'$ represents the additional cost of producing the quantity $Q'_2 - Q_2$, with domestic resources instead of importing this output at a lower price and resource cost. Economists call this loss, $GG'F'$, a protective effect. As the tariff rate is increased, the quantity of imports will continue to fall and domestic production will increase. If the tariff is sufficiently high to raise the consumer price to $P_o$, such as with $t_p$, in Figure 13.2, domestic production alone would satisfy consumer demand. At this or any higher rate, the tariff is prohibitive, blocking all imports.

## NOMINAL AND EFFECTIVE TARIFF RATES

Economists often contrast the nominal and the effective protection from a tariff rate. The **nominal rate** is the stated value of the tariff imposed on the good, as a percentage of the final price of the good. For instance, without any tariff, if a commodity sells for $20 per unit, a specific tariff of $4 would raise the final price to $24, representing a 20 percent rate of nominal protection. Note that the rate of nominal protection indicates the extent to which consumer prices are increased by the tariff.

The **effective rate of tariff protection (ERP)** measures the impact on the value added in the domestic import-competing industry from the whole tariff structure of the country.[15] Recall that value added is the difference between the selling price of a product and the cost of the intermediate goods, or the increase in value to the intermediate goods from the production process. Value added can also be expressed as the sum of the firm's factor payments plus any economic profits.

The effective rate of protection will be affected both by the existence of a tariff on the final good and by any other tariffs that fall on intermediate goods used in the production process. Thus, the ERP is measured as the percentage change in the value added in an industry from trade barriers such as tariffs.

---

[15]For a more detailed discussion of the effective rate of protection see Dennis Appleyard and Alfred Field, *International Economics*, 2d ed., Irwin, 1995, pages 232–236.

### FIGURE 13.2 | THE EFFECTS OF A SPECIFIC TARIFF

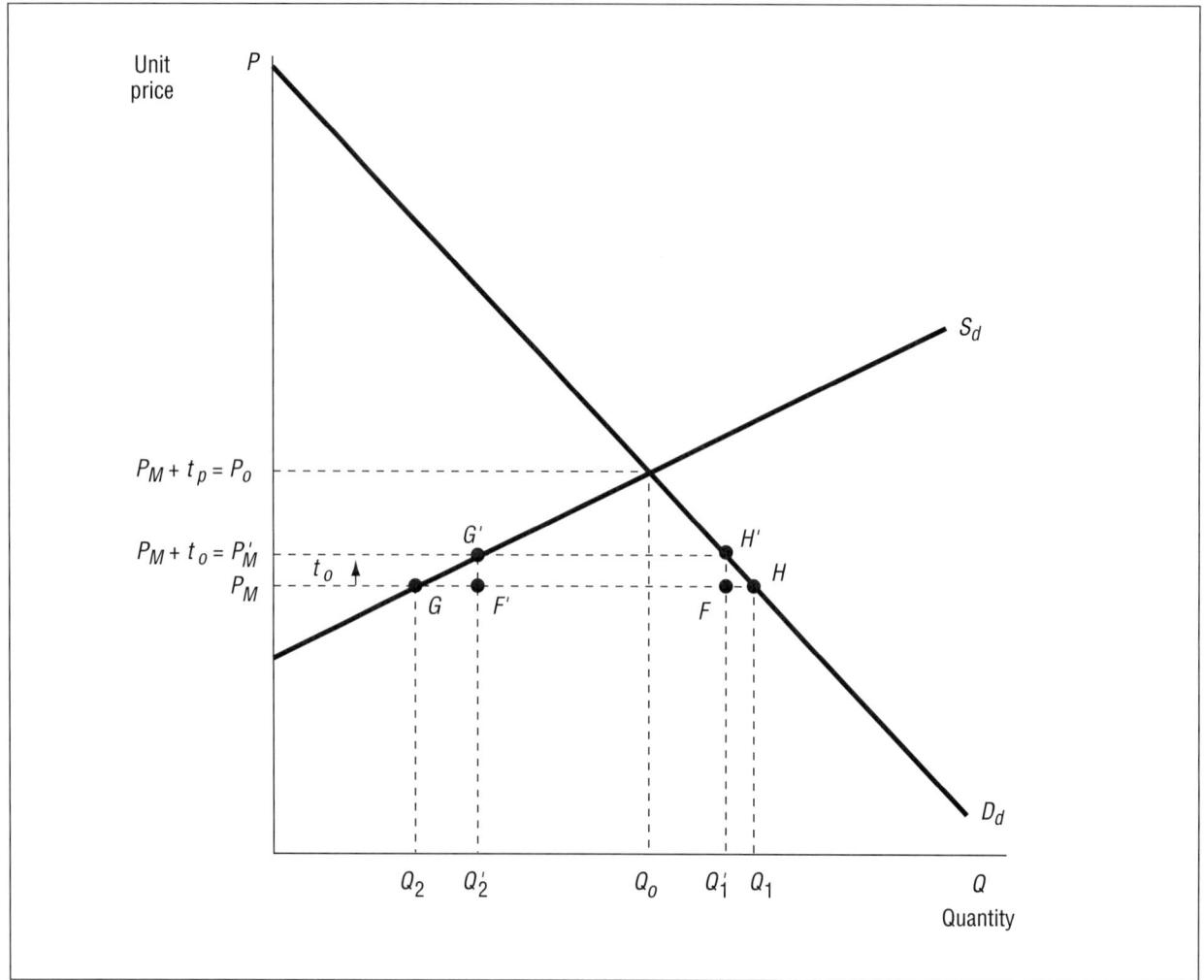

The actual calculation of effective protection would be $(VA' - VA)/VA$ where $VA$ is value added at world market prices and $VA'$ is value added at domestic prices, including the impact of the domestic tariff structure.

Consider the following example. Assume that a firm produces cotton shirts. The intermediate product, finished cotton fabric, costs $5 per shirt at world market prices; the firm sells a cotton shirt at the world market price of $8 and has $3 of value added (wages, capital costs, and profits). Now assume that to protect the domestic shirt industry, a 25 percent ad valorem tariff is imposed. The firm will now be able to sell its shirts at $10 per unit, or (1.25)($8); domestic value added could increase to $5 and still be internationally competitive. The effective rate of protection is 66.7 percent.

$$(\$5 - \$3)/\$3 = .667, \text{ or } 66.7\%$$

With no other tariffs in place, the effective rate of protection will exceed the nominal rate of protection.

Now assume that the country has a 10 percent ad valorem tariff on the imported cotton fabric. The intermediate product will now cost the firm $5.50, or (1.1)$5.00; value added will now be $4.50, or $10.00 − $5.50. The effective rate of protection falls to 50 percent.

$$(\$4.50 - \$3.00)/\$3 = .50 \text{ or } 50\%$$

With the tariff on the inputs lowering the firm's value added, the rate of effective protection falls. In this case, however, the ERP still exceeds the nominal rate. Now assume that the tariff on the cotton fabric is equal to 25 percent. In this case, the input will cost the firm $6.25; value added will be $3.75, and the effective rate of protection, 25 percent, will equal the nominal rate of protection. At any tariff rate in excess of 25 percent applied on the intermediate input, the effective rate will be lower than the nominal rate.

Economists believe that the effective rate of protection is a better measure of the degree of protection provided to a domestic industry. First, it is measured against value added or the returns to factors producing the import-substituting good. Higher returns should encourage expansion of the domestic industry, and the ERP better measures this change in value added. Second, the ERP includes the effect of the country's complete tariff structure, including levies on intermediate goods. As shown above, by imposing tariffs on the imports of intermediate goods, ceteris paribus, the country lowers its ERP on domestic value added.

From a policy point of view, if a developing country wishes to protect domestic industries that are producing final goods, the country would do well to avoid levying tariffs on those intermediate goods used in the production process. In attempting to export final goods to high-income countries, developing countries often face ERPs that exceed nominal rates of protection. Developed countries often impose tariffs on final goods but not on intermediate goods, raising their ERP to the detriment of developing countries that might otherwise have a comparative advantage in exporting those final goods. For example, the developed country is apt to have tariffs on processed food, a final good, discouraging imports of processed food. Yet the same country may have no tariff on raw materials or commodities that are used to produce the processed food, encouraging imports of raw materials and intermediate goods. The ERP on the final good will then be higher than if the same tariff rate had been applied on the inputs. To promote export growth of higher value added goods from the developing world, the industrialized countries need to be more willing to lower their high effective rates of protection.

## Quotas

An **import quota** is a physical limit on the quantity of imports within a given time period. To be effective, the quota must be set below the quantity that would otherwise be imported. Assume that an import quota equal to $VU$ in Figure 13.3 (on page 404) is imposed. In this case, price will rise from $P_M$ to $P'_M$, and the quantity consumed falls from $Q_1$ to $Q'_1$. Imports fall from $Q_1 - Q_2$ to $Q'_1 - Q'_2$ (or $VU$). With the higher price, domestic production increases from $Q_2$ to $Q'_2$. Note that a specific tariff of $t_o$ would have produced the same results: a higher consumer price, reduced imports, and increased domestic production. Here the import quota and the tariff introduce the same efficiency losses, reduced consumer surplus, and a protective effect.

### FIGURE 13.3 THE EFFECTS OF A QUOTA COMPARED TO A TARIFF

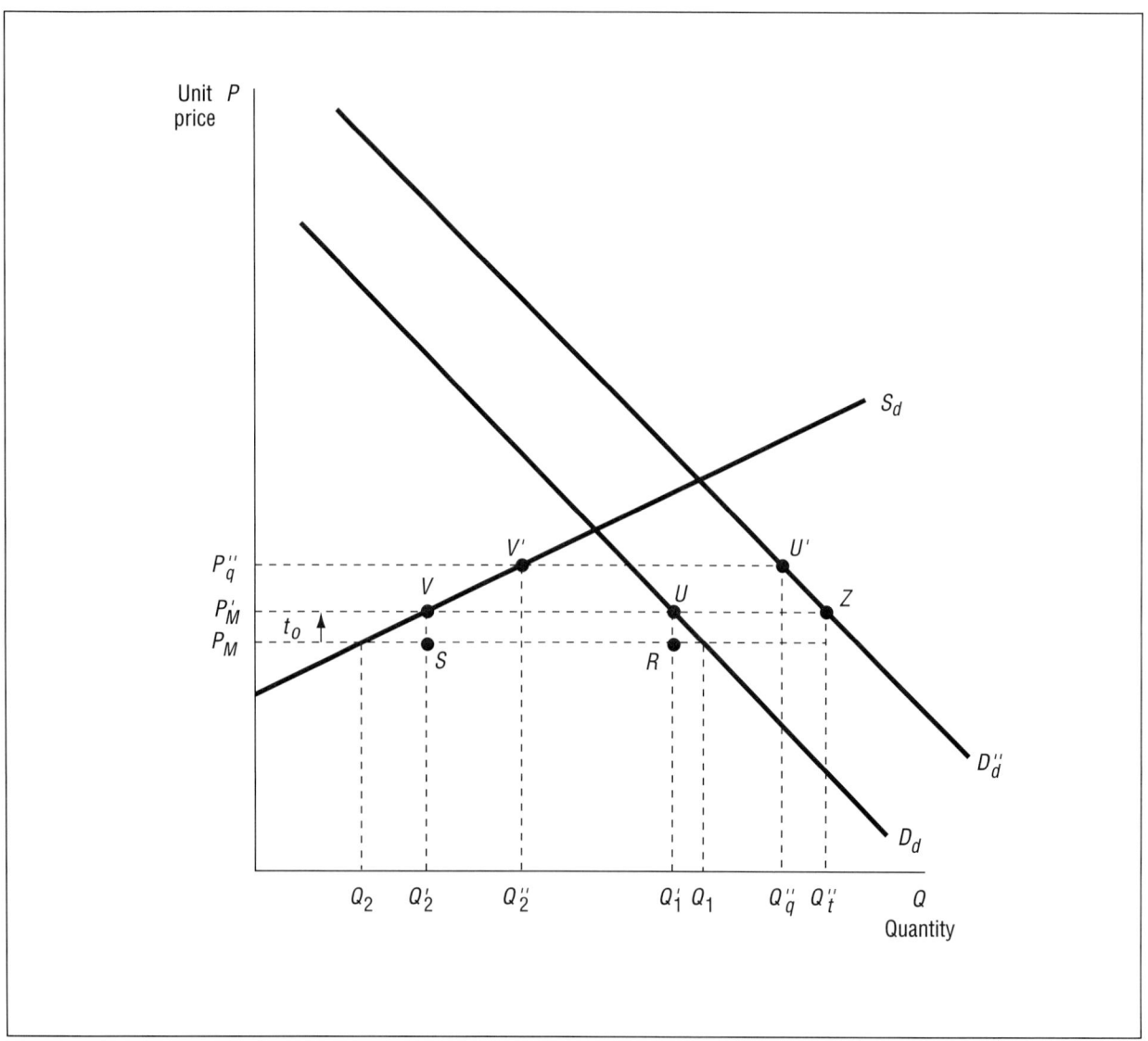

While the government collects no tariff revenues with an import quota, it does have the potential to auction quota rights to importers. The difference between the consumer price $P'_M$ and the foreign producer price $P_M$ represents the per-unit market value of an import license. An importer would pay up to this per-unit value for the right to sell in the protected market. In the event that quota rights are given away, the area $SVUR$ would represent additional profits for domestic importers. Had a tariff of $t_o$ been imposed, this area would represent the tariff revenues collected by the government.

Another significant difference between a tariff and a quota is the rigidity associated with quotas. An increase in consumer demand will lead to an increase in price but no increase in quantity imported. For instance, if demand were to shift to $D''_{d'}$ with an import quota, price would increase to $P''_q$ and consumption would increase to $Q''_{q'}$; imports would remain at the same level. Note that the distance $V'U'$ equals $VU$. Domestic production increases to $Q''_2$. In contrast, assume that a specific tariff had been used to raise price to $P'_M$. With the same increase in consumer demand, consumption would increase to $Q'_t$ and price would remain at $P'_M$. Imports would increase to $VZ$; and there would be no change in domestic production (which remains at $Q'_2$). While domestic producers benefit more from a quota than from a tariff, consumers would prefer the tariff in this case. From society's point of view the rigidity of the quota can introduce a greater efficiency loss (reduction in consumer surplus and protective effect) than the tariff.

SUBSIDIES TO DOMESTIC PRODUCERS

Alternatively, as a means to reduce imports, the government could subsidize domestic producers by providing tax concessions or reduced rates of interest on borrowed capital. The marginal cost curve for each domestic producer would shift down and the domestic-industry supply curve would shift to the right. See the shift from $S_d$ to $S'_d$ in Figure 13.4 (on page 406). The consumer price would still remain at $P_M$ with consumers purchasing $Q_1$; however, domestic production would increase from $Q_2$ to $Q'_2$. Imports would fall from $Q_1 - Q_2$ to $Q_1 - Q'_2$. Rather than tariff receipts that improve the government's fiscal balance, the government will incur the outlays from the domestic subsidies. The subsidy reduces the per unit marginal cost of production by the distance $FG'$; the $Q'_2$ units of domestic production receive the subsidy. Thus, the total cost of the domestic subsidies is measured as the area $P_S FG'P_M$. With the subsidy there is no direct loss in consumer surplus within the protected market. A protective effect (shown as $GFG'$) from replacing lower-cost imports with higher-cost domestic production still exists. Thus, on efficiency grounds, economists often prefer subsidies to tariffs. Yet subsidies require government expenditures, while tariffs generate government revenues.

In an attempt to increase the domestic supply in a protected industry, governments have extended subsidies to domestic producers and offered inducements to foreign producers to locate in the country. When successful, the entry of new firms will shift out the domestic supply function and increase the share of output produced domestically, thereby reducing imports.

AN EVALUATION OF IMPORT SUBSTITUTION

Economists tend to be skeptical of protectionism and import substitution. Given the costs to the domestic economy from limiting imports, any policy to protect domestic industry must bear a strong burden of proof. In the 1945 to 1980 period, many developing countries adopted policies aimed at promoting domestic industry with tariffs and other trade barriers, eschewing both production according to comparative advantage and world trade.

These countries hoped to accelerate the modernization process. Often, they wanted to avoid being dependent on the export of primary products in order to earn the foreign exchange to import finished industrial goods. Their intention was to produce the industrial goods domestically. Frequently, import protection was aimed first at stimulating light consumer industries, such as textiles and apparel. For these goods the production technology tends to be relatively simple and standardized, and capital

## FIGURE 13.4    Subsidizing an Import-Competing Firm

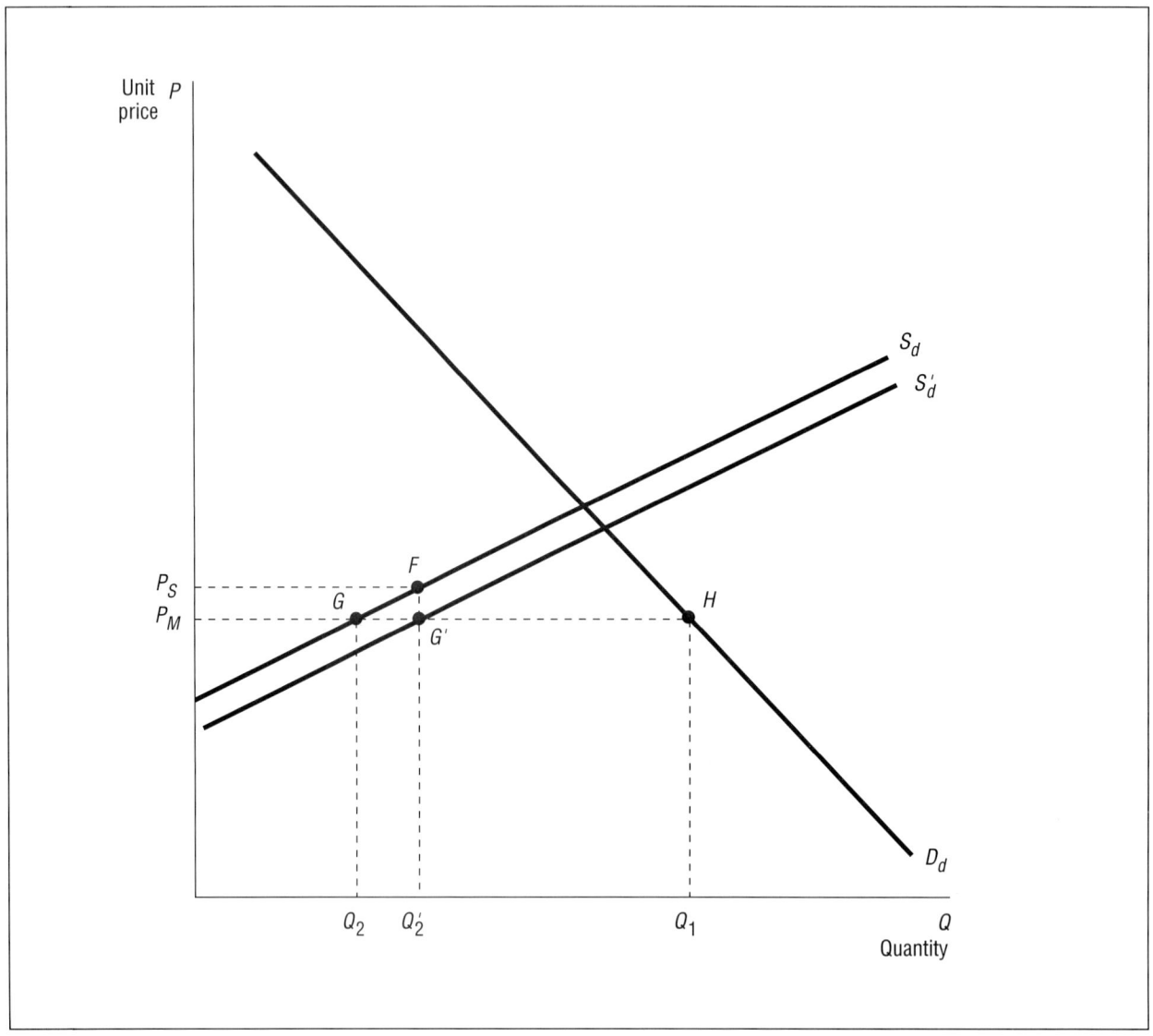

requirements tend to be modest. In many cases, imports were a significant portion of total consumer demand.

Usually, these countries suffered the costs of import substitution previously discussed: higher consumer prices, reduced output, and lack of competitive pressures to encourage efficiency. Moreover, the countries oriented their economies away from goods that could have been exported, reducing foreign exchange. In the extreme, when there are only a few domestic producers, import substitution will confer significant market power on domestic producers. Outputs could then be restricted further to increase prices. Also, domestic industries, operating behind tariff barriers, with reduced global competition, have less incentive to produce as efficiently as possible.

Finally, behind the protection of tariff walls, firms are apt to be subject to government interventions that can affect employment, costs, and pricing. For instance, "protected" firms may be subject to political pressure to increase employment, which will raise costs and further increase prices. With the protection, however, the domestic firms may still operate without a significant reduction in profits. In contrast, firms facing global competition have to resist such pressure or fear a substantial loss of sales. Most economists have concluded that redirecting production along lines of comparative advantage would benefit these economies. (See the case study at the end of this chapter which looks at import substitution in India as an example of this type of economic restructuring.)

The infant-industry argument for temporary protection against imports is more difficult to assess. If a country truly possesses a potential comparative advantage in the production of a particular good, then tariff protection, for a short period of time, has theoretical merit. In such cases, however, a clear and definitive phasing out of tariffs should be announced. The application of this argument is highly problematic. Too often, in both developed and developing countries, existing industries that lack potential comparative advantage nonetheless call for protection as an infant industry. In the developed countries, the infant-industry argument is usually cast as a "time for retooling" or a call for assistance for a "reborn" industry. Separating the truth of the argument from the self-interest of the domestic producers is the challenge for policymakers.

For reasons similar to those used to justify import substitution measures, countries have used policy measures to expand exports. Again, these arguments relate to the desire to improve the trade balance; to stimulate local industry; and to develop long-run comparative advantage. This process is called **export expansion.** Over the past decade, many developing nations have shifted emphasis to export expansion. A discussion of this outward orientation in trade follows in the next chapter.

## POLICY ISSUES CONCERNING INDUSTRY

In this section we discuss policy issues that concern industry and development. Areas of concern include the regulation of industry and public versus private production of industrial goods, particularly public utilities.

### REGULATION OF INDUSTRY

Regulation of industry within a country should address employment and working conditions, competition, and pollution. We will briefly discuss each of these concerns.

#### Employment and Working Conditions

Most of the developed countries have labor regulations that apply to industrial workers and, often, to all employees. These regulations concern minimum wages, maximum hours, job safety, job security, and unionization. Without discussing each regulation in detail, we raise two particular concerns that policymakers must balance in promoting legislation aimed at improving the quality of life of industrial workers.

Minimum wages and unionization that succeed in raising the average wage rate for workers may encourage a substitution of capital for labor within the production process. Given the goal of promoting employment within labor-surplus developing countries, legislation to protect employees from exploitation must be carefully designed to avoid providing too great an incentive for firms to replace labor within the production process. In many developing countries, modern-sector wages already exceed equilibrium levels. Contributing to higher urban wages are the inflated wage schedules that foreign firms may import into the country. Also, government wages in many of the developing countries are set too high and often spill over into the industrial sector. For this reason, international development agencies advise developing countries to monitor modern-sector wage levels to avoid discouraging employment creation. At the other extreme, there are cases where exploitative wages and working conditions require remedial action. Use of prisoners and children as labor not only may give a country an unfair wage advantage, but is considered immoral by much of the international community. Moreover, the sweatshop-type factory, described earlier in this chapter, is an example of industrial conditions that need to be remedied by government intervention.

A second concern is that overly protective labor legislation can reduce the aggregate level of economic activity and discourage the establishment of new firms. Higher wages that are not accompanied by productivity gains will raise the average cost of producing goods within a country. The increased unit costs will discourage exports and encourage imports, possibly reducing aggregate economic activity. Also, foreign firms are unlikely to locate in countries that have overly restrictive labor laws that make it difficult and costly to terminate unsatisfactory employees. (In Chapter 16 we discuss the factors that influence foreign direct investment by transnational corporations.) Clearly, countries face a delicate balancing of equity and efficiency in designing labor legislation.

### Promoting Competition

**Contestable markets** promote competition because entry by potential competitors is relatively easy. Monopoly and oligopoly, however, unchecked by contestable markets, can result in restricted output, higher prices, and reduced incentives for efficient and innovative production.[16] Effective remedies to avoid the inefficiencies of imperfect competition include relatively open markets and anti-trust legislation. With open markets, domestic industries are forced to price competitively and produce efficiently; otherwise, foreign producers can enter and undersell the uncompetitive domestic producer. We mentioned that a problem with import substitution was that tariffs would confer market power on local firms. For this reason, the burden of proof should rest on those promoting import substitution. To supplement free markets, anti-trust legislation, not yet common in the Third World, can be helpful. The existence of such

---

[16]In a contestable market, existing producers, fearing potential entrants, are inclined to price more competitively, reducing the inefficiency that could accompany a small number of producers with market power.

legislation would permit countries to break up potential monopolies; and the legislation serves as a deterrent to firms seeking market power through mergers.

POLLUTION

As discussed in Chapter 12, pollution accompanies industrial growth. Developing countries should be wary of the argument that a cleaner environment is a luxury good to be pursued only when per capita income reaches a relatively high level. Pollutants spread across borders, affecting neighboring countries. Also, pollution can impose irreversible damage both to the environment and to the health of the population. For these reasons, all countries, regardless of their level of development, need appropriate anti-pollution measures, such as taxes and regulations. As with labor regulation, however, sensible laws must be designed to avoid discouraging responsible entrepreneurship with its accompanying employment.

As a country's industrial sector grows, an increased need to address pollution concerns will develop. Also, in an attempt to accelerate economic growth, countries may be tempted to avoid anti-pollution legislation to keep production costs low and remain more competitive in international markets. The design and enforcement of appropriate legislation should reduce the incentive to lower costs by failing to internalize pollution costs.

INVESTMENT IN ECONOMIC INFRASTRUCTURE

Economic infrastructure is vital to economic growth, particularly to the widening of markets and the transformation of a society from one that is predominantly rural and self-sufficient to one that is more urban and industrial. Definitions of **economic infrastructure** or **social overhead capital** usually include:

Public utilities: power, telecommunications, piped water supply, sanitation and sewerage, solid waste collection and disposal, and piped gas
Public works: roads and major dam and canal works for irrigation and drainage
Other transport sectors: urban and interurban railways, urban transport, ports and waterways, and airports.[17]

The World Bank has noted that in the 1990s developing countries allocated nearly 20 percent of their total investment to new infrastructure.[18] While access to clean drinking water, sewerage, and electricity has increased dramatically in the Third World, an estimated one billion people are still without clean water, and two billion people without adequate sewerage or electricity. Moreover, past investments in infrastructure, such as roads in Africa, have not always been efficient—being very expensive per person served. Insufficient maintenance also has reduced the returns from past investments. According to the World Bank,

> On average 40 percent of the power-generating capacity in developing countries is unavailable.... Half the labor in African and Latin American railways is estimated to

---

[17]World Bank, *World Development Report 1994,* page 2.
[18]Ibid., page 1.

be redundant ... [and] costly investments in road construction have been wasted for lack of maintenance.[19]

The World Bank cites three broad policy recommendations to increase the effectiveness of vitally needed economic infrastructure. They include introducing sound managerial techniques into infrastructure projects; infusing competition when possible into utilities; and giving users more influence in the design and regulation of public utilities.

### Sound Management

Many public infrastructure projects are operated very inefficiently and at high cost. Plaguing public projects are excessive staffing, often as a political reward; little quality control; and shortages of needed nonlabor inputs. Replacing bureaucracies with a more cost-effective managerial approach could improve public-sector investments and widen the access to basic needs such as clean water and electricity. To be successful in such a managerial evolution, governments need to resist using public projects for political purposes and must demand quality performance from employees and providers of other inputs.[20]

### Competition and Privatization

In addition to emphasizing the need for sound management, the World Bank recommends more competition in the provision of public infrastructure.[21] In those industries that are not natural monopolies (e.g., airlines), encouraging the entry of more firms would increase output, reduce prices, and promote more cost-effective production. For industries that are natural monopolies, privatization of publicly owned enterprises can reap efficiency gains. In the privatization process the government can sell ownership rights in the enterprise to willing private investors. Typically, the government will accompany this privatization with some form of price regulation to prevent monopoly pricing and profits.

Examples of efficiency gains from telecommunications privatization can be found in Chile, Mexico, and the United Kingdom.[22] In these cases, rate schedules have been changed significantly. Higher long-distance charges had been used to subsidize local telephone service. Generally, telecommunications reform has led to higher basic service charges with a regulated local monopoly, and to lower long-distance charges with increased competition among long-distance carriers. The World Bank estimates that the sum of gains to all parties—consumers, workers, and owners of private firms—has been positive in each of these three countries. The distribution of these net benefits is harder to calculate. Low-income individuals who make few long-distance calls may actually be net losers as they pay more for local service, but receive little benefit from

---

[19]Ibid.
[20]See "Running Public Entities on Commercial Principles," World Bank, *World Development Report 1994*, Chapter 2.
[21]See "Using Markets in Infrastructure Provision," World Bank, *World Development Report 1994*, Chapter 3.
[22]Ibid., page 65.

the reduced long-distance rates. Yet, most economists would favor a move toward a pricing scheme that better reflects the marginal costs of service.

Price regulation has often involved the principle of average-cost pricing. The unregulated, profit-maximizing monopolist will produce at the point where marginal revenue is equal to marginal cost, charging a price higher than average cost. See point $U_o$ with $Q_U$ and $P_U$ in Figure 13.5 (on page 412). With average-cost pricing at $R_o$, the producer's price is set equal to the average cost of providing the service, $P_R$. With this price regulation, output will increase to $Q_R$. Costs include both direct and opportunity costs. Two problems exist with average-cost pricing, however. First, with a decreasing average cost, price, which equals average cost (LAC), will exceed marginal cost (LMC). With demand or willingness to pay above marginal cost between $Q_R$ and $Q_X$, output is inefficiently restricted, resulting in a loss of consumer surplus. Yet, marginal cost is less than average cost within the relevant output range, and marginal-cost pricing would result in an economic loss, since price, $P_X$, would be less than average cost (see point $X_o$).

The second problem with average-cost pricing is that the firm has little incentive to promote efficiencies that reduce per unit cost, since price would simply decrease. More troubling, the firm has little incentive to reduce the growth in average cost, since price would simply increase to offset the cost increase. A possible solution to this efficiency problem has been used in Britain with the privatization of previously nationalized firms. Private utilities are subject to a pricing rule, referred to as *RPI-minus-X*. With this regulation, firms are permitted to increase price "by no more than X percentage points below the rate of consumer-price inflation (RPI)."[23] For instance, if the rate of inflation were 7 percent per annum and X were set at 3 percent, then the firm could not increase price beyond 4 percent (7 percent − 3 percent). In this case, the firm has an incentive to lower costs, as economic profits will increase. The firm is not held to a break-even standard as with average-cost pricing. This approach may be desirable with public utilities; some cost reductions, such as reducing the use of nonrenewable energy or limiting the need to build additional generating capacity, can be environmentally beneficial.

One form of limited privatization is for the government to sell or to auction production rights, for a specified period of time, to potential private producers. The successful firm would then supply output, subject to price and quality controls, with any resulting profit retained by the firm. The government would benefit by receiving some auction rights and not having the burden and cost of providing the service. The profit-maximizing producing firm would have an incentive to provide high-quality service (or face the loss of future production rights) in a cost-effective manner.

## Local Participation

After sound management and increased competition and privatization, the World Bank recommends participation by local residents, particularly those who are users of services such as water and sewerage, in the design and maintenance of projects.[24] Often this participation can be best implemented when project direction is relatively decentralized, with more control at the local level and less control at the national or capital-city level. From Brazil to Indonesia, water projects that consult village leaders and

---

[23]*The Economist* (August 13, 1994), page 64.
[24]See "Beyond Markets in Infrastructure," World Bank, *World Development Report 1994*, Chapter 4.

## FIGURE 13.5 REGULATING A NATURAL MONOPOLY

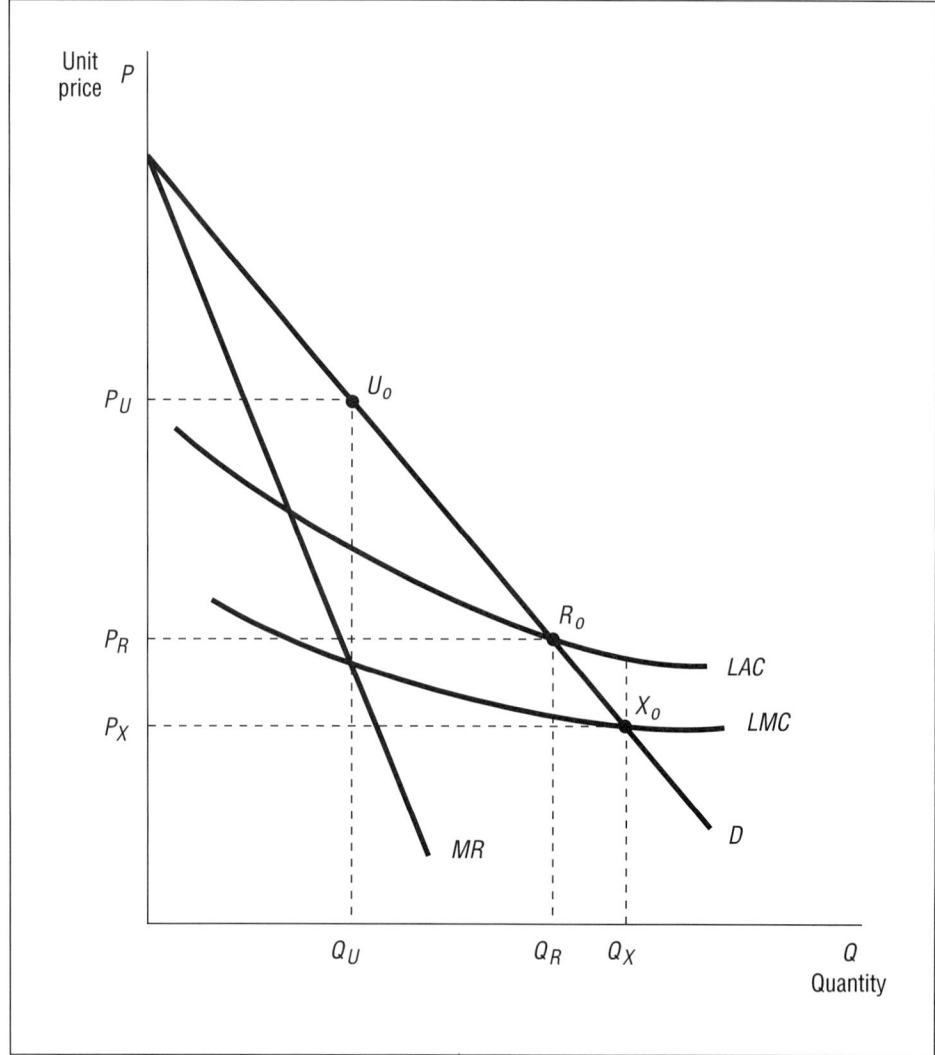

beneficiaries concerning design options and infrastructure location have reduced conflicts over land-use rights and led to lower investment costs.[25] Particularly disruptive is new irrigation infrastructure that often leads to changes in land tenure and even resettlement of whole villages. Clearly, in these cases, significant consultation with affected parties is vital to ensure both efficient and equitable outcomes.

The effective regulation of industry is a difficult challenge for the government of any country. Too little regulation risks the exploitation of workers and consumers, as well

---

[25]World Bank, *World Development Report 1994,* page 77.

as environmental degradation. In contrast, inappropriate and excessive regulation can reduce economic incentives, output, and employment. Given that the participants in the debates about regulation—owners of firms, consumers, workers, and government officials—all have an interest in the outcome, careful and balanced decision making is crucial.

## CONCLUDING NOTE

In this chapter we have raised several issues concerning industry and, to a lesser extent, services. Areas of concern for policymakers include the need to regulate aspects of industrial development; the issue of providing economic infrastructure; and the feasibility of import substitution. The following case study on development in India shows some of the difficulties with using a strategy of import substitution. We then continue our discussion of international integration in the next chapter with a more in-depth analysis of international trade and policies to expand exports.

## SUMMARY OF MAIN POINTS

1. Given that the demand for industrial products is income-elastic, while that for agricultural products is income-inelastic, with economic growth the share of industry in the economy increases, while that of agriculture decreases. Within a high-income economy, the share of services increases relative to that of industry.
2. Industry, primarily a private-sector activity, includes mining, manufacturing, construction, electricity, water, and gas. Government production or regulation of infrastructure industries that often are natural monopolies, such as electricity, is common. The degree of industry in the economy is often used as an indicator of economic development. Industry is typically more capital-intensive than other sectors of the economy and pays higher wages to employees. Industrial employment can be dangerous and is often regulated with safety laws in higher-income countries.
3. Within developing countries both informal and formal (or modern) service sectors exist. Informal services tend to be lower value-added activities such as small retail sales. Formal services, which are higher value-added activities, include computer programming and legal and financial services. With economic development, the informal service sector becomes relatively less important.
4. Input-output analysis captures the interrelationships among sectors of the economy. It shows the required output for each sector to support given levels of final demands within each sector.
5. While not considered useful as a means of allocating resources and selecting final demands, input-output analysis can be helpful in identifying constraints within the development process. The technique allows planners to calculate the additional outputs needed from supporting sectors to meet an increase in the final demands from another sector.

6. With free trade, a country will benefit from (a) exporting goods in which it has a comparative advantage (the ability to produce output at a lower domestic opportunity cost than its trading partners) and (b) importing goods in which it has a comparative disadvantage. With free trade, developing countries initially tend to export primary commodities and import finished manufactured goods.
7. Countries have often attempted to promote domestic manufacturing using tariffs, quotas, or subsidies, a process called import substitution. In those cases where a country's industry may have a long-term comparative advantage, import substitution policies can be justified. In most cases, however, such policies protect inefficient local industries to the detriment of consumer welfare.
8. To varying degrees, both developing and developed countries regulate industry to promote safer working conditions, encourage competition, and reduce pollution. While such regulation is appropriate, specific measures should be carefully designed to avoid unnecessary cost increases.
9. Governments are a logical provider of economic infrastructure, which includes public utilities, roads, other public works, and some transportation services. Developing countries need to devote more care to the effective construction and management of these services vital to economic growth.

## KEY TERMS

ad valorem tariff
comparative advantage
consistent plan
contestable market
economic infrastructure
effective rate of tariff protection (ERP)
ex ante
ex post
export expansion
import quota

import substitution
infant-industry strategy
input-output analysis
material balance process
merit goods
natural monopoly
nominal rate
social overhead capital
specific tariff
value added

## QUESTIONS

1. Choose several countries at different stages of the development process. Compare the relative importance of agriculture, industry, and services within these economies. Do you find that the sectoral shifts are as predicted by the discussion in this chapter?
2. As a policymaker within a developing country, give an example of how you would find input-output analysis useful as you were designing a development plan.
3. Assume that a country intends to use a large-scale irrigation project to open some new land for wheat production. What possible constraints would the country encounter with this development project?
4. Choose a developing country and summarize the country's use of trade barriers to protect domestic industry. Do you have reason to believe that the country is legitimately protecting an industry that will have a long-run comparative advantage? Support your argument.

5. Given the Interindustry Transactions Table (in millions of $)

|  | Intermediate-User Purchases ($) Sector | | | Final Demand | Total Demand |
|---|---|---|---|---|---|
|  | 1 | 2 | 3 |  |  |
| Sales by: |  |  |  |  |  |
| Sector 1 | — | — | 10 | 170 | 200 |
| Sector 2 | 50 | 30 | 40 | — | 150 |
| Sector 3 | 40 | 15 | 20 | 25 | — |
| Value added: | 90 | 105 | — |  |  |
| Payments to Labor | 70 | 65 | 20 |  |  |
| Payments to Capital | — | 40 | — |  |  |
| Total Supply: | 200 | 150 | — |  |  |

a. Fill in the blanks.
b. Calculate and explain the values for $a_{11}$, $a_{23}$, and $a_{31}$.
c. If there are $170 million worth of labor and $75 million worth of capital in the economy, show whether the final demands can be met.
d. Explain why an increase of $1 million in the final demand for the output of Sector 3 will increase the required gross production (total supply) in the output of Sector 3 by more than $1 million.

6. Assume that a country assembles and sells bicycles at the world market price of $40.00 per unit; each bicycle produced requires $25 of intermediate goods (parts), all of which are imported.
   a. If the country imposes an ad valorem tariff of 20 percent on bicycles, what is the effective rate of protection accorded the domestic bicycle industry?
   b. In addition to a 20 percent tariff on bicycles, if the government imposes a 10 percent tariff on the intermediate goods, what will be the effective rate of protection of the domestic bicycle industry?

7. What would it mean if the effective rate of protection were negative?

8. Assume that a country both produces and imports motor-scooter batteries. The domestic demand and supply schedules for these batteries are:

$$Q^d = 200 - 5P \quad \text{and} \quad Q^s = -10 + 4P$$

where $P$ equals the unit price of a battery (in $) and the quantities demanded and supplied are in thousands of batteries per month. Assume the country is a price-taker with respect to world trade.
   a. If the world price of batteries is $20, find the quantities demanded, domestically produced, and imported by this country under free trade.
   b. If the government of the developing nation imposes a specific tariff of $2.00 per battery on the imports of batteries, find the new consumer price and the quantities demanded, domestically produced, and imported by this country. Calculate the tariff revenues collected by the government.

c. Suppose that, instead of the specific tariff, the government sets an import quota of 12,000 batteries per month. Find the quantities demanded, domestically produced, and imported, as well as the domestic price of batteries under this import quota.

d. Assume that the price of batteries remains at $20.00 per unit with no tariff or quota. What per-unit subsidy would the government need to accord domestic producers so that battery imports would fall to 12,000 batteries per month? What would be the total costs to the government of this subsidy?

e. Assume that the domestic demand for batteries shifts to $Q^{d'} = 240 - 5P$. Compare the effects on the quantities demanded, domestically produced, and imported, as well as the domestic price under the specific tariff of $2.00 per battery and the import quota of 12,000 batteries per month.

## SUGGESTED READINGS

Chenery, Hollis, *Structural Change and Development Policy,* New York: Oxford University Press, 1979, Chapters 1–3.

World Bank, "Infrastructure: Achievements, Challenges, and Opportunities," *World Development Report 1994,* New York: Oxford University Press, 1994, Chapter 1.

## CASE STUDY

### INDIA

Following the advent of self-government in 1945, India pursued a relatively interventionist, inward-looking development strategy.[1] Under Jawaharlal Nehru, premier from 1947 to 1964, the government significantly intervened in the development process. In an attempt to promote domestic heavy industry, India embraced an import substitution strategy that included public ownership of key industries. At different times, nationalized industries included chemicals, electric power, steel, transportation, life insurance, portions of the coal and textile industries, and banking.[2] To promote these domestic industries, the government levied high tariffs; imposed import restrictions; subsidized the nationalized firms; directed investment funds; and even controlled many prices.

A recent article in *The Economist* described the situation:

> The system developed in India after independence constrained the growth of the private sector by allowing it to expand only with government permission. It reserved heavy industry for the public sector, and stunted trade by quotas and high tariffs.

---

[1] World Bank, "India," *Trends in Developing Economies,* Washington, DC, 1994, pages 223–228.

[2] Paul R. Gregory and Robert C. Stuart, *Comparative Economic Systems,* 4th ed., Boston: Houghton Mifflin, 1992, pages 255–264.

Access to foreign exchange was limited. There were controls on land use, on trade in farm products—even if the mood suited, on the price of onions.[3]

Despite such intervention, economic progress was made during this period following independence. According to the World Bank, per capita GDP grew at a respectable rate of 1.4 percent per annum from the late 1940s into the 1970s.[4] Both famine and poverty were significantly reduced during this period. Nevertheless, most economists would argue that the interventions lowered India's economic growth rates. With few major producers of many key industrial products, the concentration of domestic production was very high, inviting monopolistic pricing. Moreover, as the world economy grew, and as beneficial opportunities for growth through trade expanded, India paid an increasing price for its economic isolation.

Beginning in the early 1980s, however, economic reforms were introduced. According to the World Bank:

> Throughout the 1980s, important policy changes started to liberalize trade, industrial, and financial policies, while subsidies, tax concessions, and the depreciation of the currency improved export incentives. These measures helped GDP growth to accelerate to over 5 percent per year [or approximately 3 percent per capita] during the 1980s and reduced poverty more rapidly, but India's most fundamental structural problems were addressed only very partially. Tariffs continued to be extremely high and quantitative restrictions remained pervasive.[5]

Moreover, significant government influence continued in the allocation of credit to firms and a discouragement of foreign investment. Relatively inefficient public enterprises, controlling nearly 20 percent of GDP, remained a drag on economic growth.

In July of 1991, India launched a second major economic reform program that addressed these remaining inefficiencies. The government committed itself to promoting a competitive economy that would be open to trade and foreign investment.[6] Measures were introduced to reduce the government's influence in firms' investment decisions. According to *The Economist*:

> Much of the industrial-licensing system was dismantled, and areas once closed to the private sector were opened up—electricity generation, bits of the oil industry, heavy industry, air transport, roads and some telecommunications. Foreign investment, formerly allowed in only grudgingly and subject to arbitrary ceilings, was suddenly welcomed. Approval is now automatic for foreign equity stakes of up to 51% in most businesses; stakes up to 100% may be allowed.[7]

Greater global integration was encouraged with a significant reduction in the use of import licenses; an elimination of subsidies for exports; and the introduction of a foreign-exchange market. With successive additional monetary reforms, the rupee, in 1995, can be considered a nearly fully convertible currency at market rates. While domestic tariff

---

[3]"A Survey of India," supplement to *The Economist* (January 21, 1995), pages 4 and 7.
[4]World Bank, "India," page 223.
[5]Ibid.
[6]Ibid., page 224.
[7]*The Economist*, "A Survey of India," page 7.

rates are still quite high, the maximum nominal rate has been reduced from 400 percent to 65 percent. Also, raw materials and capital goods can be imported without restriction.[8] India currently has a much more open economy. With the more competitively priced rupee, export growth in the 1990s has been quite impressive.

India, like many developing countries that adopted a philosophy of government intervention with import substitution policies, is finding that economic reform can often be a slow, incremental process. Complications continue. Domestic producers will resist tariff reductions that subject them to increased competition. Also, many of the controls imposed on Indian firms both reduced risk and increased profits—at the expense of consumers and taxpayers. Government bureaucrats will try to maintain the power and influence that they acquired during periods of substantial government influence in economic decision making.

As reported by *The Economist*, India is still a low-income developing country.

> India has an economy slightly smaller than Belgium's. Its GDP per head is $310. Fewer than half of its 950 million people can read.... Some 14% of the population has access to clean sanitation, a lower proportion than anywhere else except for a handful of Sudans and Burkina Fasos. According to the World Bank, 63% of India's under-five-year olds are malnourished. Perhaps 40% of the world's desperately poor live in India.[9]

India has considerable economic influence and potential. The country has made major strides in establishing preconditions for successful and sustained development. In discussing Indian economic reform, *The Economist* made several observations:

> After four years of reform, the economy has moved into top gear. Industrial output-growth averaged 8.4% in 1994–95, peaking at 11.7% last March. Exports were up by 27% over a year earlier in the April–June quarter, after increasing by 19% and 18% in the two preceding years. Inflation has dipped below 10% for most of the year. The current-account deficit is below 1% of GDP, foreign-exchange reserves are high at $20 billion, and food stocks have hit an all-time high of 37m tonnes.[10]

Yet India still has proponents of economic nationalism who resent the presence of foreign firms and imported products. Large publicly-owned firms that account for nearly 50 percent of the assets of the industrial sector have not been successfully privatized nor even given sufficient autonomy to fire redundant workers.[11] Finally, the Indian government still subsidizes farmers, leading to resource misallocations and a divergence of public funds from other worthy development projects. Resolving these issues will be vital to the success of the Indian reform program.

---

[8]Ibid.
[9]Ibid., page 3.
[10]*The Economist*, "India's Economic Nationalists" (August 12, 1995), page 27.
[11]Ibid.

# PART V

# INTERNATIONAL INTEGRATION

# CHAPTER 14

# TRADE AND DEVELOPMENT

Worldwide trade has expanded by more than 6 percent a year since 1950, which is more than 50 percent faster than the growth of output.[1]

As the above statement reveals, national economies are becoming more interdependent. Despite the economic turbulence of the 1970s (including the breakdown of the prevailing international monetary system and the oil price shocks) and 1980s (external debt crises and slow, even negative, economic growth in many less developed countries), the share of exports of goods and services in the combined gross domestic products of the world increased from one in seven dollars in 1970 to more than one in five dollars in 1993.[2]

Economists have long recognized the benefits of international trade. Indeed, comparative advantage, a concept that provides the basis for trade, was introduced nearly two centuries ago by the classical economist David Ricardo, and remains one of the greatest insights of economics. A nation is said to have a **comparative advantage** in the production of a commodity if it can produce the commodity for a lower opportunity cost than its trading partner. International specialization, whereby nations produce according to their comparative advantages and trade freely, yields the most efficient allocation of resources. Nations participating in trade are able to consume beyond their production possibilities boundaries.

Considerable evidence exists that more open economies do better. For example, in an assessment of 41 developing economies for the periods 1963 to 1973 and 1973 to 1985, the World Bank concluded, "the economic performance of the outward-oriented

---

[1] World Bank, *World Development Report 1991,* New York: Oxford University Press, 1991, page 2.

[2] This statistic is derived from Table 9 in the World Bank's *World Development Report 1994,* New York: Oxford University Press, 1994; and *World Development Report 1995,* New York: Oxford University Press, 1995.

economies has been broadly superior to that of the inward-oriented economies in almost all respects."[3] Continuing success in international competition requires attention to cost minimization, innovation, and product quality. Especially for smaller countries with limited domestic markets, producing exports for the world market allows for greater economies in scale in production to be captured. Moreover, in labor-abundant, developing economies, international trade based on comparative advantages stimulates employment.

We begin this chapter with an illustration of the basis for trade that draws on the factor endowments theory of trade. With a two country–two commodity–two factor model we show how international trade can be a substitute for international factor mobility—either of which can increase the efficiency of resource utilization and the total output produced. We are also able to identify groups within the trading nations that, ceteris paribus, suffer income losses from trade, even as the general levels of consumption rise.

We then turn to a more dynamic theory of trade that explains how comparative advantages in manufactured goods can shift over time. After establishing the basis for trade, we explore trade policy, in particular, an export-oriented strategy of development. The current environment in international trade is reviewed, along with the role played by the General Agreement on Tariffs and Trade (GATT), a post–World War II institution set up to liberalize trade (and succeeded in 1995 by the World Trade Organization). A discussion of the prospects of the less developed countries in international trade concludes the chapter.

## ILLUSTRATION OF THE GAINS FROM TRADE

To illustrate the gains from trade we use a two country–two commodity–two factor model. The underlying principles, however, extend to many countries producing many commodities with additional factors of production.

Consider two countries, Norte and Sierra, producing two commodities, shoes *(s)* and rice *(r)*, using capital *(K)* and labor *(L)*. Assume that Norte has 300 units of labor and 600 units of capital.[4] Sierra has 800 units of labor and 100 units of capital. With the higher capital–labor endowment, Norte is the capital-abundant country. Sierra is the labor-abundant country.

To simplify the illustration, we will assume fixed-coefficients production functions for the commodities. That is, as you recall from Chapter 3, the input requirements for producing a given level of output are inflexible—no factor substitution is possible.

---

[3]World Bank, *World Development Report 1987,* New York: Oxford University Press, 1987, page 85. The *World Development Report 1987* focused on international trade and development. The specific performance measures examined by the World Bank were growth rates in per capita income and manufactured exports, inflation rates, and gross domestic savings rates. The greatest disparities in performance were between the strongly outward-oriented (the nations of Hong Kong, South Korea, and Singapore) and the strongly inward-oriented (16 nations in the period 1965–1973 and 14 nations in the period 1973–1985, including for both periods India, Bangladesh, Burundi, Ethiopia, Ghana, Sudan, Tanzania, Zambia, Argentina, Dominican Republic, and Peru).

[4]A *unit of labor* may be measured in person years and a *unit of capital* may be measured in hundreds of hours of use of the plant, equipment, and machinery.

Suppose that in Norte, each unit of rice requires 4 units of labor and 5 units of capital; each unit of shoes produced requires 3 units of labor and 6 units of capital.[5] In Sierra, to produce each unit of rice would take 8 units of labor and 1 unit of capital. Each unit of shoes requires 5 units of labor and 2 units of capital. We summarize these assumptions in Table 14.1.

In both countries, shoes are the capital-intensive commodity (with the higher capital–labor ratios in production) and rice is the labor-intensive commodity. The input requirements may differ between the two countries due to differences in technology (some of which may be embodied in the respective capital stocks); differences in labor skills (education, health, experience); or differences in climate and natural resource endowments. In the examples below, however, we will assume there are no qualitative differences in either the capital or labor in the two countries. Further, we will assume that there are no qualitative differences in the shoes or rice produced by each country.

From the production functions and factor endowments we can list some of the possible output combinations of rice and shoes in the countries (see Table 14.1 on page 424). For example, in Norte one possible output combination is 60 units of rice (requiring 240$L$ and 300$K$) and 20 units of shoes (requiring 60$L$ and 120$K$). With this combination there would be 180 units of capital in surplus.[6] If Norte increased shoe production from 20 to 40 units, capital and labor would have to be transferred from the production of rice; consequently rice production would decline from 60 units to 45 units (compare Combinations B and C for Norte in Table 14.1). In Norte, the capital-abundant country, production is constrained by the scarce factor, labor. For each output combination, all of the available labor is used, but there is excess capital (except in the most capital-intensive Combination F). In Sierra, the labor-abundant country, the scarce factor constraining production is capital.

We can plot the **production possibilities boundary (PPB)** for each nation[7] (see Figure 14.1 on page 425). The slope of the PPB indicates **opportunity cost,** or the loss in output of one commodity per unit increase in the production of the other commodity. With the assumption of fixed-coefficients production functions, the opportunity costs are constant. In Norte, the slope of the PPB is $-15/20 = -3/4$; or, for every decrease of 15 units of rice production, another 20 units of shoes could be produced. The opportunity cost, then, of increasing shoe production in Norte by 1 unit is 3/4 unit of rice (not produced). In Sierra, the slope of the PPB is $-20/10 = -2/1$; or, for every decrease of 20 units of rice, another 10 units of shoes could be produced. The opportunity cost of increasing shoe production by 1 unit in Sierra is 2 units of rice production.

In autarky—that is, self-sufficiency with no international trade—the opportunity cost in a nation sets the internal exchange or price ratio. In Norte, one unit of shoes would exchange for 3/4 units of rice ($1s = (3/4)r = .75r$); or equivalently, one unit of rice

---

[5] A *unit of rice* may be a thousand bushels per year; a *unit of shoes* may be a hundred pairs of shoes per year.

[6] In Norte, the surplus capital can be regarded as the available, but underutilized, plant, equipment, and machinery. In Sierra, the surplus labor can be regarded, as in Lewis's model (see Chapter 4), as the labor absorbed in a form of work-sharing, i.e., the labor is working but not really needed or contributing to production.

[7] Usually points on the production possibilities boundary imply full employment of the available resources. In contrast, here, because of the assumption of fixed-coefficients production functions, all of the output combinations on the production possibilities boundaries (except one extreme combination in each case) are consistent with an underutilization of one of the factors (capital in Norte and labor in Sierra).

| TABLE 14.1 | Two Country–Two Commodity–Two Factor Model of Trade |
|---|---|

two countries: Norte and Sierra
two commodities: rice (r) and shoes (s)
two factors: capital (K) and labor (L)

*Factor endowments:*
    Norte has 300 units of labor (300L) and 600 units of capital (600K).
    Sierra has 800 units of labor (800L) and 100 units of capital (100K).

*Production functions:*
    Norte:  Each unit of rice produced requires 4L and 5K.
            Each unit of shoes produced requires 3L and 6K.

    Sierra:  Each unit of rice produced requires 8L and 1K.
            Each unit of shoes produced requires 5L and 2K.

PRODUCTION POSSIBILITIES

| | NORTE | | | | SIERRA | | |
|---|---|---|---|---|---|---|---|
| | RICE | SHOES | SURPLUS CAPITAL | | RICE | SHOES | SURPLUS LABOR |
| A | 75<br>(300L, 375K) | 0<br>(0L, 0K) | 225K | A' | 100<br>(800L, 100K) | 0<br>(0L, 0K) | 0L |
| B | 60<br>(240L, 300K) | 20<br>(60L, 120K) | 180K | B' | 80<br>(640L, 80K) | 10<br>(50L, 20K) | 110L |
| C | 45<br>(180L, 225K) | 40<br>(120L, 240K) | 135K | C' | 60<br>(480L, 60K) | 20<br>(100L, 40K) | 220L |
| D | 30<br>(120L, 150K) | 60<br>(180L, 360K) | 90K | D' | 40<br>(320L, 40K) | 30<br>(150L, 60K) | 330L |
| E | 15<br>(60L, 75K) | 80<br>(240L, 480K) | 45K | E' | 20<br>(160L, 20K) | 40<br>(200L, 80K) | 440L |
| F | 0<br>(0L, 0K) | 100<br>(300L, 600K) | 0K | F' | 0<br>(0L, 0K) | 50<br>(250L, 100K) | 550L |

OPPORTUNITY COSTS

        $1r = (4/3)s = 1.33s$                    $1r = (1/2)s = .5s$
        $1s = (3/4)r = .75r$                     $1s = 2r$

would exchange for 4/3 units of shoes ($1r = (4/3)s = 1.33s$). In Sierra, one unit of shoes would exchange for 2 units of rice ($1s = 2r$); or equivalently, one unit of rice would exchange for 1/2 units of shoes ($1r = (1/2)s = .5s$). The difference in opportunity costs between the two countries provides a basis for trade. Here, Norte has the lower opportunity cost for the production of shoes—in terms of the sacrifice in rice production. Sierra has the lower opportunity cost for the production of rice—in terms of a sacrifice in shoe production.

## FIGURE 14.1  PRODUCTION POSSIBILITIES BOUNDARIES

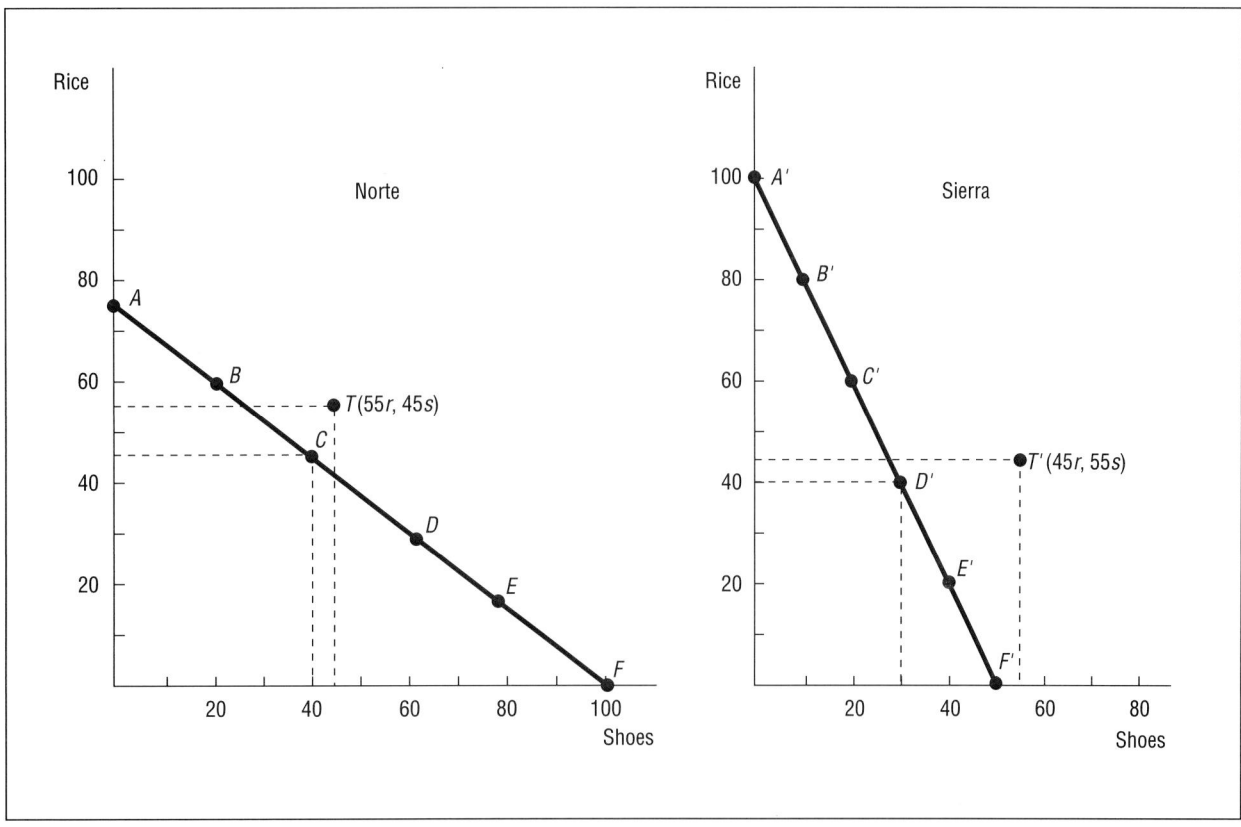

Indeed, with this simple example we can illustrate the **factor endowments theory of trade**.[8] That is, a nation will have a comparative advantage (lower opportunity cost) in the commodity whose production uses intensively the nation's abundant factor. Here Norte, the capital-abundant nation, has the comparative advantage in the production of shoes, the capital-intensive commodity. Intuitively, we would expect capital to be relatively inexpensive in a capital-abundant country. Thus, for commodities that require relatively more capital, the opportunity costs of production should be comparatively low. In contrast, in Sierra, with an abundance of labor, rice should be comparatively inexpensive, since it requires relatively more labor to produce.

### INTERNATIONAL FACTOR MOBILITY

If a nation does not engage in international trade and if factors are immobile across nations, then the nation's consumption possibilities coincide with its production

---

[8]Usually the factor endowments theory of trade (also known as the Heckscher-Ohlin theory of trade) assumes identical production functions for the two countries for a commodity. For our purposes in this example, such an assumption is not necessary. For a more formal treatment of the factor endowments theory of trade, see Chapter 8, "The Basis for Trade," in *International Economics,* 2d ed., by Dennis Appleyard and Alfred Field, Chicago: Irwin, 1995.

possibilities. Assume that before trade, Norte is producing and consuming 45 units of rice and 40 units of shoes (Combination C on Norte's production possibilities boundary), with 135 units of capital in surplus. In Norte, the average products of labor, obtained by dividing the outputs of rice and shoes by the available labor, are $(45/300)r = .15r$ and $(40/300)s = .133s$, respectively. Suppose that Sierra is producing and consuming 40 units of rice and 30 units of shoes (Combination D' on Sierra's PPB), with 330 units of labor in surplus. The average products of labor in Sierra are $(40/800)r = .05r$ and $(30/800)s = .0375s$. Correspondingly, we expect Norte to have the higher standard of living, since, with the higher capital–labor ratios (and, in all likelihood, the more advanced technologies), labor is more productive in Norte. On the other hand, the marginal productivities of capital would be higher in Sierra, the labor-abundant country. (Indeed, with surplus capital and the fixed-coefficients production functions, the marginal product of capital is zero in Norte. Additional capital would not increase output. Likewise, the marginal product of labor in Sierra is zero.)

If we allow for international factor mobility, some of the surplus labor in Sierra could migrate to Norte, where, combined with the surplus capital, output could be increased. In addition, some of the surplus capital in Norte could be shipped to Sierra to combine with the surplus labor there to increase output. To illustrate, let 60 units of labor (60$L$) migrate from Sierra to Norte and combine with 120 units of the surplus capital (120$K$) to increase the production of shoes in Norte by 20 units ($\Delta s = +20$). The remaining 15 units of surplus capital (15$K$) in Norte could be shipped to Sierra to combine with 120 units of surplus labor (120$L$) there to increase the production of rice by 15 units ($\Delta r = +15$). Therefore, the global production of shoes and rice could be increased, and the underutilization of capital and labor could be reduced (from 135 units of surplus capital to none, and from 330 units of surplus labor to 150 units). Both countries, as well as the owners of the newly employed capital and labor, would gain from this international factor mobility.[9] See Table 14.2 for a summary of the gains from factor mobility.

In fact, if no restrictions existed on international factor mobility, we would expect to see labor migrating from low-wage (labor-abundant) nations to high-wage (labor-scarce) nations. Capital would flow in the form of foreign direct investment from high-wage (capital-abundant) nations to low-wage (capital-scarce) nations. These factor flows would continue until the returns to labor and capital were equalized across nations. Nations do, however, limit immigration (and sometimes emigration), and there are restrictions on foreign direct investment and capital flows. Nevertheless, there has been a net flow of labor and population from the less developed to the developed countries, and a net flow of capital from the developed to the less developed countries. In both cases, some of the income earned abroad very likely returns to the country of origin as labor earnings remitted or profits repatriated.

We note that while outputs in both countries have increased and the underutilization of labor and capital has decreased with the international factor mobility, opposition to such factor flows may exist. The opposition would come from the scarce factor in each country. In Norte, labor is scarce, but would be less so if labor migrated in from Sierra. The inflow of labor would likely drive down the wage (returns to labor)

---

[9]Note, given the assumption of fixed-coefficients production functions, full employment of both factors would probably not occur. Here only the capital stock becomes fully utilized. Nevertheless, international factor mobility should reduce the unemployment of the capital and labor.

| TABLE 14.2 | SUMMARY OF THE GAINS FROM FACTOR MOBILITY |
|---|---|

INITIAL PRODUCTION COMBINATIONS:

Norte: 45 units of rice   (180L, 225K)   Sierra: 40 units of rice   (320L, 40K)
       40 units of shoes  (120L, 240K)           30 units of shoes  (150L, 60K)

       Surplus capital = 135K                    Surplus labor = 330L

World: 85 units of rice
       70 units of shoes
       Surplus capital = 135K
       Surplus labor = 330L

WITH INTERNATIONAL FACTOR MOBILITY:

60 units of the surplus labor migrate from Sierra to Norte, where they combine with 120 units of the surplus capital to increase the production of shoes by 20 units.

The remaining 15 units of surplus capital are sent from Norte to Sierra, where they combine with 120 units of surplus labor to increase the production of rice by 15 units.

POST-FACTOR MOBILITY PRODUCTION COMBINATIONS:

Norte: 45 units of rice   (180L, 225K)   Sierra: 55 units of rice   (440L, 55K)
       60 units of shoes  (180L, 360K)           30 units of shoes  (150L, 60K)

       No surplus capital                        Surplus labor = 150L

World: 100 units of rice  (+15 units of rice)
       90 units of shoes  (+20 units of shoes)
       Surplus capital = 0K
       Surplus labor    = 150L

in Norte. The returns to capital, in contrast, would rise in Norte, as some of the surplus capital could then be used with the additional labor from Sierra. In Sierra, with an inflow of capital, the returns to the owners of capital would fall, while the returns to labor, now less abundant, would rise.

## THE INTERNATIONAL TERMS OF TRADE AND THE GAINS FROM TRADE

Suppose instead that factors are not mobile internationally, but that the nations engage freely in trade.[10] Begin again with the given pretrade production and consumption combinations for the two countries: Norte with 45 units of rice and 40 units of shoes, and Sierra with 40 units of rice and 30 units of shoes.

---

[10]We will abstract from trade barriers and transportation costs and assume that labor and capital are internally mobile.

Recall that Norte has the lower opportunity cost for producing shoes (.75 units of rice, compared to 2 units of rice per unit of shoes in Sierra). Sierra has the lower opportunity cost for producing rice (.5 units of shoes, compared with 1.33 units of shoes per unit of rice in Norte). With trade, shoe producers in Norte would have an incentive to export shoes to Sierra (where one unit of shoes exchanges for 2 units of rice). Similarly, rice producers in Sierra would have an incentive to export rice to Norte (where one unit of rice exchanges for 1.33 units of shoes). In each country a reallocation of resources would result. Norte would increase the production of shoes, shifting capital and labor over from rice production, and export shoes to Sierra in exchange for rice. In Sierra, capital and labor would be shifted from shoe production to rice production, and rice would be exported.[11]

In Norte, increased rice would be available for consumption, since the rice imported from Sierra would more than offset the decrease in rice produced domestically. As rice became more available, the "shoe price" of rice, or the exchange ratio, in Norte would fall to less than 1.33 units of shoes per unit of rice.

In Sierra, increased shoes would be available for consumption, since the shoes imported from Norte more than make up for the decrease in domestic shoe production. Consequently, the "rice price" of shoes in Sierra would decline to less than 2 units of rice per unit of shoes. An **international terms of trade,** or common exchange ratio, would emerge as a result of the trade between the two countries. The international terms of trade would settle between the opportunity costs in Norte and Sierra, that is, between $1r = 1.33s$ and $1r = .5s$.[12]

Suppose the international terms of trade settle at one unit of rice equals one unit of shoes ($1r = 1s$). With trade Norte could completely specialize in the production of shoes, and Sierra could completely specialize in the production of rice, their respective comparative advantage commodities. Norte moves from Combination C to Combination F on its production possibilities boundary, where it produces 100 units of shoes. Assume that Norte then exports 55 units of shoes to Sierra for 55 units of rice at the international terms of trade. Norte ends up consuming 45 units of shoes (100 units produced less 55 units exported) and 55 units of rice (all imported from Sierra). See the combination represented by point T, lying beyond Norte's PPB. The gains from trade for Norte, derived by comparing the posttrade and pretrade consumption combinations, are 10 units of rice and 5 units of shoes.

Sierra shifts capital and labor to Combination A' on its production possibilities boundary, producing 100 units of rice. Sierra exports 55 units of rice for 55 units of shoes, and ends up with 45 units of rice and 55 units of shoes for consumption. See

---

[11] Note that in both countries the assumption of constant opportunity cost implies that all units of capital and labor are equally well-suited for producing rice and shoes. That is, as long as the input requirements set by the fixed-coefficients production functions are met, labor and capital can be readily shifted between the production of rice and shoes.

[12] Intuitively, given no qualitative differences in rice or shoes regardless of where produced, Sierra would import shoes only if the rice price were less than $2r = 1s$. Norte would export shoes only if the rice price were greater than $.75r = 1s$. Thus, for trade to be mutually beneficial, the international terms of trade would have to fall between the opportunity costs of the two countries. To determine the exact international terms of trade we would need additional information, such as the relative tastes and preferences for rice versus shoes in the two countries. Implicitly we assume in this example that tastes and preferences in the two countries are similar. To keep the math simple, we will assume that the international terms of trade settle at $1r = 1s$.

| TABLE 14.3 | SUMMARY OF GAINS FROM TRADE |

NORTE
    Pretrade:
        Production and consumption:  45 units of rice      (point C on PPB)
                                                    40 units of shoes

    Posttrade:
        Production:    0 units of rice      (point F on PPB)
                          100 units of shoes
        Export:  55 units of shoes
        Import:  55 units of rice
        Consumption:  55 units of rice      (point T beyond PPB)
                               45 units of shoes

    Gains from trade:  10 units of rice
                               5 units of shoes

SIERRA
    Pretrade:
        Production and consumption:  40 units of rice      (point D' on PPB)
                                                    30 units of shoes

    Posttrade:
        Production: 100 units of rice      (point A' on PPB)
                            0 units of shoes
        Export:  55 units of rice
        Import:  55 units of shoes
        Consumption:  45 units of rice      (point T' beyond PPB)
                               55 units of shoes

    Gains from trade:  5 units of rice
                               25 units of shoes

NOTE: The international terms of trade are one unit of rice for one unit of shoes.

point T' beyond Sierra's PPB. Sierra's gains from trade are 5 units of rice and 25 units of shoes. Table 14.3 summarizes the gains from trade for the two countries.

Note that in this example with complete specialization in the production of the comparative advantage commodities, all the factors are fully utilized—no surplus labor or capital exists. While this ideal case would probably not hold in practice, trade based on comparative advantages should increase the employment of the abundant factors in the nations. Earlier we illustrated the gains from international factor mobility, whereby some of the surplus labor from Sierra could migrate to Norte, and some of the surplus capital in Norte could be sent to Sierra so that production in both countries could increase. Trade in goods embodies such a transfer of factors. Norte, by exporting the capital-intensive commodity (shoes) for the labor-intensive commodity (rice), in effect has exported capital for labor. Similarly, Sierra has exported surplus labor (in the form of the labor-intensive commodity rice) and imported scarce capital (in the form of the capital-intensive commodity shoes).[13]

## GENERAL PRINCIPLES OF TRADE

Before reviewing the important principles of international trade, we should note the simplifying assumptions of this numerical example.

### Simplifying Assumptions of the Model

First, to make the analysis easier to follow, we assumed fixed-coefficients production functions, which yielded **constant opportunity costs** (and linear production possibilities boundaries). In our examples, Norte, the capital-abundant country, had the more capital-intensive production functions for both commodities. With constant opportunity costs, labor and capital are assumed to be easily shifted from the production of one commodity to the production of the other; in other words, all the units of labor (capital) are equally well-suited for both types of production.

In practice, there usually are possibilities for factor substitution—different capital–labor combinations can be used to produce a given level of output.[14] Moreover, constant opportunity costs are unlikely to prevail to the extent implied in this model. More realistically, **increasing opportunity costs** will be encountered as the production of either commodity is increased; thus, the production possibilities boundaries will not be linear, but concave in curvature. The underlying reason is that not all units of labor (or capital or other factors) will be equally well-suited for different types of production. Here rice farmers and shoe-factory workers would probably not be perfectly interchangeable. Similarly, some machines and equipment are specifically designed for the production of certain commodities, for example, tillers for farming and leather-tanning tools for shoes. Thus, shifting factors within nations with the changes in production combinations arising from trade will usually entail adjustment costs—in particular, some unemployment of labor and some underutilization of the existing physical capital stocks.

With two economies of roughly the same size, as in this example, trade allowed for complete specialization in the production of the comparative advantage commodities. With the more likely condition of increasing opportunity costs, countries would tend not to specialize completely. Furthermore, in practice, countries have been reluctant

---

[13]Consider, for Sierra to produce directly 45 units of rice and 55 units of shoes (its posttrade consumption combination), it would require 635 units of labor, i.e., $(8L)(45) + (5L)(55) = 635L$, and 155 units of capital, i.e., $(1K)(45) + (2K)(55) = 155K$, given its production functions. This is 55 more units of capital than Sierra has. Sierra, however, is able to consume this combination of 45 units of rice and 55 units of shoes through trade by producing 100 units of rice, which requires 800 units of labor and 100 units of capital. In effect, Sierra has exported 165 units of labor ($800L - 635L$) for 55 units of capital ($155K - 100K$).

[14]Recall from Chapter 3 that Solow "solved" the knife-edge problem of the fixed-coefficients Harrod-Domar growth model by allowing for substitution between capital and labor. A consequence of the fixed-coefficients production function used in this illustration of the gains from trade is the underutilization of one of the factors of production in each country—except, as it turns out here, in the case of complete specialization in the production of the comparative advantage commodity.

to rely entirely on imports for essential commodities—even when domestic production of the commodities is at a significant comparative disadvantage.

Finally, we assumed free trade and identical commodities; ignored transportation costs; and expressed exchange ratios and the international terms of trade in physical units. Trade barriers and transportation costs can offset, at least in part, underlying comparative advantages in production. Due to differences in product qualities and tastes and preferences, nations often export and import the same commodities (e.g., French and Italian wines, German and Japanese automobiles). In addition, international trade involves transactions in different currencies, thus the need for exchange rates. In Chapter 15 we will discuss how exchange rates are determined and how trade is affected.

### Comparative Advantage

The simplifying assumptions of this basic two country–two commodity–two factor model do not compromise the important principles that have been illustrated. One, comparative advantage, indicated by lower opportunity cost, forms a basis for international trade. Differences in factor endowments can account for the comparative advantages. Here we showed how the capital-abundant country (Norte) would have the comparative advantage in producing the capital-intensive commodity (shoes), and the labor-abundant country (Sierra) would have the comparative advantage in producing the labor-intensive commodity (rice).

### Gains from Trade

The gains from trade result from a more efficient allocation of resources as countries increase the production of the commodities in which they have the lower opportunity costs. In fact, international trade in goods can be a substitute for international factor flows. By exporting capital-intensive commodities and importing labor-intensive commodities, capital-abundant nations effectively are exporting capital and importing labor. Similarly, labor-abundant nations can relax the constraint on their consumption possibilities imposed by their production possibilities from the relative scarcity of capital, through importing capital-intensive commodities in exchange for labor-intensive commodities. In short, with trade, nations can consume some combinations of outputs that are beyond their production possibilities boundaries.

### Trade and the Distribution of Income

This example illustrates how two nations—one (Norte) with much higher average products of labor and standard of living—could nevertheless mutually benefit from trade. While the world wins from the increases in outputs with the more efficient allocation of resources and as consumers in the trading nations benefit (especially consumers of the imported goods), there are "losers" from freer trade and consequences for the distributions of income within the trading nations. From the factor endowments theory, we see that the returns to the owners of the scarce factor will fall, while the returns to the owners of the abundant factor will rise.

In labor-abundant Sierra, for example, with international trade, resources will be shifted to the production of the labor-intensive commodity, rice. On net, the demand for labor increases, while the use of the scarce factor, capital, is conserved. The constraint imposed by the relative scarcity of capital in Sierra is relaxed through trade, as Sierra imports capital in the form of the capital-intensive commodity, shoes. Just as if capital had been imported directly from Norte, the importation of shoes depresses the returns to the owners of capital in Sierra. Wages in Sierra are bolstered by the increased production of the labor-intensive commodity, rice. Conversely, in Norte, the scarce factor labor experiences a decline in wages as the labor-intensive rice is imported and domestic production shifts to the capital-intensive shoes.

### THE LESS DEVELOPED AND DEVELOPED ECONOMIES

In this example, Sierra, with an abundance of labor and a reliance on more labor-intensive production processes, is representative of a less developed country. Sierra should have a comparative advantage in producing labor-intensive commodities. Norte, with an abundance of capital and a reliance on relatively capital-intensive production processes, is indicative of a developed country, where the comparative advantage would be in the production of capital-intensive commodities.

On net, labor has migrated from the LDCs to the DCs, where the relative scarcity of labor is reflected in higher capital–labor ratios and higher real wages. On net, capital has flowed from the DCs to the LDCs, where the capital–labor ratios are lower and the marginal products of capital are higher. Furthermore, although sometimes frustrated by trade barriers, the LDCs have exported labor-intensive commodities to the DCs—and not just agricultural products such as rice, but labor-intensive manufactures such as textiles and apparel. In return, LDCs have imported capital-intensive manufactures such as machinery and heavy equipment from the DCs.

One problem or limitation of the static factor endowments theory of trade discussed above could be the implication that comparative advantages are more or less set. For natural resource–intensive products for which the endowments of fertile soils, favorable climates, forests, or mineral deposits are especially important inputs, comparative advantages may, in fact, be difficult to change. It does not follow, however, that comparative advantages in manufactured commodities are unchanging. True, wealthier nations would generally be able to save and invest a higher percentage of income and thus maintain higher capital–labor ratios. (Whether wealthier nations actually continue to save and invest more is another issue.) Given fixed-coefficients production functions and unchanging technology, higher capital–labor ratios would translate into a lower opportunity cost, hence a comparative advantage, in producing capital-intensive commodities. As we noted, however, factor substitutions are usually possible, and technological progress occurs. Further, there are more than just the two factors of production, capital and labor, used in this illustration. For example, in addition to natural resources, there are different types of labor—such as entrepreneurs, skilled labor, and unskilled labor. In short, less developed countries seeking to establish industrial bases need not accept permanent comparative disadvantages in manufactured commodities.

Recall from Chapter 11 that the long-term trend in the agricultural terms of trade has been downward, due mainly to the increased supplies driven by technological advances and the income-inelastic nature of the demands for most agricultural goods. The LDCs have not wanted to be locked into a position of exporting relatively low value-added primary products for the higher value-added manufactured goods. Over time the comparative advantage in the production of some manufactured goods will shift, as production functions change and technologies become diffused across economies. A more dynamic theory that describes this evolution follows.

## THE PRODUCT CYCLE THEORY OF TRADE

The main insight from the **product cycle theory of trade** is that manufactured goods, particularly new products, move through stages in trade—from being produced and consumed only domestically, to being exported, and then even to being imported.[15] If so, then comparative advantage for manufactured goods is appropriately viewed as a dynamic process.

New products tend to originate in high-income nations, such as the United States, with a relative abundance of scientists and engineers. These nations can afford to devote substantial resources to research and development, and thus have a comparative advantage in generating new products. The new products, at least initially, are expensive and necessarily aimed at high-income consumers. Moreover, consistent with the factor endowments theory of trade, the new products developed in labor-scarce, high-wage countries are often labor-saving. Examples include power mowers and power leaf blowers, car vacuums, hand calculators and personal computers, videocassette recorders, and cellular telephones for cars.

The new products are initially marketed domestically, where consumer reactions can be more easily monitored and necessary modifications in the product design can be made. If the product is accepted in the domestic market, then the possibility of exporting to other high-income, labor-scarce nations is considered. As the volume of output increases, economies of scale will bring down the average cost of production. For one, the initial research and development costs will be spread out over greater sales. Further, as the manufacturing of the good becomes more standardized, mass production allows for the substitution of capital (high-speed equipment) for labor. With decreases in the average cost, the product becomes more affordable and increasingly accepted. Even when patents are involved, competitors may develop similar versions of the product.

The increasing price competition erodes the market power enjoyed by the initiator of the product. Attention to cost minimization, in particular, reducing further the labor costs of assembly and seeking cheaper sources for the manufacture of the standardized components, becomes more important. In this stage companies may look for foreign production bases. Those less developed countries with an abundance of semiskilled labor may be attractive options for foreign subsidiaries. Thus, the nation that developed the product, then expanded sales through exports, may end up as a net importer of that product.

For example, components of personal computers are manufactured and assembled abroad and imported into the United States. For the more advanced of the LDCs (in particular, the newly industrializing countries of East Asia), some other fairly sophisticated products such as videocassette recorders, televisions, and stereo equipment are being manufactured and exported to the developed countries.

Indeed, the product cycle theory of trade applies to more than just new products. As technologies become standardized and internationally diffused, and as less developed countries build up their industrial capacities and their labor forces gain skills,

---

[15]For a discussion of the product cycle theory of trade, as well as other trade theories, see Chapter 10, "Alternative Theories of Trade and Intra-Industry Trade," in Dennis Appleyard and Alfred Field, *International Economics*, 2d ed., Chicago: Irwin, 1995. The product cycle theory of trade was introduced by Raymond Vernon in "International Investment and International Trade in the Product Cycle," *Quarterly Journal of Economics*, vol. 80, no. 2 (May 1966), pages 190–207.

the comparative advantages in many manufactured goods are shifting. The product cycle theory can be extended to well-established products such as shoes, toys, sporting equipment, textiles, and apparel, which are fairly labor-intensive and well suited for manufacturing in the LDCs. Even more capital-intensive, heavy manufactures, such as steel and automobiles, can now be produced competitively by some of the upper-middle income developing economies.

An interesting implication of the product cycle theory is that the high-income economies will only be able to maintain their international competitiveness in manufacturing by continually developing new and improved products. As the manufacturing processes become standardized, comparative advantages may shift in favor of the lower-cost producers in developing countries.

South Korea offers an illustration of the changes in comparative advantage with the technological upgrading of its exports. As Larry Westphal explains:

> In 1960, the Korean economy was dominated by agriculture and mining. With few exceptions, the manufacturing sector supplied only simple consumer products. Exports amounted to about 3 percent of GNP and consisted almost entirely of primary products such as seaweed, ginseng (a medicinal herb), and various minerals. Today the economy is dominated by the manufacturing sector. Major industries established since 1960 range from chemicals and electronics to automobiles and heavy electrical equipment. Exports exceed 40 percent of GNP, with manufactured products constituting over 90 percent of the total.
>
> The composition of Korea's manufactured exports has changed dramatically over the past 30 years. Early export successes in simple manufactures such as wigs, textiles, and plywood were followed by rapid gains in other products like shoes, steel, ships, and electronic products. More recently, Korea has penetrated markets for sophisticated durable goods such as automobiles and computers (including memory devices). Multinational corporations have played a distinctly supporting role in the evolution of Korea's comparative advantage.[16]

Before discussing the components of an export expansion strategy of development, we review recent performances in international trade.

## RECENT EXPERIENCE IN TRADE

In Tables 14.4 and 14.5. we present statistics on the growth and composition of merchandise trade for the less developed countries. We see that merchandise exports, on average, accounted for 12 to 17 percent of gross domestic products of the low- and middle-income economies (other than India and China) and the high-income economies in 1993. Regionally, however, greater disparities are evident. In East Asia and the Pacific and in sub-Saharan Africa, 22 to 24 percent of the GDPs are contributed by merchandise exports. For the less developed countries of Europe and Central Asia, South Asia (the latter region dominated by India), and Latin America and the

---

[16] Larry Westphal, "Industrial Policy in an Export-Propelled Economy: Lessons from South Korea's Experience," *Journal of Economic Perspectives*, vol. 4, no. 3 (summer 1990), page 43. Westphal, however, doubts whether South Korea's amazing success in export expansion can be easily replicated. Far from taking a free market, hands-off approach, the government of South Korea actively intervened and ably directed the export-led growth.

| TABLE 14.4 | SELECTED STATISTICS ON MERCHANDISE TRADE | | | | | | |
|---|---|---|---|---|---|---|---|
| | RATIO OF MERCHANDISE EXPORTS TO GDP (%) | AVERAGE ANNUAL GROWTH RATES (%) | | | | TERMS OF TRADE (1987=100) | |
| | | MERCHANDISE EXPORTS | | MERCHANDISE IMPORTS | | | |
| | 1993 | 1970–1980 | 1980–1993 | 1970–1980 | 1980–1993 | 1985 | 1993 |
| **INCOME GROUP** | | | | | | | |
| India | 9.6 | 5.9 | 7.0 | 4.5 | 4.2 | 96 | 92 |
| China | 21.6 | 8.7 | 11.5 | 11.1 | 9.7 | 109 | 101 |
| Other low-income | 12.7 | .4 | 1.4 | 5.7 | –2.6 | 112 | 93 |
| Middle-income | 16.7 | … | … | … | … | … | … |
| High-income | 15.9 | 6.0 | 5.1 | 5.2 | 5.8 | 94 | 99 |
| **REGION** | | | | | | | |
| sub-Saharan Africa | 22.9 | 1.0 | 2.5 | 3.2 | –2.2 | 110 | 95 |
| Middle East & North Africa | … | –.8 | –1.0 | 16.6 | –3.9 | 147 | 98 |
| Europe & Central Asia | 14.7 | … | … | … | … | … | … |
| South Asia | 10.8 | 4.2 | 7.3 | 4.3 | 3.7 | 112 | 96 |
| East Asia & Pacific | 24.0 | 9.0 | 10.8 | 9.7 | 9.2 | 111 | 101 |
| Latin America & the Caribbean | 9.6 | .9 | 3.4 | 4.7 | 0.3 | 111 | 97 |
| **SELECTED COUNTRIES** | | | | | | | |
| Ghana | 17.3 | –8.0 | 5.3 | –1.1 | 2.7 | 93 | 65 |
| Sri Lanka | 30.9 | –1.4 | 7.3 | 2.6 | 4.0 | 106 | 86 |
| Egypt | 6.3 | –1.7 | .8 | 9.6 | –1.5 | 147 | 99 |
| Poland | 16.3 | … | 2.8 | … | 2.8 | 95 | 95 |
| Costa Rica | 26.4 | 5.3 | 5.6 | 4.2 | 4.9 | 111 | 94 |
| Brazil | 8.7 | 8.6 | 5.2 | 5.8 | –.8 | 101 | 97 |
| South Korea | 24.9 | 22.7 | 12.3 | 13.2 | 11.4 | 94 | 100 |

NOTES: Lack of data is indicated by …
The *terms of trade* is the ratio of a country's index of average export prices to its index of average import prices (relative to a base year, 1987, where the terms of trade are set equal to 100).
FROM: World Bank, *World Development Report 1995*, New York: Oxford University Press, 1995, Tables 3, 13.

Caribbean, only from 9 to 15 percent of GDPs are represented by merchandise exports. For the seven countries selected in Table 14.4, the 1993 merchandise export shares range from 6.3 percent for Egypt to 30.9 percent for Sri Lanka.

Even greater variation can be found in the average annual growth rates for merchandise trade over the periods 1970 to 1980 and 1980 to 1993. For the earlier period, merchandise imports grew faster than exports for the other low-income economies and for all regions of the developing world. During the second period (1980–93), for all the developing economies aggregated by income and region, merchandise exports grew faster than imports, as external debt crises forced many nations to accept economic tightening and structural adjustments. (For the Middle East and North Africa, imports declined faster than exports.)

Finally, in Table 14.4, we can see over the latter part of the 1980s and into the 1990s a considerable deterioration in the **terms of trade** (the ratio of average export prices to average import prices) for all the income groups and regions of the developing world, especially for the nations of the Middle East and North Africa dependent on petroleum exports.

For the seven countries selected, few consistencies are found in the merchandise trade patterns over these two decades. To begin, the performances in merchandise exports varied widely. South Korea's export expansion is remarkable. In the case of Ghana, the deterioration in exports over the 1970s reflected steep decreases in revenues from cocoa, a primary commodity that continued to account for nearly 80 percent of total exports in 1980. Both Ghana and Sri Lanka dramatically improved their merchandise export performances in the 1980 to 1993 period. Correspondingly, their merchandise import growth rates rose. In contrast, for Egypt and Brazil, merchandise import growth rates were negative in this second period. Ghana, Sri Lanka, Egypt, and Costa Rica all experienced sharp declines in their terms of trade from 1985 to 1993. South Korea's terms of trade, in contrast, improved somewhat.

In Table 14.5 statistics on the structure of merchandise exports provide another dimension of trade. Since averages for the income groups and regions were not available at the time, we use the sample of 20 nations from Table 13.1. In general, with economic development a shift occurs from a reliance on natural resource–intensive products (such as fuels, minerals, metals, forestry products and agricultural commodities) to manufactures—beginning with light manufactures (such as textiles and clothing) and progressing up to heavy manufactures (such as machinery and transport equipment). From 1970 to 1993 the share of *other primary commodities* (including food and inedible crude materials) fell, sharply in many countries. In contrast, the share of manufactures in merchandise exports generally increased. For some countries the conversions were dramatic. For instance, *other primary commodities* dropped from 98 percent to 27 percent of merchandise exports for Sri Lanka, while the share of *other manufactures* (primarily textiles and clothing) rose from one percent to 71 percent. On the other hand, for Honduras, the merchandise export share of *other primary commodities* was unchanged at 83 percent.

As we discussed in Chapters 11 and 12, natural resource–intensive products are subject to boom-and-bust cycles in export revenues. For fuels, minerals, metals, and forestry products, revenues fluctuate largely with demand conditions in the developed countries. For agricultural commodities, supply-side shocks are the primary source of revenue instability. For both commodity groups, the long-run terms of trade have generally been declining—compared to manufactures. The less developed countries have attempted to diversify their exports into manufactures, with textiles and clothing and other labor-intensive light manufacturing typically at the forefront of the export expansion. Their progress, however, has often been stymied by barriers to trade. In the final section of the chapter we discuss the environment for international trade. We now examine the key ingredients of export expansion strategies.

## EXPORT EXPANSION

One of the major policy decisions in economic development is trade orientation, in particular the degree to which industrialization is promoted through international trade. We find two basic strategies.

One, **import substitution (IS),** is an inward orientation in which the government attempts to redirect domestic demand from imports to domestic production. As explained in the last chapter, with import tariffs and quotas and subsidies to domestic

| TABLE 14.5 | STRUCTURE OF MERCHANDISE EXPORTS FOR SELECTED COUNTRIES |

| | PERCENTAGE OF MERCHANDISE EXPORTS | | | | | | | | | |
|---|---|---|---|---|---|---|---|---|---|---|
| | FUELS, MINERALS, AND METALS | | OTHER PRIMARY COMMODITIES | | MACHINERY AND TRANSPORT EQUIPMENT | | OTHER MANUFACTURING | | TEXTILE FIBERS, TEXTILES, AND CLOTHING | |
| | 1970 | 1993 | 1970 | 1993 | 1970 | 1993 | 1970 | 1993 | 1970 | 1993 |
| **LOW-INCOME** | | | | | | | | | | |
| India | 13 | 7 | 35 | 18 | 5 | 7 | 47 | 68 | 27 | 30 |
| Nigeria | 62 | 94 | 36 | 4 | 0 | 0 | 1 | 2 | 2 | ... |
| Pakistan | 2 | 1 | 41 | 14 | 0 | 0 | 57 | 85 | 75 | 78 |
| Ghana | 13 | 25 | 86 | 52 | 0 | 0 | 1 | 23 | ... | ... |
| China | ... | 6 | ... | 13 | ... | 16 | ... | 65 | ... | 31 |
| Sri Lanka | 1 | 1 | 98 | 27 | 0 | 2 | 1 | 71 | 3 | 52 |
| Honduras | 10 | 3 | 83 | 83 | 0 | 0 | 8 | 13 | 3 | 3 |
| Egypt | 5 | 55 | 68 | 12 | 1 | 1 | 26 | 32 | 65 | 20 |
| **MIDDLE-INCOME** | | | | | | | | | | |
| Senegal | 12 | 25 | 69 | 54 | 4 | 2 | 15 | 19 | 7 | 4 |
| Colombia | 11 | 26 | 81 | 34 | 1 | 6 | 7 | 34 | 7 | 10 |
| Algeria | 73 | 96 | 21 | 1 | 2 | 1 | 5 | 2 | 1 | 0 |
| Poland | ... | 22 | ... | 18 | ... | 19 | ... | 41 | ... | 7 |
| Costa Rica | 1 | 1 | 80 | 66 | 3 | 4 | 17 | 29 | 4 | 5 |
| Brazil | 11 | 12 | 75 | 28 | 4 | 21 | 11 | 39 | 9 | 4 |
| Mexico | 19 | 34 | 49 | 13 | 11 | 31 | 22 | 21 | 11 | 3 |
| South Korea | 7 | 3 | 17 | 4 | 7 | 43 | 69 | 51 | 41 | 19 |
| **HIGH-INCOME** | | | | | | | | | | |
| Australia | 28 | 36 | 53 | 29 | 6 | 8 | 13 | 28 | 17 | 9 |
| Finland | 4 | 6 | 29 | 11 | 17 | 32 | 50 | 51 | 6 | 2 |
| Austria | 6 | 4 | 14 | 7 | 24 | 38 | 56 | 52 | 12 | 8 |
| Japan | 2 | 2 | 5 | 1 | 41 | 68 | 53 | 29 | 13 | 2 |

NOTES: Lack of data is indicated by ...
*Other primary commodities* include food and live animals, beverages and tobacco, inedible crude materials (except fuels), and animal and vegetable oils and fats.

*Textile fibers, textiles, and clothing* include also yarns, fabrics, made-up articles, and related products. Textile fibers are a subgroup of *other primary commodities*. Textiles and clothing are a subgroup of *other manufactures*.

FROM: World Bank, *World Development Report 1995*, New York: Oxford University Press, 1995, Table 15.

producers, foreign commodities become more expensive. The objectives are to boost spending on national output; increase employment; and improve the trade balance through a reduction of imports and conservation of foreign exchange.

The second, **export expansion (EE),** is outwardly oriented. Here domestic production is directed toward foreign markets. National output and employment are stimulated and the trade balance improved by increasing exports. By generating foreign exchange, export expansion allows for greater imports, including access to intermediate and capital goods of higher quality and lower cost than are produced domestically.

### Experience with Import Substitution

The import substitution (IS) strategy was popular in the three decades following World War II. The infant-industry argument was widely embraced as the quickest path to industrialization.

Initially, countries adopting an IS strategy would experience gains in output and employment in the protected domestic industries. Eventually, unless the infant industries became internationally competitive, growth would be limited by the size of the domestic market. All too often, domestic production languished behind the import barriers—especially for state-owned enterprises staffed with political appointees with neither the expertise nor the incentive to promote efficiency.

Given the relative inexperience of their labor forces in modern manufacturing and the usual shortages of skilled managers, it is not surprising that developing economies would begin with import substitution. The key, however, is in making the transition to export expansion. To some extent, the foundation must be laid early. Recall Adelman's depauperization strategy (presented in Chapter 5), and in particular, the second and third stages of extensive human capital formation followed by rapid growth led by the expansion of labor-intensive manufactured exports. The East Asian nations of Japan, South Korea, Taiwan, and Singapore were four of the five countries (Israel being the other) cited as examples.

### The Shift to Export Expansion

In the 1980s, the pendulum swung back. External debt crises and the stark contrast between the generally poor performances of the inward-oriented Latin American economies and the robust growth of the outward-oriented East Asian nations contributed to more market-based approaches to development. Moreover, the International Monetary Fund and World Bank made loans to the less developed countries contingent on market reforms consistent with improving international competitiveness.[17]

As discussed earlier in this chapter, labor-abundant developing countries would be expected to have a comparative advantage in labor-intensive manufacturing. To realize this advantage, unit labor costs (the ratio of wages to the average product of labor) must be kept competitive. Wages should reflect the abundance of labor and not be set artificially high by labor unions or legislation. Earlier investments in primary education should yield a labor force that is literate and adaptable to the disciplines of modern manufacturing. To promote efficiency in resource allocation, interest rates, like wages, should reflect the relative scarcity of capital.

### A Competitive Exchange Rate

Often a first priority in implementing an export expansion (EE) strategy is to "get the exchange rate correct." Frequently, due to an inability to control inflation, an

---

[17]See Sebastian Edwards, "Openness, Trade Liberalization, and Growth in Developing Countries," *Journal of Economic Literature*, vol. 31, no. 3 (September 1993), pages 1358–1393. In this survey article on trade and development, Edwards also discusses the difficulties in measuring trade orientation and in evaluating the contribution of trade policy to economic development. For another useful article, see Rudiger Dornbusch, "The Case for Trade Liberalization in Developing Countries," *Journal of Economic Perspectives*, vol. 6, no. 1 (winter 1992), pages 69–85.

## FIGURE 14.2 — EFFECTS OF AN OVERVALUED CURRENCY ON INTERNATIONAL COMPETITIVENESS

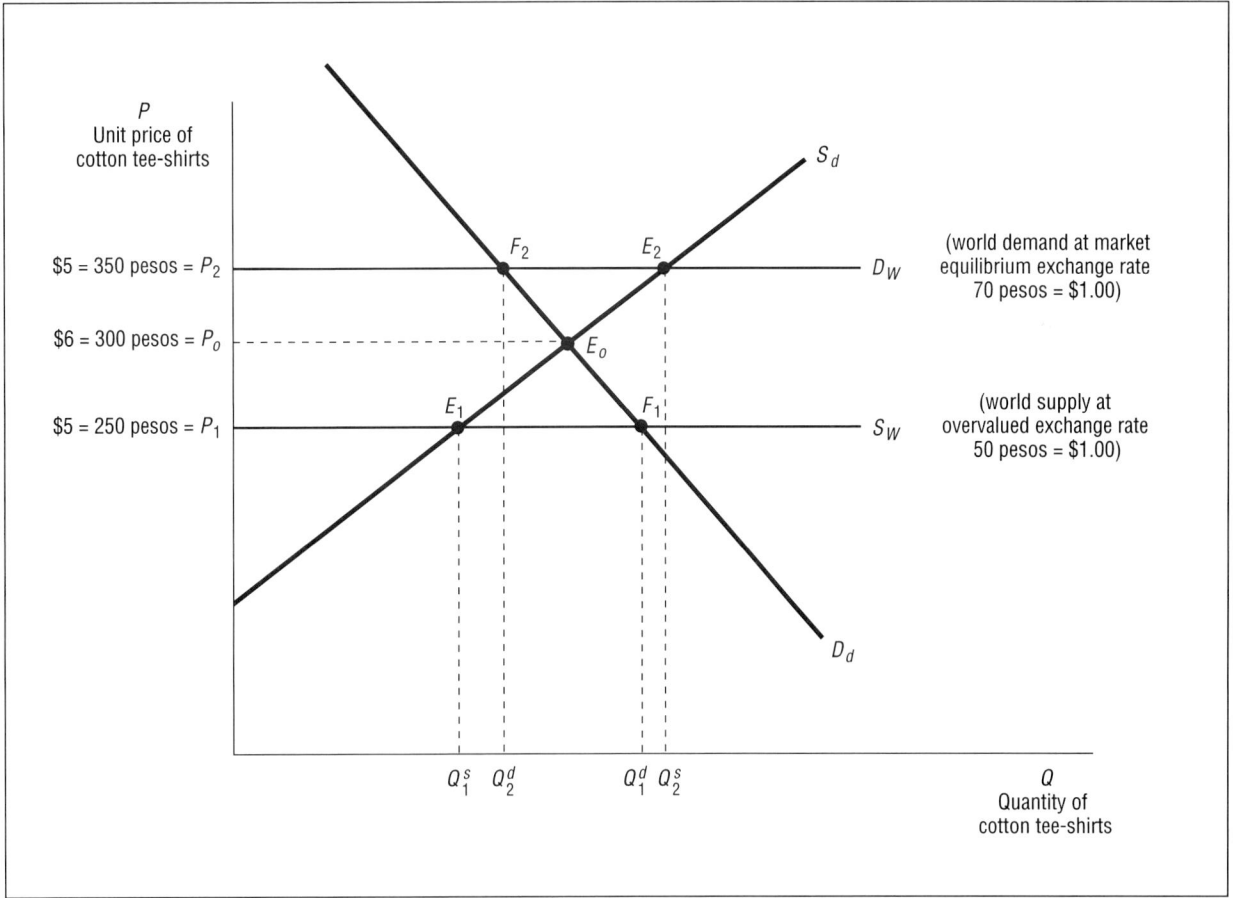

unwillingness to allow the exchange rate to be determined by market forces, or a policy of encouraging the imports of needed intermediate and capital goods, developing nations operate with official exchange rates that overvalue the domestic currency. An overvalued currency acts like a tax on exports and a subsidy to imports. Thus, a devaluation, or a decrease in the official exchange value of the currency, is often required to restore international competitiveness—and to indicate a shift in policy toward export expansion.

To illustrate, consider a small developing country, call it Tico, with a domestic demand $(D_d)$ and supply $(S_d)$ for cotton tee-shirts as depicted in Figure 14.2. Assume that Tico is an international price-taker, too small to influence the world market price for tee-shirts with any variation in its consumption or production. If the market-clearing domestic price, $P_o$, in Tico is higher than the world price, $P_w$, then Tico would be an importer of cotton tee-shirts; the supply curve of imports would be perfectly elastic at the world price. If the market-clearing price in Tico were lower than the world price, however, Tico would be an exporter of cotton tee-shirts; the foreign demand for Tico's exports would be perfectly elastic at the world price.

Suppose the world price for cotton tee-shirts is $P_w = \$5$, and the market-clearing domestic price in Tico (expressed in pesos, the national currency) is 300 pesos. If the official exchange rate in Tico were set at 50 pesos = $1.00 (or 1 peso = $.02), then Tico's domestic price of 300 pesos $(P_o)$ translates into $6.00. Tico would be an importer of cotton tee-shirts (see $P_1 = 250$ pesos). In Figure 14.2, imports equal $Q_1^d - Q_1^s$, represented by the line segment $E_1F_1$. Suppose, however, the peso is overvalued at the official exchange rate, and that the market equilibrium exchange rate is 70 pesos = $1.00 (or 1 peso = $.0143). A devaluation of the peso to the market equilibrium rate would convert Tico into an exporter of cotton shirts (see $P_2 = 350$ pesos). With the devaluation the domestic quantity produced increases from $Q_1^s$ to $Q_2^s$, and the quantity demanded declines from $Q_1^d$ to $Q_2^d$. Tico would export $Q_2^s - Q_2^d$ (or $F_2E_2$) units of cotton tee-shirts. The improvement in Tico's trade balance is the increase in export revenues, $5(Q_2^s - Q_2^d)$, plus the decrease in import payments, $5(Q_1^d - Q_1^s)$.

Note that as domestic producers in Tico gear up production in response to the devaluation, the peso supply price rises to 350 pesos, where, at the market equilibrium exchange rate, it equals the world price of $5. With trade, nations orient to the world prices. To maintain the international competitiveness gained by the devaluation, Tico has to prevent domestic inflation from appreciating the peso in real terms.

Recall from Chapter 12 that the real exchange rate $(er^*)$ is equal to the nominal exchange rate $(er)$ times the ratio of the domestic price level $(P_d)$ to the foreign price level $(P_f)$. If the devaluation of the peso from 50 to 70 pesos to the dollar (or, equivalently, from $.02 to $.0143 to the peso) is accompanied by a 40 percent rise in the domestic price level and nominal income (so that the $S_d$ and $D_d$ curves in Figure 14.2 shift up by 40 percent), then there would be no effect on the balance of trade with the devaluation. The real exchange rate would be unchanged. For example, suppose the domestic and foreign price levels are initially $P_d = 100 = P_f$. Then a devaluation of the peso from $.02 to $.0143 (1/50 to 1/70 of a dollar) could be offset by a 40 percent rise in the domestic price level (with no change in the domestic production of cotton tee-shirts or the trade balance).

$$er^* = er(P_d/P_f) = (1/50)(100/100) = .02 = (1/70)(140/100) = er'(P_d'/P_f)$$

Thus, monetary restraint is usually required with a devaluation to prevent the erosion of the competitive advantage by domestic inflation.

### Export Subsidies

Even with the devaluation, the government of the developing country may decide to subsidize domestic producers with tax breaks, marketing assistance, or low-interest loans. The consequences of a per-unit subsidy of $s$ on the exports of cotton tee-shirts are illustrated in Figure 14.3. With the export subsidy, domestic producers receive the world price $(P_2)$ plus the per unit subsidy $(s)$ on cotton tee-shirts exported. With the increased incentive to export, domestic production rises to $Q_2^{s\prime}$. Part of the production is diverted from the domestic market, since domestic consumption of cotton tee-shirts declines to $Q_2^{d\prime}$ as the domestic market price increases to $P_2'$. Exports increase to $Q_2^{s\prime} - Q_2^{d\prime}$ and export revenues to $P_2(Q_2^{s\prime} - Q_2^{d\prime})$. The cost of the export subsidy to the government is $s(Q_2^{s\prime} - Q_2^{d\prime})$.

To provide incentives to domestic producers to become more efficient, the subsidy should be phased out over time. The intent would be for gains in domestic productivity (resulting in downward shifts in the domestic supply curve) to more than offset the decrease in the subsidy.

### FIGURE 14.3  EFFECTS OF AN EXPORT SUBSIDY

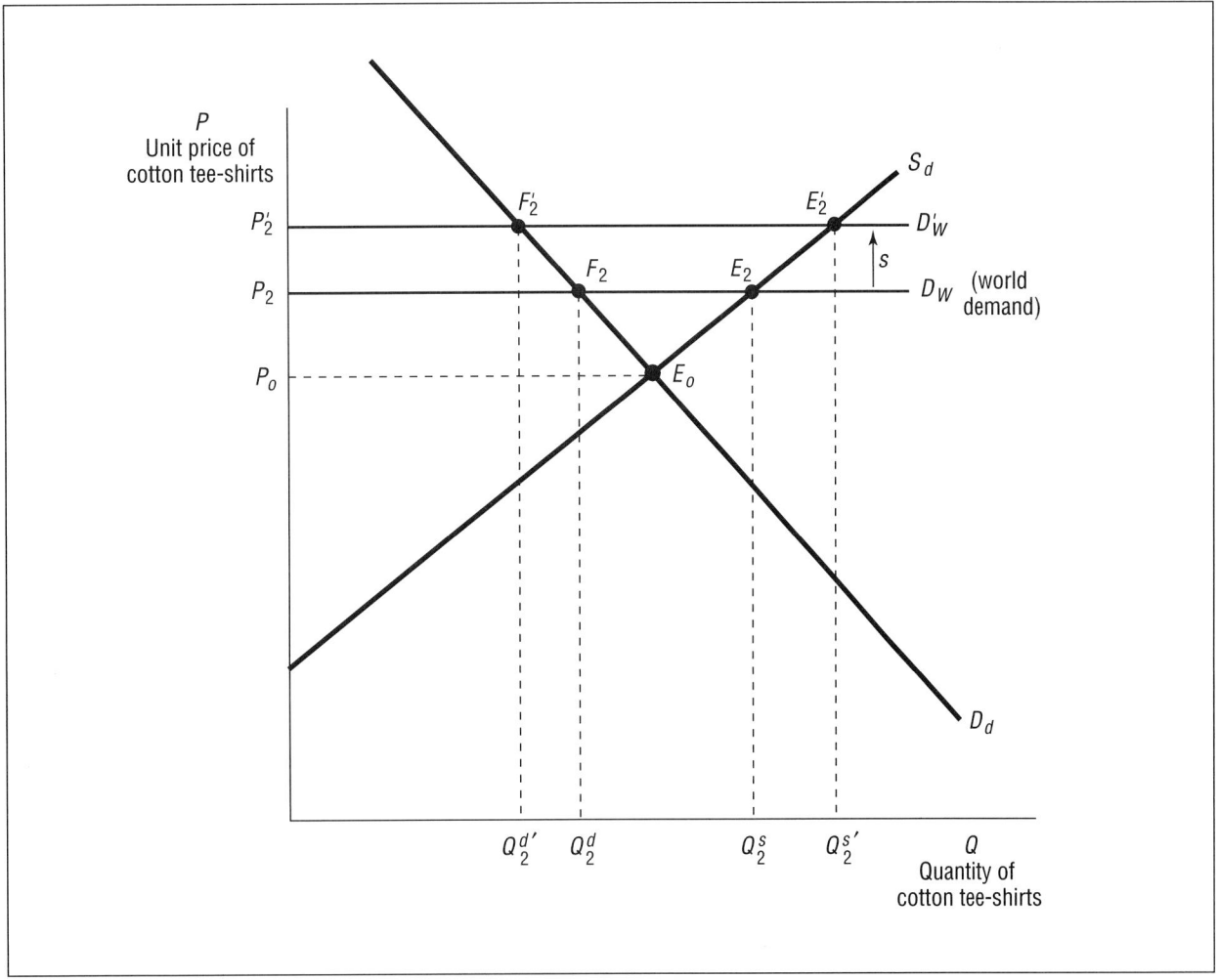

### ACHIEVING SUCCESS WITH EXPORT EXPANSION

The success of a strategy of export expansion in manufactures depends on a number of factors. One is being able to draw on a labor force that is literate and adaptable to the regimen of modern manufacturing—including punctuality and reliability in conforming to a fixed work schedule; the capacity to learn new tasks and to operate complex machinery; and the ability to work expediently while attaining international standards of quality.

Also important is the competence of the government in maintaining macroeconomic stability while promoting competition. A realistic exchange rate first must be determined and then not undermined by inflation. Large budget deficits whose financing either crowds out private investment expenditures through high real interest rates or contributes to inflation when the money supply is expanded, need to be avoided.

Frequently LDCs need help in gaining footholds in developed-country markets, in negotiating trade barriers and customs regulations, and in establishing sales outlets. Transnational corporations with their extensive connections in marketing can be useful here. In fact, the success of an outward-looking strategy of industrialization depends on access to foreign markets. All too often, LDCs with existing or potential comparative advantages in manufactures have been thwarted by trade barriers. Labor-intensive light manufactures, such as textiles and apparel, which could be produced and exported by the developing economies, run into heavy protection in the developed countries. In the concluding section of this chapter we will review the post-war history of trade barriers and the recent advances in trade liberalization. In Chapter 17 we will discuss the remarkable success of the East Asian nations in their export-led economic development.

## IMPLEMENTING THE TRADE STRATEGY

The appropriate trade strategy depends on the particular circumstances of the developing nation. For instance, is the nation favorably endowed with natural resources that not only could be directly exported, but could be further processed and form the basis for industrial development? Examples might be cotton crops for clothing, iron ore for steel, and mahogany forests for wood furniture. Has the nation undertaken the earlier investments in human capital needed for an industrial labor force? Can, or should, transnational corporations and foreign direct investment be used to expedite the industrialization? Is the domestic market sufficiently large to capture all the economies of scale in production? (Import substitution may be more viable for bigger countries.) Can a free trade area be formed with other nations to enhance the development of comparative advantages in manufacturing?

In general, a dynamic strategy of selective import substitution and export expansion, with diversification, may be in order. Perhaps the major shortcoming of IS strategies has been the failure to identify and develop genuine infant industries. Sometimes too many industries have been initially targeted, so that monitoring progress has been difficult. Similarly, the incentives to become efficient have often been insufficient. As noted in Chapter 13, typically chosen in the early stages of IS are consumer-goods industries, where domestic demands are being met by imports, where the production technologies are fairly standardized, and where the physical and human capital requirements are relatively modest. Growth in these final-stage industries is intended to stimulate growth in other sectors through backward linkages (e.g., chemicals for fertilizers or looms for textiles). While providing access to subsidized imports of intermediate goods and capital goods is intended to bolster the profitability of the protected domestic producers, it may also discourage the development of backward linkages and further shield the domestic IS industries from international competition. Furthermore, the owners of the firms in the infant industries, rather than devoting their energies to becoming more productive, may find it more profitable to seek continued protection and subsidization.

If a phase of import substitution were necessary, tariffs should be used for the protection of the domestic producers with a clearly defined schedule for decreasing tariff rates. Dornbusch suggests:

> A gradual path to trade liberalization should occur in two steps. In a first round, the country should move from quotas and licenses and other nontariff barriers to a

uniform, high tariff of (say) 50 percent. Later, as the economy grows and the external balance can support liberalization without the risk of a foreign exchange crisis, tariffs can be taken down to (say) 10 percent.[18]

To encourage labor-intensive production consistent with the labor-abundant conditions found in most developing economies, real interest rates should be positive and reflect the relative scarcity of capital. If access to credit on more favorable terms is used to help infant industries, it should be based competitively on market performances. To discourage consumption and conserve foreign exchange, high tariffs (say over 50 percent) could be placed on imports of income-elastic or luxury consumer goods. The tariff revenues could be used to subsidize infant industries. Vocational training and higher education should be geared to generating the skills needed for industrial development.

For those LDCs still predominantly reliant on primary exports, the initial areas for export expansion usually are labor-intensive light manufactures such as textiles, apparel, shoes, toys, sporting equipment, and even simple consumer electronics. Within these labor-intensive light manufactures, degrees of product sophistication would exist. As the skills of the labor forces improve and physical capital accumulates, the product lines could be upgraded—consistent with export expansion and diversification. For example, a developing country might progress from manufacturing inexpensive sandals to manufacturing running shoes.

For the more advanced of the developing nations, import substitution could be used to start heavier manufacturing. Examples of possible product evolutions would be bicycles to motor scooters to motorcycles to economy cars; transistor radios to stereos to televisions to videocassette recorders to computers; or simple tools such as hammers, shovels, and handsaws to power equipment such as drills, table saws, and lawnmowers. So too, this phase of IS would be well defined and limited, with a transition to export expansion and diversification as goals.

According to the product cycle theory of trade, the developed nations need not cede any product line entirely; rather, degrees of technological sophistication would exist within each commodity group. For example, at the upper end of the apparel industry for which fashion, style, and customized fit are important, the developed nations would probably maintain their comparative advantages. Consider designer blue jeans that are adjusted by computer to fit individual body dimensions.

## GATT AND TRADE LIBERALIZATION

As noted at the outset of the chapter, world trade has expanded faster than output since World War II. A considerable share of the credit for the greater openness of national economies must be given to GATT, the General Agreement on Tariffs and Trade. Established in 1947, GATT, along with the International Monetary Fund (IMF) and International Bank for Reconstruction and Development (World Bank), was intended to promote economic cooperation among nations in the post-war era.[19] The charge of

---

[18]Dornbusch, page 82.

[19]The IMF and the World Bank, both created in 1944 at Bretton Woods, New Hampshire, will be discussed in Chapters 15 and 16. For a concise history of GATT, see Douglas Irwin, "The GATT in Historical Perspective," *American Economic Review*, vol. 85, no. 2 (May 1995), pages 323–328.

GATT was to furnish a framework for liberalizing trade, in order to avoid the kind of destructive protectionism that had contributed to deepening the international depression during the 1930s.

GATT provided both a code of conduct for trade practices and a mechanism for resolving trade disputes. It also sponsored multilateral trade negotiations in which all the member nations jointly reduced trade barriers. The latest example was the Uruguay Round, begun in 1986 and concluded in 1993. Prior negotiations were the Kennedy Round in the 1960s and the Tokyo Round in the 1970s.

Two principles undergird GATT and its successor, the World Trade Organization (WTO). The first is **reciprocity**, which serves as the basis for negotiations between nations. If one nation, say Sweden, reduces trade barriers to a second nation, say Norway, then Norway should respond in kind and reduce its trade barriers against Sweden. Thus, trade negotiations would produce mutually beneficial concessions. The second principle is **most-favored nation**, a status conferred on all the member nations. Any reductions in trade barriers between nations should be extended to all other members. However, exceptions are allowed. For example, nations can form **free trade areas**, which require the removal or phasing-out over time of trade barriers between members; individual trade barriers against other nations are maintained. Extensions of free trade areas include **customs unions**, or free trade areas in which the members adopt common external tariffs and nontariff barriers against other nations; and **common markets**, or customs unions allowing free flows of factors (capital and labor) across the borders of member nations.[20]

Free trade areas (FTA) are a second-best type of trade liberalization. While within the FTA, trade is created and resource allocations become more efficient, trade may also be diverted from more efficient nonmember nations. To illustrate, suppose Japan could produce microcircuits for $20 per unit, the United States for $25 per unit, and Venezuela for $40 per unit. Even if Venezuela had a 50 percent tariff on all imports of microcircuits, it would still import microcircuits from Japan since the Japanese import price of $30, or $20(1 + .5), would still be less than the Venezuelan domestic price. Now, if Venezuela and the United States form a free trade area, and Venezuela drops the 50 percent tariff against imports from the United States, then imports of microcircuits from the United States (at $25 per unit) would displace those from Japan, the more efficient producer. In short, unless the free trade area includes the most efficient world producers, some trade diversion will take place along with the trade creation within the area. Needless to say, the optimal free trade area is the world.

Other exceptions to the principles of reciprocity and most-favored nation intended to help the LDCs have included special allowances for developing economies to protect their domestic markets with import barriers and to subsidize their exports. In addition, the **Generalized System of Preferences (GSP)** permits favorable treatment of exports from the LDCs. Under GSP the developed countries, primarily the United States and

---

[20]The recent momentum in favor of free trade arrangements was profiled in an article in *The Economist*, "The Right Direction?" (September 16, 1995), pages 23–27. From page 23 of the article:

> According to the WTO [World Trade Organization], 109 regional deals were notified to the GATT between 1948 and the end of last year. Nearly one-third of those were signed between 1990 and 1994... January 1st this year [1995] saw the accession to the European Union (EU), the world's biggest trading block, of Austria, Finland, and Sweden, and the creation of Mercosur, a customs union between Argentina, Brazil, Paraguay and Uruguay.

the nations of the former European Economic Community (now European Union), offer unilateral trade concessions to the LDCs, lowering or even eliminating tariffs on selected commodities. Due to a fairly limited scope on the products covered and the low levels of the tariffs effectively cut, the GSP has been only marginally beneficial for the majority of the developing nations.

Furthermore, GATT's notable success in reducing tariffs over the years has been compromised by the rise of **nontariff barriers to trade (NTBs).** In addition to import quotas, voluntary export restraints have been used, as well as orderly marketing agreements; domestic-content legislation; government-procurement policies that favor domestic producers; and discriminatory health and safety standards, often reflected in costly inspections of imports at the borders. Offensive trade barriers have included export subsidies.

### Nontariff Barriers to Trade

As indicated, nontariff barriers to trade come in many forms. **Voluntary export restraints (VERs)** are export quotas whereby nations "voluntarily" agree to limit exports to specific markets, usually under the implicit (or explicit) threat of more severe import quotas. **Orderly marketing agreements** are typically a series of bilateral quotas negotiated with other nations in which the growth of imports in a particular market is controlled or limited to a certain percentage of total sales. **Domestic-content legislation** requires that minimum percentages of the market value of designated commodities come from domestic inputs, providing protection to domestic suppliers of intermediate goods. **Government-procurement policies** often make it difficult for foreign producers to bid on, or compete for, government contracts. In the most transparent form, government agencies would only deal with domestic producers. Health and safety standards may be designed to discourage imports, since the high costs of compliance place imports at a competitive disadvantage.

Finally, as an example of an offensive trade barrier, developed nations with farm policies that heavily subsidize domestic production have dumped (i.e., sold below domestic prices) the surplus agricultural commodities in foreign markets—often in the less developed countries, driving down farm prices there and discouraging local farmers. In fact, the successful conclusion of the Uruguay Round was delayed for over two years, largely due to the dispute between the United States and the European Union over the subsidization of agricultural exports.

NTBs have proven difficult to reduce due to their complexity, diversity, and relative opaqueness. For example, the impacts of published tariff rates on import prices is readily apparent. Determining the effects of import quotas, or domestic-content legislation, or the bias of governments in purchasing from domestic producers is more difficult. Similarly, it may be relatively straightforward to implement across-the-board cuts in tariff rates by a certain percentage; however, given the different circumstances defining the NTBs, simple formulas for liberalization may not be feasible. Moreover, voluntary export restraints and orderly marketing agreements are often promoted under the guise of international cooperation, when actually an element of coercion is present.

In whatever form, NTBs, like tariffs, reduce or distort trade flows and result in a less efficient allocation of global resources. Typical of international organizations, GATT was hampered by the lack of an enforcement mechanism for member nations engaging in unfair trade practices. The new World Trade Organization, a product of the Uruguay Round, is intended to bolster compliance.

LDCs, GATT, AND THE URUGUAY ROUND

Despite the Generalized System of Preferences and special dispensation to use import barriers and export subsidies, the LDCs were generally disappointed with GATT. Like the IMF and World Bank, GATT was criticized by developing nations as an organization controlled by, and in the interests of, the rich nations. Indeed, GATT's record in trade liberalization in the areas of greatest interest to the developing nations was not impressive. Agriculture and labor-intensive manufacturing (in particular, textiles and apparel) in which the LDCs tend to enjoy comparative advantages, have been among the most heavily protected areas in international trade.

Stymied in their attempts to secure a foothold in the markets of the developed countries for labor-intensive manufactures, or even to expand exports of basic agricultural products like peanuts, sugar, and rice, some of the poorer developing nations have continued to rely on those primary commodities (e.g., coffee, tea, cocoa, lumber, rubber, minerals) that are either not produced or in short supply in the developed countries. Not only does this concentration in primary exports fail to advance the industrialization process in these nations, but trade in these same products is subject to instability in export revenues in the short run and to terms-of-trade deterioration in the long run. Reliance on a narrow group of primary commodities for the bulk of export revenues makes a nation vulnerable to highly variable foreign exchange receipts, with accompanying fluctuations in income, employment, and tax revenues. Under such uncertain conditions, development planning becomes more difficult.

The Uruguay Round, however, did make some progress in addressing these concerns. Not only are tariff rates to be cut by over a third (a substantial decrease in absolute terms for high-tariff countries), but nontariff barriers to trade in agriculture and labor-intensive manufactures are to be reduced significantly. For their part, the developed countries pushed the LDCs to open wider their own markets, where high trade barriers are still prevalent. In addition, for the first time in GATT negotiations, trade liberalization in services (such as transportation, banking, insurance, and finance) and stricter enforcement of intellectual property rights (patents and copyrights) were addressed.

Indeed, with this increased international integration of economies and the rise in the shares of services in national outputs with economic development, we might expect that trade in services will grow in relative importance. The developed countries will have the initial comparative advantage in the higher technology services in communications and information management. Further, increased foreign direct investment may occur in the LDCs with transfers of skilled labor to provide those services not easily traded across borders (e.g., branch banking, health insurance, environmental clean-ups, and even public utilities).

Nevertheless, the movement to freer trade is not without some uncertainties. For one, China was not a member of GATT, and will probably not be admitted to the World Trade Organization until it further reduces its considerable barriers to trade.[21] How effective the WTO will be in adjudicating the new commercial order—especially if conflicts arise over differing environmental standards and labor practices across nations—remains to be seen.

---

[21]In early 1995, China and the United States came to the brink of a trade war over China's failure to crack down on copyright and patent infringements of U.S. products. China has promised to be more vigilant in the future.

## CONCLUDING NOTE

As the twentieth century draws to a close, the movement toward free trade is gaining momentum. The developing countries account for the fastest growing component of world trade. The trade liberalization forthcoming from the Uruguay Round could increase the aggregate output of the LDCs by some $80 billion a year.[22]

The early indications from NAFTA (the North American Free Trade Agreement) were positive, with growing volumes of exports among Canada, the United States, and Mexico.[23] Chile may soon join NAFTA, and other Latin American countries may follow. In fact, a hemispheric free trade area for the Americas has been proposed. The United States and nations in Asia and the Pacific are also moving toward a free trade agreement. We may expect the European Union to continue to grow, including not only some of the northern European countries, but some former socialist nations of Eastern Europe.

The movement to freer trade will require many adjustments within nations—as comparative advantage industries expand and comparative-disadvantage industries contract. There will be resistance and significant dislocation costs. The gains ultimately realized from the increased efficiencies in resource allocation and greater competition, however, should more than justify the costs.

In Chapter 15 we continue with the focus on international integration by examining balance of payments and exchange rate practices. We also address the external debt problems of the less developed countries.

## SUMMARY OF MAIN POINTS

1. A nation has a comparative advantage when it can produce a commodity for a lower opportunity cost than a trading partner.
2. With international trade the gains in efficiency are reflected in greater global outputs. Trading nations can consume commodity combinations lying beyond their respective production possibilities boundaries.
3. According to the factor endowments theory of trade, labor-abundant (capital-abundant) nations should have a comparative advantage in labor-intensive (capital-intensive) commodities.

---

[22]World Bank, "Learning from the Past, Embracing the Future," Washington, DC, July 1994, page 11. For detailed estimates of the gains from the trade liberalization, see Glenn Harrison, Thomas Rutherford, and David Tarr, "Quantifying the Outcome of the Uruguay Round," *Finance and Development*, vol. 32, no. 4 (December 1995), pages 38–41.

[23]The peso crisis that emerged in late 1994 and the ensuing sharp recession in Mexico did depress intra-NAFTA trade and investment. Nevertheless, once the Mexican economy recovers, trade and investment should rebound, and NAFTA should prove to be mutually beneficial to the member nations. For an assessment of Mexico's prospects, see "A Survey of Mexico," *The Economist* (October 28, 1995).

4. By importing capital-intensive (labor-intensive) commodities, labor-abundant (capital-abundant) nations, in effect, import capital (labor). Consequently, with trade, the returns to the owners of the scarce factor in each nation decline.
5. According to the product cycle theory of trade, comparative advantages in manufactured products can change over time. Advanced countries enjoy a temporary comparative advantage in the new manufactured products they develop. As the products become widely accepted and standardized, the need to reduce labor costs grows in importance, and the comparative advantage in production may shift to those developing nations with an abundance of semiskilled labor.
6. Economies are becoming more dependent on international trade, evidenced by the rising shares of exports in national outputs. Regionally, East Asia and the Pacific and sub-Saharan Africa rely relatively more on merchandise exports than do Europe and Central Asia, South Asia, or Latin America and the Caribbean.
7. With economic development the composition of merchandise exports changes—from primarily natural resource–intensive products (minerals, metals, fuels, forestry products, and agricultural commodities) to light manufactures (especially textiles and clothing) to heavy manufactures (including machinery and transport equipment).
8. Export expansion seems to be superior to import substitution as a strategy for industrialization. The essential components of a successful export expansion in manufactures are a competitive exchange rate, a skilled labor force, and access to foreign markets. Most developing economies, however, begin with import substitution, whereby domestic industries are protected from foreign competition. In either case, the goal is to develop domestic industries that are internationally competitive.
9. The General Agreement on Tariffs and Trade (GATT) (since 1995, the World Trade Organization [WTO]) has contributed to the increasing openness of economies in the post–World War II era by sponsoring multilateral trade negotiations and providing a code of conduct for trade relations based on the principles of reciprocity and most-favored-nation status. GATT's success in reducing tariffs has been offset, in part, by the rise in nontariff barriers to trade, such as voluntary export restraints and orderly marketing agreements.
10. Despite special allowances such as the Generalized System of Preferences, the LDCs have been disappointed with the relative lack of trade liberalization in areas in which they enjoy comparative advantages, especially agriculture and labor-intensive manufactures. Progress from the Uruguay Round, however, may improve the export prospects in these areas for the LDCs.

## KEY TERMS

common market
comparative advantage
constant opportunity cost
customs union
domestic-content legislation
export expansion (EE)
factor endowments theory of trade
free trade area
Generalized System of Preferences (GSP)

government-procurement policies
import substitution (IS)
increasing opportunity cost
international terms of trade
most-favored nation
nontariff barriers to trade (NTBs)
opportunity cost
orderly marketing agreements
product cycle theory of trade

**production possibilities boundary**  
**reciprocity**

**terms of trade**  
**voluntary export restraints (VERs)**

## QUESTIONS

1. Discuss why less developed countries might find import substitution initially to be an easier strategy to implement than export expansion.
2. An implication of the product cycle theory of trade is that the less developed countries are consigned to operating at the lower end of the scale in technology. Is this necessarily true? Should a less developed country try to "leapfrog" the product cycle by investing in state-of-the-art technology in certain manufactures? Discuss.
3. Should less developed countries be given special privileges in international trade? If not, why not? If so, what privileges and why?
4. Given the domestic demand and supply schedules for ballpoint pens in Ashanti, a small less developed country that can be considered an international price-taker,

$$Q^d = 720 - 6P \quad \text{and} \quad Q^s = -80 + 4P$$

   where $Q^d$ and $Q^s$ are the quantities demanded and supplied of pens (in thousands of boxes per week) and $P$ is the price of a box of pens in cedi, the Ashanti currency.
   
   a. Sketch the domestic demand and supply curves and determine the domestic market-clearing price and quantity transacted in autarky.
   b. Suppose the official exchange rate is 80 cedi = $1.00 and that the world price of a box of ballpoint pens is $.90. Determine whether Ashanti is an exporter or importer of pens and calculate the export revenues or import payments, both in cedi and dollars.
   c. Now suppose Ashanti devalues the cedi to a market-equilibrium rate of 100 cedi = $1.00. Determine whether Ashanti is an importer or exporter of ballpoint pens and calculate the export revenues or import payments, both in cedi and dollars. Calculate the change in Ashanti's trade balance with the devaluation of the cedi.
   d. In addition to using the market equilibrium exchange rate of 100 cedi = $1.00, suppose that the government of Ashanti pays a subsidy of 5 cedi per box of ballpoint pens exported. Calculate the new export revenues in cedi and dollars and the total cost of the export subsidy in cedi.

5. Given two countries, Atlantica and Pacifica; two commodities, cloth (c) and wine (w); and two factors of production, capital (K) and labor (L); and the following factor endowments and fixed-coefficients production functions:

   Factor endowments:
   Atlantica has 1000 units of labor (1000L) and 600 units of capital (600K).
   Pacifica has 400 units of labor (400L) and 1250 units of capital (1250K).
   
   Production functions:
   Atlantica:  Each unit of cloth produced requires 10L and 10K.
                Each unit of wine produced requires 6L and 4K.
   Pacifica:  Each unit of cloth produced requires 4L and 12K.
               Each unit of wine produced requires 4L and 8K.
   
   a. In the table below, fill in the blanks for output combinations on the production possibilities boundaries.

b. Determine the opportunity costs in each country. Which nation has the comparative advantage in wine? Why? How does this illustrate the factor endowments theory of trade?

c. Suppose that in autarky, Atlantica is producing and consuming Combination C (90 units of wine and 24 units of cloth). The international terms of trade are given to be $1w = .8c$ (or $1.25w = 1c$). If Atlantica then decides to specialize completely in its comparative advantage commodity, and exports one-third of its production of this commodity to Pacifica, determine Atlantica's posttrade consumption combination and its gains from trade.

d. If Pacifica is initially producing and consuming Combination D' (40 units of wine and 60 units of cloth) in autarky, determine its posttrade production and consumption combinations and its gains from trade with Atlantica.

e. After this trade takes place, are further gains still possible from international factor mobility? Discuss and give an example.

f. Who benefits from trade? In this example, would any group oppose trade between Atlantica and Pacifica? Why?

g. Is it possible for all groups within a nation to be better off with trade? Discuss.

## PRODUCTION POSSIBILITIES

|   | ATLANTICA | | | | PACIFICA | | |
|---|---|---|---|---|---|---|---|
|   | WINE | CLOTH | SURPLUS LABOR | | WINE | CLOTH | SURPLUS CAPITAL |
| A | 150<br>(900L, 600K) | 0<br>(0L, 0K) | 100L | A' | 100<br>(400L, 800K) | 0<br>(0L, 0K) | 450K |
| B | ____<br>(____,____) | 12<br>(120L, 120K) | ____ | B' | 80<br>(320L, 640K) | ____<br>(____,____) | ____ |
| C | 90<br>(540L, 360K) | 24<br>(240L, 240K) | 220L | C' | 60<br>(240L, 480K) | 40<br>(160L, 480K) | 290K |
| D | 60<br>(360L, 240K) | 36<br>(360L, 360K) | 280L | D' | 40<br>(160L, 320K) | 60<br>(240L, 720K) | 210K |
| E | 30<br>(180L, 120K) | 48<br>(480L, 480K) | 340L | E' | 20<br>(80L, 160K) | 80<br>(320L, 960K) | 130K |
| F | 0<br>(0L, 0K) | 60<br>(600L, 600K) | 400L | F' | 0<br>(0L, 0K) | 100<br>(400L, 1200K) | 50K |

## SUGGESTED READINGS

Appleyard, Dennis, and Alfred Field, "The Basis for Trade," Chapter 8 in *International Economics*, 2d ed., Chicago: Irwin, 1995.

Dornbusch, Rudiger, "The Case for Trade Liberalization in Developing Countries," *Journal of Economic Perspectives*, vol. 6, no. 1 (winter 1992), pages 69–85.

Edwards, Sebastian, "Openness, Trade Liberalization, and Growth in Developing Countries, *Journal of Economic Literature*, vol. 31, no. 3 (September 1993), pages 1358–1393.

World Bank, *World Development Report 1987*, New York: Oxford University Press, 1987.

CHAPTER 15

# BALANCE OF PAYMENTS, EXCHANGE RATES, AND EXTERNAL DEBT

The LDC debt crisis has been called the "dominant factor in North–South relations" during the 1980s.[1] External debt for developing economies, however, is not a recent phenomenon. Indeed, a common feature of developing economies is the accumulation of foreign debt—in part to finance public investment in economic infrastructure that cannot be funded by domestic saving. The crisis erupted in August of 1982 when Mexico suspended repayments on its foreign debt. Fears of other highly indebted developing nations following suit sent shudders through the international banking system.

While in the last few years the debt crisis may have been downgraded to a debt problem, a general consensus remains that high levels of foreign debt hinder economic progress in the developing nations. In this chapter we examine the origins, consequences, and proposed remedies to the debt problem. To do this, we need to understand balance of payments and exchange rates. Thus, we begin with balance of payments accounting, which leads naturally to the determinants of exchange rates. We compare the basic types of exchange rate systems (fixed, adjustable, managed float, and flexible), and discuss the factors that might be considered by a developing nation in selecting an exchange rate practice. With this theoretical foundation, we can better analyze the debt problem.

## BALANCE OF PAYMENTS ACCOUNT

International trade and investment allow residents of different nations to exchange goods, services, and assets. (A *resident* of a nation is any individual, business, or

---

[1]Kenneth Rogoff, "Symposium on New Institutions for Developing Country Debt," *Journal of Economic Perspectives*, vol. 4, no. 1 (winter 1990), page 3.

government agency for whom the nation is legal domicile.) Derived from the demands for foreign goods, services, and assets are demands for foreign currencies to serve as mediums of exchange. To facilitate these international transactions, foreign exchange markets exist in which the currencies of nations are traded.

For example, consider a nation, Tico, whose domestic currency is the peso. Residents of Tico desiring to purchase goods, services, or assets from, say, the United States, would need to obtain U.S. dollars, since the U.S. sellers have expenses in dollars (e.g., payments to labor and interest on loans). To obtain the necessary dollars, the residents of Tico would supply or sell pesos in the foreign exchange market. The amount of pesos required to purchase one dollar would depend upon the peso–dollar exchange rate. Conversely, the U.S. demand for goods, services, and assets from Tico would generate a demand for Tican pesos and a supply of dollars in the foreign exchange market.

To keep track of all the international transactions, balance of payments accounts are kept. For any nation, the **balance of payments account (BPA)** is a summary statement of the economic transactions between its residents and the rest of the world over a given period of time, usually a year. Refer to Figure 15.1, in which a simplified version of a BPA for Tico is illustrated.

The BPA is typically presented with two sides. On the left-hand side are the **credits,** representing the value of the goods, services, and assets exported or transferred to the rest of the world by Tico. Credits account for the supply of foreign currencies to Tico and the foreign demand for Tico's pesos. On the right-hand side are **debits,** representing the value of the goods, services, and assets imported or acquired by Tico from the rest of the world. Debits account for Tico's demand for foreign currencies and the supply of Tican pesos on the foreign exchange market.[2]

By definition, the value of total credits equals the value of total debits on the BPA.[3] Thus, the bottom line of the BPA simply indicates an accounting identity, and so reveals no insight about a nation's international payments position. To obtain such information, we must look at subaccounts of the BPA.

Three subaccounts are identified here: the current account (CA), the capital account (KA), and the official settlements account (OSA). Unlike the overall balance of payments account, these individual accounts do not have to balance. On any of these accounts, there may be surpluses (the value of the credits exceeding the value of the debits) or deficits (an excess of debits over credits). Below we examine the components of these subaccounts in some detail, beginning with the current account.

## CURRENT ACCOUNT

The **current account (CA)** records a nation's international trade in goods and services, flows of investment income, and unilateral transfers. The major category in the CA is usually *merchandise trade,* which includes trade in raw materials, minerals, agricultural

---

[2]As we will illustrate later, sometimes the BPA is presented in a single column, with credit items indicated by a plus (+) and debit items indicated by a minus (–).

[3]In theory, every international exchange would generate an entry of identical value on the credit and debit sides of the BPA, indicating a real transfer of a good, service, or asset and the corresponding payment. Thus, for any accounting period the value of credits would have to equal the value of debits. Lags between the shipment of goods or the consumption of services or the acquisition of assets and the subsequent payments, however, mean that at any point in the accounting period, actual credits and debits may not match exactly.

## FIGURE 15.1    TICO'S BALANCE OF PAYMENTS (SIMPLIFIED)

| CREDITS | DEBITS |
|---|---|
| (a) Tico's exports of goods<br>(b) Tico's exports of services<br>(c) Tico's investment income receipts<br>(d) Unilateral transfers received by Tico | (a') Tico's imports of goods<br>(b') Tico's imports of services<br>(c') Tico's investment income payments<br>(d') Unilateral transfers made by Tico |
| (e) Foreign direct investment in Tico<br>(f) Foreign portfolio investment in Tico | (e') Tico's direct investment in the rest of the world<br>(f') Tico's portfolio investment in the rest of the world |
| (g) Decrease in Tico's official assets<br>(h) Increase in foreign official assets in Tico | (g') Increase in Tico's official assets<br>(h') Decrease in foreign official assets in Tico |
| Total credits   =   Total debits | |

*Credits* indicate outflows of value (Tico's goods, services, and assets) which usually involve payment from foreigners → foreign demand for Tico's currency → supply of foreign currencies to Tico

*Debits* indicate inflows of value (foreign goods, services, and assets) which usually involve payment to foreigners → Tico's demand for foreign currencies → supply of Tico's currency to the rest of the world

Current account = balance on merchandise trade (a – a')
    + balance on invisible trade (b – b')
    + net investment income receipts (c – c')
    + net unilateral transfers received (d – d')

Capital account = net foreign direct investment in Tico (e – e')
    + net foreign portfolio investment in Tico (f – f')

Official settlements account = net decrease in official assets (g – g')
    + net increase in foreign official assets in Tico (h – h')

goods, and manufactures. See line items (a) and (a') in Figure 15.1. For some of the least developed economies, exports consist predominantly of minerals, forestry products, or agricultural commodities. Most of the LDCs are still net importers of manufactured goods.

Trade in services, sometimes known as *invisible trade,* is recorded in line items (b) and (b'). Included here would be items such as transportation, insurance, banking, and tourist expenditures. The **balance of trade (BT)** is the difference between the sum of the credits and the sum of the debits on merchandise and service trade. Unless favorably endowed with natural resources, economies tend to incur large balance of trade deficits (BT–) in the early stages of development, as the substantial import requirements for intermediate inputs and capital goods, in addition to the imports of manufactured consumer goods, exceed the export revenues.

The next line item on the CA records investment income flows, (c) and (c'), or the receipts of interest and dividends by residents of Tico on the foreign assets owned (credits) and the payments of interest and dividends to foreign owners of assets in Tico (debits). For nations with large external debts (most of the LDCs), net investment income flows are usually negative, reflecting the substantial interest payments on the foreign debt.

The fourth component of the CA, **unilateral transfers,** indicates the transfers of goods, services, or assets for which no payment is expected in return. Most LDCs are net recipients of international transfers, including official foreign aid and private charities. Note that if residents of Tico working abroad send part of their earnings back to families in Tico, then unilateral transfers received by Tico would also rise. See Credits (d).

The **current account balance** is the difference between the credit and debit entries on the first four line items on the BPA.

$$\text{CA balance} = (a + b + c + d) - (a' + b' + c' + d')$$

A current account surplus (CA+) must be offset by a corresponding deficit on the rest of the balance of payments account. Similarly, a current account deficit (CA–) will be offset by a surplus in the remainder of the BPA.

The current account balance indicates a nation's net international investment condition over the accounting period. A current account surplus means that the nation has acquired net claims on the rest of the world (or reduced its net liabilities to the rest of the world). In other words, a nation with a CA+ has, on net, imported assets over that period.

On the other hand, a current account deficit indicates that the rest of the world has acquired claims on that nation's assets. Since imports of goods and services, investment income payments, and transfers to the foreigners have exceeded its exports of goods and services, investment income receipts and transfers from the foreigners, the nation, on net, has reduced its ownership of assets.

## CAPITAL ACCOUNT

The **capital account (KA)** records the exchange of assets between residents of different nations. We identify two basic types of foreign private investment. **Foreign direct investment** refers to the private acquisition of real assets, such as property and ownership of foreign enterprises. Refer to Figure 15.1. Examples of foreign direct investment in Tico would be the purchase of a Tican company by a Japanese investor or the construction of a factory in Tico by a British transnational corporation. While these would be credit items on Tico's KA, see line item (e), they would be debit entries on the capital accounts of Japan and Great Britain.

The second type, **foreign portfolio investment,** refers to the private acquisition of financial assets, including stocks (where the investor does not have significant control over the corporation), bonds, loans, and bank deposits. For example, if managers of a private pension fund in Australia purchased bonds issued by the government of Tico, or if a French commercial bank made a loan to a business in Tico, or if an Italian importer deposited pesos in a bank in Tico, then there would be corresponding credit entries on Tico's KA, under line item (f). These same transactions would be recorded as debit entries on the capital accounts of Australia, France, and Italy as residents of these nations have acquired assets in Tico.

Foreign direct investment or foreign portfolio investment by residents of Tico, indicating the purchase of real or financial foreign assets, would be debit entries on Tico's capital account, under the line items (e') and (f'). Note that we are restricting capital account transactions to those of an unofficial nature or to those involving private investment for economic gain. Official transactions, those between governments or involving the monetary authorities in the foreign exchange market, are recorded on the official settlements account (explained below).

Note also that while the purchase of foreign assets is recorded on the capital account, subsequent flows of investment income, the interest and dividends, are recorded on the current account. For example, if a Brazilian investor purchased 100 shares of stock in a Tican corporation for 50,000 pesos, the credit side of the KA of Tico increases by 50,000 pesos, line item (f). A subsequent payment of 2000 pesos in dividends by the Tican corporation to the Brazilian stockholder is entered as a debit for 2000 pesos on Tico's CA, line item (c').

The **capital account balance** is given by the difference between the credits and debits in line items (e) and (f).

$$KA \text{ balance} = (e + f) - (e' + f')$$

For most LDCs the capital account is usually in surplus, indicating net foreign investment in the economy. Alternatively, a KA+ indicates that the nation is a net exporter of private assets to the rest of the world over that period.

The balance of payments position of a country is determined by the sum of the balances on the current and capital accounts. A **balance of payments surplus, BP+,** indicates an excess of credits over debits on the combined current and capital accounts. Recall that the foreign demand for a nation's currency is derived from the foreign demand for that nation's goods, services, and assets (the credit items on that nation's BPA). Thus, a BP+ also indicates an excess demand for that nation's currency, or an excess supply of foreign currencies to the nation. Consequently, with a BP+, the international exchange value of the nation's currency tends to increase, or the currency tends to appreciate.

In contrast, a **balance of payments deficit, BP–,** would mean that debits exceed credits on the current and capital accounts. A BP– indicates an excess demand for foreign goods, services, and assets; an excess demand for foreign currencies; and an excess supply of the nation's currency in the foreign exchange market. With a BP–, we would find downward pressure on the international exchange value of the nation's currency, or a tendency for the currency to depreciate.

We say "a tendency" for an appreciation (with a BP+) or depreciation (with a BP–) because limits may be placed on the movements in the exchange rates. As we will discuss in greater detail later, under a flexible exchange rate system, any imbalance between credits and debits will be eliminated by changes in the exchange rate. The current and capital accounts, therefore, are always offsetting.

In contrast, under a fixed exchange rate system, official exchange rates are established and limits set for the range of fluctuation allowed.[4] The monetary authorities of the nations have the responsibility of maintaining the official exchange values of the currencies. With fixed exchange rates, however, the current and capital accounts need not offset each other, in which case we have a need for an official settlements account.

## OFFICIAL SETTLEMENTS ACCOUNT

The **official settlements account (OSA)** measures the movement of official assets involving monetary authorities (usually the central banks) or between governments of nations. Some of the official assets are **official reserve assets.** These are the gold and foreign currencies held by the monetary authorities, Special Drawing Rights, and the reserve position of the nation at the International Monetary Fund (IMF).

For most nations the stock of foreign currencies held by the monetary authorities constitutes the majority of the owned international reserves. Gold no longer plays a major role as an international reserve asset. All members of the IMF have quotas or required contributions of both foreign currencies and their own currencies—adjusted for the size of the national economies. This pool of currencies of the IMF is available to nations needing to borrow foreign exchange. **Special Drawing Rights (SDRs)** are an international currency created by the IMF and allocated to member nations to enhance official intervention in foreign exchange markets.[5]

As stated above, any imbalance on the current and capital accounts will be offset by the official settlements account. Credits on the OSA of a nation reflect either a decrease in official assets held by the nation or an acquisition of the nation's assets by foreign officials.

To illustrate, return to Figure 15.1 and the example of Tico's BPA. Suppose Tico has a balance of payments deficit, an excess of debits over credits on the current and capital accounts. Reflecting the BP–, an excess supply of pesos exists on the foreign exchange market. To prevent the peso from depreciating, or falling in value, the Central Bank of Tico could enter the foreign exchange market and purchase the surplus pesos, paying with foreign currencies it holds (for example, U.S. dollars). This foreign exchange intervention would be recorded on Tico's OSA as a credit, under line item (g). Alternatively, central banks in other nations with balance of payments surpluses, say the Federal Reserve of the United States, could buy up the surplus pesos, which, when

---

[4]Other types of exchange rate systems are found between the extremes of perfectly flexible and fixed, such as managed floats and adjustable pegs. We will also address some of these hybrid systems later in the chapter.

[5]Created in the late 1960s to add liquidity to the international monetary system, SDRs have been the subject of controversy. The initial and subsequent allocations of SDRs by the IMF have been based on the nations' quotas, thus the biggest-quota nations (such as the United States) received the most SDRs. The less developed countries have argued that SDRs should be distributed as foreign aid so that the poorer nations would receive the larger allocations. In any case, SDRs have yet to become a major international reserve asset as originally intended by the IMF.

placed in banks in Tico, would count as official reserve assets for the United States. On Tico's BPA, such an increase in official liabilities would be recorded as a credit, under line item (h).[6]

Suppose instead that Tico has a balance of payments surplus. The official settlements account of Tico would show an offsetting deficit, allowing Tico to add to its holdings of official assets or reduce its liabilities to foreign officials. A BP+ for Tico would put upward pressure on the Tican peso. As we will see, if allowed, the appreciation of the peso would work to eliminate the BP+. To prevent the peso from appreciating, Tico's central bank could supply or sell pesos in the foreign exchange market for foreign currencies, resulting in an increase in official reserve assets held by Tico—see line item (g') in the OSA. Alternatively, other central banks could sell their pesos in the process of purchasing back their currencies. These actions would also be recorded as debits on Tico's OSA, under line item (h'), decrease in foreign official assets in Tico.

In Table 15.1 (on page 458), we illustrate a balance of payments account for Costa Rica in 1992. We follow the model BPA shown in Figure 15.1, although we use a single-column format, with credits indicated by pluses (+) and debits indicated by minuses (−).[7]

In 1992 Costa Rica had a merchandise trade deficit of $497.6 million. (Of the total value of the merchandise exports, 28 percent and 12 percent were accounted for by bananas and coffee, respectively.) A surplus in trade existed in services of $174.4 million, and Costa Rica, on net, received $170.4 million in transfers. Investment income payments, however, exceeded receipts by $208.6 million. Overall the current account balance for Costa Rica showed a deficit of $361.4 million.

There was net foreign private investment, both direct and portfolio, in Costa Rica in 1992, giving a capital account surplus of $363.1 million. With all macroeconomic data, errors in measurement are bound to happen. In the BPA, some of the unrecorded and inaccurately measured international transactions may be due to circumvention of exchange controls and trade barriers and other illegal activities. Most of the errors and omissions probably reflect the less-than-universal coverage and the imperfect measurement of international financial and commercial transactions.

Including the net errors and omissions with the current and capital account balances, Costa Rica had a balance of payments surplus in 1992 of $129.5 million. Costa Rica increased its official assets by $141.1 million (mostly with an increase in its official holdings of foreign currencies). This was slightly offset by a net increase in foreign official assets in Costa Rica of $11.6 million (mostly in the form of a net increase in foreign official loans). Thus, Costa Rica had an official settlements account deficit of $129.5 million.

This BPA may be fairly representative of a developing economy—with a large balance of trade deficit; net payments of investment income; net receipts of unilateral transfers; and net foreign private investment in the country.

---

[6] If the U.S. Federal Reserve used the just-purchased pesos to buy bonds issued by the government of Tico, then the United States would have acquired official assets (Tican government bonds), but not official reserve assets (as were the Tican pesos). Nevertheless, the entry on the OSA of Tico is the same, line item (h), an increase in foreign official assets in Tico.

[7] We should note that the balance of payments accounts as conventionally presented do not distinguish the official settlements account as we do in this chapter. Rather the OSA is encompassed in the overall capital account.

### TABLE 15.1  BALANCE OF PAYMENTS ACCOUNT FOR COSTA RICA IN 1992 (MILLIONS OF $)

| | | | |
|---|---|---|---|
| CURRENT ACCOUNT BALANCE | | | − $361.4 |
| (a) | Merchandise exports | + $1714.3 | |
| (a′) | Merchandise imports | − $2211.9 | |
| (b) | Exports of services | + $ 858.6 | |
| (b′) | Imports of services | − $ 684.2 | |
| (c) | Investment income receipts | + $ 91.4 | |
| (c′) | Investment income payments | − $ 300.0 | |
| (d − d′) | Net unilateral transfers received | + $ 170.4 | |
| CAPITAL ACCOUNT BALANCE | | | + $363.1 |
| (e − e′) | Net foreign direct investment in Costa Rica | + $ 217.3 | |
| (f − f′) | Net foreign portfolio investment in Costa Rica (including other long-term and short-term net capital inflows) | + $ 145.8 | |
| NET ERRORS AND OMISSIONS | | | + $127.8 |
| OFFICIAL SETTLEMENTS ACCOUNT BALANCE | | | − $129.5 |
| (g − g′) | Net decrease in Costa Rica's official assets | − $ 141.1 | |
| (h − h′) | Net increase in foreign official assets in Costa Rica | + $ 11.6 | |

Addendum: Merchandise trade balance = − $497.6
Invisible trade balance = + $174.4
Balance of trade in goods and service = − $323.2
Balance of payments (the sum of the current and capital accounts and net errors and omissions) = + $129.5

SOURCE: This presentation of the balance of payments account for Costa Rica for 1992 was derived from International Monetary Fund, *Balance of Payments Statistics Yearbook*, vol. 44, Part I, 1993, pages 171–176.

## RELATIONSHIP BETWEEN THE BALANCE OF PAYMENTS AND EXCHANGE RATE

As stated earlier, an exchange rate is a price: the number of units of one currency required to purchase one unit of a second currency. Under a **flexible exchange rate system,** exchange rates are determined by the demands and supplies of the currencies in the foreign exchange market.

To illustrate, consider again the hypothetical developing country, Tico, and its currency, the peso. Since for each currency an exchange rate exists with every other currency, we will simplify and use the United States dollar ($) to represent all foreign currencies or foreign exchange in general. For our analysis, then, the relevant exchange rate is the peso price of the dollar $(p/\$)$. A rise in the exchange rate $(p/\$)\uparrow$ signifies a **depreciation** of the peso—since it requires more pesos to purchase one dollar. Conversely, a fall in the exchange rate $(p/\$)\downarrow$ indicates a decrease in the peso price of the dollar and an **appreciation** of the peso.

## THE DEMAND FOR FOREIGN EXCHANGE

In Figure 15.2 on page 460, the demand and supply of dollars (representative of foreign currencies in general) for Tico are given. The demand for dollars $(D_\$)$ by residents of Tico reflects the debit items on the Tican balance of payments account, that is, the Tican demand for foreign goods, services, and assets. The demand curve is downward-sloping. Ceteris paribus, an appreciation of the peso (decrease in the peso price of the dollar) would increase the quantity demanded of dollars.

For example, suppose the exchange rate were 25 pesos = $1.00 $(er_o = 25)$. To import a transistor radio produced for $10 would cost 250 pesos. If the peso appreciated to 20 pesos = $1.00 $(er_1 = 20)$, then the $10 transistor radio would cost only 200 pesos. Consequently, the quantity demanded of imported transistor radios would rise, and so would the quantity demanded of dollars (see the movement from $E$ to $A$ along the $D_\$$ curve in Figure 15.2).[8]

The demand-for-dollars curve is drawn holding constant, among other factors, real income in Tico $(Y_T)$; the aggregate price level in Tico relative to the foreign price level $(P_T/P_f)$; the interest rate in Tico relative to the foreign interest rate $(i_T/i_f)$; the expected exchange rate $(er^e)$; and official intervention in the foreign exchange market. Changes in any of these factors would shift the demand curve for dollars.

For example, an increase in the demand for dollars and a rightward shift in the $D_\$$ curve, could be caused by:

A rise in real national income in Tico $(Y_T)\uparrow$, which increases Tican expenditures on all normal goods and services, including imports.

A rise in the relative price level in Tico $(P_T/P_f)\uparrow$, meaning that foreign goods and services have become relatively less expensive.

A fall in the relative interest rate $(i_T/i_f)\downarrow$, meaning that the yield on foreign assets (such as bonds and certificates of deposit) has become relatively more attractive.

An expected depreciation of the peso $(er^e)\uparrow$, causing speculators to purchase dollars in the anticipation of a rise in the peso price of the dollar.

Official intervention, say, in the form of the Central Bank of Tico purchasing dollars to keep the peso from appreciating.

---

[8]Note that this inverse relationship between the peso price of the dollar and the quantity demanded of dollars holds regardless of the underlying price elasticity of Tican demand for foreign goods and services.

## FIGURE 15.2 THE DEMAND AND SUPPLY OF FOREIGN CURRENCIES

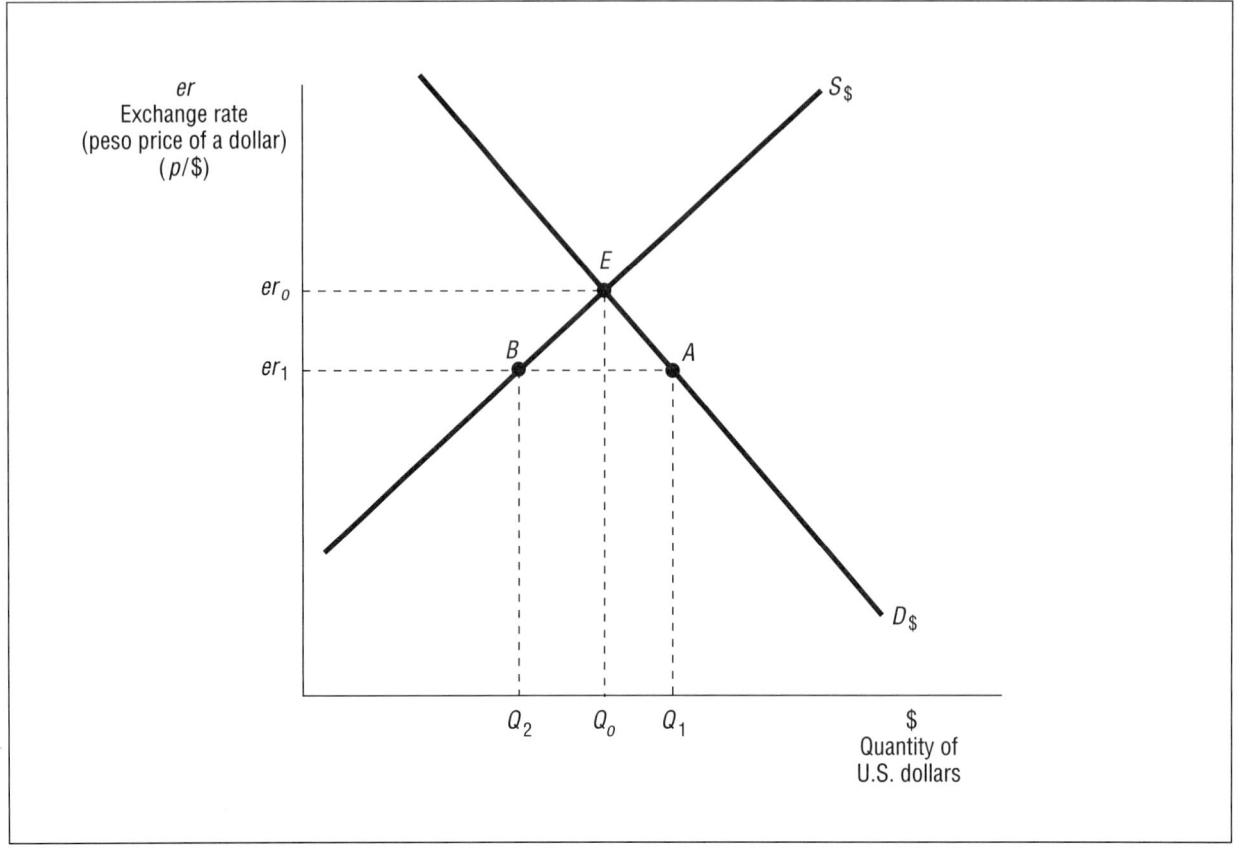

### THE SUPPLY OF FOREIGN EXCHANGE

The supply of foreign currencies to a nation, derived from the foreign demands for that nation's goods, services, and assets, reflects the credit items on the nation's balance of payments account. Refer to Figure 15.2, in which the supply-of-dollars curve, $S_\$$, to Tico is illustrated.

We have drawn the dollar supply curve as upward-sloping, indicating a positive relationship between the exchange rate (peso price of the dollar) and the quantity of dollars supplied. As the peso appreciates, the prices of Tican goods and services when converted into foreign currencies rise, prompting a decrease in the foreign quantities demanded of the Tican goods and services. If the foreign demand for Tican goods and services is price-elastic, then an appreciation of the peso would result in a decrease in the total expenditures by foreign consumers and a decrease in the quantity supplied of foreign currencies to Tico. This is the usual case and will be assumed here.

Consider the following example: Let the initial exchange rate be 25 pesos to the U.S. dollar (or 1 peso = $.04). Suppose a bushel of coffee beans in Tico costs 100 pesos to produce, or $4 when converted at the present exchange rate. If the peso appreciates to 20 pesos to the dollar (or 1 peso = $.05), then the 100-peso bushel of coffee beans would cost $5. As long as the foreign demand for Tican coffee beans is price-elastic, then the increase of 25 percent in the dollar price of coffee beans (due to the 25 percent appreciation of the peso) would result in a decrease of more than 25 percent in the quantity demanded of the beans. Decreases would occur, therefore, in total foreign expenditures and the quantity of dollars supplied. In Figure 15.2, the movement along the supply-of-dollars curve from $E$ to $B$ is consistent with an appreciation of the peso (from $er_0$ to $er_1$), resulting in a decrease in the quantity supplied of dollars (from $Q_0$ to $Q_2$).[9]

The supply curve of dollars is conditional upon many of the same factors as the demand curve for dollars. The supply curve of dollars, indicating the relationship between the peso price of dollars and the quantity supplied of dollars to Tico, is drawn holding constant real foreign income $(Y_f)$; the aggregate price level in Tico relative to the foreign price level $(P_T/P_f)$; relative interest rates $(i_T/i_f)$; the expected exchange rate $(er^e)$; and official intervention in the foreign exchange market. With a change in any of these underlying factors the supply curve would shift.

For example, an increase in the supply of dollars to Tico (a rightward shift in the $S_\$$ curve) could be caused by:

A rise in real foreign income, increasing the foreign demand for Tican goods and services $(Y_f)\uparrow$

A fall in the relative price level $(P_T/P_f)\downarrow$, making Tican goods more competitive at any given exchange rate.

A rise in the relative interest rate in Tico $(i_T/i_f)\uparrow$, increasing the foreign investment in Tican assets.

An expected appreciation of the peso $(er^e)\uparrow$, increasing the attractiveness of holding pesos that are expected to rise in value.

Official intervention in the foreign exchange market, for example, by the Central Bank of Tico selling dollars (to keep the peso from depreciating).

## DETERMINING THE EQUILIBRIUM EXCHANGE RATE

The market equilibrium exchange rate equates the quantities demanded and supplied of foreign currencies. In Figure 15.2 the market equilibrium exchange rate is $er_0$, the point at which the demand and supply curves of dollars intersect.

---

[9]On the other hand, were the foreign demand for Tican goods and services price-inelastic, then an appreciation of the peso would be associated with an increase in the quantity supplied of dollars and a downward-sloping supply-of-dollars curve. In this case the increase in the foreign currency price of Tican coffee beans by 25 percent would dominate (rather than be dominated by) the decrease in the foreign quantities demanded of Tican coffee beans. Thus the total dollar expenditures by foreigners and the quantity supplied of dollars to Tico would increase with an appreciation of the peso. In general, the price-elasticity of foreign demand depends on the degree of substitutability between Tican and foreign goods and services. In this chapter we will assume that the degree of substitutability is high, so the foreign demand for Tican goods and services is price-elastic and the supply curve of dollars to Tico is upward-sloping.

Changes in the exchange rate reflect changes in the factors underlying the demand and supply curves, e.g., real income levels, relative prices, relative interest rates, expected exchange rates, and official intervention. How much the exchange rate will adjust for a given change in an underlying factor may depend on the exchange rate system in operation. Below we illustrate the two basic types of exchange rates, fixed and flexible.

## FLEXIBLE EXCHANGE RATES

Under a perfectly flexible exchange rate system, the exchange values of currencies are determined entirely by market forces. To illustrate, refer to Figure 15.3 and assume that the Tican balance of payments is initially in equilibrium at an exchange rate of $er_o$. That is, any imbalance in the current account is exactly offset by an imbalance in the capital account, so the peso price of the dollar is stable at $er_o$.

Suppose now that Tico experiences inflation, and that the aggregate price level in Tico increases relative to the foreign price level $(P_T/P_f)\uparrow$. The Tican demand for dollars would increase in order to purchase the foreign goods and services that have become relatively less expensive. The supply of dollars to Tico falls as foreigners substitute away from the higher-priced Tican goods and services. See the shifts in the demand and supply curves to $D'_\$$ and $S'_\$$. As the imports of Tico rise and its exports decline, the current account deteriorates. A balance of payments deficit (BP–) emerges. At the initial equilibrium exchange rate of $er_o$, we find an excess demand for dollars (equal to $Q_1 - Q_2$) indicative of the BP–. Consequently, the peso begins to depreciate.

Under a flexible exchange rate system, the depreciation of the peso would continue until a balance of payments equilibrium is regained. In Figure 15.3, the new equilibrium exchange rate would be $er_1$. As the peso depreciates, the quantity demanded of dollars decreases (see the movement from $A$ to $E'$ along the new demand curve $D'_\$$). For residents of Tico the weaker peso offsets the relatively lower foreign price level. Similarly, as the peso depreciates, the quantity supplied of dollars increases (see the movement from $B$ to $E'$ along the new supply curve $S'_\$$). For foreigners, the stronger dollar offsets the relatively higher price level in Tico. The deterioration in the current account is reversed as Tico's imports decline and its exports rebound. The peso depreciates until the initial condition of the current account is restored.

On net, the inflation in Tico has been offset by the depreciation in the peso. The real exchange rate, $er^*$ (which, recall, is equal to the product of the nominal exchange rate, $er$, and the ratio of the foreign price level to the price level in Tico, $P_f/P_T$), is unchanged.

## FIXED EXCHANGE RATES

Under a **fixed exchange rate system,** official exchange values for currencies are established. The monetary authorities are supposed to maintain these official exchange rates within a prescribed range through intervention in the foreign exchange market and the adoption of appropriate monetary policies.

In Figure 15.4 on page 464, we again begin with an initial balance of payments equilibrium for Tico at $E$, with an exchange rate of $er_o$. Suppose further that $er_o$ is the official peso–dollar exchange rate, which can fluctuate between $\overline{er}$ and $\underline{er}$, the upper and lower bounds. As before, with the inflation in Tico and the resulting increase in the demand for dollars and decrease in the supply of dollars, the peso begins to depreciate. Once the peso depreciates to the upper bound, $\overline{er}$, the monetary authorities in Tico must intervene and sell dollars. At $\overline{er}$, the depreciation of the peso has not been

## FIGURE 15.3  EFFECTS OF INFLATION: FLEXIBLE EXCHANGE RATES

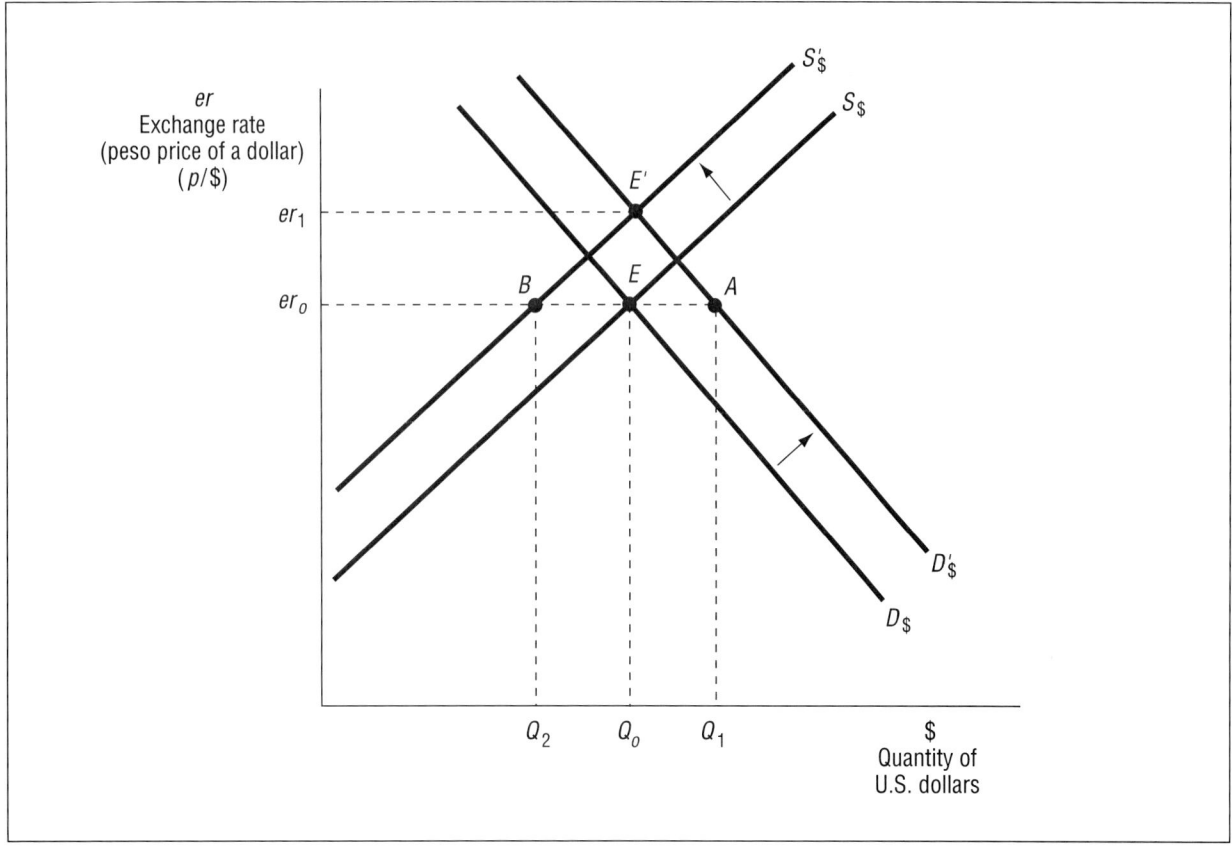

sufficient to eliminate the balance of payments deficit, indicated by the excess demand for dollars of $Q'_1 - Q'_2$.

The Central Bank of Tico would sell at least enough of its holdings of dollars to meet the excess demand for dollars at $\overline{er}$. To hold the exchange rate at $\overline{er}$, $(Q'_1 - Q'_2)$ dollars would have to be sold, shifting the supply curve of dollars $S'_\$$ to the right to $S''_\$$. (To push the exchange rate back down to $er_{o'}$ the official intervention would have to be greater. The Central Bank of Tico would have to sell enough dollars to shift the supply curve $S'_\$$ to the right by the distance $BA$.) The sale of dollars by the Central Bank of Tico would be recorded as a credit on Tico's official settlements account as a decrease in official reserve assets. See line item (g) in Figure 15.1. The surplus in the OSA is required to offset the BP−.

### EXCHANGE CONTROLS

If Tico did not have sufficient international reserves (here, dollars) to support its official exchange rate at $er_{o'}$ it might resort to exchange controls. Under **exchange controls** the Central Bank of Tico rations the available foreign exchange. All foreign currencies received by residents of Tico would be turned over to the monetary authorities, for an equivalent amount of pesos at the official exchange rate. With the inflation in Tico, the quantity supplied of dollars at $er_o$ is $Q_2$. The quantity demanded, however, is $Q_1$. The

## FIGURE 15.4  EFFECTS OF INFLATION: FIXED EXCHANGE RATES

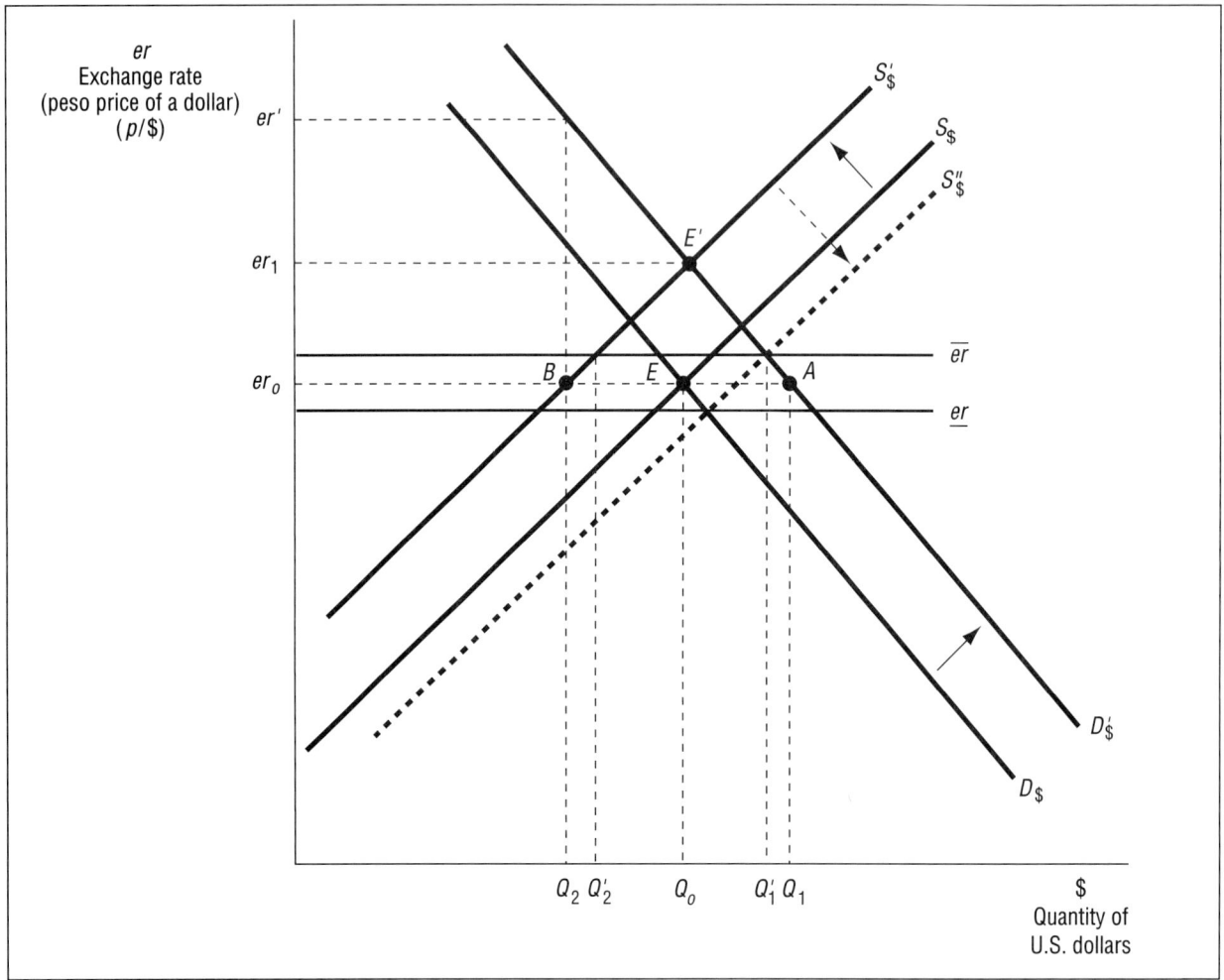

Central Bank of Tico would control access to the available dollars. For example, all importers would have to obtain import licenses entitling them to the dollars needed to pay for the allowed imports.

Several problems are associated with exchange controls. First, the balance of payments deficit is not corrected—rather, the excess demand for dollars is maintained at $Q_1 - Q_2$ through a rationing of the dollars available. Second, resources must be devoted to operating the exchange control system and criteria must be established for allocating the dollars. Third, as with any price ceiling, a black market (or parallel market) is bound to emerge. Given the $Q_2$ amount of dollars available and the demand for dollars of $D'_\$$, the black market exchange rate could rise to $er'$. Indeed, in many developing countries with officially overvalued currencies, the black market exchange rate is significantly higher than the official rate. Consequently, rent seeking arises in which individuals find it more profitable to gain access to the scarce foreign exchange at the official exchange rate (but with a considerably higher market value), than to engage in more productive economic activity.

Fourth, exchange controls can be used as a barrier to trade and investment by restricting the ability to import goods and purchase foreign assets. In sum, exchange controls are not an appropriate solution to balance of payments deficits.

BORROWING FROM THE IMF

To reduce the need to impose exchange controls or trade barriers to deal with balance of payments deficits, the International Monetary Fund provides member countries with access to additional reserves for intervention. A nation with a BP– and a need to buy up its excess currency in the foreign exchange market can borrow foreign currencies from the IMF. (Recall that the IMF maintains a pool of currencies that have been deposited by member nations.) The IMF may impose conditions on borrowing, however, requiring the nation to adopt tighter economic policies to address the underlying causes of the balance of payments deficits. Special windows or loan programs are also available for developing countries with balance of payments problems due to particular circumstances, such as significantly higher prices for oil imports or sharp declines in export revenues from a fall in primary product prices that swell current account deficits.

BALANCE OF PAYMENTS DEFICITS AND ECONOMIC POLICY

Balance of payments deficits indicate the need for tighter economic policies. The BP– brought on by inflation in Tico calls for contractionary monetary policy. The sale of dollars by the Central Bank of Tico should reduce the Tican money supply, since individuals who purchase the dollars in the foreign exchange market would pay by writing checks on their peso deposits in Tican banks. The decrease in the money supply, in turn, would set off internal adjustments that help to correct the BP–.

As the money supply falls, interest rates in Tico should rise. The higher interest rates may attract foreign capital and improve Tico's capital account. Tighter credit in Tico would also discourage interest-sensitive spending, such as business fixed investment, residential construction, and the purchase of consumer durables. The decline in spending would reduce real national output and income and put downward pressure on the price level. Lower real income would reduce spending on imports, and lower prices would improve Tico's international competitiveness. The deflationary pressure should help Tico's current account balance.

The improvement in Tico's balance of payments with the tighter monetary policy would be enhanced by tighter fiscal policy, such as reduced government spending and higher taxes. Indeed, one of the primary causes of inflation in developing nations is an overexpansion of the money supply to finance large government budget deficits.

The consequences of a higher interest rate, lower real income, and reduced inflation in Tico would be to increase the supply of dollars (in Figure 15.4, a rightward shift in the $S'_\$$ curve) and decrease the Tican demand for dollars (a leftward shift in the $D'_\$$ curve). The balance of payments deficit should be corrected and the equilibrium exchange rate brought back within the range allowed around the official exchange rate—although domestically unemployment would likely rise with the contractionary policy.

In sum, under a fixed exchange rate system, a balance of payments deficit calls for a decrease in the money supply—set off by the intervention in the foreign exchange market to soak up the excess domestic currency. This, in turn, should trigger the necessary internal adjustments in the economy to restore the balance of payments equilibrium. The official intervention in the foreign exchange market should only be temporary—to buy time for the internal adjustments in interest rates, prices, and incomes to take place.

Conversely, a nation with a balance of payments surplus would experience an appreciation of its currency. As the exchange rate approached its lower bound, the monetary authorities should intervene in the foreign exchange market and buy up the surplus foreign currencies, providing the domestic currency in exchange. The resulting increase in the domestic money supply would reduce the interest rate and stimulate the domestic economy. The rise in real national income and the domestic price level, along with the lower interest rate, would reduce the supply of foreign currencies and increase the demand for foreign currencies. The BP+ would be corrected and the appreciation of the domestic currency reversed—although if the domestic economy were at full employment, inflation may become problematic with the expansion in money supply.

## FIXED VERSUS FLEXIBLE EXCHANGE RATES

One of the most important decisions for a nation is the selection of an exchange rate system. In this chapter we have illustrated adjustments to balance of payments disequilibria under flexible and fixed exchange rates, the two basic types of exchange rate systems. Advantages and disadvantages are cited for each. Not surprisingly, the advantages claimed for one are usually the perceived disadvantages of the other.

### Advantages of Flexible Exchange Rates

The case for flexible exchange rates is drawn from the efficiencies found in the market mechanism, whereby prices adjust to clear markets. Under flexible exchange rates, any balance of payments disequilibrium would result in a self-correcting change in the exchange rate. With a BP–, the currency would depreciate; with a BP+, the currency would appreciate. Having one price, the exchange rate, adjust automatically and continuously to BP disequilibria is more efficient than having the internal adjustments in the network of interest rates, input and output prices, production and employment required under a fixed exchange rate system.

Moreover, since the BP would always tend toward equilibrium, monetary policy would be freed up to address the internal balance of full employment and price stability. The monetary authorities would not have to hold foreign currencies for intervention in the foreign exchange market to maintain an official exchange rate.

### Advantages of Fixed Exchange Rates

Exchange rates should be more stable under a fixed exchange rate system. In fact, one of the major arguments against flexible exchange rates is the potential for excessive volatility. Speculative attacks on a currency triggered by a depreciation may become self-fulfilling, resulting in large sales and further depreciation of the currency. With a flexible exchange rate there is no limit to how far the currency can depreciate, since the monetary authorities are not obliged to support any exchange rate.

Volatility in exchange rates can reduce the volumes of both international trade and investment—due to the uncertainty about the relative purchasing powers of the foreign currencies in which international payments and receipts are made. While possibilities exist for hedging and eliminating foreign exchange risk using forward and futures markets, the costs of doing so reduce the incentives to engage in international transactions. The reduced volumes of trade and investment, in turn, result in a less efficient allocation of global resources. Furthermore, variability in exchange rates can alter international price differentials, even when the underlying comparative advantages remain unchanged. Two examples might help to illustrate.

Suppose the Zephyr Company, a U.S. corporation that manufactures computer keyboards, can produce a keyboard for $100. Its Japanese competitor can produce virtually identical keyboards for 11,000 yen (or ¥11,000). If the current exchange rate is ¥100 = $1.00, then the U.S. corporation would have the price advantage and, abstracting from transportation costs and trade barriers, would be able to sell computer keyboards to Japan for an import price of ¥10,000. If the dollar were to appreciate to, say ¥125 = $1.00, then Zephyr Company would no longer have the competitive advantage. Japan would export keyboards to the United States for $88 (11,000 yen / 125 yen per dollar). In general, output and employment in the United States would fall with the appreciation of the dollar. Thus, in trade-sensitive sectors, variability in the exchange rate can result in variability in profits, production, and employment. Moreover, whether the Zephyr Company expands by building additional plants in the United States (or abroad) to manufacture keyboards will depend, in part, on expected exchange rates. The greater the uncertainty about future exchange rates, the more tentative Zephyr and other companies might be about undertaking such investments.

Now suppose the Zephyr Company decides to invest in a foreign subsidiary to assemble computer keyboards for export back to the United States. The choice comes down to locating in Tico, where keyboards can be assembled for 1000 pesos or Costa Rica, where the keyboards can be assembled for 4200 colones (the Costa Rican currency). At the current exchange rates of 25 pesos = $1.00 and 120 colones = $1.00, the foreign subsidiary would be established in Costa Rica, where the export price in dollars would be lower, $35 (or 4200 colones / 120 colones per dollar) compared to $40 (or 1000 pesos / 25 pesos per dollar). However, if the Tican peso were expected to depreciate to, say 32 pesos = $1.00, then the export price of a Tican-assembled keyboard would be $31.25 (or 1000 pesos / 32 pesos per dollar). In this case, Zephyr would build the factory in Tico. Again, uncertainty in future exchange rates, a potential characteristic of a flexible exchange rate system, can complicate, even discourage, international trade and investment.

The second major advantage for fixed exchange rates is the discipline imposed on the monetary authorities of having to maintain the official exchange rates. Recall, under a fixed exchange rate, a BP deficit, indicating an excess supply of the domestic currency on the foreign exchange market, would work to depreciate the domestic currency. The monetary authorities would have to intervene in the foreign exchange market and buy up their surplus currency. Doing so would reduce the domestic money supply, push up interest rates, and generally deflate the economy. Such are the "rules of the game" under a fixed exchange rate system. The monetary authorities are supposed to accept the discipline and avoid excessive growth in the money supply that produces inflation and balance of payments deficits.

Some nations, most notably Argentina, have attacked chronically high inflation by adopting fixed exchange rates and **currency boards,** which limit the amount of domestic currency issued to an equivalent amount of official reserves of foreign currencies on hand. In 1991, Argentina pegged its exchange rate at one peso equal to one U.S. dollar and established a currency board. Subsequently, the inflation rate in Argentina was slashed from over 1000 percent for 1990 to under 5 percent in 1994.[10]

---

[10]See "Creating Credibility," in *The Economist* (July 2, 1994), page 76; and Edward Schumacher, "Shades of the Past in Argentina's Economic Boom," *Wall Street Journal* (February 25, 1994), page A15.

Advocates of currency boards cite the fiscal discipline also promoted by the strict control of the domestic money supply. In particular, fiscal deficits can no longer be easily financed by the central bank printing money. On the other hand, the danger continues of overvaluation of the currency when the domestic inflation rate, albeit reduced, outpaces the inflation rate of the country to which the currency is tied. With a fixed exchange rate and currency board, the option of devaluation to deal with an overvalued currency is not available.

Under flexible exchange rates, however, no such discipline is imposed. Countries with relatively high inflation, for example, due to excessive money supply growth to accommodate large budget deficits, would simply find their currencies depreciating. The monetary authorities must exercise self-discipline, which may be difficult if the fiscal authorities cannot exercise restraint in spending. Failure to control inflation can result in a cycle of inflation and depreciation.

### THE INFLATION–DEPRECIATION CYCLE

Recall the earlier example of inflation in Tico leading to a deterioration in the current account, since, for any nominal exchange rate, Tico's exports become less competitive and imports to Tico become relatively cheaper. The increase in Tico's demand for foreign currencies and the decrease in the supply of foreign currencies to Tico would depreciate the peso. The depreciation of the peso should serve to counter the initial inflation and restore the current account balance. If the depreciation generates more inflation, however, the current account deterioration may not be reversed, and further depreciation of the peso may occur.

Why might depreciation induce inflation? For one, the weaker peso gives domestic producers in Tico room to raise their prices and profit margins and still compete with the more expensive imports. Second, the depreciation raises the peso price of the inputs of the raw materials, intermediate goods, and capital goods that need to be imported (i.e., that are not produced in sufficient quantities domestically). The higher costs of the imported inputs raise the costs of production in Tico and contribute to inflation. Third, the weaker peso raises the prices of imported foodstuffs and consumer goods, which can undermine real wages in Tico. Especially in urban areas where labor unions may be strong, higher prices for consumer goods could put upward pressure on peso wage rates.

Inflation, especially when it escalates into hyperinflation, can be harmful to an economy. As illustrated in Chapter 10, if nominal interest rates (which may be set by the monetary authorities) do not keep pace with inflation, then real rates of interest can become negative, discouraging saving and limiting investment. In particular, uncertainty about the future purchasing power of funds invested increases with high and variable rates of inflation. Significantly reduced is the willingness to enter into the long-term financial contracts important for physical capital formation. Moreover, not all wages and prices are equally flexible and able to adjust with inflation. Consequently, relative prices, the distribution of income, and the allocation of resources will be affected, in ways that usually add to the poverty.

For a nation, depreciation reduces the purchasing power of its exports, resulting in a deterioration in the terms of trade. To illustrate, suppose the exchange rate between the Tican peso and U.S. dollar is initially 20 pesos = $1.00 (or 1 peso = $.05). Assume that cotton shirts, a main export of Tico, cost 100 pesos (or $5.00) each to manufacture, and that the laptop computers exported by the United States cost $300 (or 6000 pesos) to produce. The terms of trade for Tico would be 60 cotton shirts per one laptop computer. If the peso depreciates to 30 pesos = $1.00 (or 1 peso = $.033), then, ceteris paribus, the 100-peso cotton shirt from Tico costs $3.33, and the terms of trade for Tico decline to 90 cotton shirts per laptop computer. In other words, a depreciation of the domestic currency means that it takes more exports to purchase a dollar's worth of imports.

In sum, there are advantages to both fixed and flexible exchange rates. The particular circumstances of a developing nation will dictate the type of exchange rate system that is most appropriate. Before exploring some of the criteria involved in the selection, we should take note of other options.

## HYBRID EXCHANGE RATE SYSTEMS

An **adjustable exchange rate** (or adjustable peg) is essentially a fixed exchange rate with provision for resetting the official exchange value of the currency. The Bretton Woods international monetary system of the 1950s and 1960s was an example. In the case of a chronic balance of payments deficit, a nation could devalue its currency. A **devaluation** is a decrease in the official exchange value of a currency. The analogue under a flexible exchange rate is a depreciation. An adjustable peg gives a nation with a BP− an option to the internal deflation of the economy.

Conversely, a nation with a persistent balance of payments surplus, rather than continually intervening in the foreign exchange market with purchases of foreign currencies and thus expanding its domestic money supply, could revalue its currency. A **revaluation** is an increase in the official exchange value of a currency. The analogue under a flexible exchange rate is an appreciation.

A **managed float** is essentially a flexible exchange rate, with market forces determining the exchange values of currencies; however, monetary authorities reserve the option of intervening in the foreign exchange market to influence or manage the extent of exchange rate movements. The IMF has established guidelines for managed floating. In the short run (i.e., on a daily or weekly basis), monetary authorities should intervene to prevent sharp or disruptive exchange rate fluctuations (for example, due to sudden political or economic crises). In the longer run (i.e., on a monthly or quarterly basis), the monetary authorities might intervene to temper the trends in exchange rates by offering modest resistance to market forces. The primary objective is orderly or stable exchange rates. In all cases, monetary authorities should not manipulate their currencies to gain an unfair advantage in trade through, for example, aggressive depreciation.

A third option, albeit little used, is known as a **crawling peg.** Here the exchange value of a currency is adjusted frequently at specified intervals by fixed amounts. Some Latin American nations with a propensity for high inflation have adopted crawling pegs to reduce the stigma and soften the shocks from less frequent, but much larger, devaluations.

## PRESENT EXCHANGE RATE ARRANGEMENTS

In Table 15.2 (on page 470) we summarize the exchange rate arrangements of the 179 members of the International Monetary Fund as of mid-1995. More than half of the nations have floating exchange rates, with various degrees of management. Included in the 36 classified as "managed floating" are China, Egypt, Poland, South Korea, and Turkey. Fifty-nine nations, including all the developed countries outside of the European Monetary System, are "independently floating." Nevertheless, these countries

| TABLE 15.2 | EXCHANGE RATE ARRANGEMENTS OF THE 179 IMF MEMBER NATIONS (JUNE 30, 1995) |

FIXED EXCHANGE RATE (71):

Currency pegged to:

*U.S. dollar* (27): Antigua and Barbuda, Argentina, The Bahamas, Bahrain, Barbados, Belize, Djibouti, Dominica, Grenada, Iraq, Liberia, Lithuania, Marshall Islands, Federated States of Micronesia, Nigeria, Oman, Panama, Qatar, Saudi Arabia, St. Kitts and Nevis, St. Lucia, St. Vincent and the Grenadines, Syrian Arab Republic, Turkmenistan, United Arab Emirates, Venezuela, Republic of Yemen

*French franc* (14): Benin, Burkina Faso, Cameroon, Central African Republic, Chad, Comoros, Congo, Côte d'Ivoire, Equatorial Guinea, Gabon, Mali, Niger, Senegal, Togo

*Other currency* (7): Bhutan (Indian rupee), Estonia (deutsche mark), Kiribati (Australian dollar), Lesotho (South African rand), Namibia (South African rand), San Marino (Italian lira), Swaziland (South African rand)

*Special Drawing Right* (3): Libya, Myanmar, Seychelles

*Other composite currency* (20): Bangladesh, Botswana, Burundi, Cape Verde, Cyprus, Czech Republic, Fiji, Iceland, Jordan, Kuwait, Malta, Mauritania, Morocco, Nepal, Slovak Republic, Solomon Islands, Thailand, Tonga, Vanuatu, Western Samoa

COOPERATIVE ARRANGEMENT (10):
European Monetary System: Austria, Belgium, Denmark, France, Germany, Ireland, Luxembourg, Netherlands, Portugal, Spain

CRAWLING PEG (3):
Chile, Ecuador, Nicaragua

MANAGED FLOATING (36):
Algeria, Angola, Belarus, Brazil, Cambodia, China, Colombia, Croatia, Dominican Republic, Egypt, Eritrea, Georgia, Greece, Guinea-Bissau, Honduras, Hungary, Indonesia, Israel, Lao PDR, Latvia, Macedonia, Malaysia, Maldives, Mauritius, Pakistan, Poland, Russian Federation, Singapore, Slovenia, South Korea, Sri Lanka, Sudan, Tunisia, Turkey, Uruguay, Viet Nam

INDEPENDENTLY FLOATING (59):
Afghanistan, Albania, Armenia, Australia, Azerbaijan, Bolivia, Bulgaria, Canada, Costa Rica, El Salvador, Ethiopia, Finland, The Gambia, Ghana, Guatemala, Guinea, Guyana, Haiti, India, Iran, Italy, Jamaica, Japan, Kazakhstan, Kenya, Kyrgyz Republic, Lebanon, Madagascar, Malawi, Mexico, Moldova, Mongolia, Mozambique, New Zealand, Norway, Papua New Guinea, Paraguay, Peru, Philippines, Romania, Rwanda, Sao Tomé and Principe, Sierra Leone, Somalia, South Africa, Suriname, Sweden, Switzerland, Republic of Tajikistan, Tanzania, Trinidad and Tobago, Uganda, Ukraine, United Kingdom, United States, Uzbekistan, Zaire, Zambia, Zimbabwe

SOURCE: International Monetary Fund, *International Financial Statistics* (September 1995), page 8.

may still intervene in foreign exchange markets at their discretion. Some of the less developed countries classified as independently floating are Iran, Costa Rica, India, Philippines, and Kenya.

Ten of the members of the European Union have a group float, or an adjustable exchange rate mechanism among their currencies, but with floating against nonmember currencies. Three nations, Chile, Ecuador, and Nicaragua, have a crawling peg. The remaining 71 members of the IMF have fixed exchange rates. Included in the 27 developing nations pegged to the U.S. dollar are Argentina, Panama, and Venezuela, several small Caribbean countries, and some of the major oil exporters such as Iraq, Nigeria, and Saudi Arabia. (Note: Most of the international petroleum trade is conducted in dollars.) Pegging to the French franc are former French colonies in Africa. Three countries peg to the SDR, and 20 countries peg to baskets of currencies of their choice. With all the different exchange rate practices, the present international monetary system has been referred to as a "nonsystem."

## CHOOSING AN EXCHANGE RATE SYSTEM

Each nation is free to select an exchange rate arrangement. As noted, the most monetary discipline is required with a fixed exchange rate. Maintaining the official exchange value of the currency becomes a primary responsibility of the monetary authorities. For developing nations, failure to do so usually results in an overvalued currency and exchange controls. An overvalued currency undermines a nation's competitiveness in trade and promotes current account deficits. Exchange controls only perpetuate the shortage in foreign exchange and encourage economically unproductive rent seeking.

A nation opting for a fixed exchange rate may nevertheless gain some flexibility with the choice of the peg. For example, the domestic currency may be tied to a currency (such as the U.S. dollar) or basket of currencies that floats. In general, a developing nation would want to peg to the currency of a major trading partner in order to reduce variability in exchange rates that can discourage trade and investment. More flexibility can be achieved by increasing the width of the band of allowed fluctuation around the official exchange rate. For instance, if the official exchange rate were set at 25 pesos = $1.00, then with a band of plus or minus 2 percent, the exchange rate could vary only between 24.5 and 25.5 pesos to the dollar. A band of plus or minus 8 percent would allow a range of fluctuation between 23 and 27 pesos. The larger the band, the less often the monetary authorities would probably have to intervene in the foreign exchange market.

Even more flexibility will be gained if the nation selects an adjustable peg. Criteria have to be established, however, for the actual resetting of the official exchange rate. Unless there is confidence in the monetary authorities' ability to maintain the official exchange rate, there is the danger of speculative attacks forcing continual devaluations. Large devaluations are unpopular (since the cost of living to consumers of imports rises), and have been known to incite urban riots in developing nations.

A crawling peg brings with it the need to choose a schedule for adjusting the official exchange value of the currency. In the early 1990s Mexico operated with a crawling peg by which the peso was devalued each day by 40 centavos (.4 pesos) against the dollar. With success in reducing inflation and the free trade agreement with the United States and Canada, Mexico then moved to a managed float. In early 1994, political turmoil in Mexico (including the assassination of the leading presidential candidate) prompted heavy selling of pesos on the foreign exchange market. Mexico's international reserves were significantly depleted in attempts to support the peso. Soon after the change in political administrations at the end of 1994, the peso again came under heavy speculative attack, and the new administration switched to a floating exchange rate.[11]

As suggested, a floating exchange rate requires self-imposed monetary discipline to prevent the cycle of inflation and depreciation. Mexico's move to a floating exchange rate was accompanied by economic reforms designed to bolster confidence in the peso. Included in the announced plan were renewed commitments to wage and price moderation, reductions in government spending, and accelerated privatization in the transportation, communications, and financial sectors. In addition, the United States and Canada took the lead in implementing a currency stabilization fund to support the peso and restore order in the foreign exchange market.[12]

Other important considerations in the selection of an exchange rate include the degree of openness of the economy; relative inflation; the synchronization of the economy with international business cycles; vulnerability to large shifts in capital flows; and even the composition of external debt. The openness of an economy can be measured by the share of exports or imports in gross domestic product. More open economies may be more willing to accept the discipline of fixed exchange rates—especially if their currencies are pegged to those of major trading partners. In particular, nations with higher marginal propensities to import require smaller changes in real national income to reduce any given import surplus. (Recall that under a fixed exchange rate system, the balance of payments adjustments occur through changes in interest rates, prices, and real incomes.)

In contrast, nations with chronically high inflation may prefer more flexibility—to avoid the need with a BP– under a fixed exchange rate to deflate periodically the domestic economy. So too, nations subject to sharp swings in international capital flows or volatility in the capital account may opt for flexible exchange rates, which could be continuously adjusting to correct the changing balance of payments.

If an economy were synchronized closely with international business cycles—or with the cycles in its major trading partners—then large balance of payments imbalances might be less likely. That is, if changes in real incomes, interest rates, and price levels are coordinated across countries, then balance of payments disequilibria should be smaller, with less pressure on the exchange rate to adjust. Consequently, a fixed exchange rate system may be more acceptable. Finally, countries with large foreign debt denominated in dollars may want to peg to the dollar in order to avoid an increase in their debt burdens from depreciation in their domestic currencies.

Clearly, many factors must be considered in choosing an exchange rate. In theory, fixed, adjustable, managed floats, and flexible exchange rates all work. How well any one system operates in practice, however, depends on the state of the international political economy; the internal consistency of nations' economic policies; and the degree of coordination between monetary authorities. We now turn to external debt and to the debt problems of the developing nations.

---

[11]For a detailed account of the events leading up to the devaluation of the peso, see David Wessel, Paul Carroll, and Thomas Vogel, "How Mexico's Crisis Ambushed Top Minds in Officialdom, Finance," *Wall Street Journal* (July 6, 1995), pages A1 and A4.

[12]For a summary of the actions taken, see "How We're Handling the Peso Crisis," by Guillermo Ortiz, Finance Minister of Mexico, in *Wall Street Journal* (January 5, 1995), page A14. For a more recent assessment, see "A Survey of Mexico," *The Economist* (October 28, 1995).

## THE EXTERNAL DEBT PROBLEM

Recall from Chapter 10 that foreign saving, reflected in current account deficits, has been an important source of funding for gross domestic investment in developing economies. When a nation runs a current account deficit, foreigners acquire claims on that nation's assets. For developing economies, current account deficits are typically the result of balance of trade deficits and net payments of investment income not offset by net receipts of unilateral transfers.

A current account deficit, however, does not necessarily mean that the nation has increased its foreign indebtedness. For any given exchange rate, a nation may finance a current account deficit by reducing its official holdings of assets (e.g., the sale of foreign currencies by the monetary authorities to produce a surplus on the official settlements account). With a flexible exchange rate, a capital account surplus would offset any current account deficit. A surplus in the capital account can reflect net increases in either equity or debt finance. Foreign direct investment and portfolio investment by which foreigners acquire stock in domestic corporations are types of **equity finance.** The foreign investor has acquired a claim on the net income generated by the domestic corporation. With equity finance, the returns to the foreign investor depend on the success of the venture. In contrast, with **debt finance,** such as bonds or loans, the borrower is obliged to repay the principal plus interest regardless of subsequent economic circumstances. When a borrower does not repay on schedule, the debt instrument is said to be *in arrears.* To the extent current account deficits are covered by debt finance, whether private or official, external debt increases.

### BRIEF HISTORY OF LESS DEVELOPED COUNTRY DEBT

From the end of World War II to the early 1970s, most capital flows to the developing nations consisted of official loans (directly from developed-country governments or channeled through multilateral agencies such as the World Bank); short-term trade credit from foreign exporters (often guaranteed by the same developed-country governments); and foreign direct investment (which, unlike official loans and trade credit, did not add to the external debt of the developing nations). In the 1950s the LDCs also began to receive substantial amounts of foreign aid, which reduced their current account deficits and the need for offsetting surpluses in their capital and official settlements accounts.[13] Even so, problems with repayment of debt did arise, and the Paris Club was set up by the developed countries in 1956 for the purpose of rescheduling debts to official creditors.

---

[13]See Chapter 6, "International Capital Flows," pages 159–202, in Joan Spero, *The Politics of International Economic Relations,* 4th ed., New York: St. Martin's Press, 1990. Another good account of the history of the debt problem is given by John Cuddington, "The Extent and Causes of the Debt Crisis of the 1980s," pages 15–44, in *Dealing with the Debt Crisis,* A World Bank Symposium, edited by Ishrat Husain and Ishac Diwan, Washington, DC: World Bank, 1989. Also, Chapter 1, "Policy Options for Global Adjustment," pages 13–39, in the World Bank's *World Development Report 1988,* New York: Oxford University Press, 1988, provides a useful overview of the events leading up to the debt crisis in the early 1980s and the subsequent economic policies of the developed and less developed countries.

The OPEC (Organization of Petroleum Exporting Countries) price hikes in late 1973 marked the beginning of the sharp increase in private commercial bank lending to the developing nations. With the higher oil prices and the short-run inelastic demand for oil, the oil-exporting nations reaped large current account surpluses, significant portions of which were deposited in Western banks.[14] The banks then extended loans to developing nations to finance the higher current account deficits brought on by the escalating oil-import bills.

The **recycling of petrodollars** seemed to be mutually advantageous. The OPEC nations did not want to bear the risk of lending directly to the LDC oil importers, preferring the safe returns on their funds deposited in Western banks. The banks, flush with deposits, were willing to make loans to the developing countries at rates of interest that were generally higher than could be earned on domestic lending. The LDC governments were eager to borrow in order to finance the import surpluses needed to keep their economies growing. Despite the higher rates of interest on the private loans, fewer conditions were attached than on official loans. In addition, inflation discounted the nominal rates charged, making the real rates of interest quite low, even negative at times. The developing nations also counted on continued growth in export revenues to service their expanding debts. From 1970 to 1975, the total debt of developing nations increased by 150 percent from $67 billion to $167 billion.[15]

By 1976, the international economy had recovered from the stagflation induced by the oil price shocks. The developed nations had followed the lead of the United States in adopting expansionary policies to deal with the rise in unemployment. For the most part, the oil-importing less-developed countries, with the financing of their current account deficits, had been able to maintain healthy rates of economic growth. Inflation, however, remained a concern. In an attempt to protect their real returns from unanticipated inflation, commercial banks began to charge variable rates of interest on their new loans.

In retrospect, the banks might not have paid enough attention to the creditworthiness of the borrowing LDC governments and to the projects funded by the loans.[16] The developing nations, in turn, may not have always used the loans in the most productive ways, that is, to increase their future capacity for repayment. We should also note that not all developing countries received commercial bank lending. The poorer countries continued to rely on foreign aid and official lending. Some of the wealthier Arab OPEC nations did increase substantially the aid given to oil-importing developing economies, especially to other Arab states.[17]

Then, in 1979, the Iranian revolution and the fall of the Shah of Iran set off panic buying to stockpile oil, a second round of oil price hikes, and another burst of inflation.[18] The surging current account deficits required renewed commercial bank lending.

In contrast to the oil price shocks in 1973 to 1974, in which the policy response in the developed countries had been to restore employment levels, the priority now was

---

[14]The international price of a barrel of petroleum quadrupled, from under $3 in late 1972 to nearly $12 by the end of 1973. Subsequently, the current account deficit of the oil-importing LDCs increased from $11.3 billion in 1973 to $46.3 billion in 1975. See Spero, pages 166 and 175.

[15]Cuddington, page 19.

[16]Ibid., page 17.

[17]Spero, page 167.

[18]Ibid., page 175. The international price of a barrel of petroleum reached a high of $35 in 1981. The total current account deficit for oil-importing LDCs rose from $31 billion in 1979 to $119 billion in 1981.

to rein in inflation. In particular, the United States, under its newly appointed chairman of the Federal Reserve, Paul Volcker, embraced contractionary monetary policy. Initially the tighter credit boosted the already elevated nominal interest rates. Interest-sensitive sectors like construction, capital goods, and consumer durables were hit hard. A recession ensued. The deflationary monetary policy, however, contrasted with the expansionary fiscal policy package of tax cuts and increased defense spending set in motion in 1981 by the Reagan administration. Federal budget deficits grew, the financing of which maintained upward pressure on interest rates. In fact, real interest rates in the United States increased, as the decline in nominal interest rates lagged behind the reduction in the inflation rate (from the tighter monetary policy). The high real interest rates attracted foreign capital to the United States, and as the capital account surplus grew, the U.S. dollar appreciated. The stronger dollar, in turn, hurt the competitiveness of the United States; consequently the U.S. current account balance sharply deteriorated into large deficits.

The severe recession of 1981–1982 in the United States spread to other industrialized nations, which were then forced to adopt tighter monetary policies to stem the outflow of savings to the United States. On several fronts the less developed economies—especially the highly indebted nations—were adversely affected.

First, the international rise in interest rates directly increased the debt burdens of the LDCs. Not only did the new loans carry higher rates of interest, but variable rates on existing loans were adjusted upward.

Second, the appreciation of the dollar directly increased the burden of the debt denominated in dollars—since more of the currencies of the developing nations would be required to pay off each appreciated dollar of foreign debt.

Third, the recession in the developed economies reduced the demands for exports from the LDCs. Moreover, a rise in protectionism in the United States and Europe further limited developing-nation exports.

Fourth, the reversal of the run-up in primary product prices from the early 1970s accelerated with the international recession. For many of the poorer developing economies, primary products accounted for the bulk of their export revenues. And, after 1981, oil prices began to fall, a reflection of both lower demands and increased supplies of oil in the world market. The oil exporters were left in a vulnerable position, especially nations like Mexico that had accumulated large foreign debt even as their export revenues were booming.

The impact of this combination of factors was succinctly captured by Mario Simonsen, a former finance minister of Brazil, who concluded that

> the central cause [of the global debt crisis that emerged in late 1982 was] the sudden and unanticipated change in sign in the difference between the growth rate of developing-country exports and international interest rates. From 1974 through 1980 a typical interest rate on developing-country loans, LIBOR [London Interbank Offer Rate] plus 1.5 percent a year spread, averaged 10.7 percent. Meanwhile, exports of nonoil-exporting developing countries were expanding at 21.1 percent, overfulfilling the weak solvency test (that nominal export growth exceed the nominal interest rate). In 1981–82 the interest rate soared to 16.3 percent, while the annual rate of growth of exports declined to 1 percent, challenging any solvency criterion.[19]

---

[19]This quotation is from Cuddington, page 16. The original source is Mario Simonsen, "The Developing-Country Debt Problem," in *International Debt and the Developing Countries,* A World Bank Symposium, edited by Gordon Smith and John Cuddington, Washington, DC: World Bank, 1985, page 120.

## THE DEBT CRISIS AND AFTERMATH

Mexico's announcement in August of 1982, after a 30 percent devaluation of the peso in February of that year, that it could not service its debt was a "shot heard 'round" the financial world. At the time, Mexico's external debt exceeded $85 billion, and included large loans from some major U.S. banks.[20] Quickly the realization set in that other highly indebted developing nations, including Brazil, Argentina, Chile, and Venezuela, were in similar predicaments. The United States responded quickly with official loans to Mexico for balance of payments support. The IMF also extended credit and pushed reluctant commercial banks to make new loans to Mexico, all conditional upon reform of Mexico's economy.

After 1982, however, voluntary commercial bank lending to developing nations was sharply scaled back. Earlier, when developing nations were unable to meet their debt service payments on time, commercial banks would roll over the loans, usually at higher rates of interest, covering the interest and principal due on the old debt with new lending. This allowed the debtor nations to avoid defaulting and kept the loans as performing assets on the balance sheets of commercial banks. Meanwhile, the debt of the developing nations mushroomed. Now, developing nations slipped into arrears, forcing numerous **debt reschedulings,** or postponements of the payments due on the outstanding debt.

Regional differences in the debt of the developing nations should be noted. The greatest exposure of the Western commercial banks was in Latin America, where much of the debt had been incurred on market terms. In sub-Saharan Africa, the other region heavily burdened by foreign debt, most of the loans were official, held by multilateral institutions and governments, usually on softer terms (i.e., concessional interest rates and more generous repayment schedules). In the Middle East and North Africa, the decline in oil prices begun in the early 1980s led to a reversal of the current account surpluses of the oil-producing nations. Asian nations, however, with generally more prudent economic policies, had largely avoided severe debt problems.

Without new lending, the indebted nations were unable to cover their current account deficits. For numerous LDCs, **capital flight** also contributed to their balance of payments difficulties. Especially in Latin America, savings were shifted abroad, not only to take advantage of the high real interest rates in the United States and other developed countries, but in anticipation of devaluations in the domestic currencies. With weak current account balances, often a reflection of overvalued domestic currencies, and insufficient official reserve assets to cover their balance of payments deficits, debtor nations turned to the International Monetary Fund.

As it had for Mexico, the IMF did extend credit to the developing nations, and even persuaded reluctant commercial banks to make additional loans. Such assistance from the IMF, however, was conditional upon the recipient nations' adopting economic reforms.

### The IMF Medicine

The standard prescription of the IMF, consistent with prevailing economic theory, was devaluation; tighter monetary and fiscal policies; and a greater reliance on the market mechanism. To redress overvalued currencies and improve international competitiveness, devaluation was recommended. Fiscal discipline was needed to improve government budget balances and, it was hoped, generate public saving.

---

[20]Spero, pages 180–181.

Tighter monetary policy was necessary to keep inflation down (and real exchange rates from appreciating) and to stimulate saving (with positive real interest rates and through a repatriation of capital from abroad).

Moreover, part of the orthodox stabilization policy involved a shift to more market-oriented policies and private enterprise. Import barriers were to be reduced and exports encouraged. Inefficient and heavily subsidized state-owned enterprises were to be privatized. Price controls were to be dismantled so that resource allocations would respond to market-determined prices. Subsidies for consumption, such as agricultural pricing policies that held down the price of food in urban areas, were to be eliminated. The underlying premise was that the adoption of such measures would not only resolve the balance of payments deficits, but create an environment conducive to sustained economic growth and debt reduction.

Indeed, to reduce foreign indebtedness, a nation has to generate current account surpluses. Recall from Chapter 10 the basic macroeconomic identity, which can be written in terms of the current account balance as:

$$(X - M - R - F) = (S - I) + (T - G)$$

| Current account balance | = | Private domestic saving–investment balance | + | Government budget balance (net public saving) |

For a current account surplus, both sides of the equation have to be positive.

Heavy debt burdens contribute to current account deficits due to the interest payments on the debt $(F\uparrow)$. Receipts of foreign aid, in contrast, work to improve the current account $(R\downarrow)$. For most developing nations, especially in the 1980s, foreign aid could not be counted on to produce current account surpluses. The primary options for improving the current account were expanding exports $(X\uparrow)$ and curbing imports $(M\downarrow)$.

A current account surplus means that the nation is a net saver over the period, that is, $(S - I) + (T - G) > 0$. For a given national income, to realize positive net private saving either personal and business saving must be increased $(S\uparrow)$ or private investment decreased $(I\downarrow)$. Dynamically, net increases in private saving would have to exceed net increases in investment so that $S - I > 0$. Tighter monetary policies that boost the real rate of interest should encourage saving and discourage investment. If real national income is declining from the austerity measures, however, the ability to save will be hampered. Moreover, given the existing low capital–labor ratios in developing economies, reducing investment and physical capital formation diminishes the potential for future growth. On the public side, given the underdeveloped tax systems and the demands for government expenditures—from education to the infrastructure to national defense—realizing a surplus in the government budget is difficult.

The IMF medicine proved tough to swallow for the developing economies. Imposing the austerity measures consistent with economic tightening in nations with low average incomes and prevailing poverty was, to say the least, politically challenging. Urban riots were sparked by the policy reforms required for IMF assistance.[21]

During recessions and periods of structural adjustment, the poor may suffer disproportionately. With little wealth to draw on, the poor are more vulnerable to income losses and cutbacks in government services. For example, evidence from Côte d'Ivoire

---

[21]The cover story for *Time* magazine (July 31, 1989) was on the developing-country debt and the role of the International Monetary Fund. See "The Debt Police," by Howard Chua-Eoan (pages 30–36), for examples of the political unrest associated with austerity measures.

| TABLE 15.3 | GROWTH RATES FOR SEVERELY INDEBTED LDCs OVER THE 1980s | | | |
|---|---|---|---|---|
| | LOW- AND MIDDLE-INCOME ECONOMIES | | SEVERELY INDEBTED COUNTRIES | |
| | 1965–80 | 1980–89 | 1965–80 | 1980–89 |
| AVERAGE ANNUAL GROWTH RATES (%) | | | | |
| Gross Domestic Product | 5.8 | 3.8 | 6.1 | 1.9 |
| Private consumption | 5.3 | 3.5 | 6.1 | 1.8 |
| General government consumption | 6.9 | 3.3 | 6.4 | 2.9 |
| Gross domestic investment | 8.2 | 2.0 | 8.3 | −2.0 |
| Merchandise exports | 3.3 | 5.4 | −.2 | 3.9 |
| Merchandise imports | 5.0 | 1.4 | 5.1 | −1.2 |

NOTES:
The *severely indebted countries* are 20 middle-income economies that are deemed to have encountered severe debt-servicing difficulties. These are defined as countries in which three of the four key ratios are above critical levels: debt to GNP (50 percent); debt to exports of goods and services (275 percent); accrued debt service to exports (30 percent); and accrued interest to exports (20 percent). The 20 countries are Argentina, Bolivia, Brazil, Chile, People's Republic of the Congo, Costa Rica, Côte d'Ivoire, Ecuador, Egypt, Honduras, Hungary, Mexico, Morocco, Nicaragua, Peru, Philippines, Poland, Senegal, Uruguay, and Venezuela.

*Private consumption* is the market value of all goods and services, including durable goods (but excluding dwellings), purchased or received as income-in-kind by households and nonprofit institutions.

*General government consumption* includes all current expenditures for the purchases of goods and services by all levels of government. Capital expenditures on national defense and security are regarded as government consumption.

*Gross domestic investment* consists of outlays on additions to the fixed assets of the economy plus net changes in the level of inventories.

FROM: World Bank, *World Development Report 1991*, New York: Oxford University Press, 1991, Tables 2, 8, 14.

over the second half of the 1980s indicates that as the economic situation deteriorated with the falling export revenues from coffee and cocoa production, the extent and degree of poverty accelerated. In particular, secondary school attendance, especially by girls from poor households, declined significantly.[22]

Furthermore, some inherent contradictions in the policy recommendations may have been perceived by the debtor nations. For one, success in promoting exports depended critically on access to the markets of the developed nations—by no means considered a given by the developing nations (refer to the discussion of international trade policy in Chapter 14). And, given the reliance on tariffs for government revenues, reducing tariff rates—consistent with the move to freer trade—may have seemed counterintuitive to improving the government budget balance.

On occasion, governments, particularly in some of the major Latin American nations, took a hard line, unilaterally announcing limits on the repayment of foreign debt. Threats of a debtor cartel, where debtor nations banded together to present a unified front to their creditors, never materialized. As illustrated by the statistics in Table 15.3, on the whole, the developing nations did adjust to their balance of payments

---

[22]See Christiaan Grootaert, "Poverty and Basic Needs Fulfilment in Africa during Structural Change: Evidence from Côte d'Ivoire," *World Development*, vol. 22, no. 10 (November 1994), pages 1521–1534.

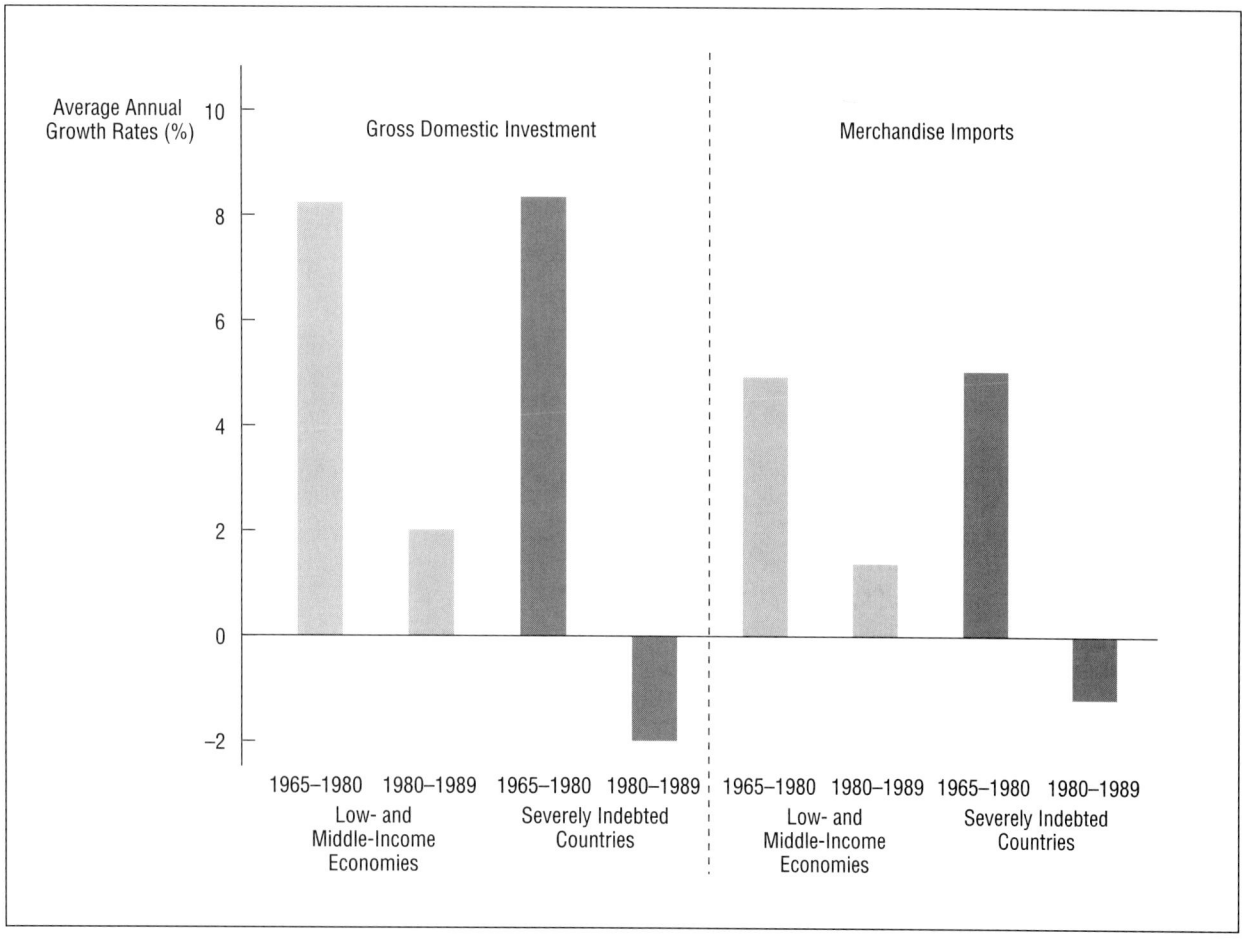

**FIGURE 15.5** AVERAGE ANNUAL GROWTH RATES IN INVESTMENT AND IMPORTS (%)

difficulties during the 1980s. For the severely indebted nations, the economic consequences were dramatic.

For all the developing nations, that is, the low- and middle-income economies, the average growth rates for gross domestic product, private and government consumption, gross domestic investment, and merchandise imports were significantly lower for 1980 to 1989 than for the 1965 to 1980 period. Only for merchandise exports did the average growth rate improve during the 1980s. For the severely indebted nations, the contrasts are even greater. In fact, reflecting the efforts to generate current account surpluses, the average growth rates for gross domestic investment and merchandise imports were negative. The reduced levels of investment spending and imports of the capital goods, intermediate goods, and raw materials needed for production and development projects, not only contributed to the declines in real per capita output, but bode ill for future economic growth.

## THE INCREASES IN EXTERNAL DEBT

Despite the adjustments undertaken and the deterioration in economic performance, the debt burden of the developing world increased. As revealed in Table 15.4, the

### TABLE 15.4    Selected Statistics on External Debt

| | | LOW-INCOME ECONOMIES | | | MIDDLE-INCOME ECONOMIES | TOTAL |
|---|---|---|---|---|---|---|
| | | CHINA | INDIA | OTHER | | |
| TOTAL EXTERNAL DEBT | | | | | | |
| (BILLIONS OF $) | 1980 | 4.5 | 20.6 | 82.9 | 428.9 | 536.9 |
| | 1993 | 83.8 | 91.8 | 264.2 | 1123.8 | 1563.6 |
| COMPOSITION OF TOTAL EXTERNAL DEBT (%) | | | | | | |
| Long-term debt | 1980 | 100 | 89 | 79 | 72 | |
| | 1993 | 84 | 91 | 86 | 78 | |
| Use of IMF credit | 1980 | 0 | 5 | 5 | 1 | |
| | 1993 | 0 | 5 | 3 | 2 | |
| Short-term debt | 1980 | 0 | 6 | 17 | 26 | |
| | 1993 | 16 | 4 | 11 | 19 | |
| SHARE OF LONG-TERM DEBT IN TOTAL ARREARS | | | | | | |
| | 1980 | 0 | 0 | 1 | 0 | |
| | 1993 | 0 | 0 | 15 | 5 | |

NOTES:
    Percentage totals may not sum exactly due to rounding error.
    The external debt of nations that are not members of the World Bank is excluded.

*Long-term debt* has three components. *Public loans* are external obligations of public debtors, including the national government, its agencies, and autonomous public bodies. *Publicly guaranteed loans* are external obligations of private debtors that are guaranteed for repayment by a public entity. *Private nonguaranteed loans* are external obligations of private debtors that are not guaranteed for repayment by a public entity.

*Use of IMF credit* denotes borrowings from the International Monetary Fund from country quotas and from special facilities of the IMF.

*Short-term debt* is debt with an original maturity of one year or less.

*Total arrears on long-term debt* denotes the principal and interest due but not paid.

FROM: These debt statistics are derived from World Bank, *World Development Report 1995*, New York: Oxford University Press, 1995, Table 20.

nominal value of the total external debt of the LDCs nearly tripled from 1980 ($537 billion) to 1993 ($1564 billion). The overwhelming majority is long term; and with the exception of China, a shift has occurred away from short-term debt (under one-year maturity)—especially for the middle-income economies. Although the IMF has played a major role in the adjustments to balance of payments deficits, the use of IMF credit remains a very small percentage of the total external debt. Finally, a sharp increase has taken place in the percentage of long-term debt in arrears—most dramatically for the other low-income countries.

Turning to measures of the debt burden in terms of ratios of debt to national income and debt service to exports, we can see additional evidence in Table 15.5 that the debt problem has not been resolved. For 1993 the ratio of the net present value of total external debt to GNP was over 75 percent for the low-income economies (other than China and India). In general, **debt-service ratios** have increased from 1980 to 1993, notably

| TABLE 15.5 | SELECTED DEBT RATIOS | | | | |
|---|---|---|---|---|---|
| | NET PRESENT VALUE OF TOTAL EXTERNAL DEBT AS A % OF GNP | TOTAL DEBT SERVICE AS A % OF EXPORTS OF GOODS & SERVICES | | MULTILATERAL DEBT AS A % OF TOTAL EXTERNAL DEBT | |
| | 1993 | 1980 | 1993 | 1980 | 1993 |
| INCOME GROUP | | | | | |
| India | 29.1 | 9.3 | 28.0 | 29.5 | 30.3 |
| China | 18.0 | 4.3 | 11.1 | .0 | 12.8 |
| Other low-income | 75.6 | 12.4 | 18.2 | 14.5 | 24.3 |
| Middle-income | 30.8 | ... | 18.8 | ... | 12.0 |
| REGION | | | | | |
| sub-Saharan Africa | 47.4 | 11.6 | 17.1 | 13.0 | 24.5 |
| Middle East & North Africa | 57.7 | 16.5 | 23.1 | 8.3 | 12.1 |
| Europe & Central Asia | 26.5 | ... | 12.4 | ... | 8.2 |
| South Asia | 31.3 | 11.9 | 24.4 | 25.1 | 35.4 |
| East Asia & Pacific | 28.5 | 13.4 | 14.4 | 8.6 | 13.1 |
| Latin America & the Caribbean | 34.0 | 36.9 | 28.1 | 5.8 | 13.2 |
| SELECTED COUNTRIES | | | | | |
| Ghana | 47.6 | 13.1 | 22.8 | 19.9 | 52.0 |
| Sri Lanka | 41.9 | 12.0 | 10.1 | 11.7 | 34.8 |
| Egypt | 70.5 | 14.7 | 14.9 | 12.6 | 8.5 |
| Poland | 49.7 | 17.9 | 9.2 | .0 | 3.2 |
| Costa Rica | 48.1 | 29.1 | 18.1 | 16.4 | 31.5 |
| Brazil | 26.3 | 63.1 | 24.4 | 4.4 | 7.1 |
| South Korea | 13.9 | 19.7 | 9.2 | 8.0 | 6.8 |

NOTES: Lack of data is indicated by ...
*Net present value of total external debt* is the discounted value of future debt service. If the discount rate used is higher (lower) than the interest rates of the loans, then the present value of the debt is less than (greater than) the nominal value of the debt.
*Total debt service* is the sum of principal repayments and interest payments on total external debt. Exports of goods and services here include workers' remittances.
*Multilateral debt* refers to the external debt held by the World Bank, regional development banks, and other multilateral and intergovernmental agencies.

FROM: World Bank, *World Development Report 1995,* New York: Oxford University Press, 1995, Table 23.

for India. For the other low-income economies and the middle-income economies, more than one in every six dollars of export receipts were required to pay off the principal and interest due on foreign debt in 1993. Despite economic tightening that helped to decrease the percentage from 36.9 percent to 28.1 percent over this period, the region of Latin America and the Caribbean still had the highest debt-service ratio.

South Asia, with sub-Saharan Africa a distant second, has the highest percentage of debt owed to multilateral agencies such as the World Bank. For all regions of the developing world, however, the share of multilateral debt rose from 1980 to 1993—in part, a reflection of the relative success of private creditors in reducing their exposures in developing economies.

The diversity in country experiences is also evident in Table 15.5: from a rise in the debt service ratio for Ghana (from 13.1 percent in 1980 to 22.8 percent in 1993) to a dramatic reduction for Brazil (from 63.1 percent in 1980 to 24.4 percent in 1993). Indicative of their respective regions, Ghana and Sri Lanka sharply increased the shares of their debts owed to multilateral agencies.

## RESOLVING THE DEBT PROBLEM

Initially when the debt crisis broke, the hope was that the combination of adverse circumstances responsible (the run-up in interest rates, the international recession, and the sharp declines in commodity prices) would pass. Once the global economy recovered and developing nations adopted appropriate economic reforms, the debt crisis would resolve itself. The immediate priority was to prevent a meltdown in the international banking system from the significant loan exposure of major Western banks in the developing economies.

By the mid-1980s, however, as debt rescheduling became common, the realization set in that the debt phenomenon was not temporary. Moreover, no grand plan or comprehensive strategy existed for dealing with Third World debt. Although recommending the same package of policy reforms for balance of payments adjustment, the IMF and commercial banks had essentially adopted a case-by-case approach, dealing with each debtor nation individually.

In addition to debt rescheduling, strategies have included debt buybacks, debt-for-equity swaps, and even debt-for-nature swaps. With **debt buybacks,** the debtor directly repurchases some of the debt at a discount (i.e., for less than the face value). With **debt-for-equity swaps,** the debtor nation exchanges domestic currency for outstanding debt, again at a discount. The currency is used by the creditor to invest in enterprises in the debtor nation. With **debt-for-nature-swaps,** a group interested in conservation will purchase the debt, and the interest due will be used by the debtor government to preserve the environment (e.g., manage a rainforest).

In 1985, U.S. Secretary of the Treasury James Baker proposed additional lending by commercial banks to select highly indebted nations adopting market-oriented economic reforms. At the 1988 economic summit of the G-7 nations (United States, Canada, Great Britain, Germany, France, Italy, and Japan) in Toronto, a plan to cancel some of the official debt of low-income nations, particularly in sub-Saharan Africa, was announced. Then, in 1989, new U.S. Treasury Secretary Nicholas Brady put forth a plan that would cancel some of the debt of those severely indebted nations embracing market-oriented reforms. The schemes, limited in funding and coverage, have made only marginal contributions to resolving the debt problem.

For their part, commercial banks in the West have been writing down (discounting) some of their outstanding loans to developing nations. Secondary markets exist for the resale of the sometimes heavily discounted external debt. The trade-off between the amount of debt owed by the developing nations and the likelihood and extent of repayment has been acknowledged. In fact, as some of the debt is cancelled (through discounting or otherwise), the expected value of the still outstanding debt obligations may rise—since, with a reduction of the debt burden, the chances for renewed economic growth may increase, as would the ability, and perhaps willingness, to pay back the remaining debt.

Significant obstacles to resolving the debt problem persist, however. Controversy abounds. For instance, should there be universal formulas for debt relief—given the different circumstances and policies of the debtor nations? In particular, should the higher-income Latin American nations, with greater proportions of debt held by private creditors, and, in some cases, with private assets held abroad that rival their external debts, receive the same treatment as the low-income African nations that have relied on official loans?[23] Would an equal percentage reduction in the public debt owed (as in the tariff-cutting formulas used in the GATT multilateral trade negotiations) be fair to those developing nations that have struggled to reduce their debts, compared to those nations that have continued their spendthrift ways?

There is also a *free-rider* problem on the creditor side. As official loans are forgiven, the ability to repay the outstanding private loans is enhanced (along with the market value of the private loans). In effect, taxpayers in the creditor countries who subsidize the multilateral institutions are also bailing out the private banks. For the same reason, some banks may hold back from any large-scale effort to write off debt, preferring to keep their loans intact, and benefiting from the reduction in claims of the participating banks.

New institutions have been proposed to deal with the debt problem. Peter Kenen suggested an International Debt Discount Corporation, established through subscriptions by the major developed countries, to exchange, at a discount, the debts of developing economies held by commercial banks for guaranteed long-term bonds.[24] Jeffrey Sachs advocates an International Debt Facility to reduce systematically the interest rates on the outstanding debt to below-market levels. Rather than a reduction of the principal through discounting, the principal would be rescheduled and fully repayable.[25]

Jeremy Bulow and Kenneth Rogoff argue against such debt relief, especially when more effective development aid might be compromised. They believe the "debt problem is better viewed as a symptom of poor growth rather than its primary cause," and further maintain that

> Development aid should be divorced from debt negotiations and instead should be tied to countries' performance in areas such as environmental policy, drug interdiction and population control. Future aid allocations should not be disguised as loan guarantees, and the massive bond obligations of existing multilateral lenders ought to be placed on the books.[26]

Whether the result of debt fatigue (a weariness brought on by the seeming intractability of the problem) or displacement by the dramatic post–Cold War changes occurring in former socialist nations, the debt crisis has moved off center stage. However, as an article appearing in the *Wall Street Journal* in October 1994 observed,

---

[23] For a contrast of the circumstances of the two groups of debtor nations of greatest concern, the low-income African nations and the highly indebted countries, see Jonathan Eaton, "Debt Relief and the International Enforcement of Loan Contracts," *Journal of Economic Perspectives*, vol. 4, no. 1 (winter 1990), pages 43–56.

[24] Peter Kenen, "Organizing Debt Relief: The Need for a New Institution," in *Journal of Economic Perspectives*, vol. 4, no. 1 (winter 1990), pages 7–18.

[25] Jeffrey Sachs, "A Strategy for Efficient Debt Reduction," *Journal of Economic Perspectives*, vol. 4, no. 1 (winter 1990), pages 19–30.

[26] Jeremy Bulow and Kenneth Rogoff, "Cleaning up Third World Debt Without Getting Taken to the Cleaners," *Journal of Economic Perspectives*, vol. 4, no. 1 (winter 1990), pages 31–42. The quotations are from page 32.

the debt crisis lingers and is worsening in many of the world's poorest countries. The World Bank lists 32 states that qualify as "severely indebted low-income countries," or Silics. The bulk of the Silics are in sub-Saharan Africa, the one region in the world where the ranks of the poor are increasing ...

and

United Nations Secretary-General Boutros-Ghali calls the debts "a millstone around the neck of Africa ... and a major obstacle to the return of private investment." In addition, heavy debt burdens make needed trade credits scarce and costly."[27]

## CONCLUDING NOTE

A satisfactory resolution to the developing-country debt dilemma remains elusive. Will substantial debt cancellation be necessary? Or will the debt burden be reduced to manageable proportions with policy reforms, economic growth, and the freer trade anticipated from the Uruguay Round? Should we even expect economic growth and development in countries with debt service ratios of 20 percent and more?

In Chapter 16 we address foreign investment and foreign aid, two highly controversial issues related to the debt of developing nations.

## SUMMARY OF MAIN POINTS

1. The balance of payments account records a nation's international economic transactions. Credits represent the value of the goods, services, and assets sold or transferred to the rest of the world. Debits represent the value of the goods, services, and assets purchased or acquired from the rest of the world.
2. The foreign demand for a nation's goods, services, and assets generates a demand for that nation's currency and a supply of foreign currencies to the nation. A nation's demand for foreign goods, services, and assets generates the nation's demand for foreign currencies and the supply of that nation's currency on the foreign exchange market.
3. Three major subaccounts are identified in the overall balance of payments account. The current account includes trade in goods and services, investment income flows, and unilateral transfers. The capital account covers the exchange of assets, both real and financial. The official settlements account records the transfer of official assets, including official reserve assets.

---

[27]Tim Carrington, "Debt Crisis in the Developing Countries Appears to be Forgotten but Not Gone," *Wall Street Journal* (October 17, 1994), page A10. For an update on the status of the LDC debt held by commercial banks, see IMF Staff, "Progress Report on Commercial Bank Debt Restructuring," *Finance and Development*, vol. 32, no. 4 (December 1995), pages 14–15.

4. A nation with a current account surplus (deficit) is a net importer (exporter) of assets over that period. That is, a nation with a current account surplus acquires net claims on the assets of the rest of the world; while for a nation with a current account deficit, the rest of the world acquires net claims on that nation's assets.
5. A balance of payments surplus (deficit) indicates an excess of credits (debits) over debits (credits) on the combined current and capital accounts of a nation. A balance of payments surplus (deficit) must be offset by a deficit (surplus) on the official settlements account.
6. An exchange rate is the price of one currency expressed in units of a second currency. Under a flexible exchange rate system, the demand and supply of that nation's currency in the foreign exchange market, reflecting the credits and debits, respectively, on the nation's balance of payments account, determine the exchange value of the nation's currency. Under a fixed exchange rate system, the government sets an official exchange value for its currency, which, in theory, it is obligated to maintain.
7. A depreciation (appreciation) of a currency reflects a fall (rise) in its foreign exchange value due to an excess supply (demand) of the currency on the foreign exchange market—in turn, an indication of a balance of payments deficit (surplus) for the nation.
8. The demand curve for foreign currencies is downward-sloping, indicating an inverse relationship between the quantity demanded of foreign currencies and the price of foreign currencies (in units of the domestic currency). The supply curve of foreign currencies is upward-sloping (as long as the foreign demand for the nation's goods and services is price-elastic), indicating that a depreciation of the currency would increase the quantity supplied of foreign currencies to the nation. Underlying the demand and supply of foreign currencies to a nation are domestic and foreign real income levels, price levels, and interest rates, the expected exchange rate, and official intervention in the foreign exchange market.
9. Exchange controls have been used to ration the excess quantity demanded of foreign currencies when a nation has a balance of payments deficit and a fixed exchange rate. Adverse consequences from exchange controls include rent seeking, the emergence of a black market in foreign exchange, and the postponement of the internal economic adjustments necessary to correct the balance of payments deficit.
10. Balance of payments deficits indicate a need for tighter economic policies, in particular, contractionary monetary policy to increase interest rates, reduce inflation, and lower the growth rate of real national income. Balance of payments surpluses, in contrast, call for expansionary economic policies.
11. The advantages of flexible over fixed exchange rates include the automatic and continuous adjustment of the exchange rate to restore a balance of payments equilibrium and the freeing of monetary policy to promote price stability and full employment. The primary disadvantages of a flexible exchange rate are volatility in exchange rates, which can dampen international trade and investment, and an inflationary bias, due to the lack of monetary discipline.
12. An adjustable exchange rate is basically a fixed exchange rate that can be adjusted or reset in the case of a persistent balance of payments disequilibrium. A managed float is basically a flexible exchange rate with the monetary authorities intervening in the foreign exchange market to modify movements in the exchange rate.
13. Under the present international monetary system, each nation can select its exchange rate practice. Factors that favor a flexible exchange rate include a

relatively closed economy; comparatively high inflation; a high degree of vulnerability to volatile capital flows; and an economy not in synchronization with the business cycles of its major trading partners.

14. The external debt problems of less developed countries had their origins in the 1970s, with the recycling of petrodollars following the oil price shocks. The debt problems became a crisis in the early 1980s with the general rise in international interest rates; the appreciation of the U.S. dollar; and the recessions in the developed nations that reduced the demands for LDC exports. The developing economies, particularly in Latin America, experienced economic stagnation during the 1980s with the adoption of austerity programs to improve their balance of payments.

15. Numerous proposals have been advanced for resolving the debt problems of the less developed countries, including debt buybacks, debt-for-equity swaps, debt-for-nature swaps, and debt cancellation for the adoption of economic reforms. No comprehensive solution to the debt problems of the developing nations, however, has been adopted. Instead, a case-by-case approach has typically been used.

## KEY TERMS

adjustable exchange rate
appreciation
balance of payments account (BPA)
balance of payments deficit (BP–)
balance of payments surplus (BP+)
balance of trade (BT)
capital account (KA)
capital account balance
capital flight
crawling peg
credits
currency board
current account (CA)
current account balance
debits
debt buybacks
debt finance
debt-for-equity swaps

debt-for-nature swaps
debt rescheduling
debt-service ratio
depreciation
devaluation
equity finance
exchange controls
fixed exchange rate system
flexible exchange rate system
foreign direct investment
foreign portfolio investment
managed float
official reserve assets
official settlements account (OSA)
recycling of petrodollars
revaluation
Special Drawing Rights (SDRs)
unilateral transfers

## QUESTIONS

1. What does a current account deficit indicate in terms of the basic macroeconomic identity? What does a current account deficit indicate within the overall balance of payments account? Should developing economies seek to avoid current account deficits at all costs? Discuss.

2. What is a balance of payments deficit? What are the consequences for an economy with a balance of payments deficit and a flexible exchange rate? What are the consequences for an economy with a balance of payments deficit and a fixed exchange rate?

3. Select a less developed country and, given its economic conditions, recommend whether a fixed or flexible exchange rate should be adopted. Justify your recommendations.
4. For a less developed country with the rupee as its currency, and using the supply and demand curves for dollars (representing foreign currencies in general), illustrate graphically the ways a depreciation in the rupee could occur.
5. For a less developed country with the rupee as its currency, and given the demand and supply curves for dollars (representing foreign currencies in general)

$$Q_\$^d = 500 - 10P_\$ \quad \text{and} \quad Q_\$^s = -100 + 20P_\$$$

where $Q_\$^d$ and $Q_\$^s$ are the quantities demanded and supplied of $ (in thousands of dollars per day) and $P_\$$ is the rupee price of the dollar or the exchange rate.
  a. Determine the market equilibrium exchange rate.
  b. Now suppose new demand and supply curves exist for dollars, given by

$$Q_\$^{d'} = 600 - 10P_\$ \quad \text{and} \quad Q_\$^{s'} = -300 + 20P_\$$$

  What could cause such shifts in the demand and supply curves of dollars? If the nation had a flexible exchange rate, find the new market equilibrium exchange rate.
  c. Suppose instead that the nation had a fixed exchange rate of 20 rupees equals $1.00 and an allowed band of fluctuation from 15 to 25 rupees to the dollar. What would the monetary authorities of the nation have to do in terms of foreign exchange intervention in the short run given the new demand and supply curves for dollars in Question 5b? Be specific. In the longer run, what economic policies are suggested? Why?
  d. Explain how exchange controls would work in Question 5c. Discuss the consequences of exchange controls.
6. Is the IMF medicine justified for a developing economy with large balance of payments deficits? Discuss.
7. Should a multilateral debt conference be held to discuss a comprehensive and uniform solution to the debt problems of the less developed countries? Or should the case-by-case approach be continued? Discuss.
8. What would you propose to deal with the external debt problems of the LDCs? Why?

## SUGGESTED READINGS

Bulow, Jeremy and Kenneth Rogoff, "Cleaning up Third World Debt Without Getting Taken to the Cleaners," *Journal of Economic Perspectives*, vol. 4, no. 1 (winter 1990), pages 31–42.

Chua-Eoan, Howard, "The Debt Police," *Time* (July 31, 1989), pages 30–36.

Cuddington, John, "The Extent and Causes of the Debt Crisis of the 1980s," *Dealing with the Debt Crisis, A World Bank Symposium*, edited by Ishrat Husain and Ishac Diwan, Washington, DC: World Bank, 1989, pages 15–44.

Eaton, Jonathan, "Debt Relief and the International Enforcement of Loan Contracts," *Journal of Economic Perspectives*, vol. 4, no. 1 (winter 1990), pages 43–56.

Kenen, Peter, "Organizing Debt Relief: The Need for a New Institution," *Journal of Economic Perspectives*, vol. 4, no. 1 (winter 1990), pages 7–18.

Rogoff, Kenneth, "Symposium on New Institutions for Developing Country Debt," *Journal of Economic Perspectives*, vol. 4, no. 1 (winter 1990), pages 3–6.

Sachs, Jeffrey, "A Strategy for Efficient Debt Reduction," *Journal of Economic Perspectives*, vol. 4, no. 1 (winter 1990), pages 19–30.

Spero, Joan, "International Capital Flows," *The Politics of International Economic Relations*, 4th ed., New York: St. Martin's Press, 1990, pages 159–202.

World Bank, "Policy Options for Global Adjustment," *World Development Report 1988*, New York: Oxford University Press, 1988, pages 13–39.

# CHAPTER 16

# FOREIGN DIRECT INVESTMENT AND FOREIGN AID

The Third World is the creation of foreign aid: without foreign aid there is no Third World.[1]

If economic growth and development are constrained by shortages of physical capital, technology, foreign exchange, entrepreneurship, and public administrative skills, then why are foreign direct investment and foreign aid—vehicles for transferring these scarce factors—controversial? In truth, we find both vocal advocates and opponents of foreign investment and aid. There are also vast numbers in a middle camp who acknowledge the potential for both good and ill from the foreign investment and aid.

We begin with foreign direct investment. An overview of the extent of foreign direct investment in the contemporary developing economies is provided. We then focus on transnational corporations and the factors determining their location of foreign subsidiaries in developing economies. The advantages and disadvantages of foreign direct investment are discussed from the perspectives of both the transnational corporations and host countries.

Then we examine foreign aid, or official development assistance. The arguments for and against foreign assistance are reviewed, with examples in support of both positions. A brief history of aid in the post–World War II era is given, and the major international agencies involved in aid are identified. The special assistance provided through nongovernmental organizations is also addressed. We conclude the chapter with an assessment of the effectiveness of foreign aid and with proposals for reform.

---

[1]P. T. Bauer, "Foreign Aid and Its Hydra-Headed Rationalization," in *Equality, the Third World, and Economic Delusion,* Cambridge, MA: Harvard University Press, 1981, page 87.

## FOREIGN DIRECT INVESTMENT

As stated in Chapter 15, **foreign direct investment (FDI)** refers to the acquisition of real (or tangible) assets in a foreign country. The purchase of a domestic firm by a foreign investor, including the purchase of stock in domestic corporations in which the foreign investor has significant equity (usually defined as ownership of 10 percent or more of the company) is one example. The establishment of a new business in a foreign country is a second. Other examples are the construction of a new plant or additions to the existing stocks of machinery and equipment by foreign investors. In each case, the potential for profits provides the primary incentive for investment.[2]

The 1990s have witnessed rapid growth in foreign direct investment in the less developed countries. In 1993 developing economies received about 40 percent of world FDI flows, up from 33 percent in 1992—the highest shares of FDI going to the LDCs in over two decades.[3] Reasons for the increased FDI in the developing nations include the successful conclusion of the Uruguay Round of multilateral trade negotiations; the adoption of economic liberalization measures by many LDCs (in particular, the encouragement of foreign investment); and the growing recognition in the developed nations of the potential for rapid growth in these emerging markets.

The flows of FDI to the developing nations, however, have been unevenly distributed. The Asian-Pacific and Latin American-Caribbean regions have been the favored recipients, accounting for some 80 percent of the FDI flows to developing nations in the early 1990s.[4] With a few exceptions, the former socialist states of Eastern Europe and the Soviet Union have not attracted much FDI—due to the more-difficult-than-anticipated conversions to market-oriented systems and economies characterized by, among other factors, declining outputs, high inflation, and weak financial and legal institutions. Africa and the least developed countries in all regions have lagged well behind in FDI inflows. (In Chapter 18 we specifically address the development challenge in Africa.) The reasons for the poor performance in attracting FDI in the least developed countries include:

> the falling global demand for most of their primary exports, often coupled with high levels of external indebtedness; their persistently small domestic investment and slow economic growth; their small domestic markets; their poorly developed physical infrastructure, often including difficult and expensive transport and communication links with the outside world; and a poorly skilled labor force. In a number of least

---

[2]The acquisition of property or real estate by foreigners for residential purposes would also be considered foreign direct investment, although the primary motivation may be personal consumption.

[3]From *World Investment Report 1994: Transnational Corporations, Employment and the Workplace,* United Nations Conference on Trade and Development, Division on Transnational Corporations and Investment, New York: United Nations, 1994, pages 9–11. Globally, foreign direct investment has increased five times faster than international trade and 10 times faster than world output since 1983. See "A Survey of Multinationals," *The Economist* (June 24, 1995), page 3. For a concise overview of recent trends in FDI, see Joel Bergsman and Xiaofang Shen, "Foreign Direct Investment in Developing Countries: Progress and Problems," *Finance and Development,* vol. 32, no. 4 (December 1995), pages 6–8.

[4]United Nations Conference on Trade and Development. These statistics are derived from Table I.8, page 19.

| TABLE 16.1 | SELECTED STATISTICS ON FOREIGN DIRECT INVESTMENT IN THE LDCs | | | |
|---|---|---|---|---|
| | NET FOREIGN DIRECT INVESTMENT (MILLION $) 1993 | POPULATION (MILLIONS) 1993 | NET FOREIGN DIRECT INVESTMENT PER CAPITA ($) 1993 | GNP PER CAPITA ($) 1993 |
| INCOME GROUP | | | | |
| India | 273 | 898.2 | 0.3 | 300 |
| China | 25,800 | 1178.4 | 21.9 | 490 |
| Other low-income economies | 2,757 | 1016.1 | 2.7 | 300 |
| Middle-income economies | 35,699 | 1596.3 | 22.4 | 2480 |
| Total | 64,529 | 4689.0 | 13.8 | 1090 |
| TOP 10 NATIONS (AFTER CHINA) | | | | |
| Argentina | 6,305 | 33.8 | 186.5 | 7220 |
| Mexico | 4,901 | 90.0 | 54.5 | 3610 |
| Malaysia | 4,351 | 19.0 | 229.0 | 3140 |
| Thailand | 2,400 | 58.1 | 41.3 | 2110 |
| Hungary | 2,349 | 10.2 | 230.3 | 3350 |
| Indonesia | 2,004 | 187.2 | 10.7 | 740 |
| Poland | 1,715 | 38.3 | 44.8 | 2260 |
| Portugal | 1,301 | 9.8 | 132.8 | 9130 |
| Czech Republic | 950 | 10.3 | 92.2 | 2710 |
| Nigeria | 900 | 105.3 | 8.6 | 300 |

NOTES:

*Net foreign direct investment* is defined as investment that is made by foreigners in the country to acquire a lasting interest (usually 10 percent of the voting stock) in an enterprise operating in the country. The purpose of the investment is to acquire an effective voice in the management of the enterprise.

FROM World Bank, *World Development Report 1995*, New York: Oxford University Press, 1995, Tables 1 and 22.

developed countries political instability and, in some cases, violence and civil strife have become prohibitive deterrents to FDI.[5]

In Table 16.1 we present some recent statistics on FDI in the low- and middle-income economies. In general, the top recipients of net foreign direct investment are the more populous countries and the higher-income economies that offer the bigger markets. China alone attracted roughly two out of every five dollars of net FDI in the developing economies in 1993. After China, the next top 10 recipients accounted for 70 percent of the remaining FDI.[6] All but one of these 10 nations, Nigeria, were

---

[5]Ibid., page 62.

[6]From 1981 to 1992 the share of the top 10 recipients in annual flows of FDI to the developing nations has varied between 66 percent and 81 percent. See United Nations Conference on Trade and Development, page 13.

middle-income economies. Clearly the distribution of foreign direct investment in the developing world is highly concentrated.

Of the top 11 LDCs, the per capita receipts of FDI in 1993 ranged from $8.6 for Nigeria to $230.3 for Hungary. Fifteen of the 102 low- and middle-income economies with populations over one million had zero net foreign direct investment, and four LDCs had negative net foreign direct investment.[7]

## TRANSNATIONAL CORPORATIONS

The most obvious manifestations of foreign direct investment are the foreign subsidiaries established by transnational corporations (TNCs), also known as multinational corporations (MNCs). Transnational corporations are major players in the international economy.

> During the early 1990s, at least 37,000 parent firms controlled over 206,000 foreign affiliates. Over 90 per cent of these parent firms are based in developed countries—a share broadly similar to these countries' share of outward FDI stocks and flows.[8]

In fact, an estimated one-third of international trade is intrafirm, or between foreign subsidiaries and the parent companies. Roughly 80 percent of international payments for royalties and fees, indicative of technology transfers, are on an intrafirm basis.[9]

A corporation becomes transnational when its production and sales extend across countries. As such, legal status and political jurisdiction become complex.

> Because firms cannot be incorporated through a global charter, the TNC as a whole has no legal personality and therefore possesses no formal nationality. Politically, TNCs are generally associated with the State in which their parent firms' headquarters are located, an image that can be reinforced if that country also claims some extraterritorial jurisdiction over the parent firms' foreign operations. On the other hand, individual foreign affiliates gain legal standing as conferred by each host country's government under the laws of that State.[10]

A desire for better integration of operations often drives foreign direct investment. **Vertical integration** involves different stages of production of a final good. With *backward integration* foreign subsidiaries may be established to supply inputs (e.g., needed raw materials or intermediate goods) on favorable terms. Examples may be oil companies such as Exxon with its own overseas refineries, and automobile companies such as Ford with parts factories located abroad. With *forward integration*, foreign subsidiaries may be used for the assembly of imported components

---

[7]The four countries with negative net foreign direct investment for 1993 are Jordan (−$34 million); Panama (−$41 million); Iran (−$50 million); and Cameroon (−$81 million). Negative net foreign direct investment denotes a withdrawal of foreign direct investment or foreign disinvestment in a country. See World Bank, *World Development Report 1995,* New York: Oxford University Press, 1995, Table 22.

[8]United Nations Conference on Trade and Development, page 3.

[9]Ibid., pages xxi–xxii.

[10]Ibid., page 320.

for re-export back to the home country (such as IBM might do with computer keyboards).

**Horizontal integration** involves replication of a given stage of production. Here foreign subsidiaries may be spin-offs of the parent company and produce essentially the same good or service, with perhaps modifications to cater to local demands. Examples would be McDonald's restaurants or Blockbuster video stores in foreign countries.

The decision to undertake FDI reflects a number of considerations. For example, in the case of manufactured products, say bicycles, a company headquartered in France has the option of producing at home and exporting to Ghana, or opening up production facilities in Ghana. Assuming the demand for bicycles in Ghana is sufficiently high, then distance to the markets and the attendant transportation costs—a function of the weight and bulkiness of the products to be shipped—become factors. So, too, if Ghana has adequate input supplies (e.g., steel and rubber for the bicycle frames and tires), then it becomes more attractive to set up production in the local economy.

If trade barriers exist, such as import tariffs or quotas on bicycles, then locating production facilities in Ghana may be advantageous. Indeed, a motivation for much foreign direct investment has been to get behind tariffs and quotas. With the signing of NAFTA, Mexico attracted additional interest from TNCs seeking favorable access to the United States and Canadian markets.

## LOCATION OF FOREIGN SUBSIDIARIES

Given the decision to integrate operations across national borders, where to locate depends on a comparison of economic and political conditions. While labor typically constitutes the major cost of production, it is not the case that FDI will automatically go to the low-wage countries. The relevant comparison is based on **unit labor costs,** or the comprehensive labor cost per unit of output.

$$\text{Unit labor cost} = \frac{\text{Average cost of labor}}{\text{Average product of labor}}$$

$$= \frac{\text{Comprehensive wage per unit of labor}}{\text{Output produced per unit of labor}}$$

The average cost of labor encompasses not only the compensation directly received by the workers, but the associated employer costs, including social insurance taxes, pension fund contributions, and health-care benefits. The average product, or labor productivity, reflects not only the education and skills of the employees, but the complementary input of physical capital; the level of technology; essential services such as electricity and water; the adequacy of the transportation and communications systems; and local labor conditions, especially the frequency of work stoppages.

Consider a widget producer that has narrowed the choice of locating a manufacturing plant down to three countries. The expected labor costs and productivities are listed below. We assume the quality of the widgets produced is identical in all three locations.

|  | Country 1 | Country 2 | Country 3 |
|---|---|---|---|
| Average cost of labor ($ per hour) | $1 | $4 | $10 |
| Average product of labor (widgets per hour) | 5 widgets | 40 widgets | 80 widgets |
| Unit labor cost ($ per widget) | $.20 per widget | $.10 per widget | $.125 per widget |

Ceteris paribus, the company would locate in Country 2, which has neither the lowest wage nor the highest labor productivity, but does have the lowest unit labor cost, at $.10 per widget.

The returns to foreign direct investment are also determined by tax rates and government regulations in the host country. Differing markedly across countries can be the effective tax rate on company profits; restrictions on the repatriation of profits; access to foreign exchange; requirements for the hiring of local labor; and environmental, health, and safety regulations.

Economic and political risk assessments are crucial in the decision to locate foreign subsidiaries. Is the national economy stable? Will inflation be kept under control? Do inefficient or corrupt government bureaucracies significantly add to the cost of doing business in the country? Is the political system stable? Will future governments in the country be as receptive to foreign investment? Are cultural conditions so different or the lack of amenities so severe as to be unacceptable for the expatriate managers of the foreign subsidiary? Clearly these questions have to be addressed before a company undertakes significant foreign direct investment in any nation, particularly in the developing countries, where, typically, the uncertainty is greater.

## FOREIGN DIRECT INVESTMENT AND THE LESS DEVELOPED COUNTRIES

International factor mobility enhanced through foreign direct investment should promote a more efficient allocation of resources. To the extent that factors are employed in their most productive uses, irrespective of national borders, gains in output and income are realized. As we illustrated in Chapter 14, the higher returns to capital, reflecting its relative scarcity, should attract foreign direct investment to labor-abundant, developing economies. We noted that the motivation for foreign investment by transnational corporations is the enhancement of profits. We turn now to the benefits for less developed countries receiving FDI.

### Advantages of FDI for Developing Economies

Perhaps the primary advantage of foreign direct investment for a country is the inflow of scarce factors. TNCs, as a primary vehicle for foreign direct investment, bring not only physical capital, but new technology, managerial talent, international marketing expertise, and increased access to international financial capital. Output and employment in the host or recipient country should be stimulated, directly from the production and hiring by the foreign subsidiary and indirectly with the multiplier effects from the spending of the income generated in the economy.

Derived demands may be created, especially through backward linkages to other sectors of the economy. For example, the manufacturing of bicycles or motor scooters would increase the demands for steel, rubber, and plastics, and for nuts and bolts, helmets, and tire pumps.

Foreign direct investment should initially improve the balance of payments, with the credits on the capital account helping to offset current account deficits. Furthermore, if the subsidiary produces for export or replaces imports, the balance of trade and the current account will be bolstered. In short, the TNC may help developing economies generate foreign exchange.

The transnational corporation should also generate tax revenues, not only on the subsidiary's profits and salaries of employees, but from the sales taxes on the output produced. Consequently, the government budget balance should improve.

Additional physical capital formation will occur in the economy if the TNC reinvests the profits of the foreign subsidiary to expand plant and machinery. Human capital formation will take place with the training of labor hired by the foreign subsidiary. The labor skills acquired may diffuse throughout the economy if workers leave the employment of the TNC for local businesses. So, too, there may be a general transfer of technology if the knowledge brought in by the TNC disseminates throughout the economy.

## POTENTIAL DISADVANTAGES OF FDI FOR DEVELOPING ECONOMIES

With the arrival of transnational corporations comes a sacrifice of some control over the national economy to foreigners. When objectives conflict, potential for discord exists. Typically, the TNC seeks to maximize profits of the parent corporation, and not necessarily the profits of each foreign subsidiary. The host country, in turn, has development objectives, including expanding employment, generating income, and improving the balance of payments. In addition, other national concerns may be important, such as environmental preservation and respect for local culture and traditions. The different agendas of the TNC and government of the host country may clash.

In general, from the point of view of the host country, the benefits of FDI and the presence of transnational corporations are diminished when the foreign subsidiaries displace or discourage local or indigenous businesses. For instance, neither employment gains nor new capital formation may occur when a domestic enterprise comes under the control of foreign investors—indeed, less of a reliance on local management and labor may actually result. The TNC, with superior resources, is often a better credit risk, and may be a heavy demander of loanable funds, crowding out domestic firms seeking to borrow. The TNC may set wage rates for its employees well above market equilibrium levels in order to attract and retain the most qualified labor. The wage scale of the transnational corporation may put upward pressure on urban wages, restricting urban employment while increasing the attractiveness of labor migration from rural areas.

If the developing country makes tax concessions to attract FDI, then any hoped-for improvement in the government budget balance would be less. The technology brought by the transnational corporation may reflect the capital-abundant conditions in the country of the parent company, and may well be inappropriate for the labor-surplus developing economies. If the foreign subsidiary relies on imported intermediate and capital goods, improvement in the current account balance and the establishment of backward linkages to domestic enterprises may be undermined. In effect, the TNC may create a modern enclave of high-technology, capital-intensive production that is isolated from the rest of the developing economy.

The foreign subsidiary's expatriates and their families may not respect local customs and thus engage in disruptive and culturally offensive behavior. Moreover, the lifestyle and consumption standards of the expatriates may have an unhealthy demonstration effect on the local population, thereby creating unrealistic consumer aspirations and tension. The importation of consumer goods for the expatriates would reduce the ability of the nation to import more productive goods.

A widely publicized example of inappropriate and even dangerous conduct involved the Swiss transnational corporation Nestlé, and the aggressive marketing of infant formula in less developed countries during the early 1970s. At the time, concern over the decline of breastfeeding in the Third World was associated, in part, with the promotion of infant formula. (As discussed in Chapter 8, substantial nutritional, health, and economic benefits come from breastfeeding, particularly in environments in which incomes are low and sanitary conditions poor.) Free samples of infant formula were distributed and mothers were exhorted to switch to more "modern methods of infant care." To save money, some mothers stretched the formula by diluting it with water, often contaminated. Lack of refrigeration contributed as well to the unsanitary preparation and storage of the formula. Stories of infants fed with formula becoming malnourished, ill, and even dying, surfaced. Nestlé was roundly condemned. The controversy simmered for years. In 1981, at an international forum, a code of conduct drafted by the World Health Organization for the marketing of infant formula was approved overwhelmingly, with only one nation, the United States, abstaining.[11]

The transnational corporation may take advantage of lax environmental, health, and safety regulations in order to gain a competitive advantage in trade. Rather than reinvesting the profits of the foreign subsidiary to expand the physical capital stock in the domestic economy, the TNC may withdraw profits. Even if the host country has capital controls, through intrafirm trade and transfer pricing the TNC can shift profits back to the parent corporation.

**Transfer pricing** refers to the manipulation of invoices on intrafirm international trade to shift profits between nations. To illustrate, suppose a transnational corporation, International Widget, wants to withdraw $16 million in profits from its foreign subsidiary in Tico. Perhaps the tax rates on profits are higher in Tico than in the home country or perhaps International Widget desires to reinvest the profits elsewhere. If Tico has a limit on the repatriation of profits of $10 million per year, and if there are substantial flows of trade between the parent company and the foreign subsidiary, then the additional $6 million in profits could be transferred out of Tico, for example, by overstating the invoice value of the goods and services sold by the parent company to its subsidiary by, say $4 million, and understating the invoice value of the exports from the foreign subsidiary to the parent company by $2 million. In effect, the exports of Tico

---

[11]For Nestlé's account of the controversy, see "The Dilemma of Third World Nutrition: Nestlé and the Role of Infant Formula," A Report prepared for Nestlé S.A. by Maggie McComas, Geoffrey Fookes, and George Taucher, 1983.

are deflated or undervalued, while the imports to Tico are inflated or overvalued. Not only does transfer pricing allow the circumvention of capital controls, but the trade balance of Tico has deteriorated.

Finally, some TNCs are very powerful, with annual sales that may be greater than the gross domestic products of the host developing nations. TNCs may interfere with domestic politics, lobbying for favorable legislation. In extreme cases, TNCs may even undermine the authority of the national government.

A particularly grievous example occurred in Chile with the United States transnational corporation, International Telephone & Telegraph (ITT). In 1970 Salvador Allende became president of Chile and the first freely elected Marxist leader in the Americas. Fearful of socialist policies, in particular, nationalization of its profitable Chilean affiliate, Chiltelco, ITT opposed Allende before the election and sought to disrupt the Chilean economy after Allende took power. ITT's unethical and illegal attempts to destabilize the Allende government even involved the U.S. Central Intelligence Agency. In September of 1973 Allende lost his life in a military coup that toppled the government.[12]

## POTENTIAL DISADVANTAGES OF FDI FOR TRANSNATIONAL CORPORATIONS

We noted the factors considered by TNCs in locating foreign subsidiaries. Though difficult to quantify and open to speculation, political risk is a major variable in the decision.

The biggest fear of TNCs may be **nationalization,** or a seizure of their assets by the host country. Increasingly, there are concerns with terrorism, whereby the employees and property of the TNC are vulnerable to attacks, for example from groups protesting against the foreign policy of the government of the parent corporation. While less severe than nationalization and terrorism, increased demands may be placed over time on the TNC to hire and train local labor, for shares in management, or for reinvestment of profits into the domestic economy. In fact, the leverage of the host country's government tends to increase with the investment made by the TNC in the domestic economy. Any such actions against TNCs, however, would very likely discourage further foreign investment in the nation.

As a way of reducing vulnerability, transnational corporations, even if not so restricted, may prefer joint ventures.[13] With **joint ventures,** the ownership, control, and often management of the enterprise are shared between domestic and foreign investors. There may even be initial maximums for the share of foreign equity, with provisions for a phasing out of foreign control over time.

Finally, TNCs realize the potential for losses in the investments made in training local labor, when those employees leave for other firms. In fact, as a primary provider of on-the-job training in many developing countries, TNCs may subsidize the formation of labor skills.

In sum, the importance of transnational corporations in the international economy will inevitably grow with the global integration of production and consumption.

---

[12]See Joan Spero, *The Politics of International Economic Relations*, 4th ed., New York: St. Martin's Press, 1990, pages 244–245.

[13]Many nations limit, or prohibit entirely, foreign ownership in certain sectors of the economy.

Indeed, increased competition and improved information management may require TNCs to become more agile, with foreign subsidiaries given greater autonomy to respond to local conditions.[14] Whether the relationships between TNCs and host countries, particularly for the developing economies, are harmonious depends on the particular circumstances. While incidents such as Nestlé (and the infant formula controversy) and ITT (and the Allende government of Chile) certainly tarnish the image of transnational corporations, there now seems to be a widely shared recognition of the mutual benefits from foreign direct investment. Certainly the potential for significant gains in efficiency and equity exist. Moreover, TNCs are adopting internal codes of conduct for socially responsible behavior and may be a force for positive change in the host countries.[15] For example, Levi Strauss, the world's largest apparel manufacturer, is widely recognized for its corporate responsibility:

> In one difficult case, Levi Strauss & Co. became aware that two of its foreign contractors in Bangladesh were employing children under 14 years old, reportedly legal under local law but below the standards set by the company's "terms of engagement" policies. Normally the children would have to be fired if the contractors were to retain Levi's business. However, after studying the situation, the company also discovered these children were their families' only source of income and likely would turn to begging in the streets if they were not employed. In an agreement illustrating a maximal social responsibility approach to improving this situation, the contractor agreed to pay the children full wages and benefits if they attended school until age 14. Levi Strauss pays for the children's tuition, books and school uniforms. When the children reach age 14, they will be offered the choice of returning to work in the factory.[16]

While controversy over foreign direct investment and the activities of transnational corporations may have abated somewhat with the increased interdependence of national economies, the same cannot be said about foreign aid.

## FOREIGN AID

At the most basic level, foreign aid, or **official development assistance (ODA),** involves the unilateral transfer of resources from donor to recipient nations for the express purpose of promoting economic development. ODA does not include military assistance, although in practice it may be difficult sometimes to distinguish economic from military aid; one example would be the construction of an airport for both civilian and military purposes. ODA also does not include the private contributions to charitable organizations working in developing countries.

Foreign aid can take several forms: cash grants, commodity transfers (e.g., capital equipment, construction materials, food, and medicines), technical assistance (e.g., consultants, relief workers, Peace Corps volunteers), and the concessional portion of loans

---

[14]See "A Survey of Multinationals," *The Economist* (June 24, 1995), pages 3–22.

[15]Ibid., page 15.

[16]United Nations Conference on Trade and Development, page 325.

(i.e., loans on softer terms, such as below-market interest rates with grace periods before payback). Foreign aid can be given for specific projects (e.g., construction of a water treatment plant) or for program support (e.g., macroeconomic reforms). Foreign aid can be dispensed *bilaterally* (i.e., government-to-government), or *multilaterally*, whereby donor nations pool their funds for aid programs administered through international organizations, such as the World Bank or agencies of the United Nations.

As suggested at the outset of this chapter, foreign aid is an emotionally charged issue with both ardent proponents and critics. We begin with a review of the arguments for official development assistance.

## THE CASE FOR FOREIGN AID

Both moral and economic arguments are offered for aid. The former are clearly normative, or value-laden, with no real possibilities for assessing their validity. In contrast, evidence can be assembled to test the economic consequences of aid—although different interpretations of the evidence are always possible and disagreements over the conclusiveness of the tests are common.

### THE MORAL BASIS FOR AID

The moral basis for aid rests on three propositions.[17] First is the *absolute argument* for aid, reflecting altruism, or concern for the welfare of others. Essentially, human beings have basic needs that must be met for a decent existence. (Recall the basic needs approach to development discussed in Chapter 5.) When possible, efforts to relieve human suffering should be made. Therefore, foreign aid to help poor nations is justified.

Second is the *relative argument* for aid. The gaps between rich and poor nations are large and growing—as they are in many nations, between the upper- and lower-income classes. A redistribution of resources from rich to poor should subtract less from the utility of the rich than it adds to the utility of the poor. Thus, total utility may be increased with more egalitarian distributions of income and resources. Classical microeconomic theory assumes that utility is not cardinal (that is, it cannot be quantitatively measured) and that interpersonal comparisons of utility cannot be made. Common sense, however, would suggest that a shift of one dollar of purchasing power from a wealthy individual (equivalent to, say, the consumption of one less candy bar each week) to a poor person (allowing, say, four additional bowls of rice per week) would enhance the welfare of the latter more than it diminishes the standard of living of the former.

The third moral argument for aid is based on *restitution*, or redressing the past injustices inflicted on the poor nations by the rich nations during the colonial period. Recall the claims of the radical [Marxist] school of development, also discussed in Chapter 5, that the underdevelopment of the Third World nations is due to exploitation by the developed countries.[18] Thus, the developed countries are morally obliged to compensate the less developed countries for past transgressions.

---

[17]This discussion draws from "The Moral Case for Aid," Roger Riddell, *Foreign Aid Reconsidered*, Baltimore: The Johns Hopkins University Press, 1987, Chapter 3. Riddell's comprehensive study of foreign aid is recommended.

[18]Recall that the radical school also maintains that foreign aid, itself, is a form of exploitation of the poor by the rich. We will review the critique of aid from the "left" below.

In sum, the moral basis for aid is legitimized if foreign assistance does help, or has the potential for helping, to meet the needs of the poor in developing nations.[19]

### The Economic Basis for Aid

Like foreign direct investment (FDI), foreign aid can help to cover a balance of trade deficit without adding to foreign indebtedness. Recall from Chapter 15 that receipt of foreign aid is a credit on the current account of the balance of payments. Unlike FDI, whereby foreigners acquire ownership of assets of the nation, foreign aid is a unilateral transfer of resources. Like foreign direct investment, foreign aid can relax factor scarcities that are constraining growth and development. For example, grants of foreign exchange can allow recipient nations to import needed intermediate and capital goods. Transfers of trained personnel, whether development economists, agricultural extension agents, engineers, doctors, or teachers, can provide needed skills, and serve also to transmit knowledge and technology.

Not typically undertaken by the private sector are some of the investments important for economic growth and development—in the infrastructure (transportation, telecommunications, power generation, and the water and sanitation systems) and for human capital formation (public education, primary health care, and child nutrition). These costly public investments, while yielding high social returns in the long run, are often beyond the budgets of governments in developing economies. Foreign aid can be vital, therefore, especially for low-income economies, not only for the funding, but for the technical expertise in devising and implementing the development projects. Furthermore, public investments on the physical infrastructure and population should complement more directly productive private-sector investments in agriculture, mining, manufacturing, and services.

For example, investing in a high-quality public education system will yield a literate and skilled labor force available for employment in the private sector. An efficient transportation network will increase the productivity and international competitiveness of the private sector. In short, public investment can enhance and stimulate private investment, both domestic and foreign, in a nation.

Not only can foreign aid promote the growth and development of the recipient countries, but it may produce dividends for donor nations. Rising per capita incomes and expanding markets in the LDCs are good for the exports, national incomes, and employment in the developed countries. Economic progress may promote political stability. Economic liberalization, fostered through foreign aid, may encourage political liberalization and more democratic forms of government. Finally, economic development leads to lower fertility rates, relieving population pressures on resources and the environment.

Many examples exist of foreign aid that has relieved human suffering or promoted economic development: humanitarian assistance in the case of natural disasters, such as earthquakes; relief efforts to supply food and medicines to displaced people during famines and civil wars; public health campaigns to immunize children; and family planning programs that offer contraceptive services and instruction on infant care. Scores of other aid projects have transferred capital equipment; provided technical expertise; and funded investments in physical infrastructure, directly expanding employment and increasing labor productivity. One specific example that indicates the full potential of aid is the Onchocerciasis Control Project, described earlier in Chapter 8.

---

[19]Riddell, page 15.

Important factors in the success of this public health project were the cooperation and coordination among donors and multilateral agencies, and the incorporation of local personnel into the operation and management of the program.

## THE CASE AGAINST AID

Critics argue that official development assistance is unnecessary, ineffective, and even counterproductive. Moreover, the moral basis for official aid is disputed. In fact, ODA has been attacked from both ends of the ideological spectrum.[20]

### QUESTIONING THE MORAL BASIS FOR AID

Some reject the notion that nations or governments have any obligation or right to intervene, whether to relieve suffering or address basic needs or promote development. Individuals, of course, are free to contribute to charities and international agencies of their choice. Governments, however, should not impose giving on taxpayers by using tax revenues for foreign aid.

P. T. Bauer, a well-known critic of aid and the author of the quotation opening this chapter, discounts even the need for aid. Echoing popular sentiments from the Far Right that poverty is endemic and that people are poor either by choice or defect of character, Bauer states:

> A disproportionate number of the poor lack the capabilities and inclination for economic achievement, and often for cultural achievement as well.[21]

and

> The attitudes, values and beliefs which keep many people poor are often an integral part of their lives. They often also give meaning to their lives, so that attempts forcibly to eradicate them could lead to spiritual collapse.[22]

Bauer discards the absolute argument for aid, saying:

> Global egalitarianism is based on the idea that people's requirements are fundamentally the same everywhere ... this idea is obviously unfounded.[23]

Bauer dismisses the relative argument for aid, claiming:

> because the personal attributes, social institutions and economic policies which promote economic advance are much more prevalent in most donor countries than in most recipient countries, international wealth transfers reallocate resources from those who can use them more productively to those who use them less so.[24]

---

[20]See Riddell, Chapters 4–7, for an extensive discussion of the arguments.

[21]Bauer, page 20.

[22]Ibid., page 115.

[23]Ibid., page 118.

[24]Ibid., page 119. We cite Bauer to illustrate some of the arguments refuting the moral case for aid. Bauer's criticism of official development assistance, however, is sweeping, and includes charges also levelled by the Radical Left—namely that aid bolsters ineffective and corrupt governments and

*continued*

Bauer further maintains that official development assistance increases the recipient developing nations' dependency on, and hostility toward, the donor developed countries.

### CRITICISMS OF FOREIGN AID FROM THE RIGHT

In general, conservatives object to ODA as an unwelcome interference with the market mechanism. Foreign aid increases the recipient government's control over resources and reduces the incentive to implement the reforms necessary for economic growth. The surest way to alleviate poverty is with economic growth, and the appropriate vehicle for growth is private enterprise. As with the growth model approach to economic development discussed in Chapters 3 and 4, measures to increase saving and promote investment are favored. Transfers to developing economies not only increase dependencies, but shift income from high savers (taxpayers in the developed countries) to low savers (populations in the recipient nations).

Moreover, government transfers increase budget deficits in the donor nations, crowding out private investment there. In sum, the keys to improving the economies of the LDCs are international trade and private investment, both driven by the pursuit of profits—not official development assistance, no matter how well-intentioned.

### CRITICISMS OF FOREIGN AID FROM THE LEFT

While many conservatives object to aid in theory, the Radical Left criticizes aid in practice. ODA may have the potential for promoting development, but experience with aid has been disappointing. Rather than assist the populations in need, official aid, all too often, has been misallocated, mismanaged, and even misappropriated. Although most of the criticism is directed at bilateral aid, inequities and inefficiencies also permeate multilateral aid.

First, the underlying premise that donor governments are genuinely interested in alleviating poverty and improving living conditions in developing nations is challenged. The allocation of bilateral assistance, in particular, seems to correspond more closely to the strategic and economic interests of the donor nations than to the needs of the poor.[25] Bilateral aid is perceived as "influence buying." This was especially true during the first two decades of the Cold War when the United States and the Soviet Union competed for allies in the Third World.

Most of the aid given is conditional. Often grants of foreign exchange are tied to purchases of exports from the donor nations—in effect, reducing the real value of the aid, since the recipients are locked into purchases of donor goods that may be more expensive or of lower quality than could be bought elsewhere. Specific projects are funded that may not be high priorities, even of questionable merit, in the developing nations.

---

perpetuates underdevelopment in Third World nations. Bauer does advocate free trade, noting, "The West can contribute to Third World development by reducing its barriers against Third World exports." Ibid., page 130.

[25]In an empirical analysis of official development assistance receipts for a cross-section of some 80 less developed countries for two periods, 1969–1970 and 1978–1980, Maizels and Nissanke found that bilateral aid flows corresponded more to the perceived interests of the donors (e.g., promotion of donor exports, creation of favorable climates for foreign investment, rewarding friendly governments, gaining regional influence), while multilateral aid flows corresponded more to the needs of the recipient (e.g., relief of factor shortages, alleviation of poverty, promotion of economic growth and development). See Alfred Maizels and Machiko Nissanke, "Motivations for Aid to Developing Countries," *World Development*, vol. 12, no. 9 (1984), pages 879–900.

Aid flows may be contingent on specific economic policy reforms that may not sufficiently consider the social, cultural, and political conditions in the recipient nations. The structural adjustment programs favored by the IMF and World Bank are often criticized for being insensitive to the plight of the poor in the LDCs.

Closely related is the premise that the governments in the developing countries are committed to the alleviation of poverty and the expansion of economic opportunity. If not drawn from the ranks of the military, leaders and policymakers in the developing nations are predominantly drawn from the wealthy elite. Their overriding concerns may be maintaining authority and consolidating power.

Sometimes the leaders of developing nations have been interested in personal aggrandizement through the creation of monuments. One conspicuous example: the largest church in the world apparently is a Roman Catholic basilica built in the mid-1980s in the Ivory Coast (now Côte d'Ivoire), a West African nation with less than 15 percent of its 13 million population Catholic. Erected at a cost of over $100 million, including two acres of stained glass and seven acres of imported Italian and Spanish marble, the air-conditioned basilica was a high priority for then-President Félix Houphouët-Boigny, despite the sharply declining per capita income in his nation.[26]

Outright corruption for personal enrichment may also characterize the governments of some nations receiving foreign aid. Consider the case of Liberia, a neighbor of Côte d'Ivoire, that had come under control of Samuel Doe, a former master sergeant of the army, in a military coup in 1980. Pro-American policies generated $500 million in aid from the United States before Liberia's stagnant economy, political corruption, and human rights violations became too much to ignore.[27] In 1988 the United States Congress dispatched a team of examiners to Liberia. They discovered that Liberia had been running on two separate budgets—with gasoline and logging taxes going directly into the president's discretionary fund. In fact, President Doe personally controlled 40 percent of government revenues. Government ministers in Liberia drove Mercedes, and the national soccer team had been awarded $1 million by Doe for a victory over the national team of Ghana.[28]

Even when no overt misappropriation exists, aid may be mismanaged. Critics cite a chronic bias in official aid toward large-scale, capital-intensive projects. Often hastily conceived and inadequately administered, the projects do little to improve the welfare of the truly poor—peasant farmers, landless laborers, and urban slum dwellers. Consider the following account by Jack Shepherd, an expert on aid to Africa.

> During the 1970s African governments inaugurated a range of projects aimed at increasing domestic food production. The ones most widely-favored—funded by the United States Agency for International Development (USAID), the World Bank, and other international agencies—were large, mechanized, and highly capitalized. Moreover, investment in food production often favored crops consumed by people in the cities: wheat, rice, and sugar....
>
> Some of the schemes involved tractors, chemical fertilizers, irrigation, and large-scale state farms. Money also went into highly visible projects such as highways,

---

[26]This account is from "Ivory Coast: a Shrine ... to What?" Kathy Koch, *Christian Science Monitor* (January 23, 1989), page 6.

[27]This account is from "Treasure for Pleasure: Liberia's American Money Managers Gave Up," by Bradley Martin with Jane Whitmore, *Newsweek* (February 13, 1989), page 39.

[28]Lest we forget that government corruption and fraud are found also in developed nations, recall Watergate and U.S. President Nixon's resignation; the revolving-door governments of Italy; and the periodic scandals in Japan.

hospitals in urban areas, and convention halls. But deep plowing and the use of chemical fertilizers did not increase yields, and perhaps even threatened an African farming system that had evolved over centuries.[29]

We should not leave the impression that all agricultural aid in Africa has "failed" or that only aid from the West "failed." We can again refer to Shepherd, who, in the same article, noted a U.S. aid project for small farmers in Guinea-Bissau that helped to increase rice yields by 400 to 900 percent in two years, with nearly all the rice used for local consumption.[30] Shepherd also provides examples of mismanaged aid to Africa from the former Soviet Union:

> During the 1960s and early 1970s ... the Soviets offered big projects to the Africans. At Diamou, Mali, for example, the Russians built a cement factory with a capacity of 50,000 tons a year—and then discovered that the road and rail systems could not handle this output and that there were no markets nearby anyway. A Russian meat-canning plant in Somalia operated at only 5.3 percent of capacity, because few cattle were available (Africans generally regard cattle as investments against future hardship) and because Somalis prefer fresh meat to canned. A Soviet fish-processing plant also failed, because it was too large and too far from the sea.[31]

One particularly controversial type of assistance has been food aid. While needed to prevent hunger and starvation from famines caused by crop failures or civil wars, food aid has also been used to dispose of surplus agricultural production in the donor nations. The dumping of surplus crops, whether as aid or as a result of export subsidies given to farmers in the developed countries, can depress food prices and discourage farmers in the recipient nations. Consumers in the recipient nations may develop preferences for the imported foodstuffs, and the nation may become more dependent on food imports. Moreover, recipient governments may be less inclined to pursue policies to increase domestic food production when food aid is regularly available.[32] In truth, even during famines, food aid does not always reach the intended beneficiaries. Sometimes the donated food is seized by warring factions, or siphoned off into the black market, or simply wasted because of logistical problems in delivering the food to the needy.

Nevertheless, as part of humanitarian relief efforts, food aid contributes to averting calamities. Often nongovernmental organizations, such as the Red Cross and CARE (Cooperative for Assistance and Relief Everywhere), are well-suited for delivering emergency assistance. Furthermore, properly administered food aid can promote economic development. For example, poor households that cannot afford even the locally produced food could be fed with food aid. So could schoolchildren. During the slack growing season when food supplies are low, governments could hire the surplus labor for infrastructural projects (e.g., road construction and improvement of irrigation systems), with part of the wages paid in food aid. In all cases, however, caution should be taken that food aid does not engender dependencies.

---

[29]Jack Shepherd, "When Foreign Aid Fails," *The Atlantic Monthly* (April 1985), pages 41–46. This quotation is from page 42.

[30]Ibid., page 43.

[31]Ibid.

[32]Robert Cassen and Associates, *Does Aid Work?*, Report to an Intergovernmental Task Force, Second edition, New York: Clarendon Press, 1994, page 131.

In sum, opponents of official development assistance, just like proponents, can find evidence to support their contentions. Critics on the right may always view aid as counterproductive, even inimical to capitalism and private enterprise—the real solutions to the underdevelopment of Third World nations. Critics on the left, especially from the radical school, may always see capitalism as the problem, with ineffective aid as just one consequence of the exploitation of the Third World by the developed nations. The relevant question for policy, however, is not whether much of foreign aid has "failed" or "succeeded." The relevant question is whether official development assistance has the potential to promote economic development. If so, then how can foreign aid be reformed to become more effective?

As background to a better understanding of the role of foreign aid in development, we provide an overview of official development assistance in the post–World War II era. We then note the level and composition of contemporary foreign aid flows to the developing nations.

## A BRIEF HISTORY OF OFFICIAL DEVELOPMENT ASSISTANCE (ODA)

Following World War II three international institutions were established to promote macroeconomic stability and economic growth.[33] To oversee balance of payments and exchange rate adjustments, the International Monetary Fund (IMF) was created. To monitor commercial policy and promote trade liberalization, the General Agreement on Tariffs and Trade (GATT) was formed. And, to generate capital for economic development, the International Bank for Reconstruction and Development (IBRD, or the World Bank) was instituted.

In development, the first priority was the reconstruction of the war-torn economies of Europe. The United States contributed to the recovery of Europe with the Marshall Plan, probably the most successful U.S. aid ever given. The economic development of the low-income nations of Africa, Asia, and Latin America was relatively ignored—primarily because of the preoccupation with the rebuilding of Europe and Japan, a concern made all the more important with the onset of the Cold War. Moreover, it was believed, or hoped, that restarting the main engines of the global economy and expanding international trade and investment would advance the less developed economies. Thus, despite requests for assistance, the LDCs received little foreign aid—until the mid-1950s and the institutionalization of the Cold War, when the strategic significance of the Third World became fully appreciated. For the West, foreign aid seemed to be a good investment in the containment of communism. Aid was intended to promote economically viable and politically stable countries, oriented toward free markets and democracy. The United States took the lead. Bilateral aid was used to cement alliances, often with authoritarian, but anticommunist, rulers. So too, the Soviet Union was employing military and economic aid to bolster its client states.

By the early 1970s the superpower competition for allies in the developing world was waning—in part, a reflection of the disenchantment with the Vietnam War and the diminished position of the United States in the international economy. Emboldened

---

[33]For a good summary of foreign aid after the Second World War, see Joan Spero "International Financial Flows," in *The Politics of International Economic Relations*, 4th ed., New York: St. Martin's Press, 1990, Chapter 6, pages 159–202.

by the success of OPEC in raising oil prices, the less developed countries lobbied for a New International Economic Order, whereby they would exert greater influence in setting the international rules of the game—rules they believed had been dictated by the developed countries that controlled the IMF, World Bank, and GATT. The developed countries were encouraged to contribute .7 percent of their GNPs for official development assistance.[34] At the First International Population Conference at Bucharest, Romania, in 1974, the developing nations argued that economic development, not family planning, was required for curbing rapid population growth. More effective and reliable aid and preferential treatment in trade, finance, and investment were sought for fostering economic development.

In general, a reorientation in development policy took place in the 1970s—away from an emphasis on physical capital formation, industrialization, and economic growth and toward human capital formation, rural development, and basic needs. So too, there was a shift from bilateral to multilateral aid.

> As the United States and other developed countries gave increasing emphasis to multilateral aid, the World Bank also expanded in the 1970s. In addition to its traditional support for infrastructure projects, the bank began to make loans for basic human needs projects, including the development of subsistence farming, minimally adequate housing, and rudimentary health care. In the late 1970s, the bank increased its lending for energy development.[35]

With the 1980s, significant changes again buffeted the international political economy. The surge in inflation set off by another round of oil price hikes led to the adoption of contractionary monetary policies in the developed countries. An international recession soon followed. Conservative governments in the United States (Reagan) and Great Britain (Thatcher) embraced supply-side economic policies, in particular, tax cuts to stimulate saving, investment, and labor force participation. The arms race ratcheted upward with increased defense spending and the initiation of the Star Wars research program in the United States. Bilateral aid for strategic purposes was emphasized by the Reagan administration, while funding for multilateral aid was trimmed.

Developing nations with balance of payments problems turning to the IMF were required to adopt austerity packages as a condition of new lending. The drying up of private capital flows to the developing economies, following the Mexican debt crisis of 1982, was not offset by increased official development assistance. In fact, repayments of principal and interest, combined with capital flight, overwhelmed new foreign investment and ODA, and resulted in a net outflow of capital from the LDCs over the 1980s. Investment and economic growth in sub-Saharan Africa and Latin America especially suffered.

In Tables 16.2 and 16.3 we present statistics on official development assistance. First, we can see in Table 16.2A the recent trends in ODA from the OECD nations, the major

---

[34]This .7 percent of GNP actually represented a scaling back from a target of 1 percent of GNP for ODA suggested in the 1960s. For the OECD nations in 1965, only four (Australia at .53%, the United States at .58%, Belgium at .60%, and France at .76%) gave more than .5 percent of GNP as ODA in 1965. In 1970, only three nations (Australia at .59%, Netherlands at .61%, and France at .66%) exceeded .5 percent of GNP as ODA. These statistics are from the World Bank, *World Development Report 1994*, New York: Oxford University Press, 1994, Table 18.

[35]Spero, page 171.

## TABLE 16.2  DONORS OF OFFICIAL DEVELOPMENT ASSISTANCE

A. OECD OFFICIAL DEVELOPMENT ASSISTANCE (ODA)

|  |  | 1970 | 1975 | 1980 | 1985 | 1990 | 1993 |
|---|---|---|---|---|---|---|---|
| OECD Total ODA (billions of 1992 $) | | 35.0 | 41.0 | 47.2 | 55.0 | 59.8 | 57.1 |
| ODA as % of GNP: | OECD | .34 | .35 | .35 | .34 | .34 | .30 |
| | U.S. | .32 | .27 | .27 | .24 | .21 | .15 |
| Net bilateral flows to low-income economies as % of GNP: | OECD | ... | ... | .11 | ... | .12 | .09 |
| | U.S. | ... | ... | .07 | ... | .07 | .04 |

B. TOP FIVE DONORS OF ODA IN 1993: BY AMOUNT AND BY SHARE OF GNP

|  | ODA (BILLIONS OF $) | ODA AS % OF GNP |
|---|---|---|
| Japan | 11.26 | .26 |
| United States | 9.72 | .15 |
| France | 7.92 | .63 |
| Germany | 6.95 | .37 |
| Italy | 3.04 | .31 |

|  | ODA AS % OF GNP | ODA (BILLIONS OF $) |
|---|---|---|
| Kuwait | 1.30 | .38 |
| Denmark | 1.03 | 1.34 |
| Norway | 1.01 | 1.01 |
| Sweden | .98 | 1.77 |
| Netherlands | .82 | 2.53 |

NOTES: Lack of data is indicated by ...

*OECD official development assistance* consists of net disbursements of loans and grants made on concessional financial terms by official agencies of the members of the Development Assistance Committee of the Organization for Economic Cooperation and Development to promote economic development and welfare. ODA also includes the value of technical assistance. Net disbursements equal gross disbursements less payments to the originators of aid for amortization of past aid receipts.

*Net bilateral flows to low-income economies* exclude unallocated bilateral flows and all disbursements to multilateral institutions.

FROM World Bank, *World Development Report 1995,* New York: Oxford University Press, 1995, Table 18.

donor group. Total flows of ODA in real terms stagnated from 1965 to 1975, and the share of ODA in GNPs fell from .47 percent to .35 percent.[36] For the United States, the share of ODA in GNP was more than halved, from .58 percent to .27 percent. Since the mid-1970s, aid donations have roughly kept pace with the growth in national incomes of the OECD nations, leaving the target of .7 percent of GNP allocated for aid more than twice the actual giving. The share of bilateral aid flows to the low-income nations also declined sharply between 1965 and 1975, from .20 percent to .11 percent, and in 1993 accounted for only .09 percent of the GNPs of the OECD nations.

As shown in Table 16.2B, in absolute amounts, Japan and the United States were the leading donor nations in 1993. As a percentage of GNP, however, Kuwait was the most generous, followed by the northern European nations of Denmark, Norway, Sweden, and the Netherlands. These figures mask the donor concentrations of bilateral aid. For example, France ranks high in ODA, although most of French aid goes to former colonies in Africa. So too, the United States, outside of the considerable aid given to strategic allies, especially Israel and Egypt, has relatively favored the Latin American region. Japan has focused on Asia and the Pacific. Aid from the OPEC nations, mainly from the subgroup OAPEC (Organization of Arab Petroleum Exporting Countries) has been channelled to other Arab nations.

Turning to Table 16.3 and the receipts of ODA, we observe significant differences by income and region. Foreign aid receipts are especially important for the other low-income economies: In 1993, official development assistance averaged $23.7 per capita and 6.4 percent of GNP. Regionally, sub-Saharan Africa receives the most aid per capita ($35.7 in 1993), followed by the Middle East and North Africa ($22.9 in 1993). Despite having lower per capita incomes than sub-Saharan Africa, the very populous region of South Asia receives relatively little aid.

In Table 16.3B the leading recipients of ODA for 1993 are also listed. In terms of per capita receipts, Israel (not considered a less developed country) is at the top—due to the bilateral aid from the United States. As a share of GNP, however, the leading recipients of aid are Mozambique and Guinea-Bissau. These rankings, however, can vary dramatically from year to year depending on economic conditions and political events (e.g., famines, civil wars, foreign conflicts). For example, aid to Nicaragua sharply increased after the Marxist Sandinista government was replaced.[37]

---

[36]These statistics on official development assistance for earlier years are from World Bank, *World Development Report 1994*, Table 18.

[37]From 1990 to 1991, receipts of ODA by Nicaragua increased from $334 million to $841 million. By 1993, however, ODA receipts were back down to $323 million. We are reminded, however, of the need to exercise caution in using the reported data on official development assistance receipts. For example, in Table 19 of the World Bank's *World Development Report 1995* (New York: Oxford University Press, 1995), net receipts of official development assistance for Sierra Leone are listed as increasing from $137 million in 1992 to $1,204 million in 1993 (or $269.4 in per capita receipts and 164.4% of Sierra Leone's GNP). Similarly, for Oman the increase in ODA from 1992 to 1993 was from $54 million to $1,071 million (or $538.8 in per capita receipts and 9.2% of Oman's GNP). Conversations with a staff member of the World Bank and others convinced us that these extraordinary increases in ODA receipts were unlikely. Thus, we list in Table 16.3 only those top five recipients of ODA in 1993 for which corresponding data from the United Nations Development Programme's *Human Development Report 1995* (Table 13) are comparable. The lesson may be that macroeconomic and demographic data, even when published in authoritative sources like the *World Development Report*, should be scrutinized, and suspicious data should be double-checked, where possible, or reported with any reservations noted.

| TABLE 16.3 | RECIPIENTS OF OFFICIAL DEVELOPMENT ASSISTANCE—ALL SOURCES |

A. RECEIPTS OF OFFICIAL DEVELOPMENT ASSISTANCE (ODA) IN 1993

|  | ODA RECEIPTS PER CAPITA ($) | ODA RECEIPTS AS % OF GNP |
|---|---|---|
| INCOME GROUP |  |  |
| India | 1.7 | 0.6 |
| China | 2.8 | 0.8 |
| Other low-income economies | 23.7 | 6.4 |
| Middle-income economies | … | … |
|  |  |  |
| REGION |  |  |
| sub-Saharan Africa | 35.7 | 11.5 |
| Middle East & North Africa | 22.9 | 3.2 |
| Europe & Central Asia | … | … |
| South Asia | 4.3 | 1.5 |
| East Asia & Pacific | 6.1 | 0.8 |
| Latin America & the Caribbean | 8.6 | 0.3 |

B. TOP FIVE RECIPIENTS OF ODA IN 1993: IN PER CAPITA $ AND BY SHARE IN GNP

|  | ODA RECEIPTS PER CAPITA ($) | ODA RECEIPTS AS % OF GNP |
|---|---|---|
| Israel | 242.5 | 1.8 |
| Mauritania | 153.2 | 34.9 |
| Namibia | 105.6 | 6.2 |
| Gabon | 100.9 | 1.9 |
| Zambia | 97.3 | 23.6 |

|  | ODA RECEIPTS AS % OF GNP | ODA RECEIPTS PER CAPITA ($) |
|---|---|---|
| Mozambique | 79.2 | 77.0 |
| Guinea-Bissau | 40.3 | 94.6 |
| Tanzania | 40.0 | 33.9 |
| Mauritania | 34.9 | 153.2 |
| Burundi | 25.8 | 40.6 |

NOTES: Lack of data is indicated by …
LDC *receipts of official development assistance* are from all sources, including OECD and OPEC nations.

FROM: World Bank, *World Development Report 1995*, New York: Oxford University Press, 1995, Table 19.

## MULTILATERAL AID AGENCIES

Numerous official international organizations and thousands of nongovernmental organizations are involved in economic development. We begin with the major official institutions.[38]

### INTERNATIONAL MONETARY FUND (IMF)

Originally chartered to regulate the international monetary system and provide short-term loans to nations for balance of payments adjustment, the IMF has become increasingly involved with economic development. In the 1970s the oil price shocks led to severe current account imbalances. In the 1980s many developing nations experienced debt problems.

The IMF does not give aid, in the sense of grants or unilateral transfers of resources. Rather, nations with balance of payments deficits, who have exhausted their international reserves and who find credit in the private market either unavailable or prohibitively expensive, turn to the IMF. During the aftermath of the Mexican debt crisis in the early 1980s, the IMF also functioned as a financial intermediary, persuading commercial banks to continue lending to developing countries. IMF credit and the bank lending sanctioned by the IMF are usually conditional on the governments of the borrowing nations adopting tighter macroeconomic policies and measures to liberalize markets. As it becomes more involved with the developing economies, the IMF has worked closely with the World Bank.

### THE WORLD BANK

As with the IMF, the funds provided by the World Bank to nations are not official transfers, but loans. While IMF lending is for short-term program assistance related to balance of payments adjustment, World Bank lending is longer term and usually for specific projects to promote economic development. The World Bank borrows on the international capital market at the prevailing rates of interest and then relends to developing nations at slightly higher rates of interest. Thus, the World Bank serves to channel credit to developing nations on better terms than the same nations could obtain directly in the international capital market.

Traditionally most of the lending by the World Bank has been for large-scale projects. Investments in the physical infrastructure have been emphasized; although the World Bank has also funded many projects in human capital formation (education, health care, nutrition, and job training). Given the debt problems of the developing economies, the World Bank also began to make loans for balance of payments support. These structural adjustment loans are intended to facilitate the longer-run policy reforms necessary for improving the international competitiveness of the developing economies.

The World Bank is also a leading center for research, technical assistance, and policy advice. In addition to the annual *World Development Reports,* the staff of the World Bank publish frequent studies on economic development. Training sessions for government

---

[38]For an overview of multilateral aid agencies, see World Bank, "Official Development Assistance," pages 94–109 in *World Development Report 1985,* New York: Oxford University Press, 1985.

officials and policymakers of developing nations are provided, as well as consultations and guidance on development planning.[39]

The management and operation of the World Bank, however, have been subject to considerable criticism over the years. Michael Irwin, director of the Health Services Department of the World Bank in 1989, before resigning in frustration, characterized the World Bank as an organization "plagued by massive overstaffing, bureaucratic gridlock and staff preoccupation with further salary and benefit hikes." Irwin documents examples of extravagant spending on and by a World Bank staff that is "out of touch with both the realities and causes of poverty in the Third World."[40] We should note that similar charges are frequently made against other United Nations agencies and affiliates, including the International Monetary Fund.

Several affiliates or members of the World Bank Group exist. The International Development Association (IDA), funded through contributions by member developed countries, makes loans to the least developed countries on highly concessional terms (interest-free, small administrative charges, and long grace periods before repayment of principal). As nations develop, they graduate from IDA assistance to regular World Bank lending. While World Bank and IDA loans are to governments of developing nations, the International Finance Corporation (IFC) makes long-term loans to, and even invests in, private enterprises in developing nations. IFC loans and investments, financed mostly by borrowing in the international capital market, are intended to encourage private-sector development.[41]

Unaffiliated, but operating much like the World Bank, are regional development banks, for example, the African Development Bank, the Asian Development Bank, and the Inter-American Development Bank (for Latin America and the Caribbean). These banks make both hard loans (i.e., on market terms) and soft loans (i.e., on concessional terms) for development projects and programs to the nations within their region.

## UNITED NATIONS AGENCIES

Established in 1945, the United Nations (UN), among its many activities, manages large concessional programs through numerous specialized agencies. In fact, the IMF and

---

[39]Michael Gavin and Dani Rodrik in "The World Bank in Historical Perspective," *American Economic Review*, vol. 85, no. 2 (May 1995), pages 329–334, remark,

Thanks to its far-flung lending operations, the Bank is the single most important external source of ideas and advice to developing-country policymakers.... at least since the mid-1960s the Bank's name has always been associated with a particular set of ideas about what constitutes important development priorities facing poor countries [page 332].

[40]See Michael Irwin, "Banking on Poverty: An Insider's Look at the World Bank," *50 Years Is Enough: The Case Against the World Bank and the International Monetary Fund*, edited by Kevin Danaher, Boston: South End Press, 1994, pages 152–160. These quotations are from pages 152 and 160, respectively.

[41]We should note two additional World Bank affiliates. The International Centre for Settlement of Investment Disputes (ICSID) facilitates foreign investment in developing economies by offering mediation services for conflicts that may arise between foreign investors and governments. ICSID also offers advice and consultation on legal matters involving foreign investment. The Multilateral Investment Guarantee Agency (MIGA) provides insurance to foreign investors in developing economies against the loss of assets due to "noncommercial risk," such as nationalization or civil unrest. MIGA helps governments in developing nations devise policies to attract foreign investment. For an overview of the World Bank affiliates, see World Bank Group, "Learning from the Past, Embracing the Future," Washington, DC: World Bank, 1994.

the World Bank, while each independently organized and operated, are affiliates in the U.N. system.

The United Nations Development Programme (UNDP) coordinates and funds much of the technical assistance provided through the U.N. agencies. The United Nations Fund for Population Activities (UNFPA) assists with family planning in developing countries. UNICEF (United Nations Children's Fund) focuses on education, health care, and nutrition for children. For example, one very successful program sponsored by UNICEF was GOBI, a campaign launched in the early 1980s to reduce child mortality. Along with the promotion of breastfeeding and child immunization, GOBI advanced a simple, but highly effective, oral rehydration therapy that allows parents to intervene and stop the dehydration associated with severe diarrhea, a leading cause of death in children in the developing nations.

The World Health Organization (WHO) works to improve health-care policies; distribute medical supplies and disseminate technology; and eradicate disease around the globe. The U.N. Food and Agriculture Organization (FAO) is charged with increasing agricultural production in the developing countries and enhancing efficiency and equity in the distribution of food. The United Nations Industrial Development Organization (UNIDO) supports industrialization projects in developing economies. The International Labour Organization (ILO) promotes productive employment and improved labor conditions. These and other U.N. agencies provide funding, technical assistance, training, policy advice, and fieldwork in the less developed countries. Like the IMF and World Bank, these U.N. agencies engage in research, publish studies in development, and sponsor conferences.

In addition to the programs in economic development, the United Nations is heavily involved in aiding refugees and displaced persons, protecting human rights; peacekeeping; and crafting international agreements on the environment, resources, and security.

### Nongovernmental Organizations

Operating in the private sector and complementing the efforts of official development agencies are the thousands of nongovernmental organizations (NGOs), sometimes referred to as private voluntary organizations (PVOs). Among the better known international NGOs are CARE, OXFAM, Catholic Relief Services, International Planned Parenthood Federation, and Save the Children Fund.[42] On the national level, Sarvodaya, discussed in Chapter 5, is an example. Rural credit cooperatives and village mothers' clubs are examples of local NGOs.[43]

Financed largely by private contributions, many NGOs also receive funding from governments and official aid agencies. While the humanitarian relief efforts of some

---

[42]For example, in 1993, CARE provided $405 million in humanitarian and development assistance to people in 53 countries. Besides emergency aid, CARE is involved in improving local food production and distribution, environmental preservation, and public health care. CARE also provides financial support and technical training for starting small businesses in developing nations. See *CARE Annual Report 1993*, CARE Foundation, Atlanta, GA, 1993.

[43]See Vittorio Masoni, "Nongovernmental Organizations and Development," *Finance and Development*, vol. 22, no. 3 (September 1985), pages 38–41, and Michael Cernea, "Nongovernmental Organizations and Local Development," World Bank Discussion Papers, Washington, DC: World Bank, 1988, for discussions of NGOs.

of the international NGOs are widely recognized, more important for sustainable development would be the grassroots work, particularly in rural communities and small villages in support of education, health care, nutrition, family planning, sanitation, job training, and small-business formation.

NGOs have been very effective in reaching the poor and advancing the interests of those marginalized groups often overlooked in the large-scale development projects, such as hydroelectric dams, urban hospitals, and international airports. Like Sarvodaya, NGOs emphasize self-help and seek to mobilize individuals and communities to improve their conditions, for instance, by organizing literacy classes, marketing handicrafts, and forming credit unions.

NGOs are advocates of the poor, publicizing their plight and promoting their human rights. Governments are lobbied for programs to help the lower-income classes, e.g., rural schools and health clinics, the services of agricultural extension agents, access to clean water and adequate disposal of wastes in urban neighborhoods. NGOs work to protect the rights of the poor, for example, by securing title to property, fair prices for farm produce, and continued access to resources, including rainforest and pastureland traditionally used by indigenous groups.

Governments and multilateral agencies collaborate with NGOs. In 1982, a World Bank-NGO Committee was formed to facilitate cooperation.[44] With their extensive field experience and firsthand knowledge of the needs of the poor, NGOs are a valuable source of information for development planners—not only in identifying the present obstacles to improving the conditions of the poor, but in designing, implementing, and evaluating more effective policies and development projects. Two examples of NGO cooperation with the World Bank are given.

> Ghana is the world's third largest producer of cocoa, which accounts for about two-thirds of the country's export earnings. In an attempt to reduce its dependence on a single crop for foreign exchange, income, and employment, Ghana is trying to diversify its agricultural production. With funding from the World Bank, Ghana is expanding production of other tree crops for which it is particularly well-suited: oil palm, rubber, and robusta coffee. NGOs are assisting in the effort. Technoserve, an international NGO, is establishing 60 palm oil mills using intermediate technology throughout Ghana and training farmers to manage, operate, and maintain these mills. Traditionally, oil palm fruits are processed in large state-owned mills (usually serving large state-owned plantations) or in small, inefficient unmechanized village mills. To date some 13 new intermediate-technology mills have begun to bring improved technology and better returns to thousands of small farmers who grow oil palms for food and income.[45]

> A mere 15 percent of girls in a poor region of Pakistan are enrolled in school. In many cases parents do not even know that their children, their girls in particular, have the right to go to school. Recently, however, a World Bank–supported NGO initiative has created more than 100 new girls' schools, many with nearly 100 percent enrollment from their villages. The Society for Community Support in Primary Education

---

[44]In 1993, NGOs collaborated in approximately one-third of World Bank–supported projects. In sub-Saharan Africa and South Asia, the participation rates were greater than 40 percent. See "Working with NGOs," *The World Bank: A Global Partnership for Development,* Washington, DC: World Bank, 1994.

[45]Ibid., page 8.

in Baluchistan (SCSPEB) launched the effort, going door-to-door to organize parents' groups. These parent groups then select a school site and recruit a teacher; she should be a girl from the village with at least an eighth grade education. After the teacher has volunteered her time for three months, the SCSPEB provides training and the government provides a salary. Along with other donors, the World Bank provides support to the SCSPEB, an NGO created by a group of individuals who served as a liaison between the community and the government's Department of Education.[46]

In sum, nongovernmental organizations provide an important type of aid. Their basic needs orientation complements the larger-scale, more physically capital-intensive development projects of the official aid agencies.

## ASSESSING THE EFFECTIVENESS OF OFFICIAL DEVELOPMENT ASSISTANCE

In his comprehensive examination of foreign aid, Riddell observed that, "Foreign aid theory nowhere asserts that aid is a necessary or a sufficient condition for development to begin or to continue."[47] To expect official development assistance, by itself, to initiate and sustain rapid economic growth and development is probably unrealistic. Rather, aid, if appropriately designed and properly implemented, can enhance socioeconomic progress in the recipient nations.

To be sure, many instances of aid failures have occurred, due to ill-conceived projects and mismanaged funds. Whether these are indictments of aid or more indications of the challenges in achieving economic development in countries with chronic poverty, weak governments, insufficiently trained civil servants, and grossly inadequate infrastructures, is hard to say. But the very conditions that may call for aid also make it difficult for aid to be effective. Moreover, as we noted, much of the bilateral aid has been given to advance the economic and strategic interests of the donor nations. Thus, different agendas are found for measuring success.

Ideally, to assess the impact of aid, we would compare the course of events in a recipient country with aid to the course of events that would have occurred without the aid. Of course, such counterfactual comparisons are not possible—there is only one history. Procedures for evaluating aid projects, however, are available. Recall from Chapter 8 the discussion of the rates of return (social and private) to investments in education, and in Chapter 10, the illustration of the net present value criterion for public investments.

Assessing the contribution of an aid project to economic development is not an exact science. For one, even if the consequences of the aid could be accurately measured, how should the distribution of the benefits and costs across the population be weighed? Second, the effects of exogenous factors should be taken into consideration—whether fortuitous (for example, ideal rainfall during an agricultural extension project) or adverse (for example, an international recession that depresses the export revenues from a textile marketing project). Third, many investments, especially for human capital formation, have long payoff periods and hard-to-quantify benefits.

---

[46]Ibid., page 20.
[47]Riddell, page 102.

Perhaps the truest test of aid is whether the self-reliance of the recipient is promoted. E. F. Schumacher maintained that

> The best aid to give is intellectual aid, a gift of useful knowledge. A gift of material goods can be appropriated by the recipient without effort or sacrifice; it therefore rarely becomes "his own" and is all too frequently and easily treated as a mere windfall. A gift of intellectual goods, a gift of knowledge, is a very different matter. Without a genuine effort of appropriation on the part of the recipient, there is no gift....
>
> This, then, should become the ever-increasing preoccupation of aid programs—to make men [and women] self-reliant and independent by the generous supply of the appropriate intellectual gifts, gifts of relevant knowledge on the methods of self-help.[48]

Measuring the gains in self-reliance achieved through aid, or the sustainability of economic development after a foreign aid project has ended, is even more difficult. Nevertheless, generalizations on the effectiveness of foreign aid have been offered. Cassen, in his book titled, *Does Aid Work?*, concludes that "the majority of aid is successful in terms of its own objectives. Over a wide range of countries and sectors, aid has made positive and valuable contributions."[49] Further, Cassen, countering critics on the right, argues that foreign aid can, and has, benefited the private sector, since

> a key purpose of aid is to do things that the private sector will not do or cannot do efficiently.... Indeed, if the public sector provides the conditions in which private activity can flourish—which include infrastructure, public services, and the legal and regulatory framework, all of which can be assisted and encouraged in appropriate directions by aid and the policy dialogue—private activity should become more prominent of its own accord.[50]

Foreign aid for human capital formation and family planning also contributes to the growth of the private sector. Not only are rapid population growth rates reduced, thereby freeing up resources for private saving and investment, but more educated and productive labor forces are created.

In sum, we find a general, if by no means universal, acknowledgment of the positive role foreign aid can play in economic development. Nonetheless, the effectiveness of aid can be improved. We conclude this chapter with proposals for reform in foreign aid.

## REFORMS IN FOREIGN AID

The need for better coordination in foreign aid—both across donors and between donor groups and the recipient nations—is widely recognized. Less developed countries can be overwhelmed in dealing with the multiplicity of donors. Cassen notes

---

[48]E. F. Schumacher, *Small Is Beautiful: Economics As if People Mattered,* New York: Harper & Row, 1973, page 197.
[49]Cassen, page 225.
[50]Ibid., page 200.

that "A typical low-income country may have twenty or thirty official aid agencies working within its borders, as well as up to twice that number of nongovernmental organizations."[51]

A first priority may be, then, for each developing nation to identify its priority needs: from current constraints on growth and development down to specific projects for funding. Some nations may require technical assistance in drawing up the priority needs. Further, developing nations could designate one ministry or government agency to coordinate their aid programs with donors.

Donors, for their part, would collaborate on appropriate aid packages—to reduce, if not eliminate, inconsistencies in approach and redundancies in efforts. Indeed, greater communication and cooperation among donors may allow for comparative advantages in aid to be realized. Various donors, based on previous success and present expertise, may specialize in certain types of assistance, for example, agricultural extension services, primary health care, construction of power-generating facilities, or institution building. Better donor coordination would also reduce the burden on developing nations of having to work simultaneously with numerous donor operating and accounting procedures and donated equipment types. For instance, rather than receiving 10 brands of personal computers from 10 aid donors, each brand with a set of manuals, software, and required technical support, it would be simpler and more efficient to receive two or three compatible brands of personal computers. In short, while aid consortia and consultative groups do exist, such as the Development Assistance Committee of the OECD nations, significant gains remain to be made in donor coordination.

Most, if not all, official aid agencies engage in regular evaluation of their aid projects and programs. Vast amounts of information are available on development projects. An international clearinghouse, in which the information could be stored and lessons from the development projects shared, would be useful. The clearinghouse could also collect the individual developing country lists of priority needs and help match donor expertise with recipient requests. Priorities for research could be established and efforts coordinated, for example, research and development of wind and solar energies; or inexpensive, portable, comprehensive, single-dosage vaccines for children; or extending the Green Revolution to the African continent.

Cassen notes the opportunities in the developed nations, with declining school populations and excess educational capacity, for training students and administrators from developing nations.[52] The international clearinghouse could coordinate scholarship programs for such educational exchanges.

Greater cooperation among developing nations is also possible and desirable. Especially cost-effective may be intraregional coordination to pool resources for disease control, agricultural research and extension work, vocational and university education, and family planning.

A second area of reform, consistent with improved coordination, would be a re-emphasis on multilateral aid, provided on a regular basis, and targeted to the least developed countries. Cassen predicts that the "poorest" countries will require aid for decades, since:

---

[51]Ibid., page 242.
[52]Ibid., pages 156–157.

They lack the fundamental necessities for material development—human skills, sound administration, infrastructure. They often have unstable governments, deteriorating ecological conditions, stagnant or declining agriculture; in some cases many years of falling per capita income, even falling GNP.[53]

Multilateral aid, accounting for, perhaps, one-third of all official development assistance, is more closely correlated to the development needs of low-income nations than is bilateral aid.

A bolder proposal, made a decade ago, by Charles Ratliff, Jr., is to create a World Development Fund (WDF), a supranational agency, established by treaty, managed by both developed and developing nations, and funded by a one percent tax on the national incomes of all the participating countries.[54] The managers of the WDF would disburse the revenues from the international income tax to finance development programs and projects. Common goals could be set, for example, reducing infant mortality rates in all nations to below 50 infant deaths per thousand live births within a decade; preserving the rainforests; and ensuring a high-quality primary education for all children. Greater use could be made of those nongovernmental organizations with a demonstrated capacity for meeting the basic needs of the poor. Other priority areas for assistance would be increasing the productivity of small farmers and improving the status of females. (Recall from Chapter 1 the finding of the United Nations Development Programme that discrimination—economic and social—against females is found in all countries.) The United Nations peacekeeping missions and aid to refugees could also be funded from the WDF.

If a World Development Fund had been in existence in 1993 with just .5 percent of the gross domestic products of all nations taxed, approximately $115 billion would have been raised for development aid. Some 80 percent of the tax revenues would have come from the developed countries. The net transfer of resources to the less developed countries would probably have been some 50 percent greater than the official development assistance received in 1993.[55] Moreover, given the funding priorities of the WDF, the aid received by the least developed countries would have increased even more. Finally, a World Development Fund or greater multilateral aid, in general, would not preclude continued bilateral assistance. In sum, significant progress could be made in alleviating poverty and promoting sustainable development with more and better coordinated foreign aid.

## CONCLUDING NOTE

Foreign aid and foreign investment, along with trade liberalization and an efficient international monetary system, are important components in economic development. Many Third World nations have made impressive economic progress over the past few

---

[53]Ibid., page 226.

[54]Charles Ratliff, Jr., *A World Development Fund,* Special Studies on Global Development, no. 4, College Park, MD: World Academy of Development and Cooperation, 1987.

[55]These calculations are derived from the statistics presented in World Bank, *World Development Report 1995,* Tables 3 and 19.

decades, in some part due to foreign aid. These nations have graduated from official development assistance and are now able to attract foreign investment. Indeed, the ultimate criterion for successful aid is that it is no longer needed. For the least developed nations, however, foreign aid, in all probability, will still be necessary for some considerable time.

In the final section of the text, we explore development paths. We begin with profiles of the economic successes of the East Asian nations and the economic transitions of the former socialist states of Eastern Europe. Then in Chapter 18 we examine the development challenges in sub-Saharan Africa, a region with many of the least developed nations. In the concluding chapter, we discuss international cooperation in addressing the common concerns of maintaining peace, ensuring human rights, and promoting sustainable development.

## SUMMARY OF MAIN POINTS

1. Foreign direct investment, the acquisition of real assets in a foreign country, has grown rapidly in the last decade, especially in the Asian and Latin American regions.
2. Much of the foreign direct investment involves the establishment of foreign subsidiaries by transnational corporations seeking profitable integrations of operations. Key factors in the location of a foreign subsidiary include low unit labor costs, adequate economic infrastructure, and political stability.
3. The benefits of foreign direct investment for developing economies include the receipt of scarce factors, especially management expertise, physical capital, and modern technology; increased income, employment, and tax revenues; creation of labor skills; and the potential for improvement in the trade balance with export expansion or import substitution.
4. Among the possible disadvantages of foreign direct investment for developing economies are the sacrifice of some control over domestic resources; the creation of an enclave with few linkages to the rest of the economy; the discouragement of local entrepreneurship; political interference; and an inappropriate demonstration effect in consumption.
5. Official development assistance, the unilateral transfer of resources from a donor to a recipient nation to promote economic development, can occur bilaterally or multilaterally; be for specific projects or general programs; and take the form of cash grants, concessional loans, commodity transfers, or technical assistance.
6. The moral case for aid rests on three premises: Poverty should be alleviated where possible; poor nations would benefit more from the transfer of resources than rich donor nations would lose; and past injustices inflicted on the less developed countries by the developed countries require compensation.
7. The economic case for aid centers on the relaxation of factor scarcities and the funding of the expenditures on the infrastructure and human capital formation necessary for economic development. Moreover, to the extent development in the recipient nations is advanced, export markets and outlets for foreign direct investment for the donor nations are improved.

8. Conservative opponents of official development assistance question the right of governments to give aid, and furthermore regard foreign aid as wasteful and as interfering with private enterprise. Opponents of aid from the left argue that aid is given not to foster economic development in the recipient nations, but to advance the economic and strategic interests of the donor nations. They claim that much of the official development assistance, especially the bilateral aid, has been mismanaged and ineffective.
9. After the Second World War, the United States and the World Bank focused on the reconstruction of the economies of Europe and Japan. With the onset of the Cold War in the 1950s, the developing nations of Asia, Africa, the Middle East, and Latin America received more attention. Aid was given not only to promote economic growth and development, but to nurture strategic alliances.
10. In the 1950s and 1960s, the emphasis of aid was on generating economic growth. In the 1970s, multilateral aid grew in relative importance with more attention to basic needs projects and human capital formation. In the 1980s, a shift occurred back to bilateral aid and policy reforms to stimulate economic growth. Over the last two decades the average share of GNP given by the OECD nations for official development assistance has been between .30 and .35 percent. The share of OECD bilateral aid to the low-income economies has been significantly less—in the neighborhood of .10 percent of GNP.
11. The record of official development assistance in promoting economic development has been mixed—with both notable successes and failures. Foreign aid appears to be neither necessary nor sufficient for economic development. Properly designed and implemented aid can contribute to economic development. Chief among the reforms to increase the effectiveness of aid is better coordination across donors and between donors and recipients.

## KEY TERMS

**foreign direct investment (FDI)**
**horizontal integration**
**joint ventures**
**nationalization**

**official development assistance (ODA)**
**transfer pricing**
**unit labor costs**
**vertical integration**

## QUESTIONS

1. The very conditions that call for official development assistance may discourage foreign direct investment. Do you agree? Discuss the above statement.
2. Transnational corporations may extend the useful life of machinery and equipment by recycling it to their foreign subsidiaries in less developed countries (see "A Survey of Multinationals," *The Economist* [June 24, 1995], page 21). Should the LDCs welcome this? Discuss.
3. Why do you think China has attracted so much foreign direct investment recently? What is the primary risk to the TNCs that invest in China? Is there any risk to China? Discuss.
4. Why do you think that Nigeria, a low-income economy, has received so much foreign direct investment?

5. Comment on the following quote from Bauer *(Equality, the Third World, and Economic Delusion,* 1981, page 100):

   If the conditions for development other than capital are present, the capital required will either be generated locally or be available commercially from abroad to governments or to businesses. If the required conditions are not present, then aid will be ineffective and wasted.

6. Can the controversy over the effectiveness of aid be settled through the moral arguments for and against aid? Discuss.
7. Comment on the Ratliff proposal to create a World Development Fund. Discuss the advantages and disadvantages of a World Development Fund.

## SUGGESTED READINGS

Bauer, P. T., "Foreign Aid and Its Hydra-Headed Rationalization," *Equality, the Third World, and Economic Delusion,* Cambridge, MA: Harvard University Press, 1981, pages 86–137.

Bergsman, Joel and Xiaofang Shen, "Foreign Direct Investment in Developing Countries: Progress and Problems," *Finance and Development,* vol. 32, no. 4 (December 1995) pages 6–8.

Cassen, Robert and Associates, *Does Aid Work?,* Report to an Intergovernmental Task Force, 2d ed., New York: Clarendon Press, 1994.

Cernea, Michael, "Nongovernmental Organizations and Local Development," World Bank Discussion Papers, Washington, DC: The World Bank, 1988.

Gavin, Michael and Dani Rodrik, "The World Bank in Historical Perspective," *American Economic Review,* vol. 85, no. 2 (May 1995), pages 329–334.

Masoni, Vittorio, "Nongovernmental Organizations and Development," *Finance and Development,* vol. 22, no. 3 (September 1985), pages 38–41.

Ratliff, Charles, Jr., *A World Development Fund,* Special Studies on Global Development, no. 4, College Park, MD: World Academy of Development and Cooperation, 1987.

Riddell, Roger, *Foreign Aid Reconsidered,* Baltimore: The Johns Hopkins University Press, 1987.

Shepherd, Jack, "When Foreign Aid Fails," *The Atlantic Monthly* (April 1985), pages 41–46.

Spero, Joan, "International Financial Flows," *The Politics of International Economic Relations,* 4th ed., New York: St. Martin's Press, 1990, pages 159–202.

United Nations Conference on Trade and Development, *World Investment Report 1994: Transnational Corporations, Employment and the Workplace,* New York: United Nations, 1994.

United Nations Development Programme, *Human Development Report 1993,* "People in Community Organizations," New York: Oxford University Press, 1993, pages 84–99.

World Bank, "Official Development Assistance," in *World Development Report 1985,* New York: Oxford University Press, 1985.

# CHAPTER 17

# PROFILES IN DEVELOPMENT: ECONOMIC ACHIEVEMENT IN EAST ASIA AND ECONOMIC TRANSITION IN EASTERN EUROPE

While the economic development of each country is unique, reflecting its geography, history, culture, and extant political system, discernible patterns exist, nevertheless, in the contemporary developing economies. For instance, we have discussed at length the physical and human capital deepening required for economic growth and development; and we have examined the structural changes and population shifts that accompany the transformation from low-income, primarily agrarian economies to high-income, diversified, industrial economies. So, too, we can identify regional tendencies across the Third World. The development paths followed by the nations of East Asia differ in important ways from those followed by nations in South Asia, or the Middle East and North Africa, or sub-Saharan Africa, or Latin America.

In this chapter we profile two rather different regions: the rapidly growing economies in East Asia and the transitional economies of the former socialist states in Eastern Europe. Then, in Chapter 18, we turn to the challenges facing the nations of sub-Saharan Africa in their attempts to reduce poverty and encourage development.

The World Bank, in the *World Development Report 1991*, set forth a market-friendly strategy, one that defines complementary roles for the private and public sectors and provides a useful template for building a foundation for sustainable development. We begin with an overview of this strategy. We will see many of the policy recommendations of Chapters 7 through 16 reflected in this market-friendly strategy.

## MARKET-FRIENDLY STRATEGY OF DEVELOPMENT

Four major components compose the World Bank's market-friendly strategy (MFS) of development: a stable macroeconomy, competitive domestic markets, investments in human capital, and integration with the international economy. In Figure 17.1 we illustrate the main features of these four, mutually reinforcing components.

## STABLE MACROECONOMY

One of the primary responsibilities of the government is to maintain a stable macroeconomy. A strong central bank is needed, not only to exercise control over the money supply, but to supervise the banking system. Sound fiscal and monetary policies are crucial for macroeconomic stability. As we discussed in Chapter 9, the use of demand-management policies to achieve the macroeconomic goals of full employment, price stability, and healthy economic growth is controversial. Widely recognized, however, are the harmful effects of chronically large government budget deficits. The deficits have to be financed, either by borrowing in the bond market, resulting in higher interest rates and a crowding out of private domestic investment, or by borrowing from the central bank, in which case the money supply is expanded. Frequently, in developing economies, the second option is used, and the monetization of the government budget deficits results in inflation.

Controlling inflation, as discussed in Chapter 10, is not only important for avoiding a deterioration in the position of those with relatively fixed nominal incomes (including a decline in the real wages of unskilled labor), but for keeping real interest rates positive and encouraging saving. Further, as we related in Chapter 15, inflation can trigger an inflation-depreciation cycle. The trade balance worsens as the domestic currency appreciates in real terms. The capital account may also weaken if there is capital flight in anticipation of continuing depreciation (or devaluation). Monetary discipline becomes easier when there is fiscal discipline.

Exercising fiscal discipline, however, is difficult in developing economies. The demands for government expenditures are great—from providing public education for rapidly increasing school-age populations, to investing in the infrastructure, to securing the national defense. Thus, in addition to economy in government spending, a comprehensive system of taxation on incomes, property, and sales needs to be developed. Trade barriers, if used to generate revenues, as well as to protect domestic industries, should take the form of tariffs, rather than quotas. As the nation establishes a domestic tax system and moves toward freer trade, the tariffs should be phased out.

In sum, a stable macroeconomy, one in which large budget deficits and inflationary growth in the money supply are avoided, real interest rates are positive, and the exchange value of the currency is competitive and stable, creates an environment conducive to economic growth and development.

## COMPETITIVE DOMESTIC MARKETS

The government is also involved in the next component of the MFS—the promotion of competitive domestic markets. Here, establishing a sound institutional environment is important. There should be fair and efficient legislative and judicial processes. Property rights should be well-defined and laws should be understood and respected. Regulations to protect the environment and promote health and safety in the workplace and in the consumption of the goods and services produced should be transparent, cost-effective, and consistently enforced. A competent and honest civil service is needed to administer efficiently the functions of the public sector.

### FIGURE 17.1    COMPONENTS OF A MARKET-FRIENDLY STRATEGY OF DEVELOPMENT

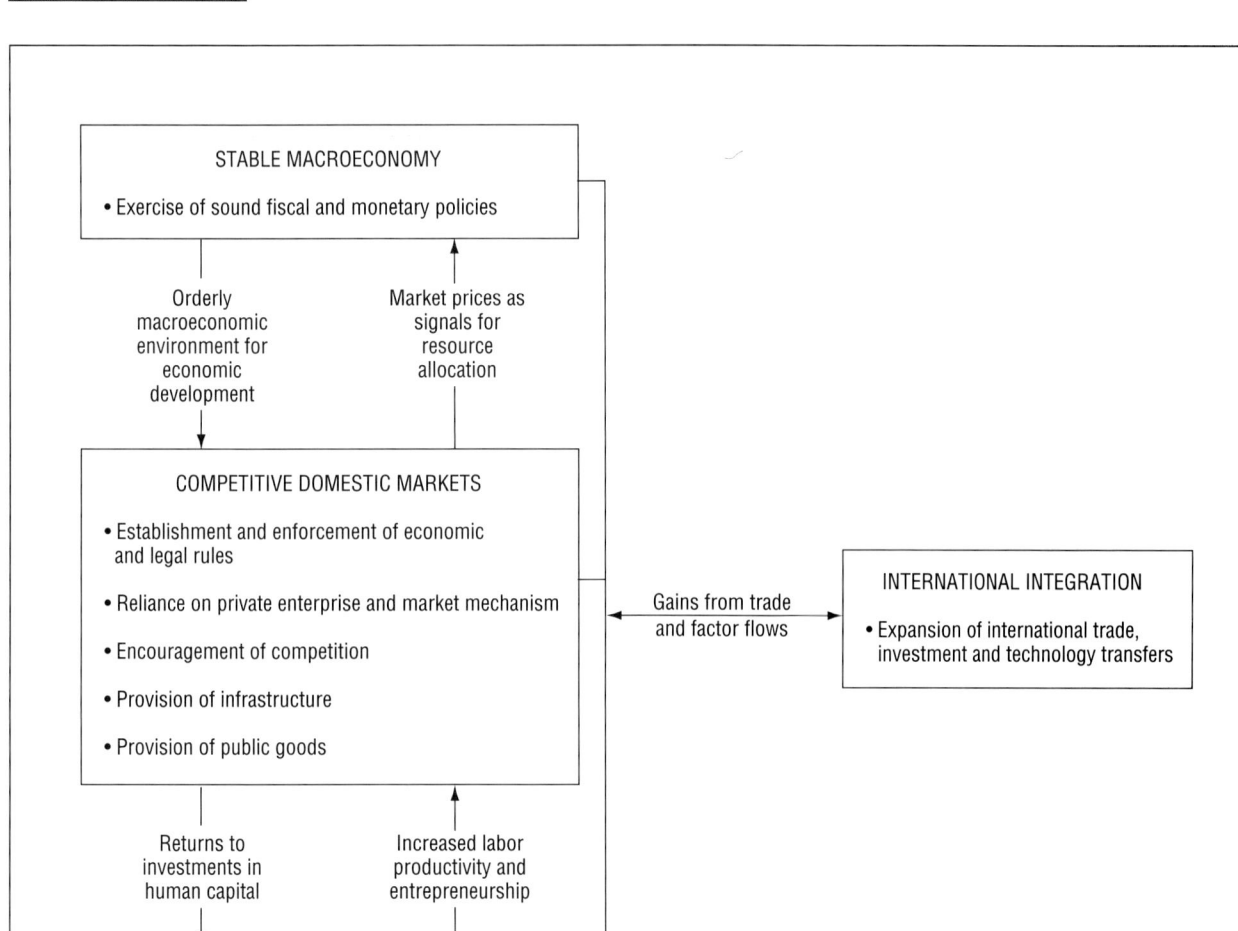

ADAPTED FROM World Bank, *World Development Report 1991*, New York: Oxford University Press, 1991, Figure 4.

Because of the inherent efficiencies in the allocation of resources—in the absence of uncorrected externalities—the market mechanism should be relied on whenever possible. For example, interest rates, wage rates, and exchange rates should be set in the market, free to respond to changes in demand and supply conditions. (Recall how interest rate ceilings and overvalued official exchange rates result in scarcities of credit and foreign exchange, respectively, and encourage unproductive, if privately profitable, rent-seeking. Recall also how institutionally set modern-sector wages restrict employment.)

Moreover, downward flexibility in wages and prices relieves the burden of adjustment on output and employment during economic recessions.

The government should promote competition through antitrust action to break up monopolies and oligopolies that restrain commerce. International trade and competition from foreign producers helps to achieve the same effect, particularly when domestic markets are too small to support many producers. There should be straightforward and streamlined procedures for forming businesses, as well as for the dissolution of bankrupt businesses.

State-owned enterprises, when inefficient and unprofitable—as is frequently the case—should be privatized. A greater role in developing economies may be found for private enterprise in the operation of public utilities, where substantial economies of scale make market competition less feasible. Regulation could be used to encourage efficiency and innovation. For example, private firms could bid on the government contracts to supply water or electricity to a given population at set user charges. Rather than regulate the rate of return earned by the private companies, the government could set standards of service. In many cases, the governments of the developing economies may have to make the initial investments in the public utility infrastructure, but private enterprise could be relied on to provide the actual services.

As discussed in Chapter 6, the government also provides public goods, such as national defense, courts, police protection, and highways. Because of the positive externalities, basic research geared to the needs of the developing economy might also be subsidized. The World Bank notes how "A strong central system of metrology, norms, standards, testing, and quality control helps an economy to upgrade and diffuse technology ... [and that] standards should conform to international specifications."[1]

Agriculture, often neglected in the early drives to industrialization, could benefit significantly from more competitive markets and additional public investment. As discussed in Chapter 11, allowing the prices received by farmers to rise to world market equilibrium levels and avoiding overvalued currencies would stimulate agricultural production. So, too, greater access to credit and agricultural extension services would boost private investment and productivity. The economies of scale in agriculture, especially for many of the food crops grown in the developing countries, are modest. Small-scale, labor-intensive farming can be efficient. Investing in the rural infrastructure—highways to markets, irrigation projects for small farmers with appropriate user fees, and storage facilities—would have high returns for the national economy. The cross-country evidence is convincing that a viable agricultural sector enhances industrial growth.

Thus, in the market-friendly strategy, the government's role includes creating an enabling environment for private enterprise by supplying the essential public goods, and carrying out public investments in the infrastructure, basic research, and human capital that augment the returns on private investment.

## INVESTMENTS IN HUMAN CAPITAL

As emphasized in the second stage of Adelman's depauperization strategy (see Chapter 5), human capital formation builds a solid foundation for sustained economic

---

[1]World Bank, *World Development Report 1991*, New York: Oxford University Press, 1991, page 92.

development. Investments in nutrition, health, and education accumulate in a beneficial cycle of improvements in the quality and quantity of life. To begin, adequate nutrition and child care should be ensured. Well-nourished and healthy children have more success in school—eventually constituting a better educated and more productive labor force. Economic mobility increases, and average wages rise. Parents have fewer children, but invest more in each child. Family planning programs to assist couples in controlling their fertility should be available. The reduced youth burden of dependency permits greater saving and additional gains in physical and human capital deepening. The returns to investments in population quality are bolstered by the more competitive domestic markets and greater opportunities for entrepreneurship.

The biases in public education and health-care expenditures often characteristic of the less developed countries were considered in Chapter 8. Gains in both efficiency and equity can be realized with a reallocation of resources, away from the heavily subsidized and expensive university education that disproportionately benefits the children of relatively well-off families and in favor of high-quality, universally available, primary education. Similarly, in public health, a shift should occur away from the costly curative medicine provided by urban hospitals toward more cost-effective, preventative medicine and basic services for the rural and poor urban populations. Opportunities for university education and graduate training and for sophisticated treatment by hospitals should still be available, but the burden of costs should be increasingly borne by the students and patients served.

Indeed, a constraint to implementing some of the institutional reforms in the market-friendly strategy is a shortage of qualified administrators and professionals within the developing nations. For example, the World Bank cites the supply of lawyers, accountants, merchant bankers, and entrepreneurs as limiting factors in the move to privatize state-owned enterprises.[2] Likewise, the implementation of comprehensive tax systems may be limited by insufficient numbers of skilled tax officials. Yet, at the same time, the ranks of the civil services may be bloated with political patrons and university graduates not absorbed by the private sector. Not only is the government bureaucracy increased, but the pressure on government budgets results in less competitive real wages for government employees (as money wages lag behind inflation). This, in turn, contributes to low morale, poor performance, and even corruption (e.g., bribes for services rendered efficiently or favors granted).[3]

A responsibility often assumed by governments has been the alleviation of poverty—in the short run through transfers and direct provision for basic needs, and in the long run through investments in human capital. In addition to more equitable access to education and health-care services, the average quality of life in developing economies could be improved by public investments in clean water supplies and sanitation systems. As illustrated in Chapter 8 by the water supplies in Lima, Peru, raising user charges to cover the costs of the services provided would allow public utilities not only to generate more revenues, but to increase their coverage. Such a restructuring of fees would mean an end to the subsidization of the upper-income consumers in

---

[2]Ibid., page 143.

[3]Ibid., pages 130–132. See also Vito Tanzi, "Corruption, Governmental Activities, and Markets," *Finance and Development* vol. 32, no. 4 (December 1995), pages 24–27, for an interesting overview of corruption in government.

urban areas. In contrast, the prices paid by the poor, who had relied on expensive private vendors, would probably fall, even as the quality of the services provided rises. Foreign aid could help with funding of the infrastructure, and nongovernmental organizations could assist in the delivery of these essential services to rural and poor urban communities.

Literate and healthy labor forces should bolster the developing nations' comparative advantages in labor-intensive manufacturing—the basis for Adelman's third stage of depauperization, rapid growth through the expansion of manufactured exports.

## INTERNATIONAL INTEGRATION

International trade is an extension of the market mechanism across national borders. As illustrated in Chapter 14, efficiency gains resulting from international specialization are realized in increased global output. Nations producing according to their comparative advantages and engaging in trade are able to consume beyond their production possibilities boundaries. National incomes and employments rise.

Recall from the factor endowments theory of trade that labor-abundant nations should increase the production and export of labor-intensive commodities while importing capital-intensive commodities. Although those factors of production employed in the comparative-disadvantage industries initially incur income losses from trade liberalization, it is possible to improve the welfare of all groups within the nations. For example, income support and assistance in retraining and relocation could be given to the labor displaced by increased import competition. Furthermore, dynamic gains from trade and international competition result, including the attention to product quality, cost efficiencies, and innovation highlighted in the product cycle theory of trade.

Also demonstrated in Chapter 14 were the gains from international factor mobility. Allowing factors to flow to their most productive uses, regardless of national borders, increases global output and employment. Restrictions on international migration limit significantly the flows of labor; however, capital is more mobile. In Chapter 16 we discussed the advantages and disadvantages of foreign direct investment. On net, we find mutual benefits from foreign direct investment, not the least of which are the transfers of skilled labor, capital, and technology. So, too, foreign portfolio investment is increasing, serving to improve developing country access to international financial capital.

The World Bank observed that

> The key to global development has been the diffusion of technological progress. New technology has allowed resources to be used more productively, causing incomes to rise and the quality of life to improve.[4]

Technology transfers can occur through merchandise trade (new technologies embodied in the imported intermediate, capital, and consumer goods); trade in services (the direct licensing of new technologies and the hiring of foreign consultants); international investment (the knowledge conveyed by the expatriate management of the foreign subsidiaries of transnational corporations); foreign aid (technical and program assistance); and the return of native students and workers from other nations.

---

[4]Ibid., page 14.

International integration not only complements, but reinforces, the other components of the market-friendly strategy. A stable macroeconomy promotes international trade and investment. As discussed in Chapter 15, avoiding large fiscal deficits and high inflation rates reduces the likelihood of serious balance of payments problems. Maintaining positive real interest rates and a stable exchange rate should reduce capital flight. Indeed, a sound, market-based macroeconomy combined with political stability should attract foreign investment. Stable national economies, in turn, contribute to a stable international environment for trade and investment.

Foreign direct investment is also attracted by an educated labor force. Early and continuing human capital formation provides the entrepreneurs and skilled labor necessary to expand exports in manufactures and services. Literate labor forces are better able to use the new technologies.

Competitive domestic markets, oriented to world prices, allow nations to reap the benefits of their comparative advantages. Adequate economic infrastructure, especially in the transportation and communication systems, are essential for success in trade and in attracting foreign investment.

In sum, the market-friendly strategy of development is based on sustained human capital formation; a stable macroeconomy with disciplined fiscal and monetary policies; competitive domestic markets, driven by private enterprise, enhanced by productive public investment in the infrastructure, complemented by the efficient provision of public goods, and grounded in fair, effective legislative and judicial systems; and an outward orientation through liberalized trade and investment policies.

## IMPLEMENTING THE MARKET-FRIENDLY STRATEGY OF DEVELOPMENT

Near the beginning of the *World Development Report 1991,* the World Bank stated, "Investing in people, if done right, provides the firmest foundation for lasting development."[5] Given the considerable lags between the investments in child nutrition, health care, and education and the subsequent payoffs in terms of improved labor quality, entrepreneurship, and lower fertility, nations that had the foresight to establish comprehensive primary education and health-care systems are now in favorable positions to implement the economic and institutional reforms consistent with the MFS. On the other hand, nations that did not undertake extensive human capital formation—as evidenced by their current low school enrollment rates, high illiteracy rates, and low life expectancies—have considerable catching up to do. For specific policy reforms in nutrition, health care, and education, refer back to Chapter 8.

In any case, special attention should be given to improving the educational and economic opportunities afforded to females. The extent of the many contributions women make to development—as caregivers, workers, managers, entrepreneurs, and community leaders—has only recently been fully appreciated. As noted by the World Bank, "Failing to raise women's level of education closer to men's detracts from the social benefits of raising men's."[6]

To implement the MFS, a dedicated, competent, and honest corps of civil servants is needed. Public-sector employees should be hired based on a competitive application process, and their promotion and compensation should similarly be based on

---

[5]Ibid., page 4.
[6]Ibid., page 55.

merit. Reducing the bureaucracy and overstaffing characteristic of many governments in developing economies is also important for achieving the fiscal discipline underlying macroeconomic stability. Public investment projects should be carefully selected, and public subsidies should be carefully targeted. In many developing nations, the share of gross domestic product going for national defense, if not the levels of real military expenditures, could be reduced. (In Chapter 19 we will examine the issue of national security and military expenditures.) Together with the revenues generated through improved tax systems, cutting government expenditures should restore budget balances, relieving the pressure on the monetary authorities for inflationary deficit-financing.

The central bank should be insulated from political pressures in order to adhere to the goal of inflation control. Adopting a fixed exchange rate imposes discipline on the monetary authorities. Under a flexible exchange rate or managed float, the monetary discipline must be self-imposed in order to avoid inflation-depreciation cycles. Either could work if properly administered.

Efforts to liberalize prices in general should be pursued, so that resource allocations reflect market forces. Indications of distortions in the economy that interfere with the efficient allocation of resources include the degree of protection (measured by the discrepancy between world prices and domestic prices for specific commodities); the premiums on foreign currencies (measured by the difference between the official and the "black market," or "parallel," exchange rates); and whether real, risk-adjusted interest rates are positive (and roughly in line with international rates).

Increased integration in the international economy will be more successful with macroeconomic stability and competitive domestic markets. Privatizing inefficient state-owned enterprises would be part of the effort to promote market competition. Similarly, as noted in Chapter 14, selective import substitution, as part of the transition to a strategy of export expansion and diversification, with gradual technological upgrading, could be pursued. Quantitative restrictions such as import quotas would be converted to tariffs, and a firm schedule for the phasing out of import tariffs and export subsidies would be put into place. The successful conclusion of the Uruguay Round and the general movement toward trade liberalization augurs well for the adoption of more outward-oriented strategies.

The World Bank suggests the following sequence for implementing the MFS:

> At the outset comes macroeconomic stabilization, which can either precede or accompany structural reform.... Next comes the liberalization of product markets, including deregulatory reform. It would be preferable not to delay domestic reforms until after trade reform. In the area of the liberalization of the external sector, the trade account best precedes the capital account. Asset markets adjust faster than goods markets, so the premature deregulation of capital flows can lead to speculation and financial instability.[7]

Through its lending for structural adjustment programs, the World Bank provides budgetary support and technical assistance to countries adopting the market-friendly strategy.

In Chapter 19 we will discuss areas of international cooperation—in debt relief, trade and finance, foreign aid, environmental preservation, and security—that complement national market-friendly strategies and are important for advancing global

---

[7]Ibid., page 118.

development. Before profiling the East Asian economies, we note some of the reservations and criticisms of the World Bank's approach.

## CONCERNS WITH THE MARKET-FRIENDLY STRATEGY

While generally well-received, the World Bank's strategy is faulted in some quarters. For example, Ajit Singh argues that "government needs to have a far bigger role in economic activity than is envisaged in the 'market-friendly' approach."[8] In particular, government guidance and coordination are important for a developing economy in devising and implementing a dynamic industrial policy. Japan and South Korea are cited as especially effective examples of state-directed industrial developments, beginning with a phase of import substitution that evolved into highly successful export promotion. Moreover, Singh observes that the emphasis of the MFS on the supply-side sources of growth "ignores altogether the role of demand factors."[9]

Albert Fishlow acknowledges the general trend in the 1990s toward economic liberalization—less government regulation and greater reliance on private enterprise and foreign trade and investment.[10] More attention, however, needs to be given to the heavy burdens of external debt under which developing countries labor. As a primary reason for the poor economic performances, Fishlow points to the declining levels of investment and imports in the 1980s, primarily in Latin America and sub-Saharan Africa, a consequence of the structural adjustments adopted to deal with external debt problems. Furthermore, the World Bank's emphasis on competitive markets and international integration may belie the difficulty of the policy challenges facing developing countries and their governments in promoting competition and expanding exports. According to Fishlow, what is needed is a "full set of rules for determining the appropriate form and changing role of government policy."[11]

In sum, the World Bank's market-friendly strategy may not set forth a guaranteed, easy-to-use recipe for economic development. While the main areas for policy reform are identified, the underlying processes of political and economic institution-building are less clearly specified. And the intervening costs of the necessary structural adjustments are not fully addressed—in particular, the costs borne by the poor if government-provided social services and support for rural development are cut back. Implementing the necessary policy changes will require capable and stable governments—by no means a given in the contemporary developing nations.

Perhaps, though, it is unrealistic to expect any one strategy to encompass all of the ramifications of economic development. Our understanding of this complex phenomenon is continually growing—informed by both the successes and failures of development experience. We turn now to a discussion of East Asia, a region widely acclaimed for its rapid economic progress and cited by the World Bank for its development strategies.

---

[8] Ajit Singh, "Openness and the Market-Friendly Approach to Development: Learning the Right Lessons from Development Experience," *World Development*, vol. 22, no. 12 (December 1994), pages 1811–1823. This excerpt is from page 1811.

[9] Ibid., page 1813.

[10] Albert Fishlow, "Economic Development in the 1990s," *World Development*, vol. 22, no. 12 (December 1994), pages 1825–1832.

[11] Ibid., page 1830.

## EAST ASIAN ECONOMIES: RAPID GROWTH WITH EQUITY

"There is no single East Asian model."[12] East Asian economies are widely heralded not only for their high growth rates in per capita incomes, but for the broad-based nature of the improvements in their standards of living. And while, as the above quotation suggests, variations are found across the East Asian nations in the specific policies pursued, defining common features also exist, including early and impressive human capital formation; strong, pragmatic governments; macroeconomic stability; and rapid export growth.

In 1993, the World Bank published a study, *The East Asian Miracle: Economic Growth and Public Policy,* that highlighted eight high-performing Asian economies (HPAEs). Along with Japan, there were the Four Tigers (Hong Kong, the Republic of Korea [or South Korea], Singapore, and Taiwan), and three newly-industrializing economies (Indonesia, Thailand, and Malaysia). Below we use this study to illustrate the "market-friendly policies [that] are the foundation of East Asia's economic success."[13]

To illustrate both the diversity and consistency across the HPAEs, in Table 17.1 we present selected statistics for South Korea and the three newly-industrializing economies. We can compare their performances with the averages for all the low- and middle-income economies, i.e., the less developed countries. Per capita GNPs for 1993 range from $740 for Indonesia, near the bottom of the middle-income economies, to $7660 for South Korea, near the top of the middle-income economies. In contrast to many developing nations, over the last decade these HPAEs achieved high economic growth and relatively low rates of inflation.[14]

The strong export performances, particularly for South Korea, Malaysia, and Thailand, allowed for high growth rates in imports. In 1993, over 90 percent of the merchandise exports of South Korea were manufactures. The newly industrializing economies, favorably endowed with natural resources, still have significant shares of merchandise exports outside of manufactures, e.g., Malaysia in timber, fuel, and rubber; Thailand in rice; and Indonesia in fuel and rubber. For South Korea and Malaysia, debt service ratios are relatively low; not so for Indonesia, where nearly a third of export revenues are required for debt service.

Also, in terms of population growth and human capital formation, we find differences as well as similarities across this subset of East Asian economies. South Korea has reduced its fertility to well below replacement level. Thailand, despite its significantly lower level of development, has attained replacement level fertility. (The positive growth rates for population in these two nations reflect population momentum.) On the other hand, Malaysia, notwithstanding its low infant mortality and relatively high female secondary school enrollment rates, still has high fertility, and consequently,

---

[12]World Bank, *The East Asian Miracle: Economic Growth and Public Policy,* A World Bank Policy Research Report, New York: Oxford University Press, 1993, page 347.

[13]Ibid.

[14]Note that the average inflation rate for the low- and middle-income economies for 1980–1993 of 35.3 percent reflects the very high inflation rate for the Latin American and Caribbean region (245 percent). For the other developing regions, the average annual inflation rates for this period are: 16.1 percent for sub-Saharan Africa, 7.1 percent for East Asia and the Pacific, 8.6 percent for South Asia, 35.3 percent for Europe and Central Asia, and 10.7 percent for the Middle East and North Africa.

| TABLE 17.1 | DEVELOPMENT INDICATORS: SELECTED EAST ASIAN NATIONS | | | | |
|---|---|---|---|---|---|
| | SOUTH KOREA | MALAYSIA | THAILAND | INDONESIA | LOW- AND MIDDLE-INCOME ECONOMIES |
| GNP per capita, 1993 ($) | 7660 | 3140 | 2110 | 740 | 1090 |
| GNP per capita, average annual growth rate 1980–93 (%) | 8.2 | 3.5 | 6.4 | 4.2 | 0.9 |
| Inflation rate, average annual 1980–93 (%) | 6.3 | 2.2 | 4.3 | 8.5 | 35.3 |
| Average annual growth rate, 1980–93 (%) | | | | | |
|     Agriculture | 2.0 | 3.5 | 3.8 | 3.2 | 2.2 |
|     Industry | 12.1 | 8.2 | 11.0 | 6.3 | 3.0 |
| Average annual growth rate, 1980–93 (%) | | | | | |
|     Merchandise exports | 12.3 | 12.6 | 15.5 | 6.7 | ... |
|     Merchandise imports | 11.4 | 9.7 | 13.8 | 4.5 | ... |
| COMPOSITION OF MERCHANDISE EXPORTS, 1993 | | | | | |
|   % Fuels, minerals, metals | 3 | 14 | 2 | 32 | ... |
|   % Other primary commodities | 4 | 21 | 26 | 15 | ... |
|   % Machinery and equipment | 43 | 41 | 28 | 5 | ... |
|   % Other manufactures | 51 | 24 | 45 | 48 | ... |
| Total debt service as a % of exports, 1993 | 9.2 | 7.9 | 18.7 | 31.8 | 18.3 |
| Population, 1993 (millions) | 44.1 | 19.0 | 58.1 | 187.2 | 4689.0 |
| Population growth rate, average annual 1980–93 (%) | 1.1 | 2.5 | 1.7 | 1.7 | 1.9 |
| Total fertility rate, 1993 | 1.7 | 3.5 | 2.1 | 2.8 | 3.4 |
| Infant mortality rate, 1993 (infant deaths per thousand live births) | 11 | 13 | 36 | 56 | 55 |
| Female life expectancy at birth, 1993 (years) | 75 | 73 | 72 | 65 | 66 |
| SCHOOL ENROLLMENT RATES, 1992 (%) | | | | | |
|   Primary    Total | 105 | 93 | 97 | 115 | ... |
|             Female | 106 | 94 | 88 | 113 | ... |
|   Secondary  Total | 90 | 58 | 33 | 38 | ... |
|             Female | 91 | 59 | 32 | ... | ... |
|   Tertiary    Total | 42 | 7 | 19 | 10 | ... |
| Adult illiteracy rate, 1990 (%) | | | | | |
|     Total | ... | 22 | 7 | 23 | 33 |
|     Female | 7 | 30 | 10 | 32 | ... |

NOTES: Lack of data is indicated by ...

The *average annual rate of inflation* is measured by the growth rate of the GDP implicit deflator. The average for all low- and middle-income economies is weighted by population shares. Excluding the high inflation region of Latin America and the Caribbean reduces the weighted average inflation rate for the less developed countries to 12.2 percent.

*Total debt service* is the sum of principal repayments and interest payments on total external debt.

*Primary school enrollment ratios* may exceed 100 percent because some pupils are younger or older than the country's standard primary-school age. The tertiary enrollment ratio is calculated by dividing the number of pupils enrolled in all post-secondary schools and universities by the population in the 20–24 age group. Pupils attending vocational schools, adult education programs, two-year community colleges, and distant education centers (primarily correspondence courses) are included.

*Adult illiteracy* is defined here as the proportion of the population over the age of 15 who cannot, with understanding, read and write a short, simple statement on their everyday life.

FROM World Bank, *World Development Report 1995,* New York: Oxford University Press, Tables 1, 2, 13, 15, 23, 25, 26, 27, 28, 29.

## FIGURE 17.2 — GROWTH RATES IN GNP PER CAPITA

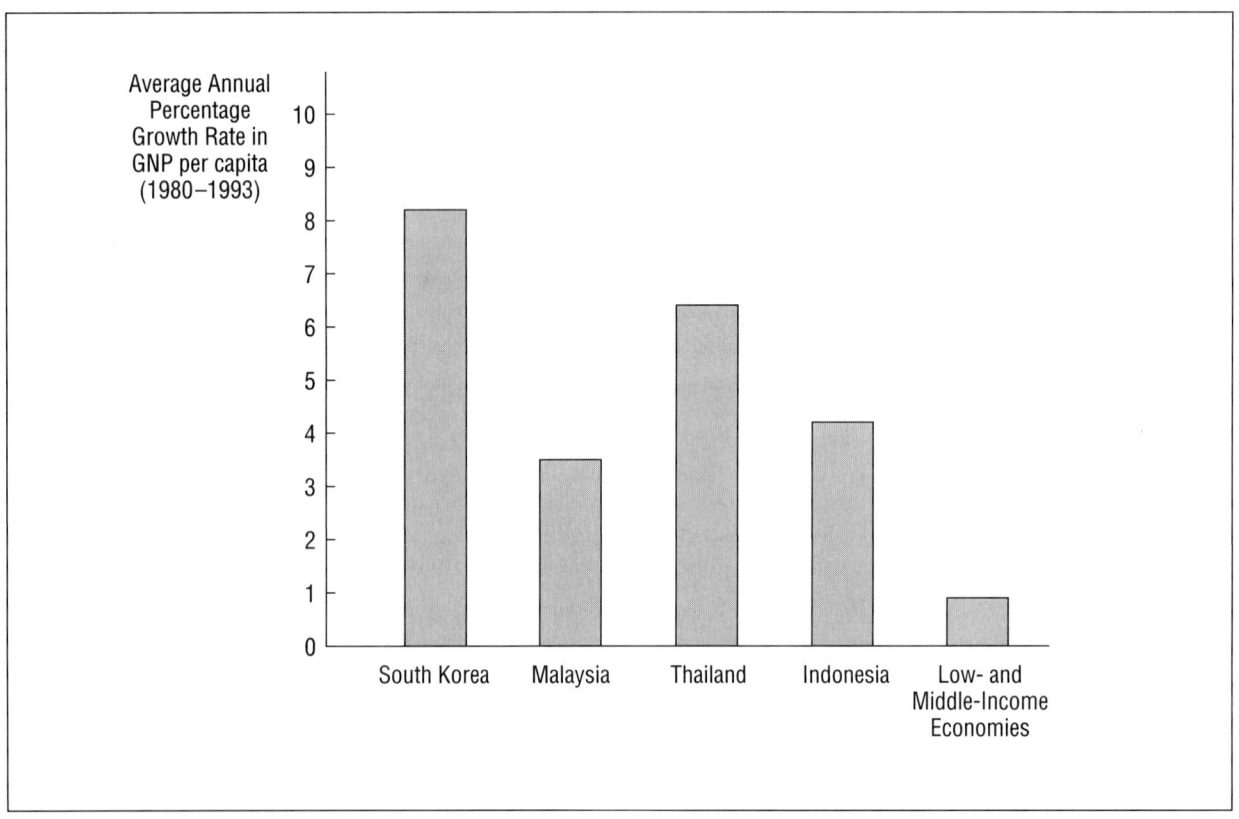

substantial population growth. School enrollment rates are strong, and adult illiteracy rates are low for these four nations. For Thailand, the record for adult literacy is particularly impressive. In general, the gaps between male and female enrollment rates are minimal or nonexistent in East Asia; Thailand, however, at the primary level is an exception.

### KEYS TO ECONOMIC SUCCESS IN EAST ASIA

We need to delve behind these selected development indicators and explore the major factors identified by the World Bank as underlying the economic achievements in East Asia. We generalize, mindful of the diversity of experiences across the nations.

#### HUMAN CAPITAL FORMATION

In the 1960s, before the initiation of rapid economic growth, the levels of human capital formation in the HPAEs were already high—compared to other developing nations. Not only was an early emphasis placed on universal primary education, but the subsequent public funding of education was not heavily skewed to expensive university education.

The allocation of public expenditures between basic and higher education is the major public policy factor that accounts for East Asia's extraordinary performance with regard to the quantity of basic education provided. The share of public expenditure on education allocated to basic education has been consistently higher in East Asia than elsewhere.[15]

High enrollments in primary school increased the demand for secondary and higher education. The attention to primary education was sustained in East Asia, in part, through merit-based restrictions on entrance to public secondary schools and universities and the expansion of private education. Rising incomes, coupled with popular demand for education, allowed for a shifting of the burden of expenses for higher education to the private sector. Roy Hofheinz and Kent Calder, in *The Eastasia Edge* (1982), note that "National policy throughout Eastasia [sic] encourages technical competence and offers incentives for training engineers and scientists, while conspicuously ignoring the liberal arts and the training of lawyers."[16]

Major dividends from the investments in education include reduced fertility rates, contributing to further human and physical capital deepening, and a literate, skilled labor force, essential for the export-expansion strategies. In fact, a highly positive relationship emerged between the expansion of manufactured exports, the absorption of technology, and human capital formation.

> Manufactured exports accelerated the acquisition and mastery of international best-practice technologies in highly imperfect international technology markets. High and rising levels of human capital in the HPAEs, especially the superior educational attainment and cognitive skills of the industrial labor force, helped to ensure that these new processes and equipment were used and adapted effectively. Thus export orientation and high human capital formed a virtuous circle; exports raised the returns from education, and education raised the returns from exporting.[17]

The emphasis on education, enhanced by policies to expand economic opportunities, contributed to the equitable growth in incomes. With its human capital formation, East Asia built a solid foundation for sustained development.

## CAPABLE ADMINISTRATIONS AND PRAGMATIC POLICIES

Economic policymaking in the HPAEs has been characterized by "pragmatic flexibility."[18] Clear objectives are set forth—whether rapid growth in manufactured exports or investment in key industrial sectors. Measures to achieve these objectives are then

---

[15] World Bank, *The East Asian Miracle*, page 199. Birdsall, Ross, and Sabot note that the expansion of school enrollments in East Asia was not at the expense of the quality of the education.

> Repetition and dropout rates—which are negatively correlated with school quality—have remained low in comparison with those in other developing regions, and East Asian children have consistently scored better in internationally comparable tests than children from other developing economies.

See Nancy Birdsall, David Ross, and Richard Sabot, "Inequality and Growth Reconsidered: Lessons from East Asia," *The World Bank Economic Review*, vol. 9, no. 3 (September 1995), pages 477–508. This quotation is from pages 481–482. Birdsall, Ross, and Sabot also observe that "The work ethic for which East Asian children and labor are well known may be less an exogenous cultural trait than an endogenous response to incentives that reward effort" (page 501).

[16] Roy Hofheinz, Jr., and Kent Calder, *The Eastasia Edge,* New York: Basic Books, 1982, page 114.

[17] World Bank, *The East Asian Miracle*, page 261.

[18] Ibid., page 86.

diligently pursued. The emphasis is on performance. Gustav Ranis observes, "What clearly marks off East Asia from the average developing-economy case is the remarkable ability of the authorities to recognize mistakes and quickly take appropriate corrective action."[19]

Consistent with the market-friendly strategy, competition and private enterprise are encouraged, although the guiding hand of government is often felt. Information is shared, and investment plans are coordinated between the public and private sectors. Policymakers, government administrators, and civil servants are competent, motivated, and largely insulated from the influence of special interest groups.

Factor markets are not entirely free of government interference—although relative factor prices reflect relative factor scarcities. There has been mild financial repression, (i.e., nominal interest rates held below market equilibrium levels), yet real interest rates usually are positive and credit is allocated based on market performance. Labor unions are not powerful, although real wages rise with productivity.

The overall strategies are balanced and equitable. The importance of small- and medium-scale enterprises is recognized with access to credit and new technologies. Foreign direct investment and technology transfers are sought, consistent with the upgrading of industry and labor skills.

Agriculture has not been slighted. On the contrary ...

> Agriculture has played a more central role in the HPAEs than in many other low- and middle-income economies. Wide adoption of Green Revolution technology, high investment in rural infrastructure, and limited direct and indirect taxation of agriculture meant that rural incomes and productivity rose more rapidly in East Asia than in other regions.[20]

Hofheinz and Calder argue that the successful land reforms in East Asian nations have not only promoted a more equitable distribution of wealth, but contributed to political stability.[21]

The contribution of the Confucian culture, especially the respect for authority, to political stability, is also highlighted by Hofheinz and Calder:

> No people builds authority structures more elaborately, or respects them, once clearly established, with as much commitment. No people so consistently subordinates individual interests to those of the group. And no people remains as loyal to the nation or the state, even in times of deep trouble. In many respects, the miracle of Eastasian [sic] economic performance is squarely based on an even more remarkable phenomenon of political coherence.[22]

### MACROECONOMIC STABILITY

The twin pillars of macroeconomic stability are fiscal responsibility and monetary discipline. For the most part, large government budget deficits have been avoided by the

---

[19] Gustav Ranis, "Another Look at the East Asian Miracle," *The World Bank Economic Review*, vol. 9, no. 3 (September 1995), pages 509–534. This quotation is from page 531.

[20] World Bank, *The East Asian Miracle*, page 352. Ranis (1995) provides a good overview of the importance of agriculture to the development of Taiwan, which early on pursued a strategy akin to Adelman's agricultural demand–led industrialization (refer back to the discussion in Chapter 5).

[21] Hofheinz and Calder, page 92.

[22] Ibid., page 217.

HPAEs. Reduced fertility and lower youth burdens of dependency have relieved the pressure on governments for social welfare expenditures. Rapid income growth and comprehensive tax systems helped by generating government revenues. Such fiscal responsibility made it easier to exercise monetary discipline. Low inflation kept real interest rates positive and real exchange rates competitive. Positive real interest rates and sound banking systems, including deposit insurance, stimulated saving.

> Between 1960 and 1990, both saving and investment increased markedly in the HPAEs, outstripping the performance of other developing regions.... The HPAEs are the only group of developing economies in which saving exceeds investment, making them exporters of capital.[23]

Net exports of capital are reflected in current account surpluses. In sum, macroeconomic stability makes export expansion strategies more feasible.

## Export Expansion

The hallmark of East Asia's economic successes has been the rapid, even phenomenal, growth of manufactured exports. Drawing on educated labor forces and following sound macroeconomic policies, the HPAEs, especially the Four Tigers (South Korea, Singapore, Hong Kong, and Taiwan) have used exports as an engine of growth. In addition to getting internal factor prices in line with relative factor scarcities to enhance their comparative advantages and maintaining competitive exchange rates, East Asian governments actively promote exports.

With the exception of Hong Kong, the HPAEs began with import substitution, and made the transition to export expansion. The World Bank identifies three different export strategies in the region.[24] Hong Kong and Singapore basically adopted a free trade approach, with very limited government intervention, although Singapore did seek foreign investment in the export sectors. Korea and Taiwan, as did Japan, continued protection of domestic industries, while more aggressively pushing exports—with prefential access to credit and foreign exchange, tax incentives, and technical and marketing assistance for exporters. Indonesia, Thailand, and Malaysia, the newly-industrializing economies in Southeast Asia, have taken an intermediate approach, combining gradual import liberalization, support for exporters, and export-oriented foreign investment.

As the World Bank notes, "An essential feature of the East Asian export push has been the ability to adapt to the global environment."[25] Reflected in this adaptability has been the alignment of domestic prices to world prices; the accommodation of foreign direct investment; the adoption of modern technology; the upgrading of the product sophistication of exports as comparative advantages changed; and the prudent management of external debt.

In the conclusion to its study of the high-performing East Asian economies, the World Bank offers:

> What can other developing economies learn from the East Asian miracle? While there is no recipe for success, there are some positive lessons: keep the macroeconomy stable; focus on early education; do not neglect agriculture; use banks to build a sound

---

[23]World Bank, *The East Asian Miracle*, page 41.
[24]Ibid., pages 358–360.
[25]Ibid., page 366.

financial system; be open to foreign ideas and technology; and let relative prices reflect economic scarcities. And there are some negative ones: promoting specific industries or attempting to leap stages of technological development will generally fail; strongly negative real interest rates and large subsidies to borrowers debilitate the financial system; and directing credit without adequate monitoring and selection of borrowers distorts allocation. Finally, we found that a successful export push, whether it results from an open economy and strong economic fundamentals, or from a combination of strong fundamentals and prudently chosen interventions, offers high economic gains.[26]

Furthermore, the World Bank is optimistic about the widespread adoption of export-oriented strategies, believing that considerable scope still exists for expanded trade—both between the less developed and developed countries (South–North) and between the less developed countries themselves (South–South). The promise of the Uruguay Round and the new World Trade Organization bolsters this optimism.

### RESERVATIONS ABOUT THE EAST ASIAN DEVELOPMENTS

Before turning to the economic transitions of the former socialist states of Eastern Europe, we observe that economic liberalization, so far, has outpaced political liberalization in East Asia. The East Asian miracle is not yet complete.

Furthermore, in a provocative article in *Foreign Affairs,* Paul Krugman discounts the view that the recent economic successes of East Asia reflect gains in efficiency or total factor productivity due to superior development strategies effectively implemented. According to Krugman, "The newly industrializing countries of Asia, like the Soviet Union of the 1950s, have achieved rapid growth in large part through an astonishing mobilization of resources."[27] Krugman attributes the extraordinary growth in per capita incomes to increases in the shares of the populations that are employed; higher levels of education; and the greater physical capital-to-labor ratios from the high rates of domestic saving and investment. With feasible upper limits to the percentages of the population that can be employed and income that can be saved, and given the diminishing returns to human and physical capital deepening, the elevated economic growth rates of East Asian nations are bound to decline. Krugman concludes, "If there is a secret to Asian growth, it is simply deferred gratification, the willingness to sacrifice current satisfaction for future gain."[28]

## ECONOMIC TRANSITION OF THE FORMER SOCIALIST STATES

In this section we discuss the challenges that the countries of the former Soviet Union and Eastern Europe face in their economic transition to capitalism. With the demise of

---

[26]Ibid., page 367.

[27]Paul Krugman, "The Myth of Asia's Miracle," *Foreign Affairs,* vol. 73, no. 6 (November/December 1994), pages 62–78. This quotation is from page 70.

[28]Ibid., page 78.

centralized socialism, more than 20 nations that had been subjected to the Soviet system are in some stage of significant economic transition.[29] We first give an overview of the model of centralized socialism (often called the *Stalinist model*). Then we discuss issues common to economies in transition. The reform programs of these nations contain many elements of the market-friendly strategy of the World Bank. Finally, we conclude the chapter with three case studies of transitional countries: Hungary, Poland, and the Ukraine.

## CENTRALIZED SOCIALISM

The Stalinist model of centralized socialism evolved in the Soviet Union (USSR) during the 1920s. By the early 1930s, with Joseph Stalin firmly in control of the USSR, the economic elements of the Stalinist model were in place. Essentially, this model used a hierarchical system of planning to allocate resources. The mix of output was determined primarily by government planners, with little regard for the desires of consumers. Discussed below are the primary features of the Stalinist model that characterized the former Soviet Union and, to varying degrees, the countries of Eastern Europe. These features are priority to economic growth; material balance planning; lack of market pricing; and economic and political inequality.

### PRIORITY TO ECONOMIC GROWTH

Following the Russian Revolution of 1917, Vladimir Lenin assumed leadership of a nation that was underdeveloped compared to other European countries. In the aftermath of the Russian Civil War (1917–1921), Russia experimented both with state control of the economy and with more decentralized, market decision making (the New Economic Policy of 1921–1924). By the late 1920s, Stalin, having succeeded Lenin, instituted a system of rigid economic and political controls.

Stalin's economic policy was aimed at promoting economic growth and national defense. In the 1930 to 1960 period, the command model served as a relatively effective vehicle for mobilizing resources to promote the growth of heavy industry and military capability.[30] The growth process was highly extensive, relying on increased uses of labor, capital, and land. The growth of total factor productivity was much lower. Priority was given to the development of industries such as steel, coal, and oil. Major infrastructure projects to develop electricity and transportation were stressed. Between 1920 and 1970, Soviet economic growth was impressive—the country changed from a relatively underdeveloped nation into a global superpower. This type of economic transformation was purposeful and facilitated by a relatively rigid process of national planning.

---

[29]These countries include 12 of the former Soviet republics that now are loosely associated in the Commonwealth of Independent States: Russia, the Ukraine, Uzbekistan, Kazakhstan, Belarus, Azerbaijan, Georgia, Moldavia, Tajikistan, Kirghizia, Armenia, and Turkmenistan. The other three former Soviet republics are the Baltic countries of Estonia, Latvia, and Lithuania. The Eastern European countries now include Bulgaria, the Czech Republic, Hungary, Poland, Romania, and Slovakia. In January 1993, Czechoslovakia was peacefully separated into the Czech Republic and Slovakia.

[30]See Gur Ofer, "Soviet Economic Growth: 1928–1985," *Journal of Economic Literature*, vol. 25, no. 4 (December 1987), pages 1767–1833.

## Material Balance Planning

Within the Soviet economy and the command economies of Eastern Europe, a process, referred to as *material balance planning,* was used to allocate economic resources to produce targeted levels of final output. As explained in Chapter 13, every economy must achieve a consistency between sources (supply) and uses (demand). A market economy utilizes market-clearing prices to achieve such a balance. A Leontief input-output model, based on fixed-coefficient production functions and given final demands, can also be used to equate sources and uses. A third option, **material balances,** employs an iterative process of trial and error to achieve consistency for each good.

In the material balance planning process, the top political leadership and the planning agency (called *GOSPLAN* within the Soviet Union) determine output targets for key industries. It is at this stage that the leaders' preferences for heavy industry and national defense are incorporated into the planning process. The political authorities tended to accord a low priority to the growth of consumer goods. As a result, the USSR in the 1970s had achieved industrial and military might, while its population had relatively low levels of household consumption.

The planning agency then provides industry managers and individual firms with their own output targets. The firms and industry managers then assess input requirements—labor, capital, and intermediate goods—needed to produce the targeted final demands. A process of negotiation between planners, industry managers, and firm directors continues until a consistent and feasible plan is achieved. (Recall from Chapter 13 that with a consistent plan, for each good, the sum of intermediate uses and final demand must equal gross output. For a feasible plan, the availability of basic inputs such as labor and capital must be equal to the requirements to produce the gross outputs.)

While this planning process can effectively channel resources into high-priority areas identified by the political leadership, major inefficiencies characterize material balance planning. First, firms have an incentive to over-request inputs to ensure that they meet their targeted output. Second, little incentive exists to produce high-quality output since the firm's success indicator is simply the number of units of output produced. In contrast, a firm within a market system must be concerned with the quality and competitiveness of its output; since output produced but not sold raises costs but does not contribute to revenues. Finally, within a complex economy, labor and capital are consumed in the planning process itself. The opportunity costs of these resources will increase with the complexity of the planning process.

## Lack of Market Pricing

Within the planned, command economy, prices have no real allocative role. Prices simply serve an accounting function to facilitate the exchange of products between firms and between households. Typically, in a command economy output prices are artificially set, often below market-clearing levels for basic necessities such as food, clothing, and housing. As a result, excess demands or shortages persist for most consumer goods. Within the Soviet Union and Eastern Europe, the authorities rarely used formal rationing. Rather, lines (first-come–first-served) existed for many goods. Also, sellers' preference in allocating available goods, often to friends or favored individuals, was quite common.

Market pricing does exist for some goods within most command economies. Often agricultural goods, particularly vegetables and fruits, are legally sold in private markets. Also, second-hand goods and services, such as household repairs, are available through private initiative with market pricing. Illegal markets for foreign currency and goods diverted from the state marketing network also exist.

## Economic and Political Inequality

Despite their socialist features, none of the command economies of the former Soviet Union or Eastern Europe could be considered as truly egalitarian. Nevertheless, the distribution of income in these countries, while unequal, was more equal than in the high-income, capitalist economies. The absence of any income accruing from the private ownership of capital tended to narrow income differentials. Also, the state generally guaranteed employment within the planned economies. Finally, basic education and health care were provided to all citizens within the Soviet economic bloc.

Inequality, however, manifested itself in different ways. First, salaries were administratively set and varied considerably. High government officials, prominent doctors, entertainers, athletes, and directors of state firms were at the high end of the wage scale, receiving several times the salary of unskilled workers. Also, these favored individuals tended to have access to scarce goods, such as imported consumer items, and better-quality services, such as health care. Clearly, government officials used their political position for their own personal advantage.

## The Failure of the Stalinist System

By the late 1970s the economic inefficiencies and the low standards of living characterizing the command economies became more critical. In 1986, when Mikhail Gorbachev assumed power in the Soviet Union, he launched a political and economic reform program aimed at increasing political dialogue **(glasnost)** and restructuring the command economy **(perestroika).** While significant political debates and the beginnings of multiparty legislative elections occurred, economic change was slow. During the Gorbachev years, some prices were raised toward market levels and some private, for-profit cooperatives began offering services. Large state enterprises, however, continued to dominate the economy.

In the early 1990s, however, the Stalinist systems of Eastern Europe and the Soviet Union began to unravel. With the collapse of the Berlin Wall in November 1989, East Germany (the Democratic Republic of Germany) began the process of reunification with West Germany (the Federal Republic of Germany). On September 12, 1990, the final treaty for the reunification of Germany was signed. Concurrently, the other nations of Eastern Europe proclaimed their economic and political independence from Moscow. These nations included Hungary, Romania, Poland, Bulgaria, and Czechoslovakia.

In the autumn of 1991, the three Baltic republics of Estonia, Latvia, and Lithuania declared their independence from Moscow. By the end of 1991 the Soviet Union had formally disbanded. Russia and the other 11 republics (minus the three Baltic states) are now united in a loose economic and political federation called the Commonwealth of Independent States (CIS).

We now turn to the economic issues that these nations face in their transition from centralized socialism.

## THE ECONOMICS OF TRANSITION

With the exception of the former East Germany, each of the countries in transition has to decide what type of economic system it eventually would like. In proposing economic reforms in the Soviet Union, Gorbachev argued that he wanted a participatory market socialism, but not necessarily capitalism. (Models of decentralized socialism, however, have not been truly operational in the contemporary world. For a brief period of time, Yugoslavia was held together with a form of decentralized socialism.) Boris Yeltsin, elected president of Russia in June 1991, countered Gorbachev, the leader of the USSR, arguing that capitalism must be the eventual goal. His bolder program for economic transition ultimately was more appealing to a majority of Russian citizens and contributed to the collapse of the Soviet Union in late 1991.

Yet, within the former Soviet Union—including Russia and Eastern Europe—powerful elements continue to argue for reformed socialism, avoiding some of the harsher aspects of capitalism. As we discuss the elements of a transitional program aimed at promoting capitalism, the concerns of those opposed to capitalism will be indicated.[31]

### Use of Consumer Markets

Within the centralized systems, output in physical units and the price per unit were both set. Typically, the set price was below the market-clearing level. Introducing market-clearing prices is a vital initial step in transforming the planned economy into a market economy. Consider the market for butter shown in Figure 17.3. At the controlled price of $P_o$, consumers purchase $Q_o^s$; there is an excess demand of $Q_o^d - Q_o^s$ or $AB$. With price decontrol, the price rises to its market-clearing level, $P_1$; quantity transacted increases to $Q_1$. If the short-run supply of output is relatively price-inelastic, then price will increase significantly, yet consumers will not receive a significant increase in output. Within a planned economy, enterprise managers have had little experience with varying supply in response to the output price. Also, critical inputs that are needed to increase short-run supply may not be readily available. For these reasons, it is likely that the supply response may be relatively price inelastic.

To the extent that a competitive environment does not exist within a market whose price has been decontrolled, an even greater price increase could result as a few producers are able to set prices above the competitive equilibrium. Consider the extreme case of a single producer within the market shown in Figure 17.3. The monopolist, to maximize profits, will set the output level at the equality of marginal revenue and marginal cost or at $Q_1'$. The monopolist then sets price from the demand curve, charging $P_1'$. Compared to the competitive equilibrium, price has increased ($P_1' > P_1$) and quantity has decreased ($Q_1' < Q_1$).

Given the relative inelasticity of short-run supply and the potential for noncompetitive price setting, some have argued that prices should be increased gradually to avoid angering consumers, impoverishing those on fixed incomes (like the elderly), and unduly enriching firms. "Gradualists" feel that concurrent supply increases and privatization efforts that will increase the number of firms should accompany upward shifts in official prices. At some point, when the economy is better acclimated to competitive market pricing, total price decontrol is implemented. Others argue, however, that the "shock" of price decontrol is needed to propel the economy into a market "mode." The underlying beliefs of those favoring rapid price decontrol are that it is

---

[31]In late 1991, a series of 11 articles on different aspects of economic transition was published in *Journal of Economic Perspectives*, vol. 5, no. 4 (fall 1991). These articles addressed a range of issues from legal reform to monetary policy within transitional economies. Moreover, the articles concern the progress of transition in seven Eastern European countries. While written before economic transition had progressed in many countries, these articles, nevertheless, provide useful background information.

## FIGURE 17.3 — PRICE LIBERALIZATION: THE MARKET FOR BUTTER

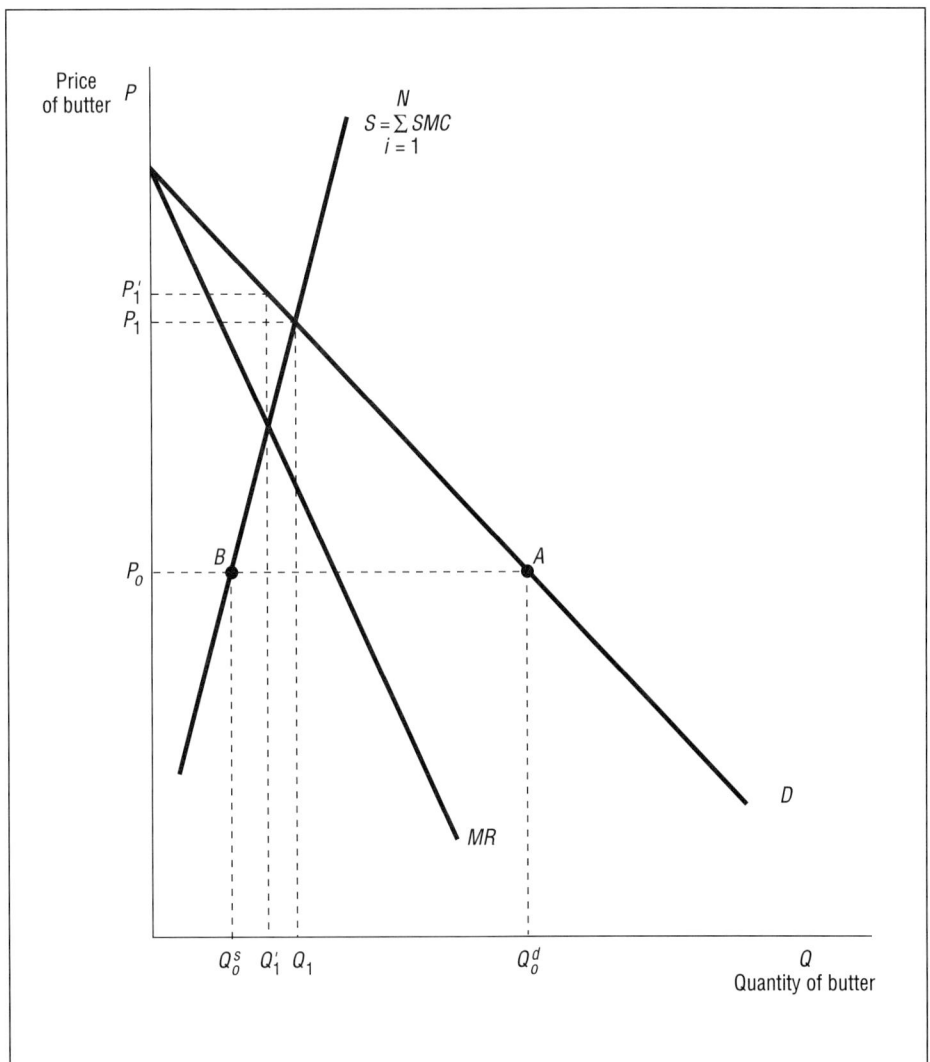

better to shock consumers only once, and the supply responses will be quicker when prices increase more rapidly. Both groups agree that market prices set by private monopolists are to be avoided.

### THE LABOR MARKET

Often within the command system both wages and employment were in excess of competitive levels. Assume that a wage is set above equilibrium at $w_0^*$ in Figure 17.4. Profit-maximizing firms would hire $L_{0'}'$ at the equality of wage and the marginal revenue product of labor. In contrast, assume that socialist firms were willing to hire all workers willing to work at $w_0^*$. The firms would hire $L_o$ units of labor at point A on the labor supply curve, $S_L$. The socialist enterprises could hire this increased quantity of labor for two reasons. First, the firms' success indicator is gross output, not profitability. The

### FIGURE 17.4 LABOR MARKET LIBERALIZATION

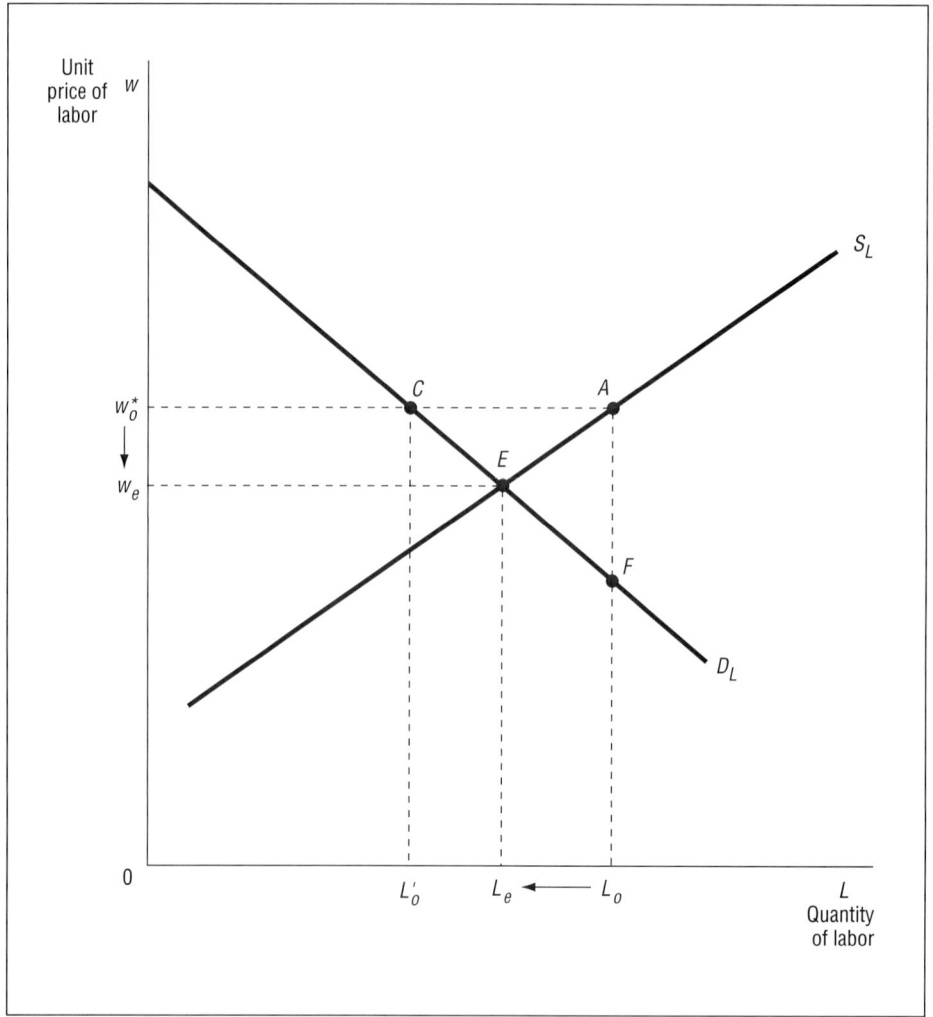

increased use of labor would raise output, as long as the marginal revenue product of labor were positive. Moreover, the government, as a full-employment measure, may mandate that firms hire all the labor willing to work at the set wage. In this case, the government may need to subsidize the losses that the enterprises may have.

The wage bill, equal to the wage rate, $w_o^*$, times the quantity of labor, $L_o$, is the area $0w_o^*AL_o$. Units of labor from $L_o'$ to $L_o$ are paid above their marginal revenue product of labor, represented by the labor demand curve, $D_L$. The area $CAF$ represents a subsidy to these units of labor and a reduction in the firms' profits (or increase in the firms' losses). In the command economy any accounting loss for an enterprise would be paid by a transfer of funds from the central government to the firm.

With a competitive labor market, however, the wage rate would fall to $w_e$ and the quantity of labor employed would fall to $L_e$. At market equilibrium, point $E$, no subsidy would be accorded to labor. If the government responds to pressure from workers to maintain wage and employment levels, it must then continue to subsidize firms that will have economic losses. In many of the transitional economies there has been a resistance to competitive labor markets. As a result, to avoid labor unrest, government budgets have been strained to subsidize firms with economic losses.

## Privatization

Within the socialist systems, capital and land were typically collectively owned, with their use directed by the state planning apparatus. Private ownership of the means of production is a cornerstone of capitalism. With private property, owners have both the right to use their property to generate income and to dispose of their property either through sale or bequest. Commercial law should permit parties to enter into agreements with the knowledge that the state, through its court system, will ensure compliance with legal business contracts. Thus, societies in transition from socialism must develop processes to privatize property and to ensure the sanctity of property ownership and the validity of business contracts.

Different means to privatize assets have been attempted in the former socialist countries. These schemes differ in the degree of property rights given, the particular groups given property claims, and the extent to which the state receives compensation for property. For instance, in Russia considerable discussion has centered on providing long-term leases of agricultural land to the households that were part of large collective farms. While these farmers could then use the land for their own profit-seeking activities, they would still not have full disposition rights of the land. The absence of full property rights would be a disincentive for making productivity-enhancing investments in the land.

The actual transfer of full ownership rights of industrial firms can proceed in different ways. All citizens can be given vouchers that permit them to acquire shares of stock in those firms that they find attractive. For instance, vouchers in Russia were given to all private citizens. Immediately, a legal market existed for these vouchers. Some citizens sold their vouchers to others who were more intent on acquiring ownership rights in firms. As large Russian firms were privatized, voucher holders exchanged their vouchers for actual shares of stock or ownership in the firms. Theoretically, these shares of stock can be traded on a stock exchange in Moscow, just as shares of stock in American firms are traded on U.S. stock exchanges. Even by 1995, however, the actual development of a fully functioning Moscow stock exchange was still in process.

Other schemes for the privatization of assets are not so egalitarian, however. In Russia, for some especially large firms, managers and workers were directly given shares of stock in the firm for which they worked. The underlying premise was that the employees of the firm deserved to have significant ownership rights. In this case, the owners of the firm became a combination of the firm's managers, the firm's workers, and shareholders who acquired ownership rights through the voucher process described above.

Both equity and efficiency problems have existed with this type of privatization. First, managers, already part of the more favored elite of the old system, were given disproportionate ownership rights. Second, the ownership rights of the managers coupled with those of the workers often gave these groups sufficient control to direct the operations of the firm. In these cases, both inefficient management and redundant labor have been retained, sometimes leading to economic losses. To avoid the social discontent of high unemployment, governments have often responded by subsidizing these inefficient firms. Given that these governments have limited abilities to tax and to borrow, the subsidies have often been financed by issuing new money. Macroeconomic stabilization then is compromised by a combination of budget deficits and inflation.

The direct auctioning of property rights to the highest bidder was not extensively used in the early stages of economic transition. Citizens of the former Soviet-style economies would generally not have financial assets that would permit them to be effective bidders in this type of auction. Those with the means to participate would be those who had been highly favored under the old system or who had enriched themselves illegally through black-market activities. Also, if there were a truly open auction, foreigners could easily become the dominant owners of the country's industry. With their greater wealth and their highly valued currency (such as U.S. dollars or German marks), foreigners could dominate any auctioning process.

The Czech Republic's auctioning of a 27 percent share of ownership in its national telephone company, Telecom, has been a notable exception, however. Five European companies bid for these ownership rights.[32] Also, Russia announced in April of 1995 that, as a means to raise government revenues, it would auction 7200 nationalized concerns to the highest bidders, domestic or foreign.[33]

Privatization has progressed in most of the former Soviet-style economies. By 1995 more than 50 percent of economic activity occurred in the private sector in nearly all the transitional economies. The biggest firms and large collective farms, primarily in the former Soviet Union, have been laggards in the privatization process. The fear of widespread unemployment and the particular difficulties of privatizing farms that can exceed 25,000 hectares have contributed to some slowdown in the process.

The former socialist states have also not done well in designing commercial legal codes, establishing independent judiciaries to enforce these codes, or in building a respect for private property. In the absence of enforceable codes, parties, particularly foreign investors, have been hesitant to make significant financial commitments in the private sectors of the transitional economies. Also, from East Europe to the former Soviet Union, economic crime has flourished. Corruption in the privatization process, bribing of government officials, protection payoffs, and contracting irregularities are frequent.[34] The costs of this lack of respect for law and property are very high. Higher product prices, reduced output, reduced employment, and lower investment are all consequences of crime.

Additionally, in many of the countries of the former Soviet Union, including Russia and the Ukraine, there is considerable resentment of those who have been financially successful during this transitional period. Historically, whether during the Tsarist period or later under communism, those who have been in positions of power, either political or economic, have tended to be resented. The underlying premise was that any gain was both ill-founded and undeserved. The inequality of result in the market system is reviving many of these same feelings. Continued corruption and the ostentatious display of wealth by the successful have fueled social discord. The economic consequences of this resentment are not only calls for confiscatory taxation, but rising crime.

---

[32]"No Other Way," *The Economist* (March 25, 1995), pages 74–75.

[33]Richard Holman, "Russia Plans More Sell-Offs," *Wall Street Journal* (April 14, 1995), page A6.

[34]"Free to Cheat in Eastern Europe," *The Economist* (March 11, 1995), page 54.

Foreign investors have been dissuaded by both consequences. Clearly, attitudinal change is needed. The risk of market activities and the inevitable inequality of results must be accepted and weighed against the efficiencies of market capitalism. The fair enforcement of commercial laws and some modest redistribution might aid in this transformation of attitudes.

In summary, privatization programs are in place in all the former Soviet-style countries. Yet much remains to be done. The harder "cases"—very large firms with outdated equipment and bloated employment levels, as well as the large collective farms—remain to be addressed in many countries. More important, the legal and social climate must be drastically altered to unleash the economically beneficial effects of private property and capitalism.

## Financial Intermediation

The former socialist countries generally had little need for a banking system. Central banks, such as GOSBANK in the Soviet Union, tended to print money as needed and to hold deposits for firms and households. No real system of financial intermediation existed by which the funds of depositors were allocated across a portfolio of assets such as business and household loans or government bonds.

The transitional countries need to establish central banks that will be responsible for the control of the domestic money supply. While most countries do have operating central banks, they have not been particularly successful in controlling the issuance of new money. In both Russia and the Ukraine, newly printed money has been used to subsidize inefficient publicly-owned firms and to provide transfer payments to citizens. This monetary creation has been highly inflationary, with these countries experiencing annual inflation rates as high as 5000 percent. International agencies such as the IMF are making loans conditional on a tighter control of the money supply.

Developing a private financial sector with commercial banks and functioning equity markets has also been difficult in many countries. In a modern economy, a functioning commercial bank needs large capital subscriptions and trusting depositors for the bank to begin making long-term investment loans to private businesses. To date, the more successful initiatives with private banking have been limited to smaller-scale credit union–type enterprises. While these can be very helpful, particularly in rural areas, large-scale industrial development requires a more sophisticated banking system.

Equity or stock markets in which shares of ownership in private companies are bought and sold have developed in most transitional economies. Such markets are often called **secondary markets** since they facilitate the sale of existing shares of ownership. A firm's issuance of new stock, as a means to raise investment funds, usually involves investment banks that serve as initial sellers of new issues. As with commercial banking, the growth of investment banking has been limited in the transitional economies.

## Global Integration

As stressed in this text, trade and appropriate foreign investment can fuel sustained economic development. To promote such economic integration, a country needs a convertible currency. The transitional countries have succeeded in introducing market rates for their currencies. Some countries such as Russia have used flexible exchange rates, while others such as Hungary have used fixed regimes that are periodically adjusted when warranted by market forces.

The transitional countries are slowly orienting their economies toward international trade. Certain obstacles to trade continue to exist. First, when fixed-rate currencies are overvalued, the competitiveness of a country's exports suffers. Second, many countries do not have business people who have long experience in negotiating international transactions. Also, the products of some countries are not yet widely accepted on world markets, restraining exports. Finally, some countries, such as Russia, have tried to tax exports as a means to raise government revenues; such levies reduce export quantities and earnings.

Foreign direct investment has been hindered in many countries by bureaucratic regulations and excessive taxation of profits. Countries that until 10 years ago were strongly communist in their ideology still are struggling with the issue of foreign, capitalist ownership. While many countries, such as Poland and the Baltic states, have made clear commitments to welcome foreign investment, others are using economic barriers to gain time, as they assess the merits of foreign ownership. The market-friendly strategy of the World Bank clearly encourages the economic integration that the transitional economies are beginning to embrace.

We have considered the particular economic issues that transitional countries need to address as they move from centralized socialism to market capitalism. We now turn to three countries, Hungary, Poland, and the Ukraine, that provide contrast in both the pace and success of economic reform.

## COUNTRY STUDIES

Hungary first began experimenting with economic reforms in the 1950s and has the longest experience with economic transition. From the late 1970s, Poland, more than any other country of Eastern Europe, offered serious political resistance to the Soviet Union. Finally, the Ukraine, the second largest of the former Soviet republics, is a country that has not been successful in making the significant decisions that are needed for effective economic transition. Table 17.2 provides current economic indicators for these three countries.

Compared to all developing countries, the transitional economies have several advantages. They have lower rates of population growth, averaging less than one percent per year for the three countries considered here. Living standards tend to be higher. The GNP per capita for Hungary is three times that for all low- and middle-income countries; Poland and the Ukraine have per capita income levels that are double the mean for all developing countries. As indicated by female life expectancy at birth and, particularly, by the infant mortality rate, the health status of the populations of the transitional economies is also above that for all developing countries. Of interest is that male life expectancy at birth does not differ greatly among the three transitional countries and all developing countries. By comparison alcoholism, poor diets, and crime have resulted during the last 10 years in a lowered male life expectancy in the other former Soviet-bloc countries. Finally, as shown by school enrollment figures, the former socialist countries have relatively high educational levels.

Despite these advantages, each of the three transitional economies faces difficult challenges. A common aspect of the transitional process in Eastern Europe, as in Russia, is the difficulty in privatizing the very large firms created under socialism. Currently, many of these inefficient firms are being subsidized by governments to avoid disruptive unemployment. As a result, macroeconomic stability within the transitional economies has been elusive. As stated by Olivier Blanchard and his colleagues:

| TABLE 17.2 | DEVELOPMENT INDICATORS: SELECTED FORMER SOCIALIST STATES | | | |
|---|---|---|---|---|
| | HUNGARY | POLAND | THE UKRAINE | LOW- AND MIDDLE-INCOME ECONOMIES |
| Population, 1993 (millions) | 10.2 | 38.3 | 51.6 | 4689.0 |
| Population growth rate, average annual, 1980–93 (%) | −0.4 | 0.6 | 0.2 | 1.9 |
| GNP per capita, 1993 ($) | 3350 | 2260 | 2210 | 1090 |
| GNP per capita, average annual growth rate, 1980–93 (%) | 1.2 | 0.4 | 0.2 | 0.9 |
| Male life expectancy at birth, 1993 (years) | 65 | 67 | 64 | 63 |
| Female life expectancy at birth, 1993 (years) | 74 | 76 | 74 | 66 |
| Infant mortality rate, 1993 (infant deaths per thousand live births) | 15 | 15 | 16 | 55 |
| Share of GDP, 1993 (%) | | | | |
|     Agriculture | 6 | 6 | 35 | ... |
|     Industry | 28 | 39 | 47 | ... |
| Defense expenditures as % of GDP, 1992 | 3.5 | 2.3 | 3.8 | 3.8 |
| Public expenditures on education as % of GDP, 1991 | 6.2 | 4.9 | ... | ... |
| Health expenditures as % of GDP, 1991 | 6.0 | 5.1 | 3.3 | ... |
| School enrollment percentage rates, 1991 | | | | |
|     Primary    Total | 89 | 98 | ... | ... |
|                 Female | 89 | 97 | ... | ... |
|     Secondary Total | 81 | 83 | ... | ... |
|                 Female | 81 | 86 | ... | ... |
|     Tertiary    Total | 15 | 23 | ... | ... |
| External debt as % of GNP, 1993 | 66.9 | 49.7 | 3.1 | 32.1 |
| Total debt service as % of exports, 1993 | 38.8 | 9.2 | 1.3 | 18.3 |

NOTES: Lack of data is indicated by ...

FROM World Bank, *World Development Report 1995,* New York: Oxford University Press, 1995, Tables 1, 3, 23, 25, 27, 28, 29; and United Nations Development Programme, *Human Development Report 1995,* New York: Oxford University Press, 1995, Tables 24, 25, 31.

Eastern European countries have entered the post-communist era with fiscal deficits and excessive money creation. Details vary across countries, but the origins can always be traced to a combination of half-hearted attempts at reform (giving firms more control over their finance and wage payments), soft budget constraints, and political pressure to appease workers. The standard stabilization principles apply here: fiscal deficits must be eliminated, money creation controlled.[35]

We now examine how each of the three countries is proceeding in the reform process.

---

[35]Olivier Blanchard, Rudiger Dornbusch, Paul Krugman, Richard Layard, and Lawrence Summers, *Reform in Eastern Europe,* Cambridge, MA: The MIT Press, 1991, page xii.

## Hungary

Following the dissolution of the Austro-Hungarian empire at the conclusion of World War I, Hungary became a separate national entity. Prior to World War II, the economy of Hungary was a relatively advanced market economy oriented toward Western Europe. After the war, Hungary fell into the Soviet sphere of influence; the Communist People's Republic was formally established in August 1949. In October 1956, an anti-Soviet rebellion occurred in Hungary; Soviet troops restored order and Hungary remained politically calm until the end of the Soviet era in 1989. The current Hungarian Republic was established on October 18, 1989, with an elected national assembly and president.

Even during the Soviet era, Hungary, more than any Eastern European country, experimented with economic reform. With political rebellion crushed in Hungary, the Soviets did not seem to view Hungarian economic reform as a major threat. It also is probable that the Soviets, concerned about their own economic stagnation, were eager to assess the results of Hungarian reforms. Thus, in 1969, Hungary introduced the **New Economic Mechanism (NEM).** In brief, the NEM reduced the role of central planning and gave firms greater discretion over output levels. Under the NEM, profits—a large portion of which firms could retain for employee bonuses—became a more important success indicator than output levels. Further, Hungarian firms were encouraged to export output to capitalist nations at market prices.

The NEM met with mixed success. In reality, the government did not surrender as much discretion to individual firms as had been envisioned. Also, price flexibility, particularly in the labor market, was not widely used. Market-determined wages could have led to both lower wages and employment, promoting labor discord (see Figure 17.4). Also, Hungary became severely indebted to foreign creditors for loans that were used both for imported investment goods and consumer goods. In the early 1980s, Hungary introduced policies to limit imports and expand exports; in addition, the country joined the International Monetary Fund. The major success of the NEM was to instill a reform mentality that would contribute to true economic restructuring in the late 1980s.

The Hungarian transition has been gradual and has not been marked by ambitious government plans or major policy shifts.[36] In the late 1980s, firms increasingly were given autonomy in the selection of their directors and in their production decisions. Also, privatization was introduced, beginning with the service sector. In 1985, only an estimated 10 percent of GDP was produced in the private sector; by 1991 nearly 30 percent of GDP was of private-sector origin.[37]

Hungarian firms no longer receive extensive subsidies to keep wages and employment high. Prices are no longer controlled. As a result, workers have been subject to declining real wages and greater unemployment, reducing their purchasing power. The government has tried to avoid placing large firms in near-monopoly positions. A liberalization of the import process, with an elimination of import license requirements, has led to a more competitive economy. Domestic

---

[36]The most complete analysis of the transition process in Hungary is an edited work by Istvan P. Szekely and David M. G. Newbery, *Hungary: An Economy in Transition*, Glasgow: Cambridge University Press, 1993. This volume contains individual articles on foreign trade, privatization, finance and banking, external debt and monetary policy, tax reform, and labor markets.

[37]Paul R. Gregory and Robert C. Stuart, *Comparative Economic Systems*, Fifth edition, Boston: Houghton Mifflin, 1995, page 438.

producers are being forced to operate more efficiently as a result of increased foreign competition.[38]

Hungary's economic performance since 1990 has been somewhat disappointing. With a relatively longer experience with economic reform, Hungary should have been one of the best candidates for successful economic transition. Economic restructuring has further aided in promoting Hungarian exports toward Western Europe and with more competitive exchange rates, higher prices have discouraged imports. Yet real GDP fell almost 20 percent between 1990 and 1993.[39] Contracting domestic demand and a reduction in traditional export markets in Russia and other Eastern European countries have hurt GDP growth. Also, even with real wage decreases, Hungarian unit labor costs tend to exceed those of other Eastern European countries, reducing demand for Hungarian exports. To increase its competitiveness and further reduce current account deficits, Hungary devalued its currency, the Hungarian forint, by 9 percent in March 1995.

Hungary's privatization program has slowed considerably. Officials are debating which of the largest enterprises should remain under state control, primarily as a means to protect employment. Investors have shown little interest in purchasing many of these firms that seem to have little long-run potential. On a positive note, Hungry has introduced effective bankruptcy and liquidations laws aimed at restructuring firms that have significant debts and poor prospects.

Hungary's longer-term outlook is unclear. Economic transition has strong political support. Progress has been made in key areas such as privatization, commercial law, and economic integration. Also, Hungary, with its longer tradition of openness to international investors, has been successful in attracting foreign direct investment from capitalist nations. There is little risk of reverting to a command-type economy.

Yet efforts seem stalled. The government is trying to restructure a weak commercial banking system that has negative net worth as a result of uncollectible loans to failed state enterprises. Some very difficult decisions concerning privatizing the large-scale industrial sector remain. Finally, the government needs to address a chronic government budget deficit that has resulted from the subsidizing of state firms and the continuation of some generous social welfare programs. In essence, many features of Hungarian socialism, particularly those with respect to employment protection and the provision of social benefits persist today.[40] A key to Hungary's ultimate economic progress will be found in the ability of the government to maintain social cohesion as it reduces subsidies and social-welfare expenditures. Long-term economic success hinges on these painful fiscal adjustments.

## POLAND

Poland has a long and proud heritage dating to its founding in the year 966 A.D. Russia and Prussia (later Germany) have contested Polish territory for centuries. Modern

---

[38]Paul G. Hare, "Hungary: In Transition to a Market Economy," *Journal of Economic Perspectives*, vol. 5, no. 4 (fall 1991), page 197.

[39]World Bank, "Hungary," *Trends in Developing Economies, 1994,* The World Bank, Washington, DC, 1994, pages 218–220.

[40]See Part Six: "Labour Markets, Unemployment, and Social Security," by Istvan P. Szekely and David M. G. Newbery, editors, *Hungary: An Economy in Transition,* Glasgow: Cambridge University Press, 1993, pages 277–325.

Polish history dates from the 1918 founding of an independent Poland, recognized by the victors of World War I. Yet Nazi and then Soviet domination of Poland occurred from 1939 until the 1980s. Poland was brought into the Soviet sphere in 1945 and had a Soviet-style planned economy through the 1980s. Political opposition to Soviet domination was very strong. Industrial workers under the leadership of Lech Walesa went on strike in 1980 to protest consumer price increases. In August of 1980, the strikes were settled with the Soviet concession to allow Solidarity an independent Polish trade union movement.

Continued opposition to the Soviet-style government of Poland under General Jaruzelski led in 1981 to the imposition of martial law and the banning of Solidarity's activities. Additional labor unrest coupled with the preoccupation of the Gorbachev government with its own problems led to the resignation of the Jaruzelski government in September 1988. Since 1989 Poland has seen contested multiparty elections. Walesa, the president of Poland until November 1995, and his Solidarity party have been primary actors in Polish politics. In recent years, a communist party, composed of officials and supporters of the Jaruzelski government, has been a strong opposition force.

Following the 1989 parliamentary elections, the Solidarity-led government introduced radical economic reform. This **shock therapy** included the freeing of nearly all consumer prices; restrained growth of the money supply; and the introduction of a convertible currency—the Polish *zloty*—pegged to a basket of five currencies (the U.S. dollar, the German mark, the British pound, the French franc, and the Swiss franc). Significant progress was made in reducing the government deficit. Small industries and services were privatized. Entrepreneurial activity was encouraged and rewarded. Fortunately for Poland, agriculture was never extensively collectivized during the Soviet years. Thus, small farmers could simply begin selling their output in private markets for profit instead of working through the state planning and distribution network. These farms, however, have not had access to modern equipment and technologies. While representing only 7 percent of GDP, Polish agriculture engages nearly 20 percent of the workforce.[41] Thus, the modernization of Polish agriculture has been a high-priority objective for the Solidarity government.

As a result of these strong measures, economic progress and hardship were simultaneously introduced. On the positive side, prices reached market-clearing levels, quickly eliminating lines and rationing. In consequence, the rate of inflation in 1990 was 585 percent.[42] The elderly and others on fixed incomes, however, were often unable to pay the higher prices for food and other basic necessities. With a reduction in subsidies, the government budget deficit decreased, reducing the expansion of the money supply. Not surprisingly, this contractionary policy resulted in reduced output and higher unemployment. In 1990 and 1991, GDP fell 11.6 percent and 7.6 percent, respectively.[43] Since the early 1990s, however, the growth of GDP has been approximately 3 percent per year, one of the best in Eastern Europe.

The economic assessment of Polish shock therapy has been mixed. While radical reform has led to many conditions that are favorable for sustained economic growth in Poland, areas of concern still remain. The government needs to finish the task of privatization, particularly that of large, unprofitable heavy industries. As Stanislaw Wellisz, writing in 1991, concludes,

---

[41]World Bank, "Poland," *Trends in Developing Economies, 1994*, page 419.
[42]Gregory and Stuart, page 443.
[43]Ibid.

> The program of the Solidarity-led government was a bold experiment. Never before has an attempt been made to liberalize and to stabilize a post-socialist economy on such a scale. For all the hardship it wrought, the program looked like a success. But now it is in danger.... Moreover, as is now amply evident, the imposition of a market discipline failed to improve the performance of public sector enterprises. The remedy that has now been decided upon is mass privatization.[44]

Wellisz's assessment of the need for continued privatization of large firms is still true.

Polish exports, which had been growing in the late 1980s, stagnated in the early 1990s due to the slow economic conditions in Western Europe and increased competition from other Eastern European countries. In 1993, Poland had a current account deficit of $2.3 billion, or about 2 percent of GDP.[45] Partially to offset this deficit, the Polish government is encouraging closer economic and political ties with Western Europe, particularly through their desire to join the European Union by the year 2000. In the 1994 to 1995 period, export growth was greatly improved, as a result of a depreciating zloty; however, the increased price of imports contributed to higher inflation. Poland is currently considering moving to a managed float of the zloty.[46]

Finally, with high unemployment and noticeable poverty—which, fortunately, is neither chronic nor severe—the social consensus within Poland is somewhat fragile.[47] It is hoped that the economic growth of the 1992 to 1995 period will convince the Polish people that their economic sacrifices will be justified. Jeffrey Sachs, an American economist who has worked closely with the Polish government on economic reform, remains confident in Poland's future. He writes

> Every time the Poles have been granted the opportunity they have accomplished marvelous things. Poland gave Europe the first written constitution in 1791 ... And it gave the world Solidarity, which ushered in the democratic and peaceful revolutions of 1989.
>
> The Poles show every evidence of displaying the same valor, energy, and skill that they have in the past, but now with even more favorable international circumstances. I believe that we will see great things from the Polish nation in the years ahead, as from many of the other long-suppressed peoples of Eastern Europe and the former Soviet Union.... The world will benefit enormously from the creativity and talents of the region, and from the opportunity of a Europe united in democracy and market economy.[48]

---

[44]Stanislaw Wellisz, "Poland under 'Solidarity' Rule," *Journal of Economic Perspectives*, vol 5, no. 4 (fall 1991), page 217.

[45]World Bank, "Poland," *Trends in Developing Economies, 1994*, page 420.

[46]"Eastern Europe's Embarrassment of Riches," *The Economist* (April 15, 1995), page 69.

[47]While an estimated 15 percent of the Polish population can be classified as poor, the average "poor" household has an income that is only 10 to 15 percent below the poverty level. Also, many of these households contain unemployed adult workers who, it is hoped, will find employment. See World Bank, "Poland," *Trends in Developing Economies, 1994*, page 460.

[48]Jeffrey Sachs, *Poland's Jump to the Market Economy*, Cambridge, MA: The MIT Press, 1993, page 114. This book, based on three lectures, looks at the Polish economic reform process from three perspectives: a brief history of the Polish economy under socialism, the 1989 to 1993 Solidarity reform program, and the remaining challenges to reaching democratic capitalism in Poland.

Sachs urges the international community to provide assistance to Poland and to other transitional economies to help them confront their many challenges. Many of the poorest developing countries, such as those in Africa, have been concerned by the increased competition from the transitional economies for scarce international economic assistance. Yet, if Sachs is correct, helping a country like Poland may eventually unleash economic forces that will benefit both developed and developing countries.

With voters concerned about the pain of economic reform, communist party candidates have been scoring election successes in many of the former Soviet bloc countries. On November 19, 1995, Aleksander Kwasniewski, a former communist party official, defeated Lech Walesa in the Polish presidential election. Kwasniewski has called for a slowing of the economic reform process and a softening of the higher prices and unemployment that have accompanied market capitalism. While pledging to keep Poland on a path toward democratic market capitalism, he feels that the pace of change has led to severe inequities. In Poland, as in other transitional economies, the recent opposition to reform poses a new and very difficult challenge: how to continue the transition to capitalism while protecting the vulnerable.

### THE UKRAINE

A Ukrainian Soviet Socialist Republic was created in December 1917. Economic and military alliances were quickly forged with the Russian Soviet Socialist Republic, and the Ukraine became one of the original republics that formed the Union of Soviet Socialists Republics in December 1922. Since then, the Ukrainian economy has been highly integrated with Russia and the other republics. As the "bread basket" of the USSR, the Ukraine exported grain to other republics, primarily in exchange for oil and natural gas from Russia. In August 1991, the Ukraine declared its independence from the USSR. It did, however, join with ten other former Soviet republics to form the Commonwealth of Independent States in 1992.

As a former republic of the USSR, the Ukraine, unlike Hungary and Poland, had little experience with economic reform, prior to independence. Also, with continued economic ties to Russia, the Ukrainian reform process was influenced by that of Russia. For instance, it originally intended to privatize state assets before freeing prices, to avoid monopoly pricing. However, with Russia pursuing price liberalization prior to privatization, it was obligated to change course, freeing about 70 percent of prices in 1992. Russians had been crossing the border, purchasing cheaper Ukrainian goods, which were still priced in rubles.[49] In 1992 the Ukraine introduced its own currency "coupons," which circulated along with Russian rubles.

In the first few years of independence, the Ukrainian economy performed very badly. The government did not have a workable plan for economic reform; former communist officials continued to dominate politically. No clear division of power existed among important political and financial institutions, such as the legislature, the central bank, and various economic ministries.[50] The real GDP fell by an estimated 40 percent between 1989 and 1993; the inflation rate, totally out of control, reached a high

---

[49]Roman Frydman, Andrzej Rapczynski, and John S. Earle, *The Privatization Process in Russia, Ukraine, and the Baltic States*, Budapest: Central European University Press, 1993, page 86.
[50]Ibid.

of 5000 percent for 1993.[51] Excessive monetary expansion, needed to pay salaries in public enterprises and to accord subsidies, was the primary cause of the inflation. Finally, with its external dependence on energy supplies, the Ukraine ran a significant trade deficit with Russia, $3 billion in 1993. As a result, the country's external debt to Russia increased significantly.

The Ukraine has not been able to fashion a coherent reform program. Leading to complete economic chaos by 1994 was pressure to retain some basic price controls, provide subsidies to consumers, maintain employment in public industries, and aggressively tax any private-sector gains. A lack of political will and internal divisions within the country have contributed to this difficult situation. For instance, Eastern Ukrainians have expressed some interest in joining with Russia, which they view as having a brighter economic future. Also, former communists hold many positions in the government and represent an important minority in the parliament. These old-time communists, often with the support of the economically-vulnerable elderly and the workers in public enterprises, confront younger reformers who wish to see a comprehensive economic reform program.

The resolution of the Ukraine's problems will be neither easy nor quick. Yet, it has good economic potential. An educated and skilled labor force, fertile agricultural land, and a strategic location between Western Europe and Russia offer many advantages. Encouragingly, a political will may finally exist to address its problems. In late 1994, President Leonid Kuchma outlined a reform package that addressed many of the country's problems. He is committed to freeing prices for many consumer goods, reducing the fiscal deficit, moving toward a convertible currency, and accelerating the stalled privatization process. The government had hoped to privatize 8000 large enterprises during 1995; by August of 1995 only 200 had been sold to private shareholders.[52] Also, the country still needs commercial and bankruptcy codes that are effectively enforced. While some firms have closed, no firm has yet to be declared officially bankrupt, permitting it to reorganize and re-employ workers.[53]

The Ukraine faces an uncertain economic future, with some sources of international support. Despite domestic opposition, Kuchma has affirmed the Ukraine's commitment to the Nuclear Nonproliferation Treaty; and the dismantling of nuclear weapons has attracted some financial support from the United States. European countries have indicated a willingness to assist the Ukraine, if the government will close the damaged nuclear power station at Chernobyl. Finally, the International Monetary Fund pledged a $1.8 billion loan if the Ukrainian government meets certain targets for fiscal and monetary restraint. In particular, the IMF asked the Ukraine to limit its 1995 budget deficit to $2.4 billion, or 3.5 percent of GDP.[54]

More than any of the countries studied, the Ukraine's future is the most uncertain. Its proximity to Russia and integration with that economy since the early 1920s constrain, to some extent, the direction and pace of Ukrainian reform. For instance, the Ukraine has been dependent on Russia for as much as 90 percent of its natural gas and 50 percent of its oil imports, often purchased on credit.[55] The prospects for the

---

[51]World Bank, "Ukraine", *Trends in Developing Economies, 1994,* page 316.

[52]"Ukraine: Better Late than Never, Maybe," *The Economist* (July 22, 1995), page 22.

[53]Ibid.

[54]Richard Holman, "Ukraine Approves Tight Budget," *Wall Street Journal* (April 7, 1995), page A-10.

[55]Stephen Larrabee, "Ukraine's Crash Landing?: A Survey of Recent Articles," *Wilson Quarterly*, vol. 19, no. 1 (winter 1995), page 151.

Ukraine are clearly related to the ultimate form of its economic and political relationship with Russia. The speculation concerning its future ranges from sustained economic growth to a reassertion of dominance by an expansionist Russia. Only time will reveal the outcome.

## CONCLUDING NOTE

A successful economic transition requires confronting many of the same problems that developing countries must address. Yet there are differences, both advantages and disadvantages. The transitional countries of Eastern Europe and the former Soviet Union have relatively well-educated populations. They also have extensive infrastructure, both physical and social, in place, although much of the infrastructure needs repair and modernization. An additional challenge for these countries is the dismantling of previously powerful governments that had repressed key features of capitalism—private property, commercial codes and laws, market prices, and tolerance for inequality. The only unambiguous and clear conclusion is that the transitional countries will reform within different time frames and with different rates of success.

From the economic successes in East Asia and the economic transitions in Eastern Europe, we turn in Chapter 18 to the challenges facing sub-Saharan Africa. Of all the regions of the developing world, sub-Saharan Africa has seen the least socioeconomic progress.

## SUMMARY OF MAIN POINTS

1. In the 1990s the World Bank set forth a market-friendly strategy of development with four major components: a stable macroeconomy, competitive domestic markets, investments in human capital, and integration with the international economy.
2. The key elements of a stable macroeconomic environment are disciplined monetary and fiscal policies. For competitive domestic markets, private enterprise should be encouraged, and the market mechanism should be relied on to allocate resources. Public investments in human capital should emphasize high-quality primary and secondary education, child nutrition, and cost-effective preventative health care. International integration involves increased openness to international trade and investment.
3. The four components of the market-friendly strategy of development are mutually reinforcing. Successful implementation of this strategy requires competent and stable domestic governments and international cooperation.
4. Concerns with the market-friendly strategy of development center on the definition of the proper role of government and the specific policy measures for institution building; the difficulties in generating sustained economic development

when operating with heavy external debt burdens, and the short-run consequences for poverty.
5. The East Asian economies are widely recognized for achieving rapid and equitable economic growth. The World Bank attributes the economic success of the East Asian nations, in part, to the implementation of market-friendly strategies.
6. Although important differences are evident across the East Asian economies, common features include strong and effective governments; early and sustained human capital formation; reduced fertility rates; attention to agriculture and rural development; and rapid expansion of merchandise exports.
7. With the demise of the Soviet Union and its economic domination of Eastern Europe, more than 20 nations are in economic transition from centralized socialism to market capitalism.
8. The Stalinist economic system that prevailed within the Soviet Union from the late 1920s until the late 1980s and in Eastern Europe during the post–World War II period, was characterized by public ownership of the means of production and central planning. Economic growth was emphasized at the expense of private consumption.
9. Other features of the Stalinist, command economy included prices often controlled below equilibrium levels (creating shortages), economic isolation (or autarky), and limited economic inequality.
10. The transition from the command economy was begun in the late 1980s by Gorbachev, who introduced modest economic and political reforms in the Soviet Union. Following an aborted coup against Gorbachev by hard-line communists in August 1991, dissatisfaction with the slow pace of economic and political liberalization led to the dissolution of the Soviet Union in late 1991. The 15 former republics became independent nations.
11. Each of the transitional economies faces common challenges: defining property rights and establishing commercial laws; introducing market pricing; privatizing state assets; integrating the domestic economy into the global economy; and promoting macroeconomic stability.
12. The transitional countries have had mixed success in meeting their objectives. Typically, the countries have been more successful in introducing market pricing and promoting international economic integration. Common failures have been problems with privatizing large state enterprises and reducing the government subsidies used to maintain employment levels.

## KEY TERMS

**glasnost**
**material balances**
**New Economic Mechanism (NEM)**
**perestroika**
**secondary markets**
**shock therapy**

## QUESTIONS

1. Which of the four major components of the World Bank's market-friendly strategy is the most essential for successful development? Discuss why.
2. Which of the four major components of the World Bank's market-friendly strategy would be the most difficult to implement? Discuss why.

3. Critique the World Bank's market-friendly strategy. To what extent does this strategy draw on the theories of development discussed in Chapters 4 and 5? What, if anything, is missing from this strategy?
4. What are the three most important lessons for development to be learned from the experiences of the East Asian nations? Discuss.
5. Will the success of the East Asian economies be easily replicated elsewhere in the developing world? Discuss.
6. To what extent do cultural and historical factors hinder the transition of the socialist countries to capitalism?
7. Choose a transitional country not studied in this chapter. Research the current obstacles faced by that country in its transition to capitalism. Comment on its progress to date.
8. In what ways should international development agencies assist the countries in transition?

## SUGGESTED READINGS

Birdsall, Nancy, David Ross, and Richard Sabot, "Inequality and Growth Reconsidered: Lessons from East Asia," *The World Bank Economic Review,* vol. 9, no. 3 (September 1995), pages 477–508.

Blanchard, Oliver, Rudiger Dornbusch, Paul Krugman, Richard Layard, and Lawrence Summers, *Reform in Eastern Europe,* Cambridge, MA: The MIT Press, 1991.

Fishlow, Albert, "Economic Development in the 1990s," *World Development,* vol. 22, no. 12 (December 1994), pages 1825–1832.

Frydman, Roman, Andrzej Rapczynski, and John S. Earle, *The Privatization Process in Russia, Ukraine, and the Baltic States,* Budapest: Central European University Press, 1993. See the Ukraine, pages 83–127.

Gregory, Paul R. and Robert C. Stuart, *Comparative Economic Systems,* 5th ed., Boston: Houghton Mifflin, 1995. See Chapters 6–7, 11–15, and 18.

Hofheinz, Roy, Jr., and Kent Calder, *The Eastasia Edge,* New York: Basic Books, 1982.

Krugman, Paul, "The Myth of Asia's Miracle," *Foreign Affairs,* vol. 73, no. 6 (November/December 1994), pages 62–78.

Ranis, Gustav, "Another Look at the East Asian Miracle," *The World Bank Economic Review,* vol. 9, no. 3 (September 1995), pages 509–534.

Sachs, Jeffrey, *Poland's Jump to the Market Economy,* Cambridge, MA: The MIT Press, 1993.

Singh, Ajit, "Openness and the Market-Friendly Approach to Development: Learning the Right Lessons from Development Experience," *World Development,* vol. 22, no. 12 (December 1994), pages 1811–1823.

Szekely, Istvan P. and David M. G. Newbery, editors, *Hungary: An Economy in Transition,* Glasgow: Cambridge University Press, 1993.

World Bank, *The East Asian Miracle: Economic Growth and Public Policy,* A World Bank Policy Research Report, New York: Oxford University Press, 1993.

World Bank, *Trends in Developing Economies, 1994,* Washington, DC, 1994. See chapters on Hungary, Poland, the Ukraine, as well as those for other countries in transition.

World Bank, *World Development Report 1991,* New York: Oxford University Press, 1991.

# CHAPTER 18

# DEVELOPMENT CHALLENGE: POVERTY IN SUB-SAHARAN AFRICA

On the eve of the twenty-first century, the world faces a particularly difficult development challenge. Approximately 560 million people—10 percent of the world's population—live in sub-Saharan Africa, where per capita income, averaging less than $600, has been virtually stagnant for the last 15 years. Writing in *The Atlantic Monthly*, journalist Robert Kaplan laments:

> West Africa is becoming the symbol of worldwide demographic, environmental, and societal stress, in which criminal anarchy emerges as the real "strategic" danger. Disease, overpopulation, unprovoked crime, scarcity of resources, refugee migrations, the increasing erosion of nation-states and international borders, and the empowerment of private armies, security firms, and international drug cartels are now most tellingly demonstrated through a West African prism.[1]

Some might argue that Kaplan is overly pessimistic and alarmist. Few, however, would deny that launching sustained development in Africa has become a global imperative: to alleviate growing poverty and to provide a future with hope for millions of young Africans.

Our analysis of the African development challenge will concentrate on the nearly 50 independent African nations that lie south of the Sahara desert (see the accompanying map of Africa). The largely Moslem countries of North Africa (Morocco, Algeria, Tunisia, Libya, and Egypt) tend to have significant cultural, historical, and political differences from those of sub-Saharan Africa. We should also note that the Republic of South Africa—a country that practiced an extreme form of political and economic segregation called *apartheid* until the early 1990s—also faces a different set of development challenges in its transition from a white-dominated to a more pluralistic society.

---

[1]Robert Kaplan, "The Coming Anarchy," *The Atlantic Monthly* (February 1994), pages 44–76. This quotation is from page 46.

## SUB-SAHARAN AFRICA

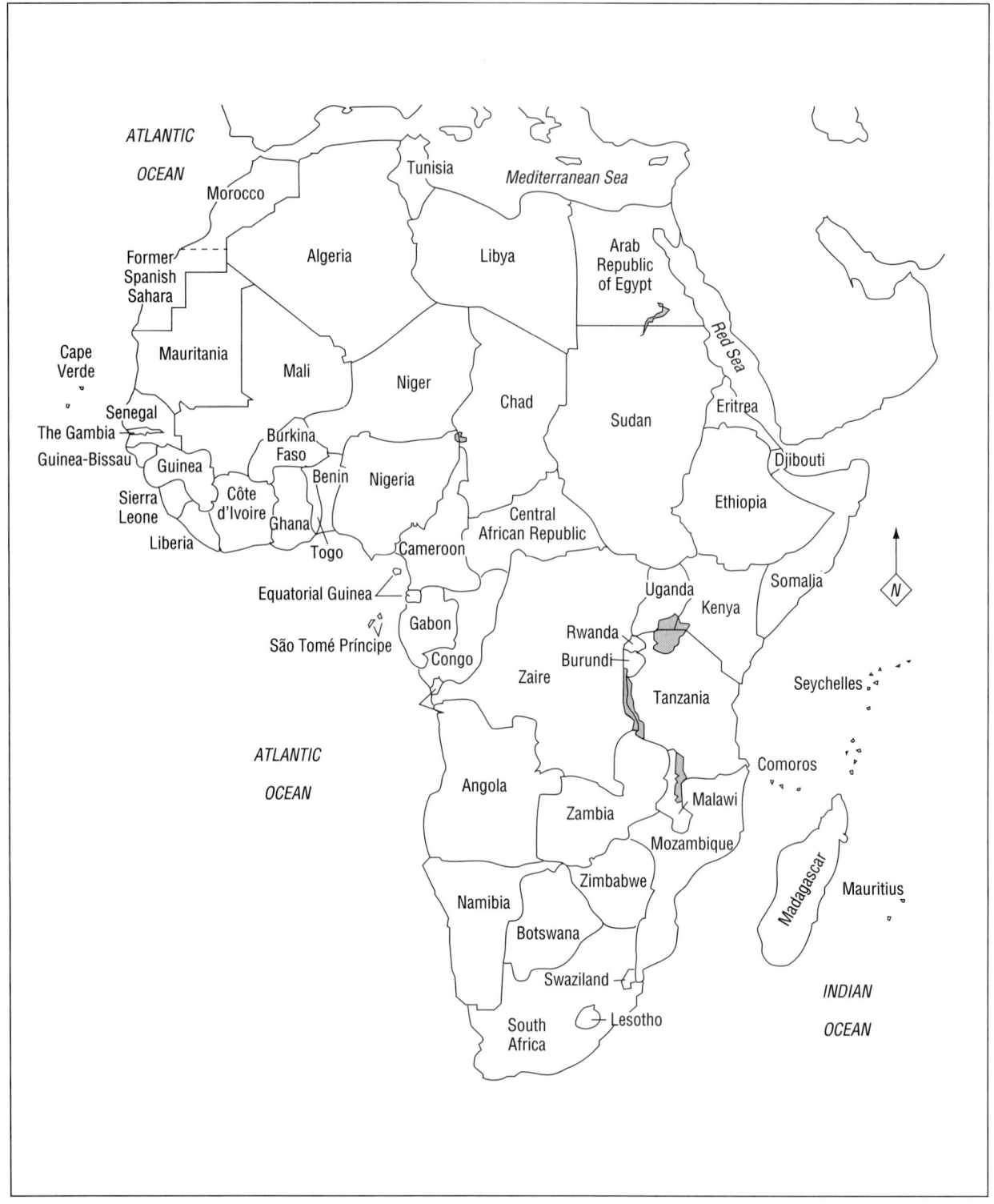

To be sure, variation exists within the countries of sub-Saharan Africa. Only about 10 percent of the African population lives in the semi-arid part of the continent that borders the Sahara Desert. This area includes the countries of Mauritania, Niger, Mali, Burkina Faso, Chad, Somalia, The Gambia, and parts of Senegal. The countries of central and southern Africa tend to have higher and more predictable rainfall levels and better natural resource endowments, including forests and minerals. For example, Nigeria, Cameroon, Congo, and Gabon have significant oil deposits.

Chronic poverty and rapid population growth continue to characterize sub-Saharan Africa. While much of the developing world has experienced a reduction in population growth, the rate of natural increase in Africa, with few exceptions, remains high. A continuation of its current average annual increase of nearly 3 percent would result in a doubling of the sub-Saharan African population, to over a billion people, by the year 2016. Most observers would argue that average living standards in 1995 are no better, and perhaps worse, than in the early 1960s, the time of independence for most African states. A recent World Bank report on sub-Saharan Africa states:

> Sub-Saharan Africa's economic growth, never spectacular, has been the weakest among developing regions. The region most in need of growth to reduce poverty has had the least. Between 1965 and 1985, its GDP per capita increased less than 1 percent a year on average. More worrisome, its economic performance actually began deteriorating in the mid 1970s.[2]

What are the causes of this stagnation? How can sustained development be nurtured in Africa? Our responses begin with a brief overview of Africa's past, from colonization to the current economic stagnation that began in the 1970s. The most critical of Africa's contemporary economic problems will then be analyzed. Finally, we will discuss policy options for sustainable development in Africa.

## FROM COLONIZATION TO ECONOMIC STAGNATION

Most of the African nations that had been colonized only gained their political independence in the late 1950s and 1960s. The national borders that emerged with political independence showed little respect for the ethnic differences of the African peoples. Thus, to understand the economic malaise of contemporary sub-Saharan Africa, we need to appreciate the colonial heritage of the African countries.

### COLONIZATION

European explorers and traders had long visited the African coast, and then ventured into the interior of the continent. Trade in arms, slaves, liquor, and foods had occurred

---

[2]World Bank, *Adjustment in Africa: Reforms, Results, and the Road Ahead,* New York: Oxford University Press, 1994, page 17.

between the Europeans and Africa's ancient kingdoms, such as the Mali kingdom, the Fulani of contemporary Nigeria, and those kingdoms that had their origins in contemporary Zimbabwe and Uganda. During the nineteenth century, with new discoveries of gold and diamonds, European colonization and settlement of Africa escalated. The French established a settlement on the Senegal River in the early 1800s; the British occupied Egypt and South Africa in the 1870s. The British and French were soon joined by German and Belgian settlers.

To forestall tension and conflict over African territory, the European powers agreed to a division of Africa with the 1884 Treaty of Berlin. Following Germany's defeat in World War I, the victors, Belgium, France, and Great Britain, acquired the German colonies in Africa. With the exception of this change in colonial rule and the ascendancy in South Africa of the Dutch Afrikaners in the pre–World War II period, colonization continued, with little substantive change, until the late 1950s. (It should be noted that the duration and conditions of colonization varied with each country. In fact, Liberia, established in 1822 [and becoming a republic in 1847] with assistance from the United States as a potential home for repatriated U.S. slaves, was never colonized. Yet even that country has clearly had its own share of ethnic troubles, much of which can be traced back to the circumstances of its founding.)

While the organization of the colonial economies differed, certain common features characterized the European domination of Africa. Most Africans remained in their traditional occupations, farming, herding, and trading. Europeans arrived, often in relatively large numbers, to serve in colonial administration, the military, and business. Cities began to emerge as centers of government and commerce between Africa and the "mother" countries in Europe. European missionaries brought Christianity to a continent that, particularly in its northern half, had already, to a large extent, embraced the Moslem religion.

Preferential trade arrangements arose between the colonial powers. For instance, in Senegal, expatriate French businessmen organized the export of groundnuts (a type of peanut that grows well in West Africa) to oil refiners in France who produced food and cooking oil for the European continent. French nationals sold French clothing, wines, and other goods to the French settlers in Africa. Since many Africans transferred land and labor from growing food crops to growing export crops (groundnuts, cotton, tea, coffee), local food production was unable to feed growing urban populations. Eventually, rice from Indochina, again sold by European traders, arrived in Africa to complement local food products such as millet, maize, and cassava.

Thus, on the eve of independence, Africans were subject to colonial administrations that had brought their own political and legal systems from Europe. Territories were divided and subdivided into administrative units. These internal borders were drawn with little regard for ethnic or geographic considerations. French West Africa had Upper Volta (now Burkina Faso), Mali, Senegal, Chad, and Niger; each of these units then had its own regions or provinces. Commerce, infrastructure, such as electrical power, and the small amount of industry were controlled and managed by Europeans. Cities, accommodating the inflow of Europeans, had grown in size. Farmers had shifted resources from local food production to export crops; imported foods such as rice, particularly in urban areas, had become a staple commodity. Few Africans had been trained for positions of leadership in either government or industry. Religious differences among Christians, Moslems, and those of more traditional faiths caused increased tensions. Ethnic hostility and mistrust were latent as different groups found themselves under a common political entity, the colonial state, which would soon become an independent nation.

The African independence movement began with the British granting independence to the Gold Coast, now Ghana, in 1957. Other British colonies were granted independence; France and Belgium also responded to local movements for autonomy and set their colonies free. The post-independent Africa of the early 1960s had great hope and enthusiasm. Unfortunately, the colonial legacy presented great hurdles to development. Mismanagement, corruption, and political instability too often replaced the exploitation and the inequities of colonization.

## THE HOPEFUL DECADE OF THE 1960s

From the early 1960s through 1970, African economic performance was not considerably different from that of the other developing countries. For example, in the early 1960s, both Africa and South Asia contained low-income countries, many of which had only recently gained independence. It is instructive to look at the relative progress of these two regions since that time period. World Bank statistics, in Table 18.1, show the relative parity in economic performance between Africa and South Asia during the 1960s.

The newly independent governments began ambitious building programs to provide economic infrastructure such as roads and electricity, and to construct health and educational facilities. This increase in government spending helped fuel growth in national outputs and employments. Typically, these facilities were located in the capital cities and modeled after those found in high-income countries. For example, school construction was biased toward higher education and the building of large, urban campuses. These government initiatives were funded with commodity exports, foreign aid, and eventually foreign debt.

The prices of primary products were relatively high and stable during the 1960s. As a result, most African countries encouraged the development of export industries. With resource endowments varying within the continent, commodities grown for export differed according to region. For example coffee was grown in Côte d'Ivoire, Burundi, Kenya, Tanzania, and Ethiopia; cocoa in Ghana and Côte d'Ivoire; sugar in Malawi; groundnuts in Senegal and The Gambia. Often, government marketing boards would purchase crops at below-market prices from farmers, continuing a system that had begun in colonization, and then export the crop for a profit.

**TABLE 18.1** COMPARISONS OF PER CAPITA INCOME GROWTH

|  | 1960–1970 | | 1970–1981 | |
| --- | --- | --- | --- | --- |
|  | AFRICA | SOUTH ASIA | AFRICA | SOUTH ASIA |
| Real GDP growth (%) | 3.8 | 4.0 | 3.2 | 3.9 |
| Population growth (%) | 2.4 | 2.4 | 2.8 | 2.2 |
| Per capita income growth (%) | 1.4 | 1.6 | 0.4 | 1.7 |
| Investment (as percent of GDP) | 15.6 | 16.7 | 21.8 | 19.4 |

NOTE: All figures are annual averages. Africa refers to sub-Saharan Africa.

FROM World Bank, *Toward Sustained Development in Sub-Saharan Africa,* Washington, DC: World Bank, 1984, Table 2.1, page 22.

Governments became an attractive source of employment, with the number of government workers increasing significantly in the newly-independent countries. Expatriate administrators needed to be replaced as countries gained independence. In many cases, however, the expatriates remained and were joined by local counterparts, further increasing the size of government. Also, many African leaders, who tended initially to acquire power in quasi-democratic ways, repaid loyal supporters with employment.

From Leopold Senghor in Senegal (president from 1960 to 1980) to Julius Nyerere in Tanzania (president of Tanganyika and then Tanzania from 1962 to 1985), most African countries committed themselves to a development path that they called "African Socialism." In this development strategy, the government was to play a significant role in key sectors. A blend of European socialist thought and Soviet economic practice, this brand of socialism emphasized the potential equity gains from public ownership and central control of the economy. Proponents of the system, however, failed to foresee the economic stagnation that would result from the self-interest of bureaucrats; the military costs of maintaining political control; and the inefficiencies of public enterprises and price controls.

In actuality, while government activity varied by country, some patterns tended to become clear. For one, the government would be heavily involved in agriculture. As noted, commodity boards would purchase export-destined crops from farmers. Governments would be the importers of food and recipients of food aid, determining the conditions under which food items would be turned over to the private sector. Finally, governments became very involved in providing inputs, such as seed and fertilizers, to farmers.

Thus, at the end of the first decade of independence, many African countries were ostensibly developing in a manner similar to that found in other parts of the Third World. In retrospect, some clear differences were being masked. First, the development process was a government-directed enterprise. Governments were becoming the preferred source of employment; jobs, in capital cities, paid relatively well and were considered secure. Little conscious effort was paid to promoting private-sector development within any African state. Also, some governments were beginning to use controlled prices, particularly on food items, to subsidize urban wages. In general, African leaders, enjoying the benefits of power, neither appreciated nor understood the efficiency gains that competitive markets could bring.

Export agriculture, since it earned foreign exchange for governments, was encouraged to the detriment of local food production. With little comparative advantage in industry and manufacturing, the African economies were not well diversified. The preponderance of economic activity was concentrated in four subsectors: commodities for export, local food production (crops, meat, and fish), low-value added commerce, and government activity. Industry and financial intermediation were two key areas of economic activity that received little attention, either from uninterested governments or from private entrepreneurs who faced significant obstacles.

Also, little attention was being paid to primary education and basic health and nutritional programs. Death rates were falling due to progress in controlling contagious diseases such as malaria, cholera, and tuberculosis, but birth rates remained quite high. The rate of growth of the sub-Saharan population was increasing and would reach an average annual rate of nearly 3 percent in the 1970s. In fact, many African governments were pro-fertility and satisfied with this high rate of population growth.

Finally, the fragility of the political systems in most African governments was tested. Coups, power struggles, and civil strife were common as individuals and groups sought power to address ethnic imbalances and to enjoy the associated prestige and wealth that government could offer. In fact, it was not until 1980, when President Abdioul Diouf replaced the voluntarily retiring Senegal President Senghor, that an African leader was legitimately replaced in a contested, relatively free election. Clearly, the economic and political conditions of the 1960s were not conducive to sustained economic development.

## ECONOMIC STAGNATION: 1970s TO THE PRESENT

Beginning in the 1970s, a development gap between Africa and other developing countries emerged. As shown in Table 18.1, between 1970 and 1981, declining GDP growth coupled with increased population growth led to minimal annual per capita income growth of .4 percent in sub-Saharan Africa, compared to the 1.7 percent per capita income increase in South Asia. Note that investment in Africa, as a percentage of GDP, exceeded that in South Asia during the 1970 to 1981 period. However, a relatively large proportion of investment in Africa originated in the public sector. The low productivity with which human and capital resources have been used by African governments has led to a lower rate of economic growth, despite a seemingly favorable level of investment.

Then, from 1980 to 1993, African per capita income fell, on average, by .8 percent per year. Tanzania, a country that had made economic progress in the 1960s before succumbing to excessive state intervention in the economy, is illustrative of the stagnation that has plagued Africa.

> Following independence in 1961, the economy, burdened with a legacy of extensive poverty, dependence on subsistence agriculture, a small industrial base, and a limited number of educated and trained personnel, still managed [an output growth of] about 6 percent a year through the late 1960s. In 1967 the government's Arusha Declaration called for the establishment of a socialist society in response to growing concerns about widespread poverty and income inequality. The public sector was given a leading role and state control was extended throughout the economy. This included nationalization of all commercial and financial firms occupying the commanding heights of the economy, collectivization of peasant farming, and granting exclusive marketing and processing rights to cooperatives and marketing boards.[3]

In the 1970s Tanzanian economic performance worsened as a result of economic inefficiencies introduced by pervasive government control. In the 1980s, the Tanzanian economy began to collapse, with real GDP per capita falling, export earnings declining, and food shortages appearing.

Thus, for Tanzania, as for most of sub-Saharan Africa, the economic stagnation and decline of the post–1970 period offset the per capita income gains of the 1960s. In other words, currently the average income level in Africa is similar to that at the time of independence in the early 1960s. Caloric consumption per capita in the late 1980s was roughly equivalent to that in 1965.[4] Several interrelated factors are most commonly cited for the poor economic performance in Africa in the post-1970 period. In general, these problems persist today and must be addressed in a comprehensive development effort for Africa.

---

[3]World Bank, "Tanzania," *Trends in Developing Economies, 1994,* Washington, D.C., 1994, page 475.

[4]See Jeffrey Herbst, "The Politics of Sustained Agricultural Reform in Africa," page 335 in *Hemmed In: Responses to Africa's Economic Decline,* ed. Thomas Callaghy and John Ravenhill, New York: Columbia University Press, 1993, page 335.

## THE ECONOMIC PROBLEMS OF AFRICA

Evidence of Africa's economic woes can be seen in Table 18.2, which provides development indicators for all developing countries and for Africa. With the high and low country values for Africa shown, we can also see the range of economic performance within the region. For instance, the infant mortality rate in 1993 for sub-Saharan Africa was 93 (per thousand live births) compared to only 55 for all developing countries. The range in Africa, however, extended from a high of 146 in Mozambique to a low of 17 in Mauritius. (As we discuss the African development challenge, refer back to Table 18.2 as needed.)

The economic problems and constraints of Africa are highly intertwined. For example, in Chapter 7 we referred to a vicious circle of low per capita income growth and high rates of population growth reinforcing each other. We will discuss Africa's high rate of population growth; the poor performance of the agricultural sector; the inattention to basic health and educational needs; and the lack of economic diversity within Africa. We begin, however, with a candid appraisal of the failure of Africa's governments and the donor community to promote economic development.

### FAILURES OF THE AFRICAN GOVERNMENTS AND THE DONOR COMMUNITY

The failure of African governments to promote sustained development is acknowledged by most observers of Africa. Rakiya Omaar, a Somali who directs the human rights group called African Rights, states "The problem in Africa has been these predatory, strong central governments that never cared about their own people."[5] From colonialism to the present, strong central authority has directed the political and economic affairs of the typical African. While colonial governments were interested in exploiting African resources for the gain of the mother country, many post-independence, African states have been used to enrich leaders and favored ethnic groups.

The most egregious example of this self-serving leadership may be Mobutu Sese Seko, ruler of Zaire since 1965. Prior to independence, resource-rich Zaire was a major exporter of agricultural and mining products. In the last 30 years, however, the Mobutu government has diverted export earnings for personal gain and military expenditures, destroying the economy in the process. In 1995, Zaire, having been expelled from the IMF, is one of the African countries considered by many to be "without a truly functioning government." The situation has been equally critical in Somalia, Rwanda, Angola, and Liberia. Other countries in Africa that have domestic clan or tribal violence of varying degrees include Niger, Mali, Sierra Leone, Ghana, Burundi, Chad, and Sudan. In Nigeria, the most populous African nation, a military dictatorship suppresses ethnic violence, while crime and graft abound.

In recent years, more African countries have experimented with democracy. Relatively free elections have been held in Senegal, Malawi, and Lesotho. Moreover, while Ghana and Uganda have achieved some degree of political stability, the peaceful,

---

[5]Keith Richburg, "A Microcosm of Disintegration," *The Washington Post National Weekly Edition*, (September 12–18), 1994, page 6.

### TABLE 18.2  DEVELOPMENT INDICATORS FOR AFRICA

| INDICATOR | LOW- AND MIDDLE-INCOME COUNTRIES | SUB-SAHARAN AFRICA | SUB-SAHARAN AFRICA (HIGH/LOW) |
|---|---|---|---|
| Population, 1993 (millions) | 4689 | 559 | Nigeria, 105.3<br>The Gambia, 1.0<br>Mauritius, 1.0 |
| Average annual population growth, 1980–93 (%) | 1.9 | 2.9 | Côte d'Ivoire, 3.7<br>Mauritius, .9 |
| GNP per capita, 1993 ($) | 1090 | 520 | Gabon, 4960<br>Mozambique, 90 |
| GNP per capita growth, 1980–93 (average annual %) | 0.9 | −0.8 | Botswana, 6.2<br>Côte d'Ivoire, −4.6 |
| Life expectancy at birth, 1993 (years) | 64 | 52 | Mauritius, 70<br>Guinea-Bissau, 44 |
| Infant mortality rate, 1993 (per thousand live births) | 55 | 93 | Mozambique, 146<br>Mauritius, 17 |
| Female-adult illiteracy, 1990 (%) | 46[a] | 62 | Burkina Faso, 91<br>Madagascar, 27 |
| Total adult illiteracy, 1990 (%) | 33 | 50 | Burkina Faso, 82<br>Madagascar, 20 |
| Distribution of GDP, 1993 (%)<br>Agriculture | ... | 20 | Ethiopia, 60<br>South Africa, 5 |
| Industry | ... | 33 | Botswana, 47<br>Lesotho, 47<br>Ethiopia, 10 |

*continued*

orderly and voluntary transition of political power—a basic hallmark of effective government—has yet to characterize much of Africa.

In the absence of a credible government, it becomes nearly impossible to design and implement effective development policies. The honest and fair collection of taxes, needed to sustain legitimate functions of government, becomes compromised by widespread corruption. Appropriate development objectives, such as enhanced rural health care and primary education, are crowded out by a combination of military spending, superfluous job creation to maintain power, and high salaries (including houses and cars) for government officials. Civil strife and violence disrupt the orderly functioning of markets, discourage private investment, and encourage human migration and capital flight. Witness the loss of life and exodus of several hundred thousand Tutsi and Hutus from Rwanda during the massacres of 1994.

Civil strife and military governments have resulted in expensive commitments of defense expenditures within Africa. In recent years, however, arms imports and military expenditures by sub-Saharan African countries have been relatively restrained. Both pressure from the international donor community and relatively high levels of

| TABLE 18.2 | DEVELOPMENT INDICATORS FOR AFRICA, continued | | |
|---|---|---|---|
| INDICATOR | LOW- AND MIDDLE-INCOME COUNTRIES | SUB-SAHARAN AFRICA | SUB-SAHARAN AFRICA (HIGH/LOW) |
| Food production per capita, 1992 (1979–1981 = 100) | 121 | 95 | Burkina Faso, 134 Liberia, 62 |
| Defense expenditures, 1992 (% of GDP) | 3.8 | 2.8 | Ethiopia, 20.1 Mauritius, 0.4 |
| Education expenditures, 1990 (% of total public expenditures) | 14.2 | 15.7 | Rwanda, 25.4 Equatorial Guinea, 3.9 |
| Public expenditures on health, 1990 (% of GDP) | 2.1 | 2.5 | Swaziland, 5.8[b] Sudan, 0.5 |
| Official development assistance, 1993 (% of GNP) | ... | 11.5 | Mozambique, 79.2 Nigeria, 0.9 |
| Official development assistance, 1993 (per capita $) | ... | 35.7 | Mauritania, 153.2 Nigeria, 2.7 |
| External debt, 1993 (% of GNP) | 32.1 | 47.4 | Mozambique, 339.4 Botswana, 13.6 |
| Total debt service, 1993 (% of exports) | 18.3 | 17.1 | Uganda, 143.6 Mali 4.5 |

NOTES: Lack of data is indicated by ...
African countries for which a full set of data are available: Benin, Botswana, Burkina Faso, Burundi, Cameroon, Central African Republic, Chad, Congo, Côte d'Ivoire, Ethiopia, Gabon, The Gambia, Ghana, Guinea, Guinea-Bissau, Kenya, Lesotho, Madagascar, Malawi, Mali, Mauritania, Mauritius, Mozambique, Namibia, Niger, Nigeria, Rwanda, Senegal, Sierra Leone, South Africa, Tanzania, Togo, Uganda, Zambia, Zimbabwe.
Other African countries for which data are available only on basic indicators, such as population and GDP: Angola, Cape Verde, Djibouti, Equatorial Guinea, Eritrea, Liberia, Reunion, Seychelles, Somalia, Sudan, Swaziland, Zaire. (See Table 1A of *World Development Report 1995*.)

SOURCES:
World Bank, *World Development Report 1995*, New York: Oxford University Press, 1995, Tables 1, 3, 19, 23, 25, 27.
[a]FROM World Bank, *World Development Report 1994*, New York: Oxford University Press, 1994, Table 1.
United Nations Development Programme, *Human Development Report 1995*, New York: Oxford University Press, 1995, Tables 8, 9, 14.
[b]FROM United Nations Development Programme, *Human Development Report 1994*, New York: Oxford University Press, 1994, Table 12.

external public indebtedness have contributed to some reduction in military expenditures within the region. For all of sub-Saharan Africa, defense expenditures averaged 2.8 percent of GDP in 1992, compared to 3.8 percent for all developing countries. Within the region, countries with particularly high military expenditures as a percentage of GDP were Angola (estimated to be in excess of 25 percent), Ethiopia (20 percent), Sudan (16 percent), and Mozambique (10 percent).[6] For these countries, all of which confront internal unrest or civil strife, military expenditures clearly have an enormous opportunity cost.

---

[6]United Nations Development Programme, *Human Development Report 1995*, New York: Oxford University Press, 1995, Table 14.

During the post-independence period, international donors, with their assistance programs, have tended to support both financially and militarily some of the worst African governments. The United States from the mid-1960s until 1990 provided relatively generous economic assistance to Mobutu in Zaire. As an avowed anticommunist, Mobutu benefited from Western aid aimed at countering any communist threat in Africa. In a similar way, France supported relatively dictatorial governments of former French colonies, including the Emperor Jean-Bedel Bokassa, the leader of the Central African Republic from 1965 to 1979.

In other cases, foreign aid, typically disbursed through the host-country government, has served as a form of financial support for administrations and rulers whose legitimacy, honesty, and effectiveness have been suspect. Donors have also supported prestigious development projects, from universities to convention centers, that have not made significant contributions to economic growth. A significant portion of this donor assistance has been in the form of loans. The African countries have high levels of public debt owed to international donors. In 1993, external debt represented 47 percent of GDP for the African countries, compared to 32 percent for all developing countries; debt service represented 17 percent of African export earnings in that year, compared to 18 percent for all developing countries (see Table 18.2). The accumulated public debts of African countries were used for projects that, in general, have not yielded recurring benefits to support the ensuing debt service. The issue of continued debt restructuring and cancellation for Africa is critical.

In short, many of the African countries have suffered a combination of political instability and repression, dishonest governments, poor economic management, and inappropriate donor policies. The unfortunate result is that now, as Africa confronts its economic challenges, the concept of government, so vital to an effective development effort, is itself highly suspect to most Africans.

## EXCESSIVE POPULATION GROWTH

From 1965 through 1980, the average annual rate of population increase in Africa was 2.7 percent; for all low-income countries the rate was 2.3 percent (see Table 18.3 and Figure 18.1). With health improvements and economic growth, crude death rates fell in the low-income countries from 16 (per thousand) to 10 between 1965 and 1993, and from 22 to 15 in Africa during the same time period. In Africa, the crude birth rate remained very high, 48 in 1965 and 44 in 1993; in all low-income countries the birth rate fell from 42 to 28.

From 1980 to 1993 Africa's population was growing at a dangerously high rate of 2.9 percent per year, while that of all low-income countries (including many African countries) has been reduced to an annual average of 2.0 percent. In South Asia, the rate of population growth slowed to an annual average rate of growth of 2.1 percent. Much of this progress is due to India's success in reducing its annual rate of population growth to approximately 2.0 percent since the mid-1980s.

As repeatedly discussed, high population growth rates place strains on available resources, from land to health services. Educational expenditures per pupil are reduced when a young population exists. The growth of income both in the aggregate, and particularly at the per capita level, is slowed with excessive population growth. Why has the African rate of population increase stayed so high? Several reasons need to be discussed. (Refer back to Chapter 7 and the discussion of fertility in sub-Saharan Africa.)

| TABLE 18.3 | DEMOGRAPHIC COMPARISONS: BIRTH AND DEATH RATES AND POPULATION GROWTH RATES | |
|---|---|---|
| | 1965 | 1993 |
| **CRUDE BIRTH RATE (PER THOUSAND)** | | |
| Africa | 48 | 44 |
| South Asia | 45 | 31 |
| Low-income countries | 42 | 28 |
| **CRUDE DEATH RATE (PER THOUSAND)** | | |
| Africa | 22 | 15 |
| South Asia | 20 | 10 |
| Low-income countries | 16 | 10 |
| | 1965–1980 | 1980–1993 |
| **AVERAGE ANNUAL POPULATION GROWTH RATE** | | |
| Africa | 2.7 | 2.9 |
| South Asia | 2.4 | 2.1 |
| Low-income countries | 2.3 | 2.0 |

NOTE: The composition of the low-income countries will vary over time.

FROM World Bank, *World Development Report 1995,* New York: Oxford University Press, 1995, Tables 25 and 26; *World Development Report 1994,* New York: Oxford University Press, 1994, Table 26; *World Development Report 1989,* New York: Oxford University Press, 1989, Tables 26 and 27.

As a starting point, are we able to assume that the demographic transition that has characterized both the high-income countries and the developing countries of Asia will apply with a similar timing and magnitude in Africa? Some development observers question this assumption. First, especially in rural Africa, children are a source of special pride for both the village, and in particular, for their family. Also, rural residents have tended to be suspicious of family planning programs that have originated with the central government in the capital city. This is particularly true when the government is dominated by an ethnic group that differs from rural ethnic groups.

The influences of Islam and Catholicism, claiming large numbers of the sub-Saharan African population, are also difficult to gauge. Both religions are pro-fertility in their discouragement of family planning and their prohibitions against abortion. Moreover, in both religions, tradition holds that children represent a gift from God and that God's will concerning family size should be respected. Polygamy, still common in Africa, also contributes to higher fertility.

Economic development should have some effect in reducing birth rates. As indicated in Chapter 7, evidence exists in Africa that increased female education and economic mobility will result in reduced fertility. It seems likely, however, that the impact of economic growth on birth rates may be slow and less pronounced, unless well-designed family planning programs that recognize traditional African values are integrated into the development process.

| FIGURE 18.1 | AVERAGE ANNUAL POPULATION GROWTH |

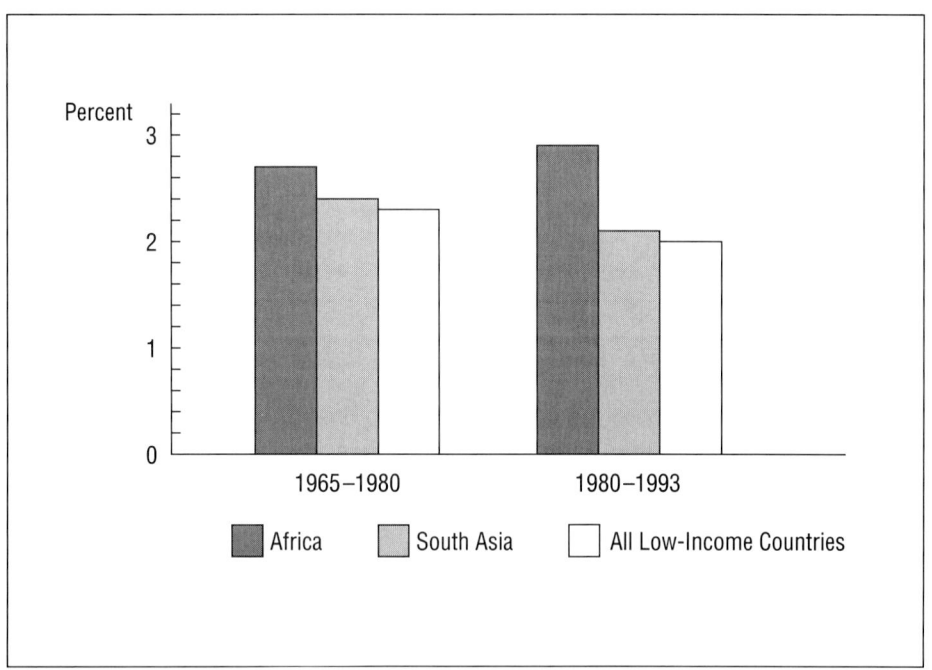

## POOR AGRICULTURAL PERFORMANCE

Economic development in Africa is crucially dependent on the performance of agriculture. As discussed in Chapter 11, agriculture is very important in low-income countries. In 1993, agriculture accounted for 20 percent of the regional GDP of sub-Saharan Africa; and the percentage of the population living in rural areas was very high, approximately 70 percent.[7] Unfortunately, agricultural performance in Africa has been hindered by several factors.

The average annual growth of agricultural output has lagged the growth in population for Africa. For instance, in the 1980 to 1993 period, while the African population grew at an average annual rate of 2.9 percent, agricultural output grew at a rate of 1.7 percent. As a consequence, African per capita food production fell throughout the time period. In contrast, for all low-income countries, agricultural output grew at a rate of 3.4 percent, while population increased at an annual average rate of only 2.0 percent (see Tables 18.2 and 18.4).

Lagging agricultural growth has serious implications for domestic food self-sufficiency. With per capita agricultural production falling, Africa has become increasingly dependent on external food sources. Commercial food imports, primarily rice, wheat, corn, and other coarse grains, increased significantly between 1980 and 1993, growing from 8.65 to 13.2 million tons. Food aid has more than tripled from 1.6 to 5.1 million tons. Thus, in

---

[7]World Bank, *World Development Report 1995*, New York: Oxford University Press, 1995, Tables 3 and 31.

## TABLE 18.4  INDICATORS OF AGRICULTURAL PERFORMANCE

| AVERAGE ANNUAL GROWTH IN AGRICULTURAL OUTPUT | 1970–1980 | 1980–1993 |
|---|---|---|
| Low-income countries | 2.0 | 3.4 |
| sub-Saharan Africa | 1.7 | 1.7 |

| | SUB-SAHARAN AFRICA | | ALL LOW-INCOME COUNTRIES | |
|---|---|---|---|---|
| | 1980 | 1993 | 1980 | 1993 |
| CEREAL IMPORTS | | | | |
| (thousand tons) | 8647 | 13,157 | 32,801 | 34,420 |
| (kilograms per capita) | 22.7 | 23.5 | 14.9 | 11.1 |

| | SUB-SAHARAN AFRICA | | ALL LOW-INCOME COUNTRIES | |
|---|---|---|---|---|
| | 1979–1980 | 1992–1993 | 1979–1980 | 1992–1993 |
| FOOD AID IN CEREALS | | | | |
| (thousand tons) | 1601 | 5079 | 6101 | 8334 |
| (kilograms per capita) | 4.2 | 9.1 | 2.8 | 2.7 |
| FERTILIZER CONSUMPTION | 138 | 149 | 528 | 1028 |
| (hundred grams per hectare) | | | 196[a] | 352[a] |

[a]Excluding China and India

FROM World Bank, *World Development Report 1995*, New York: Oxford University Press, 1995, Tables 2, 4.

1992–1993, cereal imports (including food aid) represented about 24 kilograms per person in Africa. This consumption of externally provided food grains is approximately 14 percent of an annual nutritional requirement of 175 kilograms for a cereals-based diet.

Agricultural performance in Africa has been adversely influenced by several factors. The World Bank candidly states:

> African farmers have faced the world's heaviest rates of agricultural taxation, perhaps partly because agriculture has been such a crucial source of revenue for African governments. African farmers were taxed explicitly through producer-price fixing, export taxes, and taxes on agricultural inputs. They were also taxed implicitly through overvalued exchange rates, which reduced the prices they obtained for their exports, and through high levels of industrial protection, which raised consumer prices. A study covering eighteen countries across the world showed that three broadly representative sub-Saharan countries (Côte d'Ivoire, Ghana, and Zambia) taxed their farmers 70 percent more that the average for developing countries. The high rates of taxation contributed to sub-Saharan Africa's alarming decline in the average annual rate of agricultural growth.[8]

---

[8]World Bank, *Adjustment in Africa*, page 76.

In the ensuing discussion of African agriculture, we will consider the role of export agriculture, the effects of drought and land degradation, and the lack of incentives to domestic agriculture.

### EXPORT AGRICULTURE

First, both in the colonial and post-independence periods, greater attention was paid to export agriculture as a primary source of foreign-exchange earnings. Food imports, particularly rice, had become important for urban consumption in West Africa even during the colonial period. With growing urbanization, a tendency existed for food demands to be increasingly met with imports. In urban areas, imported food, particularly rice, became preferred to local grains such as millet. Thus, while population growth was fueling food demand, domestic food production was becoming proportionately less important.

Lack of productivity growth in export agriculture coupled with adverse (from the African perspective) worldwide commodity price trends in the last 20 years, have led to unstable and often declining export earnings. The demand for primary products is relatively income-inelastic. Also, the non-African supply of primary commodities, such as coffee from Latin America, has been increasing. Thus, demand and supply conditions have not been favorable for export earnings growth in Africa during the 1970 to 1995 period. Furthermore, price fluctuations have persisted around this trend. For instance, climatic conditions can lead to periodic shortages or surpluses, with resulting sharp price changes. Countries that were particularly dependent on commodity exports, such as Ghana and Côte d'Ivoire, have experienced significant instability of export earnings as well as a declining trend to those earnings.

In addition, many African countries have had overvalued currencies. When this occurs, the price of a country's exports will be inflated to foreign buyers, reducing export demand. With African exports being sold in relatively competitive world markets, such as coffee and cocoa, the export disadvantage from an overvalued currency can be significant.

Poor performance in export agriculture can have negative effects throughout the economy. For instance, in the early 1970s, Tanzania's cashew production, in excess of 145,000 tons, represented about 30 percent of the world's production. By the late 1980s, however, the country was producing only around 17,000 tons.[9] Contributing to this decline in market output were low producer prices; a government monopoly on the marketing of cashews; and periodic blights that damaged crops. The resulting losses in agricultural income and export earnings hindered the country's development efforts.

### DROUGHT AND LAND CONSTRAINTS

The devastating droughts of the 1975 to 1985 period that primarily affected the countries of the Sahel (Burkina Faso, Niger, Chad, Mali, Mauritania, and Senegal—all bordering the Sahara Desert) demonstrated the fragility of semiarid African agriculture. A vicious cycle of drought, deforestation, and desertification has reduced the availability of good land, while growing populations have increased the demand for land. Slash-and-burn farming, coupled with a reduction in fallow cycles, has led to

---

[9]Ibid., page 82.

overcultivation in an attempt to address land shortages. The result, of course, is further land deterioration and increased pressure on existing land.

Additional negative effects from the drought have included the reduced profitability of livestock and mixed farming. During droughts, farmers and herders are forced to sell livestock; the risk-averse owners often do not replace their stock. Also, the rural to urban migration of the young has accelerated. As shown in Chapter 9, a reduction in expected rural income (even with no current increase in urban income or the probability of finding employment) will tend to increase migration to cities. From 1970 to 1993, Africa's rate of urbanization increased from 19 to 30 percent.[10] Given that modern service and manufacturing employments were not increasing at a rate to absorb this growing labor force, excessive migration has placed great strains on African governments. Finally, the drought led to sharp increases in food aid that was most easily distributed in urban areas; the availability of food aid also has reduced producer prices for locally produced food. Thus, this humanitarian effort further encouraged food dependency and urban growth.

### Lack of Incentives

As discussed in Chapter 11, a vibrant agricultural sector is encouraged with sound economic incentives for farmers. In Africa, a host of disincentives has contributed to agricultural stagnation. Most African farms are relatively small, between 2 and 10 hectares. The land, however, is often not directly titled to individual households. Land rights can be extended through traditional tribal and village channels or by governments. In the latter case, farmers, with uncertainty about the permanency of their tenancy, have an incentive to overcultivate land (and reduce fallow cycles) and refrain from longer-term investments in land.

Low producer prices have discouraged production and sale of agricultural commodities. With export crops, national commodity boards have often paid less than world-market, farm-gate prices. For food crops, countries have similarly used official producer prices with sales through marketing boards. Often, to accommodate urban residents, these official prices were set relatively low, leading to an excess demand for food. This practice discouraged production and increased the use of illegal parallel markets with risk-taking traders reaping significant economic profits. Finally, the presence of food aid as a supplement to the domestic supply of food has depressed producer food prices, reducing local production.

The Green Revolution has not really reached sub-Saharan Africa. Contributing to the relative technological stagnancy of African agriculture have been poor agricultural extension efforts by the governments; the relatively low level of education in rural Africa; the lack of drought-resistent plant varieties; and poor price incentives. Yields per hectare for major crop varieties have not shown the upward trends that have characterized agriculture in the developing countries of Asia. While average fertilizer usage (hundred grams per hectare of arable land) increased from 196 to 352 in the low-income economies (excluding China and India) between 1979–80 and 1992–93, in sub-Saharan Africa usage barely changed—from 138 to 149—during this time period.[11] Thus, African fertilizer consumption per hectare is only 43 percent of the average found in the

---

[10]World Bank, *World Development Report 1995*, Table 31.
[11]Ibid., Table 4.

low-income countries when China and India are excluded, and barely 15 percent when those two nations are included.

Without sustained development in rural Africa, the serious economic difficulties of the continent will continue. Problems linked to poor agricultural performance include high population growth; stagnant per capita income levels; land degradation; food aid dependency; and rapid urbanization.

## BASIC NEEDS: EDUCATION AND HEALTH CARE

Despite an ostensible socialist commitment to greater equality, Africa has not made significant progress in providing for the basic needs of its population in the post-independence period. In 1993, life expectancy at birth was only 52 years in sub-Saharan Africa compared to 64 years for all developing countries.[12] The percentages of the African population with access to health services (56 percent, compared to 79 percent for all developing countries) and safe water (43 percent, compared to 69 percent) are still disturbingly low.[13] Despite political rhetoric, significant development assistance, and some commitment of local government resources, Africa has a poor record of achievement in promoting basic needs or human development. Several factors are relevant.

Local governments and donors have often concentrated their activities in urban areas, where politically important groups tend to reside. Moreover, disproportionate expenditures have been allocated to more prestigious projects such as hospitals and universities rather than on small health clinics and primary schools. The beneficiaries of these efforts have primarily been higher-income, politically-connected members of the society.

The opportunity costs of these types of health and educational efforts have been high. Health clinics in rural areas, vaccination programs, primary education, and vocational education—projects that often have very high rates of return—have been neglected. As noted in Chapter 16, in many countries, nongovernmental organizations (NGOs) have attempted to address some of these critical needs.

Africa has also suffered many natural disasters and human calamities that have resulted in high levels of emergency spending by donors and local governments. Periodic famines have diverted development funds aimed at projects into emergency food aid. The mass movement of political refugees—such as the 1994 exodus of Rwandans into Zaire and Kenya—imposes significant costs for feeding and emergency health care. Unfortunately, these humanitarian efforts, while requiring large commitments of funds, do little to generate sustained economic development.

Currently the woes of Africa have been increased with the alarmingly high incidence of AIDS and HIV infection. Reliable estimates of the numbers of Africans infected with HIV are difficult to find. In 1995, as many as 10 million Africans may be infected with the HIV virus.[14] Thus, nearly 70 percent of the world's HIV-infected may reside in Africa. The rates in Central Africa are undoubtedly higher than in any other part of the world. Unlike other geographic regions, in Africa women and men are

---

[12]Ibid., Table 1.

[13]United Nations Development Programme, *Human Development Report 1995*, Table 2.

[14]Population Reference Bureau, "Women, Children, and AIDs," *Population Today*, vol. 23, no. 4 (April 1995), page 3.

infected at a relatively similar rate. In fact, in 1994, more African women, compared to men, died of AIDS. Neither local governments nor donors have made a major effort to address this issue.

In sum, the human development profile for Africa is as discouraging as its economic performance. As we have shown previously, low levels of income and education contribute to high population growth. Poor nutrition and inadequate health care help to perpetuate high infant mortality and high fertility. A major commitment to basic needs must characterize any true development effort for Africa.

## LACK OF ECONOMIC DIVERSITY

The national outputs of most African states continue to be dominated by agriculture, informal services, and government activity. Industry and modern services such as finance and insurance have lagged in the development process. The countries of sub-Saharan Africa have not been able to establish even the low-technology industries, such as textiles, footwear, and food processing that characterize countries within the early stages of the development process. To put this in some perspective, while the developed nation of Sweden, with under 9 million inhabitants, produced $51.7 billion of industrial goods in 1993, all of sub-Saharan Africa with its population of 559 million produced only $88.9 billion of industrial goods in that year.[15]

In the post-independence period, African governments, trying to avoid a form of neocolonialism involving excessive foreign ownership of productive assets, were often reluctant to encourage foreign investors. During the economic decline of the 1980s, however, many African countries introduced legislation encouraging industrial development. Specifically, between 1982 and 1987, nearly half the African countries wrote new investment codes to attract foreign direct investment (FDI).[16] Foreign direct investment in Africa, however, has been relatively marginal, having averaged only $3 billion per year in the 1986 to 1990 period.[17] The bulk of FDI has been in oil-exporting countries such as Egypt and Nigeria.

Industrial development has been hindered by several factors. First, despite the reform of investment codes in many countries, the political instability of Africa breeds economic uncertainty. Private investors, both local inhabitants and foreigners, have been reluctant to invest with such political risk. The uncertainty ranges from the possibility of confiscation (if a new government were to have more avowed socialist principles), to adverse changes in tax laws. Local investors often allocate investment funds toward urban real estate intended for rental to higher-income individuals. Such investments tend to be more secure; high rentals, often paid by government and development agencies, result in initial investments being quickly recouped. Unfortunately, this type of real estate investment does not generate permanent industrial jobs and has limited linkages to other sectors of the economy.

In a continent that does not have well-developed regional markets, the small domestic markets of most African countries limit industrial development. That is,

---

[15]World Bank, *World Development Report 1995,* Tables 1 and 3.

[16]United Nations Conference on Trade and Development, Division on Transnational Corporations and Investment, *World Investment Report, 1994: Transnational Corporations, Employment and the Workplace,* New York: United Nations, 1994, page 93.

[17]Ibid., pages 93–94.

the inability of African countries to promote economic integration has meant that industrial initiatives, have had to rely on domestic markets that are often too small to capture fully the economies of scale. The lack of steady economic growth within most African countries has limited the perceived potential for industrial entrepreneurship. Finally, decaying infrastructure in telecommunications and transportation make much of Africa unattractive for private investment, either domestic or foreign.[18]

Many countries have high minimum-wage scales and restrictive labor legislation that make it difficult to terminate unproductive labor. Some of this legislation, as in the former French colonies, has mirrored legislation in Europe. Also, skilled industrial labor, given the countries' lack of commitment to basic literacy and technical education, has often been scarce. Concurrently, however, overemployment of civil servants has occurred alongside open unemployment of many college graduates.

To the extent that many African countries have operated with overvalued exchange rates and persistent balance of payments deficits, industry has been discouraged. The overvalued exchange rates reduce the attractiveness of many African countries to potential export industries. Also, with balance of payments deficits and the need to ration scarce foreign exchange, industrial corporations would have no guarantee of access to the foreign exchange to import the capital equipment, intermediate goods, and raw materials needed in the production process.

Without a derived demand from a growing industrial sector, the growth of modern financial and commercial services has also lagged in Africa. Large cities are typically served by a few banks that often are foreign correspondents of European banks. These banks tend to operate for the convenience of government, expatriates, local business (usually commerce), and the tourist sector. Given the risks of industry, these banks tend not to be active in industrial development, preferring to generate profits on highly secured real estate loans and relatively high, noncompetitive bank service charges. Few financial intermediaries are located in rural areas. During good agricultural years, farmers might have surplus income available for saving. Currently this rural savings is held in grain stocks, livestock, jewelry, and cash. Thus, effective financial intermediation is severely lacking throughout Africa.

Given the depth and complexity of Africa's economic problems, what development strategies are available to the countries of Africa?

## THE AFRICAN DEVELOPMENT AGENDA

Stimulating economic growth in sub-Saharan Africa is arguably the most urgent global development priority. The international donor community, following the lead of the International Monetary Fund, the World Bank, the United States, and France, has favored a coordinated effort, referred to as **structural adjustment,** to assist African

---

[18]Ibid., page 95.

countries. Other, more radical approaches to development in Africa have also been suggested.

## STRUCTURAL ADJUSTMENT

The basic hallmark of structural adjustment is that donors provide budgetary support and other forms of development assistance to current African states to support economic and political reforms. Generally, with structural adjustment, donors are less involved in funding specific projects and more involved in supporting policy reform. Both macroeconomic and microeconomic policy objectives characterize a **structural adjustment agreement (SAA).** Reduced budget deficits, tighter monetary control, and more competitive exchange rates form the core of the macroeconomic reforms. Greater use of market pricing—particularly to provide agricultural incentives—and a decentralization of economic and political power are the primary microeconomic elements of an SAA.

The structural adjustment process was initiated in the mid-1980s in response to the African economic crisis. Approximately 30 of the African countries have had structural adjustment agreements since the 1980s. A recent World Bank report on structural adjustment suggests only mixed success for the policy reform process.

> Policy reforms have been uneven across sectors and across countries. The countries studied here have generally been more successful in improving their macroeconomic, trade, and agricultural policies than their public and financial sectors. Almost two-thirds of the countries managed to put better macroeconomic and agricultural policies in place by the end of the 1980s. Improvements in the macroeconomic framework also enabled countries to adopt more market-based systems of foreign exchange allocation and fewer administrative controls over imports.
>
> However, reforms remain incomplete. No African country has achieved a sound macroeconomic policy stance—which in broad terms means inflation under 10 percent, a very low budget deficit, and a competitive exchange rate.... Social spending, while not showing an overall decline during the adjustment period, is misallocated within the health and education sectors. And the politically difficult reform of the public enterprise and financial sectors lags well behind.[19]

We now look more closely at the policy objectives of the structural adjustment process.

### MACROECONOMIC STABILIZATION

A primary goal of the SAA process is to reduce government budget deficits, typically by reducing government expenditures. Several favorable effects on the economy can follow from reduced budget deficits. Recall from Chapter 10 that governments can fund deficits by either borrowing from the public or printing money. When new government debt is issued, interest rates will tend to rise and private investment will be

---

[19]World Bank, *Adjustment in Africa*, pages 1–2. The African countries included in this study were Benin, Burkina Faso, Burundi, Cameroon, the Central African Republic, Chad, Congo, Côte d'Ivoire, Gabon, The Gambia, Ghana, Guinea, Guinea-Bissau, Kenya, Madagascar, Malawi, Mali, Mauritania, Mozambique, Niger, Nigeria, Rwanda, Senegal, Sierra Leone, Tanzania, Togo, Uganda, Zambia, and Zimbabwe.

crowded out. Printing money to fund a deficit, on the other hand, will lead to higher inflation. Reducing the budget deficit by cutting expenditures will not only ameliorate the adverse effects of deficit financing, but will lower the government's overall share in the economy, increasing the relative share of the private sector.

The World Bank reports that the SAA countries slightly decreased their median deficit (including grants) from 6.4 percent of GDP during the 1981–86 period to 5.2 percent in 1990–91.[20] However, country performance varied widely. Two middle-income African countries, Côte d'Ivoire and Cameroon, had a deteriorating fiscal situation. More recently, in Nigeria, despite promises of a balanced budget for 1994–95, the budget forecasted a deficit of $4 billion, or 12 percent of GDP.[21] Given our prior discussion about the role of government in the typical African economy, it should not be surprising that reducing government expenditures will be politically difficult.

Another macroeconomic objective is to avoid overvalued exchange rates and balance of payments difficulties. To achieve these objectives, a country can either use a flexible exchange rate or a fixed exchange rate regime with appropriate monetary discipline. Of the 29 African countries whose SAA performances were studied by the World Bank, 17 had flexible exchange rates, while 12 had fixed exchange rates.

As discussed in Chapter 15, persistent balance of payments deficits with an overvalued exchange rate introduce economic problems. Essentially, the quantity demanded for foreign currency will exceed the quantity supplied, necessitating some form of exchange controls to allocate the available foreign exchange. Such rationing can lead to less than optimal uses of foreign currency (luxury imports) and introduces prospects for rent-seeking and graft, as well as illegal parallel markets for foreign currency.

Even the 17 countries with flexible exchange rates, defined by the World Bank as those "which either devalue from time to time or have a crawling peg or a managed float," still had overvalued currencies in the 1980s.[22] According to the World Bank, for these countries "the median real effective exchange rate depreciated by 78 percent between 1981–86 and 1990–91."[23] With this currency depreciation, parallel–market premiums for foreign exchange decreased in most countries. Five of the 17 countries (Mauritania, Mozambique, Sierra Leone, Tanzania, and Zambia), however, still had parallel–market premiums in excess of 50 percent for foreign exchange, suggesting that the domestic currencies are still considerably overvalued.

Generally speaking, depreciation has been associated with economic gains as exports become more competitive and producers of export goods, often primary products, have increased sales and profits. Also, the real value of foreign assistance, typically denominated in U.S. dollars or in a European currency, increases with depreciation. In many countries, parallel markets with higher prices for imports already existed; thus, the effects of the depreciation on the domestic price levels were somewhat blunted.

The countries with fixed exchange rates are primarily former French colonies with their currency, the CFA franc, tied to the French franc (FF). The last adjustment of

---

[20]Ibid., page 45. In one sense, this assessment is biased, since development grants from international agencies to the local government, in support of the structural adjustment process, lead directly to reduced budget deficits.

[21]"About Turn," *The Economist* (January 21, 1995), page 48.

[22]World Bank, *Adjustment in Africa,* page 51.

[23]Ibid., page 55.

CFA/FF parity had been in 1948; since the mid-1980s, the CFA had been significantly overvalued. The French government and the African countries had resisted calls for devaluation, fearing that higher import prices would lead to political instability. Finally, in January 1994, the CFA franc was devalued 50 percent from 50 CFA/FF to 75 CFA/FF. As a result of this currency realignment, economic activity, from tourism to export agriculture—cotton, cocoa, and coffee—has been stimulated in countries (particularly Senegal, Côte d'Ivoire, and Mali) that have comparative advantages in these goods and services.[24] Also, with the devaluation, locally produced beef and other products are replacing imported goods. While devaluation alone will not propel these countries into sustained economic development, this currency realignment has already helped.

Sustaining a sound macroeconomic policy can be difficult. Often, a country must have several currency depreciations. After the initial impetus for an SAA, successive currency adjustments may prove difficult. Consider the case of Nigeria. The Nigerian naira had a parallel market premium of 25 percent in 1990–91.[25] By early 1995, the parallel market premium was in excess of 200 percent, with the naira, officially pegged at 22 to the U.S. dollar, trading in the parallel market at 85 per U.S. dollar.[26] The pursuit of a sound macroeconomic policy, with a low budget deficit and a properly aligned currency, requires continued vigilance and political courage.

### Market Pricing in Agriculture

All concur that equitable and sustained development in Africa necessitates a vibrant agricultural sector. As a result, all African structural adjustment programs have properly emphasized increasing the profitability of small-scale farming. A unifying aspect of these SAAs is the need for African governments to refrain from excessive taxation of agriculture and to offer farmers remunerative, market prices for their crops. In general, the call is for the governments to disengage from the agricultural sector by eliminating official prices and monopoly government marketing boards. With market-determined producer prices for both export crops and food crops, African farmers then can make rational decisions on the allocation of resources between these two types of crops. The World Bank feels that some progress has been made in this area:

> Reforms of agricultural pricing and marketing systems are under way across the continent. Almost all countries have taken steps to ensure that producer prices for Africa's major agricultural exports track world prices more closely. In a few cases, they have done this by abolishing state marketing boards; more frequently they have allowed the private sector to compete with the marketing board, or they have adopted pricing formulas with a clear link to world market prices. There has been a major retrenchment of government involvement in food crop marketing, particularly where the evasion of controls was previously widespread. But reform of the maize marketing boards in eastern and southern Africa is proceeding more slowly. And much remains to be done in both the export and food crop sectors to take advantage of entrepreneurial talent in agricultural marketing and input distribution and to create a level playing field for private traders.[27]

---

[24]"Out of Africa," *The Economist* (January 14, 1995), page 67.

[25]World Bank, *Adjustment in Africa*, Table B.5.

[26]*The Economist* (January 21, 1995), page 48.

[27]World Bank, *Adjustment in Africa*, pages 61–62.

Reform of food aid distribution is also a critical component of rural-sector development. Excessive food aid that reduces producer prices for local food crops must be curbed. Food aid should be primarily used in emergencies or droughts when local food supplies are already reduced. Also justified and relatively nondistorting of local food prices are food distributions to the very poor who, without income, would not normally be demanders of locally grown foods.

Finally, for price and marketing reforms to be effective and sustained, complementary measures are needed. As discussed in Chapter 11, a vibrant agricultural sector needs timely input deliveries, proper agricultural extension, and a good transportation network, primarily roads in Africa. Both the private and public sectors have appropriate roles in providing these services needed by farmers. Also, developing a political constituency among farmers and rural residents is vital. With their voices heard in the capital city, the economic concerns of the rural sector may receive continued attention.[28]

## Decentralization

As previously discussed, during the 1960 to 1980 period, African governments involved themselves, to an increasing degree, in the economic affairs of their nations. Public enterprises were established in nearly every sector of the economy. The World Bank reports that

> At least fifteen of the adjusting countries had seventy-five or more public enterprises by the early 1980s. Ghana, Mozambique, Nigeria, and Tanzania had more than 300. The public enterprises accounted for over 20 percent of formal sector wage employment in a number of countries.... They also accounted for a large share of public investment, domestic credit, and external loans.[29]

Most SAAs call for a withdrawal of the public sector from many aspects of economic life, particularly in agriculture. Elimination of agencies and privatization of activities are primary objectives. A greater use of NGOs and private voluntary organizations (PVOs) within the development process would also reduce the need for many government organizations that were set up and funded by international donors. Often, as they attempt to expand their activities, the PVOs meet resistance both from local governments, and even from donors.

Unfortunately, with the exception of some progress in stimulating the private sector in agriculture, the African governments have not been particularly successful in trimming the scope of government.

> Reform efforts generally have not been too successful in the areas where the state has intervened most heavily. Privatizing and reforming state-owned enterprises and creating sound financial systems have proved to be among the most difficult of the adjustment reforms. Public enterprise reforms have not yet leveled the playing field for the private sector because they have not significantly curtailed the public enterprises' privileged access to the budget, to the credit system, to tariff and non-tariff protection, to special tax status, and to regulatory protection.[30]

---

[28]See Herbst, pages 345–351.
[29]World Bank, *Adjustment in Africa,* page 101.
[30]Ibid., page 100.

Given the political difficulty in reducing employment levels within the African governments, donors may have to exert even stronger pressure to reduce the influence of government within the African economies.

### Structural Adjustment and the Poor

Those critical of structural adjustment have often argued that the poor will be disproportionately hurt by economic reforms. No truly comprehensive studies concerning the impact of structural adjustment on the distribution of income exist, however. The household data needed for such studies are not available for the African countries. In theory, the impact on the poor from structural adjustment is mixed. Small farmers stand to benefit from the increases in agricultural incomes that would come from more competitive domestic markets and exchange rates. For the urban poor, the net effects are less clear. A reduced rate of inflation should increase the real incomes of the urban poor. However, if agricultural price increases translate into higher urban food prices, the impact from price reform on urban real incomes is ambiguous. To the extent that austerity programs reduce government expenditures and employment, urban unemployment might rise. The very poorest within the urban areas, however, are not the government employees, who tend to receive above-average wages. Defenders of structural adjustment claim that any short-run impacts on the distribution of income are of secondary importance to the need to launch the sustained economic development required for the poor to achieve permanent gains in their living standards.

### The Future of Structural Adjustment

For the international donor community, particularly the World Bank and the International Monetary Fund, the structural adjustment process is the best, and really only, hope for Africa. Following the "bitter medicine" of austerity, reformed African economies will be on the path to sustained development. Generally it is felt that a reform program will be more successful if it concentrates on a few key changes. All agree that for a reform program to succeed, the government must be firmly committed to its implementation.[31] Fortunately, indications show that many African governments are recognizing the economic gains that can come from sound macroeconomic policies, competitive markets, foreign direct investment, and family planning programs.

For others, structural adjustment is fundamentally flawed. Development loans are being extended to support the very governmental structures that have contributed to economic stagnation in Africa. SAAs often contain conflicting policy advice—such as simultaneously calling for tariff reductions to increase economic integration while urging measures to reduce the budget deficit. Finally, the structural adjustment process does not do enough to promote the basic needs of the poorest of Africans. Even defenders of this reform process admit that it is too early to determine whether structural adjustment will save Africa from further economic deterioration and political chaos.

## MORE RADICAL APPROACHES

Some who feel that the structural adjustment process is not the appropriate remedy for Africa's problems propose more radical solutions. Citing the ineffectiveness and

---

[31]For a good summary of some lessons, see Callaghy and Ravenhill, pages 1–17.

unfairness of structural adjustment, in 1989 the United Nations Economic Commission for Africa (UNECA) proposed an alternative development strategy.[32] Their strategy differs from the typical World Bank/IMF structural adjustment agreement in several ways. First, it stresses greater participation in government policy by labor unions and rural workers. The UNECA also feels that the structural adjustment process, with its emphasis on reducing government deficits, is too contractionary a policy. For such poor countries, according to this argument, government should be more involved in the economy, helping to provide for basic needs and generating employment. Their program also favors greater attention to agriculture and food self-sufficiency, to reduce the use of foreign exchange for food imports. Finally, the UNECA advocates the use of multiple exchange rates to encourage imports of investment goods and needed raw materials and to discourage the import of luxury consumption items. Supporters of the structural adjustment process see the United Nations proposal as having common elements with the past, failed government-directed development initiatives of many African countries.

Others have offered even more extreme suggestions. While politically very difficult, a redrawing of national borders to define larger, but ethnically more homogeneous populations, has some appeal. Such new countries might well avoid the civil turmoil that has characterized Africa and could save the costly duplication of national governments found in the nearly 50 sub-Saharan African states that now exist.

Promoting more effective economic integration among nations has been an idea advanced for two decades. Production along lines of comparative advantage with enhanced regional trade, and ultimately a common currency, could serve Africa well. Unfortunately, prior attempts at economic integration, with the exception of the French monetary zone, have been to little avail. Risk-averse and economically jealous African states have been unwilling to surrender tariff sovereignty and to accept the inevitable imports from other African states.[33]

Others place hope in the emergence of an economically and politically powerful South Africa. With its industrial base, natural resources, and more technically educated population, South Africa could become an engine of economic growth for the southern portion of Africa. This country of 40 million people, with a per capita income of nearly $3000, however, cannot be expected to solve the economic woes of the continent, however.

A hopeful development is that the 12 countries of southern Africa are reviving the Southern African Development Community (SADC), a regional economic zone.[34] From the relatively well-off South Africa to the very poor Mozambique, these countries are promoting a more integrated regional economy. Agreements concerning regional water use have already been signed. The nations have begun discussions to reduce internal tariffs, export subsidies, and even to consider a common currency. While this

---

[32]United Nations Economic Commission for Africa, "African Alternative Framework to Structural Adjustment," in *50 Years Is Enough: The Case against the World Bank and the International Monetary Fund*, Kevin Danaher, editor, Boston, MA: South End Press, 1994, pages 169–182.

[33]Fourteen African countries have their currencies tied to the French franc. Thirteen of these countries (Benin, Burkina Faso, Central African Republic, Cameroon, Chad, Congo, Côte d'Ivoire, Equatorial Guinea, Gabon, Mali, Niger, Senegal, and Togo) use the CFA. (The current official rate is 75 CFA to one French franc.) One country, Comoros, uses the Comorian franc (KMF), valued at 100 KMF per French franc.

[34]The 12 countries are Angola, Botswana, Lesotho, Malawi, Mauritius, Mozambique, Namibia, Swaziland, South Africa, Tanzania, Zambia, and Zimbabwe. See "Southern Africa Dreams of Unity," *The Economist* (September 2, 1995), page 35.

agenda is very ambitious, the experience of the European Union shows that such integration is possible and beneficial. Moreover, a successful SADC could become a model for promoting trade and development in other regions of Africa.

## CONCLUDING NOTE

With the population of Africa growing rapidly and the physical environment deteriorating, time itself has become a very scarce resource. The lack of progress under these circumstances translates into retrogression and a growing development gap between Africa and other Third World countries. We should not be totally pessimistic about Africa, however. Some positive changes have occurred, both economically and politically. As Chester Crocker, former U.S. assistant secretary of state for Africa writes:

> It would be reckless to base our conduct toward an entire continent on selective snapshots. And it would be counter to every humanitarian impulse to write off Africa, encouraging doomsdays that do not need to happen.[35]

## SUMMARY OF MAIN POINTS

1. Africa presents, perhaps, the most urgent and complex global development challenge. For the last 15 years, the economic performance of the nearly 50 sub-Saharan African countries has been virtually stagnant. The current population of 560 million people faces a difficult and uncertain future.
2. Most of sub-Saharan Africa was colonized during the nineteenth century. With colonization, significant economic changes continued to affect Africa, even after independence. Export agriculture was encouraged; also, the rate of urbanization increased significantly during colonization. As a result, local food production became relatively less important and food imports increased.
3. The African independence movement began with Ghana's sovereignty in 1957; other colonies rapidly became independent states in the late 1950s and early 1960s. In the early years of independence, African governments, replacing colonial administrators, intervened heavily in economic decision making. This form of African socialism was not conducive to launching sustained economic development, and the economic malaise of the 1970s followed.
4. During the 1970s the economic performance of Africa began to deteriorate rapidly. Contributing to poor economic performance was a combination of ineffective government policies begun in the 1960s, falling commodity prices, and drought.

---

[35]Chester A. Crocker, "Why Africa is Important," *Foreign Service Journal* (June 1995), pages 24–33. This quotation is from page 24.

5. To address the problems of their citizens, the African nations need to have efficient and honest governments that have the confidence of the population. These governments must also limit their attempts to control the economy and permit a greater role for market forces.
6. The rate of population growth in Africa is too high and is straining both natural and fiscal resources.
7. Agricultural performance has been very weak in the last 20 years. Government intervention to profit from export agriculture and the lack of incentives for local food production have been contributing factors to the decline of this sector.
8. African governments have not been successful in promoting the basic needs of their populations. The provision of health care and education has been biased toward urban elites. Currently, the incidence of AIDS is estimated to be higher in Africa than in any other part of the world.
9. Private investment, both domestic and foreign, has been relatively low in Africa. Relatively small national markets, poor infrastructure, and an unwelcoming attitude toward private sector activity have all limited investment.
10. In response to their deteriorating economic situations, many of the African countries, in the mid-1980s, negotiated official structural adjustment agreements with international agencies such as the IMF and the World Bank. Typically, these agreements called for reduced budget deficits, tighter monetary control, more competitive exchange rates, and a greater use of market pricing, particularly in agriculture. The structural adjustment process has had mixed success in Africa.
11. Some critics of structural adjustment argue that the poor bear the disproportionate brunt of the austerity measures. Others have argued that the structural adjustment process results in providing support to the very governments that have caused the economic problems within their countries. Critics, however, do not seem able to provide a viable alternative to the structural adjustment process.

## KEY TERMS

**structural adjustment**
**structural adjustment agreement (SAA)**

## QUESTIONS

1. Discuss whether it is appropriate to consider sub-Saharan Africa as a Fourth World with development challenges that are fundamentally different than those facing other developing countries.
2. During the 1980 to 1993 period, Botswana and Côte d'Ivoire had the highest and lowest growth rates of GDP per capita in Africa. Research each country using data from the most current *World Development Report* and other sources to explain the performance of each country.
3. If the African state or government has failed its population, how, given the need for government direction in the development process, can the African countries ever initiate sustained economic development?
4. What forms of international economic assistance would seem to be the most helpful for low-income African countries?

## SUGGESTED READINGS

Callaghy, Thomas M. and John Ravenhill, editors, *Hemmed In: Responses to Africa's Economic Decline,* New York: Columbia University Press, 1993.

World Bank, *Adjustment in Africa: Reforms, Results, and the Road Ahead,* New York: Oxford University Press, 1994.

World Bank, *Sub-Saharan Africa: From Crisis to Sustainable Growth,* Washington, DC, 1989.

World Bank, *Toward Sustained Development in sub-Saharan Africa,* Washington, DC, 1984.

# CHAPTER 19

## GLOBAL DEVELOPMENT

There is no minimum absolute standard of living that will make people content. Individual wants are not satiated as incomes rise, and individuals do not become more willing to transfer some of their resources to the poor as they grow richer. If their incomes rise less rapidly than they expect, they may even feel poorer as their incomes rise.[1]

Is this so? If it is, then, given a finite earth with limited capacities for yielding resources and absorbing wastes, can a system based on relative consumption standards be sustained? Can the present population of the globe, much less the expected increases in population, ever attain the material standard of living currently enjoyed by the average citizen of the United States? If any doubt exists that technological advances will allow for continually increasing per capita consumption across the world, then there is all the more reason to use current resources wisely and to plan carefully for the future. On the other hand, if the quality of life extends beyond material consumption to encompass what E. F. Schumacher calls "right livelihood," then there may be no limits to improving the human condition. (Refer to the discussion in Chapter 5 of Schumacher's "Buddhist economics.")

Economists, while heralding the efficiencies of the market mechanism, also recognize market failures, for which government intervention may be required. In particular, with externalities, the actions of the primary parties involved have consequences for the welfare of third parties not directly involved. Externalities, as discussed in Chapters 6 and 12, may be positive or negative. Rapid population growth that perpetuates poverty and ill health and that contributes to natural resource exhaustion; the unbridled pursuit of economic growth that degrades the atmosphere, pollutes the water supplies, and threatens the survival of certain species;

---

[1]Lester Thurow, *The Zero-Sum Society*, New York: Penguin Books, 1981, page 18.

and armed aggression that catches innocent civilians in the deadly crossfire are negative externalities. So, too, gender discrimination, reflected in practices and laws that deprive females of equal access to health care, education, employment, property, and credit can be viewed as a market failure. As noted in a World Bank study, "Social returns to investments in women's education and health are significantly greater than for similar investments in men."[2]

Over the last 18 chapters we have addressed policies to promote economic development. In particular, in Chapter 17 we outlined the market-friendly strategy of the World Bank, a strategy that represents a synthesis of the lessons from four decades of development experience. In this final chapter we offer a more ambitious agenda for global development—one that requires a reorientation of priorities and new levels of international cooperation.

We begin with the concept of global development. We then focus on three areas: military spending, the environment and common resources, and international cooperation. Political stability and peace would seem to be necessary, if not sufficient, conditions for economic development. And, in the long run, so is conservation of the natural environment.

## DEFINING GLOBAL DEVELOPMENT

Is global development simply the sum of the national developments (if such aggregation were possible)? Or does global development transcend national boundaries and concern the welfare of all people, regardless of where they reside?

A start in formulating the concept of global development might be Adelman's **depauperization,** discussed in Chapter 5. According to Adelman,

> [Depauperization] is humanistic, largely spiritual, and highly dynamic. It is focused upon individual welfare, as perceived by the individual himself, with full recognition of the nonmaterial, human relations, and intergenerational aspects of personal welfare . . . and stresses the removal not only of material but equally important of social, political, and spiritual forms of deprivation.[3]

In short, depauperization is a continual process of fostering opportunities for individuals to realize their full potentials. As a minimum it encompasses the universal satisfaction of basic needs in food, water, shelter, clothing, health care, and primary education. The exercise of the human and civil rights is necessary for a dignified existence. These rights include: freedom from persecution, from discrimination, and from violence; and the freedom to worship, to participate in the democratic process, and to

---

[2]World Bank, "Toward Gender Equality: The Role of Public Policy," Washington, DC, 1995, page 3. This study not only gives an overview of the widespread discrimination against girls and women, but offers policy prescriptions.

[3]Irma Adelman, "Development Economics—A Reassessment of Goals," *American Economic Review*, vol. 65, no. 2 (May 1975), page 306.

enjoy the fruits of one's labors.[4] Important for sustainable development is the recognition of the responsibility of each generation to future generations to pass on a natural environment that is at least as viable as the one inherited.

Major obstacles to achieving depauperization are internal violence and external conflict. Clearly, the devastation and misery caused by war are a human tragedy. Increasingly, civilians in the less developed countries are the victims. And, increasingly the conflicts are internal.

> At the beginning of this century, around 90% of war casualties were military. Today, about 90% are civilian—a disastrous shift in the balance.

and

> Of the 82 armed conflicts between 1989 and 1992, only three were between states. . . . Most conflicts are in developing countries. During 1993, 42 countries in the world had 52 major conflicts, and another 37 had political violence. Of these 79 countries, 65 were in the developing world.[5]

How can a global strategy of development embodying the general principles of depauperization be implemented? Specific goals could be set, and in some cases have been set, by international agreement, such as reducing air pollution and limiting nuclear weapons. Much of the depauperization approach, however, cannot be easily quantified. Moreover, some may object to the underlying concept of global development and discount the utopian ideals of depauperization. Even for those who subscribe, there are likely to be different interpretations of the objectives and debate over the means for achieving depauperization.

The United Nations Development Programme (UNDP) in the *Human Development Report 1994* argues for a shift in emphasis from national security to human security. At the individual level, human security means freedom from fear and freedom from want. And, "At the global level, human security ... means responding to the threat of global poverty travelling across international borders in the form of drugs, HIV/AIDS, climate change, illegal immigration and terrorism."[6]

For example, the UNDP reports that trade in narcotic drugs ranks second only to arms trade, with the total volume of international drug trafficking estimated at $500 billion a year.[7] Crime and violence accompany the trade and use of drugs. International terrorism, frequently targeted at civilians, is another affront to human security. Between 1975 and 1992, an average of 500 international terrorist attacks occurred annually, with bombings the most common.[8]

As a complement to our discussion of economic development in Chapters 1 through 18, we examine in this final chapter some of these other dimensions of global development. We begin with national securities and military spending.

---

[4] "According to a 1993 survey by Amnesty International, political repression, systematic torture, ill treatment or disappearance was still practiced in 110 countries." United Nations Development Programme, *Human Development Report 1994*, New York: Oxford University Press, 1994, page 32.

[5] Ibid., page 47.

[6] Ibid., page 24.

[7] Ibid., pages 36–37.

[8] Ibid., page 37.

## MILITARY SPENDING

Probably the least controversial role for a national government is providing for national security. Defining national security, however, and determining the appropriate resource allocations for attaining a given level of security are more contentious. At a minimum, national security means protecting the physical wellbeing and property of citizens and preserving the independence of a nation. Traditionally, national security has been identified with armed forces and armaments, with the adequacy of resource commitments to security evaluated relative to resource commitments of adversary or unfriendly nations. International terrorism and internal strife have become major concerns in national security—and for most nations, more real than the threat of foreign aggression.

For developing economies, the opportunity costs of military spending can be especially high. From the United Nations Group of Consultant Experts:

> The general negative effects of resource diversion to military uses tend to be aggravated in developing countries because modern armed forces make heavy demands on many of the resources which are most needed for development and which constitute severe bottlenecks in many cases: foreign exchange, skilled technical and managerial manpower and maintenance, repair, and industrial production capacity.[9]

How many resources are devoted to national defense? While data are subject to considerable measurement error, the current levels of global military expenditures and personnel commitments are high. Some trends, however, are favorable.

### RECENT TRENDS

Annual world military spending is estimated to have decreased in real terms by 30 percent from 1987 to 1993, from $1,245 billion to $868 billion[10] (see Figure 19.1 for the trends in developed and developing country real military expenditures from 1983 to

---

[9]United Nations Group of Consultant Experts, "Economic and Social Consequences of the Arms Race," in *Armaments, Arms Control and Disarmament,* UNESCO Press, 1981, reprinted in *Disarmament and Development: A Global Perspective,* P. K. Ghosh, Editor, Westport, CT: Greenwood Press, 1984, page 96.
  Earlier work on military spending in developing economies, however, has suggested that defense spending may promote economic growth. Emile Benoit offered that the vocational training and skill formation acquired in the military could be useful for the civilian economy; that some of the defense spending may contribute to the physical infrastructure (e.g., roads, dams, airports, communications networks); that the military might be a force for modernization in a developing economy; and that important derived demands may come from military spending for industrial output. See, for example, Emile Benoit, "Growth and Defense in Developing Countries," *Economic Development and Cultural Change,* vol. 26, no. 2 (January 1978), pages 271–280. For a review of the literature and an empirical analysis of the relationship among military spending, economic growth, and economic development, see Peter Hess, "The Military Burden, Economic Growth, and the Human Suffering Index: Evidence from the LDCs," *Cambridge Journal of Economics,* vol. 13, no. 4 (December 1989), pages 497–515.

[10]The statistics in this paragraph are from U.S. Arms Control and Disarmament Agency, *World Military Expenditures and Arms Transfers 1993–1994,* Washington, DC: February 1995, Table I. Note that the division between developed countries and developing countries used by the U.S. Arms Control and Disarmament Agency (USACDA) is not the same as the World Bank's division between the high-income economies and the low- and middle-income economies. The main difference is the inclusion of Russia in the developed countries by the USACDA.

**FIGURE 19.1** REAL MILITARY EXPENDITURES: TRENDS

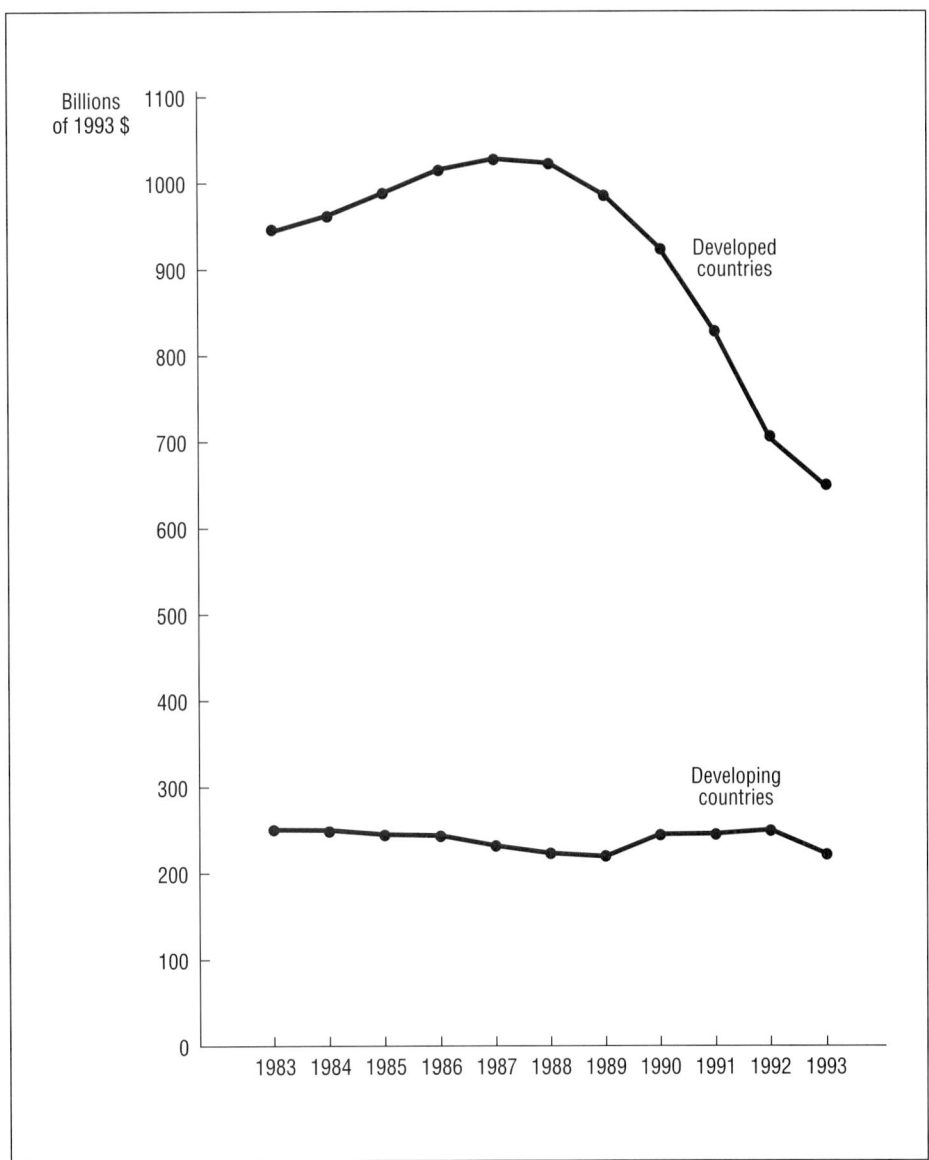

FROM U.S. Arms Control and Disarmament Agency, *World Military Expenditures and Arms Transfers 1993–1994*, Washington, DC, February 1995, Tables I and II.

1993). The decrease was due to cutbacks in defense expenditures by the developed countries (including here the Western industrialized economies and the former Soviet Union and other Warsaw Pact members). In particular, the former Warsaw Pact nations accounted for $308 billion (or almost 82 percent) of the global decline. Real military spending in the developing countries increased in 1990, 1991, and 1992, reversing a downward trend that began in 1983. The LDC increase, however, was concentrated in the Middle East and reflected the 1991 Gulf War.

| TABLE 19.1 | SELECTED STATISTICS ON MILITARY EXPENDITURES: DEVELOPED AND DEVELOPING COUNTRIES (1983–1993) |

| ANNUAL AVERAGES | DEVELOPED COUNTRIES | DEVELOPING COUNTRIES | WORLD |
|---|---|---|---|
| Share of military expenditures in gross national product (%) | | | |
| 1983–87 | 5.4 | 5.4 | 5.4 |
| 1988–93 | 4.3 | 4.0 | 4.2 |
| Real military expenditures per capita (1993 $) | | | |
| 1983–87 | 878 | 66 | 255 |
| 1988–93 | 758 | 56 | 205 |
| Armed forces per thousand population | | | |
| 1983–87 | 9.2 | 4.8 | 5.8 |
| 1988–93 | 7.9 | 4.3 | 5.0 |
| Real arms imports (in billions of 1993 $) | | | |
| 1983–87 | 15.7 | 54.7 | 70.4 |
| 1988–93 | 9.9 | 32.3 | 42.2 |

NOTES:
There are 28 countries classified as *developed* by the U.S. Arms Control and Disarmament Agency: all members of NATO, except Greece, Spain, and Turkey; all (former) Warsaw Pact members, except Bulgaria and the successor states of the Soviet Union (other than Russia) and Czechoslovakia; Austria, Finland, Ireland, Sweden, and Switzerland in Europe; and Australia, Japan, New Zealand, and South Africa. All other nations are classified as *developing*.

*Military expenditures* generally refer to expenditures of the ministry or department of defense. Military expenditure data are of uneven accuracy and completeness.

*Armed forces* refer to active-duty military personnel, including paramilitary forces, if those forces resemble regular units in their organization, equipment, training, or mission. Reserve forces are generally not included.

*Arms imports* represent the international transfer (under terms of grant, credit, barter, or cash) of military equipment, including weapons of war, ammunition, support equipment, and other commodities designated for military use.

FROM U.S. Arms Control and Disarmament Agency, *World Military Expenditures and Arms Transfers 1993–1994,* Washington, DC: February 1995, Tables I and II.

Although the downward trend in global military expenditures that began in 1988 is encouraging, the total resource commitments to national defense are still substantial. As illustrated in Table 19.1, for the period 1988 to 1993, the developing countries collectively allocated an average of 4.0 percent of gross national product for military expenditures—somewhat less than the 4.3 percent of the GNPs for the developed countries.[11] In Figure 19.2 pie charts depict the average annual shares of the developed

---

[11]We should caution that data on military expenditures are subject to considerable measurement error, with varying degrees of accuracy and coverage across countries. Often for strategic reasons, or even domestic political sensitivities, data on military expenditures and personnel may be understated. See the discussion in U.S. Arms Control and Disarmament Agency (1995), pages 165–172.

| FIGURE 19.2 | SHARES OF DEVELOPED AND DEVELOPING COUNTRIES IN WORLD RESOURCE COMMITMENTS TO THE MILITARY: ANNUAL AVERAGES (1988–1993) |

FROM U.S. Arms Control and Disarmament Agency, *World Military Expenditures and Arms Transfers 1993–1994*, Washington, DC, February 1995, Tables I and II.

and developing countries in world military spending, armed forces, and arms trade (imports and exports) for the period 1988-1993.

The share of military expenditures in GNP, known as the **military burden,** varies widely across and even within regions of the world (see Table 19.2 for the regional statistics). For example, in South Asia, the 1993 military burdens for Pakistan and Bangladesh were 6.4 percent and 1.5 percent, respectively. Furthermore, the military burden can vary dramatically from one year to the next with changing circumstances. The military burden in Kuwait increased from 6.1 percent in 1989 to 53.1 percent in 1990 and to 101.8 percent in 1991, due to the invasion of Iraq and the subsequent repayments to the United States and allies for successfully waging the Gulf War and restoring Kuwaiti independence. The Kuwaiti military burden declined to 80.9 percent in 1992 and then to 13.3 percent in 1993.[12]

In short, military burdens differ across countries and over time for economic reasons (e.g., differences in national incomes, fiscal constraints, foreign exchange availability); for strategic reasons (e.g., foreign conflicts, military alliances, regional tensions); and internal reasons (e.g., domestic unrest or violence, and types of government, such as military or civilian, authoritarian or democratic).

Other measures of resource commitments to national defense also exist. As shown in Table 19.1, real military expenditures per capita also declined, on average, for both developed and developing countries for 1988–1993. Again, for the developing countries, the situation is a bit more complex. The surge in military spending with the Gulf War in the Middle East went against the trend in most of the rest of the developing world. In East Asia and South Asia, however, real military expenditures per capita also slightly increased over this period.

Real military expenditures per capita can decrease either from nominal expenditure decreases, or inflation outpacing nominal expenditure increases, or the rate of population growth exceeding the rate of increase in real military expenditures. Real military expenditures per capita may rise even as the military burden falls. Despite declining absolutely, average real military expenditures per capita for the developed countries increased relative to the average for the developing countries.

Armed forces per thousand population, known as the **force ratio,** on average, is nearly twice as high for the developed countries as for the developing countries—additional evidence that, ceteris paribus, military expenditures and personnel commitments have been income-elastic.[13]

Finally, an indicator of the foreign exchange commitment to the military—the average annual real import expenditures on arms and military equipment—has also steadily declined in the world—from $74.3 billion in 1987 to $22.0 billion in 1993. In fact, by 1993, world arms trade (in real dollars) had decreased to its lowest level since the early 1970s.[14] In 1993, the developing nations accounted for 78 percent of arms imports in the world. Given the balance of payments difficulties in many developing nations, the use of scarce foreign exchange for importing arms and military equipment likely

---

[12]These statistics are derived from U.S. Arms Control and Disarmament Agency (1995), Table I. Note, in part, Kuwait's exploding military burden in 1990 and 1991 reflected declining national output. Kuwait's real gross national product fell by an estimated 25 percent in 1990 and by a further 39 percent in 1991.

[13]For evidence of the income-elasticity of military expenditures, see Daniel Hewitt, "What Determines Military Expenditures?" *Finance and Development*, vol. 28, no. 3 (December 1991), pages 22–25.

[14]U.S. Arms Control and Disarmament Agency, 1995, page 9 and Table II.

| TABLE 19.2 | SELECTED STATISTICS ON MILITARY EXPENDITURES BY REGION | | | |
|---|---|---|---|---|
| | ANNUAL AVERAGES (1988–1993) | | | |
| | SHARE OF MILITARY EXPENDITURES IN GROSS NATIONAL PRODUCT (%) | REAL MILITARY EXPENDITURES PER CAPITA (1993 $) | ARMED FORCES (PER THOUSAND POPULATION) | REAL ARMS IMPORTS (IN MILLIONS OF 1993 $) |
| sub-Saharan Africa | 3.0 | 9 | 2.3 | 1,802 |
| North Africa | 5.0 | 87 | 6.9 | 1,048 |
| Middle East | 14.0 | 371 | 15.3 | 14,668 |
| South Asia | 3.6 | 10 | 1.8 | 4,777 |
| East Asia | 2.0 | 73 | 4.6 | 5,367 |
| Oceania | 2.4 | 286 | 3.5 | 642 |
| Latin America | 1.5 | 45 | 3.5 | 2,109 |
| NATO | 4.0 | 764 | 8.3 | 7,998 |
| (Former) Warsaw Pact | 9.7 | 753 | 10.9 | 2,075 |

NOTES:
*North Africa* excludes Egypt, which is considered with the Middle East.
*Middle East* includes Egypt and Israel, as well as 14 other developing nations in the Middle East.
*South Asia* includes Afghanistan, Bangladesh, India, Nepal, Pakistan, and Sri Lanka.
*East Asia* includes Japan, China (both mainland and Taiwan), and 11 other developing countries in East Asia.
*Oceania* includes Australia, Fiji, New Zealand, and Papua New Guinea.
*Latin America* refers to Latin America and the Caribbean (including Cuba).
*NATO* (North Atlantic Treaty Organization) consists of Belgium, Canada, Denmark, France, Germany, Greece, Iceland, Italy, Luxembourg, the Netherlands, Norway, Portugal, Spain, Turkey, the United Kingdom, and the United States. The data for 1991 and later are for Unified Germany; prior to 1991 the data are for West Germany.
The (former) *Warsaw Pact* includes Bulgaria, (former) Czechoslovakia, (former) East Germany (before 1991), Hungary, Poland, Romania, and (former) Soviet Union.

FROM U.S. Arms Control and Disarmament Agency, *World Military Expenditures and Arms Transfers 1993–1994*, Washington, DC: February 1995, Tables I and II.

has high opportunity costs—unless covered by foreign military assistance. The developed countries accounted for 92 percent of the world's arms exports. The United States had 47 percent of the total of arms exported, up from a 23 percent share in 1987.[15]

Turning to Table 19.2, we can see sharp differences in recent resource commitments to the military across the regions of the world. For the period 1988-1993, by far the highest average military burden (14.0 percent) is for the Middle East—which is not surprising given the long-standing tensions in the region. By 1993, however, the military burden for the Middle East had declined to 9.0 percent. The (former) Warsaw Pact nations, dominated by the former Soviet Union, had the second highest military burden, with an average of 9.7 percent of GNP allocated toward military spending

---

[15]Ibid., pages 9, 14, and 15.

(reduced to 7.6 percent in 1993). The high military burdens may complicate the transition of these former socialist states to more competitive and market-oriented economies.

Per capita real military expenditures, however, are greatest for the NATO (North Atlantic Treaty Organization) nations, in large part due to the high levels of spending in the United States. (U.S. real per capita military expenditures in 1993 were $1153.) Again, the (former) Warsaw Pact nations are second, with relatively low per capita incomes offset by higher military burdens.

The Middle East also has the highest force ratio for this period, with the (former) Warsaw Pact nations and NATO following, in order. The substantial resource commitments to the military in the Middle East may explain, in part, why more economic development has not occurred in this region of relatively high per capita incomes. Moreover, the Middle East spends the most on arms imports, accounting for nearly 43 percent of total arms imports for the world in 1993. Nevertheless, here too, the trends are encouraging. In 1993, real arms imports into the Middle East were just over one-third of the annual average for 1983–87.[16]

In sum, there does seem to be a global demilitarization underway. Even so, present resource commitments to the military, especially for many of the LDCs, are substantial. To illustrate with specific examples the opportunity costs of military spending for human development, consider that in 1992: India's order for 20 MiG-29 fighter aircraft from Russia instead could have funded basic education for all of the 15 million girls in India then not in school. Or, in 1992, Nigeria purchased 80 battle tanks from the United Kingdom for an amount that could have provided immunizations to all of the 2 million then-unimmunized children, and family planning services to nearly 85 percent of the 20 million couples in Nigeria who still lack such services.[17]

## NATURAL RESOURCES AND THE ENVIRONMENT

The willingness to conserve resources and protect the environment is predicated, first, on knowledge of existing conditions in nature and the likely consequences of continuing current trends; and second, on an evaluation of the expected net benefits from altering present behavior. The consequences of human behavior, however, for the natural resource base and the environment are not known with certainty, and depend on, among other factors, possible discoveries of new resources and technological progress that brings new products and processes. Moreover, any evaluation of a course of action reflects the perceived distribution of the benefits and costs, and, in the case of the environment and natural resource base, the importance attached to the welfare of future generations.

The issue has been cast as a conflict between economic growth and the preservation of the environment. For some, economic growth and rising consumption are paramount. They argue that economic growth and the technological change stimulated by it provide the means to care for the environment. Further, the market mechanism,

---

[16]Ibid., page 9 and Table II.
[17]United Nations Development Programme, *Human Development Report 1994*, page 54.

not government control, adequately addresses resource scarcity through rising relative prices that induce conservation, substitution, and the development of alternatives.

In contrast, some reject the notion that economic growth or population growth can continue indefinitely in a world of finite natural resources and limits to the capacity of the environment to absorb wastes. Externalities such as pollution, deforestation, and overfishing are market failures. Further, they ask, "Can a price be placed on the loss of a species through extinction?"

To reduce the issue to a conflict between growth and the environment, however, is not only an oversimplification, but a distortion. Greater consensus can be found that poverty, reflecting a lack of economic growth and development, both perpetuates and is perpetuated by environmental deterioration. The World Bank observes:

> The poor are both victims and agents of environmental damage. Because they lack resources and technology, land-hungry farmers resort to cultivating erosion-prone hillsides and moving into tropical forest areas where crop yields on cleared fields usually drop sharply after just a few years. Poor families often have to meet urgent short-term needs, prompting them to "mine" natural capital through, for example, excessive cutting of trees for firewood and failure to replace soil nutrients.[18]

To expect the poor to renounce growth and forsake improvements in their low standards of living in order to conserve natural resources or protect the environment seems unrealistic and even unfair. It would seem that those already enjoying high rates of consumption would be in the best position to make adjustments.

To begin, a better accounting of the natural resources and condition of the environment needs to be taken. Much attention is given to the widely published national outputs, incomes, and expenditures. The other side of the ledger, including the costs in resource depletion, environmental deterioration, species loss, and hours toiled, is relatively neglected. Economic policymaking would be better informed with consideration of national, regional, and global accounts for land use; changes in the stocks of renewable and nonrenewable resources; food production per capita; the quality of the environment; and the disposal of hazardous wastes, such as those published in the World Resources Institute's annual reports.

For example, see Table 19.3, which presents some global statistics on resources and the environment. Over the last decade, from 1979–81 to 1989–91, small gains were achieved in cropland and permanent pasture at the expense of forest and woodland (which declined at an average annual rate of nearly .8 percent). The largest increase in land use, though, was for "other land," a category that includes land either lost to urbanization, roads, and settlements, or otherwise no longer suitable for cultivation.

Globally, food production barely kept pace with population growth. Not shown are regional extremes: The 1990–92 index of per capita food production varied from 94 for Africa to 121 for Asia (1979–81 = 100). Future gains in food production will largely come from improved yields, not the cultivation of more land. Average fertilizer use was up from 81 kilograms per hectare of cropland for 1979–81, to 96 kilograms per hectare for 1989–91. The sharpest rise and highest levels of fertilizer use are found in Asia. In the Americas, Europe, and the former Soviet Union, fertilizer consumption per hectare of cropland actually declined over this period. Irrigated land as a percentage of total cropland increased marginally over the decade.

---

[18]World Bank, *World Development Report 1992,* New York: Oxford University Press, 1992, page 7.

| TABLE 19.3 | SELECTED STATISTICS ON RESOURCES AND THE ENVIRONMENT | |
|---|---|---|
| | **WORLD** | |
| | MILLION HECTARES 1989–91 | % CHANGE 1979–81 TO 1989–91 |
| LAND USE | | |
| Cropland | 1,441 | +1.8% |
| Permanent pasture | 3,357 | +2.4% |
| Forest and woodland | 3,898 | −7.8% |
| Other land | 4,345 | +5.5% |
| INDEX OF FOOD PRODUCTION (1979–81 = 100) | TOTAL 1990–92 | PER CAPITA 1990–92 |
| | 127 | 105 |
| USE OF AGRICULTURAL INPUTS | 1979–81 | 1989–91 |
| Irrigated land as a % of total cropland | 15 | 17 |
| Average annual fertilizer use (kilograms per hectare of cropland) | 81 | 96 |

*table continued*

At present, the global supply of food is sufficient. The UNDP notes, "There is enough food to offer everyone in the world around 2500 calories a day—200 calories more than the basic minimum." [19] The hunger and undernutrition that exist across the world reflect poverty (or lack of purchasing power) and turmoil (often due to civil war).

The Worldwatch Institute warns of emerging constraints on the growth in global food production. In agriculture, we see signs of reaching sharply diminishing returns to fertilizer use, especially in Asia. So, too, concerns have arisen over limits to the expansion of irrigation, as water tables are drawn down and more water is diverted to industry and urban populations. Rapidly rising incomes and population momentum in China will create domestic food deficits that will, in all likelihood, add significantly to the growing consumer demand for grain imports and push up real international prices for grains.[20]

While the per capita food supply from fish and seafood did increase between 1978–80 and 1988–90, fish catches have been relatively constant since.[21] Overfishing (fishing beyond the capacity of fish stocks to regenerate), pollution, and habitat destruction have contributed to the slowdown. Over the past two decades, even as

---

[19] United Nations Development Programme, *Human Development Report 1994*, page 27.

[20] Lester Brown, "Nature's Limits," *State of the World 1995*, Worldwatch Institute, New York: W. W. Norton, 1995, pages 3–20.

[21] After 1989, the global oceanic catch of fish, crustaceans, and mollusks fell 5 percent and stagnated. See Peter Weber, "Protecting Oceanic Fisheries and Jobs," *State of the World 1995*, pages 21–37. The information in this paragraph is from Weber's study.

| TABLE 19.3 | SELECTED STATISTICS ON RESOURCES AND THE ENVIRONMENT, *continued* | | |
|---|---|---|---|

| | WORLD | |
|---|---|---|
| PER CAPITA ANNUAL FOOD SUPPLY FROM FISH AND SEAFOOD (KILOGRAMS) | TOTAL 1988–90 | % CHANGE 1978–80 TO 1988–90 |
| | 13.2 | +16.8 |

| CARBON DIOXIDE EMISSIONS | LOW- AND MIDDLE-INCOME ECONOMIES | HIGH-INCOME ECONOMIES | WORLD |
|---|---|---|---|
| Total emissions from fossil fuels and cement manufacture, 1989 (millions of tons of carbon) | 2013 | 2702 | 5822 |
| Average annual growth rate in total emissions, 1980–89 (%) | 3.8 | .5 | 1.8 |
| Total emissions (tons of carbon): | | | |
| Per capita, 1989 | .50 | 3.26 | 1.12 |
| Per million dollars of GDP, 1989 | 614 | 186 | 327 |

NOTES:

*Cropland* includes land under temporary and permanent crops, temporary meadows, market and kitchen gardens, and land that is temporarily fallow.

*Permanent pasture* is land used for five or more years for forage, including natural crops and cultivated crops, and wild land used for pasture.

*Forest and woodland* includes land under natural or planted stands of trees, as well as logged-over areas that will be reforested in the near future.

*Other land* includes uncultivated land, grassland not used for pasture, built-up areas, wetlands, wastelands, and roads. Built-up areas can refer to residential, recreational, and industrial lands and areas covered by roads and other transport systems, as well as quarries and technical infrastructure.

The *food production index* covers all edible agricultural products that contain nutrients. Coffee and tea have virtually no nutrient value and thus are excluded.

*Irrigated land as a percentage of cropland* refers to areas purposely provided with water, including land flooded by river water for crop production or pasture improvement, whether the area is irrigated several times or only once during the year.

*Average annual fertilizer use* refers to application of nutrients in terms of nitrogen, phosphate, and potash.

*Per capita annual food supply from fish and seafood* is the quantity of both freshwater and marine fish and fish products available for human consumption.

For carbon dioxide emissions, the difference between the totals for the world and the sum of the totals for the low- and middle-income and high-income economies is primarily due to the former Soviet Union. *Total emissions* consist of the sum of the carbon dioxide released in the consumption of solid, liquid, and gas fuels, in gas flaring, and in the production of cement.

FROM World Resources Institute, *World Resources 1994–95: A Guide to the Global Environment*, New York: Oxford University Press, 1995, Tables 17.1, 18.1, 18.2, and 22.5 (for land use, index of food production, use of agricultural inputs, and per capita annual food supply from fish and seafood); and World Bank, *World Development Report 1992*, New York: Oxford University Press, 1992, Table A.9 (for carbon dioxide emissions).

signs of limits to growth appeared in marine fishing, fleets were increasing and the technology was becoming more advanced. Furthermore, governments often subsidize the fishing industry, favoring the large-scale enterprises, despite the fact that over 90 percent of the fishers are small-scale operators. While the Law of the Seas created 200 nautical-mile exclusive economic zones (EEZs) off the shores of coastal nations, fishing in the open seas is still not under effective international jurisdiction.

Turning to the release of wastes, in Table 19.3 we also present statistics on carbon dioxide emissions which in sufficient amounts, contribute to global warming. The high-income economies, with roughly 15 percent of the world's population and 80 percent of the world's gross domestic product, accounted for nearly half (46 percent) of the total emissions of carbon dioxide in 1989. While carbon dioxide emissions per capita were over five times greater for the high-income economies, the average annual growth rate for carbon emissions and carbon emissions per million dollars of GDP (a standardized measure of the air pollution generated in the production of output) were much higher in the low- and middle-income economies. With the expected industrial growth and population increases (particularly if accompanied by deforestation), carbon emissions from the LDCs are likely to continue to rise rapidly.

In addition to the phenomenon of global warming, threats to species are increasing. According to the UNDP, "Biological diversity is more threatened now than at any time in the past. Tropical deforestation is the main culprit, but the destruction of wetlands, coral reefs and temperate forests also figures heavily."[22] The costs associated with these losses may be hidden or not well known. For example, Tietenberg notes that "Approximately one-quarter of all prescription drugs have been derived from substances found in tropical plants."[23]

# INTERNATIONAL COOPERATION

A fundamental weakness of international treaties, conventions, or agreements is that national participation is usually voluntary. Furthermore, monitoring of compliance can be difficult and expensive. Sanctions on offenders tend to be ineffective unless widely supported. Nevertheless, some progress has been made in fostering international cooperation in the areas of security, common resources, and the environment.

## SECURITY AGREEMENTS

With the end of the Cold War, the danger of a nuclear holocaust has receded. Indeed, the two superpowers had begun to dismantle their large stockpiles of nuclear weapons even before the dissolution of the Soviet Union. The threat of nuclear terrorism, in which rogue states or radical organizations acquire and use nuclear weapons, however, may now be greater.

The Nuclear Nonproliferation Treaty (NPT), initiated in 1970 and renewed indefinitely in 1995, has been fairly successful in limiting the spread of nuclear weapons beyond the five original nuclear powers (United States, former Soviet Union, United Kingdom, France, and China). The breakup of the Soviet Union, however, added some

---

[22]United Nations Development Programme, *Human Development Report 1994,* page 36.

[23]Tom Tietenberg, *Environmental and Natural Resource Economics,* 3d ed., New York: HarperCollins, 1992, page 287.

former republics to the nuclear club. Several other countries are assumed to have nuclear weapons capability (including Israel, India, and Pakistan), and a few appear to be actively seeking such capability (including North Korea, Iraq, and Iran).

Over 170 nations supported the extension of the NPT, although some in the developing world expressed dissatisfaction that the five nuclear powers have not reduced their arsenals more. The Arab nations in the Middle East remain wary of Israel's nuclear capability. Moreover, the five nuclear powers are among the leaders in exporting conventional arms to the developing world—a mixed message, at best.

In addition to the NPT, international agreements exist that prohibit the production, possession, or use of biological and chemical weapons. Not all nations are parties to these agreements; in particular, evidence indicates that Iraq may have resorted to biological or chemical weapons in its recent conflicts.

As noted, international trade in conventional weapons, notwithstanding the downward trend over the last decade, continues to be largely unregulated. In fact, the cutbacks in domestic defense spending in the United States and former Soviet Union have diverted sales to foreign markets. Stronger measures to reduce the trade in conventional weapons are in order. The United Nations Development Programme suggests that the U.N. Security Council restrict certain weapons and technologies from international trade.[24] International taxes on arms trade have also been proposed.

The peace dividends that come to nations, from shifting resources away from the military without sacrifices in national security, while welcome, are not costless. Just as with the movement to freer trade, the conversion of resources from military to civilian uses requires adjustments. The related costs of demilitarization include the retraining of the labor released from the armed forces and from employment in the military-industrial sector; the conversions of military bases, factories manufacturing military equipment, and businesses providing services to the military; and the dismantling and destruction of arms.[25] Oscar Arias, former president of Costa Rica and winner of the 1987 Nobel Peace Prize, proposed the establishment of a Global Demilitarization Fund to assist nations in disarming and demobilizing. Specifically, Arias called for all nations to reduce their military spending by 3 percent per year for five years. A portion of the savings would be contributed to the Global Demilitarization Fund, placed under international administration and used to promote disarmament, conversion, peace, and human security.[26]

For example, one particularly dangerous legacy of the many conflicts in developing countries is the land mine. The UNDP reports that more than 105 million unexploded land mines remain buried in over 60 countries and continue to maim and kill innocent civilians even after hostilities have ceased.[27] The estimated cost of removing these mines, ranging from $200 billion to $300 billion, could be covered by a demilitarization fund.

Additional measures to advance international security will be offered in the agenda for global development. Before presenting this agenda, we provide an overview of international agreements on the environment.

---

[24]United Nations Development Programme, *Human Development Report 1994*, page 56.
[25]See Michael Renner, "Budgeting for Disarmament," *State of the World 1995*, pages 150–169.
[26]United Nations Development Programme, *Human Development Report 1994*, page 59.
[27]Ibid., page 56.

## AGREEMENTS ON NATURAL RESOURCES AND THE ENVIRONMENT

As with arms control—at least for nuclear, biological, and chemical weapons—some progress in protecting common resources and preserving the global environment has been made over the past quarter century. More than 175 nations and hundreds of nongovernmental organizations were represented at the U.N. Conference on the Environment and Development, or the "Earth Summit," held in June of 1992 in Rio de Janeiro. The centerpiece of the conference was Agenda 21, a detailed plan to promote sustainable development into the twenty-first century. A U.N. Commission on Sustainable Development was created to provide a forum for the implementation of Agenda 21.[28]

Also passed at the Earth Summit were agreements on climate change and biological diversity. The Convention on Climate Change calls for the developed countries to stabilize their emissions of carbon at 1990 levels by the year 2000. Developing countries are urged to monitor their carbon emissions and, where possible, reduce them. Excess carbon emissions, due mainly to the burning of fossil fuels, increase the level of carbon dioxide in the atmosphere, which can trap the earth's heat and raise global temperatures. Higher global temperatures can affect agricultural output and may even melt polar ice caps, raising sea levels and endangering low-lying coastal nations like Bangladesh. The Convention on Biological Diversity seeks to maintain the wealth of species and allows nations to charge for commercial access to gene pools.

Earlier international agreements include the Convention on the Law of the Seas, finally ratified by a sufficient number of nations some 20 years after negotiations began. As noted earlier, the Law of the Seas established 200-mile exclusive economic zones to encourage nations to manage more carefully their coastal resources.

In some cases, the effective implementation of international agreements may occur at the local level. According to Hilary French, "Achieving sustainable development requires protecting the rights of local people to control their own resources—whether it be forests, fish, or minerals." [29] Peter Weber relates how developing nations have reserved some of their coastal zones for traditional fishers. For example, in the Philippines the government gives local communities 25-year contracts to manage sections of the coastline.[30]

Under the 1987 Montreal Protocol on the Depletion of the Ozone Layer, the developed countries are to phase out chlorofluorocarbons (CFCs) that are released by aerosol sprays and refrigerants. CFCs have contributed to the thinning of the ozone layer, permitting dangerous ultraviolet rays to pass through, increasing the risk of skin cancer and cataracts, and perhaps decreasing the productivity of farming and fishing. As in other international agreements, the developing nations are allowed a more liberal schedule for complying. As a result of this treaty, global CFC emissions have decreased by 60 percent from the peak in 1988.[31]

---

[28]See Hilary French, "Forging a New Global Partnership," pages 170-189 in *State of the World 1995;* "International Institutions," pages 223–234 in World Resources Institute, *World Resources 1994–95: A Guide to the Global Environment,* New York: Oxford University Press, 1995; and "International Environmental Concerns," pages 153–169 in World Bank, *World Development Report 1992,* for further discussion of international cooperation on common resources and the environment.

[29]French, page 179.

[30]Weber, page 37.

[31]French, page 172.

The killing of elephants in Africa dropped significantly with the 1990 ban on commercial trade in ivory (part of the Convention on International Trade in Endangered Species). In 1991, a Global Environmental Facility (GEF) was created to help preserve the global commons—the oceans, atmosphere, and species. The GEF, under the management of the World Bank, United Nations Development Programme, and United Nations Environmental Programme, channels funds to nations for environmental preservation projects. Also, under a 1991 accord, mining exploration and development in Antarctica were prohibited for 50 years.[32]

In the fall of 1994, a Convention on Desertification was signed by some 100 nations to stem the degradation of cropland and pastureland through overuse and poor management. Originally proposed at the Earth Summit, the desertification agreement addresses a problem especially severe in Africa, where yields on arid land are diminishing due to the intense usage, lack of irrigation, and deforestation.[33] In the summer of 1995 an international treaty to regulate fishing for several vulnerable species, including cod and tuna, was adopted by 99 nations. The treaty, which sets forth strict inspection and enforcement procedures, applies not only to fishing in international waters, but within the 200-mile exclusive economic zones of nations.[34]

Numerous other international agreements have been negotiated on common resources and the environment. As French observes,

> The broad framework of international agreements needed to protect the global environment is now in place. The challenge for the future is thus to see that existing agreements are translated into action around the world.[35]

## AN AGENDA FOR GLOBAL DEVELOPMENT

Throughout this text, policy changes that could contribute to sustained economic development have been suggested. Generally these recommendations have assumed a continuation of current institutional arrangements based on autonomous nation-states and contemporary multilateral development, trade, and finance organizations, such as the World Bank, World Trade Organization, and International Monetary Fund. Additionally, the market-friendly strategy of development promoted by the World Bank tends to favor market capitalism with individual national autonomy. It is, however, appropriate to question whether significant reform and more generous levels of assistance can be advanced within this relatively "nationalistic" environment. Sustained and equitable development may require more radical geopolitical change.

---

[32]Ibid., page 172.

[33]See Mailise Simons, "Nations Sign An Agreement to Halt Spread of Deserts," *New York Times* (October 16, 1994), page Y11.

[34]See William Branigin, "99 Nations Reach Accord on Fishing Regulations," *Charlotte Observer* (August 4, 1995), page 17A.

[35]French, page 173.

In particular, stronger regional cooperation of countries at different stages of development might be beneficial. Clearly, significant political and cultural difficulties would be associated with any reduction in national autonomies. Further, institutional changes of this degree will necessitate substantial negotiation and transition. Yet, from NAFTA to the European Union, countries are realizing the potential benefits from greater cooperation.

In this last section of the final chapter, an agenda for regional cooperation is offered. Five areas of integration are addressed. Consider the possible net benefits that could accrue to the citizens of participating countries, as well as the present obstacles to moving toward such a new international order.

## REGIONAL GROUPS

One possibility for global development would have three regional zones of cooperation in an international system. The American zone would include the United States, Canada, Latin America and the Caribbean—roughly 15 percent of the world's population and 35 percent of world output. The Euro-African zone would encompass Europe, Africa, and the former Soviet Union—roughly 30 percent of the population and 40 percent of the output of the world. The nations of Asia, the Pacific, and the Middle East would comprise the Asian zone—with some 55 percent of the population and 25 percent of the output.[36]

Although there are significant differences in the shares of world population and output, each zone stretches over the northern and southern hemispheres and includes nations at all levels of economic development. Nations, of course, would have the option of joining the regional alliances. Moreover, the present international institutions, such as the United Nations (UN), International Monetary Fund (IMF), World Trade Organization (WTO), and World Bank would still function much as they do now. Trade, aid, and investment would still occur on a global basis, although it might be expected that increased intrazonal trade would displace some trade across zones—which, for merchandise trade, would serve to reduce transportation costs. The underlying premise is that nations will more easily recognize the mutual benefits of cooperation when divided into geographical zones.

The five areas for reform are trade, finance, economic assistance, the environment, and security. At some point in the future, say the year 2005, the members of zones would begin 10-year transitions to economic, environmental, and security alliances.

## TRADE

In trade, regional free trade areas would be formed. For example, in the American zone, NAFTA would be extended to cover the Latin American and Caribbean nations by the year 2005. At that point, any remaining nontariff barriers to the rest of the world would be converted to equivalent tariffs, with scheduled reductions of 10 percent a

---

[36]The ratio of population to output is so high in the Asian zone because it includes China and India, low-income economies with over a third of the world population. This zone, however, also includes some of the fastest growing economies in the world.

year until elimination by the year 2015. Half of the revenues from the external tariffs would be retained by nations for retraining workers and subsidizing the conversion of factories in import-sensitive sectors. The other half of the tariff revenues would go toward financing the operation of the World Trade Organization and for investments by the International Finance Corporation of the World Bank in new, environmentally sound products and technologies in the private sectors of member developing nations. The role of the World Trade Organization would be to assist in the trade liberalization process in each of the three zones and to arbitrate trade disputes between nations in different zones.

## FINANCE

In finance, each zone would establish a monetary system, with the European Monetary System serving as a model. Exchange rates would be adjustable, with fairly wide bands and par values expressed in terms of the Special Drawing Right (SDR). Half of the member nations' quotas to the IMF would go to the regional monetary fund, providing a first pool of currencies for official exchange intervention. A primary responsibility of the national monetary authorities would be to maintain the convertibility of the currencies within the allowed range of fluctuation around the par values. The goal of the regional monetary systems would be to harmonize monetary-fiscal policy mixes so that large balance of payments discrepancies and disruptive exchange rate fluctuations could be avoided. The IMF would not only serve as a back-up fund, providing longer term balance of payments support, but would coordinate the three regional monetary systems.

James Tobin, recipient of the 1981 Nobel Prize in Economics, has proposed an international tax on foreign exchange transactions.[37] The overwhelming majority of foreign exchange transactions involve the transfer of financial assets, and much of these are driven by short-term speculation. Even a very modest tax rate (Tobin suggested .5 percent) would help to stabilize exchange rates by increasing the transactions costs of speculation. Moreover, significant tax revenues would be generated, and could be used to retire some of the foreign debt of developing nations and to improve their financial institutions and capital markets. The tax revenues could also be used to fund international efforts to reduce drug trafficking, including help to farmers in developing countries in converting from illegal crop growing, the basis for drug trade. Indeed, the revenues from an international tax on foreign exchange transactions, even if merchandise trade were exempt, may be so great as to fund other development programs, such as the care and resettlement of refugees, demilitarization, and environmental cleanup.

## ECONOMIC ASSISTANCE

Each zone would have a development bank. Existing regional development banks within any zone would be combined. The zonal development bank would serve as an aid clearinghouse: identifying priorities and coordinating projects across donors and

---

[37]For an outline of Tobin's proposal, see United Nations Development Programme, *Human Development Report 1994*, page 70.

recipients, and assessing the successes and failures of the development projects so that future efforts would be better informed. Each member nation within a zone would contribute a tenth of one percent (.1 percent) of its gross national product to three organizations: the zonal development bank; the World Bank (for lending with an emphasis on environmentally sound projects that contribute to the economic infrastructure: from public transportation systems to improving the sanitation conditions in rural villages); and the United Nations Development Programme (for the funding of human capital formation in nutrition, health care, and education).

Greater use should be made of nongovernmental organizations (NGOs) that have a demonstrated ability to mobilize communities to help themselves. The Sarvodaya Shramadana Movement in Sri Lanka is an example of an indigenous NGO that has energized rural development. The lending and aid administered through the World Bank and United Nations would help to address the discrepancies in development in nations both across and within the zones. The allocation of development assistance would reflect common goals, such as the universal inoculation of children against the major infectious diseases; access to safe water; and the provision of family planning services. While giving a total of three-tenths of one percent of GNP for multilateral aid, nations would still have the option of providing additional bilateral aid.

## THE ENVIRONMENT

The fourth area for cooperation would be the environment. First, developing nations would be allowed to cancel part of their foreign debts in exchange for managing resources that provide external benefits, for example, rain forests and endangered plant and animal species. Part of the foreign debt problems of the LDCs reflects external factors, including the oil price hikes in the 1970s, followed by a run-up in interest rates, international recession, and rising protectionism in the first half of the 1980s. Thus, swaps of debt for ecological conservation seem in order.

Second, international taxes could be levied on the extraction of nonrenewable resources and on those commodities whose production or consumption degrade the environment.[38] For example, logging companies would be required to pay a stump deposit, with refunds available (with interest) when new trees are planted and allowed to mature. Any net revenues from these taxes would be used to fund research and development of renewable and clean energies (solar, wind, tidal) and environmentally safe products (biodegradable, nontoxic, recyclable). The revenues from these natural resource taxes could also be used to manage common resources in the ocean, polar caps, and space, and for partial compensation to the holders of the cancelled LDC debt.

## SECURITY

Common security alliances would be the fifth area of cooperation. In each zone, member nations would contribute a quota of personnel and funds, based on population

---

[38]See James Poterba, "Global Warming Policy: A Public Finance Perspective," *Journal of Economic Perspectives,* vol. 7, no. 4 (fall 1993), pages 47–63, for an analysis of a carbon tax to curb global warming.

sizes and gross national products, for the regional peacekeeping forces. With bases distributed throughout the zone, each regional security force would be able to intervene quickly—as a buffer in civil wars and border conflicts and for emergency relief in natural disasters. On a more permanent basis, the regional peacekeeping forces might help police against international terrorism and drug trafficking.

Unlike the voluntary membership in the trade, monetary, aid, and environmental alliances, national membership in the security alliance would be conditional on democratic forms of government and respect for human rights. Member nations would have the right, at any time, to call for regional security forces for temporary use. Longer-term utilization of the peacekeeping forces would require consent of the United Nations Security Council. The rules of engagement for the regional security forces would be spelled out in advance, and would probably extend beyond the limited role presently played by the U. N. peacekeeping forces.

To reduce the present arsenals, which in many cases exceed deterrence needs, nations would be allowed to turn over weapons to the regional security forces in exchange for credits on the financial quotas for the security alliance. To reduce the production and trade of new weapons, an international tax of, say, 50 percent, would be placed on all arms imports, with the proceeds going to fund international peacekeeping efforts and the demilitarization of national economies.

## REFORMING THE INTERNATIONAL ORDER

Pursuing international reform is bound to be very controversial. Some might dismiss the agenda outlined above as utopian and hopelessly far-fetched, given human nature and present political, cultural, and economic realities. Others will reject any infringements on national autonomies, free enterprise, and the individual pursuit of wealth.

Nevertheless, the key features of this proposed new international order are:

1. An emphasis on regional cooperation under the superstructure of the existing international institutions
2. A movement to freer trade and greater monetary coordination
3. Incentives for preserving the environment, conserving natural resources, and developing ecologically compatible products
4. Enhanced prospects for reallocating resources from military to civilian uses
5. Increased resources for economic development and human capital formation in the poorer nations

While taxes are relied on to fund most of these initiatives, the burden of the taxes should diminish with the success of the proposed reforms. Indeed, there may be more agreement on the goals of the agenda than on the specific mechanisms proposed.

No one should underestimate the difficulty in implementing this agenda, or one like it. Unprecedented levels of international cooperation would be necessary. Whether such profound changes in the international order, as sketched here are possible, or even necessary, is open to speculation. Yet we see signs of greater cooperation among nations—and in parts of the world where such cooperation might have seemed highly improbable a decade ago. Consider the Southern African Development Community, 12 nations in southern Africa, including South Africa, that have agreed to work toward a free trade area by the year 2000. The Central European Free Trade Agreement, formed in 1992 with Hungary, Poland, the Czech Republic, and Slovakia, intends to expand to include Slovenia, Bulgaria, and Romania by 1996. Seven South Asian nations, including India and Pakistan, are reducing tariffs to boost trade within this region of the developing world.[39]

## CONCLUDING NOTE

As the twentieth century draws to a close, the challenge of providing for a satisfying existence for a growing global population looms as large as ever. A more efficient, equitable, secure, and sustainable global economy is attainable. We have the means and the knowledge to promote development, reduce poverty, improve human security, and care for the environment. Do we have the will?

## SUMMARY OF MAIN POINTS

1. Global development encompasses not only sustainable improvements in the achievements and standards of living of all populations, but the exercise of basic human and civil rights, the maintenance of peaceful relations, and the safeguarding of the environment.
2. Numerous challenges must be overcome to advance global development, including periodic wars between nations; violence within nations; terrorism; abject poverty; trade in illegal drugs; rapid population growth; HIV/AIDS; and the degradation of the environment.
3. Real military spending has declined significantly since 1987 in the developed countries, especially in the former Soviet Union and the other nations of the former Warsaw Pact. By 1993, the annual real value of arms trade had dropped to its lowest level in over two decades.
4. Regionally the Middle East has the highest average military burden, force ratio, and total spending on arms imports. On a per capita basis, however, real military expenditures are the highest in the NATO and former Warsaw Pact nations.
5. Despite the demilitarization over the last decade, resource commitments to the military are still substantial. For the LDCs, in particular, the opportunity costs of military spending can be high in terms of forgone expenditures for human capital formation or investments in economic infrastructure.
6. Economic growth and the preservation of the natural environment should not be viewed as mutually exclusive. Nevertheless, market failures result from economic

---

[39]See "Southern Africa Dreams of Unity," *The Economist* (September 2, 1995), page 35; "Concrete Heads," *The Economist* (September 16, 1995), page 60; and "World Wire," *Wall Street Journal* (October 4, 1995), page A11.

growth, population pressure, and the careless use of resources that threaten the natural environment and undermine sustainable development.
7. Increasingly nations are cooperating on shared concerns, such as the proliferation of weapons and the care and management of the global commons.
8. An agenda for global development is offered based on greater regional cooperation in trade, finance, aid, the environment, and national securities. The proposal includes measures to promote freer trade; greater monetary coordination and exchange rate stability; more reliable and effective development aid; the preservation of the environment and conservation of natural resources; and continued progress in demilitarization.

## KEY TERMS

**depauperization**
**force ratio**
**military burden**

## QUESTIONS

1. Is global development a useful concept? If not, why not? If so, what are the present obstacles to achieving global development? Which are the most serious? Discuss why.
2. Which of the theories of economic development presented in Chapters 3, 4, and 5 are the most useful for global development? Discuss why.
3. Critique the agenda for global development proposed in this chapter. In your essay, address the following questions:
   *a.* Is such an agenda necessary? Desirable? Feasible?
   *b.* Of the five areas (trade, finance, aid, environment, and security) which are the most important and the least important for global development? Discuss why.
   *c.* Which of the five areas are the most likely and the least likely to have reforms implemented? Discuss why.
   *d.* Can any of the five areas for reform be adopted without the others? Is the ordering of reform in the five areas important? That is, should reform in some areas precede reform in others? Discuss.

## SUGGESTED READINGS

Brown, Lester, "Nature's Limits," *State of the World 1995,* Worldwatch Institute, New York: W. W. Norton, 1995, pages 3–20.

French, Hilary, "Forging a New Global Partnership," *State of the World 1995,* Worldwatch Institute, New York: W. W. Norton, 1995, pages 170–189.

Poterba, James, "Global Warming Policy: A Public Finance Perspective," *Journal of Economic Perspectives*, vol. 7, no. 4 (fall 1993), pages 47–63.

United Nations Development Programme, "New Dimensions of Human Security," *Human Development Report 1994*, New York: Oxford University Press, 1994, pages 22–40.

United Nations Development Programme, "Capturing the Peace Dividend," *Human Development Report 1994*, New York: Oxford University Press, 1994, pages 47–60.

Weber, Peter, "Protecting Oceanic Fisheries and Jobs," *State of the World 1995,* Worldwatch Institute, New York: W. W. Norton, 1995, pages 21–37.

World Bank, "International Environmental Concerns," *World Development Report 1992,* New York: Oxford University Press, 1992, pages 153–169.

World Resources Institute, "International Institutions," *World Resources 1994–95: A Guide to the Global Environment,* New York: Oxford University Press, 1994, pages 223–234.

# GLOSSARY

**Adjustable exchange rate**  A fixed exchange rate with provision for changing the official exchange value of a currency in the case of a persistent disequilibrium in the balance of payments.

**Adjusted coefficient of determination**  A standardized measure of the coefficient of determination that adjusts for the number of explanatory variables included in the sample regression equation.

**Ad valorem tariff**  A tax of a fixed percentage on an imported commodity.

**Aggregate demand**  The relationship between the quantity of real national output demanded and the aggregate price level.

**Aggregate supply**  The relationship between the quantity of real national output supplied and the aggregate price level.

**Agricultural-demand-led-industrialization (ADLI)**  Adelman's strategy of development in which investment in the agricultural sector is emphasized and small to medium-scale farming is promoted.

**Appreciation**  An increase in the value of an asset; a rise in the foreign exchange value of a currency.

**Balance of payments account (BPA)**  A summary statement of all the economic transactions between residents of a nation and the rest of the world over a period of time.

**Balance of payments deficit**  An excess of debits over credits in the combined current and capital accounts of the balance of payments account of a nation.

**Balance of payments surplus**  An excess of credits over debits in the combined current and capital accounts of the balance of payments account of a nation.

**Balance of trade**  The difference between the value of the exports of goods and services and the value of the imports of goods and services for a nation over a period of time.

**Basic macroeconomic identity**  An accounting identity showing the major expenditures on Gross Domestic Product and the primary uses of the income generated in the production of Gross Domestic Product over a year.

**Basic needs**  An orientation to economic development that stresses the fulfillment of the essential human requirements for food, water, clothing, shelter, and health care as a first priority.

**Black market**  An illegal market in which goods or services are sold at prices above the legal maximum or price ceiling; sometimes called a *parallel market*.

**Buddhist economics**  Schumacher's philosophy of development based on small-scale enterprise, respect for the environment, creative employment, intermediate technology, and the pursuit of right livelihood.

**Buffer stocks**  Inventories of agricultural commodities used to stabilize prices. In times of reduced (increased) supply, stocks are sold (bought) to mitigate the increase (decrease) in the price of a commodity.

**Burden of dependency**  The ratio of the sum of the populations under age 15 and over age 64 to the population from ages 15 through 64; a measure of the age structure of a population that is roughly the ratio of net consumers to net producers.

**Capital account**  The subaccount of the balance of payments account that records the transactions in assets between the residents of a nation and the rest of the world.

**Capital account balance**  The difference between the credits (private foreign acquisition of a nation's assets) and debits (private acquisition of foreign assets) for a nation on the capital account of its balance of payments account.

**Capital flight**   A sharp and substantial outflow of financial capital from a nation, often prompted by political instability in the nation or an expected devaluation of the nation's currency.

**Capitalist sector**   The modern, industrial sector in Lewis's model, characterized by more advanced technology and higher capital–labor ratios than in the subsistence, or traditional, sector.

**Capitalist surplus**   In Lewis's model, the difference between the value of output and the total costs of labor. Any residual from the capitalist surplus, after covering the costs of materials and the fixed costs of capital, is profit.

**Centralized socialism**   An economic system in which the means of production are owned collectively, and output levels and resource allocations are determined by planners.

**Coefficient of determination**   In a sample regression equation, a statistic that measures the percentage of the total variation in the values of a dependent variable that is accounted for by the variation in the values of a set of explanatory variables.

**Common market**   A customs union with free mobility of factors (labor and capital) across the borders of member nations.

**Comparative advantage**   The ability to produce a good or provide a service for a lower opportunity cost than a trading partner.

**Consistent plan**   Within input-output analysis, a projection of outputs such that uses or demand (for consumption, intermediate use, and export) equal sources or supply (domestic production and imports).

**Constant opportunity cost**   The opportunity cost of production for a commodity that is invariant to the number of units produced.

**Constant returns to scale**   A proportional change in inputs that yields an equally proportional change in output.

**Contestable market**   A market in which no significant barriers to entry exist, such as high, nonrecoverable entry costs.

**Crawling peg**   A variant of an adjustable exchange rate wherein the official exchange value of a currency is changed according to a predetermined schedule.

**Credit cooperative**   An organization formed to pool savings and extend credit to the members.

**Credits**   On a balance of payments account, the value of the goods, services, and assets provided to the rest of the world, usually resulting in an inflow of foreign payments.

**Crude birth rate (CBR)**   The number of births in a population in a year per thousand population at mid-year.

**Crude death rate (CDR)**   The number of deaths in a population in a year per thousand population at mid-year.

**Crude rate of natural increase (CRNI)**   The difference between the crude birth rate and the crude death rate; the CRNI plus the net in-migration rate equals the population growth rate.

**Currency board**   A government agency that controls the money supply of a nation, usually limiting the amount of domestic currency issued to the amount of international reserves held.

**Current account**   The subaccount of a balance of payments account that records the trade in goods and services, investment income flows, and the unilateral transfers between the residents of a nation and the rest of the world.

**Current account balance**   The difference between the credits (exports of goods and services, investment income receipts, unilateral transfers received) and the debits (imports of goods and services, investment income payments, and unilateral transfers made) for a nation on the current account of its balance of payments account.

**Customs union**   A free trade area with common trade barriers against nonmember nations.

**Debits**   On the balance of payments account, the value of the goods, services, and assets received from the rest of the world, usually requiring payment to foreigners.

**Debt buybacks**  Repurchases by a debtor of outstanding debt from a creditor, usually at a discount.
**Debt finance**  Borrowing to cover a deficit or excess expenditures; borrowing from foreigners through the bonds issued or the loans taken to cover a current account deficit on the balance of payments account.
**Debt-for-equity swaps**  The exchange of outstanding debt by a creditor for domestic currency of the debtor, which is then invested in enterprises in the debtor nation.
**Debt-for-nature swaps**  The purchase of outstanding debt of a nation by a party in exchange for the debtor nation using the interest that would have been paid on the debt to maintain or preserve some part of its environment (e.g., tropical rain forest).
**Debt rescheduling**  A postponement of the scheduled repayment of the principal on outstanding debt.
**Debt–service ratio**  A measure of the external debt burden of a nation, given by the ratio of the repayments of principal and interest on the outstanding external debt to export revenues.
**Demographic transition**  The transition from a traditional demographic equilibrium of high birth rates offsetting high death rates to a modern demographic equilibrium of low birth rates offsetting low death rates.
**Depauperization**  Adelman's philosophy that the ultimate goal of economic development should be increasing the opportunities for the realization of individual potential.
**Depreciation**  A decrease in the value of an asset; a decline in the foreign exchange value of a currency; a loss in the value of physical capital stock due to wear and tear and technological obsolescence.
**Derived growth sector**  In Rostow's model, a sector that benefits from the overall growth and diversification of the economy as per capita incomes and consumer demands rise.
**Devaluation**  A decrease in the official foreign exchange value of a currency.
**Developed countries (DCs)**  High-income nations with advanced, industrial economies. The DCs include the United States, Canada, Japan, Australia, New Zealand, and most of the Western European nations.
**Devolution**  The process by which functions of government are transferred to lower levels of government, as from the national to the state level.
**Dirigism**  Within managed capitalism, the significant role played by the state, using taxes and subsidies, to influence resource allocation.
**Disability-adjusted life years**  A standardized measure, expressed per thousand population, of the years of productive life lost due to disease and premature death, based on the prevailing morbidity and mortality rates of the population compared to a low-mortality population.
**Domestic-content legislation**  A trade barrier that requires a minimum percentage of the production value of a designated commodity be inputs of domestic origin.
**Dutch disease**  Rapid, but unbalanced, growth, set off by an export boom in a natural resource–intensive sector, that is accompanied by rising government budget deficits, increased external indebtedness, high inflation, real appreciation of the domestic currency, and a loss in international competitiveness in other sectors of the economy.

**Economic development**  A process of economic growth and structural change in which primarily agrarian economies are transformed into diversified industrial economies with widespread improvements in human capital and the standard of living.
**Economic efficiency**  The least-cost combination of inputs for producing a given level of output.
**Economic growth**  Increases in per capita national output and real per capita national income.
**Economic infrastructure**  The roads, transportation network, communications system, and public utilities needed for economic growth and development.
**Economies of scale**  A decrease in the long-run average cost of production as output is increased, due to the gains in efficiency from the division of labor or the substitution of capital for labor.

**Effective labor** The input of physical labor adjusted by an index of labor productivity (or the quality of labor) that reflects the average levels of education, health, and experience.

**Effective rate of tariff protection** The change in value added for a domestically produced good resulting from a country's tariff structure that includes levies on both competing imported final goods and imported inputs.

**Employed** Individuals in the labor force who are working.

**Entrepreneur** An individual who initiates and organizes a business venture or who otherwise assumes risk in the pursuit of profitable opportunities.

**Entrepreneurship** The process of initiating the production process and taking the risk of being a residual claimant to any economic profit.

**Entropy** A concept central to Daly's theory of steady-state economics; a measure of the energy no longer capable of being converted into work.

**Equity finance** The sale of assets, with the purchaser acquiring ownership rights in an enterprise, to cover a deficit or excess expenditures; the foreign direct investment and foreign portfolio investment through purchases of stock in domestic corporations that can cover a current account deficit for a nation on its balance of payments account.

**Ex ante** Before the event; with input-output analysis, the planning of consistent output levels that will occur in the future.

**Ex post** After the event; with input-output analysis, the assessing of interrelationships among sectors of the economy after production has occurred.

**Exchange controls** Restrictions on access to foreign exchange, usually invoked when there is a shortage of foreign exchange due to an overvalued domestic currency.

**Export expansion** A policy to promote exports through subsidies, tax concessions, a competitive exchange rate, marketing assistance, or other measures.

**Export tax** A duty, either specific or ad valorem, that is imposed on each unit of a commodity that is exported.

**Extensive growth** Economic growth that results from the use of more inputs with unchanged factor productivity.

**Externality** A divergence between the private and social net benefits of an action; may be positive or negative.

**Factor endowments theory of trade** The theory that a nation has a comparative advantage in the production of those commodities that are intensive in the nation's abundant factors.

**Family planning programs** Organized efforts that provide contraceptive information and services to assist couples in controlling their fertility.

**Farm-gate price** The producer price equivalent to the farmer of a commodity, given the world market price of the good and transportation costs from the point of consumption.

**Female secondary school enrollment rate** The ratio of females enrolled in secondary school to the eligible population of females of secondary school age (generally 12 to 17 years of age).

**Financial capital** The money funds available for investment.

**Financial intermediation** A function provided by banks, credit unions, insurance companies, pension funds, stock markets and bond markets that channel the supply of loanable funds to the demanders of loanable funds.

**First World** A label used to designate high-income market economies (the United States, Canada, Japan, Australia, New Zealand, and the Western European nations).

**Fixed-coefficients production function** A production function characterized by a fixed, or inflexible, relationship between output and the required factors. No substitution can occur among the factors of production.

**Fixed exchange rate system** An exchange rate system in which official foreign exchange values (par values) exist for currencies that are to be maintained by the monetary authorities of the nations.

**Flexible exchange rate system** An exchange rate system in which the foreign exchange values of currencies are determined by the demands and supplies of the currencies in the foreign exchange market.

**Food aid** Raw or processed food commodities given (or sold below world market prices) to developing countries.

**Force ratio** An indicator of the resource commitment of a nation to the military, given by the number of armed forces per thousand population.

**Foreign direct investment** The private acquisition of real assets (e.g., property, significant equity in an enterprise) by residents of one nation in a second nation.

**Foreign portfolio investment** The private acquisition of financial assets (e.g., bonds, bank balances, stocks) by residents of one nation in a second nation.

**Fourth World** A label used to distinguish the least developed countries, a subset of the Third World, which includes many of the nations of sub-Saharan Africa and the poorer nations of South Asia.

**Free trade area** An agreement among nations to eliminate their trade barriers against each other, but to retain individual trade barriers against nonmember nations.

**Frictionally unemployed** Individuals in the labor force who are currently between jobs.

**Full employment** A condition in which only frictional unemployment exists, with no cyclical or involuntary unemployment resulting from deficient aggregate demand.

**Fundamental equation of the Solow model** The condition for steady-state equilibrium in which the per capita saving forthcoming is just equal to the per capita investment needed to maintain the capital–labor ratio.

**Generalized System of Preferences** The preferential treatment given to less developed countries by the United States and the European Union in the form of reduced tariffs on designated imports from the LDCs.

**Glasnost** The process of political openness and debate introduced during the Gorbachev years in the former Soviet Union.

**Government-procurement policies** Favoritism given to domestic producers by governments in their purchases of goods and services.

**Green Revolution** The introduction of high-yielding seeds with accompanying packages of fertilizer, pesticides, and herbicides; the primary cause of significant yield increases for food grain crops in Asia since the 1970s.

**Gross Domestic Product (GDP)** The market value of all the final goods and services produced within the borders of a nation over a year.

**Gross National Product (GNP)** The market value of all the final goods and services produced by the residents of a nation over a year.

**Growing economy** The post–take-off stage of Rostow's model in which economic growth can be sustained and economic activity is increasingly diversified.

**High-income economies** A classification used by the World Bank for nations with the highest per capita GNPs in a given year. (In 1993 the high-income economies had per capita GNPs in excess of $8625.)

**Horizontal integration** The expansion by a transnational corporation through foreign subsidiaries to replicate the production of a given commodity.

**Human capital formation** Investment in people, reflected in increases in education, health, and nutritional status.

**Human Development Index (HDI)** An index of economic development devised by the United Nations Development Programme. The components of the HDI are the adult literacy rate; the primary, secondary, and tertiary enrollment rates; life expectancy at birth, and per capita GDP (in international dollars and adjusted to reflect an assumption that the contributions of higher incomes to human welfare are sharply diminishing).

**Imperialism** The economic and political domination of one nation by another nation.

**Import quota**   A legal limit on the number of units of a commodity that may be imported; a type of nontariff barrier to trade.

**Import subsidy**   A transfer from the government to a firm that is producing output in an import-competitive industry.

**Import substitution**   A policy to replace imports with domestic production, initially requiring the use of import barriers.

**Income**   The value created in the production of output; the compensation received for factor services rendered; and the revenue earned from the sale of commodities.

**Income effect**   With a wage increase (decrease), the tendency to work fewer (more) hours and consume more (less) leisure, since the income earned from an hour's labor has increased (decreased).

**Increasing opportunity cost**   The condition in which the opportunity cost of producing a commodity rises with its rate of production.

**Increasing returns to scale**   A proportional increase (decrease) in inputs or factors that yields a more-than-proportional increase (decrease) in output.

**Incremental capital–output ratio (ICOR)**   The ratio of a change in the physical capital stock (i.e., net fixed investment) to the associated change in real output produced.

**Infant industry**   An industry with potential long-run comparative advantage and needing protection to develop into an effective competitor.

**Infant mortality rate (IMR)**   The number of infants who die before reaching age one, expressed per thousand live births in a year.

**Informal credit markets**   Transactions involving the extension of credit that occur outside the organized money market or formal banking system.

**Input-output analysis**   An accounting process that shows interrelationships between sectors of the economy, used either for ex-ante planning or an ex-post assessment of economic transactions.

**Intensive growth**   Economic growth that results from an increase in factor productivity with no change in the quantities of inputs used.

**Interest rate ceiling**   A maximum interest rate (usually in nominal terms) set by the government or monetary authorities.

**Intermediate technology**   Schumacher's concept of a technology that lies between the most advanced, capital-intensive technology found in the developed countries, and the primitive, labor-intensive technology found in traditional societies.

**Internal rate of return**   The interest rate at which the net present value of an investment project equals zero.

**International terms of trade**   The ratio of exchange between two traded commodities on the world market.

**Involuntary unemployment**   A situation in which individuals who are willing to work at current wage levels are unable to find work due to insufficient demand for labor.

**Isoquant**   The combinations of inputs capable of producing a given level of output.

**Joint venture**   Cooperation between firms in a given project or enterprise; a partnership between a foreign company and a domestic company.

**Knife-edge problem**   The dynamically unstable condition for steady-state equilibrium in the Harrod-Domar growth model that requires the warranted rate of growth (given by the exogenously determined ratio of the saving rate to the capital–output ratio) to equal the exogenously determined natural growth rate of the labor force. Unless this condition is satisfied, the Harrod-Domar model is out of steady-state equilibrium, with no inherent adjustment mechanism to return.

**Labor force**   Those individuals who are either working or actively seeking employment; the sum of the employed and the unemployed.

**Laissez-faire capitalism** The system of private ownership of the means of production that uses markets, with no government intervention, to determine outputs and allocate inputs.

**Latifundia** Large, privately owned, Latin American farms that depend on hired labor.

**Less developed countries (LDCs)** The low- and middle-income nations of Asia, Africa, Latin America, and the Middle East; also referred to as the *Third World* or *developing nations*.

**Life-cycle theory** A theory of consumption behavior. Individuals seeking to maintain a stable level of consumption over their lifetime will need to save some of their income during the working years to provide for their dissaving during retirement years.

**Life expectancy at birth** The number of years, on average, that a newborn could expect to live, given the age-specific death rates prevailing at the time of birth.

**Line of best fit (or sample regression equation)** A linear equation that best represents a sample of observations on a dependent variable and the explanatory variable(s).

**Low-income economies** A classification used by the World Bank for the nations with the lowest per capita GNPs in a given year. (In 1993 the low-income economies had per capita GNPs of less than $696.)

**Low-level equilibrium trap** An equilibrium characterized by poverty and economic stagnation. When in the trap, any increases in income are subsequently overwhelmed by population growth (primarily due to lower death rates) that pulls the economy back to the low-level equilibrium.

**Malnutrition** Poor nutritional status due to an unbalanced diet, unhealthy preparation of food, or inadequate assimilation of food.

**Managed capitalism** The system of private ownership of the means of production that uses markets and selective government direction for resource allocation.

**Managed float** A flexible exchange rate system in which the monetary authorities intervene at their discretion in the foreign exchange market to influence the range of exchange rate movements.

**Marginal rate of factor substitution** The rate at which one factor (e.g., capital) can substitute for another factor (e.g., labor) and maintain the same rate of production; reflected in the slope of an isoquant.

**Marginal rate of substitution** The rate at which a consumer is willing to trade off the consumption of one commodity for another commodity, holding constant the level of total utility; reflected in the slope of an indifference curve.

**Material balances** The accounting technique within centralized socialism that equates sources and uses for each commodity.

**Material balance process** A planning process within centralized socialism that relies on establishing by iteration an equality of sources and uses (material balance) for each commodity.

**Medium of exchange** An asset, such as money, that is readily acceptable as a means of payment, thus facilitating the exchange of goods and services.

**Merit goods** Commodities or services, such as health care or education, to which society deems that all citizens have a claim regardless of ability to pay.

**Middle-income economies** A classification used by the World Bank for the nations with moderate per capita GNPs in a given year. (In 1993, the middle-income economies had per capita GNPs between $696 and $8626.)

**Military burden** An indicator of the resource commitment of a nation to the military, given by the share of military expenditures in gross national product.

**Minifundia** Small subsistence landholdings in Latin America.

**Mixed farming** An agricultural enterprise that has fields for growing crops and raising livestock.

**Money** An asset that serves as a medium of exchange, store of value, and unit of account. In the aggregate for a nation, the *money supply* is narrowly defined as the sum of currency in circulation and checkable deposits.

**Most-favored nation**  A fundamental principle of the General Agreement on Tariffs and Trade (GATT) that all member nations should receive the most favorable trading privileges.

**Nationalization**  The seizure of the assets of a private enterprise by the government.

**Natural fertility**  The average number of children born to a woman who did not consciously attempt to influence her fertility, but abided by the prevailing social customs.

**Natural monopoly**  A firm that has economies of scale (decreasing long-run average cost) over a range of output sufficient to satisfy market demand. To minimize the average cost of production there should be only one producer.

**Natural resources**  The factors of production available in the natural environment, including the land, forests, minerals, energy sources, bodies of water, and wildlife.

**Net factor payments**  The payments of factor income (wages and salaries to labor, interest and profits on the invested capital) made by a nation to foreigners less the receipts of factor income by the residents of a nation from foreigners. The difference between GDP and GNP is equal to net factor payments.

**Net in-migration rate**  The difference between the immigrants to an area and the emigrants from an area over a year per thousand population in the area at mid-year.

**Net present value**  The discounted value of a stream of future net benefits (benefits less costs).

**New Economic Mechanism**  A series of market reforms introduced in Hungary in 1968.

**Newly industrializing countries (NICs)**  The more advanced, rapidly growing LDCs, including a number of the East Asian economies.

**Nominal exchange rate**  The price of one currency expressed in units of a second currency.

**Nominal rate**  The stated value of a tariff expressed as a percentage of the final price of the good.

**Nonrenewable resources**  Natural resources with finite stocks over the forseeable planning horizon.

**Nontariff barriers to trade**  Any impediments to trade other than a tariff, including import quotas, voluntary export restraints, orderly marketing agreements, domestic-content legislation, discriminatory health and safety standards for imports, and government-procurement policies.

**North**  A label used to denote the developed countries, that, in most cases, are located in the northern hemisphere.

**Official development assistance (ODA)**  A unilateral transfer of resources from a government to promote economic development; also known as *foreign economic aid.*

**Official producer prices**  Legally set prices that are to be paid for output by market intermediaries. In developing countries, such set prices have often been used in the agricultural sector.

**Official reserve assets**  The gold, foreign currencies, and Special Drawing Rights held by the monetary authorities of a nation and the reserve position of the nation at the International Monetary Fund.

**Official settlements account**  The subaccount on the balance of payments account that records the transfer and acquisition of official assets by the monetary authorities or governments of nations.

**Opportunity cost**  The best alternative use of given resources, indicated by the goods or services that are not produced or consumed when resources are committed to a given endeavor.

**Orderly marketing agreement**  Bilateral quotas that limit import sales to a certain percentage of total market sales or to a specified rate of growth.

**Output-expansion path**  For a given set of factor prices and technology, the least-cost combinations of factors for producing varying levels of output.

**Overvalued currency** A nation's monetary unit that officially exchanges for more units of a foreign currency than would occur at a market equilibrium rate.

**Partial output elasticity** The percentage change in output due to a percentage change in a factor, holding constant the levels of all the other factors of production and technology.

**Perestroika** Economic reform and reorganization introduced by Gorbachev in the former Soviet Union during the late 1980s.

**Permanent income** The discounted future income an individual expects to receive based on his or her education, employment, and financial wealth.

**Permanent income hypothesis** A theory of consumption behavior which holds that individuals tend to consume a stable proportion of permanent income. Any discrepancy between the actual income received and permanent income, known as *transitory income*, is largely saved (if positive) or dissaved (if negative).

**Physical capital stock** The human-made aids to production, including the plant, equipment, and machinery; the residential structures and other buildings; and the economic infrastructure of the transportation and communication systems.

**Physical labor** The human factor of production, usually measured in hours of work.

**Population momentum** The potential for increase in the size of a population after the onset of replacement-level fertility. Populations with high fertility and a young age structure have population momentum.

**Population policy** Measures to influence the growth rate, composition, or distribution of a population.

**Population pyramid** A bar graph depicting the age–sex structure of a population. For each age interval on opposite sides of a vertical line, the length of the bar indicates the size of the male or female populations.

**Positive checks** In Malthus's theory, the checks to population growth that operate through the death rate. Malthus distinguished between positive checks resulting from vice (wars, murder, violence) and from misery (famine, disease, natural disaster).

**Prediction error** The difference between the actual value of a dependent variable and the value predicted by a sample regression line.

**Pre–take-off economy** The stage in Rostow's model in which the preconditions (improvements in agricultural productivity; investments in the economic infrastructure; and increased imports of capital goods) for a successful take-off are in place.

**Preventative checks** In Malthus's theory, the checks to population growth that operate through the birth rate. Malthus distinguished between preventative checks resulting from vice (birth control and unnatural passions) and from moral restraint (delay of marriage and limits on family size according to the ability to provide for children).

**Primary growth sector** In Rostow's model, a leading sector during economic development, in which rapid growth in output, employment, and income induce expansion in other sectors of the economy.

**Product cycle theory of trade** A dynamic theory of trade that explains shifts in comparative advantage for manufactured products. New manufactured products are developed in high-income nations; then, if successful domestically, are exported to similar markets; and finally, may be produced abroad and imported back to the nation that originated the product.

**Production possibilities boundary (PPB)** The combination of outputs that can be produced in an economy over a given period of time using all the available resources fully and efficiently.

**Pure public good** A commodity for which the consumption by one individual does not reduce the consumption of others, such as a lighthouse or national defense. Consumers have a tendency to "free-ride" and avoid paying for their consumption; thus, the government often produces the good and uses general tax revenues to pay production costs.

**Quality of children**  Becker's term for average expenditures per child by parents, both in terms of income and commitment of time.

**Rate of labor force participation**  Percentage of the population over a specified age, usually 16, who are either employed or unemployed but seeking employment.

**Rate of unemployment**  The number of unemployed as a percentage of the labor force (employed and unemployed).

**Real exchange rate**  The nominal exchange rate adjusted for the relative price levels for internationally traded goods and services in the two nations.

**Reciprocity**  A fundamental principle of the General Agreement on Tariffs and Trade (GATT) that a nation receiving trade concessions from another nation should respond in kind and grant trade concessions to that other nation.

**Recycling of petrodollars**  The lending by Western commercial banks of the funds deposited by oil-exporting nations to oil-importing developing nations to cover their increased current account deficits in the 1970s due to the higher oil prices.

**Renewable resources**  Natural resources with stocks that can be replenished with proper care.

**Replacement-level fertility**  A fertility rate consistent with each generation replacing itself, so that in the long run the crude rate of natural increase would be zero.

**Revaluation**  An increase in the official foreign exchange value of a currency.

**Sample regression line**  See *line of best fit*.

**Scatter diagram**  A plot of ordered pairs of observations for a dependent variable and an explanatory variable.

**Second World**  A label used to designate the command or nonmarket economies of the former Soviet Union and Eastern Europe.

**Secondary markets**  Markets in which previously issued shares of stock or debt instruments are traded.

**Shock therapy**  The rapid decontrol of prices within a transitional economy, first used by Poland in the 1990 to 1992 period.

**Social overhead capital**  The roads, transportation network, communications system, and public utilities in an economy; also known as *economic infrastructure*.

**South**  A label used to designate the less developed countries, many of whom are in the southern hemisphere.

**Specific tariff**  A tax of a fixed monetary amount imposed on each unit of a commodity that is imported.

**Special Drawing Rights (SDRs)**  An international currency created by the International Monetary Fund and allocated to member nations to supplement the ability of nations with balance of payments deficits to intervene in the foreign exchange market in support of their currencies.

**Steady-state economy (SSE)**  Daly's concept of a sustainable economic system with zero population growth; limits on natural resources consumption consistent with environmental thresholds; and bounds on individual income and wealth.

**Steady-state equilibrium**  A condition for equilibrium in the growth models in which output, capital, and labor are growing at constant rates and there is product market equilibrium, full employment of labor, and full utilization of the capital stock.

**Store of value**  A function provided by an asset that serves as a stock of purchasing power or command over goods and services.

**Structural adjustment**  The introduction of economic reforms, often market-friendly, within a developing country.

**Structural adjustment agreement**  The process by which an international agency, such as the World Bank, negotiates a series of economic reforms with a developing country. Often the donor agency commits financial support to the country as part of the agreement.

**Structurally unemployed**   Individuals in the labor force who are unable to find employment since they possess skills different from those required for the job openings.

**Stunting**   A malady indicative of chronic malnutrition, in which a child's height-to-age ratio is significantly below normal.

**Subsidy**   A transfer from the government to a firm to increase output or lower production costs. In other cases, a transfer of funds to a firm to cover any accounting losses, as in the case of support for state enterprises within the transitional economies.

**Subsistence agriculture**   Small-scale agriculture in which producers primarily grow crops to feed their families; little marketable surplus exists.

**Subsistence sector**   In Lewis's model, the primarily agrarian sector, in which the technology is traditional, capital–labor ratios are low, and the marginal product of labor is near or equal to zero.

**Substitution effect**   In response to a wage increase (decrease), the tendency to take less (more) leisure as the opportunity cost of leisure increases (decreases).

**Supplementary growth sector**   In Rostow's model, a sector, linked to a primary growth sector (e.g., as a source of inputs), that expands as a direct result of the increased output of the primary growth sector.

**Surplus value**   In Marx's theory, the difference between the value of output produced by labor and labor's compensation; a measure of the exploitation of labor by capitalists.

**Sustainable development**   A development in which the needs of the present generation are met without compromising the ability to meet the needs of future generations.

**Take-off**   The key stage in Rostow's model, lasting two or three decades, in which accelerated capital formation and rapid structural change propel the economy into sustained economic growth.

**Technical efficiency**   A condition in which no more of any factor is used than is necessary to produce a given level of output; that is, the marginal product of each factor is positive for given levels of the other inputs.

**Technology**   The stock of knowledge applicable to the production of goods and services.

**Terms of trade**   In international trade, the ratio of an index of a nation's export prices to an index of its import prices.

**Third World**   A label used to designate the less developed countries or developing economies of Asia, Africa, the Middle East, and Latin America.

**Total factor productivity**   The contribution to output not directly attributable to the factors of production.

**Total fertility rate**   The number of children a woman would have, on average, if she lived through the child-bearing years and were subject to the prevailing age-specific birth rates.

**Traditional economy**   One of the classifications of economies in Rostow's model; an economy with a low level of technology, low capital–labor ratios, and low incomes. Usually, subsistence agriculture dominates in a traditional economy.

**Transfer pricing**   The manipulation of invoices on intrafirm trade to overstate or understate receipts for the purpose of shifting profits between countries.

**Transitory income**   The difference between the actual income received and permanent income in any period of time.

**Underemployment**   A condition in which an individual is working fewer hours per week than desired or working in a position below his or her skill level.

**Undernutrition**   Poor nutritional status due to general deficiencies or shortfalls in food intake.

**Unemployed**   Individuals in the labor force who are looking for work but unable to find it.

**Unemployment**   The situation of individuals who are not working, but actively seeking employment.

**Unilateral transfers**   Transfers of goods, services, or assets from one nation to another.

**Unit of account**  A function provided by an asset that serves as a common standard of value.
**Unit labor costs**  The labor cost per unit of output, equal to the ratio of the average cost of labor to the average product of labor.

**Value added**  The difference between the value of a firm's output and the value of inputs (intermediate goods) purchased from other firms.
**Value of marginal product of labor**  Marginal revenue product of labor within a perfectly competitive industry, equal to the price of output multiplied by the marginal product of labor.
**Vertical integration**  The expansion by a transnational corporation through foreign subsidiaries that are involved in different stages of production. Vertical integration may be either backward (e.g., foreign subsidiaries supply inputs to later stages of production) or forward (e.g., foreign subsidiaries assemble components of a final product).
**Voluntary export restraint**  A limit on exports to a market accepted by a nation, usually under the threat of an imposed import quota.

**Warranted rate of growth**  The steady-state equilibrium rate of growth for output (as well as for physical capital and labor) in the Harrod-Domar model, equal to the saving rate divided by the capital–output ratio.
**Wasting**  A malady, indicative of acute or short-term malnutrition, whereby a child's weight-to-height ratio is significantly below normal.
**World reserve base life index**  Based on current production rates, an estimate of the number of years of reserves left for a nonrenewable resource.

# ANSWERS TO SELECTED NUMERICAL QUESTIONS

## CHAPTER 1

5. Atlantica's GDP equals $99.8 million.
6. Pacifica's GNP per capita equals $500 at the official exchange rate.
   Pacifica's GNP per capita equals $1250 in international dollars.

## CHAPTER 2

3. The CDR equals 22 deaths per thousand population. The annual population growth rate equals 3 percent (30 per thousand). The approximate doubling time for the population is 24 years.
4. The TFR equals 3.965 or nearly four live births per woman.
5. Population B, with the expansive population pyramid, most resembles a developing economy with high fertility. Population A resembles a stationary population with replacement level fertility and zero population growth. Population C has below replacement level fertility.

## CHAPTER 3

1a. $Y_o = 25$ (output in time period 0)
    $K_1 = 101.5$ (physical capital stock in time period 1)
    $L_1 = 304.5$ (physical labor force in time period 1)
    $Y_1 = 25.375$ (output in time period 1)
1b. If the natural growth rate of labor increased to 2 percent ($n' = .02$), then in period 1 there would be an excess supply of labor (unemployment) equal to 1.5 units of labor. Capital would be the scarce factor constraining output growth.
2. The saving rate would need to increase to 8 percent ($s' = .08$) to maintain steady-state equilibrium when the natural growth rate of labor increased to 2 percent. In the new distribution of income, the share of wages in national income would be 62.5 percent, while the share of profits in national income would be 37.5 percent. $(W/Y)' = .625$ and $(P/Y)' = .375$.
3a. The fundamental equation of the Solow model is: $dk = .2k^{.5} - .025k$.
    The equilibrium capital-labor ratio is $k_o^* = 64$.
    Output per unit of labor is $y_o^* = 16$.
    The capital-output ratio is $v_o = 4$.
3b. The equilibrium capital-labor ratio is $k_1^* = 144$.
    Output per unit of labor is $y_1^* = 24$.
    The capital-output ratio is $v_1 = 6$.
3c. The equilibrium capital-labor ratio is $k_2^* = 100$.
    Output per unit of labor is $y_2^* = 20$.
    The capital-output ratio is $v_2 = 5$.

## CHAPTER 7

1a. The utility maximizing combination is 6 children and 40 units of other goods and services. $C_o = 6$ and $X_o = 40$.

**1c.** The new utility maximizing combination is 3 children and 120 units of other goods and services. $C_1 = 3$ and $X_1 = 120$.

## CHAPTER 9

**1a.** With the price decontrol, the price of corn will increase to the market-clearing level. At the higher price, the value of marginal product of labor in corn production will increase and the demand for labor curve will shift out, leading to a higher wage and an increase in the quantity of labor employed.

**1b.** With an increase in the supply of rice, the price of rice will fall. The demand for the substitute good, corn, will decrease; and the equilibrium price and quantity transacted of corn will fall. With a decrease in the price of corn, the value of marginal product of labor in corn production will decrease and the demand for labor curve will shift in, leading to a lower wage and a decrease in the quantity of labor employed.

**1c.** The assumption is that the price of corn will rise to the world market price, increasing the value of marginal product of labor, shifting out the demand for labor curve, and increasing the wage and employment.

## CHAPTER 10

**1.** The required saving rate is equal to 9 percent. $s = .09$.

**1a.** The required steady-state saving rate rises to 12 percent when the natural growth rate of the labor force increases to 2 percent. $s' = .12$.

**1b.** The required steady-state saving rate rises to 12 percent when the growth rate in labor productivity increases to 3 percent. $s'' = .12$.

**4a.** The market-equilibrium rate of interest is equal to 11 percent and the quantity of loanable funds is equal to 36 units. The rate of interest received by depositors is equal to 8 percent. $i_o^l = 11$, $F_o = 36$, and $i_o^d = 8$.

**4b.** The new market equilibrium rate of interest is equal to 10 percent and the quantity of loanable funds is equal to 40 units. The rate of interest received by depositors is equal to 8.67 percent. $i_1^l = 10$, $F_1 = 40$, and $i_1^d = 8.67$.

**5.** With an interest rate ceiling of 10 percent, the quantity of loanable funds available is equal to 30 ($F_1 = 30$), and the excess quantity demanded of credit is equal to 40 ($F_2 - F_1 = 40$). The rate of interest received on bank deposits is equal to 7 percent ($i_1^d = 7$).

**7a.** Using the unit factor prices in set I, the $NPV_A$ is equal to +$398.34 and the $NPV_B$ is equal to +$89.25. Therefore, although both projects have positive net present values, Project A would have the higher priority and would be funded over Project B. Using the unit factor prices in set II, the $NPV'_A$ is equal to -$86.78 and the $NPV'_B$ is equal to +$86.78. Thus, Project B would be funded. With a negative net present value, Project A should not be undertaken, even if the funds were available.

## CHAPTER 11

**6a.** At the exchange rate of 10 rupees equal $1.00, the world price of rice in rupees is 7 rupees per bushel. The domestic quantities demanded and supplied equal 8 million bushels and 18 million bushels, respectively. The quantity exported equals 10 million bushels. Export revenues are 70 million rupees or $7 million.

Total expenditures by domestic consumers are 56 million rupees. Total revenues for domestic rice farmers are 126 million rupees.

**6b.** At the exchange rate of 8 rupees equal $1.00, the world price of rice in rupees is 5.6 rupees per bushel. The domestic quantities demanded and supplied equal 16.4 million bushels and 10 million bushels, respectively. The quantity imported equals 6.4 million bushels. Import payments are 35.84 million rupees or $4.48 million. Total expenditures by domestic consumers are 91.84 million rupees. Total revenues for domestic rice farmers are 50 million rupees.

**6c.** The domestic quantities demanded and supplied equal 8 million bushels and 18 million bushels, respectively. The government purchases 4 million bushels. The quantity exported equals 6 million bushels. Export revenues are 42 million rupees or $4.2 million. Total expenditures by domestic consumers are 78.4 million rupees (including expenditures of 22.4 million rupees by the poor). Total revenues for domestic rice farmers are 126 million rupees. The cost of the government rice subsidy program is 5.6 million rupees.

## Chapter 12

**5.** The dollar price of a rupee is equal to $.025.

**5a.** A depreciation in the nominal exchange value of the rupee by 10 percent results in a new nominal exchange rate of 1 rupee equal to $.0225. The new real exchange rate is 1 rupee equal to $.0225 or 44.44 rupees equal to $1.00.

**5b.** An increase in the foreign price level by 10 percent results in a new real exchange rate of 1 rupee equal to $.0227 or 44 rupees equal to $1.00.

**5c.** An increase in the domestic price level by 10 percent results in a new real exchange rate of 1 rupee equal to $.0275 or 36.36 rupees equal to $1.00. The international price competitiveness of the rupee currency country is improved with both a nominal depreciation of the rupee and an increase in the foreign price level.

**6a.** The market equilibrium price and quantity transacted are equal to 5 and 15 units respectively. $P_o = 5$ and $Q_o = 15$.

**6b.** The new market equilibrium price and quantity transacted are equal to 6 and 10 units respectively. $P_1 = 6$ and $Q_1 = 10$.

## Chapter 13

**5a.** The sales from sector 1 to sector 1 equal $20 million. The sales from sector 1 to sector 2 equal $0. The final demand for the output of sector 2 equals $30 million. The total demand for the output of sector 3 equals $100 million. The total value added in sector 3 equals $30 million. The value added by capital in sector 1 equals $20 million. The value added by capital in sector 3 equals $10 million. The value of the total output (total supply) of sector 3 is $100 million.

**5b.** $a_{11} = .1$
Each $1 of output of sector 1 requires $.10 of output from sector 1.
$a_{23} = .40$
Each $1 of output of sector 3 requires $.40 of output from sector 2.
$a_{31} = .20$
Each $1 of output of sector 1 requires $.20 of output from sector 3.

**5c.** The final demands can be met. Payments to labor equal $155 million. Payments to capital equal $70 million.

**5d.** An increase of $1 million in the final demand for the output of sector 3 will require more than an increase of $1 million in the gross production of sector 3 since there will be increases in the intermediate demands from sectors 1, 2, and 3 for the output of sector 3 as these sectors increase their productions in response to the increased production of sector 3.

**6a.** The effective rate of production for the domestic bicycle industry equals 53.3 percent.

**6b.** The new effective rate of production for the domestic bicycle industry equals 36.67 percent.

**8a.** With free trade, the quantities demanded and supplied domestically equal 100 thousand batteries and 70 thousand batteries, respectively. The quantity imported equals 30 thousand batteries.

**8b.** With the specific tariff, the new consumer price equals $22. The quantities demanded and supplied domestically equal 90 thousand batteries and 78 thousand batteries, respectively. The quantity imported equals 12 thousand batteries. The tariff revenues collected by the government equal $24 thousand.

**8c.** With the import quota, the consumer price equals $22. The quantities demanded and supplied domestically equal 90 thousand batteries and 78 thousand batteries, respectively. The quantity imported equals 12 thousand batteries.

**8d.** With the government subsidy, the consumer price equals $20. The quantities demanded and supplied domestically equal 100 thousand batteries and 88 thousand batteries, respectively. The quantity imported equals 12 thousand batteries. For domestic production to equal 88 thousand batteries, the price received must be $24.50. Thus, a subsidy of $4.50 per battery is needed, for a total subsidy cost of $396 thousand.

**8e.** With the increase in demand, under the tariff, the consumer price is $22; the quantities demanded and supplied domestically are 130 thousand batteries and 78 thousand batteries, respectively; and the quantity imported equals 52 thousand batteries. Under the quota, the consumer price is $26.44; the quantities demanded and supplied domestically are 107.78 thousand batteries and 95.78 thousand batteries, respectively; and the quantity imported equals 12 thousand batteries.

## Chapter 14

**4a.** The domestic market-clearing price and quantity transacted in autarky are equal to 80 cedi and 240 thousand boxes. $P_o = 80$ and $Q_o = 240$.

**4b.** Ashanti is an importer of pens, importing 80 thousand boxes. Import payments are $72 thousand or 5,760 thousand cedi.

**4c.** Ashanti is now an exporter of pens, exporting 100 thousand boxes. Export revenues are $90 thousand or 9,000 thousand cedi. Ashanti's trade balance has improved by $162 thousand or 14,760 thousand cedi.

**4d.** Export revenues increase to $135 thousand or 13,500 thousand cedi. The total cost of the export subsidy is 750 thousand cedi.

**5a.** Output combination B for Atlantica is 120 units of wine and 12 units of cloth. The 120 units of wine require 720 units of labor and 480 units of capital. With this output combination, Atlantica has 160 units of surplus labor. Output combination B′ for Pacifica is 80 units of wine and 20 units of cloth. The 20 units of cloth require 80 units of labor and 240 units of capital. With this output combination, Pacifica has 570 units of surplus capital.

*5b.* In Atlantica, the opportunity cost of 1 unit of wine is 4 units of cloth (1w = .4c or 2.5w = 1c). In Pacifica, the opportunity cost of 1 unit of wine is 1 unit of cloth (1w = 1c). Atlantica, the labor-abundant country, has the comparative advantage (lower opportunity cost) in wine, the labor-intensive commodity.

*5c.* Atlantica produces 150 units of wine (and no cloth), and exports 50 units of wine to Pacifica for 40 units of cloth. Atlantica's post-trade consumption combination is 100 units of wine and 40 units of cloth. The gains from trade for Atlantica are 10 units of wine and 16 units of cloth.

*5d.* Pacifica produces 100 units of cloth (and no wine), and exports 40 units of cloth for 50 units of wine. Pacifica's post-trade consumption combination is 60 units of cloth and 50 units of wine. The gains from trade for Pacifica are 10 units of wine.

## CHAPTER 15

*5a.* The market equilibrium exchange rate is 20 rupees equal to $1.00.
*5b.* The new market equilibrium exchange rate is 30 rupees equal to $1.00.
*5c.* In the short run, when the rupee depreciates to the upper limit of 25 rupees equal to $1.00, the monetary authorities would have to intervene in the foreign exchange market and supply or sell $150 thousand per day.

# CREDITS

CHAPTER 4

FOOTNOTE 20  Reprinted by permission of the *Wall Street Journal,* © 1995 Dow Jones & Company, Inc.  All rights reserved worldwide.

CHAPTER 10

FOOTNOTE 3  Reprinted by permission of the *Wall Street Journal,* © 1985 Dow Jones & Company, Inc.  All rights reserved worldwide.

FOOTNOTE 17  Reprinted by permission of the *Wall Street Journal,* © 1994 Dow Jones & Company, Inc.  All rights reserved worldwide.

CHAPTER 15

FOOTNOTE 27  Reprinted by permission of the *Wall Street Journal,* © 1994 Dow Jones & Company, Inc.  All rights reserved worldwide.

# INDEX

Entries and page numbers in bold indicate defined terms. Page numbers followed by *n* indicate footnote references.

## A

Abeysekera, Gamini, 150*n*
Abortion, 192, 203
**Ad valorem tariff, 401**
Adelman, Irma, 121*n*, 122*n*, 145, 146, 588*n*
Adelman's depauperization, 120–121, 526–527
    agricultural demand-led industrialization, 122–123
    global development and, 588–589
    growth with equity, 121–122
**Adjustable exchange rate, 469,** 471
Adjusted coefficient of determination, 28
Africa
    agriculture in, 327–329, 345
    AIDS and HIV virus in, 575–576
    birth and death rates versus population change, 570
    birth rates in, 48
    Catholicism in, 570
    death rates in, 48
    debt problem in, 481–483
    deforestation in, 359–360
    demographic transition in, 47–49, 570
    developing economies of, 10, 60
    developing nations of, 5–6
    development indicators in, 567–568
    economic integration in, 577
    education in, 240, 564, 568
    exchange rates in, 579–580
    external debt in, 569
    famine in, 575
    foreign aid to, 503–504, 505, 569
    foreign direct investment in, 576
    GDP growth decline in, 563, 565
    Green Revolution in, 333, 574–575
    health and nutritional programs in, 564, 568
    illiteracy in, 240
    Islam in, 570
    killing of elephants in, 603
    labor as producer in, 258–259
    mixed socialist economies in, 161
    North
        agriculture in, 325
        fertility in, 48, 49
        foreign aid to, 509
        gross domestic investment and gross domestic savings in, 292
        land and water in, 375, 376
        merchandise trade in, 435
        military expenditures, 595
        population and labor force in, 274
        renewable water resources in, 375, 376, 377
    per capita food production in, 597
    political refugees in, 575
    political systems in, 564–565
    public debt in, 569
    rural-to-urban migration in, 271
    Southern African Development Community, 583–584
    sub-Saharan, 559–561
        agriculture in, 325
        arms imports and military expenditures in, 567–568
        colonization, 561–563
        contraceptive use in, 204–205
        development indicators in, 567–568
        disability-adjusted life years in, 231
        doctor/population ratio in, 228–229, 230
        economic development in, 13, 187
        economic performance in 1960s, 563–565
        economic stagnation (1970s to present), 565
        education and health care, 575–576
        education in, 239, 240
        excessive population growth, 569–571
        failures of governments and donor community, 566–569
        foreign aid to, 508, 509
        gross domestic investment and gross domestic saving in, 292
        lack of economic diversity in, 576–577
        land and water in, 375–376
        life expectancy in, 229
        merchandise trade in, 435
        military expenditures, 595
        per capita income growth in, 563, 565

Africa, *(continued)*
    poor agricultural performance, 571–575
        drought and land constraints, 573–574
        export agriculture, 573
        lack of incentives, 574–575
    population and labor force in, 274
    renewable water resources in, 377
    returns to investment in education, 244, 245
    selected health statistics, 230, 231
    stunting of children in, 223, 224, 225
African development agenda, 577–578
    more radical approaches, 582–584
    structural adjustment, 578
        decentralization, 581–582
        future of, 582
        macroeconomic stabilization, 578–580
        market pricing in agriculture, 580–581
        poor and, 582
African Development Bank, 511
African Rights, 566
"African Socialism," 564
Agarwala, A. N., 97n, 116, 117n
Age-specific birth rates, 37
Age-specific death rates, 35–37
**Aggregate demand (AD) curve, 262,** 263
**Aggregate supply (AS) curve, 263,** 263–264
**Agricultural demand–led industrialization (ADLI), 122–123**
Agricultural extension, 344–345
Agricultural output, declining price of, 334
Agricultural product price inelasticity, 331, 332
Agricultural productivity, 99
    in basic needs approach, 128
Agricultural Revolution, 44
Agricultural taxation, 572
Agriculture, 323–324
    average annual growth rate of, 324, 325
    characteristics of in LDCs, 327
        Africa, 571–573
        income-elasticity of food, 334–336
        long-run trend in agricultural terms of trade, 332–333
        seasonality and risk, 330–332
        type and size of farms, 327
            household as producer, 328–329
            large-scale agriculture, 329–330
    compared to other natural resource-intensive sectors, 357–360
    constraints to agricultural development, 336
        access to fertile land, 336
        agricultural pricing policy, 337–340
        availability of inputs and credit, 340–341
    export agriculture, 564, 573
    fourth phase of, 327n
    importance of, 324–326
    integration of with industry, 327
    market pricing in, 580–581
    in market-friendly development strategy, 526, 536
    mixed, 329
    policy reform, 341
        clear objectives, 342
        increasing profitability, 343
            agricultural extension, 344–345
            credit, 343–344
            infrastructure, health, education, research, 344
            opportunities for women, 345–346
            price policy, 343
            promoting full employment in off-season, 345
        land access, 342–343
    post-subsistence phase of, 326–327
    role of in high-income countries, 327n
    subsistence, 326
    transformation of agricultural sector, 326–327
AIDS (Acquired Immune Deficiency Syndrome)
    in Africa, 575–576
    deaths from, 227n
    economic impact of, 227
    mothers afflicted with, 224
Ainsworth, Alice, 380n
Akin, John, 232n, 236n, 250
Albania, centralized socialism in, 161
Alcohol, consumption of, 228
Alesina, Alberto, 169n, 173
Algeria
    merchandise export structure, 437
    sectoral shares in, 389
Allen, R. G. D., 64n, 81
Allende, Salvador, 497
Alwang, Jeffrey, 326n, 330n
Amartya, Sen, 21
Amazon Rain Forest, 376
Angola, dysfunctional government in, 566
Antarctica, restriction on mining exploration and development in, 603
Apartheid, 559

Appleyard, Dennis, 401, 425*n*, 433*n*, 450
**Appreciation, 364, 459**
Argentina
  devaluation in, 476
  foreign direct investment in, 491
  inflation in, 467
Arias, Oscar, 601
Ariyaratne, A. T., 139*n*
Armenia, economic growth in, 538–548
Arms trade, 589
  international taxation of, 601
Asia
  agriculture in, 327–329, 330, 345
  birth rates in, 48
  Central
    agriculture in, 325
    average income in, 13
    foreign aid to, 509
    gross domestic investment and gross
      domestic savings in, 292
    merchandise trade in, 435
    population and labor force in, 274
  death rates in, 47
  demographic transition in, 47–49
  developing economies of, 10, 60
  doctor/population ratio in, 228, 230
  East
    agriculture in, 325
    depauperization in, 121–123
    economic growth in, 532–534
      capable administrations and
        pragmatic policies, 535–536
      export expansion, 537–538
      human capital formation, 534–535
      macroeconomic stability, 536–537
      reservations, 538
    economic growth rates in, 11
    fertility in, 48, 49
    foreign aid to, 509
    Green Revolution in, 333
    gross domestic investment and gross
      domestic saving in, 292
    human capital formation in, 12–13
    merchandise trade in, 435
    military expenditures, 595
    renewable water resources in, 377
  economic growth rates in, 10
  education in, 240
  fertilizer use in, 597
  foreign aid to, 508, 509
  foreign direct investment in, 490
  Green Revolution in, 333
  health statistics, 228–230, 231
  labor as producer in, 258–259
  life expectancy in, 229
  modern-sector manufacturing
    employment in, 260–261
  nutrition statistics for, 224, 225
  per capita food production in, 597
  public health expenditures in,
    229–230
  returns to investment in education, 244
  South
    agriculture in, 325
    birth and death rates versus
      population change, 570
    deforestation in, 359–360
    economic development in, 13
    education in, 240
    fertility in, 48, 49
    foreign aid to, 509
    gross domestic investment and gross
      domestic savings in, 293
    illiteracy in, 239
    land and water in, 375, 376
    life expectancy in, 229
    merchandise trade in, 435
    military expenditures, 595
    per capita income growth in, 563
    renewable water resources in, 377
    stunting/wasting of children in, 223,
      224, 225
Asian Development Bank, 511
Asset redistribution
  in basic needs approach, 127–128
  in depauperization, 121–122
Aturupane, Harsha, 16*n*, 21
Australia
  economy of, 4, 5
  as First World country, 10
  merchandise export structure, 437
  natural resource reserves in, 355
  population growth in, 32
  sectoral shares in, 389
Austria
  merchandise export structure, 437
  sectoral shares in, 389
Autarky, 423–424
Average cost in the long run, 400*n*
Average-cost pricing, 411

# B

Baby booms, 37, 46*n*, 186*n*
Backward integration, 492
Baer, Werner, 179*n*, 181*n*
Baker, James, 482
**Balance of payments account, 451–452,
  452**
  capital account, 454–456

**Balance of payments account,** (continued)
  current account, 452–454
  deficits in and economic policy, 465–466
  official settlements account, 456–458
  relationship to exchange rates, 458–461
  *See also* Exchange rates
**Balance of payments deficit, 455**
**Balance of payments surplus, 455**
BancoSol, 312
Bandaranaike, S. W. R. D., 151–153
Bangladesh
  Grameen Bank of, 312
  military burden in, 594
Bank credit, loanable funds and, 297
Bank reserves, 296$n$
Bardhan, Pranab, 157$n$, 160$n$, 173, 257$n$, 278
Barnum, Howard, 329$n$
Barro, Robert, 169$n$
**Basic macroeconomic identity,** 288–290, **288**
**Basic needs, 123,** 158–159
Basic needs approach to economic development, 123
  implementation of, 128–129
  managed capitalism and, 158–159
  policies of, 123–124
    access to resources, 127–128
    employment generation, 124–127
    human capital formation, 128
Bauer, P. T., 489$n$, 501–502, 501$n$, 502$n$, 520
Beason, Richard, 159$n$
Becker, Gary, 193, 193$n$, 194$n$, 213, 239$n$, 250
Begley, Sharon, 185$n$
Behrman, Jere, 226$n$
Belisle, François J., 384$n$
Benoit, Emile, 590$n$
Bergsman, Joel, 520
Berlin Wall, 541
Bilateral aid, 168
Biological diversity, 600, 602
Birdsall, Nancy, 215$n$, 232$n$, 236$n$, 250, 535$n$, 558
Birth control, 47, 48, 94–95, 187
  Easterlin's supply-demand synthesis and, 202–204
  opposition to, 192
  in sub-Saharan Africa, 204–205
  *See also* Family planning
Birth licenses, 209
Birth rate
  age-specific, 37
  crude, 33, 34, 35, 39
  declines in, 46
**Black market, 298**
Blanchard, Olivier, 549$n$, 558
Bloom, David, 272$n$, 278
Blount, Jeb, 312$n$
Bokassa, Emperor Jean-Bedel, 569
Bolivia
  BancoSol of, 312
  inflation in, 285
  land reform in, 330
Bongaarts, John, 200$n$, 214
Bos, Eduard, 51$n$
Brady, Nicholas, 482
"Brain drain," 247–248
Branigin, William, 603$n$
Brazil
  agriculture in, 325
  coffee economy of, 179
  devaluation in, 476
  education in, 240
  government direction of economic development in, 179–182
  gross domestic investment and gross domestic saving in, 292
  growth and development in, 14, 15
  import-substitution industrialization (ISI) in, 180
  life expectancy in, 229
  merchandise export structure, 437
  merchandise trade in, 435
  natural resource reserves in, 355
  per capita GNP, 18
  population and labor force in, 274
  privatization in, 181–182
  Real Plan in, 181–182, 182$n$
  sectoral shares in, 389
  stagflation in, 181
Breastfeeding
  as natural contraceptive, 202, 225
  nutritional benefits of, 224–225
Brender, Adi, 272$n$, 278
Bretton Woods conference, 117, 135$n$, 469
Briscoe, John, 235$n$
Brown, Lester, 4$n$, 21, 189$n$, 336$n$, 598$n$, 609
Bruton, Henry, 150$n$
**Buddhist economics, 135–138, 136,** 587
  Sarvodaya Shramadana movement, 138–140, 512, 606
Budget deficits, financing, 295–296
**Buffer stocks, 332**
Bulatao, Rodolfo, 51$n$, 200$n$, 206$n$, 214, 215$n$
Bulgaria, 608
  centralized socialism in, 161

Bulow, Jeremy, 483, 483*n*, 487
**Burden of dependency, 40,** 51*n*
Burkina Faso, 561
   drought in, 573–574
   village work groups in, 345
Burton, Thomas, 237*n*
Burundi
   export commodities in, 563
   foreign aid to, 509
   tribal violence in, 566
Business saving, 305–306

## C

Calder, Kent, 535, 535*n*, 536*n*, 558
Caldwell, John, 49–51, 50*n*, 54, 204*n*
Caldwell's net intergenerational wealth flows, 49–51
Caldwell, Pat, 204*n*
Callaghy, Thomas, 565*n*, 582*n*, 586
Cameroon, 561
   deteriorating fiscal situation in, 579
Canada
   economy of, 4, 5
   as First World country, 10
   natural resource reserves in, 355
   population growth in, 32
Capital
   partial output elasticity of, 62, 63*n*
   substitution of labor for, 62–64
**Capital account,** 454–456, **454**
**Capital account balance, 455**
**Capital flight, 476**
Capital formation
   in modern sector, 105
   in public sector, 104–105
Capital goods, imports of, 99
Capital stock
   growth in, 66–67
   investment and growth in, under laissez–faire capitalism, 157, 158
Capital-intensive projects, 267–268
Capital–labor ratio, 61
   diminishing returns to, 106, 107
   in endogenous growth theory, 110–112
   increases in, 76
   in Lewis's two-sector model, 102
   Solow's model of, 70–74, 71*n*, 105–106
Capital-saving technologies, 314
Capitalism, radical critique of, 132–135
**Capitalist sector, 102**
   growth in, 103
**Capitalist surplus, 103,** 104
CARE (Cooperative for Assistance and Relief Everywhere), 504, 512

Caribbean
   agriculture in, 325
   developing nations of, 5–6
   education in, 240
   foreign aid to, 509
   foreign direct investment in, 490
   gross domestic investment and gross domestic saving in, 292
   health statistics, 230, 231
   land and water in, 375, 376
   life expectancy in, 229
   merchandise trade in, 435
   nutrition statistics for, 224, 225
   population and labor force in, 274
   renewable water resources in, 377
   returns to investment in education, 244
Carrington, Tim, 178*n*, 313*n*, 346*n*, 484*n*
Carroll, Paul, 472*n*
Carter, Jimmy, 279
Cassen, Robert, 504*n*, 515, 515*n*, 520
Catholic Relief Services, 512
Catholicism, influence of in Africa, 570
Catsambas, Thomas, 237*n*
Central African Republic, 569
Central American Common Market, 351
Central Asia. *See* Asia
Central bank, in market-friendly strategy of development, 524, 530, 547
Central European Free Trade Agreement, 607–608
**Centralized socialism, 160–162,** 539
   commitment to meeting basic needs, 167
   economic and political inequality, 541
   failure of Stalinist system, 541
   lack of market pricing, 540–541
   macroeconomic stability in, 167
   material balance planning, 540
   priority to economic growth, 539
   resource allocation in, 162–163
   transition to more market capitalist system, 161–162
Cereal grains, world consumption of, 358
Cernea, Michael, 512*n*, 520
Céspedes, Victor Hugo, 349*n*, 351*n*
Chad, 561, 562
   drought in, 573–574
   tribal violence in, 566
Chen, Kathy, 210*n*
Chenery, Hollis, 77*n*, 226*n*, 256*n*, 268*n*, 324*n*, 387, 387*n*, 397*n*, 416
Chernobyl, 555
Chhibber, Ajay, 178*n*
Chiang Kai-shek, 174

Child labor. *See* Labor
Children
  causes of mortality in, 220, 227, 241
  demand for
    consumer behavior model of, 193–201
    Easterlin's supply-demand synthesis, 201–204
  health education of, 234
  immunization of, 238
  importance of good nutrition for, 223
  preference for males, 228
  quality of, 194
  reduction of mortality in, 512
  stunting/wasting of, 222, 223–224, 225
  World Summit for, 238
Chile
  Allende regime in, 497
  devaluation in, 476
  privatization in, 410
Chiltelco, 497
China
  agriculture in, 324, 325
  average annual growth of GDP, 176
  average annual growth rate in gross domestic investment, 293
  birth control in, 208–210
  birth licenses, 209
  centralized socialism in, 160–162
  crude birth rate in, 34, 48, 209
  Cultural Revolution, 175
  disability-adjusted life years in, 231
  doctor/population ratio in, 228, 230
  economic growth in, 10
  education in, 240
  foreign aid to, 509
  foreign direct investment in, 491
  GATT and, 446
  government direction of economic development in, 174–177
  Great Leap Forward, 175, 209
  gross domestic investment and gross domestic saving in, 292
  health care in, 209
  health statistics, 230, 231
  human capital formation in, 12–13
  life expectancy in, 229
  Marriage Law of 1950, 209
  merchandise export structure, 437
  merchandise trade in, 435
  natural resource reserves in, 355
  nutrition statistics for, 224, 225
  "One Child Campaign," 209
  per capita GNP, 176
  population and labor force in, 274
  privatizing of state enterprises in, 176
  public health expenditures in, 229–230
  sectoral shares in, 389
  stunting of children in, 223, 224, 225
  total fertility rate in, 208
Chlorofluorocarbons (CFCs), 602
Chua-Eoan, Howard, 477$n$, 487
Chun Doo Hwan, General, 148
Classical economics, 167
Coale, Ansley, 47$n$, 54, 193, 193$n$, 194$n$
Cobb-Douglas production function, 63$n$
Coefficient of determination, 26–27, 27$n$
  adjusted, 28
Cold War, 502, 505, 600
Colombia
  merchandise export structure, 437
  sectoral shares in, 389
Colonization, in Africa, 561–563
Columbus, Christopher, 349
Command economy, 160–162
Commercial bank credit, loanable funds and, 297
Commodity indexes, 335
**Common markets, 444**
Commonwealth of Independent States (CIS), economic growth in, 538–548, 539$n$
*Communist Manifesto*, 132
**Comparative advantage, 398–399, 421, 431**
Competition
  in economic infrastructure development, 409–411
  promotion of, 408–409
Competitive exchange rate, 438–440
Competitive labor market, theory of, 252
  demand for labor, 252–254
  labor-market equilibrium, 255–256
  supply of labor, 254–255
Competitive rural labor market, 256–257
Congo, 561
**Consistent plan, 394**
**Constant opportunity costs, 430**
**Constant returns to scale, 61**
Consumer equilibrium, 196, 197
Consumer markets, in market-friendly development strategy, 542–543
Contraception. *See* Birth control
Convention on Biological Diversity, 602
Convention on Climate Change, 602
Convention on Desertification, 603
Convention on International Trade in Endangered Species, 603
Convention on the Law of the Seas, 602
Costa Rica, 601

agriculture in, 324, 325, 349
balance of payments account for, 458
bananas as export of, 350, 352
coffee as export of, 349
early history of, 349
economic growth in, 350–352
education in, 240
gross domestic investment and gross domestic saving in, 292
growth and development in, 14, 15
import-substitution industrialization in, 350–351
life expectancy in, 229
manufacturing in, 350–351
merchandise export structure, 437
merchandise trade in, 435
National Production Council of, 350
population and labor force in, 274
sectoral shares in, 389
social indicators in, 349
United Fruit Company in, 350
Côte d'Ivoire
agricultural price subsidies in, 338–339
deteriorating fiscal situation in, 579
export commodities in, 563
Cowley, Geoffrey, 380$n$
**Crawling peg, 469,** 471–472
Credit
agricultural policy reform and, 343–344
extension of to women, 313
improving popular access to, 311–313
loans to the poor, 312, 313
**Credit cooperative, 305**
Credit markets
commercial banks, 297
informal, 299–300
**Credits, 452**
Crimmins, Eileen, 201$n$
Crocker, Chester, 584, 584$n$
Crosswell, Michael, 123$n$, 146
**Crude birth rate, 33,** 35, 39
in China, 34, 209
**Crude death rate, 33,** 35
**Crude rate of natural increase, 33**
Cuba
centralized socialism in, 161
land reform in, 330
Cuddington, John, 473$n$, 474$n$, 475$n$, 487
Cultural Revolution (China), 175
Curative medicine, 232, 233, 527
Currency
in global integration, 547–548
overvalued, 338, 439
**Currency boards, 467–468, 467**

**Current account,** 452–454, **452**
**Current account balance, 454**
**Customs unions, 444**
Czech Republic, 608
foreign direct investment in, 491
privatization in, 546
Czechoslovakia, centralized socialism in, 161

# D

Daly, Herman, 140–143, 140$n$, 142$n$, 146
Danaher, Kevin, 511$n$, 583$n$
Dasgupta, Partha, 169$n$, 173
*Das Kapital*, 132
Datta-Chaudhuri, Mrinal, 172$n$, 174
Davies, Omar, 384$n$, 385$n$
Davis, Kingsley, 48$n$, 54
Death rate
age-specific, 35–37
crude, 33–34
declines in, 46
low-level equilibrium trap and, 93
**Debits, 452**
**Debt buybacks, 482**
Debt crisis, 451, 476–482, 510
*See also* External debt problem
**Debt finance, 473**
Debt ratios, 481
**Debt rescheduling, 476**
**Debt-for-equity swaps, 482**
**Debt-for-nature swaps, 482**
**Debt-service ratios, 480**
Decentralization, in Africa, 581–582
Deforestation, 336, 359–360
Demand
for children, 193–198
determinants of, 198–199
evidence from Mexico, 199–201
relative status, 199
Easterlin's supply-demand synthesis, 201–204
measures to reduce for sustainable development, 373
Demilitarization, 600–601
Democracy, role of in promoting economic growth, 169
Democratic Republic of Germany, 541
centralized socialism in, 161
**Demographic transition, 43–44**
in Africa, 47–49, 570
fertility declines in, 214
in LDCs, 47–49
population growth in, 186–187, 192
Western experience, 44

**Demographic transition,** *(continued)*
    Malthusian population theory, 44–45
    stages of, 45–47
Deng Xiaoping, 175
Denmark, as official development assistance donor, 507
Deolalikar, Anil, 226$n$
**Depauperization,** 120–123, **121,** 526–527
    agricultural demand-led industrialization, 122–123
    global development and, 588–589
    growth with equity, 121–122
Dependent variable, 23
**Depreciation, 306, 364, 459**
**Derived growth sectors, 101**
Desertification, 603
**Devaluation, 469**
**Developed countries (DCs), 9**
    factor endowments theory of trade in, 432
    military expenditures in, 591–596
    population growth in, 32, 35–37
Development project, net present value criterion for, 307–311
**Devolution, 168**
Diarrheal diseases, 227
Diouf, Abdioul, 565
**Dirigism, 157**
**Disability-adjusted life years (DALYs), 230–231**
Diwan, Ishac, 473$n$, 487
Doctor/population ratio, in less developed countries, 228–229, 230
Doe, Samuel, 503
*Does Aid Work?*, 515
Domar, Evsey, 64$n$
**Domestic-content legislation, 445**
Domestic investment
    measures to promote, 313–315
    sources of funds for, 288
        basic macroeconomic identity, 288–290
        foreign savings, 291
        gross domestic investment and growth in national output, 291–292, 293
Domestic markets, in market-friendly development strategy, 524–526
Domestic producers, subsidies to, 405
Domestic savings
    business saving, 305–306
    constraints on in LDCs, 302
        government (public) savings, 306–307
        household savings, 302–305

Dornbusch, Rudiger, 438$n$, 443$n$, 450, 549$n$, 558
Drip systems, 380
Drought, in Africa, 573–574
Drug trade, 589
Drugs, purchase of at competitive prices, 237
Dummy variable, 87$n$
Durning, Alan, 21
**Dutch disease,** 361, 363, 363$n$, **365**
    avoiding, 368–369
    evidence from Mexico, 366–368
    illustration of, 365–366
    real and nominal exchange rates, 363–365

# E

Earle, John S., 554$n$
Earth Summit, 3, 602
East Asia. *See* Asia
*East Asian Miracle: Economic Growth and Public Policy*, 532
East Germany. *See* Democratic Republic of Germany
*Eastasia Edge, The*, 535
Easterlin, Richard, 201$n$
Easterlin's supply-demand synthesis of declines in fertility, 201–205
Eaton, Jonathan, 483$n$
Economic assistance, in global development, 605–606
**Economic development, 8**
    alternative approaches to
        Adelman's depauperization, 120–123, 526–527, 588–589
        basic needs approach, 123–129
        Daly's steady-state economics, 140–143
        laissez-faire capitalism, 156–157
        radical critique, 132–135
        Schumacher's Buddhist economics, 135–140
    countries classified by income group, 11
    decrease in demand for children and, 197–198
    human capital formation and, 220–222
    indicators of, 9
        characteristics of developing economies, 11–14
        classification of nations, 9–11
        differences in development, 14–17
        gender equity, 17
        per capita income and

development, 18–19
market-friendly strategy of, 143, 523–531
Marxist view of, 192
slippage in, 11
structural changes as part of, 12
urban bias in policies, 120
**Economic efficiency, 61***n*
**Economic growth, 6**
  average annual rate of, 479
  constraints on, foreign exchange and human capital, 76–78
  countries classified by income group, 11
  distribution of income and, 118–120
  equity and, 121–123
  gross domestic product and gross national product, 7–8
  income inequality and, 130–131
  incremental capital–output ratios and, 287–288
  limited income inequality and, 170
  market capitalism and, 170
  military spending and, 590*n*
  models of
    endogenous growth theory, 109–113
    Harrod-Domar growth model, 64–67, 82–84
    Lewis's two-sector model, 101–105
    low-level equilibrium trap, 89–96
    policy implications, 75–76
    saving rate and distribution of income, 68–70, 100
    Solow's factor substitution, 70–74
    take-off into self-sustaining growth, 96–100
  natural resources and, 354–369
  physical capital deepening and, 84–88
  political stability and, 170
  poverty and, 187–190
  savings rate and, 286–287
  in severely indebted LDCs, 478
  sources of output growth, 6–7
  in steady-state economy, 140–143
  sustaining, 105–106
    variable population growth, 106–107
  undernutrition and, 225
**Economic infrastructure, 98–99, 103, 409–410**
  investment in, 409–413
Economic integration, 583
Economic migration, 268–272
Economic policy, balance of payments deficits and, 465–466
Economic reform, in Third World countries, 160
Economic regulation, 163
  externalities, 163–165
  labor markets, 165–166
Economic systems
  centralized socialism, 160–162
  choice of, 169–171
  laissez-faire capitalism, 156–157
  managed (authoritarian) capitalism, 158–160
Economic theories, statistical testing of, 22–30
Economic transition, from centralized socialism to market capitalism, 161–162
**Economies of scale, 7, 7***n*
Economy
  growing, 97
  pre-take-off, 97
  sectoral linkages within, 392–398
  take-off, 97
  traditional, 97
Education, 120, 238
  in Africa, 575–576
  agricultural policy reform and, 344
  in basic needs approach, 128
  benefits of, 240–241
  "brain drain" and, 247–248
  costs of, 241–242
  in depauperization, 121
  economic mobility of females and, 196
  educational policy reform, 245–248
  employment policies and, 275
  entrepreneurship and, 246–247
  high attrition rates in, 239, 240
  as human capital investment, 239–240
  in less-developed countries, 166–167, 239, 240
  in market-friendly development strategy, 527
  opportunity cost of, 242
  primary, 241–242
  private and social rates of return of, 242–245
  research agenda for, 248
  returns to, 242–245
  selected statistics on, 239, 240
  vocational training as, 247
Edwards, Sebastian, 438*n*, 450
**Effective labor, 108–109, 108**
**Effective rate of tariff protection (ERP), 401–403, 401**
Efficiency wage theory, 124*n*, 257–258
Egypt
  agriculture, 280

Egypt, *(continued)*
  agriculture in, 325
  early history, 278–279
  economic development, 279–280
  education in, 240
  gross domestic investment and gross domestic saving in, 292
  growth and development in, 14, 15
  Islamic fundamentalism, 281
  Israeli-Egyptian peace treaty, 279
  life expectancy in, 229
  merchandise export structure, 437
  merchandise trade in, 435
  nationalism, 279
  official development assistance, 279
  population and labor force in, 274
  sectoral shares in, 389
  Six-Day War, 279
  strategic location, 279
  structural adjustment, 280
  Suez Canal, 279
Ehrenberg, Ronald G., 250, 252$n$
Elephants, killing of, 603
**Employed, 261**
Employment, 251–252, 407–408
  full, **264**
  generation of in basic needs approach, 124–127
  policies to promote, 272–273
    education, 275
    labor-market policy, 273–275
    macroeconomic policy, 275
  under managed capitalism, 159
  *See also* Underemployment; Unemployment
Endangered species, 603
Endogenous growth theory, 109–113
Energy consumption, per capital income and, 86
Engel, Ernst, 334
**Entrepreneur, 6**
**Entrepreneurship,** 246–247, **246**
**Entropy, 140–141**
Environmental issues, 3, 4, 353–354
  biological diversity, 600
  global development and, 596–600, 606
  global warming, 600
  in market-friendly development strategy, 524
  *See also* Natural resources
Equity
  economic growth with, 121–122
  in health care, 233, 233$n$, 235–236
  in steady-state economy, 142

**Equity finance, 473**
Equity markets, 547
Error term, 23, 25–26
*Essay on the Principle of Population,* 44–45
Ethiopia, export commodities in, 563
Europe
  agriculture in, 325
  average income in, 13
  demographic transition in, 46–47
  Eastern, 6, 135
    centralized socialism in, 161, 539–541
    economic reforms in, 4
    economic transition, 541–548
      financial intermediation, 547
      global integration, 547–548
      labor market, 543–545
      privatization, 545–547
      use of consumer markets, 542–543
    health statistics, 230, 231
    move toward market capitalism in, 169
    nutrition statistics for, 224
  education in, 240
  fertilizer use in, 597
  foreign aid to, 509
  gross domestic investment and gross domestic saving in, 292
  life expectancy in, 229
  merchandise trade in, 435
  population and labor force in, 274
  post–World War II economic reconstruction in, 59–60
  renewable water resources in, 377
  returns to investment in education, 244
**Ex ante, 393**
**Ex post, 392**
**Exchange controls,** 463–465, **463**
Exchange rates, 118–119
  adjustable, 469
  choosing a system, 471–472
  competitive, 438–440
  flexible exchange rate system, 458–459
  hybrid systems, 469
  market equilibrium, 461–462
    fixed exchange rates, 462–466, 579–580
    fixed versus flexible exchange rates, 466–468
    flexible exchange rates, 462, 463
    inflation-depreciation cycle, 468–469
  present arrangements, 469–471
  real and nominal, 363–365
Exclusive economic zones, 599
Expanded Programme on Immunization, 238

Expansionary fiscal and monetary
    policies, 264–266
Expectant mothers, health care services
    for, 220
Export agriculture, 564, 573
Export commodities, in Africa, 563
**Export expansion, 407,** 436–438, **437**
    achieving success with, 441–442
    competitive exchange rate, 438–440
    experience with import substitution, 438
    in East Asia, 537–538
    shift to, 438
Export subsidies, 440, 441
**Export tax,** 338
    on natural resource-intensive products,
        360–362
**Extensive growth, 161**
External debt problem, 473
    debt crisis and aftermath, 476
        IMF medicine, 476–479
        increase in external debt, 479–482
    less-developed country debt, 473–475
    resolving, 482–484
    selected statistics on, 480
**Externalities, 163**
    in laissez-faire capitalism, 157
    in market-friendly development
        strategy, 525
    negative, 163–165
    positive, 165

## F

**Factor endowments theory of trade,**
    422–425, **425,** 425n
Factor mobility, 425–427, 528–529
Factor price ratios, 124–127
Factor substitution, 62–64
    isoquants for, 63
    least-cost factor combinations, 124–127
    in microeconomic explanations of
        unemployment, 268
    Solow's model of, 70–74
Family planning, 187
    *See also* Birth control
**Family planning programs (FFP),**
    **206–207,** 214–215
Famine, in Africa, 575
**Farm gate prices,** 337
Farming. *See* Agriculture
Federal Republic of Germany, 541
Federal Reserve, 475
**Female secondary school enrollment
    rate, 12**

Females
    agricultural opportunities for, 345–346
    economic mobility of, 196
    education of as determinant of fertility,
        214–215, 241
    longer life expectancy of, 228, 229
    market-friendly development strategy
        and opportunities for, 529
    rate of return of education of, 245
Fertility
    determinants of, 214–218
    Easterlin's supply-demand synthesis
        and, 201–204
    effect of education on, 241
    female education as determinant of,
        214–215
    high
        and age structure of society, 190
        related to high rates of infant and
            child mortality, 228
    measures of, 34, 37–39
    natural, 202
    net intergenerational wealth flows and,
        49–51
    per capita income and, 95–96
    preconditions for sustained decline in,
        193
Fertilizer, use of, 597, 598
Field, Alfred, 401n, 425n, 433n, 450
**Financial capital, 284**
    interest rates and, 313–314
    money and, 284–286
**Financial intermediation,** 101, 294–295, **294**
    efficiencies in, 296–298
    financing government budget deficits,
        295–296
    inflation and market for loanable funds,
        300–302
    informal credit markets, 299–300
    interest rate ceilings, 298–299
    loanable funds and, 295
    for small savers and borrowers, 315
Findlay, Ronald, 384n
Finland
    merchandise export structure, 437
    sectoral shares in, 389
First International Population Conference,
    187, 192, 506
**First World, 10**
Fiscal policy, expansionary, 264–266
Fishing, 357–358
Fishlow, Albert, 531, 531n, 558
**Fixed exchange rate system,** 462–463, **462,**
    471

**Fixed exchange rate system,** *(continued)*
   balance of payments deficits and economic policy, 465–466
   borrowing from the IMF, 465
   compared to flexible exchange rates, 466–469
   exchange controls, 463–465
   inflation-depreciation cycle, 468–469
**Fixed-coefficients production function, 60–62,** 83
   Isoquants for, 62
**Flexible exchange rate system, 458–459,** 462, 463, 472
   compared to fixed exchange rate, 466–469
   inflation-depreciation cycle, 468–469
Food
   demand for, 331–332
   income inelasticity of, 334–336
   production of and population growth, 597–599
   safe preparation of, 226
Food and Agriculture Organization (FAO), 512
**Food aid,** 166, **338,** 504
Food fortification, 226
Food subsidy programs, 226
Fookes, Geoffrey, 496*n*
**Force ratio, 594,** 596
Foreign aid, 498–499
   assessing effectiveness of, 514–515
   brief history of, 505–509
   case against, 501
      criticisms from the left, 502–505
      criticisms from the right, 502
      questioning moral basis, 501–502
   case for, 499
      economic basis, 500–501
      moral basis, 499–500
   donors of, 507
   multilateral aid agencies, 510
      International Monetary Fund, 510
      nongovernmental organizations, 512–514
      United Nations agencies, 511–512
      World Bank, 510–511
   radical critique of, 134–135, 502–505
   reforms in, 515–517
**Foreign direct investment, 454,** 490–492, **490**
   in Africa, 576–577
   less developed countries and, 494
      advantages of FDI, 494–495
      potential disadvantages of FDI, 495–497
   in market-friendly development strategy, 529
   transnational corporations, 492–494
      potential disadvantages of FDI for, 497–498
Foreign exchange, 76–78
   demand for, 459–460
   supply of, 460–461
Foreign exchange transactions, international tax on, 605
**Foreign portfolio investment, 455**
Foreign saving, 291
Forestry, 359–360
Forward integration, 492–493
Foster, Susan, 237*n*
Four Tigers, 532, 537
**Fourth World, 11**
France
   African colonization by, 562
   mortality in, 47
   as official development assistance donor, 507
   structural adjustment approach to African development agenda, 577–582
   support for dictatorial African governments, 569
Free enterprise, radical critique of, 132–135
Free market view of population growth and economic development, 192
Free trade, 398–399
   in laissez-faire capitalism, 157
**Free trade area, 444**
Free-rider problem, 483
French, Hilary, 602, 602*n*, 603*n*, 609
French West Africa, 562
**Frictionally unemployed, 264**
Friedland, Jonathan, 113*n*
Friedrich, Otto, 190*n*
Froyen, Richard, 64*n*
Frydman, Roman, 554*n*, 558
**Full employment, 264**
   in agricultural off-season, 345
**Fundamental equation of Solow model, 72–73**

## G

G-7 nations, 482
Gabon, 561
   foreign aid to, 509
Gains from trade. *See* Trade
Gambia, The, 561
   export commodities in, 563

Gardner, H. Stephen, 174n, 175n
GATT. *See* General Agreement on Tariffs and Trade (GATT)
Gaud, William, 326n
Gavin, Michael, 511n, 520
Gender equity, 17
General Agreement on Tariffs and Trade (GATT), 3, 59n, 134
　Kennedy Round, 444
　official development assistance and, 505
　Tokyo Round, 444
　trade liberalization and, 443–445
　Uruguay Round, 123, 444
child labor, 259
**Generalized System of Preferences, 444–445**
Germany
　African colonization by, 562
　East, 541
　mortality in, 47
　as official development assistance donor, 507
Gersovitz, Mark, 319
Ghana
　agriculture in, 325
　diversification of agricultural production in, 513
　education in, 240
　export commodities in, 563
　exports of, 177
　GDP, 178
　GNP, 178
　government direction of economic development in, 177–178
　gross domestic investment and gross domestic saving in, 292
　growth and development in, 14, 15
　life expectancy in, 229
　merchandise export structure, 437
　merchandise trade in, 435
　political stability in, 566–567
　population and labor force in, 274
　Rawlings Economic Recovery Program, 178
　sectoral shares in, 389
　subsistence farming in, 13–14
　tribal violence in, 566
Gillis, Malcolm, 363n
**Glastnost, 541**
Glewwe, Paul, 16n, 21, 246n
Global Demilitarization Fund, 601
Global development, 587–588
　agenda for, 603–604
　　economic assistance, 605–606

　　environment, 606
　　finance, 605
　　reforming the international order, 607–608
　　regional groups, 604
　　security, 606–607
　　trade, 604–605
　defining, 588–589
　international cooperation, 600
　　natural resources and environmental agreements, 602–603
　　security agreements, 600–601
　military spending, 590–596
　natural resources and the environment, 596–600
Global industrial integration, 398–407, 547–548
Global warming, 600, 602
GOBI, 512
Gold Coast, 563
　*See also* Ghana
González-Vega, Claudio, 349n, 351n
GOSPLAN, 540
Goulet, Denis, 139n, 146
Government
　role of in economic development, 162
　　economic regulation, 163
　　　externalities, 163–165
　　　labor markets, 165–166
　　income maintenance and redistribution, 166–167
　　macroeconomic stability, 167
　　policy coordination, 168–169
　　resource allocation, 162–163
　wages paid by, 266–267
**Government procurement policies, 445**
Government saving, 306–307
Grameen Bank, 312
Great Leap Forward (China), 175, 209
**Green Revolution,** 99, 324, 326, 326n, 327, 332–333, **332**, 357
　in Africa, 333, 574–575
Gregory, Paul R., 174, 416n, 550n, 552n, 558
Griffin, Keith, 133n, 134n, 135n, 146
Grootaert, Christiaan, 478n
Gross domestic investment (GDI), 291–293
　average annual growth rates in, 293
**Gross Domestic Product (GDP),** 7–8, **7**
　agriculture as percentage of, 324–325
　health expenditures in, 229–230
Gross domestic saving (GDS), 70n, 291–293, 291n
Grossman, Gene, 89n, 110n, 112n, 116

**Gross National Product (GNP),** 7–8, **7**
  of less developed countries, 84*n*, 86
  as measure of economic development or average standard of living, 11–12, 14–15
  United Nations International Comparison Programme, 15–16
"Groupements Naam," 345
**Growing economy, 97**
Growth
  extensive, 161
  intensive, 161
Guilkey, David, 199*n*, 201*n*
Guinea-Bissau, foreign aid to, 509
Gulf War, 591, 594
Gurley, John, 133*n*, 134*n*, 135*n*, 146

## H

Habib, Masooma, 250
Hansen, Alvin, 186*n*
Hardin, Garrett, 146
Hare, Paul G., 551*n*
Haiti, Duvalier rule of, 160
Harrison, Glenn, 447*n*
Harrod-Domar growth model, 64–67, 430*n*
  numerical example of, 82–84
Harrod, Roy, 64*n*
Haub, Carl, 31
Health, 227
  agricultural policy reform and, 344
  conditions in LDCs, 227–231
  health-care policy, 231–232
    integrated health-care system, 236–238
    need for reform, 232–233
    recommendations, 233–236
  *See also* Medicine
Health-care services, 120
  in Africa, 575–576
  in basic needs approach, 128
  for expectant mothers, 220, 221
  expenditures on as share of GDP, 229–230
  for infants, 215
  as positive externality, 165
  primary, 236–238
Heckscher-Ohlin theory of trade. *See* Factor endowments theory of trade
Heilbroner, Robert, 54, 132*n*, 146
Helpman, Elhanan, 89*n*, 110*n*, 112*n*, 116
Herbst, Jeffrey, 565*n*, 581*n*
Herz, Barbara, 245*n*, 250
Hess, Peter, 146*n*, 199*n*, 201*n*, 204*n*, 590*n*

Hewitt, Daniel, 594*n*
**High-income economies,** 10, **11**
Higher education
  resources used for, 247
  social rate of return for, 244
  *See also* Education
HIV infection, in Africa, 575–576
Hofheinz, Roy, 535, 535*n*, 536*n*, 558
Hollerbach, Paula, 200*n*, 214
Holman, Richard, 546*n*, 555*n*
Holmes, Kim, 169*n*
Honduras
  merchandise export structure, 437
  sectoral shares in, 389
Hong Kong, 532, 537
**Horizontal integration, 493**
Household, as agricultural producer, 328–329
Household saving, 303–304
  demographic factors, 302–303
  income effects, 303–304
  instruments for, 305
  return to saving, 304–305
Human capital, 76–78
  education as investment in, 239–240
  in market-friendly development strategy, 526–528
Human capital formation, 219
  in basic needs approach, 128
  in depauperization, 121–122
  economic development and, 220–222
  in market-friendly development strategy, 534–535
**Human Development Index (HDI),** 16–17
Human security, versus national security, 589
Hungary, 548, 550–551, 608
  centralized socialism in, 161
  development indicators in, 549
  foreign direct investment in, 491
  New Economic Mechanism in, 550
Husain, Ishrat, 473*n*, 487
Hybrid exchange rate systems, 469

## I

Illiteracy, in less-developed countries, 239, 240
Immunization, programs for, 234
**Imperialism, 133**
**Import quota, 403–405**
**Import subsidy, 338**
**Import substitution,** 399–400, **399, 436**
  evaluation of, 405–407

experience with, 438
nominal and effective tariff rates, 401–403
quotas, 403–405
subsidies to domestic producers, 405
tariffs, 401
Import-substitution industrialization (ISI), 180, 350–351
**Income, 284**
distribution of, 68–70
economic growth and, 118–120
in laissez-faire capitalism, 156
trade and, 431–432
maintenance of, 166–167
per capita, 18–19, 23, 131
permanent, 303
redistribution of, 166–167
shares of received by lowest 40 percent of population (selected countries), 131
transitory, 303
**Income effect, 254**
Income inequality
economic growth and, 130–131, 170
optimal degree of, 170
**Increasing opportunity costs, 430**
**Increasing returns to scale, 7, 7n**
**Incremental capital-output ratio, 287–288, 287**
Independent variable, 23
India
agriculture in, 325
average annual growth rate in gross domestic investment, 293
economic growth in, 10
economic nationalism, 418
economic progress, 417
economic reforms, 417, 418
education in, 240
foreign aid to, 509
foreign direct investment in, 491
gross domestic investment and gross domestic saving in, 292
health statistics, 230, 231
import substitution policies, 416, 418
life expectancy in, 229
merchandise export structure, 437
merchandise trade in, 435
nationalized industries, 416–417
nutritional statistics for, 224, 225
population and labor force in, 274
privatization, 418
sectoral shares in, 389
self-government, 416
Indifference mapping, 195

for demand for children, 196–198
Indonesia, 532, 537
foreign direct investment in, 491
natural resource reserves in, 356
Industrial policy, of managed capitalism, 159–160
Industrial Revolution, 44, 99
Industrialization, in LDCs, 120
Industry, integration of with agriculture, 327
Industry and services, 387–388
global industrial integration, 398
free trade, 398–399
import substitution, 399–407
industrial sector, 388–390
policy issues, 407
investment in economic infrastructure, 409–410
competition and privatization, 410–411
local participation, 411–412
sound management, 410
regulation of industry, 407
competition, 408–409
employment and working conditions, 407–408
pollution, 409
public production of industry and services, 391–392
sectoral linkages within an economy, 392
input-output model, 392–398
service sector, 390
informal, 390–391
modern, 391
Inequality, political and economic, 541
**Infant industries, 159**
**Infant-industry strategy, 400, 407**
**Infant mortality rate (IMR), 12, 215–218**
Infants
immunization rate for, 230
importance of nutrition for, 222
Inflation, 100
effect of on loanable funds market, 300–302
in market-friendly strategy of development, 524
overexpansion of money supply and, 266, 285
real rate of interest and, 314
Inflation-depreciation cycle, 468–469
**Informal credit markets, 299–300, 299**
Informal service sector, 390–391
Infrastructure
agricultural policy reform and, 344

Infrastructure, *(continued)*
    investments in, 158, 500
**Input-output analysis,** 392–394, **392**
    change in final demands, 397
    current uses of, 397–398
    plan feasibility, 395–397
    sectoral consistency with, 394–395
Input-output relationships, 395
    following a change in final demand for agricultural output, 396
**Intensive growth, 161**
Inter-American Development Bank, 511
Intercept term, 23
**Interest rate ceilings,** 298–299, **298**
Interest rates, financial capital and, 313–314
**Intermediate technology, 137**
**Internal rate of return (IRR), 243**
International Bank for Reconstruction and Development, 59, 59$n$, 505
    *See also* World Bank
International Centre for Settlement of Investment Disputes (ICSID), 511$n$
International Debt Discount Corporation, 483
International Debt Facility, 483
International development agencies, 168
International Development Association (IDA), 511
International factor mobility, 425–427
International Finance Corporation (IFC), 511, 605
International integration, 528–529
International Labour Organization (ILO), 123, 512
    current employment prospects in LDCs, 252
International Monetary Fund (IMF), 59$n$, 134, 178
    borrowing from, 465
    establishment of, 135$n$
    exchange rate arrangements of member countries, 469–471
    market-friendly development strategy of, 157
    official development assistance by, 505, 510
    prescription for solving international debt crisis, 476–479
    Special Drawing Rights, 456, 456$n$
    structural adjustment policy of, 577–582
International monetary system, 117, 134, 134$n$
International order, reformation of, 607–608
International Planned Parenthood Federation, 207, 512
International Telephone & Telegraph (ITT), 497
**International terms of trade,** 427–430, **428**
Invisible trade, 454
**Involuntary unemployment, 256**
Iodine deficiency, 223, 234
Iran, Islamic fundamentalism in, 99
Iron deficiency, 223
Irrigation, 328
Irwin, Douglas, 443$n$
Irwin, Michael, 511$n$
Isenman, Paul, 16$n$
Islam, influence of in Africa, 570
Islamic fundamentalism, 281
**Isoquant, 61**
Israel, foreign aid to, 509
Israeli-Egyptian peace treaty, 279, 280
Italy, as official development assistance donor, 507
Ivory, ban on commercial trade in, 603
Ivory Coast. *See* Côte d'Ivoire

# J

Jacoby, Haran, 246$n$
*Jaebol*, 149
Jamaica, 383–384
    agricultural sector, 384–385
    bauxite-alumina industry, 385
    budget deficits, 385
    economic boom, 384
    foreign investment, 384
    loan agreements with IMF, 386
    real gross domestic product, 384
    socialism in, 385
    tourism, 386
Japan
    economic growth in, 69–70
    economy of, 4, 5
    expansion of labor-intensive manufactured exports in, 122
    fertility rate in, 39
    as First World country, 10
    managed capitalism in, 159–160
    merchandise export structure, 437
    as official development assistance donor, 507
    population growth in, 32
    post-World War II economic reconstruction in, 59–60
    relations with South Korea, 146–147, 148–149
    saving rate in, 69–70
    sectoral shares in, 388, 389

Jayewardne, J. R., 152
Jingneng, Li, 208n, 214
**Joint ventures, 497**

# K

Kaldor model of savings rate and distribution of income, 68–70, 100, 158, 303
Kaldor, Nicholas, 68, 68n, 81
Kalish, Susan, 208n
Kaplan, Robert, 559, 559n
Kelley, Allen, 191, 191n, 214
Kenen, Peter, 483, 483n, 487
Kenya
   crude birth rate in, 48
   export commodities in, 563
Keyfitz, Nathan, 208n, 214
Keynesian economics, 167
Khmer Rouge, 99
Khomeini, Ayatollah, 99
**Knife-edge problem, 67,** 430n
   Solow's solution to, 70–74
Knodel, John, 47n, 54
Koch, Kathy, 503n
Korea
   Japanese relations with, 146–147, 148–149
   See also South Korea
Korean War, 147
Krueger, Anne, 160, 160n, 174, 337n
Krugman, Paul, 538, 538n, 549n, 558
Kuchma, Leonid, 555
Kuwait
   military burden in, 594
   as official development assistance donor, 507

# L

Labor
   child, 259–260
   demand for, 252–254
   migration of, 268–272
   partial output elasticity of, 62, 63n
   as producer, 258–259
   substitution of capital for, 62–64
   supply of, 254–255
   See also Competitive labor market, theory of
**Labor force, 261**
   growth rate of, 66–67, 75, 91–92, 93, 251
   natural growth rate in, 67, 69, 75
   warranted growth rate in, 67
Labor legislation, 408

**Labor market**
   in developing countries, 256
      modern-sector employment, 260–261
      rural labor markets, 256
         competitive rural labor market, 256–257
         labor as producer, 258–259
         surplus labor models, 257–258
      urban informal labor markets, 259–260
   in market-friendly development strategy, 543–545
   policies to promote employment, 272–275
Labor productivity, growth in, 108–109, 110
Labor unions, 267
Labor-intensive manufactured exports, expansion of, 122
Labor-intensive technologies, 314
Labor-market equilibrium, 255–256
Lachicha, Eduardo, 272n
**Laissez-faire capitalism, 156–157, 156**
   externalities in, 163–165
   income maintenance and redistribution in, 166–167
   policy coordination in, 168–169
   public goods in, 162–163
Land, access to fertile, 336, 342–343
Land redistribution, 128
Land reform, 121, 329–330
Laos, crude birth rate in, 48
Lapham, Robert J., 215n
Larrabee, Stephen, 555n
**Latifundias, 329**
Latin America
   agriculture in, 325, 327–330
   birth rates in, 48, 49
   crawling peg used in controlling inflation, 469
   death rates in, 48, 49
   debt problem in, 483
   deforestation in, 359–360
   demographic transition in, 47–49
   developing economies of, 13, 60
   developing nations of, 5–6
   economic liberalization in, 307
   economic progress of, 187
   education in, 240
   fertilizer use in, 597
   foreign aid to, 505, 509
   foreign direct investment in, 490
   gross domestic investment and gross domestic saving in, 292
   health statistics, 230, 231

Latin America, *(continued)*
  inflation in, 469
  land and water in, 375, 376
  life expectancy in, 229
  life expectancy and infant mortality in, 349*n*
  merchandise trade in, 435
  military expenditures in, 595
  nutrition statistics, 224, 225
  population and labor force in, 274
  renewable water resources in, 377
  returns to investment in education, 244
Law of the Seas, 599, 602
Layard, Richard, 549*n*, 558
Lead exposure, as health hazard, 370
Least squares criterion, 26, 28
Least-cost factor combinations, 124–127
Lee, Ronald, 200*n*, 214
Leechor, Chad, 178*n*
Leibenstein, Harvey, 199*n*, 257*n*
Leipziger, Danny, 123*n*
Lenin, Vladimir, 133
Leontief, Wassily W., 392, 392*n*
Lesotho, political stability in, 566, 568
**Less developed countries (LDCs), 4, 9**
  agriculture in, 323–326, 327–336, 336–343
  crude birth rates in, 48–49
  crude death rates in, 48–49
  death rates in, 47
  debt crisis and recovery in, 451, 473–484
  defense and military spending in, 591, 592–594
  demographic transition in, 47–49
  determinants of fertility in, 217–218
  devolution in, 168–169
  disease control in, 47
  domestic saving constraints in, 302–307
  economic growth in, 12–14, 15, 479
  education in, 166–167, 239, 240
  employment in, 251–252
  endogenous growth theory and, 111
  export expansion in, 436–442
  external debt in, 473–484
  factor endowments theory of trade in, 432
  foreign direct investment in, 494–498
  foreign saving, in, 291
  GATT and trade liberalization, 443–445
  gross domestic investment and growth in national output, 291–293
  health care in, 166–167
  health care reform in, 232–233, 236–238
  health conditions in, 227–231, 238
  incremental capital-output ratios in, 287–288
  industrialization in, 120
  labor force growth in, 251
  literacy and numeracy in, 246
  low-level equilibrium trap in, 93
  net present value criterion for development projects in, 307–311
  nutrient disorders in, 222–223
  per capita GNPs of, 84*n*, 86
  policy coordination in, 168–169
  population growth in, 32–34, 186
    cycle of poverty and rapid population growth, 187–190
    historical setting, 186–187
  population and labor force in, 273, 274
  population momentum in, 42–43
  preference for male children in, 228
  radical economists' view of, 134
  research agenda for universities in, 248
  sanitation in, 380
  sustainable development in, 376–381
  trade deficits in, 291
  trade strategy implementation in, 442–443
  unemployment in, 261, 262
Levi Strauss, 498
Lewis, W. Arthur, 101–102, 102*n*, 116, 117, 117*n*
Lewis's two-sector model of economic development, 101–102, 129
  agriculture and food prices in, 119
  growth of modern sector, 103
  policy implications, 103–105
  surplus labor in, 257
Liberia, 562
  dysfunctional government in, 566
  economic corruption in, 503
Liese, Bernhard, 235*n*
**Life cycle theory, 303**
**Life expectancy at birth, 36–37**
  perception of, 232
  selected statistics, 229
  as sign of human capital formation, 220
Lima, water and sewer usage in, 235
Line of best fit, 26
Literacy, 246
Loanable funds
  commercial bank credit and, 297
  demand and supply of, 118–119
  effect of inflation on, 300–302
  financial intermediation and, 295
Logging, 359
  *See also* Deforestation; Forestry

**Low-income economies,** 10, **11**
**Low-level equilibrium trap, 89–90,** 94, 106–107*n*
  escaping, 92–96
  growth rate of labor, 91–92, 93
  growth rate of physical capital, 90–91
Lutz, Wolfgang, 31–32, 32*n*, 54

## M

MacKenzie, G. A., 315*n*
Macroeconomic identity, 65*n*
Macroeconomic policy, employment and, 275
Macroeconomic stability, 167
  in market-friendly development strategy, 524, 536–537
  as part of structural adjustment approach, 578–580
Macrostability, 141–142
Macy, Joanna, 139*n*, 140*n*
Mahaweli Ganga Development Scheme, 152
Maizels, Alfred, 502*n*
Malaria, 227, 235
Malawi
  export commodities in, 563
  political stability in, 566, 568
Malaysia, 532, 537
  foreign direct investment in, 491
Males, life expectancy of, 228, 229
Mali, 561, 562
  drought in, 573–574
  population pyramid for, 41, 42
  tribal violence in, 566
**Malnutrition, 222**
  summary statistics on, 223–224, 225
  *See also* Nutrition
Malthus, Thomas, 4–5, 32
Malthusian population theory, 44–45, 45*n*
**Managed capitalism, 158**
  industrial policy or sectoral development, 159–160
  promoting investment and growth, 158
  providing basic needs, 158–159
  resource allocation in, 163
**Managed float, 469**
Management, of public infrastructure projects, 410
Manley, Michael, 385, 386
Mao Zedong, Chairman, 174–175
**Marginal rate of factor substitution, 124,** 124–127
**Marginal rate of substitution, 196**

Marginal revenue product of labor, 253*n*
Market capitalism
  as economic system, 169
  transition of centralized socialism to, 161–162, 169
Market economies
  health statistics, 228–231
  nutrition statistics, 224, 225
Market equilibrium exchange rate. *See* Exchange rates
Market failure, 371
Market pricing, 540–541
Market-friendly development strategy, 143, 157, 523–524, 525
  competitive domestic markets, 524–526
  concerns with, 531
  global development and, 603
  implementation of, 529–531
  international integration, 528–529
  investments in human capital, 526–528
  stable macroeconomy, 524
Marriage Law of 1950 (China), 209
Marshall Plan, 505
Martin, Bradley, 503*n*
Marx, Karl, 132–133
Marxist view of population growth and economic development, 192
Masoni, Vittorio, 512*n*, 520
Massiah, Ernest, 51*n*
**Material balance process, 397,** 540
**Material balances, 540**
Mauldin, Paul, 215*n*
Mauritania, 561
  drought in, 573–574
  foreign aid to, 509
  parallel-market premiums for foreign exchange, 579
Mazumdar, D., 257*n*
McCartney, Scott, 113*n*
McClelland, David, 246*n*
McComas, Maggie, 496*n*
Medicine
  curative, 232, 233, 527
  preventative, 227, 237, 527
  research, 237–238
  traditional, 237
  *See also* Health
**Medium of exchange, 284**
Meier, Gerald M., 246*n*
Merchandise trade
  current balance of payments account and, 452–453
  selected statistics on, 434–436, 437

**Merit goods, 391**
Mexico
   crawling peg used in, 471–472
   demographic survey of, 199–201
   devaluation of peso, in, 476, 510
   foreign direct investment in, 491
   land reform in, 330
   management of common resources, 378–379
   merchandise export structure, 437
   oil exports from, 366–368
   privatization in, 410
   sectoral shares in, 389
   selected statistics from, 367
   transnational corporations in, 493
Mexico City, population growth and conditions in, 189–190
Microvariability, 141–142
Middle East
   agriculture in, 325
   birth rates in, 48
   death rates in, 48
   demographic transition in, 47–49
   developing economies of, 10, 60
   developing nations of, 5–6
   fertility in, 48, 49
   foreign aid to, 509
   gross domestic investment and gross domestic saving in, 292
   illiteracy in, 239
   land and water in, 375, 376
   merchandise trade in, 435
   military expenditures, 595, 596
   population and labor force in, 274
   renewable water resources in, 377
   returns to investment in education, 244
**Middle-income economies, 10, 11**
Migration, 268
   economic, 268–272
**Military burden, 594**
Military spending, global development and, 590–596
Mineral production, country shares of, 356
**Minifundias, 329**
Minimum wages, 266–267, 407–408
Mining, 357
**Mixed agriculture, 329**
Modern sector
   economic growth and distribution of income in, 118–120
   employment in, 260–261
   growth of, 103
Modern service sector, 391
Monetary policy
   expansionary, 264–266
   in global development, 605
**Money, 284**
   financial capital and, 284
   functions of, 284–286
   supply of in market-friendly development strategy, 524
Monopsony, 338
Montreal Protocol on the Depletion of the Ozone Layer, 602
Morbidity rates, nutrition and, 220–221
Mortality
   child, 190
   indicators of, 34, 35–37
   lowering of as precondition for adoption of birth control and lower fertility, 232
**Most-favored nation, 444**
Mozambique
   foreign aid to, 509
   parallel market premiums for foreign exchange, 579
Mubarak, Hosni, 279
Mueller, Eva, 200$n$, 214
Multilateral aid, 168
Multilateral Investment Guarantee Agency (MIGA), 511$n$

## N

NAFTA. *See* North American Free Trade Agreement (NAFTA)
Namibia, foreign aid to, 509
Nasser, Gamal Abdel, 279
National Demographic Survey (Mexico), 199–201
National security, versus human security, 589
Nationalist (Guomindang) Party, 174
**Nationalization, 497**
NATO nations, military expenditures by, 595–596
**Natural fertility, 202**
**Natural monopoly, 391**
   regulation of, 411
Natural resource-intensive products
   export tax on, 362
   exports of, 360–362
**Natural resources, 7, 353–355**
   diversity in resource endowment and utilization, 375–376
   economic growth and, 354–355
      agriculture and other natural resource-intensive sectors, 357
      fishing, 357–358

forestry, 359–360
    mining, 357
Dutch disease, 363
    avoiding, 368–369
    evidence from Mexico, 366–368
    illustration of, 365–366
    real and nominal exchange rates, 363–365
    exports of natural resource-intensive products, 360–362
        tradeoffs in short and long run, 362–363
    resource scarcity, 355–356
    export revenue instability in, 361
    global development and, 596–600
Nazario, Sonia, 285n
Negative externalities, 163–164
    market failure and, 370–372
    reduction in demand and, 373–374
Nehru, Jawaharlal, 416
Nelson, Joan, 160, 160n, 168n, 174
Nelson, Richard, 90, 90n, 116
Neoclassical economics, 166
Nestlé, 496
**Net factor payments, 8**
**Net in-migration rate, 33**
Net intergenerational wealth flows, 49–51
Net investment, rate of, 100
**Net present value, 242–243, 308**
Net present value criterion for development projects, 307–311
Net savings rate, 93n
Netherlands, as official development assistance donor, 507
Neumann, Holly, 379n
Newbery, David M. G., 550n, 551n, 558
Newborns, effect of human capital formation on cohort of, 221
**New Economic Mechanism (NEM), 550**
New International Economic Order, 506
**Newly Industrializing Countries, 11**
New Zealand
    economy of, 4, 5
    as First World Country, 10
    population growth in, 32
Nicaragua, foreign aid to, 508
Niger, 561, 562
    crude birth rate in, 48
    drought in, 573–574
    tribal violence in, 566
Nigeria, 561
    budget deficit in, 579
    foreign direct investment in, 491
    macroeconomic policy in, 580
    merchandise export structure, 437

    military dictatorship in, 566
    sectoral shares in, 389
Nissanke, Machiko, 502n
**Nominal exchange rate, 363–365, 363**
**Nominal rate, 401**
Nongovernmental organizations (NGOs), 512–514
    in global development, 606
**Nonrenewable resources, 354, 355**
    optimal rate of depletion of, 369n
**Nontariff barriers to trade, 445**
**North, 9**
North American Free Trade Agreement (NAFTA), 123, 368, 493, 604
North Korea, centralized socialism in, 161
Norton, George W., 326n, 330n
Norway, as official development assistance donor, 507
Nuclear Nonproliferation Treaty, 555, 600–601
Nuclear weapons capability, 600–601
Nugent, Jeffrey, 393n
Numeracy, 246
Nutrition, 222
    importance of, 222–224
    improvements in that contribute to declines in morbidity rates, 220–221
    malnutrition, 222
    policy of, 224–226
    undernutrition, 222, 225
Nyerere, Julius, 564

# O

OAPEC. *See* Organization of Arab Petroleum Exporting Nations (OAPEC)
Oceania, military expenditures in, 595
Ofer, Gur, 539n
**Official development assistance (ODA), 279, 498**
    *See also* Foreign aid
**Official producer prices, 338**
**Official reserve assets, 456**
**Official settlements account, 456–458, 456**
Omaar, Rakiya, 566
Onchocerciasis Control Programme, 234–235, 235n, 500–501
"One Child Campaign" (China), 209–210
OPEC. *See* Organization of Petroleum Exporting Countries (OPEC)
Opportunity costs
    constant, 430
    increasing, 430

Optimal rate of depletion of nonrenewable resources, 369n
**Orderly marketing agreements, 445**
Organization of Arab Petroleum Exporting Countries (OAPEC), 508
Organization for Economic Cooperation and Development (OECD), 10
  official development assistance by, 507
Organization of Petroleum Exporting Countries (OPEC), 117, 363n, 505–506
  embargo by, 365–366, 366n
  external debt problem and, 474
Ortiz, Guillermo, 472n
Orubuloye, I. O., 204n
Outliers, 30
**Output-expansion path, 61**
**Overvalued currency, 338**
OXFAM, 512
Ozone layer, depletion of, 602

# P

Pacific
  agriculture in, 325
  developing nations of, 5–6
  education in, 240
  foreign aid to, 509
  foreign direct investment in, 490
  Green Revolution in, 333
  gross domestic investment and gross domestic saving in, 292
  health in, 230, 231
  life expectancy in, 229
  merchandise trade in, 435
  military expenditures, 595
  nutrition in, 224, 225
  population and labor force in, 274
  renewable water resources in, 377
Pack, Howard, 110n, 116
Pakistan
  crude birth rate in, 48
  education in, 513–514
  merchandise export structure, 437
  military burden in, 594
  sectoral shares in, 389
Paris Club, 473
Park Chung Hee, General, 99, 147
**Partial output elasticity, 62**
People's Republic of China
  establishment of, 174, 209
  *See also* China
Per capita income
  energy consumption and, 86
  fertility rate and, 95–96
  subsistence level of, 93n
Per capita output, percentage change in, 8
**Perestroika, 541**
Perkins, Dwight, 176n, 363n
**Permanent income, 194, 194n, 303**
**Permanent income hypothesis, 303–304, 303**
Perotti, Roberto, 169n
**Petrodollars, recycling of, 474**
Petroleum, exports of, 363n, 365–366
Petry, Joseph, 181n
**Physical capital, 284**
  growth rate of, 90–91
Physical capital deepening, 84–88, 100
Physical capital formation, 101, 104–105, 283–284
  constraints on domestic savings, 302–307
  domestic investment, sources of funds for, 288–293
  financial intermediation, 293–302
  generation of employment and, 124–127
  improving access to credit, 311–313
  incremental capital-output ratios, 287–288
  money and financial capital, 284–286
  net present value criterion for development projects, 307–311
  saving rate and economic growth, 286–287
**Physical capital stock, 6–7**
**Physical labor, 6**
Poland, 548, 551–554, 608
  agriculture in, 325
  centralized socialism in, 161
  development indicators in, 549
  education in, 240
  foreign direct investment in, 491
  gross domestic investment and gross domestic saving in, 292
  growth and development in, 14, 15
  life expectancy in, 229
  merchandise export structure, 437
  merchandise trade in, 435
  population and labor force in, 274
  sectoral shares in, 389
  shock therapy in, 552–553
Policy coordination, 168–169
Political migration, 272
Political refugees, in Africa, 575
Political revolution, 99
Political stability, economic growth and, 170

Pollution, 409
Pomfret, Richard, 59$n$, 81
Ponnambalam, Satchi, 150$n$, 151$n$
Population
  doubling time of, 33
  increases in, 7
  positive checks on, 45
  preventative checks on, 45
  world, 4–5
Population Conferences, 187
Population growth, 31–32, 55–56, 185–186
  average annual rates, 1980–1993, 191$n$
  climatic changes and, 189
  components of population change, 32–34
    fertility, 37–39
    mortality, 35–37
  demand for children and, 193–201
    Easterlin's supply-demand synthesis, 201–204
  economic development and, 190–193
  employment and, 251
  Marxist view of, 192
  potential consequences of in LDCs, 186–190
  reduction of mortality rates and, 232
  in steady-state economy, 141–142
  in sub-Saharan Africa, 569–571
  variable (in Solow model), 106–107
**Population momentum, 40–43, 40**
**Population policy, 205**
  birth control in China, 208–210
  range of, 205–206
    economic incentives and other measures, 207–208
    family planning programs (FPP), 206–207
**Population pyramid, 40–41, 42**
Portugal, foreign direct investment in, 491
**Positive checks** (on population), **45**
Positive externality, 165
  in public production of industry and services, 391
Post-subsistence phase of agriculture, 326–327
Poterba, James, 606$n$, 609
Poverty, 13–14, 117–118
  alleviation of, 527–528
  economic growth and, 130
  as primary explanation for undernutrition, 225
  rapid population growth and, 187–190
  in steady-state economy, 142
**Pre-take-off economy, 97**

Predatory state, 160
**Prediction error, 26**
**Preventative checks** (on population), **45**
Preventative medicine, 237, 527
Price liberalization, 530, 542–543
Price regulation, 411
Price signals, 376–378
Primary education
  costs of, 241–242
  rate of return for, 244
  *See also* Education
**Primary growth sectors, 100**
Private market, 371
  initial demand in, 374
  reduced demand in, 374
Private rate of return of education, 242–245
Privatization
  in Brazil, 181
  in China, 176
  of economic infrastructure, 410–411
  in market-friendly development strategy, 526, 545–547
**Product cycle theory of trade, 433–434, 433**
Production functions, 60
  Cobb-Douglas, 63$n$
  with factor substitution, 62–64
  fixed-coefficients production function, 60–62
  Harrod-Domar growth model, 64–67
**Production possibilities boundary (PPB), 6, 423–425, 423**
Property rights, 378–379
  in laissez-faire capitalism, 156–157
  in market-friendly development strategy, 524
Psacharopoulos, George, 243–244, 245, 250
Public goods, 156
  in market-friendly development strategy, 526
Public health. *See* Health; Health-care services
Public infrastructure projects
  competition and privatization, 410–411
  local participation, 411–412
  management of, 410
Public saving, 306–307
**Pure public good, 162**

# Q

Qin dynasty, 174
**Quality of children, 194**

## R

Radical critique
  of economic development theory, 132
    Marxian foundation, 132–133
    radical school, 133–135
  of foreign aid, 502–505
Raney, Laura, 245n, 250
Ranis, Gustav, 536n, 558
Rapczynski, Andrzej, 554n
**Rate of labor force participation (LFP), 261**
**Rate of unemployment (UNP), 262**
Ratliff, Charles, Jr., 517, 517n, 520
Ratnapala, Nandesena, 139n
Ravenhill, John, 565n, 582n, 586
Rawlings Economic Recovery Program, 178
Rawlings, Jerry, 177–178
**Real exchange rate, 364–366**, 367–368, 367n
Real Plan, 181–182, 182n
**Reciprocity, 444**
**Recycling of petrodollars, 474**
Red Cross, 504
Refugees, 272
Regional development banks, 605–606
Regional zones of cooperation, 604
Regression equations, 26–30
**Renewable resources, 354**, 355
Renner, Michael, 601n
**Replacement-level fertility, 38**
Republic of South Africa, 559, 583
Research
  agricultural policy reform and, 344
  educational, 248
Reserves, bank, 296n
Resident, of nation, 451–452
Resource allocation, 162–163
Resource scarcity, 355–356
Respiratory infections, 227
**Revaluation, 469**
Rhee, Syngman, 147
Ricardo, David, 421
Richburg, Keith, 566n
Riddell, Roger, 499n, 500n, 501n, 514n, 520
"Right livelihood," 137, 138, 587
Riverblindness, 227, 234–235
  Onchocerciasis Control Programme, 234–235, 235n, 500–501
Rodrik, Dani, 511n
Roemer, Michael, 363n
Rogoff, Kenneth, 483, 483n, 451n, 487
Roh Tae-Woo, General, 148
Romania, 608
  centralized socialism in, 161
Romer, Paul, 110n, 111n, 116
Rosenzweig, Mark R., 256n
Ross, David, 558
Rostow, W. W., 96–97, 97n, 116
Rostow's take-off into self-sustaining growth, 96–101, 294–295
Rural labor markets, 256–259
Russia
  economic growth in, 169
  natural resource reserves in, 355
  privatization in, 545, 546
  Start II Treaty, 3–4
Russian Civil War, 539
Russian Revolution, 539
Russo-Japanese War, 146
Rutherford, Thomas, 447n
Rwanda
  dysfunctional government in, 566
  tribal massacres in, 567

## S

Sabot, Richard, 535n, 558
Sachdeva, Paramjit, 235n
Sachs, Jeffrey, 483, 483n, 487, 553, 553n, 554, 558
Sadat, Anwar, 279
Sample regression equation, 26
Sanderatne, Nimal, 150n
Sandinista government, 508
Sarin, Seema, 50n
Sarvodaya Shramadana movement, 138–140, 512, 606
Save the Children Fund, 512
Saving
  business, 305–306
  domestic, 302–307
  foreign, 291
  government (public), 306–307
  household, 302–305
  return to, 304–305
Saving rate, 68–70
  economic growth and, 286–287
  in laissez-faire capitalism, 156
Scatter diagram, 23, 25
Schiff, Maurice, 337n
Scholarship programs, 247
Schultz, Theodore, 102n, 219, 219n, 238, 238n, 323, 323n
Schumacher, E. F., 135–140, 136n, 146, 311–312, 311n, 467n, 515, 515n, 587
Schumacher's Buddhist economics, 135–140, 587

Seaga, Edward, 386
Second International Population Conference, 187
**Second World, 10**
**Secondary markets, 547**
Sectoral development, in managed capitalism, 159–160
Security alliances, 606–607
Seko, Mobutu Sese, 566
Self-sustaining growth, take-off into, 96–101
Senegal, 561, 562, 565
    "African Socialism" in, 564
    drought in, 573–574
    export commodities in, 563
    merchandise export structure, 437
    political stability in, 566
    sectoral shares in, 389
Senghor, Leopold, 564, 565
Service sector. *See* Industry and services
Sewage treatment, 226, 228, 235
Sheahan, John, $350n$, $351n$
Shen, Xiaofang, $490n$, 520
Shepherd, Jack, 503–504, $504n$, 520
**Shock therapy, 552–553, 552**
Shome, Parthasarathi, $307n$
Short, Kathleen, $200n$, 214
Sierra Leone
    parallel market premiums for foreign exchange, 579
    tribal violence in, 566
Simons, Mailise, $603n$
Simonsen, Mario, 475, $475n$
Simpson, Murray S., $181n$
Singapore, 532, 537
    expansion of labor-intensive manufactured exports in, 122
Singh, Ajit, 531, $531n$, 558
Singh, S. P., $97n$, 116, $117n$
Six-Day War, 279
Slovakia, 608
Slovenia, 608
*Small Is Beautiful: Economics As If People Mattered*, 135–136, 138, 311
Smith, Adam, 156
Smith, Gordon, $475n$
Smith, Robert S., 250, $252n$
Snodgrass, Donald, $363n$
Social market, negative externality in, 371
**Social overhead capital, 409**
Social rate of return of education, 242–245
Social security, 266–267
Society for Community Support in Primary Education in Baluchistan, 513–514

Soil erosion, 380
Solar box cooker, 380
Solow model, 70–74, $430n$
    fundamental equation of, 72
    variable population growth in, 106–107
Solow, Robert, 70, $70n$, 81, $106n$, $110n$, 116, $430n$
Somalia, 561
    dysfunctional government in, 566
Song, Byung-Nak, $146n$, 149
**South, 9**
South Africa. *See* Republic of South Africa
South Korea, 532, 537
    agriculture in, 325
    case study of economic development in, 146–149
    education in, 240
    expansion of labor-intensive manufactured exports in, 122
    GNP, 148
    gross domestic investment and gross domestic saving in, 292
    growth and development in, 14, 15
    life expectancy in, 229
    managed capitalism in, 159–160
    merchandise export structure, 437
    merchandise trade in, 435
    population and labor force in, 274
    product cycle theory of trade and, 434
    sectoral shares in, 389
    take-off in, 99
Southern African Development Community, 583–584, 607
Soviet Union (former), 6
    average income in, 13
    centralized socialism in, 160–162, 539–541
    dissolution of, 135, 169
    economic reforms in, 4
    economic transition in, 538–539, 541–542
        financial intermediation, 547
        global integration, 547–548
        labor market, 543–545
        privatization, 545–547
        use of consumer markets, 542–543
    fertilizer use in, 597
    military burden in, 595–596
    military and economic aid offered by, 505
    nuclear weapons capability, 600–601
**Special Drawing Rights, 456**, $456n$, 605
**Specific tariff, 401**

Spero, Joan, 473n, 474n, 476n, 487, 497n, 505n, 506n, 520
Squire, Lyn, 329n
Sri Lanka
  agriculture in, 325
  case study of economic development in, 150–153
  crude birth rate in, 48
  education in, 240
  GDP, 152–153
  gross domestic investment and gross domestic saving in, 292
  growth and development in, 14, 15
  life expectancy in, 229
  merchandise export structure, 437
  merchandise trade in, 435
  per capita GNP, 18
  population and labor force in, 274
  Sarvodaya Shramadana movement in, 138–140, 512, 606
  sectoral shares in, 389
Sri Lanka Freedom Party (SLFP), 151, 152
Srinivasan, T. N., 16n, 21, 226n, 256n, 268n, 324n
Stalin, Josef, 539
Stalinist system, 539
  failure of, 541
  *See also* Centralized socialism
Start II Treaty, 3–4
*Steady-State Economics: The Economics of Biophysical Equilibrium and Moral Growth*, 140
**Steady-state economy (SSE), 140–141, 141**
  institutions for, 141–143
**Steady-state equilibrium, 66–67, 89**
  growth in labor productivity and, 108–111
  in Solow model, 74
Stern, Nicholas, 21
Stiglitz, J. E., 258n
Stock markets, 547
Stone, Carl, 384n, 385n, 386n
**Store of value, 285**
Streeten, Paul, 16n, 22, 128n, 146
Strout, Alan, 77n
**Structural adjustment, 577–578**
  decentralization, 581–582
  future of, 582
  macroeconomic stabilization, 578–580
  market pricing in agriculture, 580–581
  poor and, 582
**Structural adjustment agreement, 578**
*Structural Change and Development Policy*, 387

Structural changes, as part of economic development process, 12
**Structurally unemployed, 264**
Stuart, Robert C., 174, 416n, 550n, 552n, 558
Student-teacher ratio, 239, 240
**Stunting, 223–224, 223, 225**
Subbarao, K., 245n, 250
**Subsidy, 337–338, 337**
  to domestic producers, 405
  to import-competing firms, 406
**Subsistence agriculture, 326**
**Subsistence sector, 102**
**Substitution effect, 254**
Sudan, tribal violence in, 566
Suez Canal, 279
Summers, Lawrence, 549n, 558
Sun Yat-sen, 174
**Supplementary growth sectors, 100**
Supply, measures to reduce for sustainable development, 372–373
Surplus labor models, 257–258
**Surplus value, 132**
**Sustainable development, 369**
  diversity in resource endowment and utilization, 375–376
  market failures and government regulation, 369–372
  measures to reduce demand, 373
  measures to reduce supply, 372–373
  policies for, 376
    price signals, 376–378
    property rights, 378–379
    technology, 379–381
Swardson, Anne, 358n
Sweden
  as official development assistance donor, 507
  population pyramid for, 41, 42
Szekely, Istvan P., 550n, 551n, 558

# T

*t* statistic, 29n
*t* tests, 29n
Taiwan
  economic growth in, 532
  expansion of labor-intensive manufactured exports in, 122
**Take-off, 97, 98**
  initiation, 99
  into self-sustaining growth, 96–97
  classification of economies, 97–98
  preconditions, 98–99
  sustaining, 100–101

Tanganyika, 564
Tanouye, Elyse, 235*n*
Tanzania
　"African Socialism" in, 564
　economic stagnation in, 565
　export commodities in, 563
　foreign aid to, 509
　parallel–market premiums for foreign exchange, 579
Tanzi, Vito, 527*n*
Tariffs, 401
　ad valorem, 401
　compared to import quotas, 404
　in market-friendly strategy of development, 524
　nominal and effective tariff rates, 401–403
　specific tariff, 401
Tarr, David, 447*n*
Taucher, George, 496*n*
**Technical efficiency, 61***n*
Technological change, 76
Technological progress, 61, 75–76
　in endogenous growth theory, 111–112
　low-level equilibrium trap and, 94
**Technology, 7**
　intermediate, 137
　shifts in, 126–127
　in sustainable development, 379–381
　transfers of, 528
Technoserve, 513
Teitelbaum, Michael, 47*n*, 54
Telecommunications, privatization of, 410
**Terms of trade, 435–436**
Terrorist attacks, 589
Thailand, 532, 537
　foreign direct investment in, 491
Third International Population Conference, 187
**Third World, 10**
　economic development in, 564
　economic reform in, 160
Thurow, Lester, 587*n*
Tianlu, Zhang, 208*n*, 214
Tien, H. Yuan, 208*n*, 209*n*, 210*n*, 214
Tietenberg, Tom, 359*n*, 360*n*, 378*n*, 383*n*, 600*n*
Timmer, C. P., 324, 324*n*, 327*n*, 328*n*
Tobacco, use of, 228
Tobin, James, 605, 605*n*
Todaro, Michael, 269*n*
Torres, Craig, 291*n*
**Total factor productivity, 7**
**Total fertility rate, 37,** 39, 95–96, 215, 216, 217–218

　in China, 208
Trade, 421–422
　factor endowments theory of, 422–425
　gains from, 422–425
　export expansion, 436–437
　　achieving success with, 441–442
　　competitive exchange rate, 438–440
　　experience with import substitution, 438
　　export subsidies, 440, 441
　　shift to, 438
　GATT and trade liberalization, 443–445
　　LDCs, GATT, and the Uruguay Round, 446
　　nontariff barriers to trade, 445
　implementing trade strategy, 442–443
　international factor mobility, 425–427
　international terms of trade, 427–430
　principles of trade, 430
　　comparative advantage, 431
　　gains from trade, 431
　　less developed and developed economies, 432
　　simplifying assumptions of the model, 430–431
　　trade and distribution of income, 431–432
　recent experience, 434–436
　global development and, 604–605
　international terms of, 427–430
　invisible, 454
　product cycle theory of, 433–434
　in services, 454
Trade deficits, 291
**Traditional economy, 97**
Traditional medicine, 237
Traditional sector, 103
**Transfer pricing, 496–497, 496**
**Transitory income, 303**
Transnational corporations
　foreign direct investment by, 492–493
　　location of foreign subsidiaries, 493–494
　foreign investment through, 120
　mining as leading sector for, 357
　in radical critique of economic development theory, 134
Transportation, 98–99
Treaty of Berlin, 562
Turchin, Boone, 199*n*, 201*n*
Two-sector model of economic development, 101–105, 129, 257

## U

Uganda, political stability in, 566
Ukraine, The, 548, 554–556
   economic indicators in, 549
   IMF loan to, 555
**Underemployment, 261**
   *See also* Employment; Unemployment
**Undernutrition, 222**
   poverty as primary explanation for, 225
   *See also* Nutrition
**Unemployed,** 261
**Unemployment,** 261–262, **261**
   frictional, 264
   involuntary, 256
   macroeconomic analysis of, 262–266
   microeconomic analysis of, 266
      bias toward capital-intensive projects, 267–268
      limited factor substitution, 268
      minimum wages, social security, and unions, 266–267
   rate of, 262
   structural, 264
UNICEF. *See* United Nations Children's Fund (UNICEF)
**Unilateral transfers, 454**
Unionization, 408
**Unit of account, 285**
**Unit labor costs, 493**
Unit of Real Value (URV), 182$n$
United Fruit Company, 350
United Kingdom, privatization in, 410
United National Party (UNP), 151, 152, 153
United Nations, agencies of, 511–512
United Nations Children's Fund (UNICEF), 237, 512
United Nations Conference on the Environment and Development, 602–603
United Nations Development Programme (UNDP), 16–17, 234, 272–273, 512, 589, 601
United Nations Economic Commission for Africa (UNECA), 583
United Nations Fund for Population Activities (UNFPA), 512
United Nations Group of Consultant Experts, 590
United Nations Industrial Development Organization (UNIDO), 512
United Nations International Comparison Programme, 15–16
United Nations Population Fund, 207
United Nations Security Council, 601, 607
United States
   demographic transition in, 186
   economy of, 4, 5
   Federal Reserve, 475
   as First World country, 10
   nutrition statistics for, 224, 225
   as official development assistance donor, 507
   population growth in, 32, 186
   position of in international economy, 505
   recession of 1981–1982 in, 475
   relations with Korea, 147, 148–149
   Start II Treaty, 3–4
   structural adjustment approach to African development agenda, 577–582
Upper Volta, 562
Urban informal labor markets, 259–260
U.S. Agency for International Development, 326$n$

## V

Valdes, Alberto, 337$n$
**Value added, 390,** 390$n$, 395, 396
**Value of marginal product of labor, 253,** 254
van de Walle, Etienne, 47$n$, 54
Variables
   dependent, 23
   independent, 23
Vernon, Raymond, 433$n$
Verspoor, Adriaan, 239, 239$n$, 245$n$, 250
**Vertical integration, 492**
Vietnam War, 505
Vitamin A deficiency, 223, 234
Vocational training, 247
Vogel, Thomas, Jr., 291$n$, 472$n$
Volcker, Paul, 475
**Voluntary export restraints, 445**
Vu, My T., 51$n$

## W

Wages, government, 266–267
Walesa, Lech, 552
War, global development and, 589
**Warranted growth rate, 66**
Warsaw Pact nations, 591
   military expenditures in, 595–596
**Wasting,** 223–224, **223**, 225
Water

renewable resources per capita, 377
safe supply of, 226, 227–228, 235
Weber, Peter, 598n, 602n, 610
Weeks, John, 39
Weinstein, David, 159n
Wellisz, Stanislaw, 384n, 385n, 386n, 552–553, 553n
Wessel, David, 472n
West Germany. *See* Federal Republic of Germany
Western cultures
  demographic transition in, 44–47
  intergenerational wealth flow in, 49–51
Western Europe
  crude birth rates in, 48
  demographic transition in, 47–49
  First World status, 10
  population growth in, 32
  share of world output, 4, 5
Westphal, Larry E., 159n, 174, 434n
Whitmore, Jane, 503n
Williamson, Jeffrey G., 268n
Winter, David, 246n
Wood, used for cooking, 379–380
Working conditions, 407–408
World Bank, 59, 59n
  agricultural pricing policy, 337, 338
  agriculture in Africa, 572
  causes of famine in recent years, 5
  competition in financial markets, 313–314
  data published by, 9
  deforestation, 359
  economic benefits of trade, 421–422
  economic infrastructure, 409–413
  education and economic growth, 242
  establishment of, 135n
  estimate of total burden of disease in a country, 230–231
  family planning study, 206
  in Ghana, 178
  income classifications, 10, 11
  International Finance Corporation of, 605
  lead exposure, 370
  market-friendly development strategy of, 143, 157, 523–531, 603
  natural resources, 355–356
  official development assistance by, 510–511
  public health package outlined by, 234
  radical critique of, 135
  Structural Adjustment Agreements (SAA), 168
  structural adjustment policy of, 577–582
  world consumption of cereal grains, 358
World commodity price indexes, 335
World Development Fund, 517
*World Development Reports*, 9, 131, 223, 242, 510, 523–531 *passim*
World Employment Conference (1976), 123
World Health Organization (WHO)
  code of conduct for marketing infant formula, 496
  essential drugs available in generic form, 237
  estimation of total burden of disease in a country, 230–231
  official development assistance by, 512
  riverblindness prevention, 234–235, 235n
World merchandise exports, 5
World output, 5
**World reserve base life index, 355**
World Resources Institute, 192
  world food production, 323–324
World Summit for Children, 238
World Trade Organization, 446, 605
  child labor concerns, 260
Worldwatch Institute, 189
  estimate of earth's forest cover, 336
  growth in global food production, 598
Worm infections, 226, 234

# Y

Yotopoulos, Pan, 393n
Yu, Ping, 208n, 214
Yusof, Zainal Aznam, 150n

# Z

Zaire
  ineffective government in, 566
  Mobutu government of, 160, 566, 569
Zambia
  foreign aid to, 509
  parallel–market premiums for foreign exchange, 579
Zhongtang, Liang, 208n, 214